A-Z BRISTOL & NORTH SOMERSET

Key to Map Pages	2-3
Large Scale Bristol City Centre	4-5
Large Scale Bath City Centre	6-7
Map Pages	8-159

Postcode Map	
Index to Streets, Towns, Villages, Stations & selected Places of Interest	162-207
Index to Hospitals, etc.	208

REFERENCE

Motorway	M5
Primary Route	A4
A Road	A36
B Road	B4055
Dual Carriageway	
One-way Street Traffic flow on A Roads is also indicated by a heavy line on the driver's left.	
Road Under Construction Opening dates are correct at the time of publication.	
Proposed Road	
Restricted Access	
Pedestrianized Road	
City Centre Loop	
Track / Footpath	
Residential Walkway	
Railway	Station / Tunnel / Level Crossing / Heritage Sta.
Built-up Area	MILL ST
Local Authority Boundary	
Posttown Boundary	
Postcode Boundary (within Posttown)	
Map Continuation	86 — Large Scale City Centre 4
Airport	
Car Park (selected)	P

Church or Chapel	†
Cycleway (selected)	
Bristol Ferry Waterbus Stop	F
Fire Station	■
Hospital	H
House Numbers (selected roads)	13 8 25
Information Centre	i
National Grid Reference	360
Park & Ride	Portway P+R
Police Station	▲
Post Office	★
Safety Camera (with Speed Limit) Fixed cameras and long term road works cameras. Symbols do not indicate camera direction.	30
Toilet: without facilities for the Disabled with facilities for the Disabled Disabled use only	▽ ▽ ▽
Viewpoint	
Educational Establishment	
Hospital or Healthcare Building	
Industrial Building	
Leisure or Recreational Facility	
Place of Interest	
Public Building	
Shopping Centre or Market	
Other Selected Buildings	

SCALE

Map Pages 8-159 1:14,908	Map Pages 4-7 1:7,454
0 ¼ ½ Mile	0 ⅛ ¼ Mile
0 250 500 750 Metres	0 100 200 300 400 Metres
4¼ inches (10.8 cm) to 1 mile 6.71 cm to 1 km	8½ inches (21.6) to 1 mile 13.42 cm to 1 km

registered trade marks of Geographers' A-Z Map Company Ltd

www./az.co.uk

EDITION 5 2015
Copyright © Geographers' A-Z Map Co. Ltd.
Telephone: 01732 781000 (Enquiries & Trade Sales)
01732 783422 (Retail Sales)

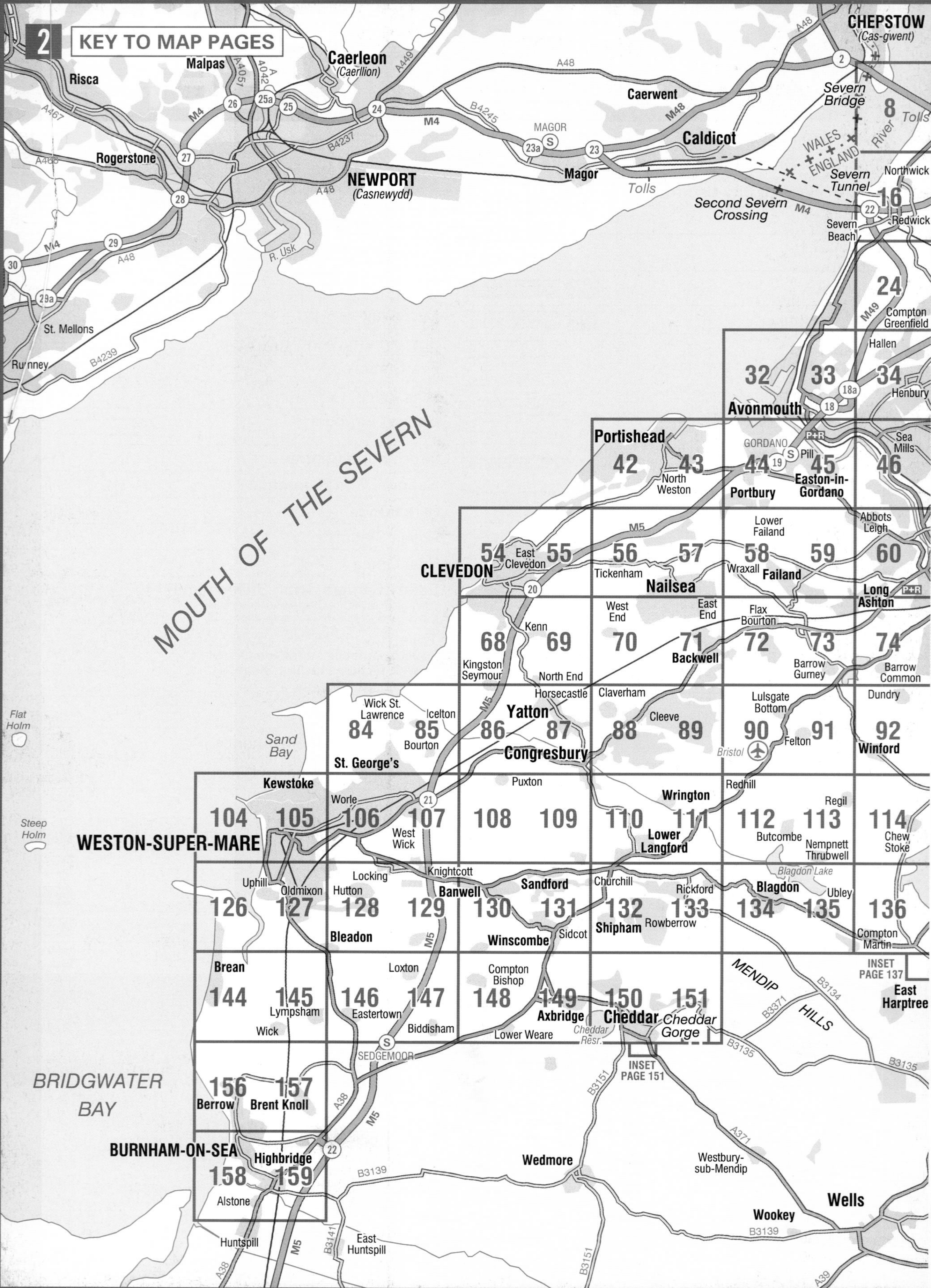

KEY TO MAP PAGES

2

Risca
Malpas
Caerleon *(Caerllion)*
Rogerstone
NEWPORT *(Casnewydd)*
St. Mellons
Rumney
Caerwent
MAGOR
Magor
Caldicot
CHEPSTOW *(Cas-gwent)*
Severn Bridge
8
Tolls
River
WALES
ENGLAND
Second Severn Crossing
Severn Tunnel
Severn Beach
Northwick
16
Redwick

MOUTH OF THE SEVERN

24
Compton Greenfield
Hallen
Henbury

32 **33** **34**

Avonmouth
GORDANO
Pill
Easton-in-Gordano
Portbury
Sea Mills
46

Flat Holm

Steep Holm

Portishead
42 **43** **44** **45**
North Weston

Abbots Leigh
60

Clevedon
54 **55** **56** **57** **58** **59**
East Clevedon
Tickenham
Nailsea
Wraxall
Failand
Lower Failand
Long Ashton

68 **69** **70** **71** **72** **73** **74**
Kenn
West End
East End
Flax Bourton
Backwell
Barrow Gurney
Barrow Common
Kingston Seymour
North End
Horsecastle

Sand Bay

Wick St. Lawrence
Icelton
Yatton
Claverham
Cleeve
Lulsgate Bottom
Dundry
84 **85** **86** **87** **88** **89** **90** **91** **92**
Bourton
Congresbury
Bristol
Felton
Winford

St. George's
Puxton
Redhill
Regil
Kewstoke
Worle
Wrington
Butcombe
Nempnett Thrubwell
Chew Stoke
104 **105** **106** **107** **108** **109** **110** **111** **112** **113** **114**
West Wick
Lower Langford

WESTON-SUPER-MARE

Uphill
Oldmixon
Locking
Hutton
Knightcott
Sandford
Churchill
Rickford
Blagdon
Ubley
Compton Martin
126 **127** **128** **129** **130** **131** **132** **133** **134** **135** **136**
Banwell
Sidcot
Shipham
Rowberrow
Bleadon
Winscombe
INSET PAGE 137
East Harptree

Brean
Loxton
Compton Bishop
MENDIP
144 **145** **146** **147** **148** **149** **150** **151**
Lympsham
Eastertown
Biddisham
Axbridge
Cheddar
Cheddar Gorge
HILLS
Wick
Lower Weare
Cheddar Resr.
SEDGEMOOR

BRIDGWATER BAY
Berrow
Brent Knoll
INSET PAGE 151
156 **157**

BURNHAM-ON-SEA
Highbridge
158 **159**
Alstone
Wedmore
Westbury-sub-Mendip
Wells
Huntspill
East Huntspill
Wookey

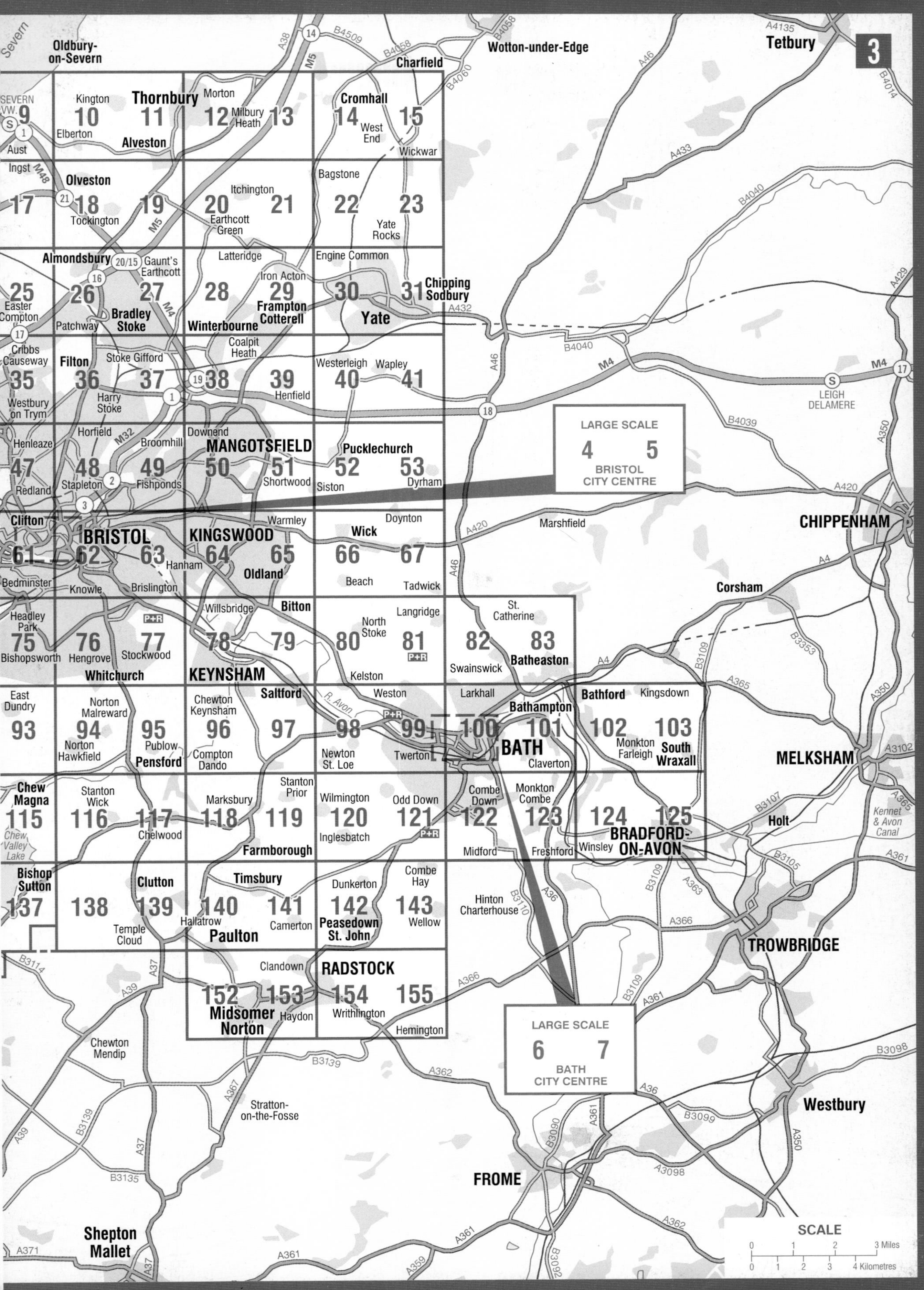
Severn
Oldbury-
on-Severn
Wotton-under-Edge
Tetbury
Charfield
SEVERN
VW.
9
Aust
Kington
10
Elberton
Thornbury
11
Alveston
Morton
12
Milbury
Heath
13
Cromhall
14
West
End
15
Wickwar
Ingst
17
Olveston
18
Tockington
19
Itchington
20
Earthcott
Green
21
Bagstone
22
Yate
Rocks
23
Almondsbury
Gaunt's
Earthcott
25
Easter
Compton
26
Patchway
Bradley
Stoke
27
Latteridge
28
Winterbourne
Iron Acton
29
Frampton
Cotterell
Engine Common
30
Yate
31
Chipping
Sodbury
Cribbs
Causeway
35
Westbury
on Trym
Filton
36
Harry
Stoke
Stoke Gifford
37
Coalpit
Heath
38
39
Henfield
Westerleigh
40
Wapley
41
LEIGH
DELAMERE
LARGE SCALE
4
5
BRISTOL
CITY CENTRE
Henleaze
47
Redland
Horfield
48
Stapleton
Broomhill
49
Fishponds
Downend
MANGOTSFIELD
50
51
Shortwood
Pucklechurch
52
Siston
53
Dyrham
Clifton
61
Bedminster
BRISTOL
62
Knowle
63
Hanham
Brislington
KINGSWOOD
64
65
Oldland
Warmley
Wick
66
Beach
Doynton
67
Tadwick
Marshfield
CHIPPENHAM
Corsham
Headley
Park
75
Bishopsworth
76
Hengrove
77
Stockwood
Whitchurch
Willsbridge
78
KEYNSHAM
Bitton
79
North
Stoke
80
Langridge
81
Kelston
St.
Catherine
82
Swainswick
83
Batheaston
East
Dundry
93
Norton
Malreward
94
Norton
Hawkfield
95
Publow
Pensford
Chewton
Keynsham
96
Compton
Dando
Saltford
97
R. Avon
98
Newton
St. Loe
Weston
99
Twerton
Larkhall
100
BATH
Bathampton
101
Claverton
Bathford
102
Monkton
Farleigh
Kingsdown
103
South
Wraxall
MELKSHAM
Chew
Magna
115
Chew
Valley
Lake
Stanton
Wick
116
117
Chelwood
Marksbury
118
Stanton
Prior
119
Farmborough
Wilmington
120
Inglesbatch
Odd Down
121
Combe
Down
122
Midford
Monkton
Combe
123
Freshford
124
Winsley
125
BRADFORD-
ON-AVON
Holt
Kennet
& Avon
Canal
Bishop
Sutton
137
138
Clutton
139
Temple
Cloud
Hallatrow
140
Paulton
Timsbury
141
Camerton
Dunkerton
142
Peasedown
St. John
Combe
Hay
143
Wellow
Hinton
Charterhouse
TROWBRIDGE
Clandown
152
Midsomer
Norton
153
Haydon
RADSTOCK
154
Writhlington
155
Hemington
LARGE SCALE
6
7
BATH
CITY CENTRE
Chewton
Mendip
Stratton-
on-the-Fosse
Westbury
FROME
Shepton
Mallet
SCALE
0
1
2
3 Miles
0
1
2
3
4 Kilometres

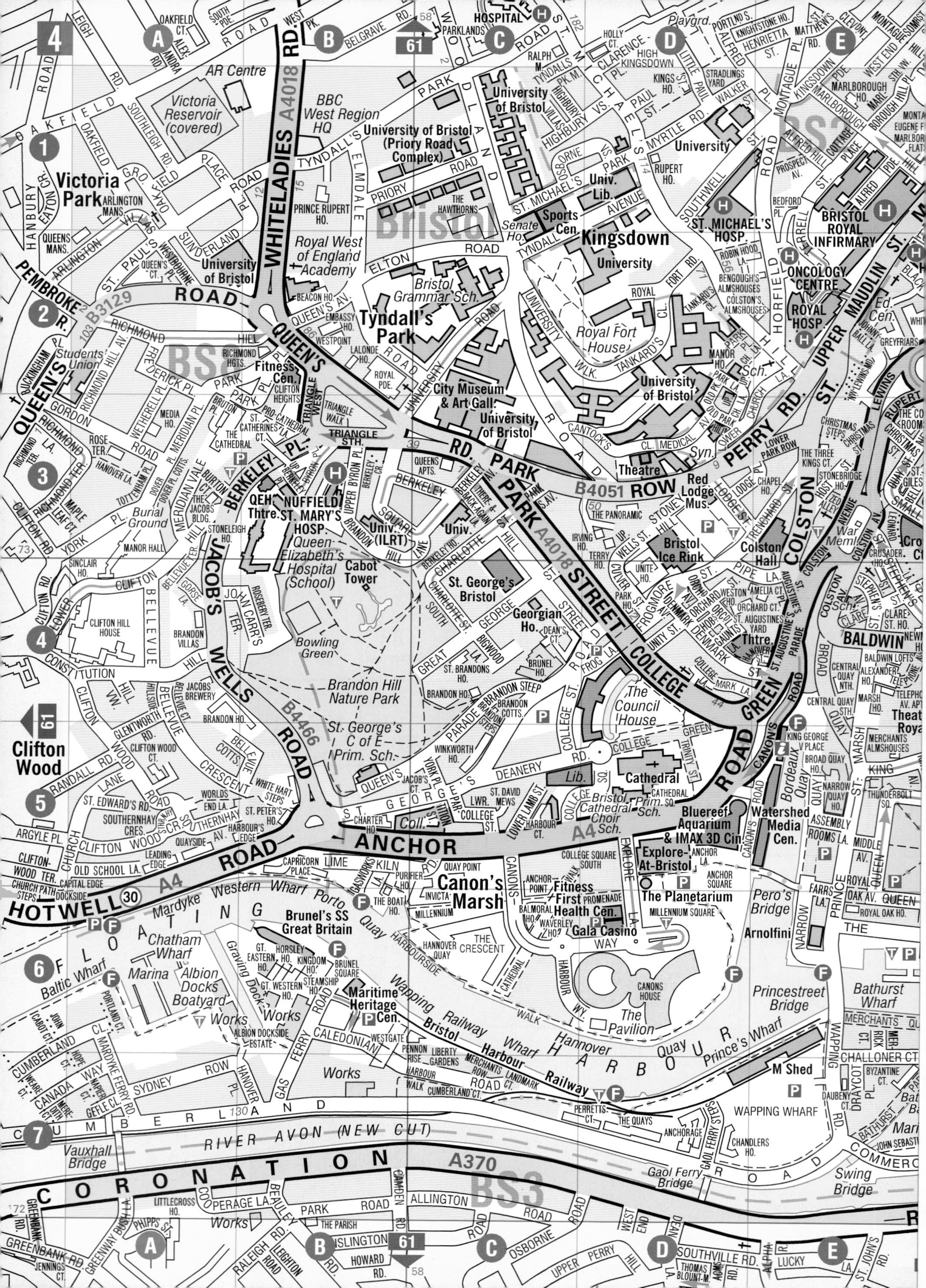

4
A
B
C
D
E
1
2
3
4
5
6
7
61
58
Victoria Park
Victoria Reservoir (covered)
AR Centre
BBC West Region HQ
University of Bristol (Priory Road Complex)
University of Bristol
WHITELADIES RD.
A4018
PEMBROKE R.
QUEEN'S RD.
B3129
RICHMOND HILL
Students' Union
Fitness Cen.
Royal West of England Academy
Bristol Grammar Sch.
Tyndall's Park
Bristol
BS8
Kingsdown
Univ. Lib.
Sports Cen.
Senate Ho.
Royal Fort House
ST. MICHAEL'S HOSP.
BRISTOL ROYAL INFIRMARY
ONCOLOGY CENTRE
ROYAL HOSP.
UPPER MAUDLIN ST.
City Museum & Art Gall.
University of Bristol
Theatre
Syn.
PERRY RD.
B4051
RED LODGE MUS.
PARK ROW
PARK ST.
Cabot Tower
QEH Thtre.
NUFFIELD ST. MARY'S HOSP.
Queen Elizabeth's Hospital (School)
Univ. (ILRT)
Univ
St. George's Bristol
Georgian Ho.
Bristol Ice Rink
Colston Hall
COLSTON AVENUE
War Meml.
Burial Ground
JACOB'S WELLS ROAD
B4466
Bowling Green
Brandon Hill Nature Park
St. George's C of E Prim. Sch.
The Council House
COLLEGE GREEN
Cathedral
Lib.
Bristol Cathedral Prim. Sch.
Bristol Cathedral Choir Sch.
Thtre.
BALDWIN
Clifton Wood
CLIFTON
CONSTITUTION HILL
HOTWELL ROAD
A4
ANCHOR ROAD
Blureef Aquarium & IMAX 3D Cin
Explore-At-Bristol
The Planetarium
Canon's Marsh
Fitness First Health Cen.
Gala Casino
Watershed Media Cen.
Bordeaux Quay
Pero's Bridge
Arnolfini
Theatre Royal
F L O A T I N G   H A R B O U R
Mardyke Western Wharf
Porto Quay
Brunel's SS Great Britain
Chatham Wharf
Baltic Wharf
Marina
Albion Docks Boatyard
Graving Dock
Works
Maritime Heritage Cen.
Wapping Railway Wharf
Bristol Harbour Railway
Hannover Quay
The Pavilion
Canons House
Princestreet Bridge
Prince's Wharf
Bathurst Wharf
M Shed
WAPPING WHARF
CUMBERLAND ROAD
RIVER AVON (NEW CUT)
Vauxhall Bridge
CORONATION ROAD
A370
BS3
Gaol Ferry Bridge
Swing Bridge
COMMERCIAL ROAD
GREENBANK RD.
ALLINGTON ROAD
PARK ROAD
OSBORNE ROAD
SOUTHVILLE RD.

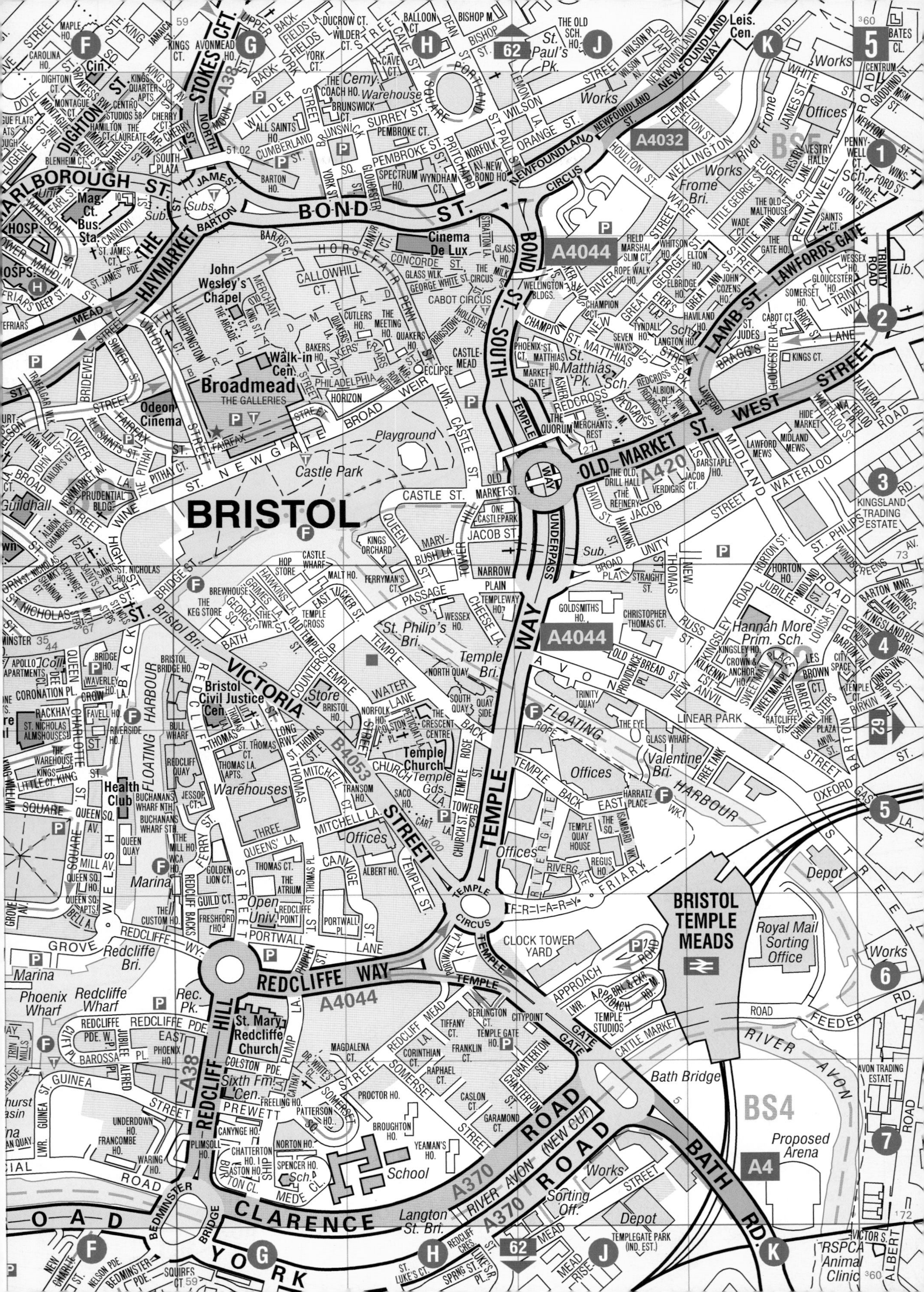

F
G
H
J
K
5
62
BRISTOL
Broadmead
THE GALLERIES
Odeon Cinema
Cinema De Lux
John Wesley's Chapel
Walk-in Cen.
Castle Park
Playground
St. Paul's Pk.
St. Matthias Pk.
Cabot Circus
BOND ST.
HAYMARKET
MARLBOROUGH ST.
NEWFOUNDLAND WAY
NEWFOUNDLAND CIRCUS
A4032
A4044
A420
A38
B4053
A370
A4
OLD MARKET ST.
WEST STREET
LAWFORDS GATE
LAMB ST.
TEMPLE WAY
TEMPLE WAY UNDERPASS
VICTORIA STREET
REDCLIFFE WAY
REDCLIFF HILL
CLARENCE ROAD
YORK ROAD
BATH RD.
TEMPLE CIRCUS
BRISTOL TEMPLE MEADS
Royal Mail Sorting Office
Bristol Civil Justice Cen.
St. Mary Redcliffe Church
Temple Church
Temple Gds.
St. Philip's Bri.
Temple Bri.
Valentine Bri.
Redcliffe Bri.
Langton St. Bri.
Bath Bridge
FLOATING HARBOUR
RIVER AVON
Hannah More Prim. Sch.
Proposed Arena
BS4
BS5
Guildhall
Marina
Health Club
Warehouses
Offices
Works
Depot
Sixth Fm. Cen.
School
Open Univ.
RSPCA Animal Clinic
Lib.
1
2
3
4
5
6
7

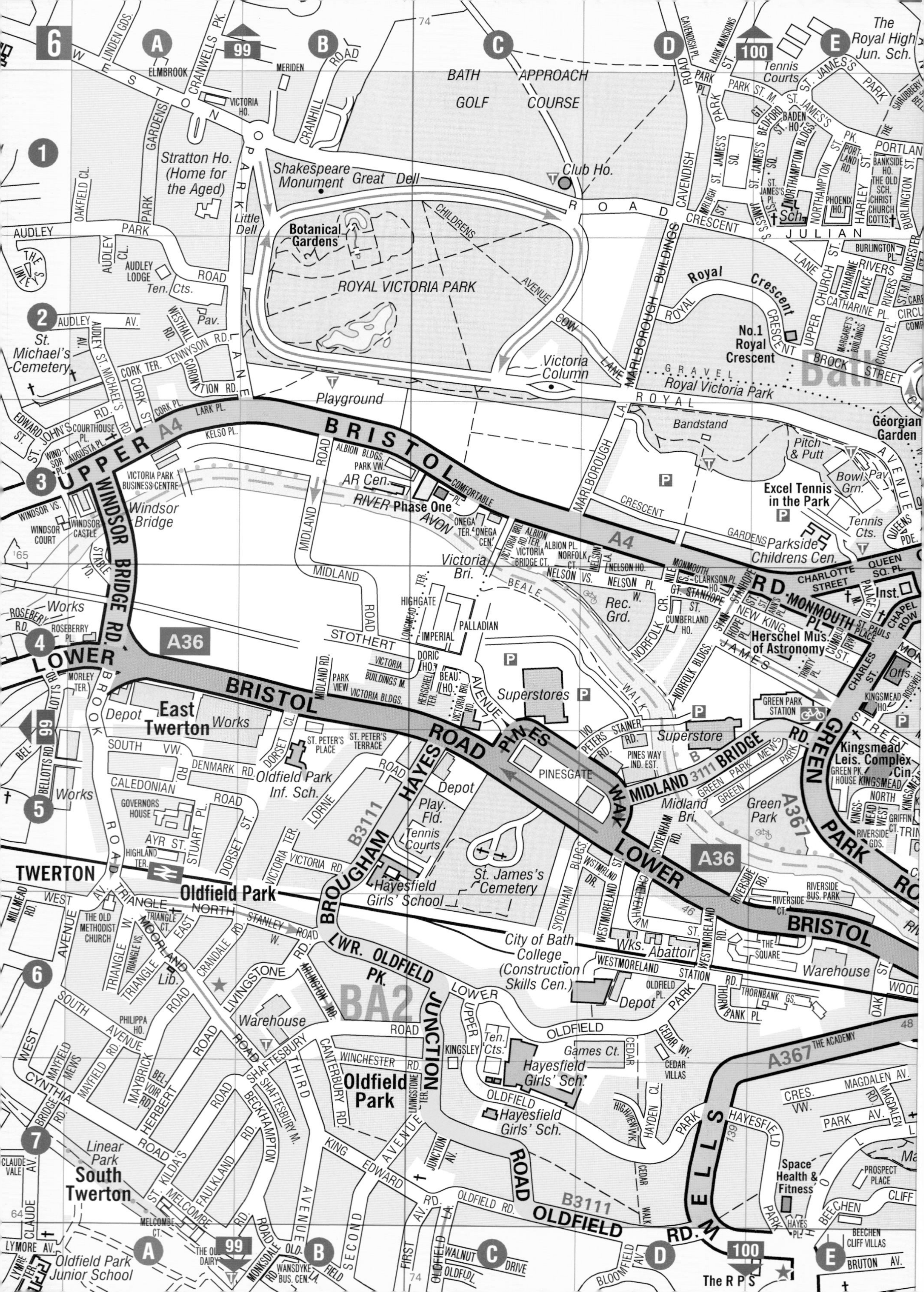
BATH APPROACH GOLF COURSE
Club Ho.
Shakespeare Monument
Great Dell
Little Dell
Botanical Gardens
ROYAL VICTORIA PARK
Stratton Ho. (Home for the Aged)
Royal Crescent
No.1 Royal Crescent
Victoria Column
Playground
Royal Victoria Park
Bandstand
Georgian Garden
Pitch & Putt
Excel Tennis in the Park
Parkside Childrens Cen.
The Royal High Jun. Sch.
St. Michael's Cemetery
Windsor Bridge
Victoria Park Business Centre
Phase One
AR Cen.
Victoria Bri.
Rec. Grd.
Herschel Mus. of Astronomy
Superstores
Superstore
Green Park Station
Kingsmead Leis. Complex
Midland Bri.
Green Park
East Twerton
Works
Depot
Oldfield Park Inf. Sch.
Play. Fld.
Tennis Courts
St. James's Cemetery
Hayesfield Girls' School
TWERTON
Oldfield Park
City of Bath College (Construction Skills Cen.)
Abattoir
Warehouse
BA2
Hayesfield Girls' Sch.
Games Ct.
Oldfield Park
Linear Park
South Twerton
Oldfield Park Junior School
Space Health & Fitness
The R P S
UPPER BRISTOL ROAD
LOWER BRISTOL ROAD
WINDSOR BRIDGE RD.
BROUGHAM HAYES
MIDLAND BRIDGE
PINES WAY
GREEN PARK ROAD
WELLS RD.
OLDFIELD ROAD
A4
A36
A367
B3111
99
100
74

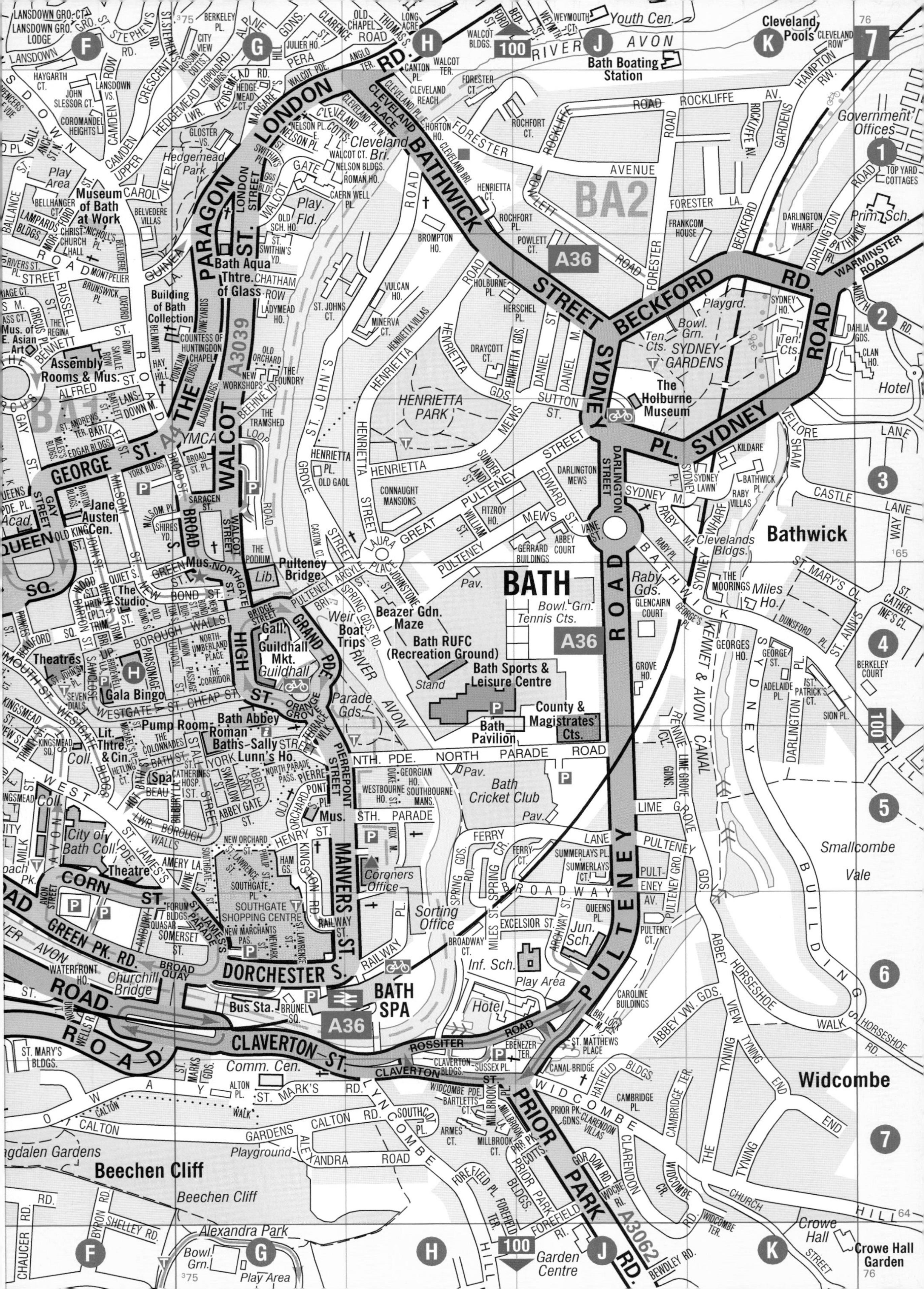

F
G
H
J
K
7
76
375
100
Youth Cen.
Cleveland Pools
RIVER AVON
Bath Boating Station
LONDON RD.
WALCOT BLDGS.
WALCOT TER.
CLEVELAND PLACE
CLEVELAND REACH
Cleveland Bri.
BATHWICK STREET
FORESTER RD.
ROCKLIFFE AV.
ROCKLIFFE RD.
HAMPTON RW.
Government Offices
1
TOP YARD COTTAGES
Prim. Sch.
DARLINGTON WHARF
FORESTER AVENUE
FORESTER LA.
FRANKCOM HOUSE
BA2
A36
BECKFORD RD.
WARMINSTER ROAD
NORTH RD.
2
SYDNEY GARDENS
Playgrd.
Bowl. Grn.
Ten. Cts.
The Holburne Museum
SYDNEY ROAD
SYDNEY PL.
Hotel
CLAN HO.
DAHLIA GDS.
LANSDOWN
LANSDOWN GRO. CT.
LANSDOWN GRO. LODGE
ST. STEPHEN'S RD.
CAMDEN RD.
HEDGEMEAD RD.
Hedgemead Park
Play Area
Museum of Bath at Work
BELVEDERE VILLAS
GUINEA LA.
THE PARAGON
LONDON STREET
WALCOT ST.
A3039
Bath Aqua Thtre. of Glass
CHATHAM ROW
Building of Bath Collection
COUNTESS OF HUNTINGDON CHAPEL
NEW WORKSHOPS
THE FOUNDRY
THE TRAMSHED
Play. Fld.
BROMPTON HO.
ST. JOHN'S ROAD
HENRIETTA PARK
HENRIETTA ST.
HENRIETTA RD.
HENRIETTA GDS.
HENRIETTA MEWS
DRAYCOTT CT.
HERSCHEL PL.
DANIEL ST.
SUTTON ST.
GREAT PULTENEY STREET
LAURA PLACE
WILLIAM ST.
EDWARD ST.
DARLINGTON STREET
DARLINGTON MEWS
VANE ST.
CONNAUGHT MANSIONS
3
CASTLE LANE
Bathwick
BATHWICK ST.
Clevelands Bldgs.
Raby Gds.
THE MOORINGS
Miles Ho.
ST. MARY'S CL.
ST. ANN'S
BERKELEY COURT
4
65
Mus. of E. Asian Art
Assembly Rooms & Mus.
ALFRED ST.
BA1
GEORGE ST.
A4
YMCA
BROAD ST.
GAY STREET
QUEEN SQ.
Jane Austen Cen.
MILSOM ST.
The Studio
Mus.
NORTHGATE ST.
NEW BOND ST.
THE PODIUM
Lib.
Pulteney Bridge
BATH
PULTENEY ROAD
Beazer Gdn. Maze
Bath RUFC (Recreation Ground)
Bowl. Grn.
Tennis Cts.
Bath Sports & Leisure Centre
County & Magistrates' Cts.
Bath Pavilion
Stand
Weir
Boat Trips
Gall.
Guildhall Mkt.
Guildhall
HIGH ST.
GRAND PDE.
BOROUGH WALLS
Theatres
Gala Bingo
WESTGATE ST.
CHEAP ST.
Bath Abbey
Pump Room
Roman Baths
Sally Lunn's Ho.
ORANGE GROVE
Parade Gds.
RIVER AVON
NTH. PDE.
NORTH PARADE ROAD
PIERREPONT STREET
Lit. Thtre. & Cin.
Coll.
Spa
ABBEY GATE ST.
KENNET & AVON CANAL
SYDNEY BUILDINGS
5
Smallcombe Vale
Bath Cricket Club
Pav.
LIME GROVE
Mus.
STH. PARADE
MANVERS ST.
City of Bath Coll.
Theatre
CORN ST.
Coroners Office
FERRY LANE
BROADWAY
Sorting Office
SOUTHGATE SHOPPING CENTRE
GREEN PK. RD.
Churchill Bridge
DORCHESTER ST.
BATH SPA
Bus Sta.
EXCELSIOR ST.
Jun. Sch.
Inf. Sch.
Play Area
Hotel
6
PULTENEY RD.
CAROLINE BUILDINGS
ABBEY VW. GDS.
HORSESHOE WALK
CLAVERTON ST.
ROSSITER ROAD
LOWER BRISTOL ROAD
ST. MARY'S BLDGS.
Comm. Cen.
ST. MARK'S RD.
WIDCOMBE PDE.
PRIOR PARK RD.
A3062
WIDCOMBE HILL
Widcombe
THE TYNING
7
CALTON RD.
CALTON GARDENS
Magdalen Gardens
Playground
ALEXANDRA ROAD
LYNCOMBE HILL
Beechen Cliff
Alexandra Park
Bowl. Grn.
Play Area
CHURCH ST.
Crowe Hall
Crowe Hall Garden
Garden Centre
64
BEWDLEY RD.

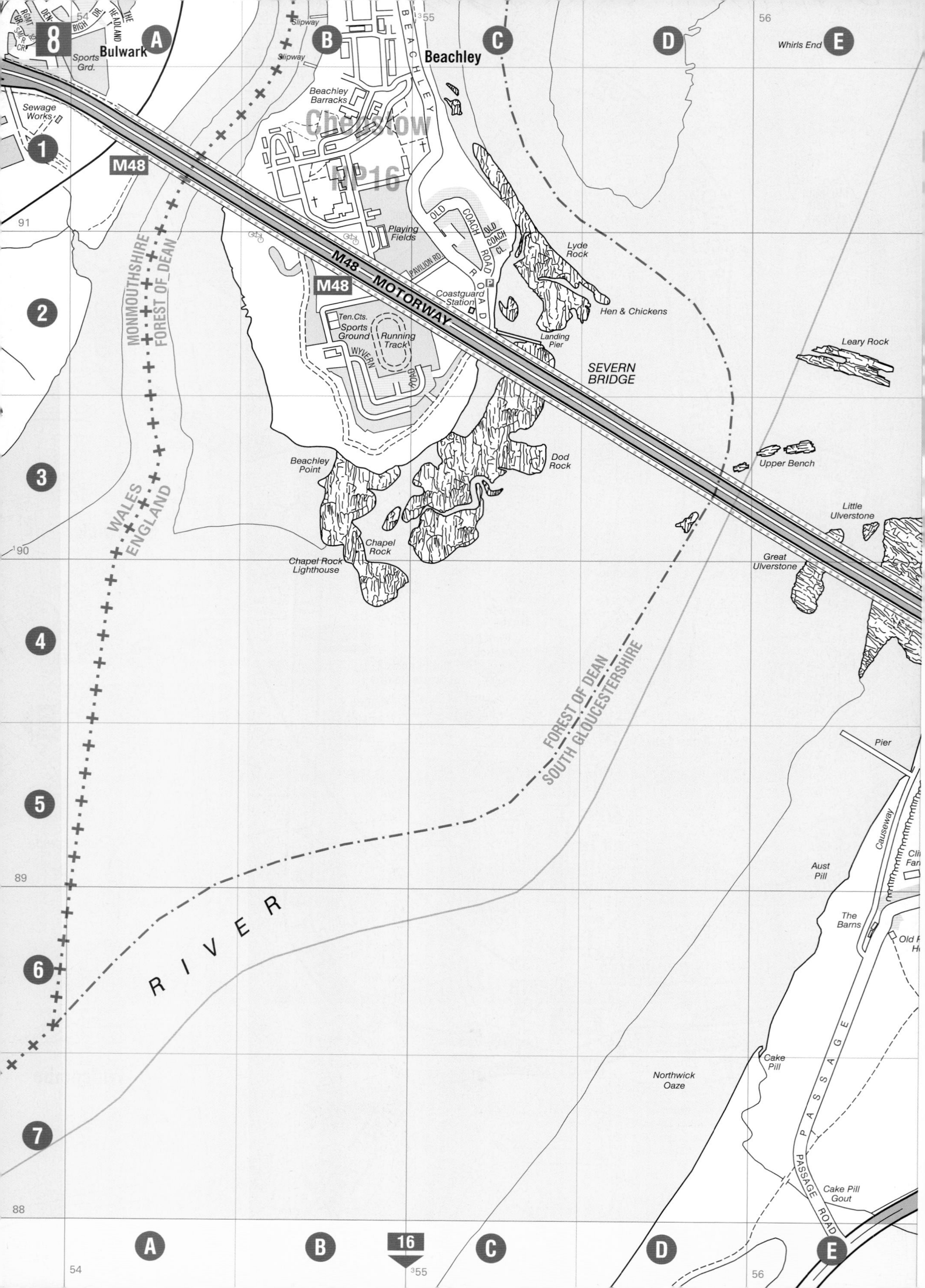

Bulwark
Sports Grd.
Sewage Works
M48
Slipway
Slipway
Beachley
Beachley Barracks
Chepstow
NP16
BEACHLEY
OLD COACH ROAD
OLD COACH CL.
PAVILION RD.
Playing Fields
M48 MOTORWAY
Coastguard Station
Ten.Cts.
Sports Ground
Running Track
WYVERN ROAD
Landing Pier
Lyde Rock
Hen & Chickens
SEVERN BRIDGE
Leary Rock
Upper Bench
Little Ulverstone
Great Ulverstone
Dod Rock
Beachley Point
Chapel Rock
Chapel Rock Lighthouse
MONMOUTHSHIRE
FOREST OF DEAN
WALES
ENGLAND
FOREST OF DEAN
SOUTH GLOUCESTERSHIRE
RIVER
Whirls End
Pier
Causeway
Aust Pill
The Barns
Cake Pill
Northwick Oaze
PASSAGE
PASSAGE ROAD
Cake Pill Gout
54
355
56
91
90
89
88
A
B
C
D
E
1
2
3
4
5
6
7

16

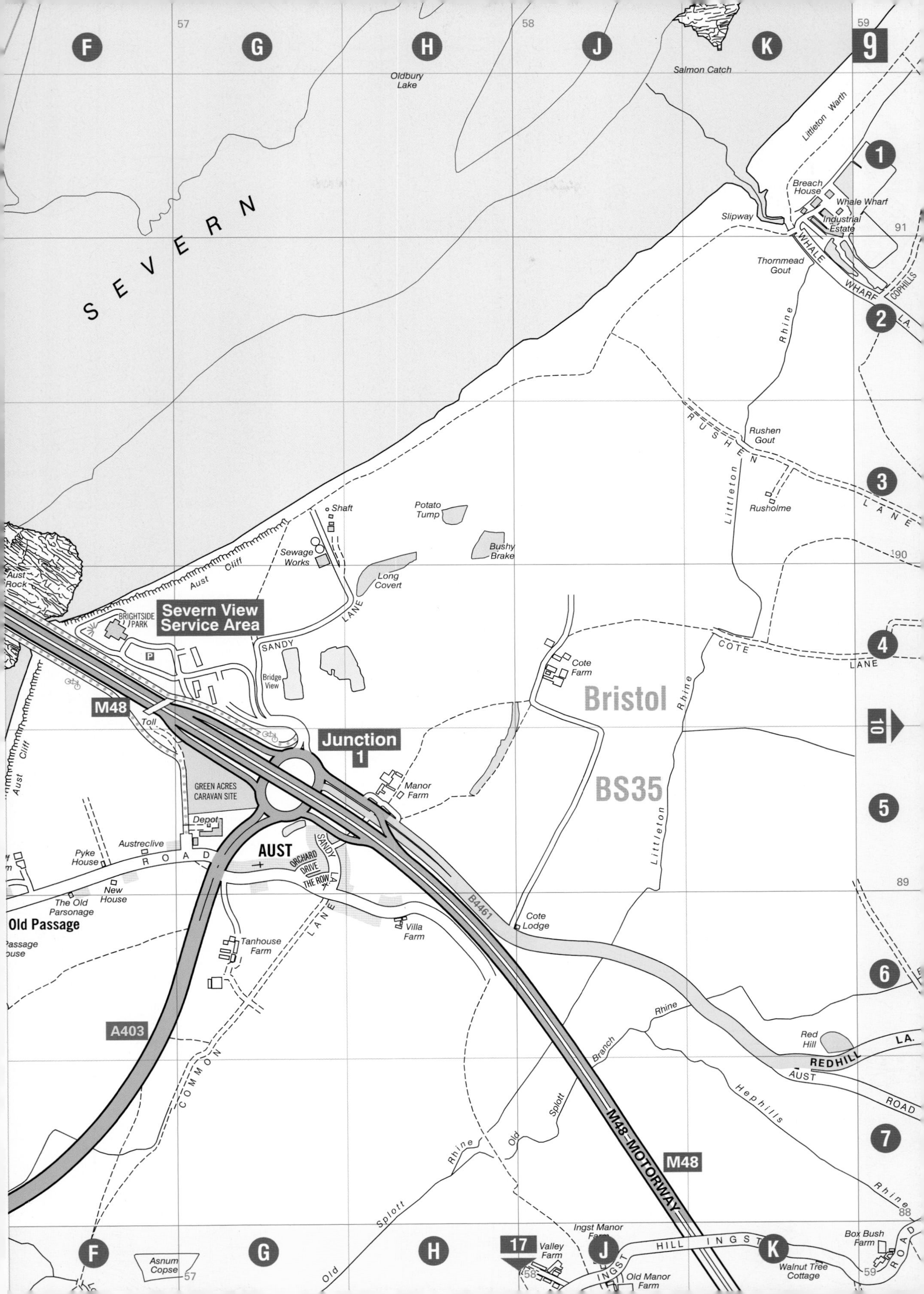

9
F
G
H
J
K
57
58
59
Oldbury Lake
Salmon Catch
SEVERN
Littleton Warth
Breach House
Whale Wharf
Industrial Estate
Slipway
Thornmead Gout
WHALE WHARF LA.
COPHILLS
Rhine
Rushen Gout
RUSHEN LANE
Littleton
Rusholme
91
190
89
88
Potato Tump
Bushy Brake
Shaft
Sewage Works
Long Covert
Aust Cliff
Aust Rock
BRIGHTSIDE PARK
Severn View Service Area
SANDY LANE
Bridge View
COTE LANE
Cote Farm
Bristol
BS35
M48
Toll
Junction 1
Manor Farm
GREEN ACRES CARAVAN SITE
Depot
AUST
ORCHARD DRIVE
THE ROW
SANDY LA.
Austreclive
Pyke House
ROAD
New House
The Old Parsonage
Old Passage
Passage House
B4461
Cote Lodge
Villa Farm
Tanhouse Farm
LANE
A403
COMMON
Rhine
Branch
Red Hill
REDHILL LA.
AUST ROAD
Hephills
Rhine
Splott
Old
M48-MOTORWAY
Old Splott
Ingst Manor Farm
INGST HILL
INGST
Valley Farm
17
Old Manor Farm
Asnum Copse
Walnut Tree Cottage
Box Bush Farm
ROAD
10
1
2
3
4
5
6
7

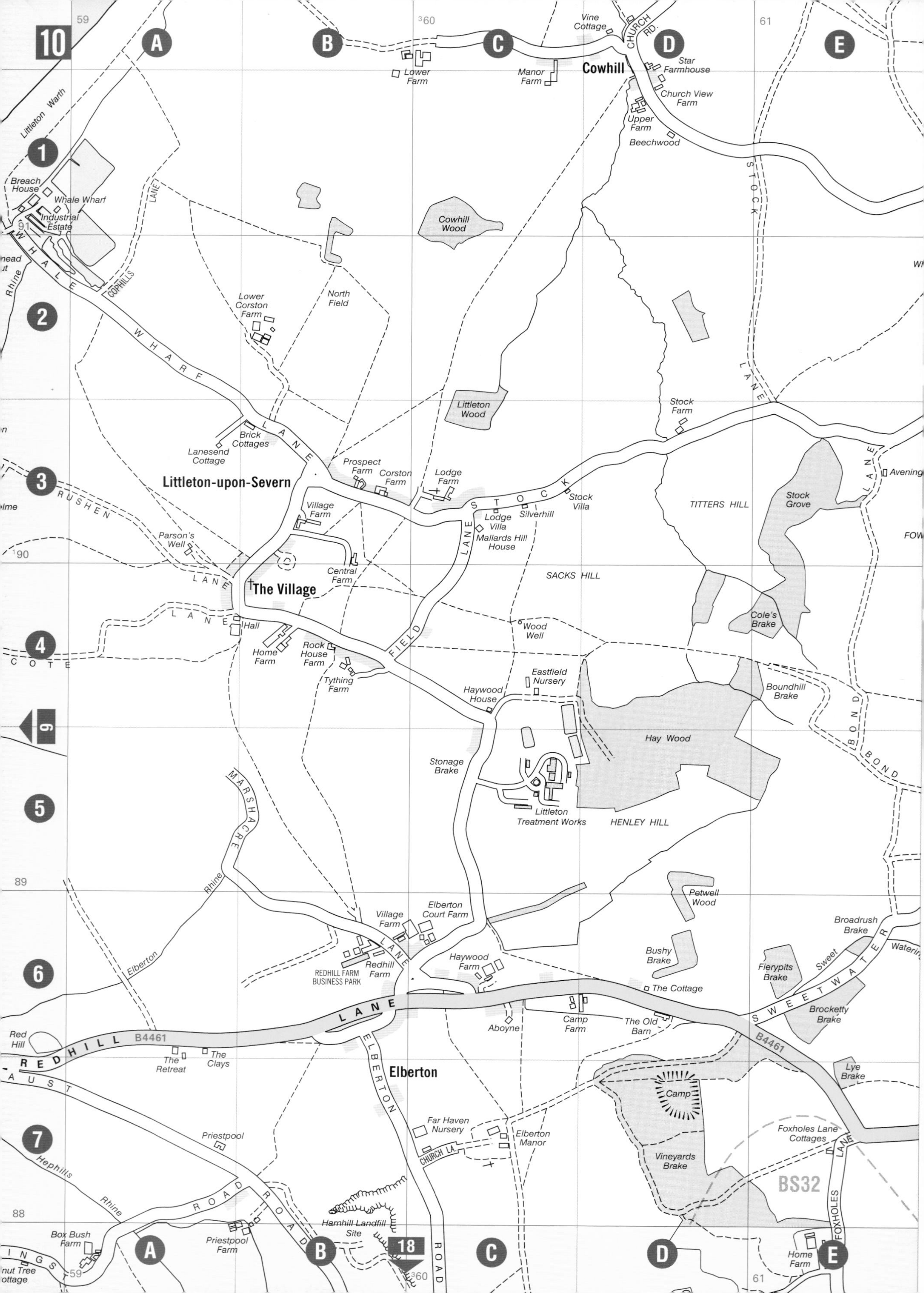
Littleton Warth
Breach House
Whale Wharf
Industrial Estate
WHALE
COPHILLS
LANE
WHARF
LANE
Lower Farm
Manor Farm
Cowhill
Vine Cottage
CHURCH RD.
Star Farmhouse
Church View Farm
Upper Farm
Beechwood
STOCK
LANE
Cowhill Wood
Lower Corston Farm
North Field
Littleton Wood
Stock Farm
Brick Cottages
Lanesend Cottage
Littleton-upon-Severn
Prospect Farm
Corston Farm
Lodge Farm
RUSHEN
Village Farm
Lodge Villa
Silverhill
Stock Villa
STOCK
Mallards Hill House
TITTERS HILL
Stock Grove
Avening
Parson's Well
LANE
The Village
Central Farm
SACKS HILL
Cole's Brake
LANE
Hall
Home Farm
Rock House Farm
Tything Farm
FIELD
Wood Well
COTE
Eastfield Nursery
Haywood House
Boundhill Brake
BOND
Hay Wood
Stonage Brake
MARSHACRE
Littleton Treatment Works
HENLEY HILL
Rhine
Petwell Wood
Village Farm
Elberton Court Farm
Broadrush Brake
Elberton
Haywood Farm
Bushy Brake
Fierypits Brake
Sweet
SWEETWATER
REDHILL FARM BUSINESS PARK
Redhill Farm
LANE
The Cottage
Camp Farm
Aboyne
The Old Barn
Brocketty Brake
Red Hill
REDHILL
B4461
The Retreat
The Clays
B4461
AUST
Elberton
ELBERTON
Lye Brake
Camp
Far Haven Nursery
Elberton Manor
Foxholes Lane Cottages
Priestpool
CHURCH LA.
Vineyards Brake
LANE
Hephills
Rhine
ROAD
ROAD
BS32
FOXHOLES
Box Bush Farm
Priestpool Farm
Harnhill Landfill Site
18
ROAD
Home Farm
A
B
C
D
E
1
2
3
4
5
6
7
59
360
61
91
90
89
88
9

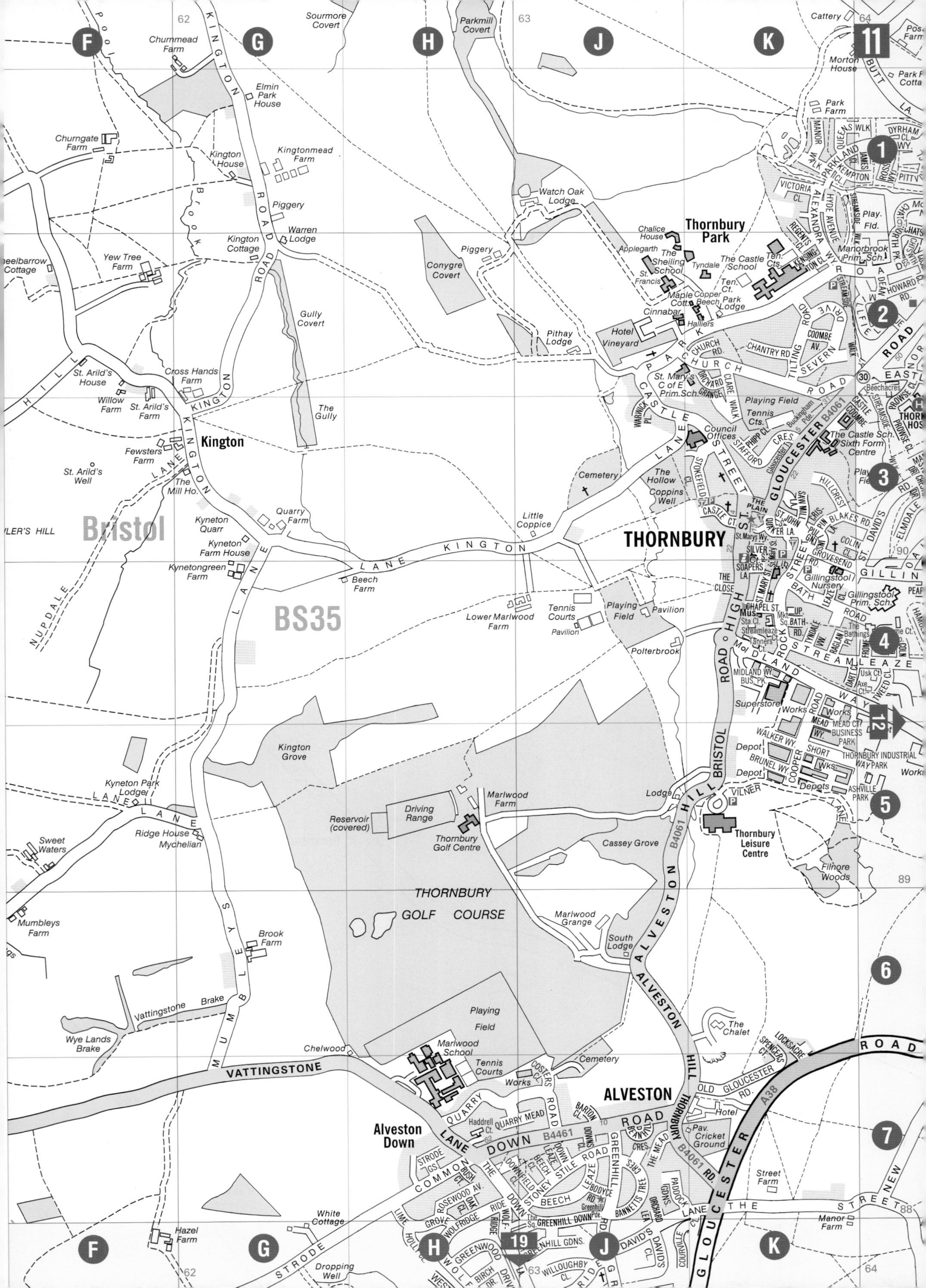
Thornbury
Thornbury Park
THORNBURY
Kington
Alveston
Alveston Down
Bristol
BS35
THORNBURY GOLF COURSE
Thornbury Leisure Centre
Kington Grove
Conygre Covert
Gully Covert
Cassey Grove
Filnore Woods
12
19

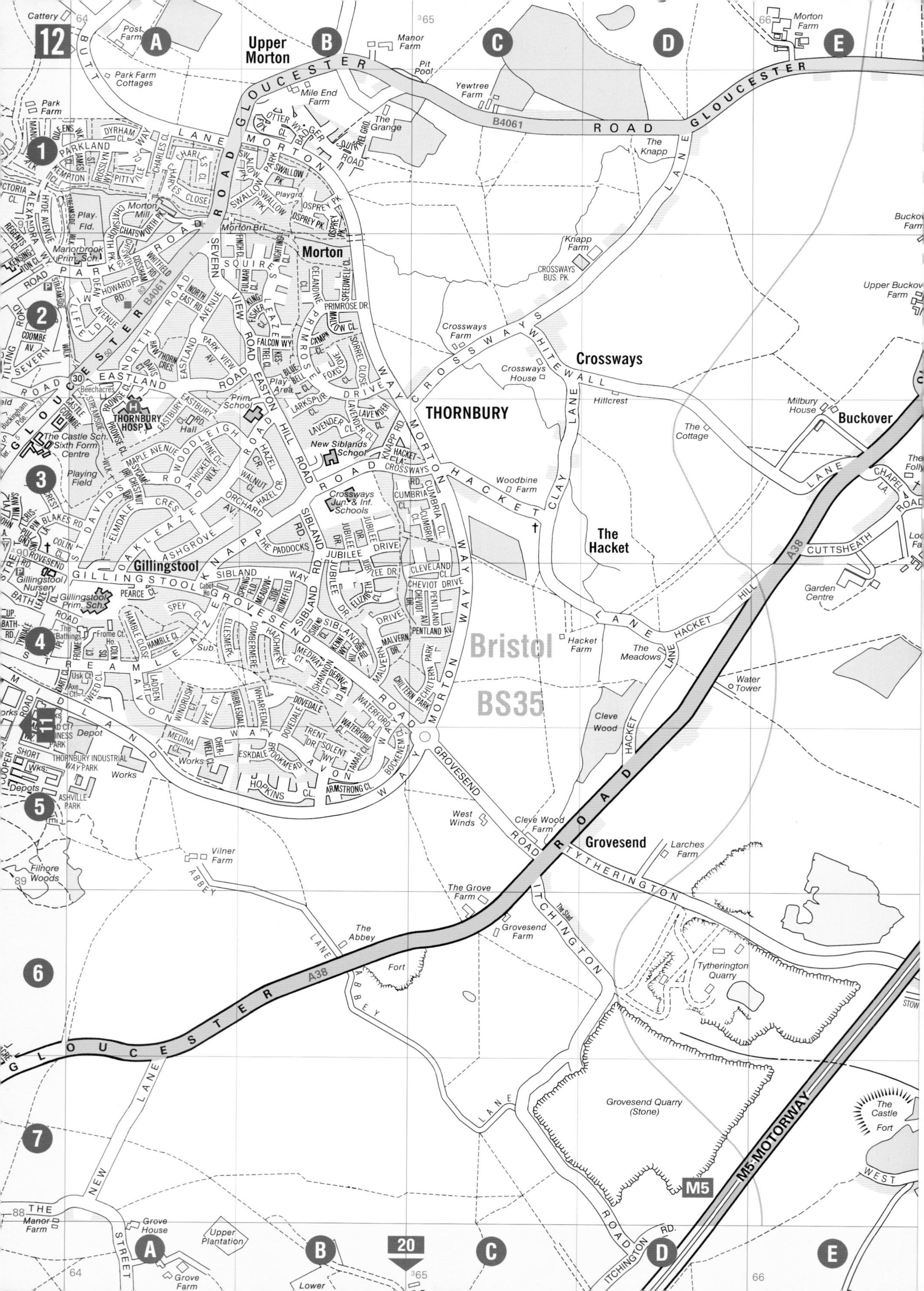

Cattery
Post Farm
Upper Morton
Manor Farm
Pit Pool
Morton Farm
Park Farm Cottages
Mile End Farm
Yewtree Farm
Park Farm
GLOUCESTER ROAD
B4061
The Grange
The Knapp
MORTON LANE
PARKLAND
KEMPTON
ROSSLYN
PITTVILLE
CHARLES CL.
DYRHAM CL.
QUEENS WK.
JAMES ST.
HYDE AVENUE
ALEXANDRA
VICTORIA CL.
STREAMSIDE
Play. Fld.
Morton Mill
CHATSWORTH PK.
CHATSWORTH
SWALLOW PARK
SWALLOW PK.
OSPREY PK.
OTTER WY.
FOX CL.
BADGER
SQUIRREL GRO.
Playgrd.
Morton Bri.
Morton
Knapp Farm
CROSSWAYS BUS. PK.
Buckover Farm
Upper Buckover Farm
Manorbrook Prim. Sch.
KENSINGTON CL.
PARK ROAD
HOWARD RD.
WHITFIELD RD.
COSSHAM ST.
DEAN AVENUE
SEVERN VIEW ROAD
SQUIRES LEAZE
NIGHTINGALE CL.
FULMAR CL.
KINGFISHER CL.
FALCON WY.
CELANDINE CL.
SPEEDWELL CL.
PRIMROSE DR.
MALLOW CL.
CAMPION CL.
PRIMROSE DRIVE
SORREL CLOSE
FOXGLOVE
BLUEBELL CL.
Play Area
COOMBE AV.
SEVERN ROAD
TILTING ROAD
NORTH EAST RD.
NORTH ROAD
EASTLAND AVENUE
PARK VIEW AV.
HAWTHORN CRES.
DAVIS ST.
EASTLAND ROAD
EASTON HILL ROAD
Crossways Farm
CROSSWAYS
WHITEWALL LANE
Crossways
Crossways House
Hillcrest
Milbury House
Buckover
The Cottage
Beechacres
Buckingham Pde.
THORNBURY HOSP.
PROWSE CL.
CASTLE COOMBE
The Castle Sch. Sixth Form Centre
EASTBURY CL.
EASTBURY RD.
Hall
Prim. School
LARKSPUR CL.
LAVENDER CL.
LAVENDER
New Siblands School
KNAPP RD.
HACKET LA.
THORNBURY
MORTON WAY
CROSSWAYS RD.
HACKET
Woodbine Farm
CLAY LANE
The Folly
CHAPEL LA.
Playing Field
MAPLE AVENUE
WOODLEIGH
PINE CL.
THICKET WLK.
SYCAMORE DR.
CHESTNUT DR.
HAZEL CR.
WALNUT CL.
HAZEL CR.
ORCHARD AV.
ELMDALE CRES.
ST. DAVID'S
BLAKES RD.
CRISPIN
COLIN CL.
ROVESEND RD.
OAKLEAZE
ASHGROVE
KNAPP ROAD
THE PADDOCKS
SIBLAND RD.
Crossways Jun. & Inf. Schools
CUMBRIA CL.
CUMBRIA RD.
JUBILEE DRIVE
JUBILEE DR.
The Hacket
CUTTSHEATH
A38
Gillingstool
GILLINGSTOOL
SIBLAND WAY
SPRINGFIELD
MEADOWSIDE
HOMEFIELD
CLEVELAND CL.
CHEVIOT DRIVE
CHEVIOT AV.
PENTLAND AV.
PENTLAND DR.
Garden Centre
Gillingstool Nursery
Gillingstool Prim. Sch.
PEARCE CL.
SPEY CL.
GROVESEND ROAD
ELIZABETH CL.
MALVERN DR.
MALVERN DRIVE
CHILTERN PARK
Bristol
BS35
Hacket Farm
The Meadows
HACKET LANE
HACKET HILL
Water Tower
BATH RD.
The Bathings
Frome Ct.
Frome Ct. Ho.
COLN CL.
HAMBLE CLOSE
HAMBLE CL.
Sub.
ELLESMERE
COMBERMERE
HATCHMERE
MEDWAY CT.
SHANNON CT.
DERWENT CL.
KENNET WY.
HILLBROOK
STREAMLEAZE
DART CL.
USK CL.
AXE CL.
TWEED CL.
LADDEN CT.
WINDRUSH CT.
WYE CT.
RIBBLESDALE
WHARFEDALE
DOVEDALE
TRENT DR.
SOLENT WY.
WATERFORD
TAMAR CL.
BOCKENEM CL.
Cleve Wood
MIDLAND WAY
Depot
THORNBURY INDUSTRIAL PARK
MEDINA CL.
CHERWELL CT.
ESKDALE
BROOKMEAD
AVON WAY
HOPKINS CL.
ARMSTRONG CL.
Works
SHORT WAY
COOPER RD.
Wks.
Depots
ASHVILLE PARK
West Winds
Cleve Wood Farm
Grovesend
Larches Farm
Vilner Farm
ABBEY LANE
Filnore Woods
The Grove Farm
Grovesend Farm
TYTHERINGTON ROAD
ITCHINGTON ROAD
The Stud
The Abbey
Fort
Tytherington Quarry
STOW
Grovesend Quarry (Stone)
The Castle Fort
M5 MOTORWAY
M5
WEST
NEW STREET
NEW LANE
THE
Manor Farm
Grove House
Upper Plantation
ITCHINGTON RD.
Grove Farm
Lower
A B C D E
1 2 3 4 5 6 7
64 65 66
88 89 90 91
11
20

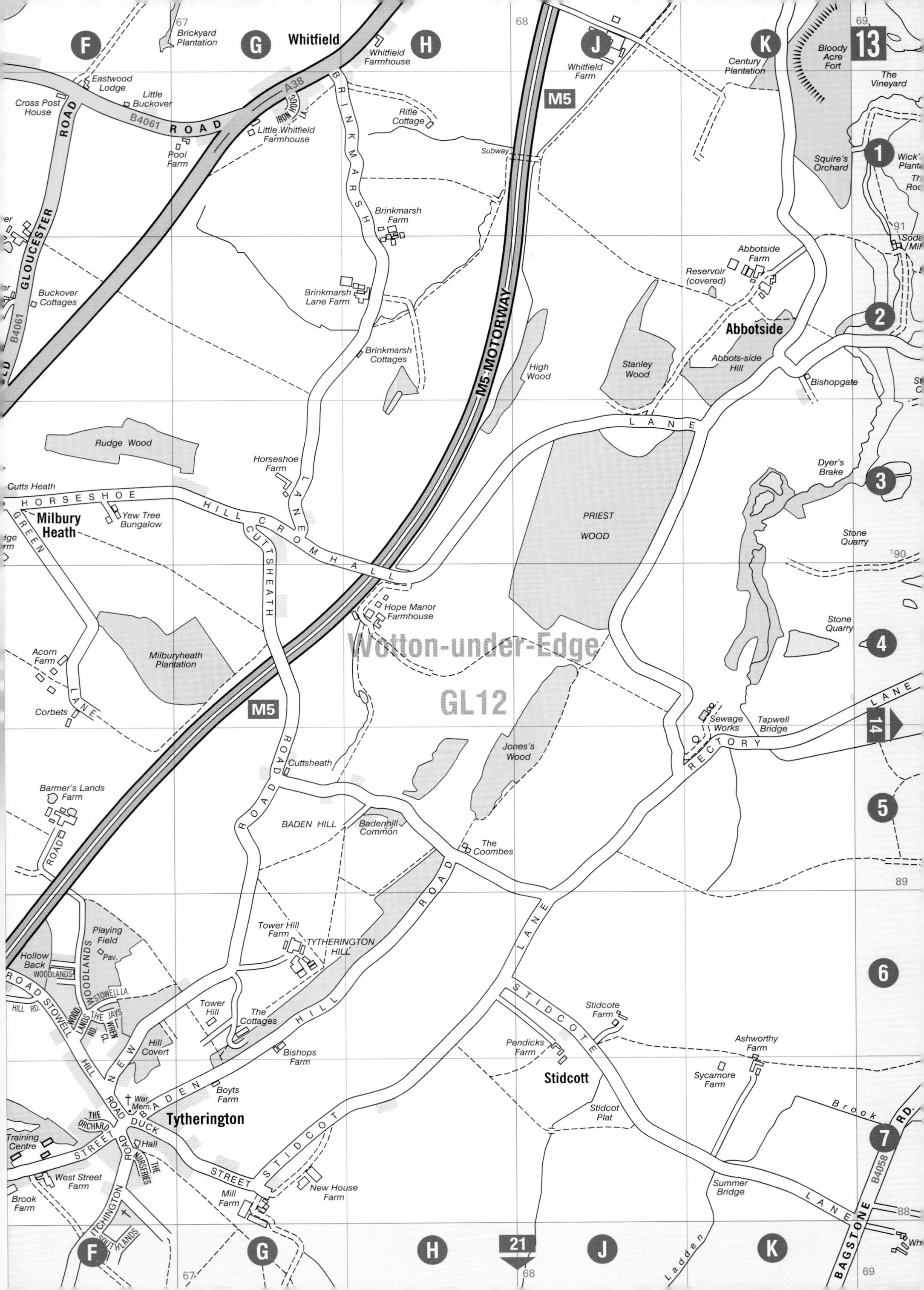

13
Whitfield
Brickyard Plantation
Whitfield Farmhouse
Whitfield Farm
Century Plantation
Bloody Acre Fort
The Vineyard
Eastwood Lodge
Little Buckover
Cross Post House
B4061 ROAD
A38
IRON HOGS LA.
Rifle Cottage
Little Whitfield Farmhouse
Pool Farm
M5
Subway
Squire's Orchard
Wick' Plant
91
GLOUCESTER ROAD
B4061
Buckover Cottages
BRINKMARSH LANE
Brinkmarsh Farm
Brinkmarsh Lane Farm
Brinkmarsh Cottages
M5 MOTORWAY
Abbotside Farm
Reservoir (covered)
Abbotside
Abbots-side Hill
Stanley Wood
High Wood
Bishopgate
Rudge Wood
Horseshoe Farm
LANE
Cutts Heath
HORSESHOE HILL
Milbury Heath
Yew Tree Bungalow
CROMHALL LANE
Dyer's Brake
PRIEST WOOD
Stone Quarry
90
CUTTSHEATH ROAD
Hope Manor Farmhouse
Wotton-under-Edge
GL12
Acorn Farm
Milburyheath Plantation
GREEN LANE
Corbets
Jones's Wood
Sewage Works
Tapwell Bridge
RECTORY LANE
14
Cuttsheath
Barmer's Lands Farm
BADEN HILL
Badenhill Common
The Coombes
ROAD
89
Playing Field
Pav.
Tower Hill Farm
TYTHERINGTON HILL
Hollow Back
WOODLANDS
STOWELL LA.
STOWELL HILL RD.
THE JAYS
WREN CL.
Tower Hill
The Cottages
Hill Covert
Bishops Farm
STIDCOTE LANE
Stidcote Farm
Pendicks Farm
Stidcott
Ashworthy Farm
Sycamore Farm
Stidcot Plat
Brook
RD.
War Mem.
BADEN HILL ROAD
Boyts Farm
Tytherington
DUCK STREET
THE ORCHARD
Training Centre
Hall
THE NURSERIES
West Street Farm
STIDCOT LANE
New House Farm
Mill Farm
Brook Farm
ITCHINGTON ROAD
SOUTHLANDS
Summer Bridge
B4058
BAGSTONE
88
Ladden
F
G
H
J
K
1
2
3
4
5
6
7
21
67
68
69

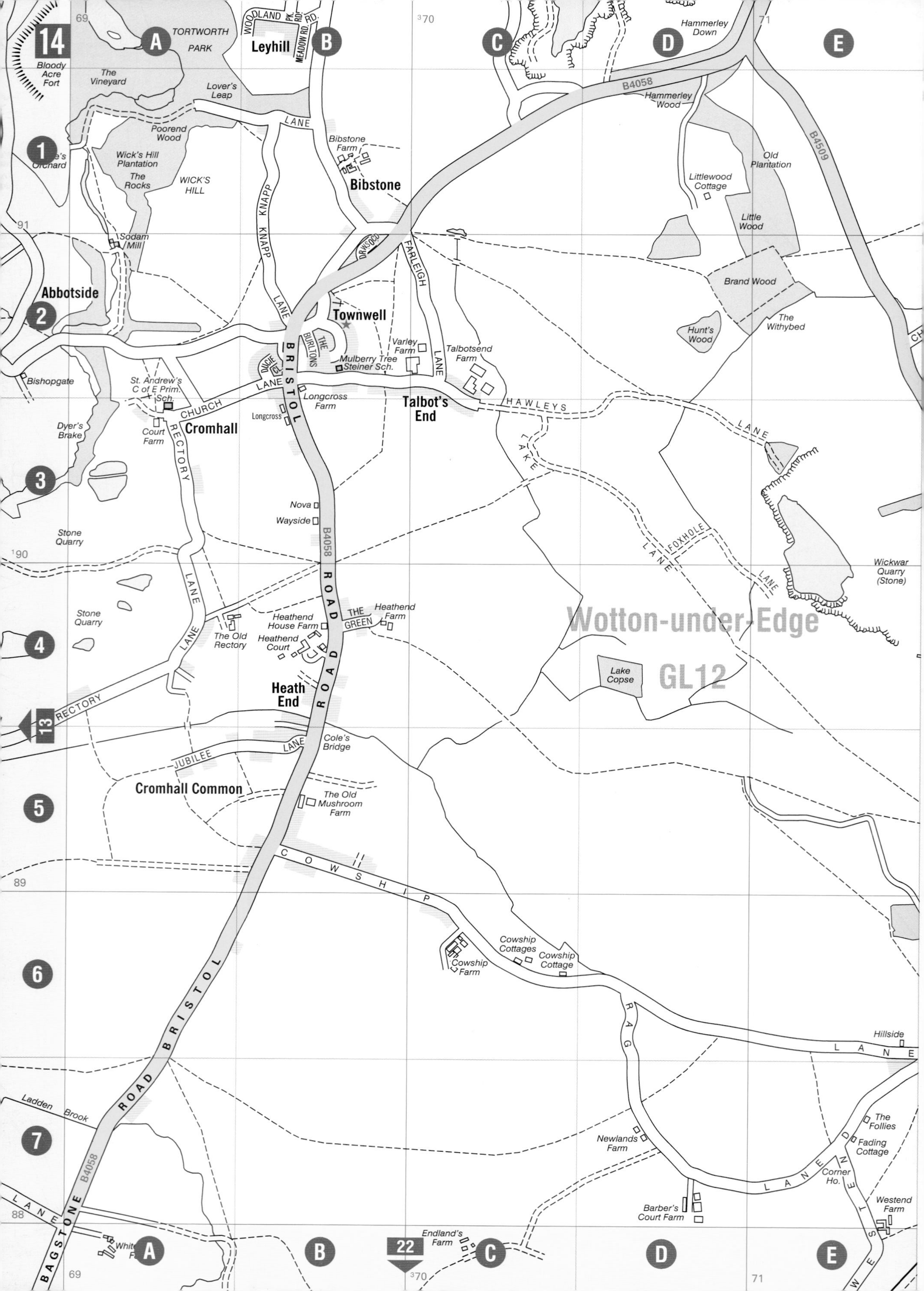

Bloody Acre Fort
TORTWORTH PARK
The Vineyard
Lover's Leap
Leyhill
WOODLAND RD.
PK. RD.
MEADOW RD.
Hammerley Down
B4058
Hammerley Wood
Poorend Wood
Wick's Hill Plantation
The Rocks
WICK'S HILL
Bibstone Farm
Bibstone
Old Plantation
B4509
Littlewood Cottage
Little Wood
Sodam Mill
Abbotside
KNAPP
LANE
FARLEIGH
DAWSCOTE
Townwell
THE BURLTONS
Varley Farm
Mulberry Tree Steiner Sch.
Talbotsend Farm
Brand Wood
The Withybed
Hunt's Wood
Bishopgate
St. Andrew's C of E Prim. Sch.
CHURCH LANE
DACIE CL.
BRISTOL
Longcross Farm
Longcross
Talbot's End
HAWLEYS LANE
Cromhall
Court Farm
RECTORY
Dyer's Brake
LAKE
Nova
Wayside
Stone Quarry
FOXHOLE LANE
Wickwar Quarry (Stone)
Heathend House Farm
Heathend Court
THE GREEN
Heathend Farm
The Old Rectory
Wotton-under-Edge
GL12
Lake Copse
Heath End
ROAD
Cole's Bridge
JUBILEE LANE
Cromhall Common
The Old Mushroom Farm
COWSHIP
Cowship Cottages
Cowship Cottage
Cowship Farm
RAG
Hillside
Ladden Brook
The Follies
Fading Cottage
Newlands Farm
Corner Ho.
Westend Farm
Barber's Court Farm
BAGSTONE LANE
WEST END
Endland's Farm
22
13

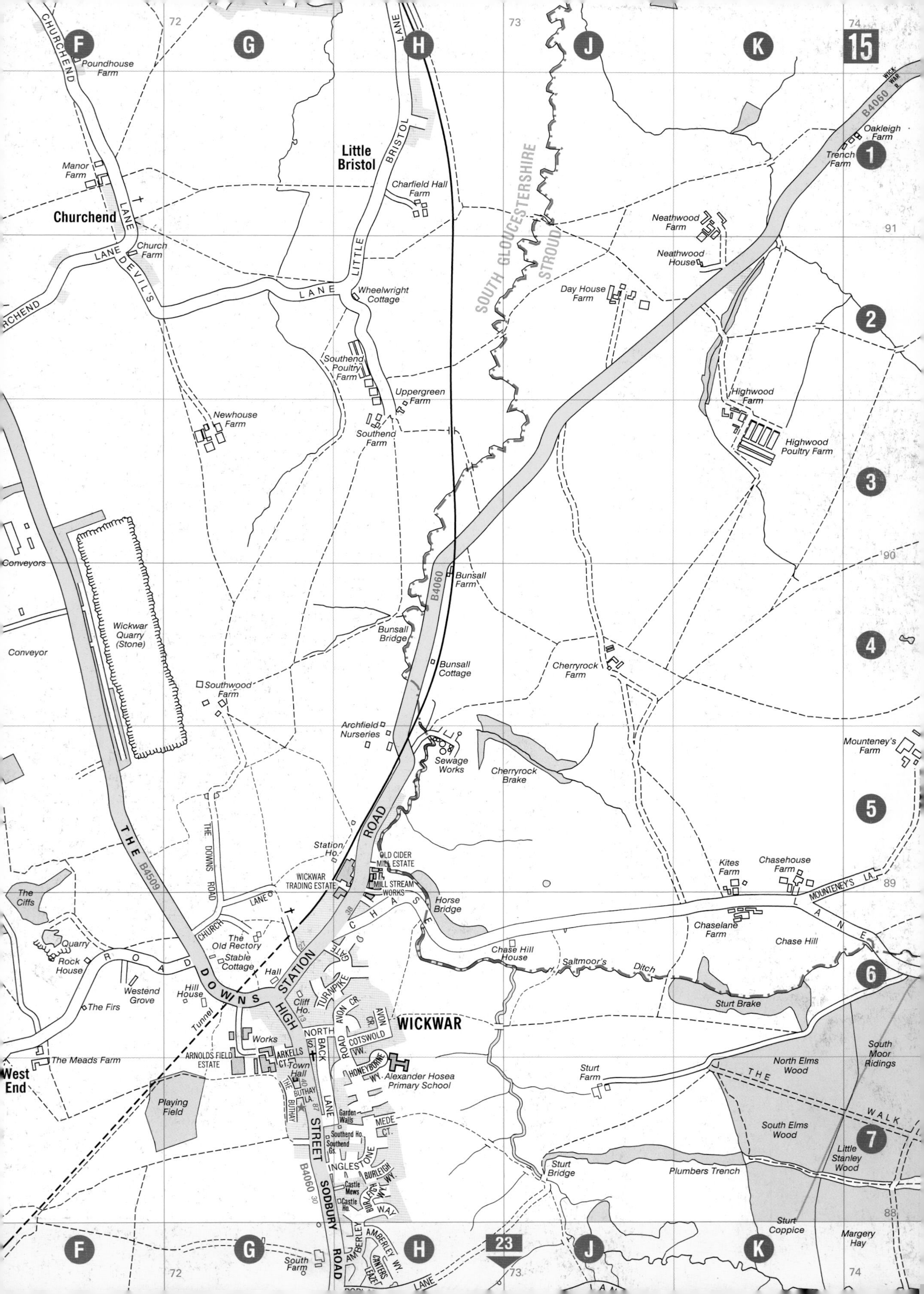
Churchend
Poundhouse Farm
Manor Farm
Church Farm
Devil's Lane
Little Bristol
Charfield Hall Farm
Wheelwright Cottage
Southend Poultry Farm
Uppergreen Farm
Southend Farm
Newhouse Farm
South Gloucestershire
Stroud
Oakleigh Farm
Trench Farm
Neathwood Farm
Neathwood House
Day House Farm
Highwood Farm
Highwood Poultry Farm
Conveyors
Conveyor
Wickwar Quarry (Stone)
Bunsall Farm
Bunsall Bridge
Bunsall Cottage
Cherryrock Farm
Southwood Farm
Archfield Nurseries
Sewage Works
Cherryrock Brake
Mounteney's Farm
Station Ho.
Old Cider Mill Estate
Wickwar Trading Estate
Mill Stream Works
Horse Bridge
Kites Farm
Chasehouse Farm
Mounteney's La.
Chaselane Farm
Chase Hill
Chase Lane
Chase Hill House
Saltmoor's Ditch
Sturt Brake
The Cliffs
Quarry
Rock House
The Old Rectory
Stable Cottage
Hall
Hill House
Westend Grove
The Firs
The Downs
Station Road
High Street
The Downs Road
Church Lane
Cliff Ho.
Turnpike
Gate
Avon Cr.
North Back Lane
Cotswold Vw.
Wickwar
Honeyborne Wy.
Alexander Hosea Primary School
Tunnel
Works
Arnolds Field Estate
Arkells Ct.
Town Hall
The Buthay
Buthay La.
The Meads Farm
West End
Playing Field
Garden Walls
Mede Ct.
Southend Ho.
Southend Gs.
Inglestone
Burleigh Wy.
Castle Mews
Castle Ho.
Burleigh Way
Amberley
Amberley Wy.
Sodbury Road
Sturt Farm
North Elms Wood
South Moor Ridings
The Walk
South Elms Wood
Little Stanley Wood
Sturt Bridge
Plumbers Trench
Sturt Coppice
Margery Hay
South Farm
B4060
B4509
Wickwar Rd.
F G H J K
1 2 3 4 5 6 7
72 73 74
88 89 90 91

23

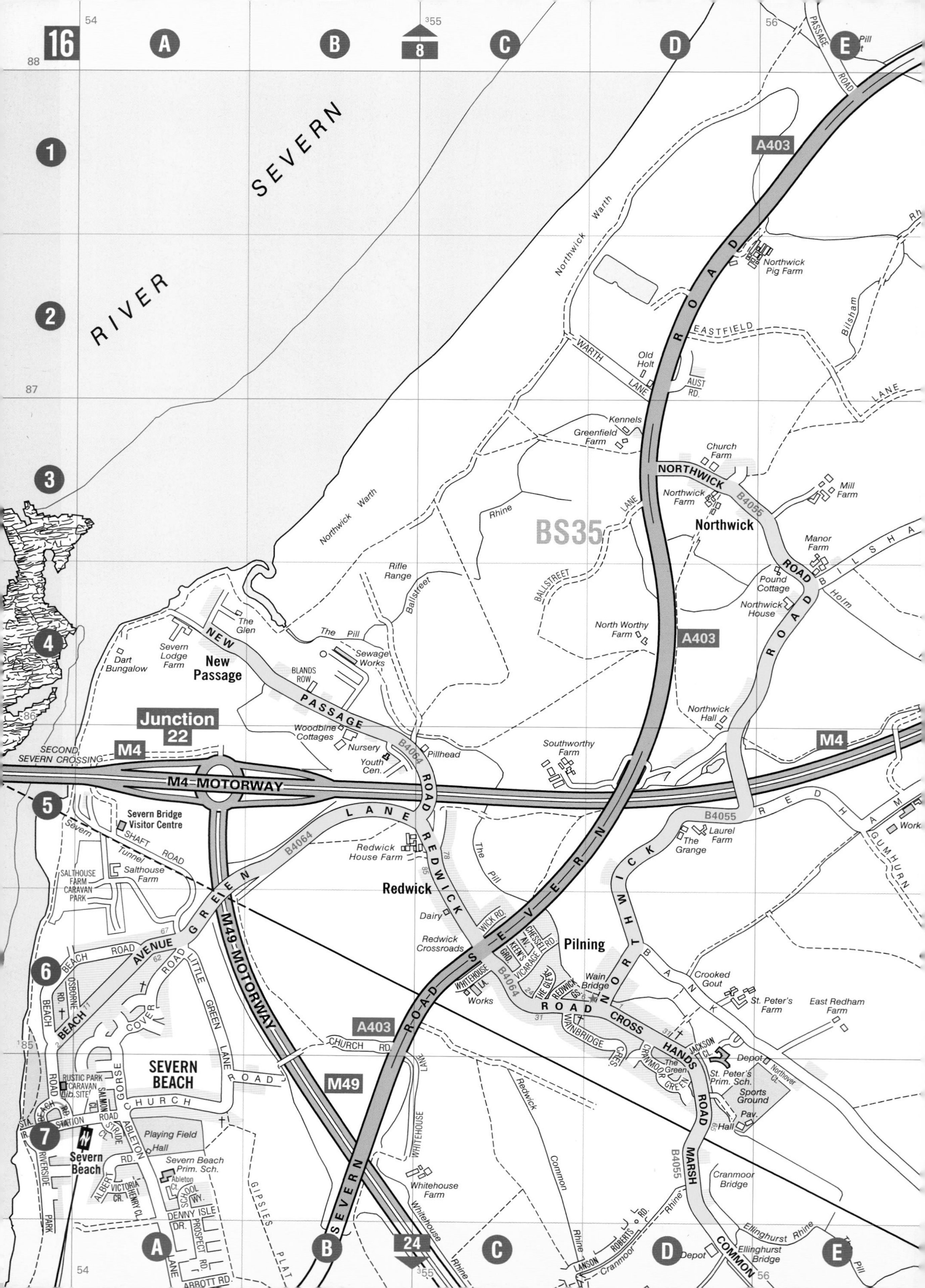
A
B
C
D
E
8
RIVER SEVERN
A403
Northwick Warth
Northwick Pig Farm
EASTFIELD
WARTH LANE
Old Holt
AUST RD.
Kennels
Greenfield Farm
Church Farm
NORTHWICK
Northwick Farm
Mill Farm
Northwick
BS35
Rifle Range
Ballstreet
BALLSTREET
Manor Farm
Pound Cottage
Northwick House
North Worthy Farm
The Glen
The Pill
Sewage Works
Dart Bungalow
Severn Lodge Farm
New Passage
NEW PASSAGE
BLANDS ROW
Woodbine Cottages
Nursery
Youth Cen.
Pillhead
Junction 22
M4
SECOND SEVERN CROSSING
M4 MOTORWAY
Northwick Hall
Southworthy Farm
Severn Bridge Visitor Centre
SHAFT ROAD
Severn Tunnel
SALTHOUSE FARM CARAVAN PARK
Salthouse Farm
LANE
REDWICK ROAD
Redwick House Farm
B4064
B4055
Laurel Farm
The Grange
REDHAM
GUMHURN
Work
Redwick
Dairy
WICK RD.
Redwick Crossroads
Pilning
SEVERN ROAD
NORTHWICK ROAD
M49 MOTORWAY
GREEN LANE
AVENUE
BEACH ROAD
OSBORNE RD.
COVE
LITTLE GREEN LANE
WHITEHOUSE LA.
Works
CHESSEL AV
KEEN'S GRO
VICARAGE RD.
THE GLEBE
REDWICK GS.
Wain Bridge
CROSS HANDS ROAD
WAINBRIDGE CRES.
BANK
Crooked Gout
St. Peter's Farm
East Redham Farm
JACKSON CL.
Depot
Northover Cl.
St. Peter's Prim. Sch.
Sports Ground
Pav.
Hall
The Green
CRANMOOR GREEN
CHURCH RD.
A403
SEVERN BEACH
RUSTIC PARK CARAVAN
Lib. SITE
SALMON CL.
GORSE
CHURCH ROAD
STATION ROAD
STRIDE CL.
ABLETON
Playing Field
Hall
Severn Beach
Severn Beach Prim. Sch.
Ableton Ct.
SCHOOL WY.
ALBERT RD.
VICTORIA CR.
HENRY CL.
DENNY ISLE DR.
PROSPECT RD.
ABBOTT RD.
RIVERSIDE PARK
GIPSIES PLAT
M49
WHITEHOUSE LANE
Whitehouse Farm
Whitehouse Rhine
Redwick Common Rhine
B4055
MARSH COMMON
Cranmoor Bridge
Ellinghurst Rhine
Ellinghurst Bridge
ROBERTS RD.
LANSON
Cranmoor Rhine
Depot
The Pill
PASSAGE ROAD
Pill
Bilsham
BILSHAM
Holm
24
54
355
56
88
87
86
85

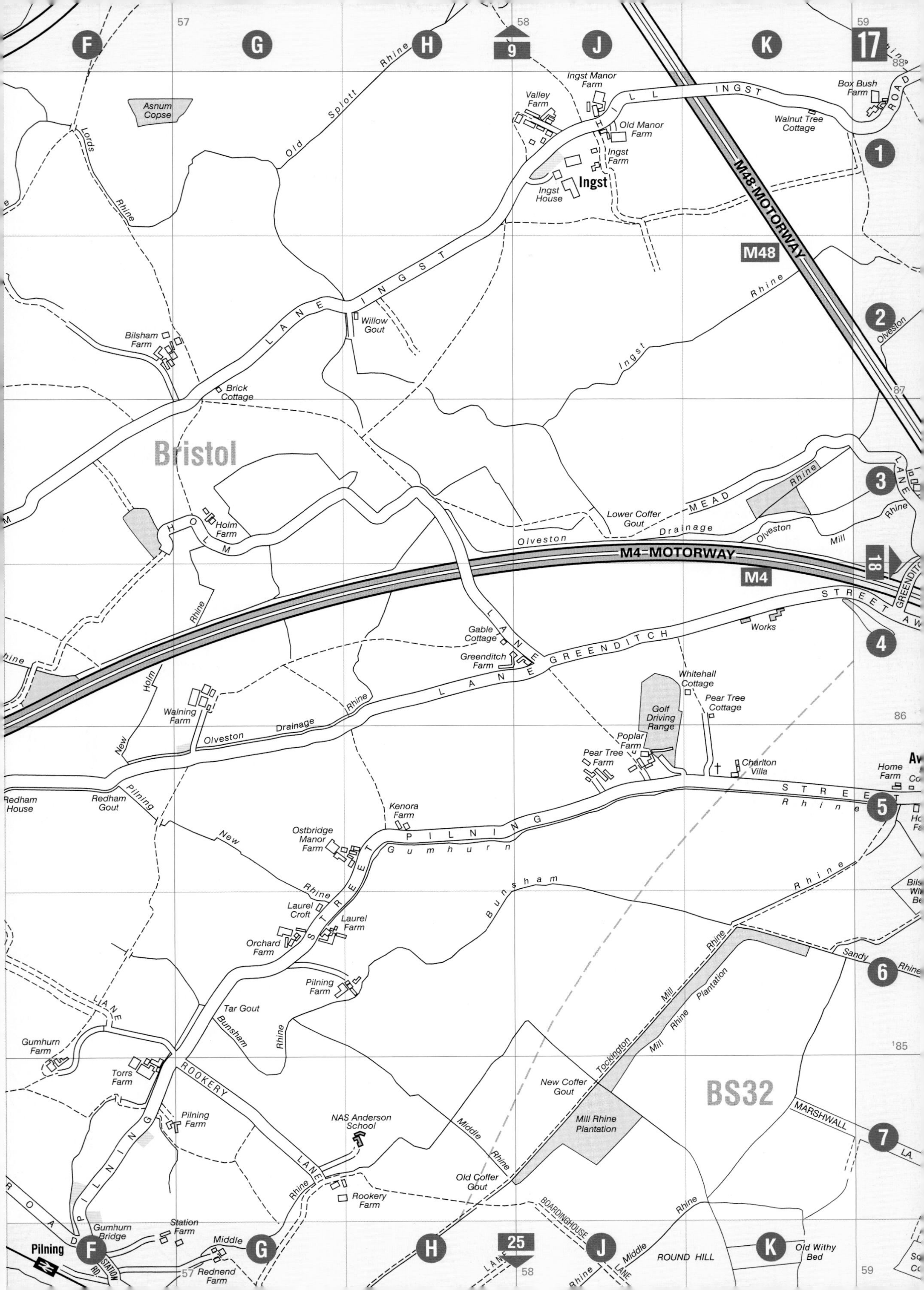
F
G
H
J
K
57
58
59
9
88
87
86
85
1
2
3
4
5
6
7
18
25
Asnum Copse
Lords Rhine
Old Splott Rhine
Ingst Manor Farm
Valley Farm
Box Bush Farm
Walnut Tree Cottage
Old Manor Farm
Ingst Farm
Ingst
Ingst House
HILL
INGST
ROAD
M48-MOTORWAY
M48
LANE INGST
Willow Gout
Bilsham Farm
Brick Cottage
Rhine
Ingst
Olveston
Bristol
Holm Farm
HOLM
Lower Coffer Gout
MEAD
Drainage
Olveston
Olveston
Rhine
Mill
LANE
M4-MOTORWAY
M4
STREET
GREENDITCH
Works
Gable Cottage
Greenditch Farm
GREENDITCH
LANE
Holm
Walning Farm
New
Olveston
Drainage
Rhine
Whitehall Cottage
Pear Tree Cottage
Golf Driving Range
Poplar Farm
Pear Tree Farm
Charlton Villa
Home Farm
STREET
Rhine
Redham House
Redham Gout
Pilning
New
Kenora Farm
Ostbridge Manor Farm
PILNING
Gumhurn
Rhine
STREET
Bunsham
Rhine
Laurel Croft
Laurel Farm
Orchard Farm
Sandy
Rhine
Mill
Rhine
Plantation
Mill
Rhine
Pilning Farm
Tar Gout
Bunsham
Rhine
LANE
Gumhurn Farm
Torrs Farm
ROOKERY
Tockington
New Coffer Gout
BS32
MARSHWALL
LA.
Pilning Farm
NAS Anderson School
Middle
Rhine
Mill Rhine Plantation
LANE
Old Coffer Gout
Rhine
Rookery Farm
BOARDINGHOUSE
ROAD
PILNING
Station Farm
Gumhurn Bridge
Middle
Pilning
STATION RD.
Rednend Farm
Rhine
Middle
LANE
ROUND HILL
Old Withy Bed

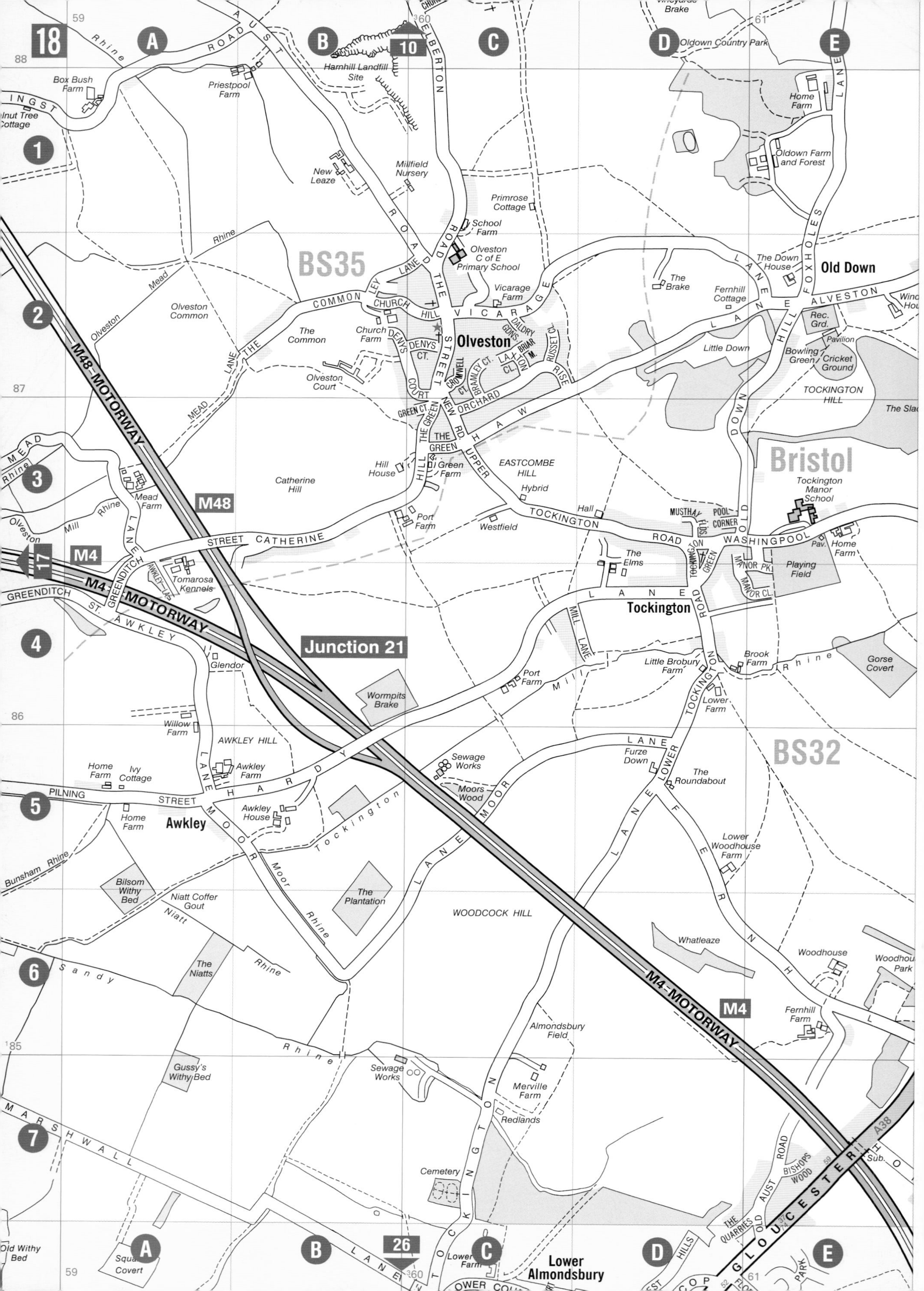

Olveston
Old Down
Tockington
Awkley
Lower Almondsbury
Bristol
BS35
BS32
Junction 21
M48 MOTORWAY
M4 MOTORWAY
M48
M4
Harnhill Landfill Site
Oldown Country Park
Box Bush Farm
Priestpool Farm
New Leaze
Millfield Nursery
Primrose Cottage
School Farm
Olveston C of E Primary School
Home Farm
Oldown Farm and Forest
The Down House
The Brake
Fernhill Cottage
Vicarage Farm
Olveston Common
The Common
Church Farm
Olveston Court
Little Down
Rec. Grd.
Pavilion
Bowling Green
Cricket Ground
TOCKINGTON HILL
Catherine Hill
Hill House
Green Farm
EASTCOMBE HILL
Hybrid
Hall
Westfield
Port Farm
Mead Farm
Tockington Manor School
Tomarosa Kennels
The Elms
Playing Field
Glendor
Wormpits Brake
Little Brobury Farm
Brook Farm
Gorse Covert
Lower Farm
Willow Farm
AWKLEY HILL
Home Farm
Ivy Cottage
Awkley Farm
Sewage Works
Moors Wood
Furze Down
The Roundabout
Awkley House
Bilsom Withy Bed
Niatt Coffer Gout
The Plantation
WOODCOCK HILL
Lower Woodhouse Farm
Whatleaze
Woodhouse
Woodhouse Park
Fernhill Farm
The Niatts
Almondsbury Field
Gussy's Withy Bed
Merville Farm
Redlands
Cemetery
Old Withy Bed
Square Covert
Lower Farm

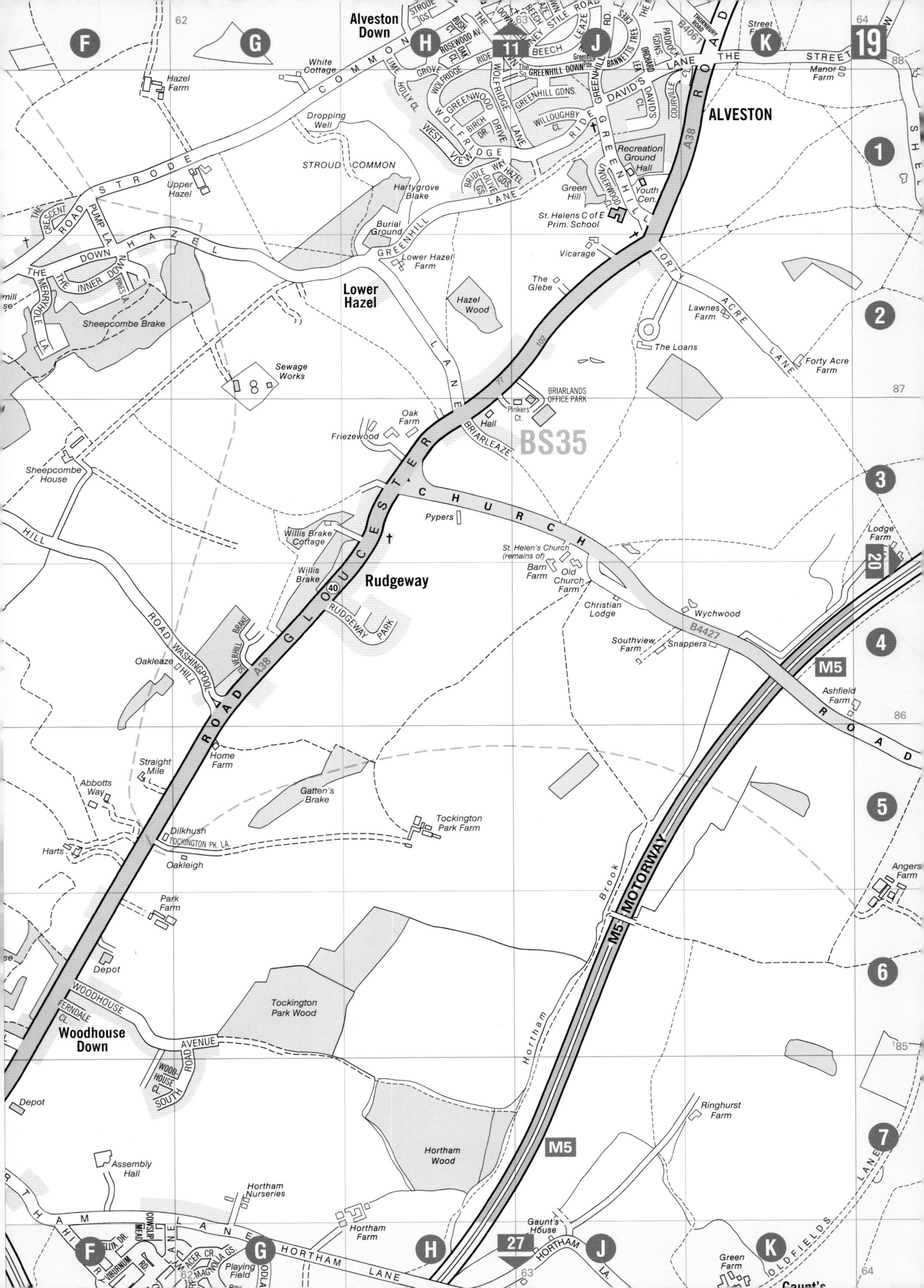
Alveston Down
Hazel Farm
White Cottage
COMMON
Dropping Well
STROUD COMMON
STRODE ROAD
Upper Hazel
Hartygrove Blake
Burial Ground
GREENHILL LANE
Lower Hazel Farm
Lower Hazel
DOWN HAZEL
THE INNER DOWN
THE MERRYHOLE LA.
PINES LA.
PUMP LA.
THE CRESCENT
Sheepcombe Brake
Sewage Works
Hazel Wood
ALVESTON
Recreation Ground Hall
Youth Cen.
Green Hill
St. Helens C of E Prim. School
Vicarage
The Glebe
FORTY ACRE LANE
Lawnes Farm
The Loans
Forty Acre Farm
Manor Farm
THE STREET
Street Farm
BRIARLANDS OFFICE PARK
Pinkers Ct.
Hall
Oak Farm
Friezewood
BRIARLEAZE
BS35
Sheepcombe House
HILL
GLOUCESTER ROAD
A38
CHURCH
Pypers
Willis Brake Cottage
Willis Brake
Rudgeway
RUDGEWAY PARK
St. Helen's Church (remains of)
Barn Farm
Old Church Farm
Christian Lodge
Wychwood
B4427
Southview Farm
Snappers
Lodge Farm
20
M5
Ashfield Farm
ROAD
WASHINGPOOL HILL ROAD
SILVERHILL BRAKE
Oakleaze
Home Farm
Straight Mile
Abbotts Way
Gatten's Brake
Tockington Park Farm
Dilkhush
TOCKINGTON PK. LA.
Harts
Oakleigh
Park Farm
M5 MOTORWAY
Brook
Angers Farm
Depot
WOODHOUSE AVENUE
FERNDALE CL.
Woodhouse Down
Tockington Park Wood
WOODHOUSE CL.
SOUTH ROAD
Hortham
Hortham Wood
Ringhurst Farm
Assembly Hall
Hortham Nurseries
Hortham Farm
HORTHAM LANE
COWSLIP MEAD
VIBURNUM RD.
ACER CR.
MAGNOLIA GS.
Playing Field
Gaunt's House
HORTHAM LA.
27
11
Green Farm
OLDFIELDS LANE
B4061
THORNBURY ROAD
GREENHILL DOWN
DAVID'S LANE
WOLFRIDGE RIDE
GREENWOOD
BIRCH DR.
WEST VIEW
HOLLY CL.
GROVE
ROSEWOOD AV.
BEECH
WILLOUGHBY CL.
GREENHILL GDNS.
BANNETTS TREE CRES.
ORCHARD LEA
PADDOCK GDNS.
COURVILLE CL.
UNDERWOOD CL.
BRIDLE WAY
OLIVE GDS.
HAZEL GDS.
62
63
64
88
87
86
85
1
2
3
4
5
6
7
F
G
H
J
K

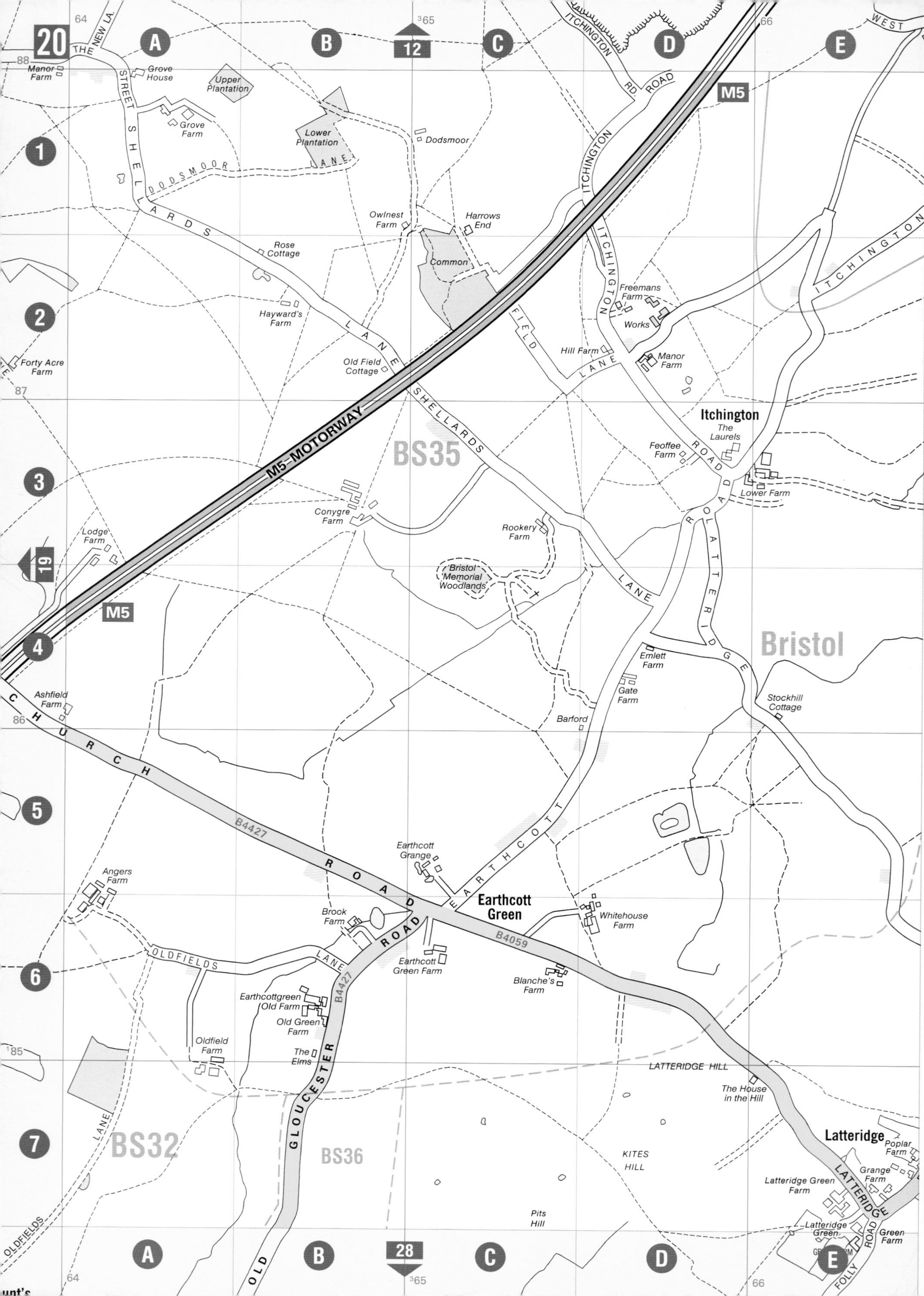

64
365
66
88
87
86
85
12
19
28
A
B
C
D
E
1
2
3
4
5
6
7
THE NEW LA.
Manor Farm
Grove House
Upper Plantation
Grove Farm
Lower Plantation
Dodsmoor
DODSMOOR LANE
STREET
SHELLARDS LANE
Owlnest Farm
Harrows End
Rose Cottage
Common
Hayward's Farm
Forty Acre Farm
Old Field Cottage
ITCHINGTON RD. ROAD
ITCHINGTON LANE
M5
M5 MOTORWAY
FIELD LANE
Freemans Farm
Works
Hill Farm
Manor Farm
WEST
ITCHINGTON
Itchington
The Laurels
Feoffee Farm
ROAD
Lower Farm
BS35
SHELLARDS
Conygre Farm
Rookery Farm
Lodge Farm
Bristol Memorial Woodlands
LANE
LATTERIDGE
Bristol
Emlett Farm
Gate Farm
Stockhill Cottage
Barford
Ashfield Farm
CHURCH ROAD
B4427
EARTHCOTT
Earthcott Grange
Angers Farm
Earthcott Green
Whitehouse Farm
Brook Farm
B4059
OLDFIELDS LANE
Earthcott Green Farm
Blanche's Farm
Earthcottgreen Old Farm
Old Green Farm
Oldfield Farm
The Elms
LATTERIDGE HILL
The House in the Hill
GLOUCESTER ROAD
BS32
BS36
KITES HILL
Latteridge
Poplar Farm
Grange Farm
Latteridge Green Farm
LATTERIDGE
Pits Hill
OLDFIELDS
OLD
Latteridge Green
Green Farm
FOLLY ROAD

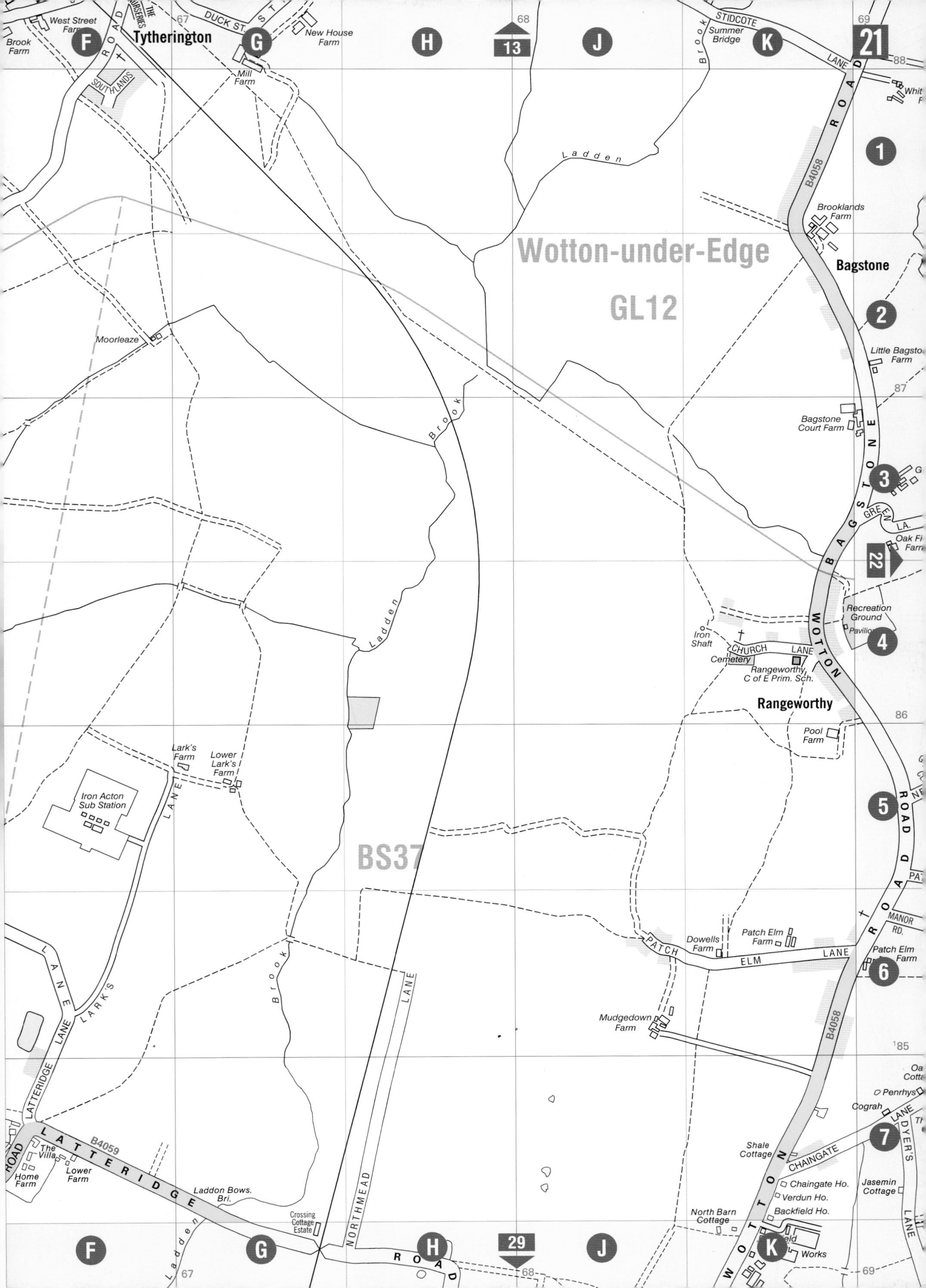

21
Tytherington
West Street Farm
Brook Farm
THE NURSERIES
ROAD
DUCK ST.
ST
New House Farm
Mill Farm
SOUTYLANDS
13
STIDCOTE
LANE
Summer Bridge
Brook
Ladden
B4058
ROAD
Brooklands Farm
Bagstone
Wotton-under-Edge
GL12
Little Bagstone Farm
Moorleaze
Brook
Bagstone Court Farm
BAGSTONE
GREEN LA.
Oak Fi Farm
22
Recreation Ground
Pavilion
WOTTON
Iron Shaft
CHURCH LANE
Cemetery
Rangeworthy C of E Prim. Sch.
Rangeworthy
Ladden
Pool Farm
Lark's Farm
Lower Lark's Farm
LANE
Iron Acton Sub Station
ROAD
BS37
MANOR RD.
Patch Elm Farm
Dowells Farm
PATCH ELM LANE
Patch Elm Farm
LARK'S LANE
Brook
NORTHMEAD LANE
Mudgedown Farm
B4058
LATTERIDGE LANE
Penrhys
Cograh
LANE
DYER'S LANE
Shale Cottage
CHAINGATE
Chaingate Ho.
Verdun Ho.
Backfield Ho.
Jasemin Cottage
LATTERIDGE
B4059
The Villa
Home Farm
Lower Farm
Laddon Bows. Bri.
Crossing Cottage Estate
North Barn Cottage
WOTTON
Works
ROAD
29
Ladden
F
G
H
J
K
1
2
3
4
5
6
7
67
68
69
88
87
86
85

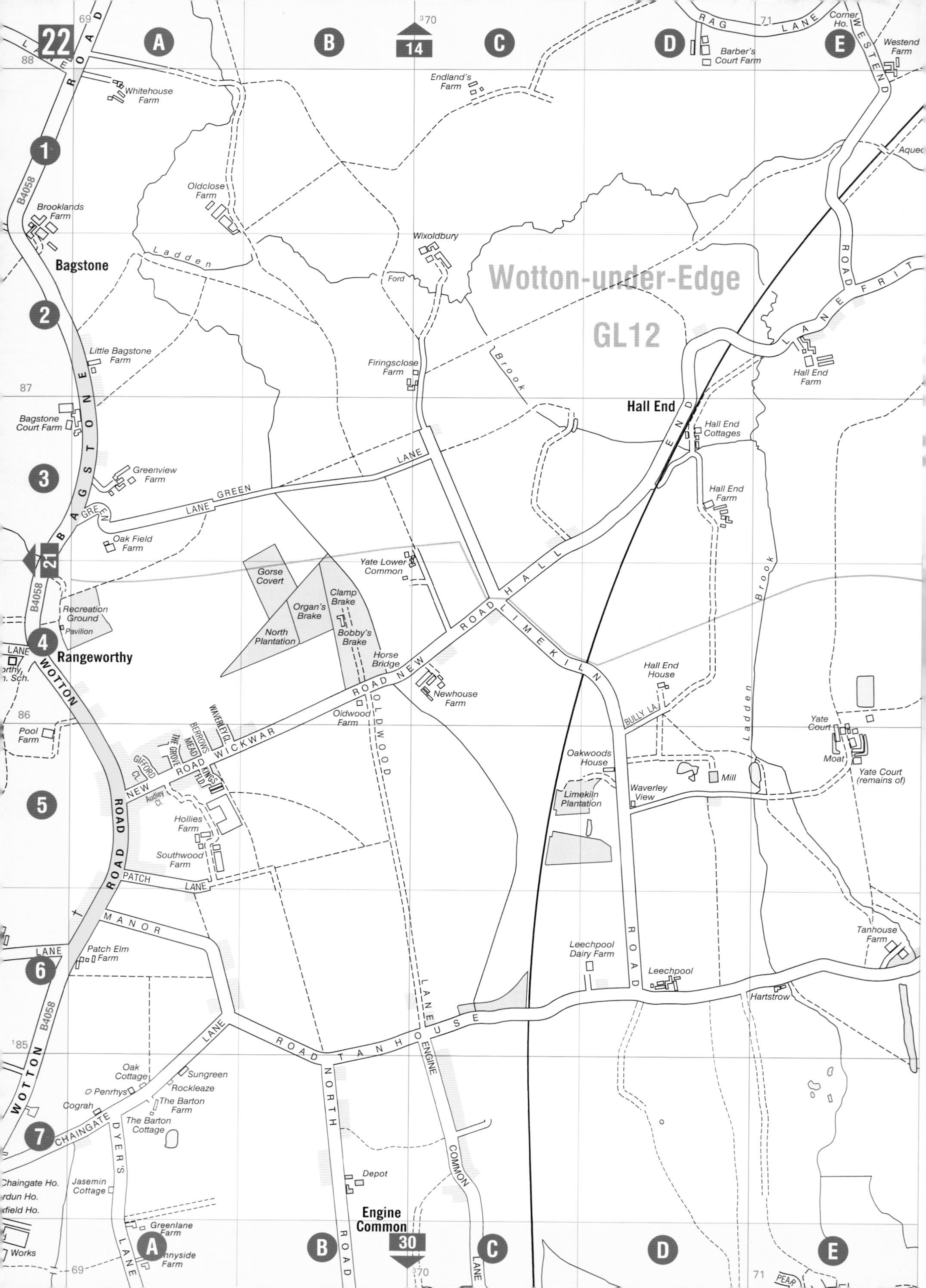
Wotton-under-Edge
GL12
Bagstone
Rangeworthy
Hall End
Engine Common
Whitehouse Farm
Brooklands Farm
Oldclose Farm
Endland's Farm
Barber's Court Farm
Westend Farm
Corner Ho.
Wixoldbury
Ford
Little Bagstone Farm
Firingsclose Farm
Bagstone Court Farm
Greenview Farm
Oak Field Farm
Hall End Farm
Hall End Cottages
Yate Lower Common
Gorse Covert
Clamp Brake
Organ's Brake
North Plantation
Bobby's Brake
Horse Bridge
Recreation Ground
Pavilion
Newhouse Farm
Oldwood Farm
Hall End House
Pool Farm
Oakwoods House
Limekiln Plantation
Waverley View
Mill
Yate Court
Moat
Yate Court (remains of)
Hollies Farm
Southwood Farm
Patch Elm Farm
Leechpool Dairy Farm
Leechpool
Hartstrow
Tanhouse Farm
Oak Cottage
Sungreen
Rockleaze
Penrhys
Cograh
The Barton Farm
The Barton Cottage
Jasemin Cottage
Chaingate Ho.
Depot
Greenlane Farm
Works
BAGSTONE ROAD
WOTTON ROAD
GREEN LANE
HALL END
NEW ROAD
WICKWAR ROAD
LIMEKILN
OLDWOOD
PATCH LANE
MANOR LANE
TANHOUSE ROAD
ENGINE COMMON LANE
NORTH ROAD
CHAINGATE
DYER'S LANE
RAG LANE
WESTEND ROAD
FRIT LANE
BULLY LA.
WAVERLEY CL.
BERROWS MEAD
THE GROVE
GIFFORD CL.
KINGS FD.
Audley Cl.
Ladden Brook
Brook
B4058
14
21
30
A
B
C
D
E
1
2
3
4
5
6
7
69
370
71
88
87
86
185

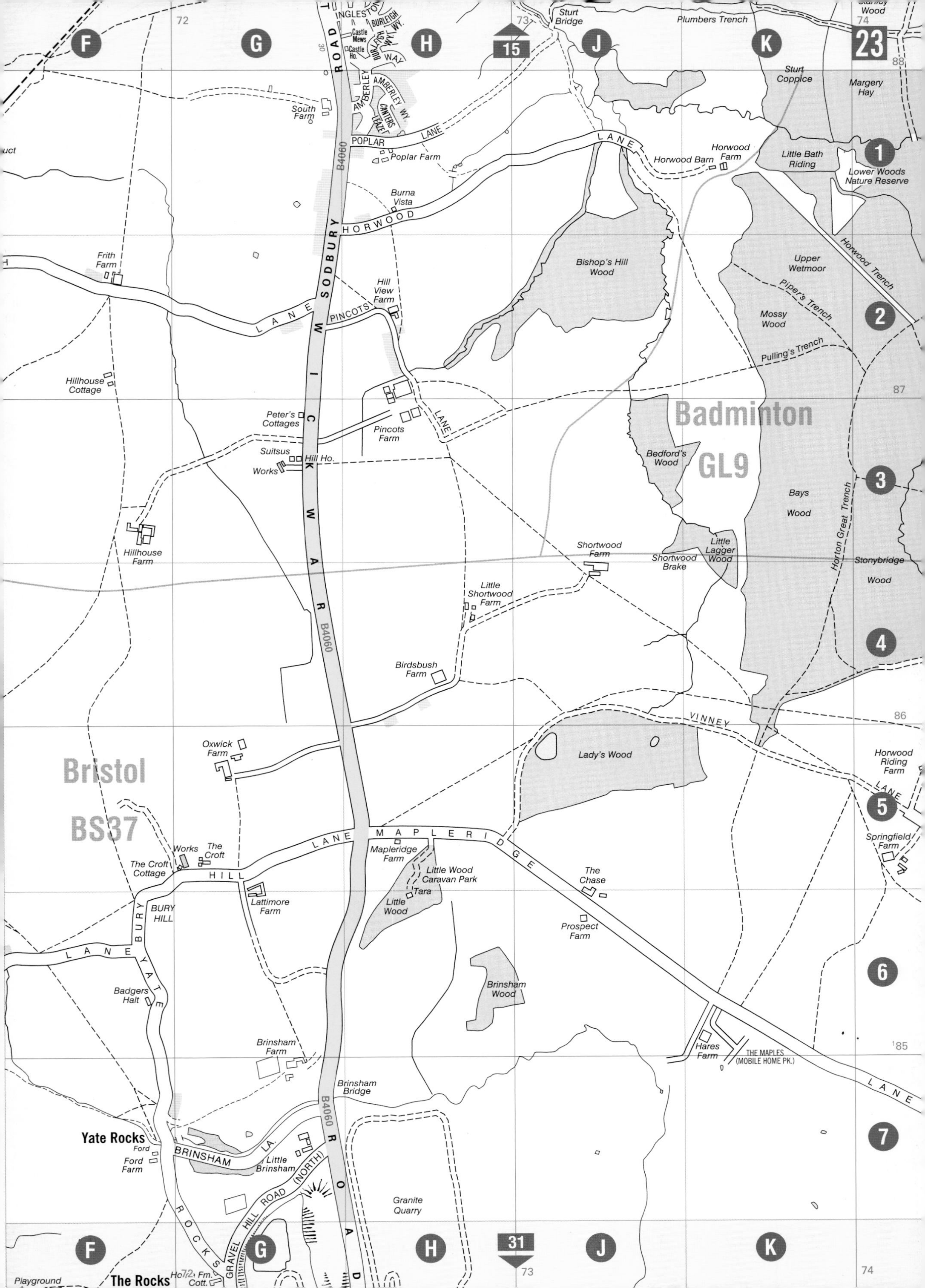
F
G
H
J
K
15
Sturt Bridge
Plumbers Trench
Stanley Wood
Sturt Coppice
Margery Hay
South Farm
POPLAR LANE
Poplar Farm
LANE
Horwood Barn
Horwood Farm
Little Bath Riding
Lower Woods Nature Reserve
Burna Vista
HORWOOD
Bishop's Hill Wood
Upper Wetmoor
Horwood Trench
Frith Farm
Hill View Farm
PINCOTS
LANE
Piper's Trench
Mossy Wood
Pulling's Trench
Hillhouse Cottage
Badminton
GL9
Peter's Cottages
Pincots Farm
LANE
Bedford's Wood
Suitsus
Hill Ho.
Works
Bays Wood
Horton Great Trench
Hillhouse Farm
Shortwood Farm
Shortwood Brake
Little Lagger Wood
Stonybridge Wood
Little Shortwood Farm
SODBURY ROAD
WICKWAR
B4060
Birdsbush Farm
VINNEY
Oxwick Farm
Lady's Wood
Horwood Riding Farm
LANE
Bristol
BS37
MAPLERIDGE LANE
Mapleridge Farm
Springfield Farm
Works
The Croft
The Croft Cottage
HILL
Little Wood Caravan Park
Tara
The Chase
Little Wood
Lattimore Farm
BURY HILL
BURY LANE
YATE
Prospect Farm
Brinsham Wood
Badgers Halt
Brinsham Farm
Hares Farm
THE MAPLES (MOBILE HOME PK.)
LANE
Brinsham Bridge
Yate Rocks
Ford
Ford Farm
BRINSHAM LA.
Little Brinsham
ROAD (NORTH)
GRAVEL HILL ROAD
Granite Quarry
ROCKS
31
Playground
The Rocks
Ho. Fm. Cott.
1
2
3
4
5
6
7
72
73
74
88
87
86
85

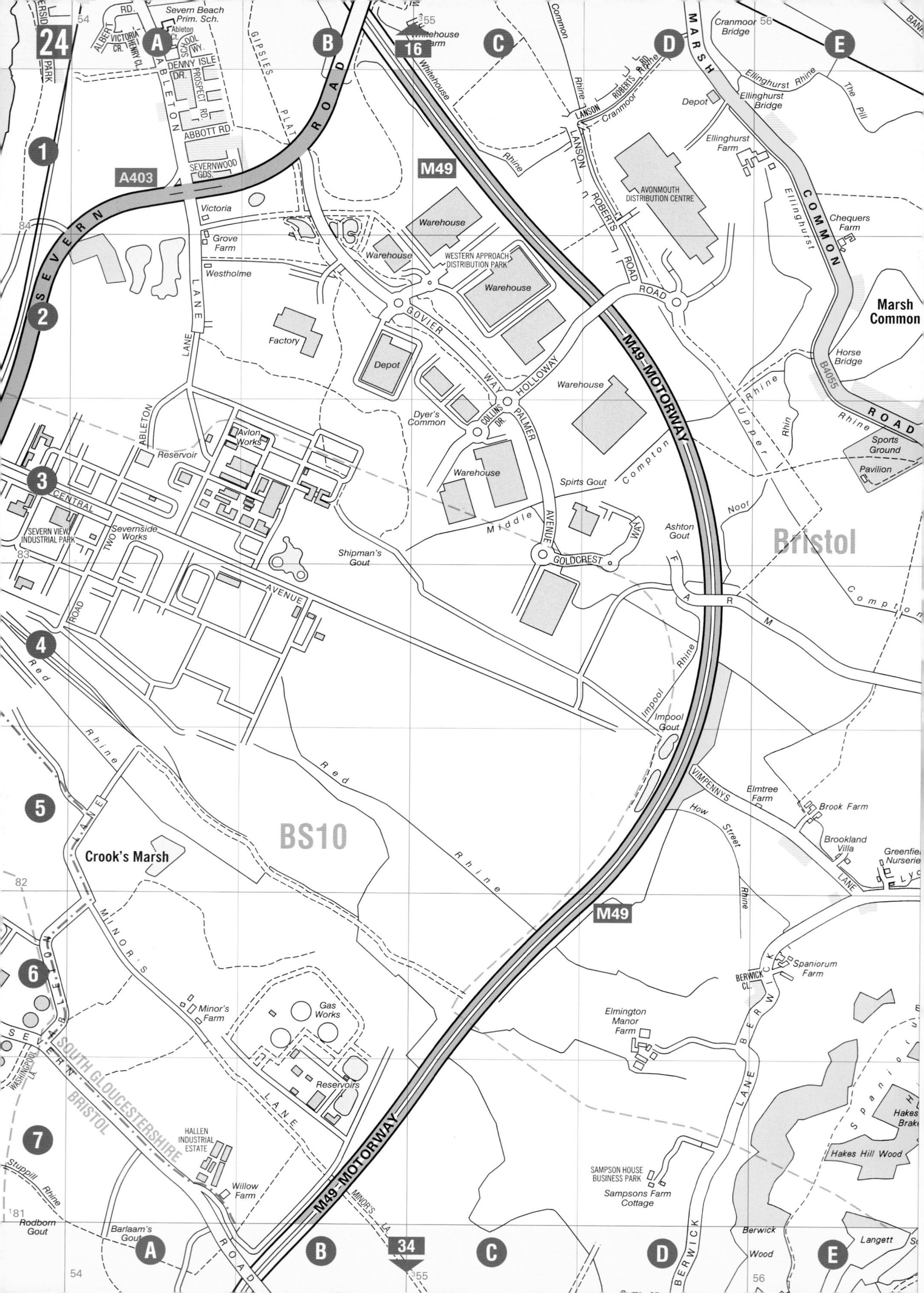
Severn Beach Prim. Sch.
Whitehouse Farm
16
Cranmoor Bridge
A403
SEVERN ROAD
M49
Victoria
Grove Farm
Westholme
Warehouse
WESTERN APPROACH DISTRIBUTION PARK
AVONMOUTH DISTRIBUTION CENTRE
Ellinghurst Bridge
Ellinghurst Farm
Depot
Chequers Farm
Marsh Common
Horse Bridge
B4055
Factory
Dyer's Common
Sports Ground
Pavilion
Reservoir
Avlon Works
SEVERN VIEW INDUSTRIAL PARK
Severnside Works
Spirts Gout
Ashton Gout
Shipman's Gout
Bristol
Impool Gout
Elmtree Farm
Brook Farm
Brookland Villa
BS10
Crook's Marsh
M49-MOTORWAY
Minor's Farm
Gas Works
Reservoirs
Spaniorum Farm
Elmington Manor Farm
HALLEN INDUSTRIAL ESTATE
Willow Farm
SOUTH GLOUCESTERSHIRE
BRISTOL
SAMPSON HOUSE BUSINESS PARK
Sampsons Farm Cottage
Hakes Hill Wood
Rodborn Gout
Barlaam's Gout
Berwick Wood
Langett
34

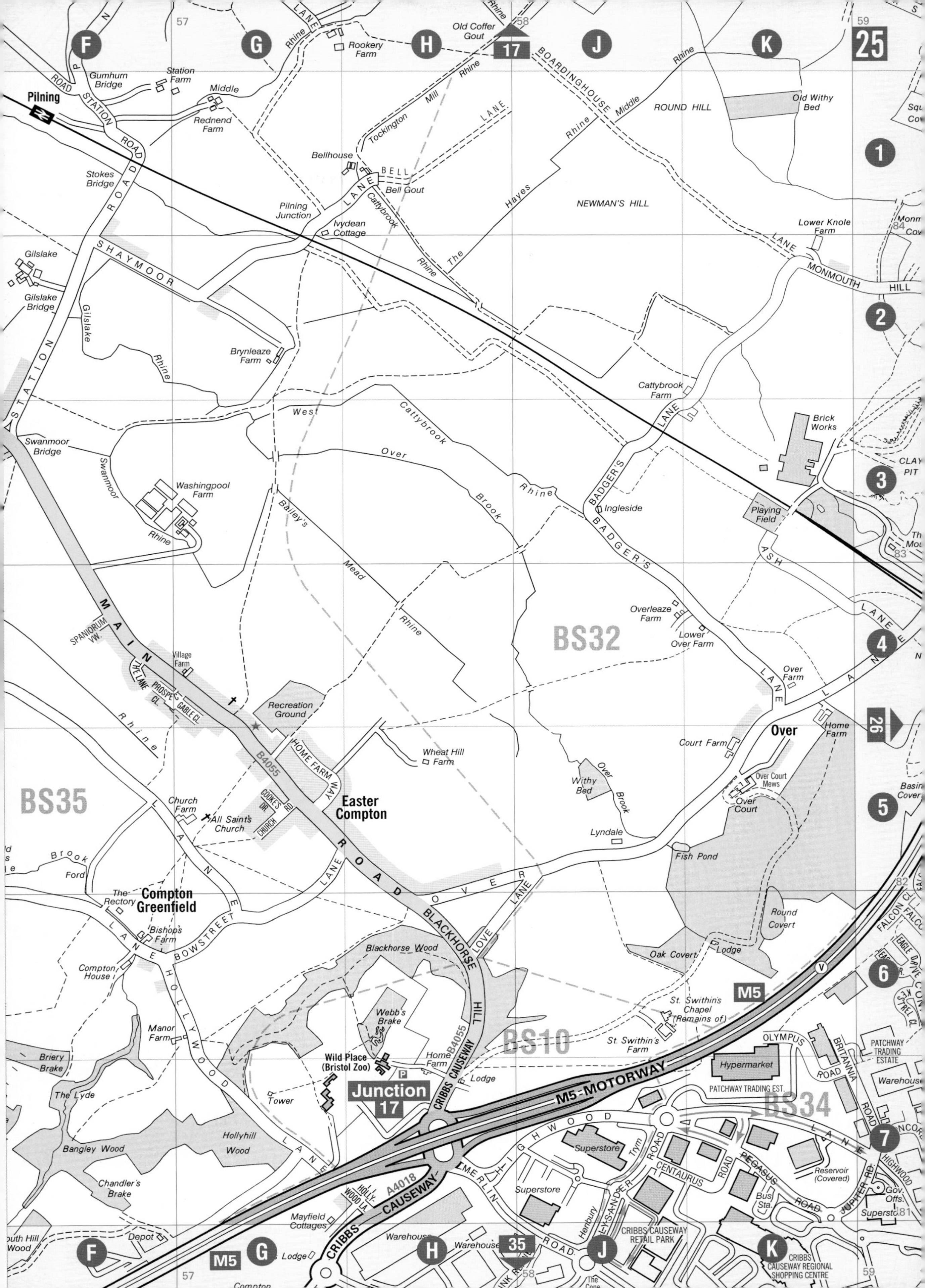

25
F
G
H
J
K
57
58
59
17
35
26
1
2
3
4
5
6
7
Pilning
Gumhurn Bridge
Station Farm
Middle
Rednend Farm
Stokes Bridge
STATION ROAD
Rookery Farm
Old Coffer Gout
Bellhouse
Bell Gout
Pilning Junction
Ivydean Cottage
Tockington Mill Rhine
BOARDINGHOUSE LANE
ROUND HILL
Old Withy Bed
NEWMAN'S HILL
The Hayes Rhine
Lower Knole Farm
MONMOUTH HILL
Gilslake
Gilslake Bridge
SHAYMOOR LANE
Brynleaze Farm
Cattybrook Farm
Brick Works
CLAY PIT
Swanmoor Bridge
Washingpool Farm
West
Cattybrook Over Brook Rhine
BADGER'S LANE
Ingleside
Playing Field
ASH LANE
Bailey's Mead Rhine
BS32
Overleaze Farm
Lower Over Farm
Over Farm
Over
Home Farm
Court Farm
SPANIORUM VW.
MAIN ROAD
Village Farm
THE LANE
PROSPECT CL.
GABLE CL.
Recreation Ground
HOME FARM WAY
Wheat Hill Farm
B4055
BS35
Church Farm
All Saint's Church
COOKE'S DR.
CHURCH RD
Easter Compton
Withy Bed
Over Court Mews
Over Court
Lyndale
Fish Pond
Brook
Ford
The Rectory
Compton Greenfield
Bishops Farm
BOWSTREET LANE
OVER LANE
BLACKHORSE HILL
LOVE LANE
Round Covert
Oak Covert
Lodge
Compton House
Blackhorse Wood
M5
St. Swithin's Chapel (Remains of)
St. Swithin's Farm
Manor Farm
HOLLYWOOD LANE
Webb's Brake
Wild Place (Bristol Zoo)
Home Farm
CRIBBS CAUSEWAY
BS10
OLYMPUS ROAD
BRITANNIA ROAD
PATCHWAY TRADING ESTATE
Hypermarket
Warehouse
Briery Brake
The Lyde
Tower
Junction 17
M5 MOTORWAY
PATCHWAY TRADING EST.
BS34
Bangley Wood
Hollyhill Wood
HIGHWOOD LANE
Superstore
Trym Road
Centaurus Road
PEGASUS ROAD
Reservoir (Covered)
JUPITER RD.
Gov. Offs.
Chandler's Brake
A4018
HOLLY WOOD LA.
MERLIN ROAD
LYSANDER ROAD
Henbury
Bus Sta.
Mayfield Cottages
Depot
Warehouse
Lodge
CRIBBS CAUSEWAY RETAIL PARK
CRIBBS CAUSEWAY REGIONAL SHOPPING CENTRE
FALCON CL.
EAGLE DRIVE
Basin Covert
Compton
The Cone

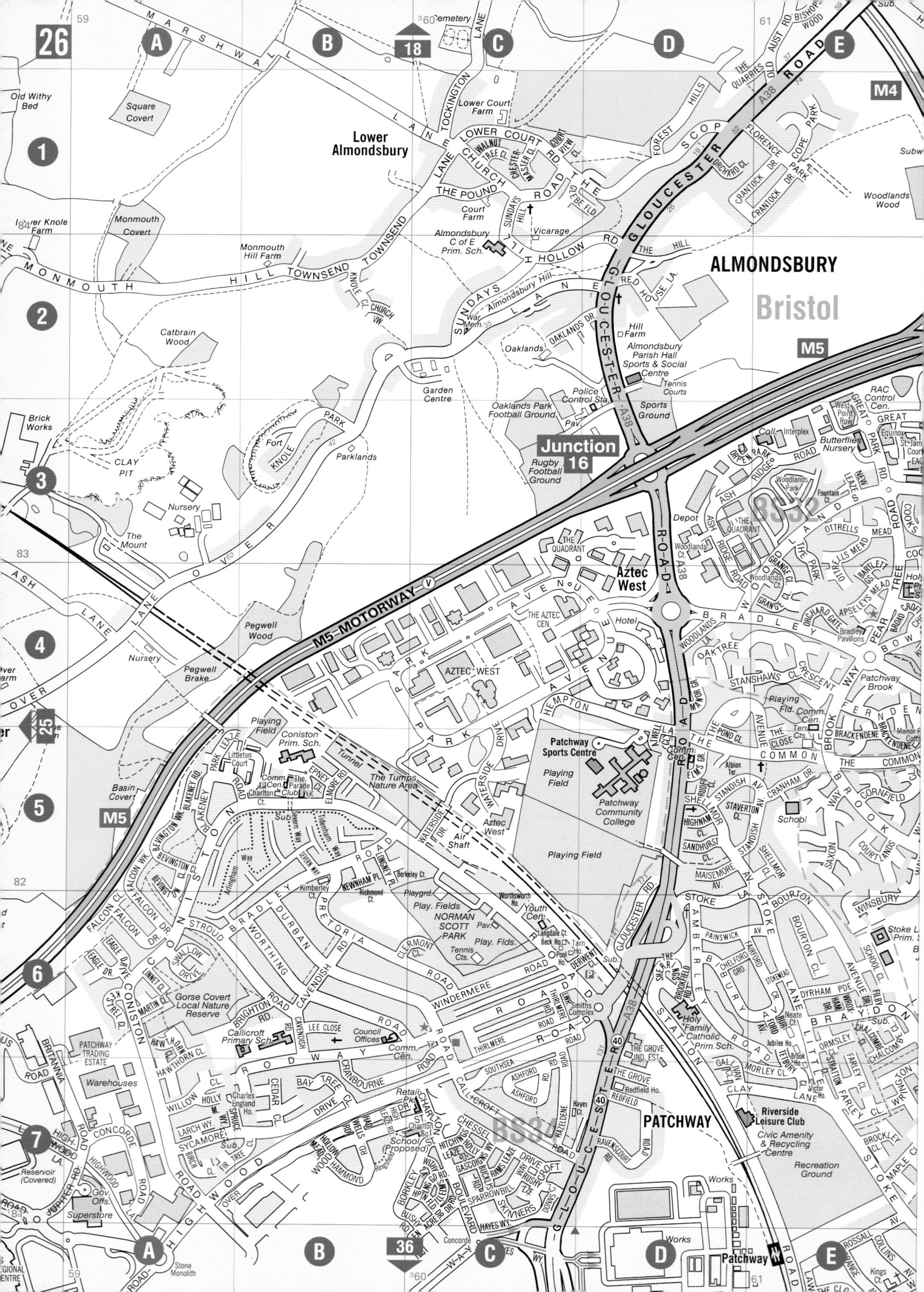
18
36
25
A
B
C
D
E
1
2
3
4
5
6
7
59
60
61
84
83
82
81
Cemetery
MARSHWALL LANE
TOCKINGTON LANE
Old Withy Bed
Square Covert
Lower Court Farm
Lower Almondsbury
LOWER COURT RD
WALNUT TREE CL.
CHESTER-MASTER CL.
COURT VIEW CL.
CHURCH ROAD
THE POUND
Court Farm
Almondsbury C of E Prim. Sch.
Vicarage
SUNDAYS HILL
GLEBE FLD.
Lower Knole Farm
Monmouth Covert
Monmouth Hill Farm
MONMOUTH HILL
TOWNSEND LANE
KNOLE CL.
CHURCH VW.
SUNDAYS HILL
HOLLOW RD
Almondsbury Hill
War Mem.
THE HILL
RED HOUSE LA.
ALMONDSBURY
Bristol
Hill Farm
Almondsbury Parish Hall Sports & Social Centre
Tennis Courts
OAKLANDS DR.
Oaklands
Catbrain Wood
Garden Centre
Police Control Sta.
Oaklands Park Football Ground
Sports Ground
Pav.
Junction 16
Rugby Football Ground
Brick Works
CLAY PIT
Fort
KNOLE PARK
Parklands
Nursery
The Mount
OVER LANE
ASH LANE
Pegwell Wood
Pegwell Brake
Nursery
Basin Covert
M4
M5
M5 MOTORWAY
GLOUCESTER ROAD
A38
THE QUARRIES
OLD AUST RD
BISHOPS WOOD
FOREST HILLS
SCOP
FLORENCE PARK
COPE PARK
ORCHARD CL.
CRANTOCK DR.
Woodlands Wood
RAC Control Cen.
West Point Row
GREAT PARK RD.
Equinox
Interplex
Butterflies Nursery
RIDGES
ORPEN PARK
ASH RIDGE ROAD
Woodlands Park
Depot
THE QUADRANT
Woodlands Ct.
BS32
WOODLANDS
GRANGE CL.
THE PARK
OTTRELLS MEAD
BARTLETT GS.
APSELEYS MEAD
PEAR TREE
ORCHARD GATE
Bradley Pavilions
BRADLEY
Aztec West
THE AZTEC CEN.
Hotel
AZTEC WEST
PARK AVENUE
HEMPTON
OAKTREE
STANSHAWS CL.
CRESCENT
Patchway Brook
BROOK WAY
Playing Fld.
Comm. Cen.
POND CL.
AVENUE
THE CLOSE
BRACKENDENE
THE COMMON
Playing Field
Coniston Prim. Sch.
Littleton Court
PARK LEAZE
Tunnel
The Tumps Nature Area
Patchway Sports Centre
Playing Field
Patchway Community College
WATERSIDE DRIVE
Aztec West
Air Shaft
Playing Field
ELMS GR.
Albion Ter.
STANDISH AV.
CRANHAM DR.
STAVERTON CL.
HIGHNAM CL.
SANDHURST CL.
SHELLMOR
MAISEMORE AV.
School
CORNFIELD
SAXON WAY
COURTLANDS
WINSBURY
BLAKENEY RD.
BEVINGTON WK.
Comm. Cen.
Charlton Ct.
The Parade Club
EPNEY CL.
ELMORE RD
Severn Way
Tidenham Way
Arlingham Way
FALCON WK.
BEVINGTON CL.
CONISTON ROAD
BRADLEY
DURBAN
PRETORIA
Kimberley Ct.
NEWNHAM PL.
LONGNEY PL.
Berkeley Ct.
Richmond Ct.
Playgrd.
Play. Fields
NORMAN SCOTT PARK
Play. Flds.
Tennis Cts.
Pav.
Worthsworth Ho.
Youth Cen.
Langdale Ct.
Beck Ho.
Tarn Ho.
Pool Ho.
DERWENT CL.
Sub.
GLOUCESTER RD.
STOKE LANE
BOURTON
STROUD
FALCON CL.
FALCON DR.
FALCON
EAGLE DR.
SWALLOW DRIVE
LINNET CL.
WORTHING ROAD
CAVENDISH
CLERMONT CL.
WINDERMERE ROAD
THIRLMERE
Smiths Complex
MARTIN CL.
Gorse Covert Local Nature Reserve
BRIGHTON RD.
LEE CLOSE
Council Offices
Comm. Cen.
Callicroft Primary Sch.
HAWTHORN CL.
RODWAY ROAD
PATCHWAY TRADING ESTATE
Warehouses
BRITANNIA ROAD
CRANBOURNE
BAY TREE CL.
WILLOW CL.
HOLLY
Charles England Ho.
CEDAR
DRIVE
LARCH WY.
SPRUCE
SYCAMORE DR.
BIRCH
FIR TREE CL.
HIGHWOOD ROAD
CONCORDE
Reservoir (Covered)
JUPITER RD.
Gov. Offs.
Superstore
Stone Monolith
Retail Pk
CHARLTON
School (Proposed)
SOUTHSEA
ASHFORD RD.
CALLICROFT
HAZELDENE
Hayes Ct.
THE GROVE
THE GROVE IND. EST.
Redfield Ho.
REDFIELD
PATCHWAY
BS34
RAVENSCOURT RD.
CHESSEL
HITCHINGS
GASCOIGNS WY.
RAMS LEAZE
RUSHY
CROFT
SPARROWBILL
SKINNERS
BORKLEY
BUSHY
HAYES WY.
BOULEVARD
Concorde
HAMMOND
HOLLOW
Ringsfield
Holy Family Catholic Prim. Sch.
STATION ROAD
BROOKFIELD
AMBERLEY
PAINSWICK AV.
CHELFORD GRO.
FAIRFORD
DYRHAM PDE.
BRAYDON
Jubilee Ho.
Brook Ho.
MORLEY CL.
TETBURY
Victor Ho.
Neate Ct.
ORMSLEY CL.
FARLEY CL.
CHALCOMBE CL.
CLAY LANE
Riverside Leisure Club
Civic Amenity & Recycling Centre
Recreation Ground
Works
Works
Patchway
Stoke Lodge Prim. Sch.
SCHOOL CL.
BROCKLEY CL.
MAPLE CL.
STOKE
ROSSALL
COLLINS
Kings Ct.

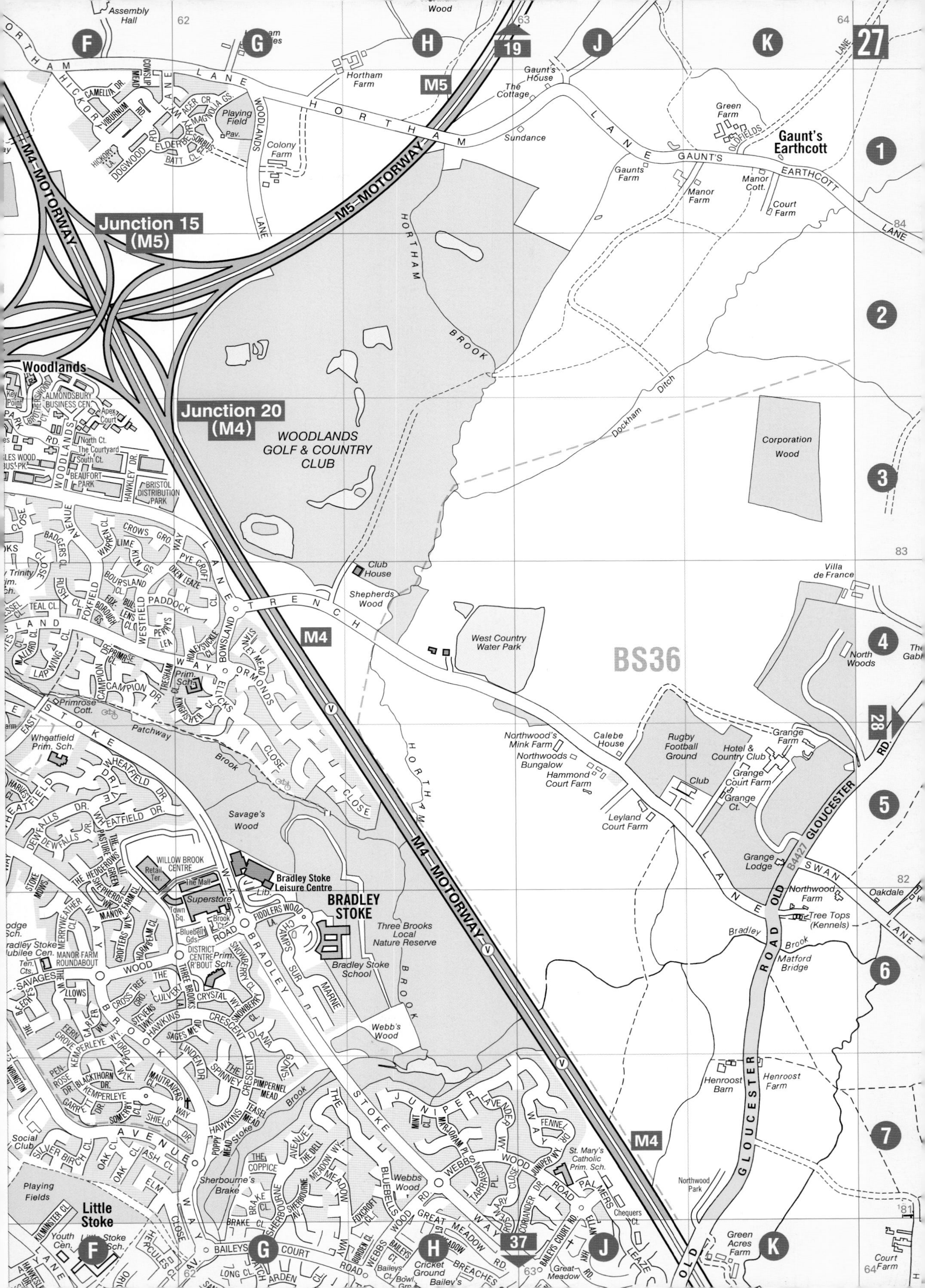

27
F
G
H
J
K
1
2
3
4
5
6
7
62
63
64
84
83
82
81
19
28
37
M5
M4
Junction 15
(M5)
Junction 20
(M4)
M5-MOTORWAY
M4-MOTORWAY
HORTHAM LANE
Hortham Farm
Gaunt's House
The Cottage
Sundance
Green Farm
Gaunt's Earthcott
GAUNT'S EARTHCOTT LANE
Gaunts Farm
Manor Farm
Manor Cott.
Court Farm
Colony Farm
Playing Field
Woodlands
WOODLANDS GOLF & COUNTRY CLUB
HORTHAM BROOK
Dockham Ditch
Corporation Wood
Club House
Shepherds Wood
TRENCH LANE
West Country Water Park
BS36
Villa de France
North Woods
Northwood's Mink Farm
Northwoods Bungalow
Calebe House
Hammond Court Farm
Rugby Football Ground
Club
Hotel & Country Club
Grange Farm
Grange Court Farm
Grange Ct.
Leyland Court Farm
Grange Lodge
GLOUCESTER RD.
B4427
OLD GLOUCESTER ROAD
SWAN LANE
Northwood Farm
Oakdale
Tree Tops (Kennels)
Bradley Brook
Matford Bridge
Henroost Barn
Henroost Farm
Northwood Park
Green Acres Farm
Court Farm
Patchway Brook
Wheatfield Prim. Sch.
Savage's Wood
WILLOW BROOK CENTRE
Bradley Stoke Leisure Centre
BRADLEY STOKE
Three Brooks Local Nature Reserve
Bradley Stoke School
Superstore
Webb's Wood
Sherbourne's Brake
Webbs Wood
St. Mary's Catholic Prim. Sch.
Chequers Ct.
Playing Fields
Little Stoke
Youth Cen.
Social Club
Cricket Ground
Great Meadow
BAILEYS COURT ROAD

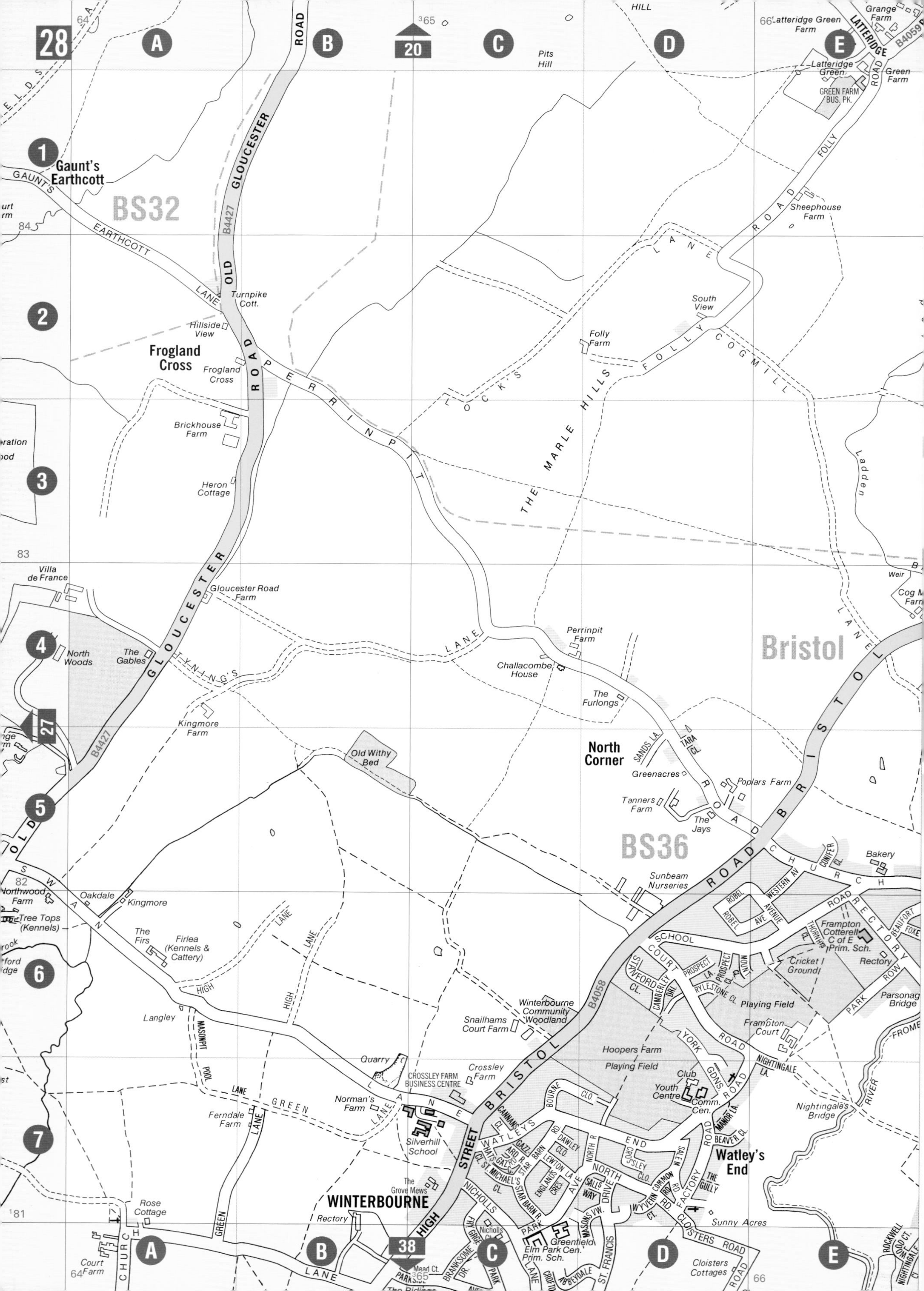
20
27
38
A
B
C
D
E
1
2
3
4
5
6
7
Gaunt's Earthcott
BS32
GAUNT'S EARTHCOTT LANE
OLD GLOUCESTER ROAD
B4427
Turnpike Cott.
Hillside View
Frogland Cross
Brickhouse Farm
Heron Cottage
PERRINPIT LANE
Pits Hill
HILL
Latteridge Green Farm
LATTERIDGE ROAD
Latteridge Green
Green Farm
GREEN FARM BUS. PK.
Grange Farm
FOLLY ROAD
Sheephouse Farm
FOLLY LANE
South View
Folly Farm
COCKS LANE
THE MARLE HILLS
COGMILL LANE
Ladden
Villa de France
Gloucester Road Farm
GLOUCESTER ROAD
North Woods
The Gables
TYNING'S LANE
Kingmore Farm
Old Withy Bed
Perrinpit Farm
Challacombe House
The Furlongs
Bristol
Weir
Cog Mill Farm
North Corner
SANDS LA.
TARA CL.
Greenacres
Poplars Farm
Tanners Farm
The Jays
BS36
BRISTOL ROAD
Bakery
CHURCH ROAD
CONIFER CL.
SWAN LANE
Northwood Farm
Oakdale
Kingmore
Tree Tops (Kennels)
The Firs
Firlea (Kennels & Cattery)
HIGH LANE
Langley
MASONPIT POOL LANE
Sunbeam Nurseries
ROBEL AVE
WESTERN AV
AVENUE
RECTORY ROAD
SCHOOL
COURT
Frampton Cotterell C of E Prim. Sch.
Rectory
Cricket Ground
PARK ROW
Parsonage Bridge
FROME
STAVORDALE
Winterbourne Community Woodland
Snailhams Court Farm
B4058
Hoopers Farm Playing Field
Playing Field
Frampton Court
YORK ROAD
NIGHTINGALE LA.
Quarry
CROSSLEY FARM BUSINESS CENTRE
Crossley Farm
Norman's Farm
GREEN LANE
Ferndale Farm
Silverhill School
Club
Youth Centre
Comm. Cen.
Nightingale Bridge
RIVER
Watley's End
WATLEYS END
NORTH ROAD
NORTH DRIVE
The Grove Mews
WINTERBOURNE
Rectory
HIGH STREET
NICHOLLS LANE
Rose Cottage
Court Farm
CHURCH
Greenfield Elm Park Cen. Prim. Sch.
ST. FRANCIS
Sunny Acres
CLOISTERS ROAD
Cloisters Cottages
Mead Ct.
BRANKSOME DR.
ROCKWELL
NIGHTINGALE
64
365
66
84
83
82
81

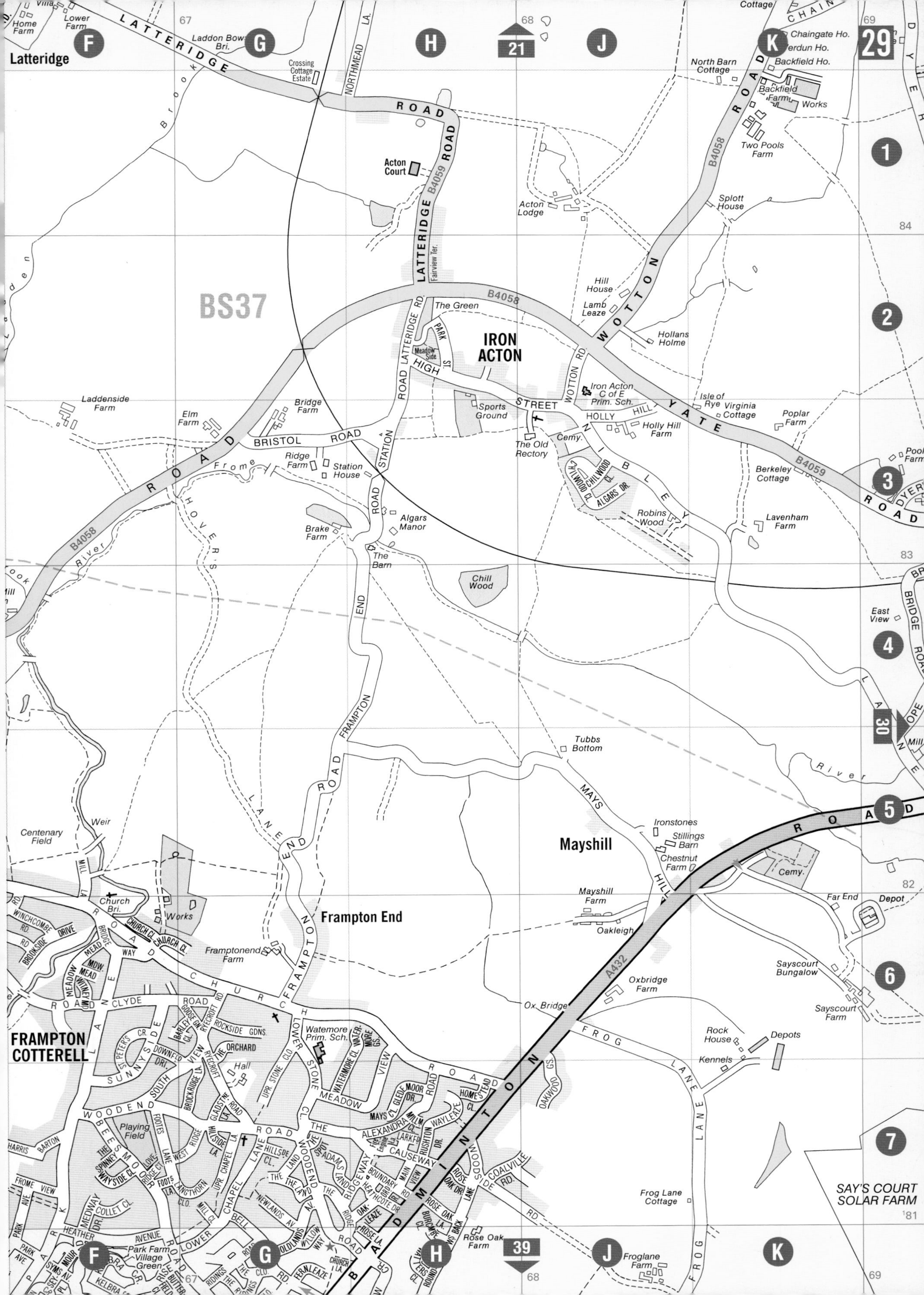
Latteridge
Lower Farm
Home Farm
Laddon Bow Bri.
LATTERIDGE ROAD
Crossing Cottage Estate
NORTHMEAD LA.
21
North Barn Cottage
Chaingate Ho.
Verdun Ho.
Backfield Ho.
Backfield Farm
Works
Two Pools Farm
Acton Court
LATTERIDGE ROAD
B4059
Acton Lodge
Splott House
Fairview Ter.
WOTTON ROAD
Hill House
Lamb Leaze
Hollans Holme
BS37
B4058
The Green
IRON ACTON
Meadow Side
PARK ST.
HIGH STREET
WOTTON RD.
Iron Acton C of E Prim. Sch.
Isle of Rye
Virginia Cottage
Poplar Farm
YATE ROAD
Laddenside Farm
Elm Farm
Bridge Farm
Sports Ground
HOLLY HILL
Holly Hill Farm
BRISTOL ROAD
The Old Rectory
Cemy.
Ridge Farm
Station House
STATION ROAD
CHILWOOD CL.
ALGARS DR.
IBLEY
Berkeley Cottage
B4059
DYER ROAD
Frome
HOVER'S LANE
Algars Manor
Robins Wood
Lavenham Farm
Brake Farm
The Barn
River
B4058
Chill Wood
East View
BRIDGE ROAD
END
FRAMPTON END ROAD
30
Tubbs Bottom
River
MAYS HILL
Centenary Field
Weir
Ironstones
Stillings Barn
Mayshill
Chestnut Farm
ROAD
Cemy.
Church Bri.
Works
Mayshill Farm
Far End
Depot
Frampton End
Oakleigh
Framptonend Farm
A432
Sayscourt Bungalow
CHURCH ROAD
CLYDE ROAD
Oxbridge Farm
Ox. Bridge
Sayscourt Farm
FRAMPTON COTTERELL
Watemore Prim. Sch.
FROG LANE
Rock House
Depots
Kennels
Hall
OAKWOOD GS.
DOWNFIELD
WOODEND ROAD
Playing Field
BADMINTON ROAD
SAY'S COURT SOLAR FARM
Frog Lane Cottage
Rose Oak Farm
39
Park Farm Village Green
Froglane Farm

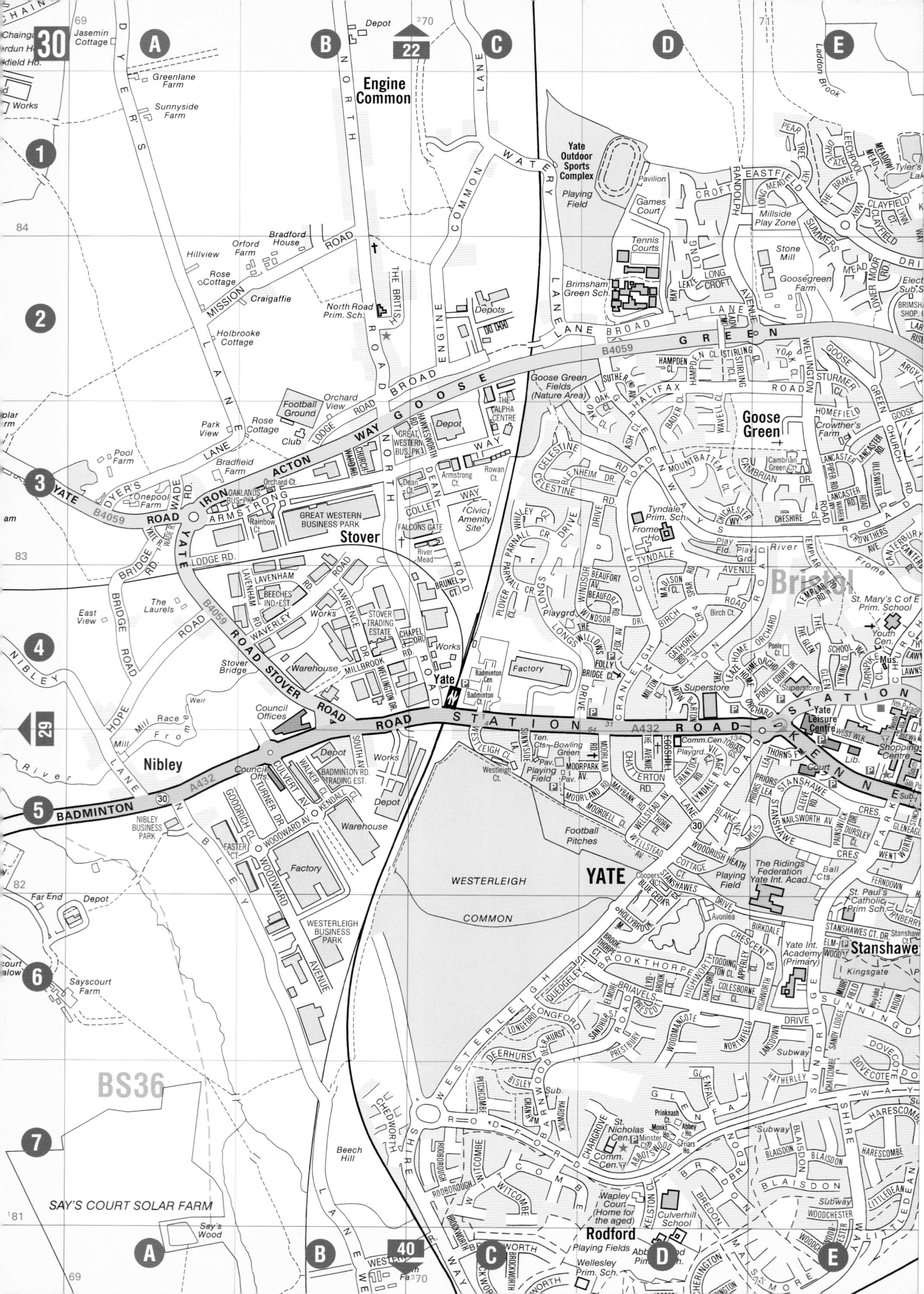
A
B
C
D
E
1
2
3
4
5
6
7
22
29
40
Engine Common
Jasemin Cottage
Greenlane Farm
Sunnyside Farm
Depot
Works
Yate Outdoor Sports Complex
Playing Field
Pavilion
Games Court
Tennis Courts
Brimsham Green Sch.
Ladden Brook
Tyler's Lake
Millside Play Zone
Stone Mill
Goosegreen Farm
Elect. Sub.Sta.
Hillview
Orford Farm
Bradford House
Rose Cottage
Craigaffie
North Road Prim. Sch.
Depots
Holbrooke Cottage
Goose Green Fields (Nature Area)
Goose Green
Crowther's Farm
Cambrian Green Ct.
Football Ground
Orchard View
Rose Cottage
Park View
Club
Pool Farm
Bradfield Farm
Onepool Farm
Great Western Bus. Pk.
The Alpha Centre
Armstrong Ct.
Rowan Ct.
Civic Amenity Site
Oaklands Bus. Pk.
Orchard Ct.
Rainbow Ct.
Great Western Business Park
Stover
Falcons Gate
River Mead
Tyndale Prim. Sch.
Frome Ho.
Bristol
St. Mary's C of E Prim. School
Youth Cen.
Mus.
Lavenham
Beeches Ind. Est.
Stover Trading Estate
Works
Warehouse
Factory
Yate
Badminton Cen.
Superstore
Yate Leisure Centre
Shopping Centre
Lib.
Court
The Laurels
East View
Stover Bridge
Weir
Mill Race
River Frome
Mill
Council Offices
Nibley
Council Offs.
Depot
Badminton Rd. Trading Est.
Westleigh Ct.
Ten. Cts.
Bowling Green
Playing Field
Pav.
Comm. Cen.
Playgrd.
Nibley Business Park
Easter Ct.
Factory
Warehouse
Football Pitches
Westerleigh Common
YATE
The Ridings Federation Yate Int. Acad.
Playing Field
Ball Cts.
St. Paul's Catholic Prim. Sch.
Avonlea
Yate Int. Academy (Primary)
Stanshawe
Kingsgate
Westerleigh Business Park
Far End
Depot
Sayscourt Farm
Beech Hill
Subway
St. Nicholas Cen.
Minster Ct.
Comm. Cen.
Prinknash Ct.
Monks Ho.
Abbey Ho.
Friars Ho.
Wapley Court (Home for the aged)
Culverhill School
Rodford
Playing Fields
Wellesley Prim. Sch.
BS36
SAY'S COURT SOLAR FARM
Say's Wood
B4059
A432
30
YATE ROAD
IRON ACTON WAY
GOOSE GREEN WAY
BROAD LANE
STATION ROAD
BADMINTON ROAD
STOVER ROAD
NORTH ROAD
DYERS LANE
MISSION ROAD
LODGE ROAD
BRIDGE ROAD
HOPE ROAD
NIBLEY LANE
WESTERLEIGH ROAD
RODFORD WAY
SHIRE WAY
KENNEDY WAY
CHURCH ROAD
COURT ROAD
WELLINGTON ROAD
RANDOLPH AVENUE
EASTFIELD DRIVE
WATERY LANE
COMMON LANE
ENGINE COMMON LANE

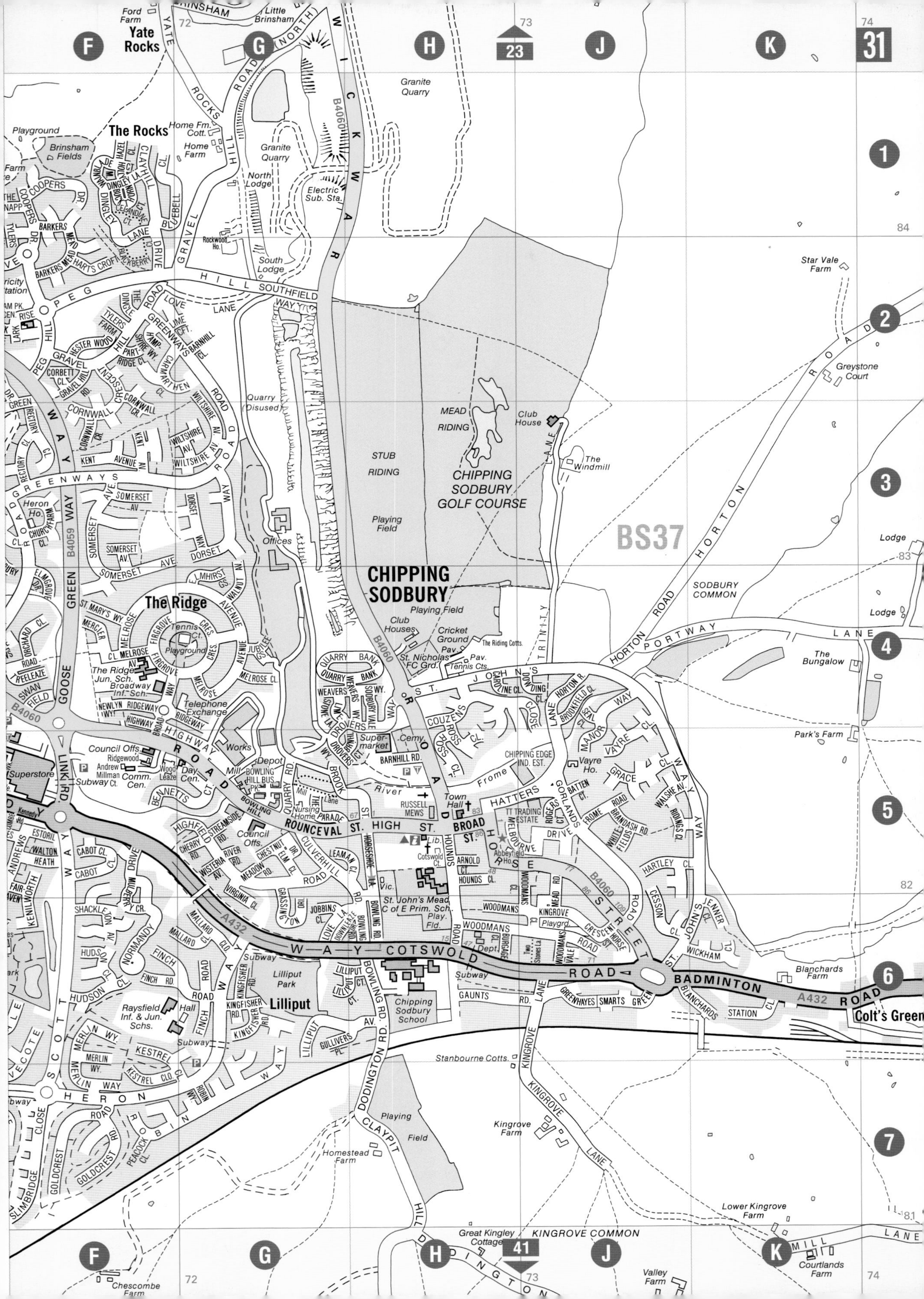

Yate Rocks
The Rocks
Brinsham Fields
Granite Quarry
North Lodge
South Lodge
Electric Sub. Sta.
Home Farm
Quarry (Disused)
Offices
MEAD RIDING
STUB RIDING
CHIPPING SODBURY GOLF COURSE
Club House
The Windmill
BS37
CHIPPING SODBURY
Playing Field
Club Houses
Cricket Ground
St. Nicholas FC Grd.
The Ridge
Tennis Ct.
Playground
The Ridge Jun. Sch.
Broadway Inf. Sch.
Telephone Exchange
Works
Council Offs.
Superstore
Depot
Town Hall
Lib.
Cotswold Ct.
Abbeyfield Ho.
TT TRADING ESTATE
CHIPPING EDGE IND. EST.
Vayre Ho.
St. John's Mead C of E Prim. Sch.
Lilliput Park
Lilliput
Chipping Sodbury School
Raysfield Inf. & Jun. Schs.
Hall
Stanbourne Cotts.
Kingrove Farm
Playing Field
Homestead Farm
Lower Kingrove Farm
KINGROVE COMMON
Great Kingley Cottage
Chescombe Farm
Valley Farm
Courtlands Farm
SODBURY COMMON
Star Vale Farm
Greystone Court
Lodge
The Bungalow
Park's Farm
Blanchards Farm
Colt's Green
COTSWOLD ROAD
BADMINTON ROAD
A432
B4060
B4059
ROUNCEVAL ST.
HIGH ST.
BROAD ST.
HORSE STREET
HORTON ROAD
PORTWAY LANE
WICKWAR ROAD
PEG HILL
SOUTHFIELD WAY
GOOSE GREEN WAY
HERON WAY
SCOTT WAY
DODINGTON RD.
CLAYPIT HILL
KINGROVE LANE
MILL LANE

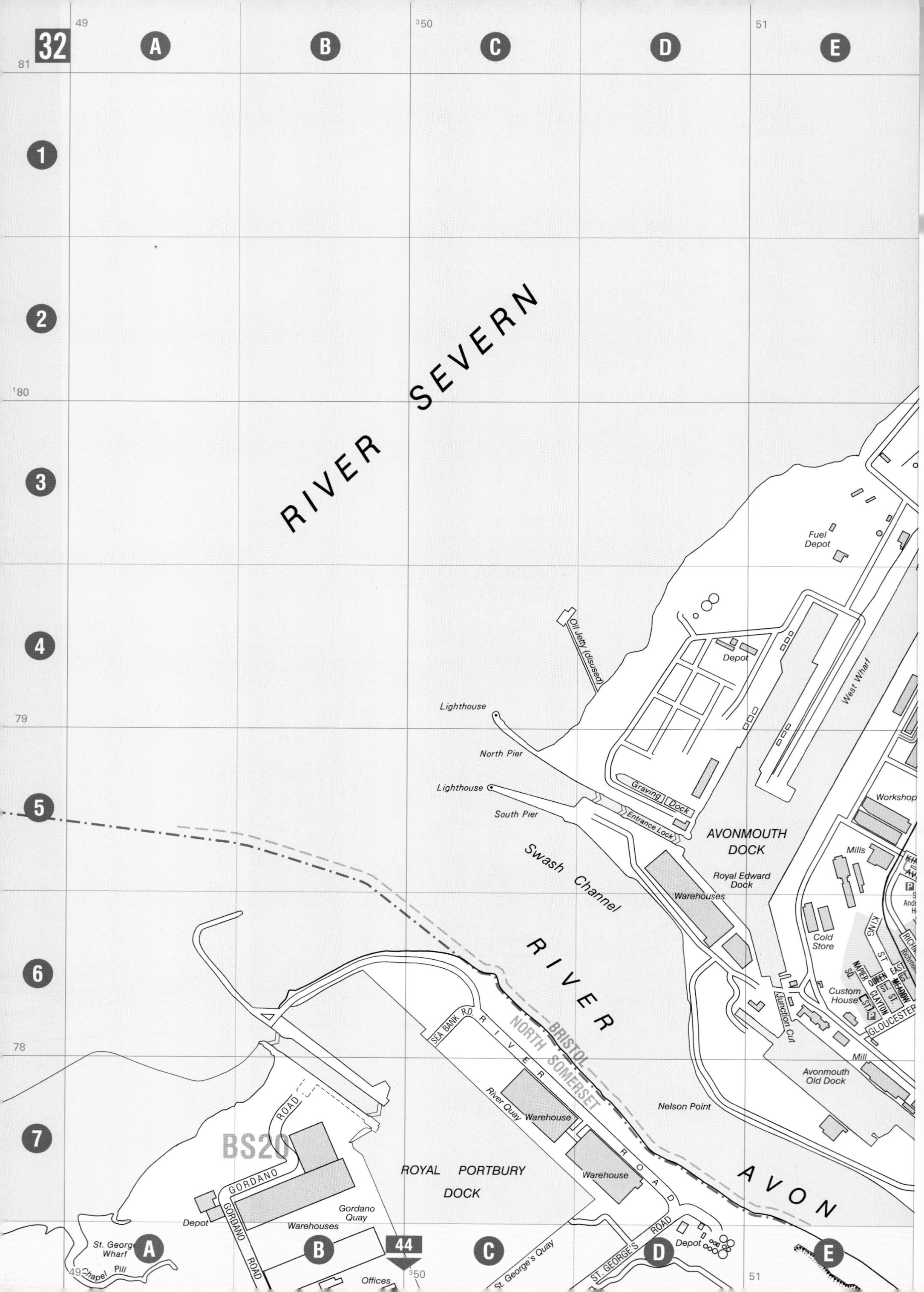

49   A   B   ³50   C   D   51   E

81

1

2

¹80

3

RIVER SEVERN

Fuel Depot

4

Oil Jetty (disused)

Depot

West Wharf

Lighthouse

North Pier

Lighthouse

South Pier

Graving Dock

79

Entrance Lock

Workshop

5

Swash Channel

AVONMOUTH DOCK

Mills

Royal Edward Dock

Warehouses

Cold Store

KING AV

St Andr H

P

RIVER

Custom House

KING ST

NAPIER SQ

QUEEN ST

CLAYTON ST

McBURROW ST

EAST ST

RICHMOND

GLOUCESTER

6

BRISTOL

Junction Cut

Mill

NORTH SOMERSET

SEA BANK RD

78

Avonmouth Old Dock

ROAD

River Quay Warehouse

RIVER

Nelson Point

7

BS20

ROYAL PORTBURY DOCK

Warehouse

ROAD

AVON

GORDANO ROAD

Depot

GORDANO ROAD

Warehouses

Gordano Quay

Depot

St George's Wharf

Chapel Pill

A

49

44

B

³50

C

St George's Quay

ST GEORGE'S ROAD

D

51

Depot

E

Offices

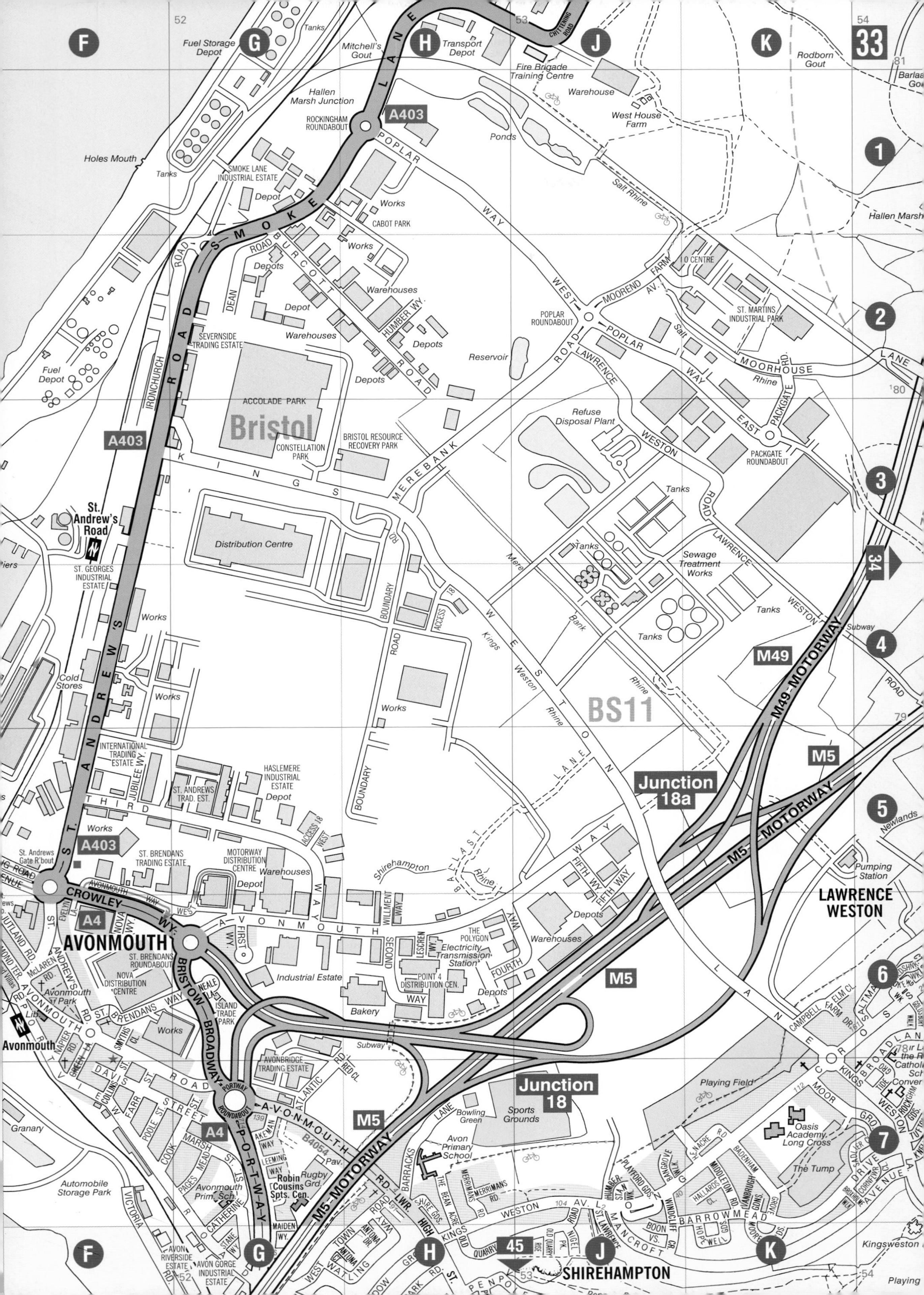
33
52
53
54
F
G
H
J
K
1
2
3
4
5
6
7
81
80
79
Fuel Storage Depot
Tanks
Mitchell's Gout
Transport Depot
CHITTENING ROAD
Fire Brigade Training Centre
Warehouse
Rodborn Gout
Hallen Marsh Junction
West House Farm
ROCKINGHAM ROUNDABOUT
A403
Ponds
Holes Mouth
SMOKE LANE INDUSTRIAL ESTATE
SMOKE LANE
POPLAR WAY WEST
Salt Rhine
Hallen Marsh
Depot
Works
CABOT PARK
BURCOTT ROAD
DEAN ROAD
Depots
Warehouses
MOOREND FARM AV.
I O CENTRE
ST. MARTINS INDUSTRIAL PARK
POPLAR ROUNDABOUT
HUMBER WY.
Reservoir
POPLAR WAY EAST
MOORHOUSE LANE
PACKGATE RD.
Rhine
SEVERNSIDE TRADING ESTATE
IRONCHURCH ROAD
ST. ANDREW'S ROAD
Fuel Depot
ACCOLADE PARK
Bristol
CONSTELLATION PARK
BRISTOL RESOURCE RECOVERY PARK
MEREBANK ROAD
LAWRENCE WESTON ROAD
Refuse Disposal Plant
PACKGATE ROUNDABOUT
KINGS WESTON LANE
St. Andrew's Road
ST. GEORGES INDUSTRIAL ESTATE
Distribution Centre
Tanks
Sewage Treatment Works
Mere Bank
34
BOUNDARY ROAD
ACCESS 18
Kings Weston Rhine
Subway
M49
M49 MOTORWAY
Cold Stores
BS11
INTERNATIONAL TRADING ESTATE
JUBILEE WY.
ST. ANDREWS TRAD. EST.
HASLEMERE INDUSTRIAL ESTATE
Junction 18a
M5
THIRD WAY
Shirehampton Rhine
BALLAST LANE
M5 MOTORWAY
Newlands
St. Andrews Gate R'bout
ST. BRENDANS TRADING ESTATE
MOTORWAY DISTRIBUTION CENTRE
WEST WAY
Pumping Station
FIFTH WAY
LAWRENCE WESTON
CROWLEY WY.
A4
AVONMOUTH WAY
AVONMOUTH
ST. BRENDANS ROUNDABOUT
NOVA DISTRIBUTION CENTRE
FIRST WY.
SECOND WAY
WILLMENT WAY
LESCREN WY.
THE POLYGON
Electricity Transmission Station
FOURTH WAY
POINT 4 DISTRIBUTION CEN.
Industrial Estate
Bakery
Avonmouth Park
ST. BRENDANS WAY
BRISTOW BROADWAY
ISLAND TRADE PARK
Avonmouth
Subway
CAMPBELL FARM DR.
Playing Field
AVONBRIDGE TRADING ESTATE
ATLANTIC RD.
Junction 18
Sports Grounds
Bowling Green
Oasis Academy Long Cross
PORTWAY ROUNDABOUT
AVONMOUTH RD.
B4054
PORTWAY
The Tump
Granary
Avon Primary School
Rugby Grd.
Robin Cousins Spts. Cen.
Automobile Storage Park
Avonmouth Prim. Sch.
BARRACKS LANE
HIGH ST.
KINGS WESTON AV.
BARROWMEAD DR.
VICTORIA RD.
AVON RIVERSIDE ESTATE
AVON GORGE INDUSTRIAL ESTATE
45
SHIREHAMPTON
Kingsweston
Playing

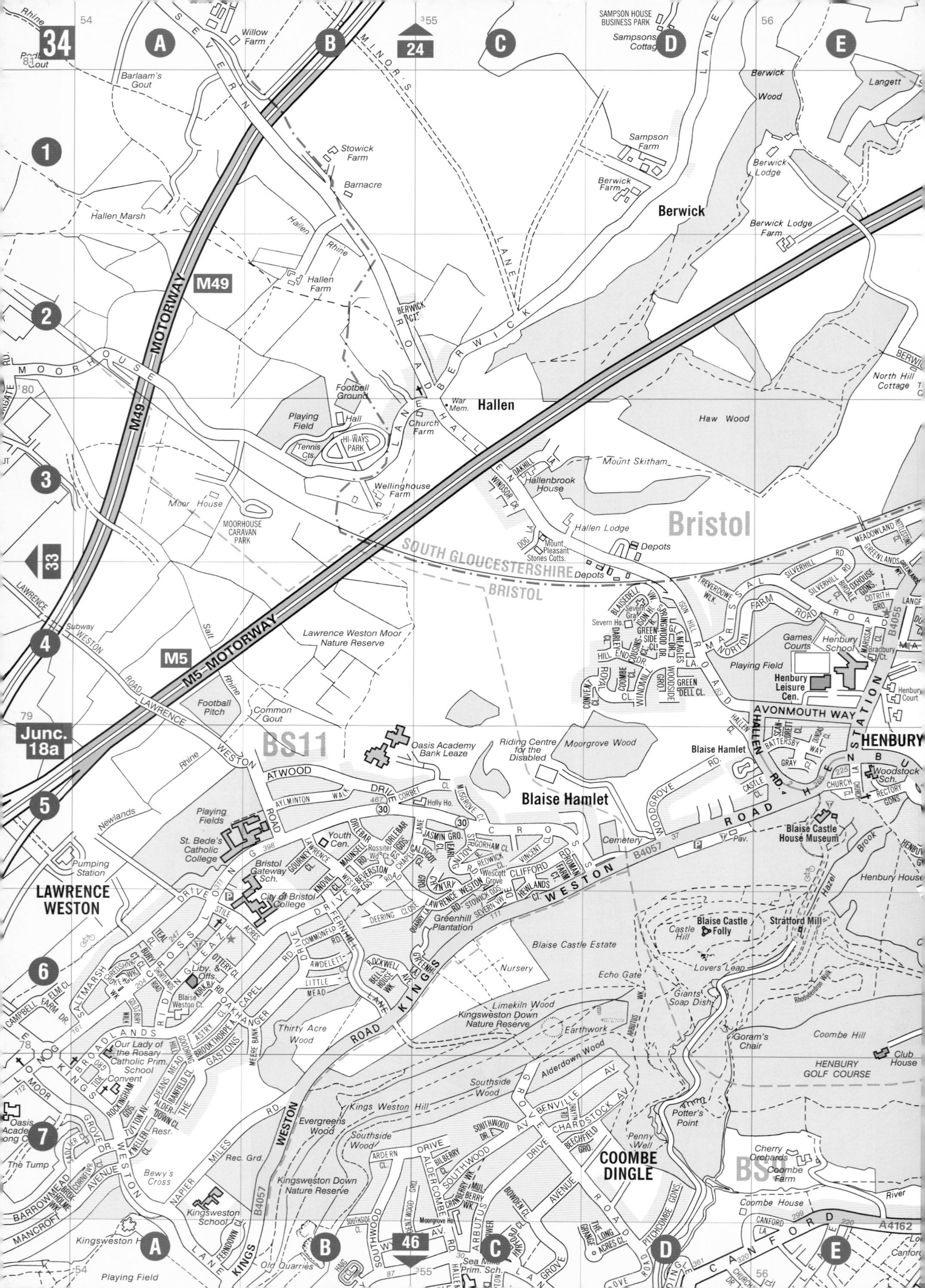
24
33
46
Hallen
Berwick
Bristol
BS11
Blaise Hamlet
HENBURY
LAWRENCE WESTON
COOMBE DINGLE
M5 MOTORWAY
M49 MOTORWAY
Junc. 18a
SOUTH GLOUCESTERSHIRE
BRISTOL
Hallen Marsh
Hallen Farm
Stowick Farm
Barnacre
Barlaam's Gout
Willow Farm
Sampson House Business Park
Sampson Farm
Berwick Farm
Berwick Wood
Berwick Lodge
Berwick Lodge Farm
Langett
North Hill Cottage
Haw Wood
Mount Skitham
Hallenbrook House
Hallen Lodge
Depots
Moor House
Moorhouse Caravan Park
Wellinghouse Farm
Church Farm
War Mem.
Football Ground
Playing Field
Hi-Ways Park
Lawrence Weston Moor Nature Reserve
Common Gout
Oasis Academy Bank Leaze
Riding Centre for the Disabled
Moorgrove Wood
Cemetery
St. Bede's Catholic College
Bristol Gateway Sch.
City of Bristol College
Pumping Station
Blaise Castle Estate
Blaise Castle Folly
Blaise Castle House Museum
Stratford Mill
Lovers Leap
Giants Soap Dish
Echo Gate
Goram's Chair
Henbury Golf Course
Coombe Hill
Club House
Henbury School
Henbury Leisure Cen.
Woodstock Sch.
Henbury House
Limekiln Wood
Kingsweston Down Nature Reserve
Earthwork
Alderdown Wood
Southside Wood
Kings Weston Hill
Evergreens Wood
Thirty Acre Wood
Greenhill Plantation
Nursery
Potter's Point
Penny Well
Cherry Orchards
Coombe Farm
Coombe House
Kingsweston School
Bewy's Cross
Rec. Grd.
Our Lady of the Rosary Catholic Prim. School
Convent
The Tump
Kingsweston House
Playing Field
Old Quarries
Sea Mills Prim. Sch.
A4162
B4057
B4055
AVONMOUTH WAY
KINGS WESTON ROAD
WESTON ROAD
LAWRENCE WESTON ROAD
HALLEN ROAD
BERWICK LANE
MOORHOUSE LANE
SEVERN ROAD
MINORS LANE
CANFORD LANE
STATION ROAD

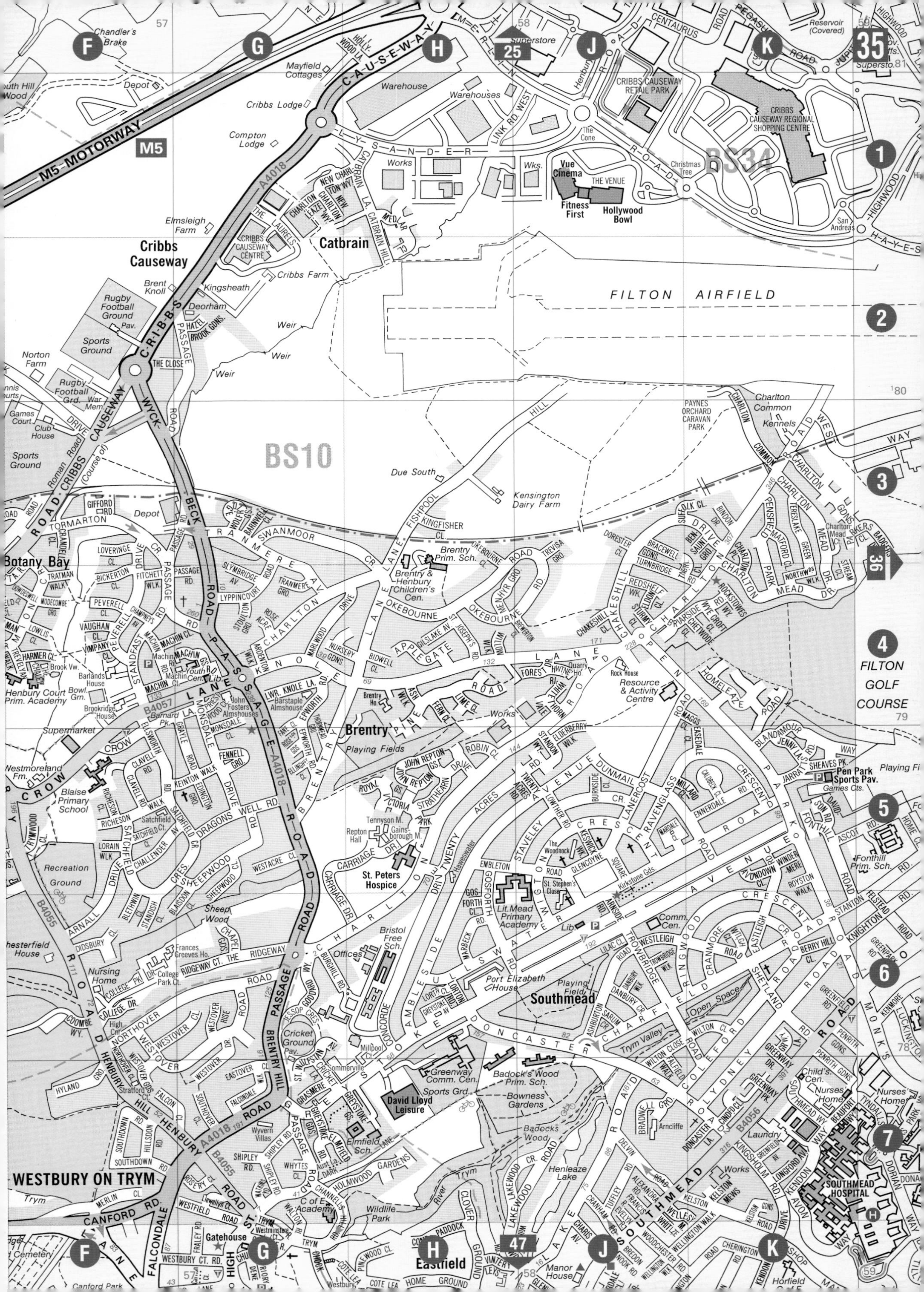
F
G
H
J
K
57
58
59
Chandler's Brake
Mayfield Cottages
Cribbs Lodge
Compton Lodge
Depot
M5-MOTORWAY
M5
CAUSEWAY
HOLLYWOOD LA.
Superstore
25
Warehouse
Warehouses
LINK RD. WEST
LYSANDER
CENTAURUS
ROAD
PEGASUS ROAD
Reservoir (Covered)
CRIBBS CAUSEWAY RETAIL PARK
CRIBBS CAUSEWAY REGIONAL SHOPPING CENTRE
The Cone
Christmas Tree
BS34
Vue Cinema
THE VENUE
Fitness First
Hollywood Bowl
Works
Wks.
HIGHWOOD
San Andreas
HAYES
Elmsleigh Farm
Cribbs Causeway
Catbrain
CATBRAIN LA.
CATBRAIN HILL
NEW CHARLTON WY.
CHARLTON LEAZE
THE LAURELS
CRIBBS CAUSEWAY CENTRE
MEDLAR
Cribbs Farm
Brent Knoll
Kingsheath
Deorham
Rugby Football Ground
Pav.
Sports Ground
Norton Farm
Rugby Football Grd.
War Mem.
Games Court
Club House
Sports Ground
FILTON AIRFIELD
Weir
HAZEL BROOK GDNS.
THE CLOSE
PASSAGE ROAD
WYCK BECK ROAD
A4018
BS10
Due South
Kensington Dairy Farm
PAYNES ORCHARD CARAVAN PARK
Charlton Common
Kennels
CHARLTON COMMON
CHARLTON ROAD WEST
WAY
Botany Bay
TORMARTON
GIFFORD RD
Depot
TRANMERE
SWANMOOR
KINGFISHER CL.
FISHPOOL HILL
Brentry Prim. Sch.
Brentry & Henbury Children's Cen.
OKEBOURNE ROAD
TREVISA GRO.
DORESTER CL.
BRACEWELL GDNS.
TURNBRIDGE
SUFFOLK CL.
BINDON DR.
PENSFIELD PARK
TERESLAKE GREEN
MATFORD CL.
MEAD
Charlton Mead Ct.
PARKERS CL.
BADGERS
NORTHWOODS WLK.
STREAM CL.
MEAD DR.
36
LOVERINGE CL.
TRATMAN WALK
BICKERTON CL.
PEVERELL CL.
VAUGHAN CL.
VIMPANY CL.
LOWLIS CL.
HARMER CL.
FITCHETT WLK.
PASSAGE RD.
SLYMBRIDGE AV.
LYPPINCOURT RD.
STOULTON GRO.
ROSE ACRE
TRANMERE GRO.
CHARLTON
OKEBOURNE
ST. JOSEPH'S RD.
GILSLAKE AV.
WILLOW WLK.
CHAKESHILL CL.
CHAKESHILL DR.
REDSHELF WK.
ROCKSTOWES
PIARSIDE
WYE CROFT CL.
CHETWODE CL.
Brook Vw.
Barlands House
Bowl. Grn.
Henbury Court Prim. Academy
Brookridge House
Machin Gdns.
Youth Cen.
Lib.
MACHIN
STANDFAST RD
KNOLE LANE
NURSERY GDNS.
BIDWELL CL.
APPLEGATE
MARLWOOD DRIVE
ARDENTON WLK.
Quarry Ho.
Rock House
Resource & Activity Centre
FOREST DR.
WHITEHORN VALE
LWR. KNOLE LA.
Barstaple Almshouse
Brentry Ho.
ASH WLK.
PINE ROAD
FERN CL.
LIME CL.
Works
HOMELEAZE
MAGGS CL.
EASEDALE CL.
Supermarket
CROW LANE
B4057
Barnard Pk.
John Fosters Almshouses
MONSDALE DRIVE
Brentry
Playing Fields
EPWORTH RD.
ELLINGHURST CL.
ROBIN CL.
STANDON WY.
ELDERBERRY WLK.
BLANDAMOUR WAY
JENNY LA.
JARRATT
SHEAVES PK.
Pen Park Sports Pav.
Games Cts.
Playing Fi
Westmoreland Fm.
Blaise Primary School
CLAVELL RD.
KEINTON WALK
FENNELL GRO.
EDINGTON GRO.
JOHN REPTON GS.
ROYAL VICTORIA PARK
STRATHEARN DR.
TWENTY ACRES RD.
AVENUE
DUNMAIL
LANERCOST
RAVENGLASS
MILLARD CL.
ENNERDALE RD
PARK RD
FONTHILL
ASCOT
Fonthill Prim. Sch.
RICHESON CL.
SATCHFIELD CR.
DRAGONS WELL RD.
Tennyson M.
Gainsborough M.
Repton Hall
CARRIAGE DR.
St. Peters Hospice
Haweswater
STAVELEY CR.
LOWTHER RD.
KESWICK WK.
The Woodnock
GLENCOYNE SQUARE
St. Stephen's Close
Kirkstone Gds.
WINDERMERE
AVONDOWN
ROYSTON WALK
STANTON RD
FELSTEAD RD.
KNIGHTON RD
Recreation Ground
CHALLENGER AV.
SHEEPWOOD RD.
WESTACRE CL.
Sheep Wood
EMBLETON
GOSFORTH RD.
Lit.Mead Primary Academy
Comm. Cen.
Lib.
CRESCENT
B4055
Chesterfield House
ARNALL DRIVE
DIDSBURY CL.
Frances Greeves Ho.
College Park Ct.
RIDGEWAY CT.
THE RIDGEWAY
Bristol Free Sch.
Offices
MARBECK RD.
ULLSWATER RD.
WESTLEIGH
LILAC CL.
TROWBRIDGE
RINGWOOD
CRANMORE
WITCH
EASTLEIGH
BERRY HILL
GREENPARK
6
Nursing Home
COLLEGE DR.
NORTHOVER
WESTOVER RISE
WESTOVER DR.
Cricket Ground Pav.
CONCORDE DR.
AMBLESIDE AV.
Port Elizabeth House
Playing Field
Southmead
Open Space
Trym Valley
DONCASTER
CHARFIELD RD.
WILTON CLOSE
SHETLAND RD.
GREENWAY RD.
KENMORE
PENRITH GDNS.
MONK'S PARK
HYLAND GRO.
Stratford Ct.
FALCON CL.
EASTOVER CL.
BRENTRY HILL
ST. WULFSTAN AV.
Sommerville
Millpool Ct.
Greenway Comm. Cen.
Badock's Wood Prim. Sch.
Bowness Gardens
Sports Grd.
David Lloyd Leisure
Child's Cen.
Nurses' Home
Nurses' Home
Laundry
7
SOUTHDOWN RD.
HILLSDON RD.
HENBURY ROAD
A4018
B4055
Wyvern Villas
GRASMERE
GREYSTOKE AV.
Elmfield Sch.
Badocks Wood
Henleaze Lake
LAKEWOOD CR.
BRADWELL GRO.
Arncliffe
DONCASTER LA.
B4056
KINGSHOLM RD.
SOUTHMEAD WY.
SOUTHMEAD HOSPITAL
WESTBURY ON TRYM
SHIPLEY RD.
WHYTES CL.
HOLMWOOD GARDENS
River Trym
Trym
MERLIN CL.
CANFORD RD.
WESTFIELD ROAD
Llewellyn Ct.
C of E Academy
Wildlife Park
CLOVER GROUND
DELVIN
ALEXANDRA RD.
SOUTHMEAD RD.
KELSTON
Works
KELSTON MEWS
Gatehouse
Westminster Ct.
PADDOCK
Eastfield
47
Manor House
CHARIS AV.
CRANHAM
WELLINGTON WALK
WOODCHESTER RD.
CHERINGTON RD.
KENDON DR.
Horfield C. of E.
FALCONDALE RD.
WESTBURY CT. RD.
HIGH ST.
TRYM CROSS
PINEWOOD CL.
COTE LEA
HOME GROUND
Canford Park
Cemetery
Westbury
1
2
3
4
5
Filton Golf Course
78
79
80
81

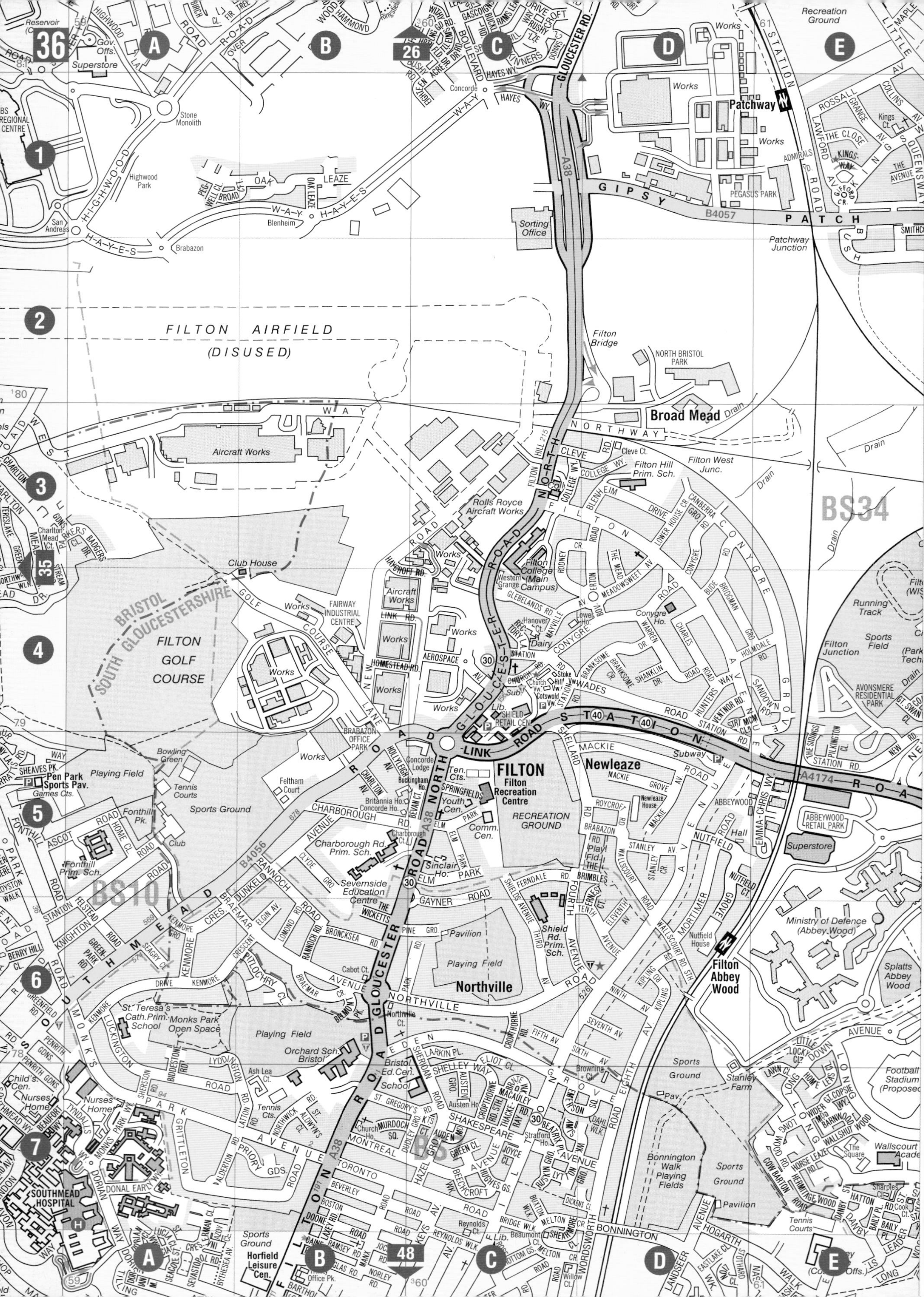

26
35
48
A
B
C
D
E
1
2
3
4
5
6
7
Reservoir
Gov. Offs.
Superstore
BS REGIONAL CENTRE
Stone Monolith
Highwood Park
San Andreas
Brabazon
Blenheim
Concorde
HIGHWOOD ROAD
HAYES WAY
HAYES WY.
GLOUCESTER RD.
A38
Works
Patchway
Recreation Ground
STATION
ROSSALL
COLLINS
GRANGE
LAWFORD AV
THE CLOSE
KINGS WAY
THE AVENUE
ADMIRALS RD.
GIFFORD CR.
PEGASUS PARK
GIPSY PATCH
B4057
Sorting Office
Patchway Junction
SMITHCOT
FILTON AIRFIELD
(DISUSED)
Filton Bridge
NORTH BRISTOL PARK
Broad Mead
Drain
NORTHWAY
WEST WAY
Aircraft Works
Rolls Royce Aircraft Works
CLEVE RD.
Cleve Ct.
COLLEGE WY.
Filton Hill Prim. Sch.
Filton West Junc.
BS34
BLENHEIM DRIVE
CANBERRA GRO
CONYGRE GROVE
LOWER HOUSE CR.
Club House
BRISTOL
SOUTH GLOUCESTERSHIRE
FILTON GOLF COURSE
GOLF COURSE LANE
FAIRWAY INDUSTRIAL CENTRE
HAYCROFT RD.
LINK RD
HOMESTEAD RD.
AEROSPACE
Filton College (Main Campus)
Western Grange
GLEBELANDS RD
MEADOWSWEET AV
Conygre Ho.
WARREN DR.
CHARLES
BRIDGMAN GRO
Running Track
Sports Field
Filton Junction
AVONSMERE RESIDENTIAL PARK
Hanover Ct.
Dairy
STATION
CHURCH RD.
Lib.
SHIELD RETAIL CEN.
WADES ROAD
BRANKSOME
SHANKLIN DR.
HUNTERS WAY
SANDOWN RD.
STATION ROAD
A4174
LINK ROAD
30
40
NEW LANE
BRABAZON OFFICE PARK
Bowling Green
Tennis Courts
Pen Park Sports Pav.
Games Cts.
Playing Field
SHEAVES PK.
Sports Ground
Fonthill Pk.
Club
Feltham Court
Concorde Lodge
Buckingham Ho.
Britannia Ho.
Concorde Ho.
CHARLTON AV.
HOLLYLEIGH AV.
BEVAN CT.
SPRINGFIELDS
Youth Cen.
Ten. Cts.
FILTON
Filton Recreation Centre
RECREATION GROUND
Comm. Cen.
Newleaze
MACKIE GROVE
Newleaze House
ROYCROFT RD.
BRABAZON RD.
STANLEY AV
NUTFIELD
ABBEYWOOD
ABBEYWOOD RETAIL PARK
Superstore
EMMA-CHRIS WY.
Subway
Hall
CHARBOROUGH RD.
Charborough Rd. Prim. Sch.
FONTHILL
ASCOT
Fonthill Prim. Sch.
BS10
B4056
SOUTHMEAD ROAD
RANNOCH
DUNKELD
CLYDE
Severnside Education Centre
THE WICKETTS
GAYNER ROAD
PINE GRO
Sinclair Ho.
ELM PARK
FERNDALE RD.
THE BRIMBLES
Shield Rd. Prim. Sch.
FOURTH AVENUE
Nutfield House
MORTIMER
WALLSCOURT RD.
Filton Abbey Wood
Ministry of Defence (Abbey Wood)
Splatts Abbey Wood
STANTON
KNIGHTON
BERRY HILL
KENMORE
BRAEMAR
CRESCENT
PITLOCHRY
Cabot Ct.
Pavilion
Playing Field
Northville
NORTHVILLE
St. Teresa's Cath. Prim. School
Monks Park Open Space
Orchard Sch. Bristol
Bristol Ed. Cen.
School
EDEN
LARKIN PL.
SHELLEY WAY
ELIOT CL.
Browning Ct.
Sports Ground
Stanley Farm
Pav.
Football Stadium (Proposed)
LUCKINGTON
LYDDINGTON ROAD
Ash Lea Ct.
Tennis Cts.
St. GREGORY'S RD.
MURDOCH SQ.
Church Ho.
SHAKESPEARE
AUSTEN
Austen Ho.
MACAULEY
Stratford Ho.
Child's Cen.
Nurses' Home
SOUTHMEAD HOSPITAL
MONKS PARK AVENUE
PRIORY GDS.
MONTREAL
TORONTO
BEVERLEY
BOSTON
DOONE
GREEN CL.
AVENUE
BEECHCROFT
Bonnington Walk Playing Fields
Sports Ground
Pavilion
Tennis Courts
Wallscourt Acad.
HATTON
DANBY
BONNINGTON
HOGARTH
LANDSEER
WORDSWORTH
Reynolds Ct.
REYNOLDS WLK
Lib.
Beaumont Ct.
MELTON
Sports Ground
Horfield Leisure Cen.
Willow Ct.
FILTON AV.

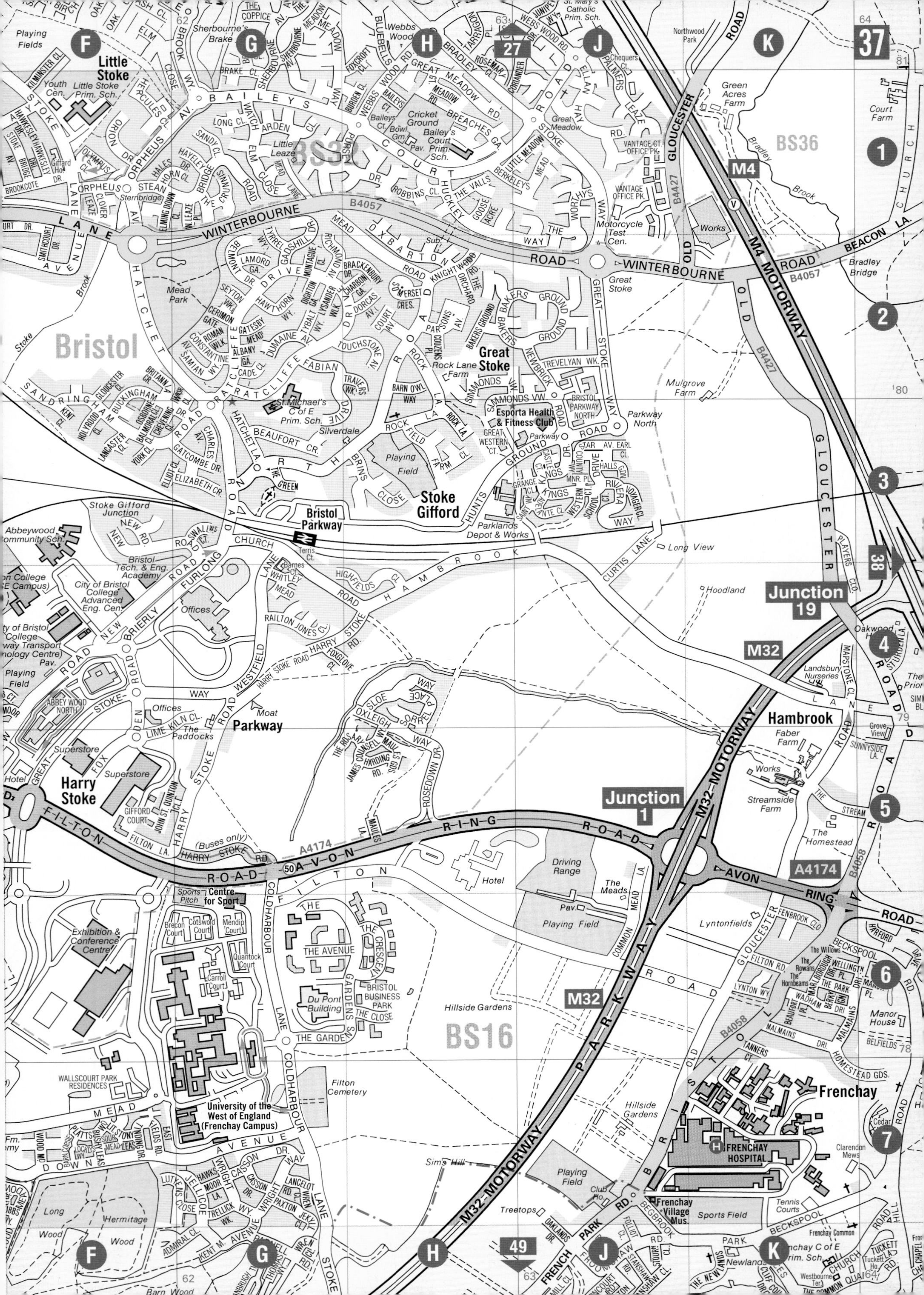

37
27
38
49
F
G
H
J
K
1
2
3
4
5
6
7
Little Stoke
Little Stoke Prim. Sch.
Youth Cen.
Playing Fields
Sherbourne's Brake
Webbs Wood
St. Mary's Catholic Prim. Sch.
Northwood Park
Green Acres Farm
Court Farm
BS36
BS34
BS16
M4
M4 MOTORWAY
B4057
B4427
B4058
A4174
M32
M32 MOTORWAY
Bradley Brook
Bradley Bridge
BEACON LA.
WINTERBOURNE ROAD
BAILEYS COURT
Cricket Ground
Bailey's Court Prim. Sch.
Little Leaze
Great Meadow
Vantage Office Pk.
Motorcycle Test Cen.
Works
Great Stoke
Mead Park
Bristol
Stoke Brook
RATCLIFFE DRIVE
St. Michael's C of E Prim. Sch.
Silverdale
Rock Lane Farm
Esporta Health & Fitness Club
Parkway North
Mulgrove Farm
Playing Field
Stoke Gifford
Bristol Parkway
Parklands Depot & Works
Stoke Gifford Junction
Abbeywood Community Sch.
Bristol Tech. & Eng. Academy
City of Bristol College Advanced Eng. Cen.
Offices
HAMBROOK LANE
CURTIS LANE
Long View
Hoodland
Junction 19
Oakwood Ho.
Landsbury Nurseries
Hambrook
Faber Farm
Streamside Farm
The Homestead
Grove View
Parkway
Moat
The Paddocks
Superstore
Harry Stoke
Gifford Court
Hotel
Playing Field
Junction 1
AVON RING ROAD
FILTON ROAD
Driving Range
The Meads
Hotel
Sports Pitch
Centre for Sport
Exhibition & Conference Centre
Brecon Court
Cotswold Court
Mendip Court
Quantock Court
Carroll Court
THE AVENUE
THE CRESCENT
Bristol Business Park
Du Pont Building
THE GARDENS
Hillside Gardens
COLDHARBOUR LANE
Filton Cemetery
Wallscourt Park Residences
University of the West of England (Frenchay Campus)
Lyntonfields
Manor House
Frenchay
FRENCHAY HOSPITAL
Clarendon Mews
Frenchay Village Mus.
Sports Field
Tennis Courts
Club Ho.
Treetops
Sims Hill
Long Wood
Hermitage Wood
Barn Wood
FRENCHAY PARK RD.
BECKSPOOL
Newlands
Frenchay Common
Frenchay C of E Prim. Sch.
DOWN AVENUE
62
63
64
78
79
80
81

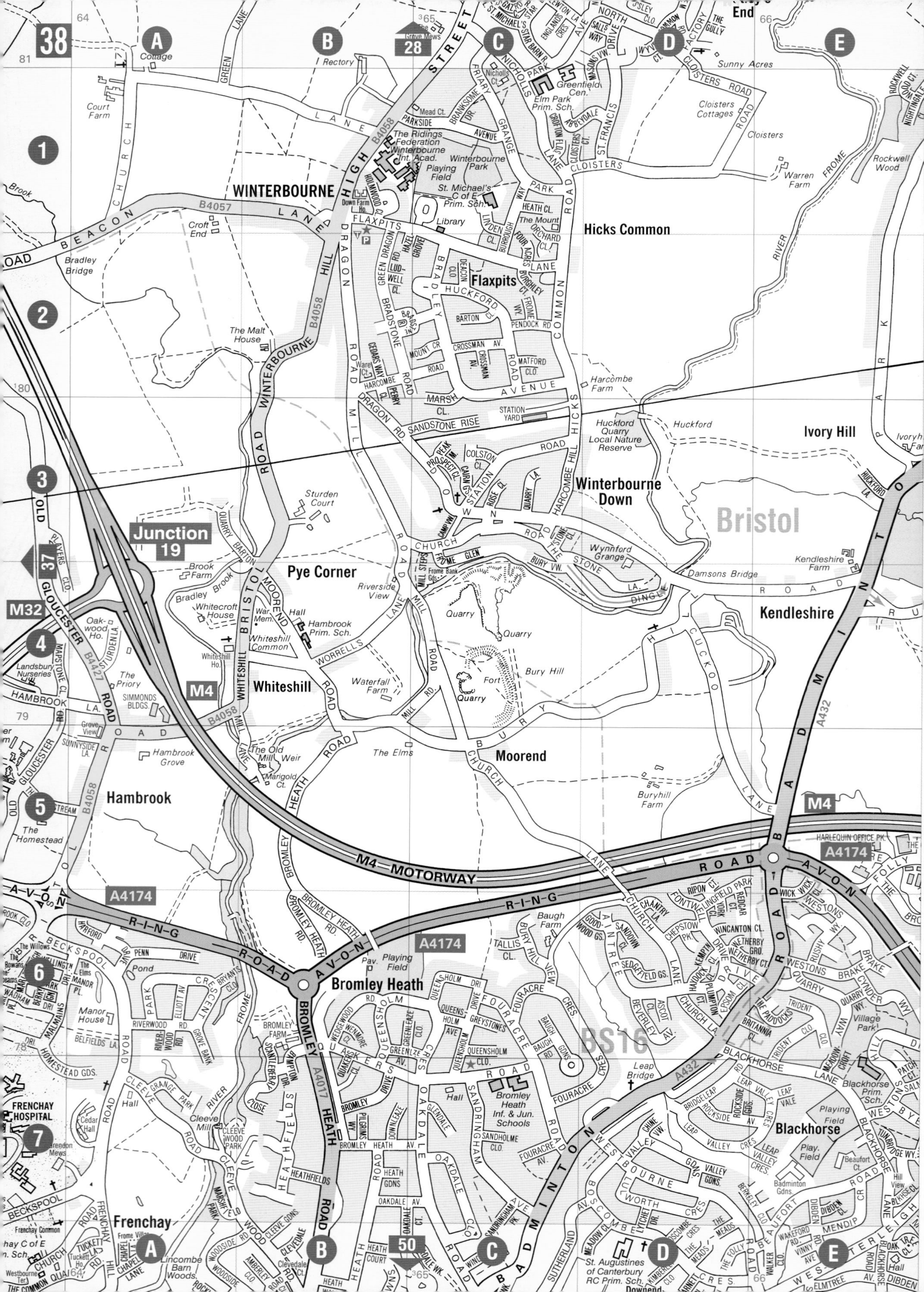

28
50
37
Junction 19
M32
M4
M4 MOTORWAY
A4174
A432
A4017
B4058
B4057
B4427
WINTERBOURNE
Winterbourne Down
Hicks Common
Flaxpits
Pye Corner
Whiteshill
Hambrook
Moorend
Kendleshire
Ivory Hill
Bristol
Bromley Heath
Blackhorse
Frenchay
FRENCHAY HOSPITAL
BS16
HIGH STREET
BEACON LANE
WINTERBOURNE ROAD
BRISTOL ROAD
GLOUCESTER ROAD
DRAGON ROAD
MILL ROAD
BURY HILL
HEATH ROAD
BROMLEY HEATH ROAD
RING ROAD
AVON RING ROAD
BADMINTON ROAD
CHURCH LANE
CLOISTERS ROAD
DINGLE ROAD
CUCKOO LANE
HICKS COMMON ROAD
HARCOMBE HILL
MARSH AVENUE
SANDSTONE RISE
HUCKFORD ROAD
Court Farm
Rectory
Cottage
Sunny Acres
Cloisters Cottages
Cloisters
Warren Farm
Rockwell Wood
Greenfield Cen.
Elm Park Prim. Sch.
The Ridings Federation Winterbourne Int. Acad.
Playing Field
Winterbourne Park
St. Michael's C of E Prim. Sch.
Library
Croft End
Bradley Bridge
The Malt House
Harcombe Farm
Huckford
Huckford Quarry Local Nature Reserve
Sturden Court
Brook Farm
Whitecroft House
Hambrook Prim. Sch.
Whiteshill Common
Riverside View
Quarry
Fort
Bury Hill
Waterfall Farm
Wynnford Grange
Damsons Bridge
Kendleshire Farm
The Elms
The Old Mill
Weir
Hambrook Grove
The Priory
Landsbury Nurseries
The Homestead
Buryhill Farm
Baugh Farm
Bromley Heath Inf. & Jun. Schools
Leap Bridge
Village Park
Blackhorse Prim. Sch.
Play. Field
Manor House
Cleeve Mill
Lincombe Barn Woods
St. Augustines of Canterbury RC Prim. Sch.
Frenchay Common
HARLEQUIN OFFICE PK.

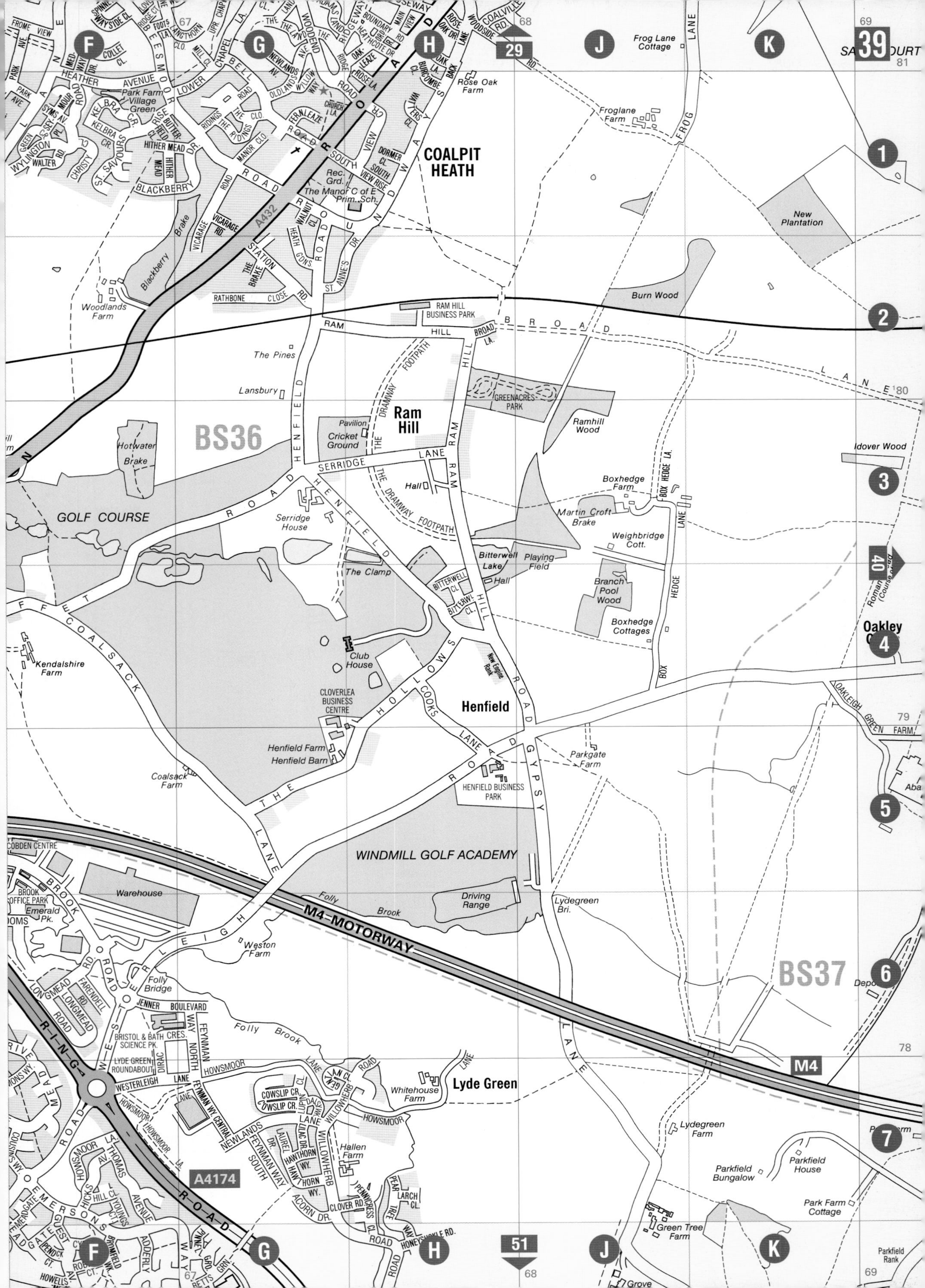
29
51
40
F
G
H
J
K
1
2
3
4
5
6
7
67
68
69
81
80
79
78
COALPIT HEATH
Ram Hill
Henfield
Lyde Green
BS36
BS37
Frog Lane Cottage
Rose Oak Farm
Froglane Farm
New Plantation
Burn Wood
RAM HILL BUSINESS PARK
The Pines
Lansbury
GREENACRES PARK
Ramhill Wood
Idover Wood
Pavilion
Cricket Ground
Hotwater Brake
GOLF COURSE
Serridge House
Hall
Boxhedge Farm
Martin Croft Brake
Weighbridge Cott.
Bitterwell Lake
Playing Field
The Clamp
Branch Pool Wood
Boxhedge Cottages
Kendalshire Farm
Club House
CLOVERLEA BUSINESS CENTRE
Henfield Farm
Henfield Barn
Coalsack Farm
HENFIELD BUSINESS PARK
Parkgate Farm
WINDMILL GOLF ACADEMY
Driving Range
Lydegreen Bri.
Folly Brook
Weston Farm
Folly Bridge
M4 MOTORWAY
M4
A432
A4174
COBDEN CENTRE
Warehouse
BROOK OFFICE PARK
Emerald Pk.
BRISTOL & BATH SCIENCE PK.
LYDE GREEN ROUNDABOUT
Whitehouse Farm
Hallen Farm
Lydegreen Farm
Parkfield Bungalow
Parkfield House
Park Farm Cottage
Green Tree Farm
Parkfield Rank
Woodlands Farm
Blackberry Brake
Rec. Grd.
The Manor C of E Prim. Sch.
Park Farm Village Green
Oakley
Depot
RAM HILL
BROAD LANE
SERRIDGE LANE
HENFIELD ROAD
THE DRAMWAY FOOTPATH
BOX HEDGE LANE
GYPSY LANE
FEET ROAD
COALSACK
THE HOLLOWS
COOKS LANE
WESTERLEIGH ROAD
RING ROAD
JENNER BOULEVARD
HOWSMOOR LANE
STATION ROAD
RATHBONE CLOSE
HEATHER AVENUE
BLACKBERRY

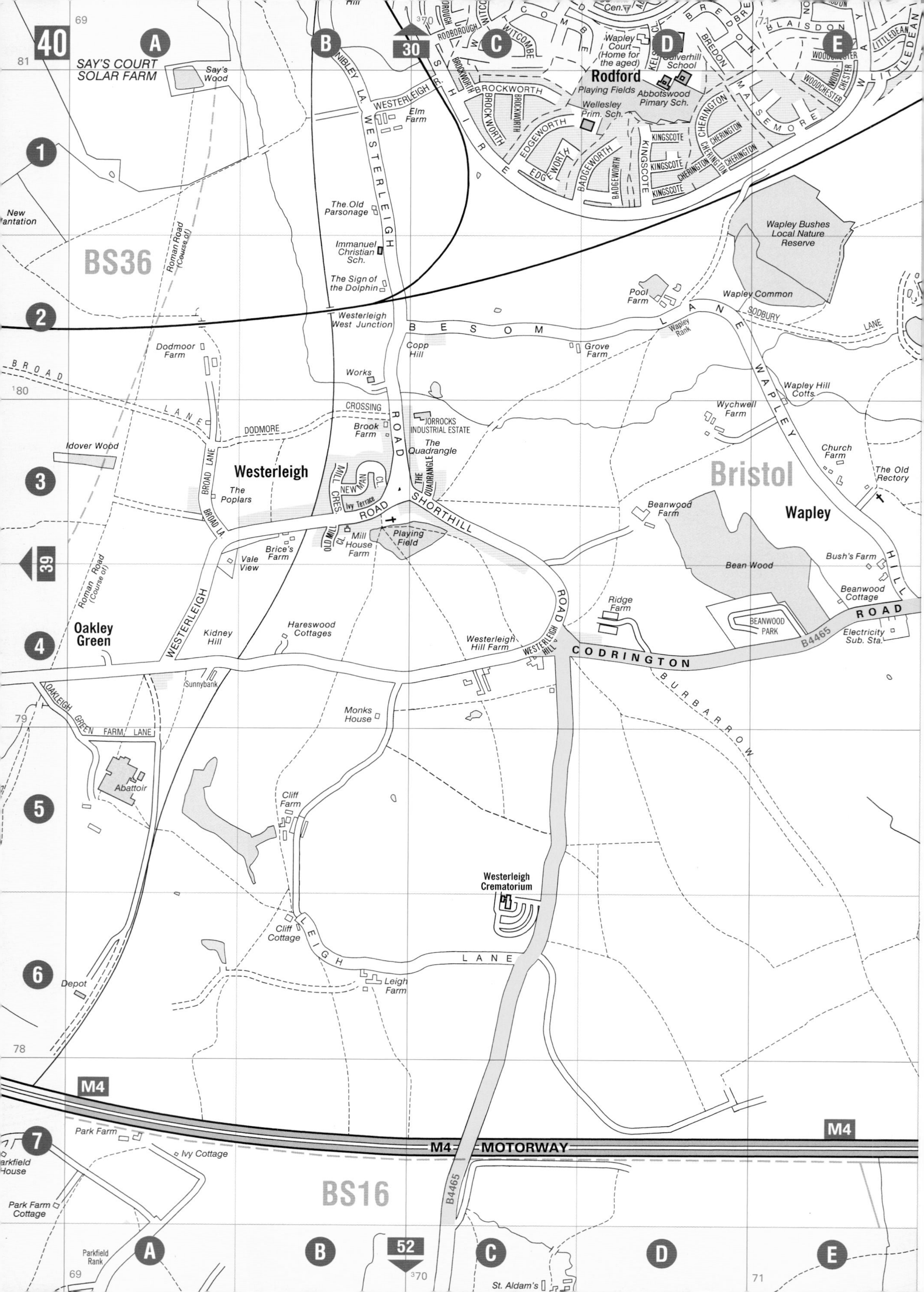
SAY'S COURT
SOLAR FARM
Say's Wood
Rodford
Playing Fields
Wapley Court (Home for the aged)
Culverhill School
Abbotswood Pimary Sch.
Wellesley Prim. Sch.
Elm Farm
New Plantation
BS36
Roman Road (Course of)
The Old Parsonage
Immanuel Christian Sch.
The Sign of the Dolphin
Wapley Bushes Local Nature Reserve
Pool Farm
Wapley Common
Westerleigh West Junction
BESOM LANE
SODBURY LANE
Wapley Rank
Dodmoor Farm
Copp Hill
Grove Farm
BROAD LANE
Works
Wapley Hill Cotts.
Wychwell Farm
CROSSING
DODMORE LANE
Brook Farm
JORROCKS INDUSTRIAL ESTATE
The Quadrangle
Idover Wood
Church Farm
Westerleigh
Bristol
The Old Rectory
The Poplars
Beanwood Farm
Wapley
MILL CRES.
NEWMAN CL.
Ivy Terrace
THE QUADRANGLE
SHORTHILL ROAD
Playing Field
Mill House Farm
Brice's Farm
Vale View
Bean Wood
Bush's Farm
Beanwood Cottage
Ridge Farm
BEANWOOD PARK
CODRINGTON ROAD
B4465
Electricity Sub. Sta.
Oakley Green
Kidney Hill
Hareswood Cottages
Westerleigh Hill Farm
WESTERLEIGH HILL
Sunnybank
OAKLEIGH GREEN FARM LANE
Monks House
BURBARROW
Abattoir
Cliff Farm
Westerleigh Crematorium
Cliff Cottage
LEIGH LANE
Depot
Leigh Farm
M4
Park Farm
Ivy Cottage
Parkfield House
M4 MOTORWAY
Park Farm Cottage
BS16
Parkfield Rank
St. Aldam's

30
39
52

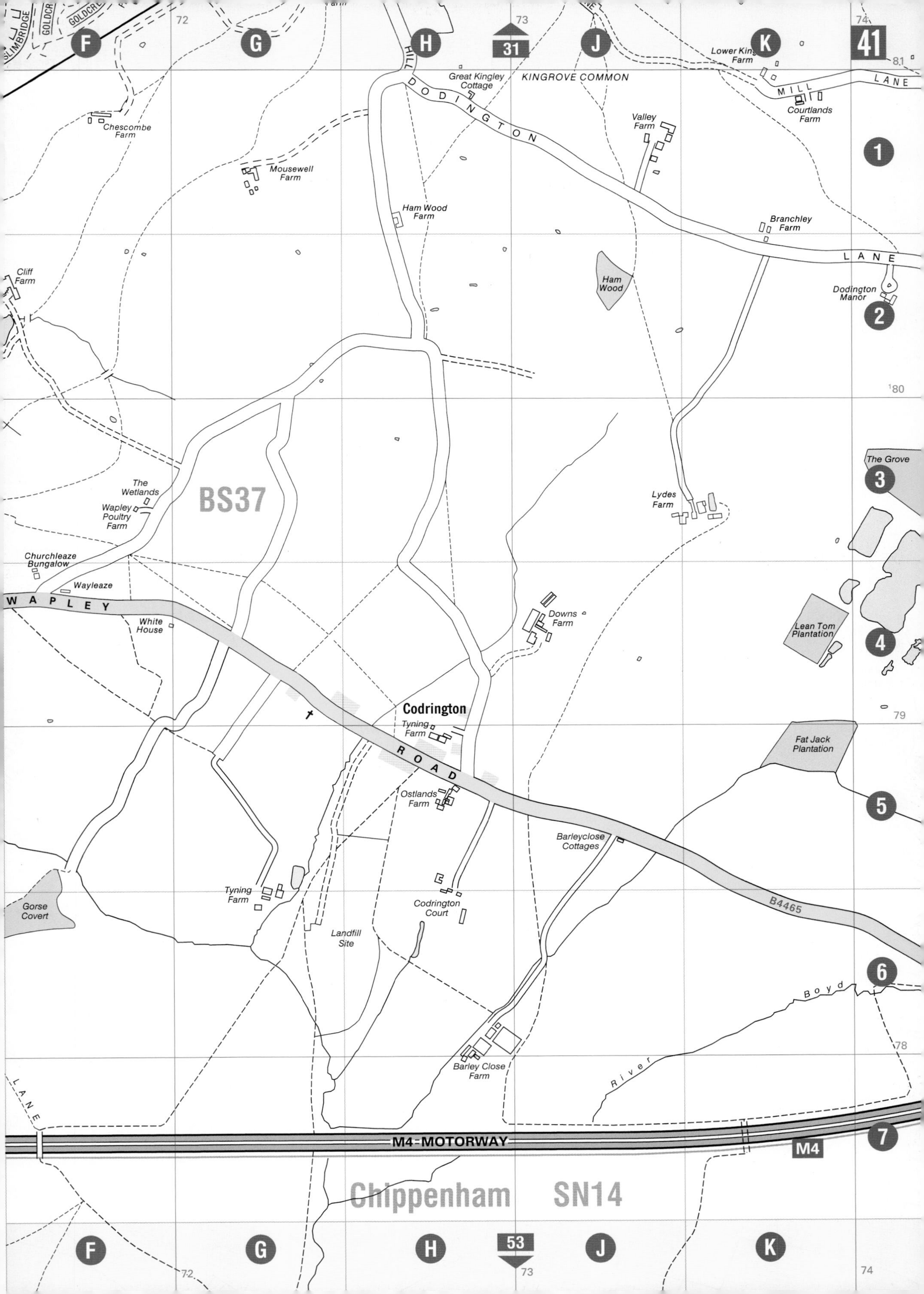

GOLDCRE
GOLDCR
72
73
74
81

Great Kingley
Cottage
KINGROVE COMMON

Lower King
Farm
MILL LANE

Chescombe
Farm

HILL DODINGTON

Valley
Farm

Courtlands
Farm

1

Mousewell
Farm

Ham Wood
Farm

Branchley
Farm

LANE

Cliff
Farm

Ham
Wood

Dodington Manor

2

80

The Grove

3

The
Wetlands

BS37

Lydes
Farm

Wapley
Poultry
Farm

Lean Tom
Plantation

4

Churchleaze
Bungalow

Wayleaze

Downs
Farm

79

WAPLEY

White
House

Fat Jack
Plantation

Codrington

Tyning
Farm

5

ROAD

Ostlands
Farm

Barleyclose
Cottages

B4465

Gorse
Covert

Tyning
Farm

Codrington
Court

6

Landfill
Site

Boyd

78

Barley Close
Farm

River

LANE

M4 - MOTORWAY

M4

7

Chippenham SN14

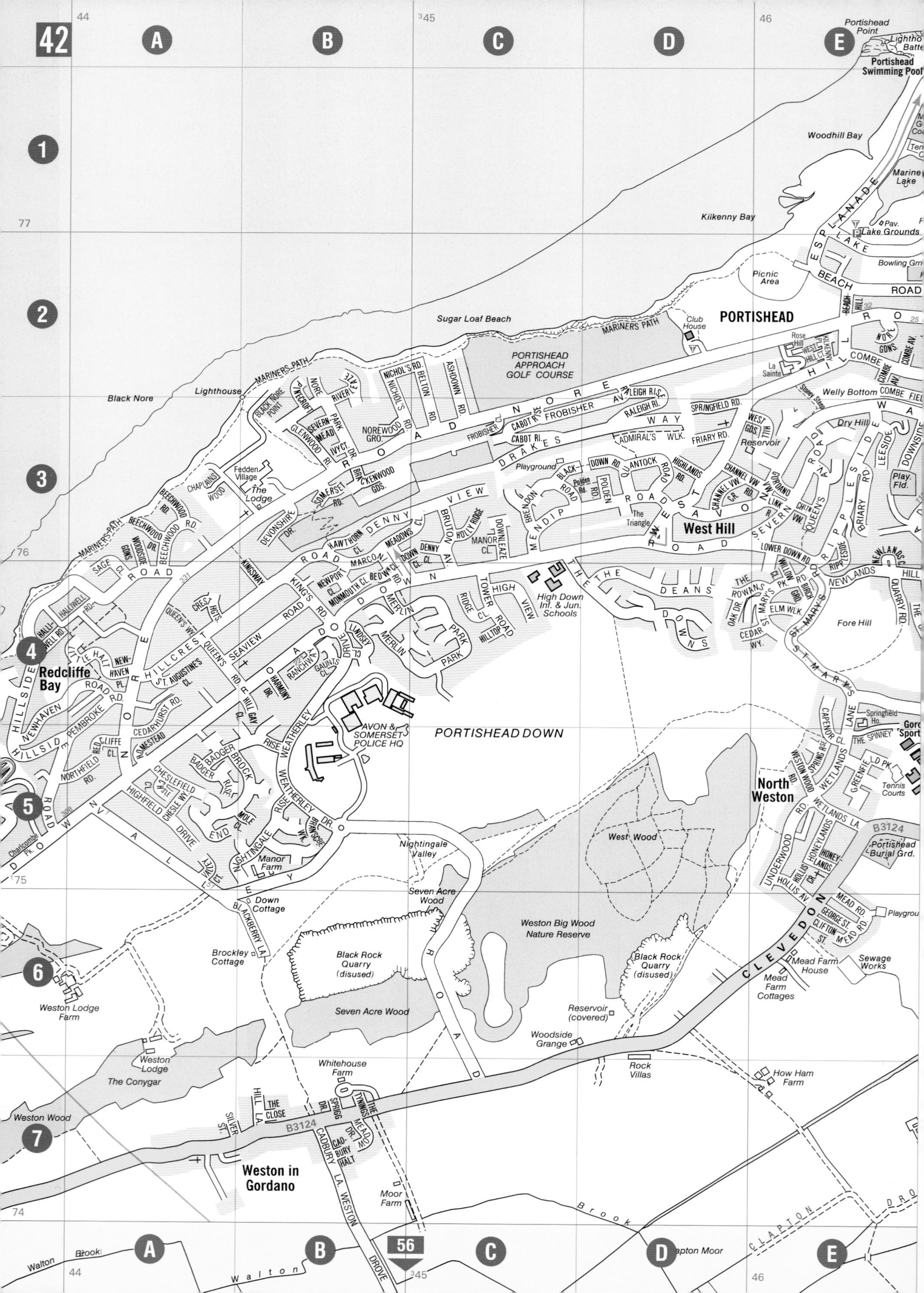

42
A
B
C
D
E
1
2
3
4
5
6
7
44
345
46
77
76
75
74
Portishead Point
Portishead Swimming Pool
Woodhill Bay
Marine Lake
Kilkenny Bay
ESPLANADE
Lake Grounds
LAKE
Bowling Grn
Picnic Area
BEACH
ROAD
Sugar Loaf Beach
Club House
PORTISHEAD
MARINERS PATH
PORTISHEAD APPROACH GOLF COURSE
Rose Hill
KILKENNY
La Sainte
COMBE
Black Nore
Lighthouse
BLACK NORE POINT
PYNECROFT
NORE PARK
RIVERLEAZE
NICHOL'S RD.
BELTON RD.
ASHDOWN RD.
NOREWOOD GRO.
SEVERN MEAD
GLENWOOD RI.
IVY CT. DR.
NORE ROAD
FROBISHER AV.
FROBISHER CL.
RALEIGH RISE
RALEIGH RI.
CABOT RISE
CABOT RI.
DRAKES WAY
ADMIRAL'S WLK.
SPRINGFIELD RD.
FRIARY RD.
Welly Bottom
Stoney Steep
Dry Hill
LEESIDE
DOWNSIDE
Play. Fld.
Reservoir
Playground
CHAPLAINS WOOD
Fedden Village
The Lodge
BRACKENWOOD GDS.
SOMERSET RD.
DEVONSHIRE DR.
BLACKDOWN RD.
QUANTOCK ROAD
HIGHLANDS RD.
CHANNEL VW.
GORDANO
BRENDON ROAD
Polden Rd.
POLDEN RD.
MENDIP ROAD
The Triangle
WEST HILL
West Hill
SEVERN ROAD
QUEEN'S RD.
RIPPLESIDE
BRIARY RD.
MARINERS PATH
BEECHWOOD RD.
BEECHWOOD DR.
WOODSIDE GDNS
SAGE CL.
HALLIWELL RD.
HALLIWELL RD.
DENNY VIEW
HAWTHORN CL.
MEADOWS CL.
BRUTON AV.
HOLLY RIDGE
DOWNLEAZE
MANOR CL.
DENNY CL.
MARCONI RD.
NEWPORT CL.
MONMOUTH CL.
BEDWIN CL.
DOWN ROAD
KINGSWAY
QUEEN'S WY.
CREST HGTS.
SEAVIEW ROAD
KING'S RD.
HIGH VIEW
TOWER ROAD
RIDGE CL.
HILLTOP
MERLIN PARK
MERLIN CL.
LINDSEY CL.
High Down Inf. & Jun. Schools
THE DEANS
THE DOWNS
LOWER DOWN RD.
THE ROWANS
WILLOW GRD.
BIRCH RD.
ELM WLK.
OAK DR.
ST. MARY'S PK. RD.
ST. MARY'S RD.
CEDAR WY.
NEWLANDS
QUARRY RD.
Fore Hill
HILL
Redcliffe Bay
LITTLE HALT
NEWHAVEN PL.
NEWHAVEN ROAD
HILLSIDE
PEMBROKE RD.
HILLCREST
ST. AUGUSTINE'S CL.
CEDARHURST RD.
HOMESTEAD
NORTHFIELD RD.
REDCLIFFE CL.
RANCHWAY
GAUNTS CL.
HARMONY DR.
HILL GAY CL.
WEATHERLEY RISE
WEATHERLEY DR.
AVON & SOMERSET POLICE HQ
PORTISHEAD DOWN
BADGER RISE
BROCK END
MOLE CL.
CHESLEFIELD
CHESLE WY.
HIGHFIELD DRIVE
NIGHTINGALE RISE
Manor Farm
BRAMBLE WLK.
DOWN ROAD
Charlcombe
VALLEY
Springfield Ho.
THE SPINNEY
CAPENOR CL.
LANE
SPRING RISE
WESTON WOOD RD.
WETLANDS
GREENFIELD PK.
Tennis Courts
North Weston
WETLANDS LA.
B3124
Portishead Burial Grd.
UNDERWOOD
HONEYLANDS
HOLLIS CR.
HOLLIS AV.
MEAD RD.
GEORGE ST.
CLIFTON ST.
Playground
Nightingale Valley
West Wood
Seven Acre Wood
Down Cottage
BLACKBERRY LA.
Weston Big Wood Nature Reserve
Brockley Cottage
Black Rock Quarry (disused)
Black Rock Quarry (disused)
Mead Farm House
Mead Farm Cottages
Sewage Works
CLEVEDON
Weston Lodge Farm
Seven Acre Wood
Reservoir (covered)
Woodside Grange
Weston Lodge
The Conygar
Rock Villas
How Ham Farm
Whitehouse Farm
Weston Wood
HILL LA.
THE CLOSE
SILVER ST.
SPRIGG DR.
THE TYNINGS
MEAD DR.
CADBURY HALT
CADBURY LA.
Weston in Gordano
Moor Farm
WESTON DROVE
Brook
CLAPTON
Clapton Moor
Walton
Walton Brook
56

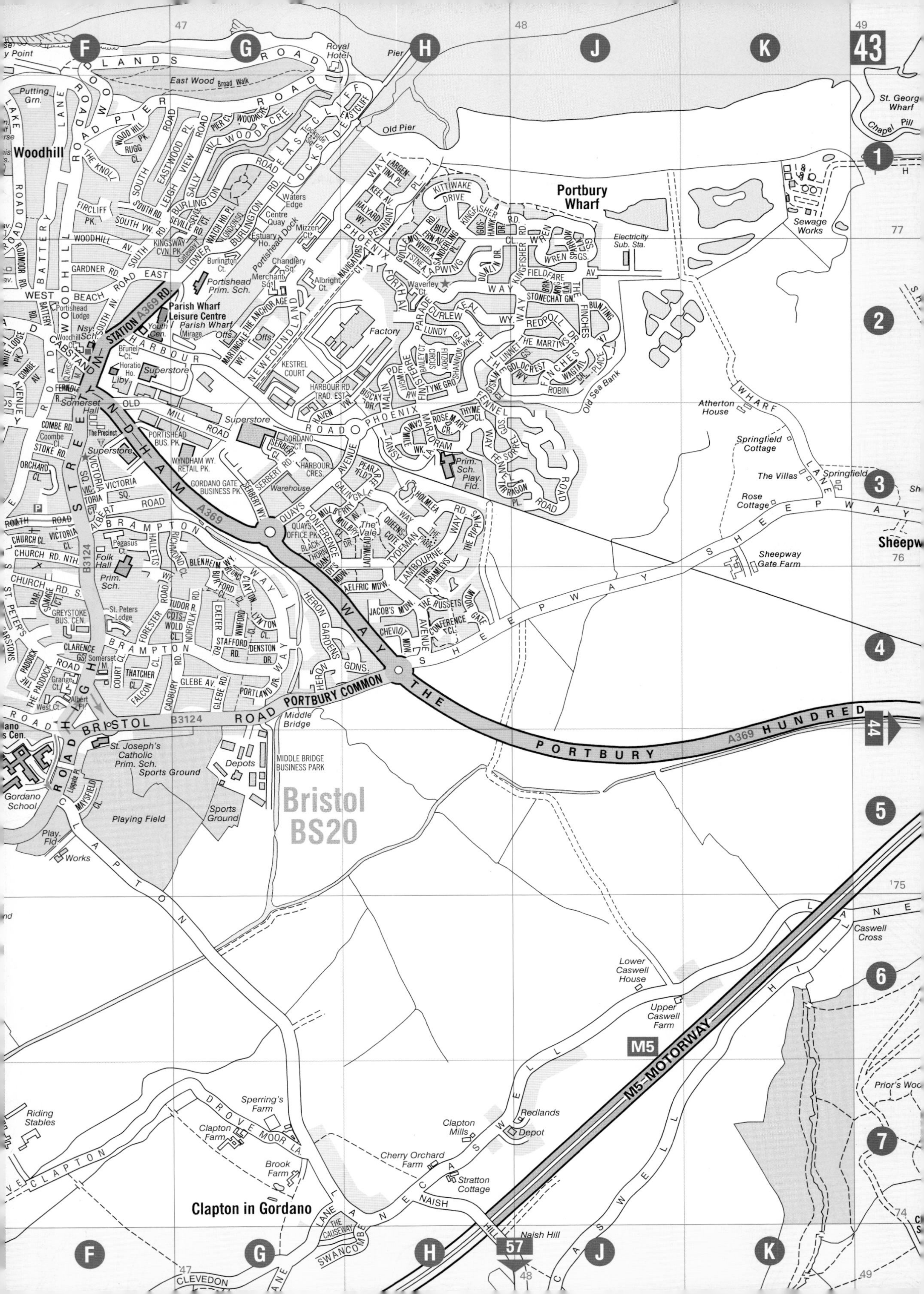
Woodhill
Portbury Wharf
Bristol BS20
Clapton in Gordano
Sheepway
Portishead Dock
Portishead Prim. Sch.
Parish Wharf Leisure Centre
Factory
Sewage Works
Electricity Sub. Sta.
Royal Hotel
Pier
Old Pier
St. George's Wharf
Atherton House
Springfield Cottage
The Villas
Springfield
Rose Cottage
Sheepway Gate Farm
Middle Bridge
MIDDLE BRIDGE BUSINESS PARK
St. Joseph's Catholic Prim. Sch.
Sports Ground
Playing Field
Gordano School
Works
Lower Caswell House
Upper Caswell Farm
Caswell Cross
M5
M5 MOTORWAY
Redlands
Depot
Clapton Mills
Cherry Orchard Farm
Stratton Cottage
Naish Hill
Sperring's Farm
Clapton Farm
Brook Farm
Riding Stables
Prior's Wood
THE PORTBURY HUNDRED
A369
B3124
44
57

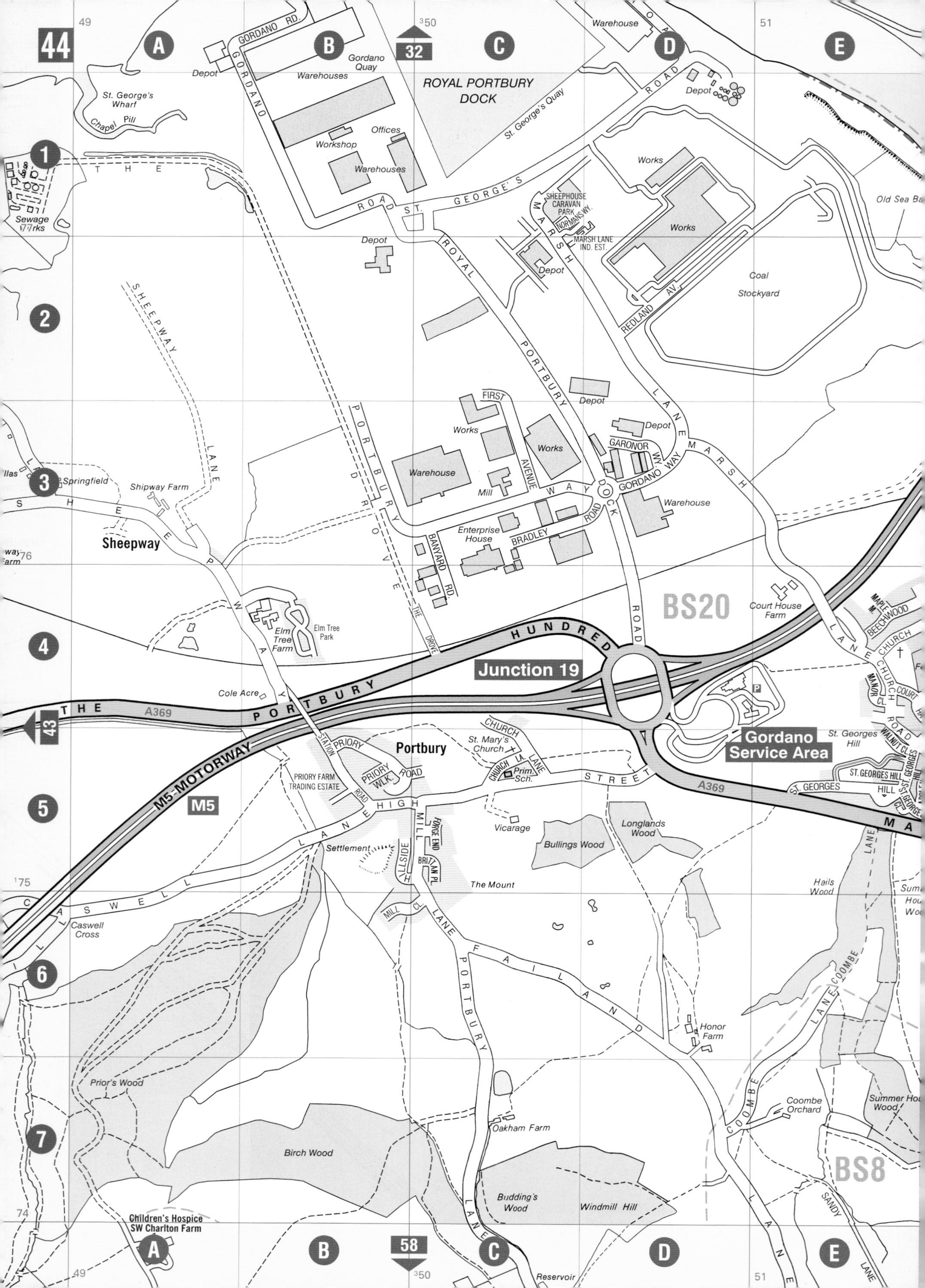

ROYAL PORTBURY DOCK
St. George's Wharf
Chapel Pill
Gordano Quay
Warehouses
Workshop
Offices
Depot
St. George's Quay
Warehouse
Works
Sewage Works
SHEEPHOUSE CARAVAN PARK
MARSH LANE IND. EST.
Coal Stockyard
Old Sea Bank
Springfield
Shipway Farm
Sheepway
Mill
Enterprise House
Elm Tree Farm
Elm Tree Park
Court House Farm
BS20
Junction 19
Cole Acre
Portbury
St. Mary's Church
PRIORY FARM TRADING ESTATE
Prim. Sch.
Vicarage
Gordano Service Area
St. Georges Hill
Longlands Wood
Bullings Wood
Settlement
The Mount
Hails Wood
Caswell Cross
Honor Farm
Prior's Wood
Coombe Orchard
Summer House Wood
Birch Wood
Oakham Farm
BS8
Budding's Wood
Windmill Hill
Children's Hospice SW Charlton Farm
Reservoir
M5-MOTORWAY
M5
A369
THE PORTBURY HUNDRED
32
43
58

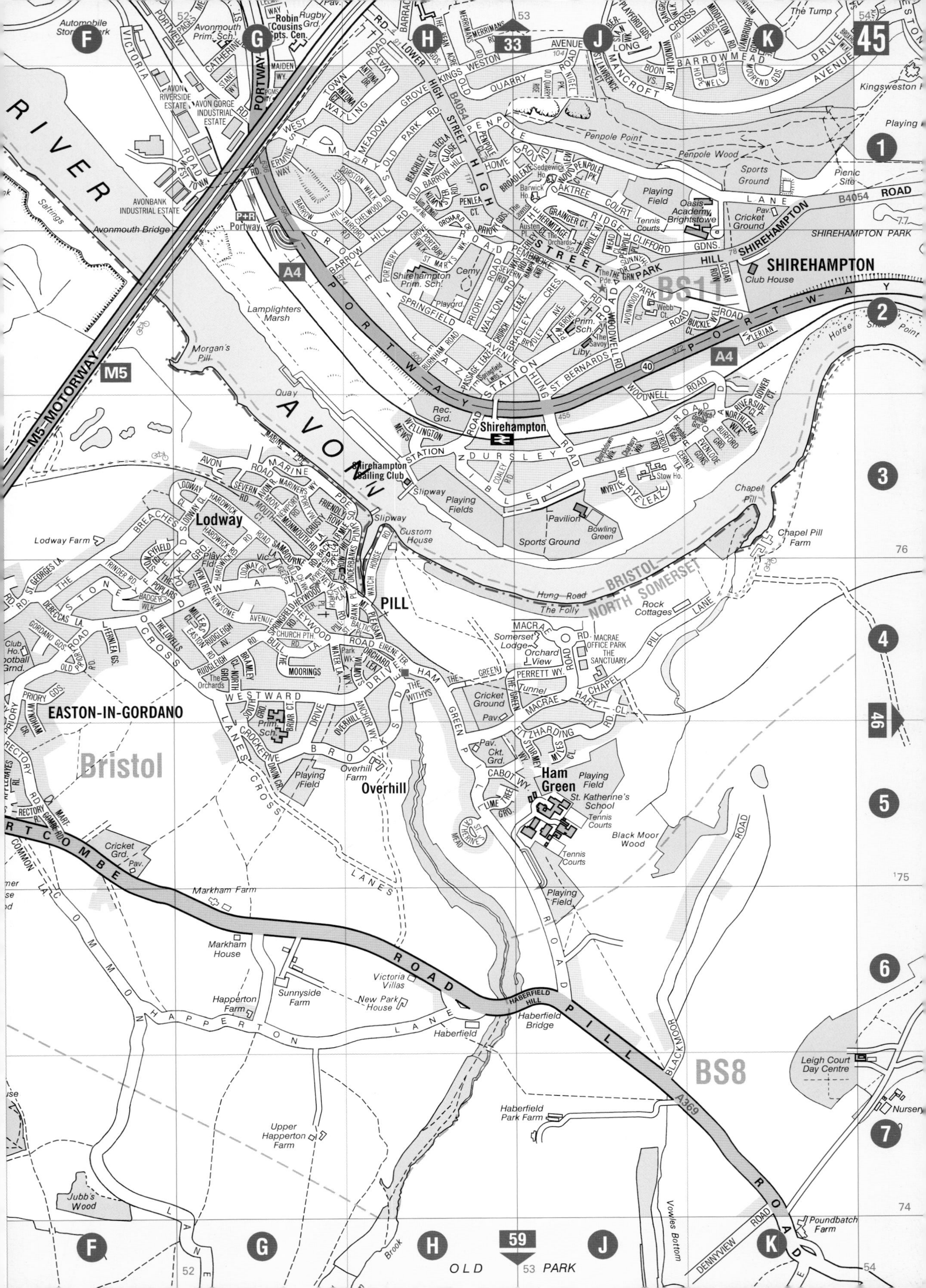

F
G
H
J
K
33
53
52
54
Automobile Storage Park
Avonmouth Prim. Sch.
Robin Cousins Spts. Cen.
Rugby Grd.
The Tump
Kingsweston
Playing
RIVER
AVON
AVON RIVERSIDE ESTATE
AVON GORGE INDUSTRIAL ESTATE
AVONBANK INDUSTRIAL ESTATE
Avonmouth Bridge
Saltings
PORTWAY
P+R Portway
M5 MOTORWAY
M5
A4
B4054
Penpole Point
Penpole Wood
Sports Ground
Picnic Site
Playing Field
Oasis Academy Brightstowe
Tennis Courts
Cricket Ground
SHIREHAMPTON PARK
SHIREHAMPTON
Club House
BS11
HIGH STREET
Shirehampton Prim. Sch.
Cemy
Playgrd.
Prim. Sch.
Liby.
Lamplighters Marsh
Morgan's Pill
Quay
Rec. Grd.
Shirehampton
Shirehampton Sailing Club
Slipway
Playing Fields
Pavilion
Bowling Green
Sports Ground
Stow Ho.
Chapel Pill
Chapel Pill Farm
Horse Shoe Point
Lodway
Lodway Farm
Custom House
PILL
BRISTOL
NORTH SOMERSET
Hung Road
The Folly
Rock Cottages
Somerset Lodge
Orchard View
MACRAE OFFICE PARK
THE SANCTUARY
Club Ho.
Football Grnd.
EASTON-IN-GORDANO
Bristol
Cricket Ground
Pav.
Prim. Sch.
Playing Field
Overhill Farm
Overhill
Ckt. Grd.
Ham Green
Playing Field
St. Katherine's School
Tennis Courts
Black Moor Wood
Cricket Grd.
Markham Farm
Markham House
Victoria Villas
New Park House
Sunnyside Farm
Happerton Farm
HABERFIELD HILL
Haberfield Bridge
Haberfield
PILL ROAD
A369
BS8
Leigh Court Day Centre
Nursery
Haberfield Park Farm
Upper Happerton Farm
Jubb's Wood
Vowles Bottom
Poundbatch Farm
DENNYVIEW ROAD
BLACKMOOR ROAD
HAPPERTON LANE
OLD PARK
Brook
46
59
1
2
3
4
5
6
7
76
75
74

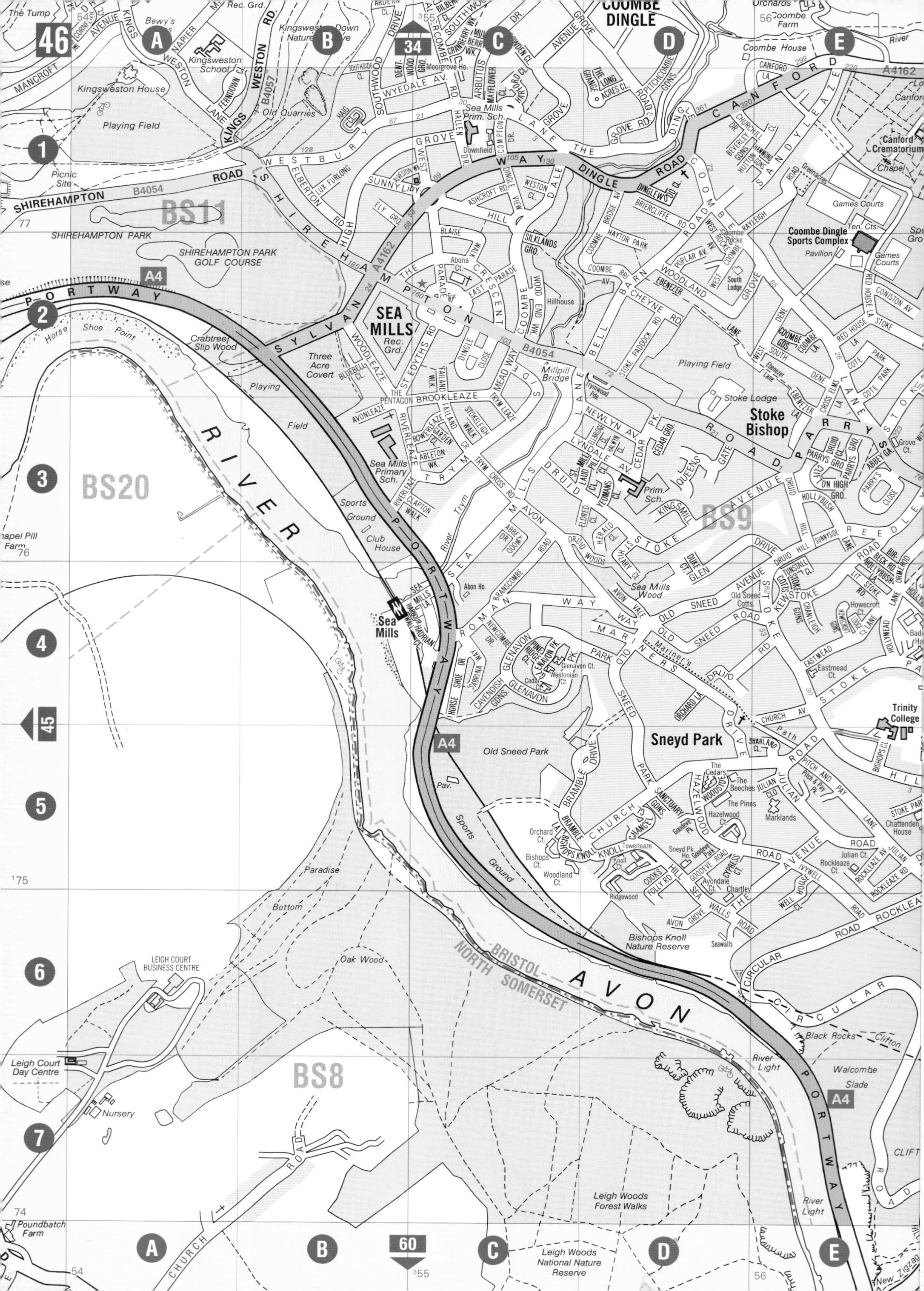

46
34
45
60
A
B
C
D
E
1
2
3
4
5
6
7
COOMBE DINGLE
SEA MILLS
Stoke Bishop
Sneyd Park
BS11
BS20
BS9
BS8
SHIREHAMPTON ROAD
SHIREHAMPTON PARK
SHIREHAMPTON PARK GOLF COURSE
PORTWAY
A4
A4162
B4054
B4057
RIVER AVON
Kingsweston House
Kingsweston School
Kingsweston Down Nature Reserve
Playing Field
Picnic Site
Old Quarries
Horse Shoe Point
Crabtree Slip Wood
Three Acre Covert
Sea Mills Rec. Grd.
Sea Mills Primary Sch.
Sea Mills Prim. Sch.
Sports Ground
Club House
Sea Mills
Sea Mills Wood
Abon Ho.
Old Sneed Park
Millpill Bridge
Stoke Lodge
Coombe Dingle Sports Complex
Canford Crematorium
Games Courts
Pavilion
Coombe House
Coombe Farm
Trinity College
Markslands
Bishops Knoll Nature Reserve
Paradise Bottom
Oak Wood
Leigh Court Business Centre
Leigh Court Day Centre
Nursery
Leigh Woods Forest Walks
Leigh Woods National Nature Reserve
NORTH SOMERSET
BRISTOL
Black Rocks
Walcombe Slade
River Light
Poundbatch Farm
Chapel Pill Farm
CIRCULAR ROAD
STOKE HILL
PARRY'S LANE
CANFORD LANE
SANDY LEAZE
DINGLE ROAD
WESTBURY LANE
SYLVAN WAY
STOKE ROAD
CHURCH ROAD
ROCKLEAZE

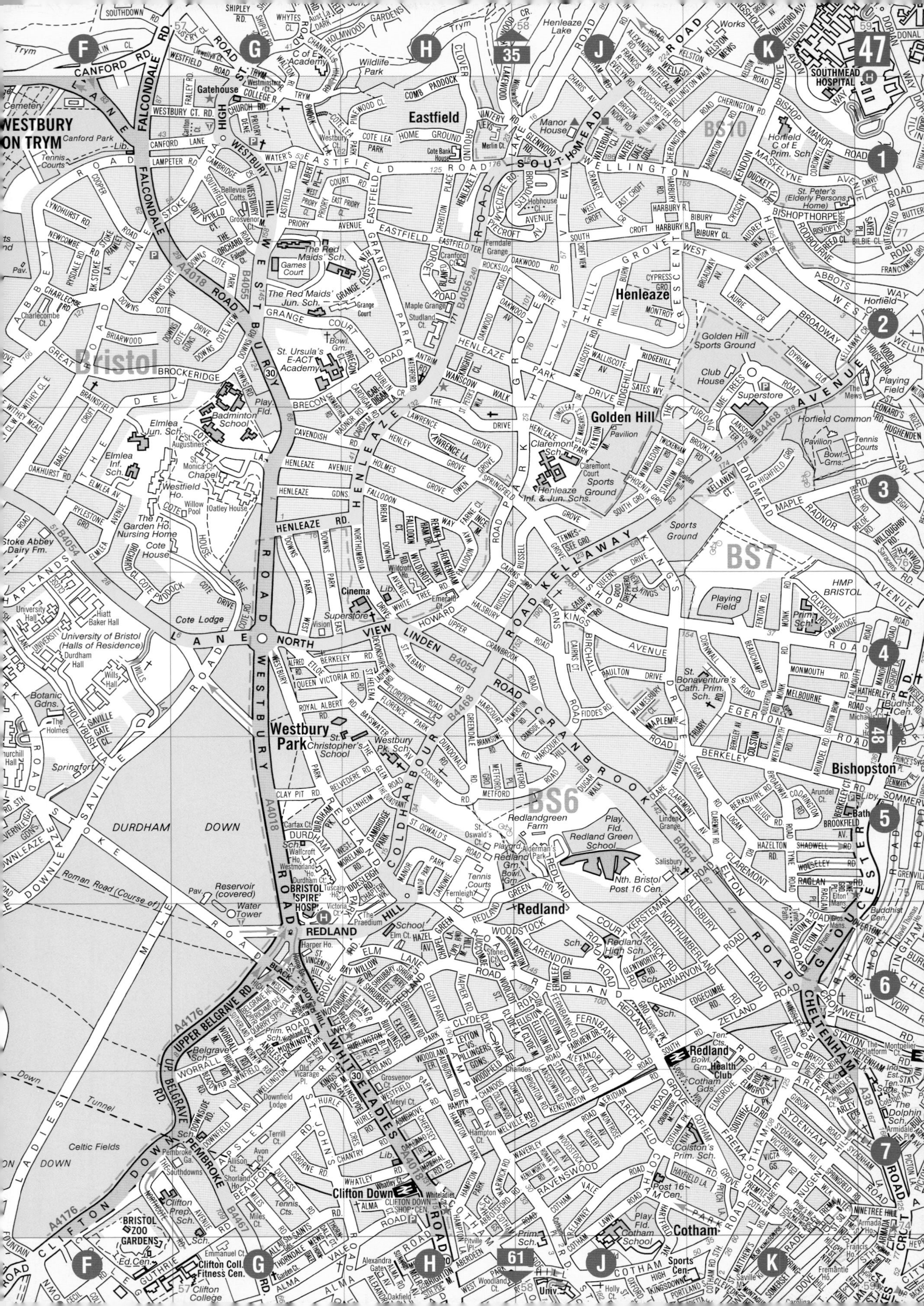

47
F
G
H
J
K
1
2
3
4
5
6
7
35
61
48
57
58
59
77
WESTBURY ON TRYM
Eastfield
Henleaze
Golden Hill
Bristol
Westbury Park
Redland
Bishopston
Cotham
Clifton Down
BS6
BS7
BS10
SOUTHMEAD HOSPITAL
Horfield Common
HMP BRISTOL
Badminton School
The Red Maids' Sch.
St. Ursula's E-ACT Academy
Elmlea Jun. Sch.
Elmlea Inf. Sch.
Westfield Ho.
Cote House
Cote Lodge
University of Bristol (Halls of Residence)
Botanic Gdns.
DURDHAM DOWN
Reservoir (covered)
Water Tower
Celtic Fields
BRISTOL ZOO GARDENS
Clifton Coll. Fitness Cen.
Clifton College
BRISTOL 'SPIRE' HOSP.
Redland Green School
Redlandgreen Farm
Golden Hill Sports Ground
Sports Ground
Superstore
Cinema
Gatehouse
Canford Park
Henleaze Lake
Wildlife Park
Manor House
Claremont Sch.
Henleaze Inf. & Jun. Schs.
St. Christopher's School
Westbury Pk. Sch.
Colston's Prim. Sch.
Cotham School
Sports Cen.
FALCONDALE RD.
WESTBURY RD.
HENLEAZE RD.
KELLAWAY AV.
SOUTHMEAD RD.
WELLINGTON RD.
EASTFIELD RD.
GLOUCESTER RD.
CHELTENHAM RD.
CRANBROOK RD.
COLDHARBOUR RD.
WHITELADIES RD.
UPPER BELGRAVE RD.
STOKE RD.
NORTH VIEW
CLIFTON DOWN
A4018
A4176
B4054
B4055
B4056
B4468
B4467
A38

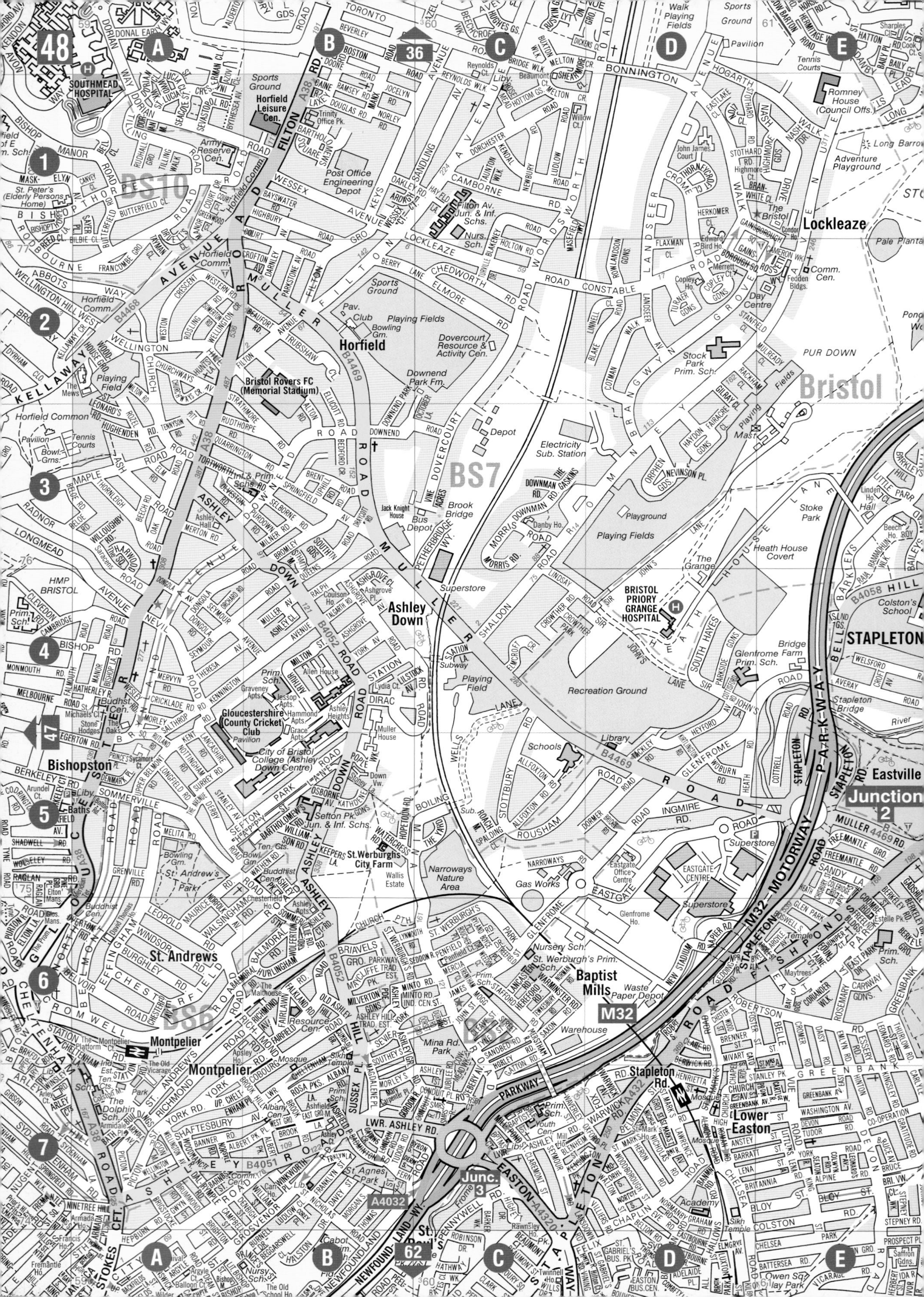
36
47
62
A
B
C
D
E
1
2
3
4
5
6
7
BS10
BS7
BS6
BS2
Bristol
Horfield
Lockleaze
Ashley Down
Bishopston
St. Andrews
Montpelier
Baptist Mills
Lower Easton
STAPLETON
Eastville
PUR DOWN
Southmead Hospital
Horfield Leisure Cen.
Sports Ground
Post Office Engineering Depot
Army Reserve Cen.
St. Peter's (Elderly Persons Home)
Horfield Comm.
Horfield Common
Playing Field
Playing Fields
Bristol Rovers FC (Memorial Stadium)
Dovercourt Resource & Activity Cen.
Downend Park Fm.
HMP BRISTOL
Gloucestershire County Cricket Club
City of Bristol College (Ashley Down Centre)
Muller House
Electricity Sub. Station
Depot
Superstore
Recreation Ground
BRISTOL PRIORY GRANGE HOSPITAL
Heath House Covert
Stoke Park
Glenfrome Prim. Sch.
Stock Park Prim. Sch.
Romney House (Council Offs.)
Adventure Playground
Colston's School
Narroways Nature Area
St. Werburghs City Farm
Gas Works
EASTGATE CENTRE
St. Andrew's Park
Mina Rd. Park
St. Agnes Park
Junction 2
Junc. 3
M32
M32 MOTORWAY
PARKWAY
A38
A4032
A4320
A432
B4051
B4052
B4058
B4468
B4469
GLOUCESTER ROAD
MULLER ROAD
FILTON AVENUE
FILTON RD.
WELLINGTON HILL WEST
KELLAWAY AV.
ASHLEY DOWN ROAD
LOCKLEAZE ROAD
CONSTABLE ROAD
WORDSWORTH ROAD
DOWNEND ROAD
GLENFROME ROAD
STAPLETON ROAD
FISHPONDS ROAD
CHELTENHAM ROAD
EASTON WAY
NEWFOUNDLAND WY.
ASHLEY ROAD
CROMWELL ROAD
ST. WERBURGH'S PARK
BONNINGTON WALK
Walk Playing Fields
Long Barrow
Pale Plantation

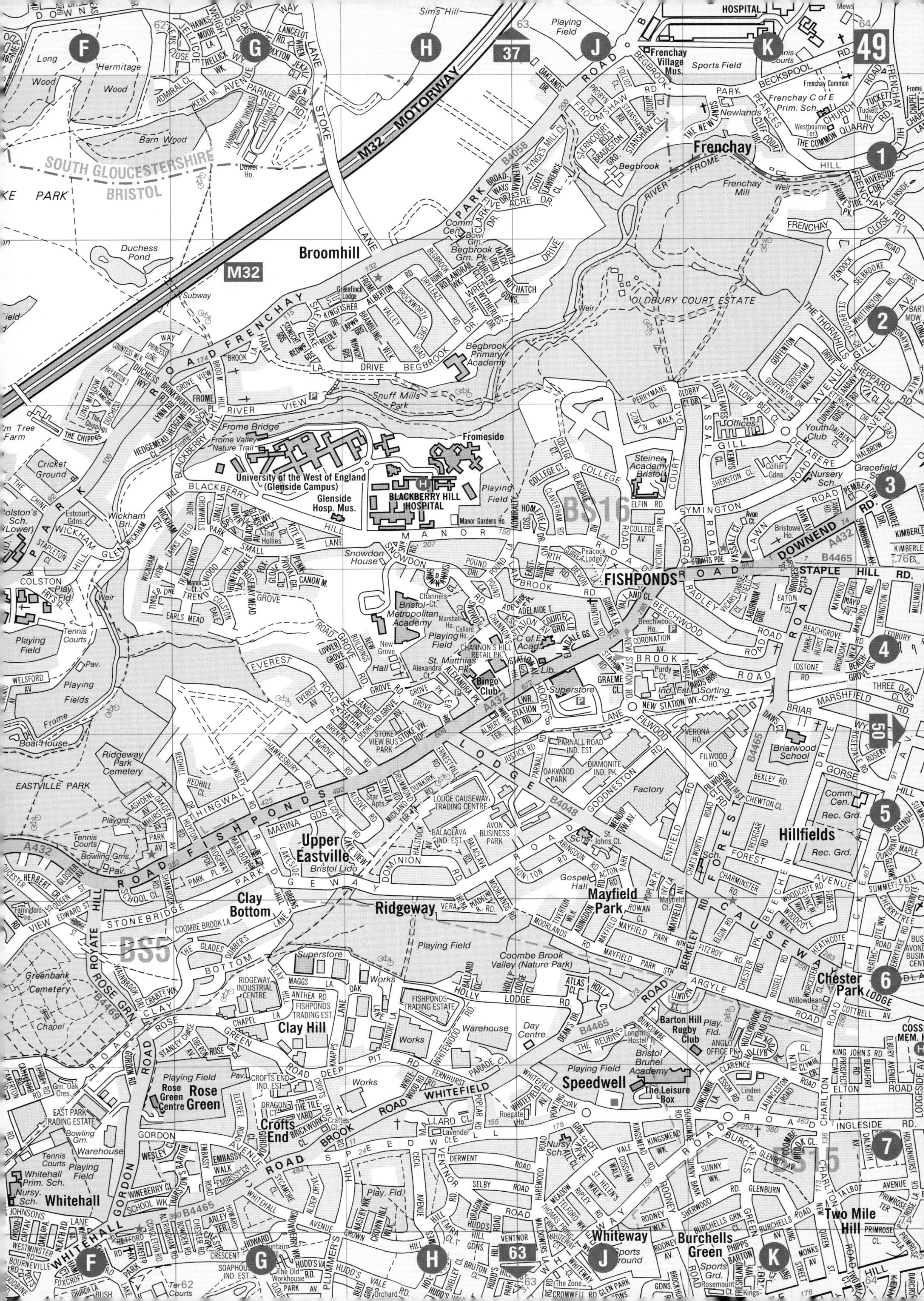
M32 MOTORWAY
SOUTH GLOUCESTERSHIRE
BRISTOL
Broomhill
Frenchay
Frenchay Mill
OLDBURY COURT ESTATE
Snuff Mills Park
Begbrook Primary Academy
University of the West of England (Glenside Campus)
Glenside Hosp. Mus.
BLACKBERRY HILL HOSPITAL
Fromeside
Steiner Academy Bristol
BS16
FISHPONDS
Bristol Metropolitan Academy
Snowdon House
Channon's Hill Retail Pk.
Bingo Club
Superstore
Lodge Causeway Trading Centre
Upper Eastville
Bristol Lido
Ridgeway Park Cemetery
EASTVILLE PARK
Clay Bottom
Ridgeway
Mayfield Park
Hillfields
Briarwood School
BS5
Greenbank Cemetery
Ridgeway Industrial Centre
Fishponds Trading Est.
Clay Hill
Fishponds Trading Estate
Coombe Brook Valley (Nature Park)
Barton Hill Rugby Club
Bristol Brunel Academy
The Leisure Box
Speedwell
Rose Green
Crofts End
Whitehall
East Park Trading Estate
Chester Park
Two Mile Hill
BS15
Whiteway
Burchells Green
FISHPONDS ROAD
DOWNEND RD.
STAPLE HILL RD.
FRENCHAY PARK ROAD
A432
B4465
B4048
B4058
B4469
37
50
63

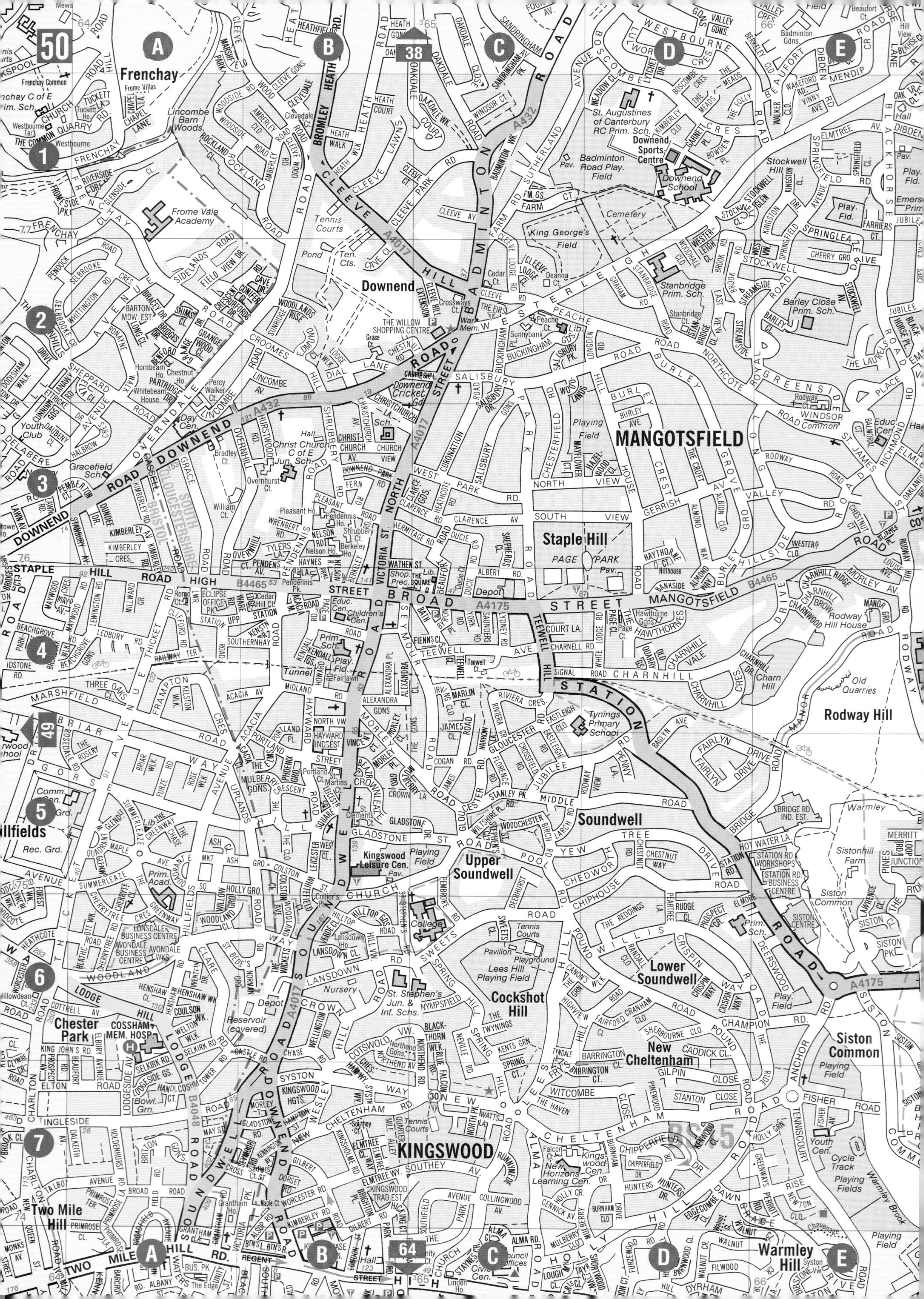
A
B
C
D
E
1
2
3
4
5
6
7
38
49
64
Frenchay
Frenchay Common
Frenchay C of E Prim. Sch.
Frome Villas
Lincombe Barn Woods
Frome Vale Academy
Downend
THE WILLOW SHOPPING CENTRE
Christ Church C of E Jun. Sch.
Gracefield Sch.
St. Augustines of Canterbury RC Prim. Sch.
Downend Sports Centre
Downend School
Badminton Road Play. Field
Cemetery
King George's Field
Stanbridge Prim. Sch.
Barley Close Prim. Sch.
MANGOTSFIELD
Playing Field
Staple Hill
PAGE PARK
Rodway Hill House
Old Quarries
Rodway Hill
Tynings Primary School
Soundwell
Upper Soundwell
Kingswood Leisure Cen.
College
St. Stephen's Jun. & Inf. Schs.
Lees Hill Playing Field
Cockshot Hill
Lower Soundwell
New Cheltenham
Siston Common
KINGSWOOD
New Horizons Learning Cen.
Kingswood Cen.
Chester Park
COSSHAM MEM. HOSP.
Two Mile Hill
Warmley Hill
Warmley Brook
Cycle Track
Playing Fields
Sistonhill Farm
BRIDGE RD. IND. EST.
STATION RD. BUSINESS CENTRE
SISTON CENTRE
LONSDALE BUSINESS CENTRE
AVONDALE BUSINESS CENTRE
HAYWARD IND. EST.
KINGSWOOD TRAD. EST.
BS15
A432
A4017
A4175
B4465
B4048
DOWNEND ROAD
BADMINTON ROAD
CLEEVE HILL
BROMLEY HEATH RD.
NORTH STREET
VICTORIA ST.
BROAD STREET
HIGH STREET
STAPLE HILL ROAD
MANGOTSFIELD ROAD
STATION ROAD
SOUNDWELL ROAD
DOWNEND ROAD
LODGE ROAD
TWO MILE HILL RD.
CHELTENHAM ROAD
SIDELANDS ROAD
OVERNDALE ROAD
WESTERLEIGH ROAD
ROYAL ROAD
BLACKHORSE ROAD
MARSHFIELD ROAD
BRIAR WAY
SOUTH GLOUCESTERSHIRE
BRISTOL

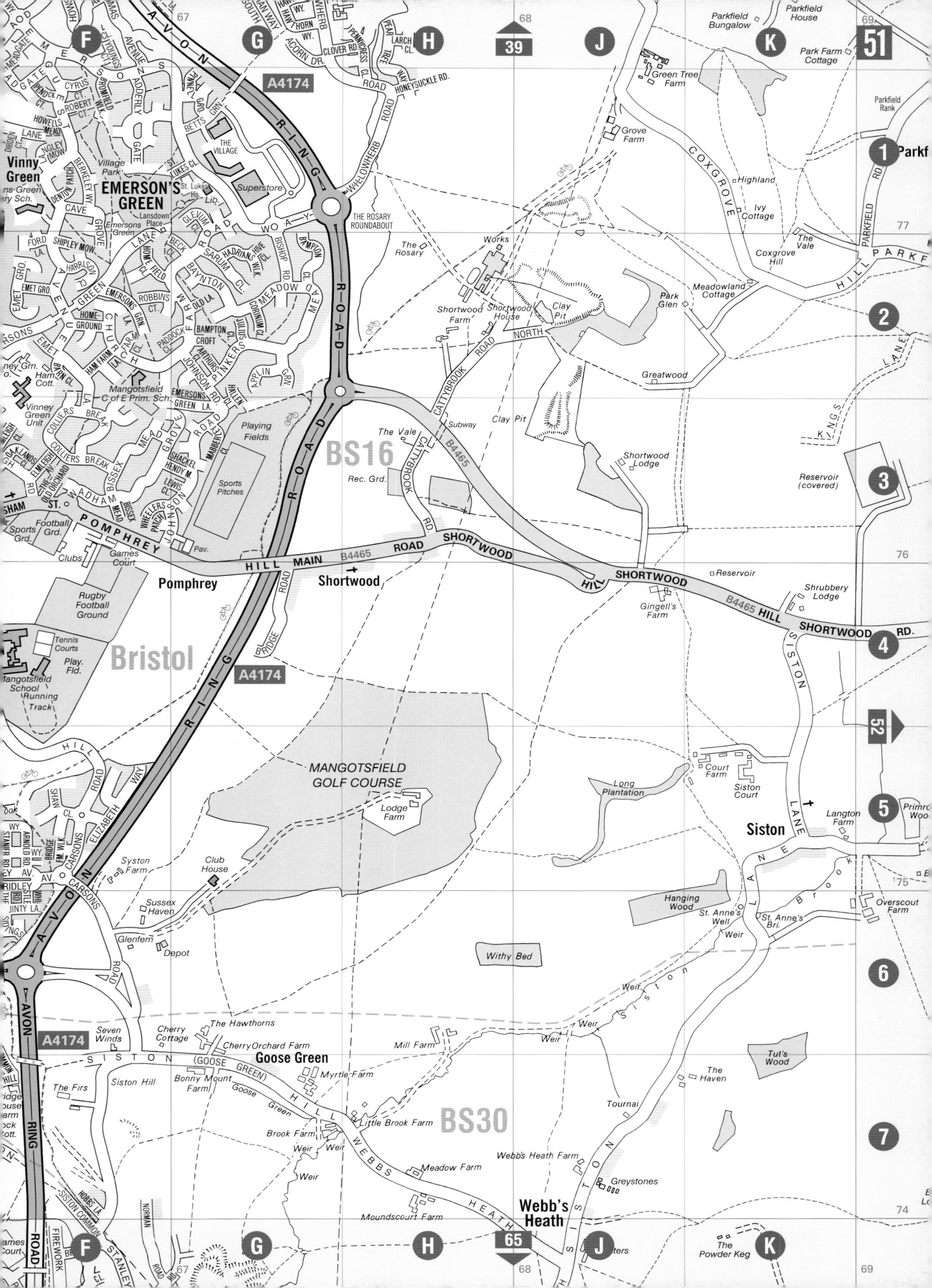

51
39
65
52
F
G
H
J
K
1
2
3
4
5
6
7
67
68
69
77
76
75
74
A4174
RING ROAD
AVON RING ROAD
B4465
BS16
BS30
Bristol
EMERSON'S GREEN
Vinny Green
Pomphrey
Shortwood
Siston
Goose Green
Webb's Heath
THE ROSARY ROUNDABOUT
THE VILLAGE
Superstore
Village Park
Lansdown Place
Emersons Green
Playing Fields
Sports Pitches
Rugby Football Ground
Tennis Courts
Play. Fld.
Mangotsfield School Running Track
Mangotsfield C of E Prim. Sch.
Vinney Green Unit
Football Grd.
Sports Grd.
Clubs
Games Court
Pav.
MANGOTSFIELD GOLF COURSE
Lodge Farm
Club House
Syston Farm
Sussex Haven
Glenfern
Depot
Seven Winds
Cherry Cottage
The Hawthorns
Cherry Orchard Farm
Bonny Mount Farm
Myrtle Farm
Little Brook Farm
Brook Farm
Meadow Farm
Moundscourt Farm
Webb's Heath Farm
Greystones
Tournai
The Haven
Tut's Wood
The Powder Keg
Withy Bed
Hanging Wood
St. Anne's Well
St. Anne's Bri.
Weir
Overscout Farm
Langton Farm
Court Farm
Siston Court
Long Plantation
Reservoir (covered)
Reservoir
Shrubbery Lodge
Gingell's Farm
Shortwood Lodge
Clay Pit
Greatwood
Park Glen
Meadowland Cottage
Coxgrove Hill
The Vale
Ivy Cottage
Highland
Grove Farm
Green Tree Farm
Parkfield Bungalow
Parkfield House
Park Farm Cottage
Parkfield Rank
Works
The Rosary
Shortwood Farm
Shortwood House
Subway
Rec. Grd.
The Firs
Siston Hill
SHORTWOOD HILL
SHORTWOOD RD.
SHORTWOOD ROAD
HILL MAIN ROAD
POMPHREY HILL
CATTYBROOK ROAD
CATTYBROOK RD.
SHORTWOOD ROAD NORTH
COXGROVE HILL
PARKFIELD RD.
KINGS LANE
SISTON LANE
SISTON HILL
WEBBS HEATH
SISTON COMMON
HOBBS LA.
FIREWORK
STANLEY
NORMAN ROAD
CARSONS AV.
CARSONS ROAD
ELIZABETH WAY
HILL ROAD
WHITTUCKS ROAD
BRIDGE ROAD
Siston Brook
EMERSONS GREEN LA.
CHURCH LA.
WADHAM ST.
COLLIERS BREAK
BISSEX MEAD
JOHNSON RD.
HONEYSUCKLE RD.
CLOVER RD.
ACORN DR.
BISHOP RD.
BAMPTON CL.
ROBBINS CT.
BAYNTON
SARUM
GLEVUM CL.
HADRIANS WLK.

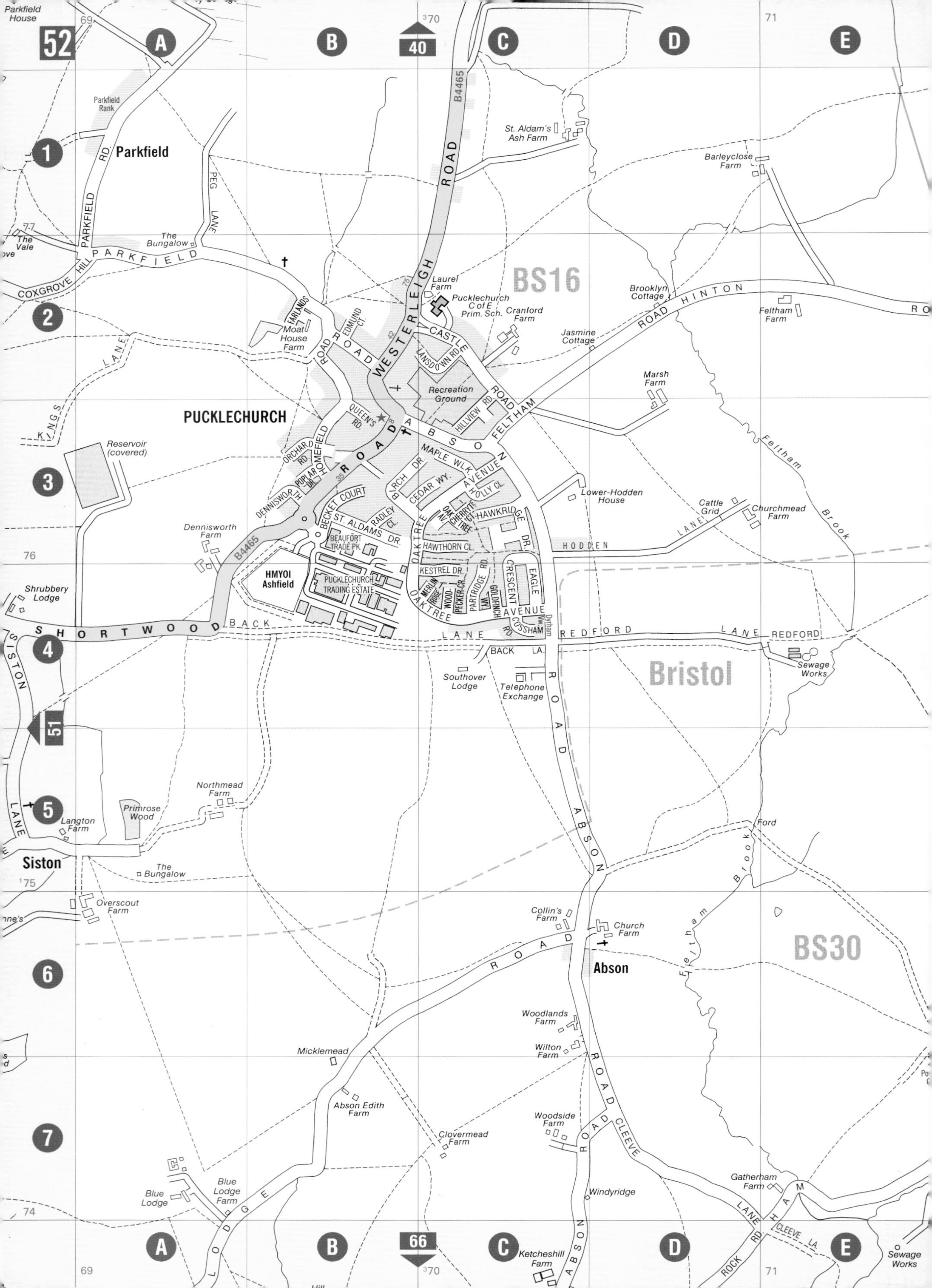

Parkfield House
Parkfield Rank
Parkfield
PARKFIELD RD.
PEG LANE
The Vale
The Bungalow
PARKFIELD
COXGROVE HILL
FARLANDS
Moat House Farm
EDMUND CT.
ROAD
WESTERLEIGH ROAD
B4465
Laurel Farm
Pucklechurch C of E Prim. Sch.
Cranford Farm
St. Aldam's Ash Farm
BS16
Barleyclose Farm
Brooklyn Cottage
HINTON ROAD
Feltham Farm
Jasmine Cottage
CASTLE ROAD
LANSDOWN RD.
Recreation Ground
HILLVIEW RD.
FELTHAM
Marsh Farm
PUCKLECHURCH
KINGS LANE
Reservoir (covered)
QUEEN'S RD.
ABSON
MAPLE WLK.
ORCHARD RD.
HOMEFIELD
POPLAR DR.
DENNISWORTH
BECKET COURT
BIRCH DR.
CEDAR WY.
AVENUE
HOLLY CL.
Lower-Hodden House
ST. ALDAMS DR.
RADLEY CL.
OAKTREE AV.
CHERRYTREE CT.
HAWKRIDGE DR.
Cattle Grid
Churchmead Farm
Feltham Brook
Dennisworth Farm
BEAUFORT TRADE PK.
HAWTHORN CL.
HODDEN LANE
HMYOI Ashfield
PUCKLECHURCH TRADING ESTATE
KESTREL DR.
MERLIN RIDGE
WOODPECKER CR.
PARTRIDGE RD.
GOLDFINCH RD.
CRESCENT
EAGLE
Shrubbery Lodge
SHORTWOOD
BACK LANE
OAKTREE AVENUE
COSSHAM
Dyrham Vw.
REDFORD LANE
REDFORD
BACK LA.
Southover Lodge
Telephone Exchange
Bristol
Sewage Works
SISTON LANE
51
Northmead Farm
Primrose Wood
Langton Farm
Siston
The Bungalow
ABSON ROAD
Ford
Overscout Farm
Collin's Farm
Church Farm
Abson
ROAD
BS30
Feltham Brook
Woodlands Farm
Wilton Farm
Micklemead
Absons Edith Farm
Clovermead Farm
Woodside Farm
ROAD
CLEEVE
Blue Lodge
Blue Lodge Farm
LODGE
Windyridge
Gatherham Farm
HAM
LANE
ROCK RD.
CLEEVE LA.
Ketcheshill Farm
ABSON
Sewage Works
40
66
A
B
C
D
E
1
2
3
4
5
6
7
69
370
71
77
76
75
74

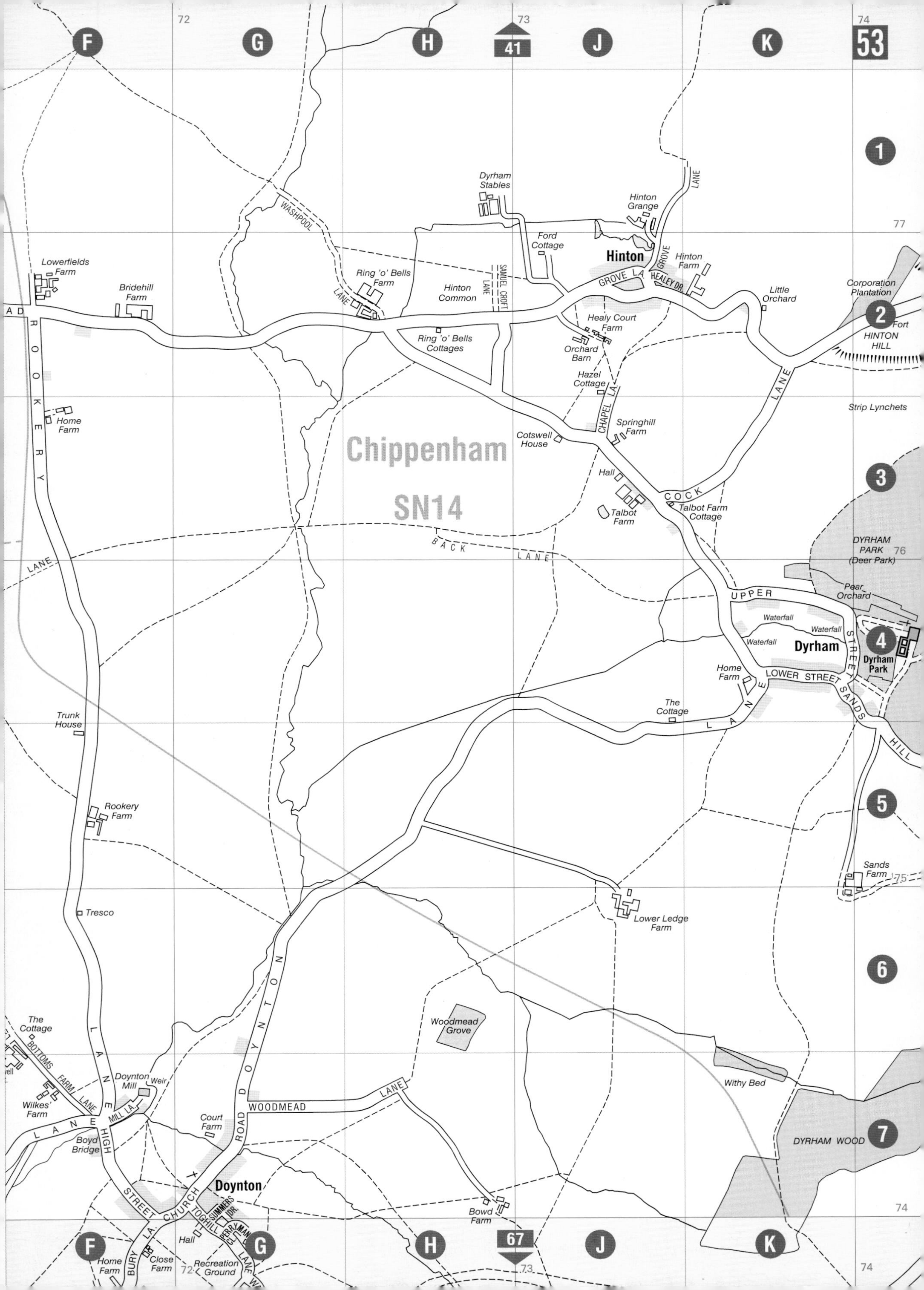
F
G
H
41
J
K
72
73
74
1
2
3
4
5
6
7
77
76
75
74
Dyrham Stables
WASHPOOL
Hinton Grange
LANE
Ford Cottage
Hinton
GROVE
Hinton Farm
GROVE LA.
HEALEY DR.
Little Orchard
Corporation Plantation
Fort
HINTON HILL
Lowerfields Farm
Bridehill Farm
Ring 'o' Bells Farm
LANE
Hinton Common
SAMUEL CROFT
LANE
Healy Court Farm
Ring 'o' Bells Cottages
Orchard Barn
Hazel Cottage
CHAPEL LA.
LANE
Strip Lynchets
ROOKERY
Home Farm
Chippenham
SN14
Cotswell House
Springhill Farm
Hall
COCK
Talbot Farm Cottage
Talbot Farm
BACK LANE
LANE
DYRHAM PARK (Deer Park)
Pear Orchard
UPPER
Waterfall
Waterfall
Waterfall
Dyrham
Dyrham Park
STREET
Home Farm
LOWER STREET
SANDS
HILL
The Cottage
LANE
Trunk House
Rookery Farm
Sands Farm
Lower Ledge Farm
Tresco
DOYNTON
Woodmead Grove
Withy Bed
The Cottage
BOTTOMS FARM LANE
LANE
Doynton Mill
Weir
Wilkes' Farm
MILL LA.
LANE
HIGH
WOODMEAD
LANE
Court Farm
ROAD
Boyd Bridge
DYRHAM WOOD
Doynton
STREET
CHURCH
TOGHILL
SUMMERS DR.
PERRYMAN CL.
Bowd Farm
Hall
BURY LA.
Home Farm
Close Farm
Recreation Ground
LANE
67

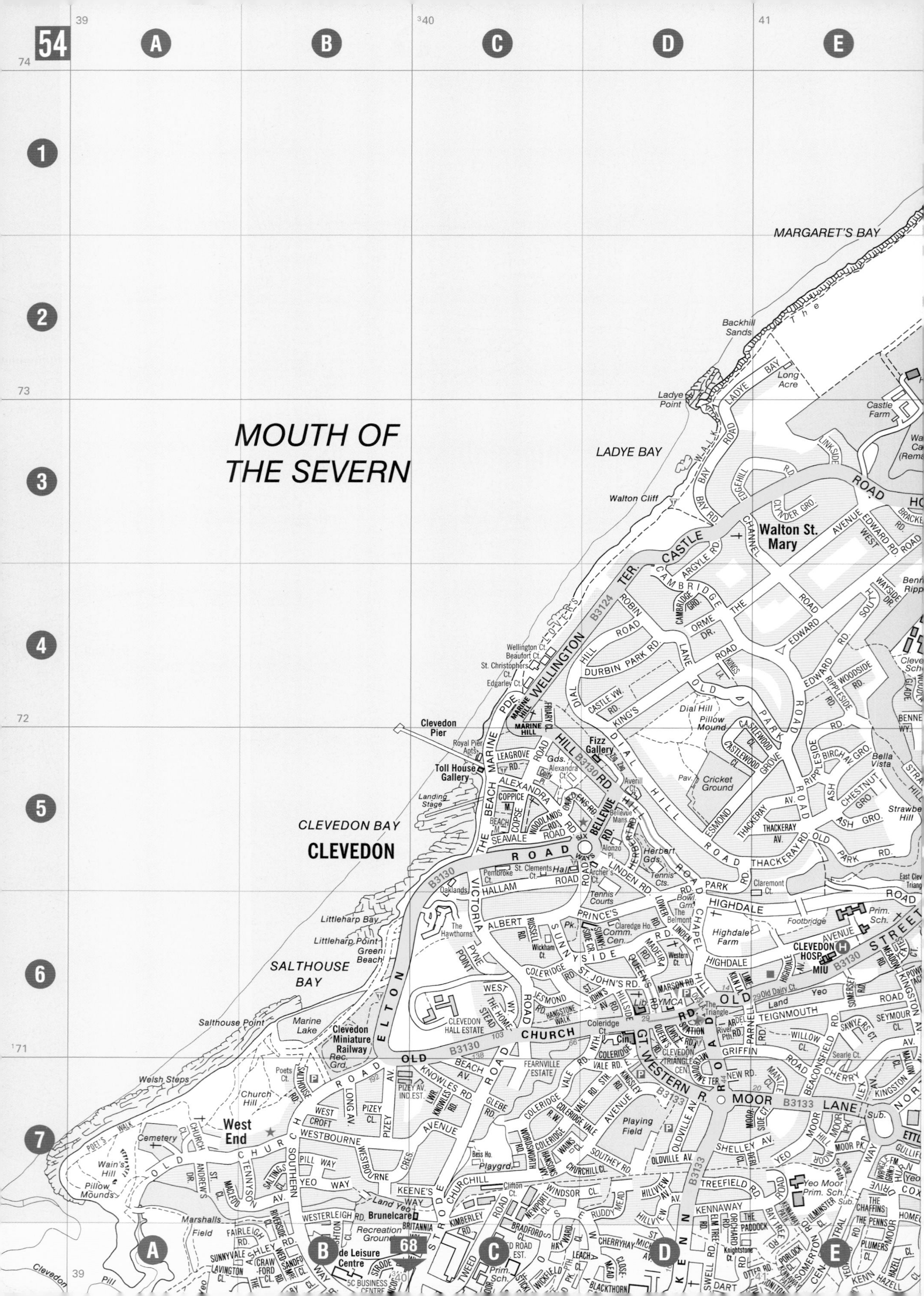
MOUTH OF
THE SEVERN
MARGARET'S BAY
Backhill Sands
Ladye Point
LADYE BAY
Walton Cliff
Long Acre
Castle Farm
Walton St. Mary
CASTLE ROAD
WELLINGTON TER.
B3124
DIAL HILL ROAD
Dial Hill
Pillow Mound
Cricket Ground
Clevedon Pier
Toll House Gallery
Fizz Gallery
Landing Stage
CLEVEDON BAY
CLEVEDON
SIX WAYS
ELTON ROAD
B3130
Littleharp Bay
Littleharp Point
Green Beach
SALTHOUSE BAY
Salthouse Point
Marine Lake
Clevedon Miniature Railway
Rec. Grd.
Welsh Steps
Church Hill
West End
Cemetery
Wain's Hill
Pillow Mounds
Marshalls Field
CLEVEDON HALL ESTATE
OLD CHURCH ROAD
FEARNVILLE ESTATE
Playing Field
Highdale Farm
CLEVEDON HOSP.
MIU
Prim. Sch.
MOOR LANE
B3133
Yeo Moor Prim. Sch.
Brunelcare
Recreation Ground
de Leisure Centre
68
Bella Vista
Strawberry Hill
Clevedon Pill

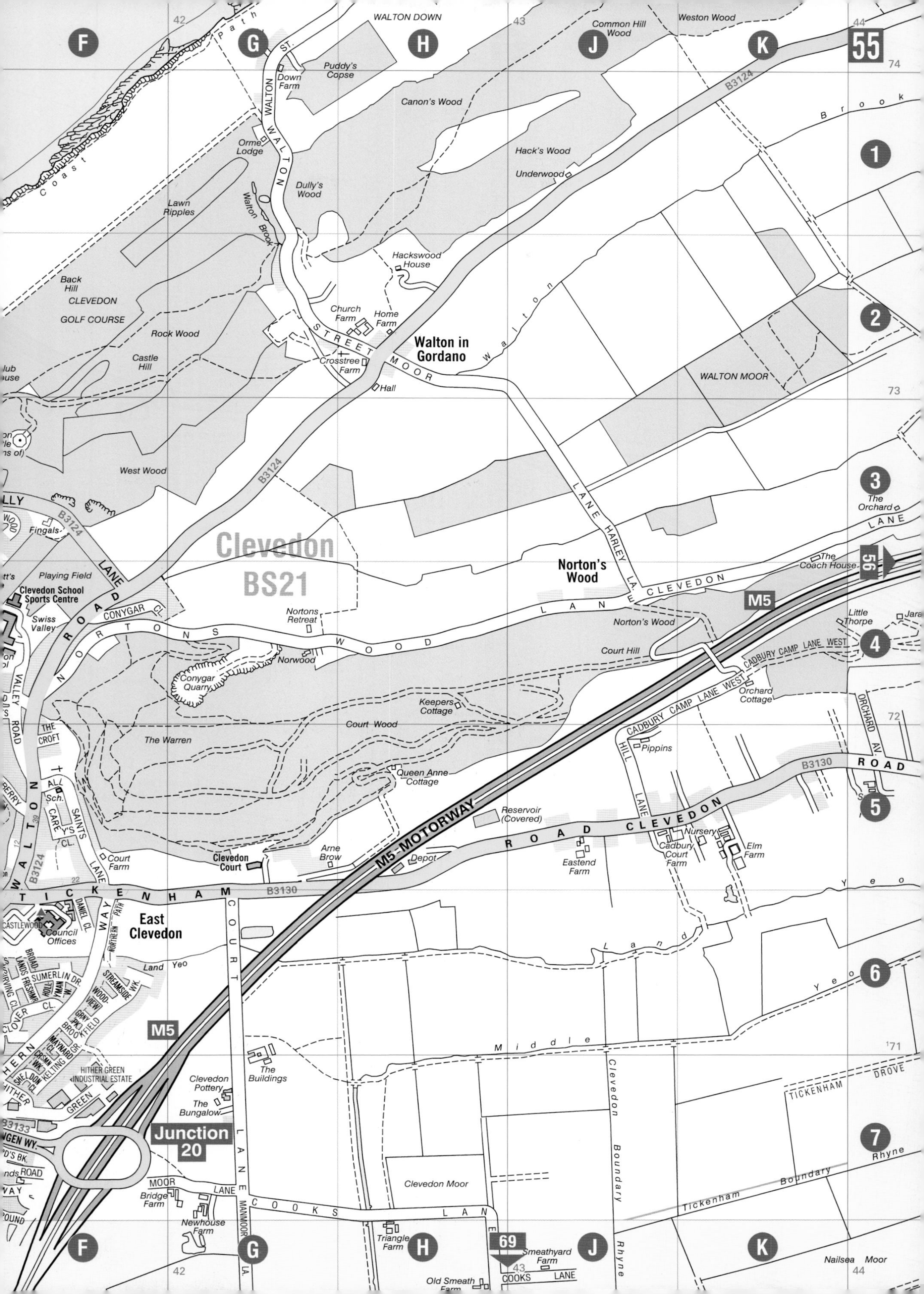

WALTON DOWN
Puddy's Copse
Down Farm
Common Hill Wood
Weston Wood
Canon's Wood
Hack's Wood
Underwood
Orme Lodge
Dully's Wood
Lawn Ripples
Walton Brook
Hackswood House
Back Hill
CLEVEDON
GOLF COURSE
Rock Wood
Castle Hill
Church Farm
Home Farm
Walton in Gordano
Crosstree Farm
Hall
STREET
MOOR
WALTON MOOR
West Wood
B3124
Fingals
Clevedon BS21
Norton's Wood
Playing Field
Clevedon School Sports Centre
Swiss Valley
CONYGAR CL.
NORTONS WOOD LANE
Nortons Retreat
Norwood
Conygar Quarry
HARLEY LA.
CLEVEDON LANE
The Orchard
The Coach House
M5
Little Thorpe
Court Hill
CADBURY CAMP LANE WEST
Orchard Cottage
Keepers Cottage
Court Wood
The Warren
THE CROFT
ORCHARD AV.
CADBURY HILL LANE
Pippins
Queen Anne Cottage
B3130
ROAD
Reservoir (Covered)
M5-MOTORWAY
CLEVEDON ROAD
Nursery
Cadbury Court Farm
Elm Farm
Eastend Farm
Depot
Arne Brow
Clevedon Court
Court Farm
ALL SAINTS LANE
WALTON ROAD
TICKENHAM ROAD
East Clevedon
Council Offices
CASTLEWOOD
DANIEL CL.
Land Yeo
Yeo
COURT LANE
Middle
Clevedon Boundary Rhyne
The Buildings
Clevedon Pottery
The Bungalow
HITHER GREEN INDUSTRIAL ESTATE
Junction 20
MOOR LANE
Bridge Farm
Newhouse Farm
COOKS LANE
MANMOOR LA.
Clevedon Moor
Triangle Farm
69
Smeathyard Farm
Old Smeath Farm
TICKENHAM DROVE
Tickenham Boundary Rhyne
Nailsea Moor
56
F G H J K
1 2 3 4 5 6 7
42 43 44
74 73 72 71

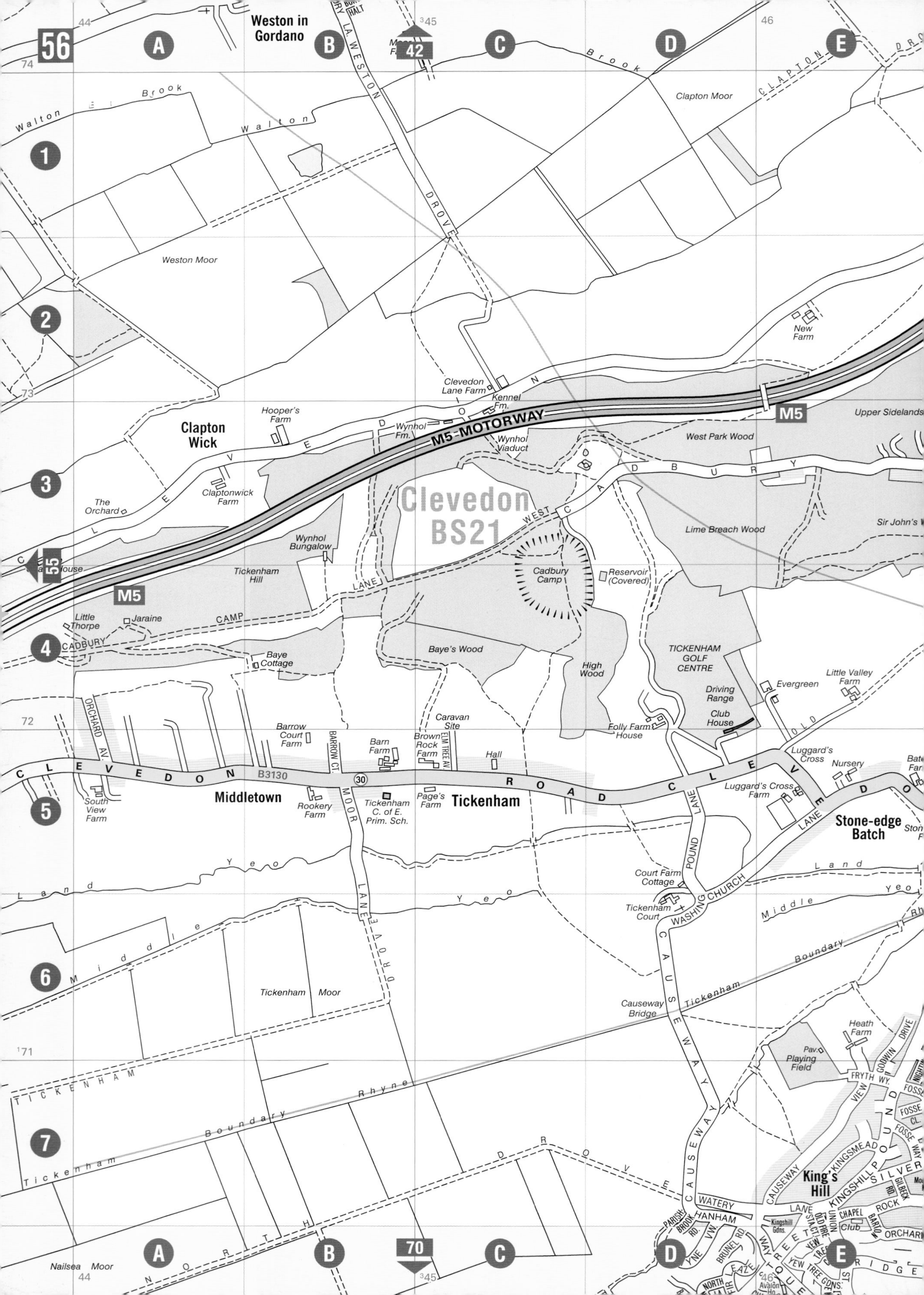
Weston in Gordano
42
Clapton Moor
Weston Moor
New Farm
Clevedon Lane Farm
Kennel Fm.
M5
Upper Sidelands
Clapton Wick
Hooper's Farm
Wynhol Fm.
M5 MOTORWAY
Wynhol Viaduct
West Park Wood
Claptonwick Farm
The Orchard
Clevedon BS21
Lime Breach Wood
Sir John's
Wynhol Bungalow
55
Tickenham Hill
Cadbury Camp
Reservoir (Covered)
M5
Little Thorpe
Jaraine
CAMP
CADBURY
Baye's Wood
TICKENHAM GOLF CENTRE
Baye Cottage
High Wood
Little Valley Farm
Evergreen
Driving Range
Club House
Caravan Site
Folly Farm House
Barrow Court Farm
Barn Farm
Brown Rock Farm
Hall
Luggard's Cross
Nursery
ORCHARD AV.
BARROW CT.
ELM TREE AV.
CLEVEDON ROAD
B3130
CLEVEDON
30
Luggard's Cross Farm
Middletown
Rookery Farm
MOOR
Tickenham C. of E. Prim. Sch.
Page's Farm
Tickenham
Stone-edge Batch
South View Farm
POUND LANE
LANE
Land Yeo
Court Farm Cottage
Tickenham Court
WASHING CHURCH
Middle
Boundary
LANE
DROVE
Tickenham Moor
Causeway Bridge
Tickenham
CAUSEWAY
Heath Farm
Pav.
Playing Field
GODWIN DRIVE
FRYTH WY.
VIEW
FOSSE CL.
FOSSE WAY
POUND
KINGSMEAD
TICKENHAM
Rhyne
Boundary
Tickenham
DROVE
King's Hill
KINGSHILL
SILVER
GILBECK RD.
ROCK
CHAPEL
BARTON
Club
ORCHARD
WATERY LANE
PARISH BROOK RD.
HANHAM
Kingshill Gdns.
UNION
OLD FIRE STA. CT.
YEW TREE
YEW TREE GDNS.
BRUNEL RD.
LYNE VW.
FIR LEAZE
NORTH
Avalon Ho.
RIDGE
ST.
NORTH DROVE
Nailsea Moor
70
A
B
C
D
E
1
2
3
4
5
6
7
44
345
46
74
73
72
71

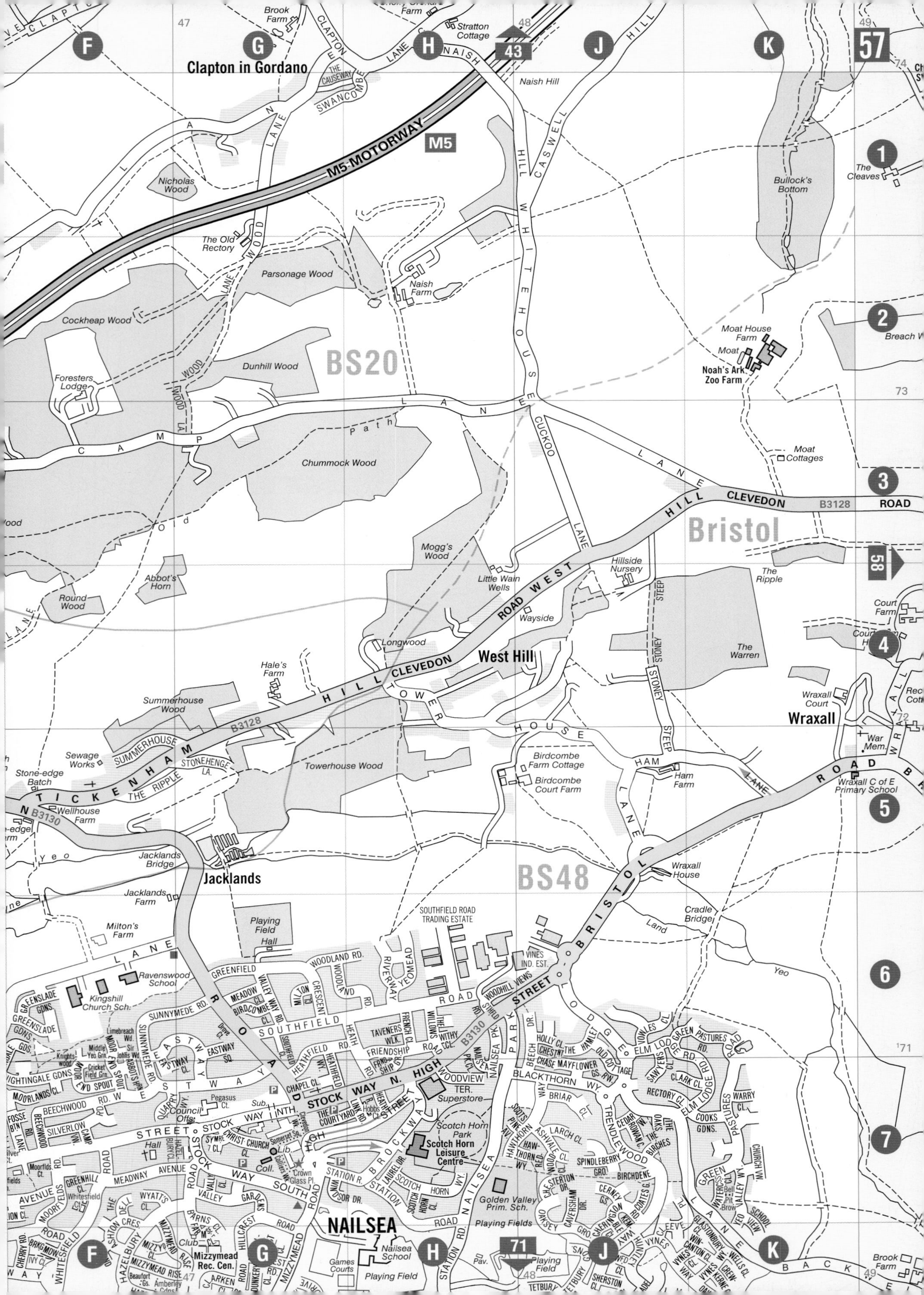
Clapton in Gordano
M5 MOTORWAY
Nicholas Wood
The Old Rectory
Parsonage Wood
Cockheap Wood
Dunhill Wood
BS20
Foresters Lodge
Naish Hill
Naish Farm
Bullock's Bottom
The Cleaves
Moat House Farm
Noah's Ark Zoo Farm
Breach
Moat Cottages
CAMP LANE
Chummock Wood
CLEVEDON ROAD
B3128
Bristol
Mogg's Wood
Little Wain Wells
Hillside Nursery
The Ripple
Abbot's Horn
Round Wood
Longwood
Wayside
The Warren
Court Farm
West Hill
Hale's Farm
Summerhouse Wood
Wraxall Court
Wraxall
War Mem.
Sewage Works
Stone-edge Batch
Towerhouse Wood
Birdcombe Farm Cottage
Birdcombe Court Farm
Ham Farm
Wraxall C of E Primary School
Wellhouse Farm
Jacklands Bridge
Jacklands
BS48
Wraxall House
Jacklands Farm
Cradle Bridge
Milton's Farm
Playing Field
SOUTHFIELD ROAD TRADING ESTATE
VINES IND. EST.
Ravenswood School
Kingshill Church Sch.
Scotch Horn Leisure Centre
Superstore
NAILSEA
Nailsea School
Golden Valley Prim. Sch.
Playing Fields
Mizzymead Rec. Cen.
Games Courts
Playing Field
Brook Farm
Stratton Cottage
43
58
71

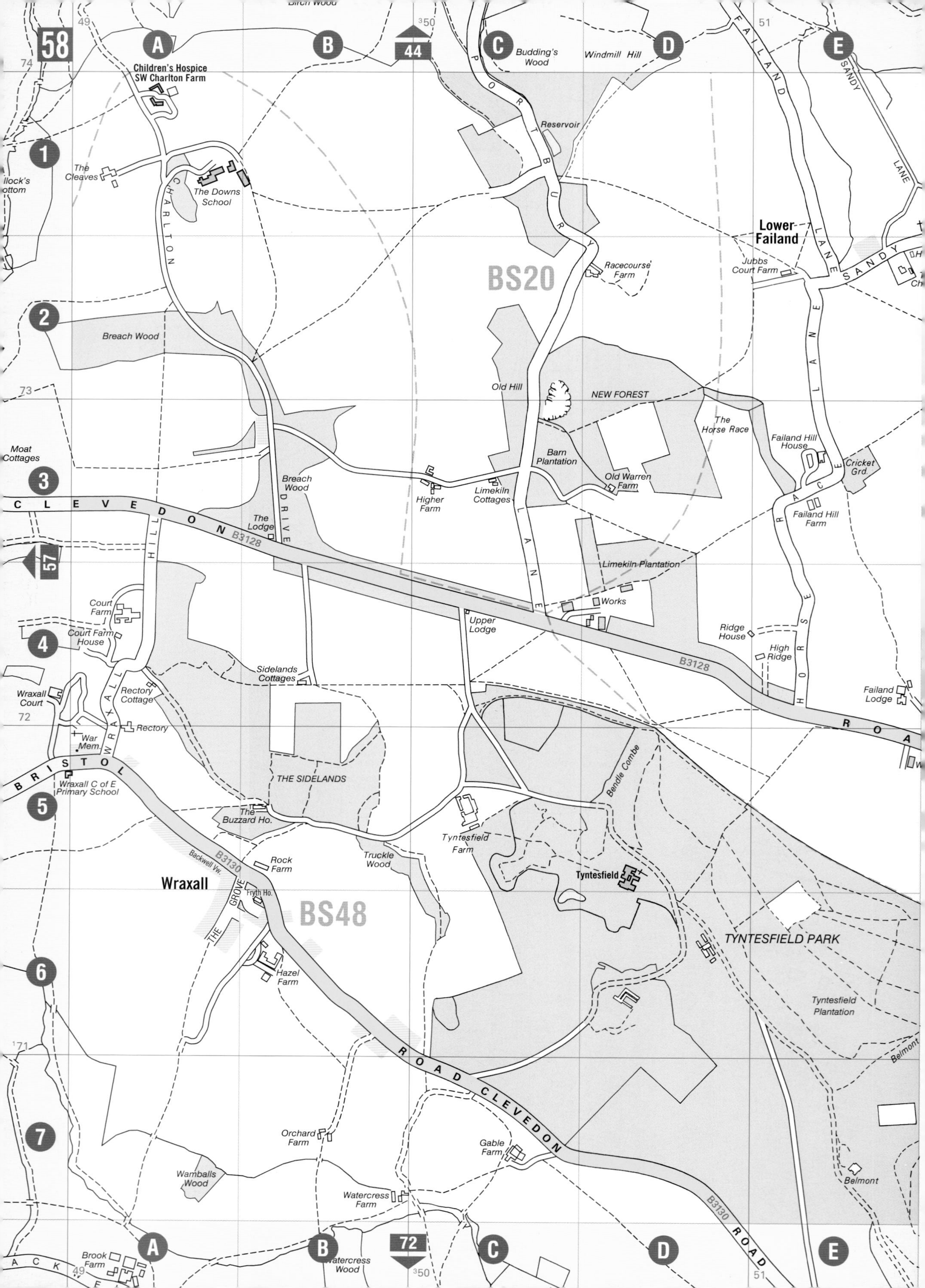

Children's Hospice
SW Charlton Farm
The Cleaves
The Downs School
CHARLTON
Budding's Wood
Windmill Hill
Reservoir
PORTBURY LANE
FAILAND LANE
SANDY LANE
Lower Failand
Jubbs Court Farm
Racecourse Farm
BS20
Breach Wood
Old Hill
NEW FOREST
The Horse Race
Failand Hill House
Cricket Grd.
Moat Cottages
Barn Plantation
Old Warren Farm
Breach Wood
Higher Farm
Limekiln Cottages
CLEVEDON ROAD
B3128
The Lodge
DRIVE
Failand Hill Farm
Limekiln Plantation
Works
Court Farm
Court Farm House
Upper Lodge
Ridge House
High Ridge
HORSE RACE LANE
Sidelands Cottages
Wraxall Court
Rectory Cottage
Rectory
WRAXALL HILL
War Mem.
Failand Lodge
BRISTOL
Wraxall C of E Primary School
THE SIDELANDS
Bendle Combe
The Buzzard Ho.
Tyntesfield Farm
Truckle Wood
Rock Farm
Backwell Vw.
B3130
Wraxall
Tyntesfield
THE GROVE
Fryth Ho.
BS48
TYNTESFIELD PARK
Hazel Farm
Tyntesfield Plantation
Belmont
ROAD CLEVEDON
Orchard Farm
Gable Farm
Wamballs Wood
Watercress Farm
Belmont
B3130 ROAD
Brook Farm
Watercress Wood

44
57
72

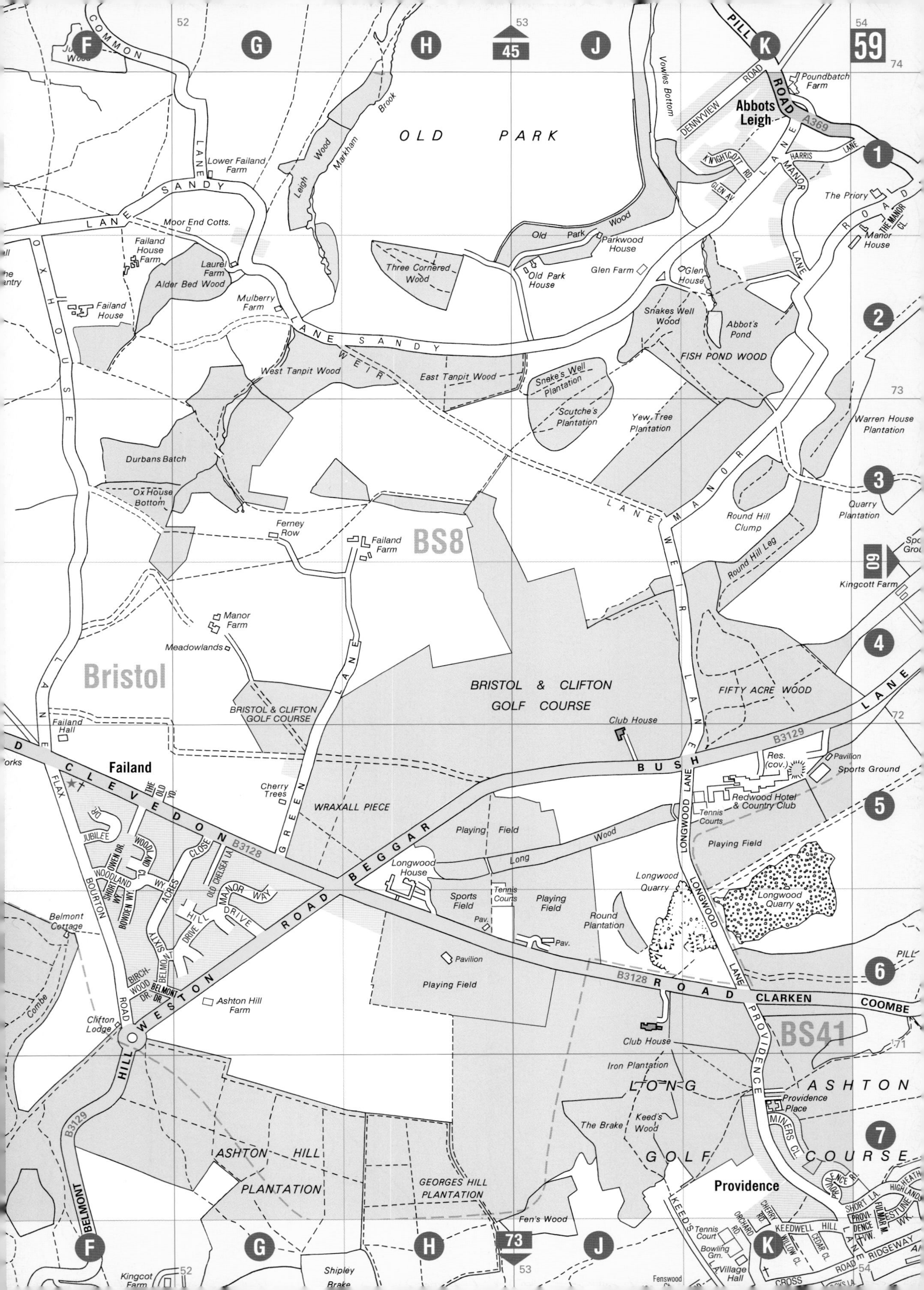
45
73
60
BS8
BS41
Bristol
Failand
Abbots Leigh
Providence
OLD PARK
BRISTOL & CLIFTON GOLF COURSE
LONG ASHTON GOLF COURSE
ASHTON HILL PLANTATION
GEORGES HILL PLANTATION
FIFTY ACRE WOOD
FISH POND WOOD
WRAXALL PIECE
Lower Failand Farm
Moor End Cotts.
Failand House Farm
Laurel Farm
Alder Bed Wood
Failand House
Mulberry Farm
West Tanpit Wood
East Tanpit Wood
Three Cornered Wood
Old Park Wood
Parkwood House
Old Park House
Glen Farm
Glen House
Snakes Well Wood
Abbot's Pond
Snake's Well Plantation
Scutche's Plantation
Yew Tree Plantation
Warren House Plantation
Quarry Plantation
Round Hill Clump
Round Hill Leg
Kingcott Farm
Durbans Batch
Ox House Bottom
Ferney Row
Failand Farm
Manor Farm
Meadowlands
Failand Hall
Club House
Res. (cov.)
Pavilion
Sports Ground
Redwood Hotel & Country Club
Tennis Courts
Playing Field
Longwood Quarry
Longwood House
Sports Field
Pav.
Round Plantation
Cherry Trees
Belmont Cottage
Clifton Lodge
Ashton Hill Farm
Iron Plantation
The Brake
Keed's Wood
Providence Place
Fen's Wood
Shipley Brake
Kingcot Farm
Village Hall
Bowling Grn.
Fenswood
Poundbatch Farm
The Priory
Manor House
Vowles Bottom
Leigh Wood
Markham Brook
Combe
SANDY LANE
OX HOUSE LANE
WEIR LANE
MANOR LANE
MANOR ROAD
HARRIS LANE
KNIGHTCOTT RD.
GLEN AV.
THE MANOR CL.
DENNYVIEW ROAD
PILL ROAD
A369
GREEN LANE
BUSH LANE
B3129
B3128
BEGGAR BUSH LANE
CLEVEDON ROAD
WESTON ROAD
LONGWOOD LANE
CLARKEN COOMBE
PROVIDENCE LANE
BOURTON ROAD
FLAX BOURTON ROAD
HILL
BELMONT HILL
THE OLD YD.
JUBILEE DR.
WOODLAND CL.
OWEN DR.
WOODLAND WY.
SHORT WY.
BOWDEN WY.
SIXTY ACRES CLOSE
OLD CHELSEA LA.
MANOR WAY
HILL DRIVE
MANOR DRIVE
BIRCHWOOD DR.
BELMONT DR.
MINERS CL.
KEEDS LA.
ORCHARD RD.
CHERRY RD.
WILLOW CL.
CEDAR CL.
KEEDWELL HILL
SHORT LA.
HIGHLANDS
FULMAR
PROVIDENCE VW.
RIDGEWAY
CROSS
Tennis Court
Works
PILL
F
G
H
J
K
1
2
3
4
5
6
7
52
53
54
71
72
73
74

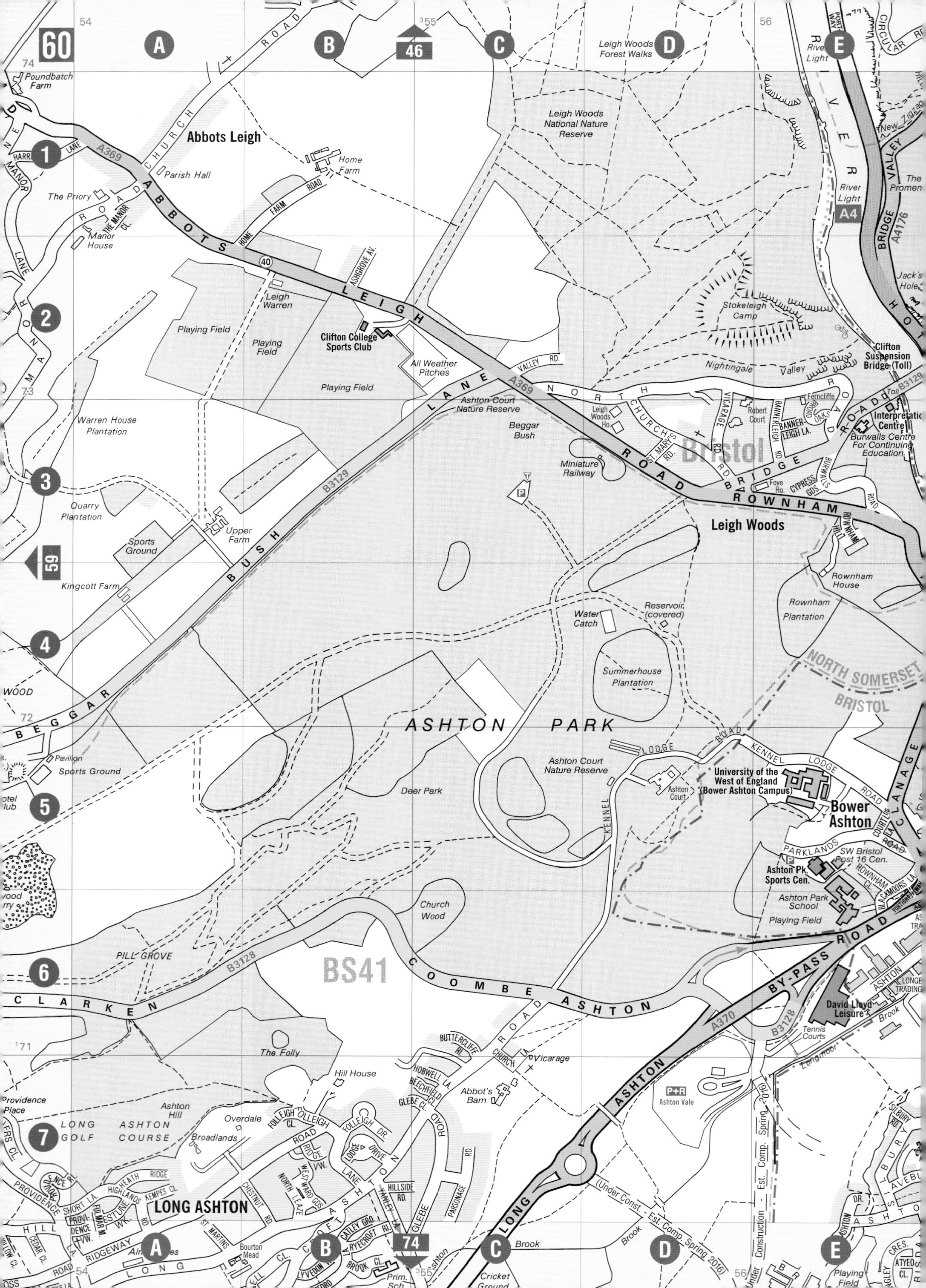
Abbots Leigh
Leigh Woods Forest Walks
Leigh Woods National Nature Reserve
Poundbatch Farm
Parish Hall
Home Farm
The Priory
Manor House
Leigh Warren
Playing Field
Clifton College Sports Club
All Weather Pitches
Stokeleigh Camp
Clifton Suspension Bridge (Toll)
Nightingale Valley
Interpretation Centre
Burwalls Centre For Continuing Education
Ashton Court Nature Reserve
Beggar Bush
Miniature Railway
Bristol
Leigh Woods
Rownham House
Rownham Plantation
Warren House Plantation
Quarry Plantation
Upper Farm
Sports Ground
Kingcott Farm
Water Catch
Reservoir (covered)
Summerhouse Plantation
NORTH SOMERSET
BRISTOL
ASHTON PARK
Ashton Court
University of the West of England (Bower Ashton Campus)
Bower Ashton
Deer Park
Pavilion
SW Bristol Post 16 Cen.
Ashton Pk. Sports Cen.
Ashton Park School
Church Wood
PILL GROVE
BS41
David Lloyd Leisure
Tennis Courts
The Folly
Vicarage
Hill House
Abbot's Barn
P+R Ashton Vale
Providence Place
Ashton Hill
Overdale
Broadlands
LONG ASHTON GOLF COURSE
LONG ASHTON
Bourton Mead
Prim. Sch.
Cricket Ground
Playing Field
(Under Const. - Est. Comp. Spring 2016)
ABBOTS LEIGH ROAD
BEGGAR BUSH LANE
CLARKEN COOMBE
ASHTON ROAD
ROWNHAM HILL
NORTH ROAD
BRIDGE ROAD
LONG ASHTON BY-PASS
CHURCH ROAD
KENNEL LODGE ROAD
PARKLANDS ROAD
RIVER AVON
A369
A370
A4
A4176
B3128
B3129
46
59
74

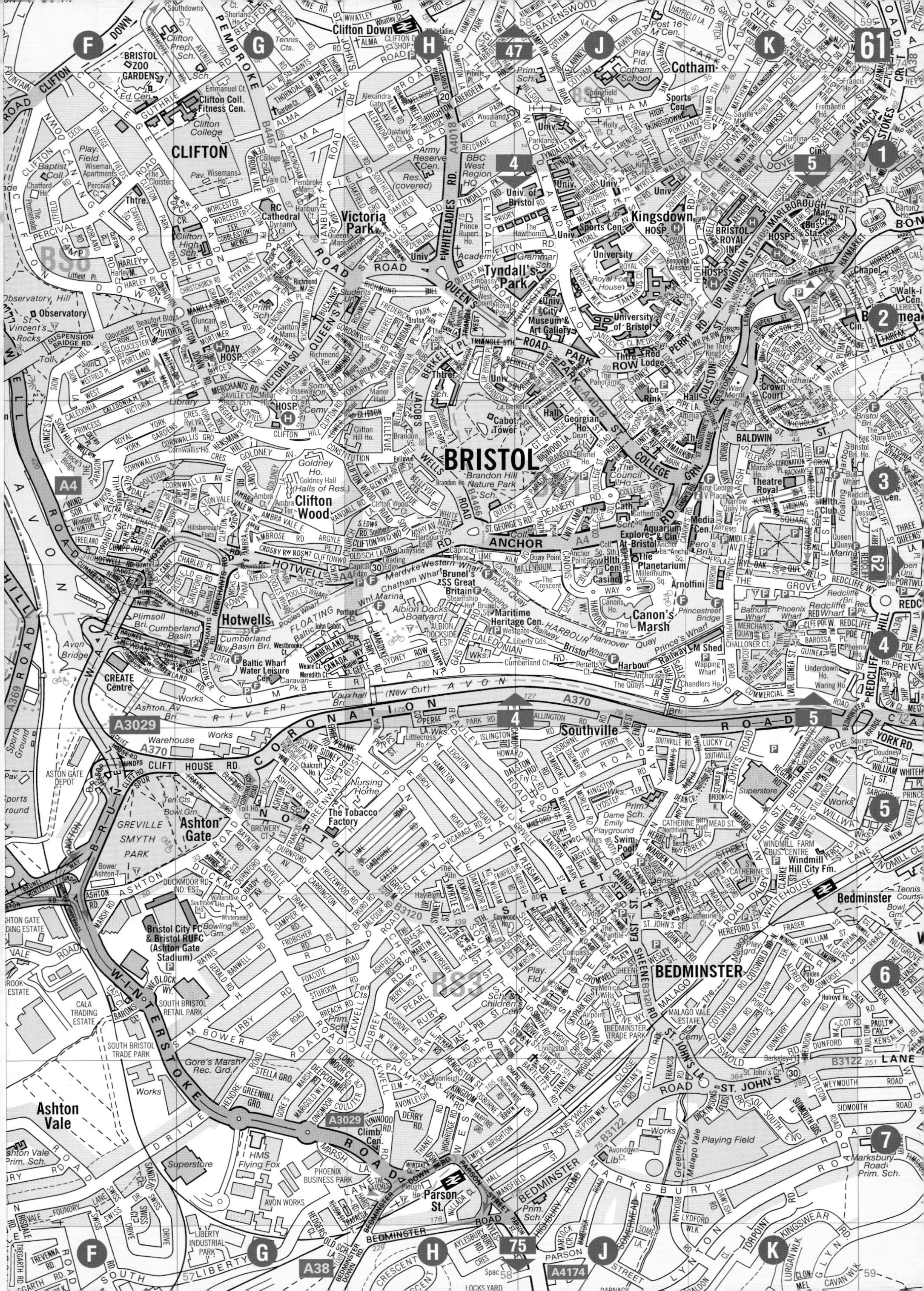
F
G
H
J
K
47
4
5
62
75
1
2
3
4
5
6
7
BRISTOL
CLIFTON
Clifton Down
BRISTOL ZOO GARDENS
Clifton Coll. Fitness Cen.
Clifton College
Cotham
Cotham School
Kingsdown
BRISTOL ROYAL INF.
Victoria Park
RC Cathedral
Tyndall's Park
University
University of Bristol
City Museum & Art Gallery
Cabot Tower
Brandon Hill Nature Park
Clifton Wood
Goldney Hall (Halls of Res.)
Observatory
St Vincent's Rocks
SUSPENSION BRIDGE RD.
Hotwells
Cumberland Basin
Baltic Wharf Water Leisure Cen.
Brunel's SS Great Britain
Maritime Heritage Cen.
FLOATING HARBOUR
Canon's Marsh
Aquarium & Cin.
Explore-At-Bristol
The Planetarium
Media Cen.
Arnolfini
M Shed
Theatre Royal
Crown Court
Council Ho.
Cath.
ANCHOR RD.
HOTWELL RD.
CUMBERLAND RD.
RIVER AVON (New Cut)
CORONATION ROAD
Southville
CREATE Centre
Ashton Gate
GREVILLE SMYTH PARK
Bristol City FC & Bristol RUFC (Ashton Gate Stadium)
SOUTH BRISTOL RETAIL PARK
The Tobacco Factory
NORTH ST.
BEDMINSTER
Bedminster
Windmill Hill City Fm.
Malago Vale
Playing Field
WINTERSTOKE ROAD
Ashton Vale
Parson St.
HMS Flying Fox
PHOENIX BUSINESS PARK
LIBERTY INDUSTRIAL PARK
SOUTH BRISTOL TRADE PARK
CALA TRADING ESTATE
ST. JOHN'S ROAD
MARKSBURY RD.
Marksbury Road Prim. Sch.
BS8
BS3
A4
A38
A370
A3029
A4018
A4174
B3120
B3122
B4466
B4467

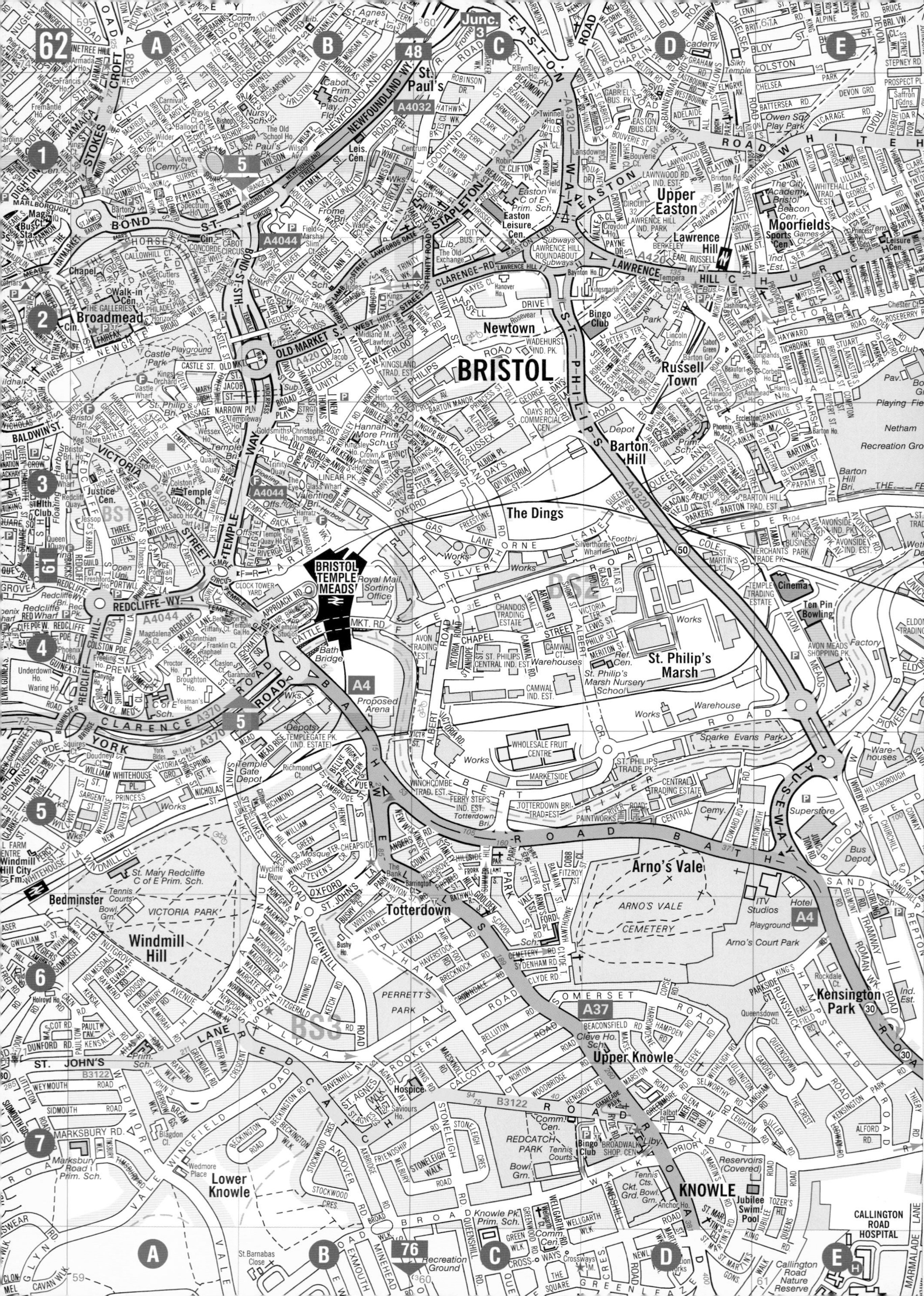
A
B
C
D
E
1
2
3
4
5
6
7
48
Junc. 3
5
61
76
A4032
A4044
A4320
A432
A420
A4
A370
A37
A38
B4053
B3122
B4465
BRISTOL
St. Paul's
Broadmead
Newtown
Upper Easton
Lawrence Hill
Russell Town
Moorfields
Barton Hill
The Dings
St. Philip's Marsh
BRISTOL TEMPLE MEADS
Royal Mail Sorting Office
Totterdown
Arno's Vale
ARNO'S VALE CEMETERY
Arno's Court Park
Kensington Park
Upper Knowle
KNOWLE
Lower Knowle
Windmill Hill
VICTORIA PARK
Bedminster
PERRETT'S PARK
REDCATCH PARK
Sparke Evans Park
WHOLESALE FRUIT CENTRE
Netham Recreation Grd.
Playing Fields
CALLINGTON ROAD HOSPITAL
Callington Road Nature Reserve
Recreation Ground
Proposed Arena
Bath Bridge
Temple Ch.
Castle Park
Cinema
Ten Pin Bowling
Superstore
ITV Studios
Hospice
Jubilee Swim. Pool
Bingo Club
BS1
BS2
BS3
BOND ST.
NEWFOUNDLAND WY.
TEMPLE WAY
VICTORIA ST.
REDCLIFFE WY.
CLARENCE ROAD
YORK ROAD
BATH ROAD
WELLS ROAD
FEEDER ROAD
ST. PHILIPS CAUSEWAY
EASTON WAY
LAWRENCE HILL
CHURCH ROAD
STAPLETON ROAD
OLD MARKET ST.
WEST ST.
WINDMILL HILL
SOMERSET ROAD
REDCATCH ROAD
BROAD WALK
WEDMORE VALE
ST. JOHN'S LANE

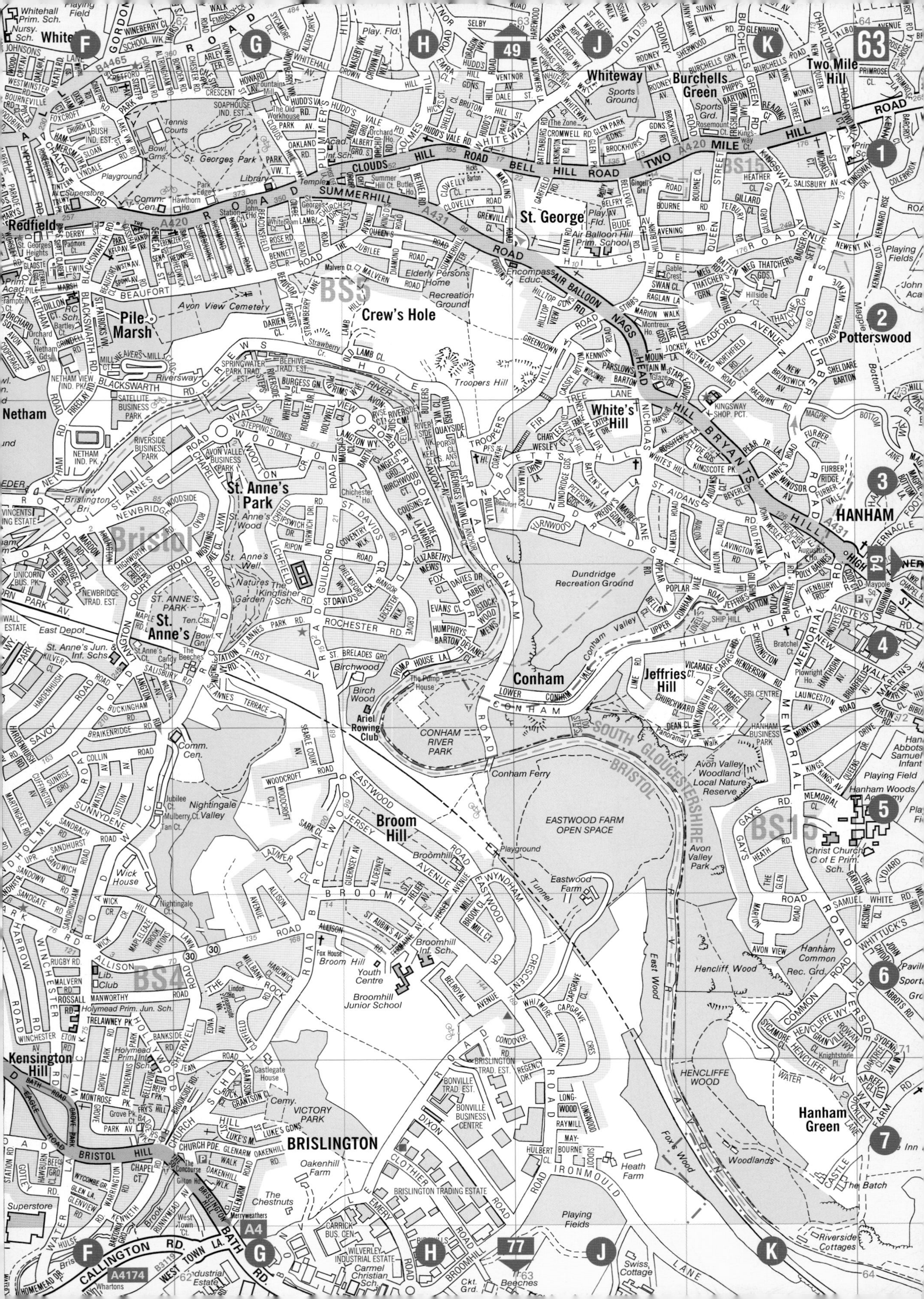

F
G
H
J
K
49
64
77
1
2
3
4
5
6
7
Whitehall Prim. Sch.
Nursy. Sch.
Playing Field
Play. Fld.
Whiteway
Burchells Green
Two Mile Hill
Sports Ground
Sports Grd.
TWO MILE HILL ROAD
A420
BS15
Redfield
St. Georges Heights
Superstore
Comm. Cen.
Library
Tennis Courts
Bowl. Grns.
St. Georges Park
Playground
SOAPHOUSE IND. EST.
The Old Workhouse
BUSH IND. EST.
Acad. Int. Sch.
Temple
Summer Hill Ct.
Butler Ho.
CLOUDS HILL ROAD
BELL HILL ROAD
SUMMERHILL ROAD
A431
St. George
Air Balloon Hill Prim. School
Encompass Educ.
AIR BALLOON RD.
NAGS HEAD HILL
BRYANTS HILL
HILLSIDE
Elderly Persons Home
Recreation Ground
BS5
Crew's Hole
Pile Marsh
Avon View Cemetery
BEAUFORT RD.
BLACKSWARTH RD.
Netham
NETHAM VIEW IND. PK.
NETHAM IND. PK.
SATELLITE BUSINESS PARK
RIVERSIDE BUSINESS PARK
AVON VALLEY BUSINESS PARK
SPRINGWATER PARK TRAD. EST.
BEEHIVE TRAD. EST.
Riversway
CREWS HOLE RD.
Troopers Hill
White's Hill
KINGSWAY SHOP. PCT.
Potterswood
Playing Fields
HANHAM
New Brislington Bri.
St. Anne's Park
St. Anne's Wood
St. Anne's Well
Natures Garden
The Kingfisher Sch.
Bristol
UNICORN BUS. PK
NEWBRIDGE TRAD. EST.
St. Anne's
ST. ANNE'S PARK
East Depot
St. Anne's Jun. & Inf. Schs
Dundridge Recreation Ground
Conham Valley
Conham
Jeffries Hill
Ship Hill
Birchwood
Birch Wood
Ariel Rowing Club
The Pump House
CONHAM RIVER PARK
Conham Ferry
SOUTH GLOUCESTERSHIRE
BRISTOL
EASTWOOD FARM OPEN SPACE
Playground
Eastwood Farm
Tunnel
Avon Valley Woodland Local Nature Reserve
Avon Valley Park
Panorama Walk
SBI CENTRE
HANHAM BUSINESS PARK
Hanham Woods Academy
Christ Church C of E Prim. Sch.
Hanham Abbots Samuel Infant
Playing Field
Broom Hill
Broomhill
Broomhill Inf. Sch.
Fox House
Youth Centre
Broomhill Junior School
Nightingale Valley
Comm. Cen.
Wick House
BS4
Lib. Club
Holymead Prim. Jun. Sch.
Holymead Prim. Inf. Sch.
Castlegate House
Cemy.
VICTORY PARK
BRISLINGTON
BRISLINGTON TRAD. EST.
BONVILLE TRAD. EST.
BONVILLE BUSINESS CENTRE
BRISLINGTON TRADING ESTATE
Heath Farm
Oakenhill Farm
The Chestnuts
Playing Fields
Kensington Hill
BRISTOL HILL
Superstore
The Concourse
Merryweathers
A4
BATH RD.
CALLINGTON RD.
A4174
B3119
WEST TOWN LA.
CARRICK BUS. CEN
WILVERLEY INDUSTRIAL ESTATE
Carmel Christian Sch.
Beeches
Swiss Cottage
RIVER AVON
East Wood
Fox's Wood
HENCLIFFE WOOD
Hencliff Wood
Hanham Common Rec. Grd.
Woodlands
Hanham Green
The Batch
Riverside Cottages

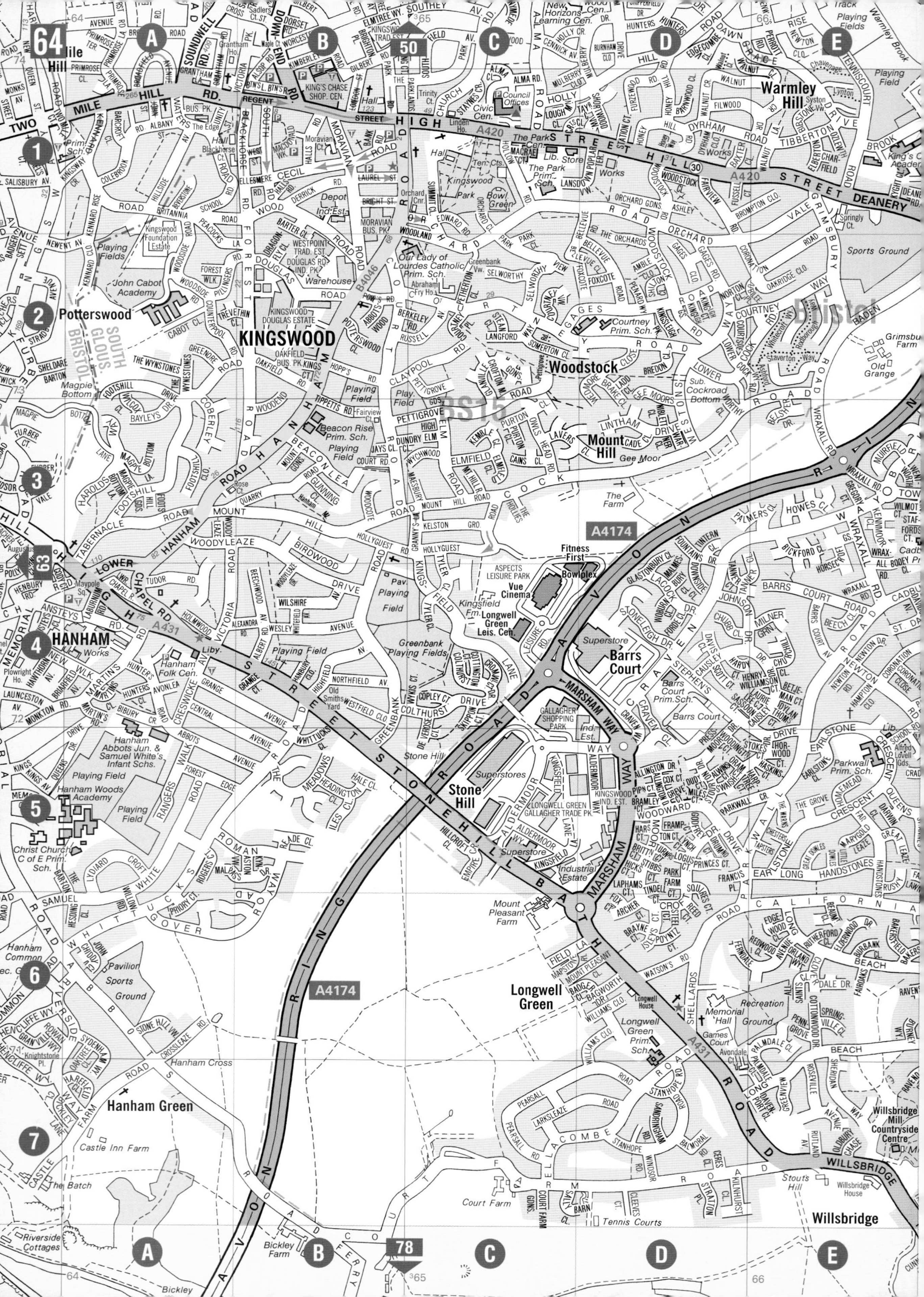
A
B
C
D
E
1
2
3
4
5
6
7
50
78
63
64
65
66
Two Mile Hill
TWO MILE HILL RD.
REGENT ST.
HIGH STREET
A420
KING'S CHASE SHOP. CEN.
Council Offices
Civic Cen.
Warmley Hill
STREET HILL
DEANERY
Playing Fields
Playing Field
Sports Ground
Potterswood
KINGSWOOD
John Cabot Academy
Kingswood Foundation Estate
SOUTH GLOUS.
BRISTOL
Magpie Bottom
B4046
KINGSWOOD DOUGLAS ESTATE
OAKFIELD BUS. PK.
Beacon Rise Prim. Sch.
Our Lady of Lourdes Catholic Prim. Sch.
Woodstock
Courtney Prim. Sch.
BS15
Mount Hill
Gee Moor
Cockroad Bottom
Old Grange
Grimsbury Farm
Bristol
The Farm
A4174
Fitness First
Bowlplex
ASPECTS LEISURE PARK
Vue Cinema
Longwell Green Leis. Cen.
Kingsfield Fm.
Superstore
Barrs Court
Barrs Court Prim. Sch.
Parkwall Prim. Sch.
HANHAM
Hanham Folk Cen.
Hanham Abbots Jun. & Samuel White's Infant Schs.
Hanham Woods Academy
Christ Church C of E Prim. Sch.
Greenbank Playing Fields
GALLAGHER SHOPPING PARK
Stone Hill
Superstores
KINGSWOOD IND. EST.
LONGWELL GREEN GALLAGHER TRADE PK
Industrial Estate
A431
STONEHILL
RING ROAD
AVON RING ROAD
MARSHAM WAY
BATH ROAD
Mount Pleasant Farm
Longwell Green
Longwell Green Prim. Sch.
Memorial Hall
Recreation Ground
Hanham Common
Pavilion
Sports Ground
Hanham Cross
Hanham Green
Castle Inn Farm
The Batch
Riverside Cottages
Bickley Farm
Court Farm
Tennis Courts
Stouts Hill
Willsbridge House
Willsbridge
Willsbridge Mill Countryside Centre
WILLSBRIDGE HILL
Bickley

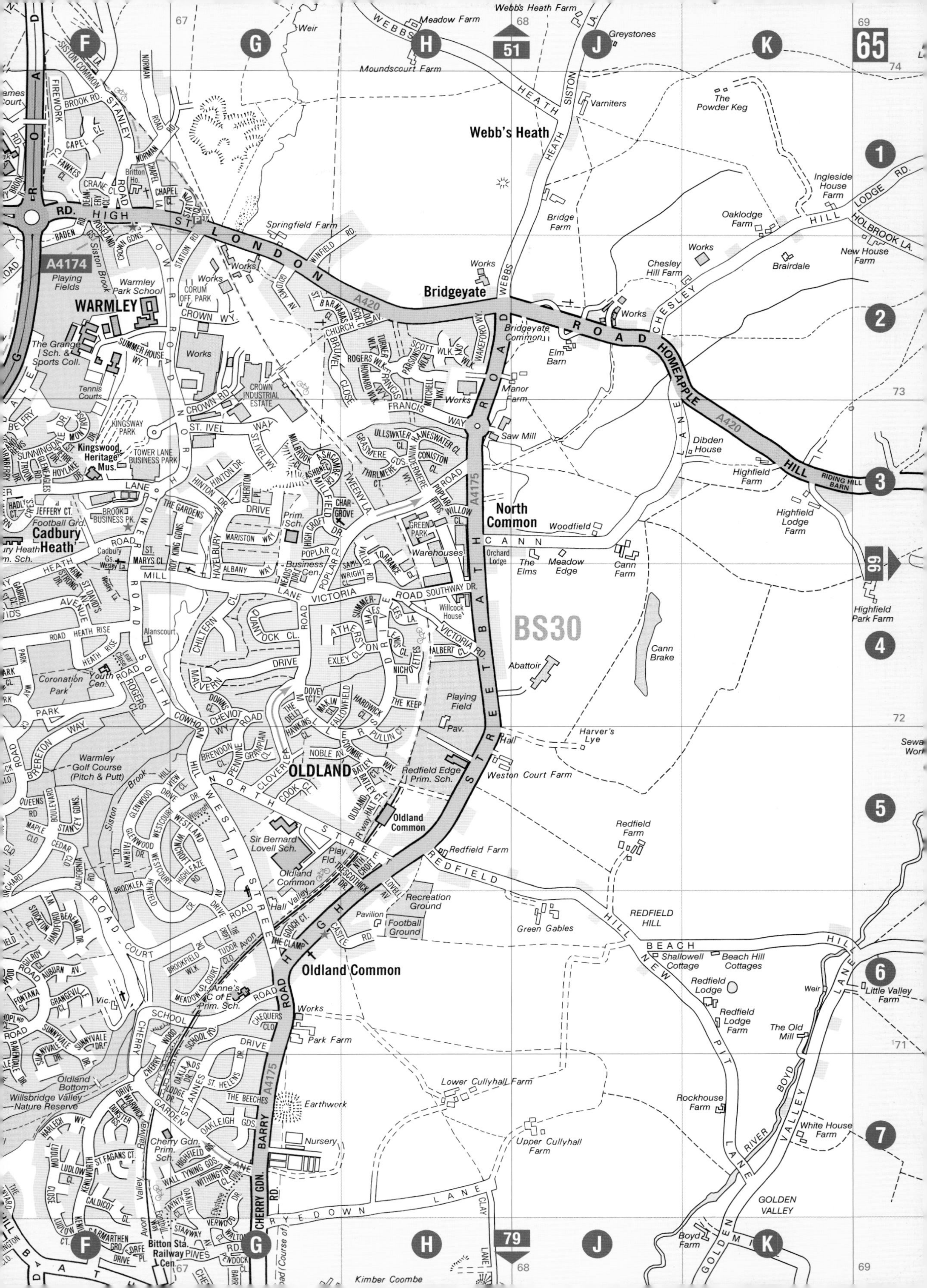
65
51
79
99
BS30
WARMLEY
Cadbury Heath
OLDLAND
Oldland Common
North Common
Bridgeyate
Webb's Heath
REDFIELD HILL
GOLDEN VALLEY
A4174
A420
A4175
LONDON ROAD
HIGH ST.
HOMEAPPLE HILL
BATH ROAD
STREET
BARRY ROAD
HIGH STREET
NORTH STREET
WEST STREET
TOWER ROAD SOUTH
TOWER ROAD NORTH
VICTORIA ROAD
CANN LANE
REDFIELD HILL
BEACH HILL
NEW PIT LANE
BOYD VALLEY
RYEDOWN LANE
CHESLEY HILL
WEBBS HEATH
SISTON LA.
Webb's Heath Farm
Meadow Farm
Moundscourt Farm
Greystones
Varniters
The Powder Keg
Ingleside House Farm
Oaklodge Farm
New House Farm
Brairdale
Chesley Hill Farm
Springfield Farm
Bridge Farm
Bridgeyate Common
Elm Barn
Manor Farm
Saw Mill
Dibden House
Highfield Farm
Highfield Lodge Farm
Highfield Park Farm
Woodfield
Orchard Lodge
The Elms
Meadow Edge
Cann Farm
Cann Brake
Abattoir
Playing Field
Harver's Lye
Weston Court Farm
Redfield Farm
Redfield Edge Prim. Sch.
Recreation Ground
Football Ground
Green Gables
Shallowell Cottage
Beach Hill Cottages
Redfield Lodge
Redfield Lodge Farm
Little Valley Farm
The Old Mill
Rockhouse Farm
White House Farm
Boyd Farm
Lower Cullyhall Farm
Upper Cullyhall Farm
Earthwork
Nursery
Park Farm
Kimber Coombe
Warmley Park School
The Grange Sch. & Sports Coll.
Kingswood Heritage Mus.
Tower Lane Business Park
Crown Industrial Estate
Kingsway Park
Coronation Park
Warmley Golf Course (Pitch & Putt)
Sir Bernard Lovell Sch.
St. Anne's C of E Prim. Sch.
Cherry Gdn. Prim. Sch.
Bitton Sta. Railway Cen.
Willsbridge Valley Nature Reserve
Oldland Bottom

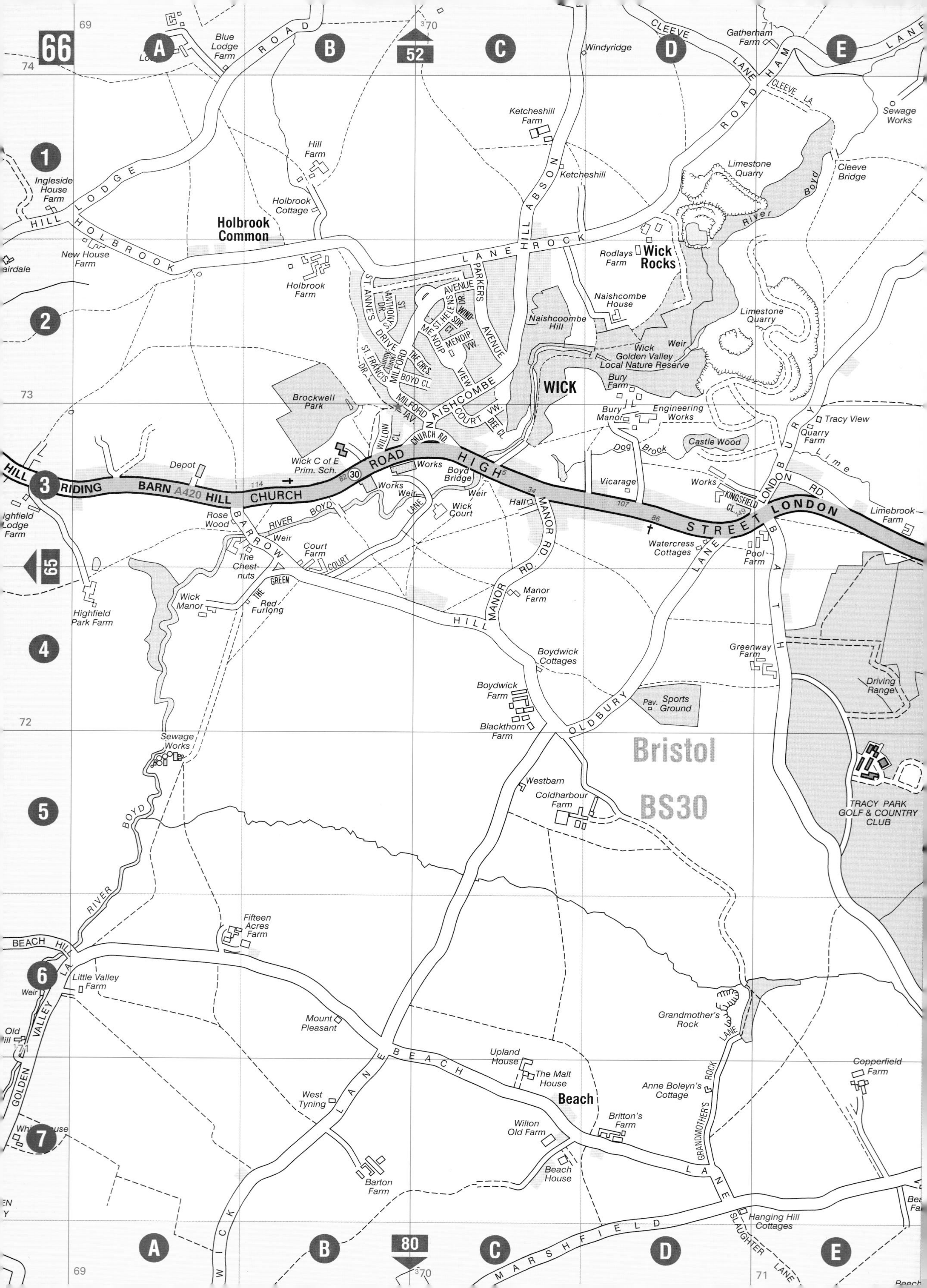

Blue Lodge Farm
Windyridge
Gatherham Farm
Cleeve Lane
Sewage Works
Ketcheshill Farm
Hill Farm
Ingleside House Farm
Limestone Quarry
Cleeve Bridge
Ketcheshill
Holbrook Cottage
Holbrook Common
New House Farm
Rodlays Farm
Wick Rocks
Holbrook Farm
Naishcombe House
Limestone Quarry
Naishcoombe Hill
Wick Golden Valley Local Nature Reserve
Brockwell Park
WICK
Bury Farm
Bury Manor
Engineering Works
Tracy View
Quarry Farm
Castle Wood
Depot
Wick C of E Prim. Sch.
Works
Boyd Bridge
Vicarage
Works
Wick Court
Hall
Limebrook Farm
Rose Wood
Watercress Cottages
Pool Farm
Court Farm
The Chestnuts
Highfield Lodge Farm
Wick Manor
Red Furlong
Manor Farm
Highfield Park Farm
Boydwick Cottages
Greenway Farm
Driving Range
Boydwick Farm
Sports Ground
Blackthorn Farm
Sewage Works
Bristol
BS30
Westbarn
Coldharbour Farm
TRACY PARK GOLF & COUNTRY CLUB
Fifteen Acres Farm
Little Valley Farm
Mount Pleasant
Grandmother's Rock
Old Mill
Upland House
The Malt House
Copperfield Farm
West Tyning
Beach
Anne Boleyn's Cottage
Britton's Farm
Wilton Old Farm
Beach House
Barton Farm
Hanging Hill Cottages
A420
Hill Lodge
Holbrook Lane
Rock Lane
Abson Hill
Ham Road
Church Road
High Street
London Road
Bath Road
Barrow Hill
Manor Rd.
Oldbury Lane
Beach Hill
Golden Valley Lane
Wick Lane
Beach Lane
Marshfield Road
Slaughter Lane
Grandmother's Rock Lane
River Boyd

52
65
80

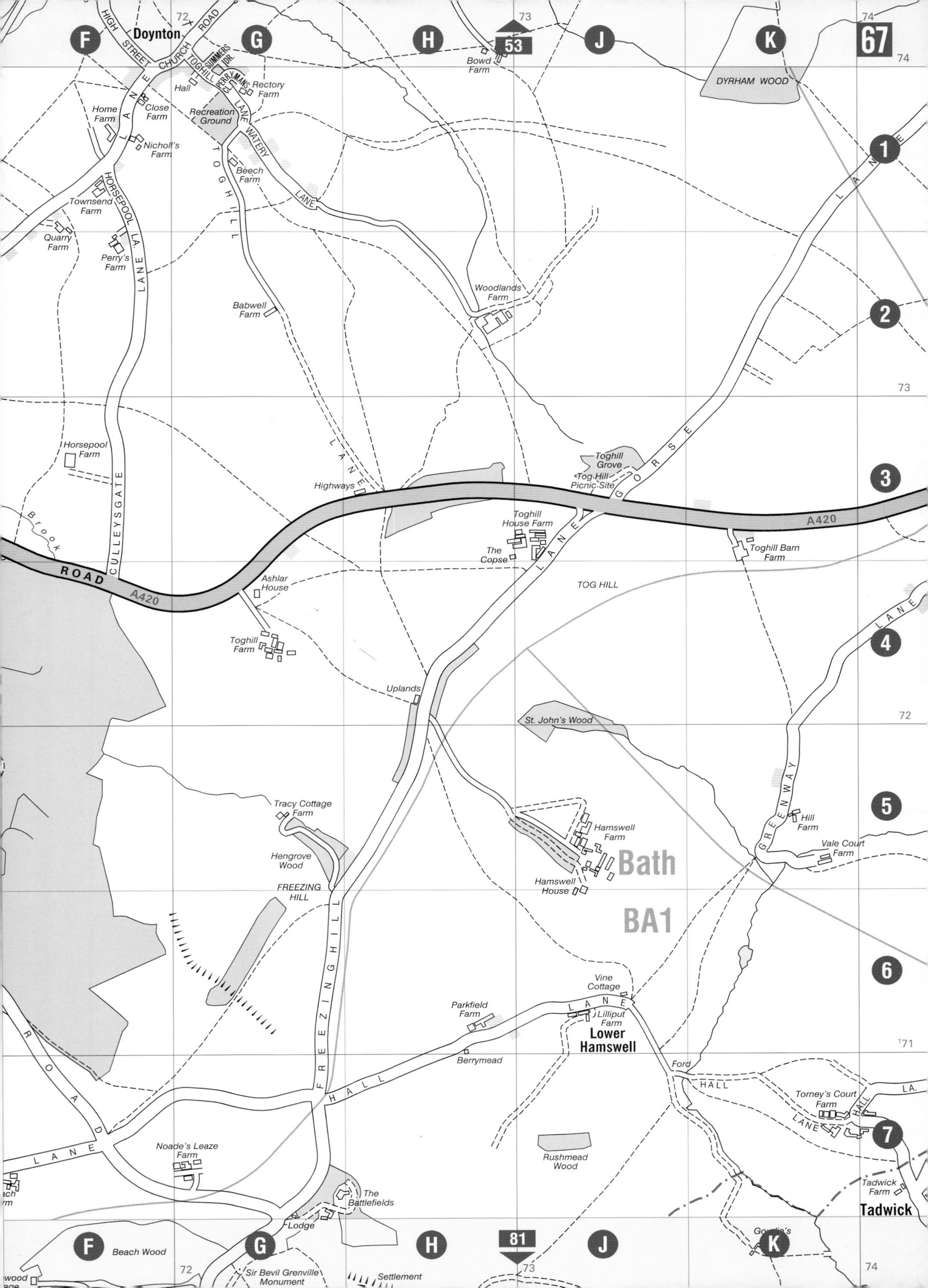

F   G   H   53   J   K

Doynton

Bowd Farm

DYRHAM WOOD

1

2

73

Home Farm

Close Farm

Hall

Rectory Farm

Recreation Ground

Nicholl's Farm

Beech Farm

Townsend Farm

Babwell Farm

Woodlands Farm

Quarry Farm

Perry's Farm

3

A420

Horsepool Farm

Highways

Toghill Grove

Tog Hill Picnic Site

Toghill House Farm

The Copse

Toghill Barn Farm

ROAD A420

Ashlar House

TOG HILL

LANE

4

72

Toghill Farm

Uplands

St. John's Wood

GREENWAY

Tracy Cottage Farm

Hamswell Farm

Bath

Hill Farm

5

Vale Court Farm

Hengrove Wood

FREEZING HILL

Hamswell House

BA1

6

FREEZING HILL

Vine Cottage

Parkfield Farm

Lilliput Farm

Lower Hamswell

Berrymead

Ford

HALL

Torney's Court Farm

HALL LA.

7

ROAD

LANE

Noade's Leaze Farm

Rushmead Wood

Tadwick Farm

Tadwick

Gaunt's

The Battlefields

Lodge

F   Beach Wood   G   H   81   J   K

Sir Bevil Grenville Monument

Settlement

72   73   74

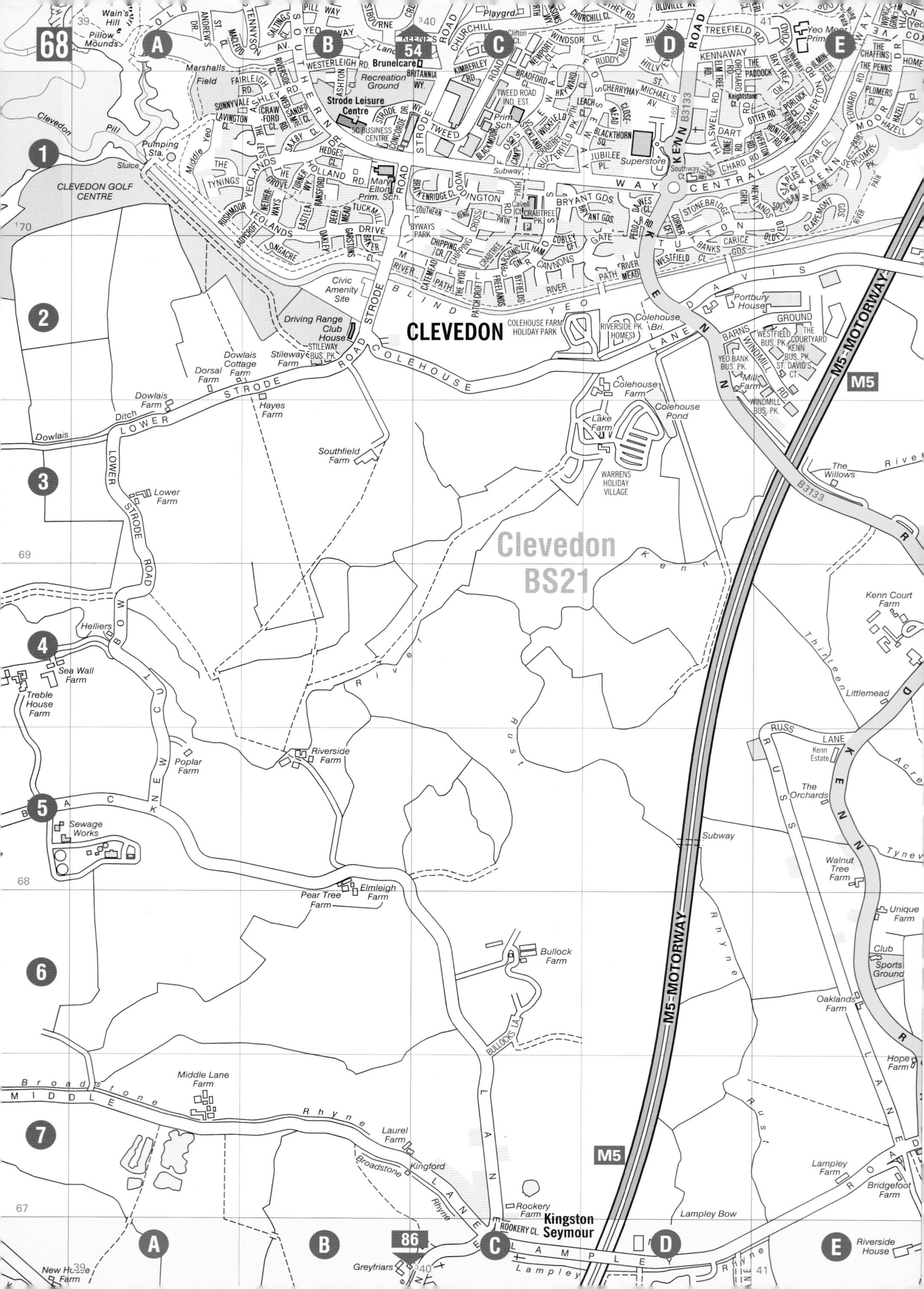
CLEVEDON
Clevedon
BS21
Wain's Hill
Pillow Mounds
Marshalls Field
Clevedon Pill
Pumping Sta.
Sluice
CLEVEDON GOLF CENTRE
Strode Leisure Centre
Recreation Ground
Brunelcare
5C BUSINESS CENTRE
Mary Elton Prim. Sch.
Tweed Road Ind. Est.
Prim. Sch.
Superstore
Southway Ct.
Civic Amenity Site
Driving Range Club House
Stileway Bus. Pk.
Stileway Farm
Dowlais Cottage Farm
Dorsal Farm
Dowlais Farm
Hayes Farm
Colehouse Farm Holiday Park
Riverside Pk. Homes
Colehouse Bri.
Portbury House
Westfield Bus. Pk.
The Courtyard
Kenn Bus. Pk.
St. David's Ct.
Yeo Bank Bus. Pk.
Mill Farm
Windmill Bus. Pk.
Colehouse Farm
Lake Farm
Colehouse Pond
Warrens Holiday Village
Southfield Farm
Lower Farm
The Willows
Kenn Court Farm
Littlemead
Kenn Estate
The Orchards
Walnut Tree Farm
Unique Farm
Club
Sports Ground
Oaklands Farm
Hope Farm
Lampley Farm
Bridgefoot Farm
Lampley Bow
Riverside House
Helliers
Sea Wall Farm
Treble House Farm
Poplar Farm
Riverside Farm
Sewage Works
Pear Tree Farm
Elmleigh Farm
Bullock Farm
Middle Lane Farm
Laurel Farm
Kingford
Rookery Farm
Kingston Seymour
Greyfriars
New House Farm
M5-MOTORWAY
M5
B3133
LOWER STRODE ROAD
STRODE ROAD
COLEHOUSE LANE
KENN ROAD
KENN MOOR DRIVE
RUSS LANE
BULLOCKS LA.
LAMPLEY ROAD
MIDDLE LANE
NEW CUT
BLIND YEO
Broadstone Rhyne
River Kenn
Thirteen Acre
Rust
Rhyne
Tynev
Dowlais Ditch
54
86
39
340
41
170
69
68
67

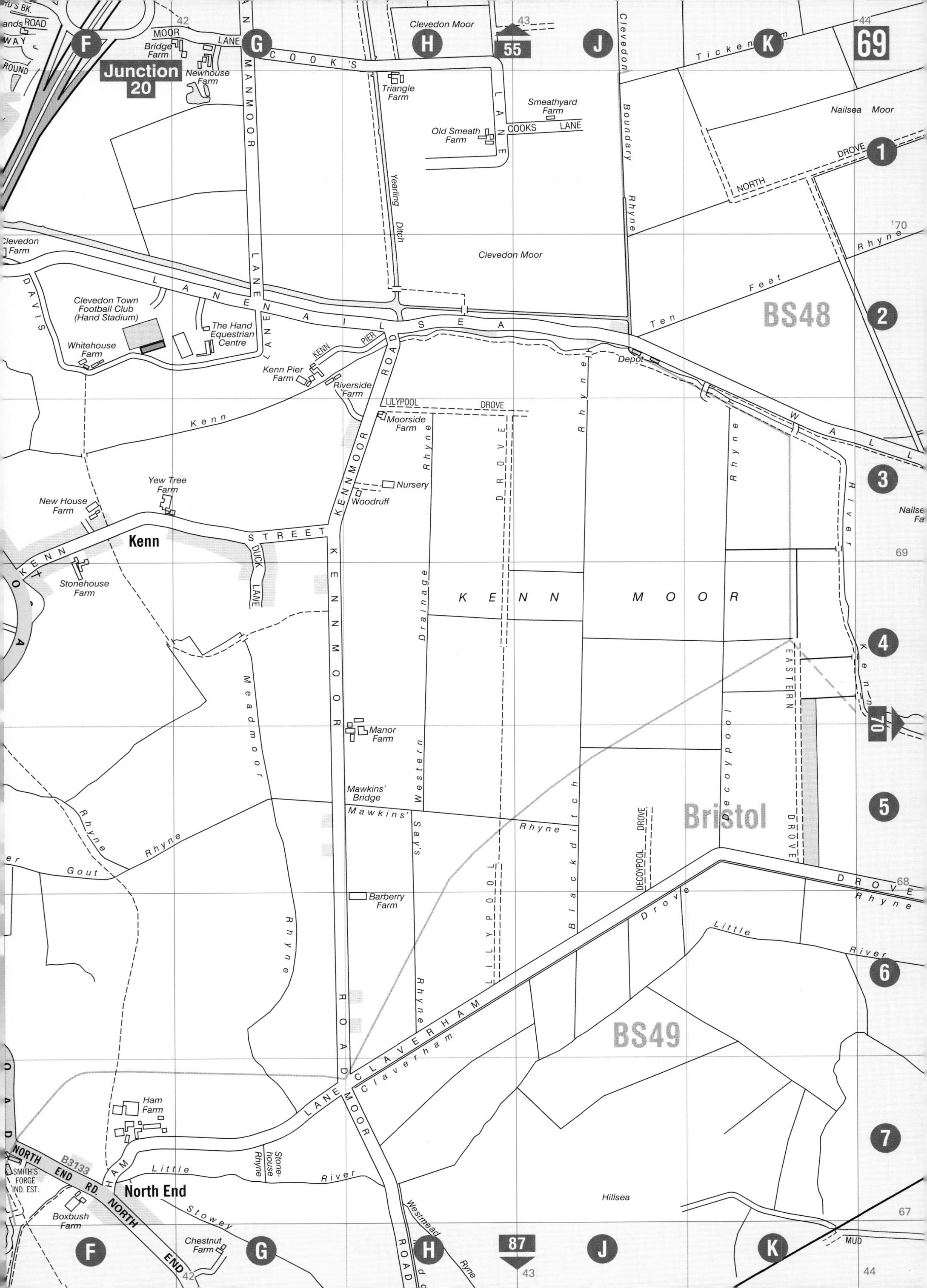

Junction 20
Moor Lane
Bridge Farm
Newhouse Farm
Cook's Lane
Triangle Farm
Clevedon Moor
55
Smeathyard Farm
Old Smeath Farm
Cooks Lane
Clevedon Boundary Rhyne
Ticken Moor
Nailsea Moor
North Drove
Manmoor Lane
Yearling Ditch
Clevedon Farm
Clevedon Moor
Rhyne
Ten Feet
BS48
Davis
Clevedon Town Football Club (Hand Stadium)
The Hand Equestrian Centre
Whitehouse Farm
Lane
Nailsea
Kenn Pier
Kenn Pier Farm
Riverside Farm
Kenn Road
Depot
Lilypool Drove
Moorside Farm
Kenn
Rhyne
Wall
Nursery
Woodruff
Yew Tree Farm
New House Farm
Kenn Street
Kenn
Duck Lane
Stonehouse Farm
Kennmoor
Drove
Drainage
River
Nailsea Farm
Kenn Moor
Meadmoor
Kennmoor Road
Manor Farm
Eastern Drove
Decoypool
Kenn
70
Western
Mawkins' Bridge
Mawkins' Rhyne
Say's
Blackditch
Bristol
Decoypool Drove
Rhyne
Gout Rhyne
Lilypool
Barberry Farm
Drove
Rhyne
Little River
BS49
Claverham Lane
Claverham
Moor
Ham Farm
North End Rd.
B3133
Smith's Forge Ind. Est.
Ham
Little River
Stonehouse Rhyne
North End
Boxbush Farm
Stowey
Chestnut Farm
Westmead
Road
Ryne
Hillsea
Mud
87
F
G
H
J
K
1
2
3
4
5
6
7
42
43
44
67
68
69
70

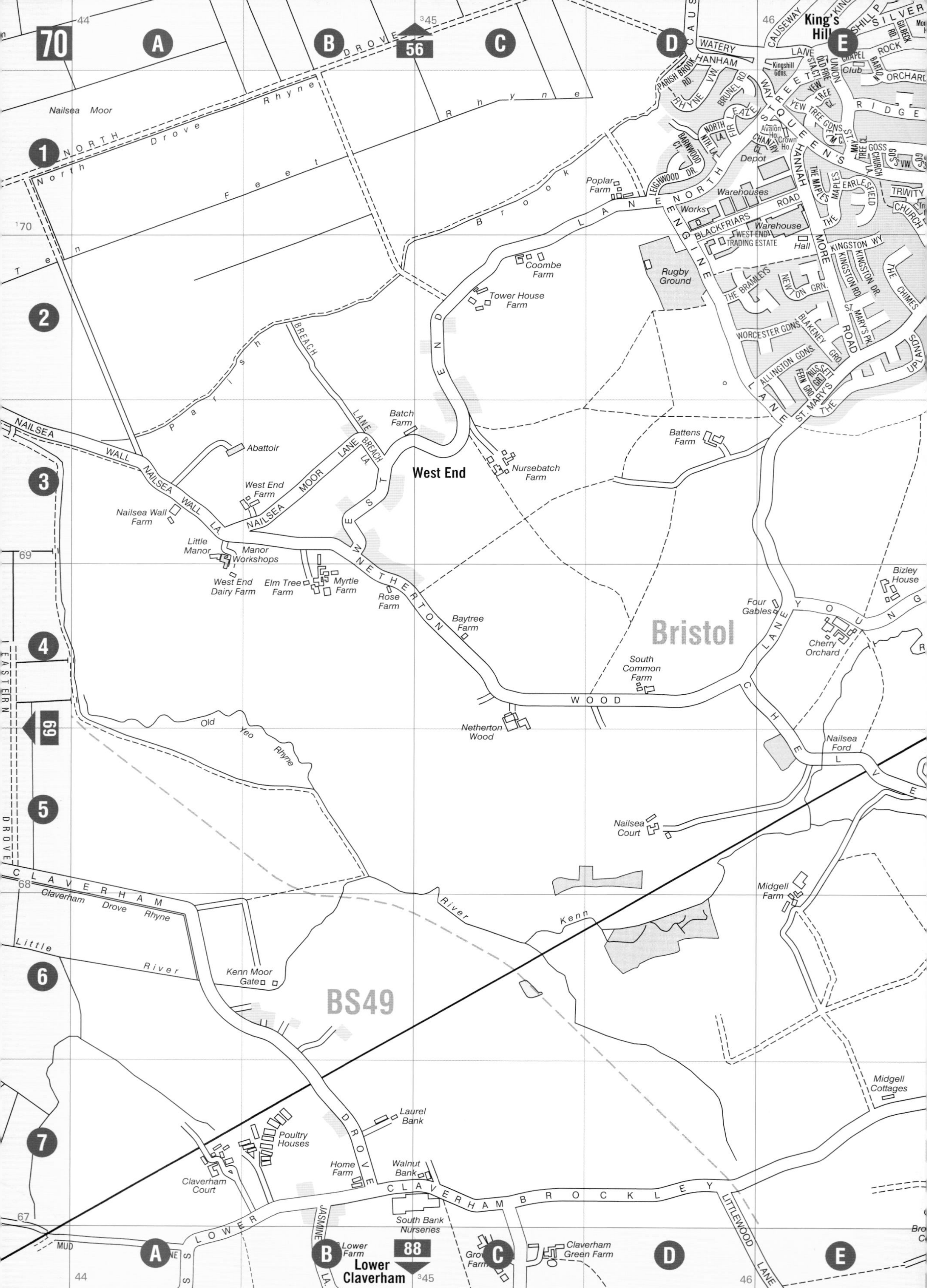

Nailsea Moor
North Drove Rhyne
North Drove
Ten Feet Rhyne
Brook
Parish
Poplar Farm
Coombe Farm
Tower House Farm
Rugby Ground
Works
Warehouses
Warehouse
West End Trading Estate
Hall
Depot
King's Hill
Batch Farm
Abattoir
West End
Nursebatch Farm
West End Farm
Nailsea Wall Farm
Little Manor
Manor Workshops
West End Dairy Farm
Elm Tree Farm
Myrtle Farm
Rose Farm
Baytree Farm
Battens Farm
Bizley House
Four Gables
Cherry Orchard
Bristol
South Common Farm
Netherton Wood
Nailsea Ford
Nailsea Court
Old Yeo Rhyne
Claverham Drove Rhyne
Little River
River Kenn
Midgell Farm
Kenn Moor Gate
BS49
Midgell Cottages
Laurel Bank
Poultry Houses
Home Farm
Walnut Bank
Claverham Court
South Bank Nurseries
Lower Farm
Claverham Green Farm
Lower Claverham
Nailsea Wall
Nailsea Wall La.
Nailsea Moor Lane
Breach Lane
West End
Netherton Wood
Engine Lane
North Lane
Youngwood Lane
Chelvey
Claverham Brockley Way
Claverham Drove
Lower Causeway
Littlewood Lane
Jasmine La.
Mud
Drove
Eastern Drove
56
88
69

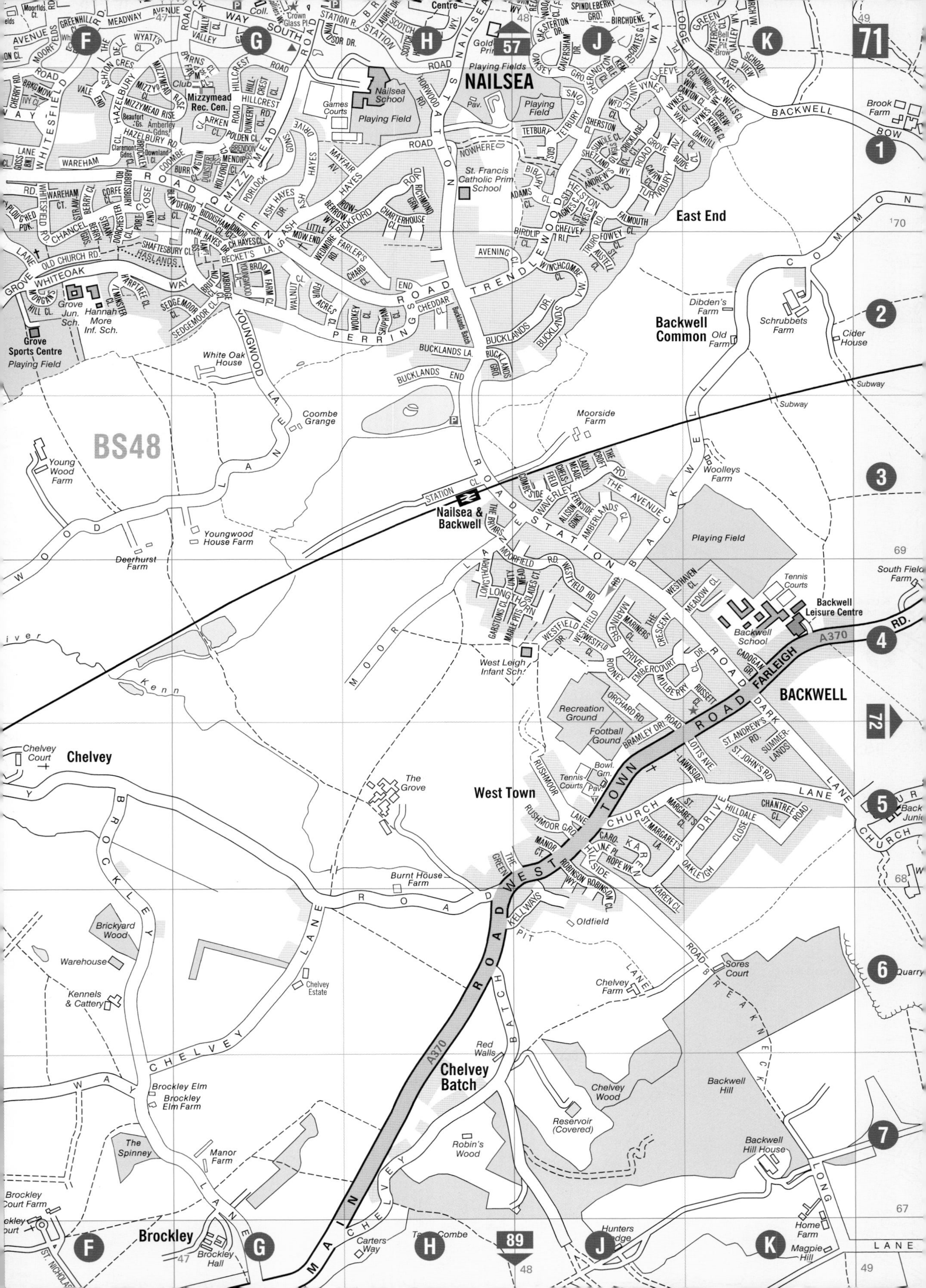
NAILSEA
East End
Backwell Common
BS48
Nailsea & Backwell
BACKWELL
West Town
Chelvey
Chelvey Batch
Brockley
Nailsea School
Playing Field
Games Courts
Mizzymead Rec. Cen.
St. Francis Catholic Prim. School
Grove Jun. Sch.
Hannah More Inf. Sch.
Grove Sports Centre
Playing Field
White Oak House
Coombe Grange
Young Wood Farm
Youngwood House Farm
Deerhurst Farm
Moorside Farm
Woolleys Farm
Dibden's Farm
Old Farm
Schrubbets Farm
Cider House
Brook Farm
South Field Farm
Backwell School
Backwell Leisure Centre
Tennis Courts
West Leigh Infant Sch.
Recreation Ground
Football Gound
Bowl. Grn.
Tennis Courts
Pav.
Chelvey Court
The Grove
Burnt House Farm
Oldfield
Sores Court
Chelvey Farm
Brickyard Wood
Warehouse
Kennels & Cattery
Chelvey Estate
Red Walls
Chelvey Wood
Backwell Hill
Reservoir (Covered)
Robin's Wood
Backwell Hill House
Brockley Elm
Brockley Elm Farm
The Spinney
Manor Farm
Brockley Court Farm
Brockley Hall
Carters Way
Hunters Lodge
Home Farm
Magpie Hill
Quarry
Subway
Kenn
River
A370
FARLEIGH ROAD
WEST TOWN ROAD
MAIN ROAD
STATION ROAD
QUEENS ROAD
TRENDLEWOOD ROAD
PERRINGS ROAD
WOOD LANE
YOUNGWOOD LA.
MOOR LANE
CHELVEY ROAD
CHELVEY LANE
CHELVEY WAY
BROCKLEY LANE
BACKWELL COMMON
BACKWELL BOW
CHURCH LANE
DARK LANE
BREAKNECK
LONG LANE
BATCH
PIT
57
89
72
F G H J K
1 2 3 4 5 6 7
47 48 49
67 68 69 70

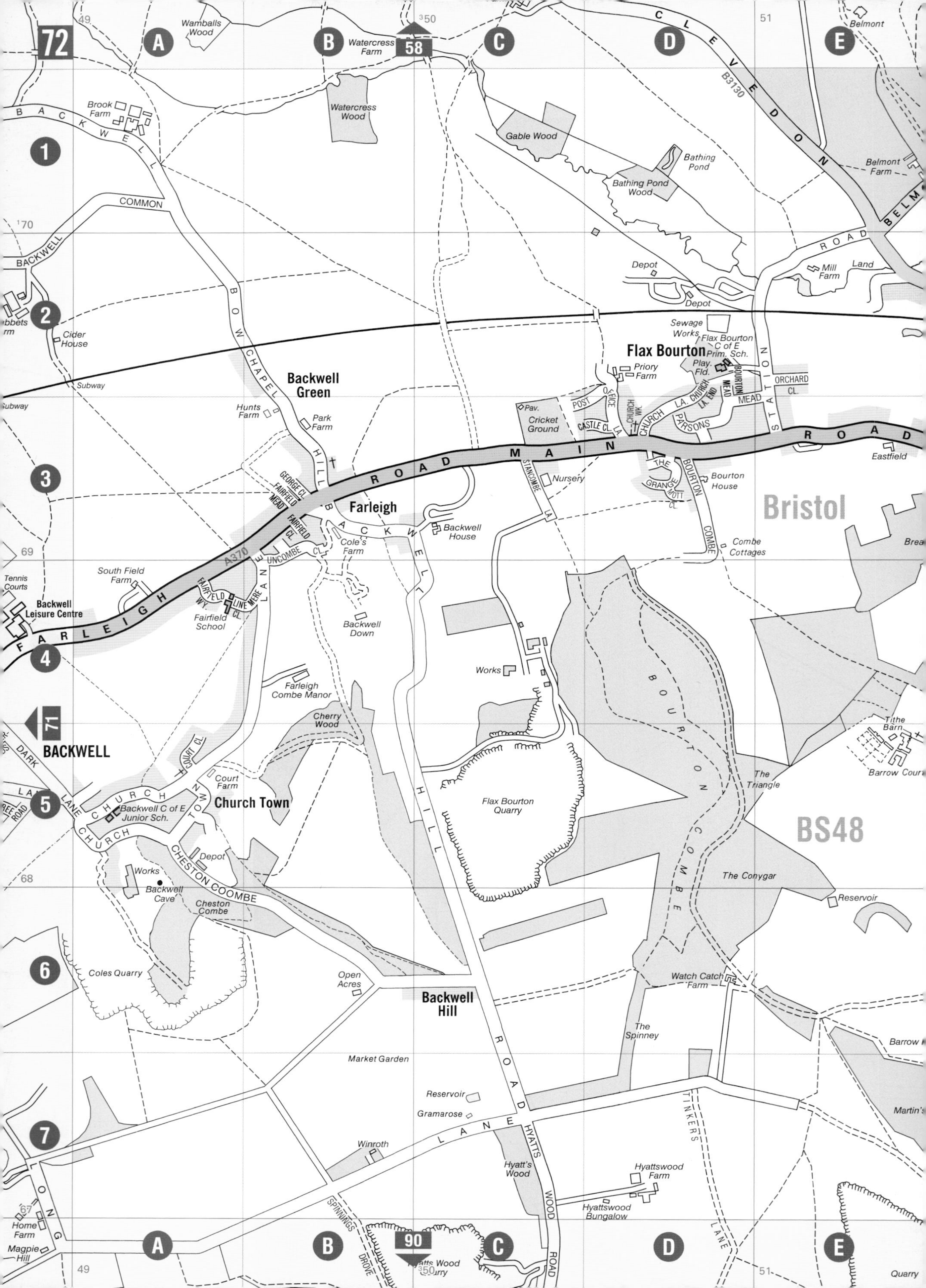

A **B** **58** **C** **D** **E**

1

Wamballs Wood

Brook Farm

Watercress Farm

Watercress Wood

BACKWELL COMMON

BOW CHAPEL HILL

Gable Wood

Bathing Pond

Bathing Pond Wood

Depot

Depot

CLEVEDON ROAD B3130

Belmont

Belmont Farm

BELM ROAD

170

2

Backwell

Cider House

Subway

Subway

Backwell Green

Hunts Farm

Park Farm

Sewage Works

Flax Bourton C of E Prim. Sch.

Flax Bourton

Priory Farm

Play. Fld.

BOURTON MEAD

ORCHARD CL.

STATION ROAD

Mill Farm

Land

3

George Cl.

Fairfield Mead

Fairfield Cl.

Farleigh

ROAD MAIN

Pav. Cricket Ground

CASTLE CL.

POST

SPICE

CHURCH LA.

CHURCH WK.

CHURCH LA. END

PARSONS

BOURTON CL.

THE GRANGE

STANCOMBE

Nursery

Bourton House

Combe Cottages

Bristol

Eastfield

69

A370

FARLEIGH

FAIRFIELD WAY

Fairfield School

South Field Farm

Tennis Courts

Backwell Leisure Centre

LINE CL.

WERE LANE

UNCOMBE CL.

Cole's Farm

Backwell House

Backwell Down

BACKWELL HILL

Works

BOURTON COOMBE

Break

Tithe Barn

Barrow Court

4

71

◄ **BACKWELL**

DARK LANE

TREE ROAD

Farleigh Combe Manor

Cherry Wood

Works

Flax Bourton Quarry

The Triangle

BS48

5

CHURCH LANE

COURT CL.

MONKTON

Court Farm

Church Town

Backwell C of E Junior Sch.

Depot

Works

Backwell Cave

Cheston Combe

CHESTON COOMBE

The Conygar

Reservoir

68

6

Coles Quarry

Open Acres

Backwell Hill

Watch Catch Farm

The Spinney

Barrow

7

LONG

Home Farm

Magpie Hill

Market Garden

Reservoir

Gramarose

Winroth

SPINNINGS DRIVE

HYATTS WOOD ROAD

LANE

Hyatt's Wood

Hyattswood Farm

Hyattswood Bungalow

TINKERS LANE

Martin's

Quarry

49

A **B** **90** **C** **D** **E**

51

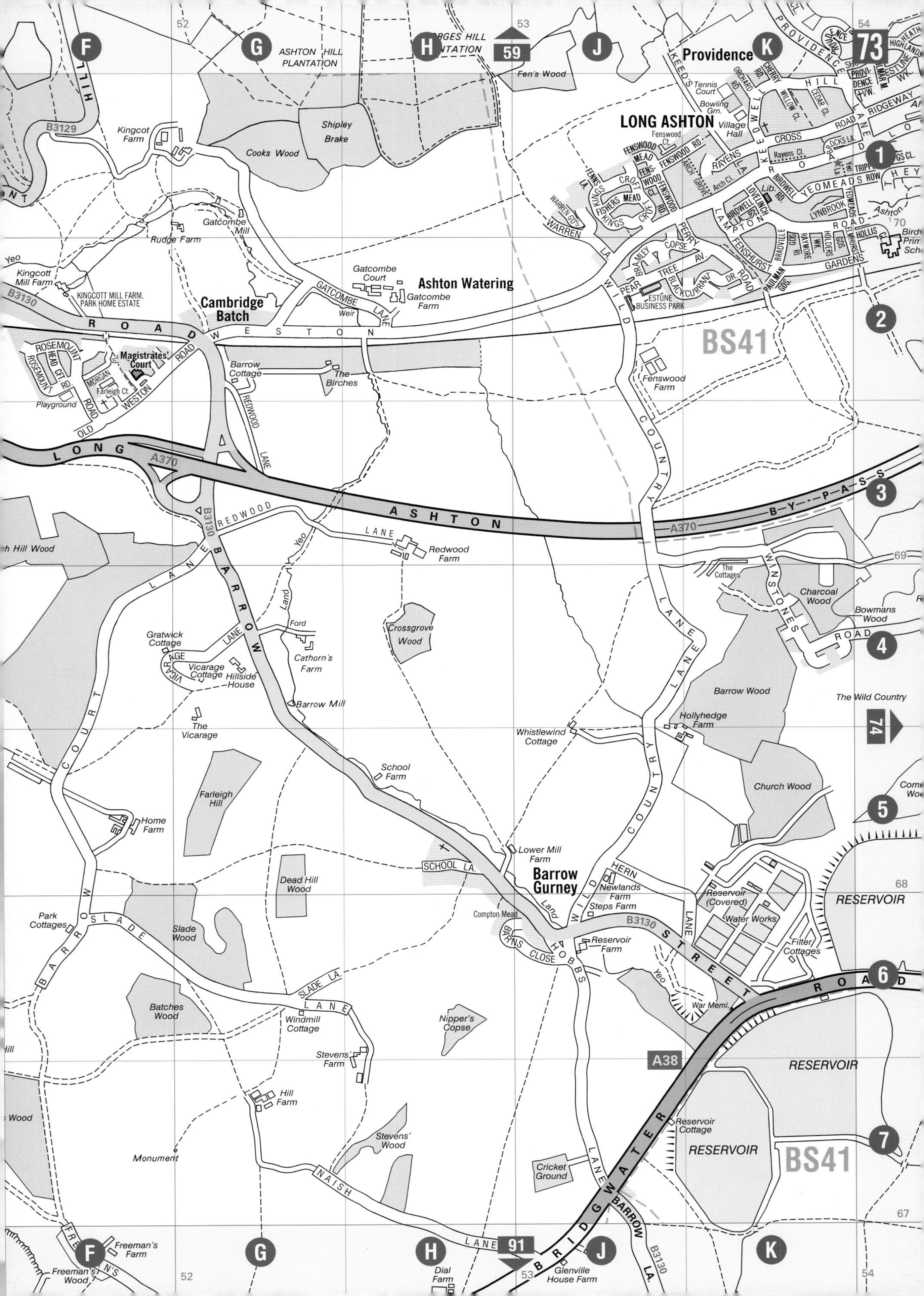

73
Providence
LONG ASHTON
Ashton Watering
Cambridge Batch
Barrow Gurney
BS41
ASHTON HILL PLANTATION
Fen's Wood
Shipley Brake
Cooks Wood
Kingcot Farm
Gatcombe Mill
Rudge Farm
Kingcott Mill Farm
KINGCOTT MILL FARM, PARK HOME ESTATE
Gatcombe Court
Gatcombe Farm
Magistrates' Court
Barrow Cottage
The Birches
Fenswood Farm
ESTUNE BUSINESS PARK
LONG ASHTON BY-PASS
A370
B3130
B3129
WESTON ROAD
REDWOOD LANE
Redwood Farm
Crossgrove Wood
Gratwick Cottage
Vicarage Cottage
Hillside House
Cathorn's Farm
Barrow Mill
The Vicarage
School Farm
Farleigh Hill
Home Farm
Lower Mill Farm
Dead Hill Wood
Park Cottages
Slade Wood
Batches Wood
Windmill Cottage
Stevens' Farm
Nipper's Copse
Hill Farm
Monument
Stevens' Wood
Cricket Ground
NAISH LANE
Freeman's Farm
Freeman's Wood
Dial Farm
Glenville House Farm
BRIDGWATER ROAD
A38
BARROW LA.
Reservoir Cottage
RESERVOIR
Filter Cottages
Water Works
Reservoir (Covered)
War Meml.
Reservoir Farm
Newlands Farm
Steps Farm
Compton Mead
Whistlewind Cottage
Hollyhedge Farm
Barrow Wood
Church Wood
Charcoal Wood
Bowmans Wood
The Cottages
WINSTONES ROAD
The Wild Country
WILD COUNTRY LANE
BARROW COURT LANE
BARROW STREET
HOBBS LANE
59
74
91

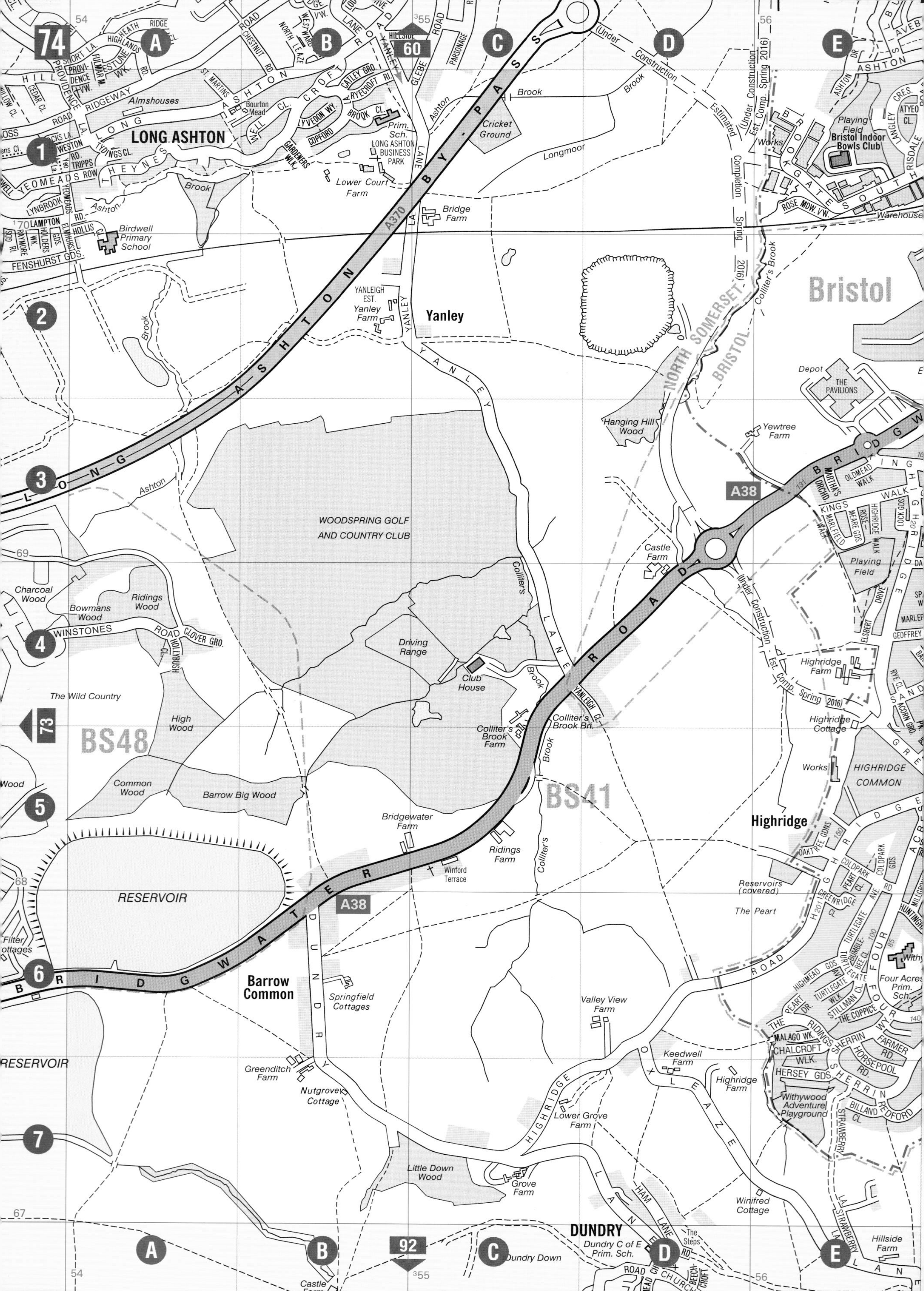
LONG ASHTON
Yanley
Bristol
BS48
BS41
Highridge
Barrow Common
DUNDRY
WOODSPRING GOLF AND COUNTRY CLUB
RESERVOIR
LONG ASHTON BY-PASS
A370
A38
BRIDGWATER ROAD
NORTH SOMERSET
BRISTOL
Bristol Indoor Bowls Club
Birdwell Primary School
Long Ashton Business Park
Lower Court Farm
Bridge Farm
Cricket Ground
Longmoor
Yanley Farm
Hanging Hill Wood
Yewtree Farm
Castle Farm
Charcoal Wood
Bowmans Wood
Ridings Wood
WINSTONES ROAD
The Wild Country
High Wood
Common Wood
Barrow Big Wood
Driving Range
Club House
Colliter's Brook Farm
Bridgewater Farm
Ridings Farm
Winford Terrace
Highridge Farm
Highridge Cottage
HIGHRIDGE COMMON
Reservoirs (covered)
The Peart
Springfield Cottages
Valley View Farm
Keedwell Farm
Greenditch Farm
Nutgrove Cottage
Lower Grove Farm
Little Down Wood
Grove Farm
Winifred Cottage
Hillside Farm
Dundry C of E Prim. Sch.
Dundry Down
Castle Farm
Four Acres Prim. Sch.
Withywood Adventure Playground
The Pavilions
Depot
Works
Playing Field
Almshouses
(Under Construction Est. Comp. Spring 2016)
60
73
92

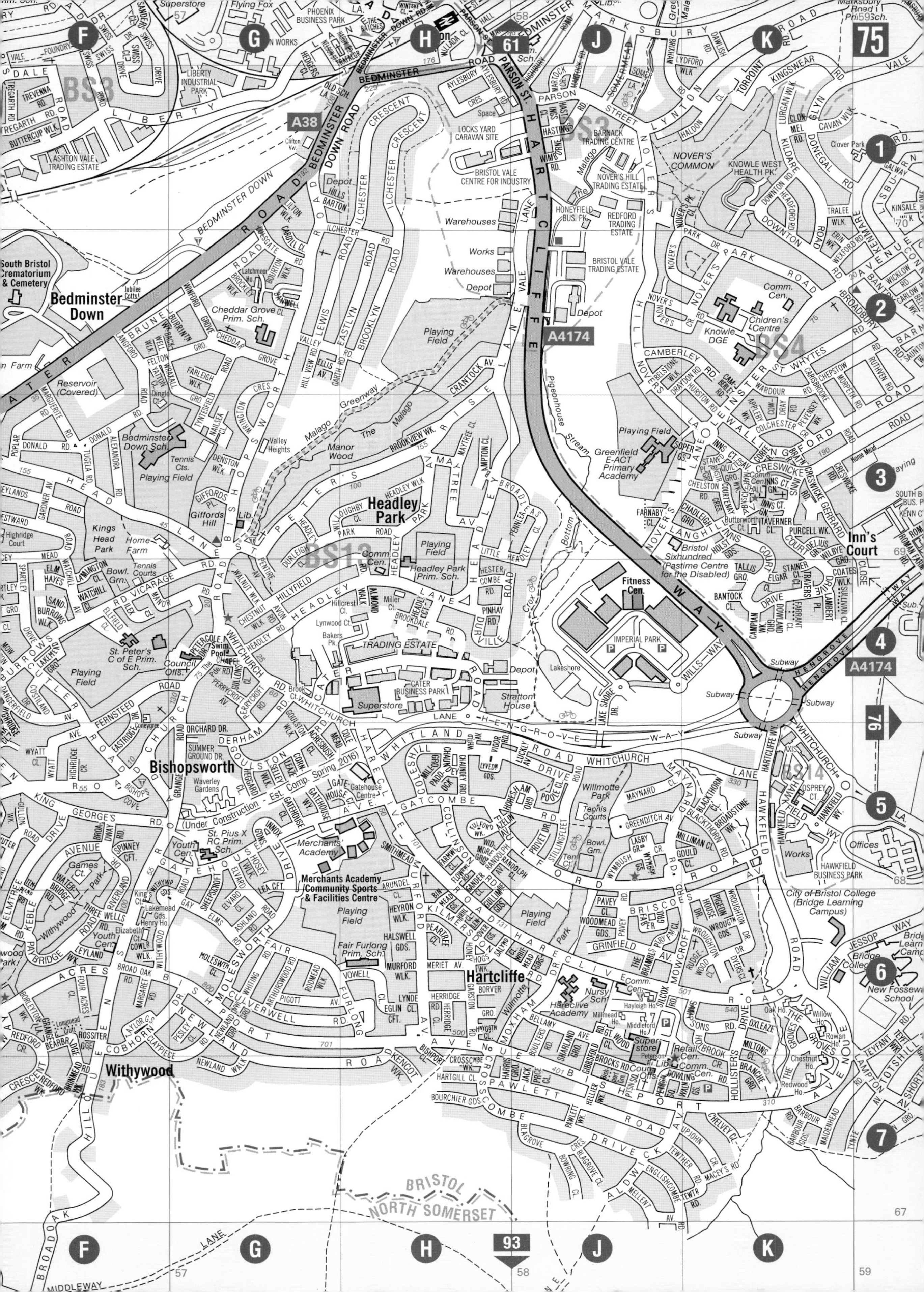
F
G
H
J
K
61
A38
A4174
BS3
BS4
BS13
BS14
Bedminster Down
Headley Park
Bishopsworth
Withywood
Hartcliffe
Inn's Court
South Bristol Crematorium & Cemetery
Liberty Industrial Park
Ashton Vale Trading Estate
Locks Yard Caravan Site
Bristol Vale Centre for Industry
Barnack Trading Centre
Nover's Common
Knowle West Health Pk.
Nover's Hill Trading Estate
Redford Trading Estate
Bristol Vale Trading Estate
Honeyfield Bus. Pk.
Cheddar Grove Prim. Sch.
Bedminster Down Sch.
Kings Head Park
Manor Wood
Headley Park Prim. Sch.
Greenfield E-ACT Primary Academy
Knowle DGE
Children's Centre
Bristol Sixhundred (Pastime Centre for the Disabled)
Fitness Cen.
Imperial Park
Cater Business Park
Trading Estate
Stratton House
St. Peter's C of E Prim. Sch.
Merchants' Academy
Merchants Academy Community Sports & Facilities Centre
Fair Furlong Prim. Sch.
St. Pius X RC Prim. Sch.
Hareclive Academy
Willmotte Park
Hawkfield Business Park
City of Bristol College (Bridge Learning Campus)
New Fosseway School
(Under Construction - Est. Comp. Spring 2016)
BRISTOL
NORTH SOMERSET
Bedminster Down Road
Hartcliffe Way
Hengrove Way
Whitchurch Lane
Bishopsworth Road
Headley Lane
Hareclive Road
Bishport Avenue
Pawlett Road
Whitland Road
Wills Way
Hengrove Way
1
2
3
4
5
6
7
76
93
57
58
59
67
68
69
70

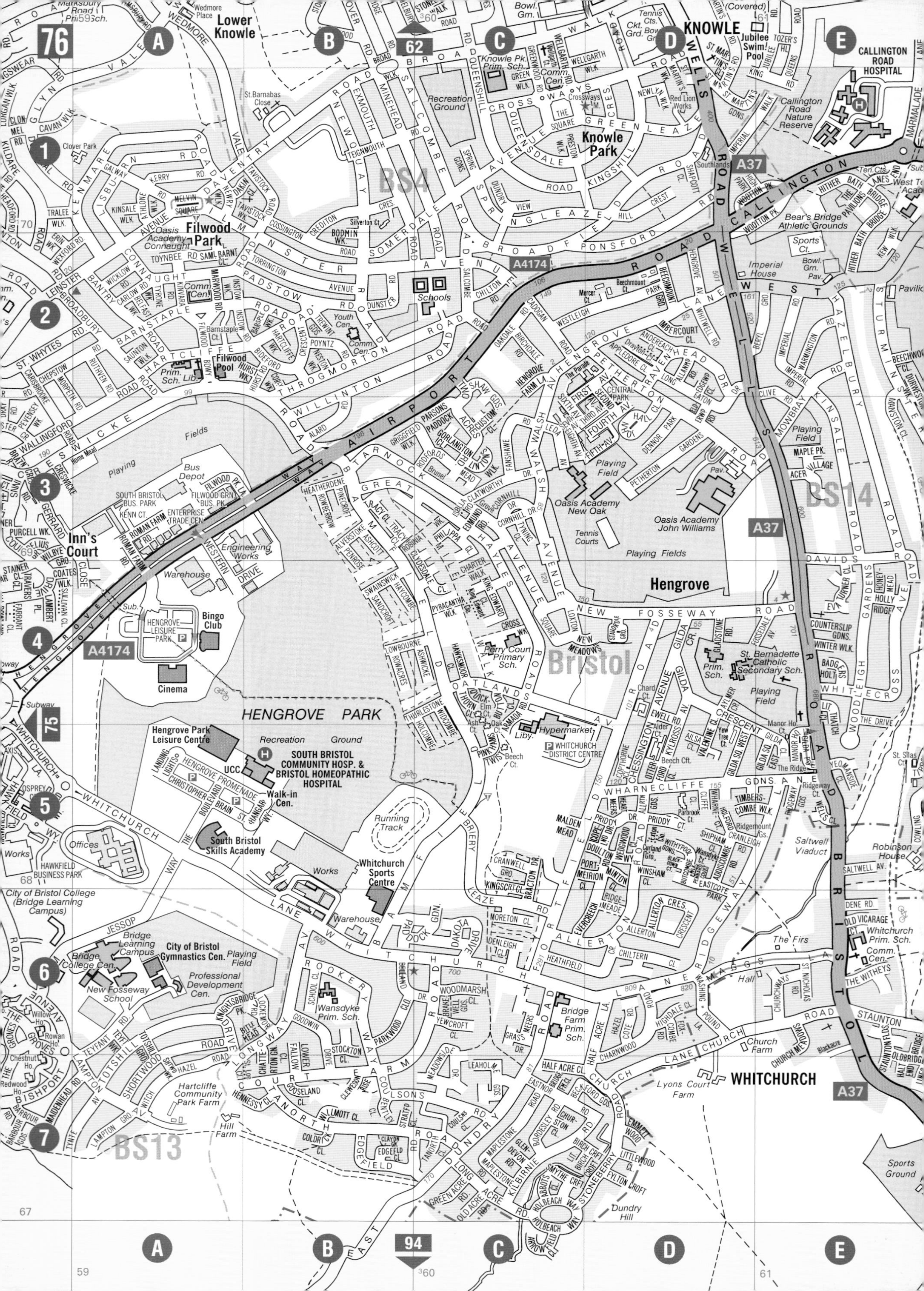

Lower Knowle
KNOWLE
Jubilee Swim. Pool
CALLINGTON ROAD HOSPITAL
Callington Road Nature Reserve
Knowle Pk. Prim. Sch.
Recreation Ground
Knowle Park
BS4
Filwood Park
Oasis Academy Connaught
Schools
Youth Cen.
Filwood Pool
Prim. Sch. Lib.
A37
A4174
A37
Bear's Bridge Athletic Grounds
Imperial House
Playing Fields
Bus Depot
SOUTH BRISTOL BUS. PARK
FILWOOD GRN. BUS. PK.
ENTERPRISE TRADE CEN.
Inn's Court
Engineering Works
Warehouse
HENGROVE LEISURE PARK
Bingo Club
Cinema
AIRPORT ROAD
HENGROVE WAY
Oasis Academy New Oak
Oasis Academy John Williams
Tennis Courts
Playing Fields
Hengrove
BS14
NEW FOSSEWAY ROAD
Perry Court Primary Sch.
Bristol
St. Bernadette Catholic Secondary Sch.
Prim. Sch.
Playing Field
HENGROVE PARK
Hengrove Park Leisure Centre
Recreation Ground
SOUTH BRISTOL COMMUNITY HOSP. & BRISTOL HOMEOPATHIC HOSPITAL
UCC
Walk-in Cen.
Hypermarket
Liby.
WHITCHURCH DISTRICT CENTRE
Running Track
South Bristol Skills Academy
Offices
Works
HAWKFIELD BUSINESS PARK
Whitchurch Sports Centre
Warehouse
City of Bristol College (Bridge Learning Campus)
Bridge Learning Campus
Bridge College Cen.
City of Bristol Gymnastics Cen.
Playing Field
Professional Development Cen.
New Fosseway School
Wansdyke Prim. Sch.
Bridge Farm Prim. Sch.
Saltwell Viaduct
Robinson House
The Firs
Whitchurch Prim. Sch.
Comm. Cen.
Church Farm
WHITCHURCH
Lyons Court Farm
Hartcliffe Community Park Farm
Hill Farm
BS13
Dundry Hill
Sports Ground
BRISTOL ROAD
WELLS ROAD
62
75
94
A
B
C
D
E
1
2
3
4
5
6
7
59
60
61
67
68
69
70

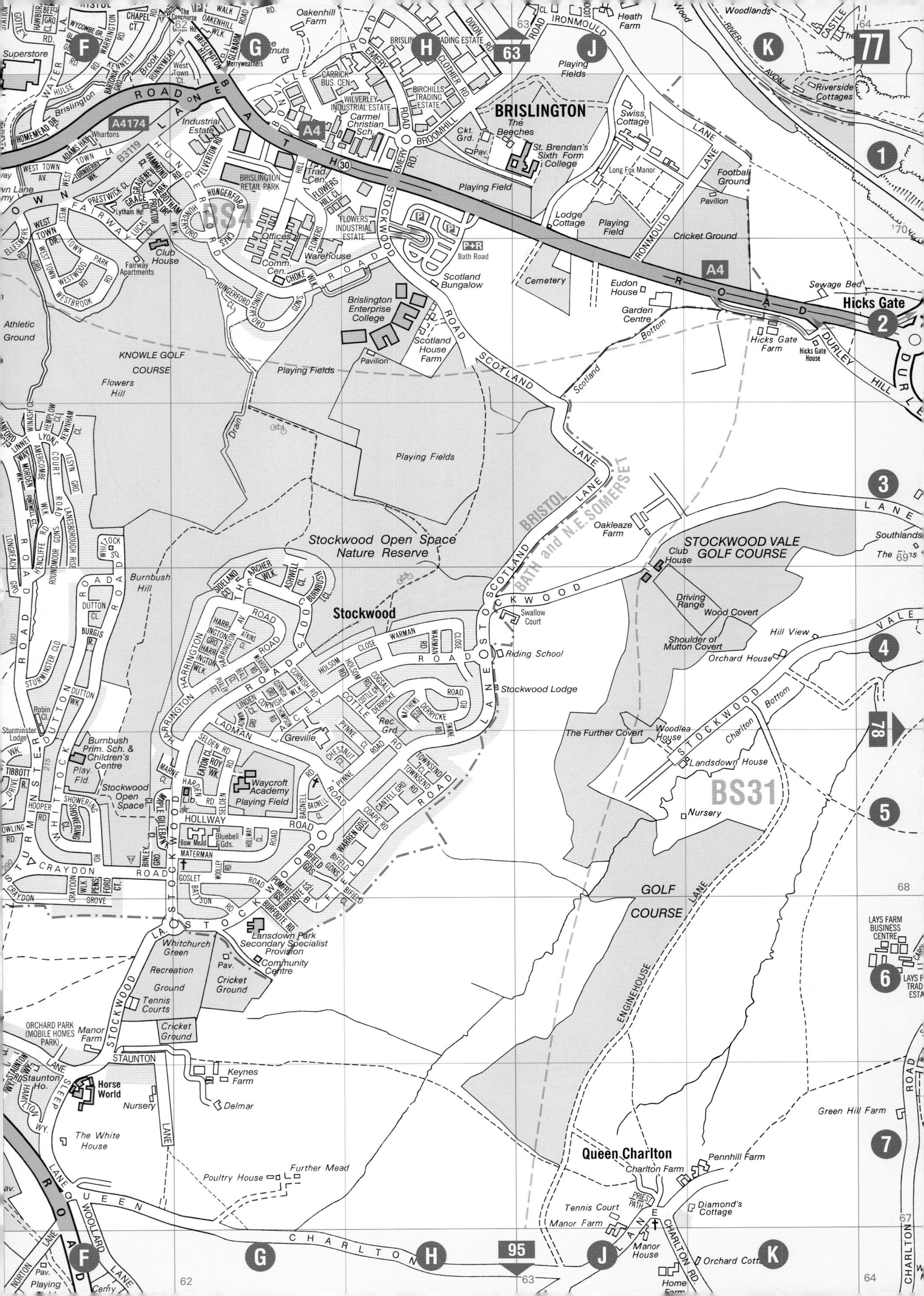
77
63
95
78
F
G
H
J
K
1
2
3
4
5
6
7
62
63
64
70
69
68
67
BRISLINGTON
BS4
BS31
Stockwood
Queen Charlton
Hicks Gate
A4
A4174
B3119
BATH ROAD
BRISTOL
BATH and N.E. SOMERSET
Superstore
Industrial Estate
Brislington Retail Park
Brislington Trading Estate
Carrick Bus. Cen.
Wilverley Industrial Estate
Carmel Christian Sch.
Birchills Trading Estate
Flowers Industrial Estate
St. Brendan's Sixth Form College
The Beeches
Ckt. Grd.
Pav.
Playing Field
Playing Fields
Cricket Ground
Football Ground
Pavilion
Long Fox Manor
Swiss Cottage
Lodge Cottage
Cemetery
Eudon House
Garden Centre
Scotland Bottom
Sewage Bed
Hicks Gate Farm
Hicks Gate House
Durley Hill
Woodlands
River Avon
Riverside Cottages
Heath Farm
Oakenhill Farm
Merryweathers
Scotland Bungalow
P+R Bath Road
Brislington Enterprise College
Scotland House Farm
Scotland Lane
Stockwood Road
Knowle Golf Course
Flowers Hill
Athletic Ground
Club House
Fairway Apartments
Offices
Warehouse
Comm. Cen.
Stockwood Open Space Nature Reserve
Burnbush Hill
Oakleaze Farm
Stockwood Vale Golf Course
Club House
Driving Range
Wood Covert
Shoulder of Mutton Covert
Hill View
Orchard House
Swallow Court
Riding School
Stockwood Lodge
The Further Covert
Woodlea House
Landsdown House
Nursery
Charlton Bottom
Stockwood Lane
Stockwood Vale
Southlands
Golf Course
Enginehouse Lane
Lays Farm Business Centre
Greville
Rec. Grd.
Waycroft Academy Playing Field
Lib.
Hollway
Burnbush Prim. Sch. & Children's Centre
Play. Fld.
Stockwood Open Space
Sturminster Lodge
Craydon Road
Whitchurch Green
Recreation Ground
Tennis Courts
Cricket Ground
Pav.
Lansdown Park Secondary Specialist Provision
Community Centre
Orchard Park (Mobile Homes Park)
Manor Farm
Staunton Lane
Staunton Ho.
Horse World
Nursery
The White House
Keynes Farm
Delmar
Poultry House
Further Mead
Queen Charlton Lane
Woollard Lane
Norton Lane
Charlton Farm
Pennhill Farm
Tennis Court
Manor Farm
Manor House
Priest Path
Diamond's Cottage
Orchard Cott.
Home Farm
Charlton Rd.
Green Hill Farm
Playing
Cemy.

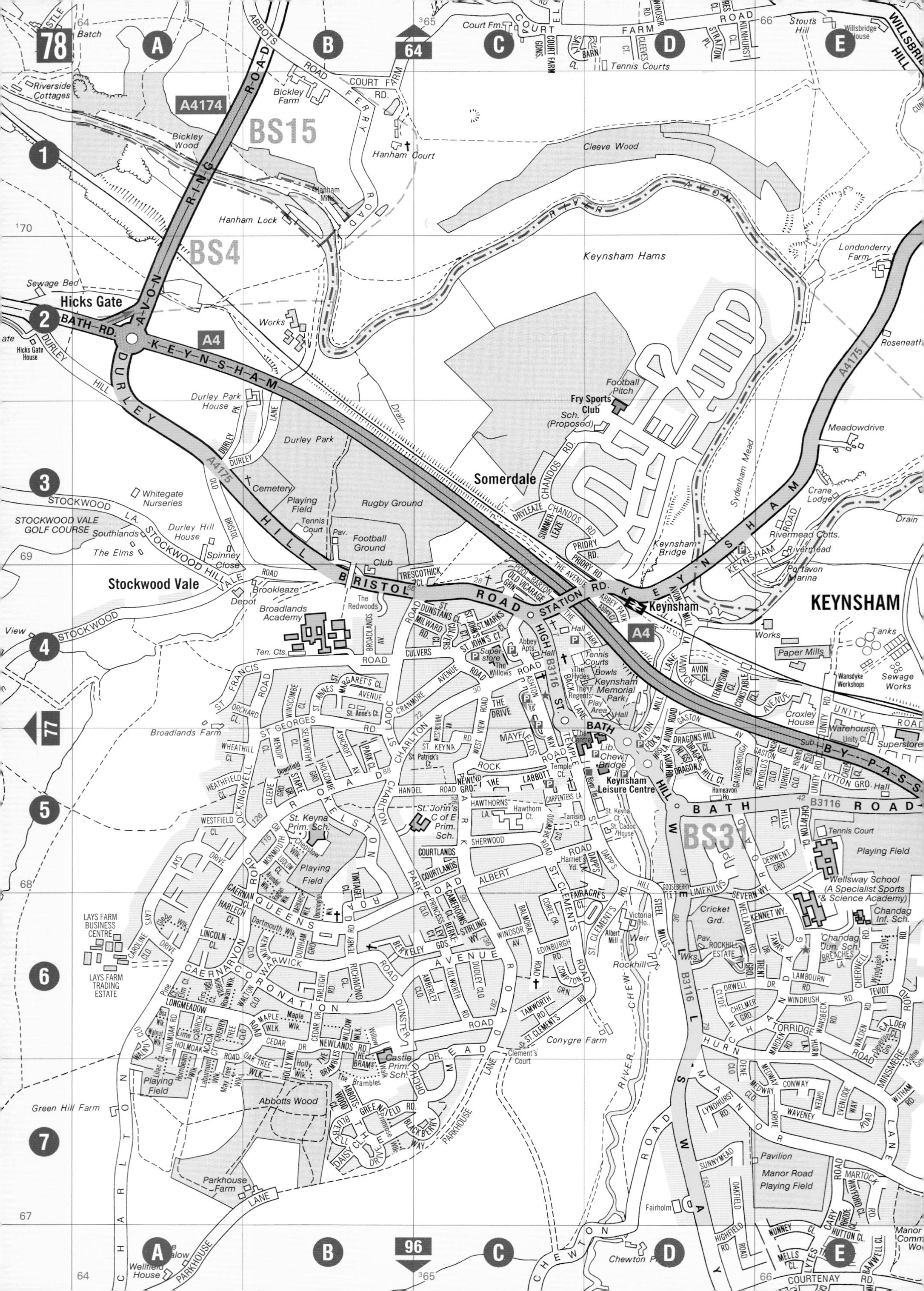
Hicks Gate
BS15
BS4
BS31
Somerdale
Stockwood Vale
KEYNSHAM
Keynsham Hams
Cleeve Wood
Hanham Court
Hanham Lock
Bickley Wood
Bickley Farm
Durley Park
Rugby Ground
Football Ground
Fry Sports Club
Broadlands Academy
Stockwood Vale Golf Course
Keynsham Leisure Centre
Wellsway School (A Specialist Sports & Science Academy)
Manor Road Playing Field
Abbotts Wood
Lays Farm Business Centre
Lays Farm Trading Estate
Green Hill Farm
Parkhouse Farm
Conygre Farm
Chewton Place
Portavon Marina
Paper Mills
Londonderry Farm
A4174
A4
A4175
B3116

64
96
77

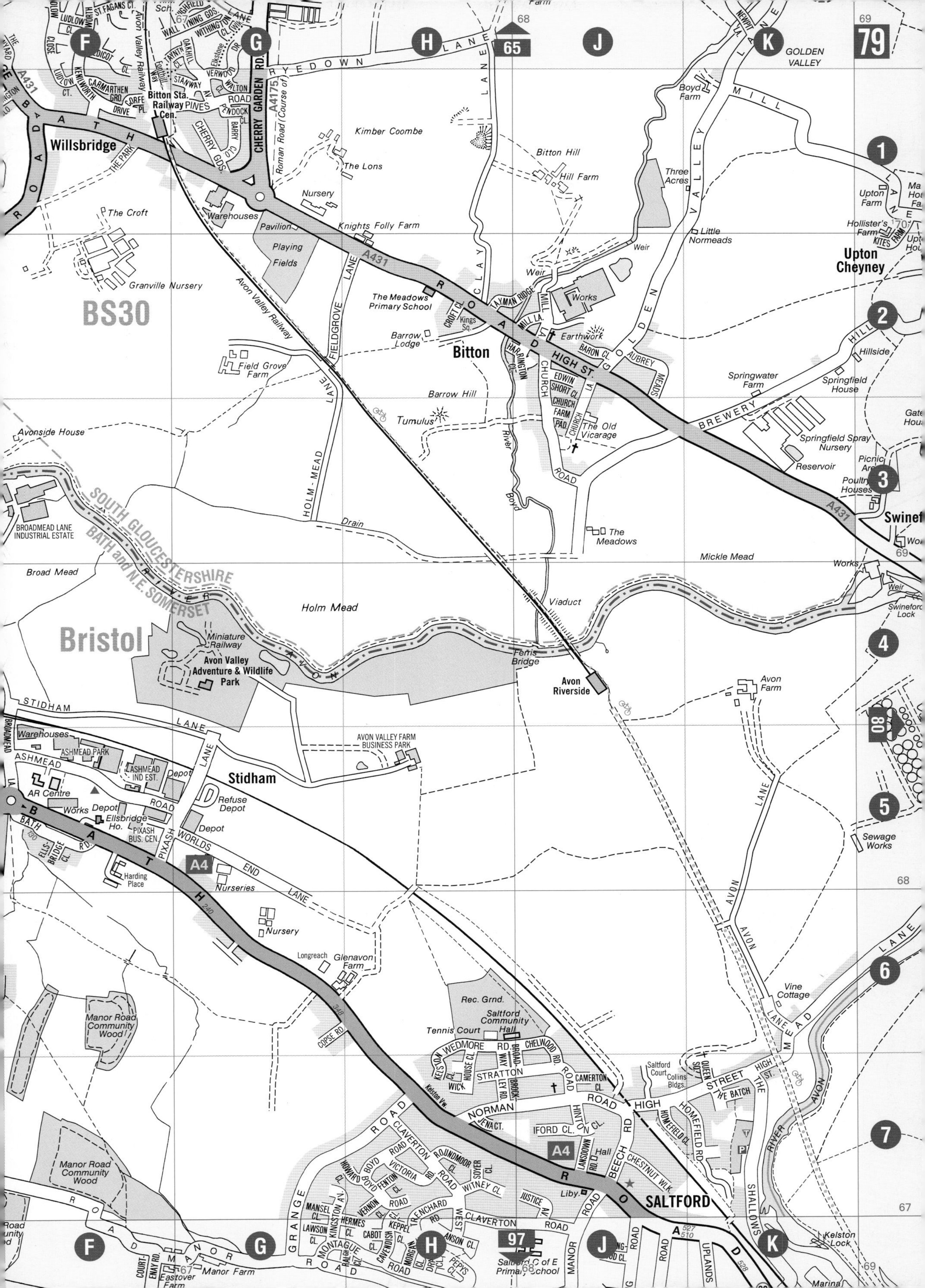

79
65
80
97
F
G
H
J
K
1
2
3
4
5
6
7
Willsbridge
Bitton Sta. Railway Cen.
Avon Valley Railway
CHERRY GARDEN RD.
A4175
Roman Road (Course of)
RYEDOWN LANE
GOLDEN VALLEY
Boyd Farm
Kimber Coombe
Bitton Hill
Hill Farm
The Lons
Nursery
Warehouses
Pavilion
Playing Fields
Knights Folly Farm
The Croft
Granville Nursery
BS30
A431
BATH ROAD
HIGH ST.
The Meadows Primary School
Barrow Lodge
Bitton
Field Grove Farm
FIELDGROVE LANE
Barrow Hill
Tumulus
Earthwork
Works
Weir
Three Acres
Little Normeads
Upton Farm
Hollister's Farm
Upton Cheyney
Springwater Farm
Springfield House
Hillside
BREWERY HILL
Springfield Spray Nursery
Reservoir
The Old Vicarage
The Meadows
River Boyd
HOLM MEAD
Drain
Mickle Mead
Avonside House
BROADMEAD LANE INDUSTRIAL ESTATE
Broad Mead
SOUTH GLOUCESTERSHIRE
BATH and N.E. SOMERSET
RIVER AVON
Holm Mead
Viaduct
Ferris Bridge
Avon Riverside
Swineford Lock
Bristol
Miniature Railway
Avon Valley Adventure & Wildlife Park
Avon Farm
STIDHAM LANE
AVON VALLEY FARM BUSINESS PARK
Stidham
ASHMEAD PARK
LASHMEAD IND EST.
AR Centre
Depot
Refuse Depot
Ellsbridge Ho.
PIXASH BUS. CEN.
WORLDS END LANE
A4
Harding Place
Nurseries
Nursery
Sewage Works
Longreach
Glenavon Farm
Manor Road Community Wood
Rec. Grnd.
Saltford Community Hall
Tennis Court
WEDMORE RD.
CHELWOOD RD.
STRATTON
NORMAN ROAD
HIGH STREET
Saltford Court
Collins Bldgs.
THE BATCH
HOMEFIELD RD.
Vine Cottage
MEAD LANE
AVON LANE
Hall
Liby.
SALTFORD
CLAVERTON ROAD
GRANGE ROAD
MANOR ROAD
Manor Farm
Eastover Farm
Saltford C of E Primary School
UPLANDS
SHALLOWS
Kelston Lock
Marina

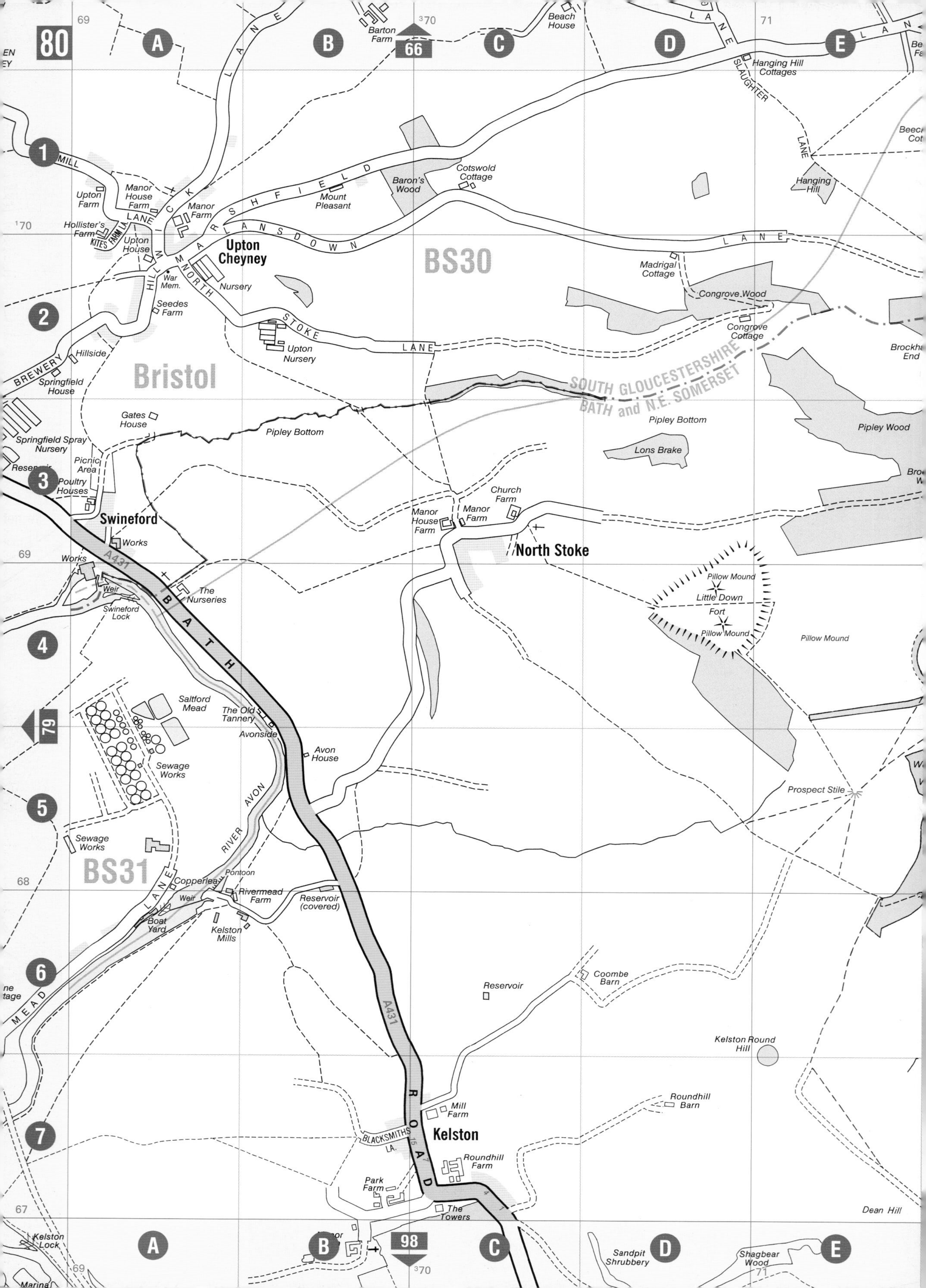

Barton Farm
Beach House
66
Hanging Hill Cottages
Upton Farm
Manor House Farm
Manor Farm
Mount Pleasant
Baron's Wood
Cotswold Cottage
Hanging Hill
Hollister's Farm
Upton House
Upton Cheyney
BS30
War Mem.
Nursery
Madrigal Cottage
Congrove Wood
Seedes Farm
Congrove Cottage
Upton Nursery
Hillside
Springfield House
Bristol
Brockham End
SOUTH GLOUCESTERSHIRE
BATH and N.E. SOMERSET
Gates House
Pipley Bottom
Pipley Wood
Springfield Spray Nursery
Lons Brake
Picnic Area
Poultry Houses
Church Farm
Manor House Farm
Manor Farm
Swineford
Works
North Stoke
Pillow Mound
Little Down Fort
The Nurseries
Weir
Swineford Lock
Saltford Mead
The Old Tannery
Avonside
Avon House
Sewage Works
79
Prospect Stile
RIVER AVON
BS31
Copperleaf
Pontoon
Rivermead Farm
Reservoir (covered)
Boat Yard
Kelston Mills
Coombe Barn
Reservoir
Kelston Round Hill
Roundhill Barn
Mill Farm
BLACKSMITHS LA.
Kelston
Roundhill Farm
Park Farm
The Towers
Dean Hill
Kelston Lock
98
Sandpit Shrubbery
Shagbear Wood
Marina
MILL LANE
KITES FARM LA.
HILL
NORTH STOKE LANE
MARSHFIELD
LANSDOWN LANE
SLAUGHTER LANE
BREWERY
A431
BATH ROAD
MEAD LANE
LANE

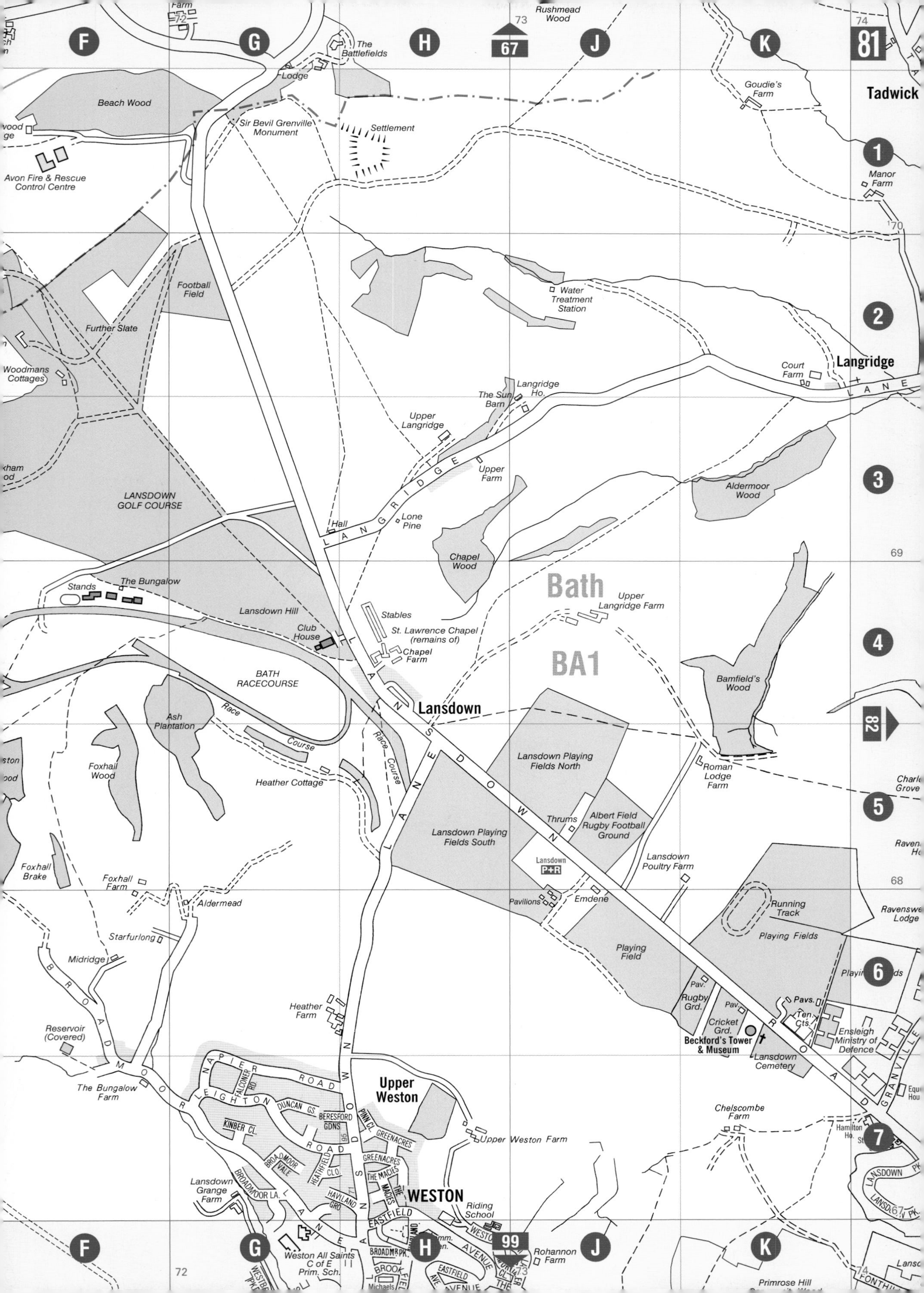

81
F
G
H
J
K
67
99
82
1
2
3
4
5
6
7
Rushmead Wood
The Battlefields
Lodge
Beach Wood
Sir Bevil Grenville Monument
Settlement
Goudie's Farm
Tadwick
Manor Farm
Avon Fire & Rescue Control Centre
Football Field
Further Slate
Woodmans Cottages
Water Treatment Station
Court Farm
Langridge
LANE
Langridge Ho.
The Sun Barn
Upper Langridge
Upper Farm
LANGRIDGE
Aldermoor Wood
LANSDOWN GOLF COURSE
Hall
Lone Pine
Chapel Wood
Bath
Upper Langridge Farm
Stands
The Bungalow
Lansdown Hill
Stables
St. Lawrence Chapel (remains of)
Club House
Chapel Farm
BA1
BATH RACECOURSE
Bamfield's Wood
Lansdown
Ash Plantation
Race Course
Foxhall Wood
Heather Cottage
Lansdown Playing Fields North
Roman Lodge Farm
Charlcombe Grove
Lansdown Playing Fields South
Thrums
Albert Field Rugby Football Ground
Foxhall Brake
Lansdown P+R
Lansdown Poultry Farm
Foxhall Farm
Pavilions
Emdene
Aldermead
Running Track
Ravenswell Lodge
Starfurlong
Playing Fields
Midridge
Playing Field
BROAD
Heather Farm
Pav.
Rugby Grd.
Pav.
Cricket Grd.
Pavs.
Ten. Cts.
Ensleigh Ministry of Defence
Reservoir (Covered)
Beckford's Tower & Museum
Lansdown Cemetery
NAPIER ROAD
MOORLEIGHTON ROAD
Upper Weston
The Bungalow Farm
FALCONER RD.
DUNCAN GS.
BERESFORD GDNS
PINN CL.
KINBER CL.
GREENACRES
Chelscombe Farm
Upper Weston Farm
Hamilton Ho.
GRANVILLE
BROADMOOR VALE
HEATHFIELD CLO.
THE MACIES
LANSDOWN PK.
Lansdown Grange Farm
BROADMOOR LA.
HAVILAND GRO.
WESTON
Riding School
EASTFIELD
WESTON AVENUE
Weston All Saints C of E Prim. Sch.
BROADMR PK.
BROOKFIELD
EASTFIELD AVE.
Rohannon Farm
Primrose Hill
72
73
74
70
69
68
67

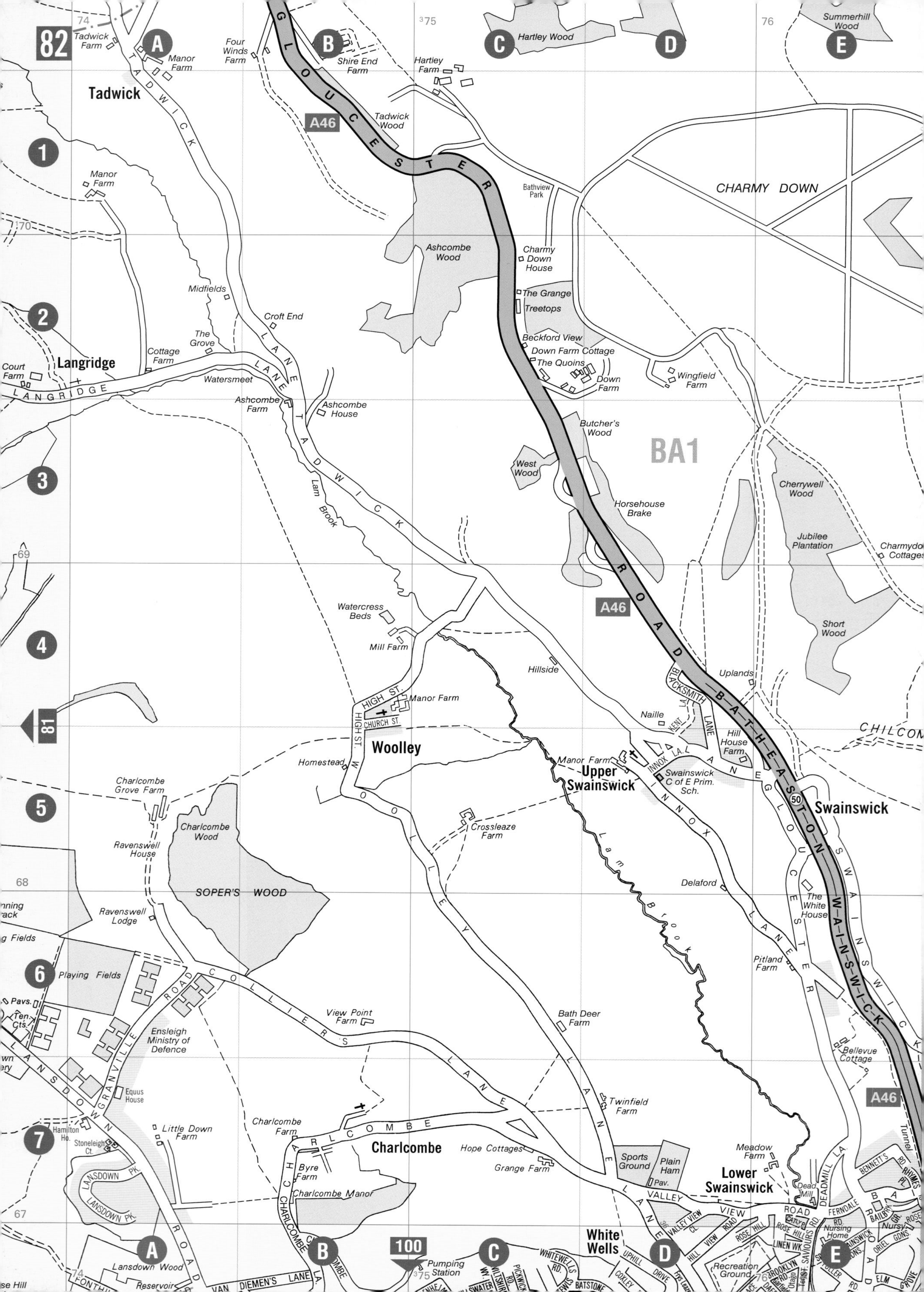
Tadwick Farm
Manor Farm
Tadwick
Four Winds Farm
Shire End Farm
Hartley Farm
Hartley Wood
Summerhill Wood
GLOUCESTER ROAD
A46
Tadwick Wood
Manor Farm
CHARMY DOWN
Bathview Park
Ashcombe Wood
Charmy Down House
Midfields
The Grange
Treetops
Croft End
The Grove
Cottage Farm
Langridge
Court Farm
LANGRIDGE
Watersmeet
Beckford View
Down Farm Cottage
The Quoins
Down Farm
Wingfield Farm
Ashcombe Farm
Ashcombe House
TADWICK LANE
Butcher's Wood
BA1
West Wood
Lam Brook
Horsehouse Brake
Cherrywell Wood
Jubilee Plantation
Charmydown Cottages
Watercress Beds
Mill Farm
Short Wood
Hillside
Uplands
HIGH ST.
Manor Farm
CHURCH ST.
Woolley
BLACKSMITH LANE
Naille
KENT LA.
Hill House Farm
CHILCOMBE
Homestead
Manor Farm
Upper Swainswick
INNOX LA.
Swainswick C of E Prim. Sch.
Swainswick
50
Charlcombe Grove Farm
Charlcombe Wood
Crossleaze Farm
WOOLLEY LANE
Ravenswell House
SOPER'S WOOD
Delaford
The White House
BATHEASTON-SWAINSWICK
Ravenswell Lodge
Playing Fields
Pitland Farm
Pavs.
Ten. Cts.
COLLIERS LANE
View Point Farm
Bath Deer Farm
GRANVILLE ROAD
Ensleigh Ministry of Defence
Bellevue Cottage
LANSDOWN ROAD
Equus House
Twinfield Farm
A46
Hamilton Ho.
Stoneleigh Ct.
Little Down Farm
Charlcombe Farm
CHARLCOMBE LANE
Charlcombe
Hope Cottages
Grange Farm
Sports Ground
Plain Ham
Pav.
Meadow Farm
Lower Swainswick
Tunnel
Byre Farm
LANSDOWN PK.
Charlcombe Manor
VALLEY VIEW ROAD
Dead Mill
DEADMILL LA.
FERNDALE RD.
Nursing Home
White Wells
UPHILL DRIVE
HILL VIEW ROAD
ROSE HILL
LINEN WK.
Recreation Ground
BROOKLYN RD.
ST. SAVIOURS RD.
Lansdown Wood
Reservoir
VAN DIEMEN'S LANE
Pumping Station
WHITEWELLS RD.
BATSTONE
COXLEY
ELM GROVE
A B C D E
1 2 3 4 5 6 7
74 75 76
70 69 68 67
81
100

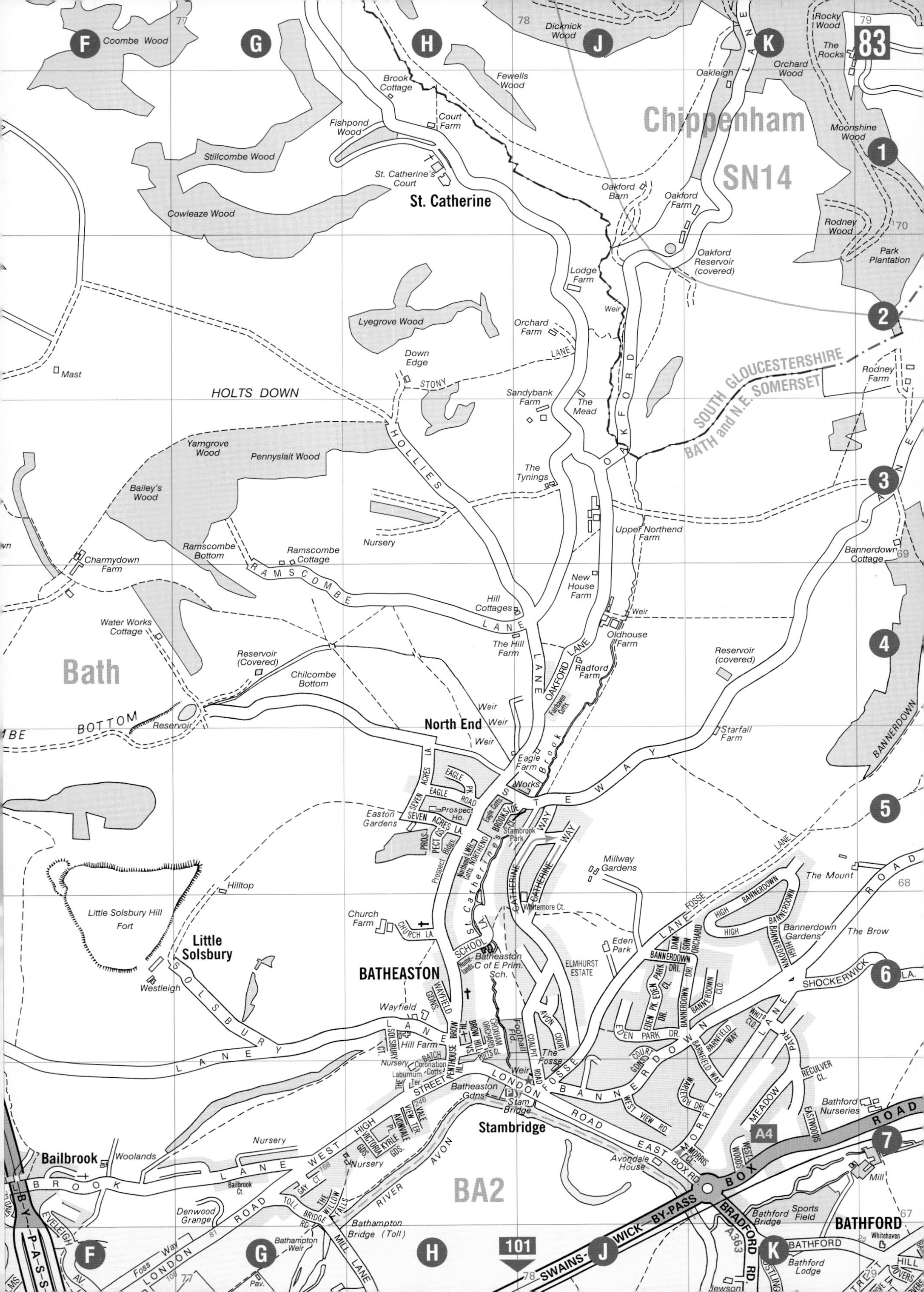

Chippenham
SN14
St. Catherine
North End
Batheaston
Little Solsbury
Bailbrook
Stambridge
Bathford
Bath
BA2
Coombe Wood
Stillcombe Wood
Cowleaze Wood
Fishpond Wood
Brook Cottage
Court Farm
St. Catherine's Court
Dicknick Wood
Fewells Wood
Oakleigh
Orchard Wood
Rocky Wood
The Rocks
Moonshine Wood
Rodney Wood
Park Plantation
Oakford Barn
Oakford Farm
Oakford Reservoir (covered)
Lodge Farm
Lyegrove Wood
Orchard Farm
Down Edge
Sandybank Farm
The Mead
Mast
HOLTS DOWN
Yarngrove Wood
Pennyslait Wood
Bailey's Wood
The Tynings
Nursery
Upper Northend Farm
SOUTH GLOUCESTERSHIRE
BATH and N.E. SOMERSET
Rodney Farm
Bannerdown Cottage
Charmydown Farm
Ramscombe Bottom
Ramscombe Cottage
RAMSCOMBE LANE
Hill Cottages
The Hill Farm
New House Farm
Oldhouse Farm
Water Works Cottage
Reservoir (Covered)
Chilcombe Bottom
Radford Farm
Reservoir (covered)
BOTTOM
Reservoir
Weir
Starfall Farm
Eagle Farm
Works
FOSSE WAY
Easton Gardens
Prospect Ho.
Stambrook Park
Millway Gardens
The Mount
Hilltop
Little Solsbury Hill Fort
Church Farm
Whitemore Ct.
Eden Park
ELMHURST ESTATE
Bannerdown Gardens
The Brow
Batheaston C of E Prim. Sch.
Westleigh
Wayfield
Hill Farm
Football Fld.
The Fosse
Nursery
Coronation Cotts
Laburnum Ter.
Batheaston Gdns
Stam Bridge
Avondale House
Bathford Nurseries
Woolands
Bailbrook Ct.
Denwood Grange
Bathampton Bridge (Toll)
Bathampton Weir
Bathford Bridge
Sports Field
Mill
Whitehaven
Bathford Lodge
Jewson
Pav.
RIVER AVON
SWAINSWICK BY-PASS
A4
A363
BRADFORD RD.
LONDON ROAD
HIGH STREET
SOLSBURY LANE
BANNERDOWN ROAD
SHOCKERWICK LA.
OAKFORD LANE
HOLLIES LANE
STONY LANE
BROOK LANE
BY-PASS
Foss Way
MILL LANE
101

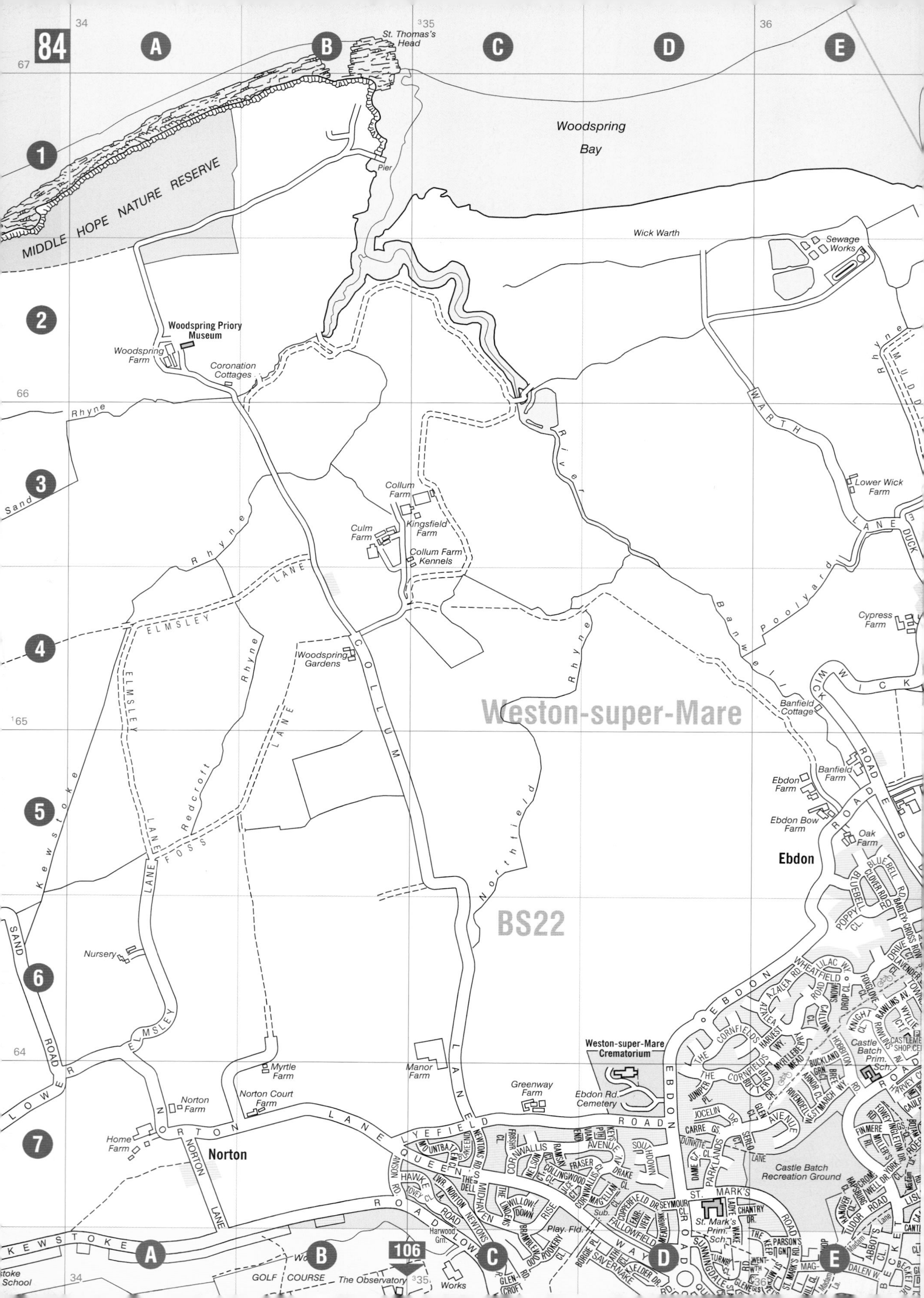

St. Thomas's Head
Woodspring Bay
MIDDLE HOPE NATURE RESERVE
Pier
Wick Warth
Sewage Works
Woodspring Priory Museum
Woodspring Farm
Coronation Cottages
Rhyne
Sand
Collum Farm
Kingsfield Farm
Culm Farm
Collum Farm Kennels
River
WARTH
Lower Wick Farm
LANE
DUCK
Poolyard
Banwell
Cypress Farm
ELMSLEY
LANE
Woodspring Gardens
COLLUM
Weston-super-Mare
Banfield Cottage
WICK
ROAD
Banfield Farm
Ebdon Farm
Ebdon Bow Farm
Oak Farm
Ebdon
Kewstoke
Redcroft
FOSS
Northfield
BS22
Nursery
SAND
ROAD
LOWER
Myrtle Farm
Manor Farm
Weston-super-Mare Crematorium
Norton Court Farm
Norton Farm
Greenway Farm
Ebdon Rd. Cemetery
Home Farm
NORTON
Norton
LYEFIELD
ROAD
CORNWALLIS
Castle Batch Prim. Sch.
Castle Batch Recreation Ground
ST. MARK'S
St. Mark's Prim. Sch.
Play. Fld.
Harwood Grn.
KEWSTOKE
GOLF COURSE
The Observatory
Works
106
stoke School

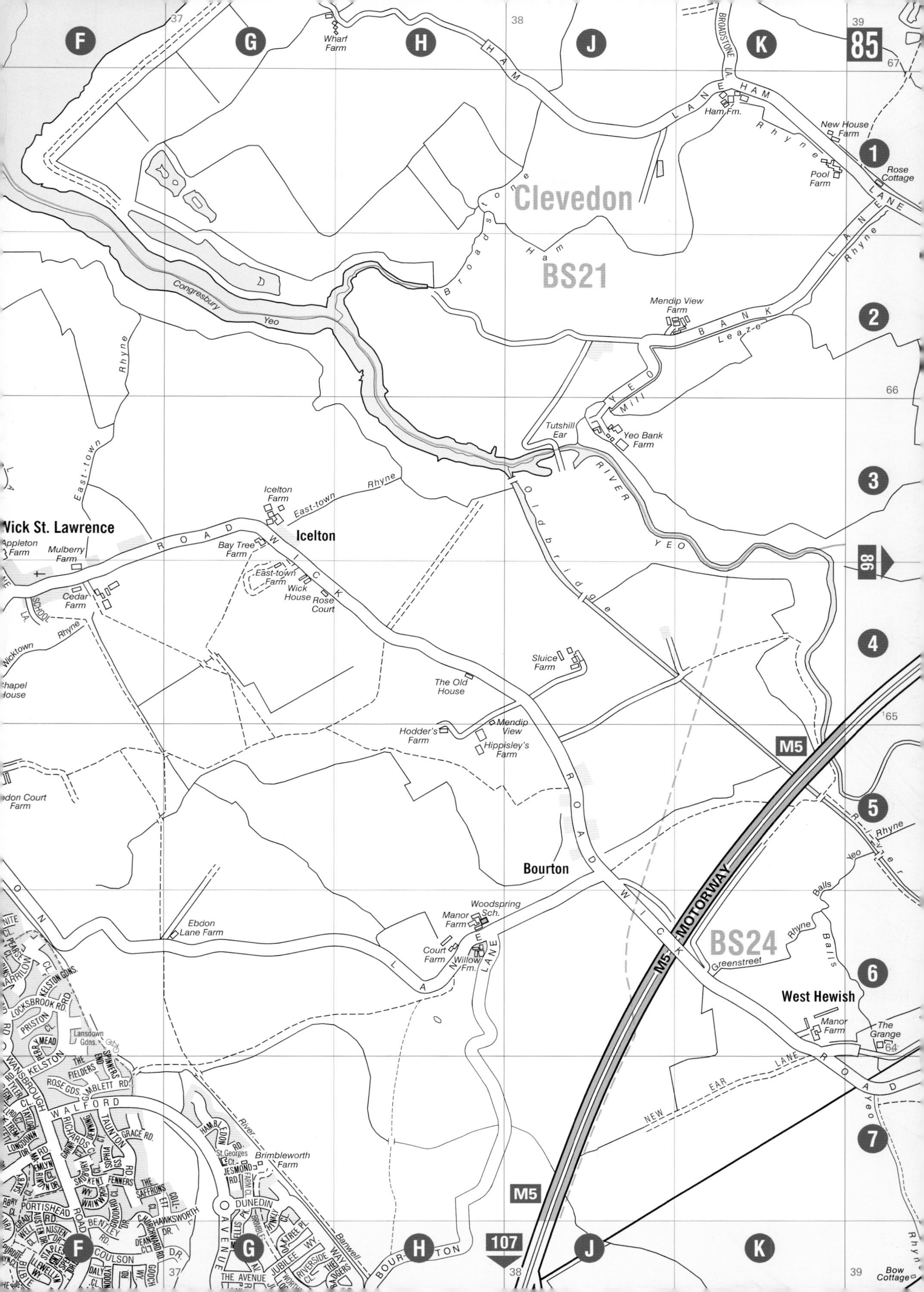

Clevedon
BS21
BS24
Wick St. Lawrence
Icelton
Bourton
West Hewish
Wharf Farm
Ham Fm.
New House Farm
Pool Farm
Rose Cottage
Mendip View Farm
Tutshill Ear
Yeo Bank Farm
Icelton Farm
Appleton Farm
Mulberry Farm
Bay Tree Farm
East-town Farm
Wick House
Rose Court
Cedar Farm
Sluice Farm
The Old House
Hodder's Farm
Mendip View
Hippisley's Farm
Ebdon Lane Farm
Manor Farm
Woodspring Sch.
Court Farm
Willow Fm.
The Grange
Brimbleworth Farm
Bow Cottage
Congresbury Yeo
RIVER YEO
Oldbridge
WICK ROAD
HAM LANE
BROADSTONE LA.
LANE
Broadstone Ham
Broadstone
Rhyne
BANK
Leaze
YEO Mill
East-town Rhyne
Wicktown Rhyne
Balls Rhyne
Greenstreet
NEW EAR LANE
M5 MOTORWAY
M5
River Banwell
BOURTON
WALFORD
PORTISHEAD ROAD
DUNEDIN
AVENUE
THE AVENUE
JUBILEE WY.
RIVERSIDE CL.
COULSON
KELSTON GDNS.
LOCKSBROOK RD.
PRISTON CL.
Lansdown Gdns.
ROSE GDS.
GIMBLETT RD.
TAUNTON
GRACE RD.
HAMBLEDON RD.
St.Georges Ct.
JESMOND RD.
THE SAFFRONS
HAWKSWORTH DR.
BENTLEY RD.
FENNERS
St.Georges
98
107

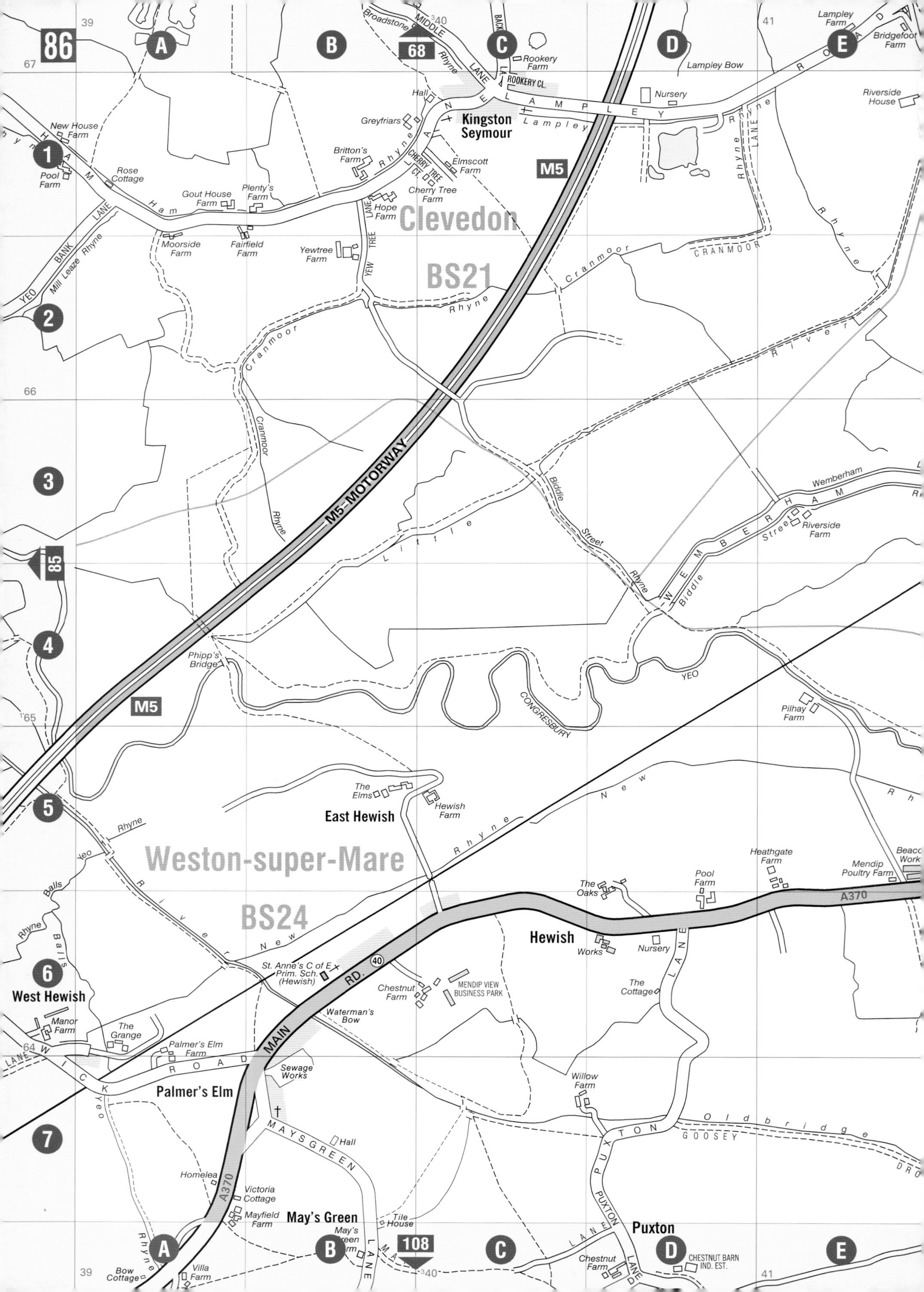

Kingston Seymour
Clevedon
BS21
M5
M5-MOTORWAY
Lampley Bow
Lampley Farm
Bridgefoot Farm
Rookery Farm
ROOKERY CL.
Nursery
Riverside House
Greyfriars
Hall
Britton's Farm
Elmscott Farm
Cherry Tree Farm
New House Farm
Pool Farm
Rose Cottage
Gout House Farm
Plenty's Farm
Hope Farm
Moorside Farm
Fairfield Farm
Yewtree Farm
Mill Leaze Rhyne
Cranmoor
Biddle Street Rhyne
Little
River
Wemberham
Riverside Farm
Phipp's Bridge
Congresbury Yeo
Pilhay Farm
The Elms
Hewish Farm
East Hewish
Weston-super-Mare
BS24
New Rhyne
River
Heathgate Farm
Pool Farm
Mendip Poultry Farm
The Oaks
A370
Hewish
Works
Nursery
The Cottage
St. Anne's C of E Prim. Sch. (Hewish)
MAIN RD.
Chestnut Farm
MENDIP VIEW BUSINESS PARK
Waterman's Bow
West Hewish
Manor Farm
The Grange
Palmer's Elm Farm
WICK ROAD
Sewage Works
Palmer's Elm
Willow Farm
PUXTON LANE
Oldbridge
GOOSEY DROVE
MAYSGREEN LANE
Hall
Homelea
Victoria Cottage
Mayfield Farm
May's Green
Tile House
Puxton
Chestnut Farm
CHESTNUT BARN IND. EST.
Bow Cottage
Villa Farm

68
85
108

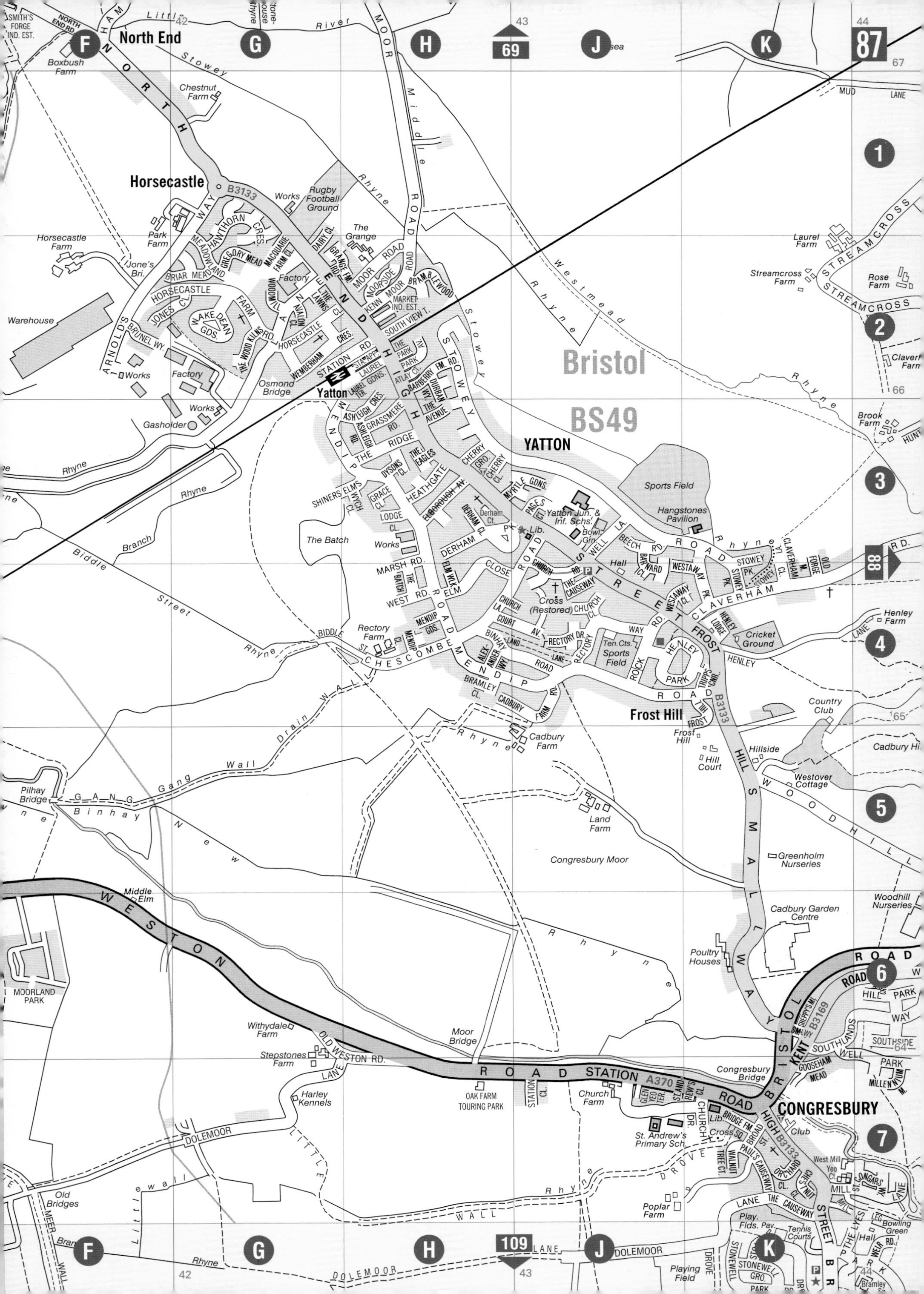
North End
Horsecastle
Yatton
YATTON
Bristol
BS49
Frost Hill
Congresbury Moor
CONGRESBURY
Horsecastle Farm
Boxbush Farm
Chestnut Farm
Park Farm
Warehouse
Works
Factory
Gasholder
Osmond Bridge
Rugby Football Ground
The Grange
Market Ind. Est.
The Batch
Rectory Farm
Sports Field
Hangstones Pavilion
Cricket Ground
Cadbury Farm
Land Farm
Laurel Farm
Streamcross Farm
Rose Farm
Brook Farm
Henley Farm
Country Club
Hillside
Hill Court
Westover Cottage
Greenholm Nurseries
Woodhill Nurseries
Cadbury Garden Centre
Poultry Houses
Pilhay Bridge
Middle Elm
Moorland Park
Withydale Farm
Stepstones Farm
Harley Kennels
Moor Bridge
Oak Farm Touring Park
Church Farm
Congresbury Bridge
St. Andrew's Primary Sch.
Poplar Farm
Old Bridges
Playing Field
Yatton Jun. & Inf. Schs.
WESTON ROAD
STATION ROAD A370
HIGH STREET
B3133
B3169
SMALLWAY
FROST HILL
BRISTOL ROAD
WOODHILL
DOLEMOOR
69
88
109

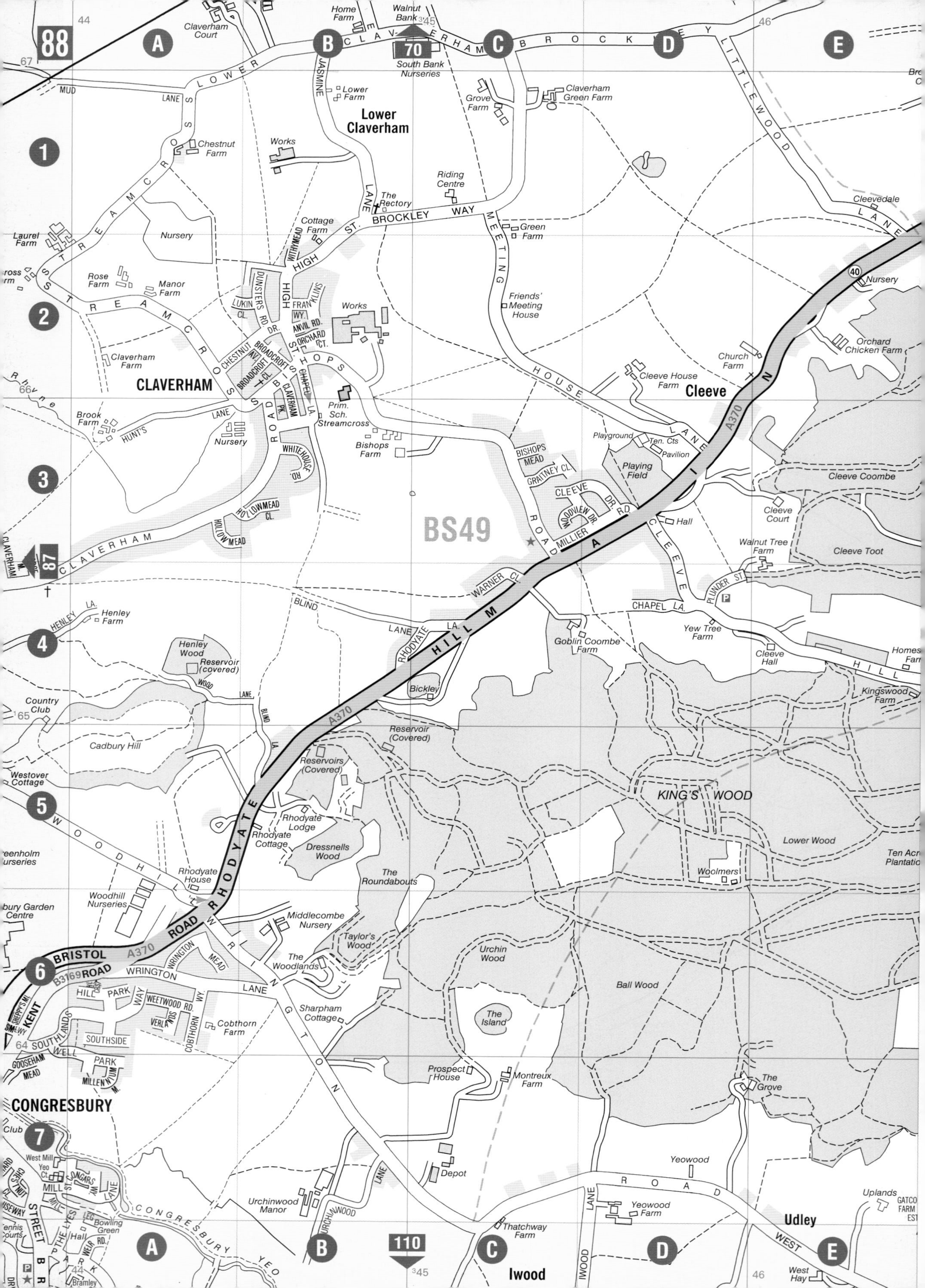

Claverham Court
Home Farm
Walnut Bank
70
South Bank Nurseries
Lower Farm
Lower Claverham
Grove Farm
Claverham Green Farm
Chestnut Farm
Works
Riding Centre
The Rectory
Cottage Farm
Nursery
Laurel Farm
Rose Farm
Manor Farm
Green Farm
Friends' Meeting House
Cleevedale
Nursery
Orchard Chicken Farm
Church Farm
Cleeve House Farm
Cleeve
Claverham Farm
CLAVERHAM
Brook Farm
Prim. Sch. Streamcross
Bishops Farm
Playground
Ten. Cts
Pavilion
Playing Field
Cleeve Coombe
Cleeve Court
Hall
BS49
Walnut Tree Farm
Cleeve Toot
87
Henley Farm
Yew Tree Farm
Goblin Coombe Farm
Cleeve Hall
Henley Wood
Reservoir (covered)
Bickley
Kingswood Farm
Country Club
Reservoir (Covered)
Cadbury Hill
Reservoirs (Covered)
Westover Cottage
KING'S WOOD
Rhodyate Lodge
Rhodyate Cottage
Dressnells Wood
Lower Wood
Ten Acre Plantation
The Roundabouts
Woolmers
Rhodyate House
Woodhill Nurseries
Middlecombe Nursery
Taylor's Wood
Urchin Wood
The Woodlands
Ball Wood
Sharpham Cottage
Cobthorn Farm
The Island
CONGRESBURY
Prospect House
Montreux Farm
The Grove
Club
West Mill
Yeo Ct.
Depot
Yeowood
Urchinwood Manor
Yeowood Farm
Uplands
Udley
Bowling Green
Hall
Thatchway Farm
110
Iwood
West Hay
LOWER CLAVERHAM BROCKLEY LITTLEWOOD LANE
JASMINE LANE
HIGH ST.
BROCKLEY WAY
MEETING HOUSE LANE
STREAMCROSS
WITHYMEAD
DUNSTERS RD.
LUKIN CL.
FRANKLINS WY.
ANVIL RD.
ORCHARD CT.
CHESTNUT AV.
BROADCROFT CL.
BISHOPS ROAD
CHAPEL LA.
CLAVERHAM PK.
HUNT'S LANE
WHITEHOUSE RD.
HOLLOWMEAD CL.
HOLLOW MEAD
CLAVERHAM ROAD
BISHOPS MEAD
GRATTNEY CL.
CLEEVE DR.
WOODVIEW DR.
MILLIER RD.
CLEEVE ROAD
WARNER CL.
PLUNDER ST
CHAPEL LA.
CLEEVE HILL
HENLEY LA.
BLIND LANE
RHODYATE LA.
HILL
A370
WOOD LANE
BLIND LA.
WOODHILL
RHODYATE ROAD
BRISTOL ROAD
B3169 ROAD
WRINGTON LANE
WRINGTON MEAD
HILL PARK
WEETWOOD RD.
VERLANDS
COBTHORN WY.
KENT
SOUTHLANDS
SOUTHSIDE
WELL PARK
GOOSEHAM MEAD
MILLENNIUM
WRINGTON
URCHINWOOD LANE
ROAD
IWOOD LANE
WEST
MILL
ST. GROUNDS
LANE
CONGRESBURY YEO
THE LYES
WEIR RD.
STREET
Tennis Courts
Bramley
A B C D E
1 2 3 4 5 6 7
44 45 46
67 66 65 64

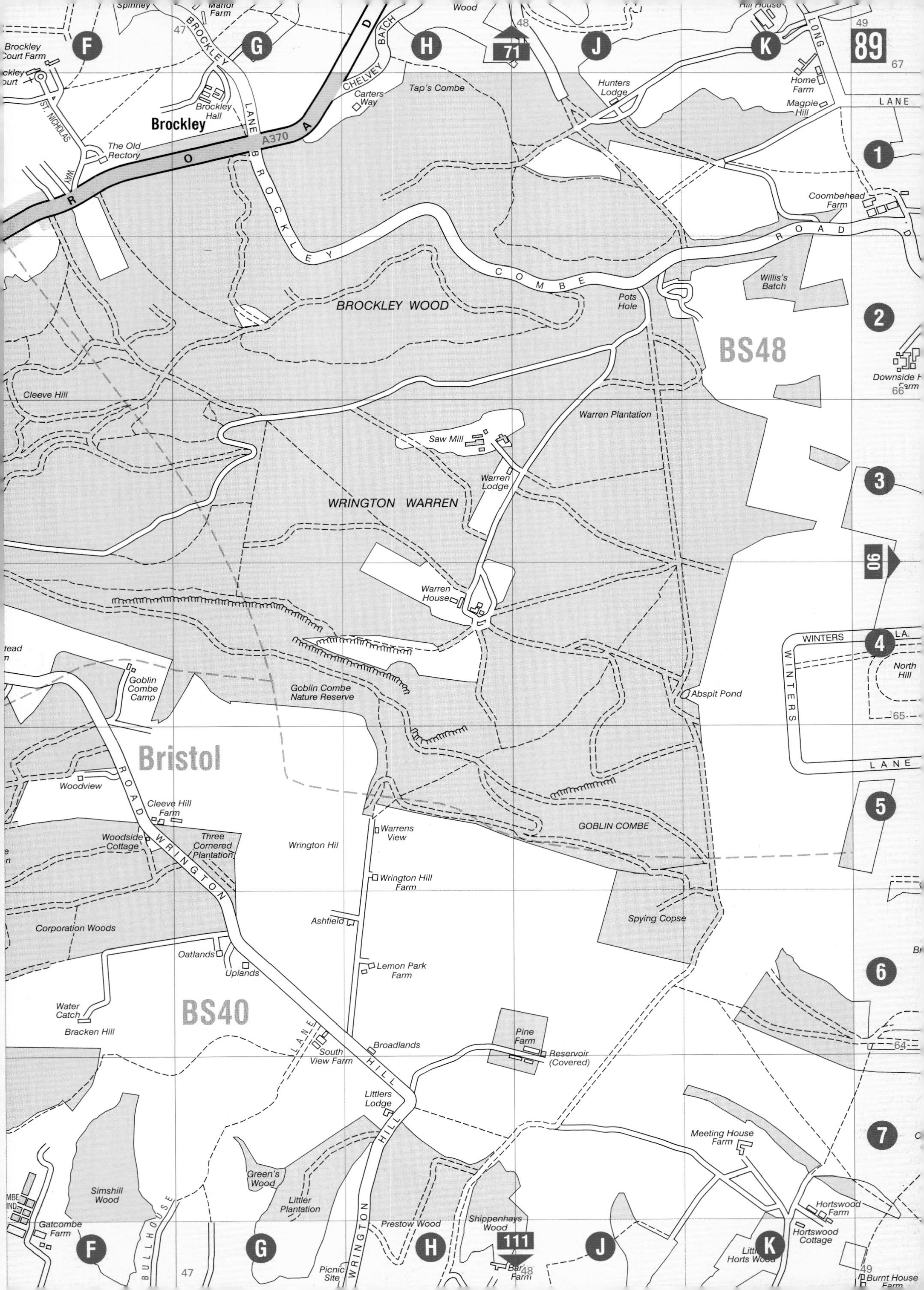

Brockley
Brockley Court Farm
Brockley Hall
The Old Rectory
Manor Farm
Spinney
Wood
Hill House
LONG
LANE
Home Farm
Magpie Hill
Hunters Lodge
Tap's Combe
Carters Way
CHELVEY BATCH
BROCKLEY LANE
ST. NICHOLAS WAY
A370
ROAD
BROCKLEY COMBE ROAD
Coombehead Farm
Willis's Batch
Pots Hole
BROCKLEY WOOD
BS48
Downside Farm
Cleeve Hill
Warren Plantation
Saw Mill
Warren Lodge
WRINGTON WARREN
Warren House
WINTERS LA.
WINTERS LANE
North Hill
Goblin Combe Camp
Goblin Combe Nature Reserve
Abspit Pond
Bristol
Woodview
Cleeve Hill Farm
Woodside Cottage
Three Cornered Plantation
WRINGTON ROAD
Wrington Hil
Warrens View
Wrington Hill Farm
GOBLIN COMBE
Ashfield
Spying Copse
Corporation Woods
Oatlands
Uplands
Lemon Park Farm
Water Catch
Bracken Hill
BS40
South View Farm
LANE
Broadlands
Pine Farm
Reservoir (Covered)
WRINGTON HILL
Littlers Lodge
Meeting House Farm
Green's Wood
Simshill Wood
Littler Plantation
Gatcombe Farm
BULLHOUSE
Prestow Wood
Shippenhays Wood
Hortswood Farm
Hortswood Cottage
Horts Wood
Burnt House Farm
Picnic Site
WRINGTON

71
90
111

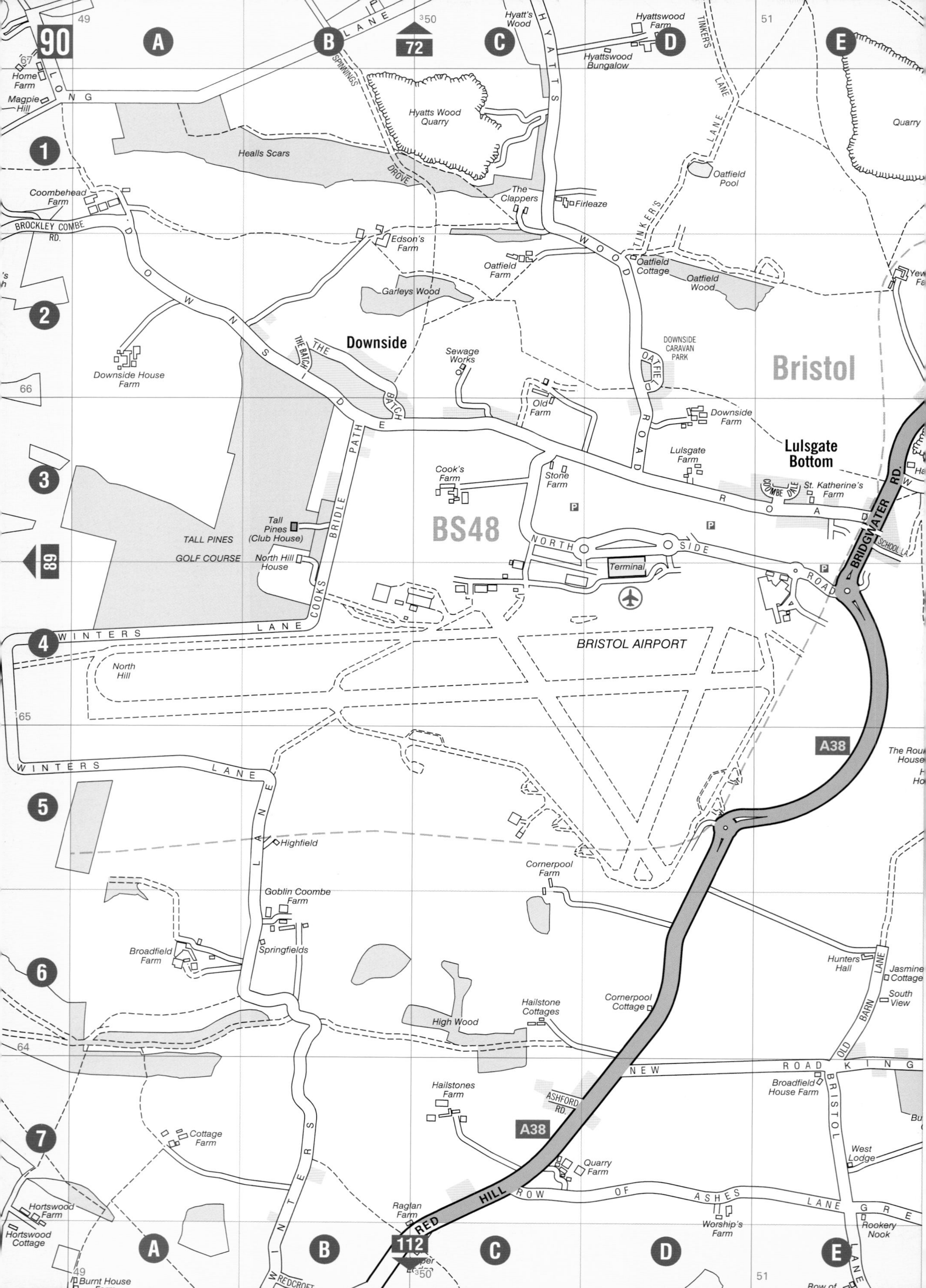
A
B
C
D
E
1
2
3
4
5
6
7
49
350
51
67
66
65
64
72
89
112
Home Farm
Magpie Hill
LONG
LANE
SPINNINGS
Hyatt's Wood
HYATTS
Hyattswood Farm
Hyattswood Bungalow
TINKERS
LANE
Hyatts Wood Quarry
Quarry
Healls Scars
DROVE
The Clappers
Firleaze
Oatfield Pool
Coombehead Farm
BROCKLEY COMBE RD.
DOWNSIDE
Edson's Farm
Oatfield Farm
WOOD
TINKER'S
Oatfield Cottage
Oatfield Wood
Yew Fa
Garleys Wood
Downside
THE BATCH
THE BATCH
Sewage Works
DOWNSIDE CARAVAN PARK
OATFIELD
Bristol
Downside House Farm
Old Farm
ROAD
Downside Farm
BRIDLE PATH
Cook's Farm
Stone Farm
Lulsgate Farm
Lulsgate Bottom
COOMBE DALE
St. Katherine's Farm
RD.
BRIDGWATER
Tall Pines (Club House)
BS48
TALL PINES GOLF COURSE
North Hill House
NORTH SIDE ROAD
Terminal
SCHOOL LA
COOKS
WINTERS LANE
North Hill
BRISTOL AIRPORT
A38
The Rou House
WINTERS LANE
LANE
Highfield
Cornerpool Farm
Goblin Coombe Farm
Springfields
Broadfield Farm
Hunters Hall
Jasmine Cottage
South View
BARN
OLD
Hailstone Cottages
Cornerpool Cottage
High Wood
NEW ROAD
KING
Broadfield House Farm
BRISTOL
Hailstones Farm
ASHFORD RD.
A38
Cottage Farm
WINTERS
West Lodge
Quarry Farm
RED HILL
ROW OF ASHES LANE
GREEN
Hortswood Farm
Hortswood Cottage
Raglan Farm
Worship's Farm
Rookery Nook
LANE
Burnt House Farm
REDCROFT
Row of

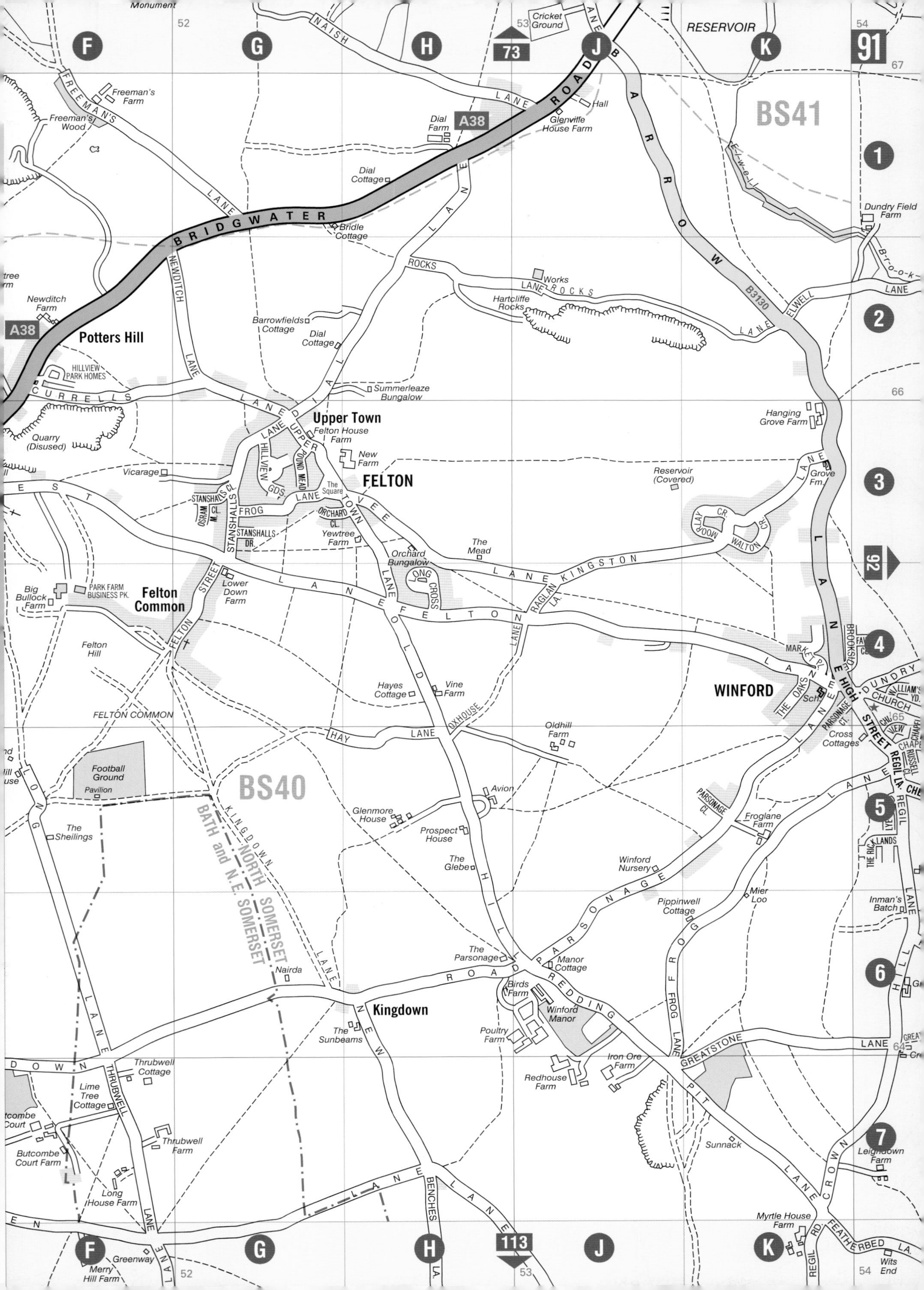

91
73
92
113
BS41
BS40
F
G
H
J
K
1
2
3
4
5
6
7
52
53
54
67
66
65
64
Monument
Cricket Ground
RESERVOIR
NAISH LANE
Freeman's Farm
FREEMAN'S LANE
Freeman's Wood
Hall
Glenville House Farm
Dial Farm
A38
BRIDGWATER ROAD
BARROW LANE
B3130
Dial Cottage
Bridle Cottage
E-l-w-e-l-l
B-r-o-o-k
Dundry Field Farm
ROCKS LANE
Works
LANE ROCKS
Hartcliffe Rocks
ELWELL LANE
NEWDITCH LANE
Newditch Farm
Potters Hill
Barrowfields Cottage
Dial Cottage
HILLVIEW PARK HOMES
CURRELLS LANE
Summerleaze Bungalow
Quarry (Disused)
Upper Town
Felton House Farm
UPPER POUND MEAD
HILLVIEW GDS.
New Farm
Hanging Grove Farm
Vicarage
FELTON
The Square
FROG LANE
TOWN
VEE
ORCHARD CL.
STANSHALLS CL.
OSRAM M.
STANSHALLS DR.
Yewtree Farm
Reservoir (Covered)
Grove Fm.
MOORLAY CR.
WALTON CR.
KINGSTON LANE
The Mead
Orchard Bungalow
LONG CROSS
RAGLAN LA.
Big Bullock Farm
PARK FARM BUSINESS PK.
Felton Common
FELTON STREET
Lower Down Farm
FELTON LANE
OLD HILL
Felton Hill
MARKET CL.
BROOKSIDE
THE OAKS
Sch
WINFORD
HIGH STREET
DUNDRY
CHURCH
WILLIAM'S YD.
PARSONAGE CT.
Cross Cottages
REGIL LA.
Hayes Cottage
Vine Farm
OXHOUSE LANE
HAY LANE
Oldhill Farm
FELTON COMMON
Football Ground
Pavilion
Avion
KINGDOWN
BATH and N.E. SOMERSET
NORTH SOMERSET
Glenmore House
Prospect House
PARSONAGE CL.
Froglane Farm
THE RICKLANDS
The Sheilings
The Glebe
Winford Nursery
PARSONAGE ROAD
Pippinwell Cottage
Mier Loo
Inman's Batch
The Parsonage
Manor Cottage
Nairda
Birds Farm
Winford Manor
REDDING
Kingdown
NEW LANE
The Sunbeams
Poultry Farm
FROG LANE
GREATSTONE LANE
Iron Ore Farm
Redhouse Farm
DOWN
Thrubwell Cottage
THRUBWELL LANE
Lime Tree Cottage
Butcombe Court Farm
Thrubwell Farm
PIT LANE
Sunnack
CROWN
Leighdown Farm
Long House Farm
BENCHES LA.
Myrtle House Farm
REGIL RD.
FEATHERBED LA.
Wits End
Greenway
Merry Hill Farm

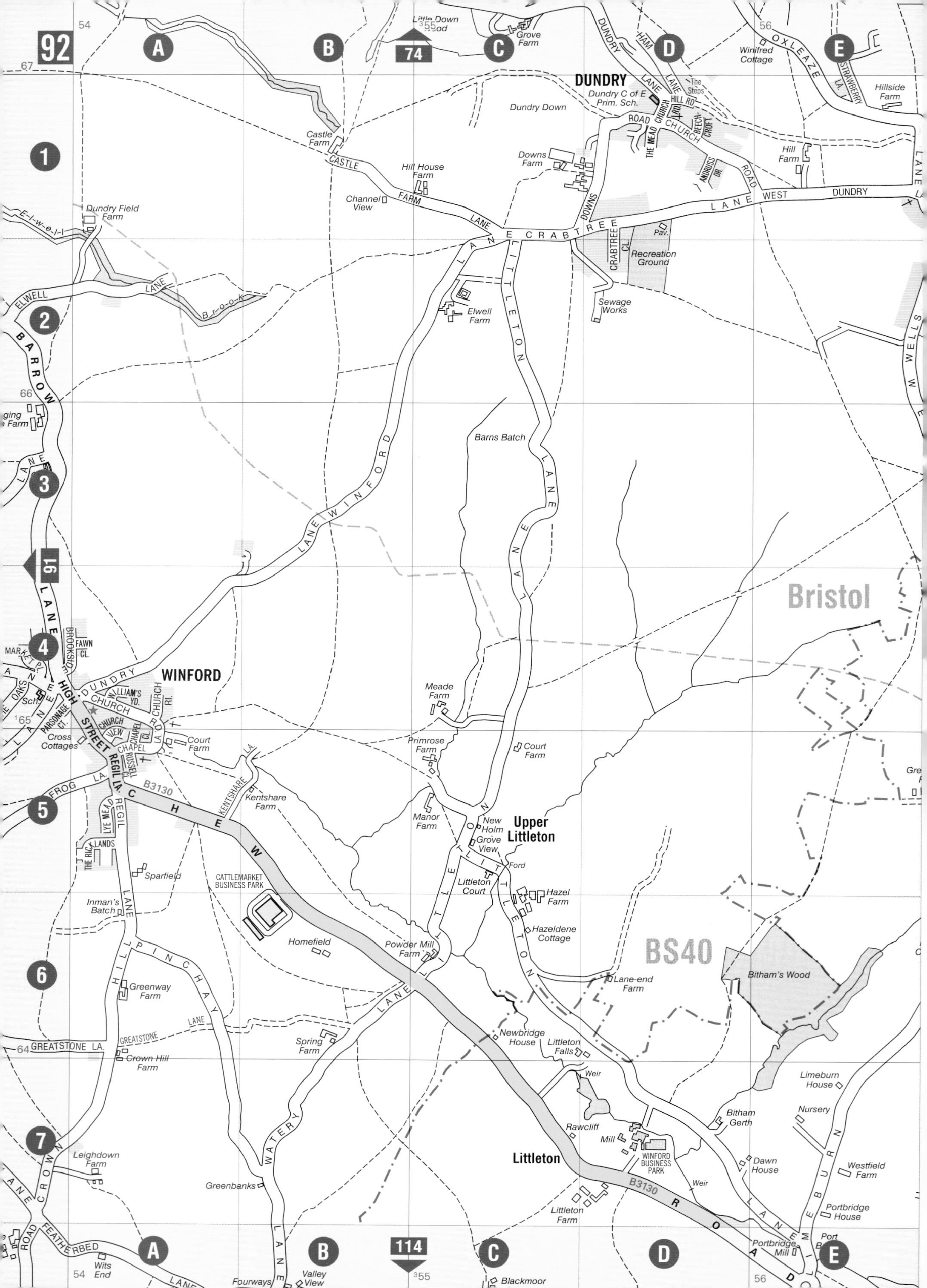

DUNDRY
WINFORD
Upper Littleton
Littleton
Bristol
BS40
Dundry Down
Castle Farm
Hill House Farm
Channel View
Dundry Field Farm
Downs Farm
Recreation Ground
Sewage Works
Elwell Farm
Barns Batch
Meade Farm
Primrose Farm
Court Farm
Manor Farm
Kentshare Farm
Sparfield
Inman's Batch
Greenway Farm
Crown Hill Farm
Leighdown Farm
Homefield
Powder Mill Farm
Spring Farm
Greenbanks
Newbridge House
Littleton Falls
Littleton Court
Hazel Farm
Hazeldene Cottage
Lane-end Farm
Bitham's Wood
Limeburn House
Nursery
Bitham Gerth
Dawn House
Westfield Farm
Portbridge House
Portbridge Mill
Rawcliff Mill
WINFORD BUSINESS PARK
CATTLEMARKET BUSINESS PARK
Littleton Farm
Wits End
Valley View
Fourways
Blackmoor
Grove Farm
Little Down Wood
Winifred Cottage
Hillside Farm
Hill Farm
Dundry C of E Prim. Sch.
Cross Cottages
B3130
CHEW ROAD
74
91
114

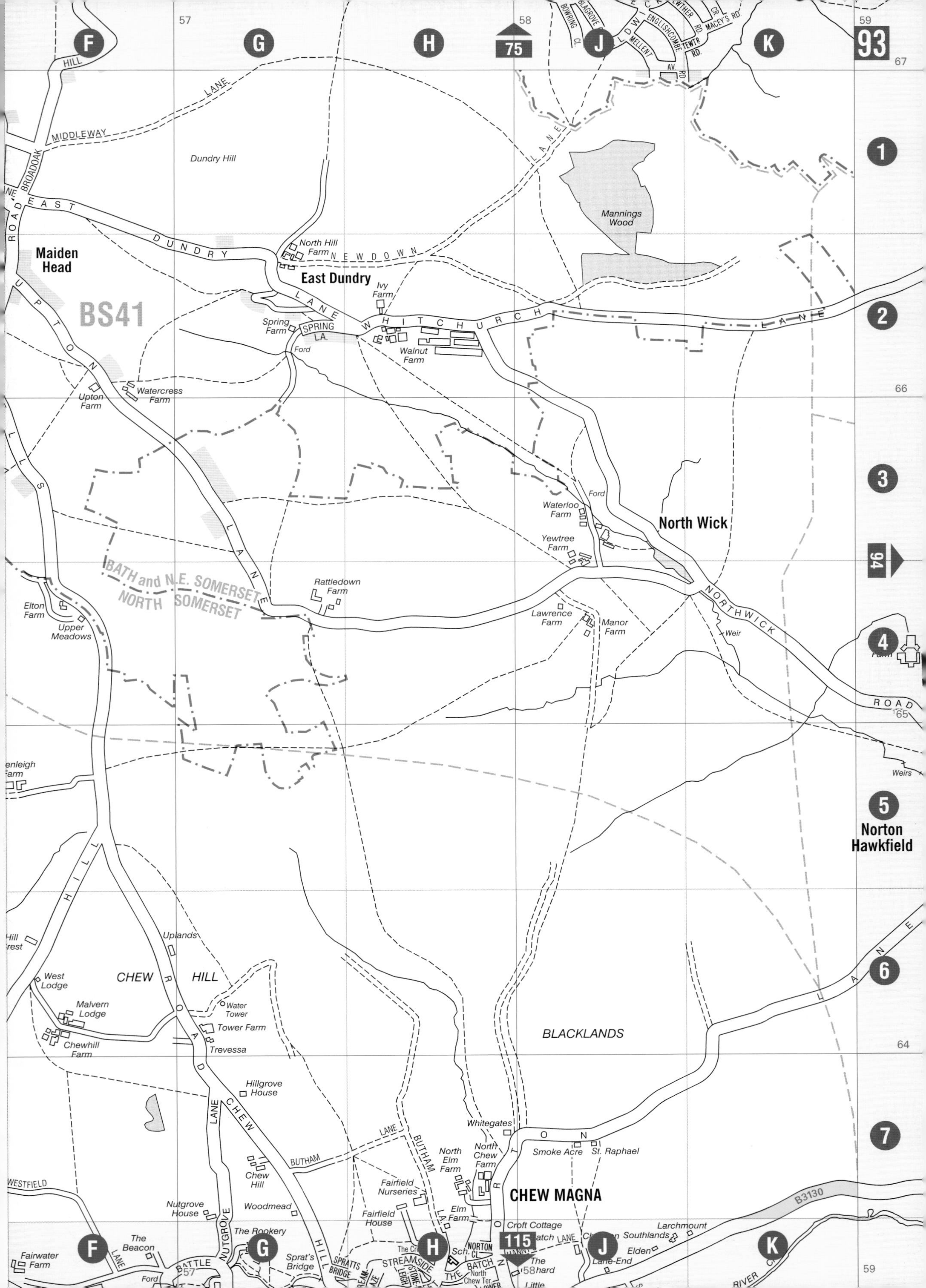
F
G
H
J
K
57
58
59
75
67
66
65
64
1
2
3
4
5
6
7
94
115
Dundry Hill
Mannings Wood
Maiden Head
East Dundry
North Hill Farm
Ivy Farm
Spring Farm
Walnut Farm
Watercress Farm
Upton Farm
BS41
MIDDLEWAY
LANE
EAST DUNDRY LANE
NEWDOWN
SPRING LA.
WHITCHURCH LANE
UPTON LANE
BROADOAK
Ford
North Wick
Waterloo Farm
Yewtree Farm
Rattledown Farm
Lawrence Farm
Manor Farm
NORTHWICK ROAD
Weir
Weirs
BATH and N.E. SOMERSET
NORTH SOMERSET
Elton Farm
Upper Meadows
Norton Hawkfield
CHEW HILL
Uplands
West Lodge
Malvern Lodge
Chewhill Farm
Water Tower
Tower Farm
Trevessa
Hillgrove House
BLACKLANDS
CHEW ROAD
NORTON LANE
Whitegates
North Chew Farm
North Elm Farm
Smoke Acre
St. Raphael
CHEW MAGNA
B3130
Fairfield Nurseries
Fairfield House
Elm Farm
Croft Cottage
Larchmount
Southlands
Elden
Lane-End
Chew Hill
Nutgrove House
Woodmead
The Rookery
The Beacon
Fairwater Farm
Sprat's Bridge
WESTFIELD
BUTHAM LANE
NUTGROVE LANE
BATTLE LANE
SPRATTS BRIDGE
STREAMSIDE
THE BATCH
SCH. CL
RIVER

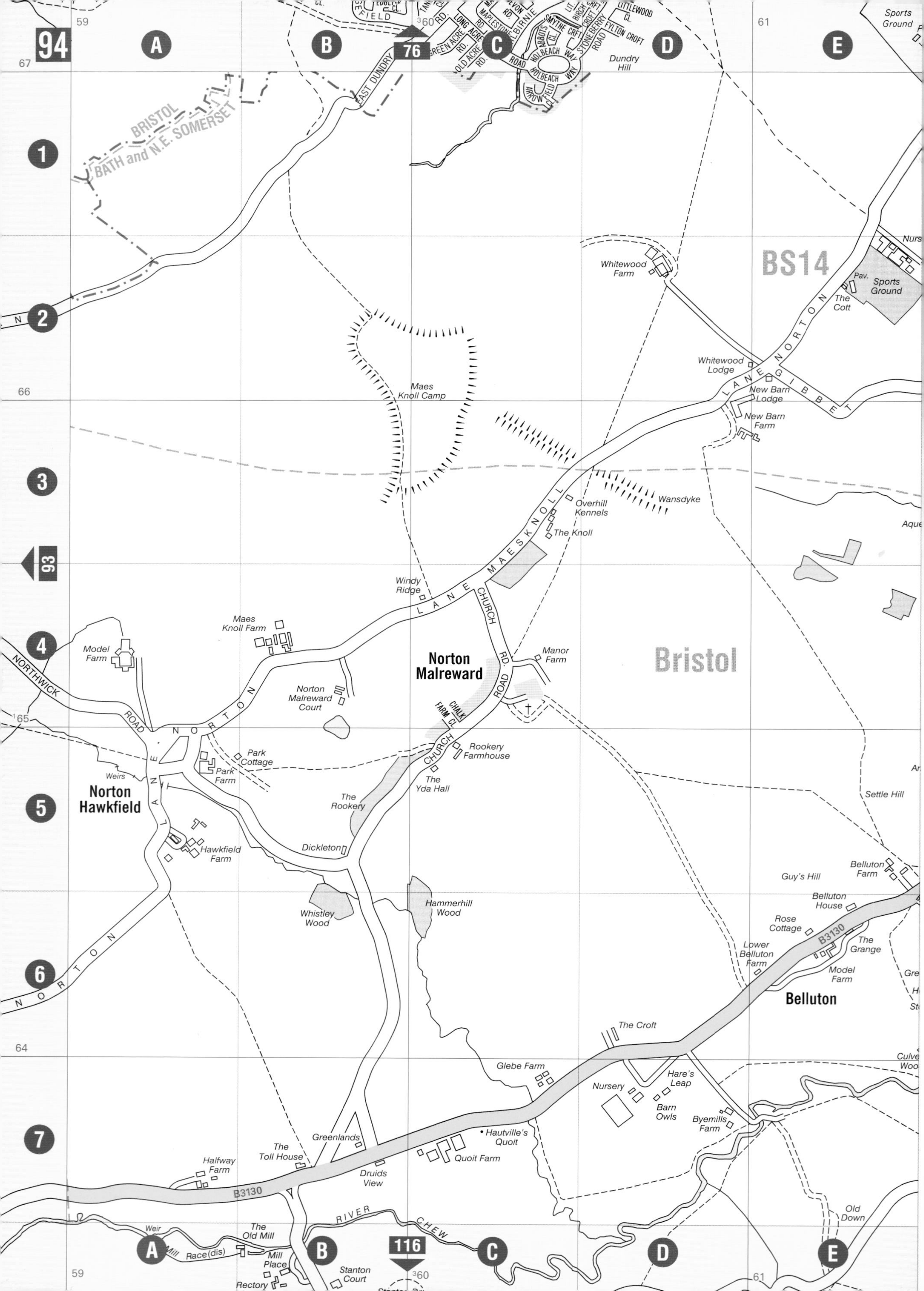
76
93
116
A
B
C
D
E
1
2
3
4
5
6
7
59
60
61
67
66
65
64
BS14
Bristol
BRISTOL
BATH and N.E. SOMERSET
Dundry Hill
Sports Ground
Whitewood Farm
Whitewood Lodge
New Barn Lodge
New Barn Farm
The Cott
Pav.
GIBBET
NORTON LANE
EAST DUNDRY
Maes Knoll Camp
Wansdyke
Overhill Kennels
The Knoll
MAESKNOLL LANE
Windy Ridge
Maes Knoll Farm
Model Farm
NORTHWICK ROAD
NORTON LANE
Norton Malreward
Norton Malreward Court
CHURCH RD.
CHURCH ROAD
CHALK FARM CL.
Manor Farm
Rookery Farmhouse
The Yda Hall
The Rookery
Park Cottage
Park Farm
Weirs
Norton Hawkfield
Hawkfield Farm
Dickleton
Whistley Wood
Hammerhill Wood
Settle Hill
Guy's Hill
Belluton Farm
Belluton House
Rose Cottage
The Grange
Model Farm
Lower Belluton Farm
Belluton
B3130
The Croft
Glebe Farm
Nursery
Hare's Leap
Barn Owls
Byemills Farm
Hautville's Quoit
Quoit Farm
Greenlands
The Toll House
Halfway Farm
Druids View
Old Down
RIVER CHEW
Weir
The Old Mill
Mill Race (dis)
Mill Place
Stanton Court
Rectory
HOLBEACH WAY
ARROWFIELD CL.
LITTLEWOOD CL.
FYLTON CROFT
STONEBERRY ROAD
GREEN ACRE RD.
OLD ACRE RD.
LONG ACRE RD.
MAPLESTONE RD.
KILBIRNIE ROAD
ABBOTS CL.
SMYTHE CRFT
BIRCH CRFT

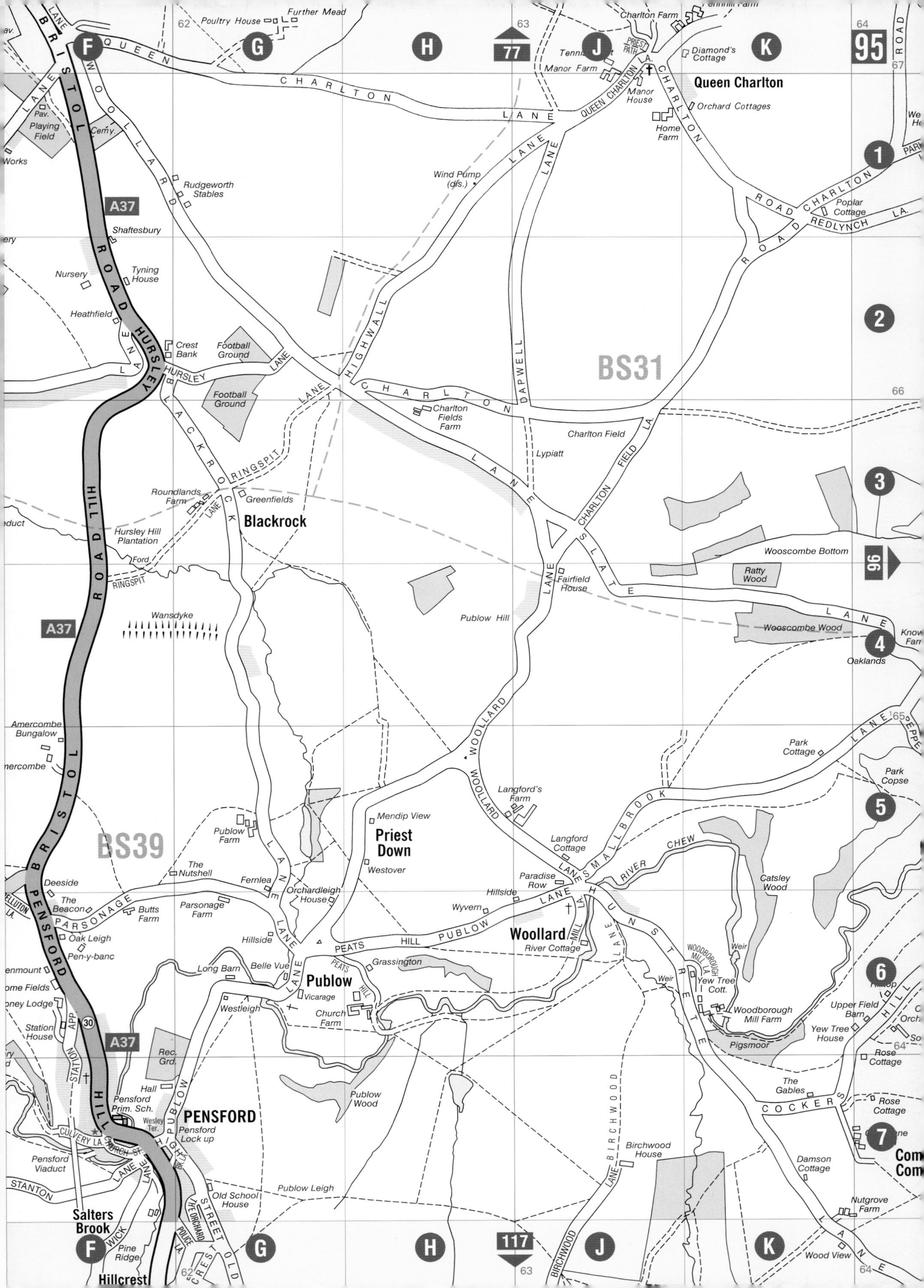
95
77
117
96
Queen Charlton
Charlton Farm
Further Mead
Poultry House
Tennis Court
Manor Farm
Manor House
Diamond's Cottage
Orchard Cottages
Home Farm
PRIEST PATH
QUEEN CHARLTON LA.
CHARLTON ROAD
CHARLTON LANE
QUEEN CHARLTON LANE
WOOLLARD LANE
BRISTOL LANE
Pav.
Playing Field
Cemy.
Works
Rudgeworth Stables
Wind Pump (dis.)
Poplar Cottage
REDLYNCH LA.
Shaftesbury
A37
Tyning House
Nursery
Heathfield
Crest Bank
Football Ground
HURSLEY LANE
BRISTOL ROAD
HURSLEY HILL
HIGHWALL LANE
DAPWELL LANE
BS31
Charlton Fields Farm
Charlton Field
CHARLTON FIELD LA.
Lypiatt
BLACKROCK LANE
RINGSPIT LANE
Roundlands Farm
Greenfields
Blackrock
Hursley Hill Plantation
Ford
RINGSPIT
Wooscombe Bottom
Ratty Wood
Fairfield House
SLATE LANE
Pablow Hill
Wooscombe Wood
Wansdyke
Oaklands
Amercombe Bungalow
Park Cottage
Park Copse
SMALLBROOK LANE
Langford's Farm
Mendip View
Priest Down
Westover
BS39
Pablow Farm
The Nutshell
Fernlea
Orchardleigh House
Langford Cottage
Paradise Row
Hillside
Wyvern
Woollard
River Cottage
RIVER CHEW
Catsley Wood
Deeside
The Beacon
Butts Farm
Parsonage Farm
PARSONAGE LA.
Oak Leigh
Pen-y-banc
PEATS HILL
PUBLOW LANE
MILL LA.
Hillside
Belle Vue
Long Barn
Grassington
Publow
Vicarage
Church Farm
Westleigh
Weir
WOODBOROUGH MILL LA.
Yew Tree Cott.
Woodborough Mill Farm
Upper Field Barn
Yew Tree House
Pigsmoor
Rose Cottage
The Gables
COCKERS HILL
Station House
STATION APP.
Rec. Grd.
Hall
Pensford Prim. Sch.
PENSFORD
Pensford Lock up
Wesley Ter.
Publow Wood
BIRCHWOOD LANE
Birchwood House
Damson Cottage
CULVERY LA.
CHURCH ST.
Pensford Viaduct
STANTON
Publow Leigh
Old School House
THE ORCHARD
Nutgrove Farm
Salters Brook
WICK
Pine Ridge
Hillcrest
POLICE LA.
CREST
OLD STREET
Wood View
LANE
STREET
62
63
64
65
66
67
F
G
H
J
K
1
2
3
4
5
6
7

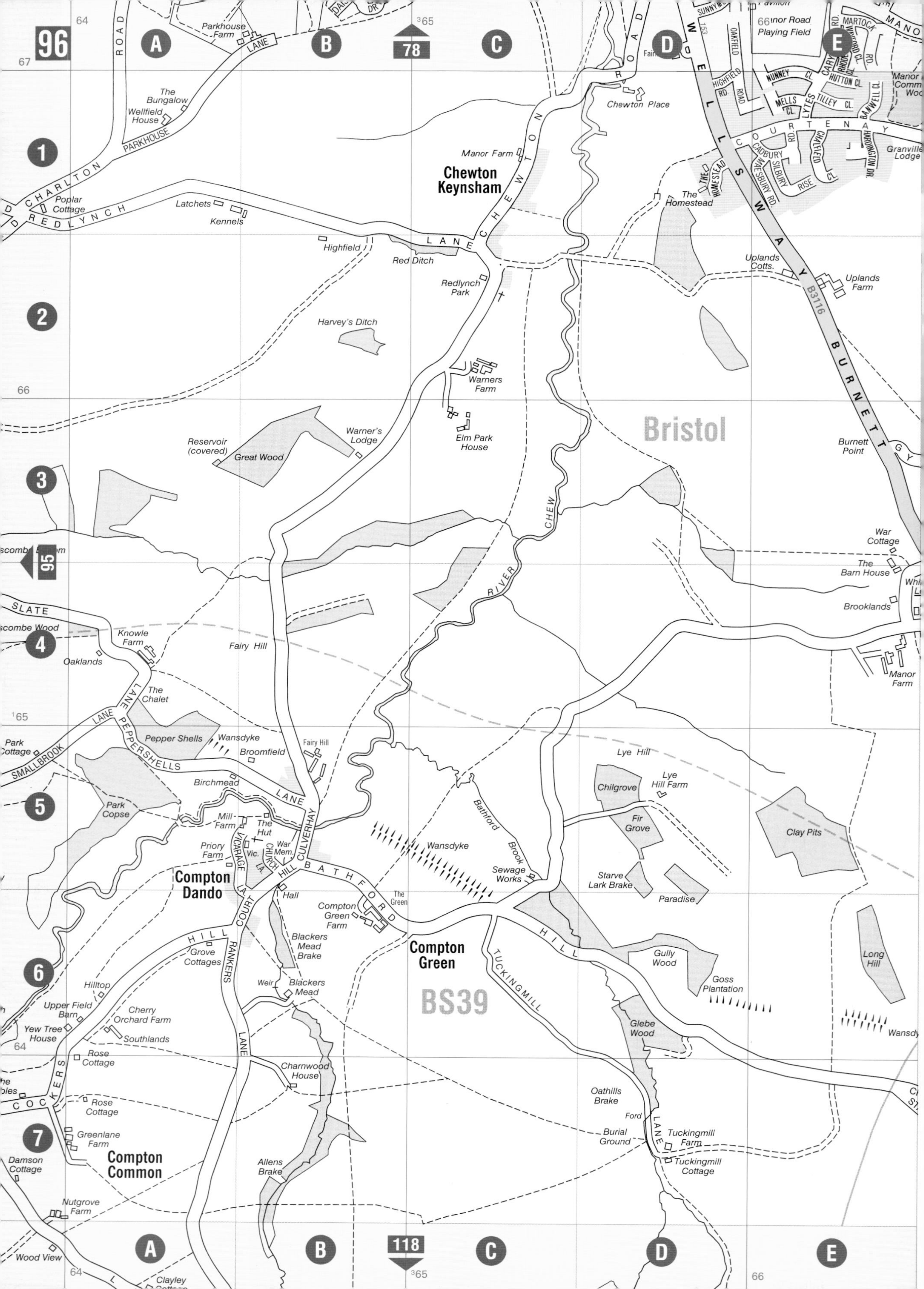
Chewton Keynsham
Compton Dando
Compton Green
Compton Common
Bristol
BS39
Manor Farm
Chewton Place
Redlynch Park
Warners Farm
Elm Park House
Warner's Lodge
Great Wood
Reservoir (covered)
Harvey's Ditch
Red Ditch
Highfield
Latchets
Kennels
Poplar Cottage
Parkhouse Farm
The Bungalow
Wellfield House
The Homestead
Uplands Cotts.
Uplands Farm
Burnett Point
War Cottage
The Barn House
Brooklands
Manor Farm
Knowle Farm
Oaklands
Fairy Hill
The Chalet
Pepper Shells
Wansdyke
Broomfield
Park Cottage
Birchmead
Park Copse
Mill Farm
The Hut
Priory Farm
War Mem.
Hall
Compton Green Farm
The Green
Blackers Mead Brake
Grove Cottages
Hilltop
Upper Field Barn
Cherry Orchard Farm
Yew Tree House
Southlands
Rose Cottage
Weir
Blackers Mead
Charnwood House
Greenlane Farm
Damson Cottage
Nutgrove Farm
Wood View
Allens Brake
Lye Hill
Lye Hill Farm
Chilgrove
Fir Grove
Clay Pits
Starve Lark Brake
Paradise
Sewage Works
Bathford Brook
Gully Wood
Goss Plantation
Long Hill
Glebe Wood
Oathills Brake
Ford
Burial Ground
Tuckingmill Farm
Tuckingmill Cottage
River Chew
B3116
Wells Way
Burnett
Courtenay
Redlynch Lane
Charlton
Parkhouse Lane
Slate Lane
Smallbrook Lane
Peppershells Lane
Culverhay
Bathford Hill
Vicarage La.
Church La.
Court Hill
Rankers Lane
Cockers Hill
Tuckingmill Lane
Manor Road Playing Field
Granville Lodge
95
78
118

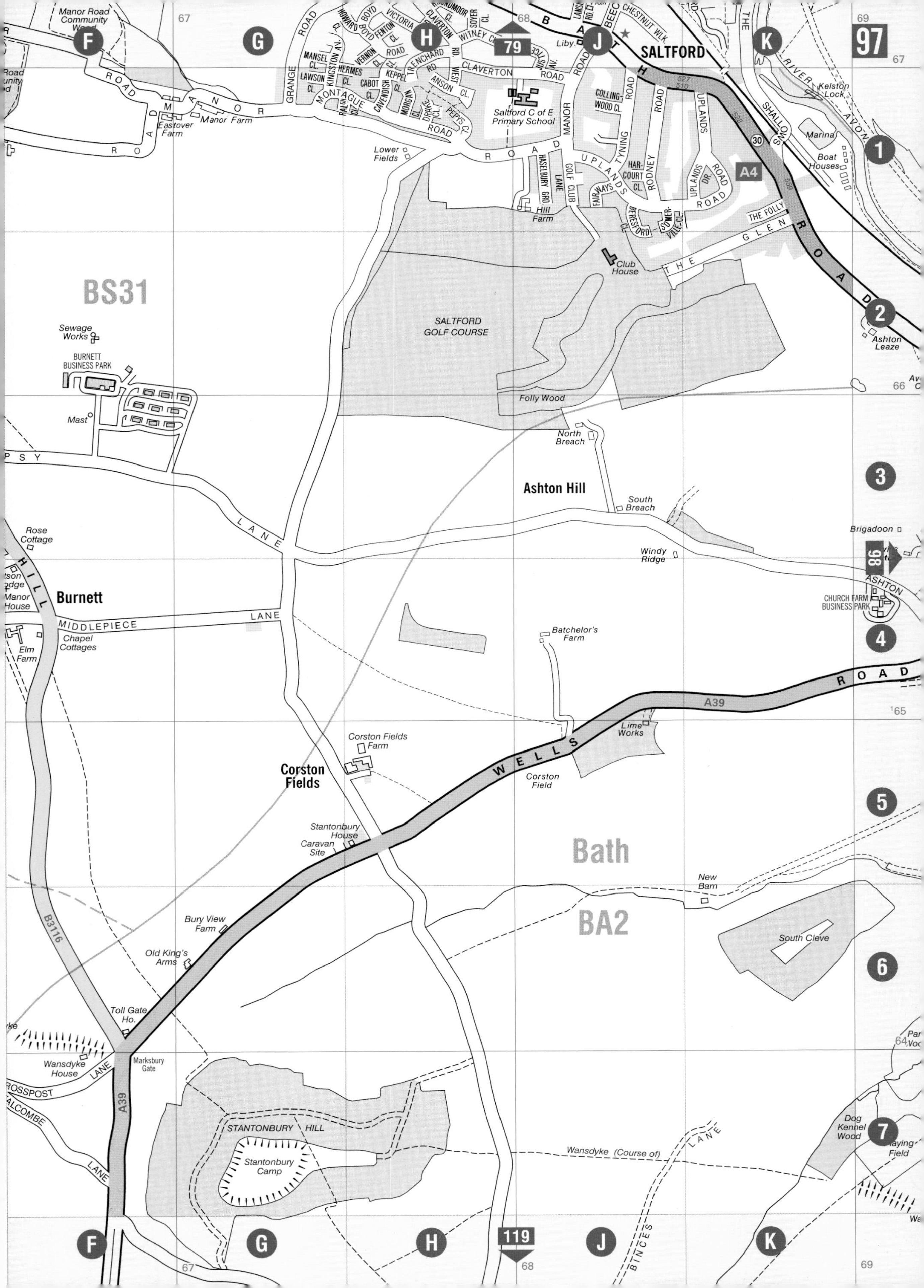
SALTFORD
BS31
Bath
BA2
Burnett
Ashton Hill
Corston Fields
Saltford C of E Primary School
SALTFORD GOLF COURSE
Folly Wood
BURNETT BUSINESS PARK
Sewage Works
Mast
Manor Road Community Wood
Manor Farm
Eastover Farm
Lower Fields
Hill Farm
Club House
North Breach
South Breach
Windy Ridge
Brigadoon
CHURCH FARM BUSINESS PARK
Batchelor's Farm
Lime Works
Corston Field
Corston Fields Farm
Stantonbury House
Caravan Site
Bury View Farm
Old King's Arms
Toll Gate Ho.
Marksbury Gate
Wansdyke House
STANTONBURY HILL
Stantonbury Camp
Wansdyke (Course of)
New Barn
South Cleve
Dog Kennel Wood
Rose Cottage
Manor House
Elm Farm
Chapel Cottages
Marina
Kelston Lock
Boat Houses
Ashton Leaze
RIVER AVON
MANOR ROAD
WELLS ROAD
A39
A4
B3116
MIDDLEPIECE LANE
CROSSPOST LANE
BINCES LANE
THE GLEN
THE FOLLY
UPLANDS ROAD
CLAVERTON ROAD
GRANGE ROAD
79
86
119

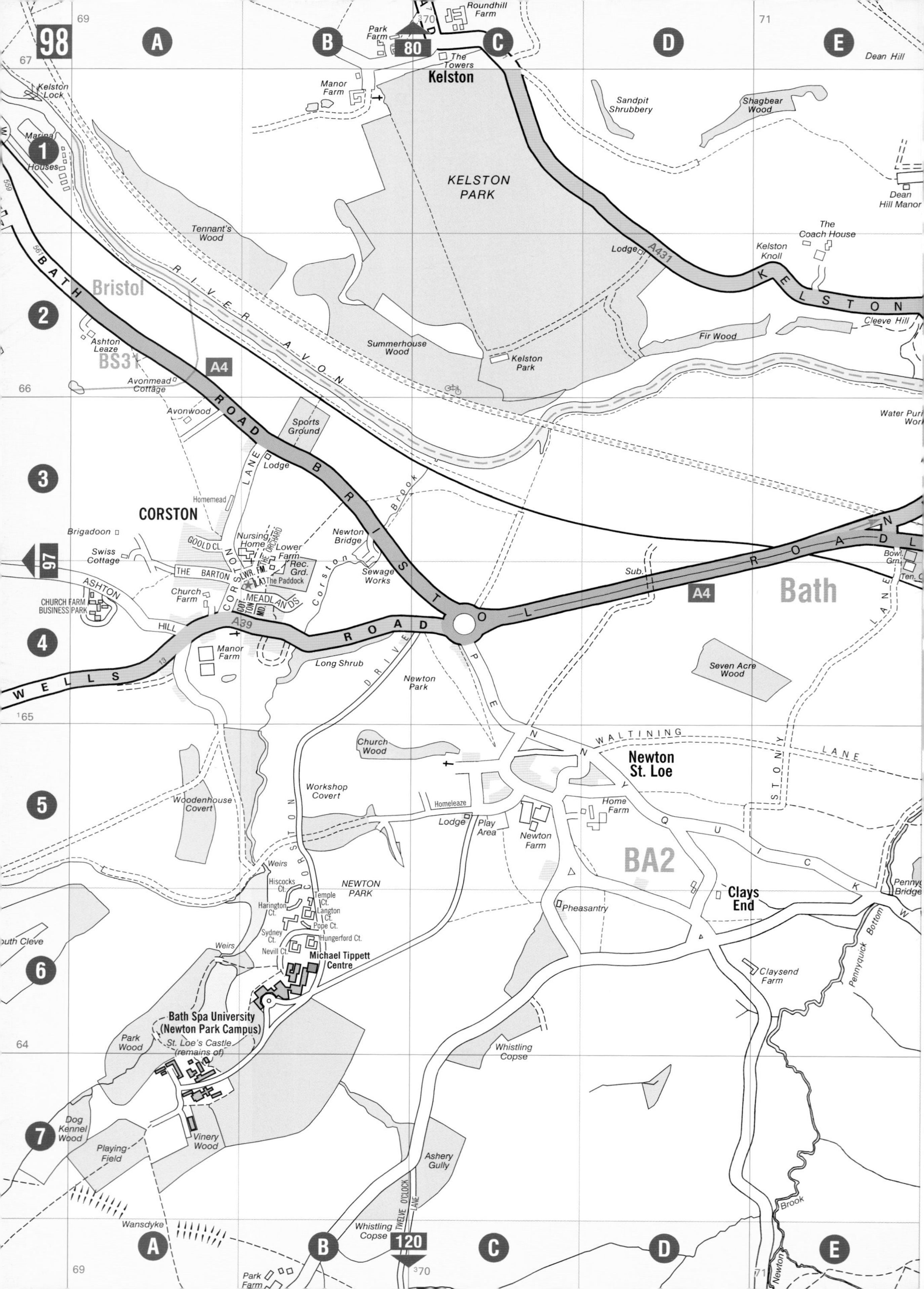

80
120
97
Kelston
Roundhill Farm
Park Farm
The Towers
Manor Farm
Kelston Lock
Marina
Houses
KELSTON PARK
Sandpit Shrubbery
Shagbear Wood
Dean Hill
Dean Hill Manor
The Coach House
Kelston Knoll
Lodge
A431
KELSTON
Cleeve Hill
Fir Wood
Kelston Park
Summerhouse Wood
Tennant's Wood
RIVER AVON
Bristol
BS31
BATH ROAD
BRISTOL ROAD
Ashton Leaze
A4
Avonmead Cottage
Avonwood
Sports Ground
Lodge
Water Puri Work
Homemead
CORSTON
Brigadoon
Swiss Cottage
GOULD CL.
Nursing Home
THE ORCHARD
Lower Farm
Rec. Grd.
The Paddock
THE BARTON
LWR. FM.
LA.
ASHTON HILL
CHURCH FARM BUSINESS PARK
Church Farm
CORSTON
MEADLANDS
Newton Bridge
Brook
Sewage Works
Corston
Sub.
Bath
Bowl. Grn.
Ten. C
A39
ROAD
WELLS
Manor Farm
Long Shrub
DRIVE
Newton Park
Seven Acre Wood
WALTINING LANE
Newton St. Loe
Church Wood
PENN
Workshop Covert
CORSTON
Homeleaze
Lodge
Play Area
Newton Farm
Home Farm
STONY LANE
QUICK
BA2
Woodenhouse Covert
Weirs
Hiscocks Ct.
Temple Ct.
Langton Ct.
Harington Ct.
Pope Ct.
Sydney Ct.
Hungerford Ct.
Nevill Ct.
NEWTON PARK
Michael Tippett Centre
Clays End
Pheasantry
Penny Bridge
Pennyquick Bottom
Claysend Farm
South Cleve
Bath Spa University (Newton Park Campus)
Park Wood
St. Loe's Castle (remains of)
Whistling Copse
Dog Kennel Wood
Playing Field
Viner Wood
Ashery Gully
TWELVE O'CLOCK LANE
Whistling Copse
Wansdyke
Brook
Newton
Park Farm

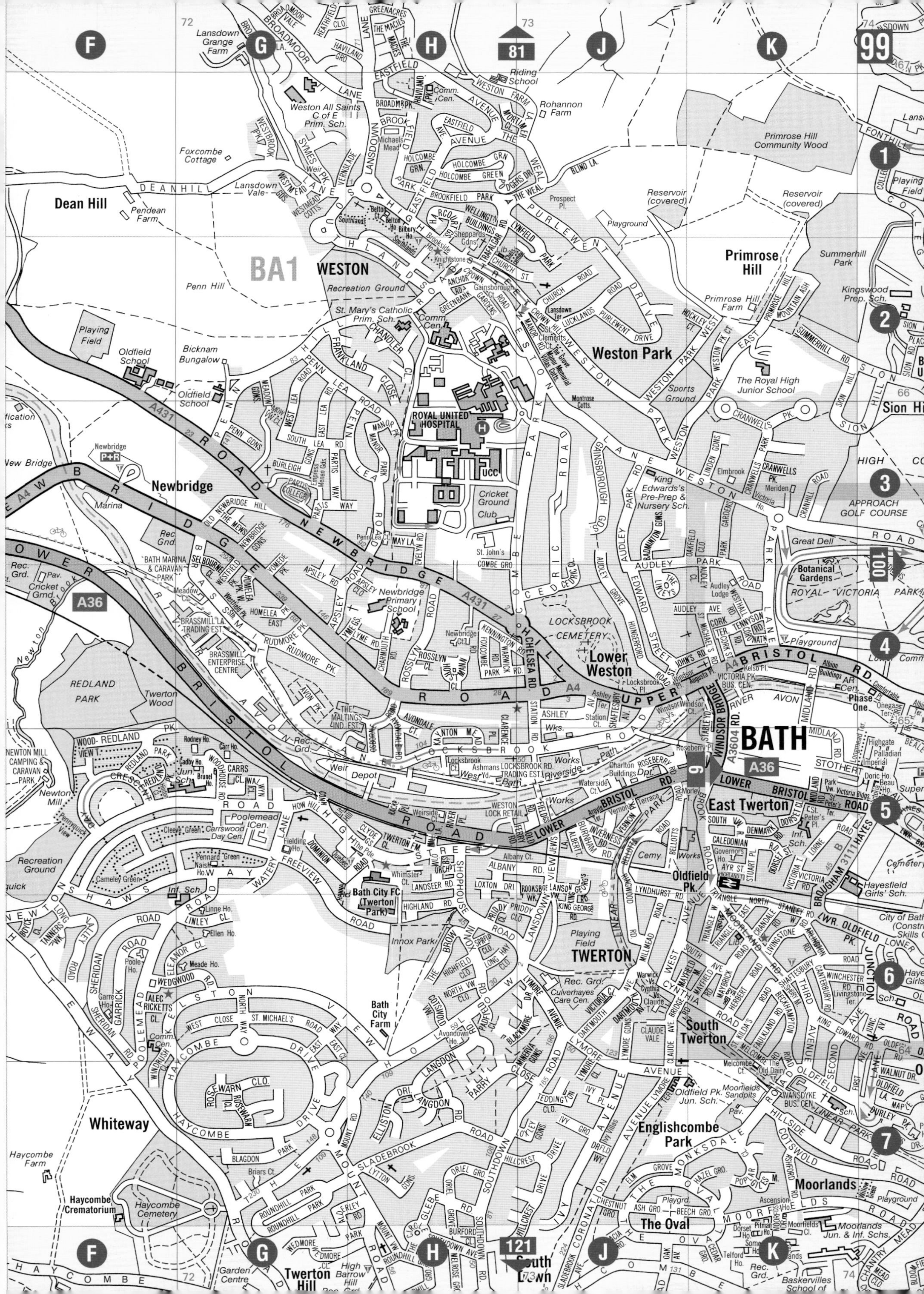

99
81
121
100
F
G
H
J
K
1
2
3
4
5
6
7
72
73
74
BA1
WESTON
BATH
Dean Hill
Newbridge
Primrose Hill
Weston Park
Lower Weston
East Twerton
TWERTON
South Twerton
Whiteway
Englishcombe Park
The Oval
Moorlands
Sion Hill
Oldfield Pk.
Twerton Hill
South Down
Lansdown Grange Farm
Weston All Saints C of E Prim. Sch.
Foxcombe Cottage
Pendean Farm
Lansdown Vale
Penn Hill
Riding School
Rohannon Farm
Primrose Hill Community Wood
Reservoir (covered)
Playground
Prospect Pl.
Summerhill Park
Kingswood Prep. Sch.
Primrose Hill Farm
The Royal High Junior School
Sports Ground
St. Mary's Catholic Prim. Sch.
Recreation Ground
Playing Field
Oldfield School
Bicknam Bungalow
ROYAL UNITED HOSPITAL
UCC
Cricket Ground Club
Newbridge P+R
Marina
BATH MARINA & CARAVAN PARK
Rec. Grd.
Cricket Grnd.
BRASSMILL LA. TRADING EST.
BRASSMILL ENTERPRISE CENTRE
Newbridge Primary School
LOCKSBROOK CEMETERY
King Edwards's Pre-Prep & Nursery Sch.
Botanical Gardens
ROYAL VICTORIA PARK
APPROACH GOLF COURSE
Great Dell
REDLAND PARK
Twerton Wood
NEWTON MILL CAMPING & CARAVAN PARK
Newton Mill
Recreation Ground
THE MALTINGS IND. EST.
LOCKSBROOK RD. TRADING EST.
WESTON LOCK RETAIL
Depot
Weir
Works
Bath City FC (Twerton Park)
Innox Park
Bath City Farm
Culverhayes Care Cen.
Rec. Grd.
Cemy.
Hayesfield Girls' Sch.
City of Bath (Construction Skills C...
Oldfield Jun. Sch.
Moorfields Sandpits
WANSDYKE BUS. CEN.
Haycombe Farm
Haycombe Crematorium
Haycombe Cemetery
Garden Centre
Moorlands Jun. & Inf. Schs.
Baskervilles School of
A4
A36
A431
A3604
LOWER BRISTOL ROAD
UPPER BRISTOL RD.
NEWBRIDGE ROAD
NEWBRIDGE HILL
WESTON LANE
HIGH STREET
LANSDOWN LANE
DEANHILL
HAYCOMBE DRIVE
WHITEWAY ROAD
NEWTON ROAD
SHAWS WAY
LINEAR PARK
WINDSOR BRIDGE
MOORFIELDS ROAD

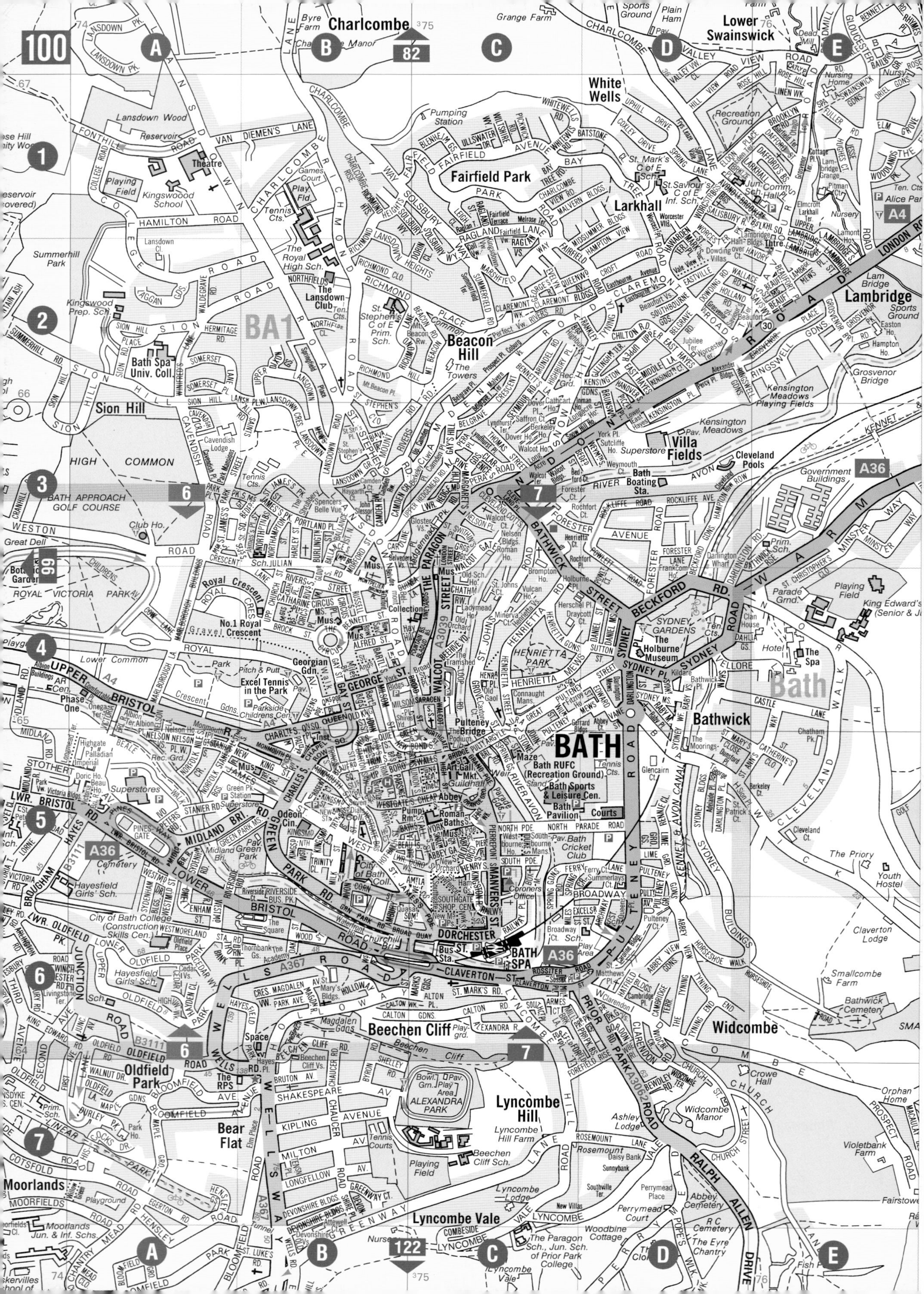
A
B
C
D
E
1
2
3
4
5
6
7
82
6
7
99
122
Charlcombe
Byre Farm
Grange Farm
Sports Ground
Plain Ham
Lower Swainswick
Lansdown Wood
Reservoir
Theatre
Playing Field
Kingswood School
Summerhill Park
Kingswood Prep. Sch.
BA1
Bath Spa Univ. Coll.
Sion Hill
HIGH COMMON
BATH APPROACH GOLF COURSE
Club Ho.
Botanic Garden
ROYAL VICTORIA PARK
Royal Crescent
No.1 Royal Crescent
Lower Common
Georgian Gdn.
Excel Tennis in the Park
The Royal High Sch.
The Lansdown Club
St. Stephen's C of E Prim. Sch.
Beacon Hill
The Towers
Fairfield Park
White Wells
Larkhall
Recreation Ground
Lambridge
Sports Ground
Kensington Meadows Playing Fields
Kensington Meadows
Villa Fields
Cleveland Pools
Bath Boating Sta.
Government Buildings
Playing Field
King Edward's (Senior & J
The Spa
Bath
Bathwick
The Holburne Museum
SYDNEY GARDENS
HENRIETTA PARK
Pulteney Bridge
BATH
Bath RUFC (Recreation Ground)
Bath Sports & Leisure Cen.
Bath Pavilion
Courts
Bath Cricket Club
Abbey
Roman Baths
Guildhall
Superstores
Green Park
Odeon Cin.
City of Bath Coll.
Hayesfield Girls' Sch.
City of Bath College (Construction Skills Cen.)
Phase One
Cemetery
Bus Sta.
BATH SPA
A36
A4
A367
A3062
A3039
B3111
Beechen Cliff
Oldfield Park
Bear Flat
The RPS
ALEXANDRA PARK
Lyncombe Hill
Lyncombe Hill Farm
Beechen Cliff Sch.
Playing Field
Lyncombe Vale
Widcombe
Widcombe Manor
Crowe Hall
Claverton Lodge
Smallcombe Farm
Bathwick Cemetery
Youth Hostel
The Priory
Cleveland Ct.
Orphan Home
Violetbank Farm
Abbey Cemetery
R C Cemetery
The Eyre Chantry
The Paragon Sch., Jun. Sch. of Prior Park College
Woodbine Cottage
Perrymead Court
Moorlands
Moorlands Jun. & Inf. Schs.
Playground
Fairfield Park
Lansdown Cl.
Widcombe

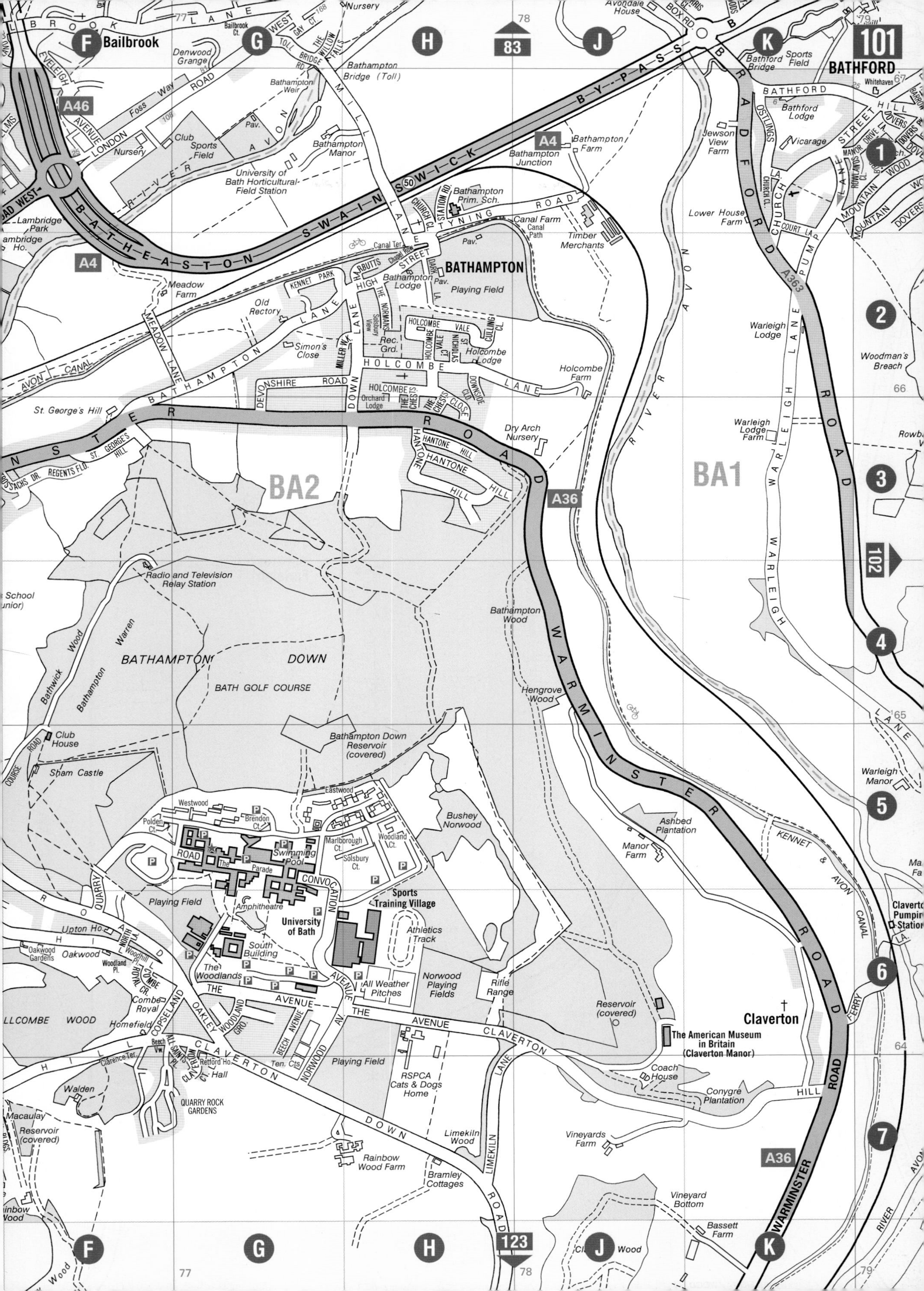
Bailbrook
Bathford
BATHFORD
BATHAMPTON
BA1
BA2
BATHAMPTON DOWN
BATH GOLF COURSE
University of Bath
Sports Training Village
Claverton
The American Museum in Britain (Claverton Manor)
BATHEASTON SWAINSWICK BY-PASS
A4
A46
A36
A363
WARMINSTER ROAD
CLAVERTON DOWN
Bathampton Down Reservoir (covered)
Radio and Television Relay Station
Sham Castle
Club House
Bathwick Wood
Bathampton Warren
Bathampton Wood
Hengrove Wood
Bushey Norwood
Norwood Playing Fields
Rifle Range
Reservoir (covered)
Limekiln Wood
Rainbow Wood Farm
Bramley Cottages
Vineyards Farm
Vineyard Bottom
Bassett Farm
Conygre Plantation
Coach House
Ashbed Plantation
Manor Farm
Warleigh Manor
Warleigh Lodge
Warleigh Lodge Farm
Woodman's Breach
Holcombe Farm
Dry Arch Nursery
Canal Farm
Timber Merchants
Bathampton Farm
Bathampton Junction
Bathampton Manor
Bathampton Bridge (Toll)
Bathampton Weir
University of Bath Horticultural Field Station
Club Sports Field
Nursery
Denwood Grange
Meadow Farm
Old Rectory
Simon's Close
Holcombe Lodge
Bathampton Lodge
Playing Field
Bathampton Prim. Sch.
Lower House Farm
Jewson View Farm
Bathford Lodge
Bathford Bridge
Sports Field
Vicarage
Lambridge Park
Lambridge Ho.
St. George's Hill
Quarry Rock Gardens
Walden
RSPCA Cats & Dogs Home
Amphitheatre
South Building
The Woodlands
All Weather Pitches
Athletics Track
Swimming Pool
Claverton Pumping Station
RIVER AVON
KENNET & AVON CANAL
83
123
102
F G H J K
1 2 3 4 5 6 7
77 78 79
64 65 66 67

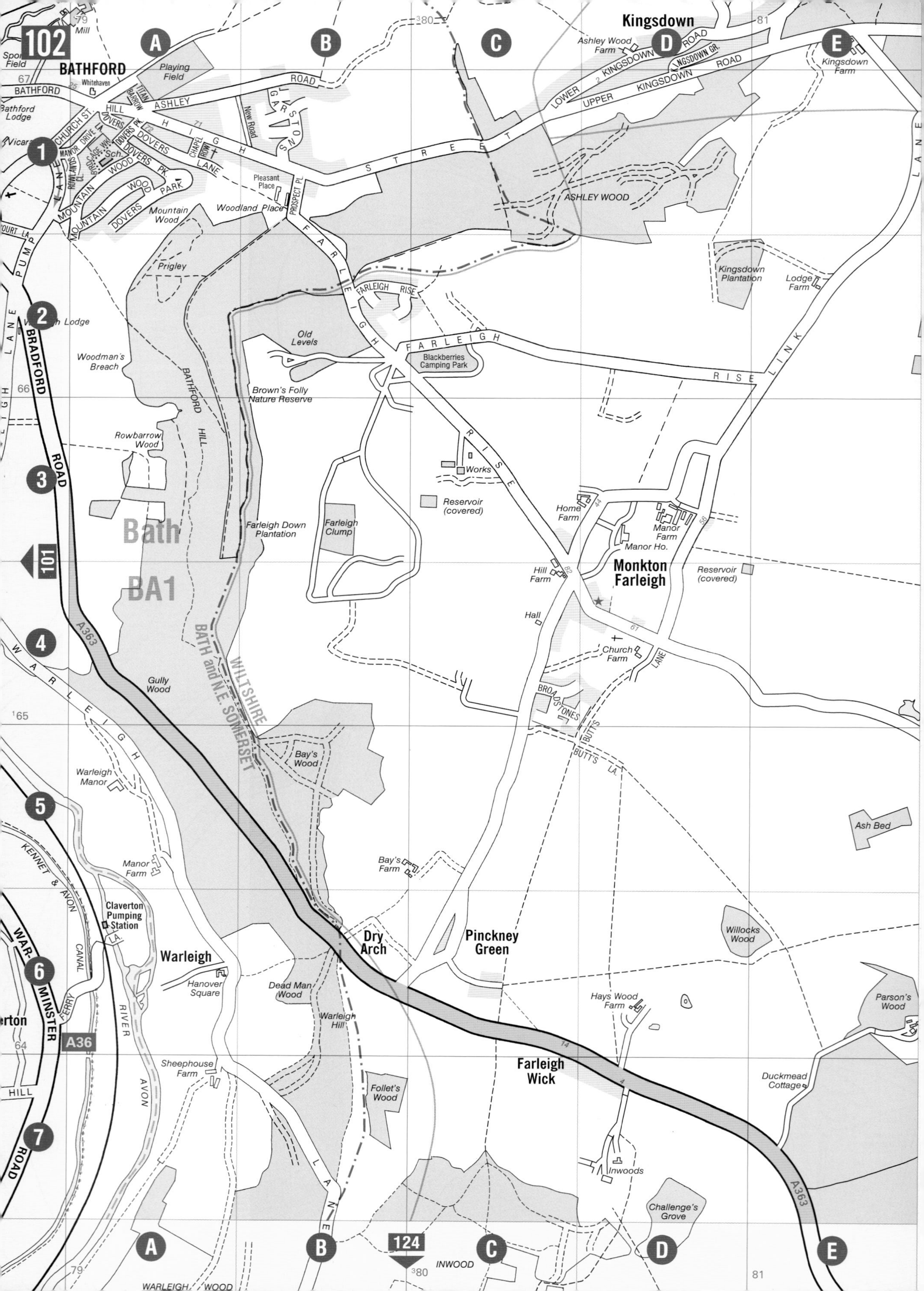

BATHFORD
Kingsdown
Playing Field
Ashley Wood Farm
Kingsdown Farm
LOWER KINGSDOWN ROAD
UPPER KINGSDOWN ROAD
KINGSDOWN GR.
ASHLEY ROAD
HIGH STREET
ASHLEY WOOD
Pleasant Place
PROSPECT PL.
Woodland Place
Mountain Wood
Prigley
FARLEIGH RISE
Kingsdown Plantation
Lodge Farm
Woodman's Breach
Old Levels
Blackberries Camping Park
LINK
Brown's Folly Nature Reserve
BATHFORD HILL
Rowbarrow Wood
Works
Reservoir (covered)
Home Farm
Manor Farm
Manor Ho.
Farleigh Down Plantation
Farleigh Clump
Bath
BA1
Hill Farm
Monkton Farleigh
Hall
Church Farm
BROADSTONES
BUTTS LA.
A363
Gully Wood
WILTSHIRE
BATH and N.E. SOMERSET
WARLEIGH LANE
Bay's Wood
Warleigh Manor
Ash Bed
Bay's Farm
KENNET & AVON CANAL
Manor Farm
Claverton Pumping Station
FERRY LA.
Dry Arch
Pinckney Green
Willocks Wood
Warleigh
Hanover Square
Dead Man Wood
Warleigh Hill
Hays Wood Farm
Parson's Wood
WARMINSTER ROAD
A36
RIVER AVON
Sheephouse Farm
Farleigh Wick
Follet's Wood
Duckmead Cottage
Inwoods
Challenge's Grove
INWOOD
WARLEIGH WOOD
101
124

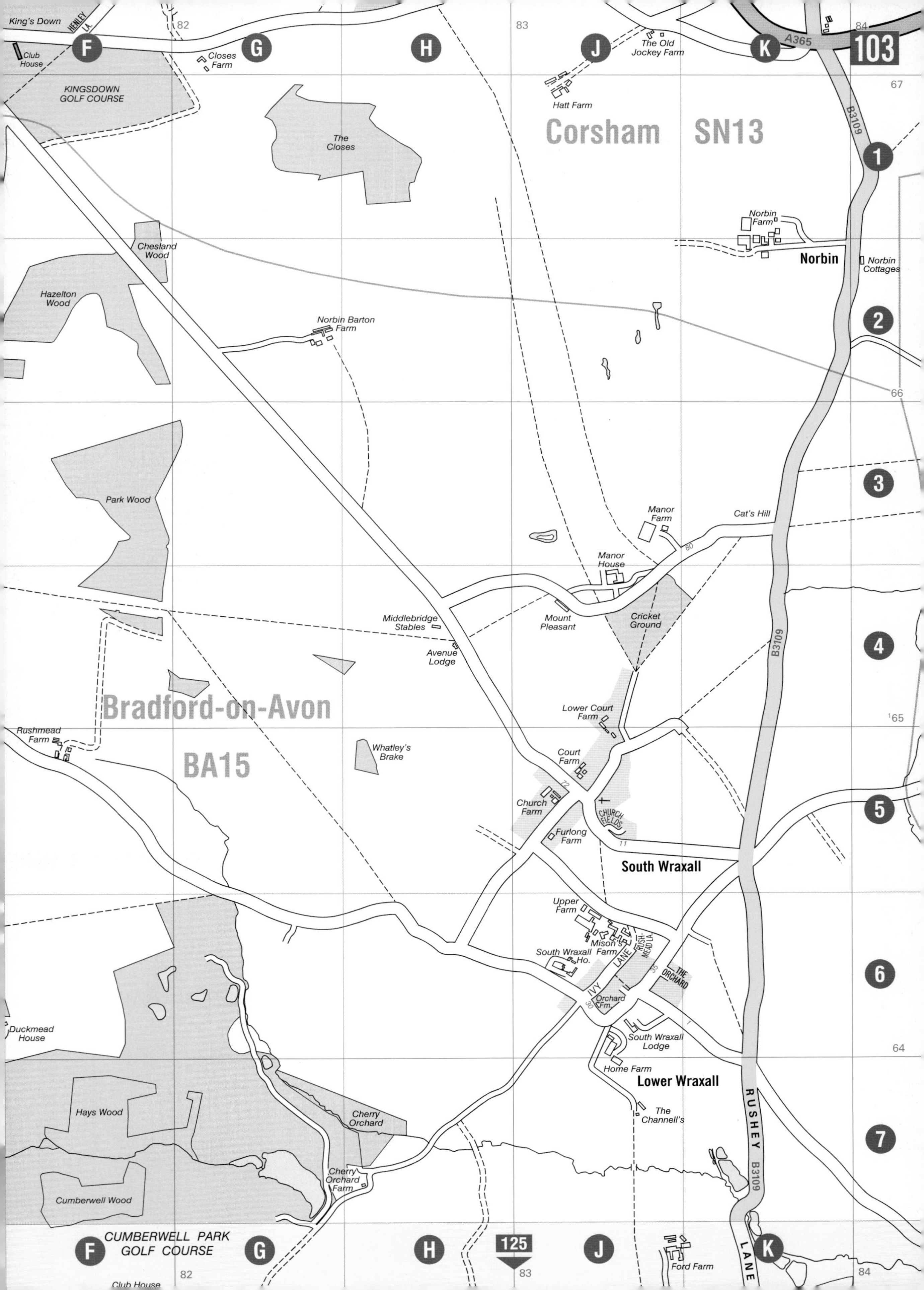

F **G** **H** **J** **K**

King's Down
HENLEY LA
82
83
84
A365
67

Club House
Closes Farm
The Old Jockey Farm

KINGSDOWN GOLF COURSE
Hatt Farm

Corsham SN13

1

The Closes

Norbin Farm

Chesland Wood

Norbin

Norbin Cottages

Hazelton Wood
66

2

Norbin Barton Farm

3

Park Wood

Manor Farm
Cat's Hill

80

Manor House

Middlebridge Stables
Mount Pleasant
Cricket Ground
4

Avenue Lodge
165

Bradford-on-Avon

Lower Court Farm

Rushmead Farm

Whatley's Brake
Court Farm

BA15

Church Farm
CHURCH FIELDS
5

Furlong Farm
11

South Wraxall

Upper Farm

Mison's Farm
RUSH-MEAD LA

South Wraxall Ho.
IVY LANE
THE ORCHARD
6

Duckmead House
Orchard Fm.
64

South Wraxall Lodge

Home Farm

Lower Wraxall

Hays Wood
Cherry Orchard
The Channell's

7

Cumberwell Wood
Cherry Orchard Farm

RUSHEY LANE B3109

F CUMBERWELL PARK GOLF COURSE **G** **H** 125 **J** **K**

Club House
82
83
Ford Farm
84

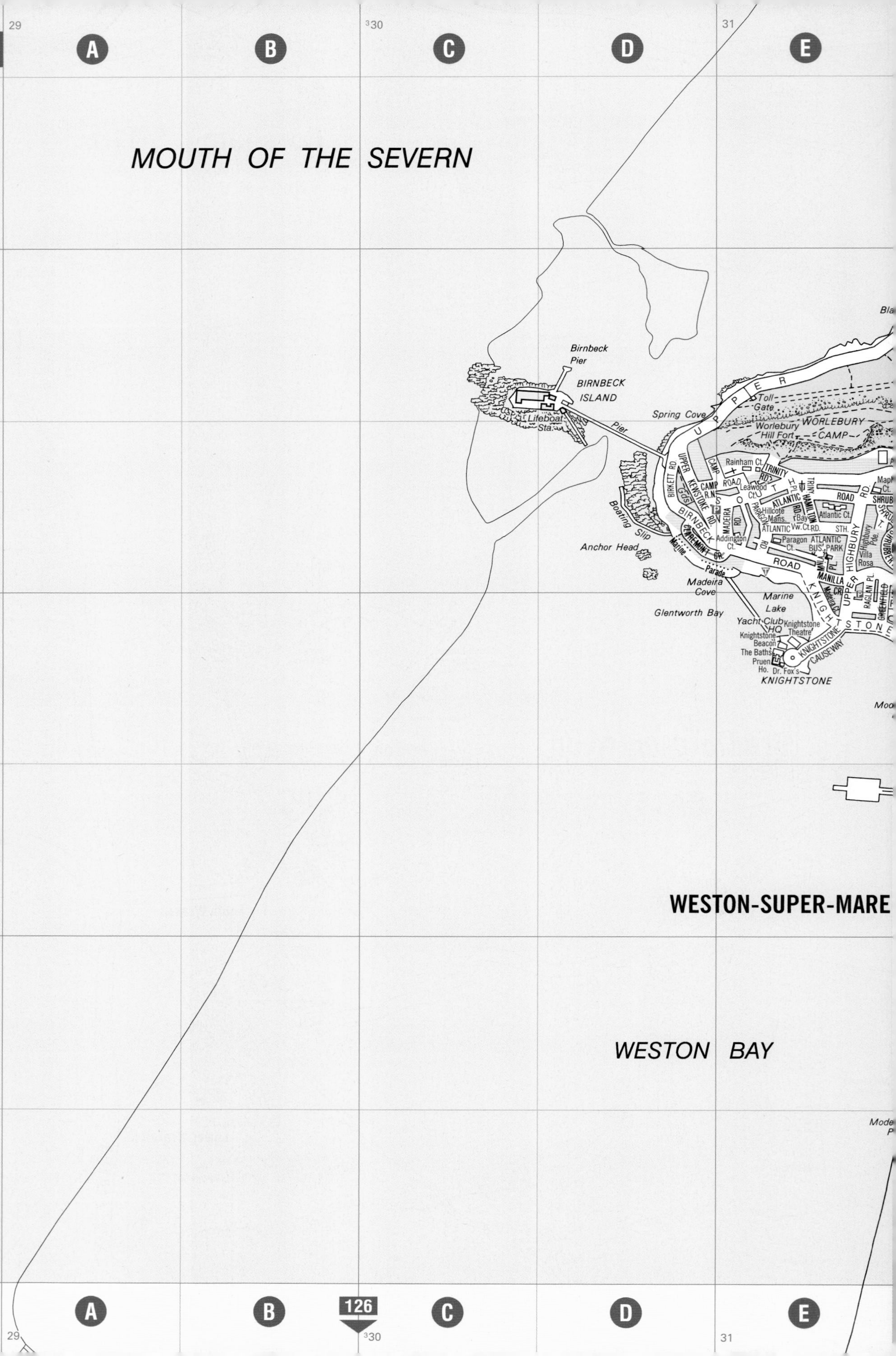

A B C D E

MOUTH OF THE SEVERN

1

63

2

Birnbeck Pier

BIRNBECK ISLAND

Spring Cove

Toll Gate

Worlebury Hill Fort **WORLEBURY CAMP**

Lifeboat Sta.

Pier

Rainham Ct.

TRINITY

ATLANTIC Mans.

Atlantic Ct.

Villa Rosa

3

Boating Slip

Anchor Head

Addington Ct.

Paragon ATLANTIC BUS PARK

ATLANTIC Vw.Ct.RD.

STH.

MANILLA

62

Marine Lake

Madeira Cove

Parade

ROAD

Glentworth Bay

Yacht Club HO

Knightstone Theatre

Knightstone Beacon

The Baths

Pruen Ho.

Dr. Fox's

KNIGHTSTONE

4

5

61

WESTON-SUPER-MARE

6

WESTON BAY

7

60

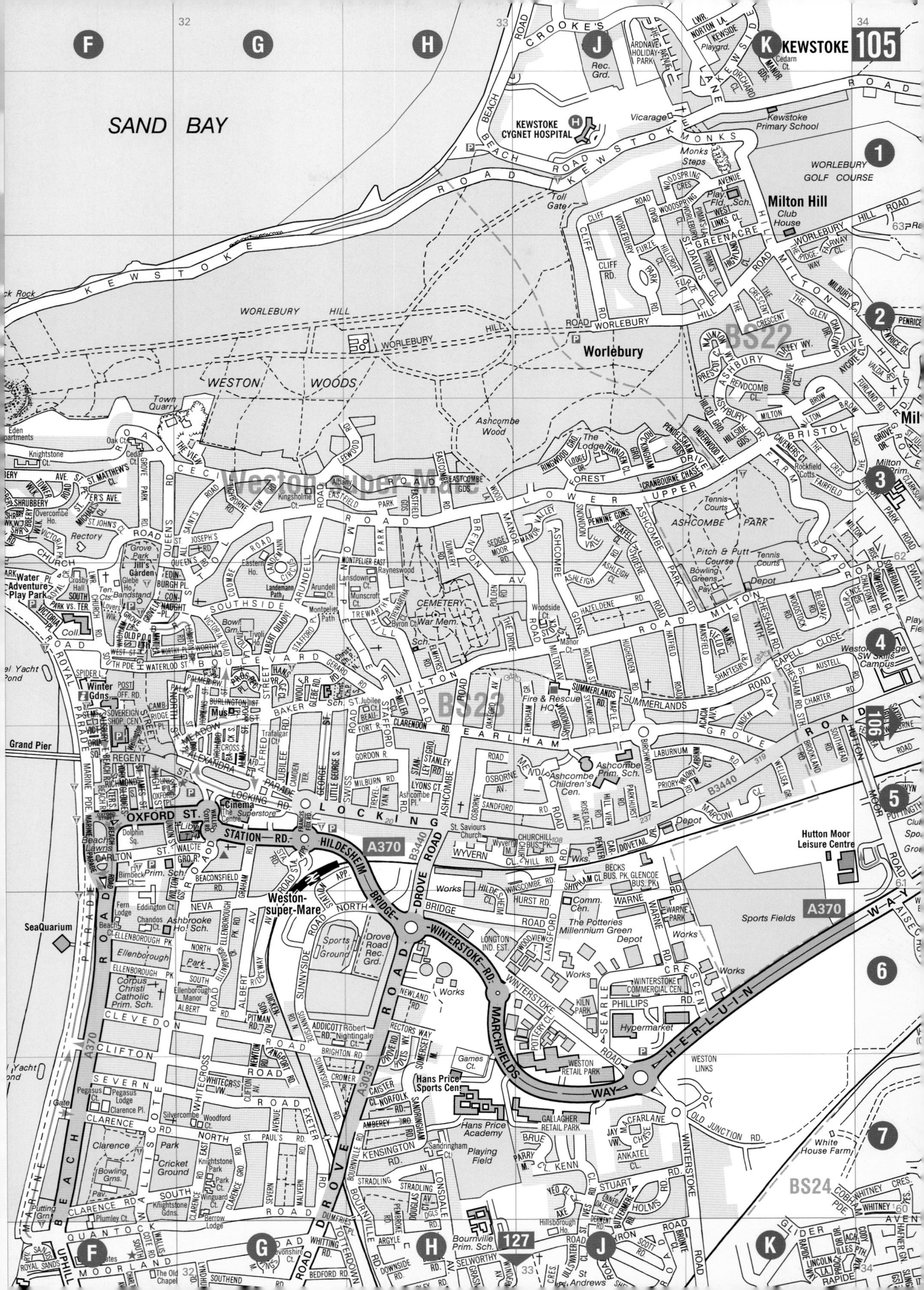
F
G
H
J
K
32
33
34
1
2
3
4
5
6
7
SAND BAY
KEWSTOKE ROAD
CROOKE'S LANE
Rec. Grd.
ARDNAVE HOLIDAY PARK
Playgrd.
Cedarn Ct.
Vicarage
Kewstoke Primary School
KEWSTOKE CYGNET HOSPITAL
MONKS HILL
Monks Steps
Toll Gate
WORLEBURY GOLF COURSE
Milton Hill
Club House
WORLEBURY HILL
WORLEBURY HILL ROAD
Worlebury
BS22
WESTON WOODS
Town Quarry
Ashcombe Wood
Weston-super-Mare
Knightstone
Water Adventure Play Park
Rectory
Jill's Garden
Grove Park
Bandstand
Coll.
Winter Gdns.
Grand Pier
SOVEREIGN SHOP. CEN.
Mus.
Cinema
Superstore
OXFORD ST.
STATION RD.
HILDESHEIM BRIDGE
A370
B3440
LOCKING ROAD
CEMETERY
War Mem.
BS23
Fire & Rescue HQ
EARLHAM GROVE
Ashcombe Prim. Sch.
Ashcombe Children's Cen.
ASHCOMBE PARK
Pitch & Putt Course
Tennis Courts
Bowling Greens
Depot
MILTON ROAD
Weston College SW Skills Campus
Hutton Moor Leisure Centre
Sports Fields
HUTTON MOOR ROAD
Weston-super-Mare
Sports Ground
Drove Road Rec. Grd.
Works
LONGTON IND. EST.
The Potteries Millennium Green
WINTERSTOKE COMMERCIAL CEN.
Hypermarket
WESTON RETAIL PARK
GALLAGHER RETAIL PARK
HERLUIN WAY
MARCHFIELDS WAY
WINTERSTOKE RD.
DROVE ROAD
A3033
SeaQuarium
Ellenborough Park
Corpus Christi Catholic Prim. Sch.
Ashbrooke Ho. Sch.
Clarence Park
Cricket Ground
Bowling Grns.
Hans Price Sports Cen.
Hans Price Academy
Playing Field
WESTON LINKS
White House Farm
BS24
Bournville Prim. Sch.
MARINE PARADE
BEACH ROAD
UPHILL ROAD
QUANTOCK RD.
MOORLAND RD.
St Andrews
The Old Chapel

106
127

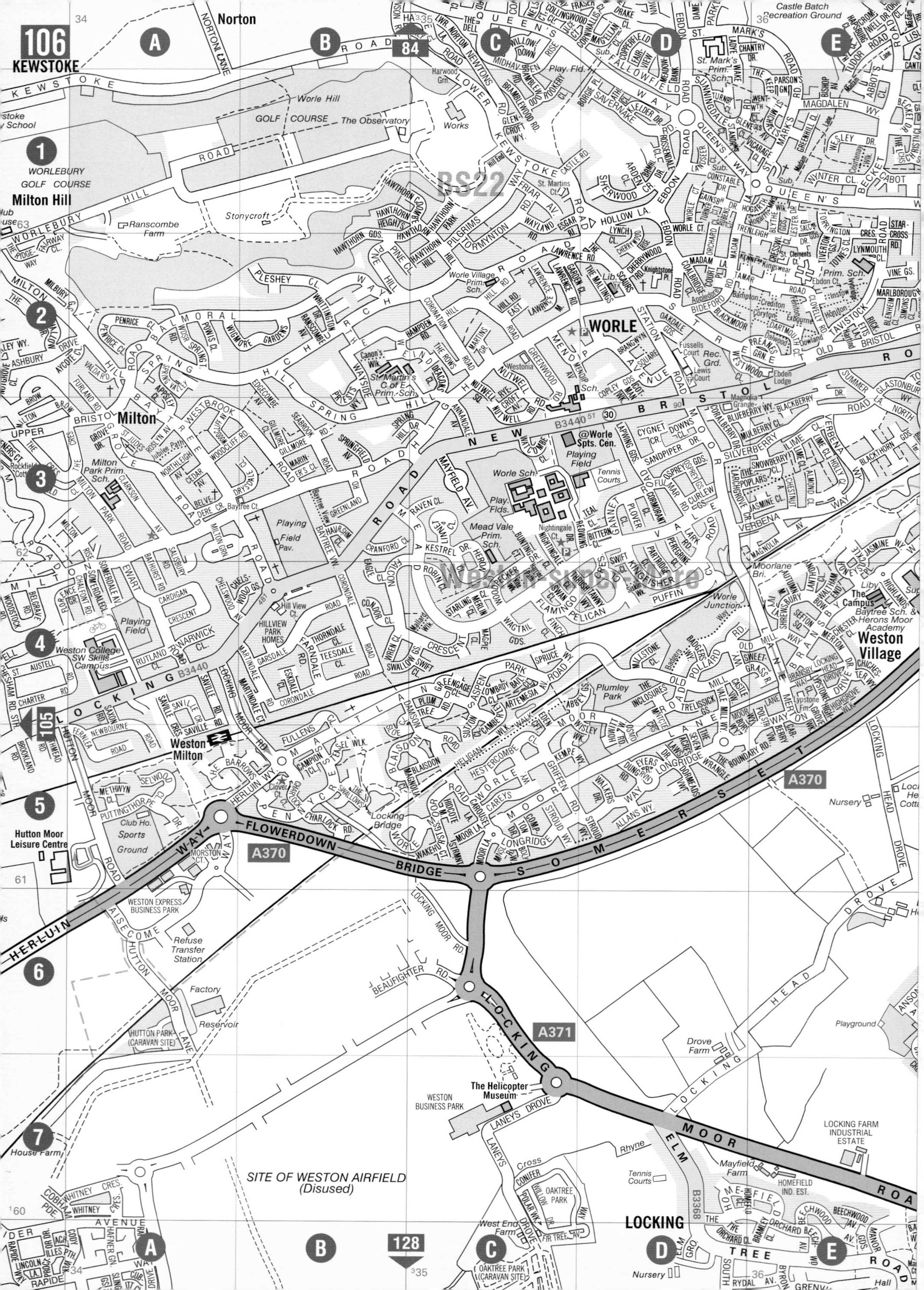
106
KEWSTOKE
Norton
Castle Batch Recreation Ground
Worle Hill
GOLF COURSE
The Observatory
WORLEBURY GOLF COURSE
Milton Hill
Ranscombe Farm
Stonycroft
Works
BS22
KEWSTOKE ROAD
WORLEBURY HILL ROAD
Worle Village Prim. Sch.
WORLE
Milton
Milton Park Prim. Sch.
St. Martin's C of E Prim. Sch.
Worle Sch.
@Worle Spts. Cen.
Playing Field
Tennis Courts
Mead Vale Prim. Sch.
Weston-super-Mare
Moorlane Bri.
Worle Junction
The Campus
Baytree Sch. & Herons Moor Academy
Weston Village
Weston College SW Skills Campus
Plumley Park
Weston Milton
Hutton Moor Leisure Centre
Sports Ground
WESTON EXPRESS BUSINESS PARK
Refuse Transfer Station
Factory
Reservoir
HUTTON PARK (CARAVAN SITE)
The Helicopter Museum
WESTON BUSINESS PARK
SITE OF WESTON AIRFIELD (Disused)
Drove Farm
LOCKING FARM INDUSTRIAL ESTATE
Mayfield Farm
HOMEFIELD IND. EST.
OAKTREE PARK
OAKTREE PARK (CARAVAN SITE)
West End Farm
LOCKING
House Farm
Nursery
Playground
A370
A371
B3440
B3368
FLOWERDOWN BRIDGE
HERLUIN WAY
SOMERSET
LOCKING MOOR ROAD
NEW BRISTOL ROAD
OLD BRISTOL ROAD
84
105
128

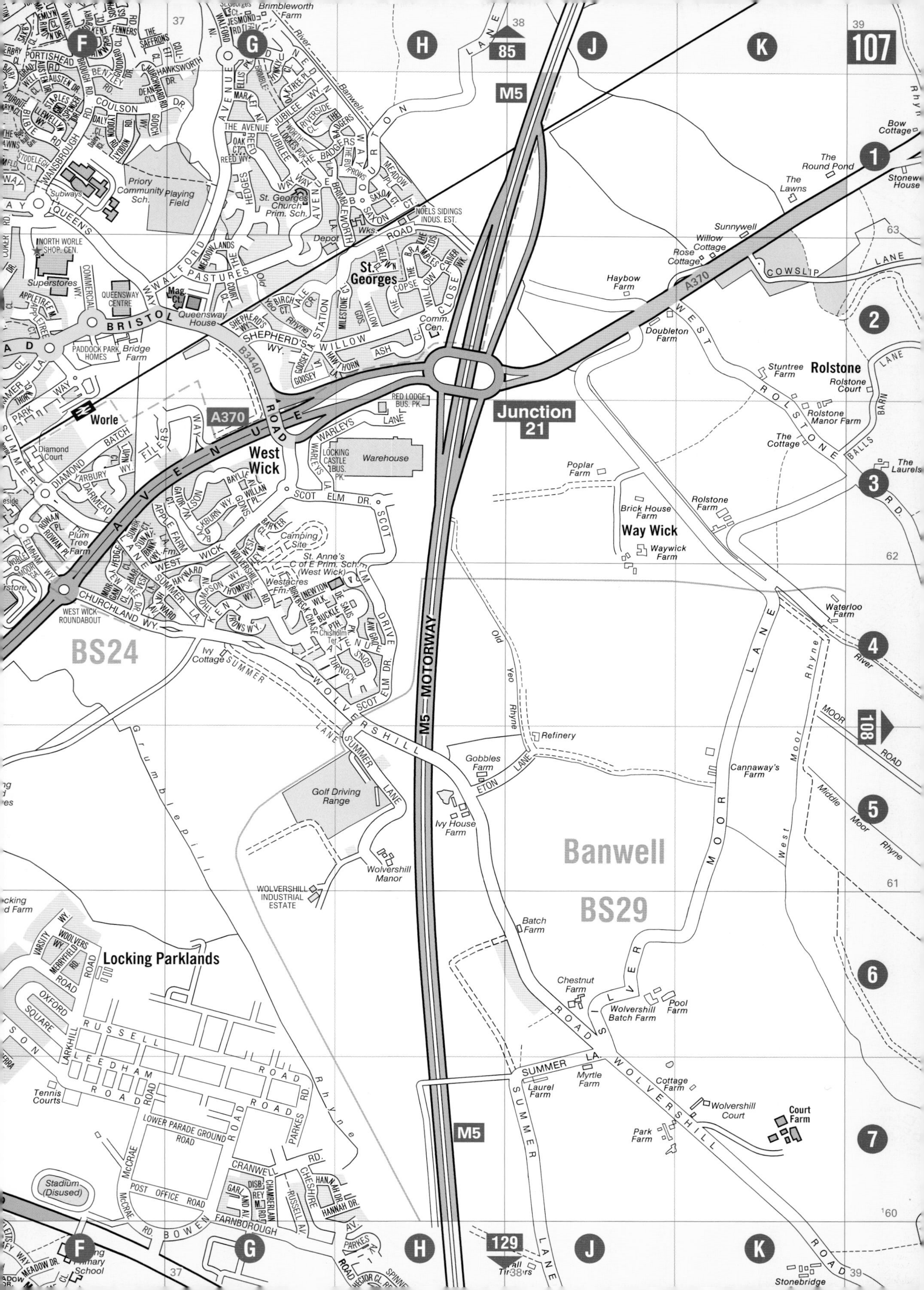

Worle
West Wick
St. Georges
Way Wick
Rolstone
Junction 21
M5 MOTORWAY
A370
B3440
BS24
BS29
Banwell
Locking Parklands
Golf Driving Range
Wolvershill Manor
WOLVERSHILL INDUSTRIAL ESTATE
Court Farm
Stonebridge
85
108
129

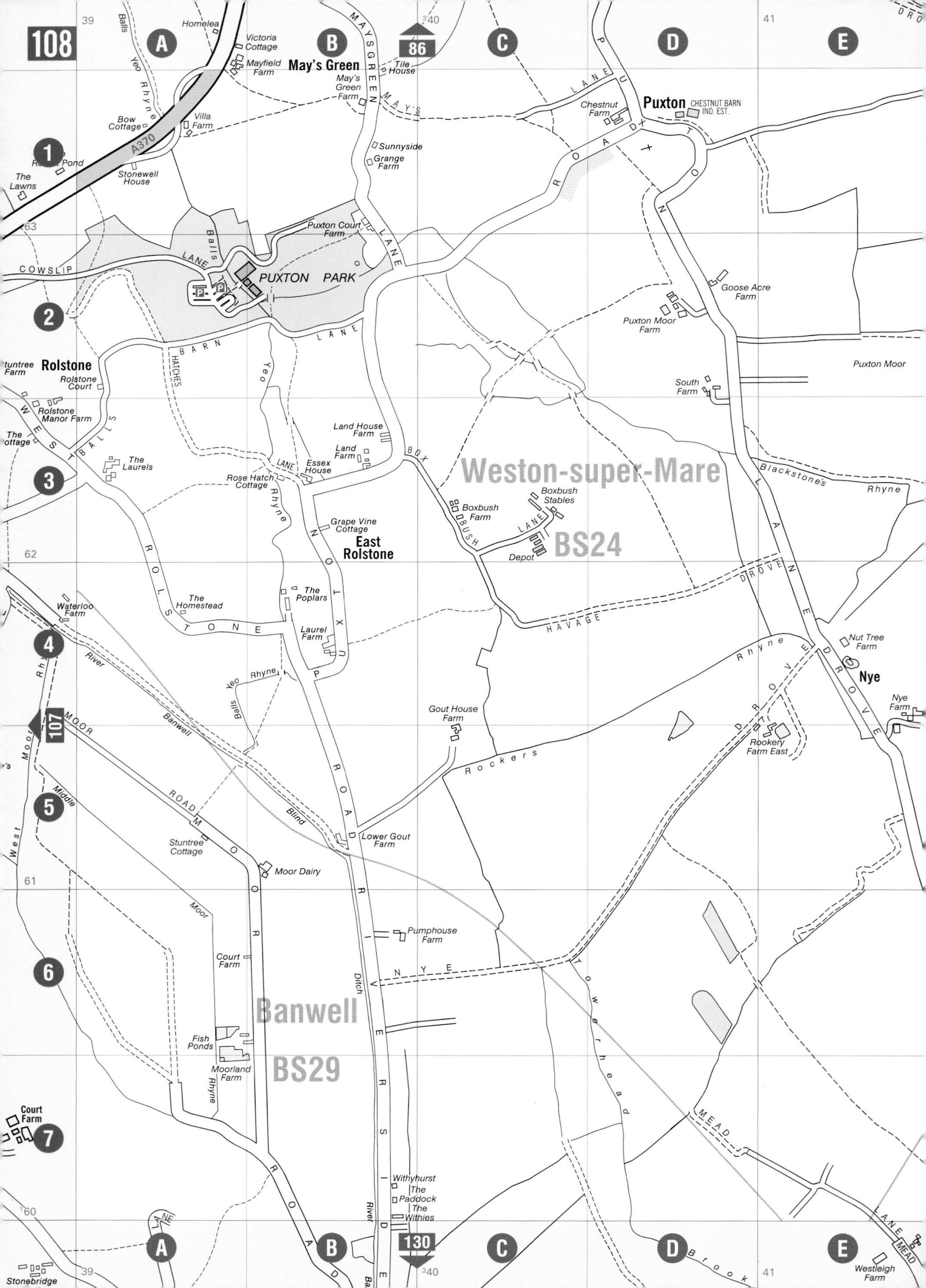
May's Green
Puxton
CHESTNUT BARN IND. EST.
PUXTON PARK
Rolstone
East Rolstone
Weston-super-Mare
BS24
Nye
Banwell
BS29
Homelea
Victoria Cottage
Mayfield Farm
May's Green Farm
Tile House
Villa Farm
Bow Cottage
Stonewell House
The Lawns
Sunnyside
Grange Farm
Puxton Court Farm
Chestnut Farm
Goose Acre Farm
Puxton Moor Farm
Puxton Moor
South Farm
Rolstone Court
Rolstone Manor Farm
The Laurels
Land House Farm
Land Farm
Essex House
Rose Hatch Cottage
Grape Vine Cottage
Boxbush Farm
Boxbush Stables
Depot
The Homestead
The Poplars
Laurel Farm
Waterloo Farm
Nut Tree Farm
Nye Farm
Rookery Farm East
Gout House Farm
Lower Gout Farm
Stuntree Cottage
Moor Dairy
Pumphouse Farm
Court Farm
Fish Ponds
Moorland Farm
Withyhurst
The Paddock
The Withies
Stonebridge
Westleigh Farm
A370
COWSLIP LANE
BARN LANE
HATCHES
BOX LANE
BOXBUSH LANE
PUXTON ROAD
MAYSGREEN LANE
MAY'S LANE
WEST BALLS
ROLSTONE
LANE
PUXTON ROAD
HAVAGE DROVE
LANE DROVE
Blackstone's Rhyne
Rhyne
Rockers
Yeo Rhyne
Balls
River Banwell
Blind
MOOR ROAD
MOOR ROAD
Middle Moor
West Moor
RIVER ROAD
NYE
River Ditch
Towerhead
Brook
MEAD
MEAD LANE
86
107
130
39
340
41
63
62
61
60

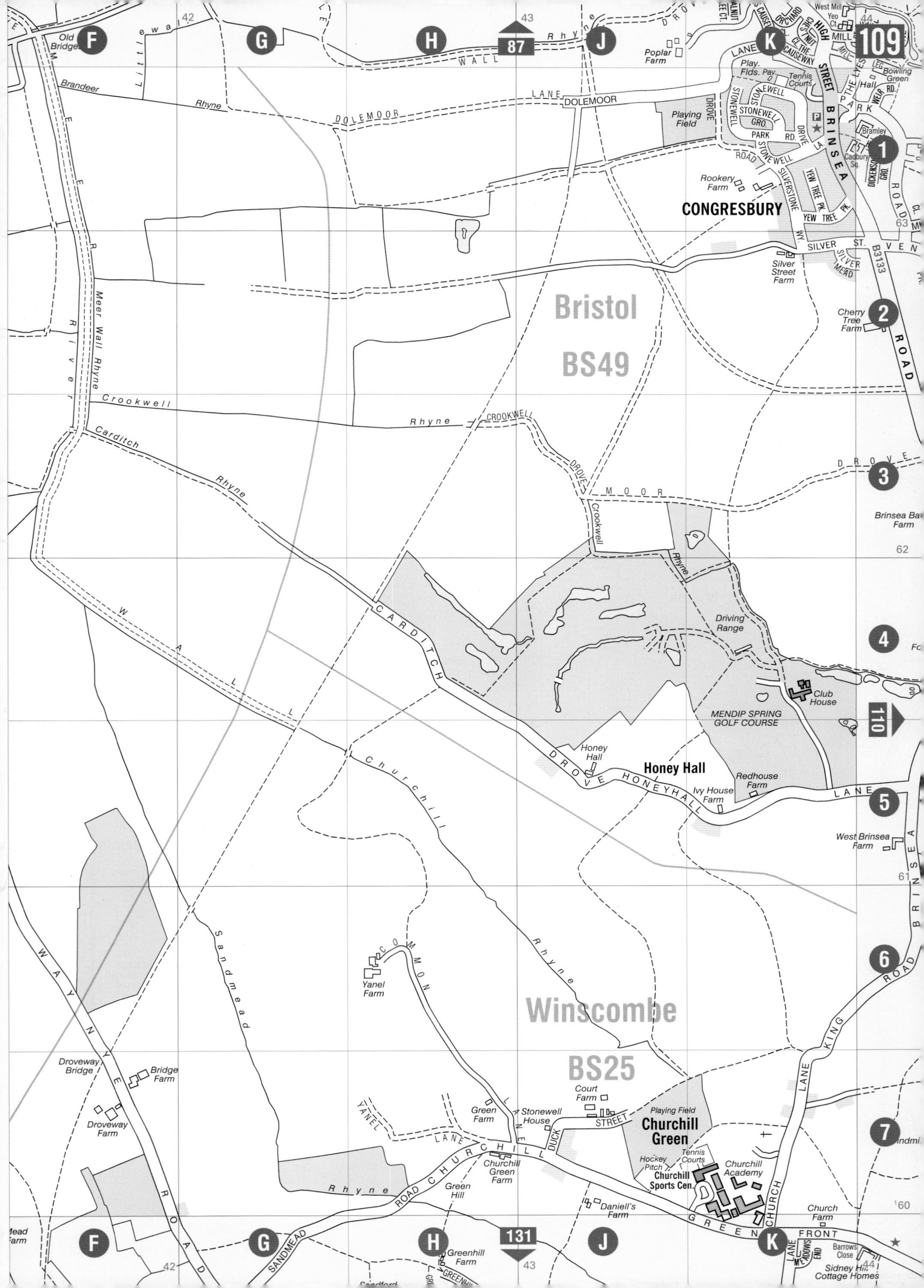
109
87
131
110
F
G
H
J
K
1
2
3
4
5
6
7
42
43
44
63
62
61
60
Old Bridge
Poplar Farm
West Mill
MILL
Play. Flds.
Tennis Courts
Bowling Green
Playing Field
DOLEMOOR LANE
WALL Rhyne
Littlewall
Brandeer Rhyne
STONEWELL
STONEWELL GRO.
PARK RD.
HIGH STREET
BRINSEA ROAD
THE CAUSEWAY
ORCHARD
CHESTNUT CL.
YEW TREE PK.
SILVERSTONE WY.
Rookery Farm
CONGRESBURY
SILVER ST.
SILVER MEAD
B3133
Silver Street Farm
Cherry Tree Farm
Bristol
BS49
Meer Wall Rhyne
River
Crookwell Rhyne
CROOKWELL DROVE
Carditch Rhyne
MOOR DROVE
Brinsea Farm
CARDITCH DROVE
Driving Range
Club House
MENDIP SPRING GOLF COURSE
Honey Hall
HONEYHALL LANE
Redhouse Farm
Ivy House Farm
West Brinsea Farm
WALL
Churchill Rhyne
Sandmead
WAYNE ROAD
COMMON
Yanel Farm
Winscombe
BS25
KING ROAD
Droveway Bridge
Bridge Farm
Droveway Farm
Court Farm
Green Farm
Stonewell House
DUCK STREET
Playing Field
Churchill Green
YANEL LANE
CHURCHILL ROAD
SANDMEAD
Churchill Green Farm
Hockey Pitch
Tennis Courts
Churchill Academy
Churchill Sports Cen.
Green Hill
Daniell's Farm
GREEN
CHURCH LANE
Church Farm
FRONT
Greenhill Farm
MEADOWS END
Barrows Close
Sidney Hill Cottage Homes
Mead Farm

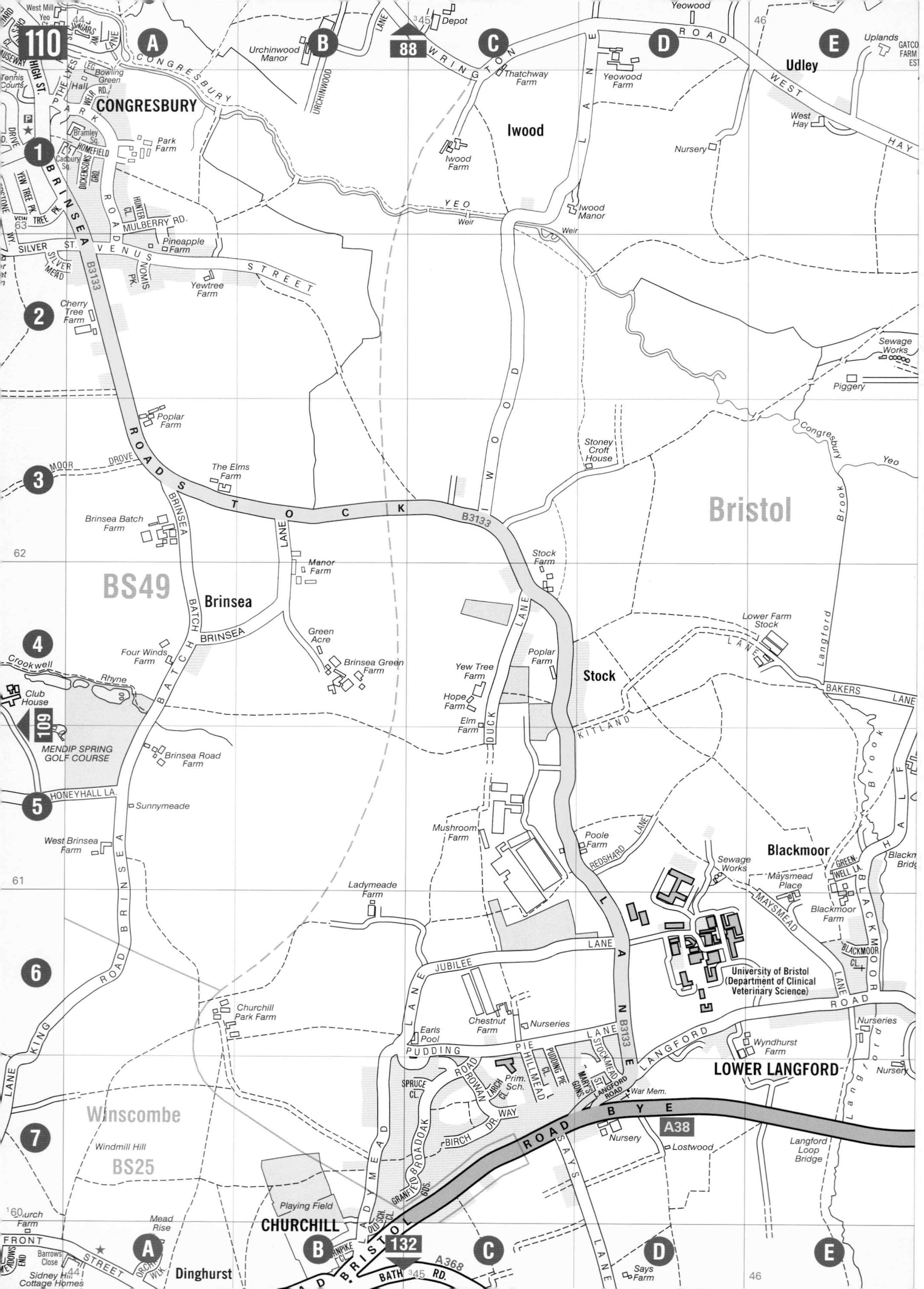
CONGRESBURY
Iwood
Udley
Bristol
BS49
Brinsea
Stock
Blackmoor
LOWER LANGFORD
CHURCHILL
Dinghurst
Winscombe
BS25
Urchinwood Manor
Thatchway Farm
Yeowood Farm
Yeowood
Depot
Uplands
West Hay
Nursery
Park Farm
Iwood Farm
Iwood Manor
Weir
Pineapple Farm
Yewtree Farm
Cherry Tree Farm
Sewage Works
Piggery
Poplar Farm
The Elms Farm
Stoney Croft House
Brinsea Batch Farm
Manor Farm
Stock Farm
Green Acre
Brinsea Green Farm
Four Winds Farm
Lower Farm Stock
Poplar Farm
Yew Tree Farm
Hope Farm
Elm Farm
Club House
MENDIP SPRING GOLF COURSE
Brinsea Road Farm
Sunnymeade
West Brinsea Farm
Mushroom Farm
Poole Farm
Maysmead Place
Blackmoor Farm
Ladymeade Farm
University of Bristol (Department of Clinical Veterinary Science)
Churchill Park Farm
Earls Pool
Chestnut Farm
Nurseries
Wyndhurst Farm
Prim. Sch.
War Mem.
Nursery
Lostwood
Langford Loop Bridge
Windmill Hill
Playing Field
Church Farm
Mead Rise
Barrows Close
Sidney Hill Cottage Homes
Says Farm
BRINSEA ROAD
STOCK LANE
B3133
A38
A368
CONGRESBURY YEO
MOOR DROVE
HONEYHALL LA.
KING LANE
JUBILEE LANE
PUDDING PIE LANE
LANGFORD ROAD
BYE ROAD
BRISTOL ROAD
BATH RD.
FRONT STREET
WOOD LANE
DUCK LANE
KITLAND
REDSHARD LANE
BAKERS LANE
HALF
WRINGTON ROAD
WEST HAY ROAD
88
109
132

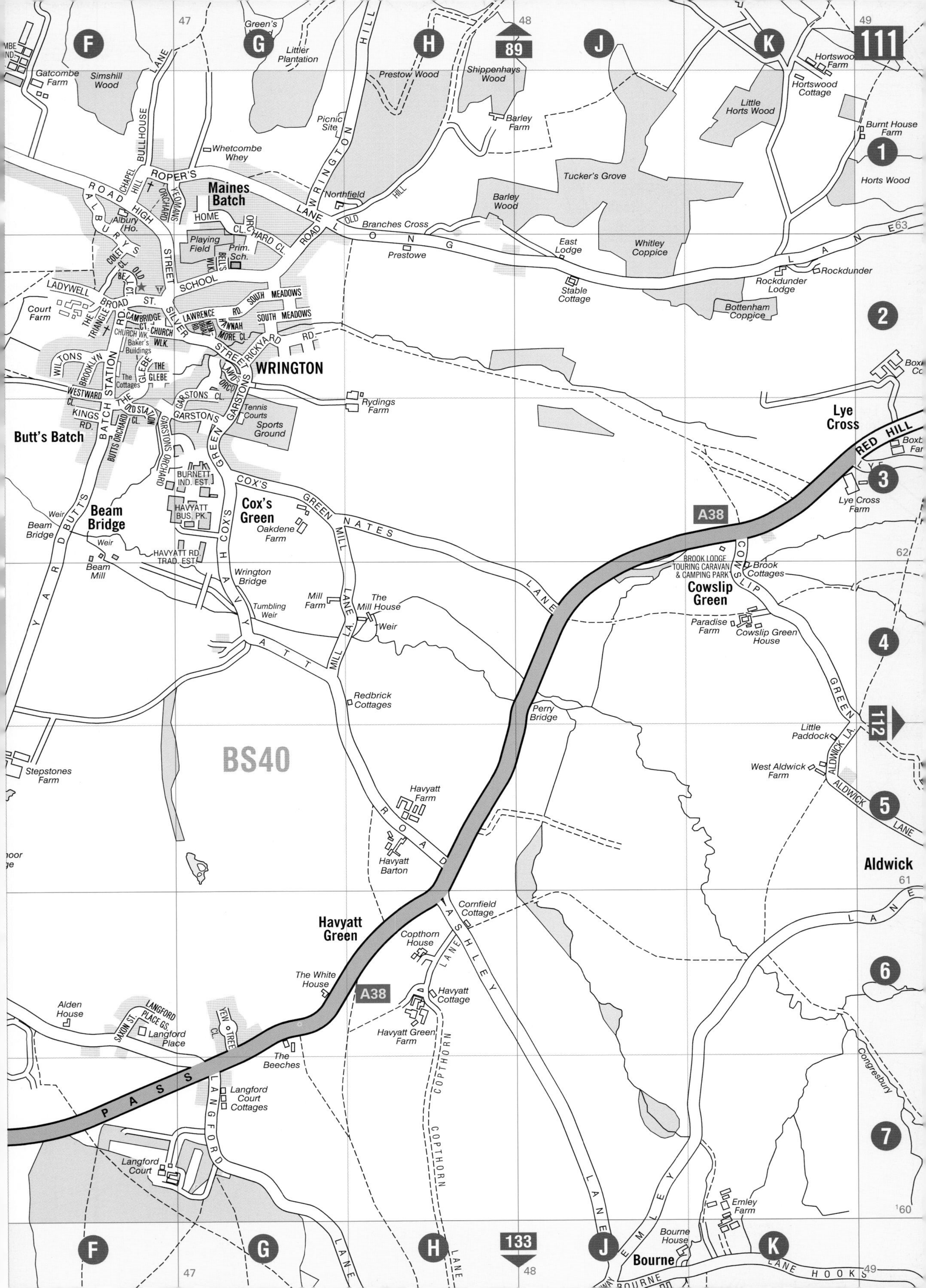
F
G
H
J
K
47
48
49
89
111
Green's
Littler Plantation
Gatcombe Farm
Simshill Wood
Prestow Wood
Shippenhays Wood
Hortswood Farm
Hortswood Cottage
Little Horts Wood
Burnt House Farm
Picnic Site
Barley Farm
Whetcombe Whey
Maines Batch
Northfield
Tucker's Grove
Barley Wood
Horts Wood
Branches Cross
Albury Ho.
Playing Field
Prim. Sch.
Prestowe
East Lodge
Whitley Coppice
Rockdunder
Rockdunder Lodge
Stable Cottage
Bottenham Coppice
Court Farm
Baker's Buildings
The Cottages
WRINGTON
Rydings Farm
Tennis Courts
Sports Ground
Lye Cross
Butt's Batch
BURNETT IND. EST.
HAVYATT BUS. PK.
Cox's Green
Lye Cross Farm
Beam Bridge
Weir
Oakdene Farm
A38
Beam Mill
HAVYATT RD. TRAD. EST.
BROOK LODGE TOURING CARAVAN & CAMPING PARK
Brook Cottages
Wrington Bridge
Mill Farm
The Mill House
Cowslip Green
Tumbling Weir
Paradise Farm
Cowslip Green House
Redbrick Cottages
Perry Bridge
112
Little Paddock
BS40
Stepstones Farm
West Aldwick Farm
Havyatt Farm
Havyatt Barton
Aldwick
Cornfield Cottage
Havyatt Green
Copthorn House
The White House
Havyatt Cottage
Alden House
Langford Place
Havyatt Green Farm
The Beeches
Congresbury
Langford Court Cottages
Langford Court
Emley Farm
Bourne House
Bourne
133
1
2
3
4
5
6
7
63
62
61
60
ROPER'S LANE
BULLHOUSE LANE
CHAPEL HILL
HIGH STREET
ORCHARD
YEOMANS
HOME
ORCHARD CL.
SCHOOL
BROAD ST.
SILVER STREET
LAWRENCE RD.
SOUTH MEADOWS
CHURCH WLK.
RICKYARD RD.
STATION RD.
GARSTONS
COX'S GREEN
NATES LANE
MILL LANE
HAVYATT ROAD
LONG LANE
WRINGTON HILL
RED HILL
COWSLIP GREEN
ALDWICK LA.
ALDWICK LANE
ASHLEY LANE
COPTHORN LANE
LANGFORD LANE
LANGFORD PLACE
SAXON ST.
YEW TREE CL.
PASS
BUTT'S YARD
EMLEY
BOURNE LANE
HOOKS LANE

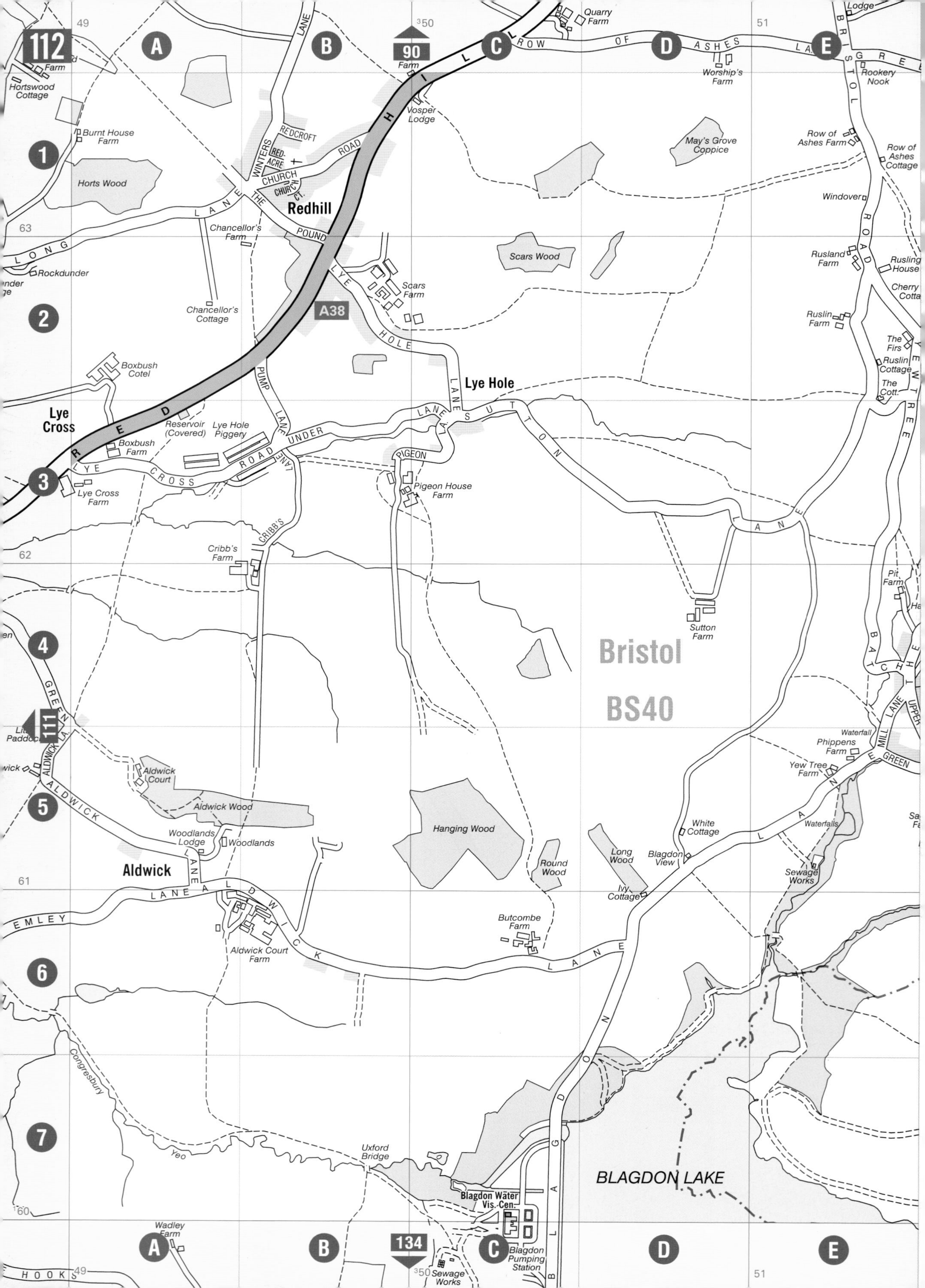
Hortswood Cottage
Burnt House Farm
Horts Wood
Redhill
Lye Hole
Lye Cross
Aldwick
Bristol
BS40
A38
Hanging Wood
Aldwick Wood
Scars Wood
May's Grove Coppice
Sutton Farm
Pigeon House Farm
Cribb's Farm
Boxbush Farm
Lye Cross Farm
Aldwick Court Farm
Butcombe Farm
Round Wood
Long Wood
BLAGDON LAKE
Blagdon Water Vis. Cen.
Blagdon Pumping Station
Sewage Works
Uxford Bridge
Wadley Farm
Worship's Farm
Quarry Farm
Vosper Lodge
Row of Ashes Farm
Rusland Farm
Ruslin Farm
Windover
Chancellor's Farm
Chancellor's Cottage
Rockdunder
Boxbush Cotel
Reservoir (Covered)
Lye Hole Piggery
Woodlands Lodge
Woodlands
Aldwick Court
White Cottage
Blagdon View
Ivy Cottage
Yew Tree Farm
Phippens Farm
Waterfall
Scars Farm
Rookery Nook
Pit Farm
90
111
134

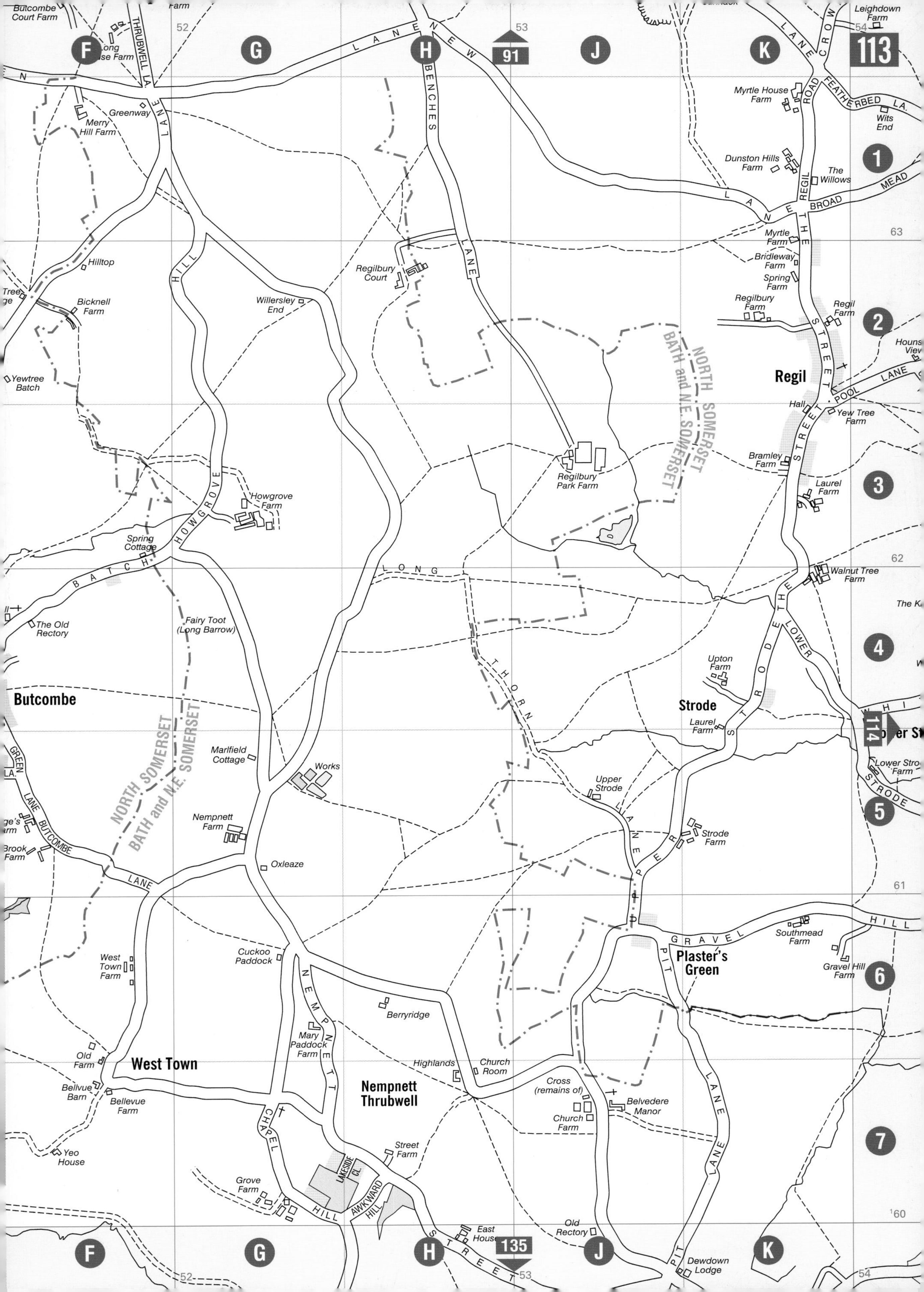

Butcombe
Court Farm

THRUBWELL LA.

Long
House Farm

Merry
Hill Farm

Greenway

Hilltop

Tree
ge

Bicknell
Farm

Yewtree
Batch

LANE

HILL

BATCH

HOWGROVE

Spring
Cottage

Howgrove
Farm

Willersley
End

Regilbury Court

NEW BENCHES LANE

LANE

Regilbury
Park Farm

LONG

THORN

NORTH SOMERSET
BATH and N.E. SOMERSET

Myrtle House
Farm

Dunston Hills
Farm

The
Willows

Wits
End

Leighdown
Farm

FEATHERBED LA.

CROW

ROAD

BROAD

MEAD

1

63

Myrtle
Farm

Bridleway
Farm

Spring
Farm

Regilbury
Farm

Hall

Regil
Farm

Regil

Houns
View

POOL LANE

2

Yew Tree
Farm

STREET

THE

Bramley
Farm

Laurel
Farm

3

62

Walnut Tree
Farm

The K

LOWER

STRODE

Upton
Farm

Strode

Laurel
Farm

4

114

Lower Stro
Farm

STRODE

5

61

Butcombe

NORTH SOMERSET
BATH and N.E. SOMERSET

GREEN

LA.

BUTCOMBE

ge's
Farm

Brook
Farm

The Old
Rectory

Fairy Toot
(Long Barrow)

Marlfield
Cottage

Nempnett
Farm

Works

Oxleaze

LANE

West
Town
Farm

Old
Farm

Bellvue
Barn

Bellevue
Farm

Yeo
House

CHAPEL

West Town

HILL

Cuckoo
Paddock

NEMPNETT

Mary
Paddock
Farm

Nempnett
Thrubwell

Berryridge

Highlands

Church
Room

Grove
Farm

LAKESIDE CL.

Street
Farm

AWKWARD

HILL

STREET

East
House

135

Old
Rectory

Cross
(remains of)

Church
Farm

Belvedere
Manor

UPPER

Upper
Strode

Strode
Farm

GRAVEL

PIT

Plaster's
Green

Southmead
Farm

HILL

Gravel Hill
Farm

6

LANE

Dewdown
Lodge

7

60

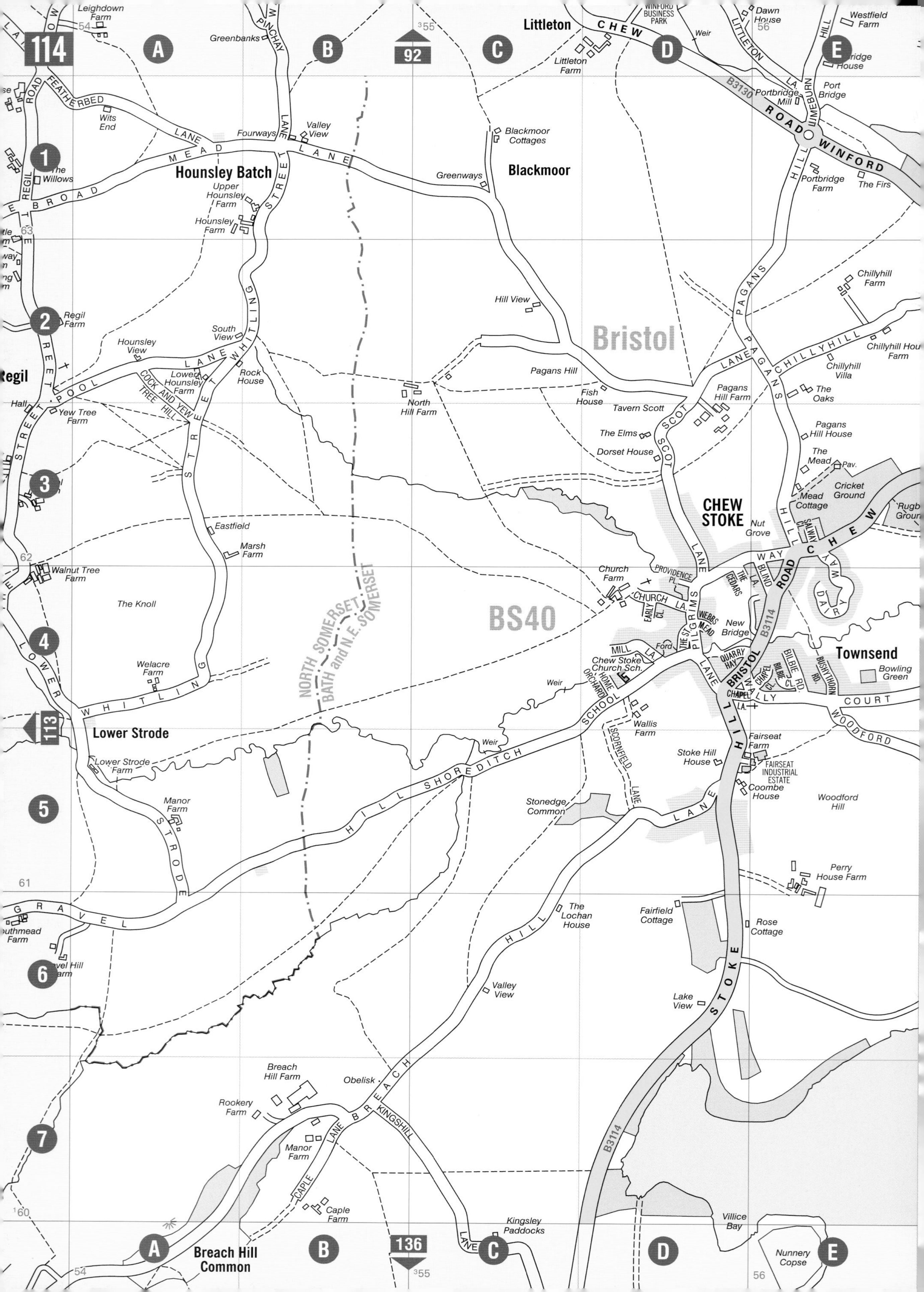

114
A
B
C
D
E
92
113
136
Littleton
Littleton Farm
WINFORD BUSINESS PARK
Leighdown Farm
Greenbanks
PINCHAY
Dawn House
Westfield Farm
Weir
CHEW
LITTLETON LA.
B3130
ROAD
WINFORD
Portbridge Mill
Port Bridge
LIMEBURN HILL
Portbridge Farm
The Firs
FEATHERBED LANE
Wits End
Fourways
Valley View
MEAD LANE
Hounsley Batch
Blackmoor Cottages
Blackmoor
Greenways
The Willows
BROAD
REGIL
Upper Hounsley Farm
Hounsley Farm
Regil Farm
Regil
Hall
Hounsley View
South View
POOL LANE
WHITLING STREET
COCK AND YEW TREE HILL
Lower Hounsley Farm
Rock House
Yew Tree Farm
Hill View
Bristol
Pagans Hill
Fish House
Tavern Scott
North Hill Farm
The Elms
Dorset House
SCOT LANE
PAGANS HILL
Pagans Hill Farm
CHILLYHILL LANE
Chillyhill Farm
Chillyhill Villa
The Oaks
Pagans Hill House
The Mead
Pav.
Cricket Ground
Mead Cottage
CHEW STOKE
Nut Grove
Eastfield
Marsh Farm
Walnut Tree Farm
The Knoll
Church Farm
PROVIDENCE PL.
CHURCH LA.
EARLY CL.
PILGRIMS
THE CEDARS
BLIND LA.
WEBBS MEAD
New Bridge
BS40
DAIRY WAY
B3114
NORTH SOMERSET
BATH and N.E. SOMERSET
MILL LA.
Ford
Chew Stoke Church Sch.
HOME ORCHARD
SCHOOL LANE
QUARRY HAY
BRISTOL
CHAPEL CL.
CHAPEL LA.
BILBIE CL.
BILBIE RD.
BUSHYTHORN RD.
Townsend
Bowling Green
COURT
WOODFORD
Welacre Farm
LOWER WHITLING
Lower Strode
Lower Strode Farm
Weir
Wallis Farm
SCORNFIELD LANE
Fairseat Farm
FAIRSEAT INDUSTRIAL ESTATE
Stoke Hill House
Coombe House
Woodford Hill
Stonedge Common
SHOREDITCH HILL
Manor Farm
STRODE
Perry House Farm
GRAVEL
Southmead Farm
Gravel Hill Farm
The Lochan House
Fairfield Cottage
Rose Cottage
STOKE HILL
Valley View
Lake View
Obelisk
Breach Hill Farm
Rookery Farm
BREACH LANE
KINGSHILL
Manor Farm
CAPLE LANE
Caple Farm
Kingsley Paddocks
Villice Bay
Nunnery Copse
Breach Hill Common
1
2
3
4
5
6
7
54
55
56
60
61
62
63

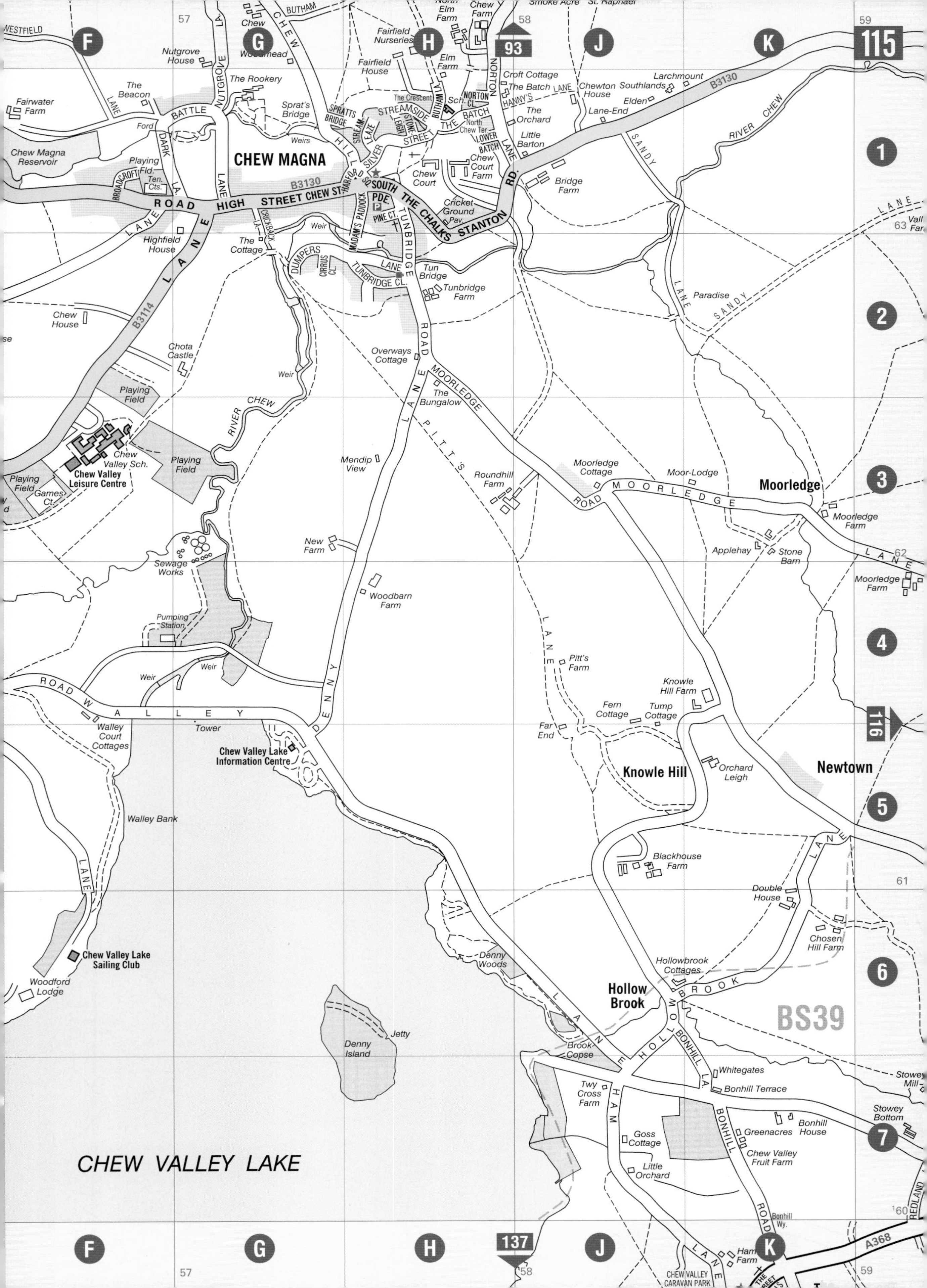
CHEW MAGNA
Chew Magna Reservoir
Fairwater Farm
The Beacon
Nutgrove House
Chew Woodmead
The Rookery
Sprat's Bridge
Fairfield Nurseries
Fairfield House
Elm Farm
North Elm Farm
Chew Farm
Croft Cottage
The Batch
Chewton House
Southlands
Larchmount
Elden
Lane-End
The Orchard
Little Barton
Chew Court
Chew Court Farm
Bridge Farm
Cricket Ground Pav.
Highfield House
The Cottage
Tun Bridge
Tunbridge Farm
Chew House
Chota Castle
Overways Cottage
The Bungalow
Paradise
Playing Field
Chew Valley Sch.
Chew Valley Leisure Centre
Games Ct.
Mendip View
Roundhill Farm
Moorledge Cottage
Moor-Lodge
Moorledge
Moorledge Farm
Applehay
Stone Barn
New Farm
Sewage Works
Woodbarn Farm
Pumping Station
Pitt's Farm
Knowle Hill Farm
Fern Cottage
Tump Cottage
Far End
Walley Court Cottages
Tower
Chew Valley Lake Information Centre
Knowle Hill
Orchard Leigh
Newtown
Walley Bank
Blackhouse Farm
Double House
Chosen Hill Farm
Chew Valley Lake Sailing Club
Woodford Lodge
Denny Woods
Hollowbrook Cottages
Hollow Brook
BS39
Denny Island
Jetty
Brook Copse
Twy Cross Farm
Whitegates
Bonhill Terrace
Stowey Mill
Stowey Bottom
Goss Cottage
Greenacres
Bonhill House
Chew Valley Fruit Farm
Little Orchard
CHEW VALLEY LAKE
Ham Farm
CHEW VALLEY CARAVAN PARK
B3130
B3114
A368
93
116
137

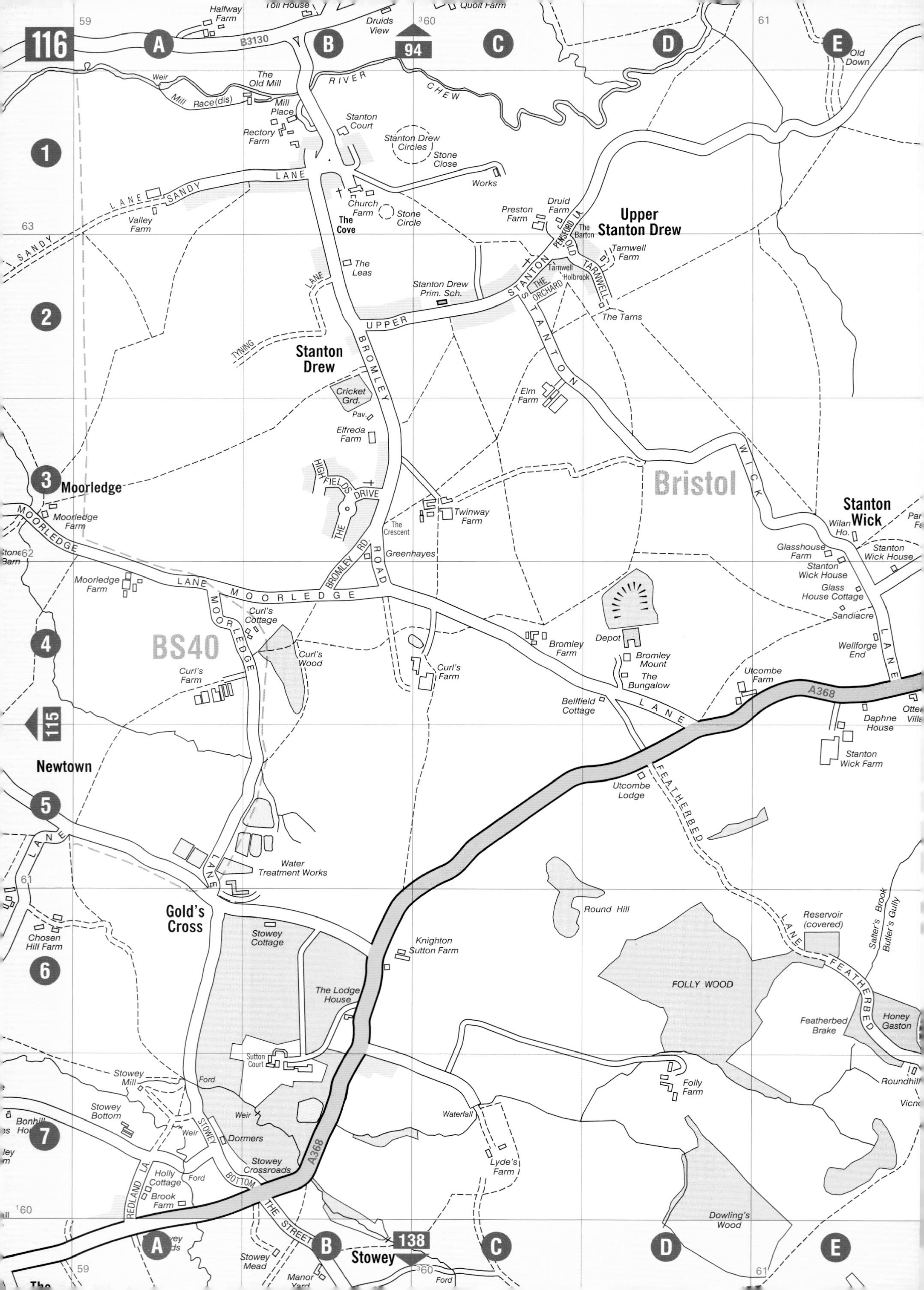
Halfway Farm
Toll House
Quoit Farm
Druids View
94
B3130
A
B
C
D
E
Old Down
59
360
61
Weir
The Old Mill
Mill Race(dis)
Mill Place
RIVER
CHEW
Stanton Court
Rectory Farm
Stanton Drew Circles
Stone Close
Works
SANDY LANE
LANE
Valley Farm
Church Farm
The Cove
Stone Circle
Preston Farm
Druid Farm
PENSFORD LA.
The Barton
Upper Stanton Drew
63
SANDY
The Leas
OLD
TARNWELL
Tarnwell Farm
Tarnwell
Holbrook
THE ORCHARD
Stanton Drew Prim. Sch.
STANTON
UPPER
The Tarns
LANE
TYNING
Stanton Drew
BROMLEY
Elm Farm
Cricket Grd.
Pav.
Elfreda Farm
HIGHFIELDS
THE DRIVE
WICK
Bristol
Moorledge
Moorledge Farm
MOORLEDGE
Twinway Farm
The Crescent
Greenhayes
Stanton Wick
Wilan Ho.
Glasshouse Farm
Stanton Wick House
Glass House Cottage
Sandiacre
Stone Barn
62
BROMLEY RD.
ROAD
Moorledge Farm
LANE
MOORLEDGE
Curl's Cottage
Depot
Bromley Farm
Bromley Mount
The Bungalow
Wellforge End
BS40
Curl's Wood
Curl's Farm
Curl's Farm
Utcombe Farm
A368
Bellfield Cottage
LANE
Daphne House
115
Stanton Wick Farm
Newtown
Utcombe Lodge
FEATHERBED
LANE
Water Treatment Works
61
Gold's Cross
Round Hill
Reservoir (covered)
Salter's Brook
Butler's Gully
Chosen Hill Farm
Stowey Cottage
Knighton Sutton Farm
FOLLY WOOD
The Lodge House
Featherbed Brake
Honey Gaston
Sutton Court
Stowey Mill
Ford
Roundhill
Stowey Bottom
Weir
Waterfall
Folly Farm
Bonhill
Weir
STOWEY
Dormers
Stowey Crossroads
Lyde's Farm
REDLAND LA.
Holly Cottage
Brook Farm
Ford
BOTTOM
THE STREET
160
Dowling's Wood
138
Stowey Mead
Stowey
Manor Yard
Ford
1
2
3
4
5
6
7

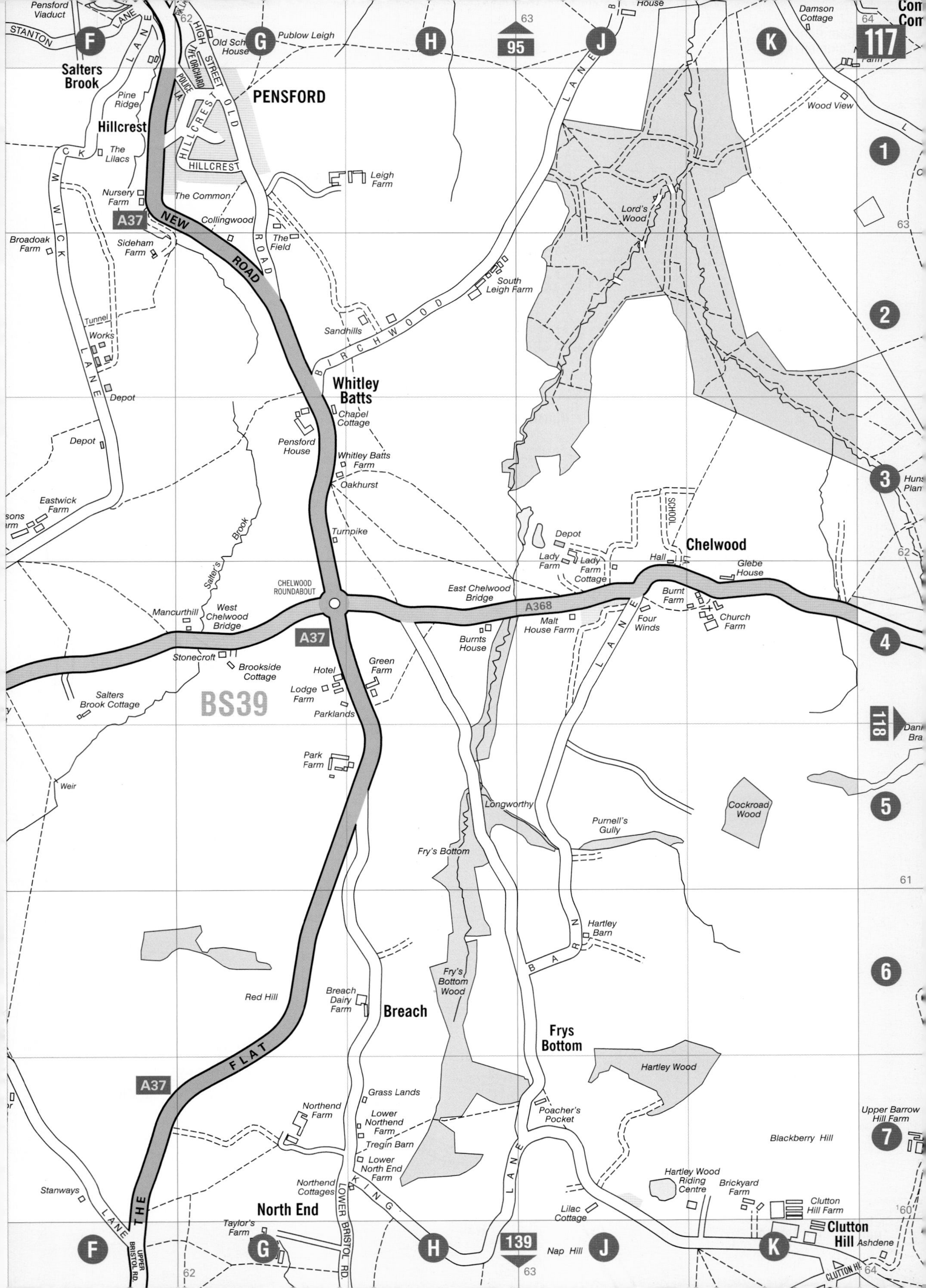

F **G** **H** **95** **J** **K** **117**

STANTON

Pensford
Viaduct

Salters
Brook

Pine
Ridge

Hillcrest

The Lilacs

Nursery
Farm

Broadoak
Farm

Sideham
Farm

The Common

A37

Collingwood

The
Field

NEW ROAD

HILLCREST

HIGH STREET

THE ORCHARD

OLD ROAD

POLICE

PENSFORD

Old School
House

Publow Leigh

Leigh
Farm

South
Leigh Farm

Sandhills

BIRCHWOOD

Whitley
Batts

Chapel
Cottage

Pensford
House

Whitley Batts
Farm

Oakhurst

Turnpike

Lord's
Wood

House

Damson
Cottage

Wood View

1

63

62

2

Chelwood

Depot

Lady
Farm

Lady
Farm
Cottage

SCHOOL

Hall

Glebe
House

Burnt
Farm

Four
Winds

Church
Farm

3

Huns
Plan

62

Tunnel

Works

Depot

Depot

Eastwick
Farm

sons
Farm

Salter's Brook

Mancurthill

West
Chelwood
Bridge

CHELWOOD
ROUNDABOUT

A37

Stonecroft

Salters
Brook Cottage

Brookside
Cottage

Hotel

Lodge
Farm

Green
Farm

Parklands

East Chelwood
Bridge

A368

Burnts
House

Malt
House Farm

4

BS39

LANE

118 Dan
Bra

Cockroad
Wood

5

61

Weir

Park
Farm

Longworthy

Fry's Bottom

Purnell's
Gully

BARN

Hartley
Barn

6

Red Hill

THE FLAT

A37

Breach
Dairy
Farm

Breach

Fry's
Bottom
Wood

Frys
Bottom

Hartley Wood

Upper Barrow
Hill Farm

Blackberry Hill

7

Northend
Farm

Grass Lands

Lower
Northend
Farm

Tregin Barn

Lower
North End
Farm

Northend
Cottages

Poacher's
Pocket

Hartley Wood
Riding
Centre

Brickyard
Farm

Clutton
Hill Farm

Stanways

Taylor's
Farm

North End

LOWER BRISTOL RD

KING LANE

139

Nap Hill

Lilac
Cottage

Clutton
Hill

Ashdene

UPPER BRISTOL RD

LANE

CLUTTON HI

62

63

64

60

F **G** **H** **139** **J** **K**

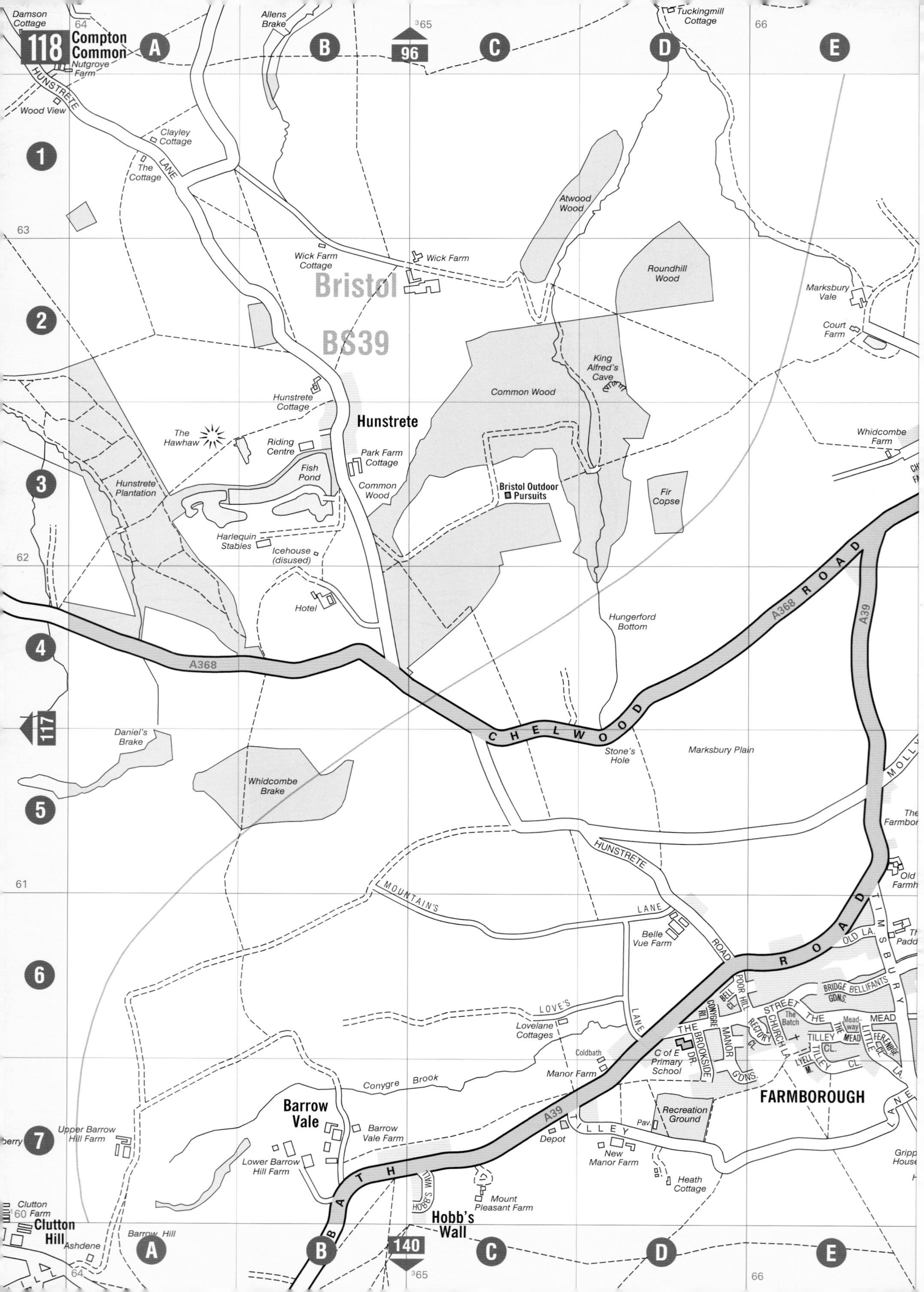
118
Compton Common
Damson Cottage
Nutgrove Farm
Wood View
Allens Brake
96
Tuckingmill Cottage
A
B
C
D
E
1
2
3
4
5
6
7
HUNSTRETE LANE
Clayley Cottage
The Cottage
Atwood Wood
Wick Farm Cottage
Wick Farm
Bristol
BS39
Roundhill Wood
Marksbury Vale
Court Farm
King Alfred's Cave
Common Wood
Hunstrete Cottage
Hunstrete
The Hawhaw
Riding Centre
Park Farm Cottage
Whidcombe Farm
Fish Pond
Common Wood
Hunstrete Plantation
Bristol Outdoor Pursuits
Fir Copse
Harlequin Stables
Icehouse (disused)
Hotel
Hungerford Bottom
A368
A368 ROAD
A39
CHELWOOD
117
Daniel's Brake
Stone's Hole
Marksbury Plain
Whidcombe Brake
HUNSTRETE ROAD
MOUNTAIN'S LANE
Belle Vue Farm
Old Farm
TIMSBURY ROAD
OLD LA.
LOVE'S LANE
Lovelane Cottages
POOR HILL
BELL CL.
CONYGRE RI.
STREET
THE BROOKSIDE DR.
MANOR GDNS.
RECTORY CL.
CHURCH LA.
The Batch
THE MEAD
Meadway
MEAD
TILLEY CL.
TILLEY
LYELL M.
LITTLE
FERNDGE CL.
BRIDGE GDNS.
BELLIFANTS
Coldbath
Manor Farm
C of E Primary School
Conygre Brook
Barrow Vale
Barrow Vale Farm
Recreation Ground
FARMBOROUGH
Upper Barrow Hill Farm
A39
TILLEY
Depot
Pav.
New Manor Farm
Lower Barrow Hill Farm
BATH
HOBB'S WALL
Mount Pleasant Farm
Heath Cottage
Clutton Farm
Clutton Hill
Ashdene
Barrow Hill
Hobb's Wall
140
64
365
66
63
62
61
60

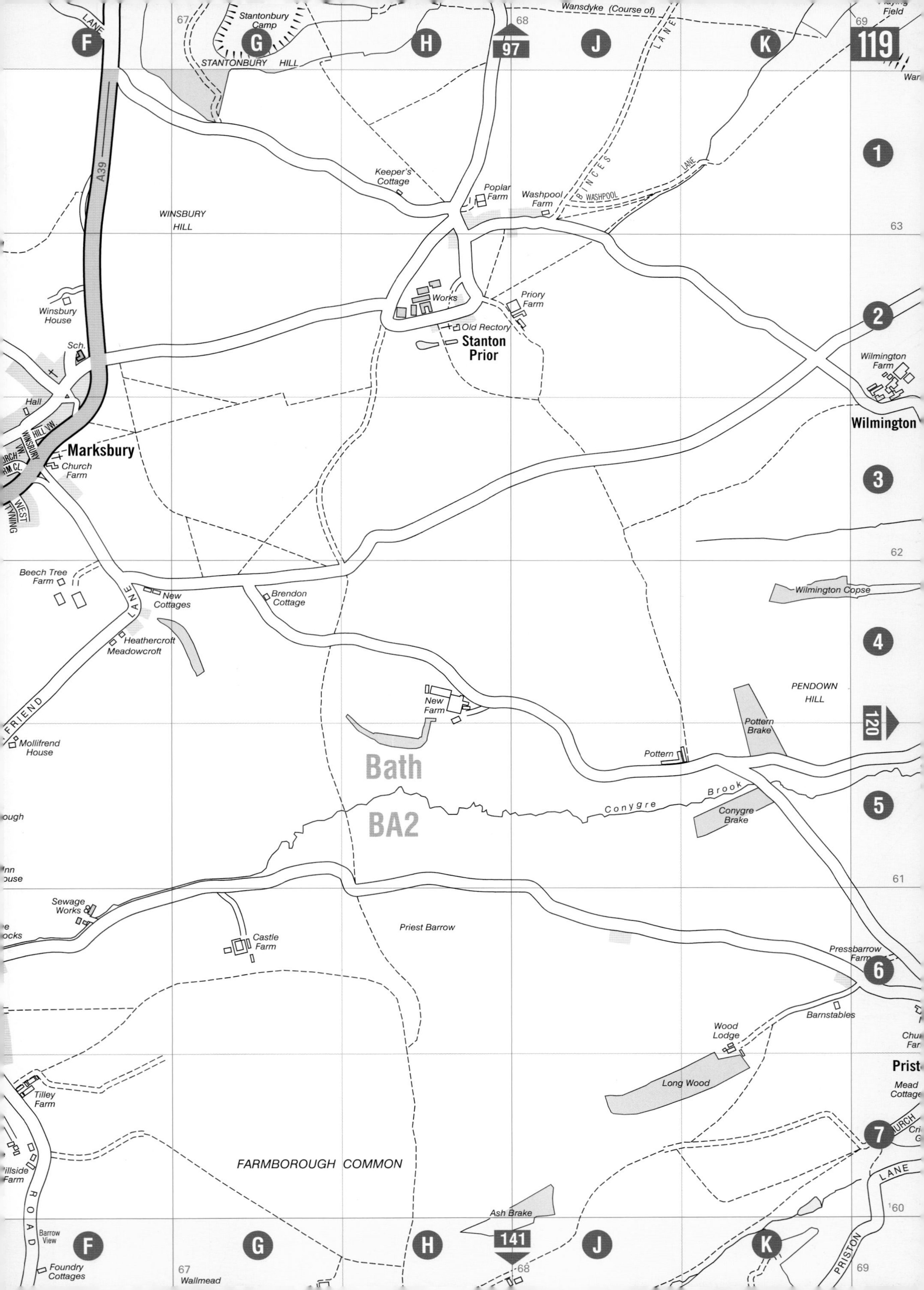

Wansdyke (Course of)

Playing
Field

War

1

63

Stantonbury
Camp

STANTONBURY HILL

Keeper's
Cottage

Poplar
Farm

Washpool
Farm

WASHPOOL

WINSBURY
HILL

A39

Winsbury
House

Works

Priory
Farm

2

Wilmington
Farm

Sch.

Old Rectory

**Stanton
Prior**

Wilmington

Hall

HILL VW.

WINSBURY

Marksbury

Church
Farm

3

62

Beech Tree
Farm

New
Cottages

Brendon
Cottage

Wilmington Copse

FRIEND LANE

Heathercroft
Meadowcroft

4

PENDOWN
HILL

120

Mollifrend
House

New
Farm

Pottern
Brake

Pottern

Bath

Conygre   Brook

5

BA2

Conygre
Brake

61

nn
ouse

Sewage
Works

Priest Barrow

ocks

Castle
Farm

Pressbarrow
Farm

6

Barnstables

Wood
Lodge

Chu
Far

Tilley
Farm

Prist

Mead
Cottage

Long Wood

7

URCH

Cri
G

illside
Farm

FARMBOROUGH COMMON

ROAD

Ash Brake

LANE

PRISTON

160

Barrow
View

Foundry
Cottages

67
Wallmead

67
68

69

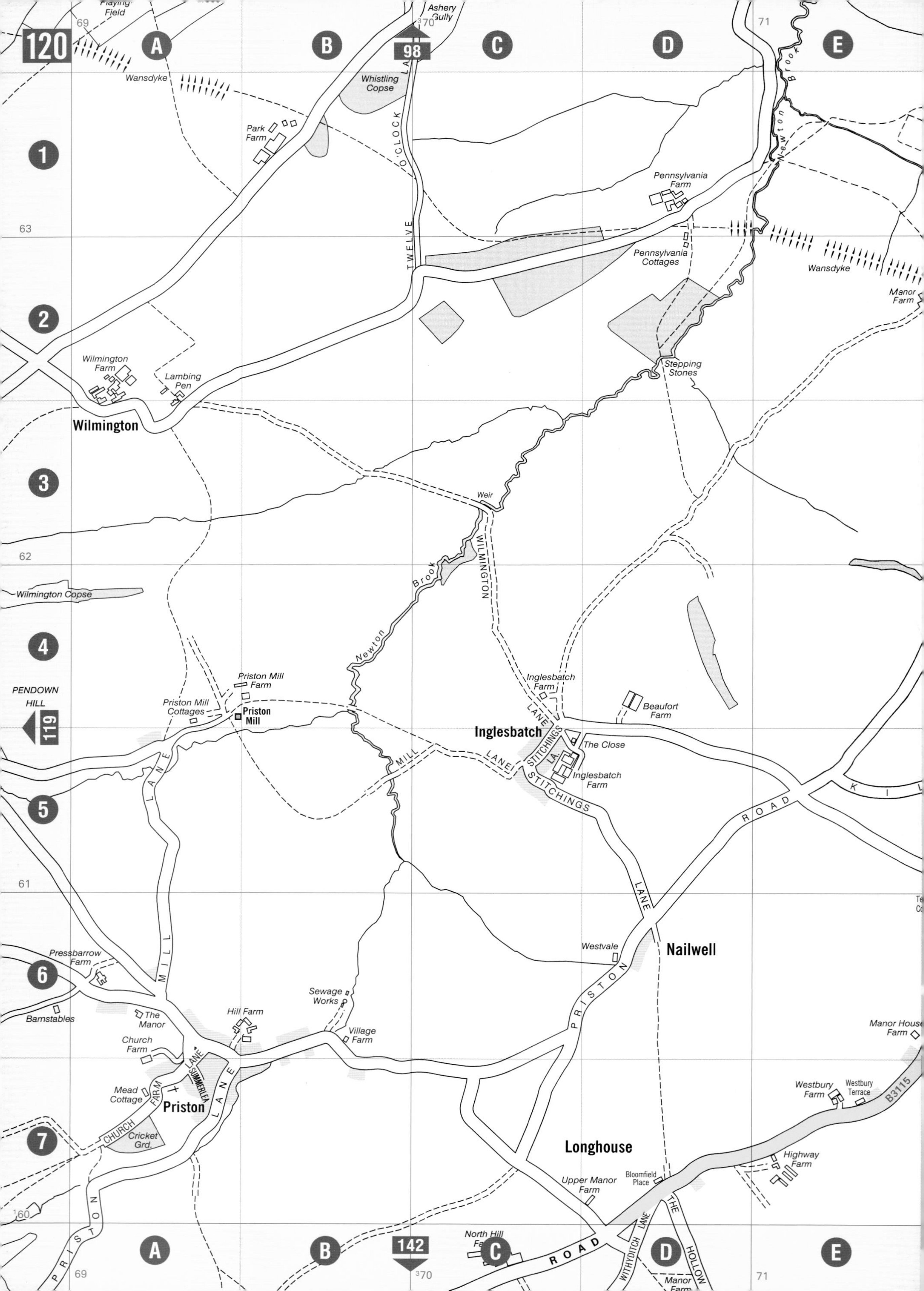

120

A B 98 C D E

1

Playing Field
Wansdyke
Whistling Copse
Park Farm
Ashery Gully
370
Pennsylvania Farm
71

63

Pennsylvania Cottages
Wansdyke
Manor Farm

2

Wilmington Farm
Lambing Pen
Stepping Stones

Wilmington

Weir

3

Wilmington Copse
Newton Brook
Wilmington Lane

62

4

PENDOWN HILL
119
Priston Mill Farm
Priston Mill Cottages
Priston Mill
Inglesbatch Farm
Beaufort Farm

Inglesbatch
The Close
Inglesbatch Farm
STITCHINGS LA
LANE STITCHINGS

5

LANE
MILL
LANE
ROAD
KI

61

6

Pressbarrow Farm
Barnstables
The Manor
Hill Farm
Sewage Works
Village Farm
Westvale
Nailwell
Manor House Farm

Church Farm

7

Mead Cottage
Priston
Cricket Grd.
CHURCH FARM SUMMERVILLE LANE
MILL LANE
Longhouse
Upper Manor Farm
Bloomfield Place
Westbury Farm
Westbury Terrace
B3115
Highway Farm

160
PRISTON LANE
69
North Hill Fm
142
370
ROAD
WITHYDITCH LANE
Manor Farm
THE HOLLOW
71

A B 142 C D E

Newton Brook
Mill Brook
PRISTON LANE

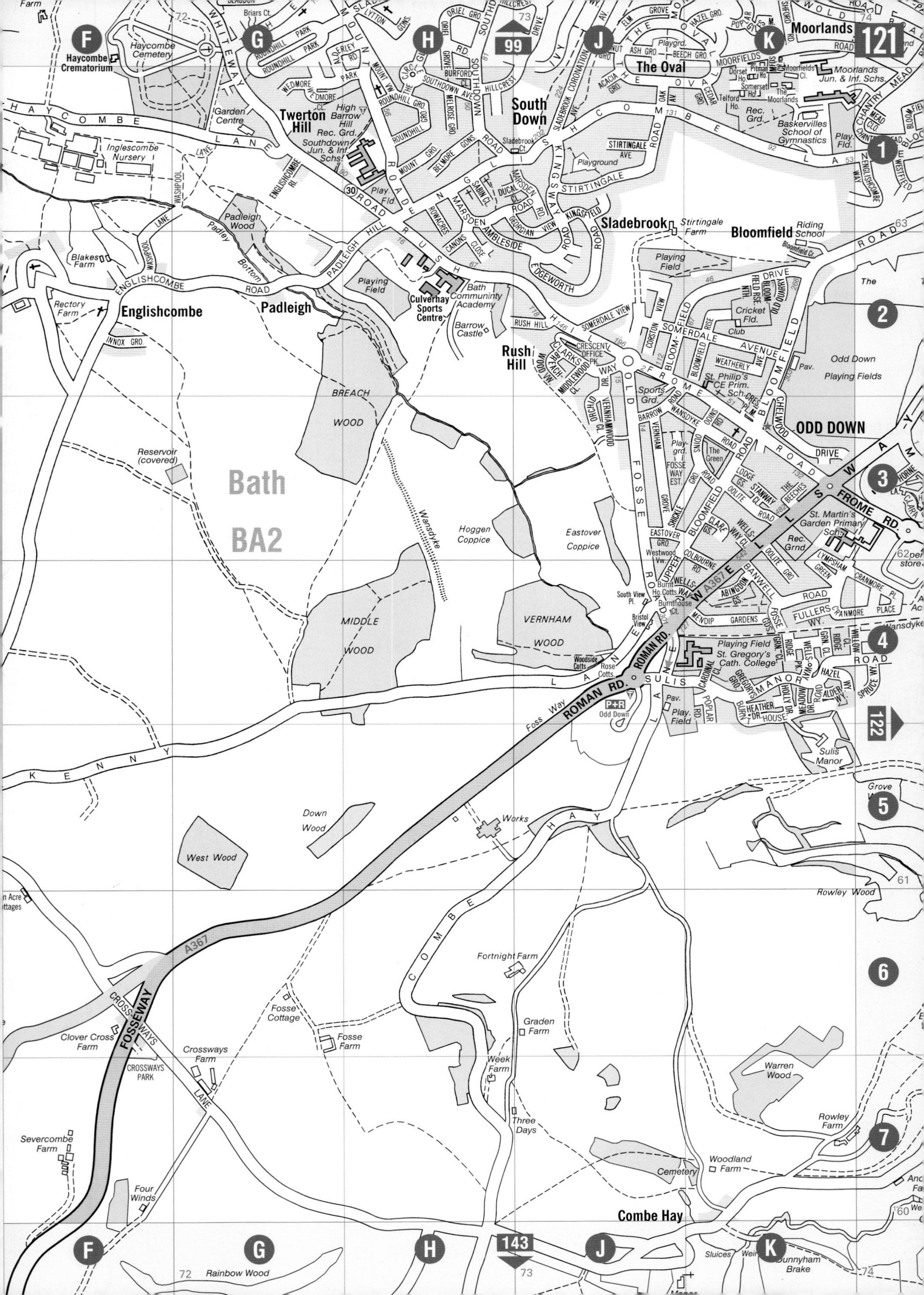

99
143
122
Bath
BA2
Haycombe Crematorium
Haycombe Cemetery
Twerton Hill
South Down
The Oval
Moorlands
Sladebrook
Bloomfield
Englishcombe
Padleigh
Rush Hill
ODD DOWN
Combe Hay
HAYCOMBE LANE
Inglescombe Nursery
Padleigh Wood
Blakes Farm
Rectory Farm
Culverhay Sports Centre
Bath Community Academy
Barrow Castle
Stirtingale Farm
Riding School
Odd Down Playing Fields
St. Philip's CE Prim. Sch.
St. Martin's Garden Primary Sch.
St. Gregory's Cath. College
Breach Wood
Middle Wood
Vernham Wood
Hoggen Coppice
Eastover Coppice
Wansdyke
Reservoir (covered)
Down Wood
West Wood
Works
Fortnight Farm
Graden Farm
Week Farm
Three Days
Woodland Farm
Cemetery
Warren Wood
Rowley Farm
Rowley Wood
Sulis Manor
Clover Cross Farm
Crossways Farm
CROSSWAYS PARK
Severcombe Farm
Four Winds
Fosse Cottage
Fosse Farm
Rainbow Wood
Sluices
Weir
Dunnyham Brake
KENNY
ROMAN RD.
FOSSEWAY
A367
Foss Way
P+R Odd Down
COMBE HAY LANE
WELLS ROAD
FROME RD.

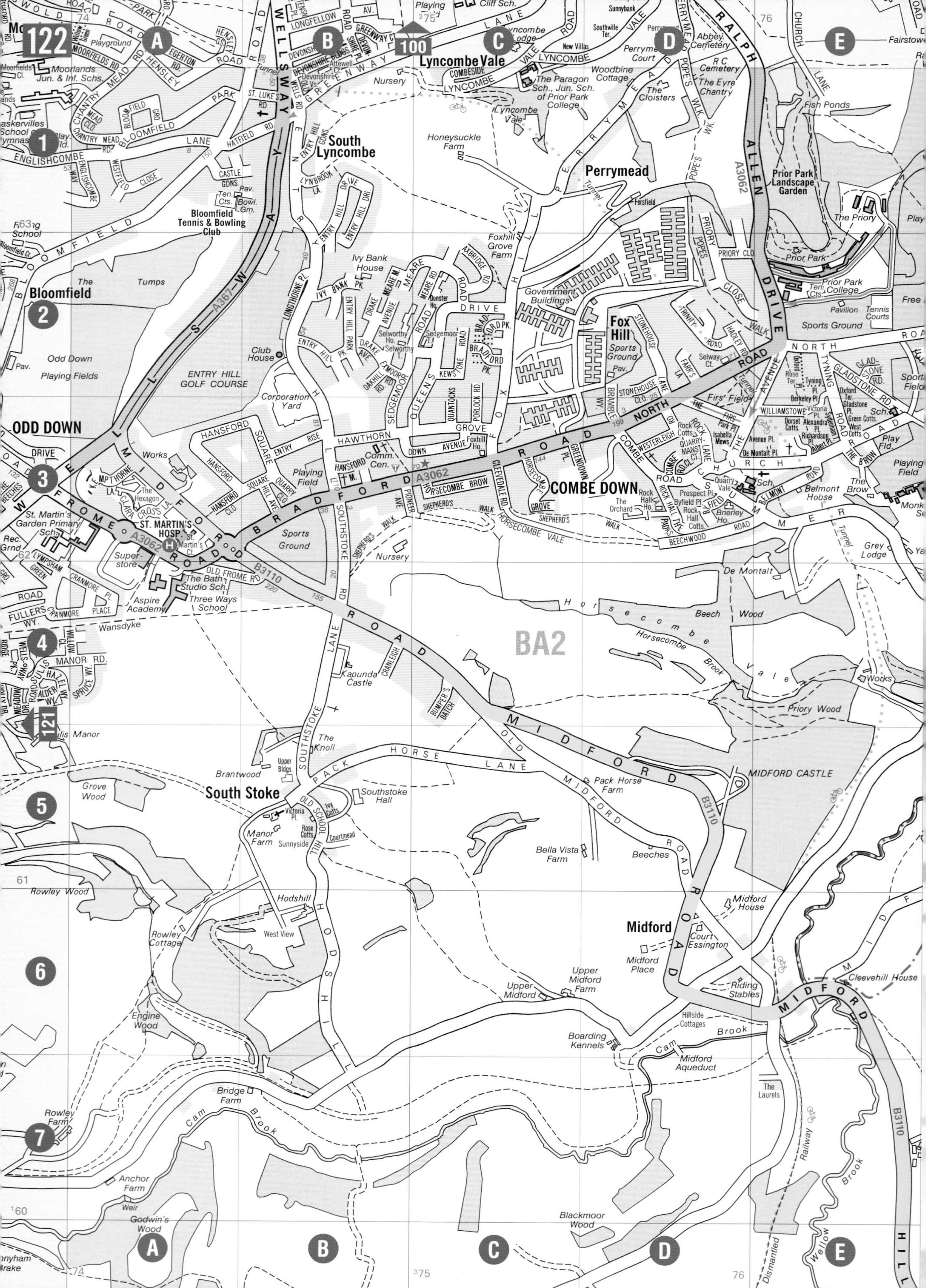

122
100
121
Lyncombe Vale
South Lyncombe
Perrymead
Bloomfield
Odd Down
Fox Hill
Combe Down
South Stoke
Midford
BA2
Wellsway
A367
A3062
B3110
Ralph Allen Drive
Bradford Road
North Road
Midford Road
Old Midford Road
Pack Horse Lane
Southstoke Road
Entry Hill
Frome Road
Longfellow Av.
Greenway Lane
Lyncombe Hill
Perrymead
Church Lane
Bloomfield Road
Englishcombe Lane
Hodshill
Southstoke Lane
Priory Close
Church Road
Hansford Square
Queens Drive
Quantocks
Porlock Rd
Bradford Pk.
Shepherd's Walk
Horsecombe Vale
Beechwood Road
Belmont
Tyning Road
Gladstone Rd.
Entry Hill Golf Course
Odd Down Playing Fields
Bloomfield Tennis & Bowling Club
Prior Park Landscape Garden
Prior Park College
The Priory
Sports Ground
Government Buildings
St. Martin's Hosp.
St. Martin's Garden Primary Sch.
The Bath Studio Sch.
Three Ways School
Aspire Academy
Super-store
Wansdyke
Kapunda Castle
Midford Castle
Pack Horse Farm
Southstoke Hall
Manor Farm
Bella Vista Farm
Midford House
Court Essington
Midford Place
Upper Midford Farm
Upper Midford
Riding Stables
Boarding Kennels
Midford Aqueduct
Cam Brook
Bridge Farm
Rowley Wood
Rowley Cottage
Rowley Farm
Engine Wood
Anchor Farm
Godwin's Wood
Blackmoor Wood
Grove Wood
Brantwood
Beech Wood
Horsecombe Brook
Priory Wood
De Montalt
Grey Lodge
Cleevehill House
Dismantled Railway
Wellow Brook
Hodshill
West View
Honeysuckle Farm
Foxhill Grove Farm
Corporation Yard
Club House
Ivy Bank House
Abbey Cemetery
R C Cemetery
The Eyre Chantry
The Cloisters
Woodbine Cottage
Perrymead Court
The Paragon Sch., Jun. Sch. of Prior Park College
Moorlands Jun. & Inf. Schs.
Fish Ponds
Nursery
A B C D E
1 2 3 4 5 6 7
74 375 76
61 60 62 63

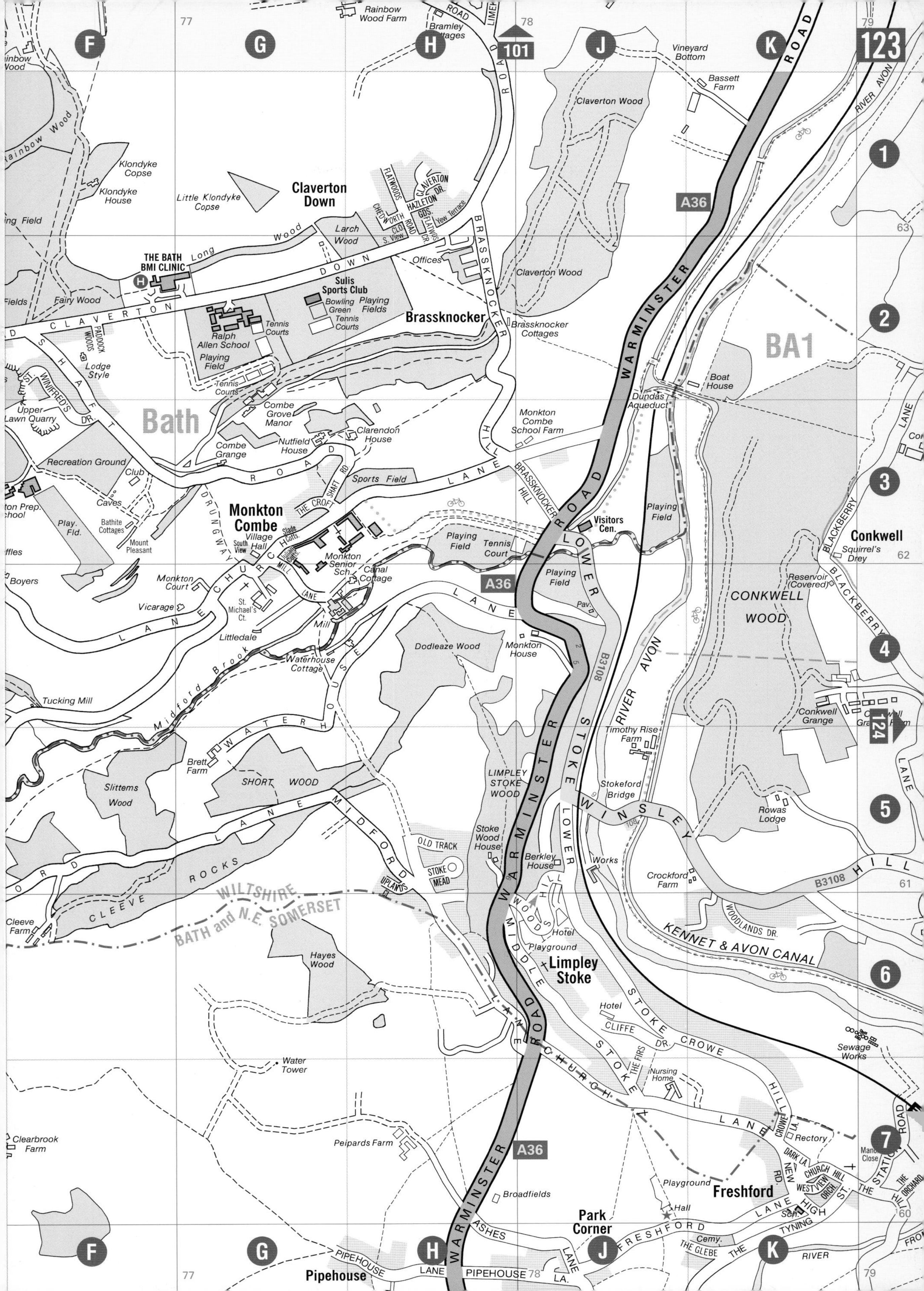

123
101
124
F
G
H
J
K
1
2
3
4
5
6
7
77
78
79
63
62
61
60
Rainbow Wood Farm
Bramley Cottages
Vineyard Bottom
Bassett Farm
Rainbow Wood
Klondyke Copse
Klondyke House
Little Klondyke Copse
Claverton Down
Claverton Wood
RIVER AVON
A36
Larch Wood
Long Wood
DOWN
THE BATH BMI CLINIC
Fairy Wood
CLAVERTON
Sulis Sports Club
Bowling Green
Playing Fields
Tennis Courts
Ralph Allen School
Playing Field
Offices
View Terrace
BRASSKNOCKER
Brassknocker
Brassknocker Cottages
BA1
Boat House
Dundas Aqueduct
Bath
Combe Grove Manor
Clarendon House
Nutfield House
Combe Grange
Recreation Ground
Club
Caves
Monkton Combe School Farm
Sports Field
THE CROFT
LANE
Monkton Combe
Village Hall
South View
Monkton Senior Sch.
Canal Cottage
Playing Field
Tennis Court
Visitors Cen.
Conkwell
Squirrel's Drey
Reservoir (Covered)
CONKWELL WOOD
BLACKBERRY
Bathite Cottages
Mount Pleasant
Monkton Court
Boyers
Vicarage
St. Michael's Ct.
Littledale
Mill
Dodleaze Wood
Monkton House
Waterhouse Cottage
Tucking Mill
Midford Brook
WATERHOUSE
B3108
RIVER AVON
Conkwell Grange
Timothy Rise Farm
Brett Farm
SHORT WOOD
Slittems Wood
LIMPLEY STOKE WOOD
Stokeford Bridge
WINSLEY
Rowas Lodge
LANE
MIDFORD
OLD TRACK
STOKE MEAD
Stoke Wood House
Berkley House
Works
Crockford Farm
HILL
ROCKS
CLEEVE
Cleeve Farm
WILTSHIRE
BATH and N.E. SOMERSET
UPLANDS
WOODLANDS DR.
KENNET & AVON CANAL
Hayes Wood
Hotel
Playground
Limpley Stoke
WARMINSTER ROAD
LOWER STOKE
MIDDLE STOKE
CLIFFE DR.
CROWE
Sewage Works
Water Tower
THE FIRS
Nursing Home
CHURCH LANE
Clearbrook Farm
Peipards Farm
Rectory
Manor Close
DARK LA.
CHURCH HILL
WESTVIEW ORCH.
THE HILL
THE ORCHARD
STATION ROAD
Broadfields
Playground
Freshford
Hall
Sch.
HIGH ST
Park Corner
FRESHFORD LANE
ASHES
Cemy.
THE GLEBE
THE TYNING
RIVER
PIPEHOUSE LANE
Pipehouse

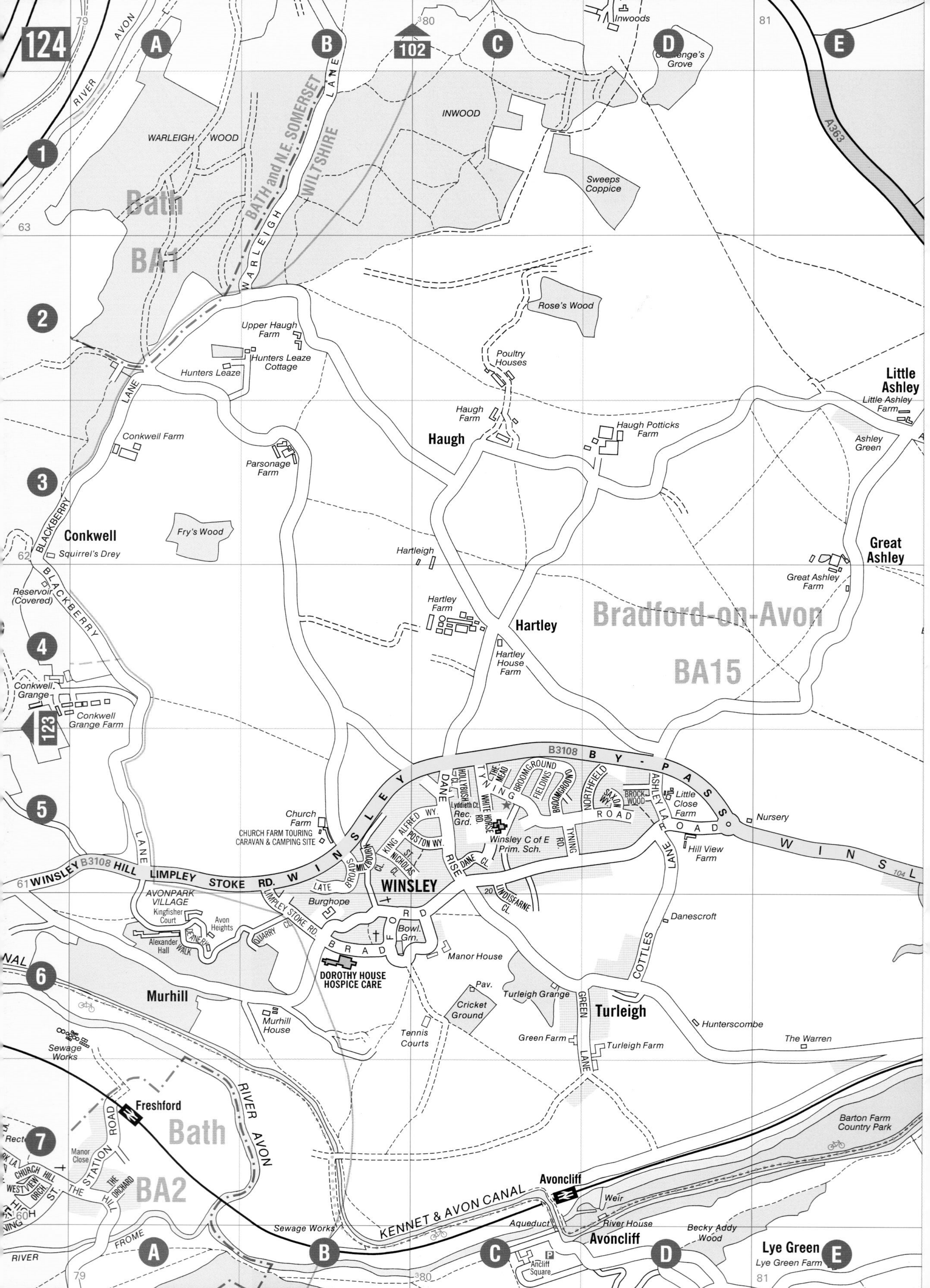

102
123
RIVER AVON
WARLEIGH WOOD
Bath
BA1
BATH and N.E. SOMERSET
WILTSHIRE
WARLEIGH LANE
INWOOD
Inwoods
Sweeps Coppice
A363
Rose's Wood
Upper Haugh Farm
Hunters Leaze Cottage
Hunters Leaze
LANE
Poultry Houses
Little Ashley
Little Ashley Farm
Haugh Farm
Haugh
Haugh Potticks Farm
Ashley Green
Conkwell Farm
Parsonage Farm
BLACKBERRY
Conkwell
Squirrel's Drey
Fry's Wood
Hartleigh
Great Ashley
Great Ashley Farm
Reservoir (Covered)
Hartley Farm
Hartley
Bradford-on-Avon
Hartley House Farm
BA15
Conkwell Grange
Conkwell Grange Farm
B3108 BY-PASS
Nursery
Little Close Farm
Church Farm
CHURCH FARM TOURING CARAVAN & CAMPING SITE
Winsley C of E Prim. Sch.
Hill View Farm
WINSLEY HILL
LIMPLEY STOKE RD.
WINSLEY
AVONPARK VILLAGE
Kingfisher Court
Avon Heights
Alexander Hall
Burghope
Danescroft
Bowl. Grn.
Manor House
DOROTHY HOUSE HOSPICE CARE
KENNET & AVON CANAL
Murhill
Murhill House
Pav.
Cricket Ground
Turleigh Grange
Turleigh
Hunterscombe
The Warren
Green Farm
Turleigh Farm
Tennis Courts
Sewage Works
Freshford
Bath
BA2
Barton Farm Country Park
Manor Close
Avoncliff
Weir
Aqueduct
River House
Becky Addy Wood
Lye Green
Lye Green Farm
Ancliff Square
RIVER FROME

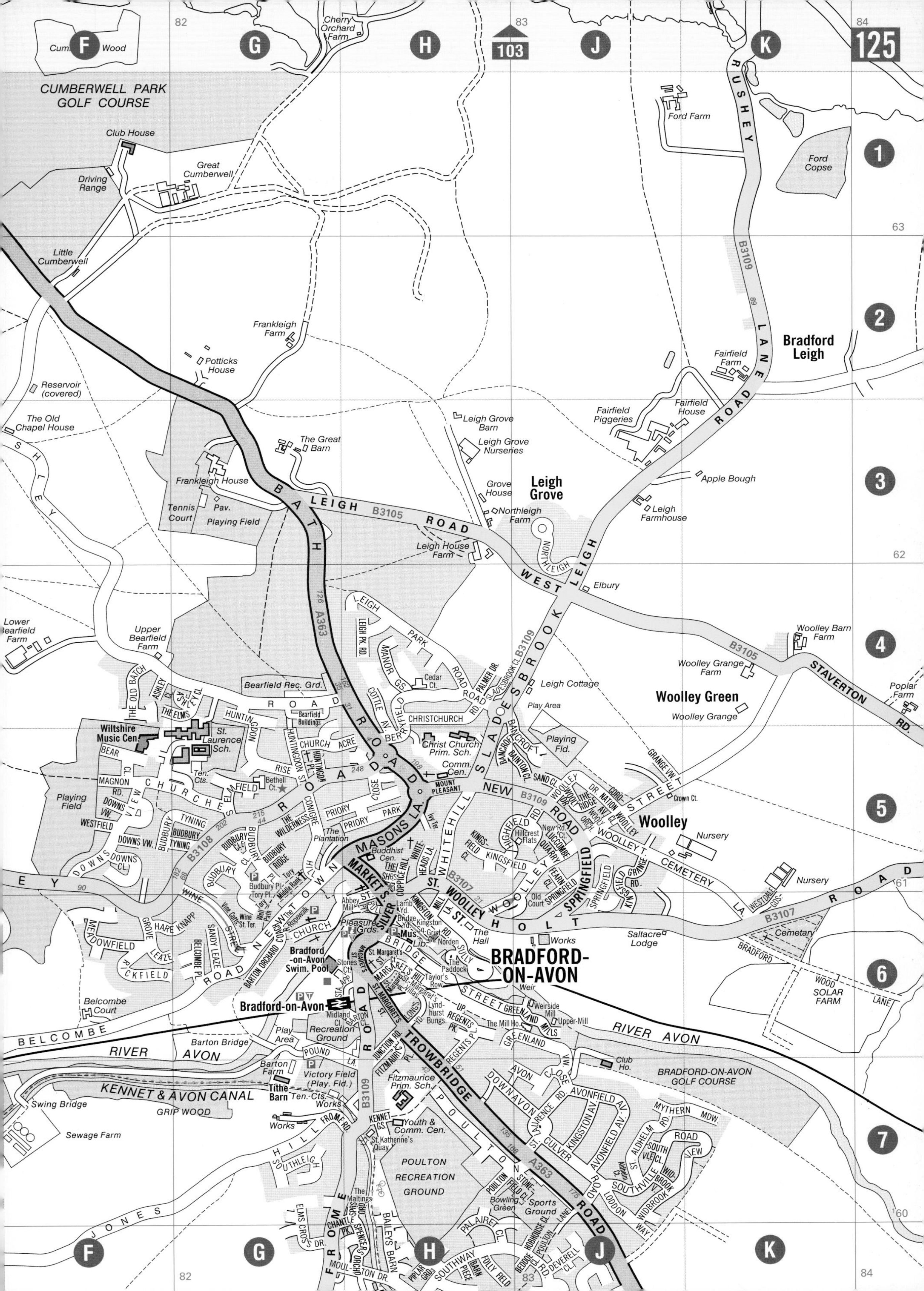
CUMBERWELL PARK
GOLF COURSE
Club House
Driving Range
Great Cumberwell
Little Cumberwell
Cherry Orchard Farm
103
Ford Farm
Ford Copse
RUSHEY LANE ROAD
B3109
Frankleigh Farm
Potticks House
Reservoir (covered)
The Old Chapel House
Bradford Leigh
Fairfield Farm
Fairfield House
Fairfield Piggeries
Leigh Grove Barn
Leigh Grove Nurseries
The Great Barn
Frankleigh House
Tennis Court
Pav.
Playing Field
Apple Bough
Leigh Farmhouse
Grove House
Leigh Grove
Northleigh Farm
LEIGH ROAD
B3105
WEST LEIGH
BATH ROAD
A363
Leigh House Farm
Elbury
Lower Bearfield Farm
Upper Bearfield Farm
Woolley Barn Farm
STAVERTON RD.
Woolley Grange Farm
Poplar Farm
Leigh Cottage
Woolley Green
Woolley Grange
Bearfield Rec. Grd.
Play Area
Playing Fld.
Wiltshire Music Cen.
St. Laurence Sch.
Christ Church Prim. Sch.
Comm. Cen.
Playing Field
Woolley
Nursery
CEMETERY LA.
Nursery
HOLT ROAD
B3107
Cemetary
Saltacre Lodge
The Hall
Works
BRADFORD-ON-AVON
Weir
Bradford-on-Avon Swim. Pool
Bradford-on-Avon
Recreation Ground
Play Area
Barton Bridge
RIVER AVON
Barton Farm
Tithe Barn
Victory Field (Play. Fld.)
KENNET & AVON CANAL
Swing Bridge
GRIP WOOD
Sewage Farm
Fitzmaurice Prim. Sch.
Youth & Comm. Cen.
St. Katherine's Quay
POULTON RECREATION GROUND
TROWBRIDGE ROAD
Club Ho.
BRADFORD-ON-AVON GOLF COURSE
WOOD SOLAR FARM
BRADFORD WOOD LANE
Bowling Green
Sports Ground
The Maltings
JONES HILL
Belcombe Court
BELCOMBE ROAD
Upper-Mill
Weirside Mill
The Mill Ho.
Taylor's Row
Lynd-hurst Bungs.
Buddhist Cen.
The Plantation
Bethell Ct.
MASONS LA.
MARKET ST.
SILVER ST.
NEWTOWN
WINE STREET
Abbey Mill
Pleasure Grds.
Mus.
Lib.
Stones Ct.
Midland Cl.
Bearfield Buildings
MOUNT PLEASANT
New Rd. Ct.
Hillcrest Flats
Old Court
Crown Ct.
Ten. Cts.
F G H J K
1 2 3 4 5 6 7
82 83 84
60 61 62 63

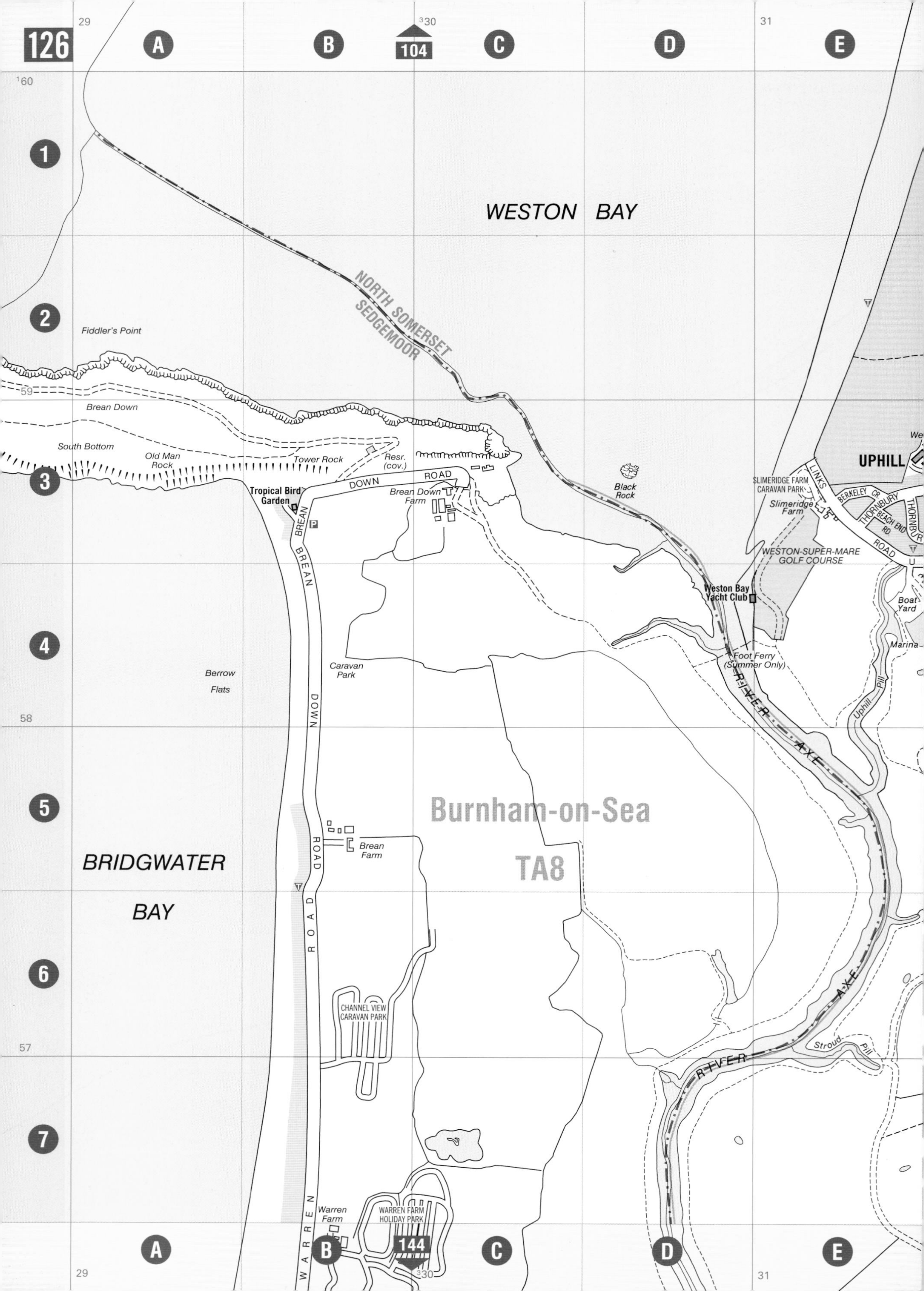

A   B   C   D   E

104

WESTON BAY

Fiddler's Point

NORTH SOMERSET SEDGEMOOR

Brean Down

South Bottom

Old Man Rock

Tower Rock

Resr. (cov.)

DOWN ROAD

Brean Down Farm

Black Rock

SLIMERIDGE FARM CARAVAN PARK

Slimeridge Farm

LINKS

BERKELEY CR

THORNBURY

BEACH END

THORNBURY RD

UPHILL

Tropical Bird Garden

BREAN

WESTON-SUPER-MARE GOLF COURSE

Weston Bay Yacht Club

Boat Yard

Marina

Berrow Flats

Caravan Park

BREAN DOWN

Foot Ferry (Summer Only)

RIVER AXE

Uphill Pill

BRIDGWATER

BAY

Burnham-on-Sea

TA8

Brean Farm

ROAD

CHANNEL VIEW CARAVAN PARK

RIVER AXE

Stroud Pill

WARREN

Warren Farm

WARREN FARM HOLIDAY PARK

144

A   B   C   D   E

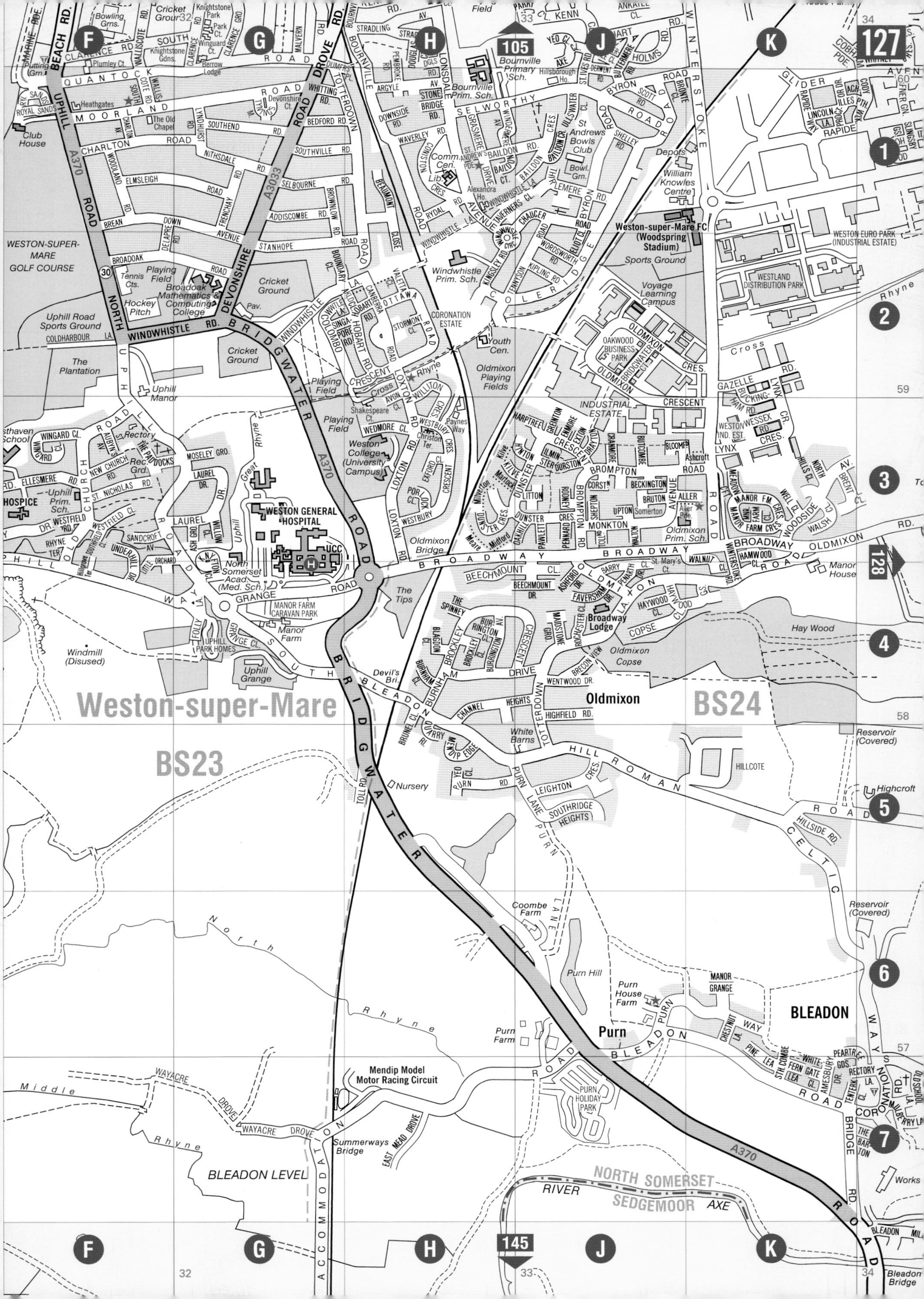
Weston-super-Mare
BS23
BS24
Oldmixon
BLEADON
Purn
WESTON-SUPER-MARE GOLF COURSE
Uphill Road Sports Ground
The Plantation
Cricket Ground
Broadoak Mathematics & Computing College
Playing Field
Tennis Cts.
Hockey Pitch
Club House
Heathgates
The Old Chapel
Devonshire Ct.
Bournville Primary Sch.
Bournville Prim. Sch.
Comm. Cen.
Lib.
Alexandra Ho.
St Andrews Bowls Club
Bowl. Grn.
Depots
William Knowles Centre
Weston-super-Mare FC (Woodspring Stadium)
Sports Ground
WESTON EURO PARK (INDUSTRIAL ESTATE)
WESTLAND DISTRIBUTION PARK
Voyage Learning Campus
OAKWOOD BUSINESS PARK
INDUSTRIAL ESTATE
WESTON IND. EST.
Windwhistle Prim. Sch.
CORONATION ESTATE
Youth Cen.
Oldmixon Playing Fields
Weston College (University Campus)
Shakespeare Ct.
Paynes Way
Christon Ter.
WESTON GENERAL HOSPITAL
UCC
North Somerset Acad. (Med. Sch.)
MANOR FARM CARAVAN PARK
Manor Farm
Uphill Manor
Uphill Grange
UPHILL PARK HOMES
Windmill (Disused)
HOSPICE
Uphill Prim. Sch.
The Tips
Devil's Bri.
Oldmixon Bridge
Oldmixon Prim. Sch.
Broadway Lodge
Oldmixon Copse
Hay Wood
Manor House
White Barns
Nursery
Reservoir (Covered)
Highcroft
HILLCOTE
Coombe Farm
Purn Hill
Purn House Farm
Purn Farm
PURN HOLIDAY PARK
Mendip Model Motor Racing Circuit
Summerways Bridge
BLEADON LEVEL
NORTH SOMERSET
SEDGEMOOR
RIVER AXE
Works
Bleadon Bridge
A370
A3033
BRIDGWATER ROAD
BROADWAY
ROMAN ROAD
CELTIC WAY
WINDWHISTLE RD.
DEVONSHIRE ROAD
UPHILL ROAD NORTH
LOXTON ROAD
BLEADON ROAD
ACCOMMODATION ROAD
WAYACRE DROVE
EAST MEAD DROVE
PURN LANE
OLDMIXON ROAD
OLDMIXON CRES.
WINTERSTOKE ROAD
COLERIDGE ROAD
SELWORTHY ROAD
MOORLAND ROAD
QUANTOCK ROAD
CHARLTON ROAD
TOTTERDOWN ROAD
BURNHAM DRIVE
HIGHFIELD RD.
LEIGHTON CRES.
SOUTHRIDGE HEIGHTS
BRIDGE RD.
North Rhyne
Middle Rhyne
Rhyne
F
G
H
J
K
1
2
3
4
5
6
7
32
33
34
57
58
59
60
105
128
145
30

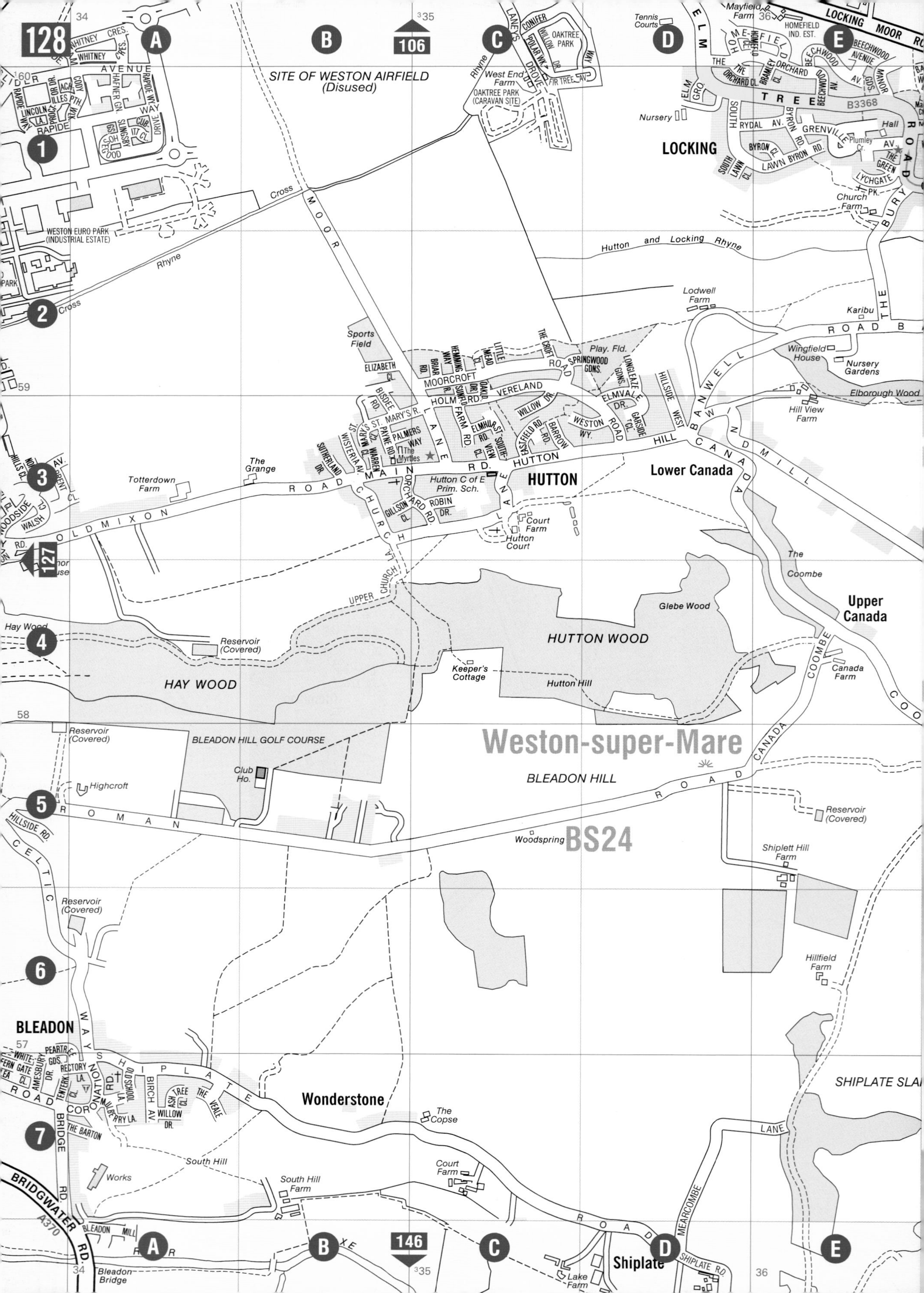
SITE OF WESTON AIRFIELD (Disused)
LOCKING
HUTTON
Lower Canada
Upper Canada
HUTTON WOOD
HAY WOOD
BLEADON HILL GOLF COURSE
BLEADON HILL
Weston-super-Mare
BS24
BLEADON
Wonderstone
Shiplate
SHIPLATE SLAIT
WESTON EURO PARK (INDUSTRIAL ESTATE)
Glebe Wood
The Coombe
Hutton Hill
Keeper's Cottage
Reservoir (Covered)
Woodspring
South Hill
Works
Bleadon Bridge
Lake Farm
Court Farm
South Hill Farm
The Copse
Hillfield Farm
Shiplett Hill Farm
Canada Farm
Hill View Farm
Elborough Wood
Wingfield House
Nursery Gardens
Lodwell Farm
Karibu
Church Farm
Totterdown Farm
The Grange
Hutton C of E Prim. Sch.
Hutton Court
Highcroft
Club Ho.
OAKTREE PARK (CARAVAN SITE)
West End Farm
Tennis Courts
Mayfield Farm
HOMEFIELD IND. EST.
LOCKING MOOR ROAD
B3368
Hutton and Locking Rhyne
Cross Rhyne
MOOR LANE
OLDMIXON ROAD
MAIN ROAD
HUTTON HILL
BANWELL ROAD
CANADA COOMBE
ROMAN ROAD
CANADA ROAD
CELTIC WAY
SHIPLATE ROAD
BRIDGWATER RD. A370
BLEADON MILL
MEARCOMBE LANE
AXE

106
127
146

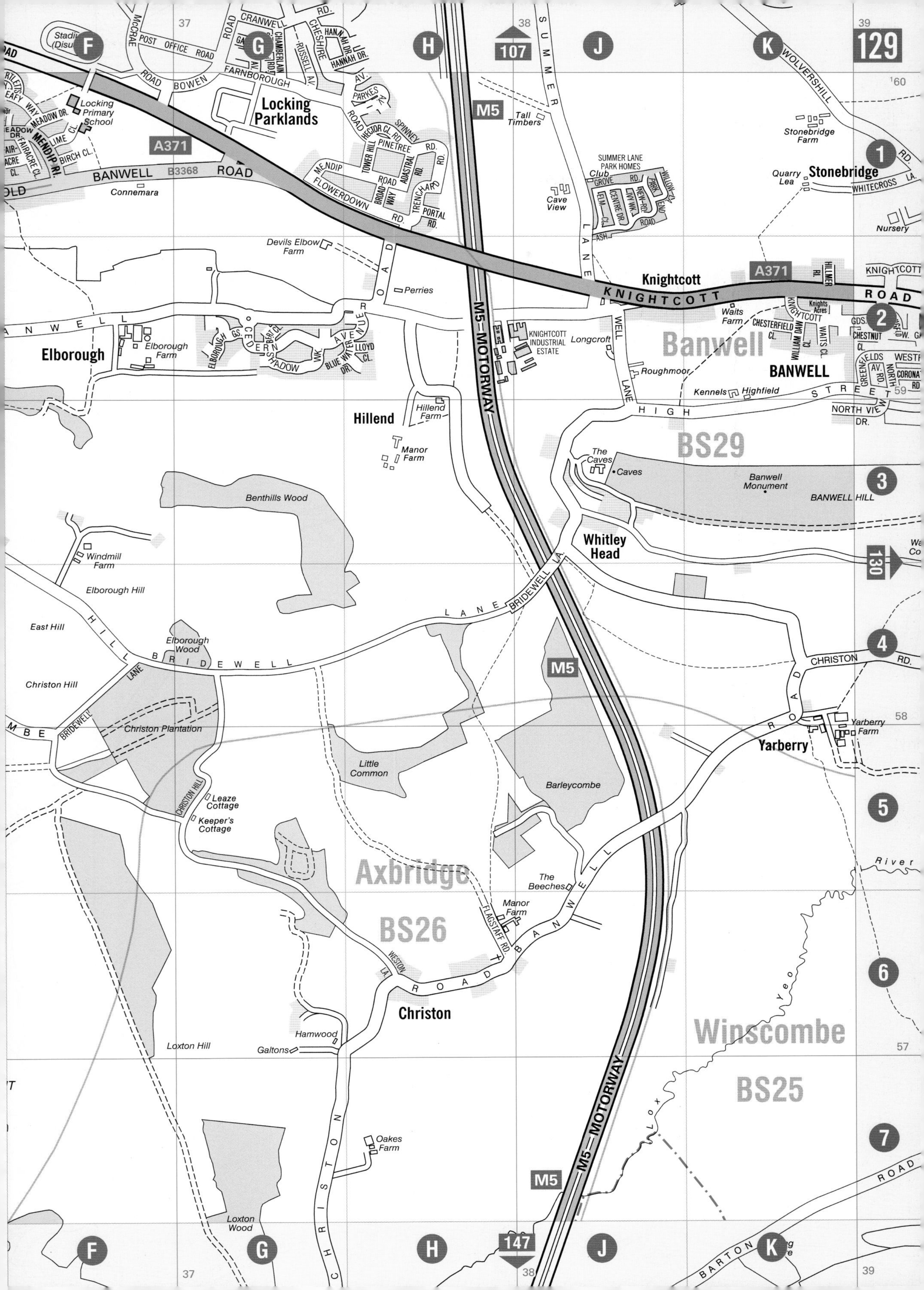

Locking Parklands
Locking Primary School
Elborough
Elborough Farm
Hillend
Hillend Farm
Manor Farm
Benthills Wood
Windmill Farm
Elborough Hill
East Hill
Elborough Wood
Christon Hill
Christon Plantation
Little Common
Barleycombe
Leaze Cottage
Keeper's Cottage
Axbridge
BS26
The Beeches
Manor Farm
Christon
Hamwood
Galtons
Loxton Hill
Oakes Farm
Loxton Wood
Tall Timbers
Cave View
SUMMER LANE PARK HOMES
Club
Knightcott
KNIGHTCOTT ROAD
KNIGHTCOTT INDUSTRIAL ESTATE
Longcroft
Waits Farm
Banwell
BANWELL
Roughmoor
Kennels
Highfield
HIGH STREET
BS29
The Caves
Caves
Banwell Monument
BANWELL HILL
Whitley Head
BRIDEWELL LA.
BRIDEWELL LANE
CHRISTON RD.
Yarberry
Yarberry Farm
River
Yeo
Lox
Winscombe
BS25
Stonebridge Farm
Stonebridge
Quarry Lea
WHITECROSS LA.
Nursery
WOLVERSHILL
Devils Elbow Farm
Perries
Connemara
BANWELL B3368 ROAD
A371
M5
M5 MOTORWAY
BANWELL ROAD
WESTON ROAD
CHRISTON
FLAGSTAFF RD.
CHRISTON HILL
BARTON ROAD
107
147
130

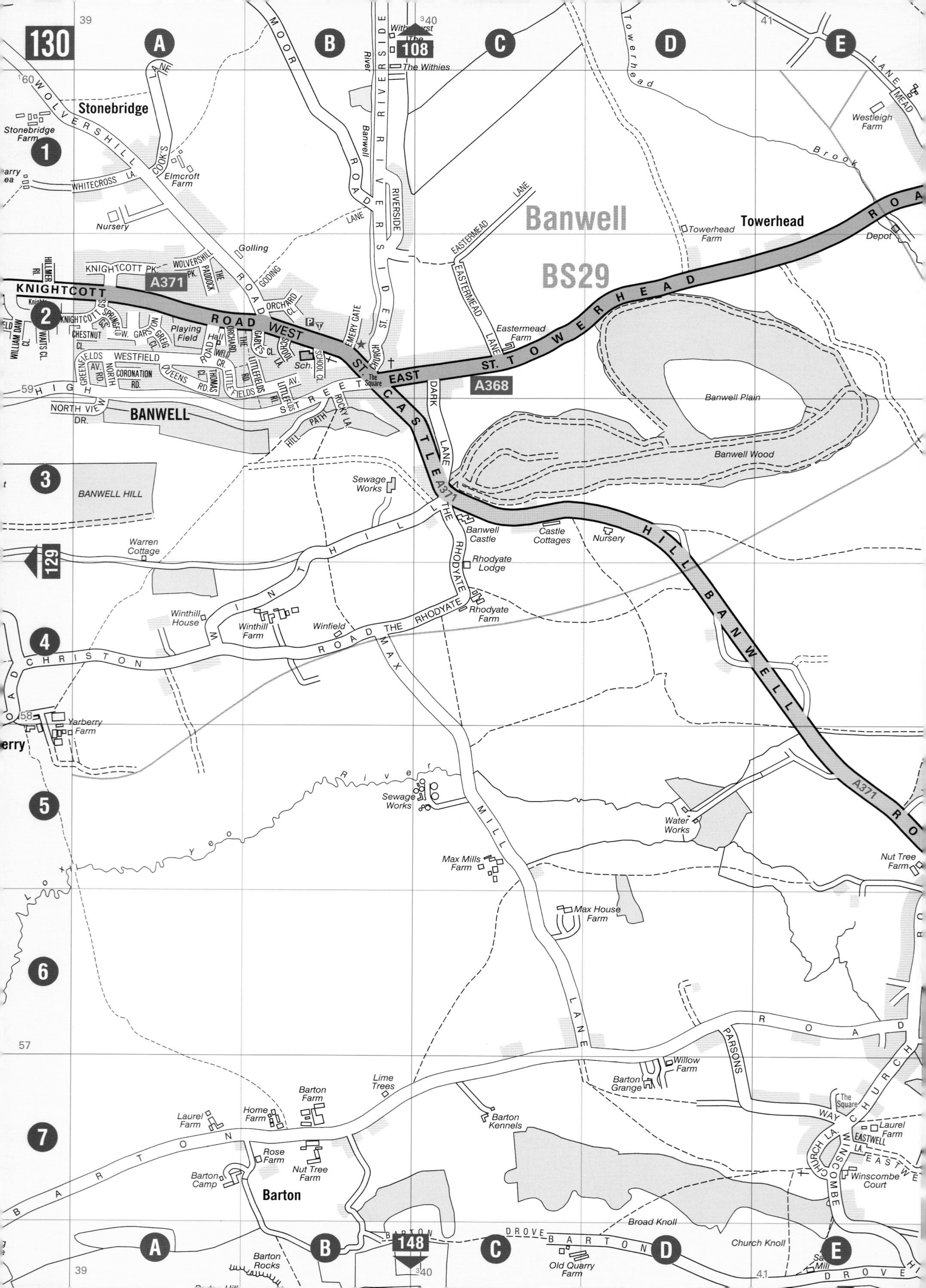

Stonebridge
Stonebridge Farm
Elmcroft Farm
Nursery
Golling
Banwell
BS29
Towerhead
Towerhead Farm
Depot
Westleigh Farm
Eastermead Farm
BANWELL
Banwell Plain
Banwell Wood
BANWELL HILL
Sewage Works
Banwell Castle
Castle Cottages
Nursery
Warren Cottage
Rhodyate Lodge
Rhodyate Farm
Winthill House
Winthill Farm
Winfield
Yarberry Farm
Sewage Works
Water Works
Max Mills Farm
Max House Farm
Nut Tree Farm
Willow Farm
Barton Grange
Lime Trees
Barton Farm
Home Farm
Laurel Farm
Barton Kennels
Rose Farm
Nut Tree Farm
Barton Camp
Barton
Broad Knoll
Church Knoll
Old Quarry Farm
Barton Rocks
Laurel Farm
Winscombe Court
The Square
A371
A368

108
129
148

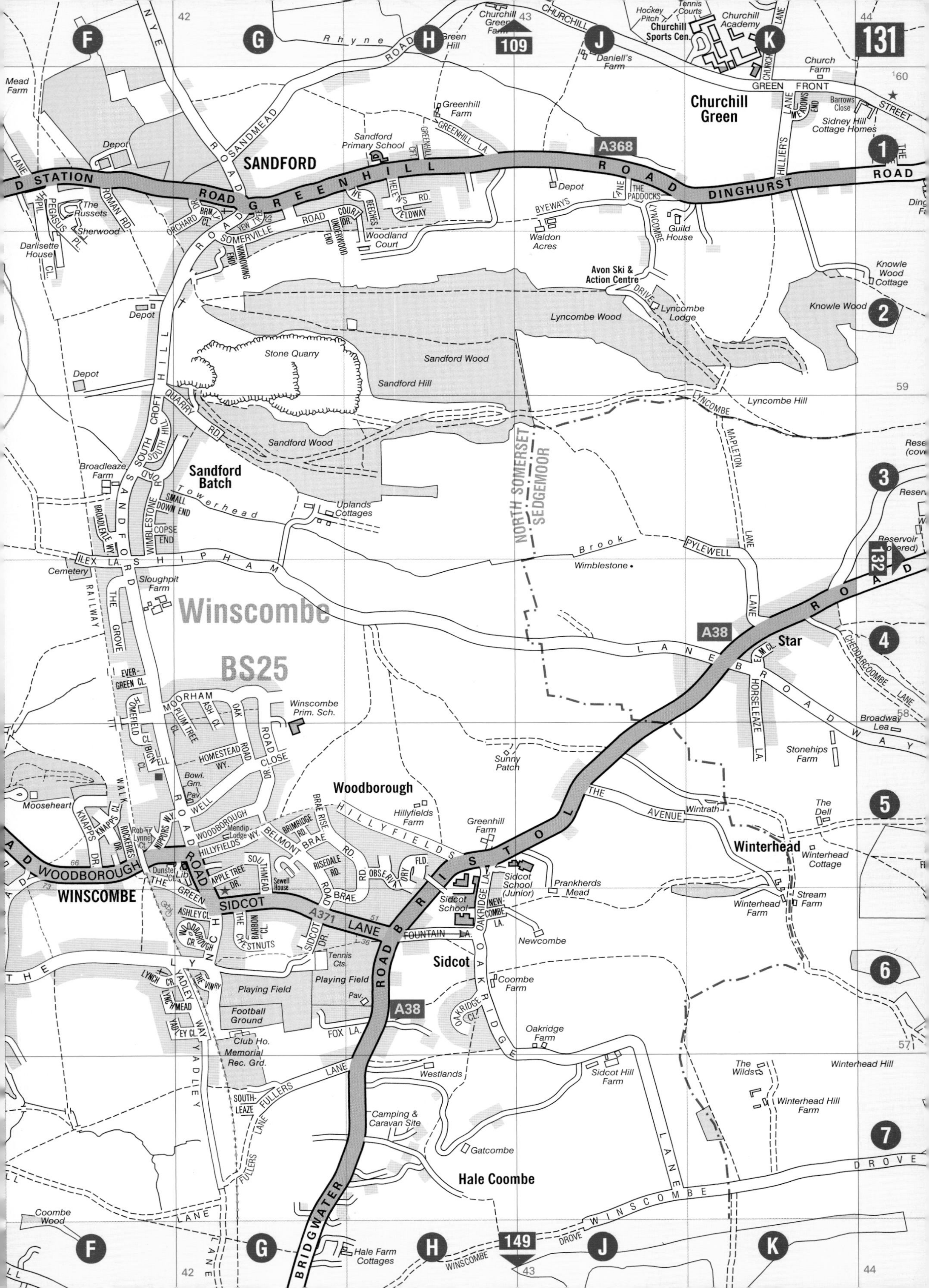
SANDFORD
Churchill Green
Sandford Batch
Winscombe
BS25
Woodborough
WINSCOMBE
Sidcot
Star
Winterhead
Hale Coombe
GREENHILL ROAD
DINGHURST ROAD
STATION ROAD
SHIPHAM LANE
BROADWAY
BRISTOL ROAD
BRIDGWATER ROAD
SIDCOT LANE
WOODBOROUGH ROAD
WINSCOMBE DROVE
A368
A38
A371
Churchill Academy
Churchill Sports Cen.
Sandford Primary School
Winscombe Prim. Sch.
Sidcot School
Sidcot School (Junior)
Stone Quarry
Sandford Wood
Sandford Hill
Lyncombe Wood
Knowle Wood
Lyncombe Hill
Winterhead Hill
Avon Ski & Action Centre
Playing Field
Football Ground
Memorial Rec. Grd.
Camping & Caravan Site
NORTH SOMERSET
SEDGEMOOR
109
132
149

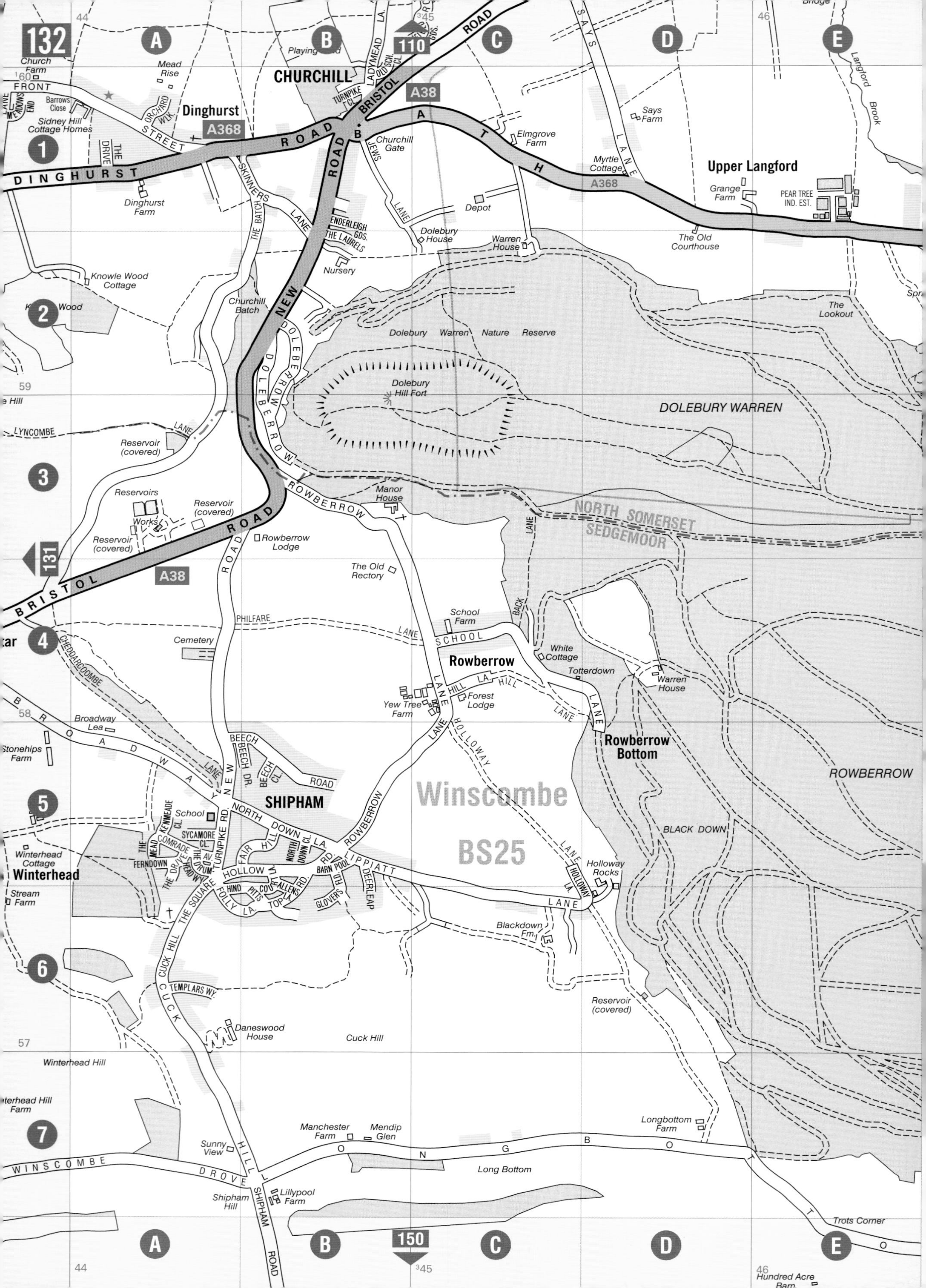
A
B
C
D
E
1
2
3
4
5
6
7
110
131
150
44
345
46
60
59
58
57
CHURCHILL
Dinghurst
Upper Langford
Rowberrow
Rowberrow Bottom
SHIPHAM
Winterhead
Winscombe
BS25
A368
A38
DINGHURST
ROAD
FRONT
STREET
NEW
BRISTOL
BATH
Church Farm
Mead Rise
Playing Field
Barrows Close
Sidney Hill Cottage Homes
ORCHARD WLK.
THE DRIVE
LADYMEAD LA.
OLD SCH. CL.
TURNPIKE CL.
Churchill Gate
JEWS LANE
Says Farm
SAYS LANE
Elmgrove Farm
Myrtle Cottage
Grange Farm
PEAR TREE IND. EST.
Langford Brook
Dinghurst Farm
SKINNERS LANE
THE BATCH
ENDERLEIGH GDS.
THE LAURELS
Nursery
Depot
Dolebury House
Warren House
The Old Courthouse
Knowle Wood Cottage
Knowle Wood
Churchill Batch
DOLEBERROW
Dolebury Warren Nature Reserve
Dolebury Hill Fort
DOLEBURY WARREN
The Lookout
LYNCOMBE LANE
Reservoir (covered)
Reservoirs
Works
Manor House
ROWBERROW
NORTH SOMERSET
SEDGEMOOR
Rowberrow Lodge
The Old Rectory
BACK LANE
School Farm
SCHOOL LANE
PHILFARE LANE
Cemetery
CHEDDARCOOMBE
White Cottage
Totterdown
Warren House
HILL LA.
HILL LANE
Forest Lodge
Yew Tree Farm
HOLLOWAY
BROADWAY
Broadway Lea
Stonehips Farm
BEECH
BEECH DR.
BEECH CL.
BEECH ROAD
NORTH DOWN LA.
School
KENNMEADE CL.
SYCAMORE CL.
COMRADE
THE MEAD
FERNDOWN
THE DRIVE
TURNPIKE RD.
FAIR HILL
NORTH DOWN CL.
BARN POOL
LIPPIATT LANE
DEERLEAP
GLOVERS FLD.
HOLLOW
HIND PITS
ALLENS RD.
TOP LA.
FOLLY LA.
THE SQUARE
CUCK HILL
ROWBERROW
BLACK DOWN
Holloway Rocks
HOLLOWAY LA.
Winterhead Cottage
Stream Farm
Blackdown Fm.
TEMPLARS WY.
Reservoir (covered)
Daneswood House
Cuck Hill
Winterhead Hill
Winterhead Hill Farm
Manchester Farm
Mendip Glen
Longbottom Farm
LONG BOTTOM
Long Bottom
Sunny View
WINSCOMBE DROVE
Shipham Hill
Lillypool Farm
SHIPHAM ROAD
Trots Corner
Hundred Acre Barn

160

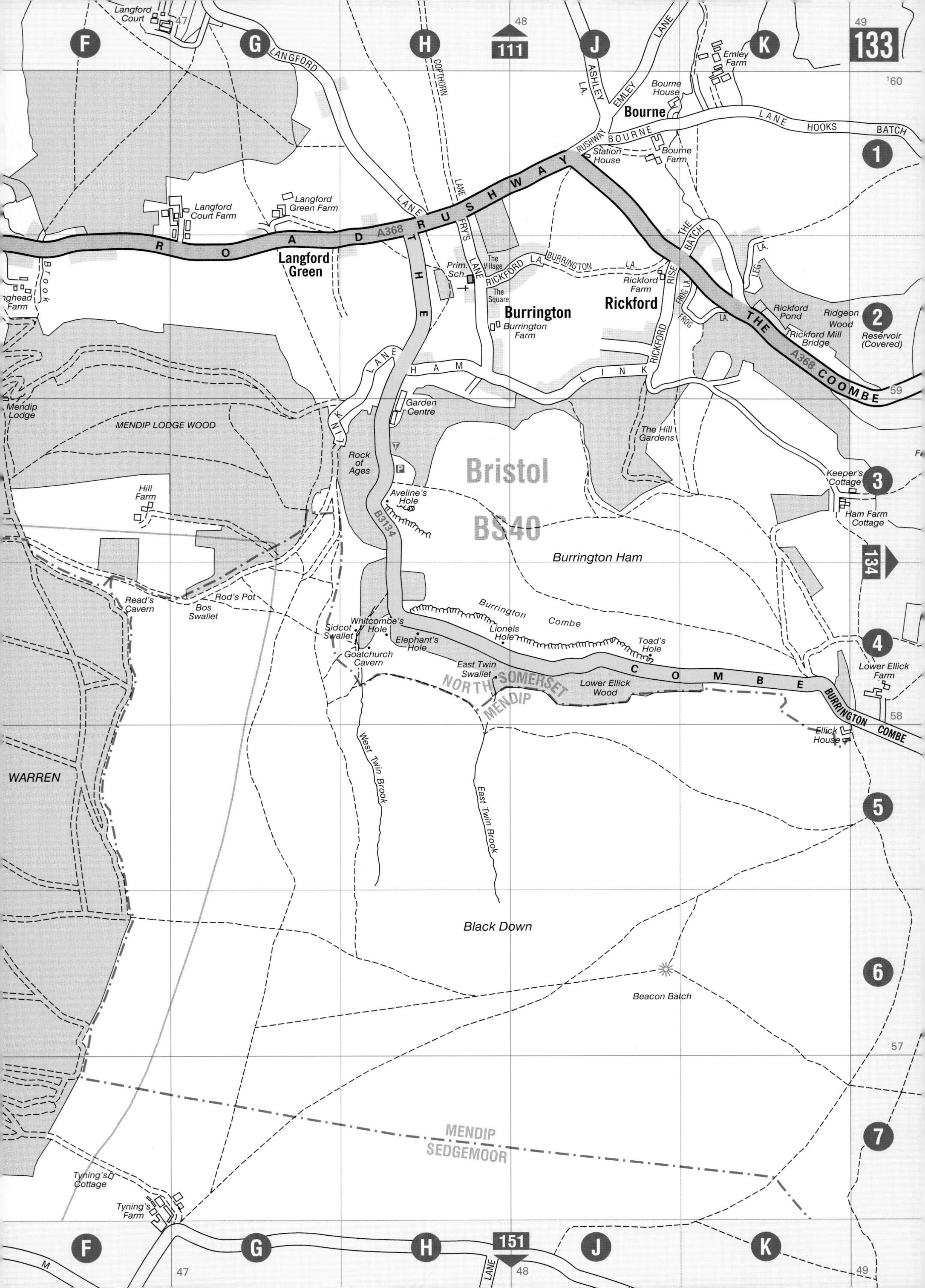

Langford Court
47
Langford
LANGFORD

COPTHORN
LANE

ASHLEY
LANE

EMLEY
LANE

Emley Farm
K

Bourne House

Bourne Farm
Bourne

Station House

BOURNE

RUSHWAY

LANE HOOKS BATCH

1

Langford Court Farm

Langford Green Farm

RUSHWAY

ROAD
A368

Langford Green

FRY'S
LANE

Prim. Sch.

The Village

The Square

RICKFORD LA.

BURRINGTON

Burrington

Burrington Farm

RICKFORD

LA.

Rickford Farm

RISE

THE

BATCH

FROG

LA.

LINK

RICKFORD

Rickford

Rickford Pond

Ridgeon Wood

Rickford Mill Bridge

A368

COOMBE

THE

2

Reservoir (Covered)
59

Brook

nghead Farm

Mendip Lodge

MENDIP LODGE WOOD

Hill Farm

LINK

LANE

HAM

LANE

Garden Centre

Rock of Ages

P

Aveline's Hole

B3134

Bristol

BS40

The Hill Gardens

Keeper's Cottage

3

Ham Farm Cottage

F

134

Burrington Ham

4

Lower Ellick Farm

58

Read's Cavern

Rod's Pot

Bos Swallet

Sidcot Swallet

Whitcombe's Hole

Goatchurch Cavern

East Twin Swallet

Elephant's Hole

Burrington

Lionels Hole

Combe

Toad's Hole

C O M B E

Lower Ellick Wood

NORTH SOMERSET

MENDIP

BURRINGTON COMBE

Ellick House

WARREN

West Twin Brook

East Twin Brook

East Twin Brook

5

6

Black Down

Beacon Batch

57

MENDIP

SEDGEMOOR

7

Tyning's Cottage

Tyning's Farm

M
47
48
49

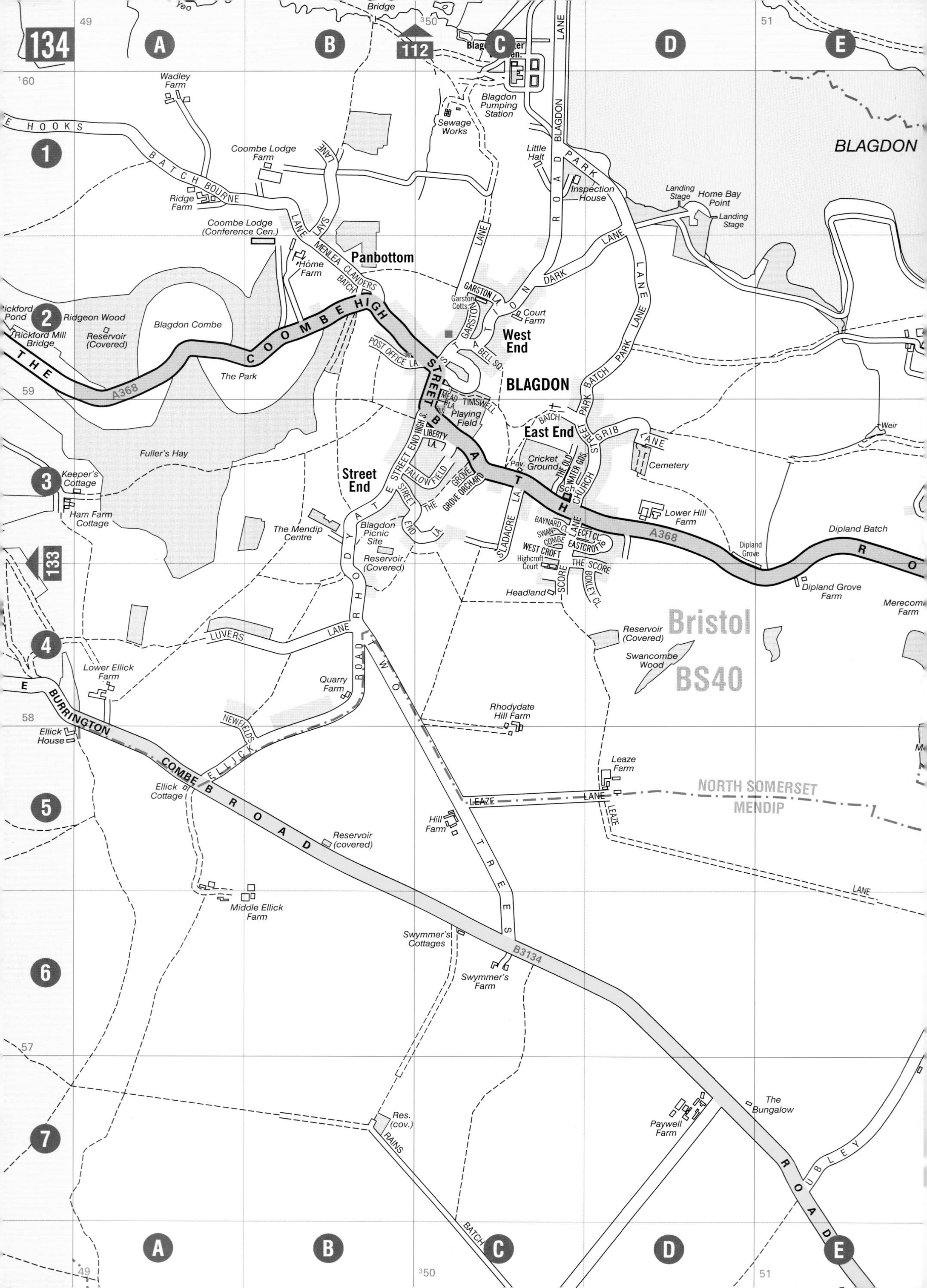

49   50   51

160

BLAGDON

1

e HOOKS

Wadley Farm

Coombe Lodge Farm

BATCH BOURNE

Ridge Farm

Coombe Lodge (Conference Cen.)

Blagdon Pumping Station

Sewage Works

Blag   er   en.

Little Halt

Inspection House

Landing Stage

Home Bay Point

Landing Stage

Home Farm

Panbottom

MENLEA CLANDERS BATCH

COOMBE HIGH

GARSTON LA.

Garston Cotts.

Court Cottage

West End

DARK LANE

PARK LANE

2

rickford Pond

Ridgeon Wood

rickford Mill Bridge

Reservoir (Covered)

Blagdon Combe

THE

A368

The Park

POST OFFICE LA.

BELL SQ.

BLAGDON

STREET

MEAD LA.
TIMSWELL

Playing Field

PARK BATCH

GRIB LANE

Weir

59

3

Keeper's Cottage

Ham Farm Cottage

Fuller's Hay

Street End

HIGH LIBERTY LA.

FALLOW FIELD

East End

THE GROVE

GROVE ORCHARD

Cricket Ground

Pav.

SLADACRE LA.

THE OLD
SCH
WATER GDNS.
CHURCH

Cemetery

A368

Lower Hill Farm

Dipland Batch

R O

133

The Mendip Centre

Blagdon Picnic Site

Reservoir (Covered)

DYE STREET END

STREET END

GATE

BAYNARD CL.
SWAN
WEST CROFT
Highcroft Court

CROFT CL.
EASTCROFT
COMBE
THE SCORE
BOXLEY CL.
SCORE

Dipland Grove

Dipland Grove Farm

Merecom Farm

4

Lower Ellick Farm

LUVERS

Quarry Farm

ROAD

Newfields

TWO

Headland

Reservoir (Covered)

Bristol

BS40

Swancombe Wood

Rhodydate Hill Farm

E

BURRINGTON

Ellick House

Ellick Cottage

ELLICK

NEWFIELDS

Leaze Farm

LEAZE
LANE

NORTH SOMERSET
MENDIP

LANE

58

5

COMBE

BROAD

Reservoir (covered)

Hill Farm

LEAZE

LANE

6

Middle Ellick Farm

Swymmer's Cottages

B3134

Swymmer's Farm

TREES

57

The Bungalow

7

Res. (cov.)

RAINS

BATCH

Paywell Farm

ROUBLEY
ROAD

49   350   51

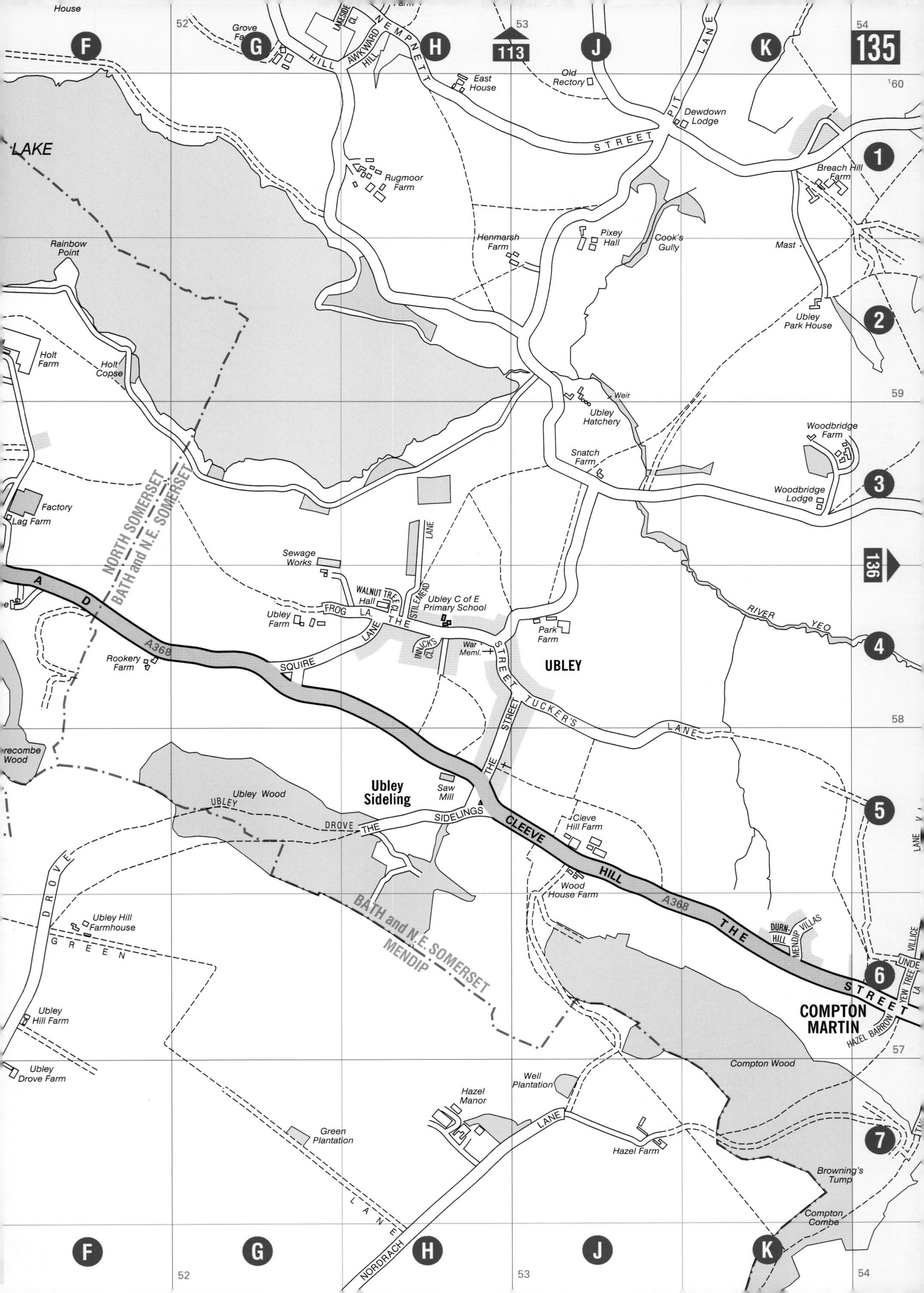

113
136
LAKE
Grove Farm
House
LAKESIDE CL.
AWKWARD HILL
NEMPNETT
HILL
East House
Old Rectory
PIT LANE
Dewdown Lodge
STREET
Rugmoor Farm
Breach Hill Farm
Mast
Henmarsh Farm
Pixey Hall
Cook's Gully
Rainbow Point
Ubley Park House
Holt Farm
Holt Copse
Weir
Ubley Hatchery
Woodbridge Farm
Snatch Farm
Woodbridge Lodge
Factory
Lag Farm
NORTH SOMERSET
BATH and N.E. SOMERSET
LANE
Sewage Works
WALNUT TREE CL.
STILEMEAD
Hall
Ubley C of E Primary School
FROG LA.
THE
LANE
Ubley Farm
Park Farm
RIVER YEO
A368
INNICKS CL.
War Meml.
STREET
UBLEY
Rookery Farm
SQUIRE
TUCKER'S LANE
THE STREET
Ubley Wood
Ubley Sideling
Saw Mill
UBLEY DROVE
THE SIDELINGS
CLEEVE HILL
Cleve Hill Farm
Wood House Farm
DROVE
Ubley Hill Farmhouse
GREEN
BATH and N.E. SOMERSET
MENDIP
THE STREET
DURN-HILL
MENDIP VILLAS
VILLICE
UNDE
YEW TREE
COMPTON MARTIN
HAZEL BARROW
Ubley Hill Farm
Ubley Drove Farm
Compton Wood
Well Plantation
Hazel Manor
LANE
Hazel Farm
Green Plantation
Browning's Tump
Compton Combe
LANE
NORDRACH
F
G
H
J
K
1
2
3
4
5
6
7
52
53
54
60
59
58
57

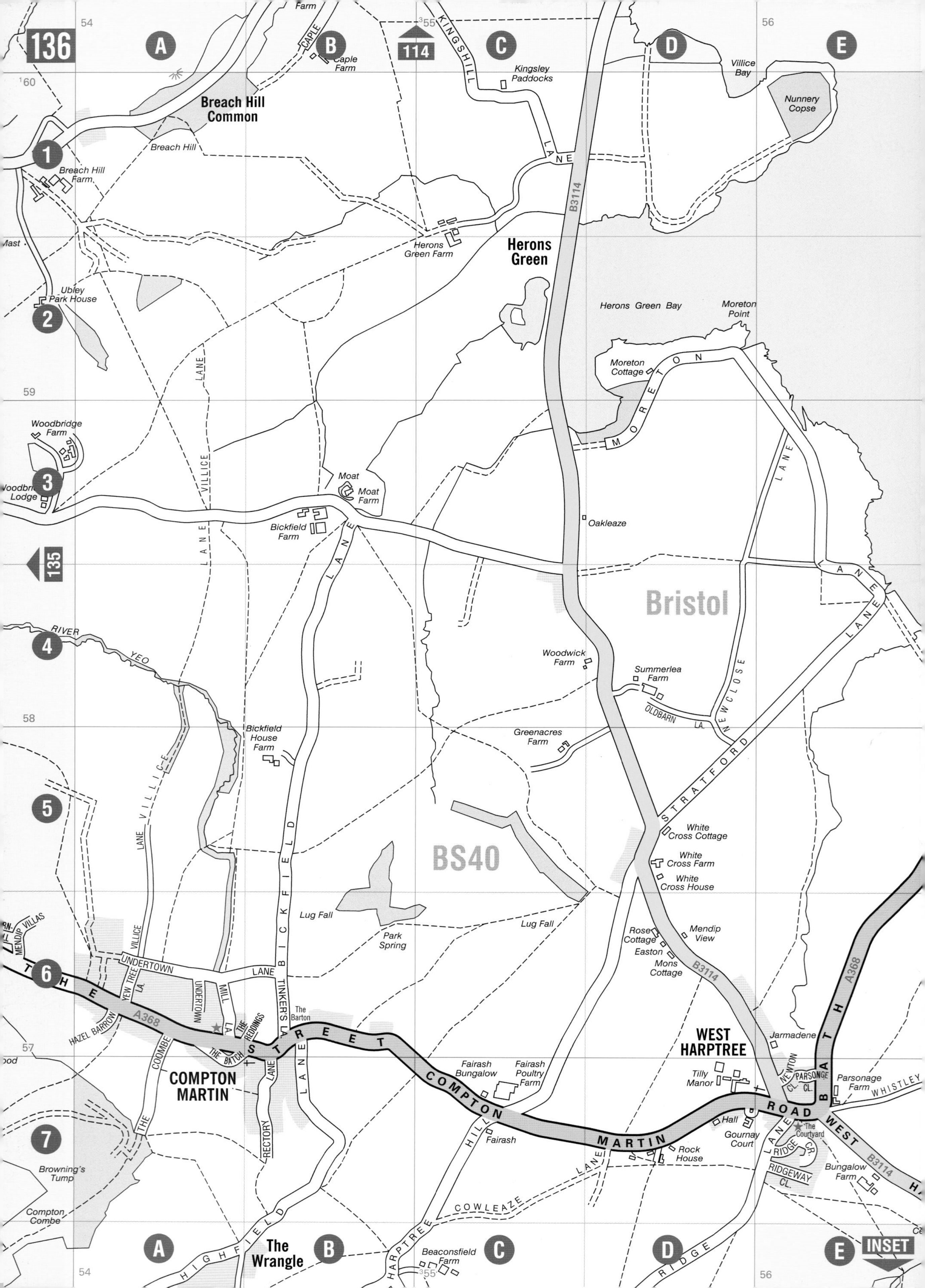

54 · A · B · 114 · C · D · 56 · E

160

Breach Hill Common

Breach Hill

1 · Breach Hill Farm

Mast

2 · Ubley Park House

Caple Farm

355 · Farm · KINGSHILL LANE

Kingsley Paddocks

Herons Green Farm

Herons Green

B3114

Villice Bay

Nunnery Copse

Herons Green Bay · Moreton Point

Moreton Cottage · MORETON LANE

59

Woodbridge Farm

3 · Woodbridge Lodge

135

VILLICE LANE

Moat · Moat Farm

Bickfield Farm

Oakleaze

Bristol

LANE

4 · RIVER YEO

58

Bickfield House Farm

Woodwick Farm

Summerlea Farm

OLDBARN LA.

NEWCLOSE LANE

LANE

5

BS40

Greenacres Farm

STRATFORD

White Cross Cottage

White Cross Farm

White Cross House

VILLICE LANE · BICKFIELD LANE

Lug Fall

Park Spring

Lug Fall

Rose Cottage · Easton · Mons Cottage

Mendip View

B3114

MENDIP VILLAS

THE · A368

6 · UNDERTOWN · YEW TREE LA. · UNDERTOWN · MILL LA. · TINKERS LA.

The Barton

The Beddings

HAZEL BARROW

57

THE COOMBE · THE BATCH · STREET

COMPTON MARTIN

RECTORY LANE

STREET

Fairash Bungalow · Fairash Poultry Farm

COMPTON MARTIN

Fairash

HILL LANE

Jarmadene

Tilly Manor

Hall

Gournay Court

WEST HARPTREE

NEWTON LANE · PARSONGE CL. · Parsonage Farm · WHISTLEY

The Courtyard

ROAD · WEST · B3114

RIDGE CL. · RIDGEWAY CL. · Bungalow Farm

7

Browning's Tump

Compton Combe

Rock House

COWLEAZE

Beaconsfield Farm

355

HARPTREE HILL LANE · RIDGE

54 · A · **The Wrangle** · B · C · 56 · D · E · **INSET**

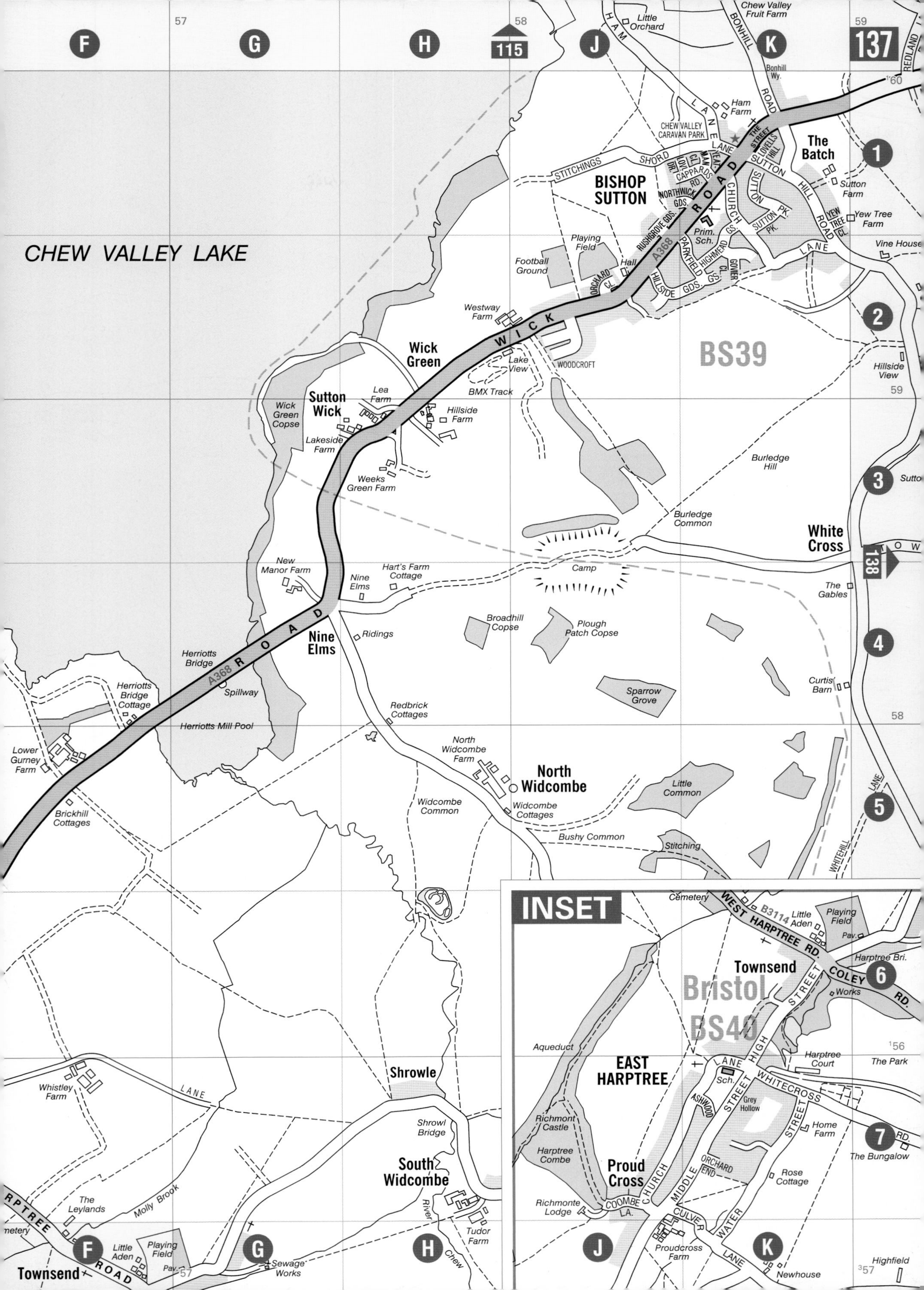

CHEW VALLEY LAKE

137

1

The Batch

Little Orchard

Chew Valley Fruit Farm

Bonhill Wy.

Ham Farm

Sutton Farm

Yew Tree Farm

Vine House

Chew Valley Caravan Park

BISHOP SUTTON

STITCHINGS

SHORD

NORTHWICK

RUSHGROVE GDS.

CAPPARDS RD.

HAM LANE

THE STREET

LOVELLS HILL

SUTTON HILL ROAD

SUTTON PK.

Prim. Sch.

HILLSIDE GDS.

HIGHMEAD

GOWER RD.

PARKFIELD

A368

CHURCH ROAD

Playing Field

Hall

ORCHARD CL.

Football Ground

Westway Farm

WICK

Lake View

BMX Track

WOODCROFT

Lake View

BS39

2

Hillside View

59

Wick Green

Sutton Wick

Wick Green Copse

Lea Farm

Lakeside Farm

Hillside Farm

Weeks Green Farm

Burledge Hill

3

Sutto

Burledge Common

White Cross

138 IOW

4

The Gables

Camp

Hart's Farm Cottage

Nine Elms

New Manor Farm

Nine Elms

Ridings

Broadhill Copse

Plough Patch Copse

Curtis Barn

58

Herriotts Bridge

A368 ROAD

Spillway

Herriotts Bridge Cottage

Herriotts Mill Pool

Sparrow Grove

Redbrick Cottages

5

Lower Gurney Farm

Brickhill Cottages

North Widcombe Farm

North Widcombe

Widcombe Cottages

Widcombe Common

Little Common

Bushy Common

Stitching

WHITEHILL LANE

INSET

Cemetery

WEST HARPTREE RD.

B3114

Little Aden

Playing Field

Pav.

Harptree Bri.

Bristol BS40

Townsend

COLEY RD.

6

Works

156

Aqueduct

HIGH STREET

Harptree Court

The Park

EAST HARPTREE

Sch.

LANE

ASHWOOD

WHITECROSS

CHURCH STREET

Grey Hollow

Home Farm

STREET

MIDDLE STREET

Shrowle

Whistley Farm

LANE

Shrowl Bridge

Richmont Castle

Harptree Combe

ORCHARD END

Rose Cottage

7 RD.

The Bungalow

South Widcombe

Richmonte Lodge

Proud Cross

COOMBE LA.

River Chew

WATER LANE

CULVER LANE

Proudcross Farm

Newhouse

Highfield

157

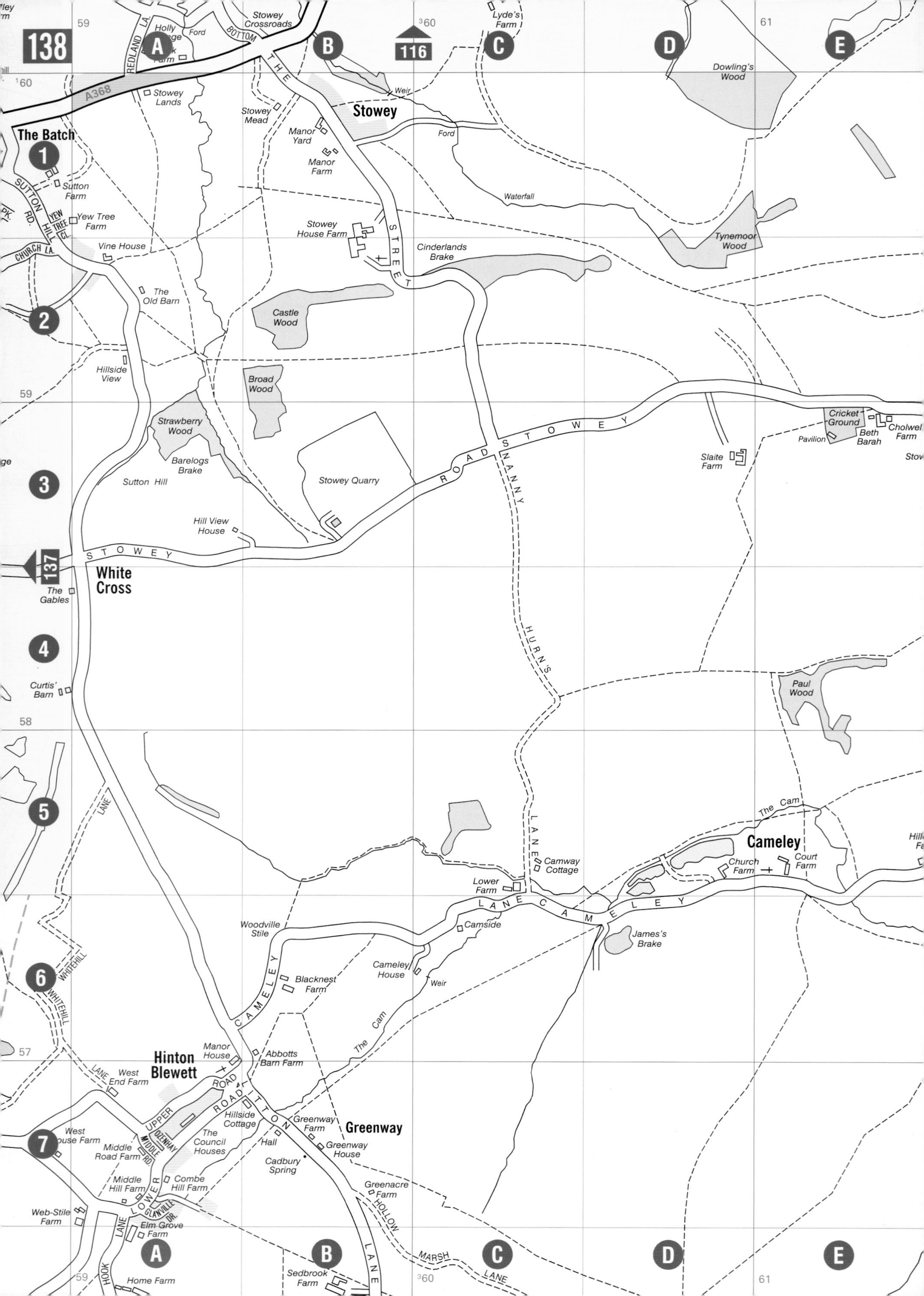
Stowey Crossroads
Holly
Ford
BOTTOM
THE
REDLAND LA.
A368
Stowey Lands
Stowey Mead
Stowey
Lyde's Farm
Weir
Ford
Dowling's Wood
The Batch
SUTTON HILL
SUTTON RD.
Sutton Farm
Manor Yard
Manor Farm
Waterfall
Yew Tree Farm
YEW TREE CL.
CHURCH LA.
Vine House
Stowey House Farm
STREET
Cinderlands Brake
Tynemoor Wood
The Old Barn
Castle Wood
Hillside View
Broad Wood
Strawberry Wood
Barelogs Brake
Sutton Hill
Stowey Quarry
ROAD
STOWEY
NANNY
Cricket Ground
Pavilion
Beth Barah
Cholwell Farm
Slaite Farm
Hill View House
White Cross
The Gables
HURN'S
Curtis' Barn
Paul Wood
LANE
Camway Cottage
Cameley
The Cam
Church Farm
Court Farm
Lower Farm
CAMELEY
Camside
James's Brake
Woodville Stile
Cameley House
Weir
Blacknest Farm
WHITEHILL
The Cam
Manor House
Abbotts Barn Farm
Hinton Blewett
West End Farm
UPPER
OZENHAY
Hillside Cottage
LITTON
Greenway Farm
Greenway
Greenway House
West House Farm
Middle Road Farm
MIDDLE RD.
The Council Houses
Hall
Cadbury Spring
Middle Hill Farm
LOWER
Combe Hill Farm
Greenacre Farm
HOLLOW
GLANVILLE DR.
Web-Stile Farm
Elm Grove Farm
HOOK LANE
MARSH LANE
Home Farm
Sedbrook Farm
116
137
59
360
61
160
58
57

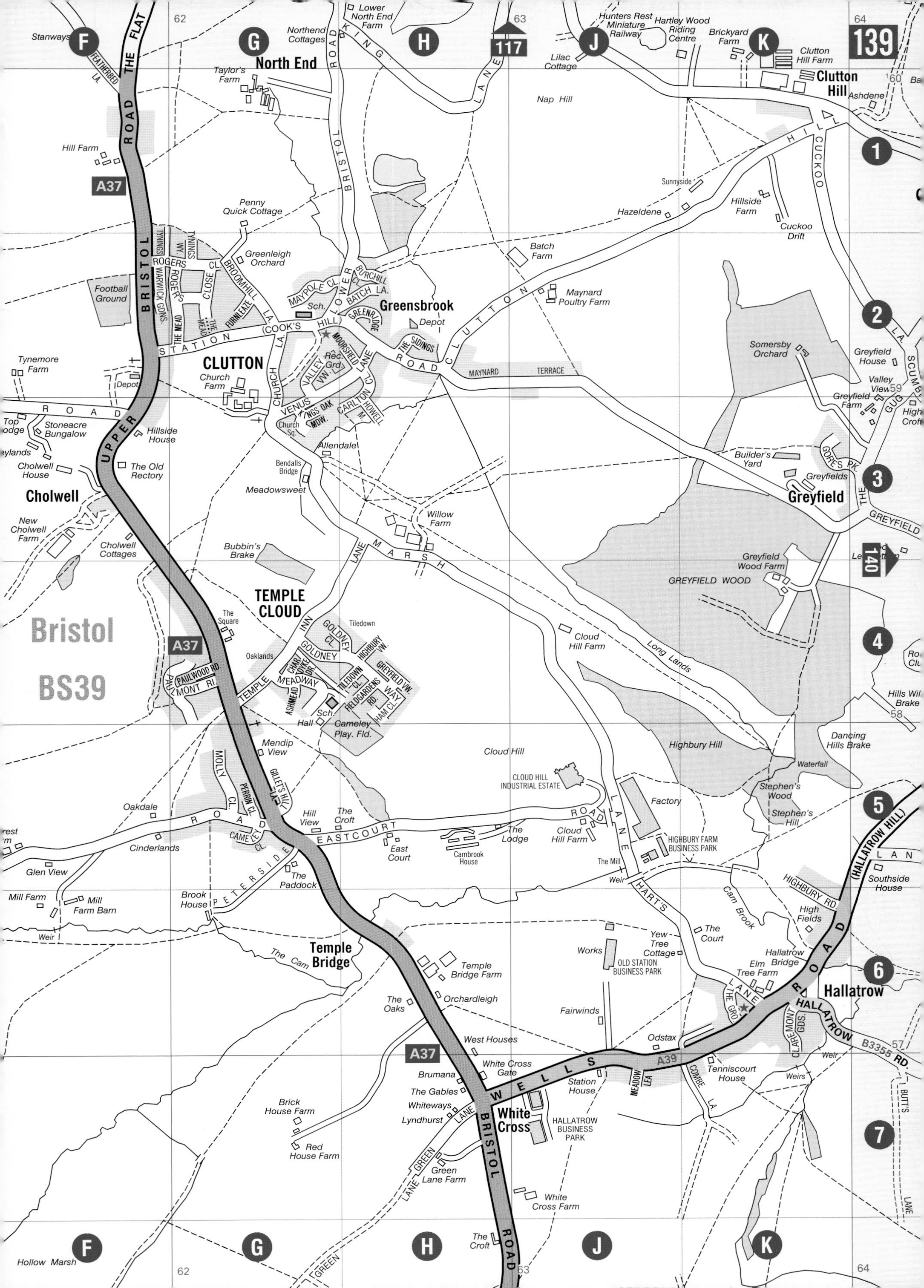

North End
Greensbrook
CLUTTON
TEMPLE CLOUD
Cholwell
Greyfield
Clutton Hill
Temple Bridge
Hallatrow
White Cross
Bristol BS39
A37
A39
B3355
117
140
F G H J K
1 2 3 4 5 6 7
62 63 64
Stanways
Northend Cottages
Lower North End Farm
Hunters Rest Miniature Railway
Hartley Wood Riding Centre
Brickyard Farm
Clutton Hill Farm
Lilac Cottage
Taylor's Farm
Nap Hill
Ashdene
Hill Farm
Sunnyside
Hillside Farm
Hazeldene
Cuckoo Drift
Penny Quick Cottage
Greenleigh Orchard
Batch Farm
Maynard Poultry Farm
Football Ground
Depot
Somersby Orchard
Greyfield House
Valley View
Greyfield Farm
Tynemore Farm
Church Farm
Top Lodge
Stoneacre Bungalow
Hillside House
Cholwell House
The Old Rectory
Allendale
Bendalls Bridge
Builder's Yard
Greyfields
Meadowsweet
Willow Farm
New Cholwell Farm
Cholwell Cottages
Bubbin's Brake
Greyfield Wood Farm
GREYFIELD WOOD
The Square
Tiledown
Oaklands
Cloud Hill Farm
Long Lands
Hills Wil Brake
Sch.
Hall
Cameley Play. Fld.
Rec. Grd.
Church Sq.
Mendip View
Cloud Hill
Highbury Hill
Dancing Hills Brake
Waterfall
CLOUD HILL INDUSTRIAL ESTATE
Stephen's Wood
Stephen's Hill
Factory
Oakdale
Hill View
The Croft
The Lodge
Cloud Hill Farm
HIGHBURY FARM BUSINESS PARK
Cinderlands
East Court
Cambrook House
The Mill
Weir
Southside House
Glen View
The Paddock
Mill Farm
Mill Farm Barn
Brook House
Cam Brook
High Fields
The Court
Yew Tree Cottage
Works
OLD STATION BUSINESS PARK
Hallatrow Bridge
Elm Tree Farm
The Cam
Temple Bridge Farm
The Oaks
Orchardleigh
Fairwinds
Odstax
West Houses
White Cross Gate
Station House
Tenniscourt House
Weirs
Brumana
The Gables
Whiteways
Lyndhurst
HALLATROW BUSINESS PARK
Brick House Farm
Red House Farm
Green Lane Farm
White Cross Farm
The Croft
Hollow Marsh
UPPER BRISTOL ROAD
THE FLAT
FEATHERBED LA.
BRISTOL ROAD
KING LANE
TYNINGS
TYNINGS WY.
ROGERS
ROGERS CLOSE
WARWICK GDNS.
THE MEAD
BROOMHILL LA.
FURNLEAZE
STATION ROAD
(COOK'S HILL)
CHURCH LA.
MAYPOLE CL.
LOWER BATCH LA.
BURCHILL CL.
GREENRIDGE
MOORSFIELD
VALLEY VW.
LANE
CARLTON CL.
HOWELL M.
VENUS
KINGS OAK MDW.
THE SIDINGS
CLUTTON ROAD
MAYNARD TERRACE
CUCKOO HILL
CUCKOO LA.
SCUMBY LA.
GUG
GORES PK.
THE GREYFIELD
MARSH LANE
INN LANE
GOLDNEY CL.
GOLDNEY
HIGHBURY VW.
GREYFIELD VW.
CHARLTON DR.
MEADWAY
ASHMEAD
TILEDOWN CL.
FIELDGARDENS RD.
WAY
HAM CL.
PAULWOOD RD.
PAULMONT RI.
TEMPLE
MOLLY CL.
PERRIN CL.
GILLETT'S HILL LA.
ROAD
CAMELEY CL.
EASTCOURT ROAD
PETERSIDE
CLOUD HILL LANE
HART'S LANE
HIGHBURY RD.
(HALLATROW HILL) ROAD
LANE
WELLS ROAD
MEADOW LEA
COMBE LA.
THE GROVE
CLAREMONT GDS.
HALLATROW RD.
BUTT'S LANE
GREEN LANE
GREEN

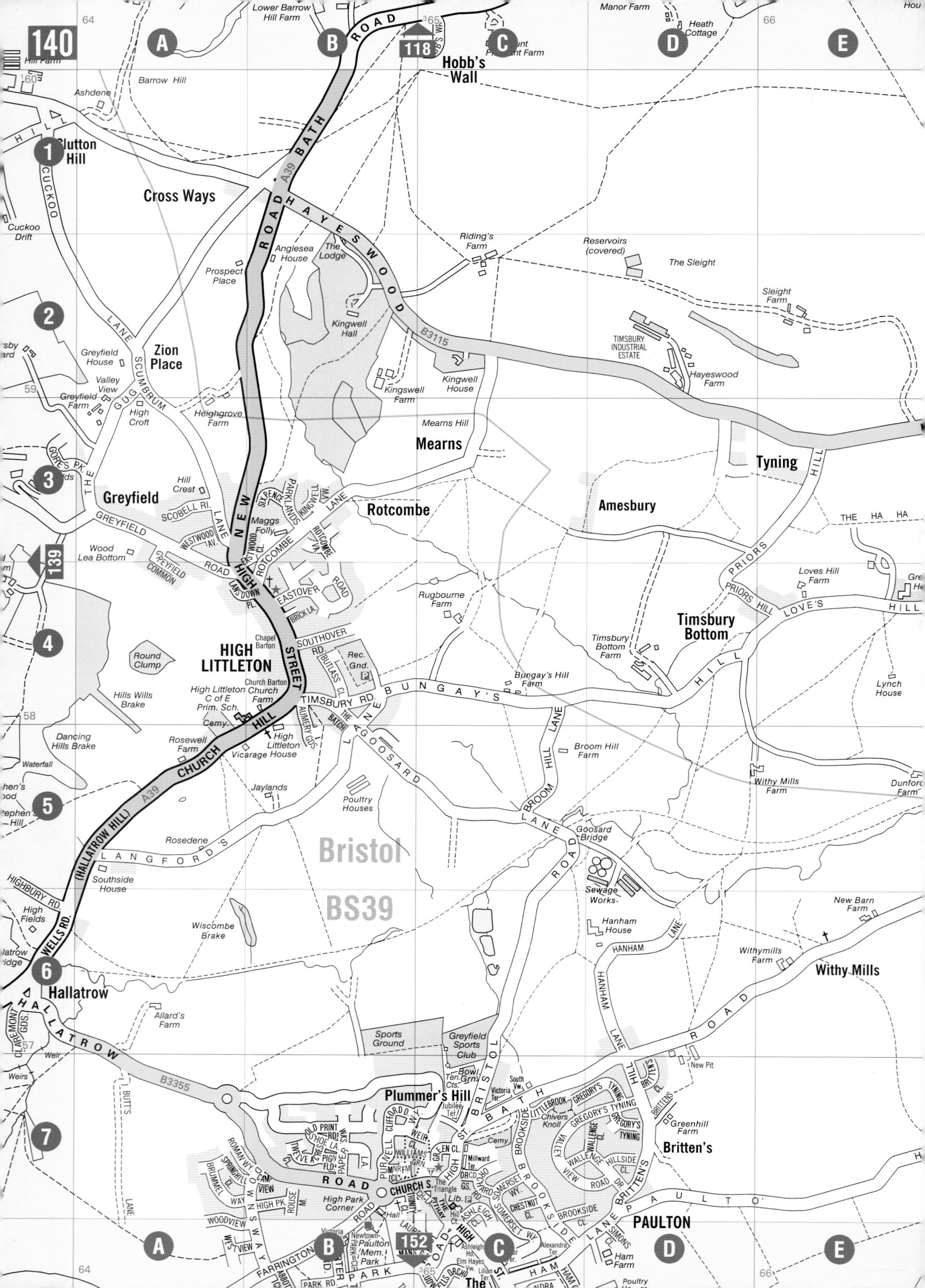

Hobb's Wall
Clutton Hill
Cross Ways
Zion Place
Greyfield
Mearns
Rotcombe
Tyning
Amesbury
HIGH LITTLETON
Timsbury Bottom
Bristol
BS39
Hallatrow
Withy Mills
Plummer's Hill
Britten's
PAULTON
Lower Barrow Hill Farm
Manor Farm
Heath Cottage
Barrow Hill
Ashdene
Cuckoo Drift
Anglesea House
The Lodge
Riding's Farm
Reservoirs (covered)
The Sleight
Sleight Farm
Prospect Place
Kingwell Hall
TIMSBURY INDUSTRIAL ESTATE
Hayeswood Farm
Greyfield House
Valley View
Greyfield Farm
High Croft
Heighgrove Farm
Kingswell Farm
Kingwell House
Mearns Hill
Hill Crest
Maggs Folly
Wood Lea Bottom
Loves Hill Farm
Rugbourne Farm
Round Clump
Chapel Barton
Rec. Gnd.
Timsbury Bottom Farm
Bungay's Hill Farm
Lynch House
Hills Wills Brake
Church Barton
High Littleton Church Farm
High Littleton C of E Prim. Sch.
Cemy.
Dancing Hills Brake
Rosewell Farm
High Littleton Vicarage House
Broom Hill Farm
Waterfall
Withy Mills Farm
Jaylands
Poultry Houses
Goosard Bridge
Rosedene
Southside House
Sewage Works
High Fields
Wiscombe Brake
Hanham House
New Barn Farm
Withymills Farm
Allard's Farm
Sports Ground
Greyfield Sports Club
New Pit
Weir
Weirs
Bowl. Grn.
Ten. Cts.
Victoria Ter.
South Vw.
Jubilee Ter.
Chivers Knoll
Greenhill Farm
Cemy.
Millward Ter.
The Triangle
Lib.
High Park Corner
Hall
Newtown
Paulton Mem. Park
Ashleigh Ho.
Elm Hayes Vw.
Lilian Ter.
Alexandra Ter.
Ham Farm
Poultry
BATH ROAD
NEW ROAD
HAYESWOOD ROAD
A39
B3115
B3355
CUCKOO LANE
SCUMBRUM LANE
GUG
GORE'S PK.
THE HIGHLANDS
GREYFIELD ROAD
SCOBELL RI.
WESTWOOD AV.
LANE
GREYFIELD COMMON
SIXPENCE
PARKLANDS
KINGWELL VW.
EASTWOOD CL.
ROTCOMBE LANE
ROTCOMBE VA.
EASTOVER ROAD
LANSDOWN PL.
BRICK LA.
HIGH STREET
SOUTHOVER RD.
BUTLASS CL.
TIMSBURY RD.
BUNGAY'S HILL
THE BATCH
AUMERY GDS.
GOOSARD LANE
CHURCH HILL
HALLATROW HILL
LANGFORD'S LANE
HIGHBURY RD.
WELLS RD.
HALLATROW ROAD
CLAREMONT GDS.
BUTTS LANE
BROOM HILL LANE
ROAD
PRIORS HILL
LOVE'S HILL
THE HA HA
HANHAM LANE
BRISTOL ROAD
PAULTON ROAD
BATH ST.
BROOKSIDE
LITTLEBROOK
GREGORY'S TYNING
VALLEY VIEW ROAD
WALLENGE DR.
HILLSIDE CL.
BRITTEN'S HILL
BRITTENS CL.
CHURCH ST.
HIGH ST.
WEIR
GREEN CL.
WILLIAMS GRN.
ORCHARD GS.
SOMERSET WY.
CHESTNUT CL.
BROOKSIDE CL.
SIMONS CL.
HAM LANE
ROMAN WY.
SPRINGHILL CL.
BRUMMEL WAY
WOODVIEW
WEST VIEW
HIGH PK.
ROUSE M.
OLD PRINT
SHOE LA.
PIGN FLD.
PAPER LA.
PURNELL WY.
CLIFFORD
FARRINGTON RD.
PARK RD.
ASHLEIGH CL.
THE PITHAY
118
139
152
64
65
66
160
59
58
57
A B C D E
1 2 3 4 5 6 7

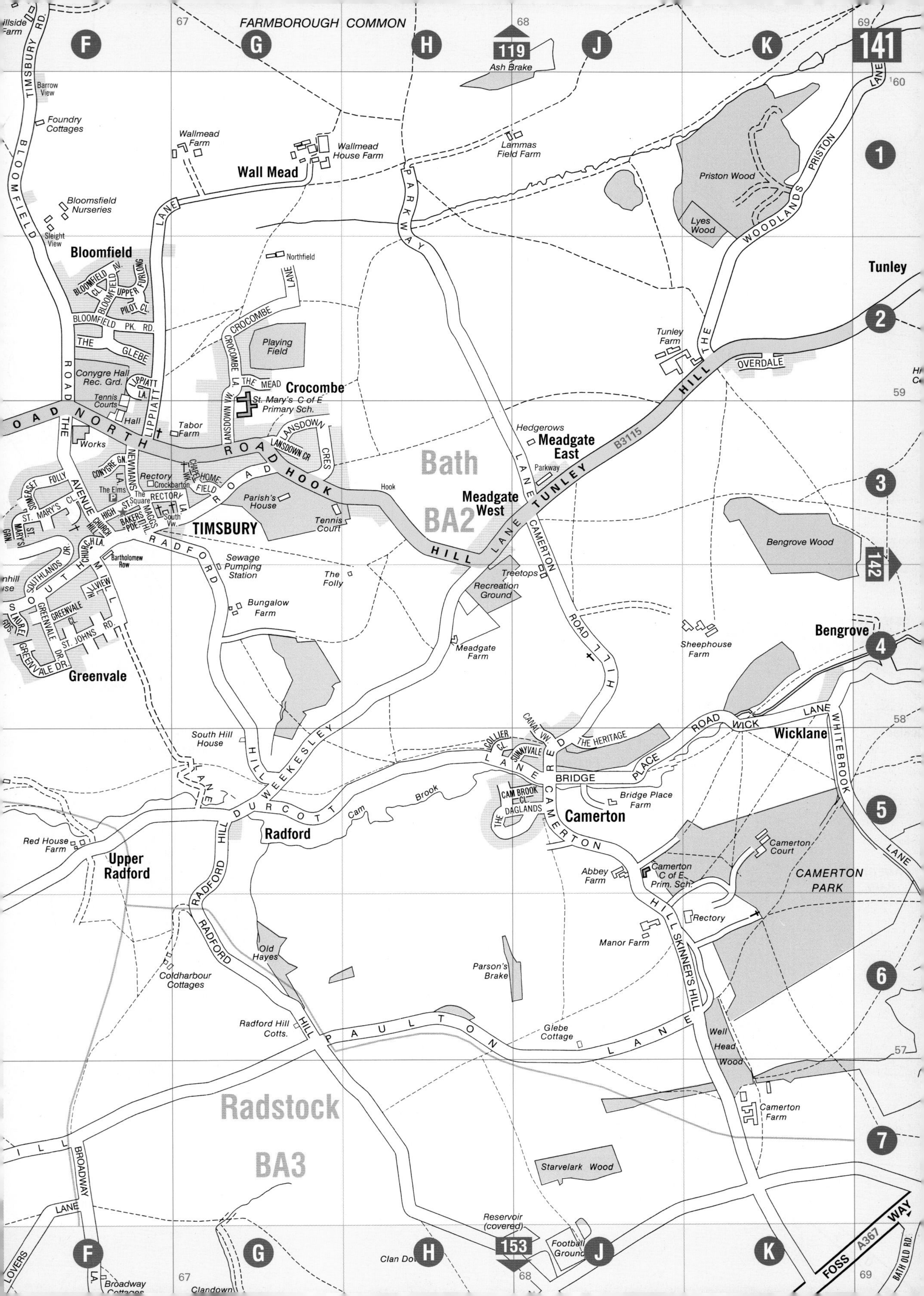
FARMBOROUGH COMMON
119
Ash Brake
Barrow View
Foundry Cottages
Wallmead Farm
Wallmead House Farm
Wall Mead
Lammas Field Farm
Priston Wood
Lyes Wood
Bloomsfield Nurseries
Sleight View
Bloomfield
Northfield
Tunley
Tunley Farm
Playing Field
Conygre Hall Rec. Grd.
Tennis Courts
Hall
Crocombe
St. Mary's C of E Primary Sch.
Tabor Farm
Works
Hedgerows
Meadgate East
Parkway
Bath
Rectory
Crockbarton
The Elms
The Square
Parish's House
Hook
Meadgate West
TIMSBURY
Tennis Court
BA2
Bengrove Wood
142
Bartholomew Row
Sewage Pumping Station
The Folly
Treetops
Recreation Ground
Bungalow Farm
Meadgate Farm
Sheephouse Farm
Bengrove
Greenvale
South Hill House
Wicklane
Bridge Place Farm
Camerton
Radford
Red House Farm
Upper Radford
Camerton Court
CAMERTON PARK
Abbey Farm
Camerton C of E Prim. Sch.
Rectory
Manor Farm
Old Hayes
Parson's Brake
Coldharbour Cottages
Radford Hill Cotts.
Glebe Cottage
Well Head Wood
Camerton Farm
Radstock
BA3
Starvelark Wood
Reservoir (covered)
153
Football Ground
Clan Down
Broadway Cottages
Clandown
FOSS WAY A367
BATH OLD RD.
B3115

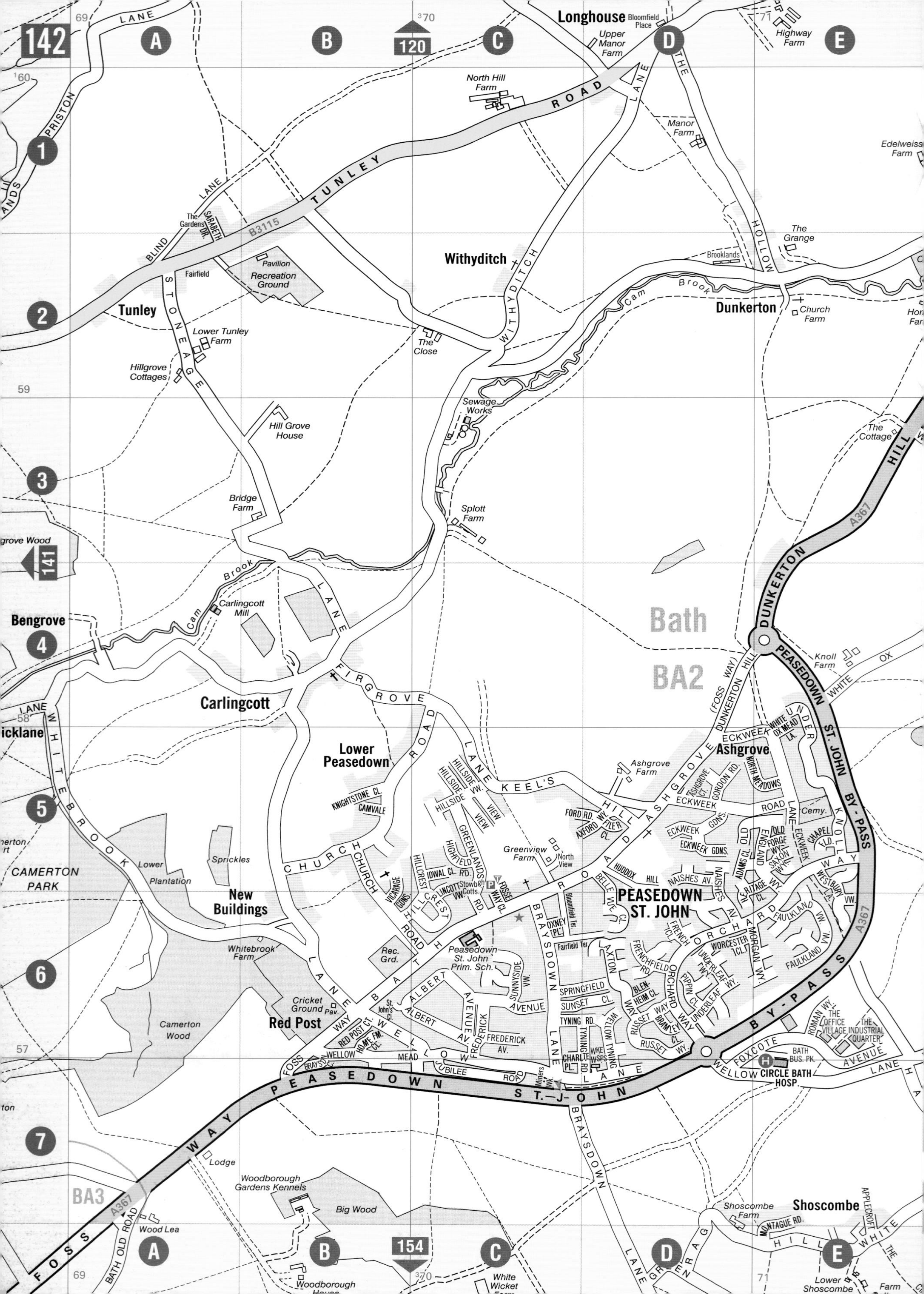

120
141
154
Longhouse
Bloomfield Place
Upper Manor Farm
Highway Farm
North Hill Farm
TUNLEY ROAD
B3115
Manor Farm
Edelweiss Farm
PRISTON
BLIND LANE
The Gardens
SARABETH DR.
Fairfield
Pavilion
Recreation Ground
Withyditch
WITHYDITCH
Brooklands
The Grange
HOLLOW
Cam Brook
Dunkerton
Church Farm
Tunley
STONEAGE
Lower Tunley Farm
Hillgrove Cottages
The Close
Sewage Works
Hill Grove House
The Cottage
Bridge Farm
Splott Farm
grove Wood
Bengrove
Carlingcott Mill
LANE
A367
DUNKERTON
Bath
BA2
Knoll Farm
WHITE OX
PEASEDOWN ST. JOHN BY-PASS
FIRGROVE
Carlingcott
(FOSS WAY)
DUNKERTON HILL
Ashgrove
Ashgrove Farm
WHITEBROOK
Lower Peasedown
KNIGHTSTONE CL.
CAMVALE
HILLSIDE VW.
KEEL'S HILL
FORD RD.
ECKWEEK ROAD
Cemy.
ECKWEEK GDNS.
NORTH MEADOWS
CAMERTON PARK
Lower Plantation
Sprickles
CHURCH ROAD
Greenview Farm
North View
HUDDOX HILL
NAISHES AV.
New Buildings
PEASEDOWN ST. JOHN
ORCHARD
BATH ROAD
BRAYSDOWN LANE
Bloomfield Ter.
OXNEY PL.
Fairfield Ter.
WESTBURY LA.
FAULKLAND VW.
Whitebrook Farm
Peasedown St. John Prim. Sch.
Rec. Grd.
ALBERT AVENUE
SUNNYSIDE VW.
SPRINGFIELD
SUNSET CL.
WORCESTER CL.
MORGAN WY.
UNDERLEAF WY.
PIPPIN CL.
Camerton Wood
Cricket Ground
Pav.
Red Post
RED POST CT.
HOME FM. CL.
FREDERICK AV.
TYNING RD.
WELLOW TYNING
RUSSET WAY
ROMAN WY.
THE OFFICE VILLAGE
THE INDUSTRIAL QUARTER
FOXCOTE AVENUE
BATH BUS. PK.
CIRCLE BATH HOSP.
WELLOW MEAD
JUBILEE ROAD
WELLOW LANE
FOSS WAY
PEASEDOWN ST. JOHN
Lodge
BRAYSDOWN LANE
BA3
Woodborough Gardens Kennels
Big Wood
Wood Lea
BATH OLD ROAD
Shoscombe Farm
Shoscombe
MONTAGUE RD.
WHITE HILL
APPLECROFT
Woodborough House
White Wicket
Lower Shoscombe
Farm
GREEN

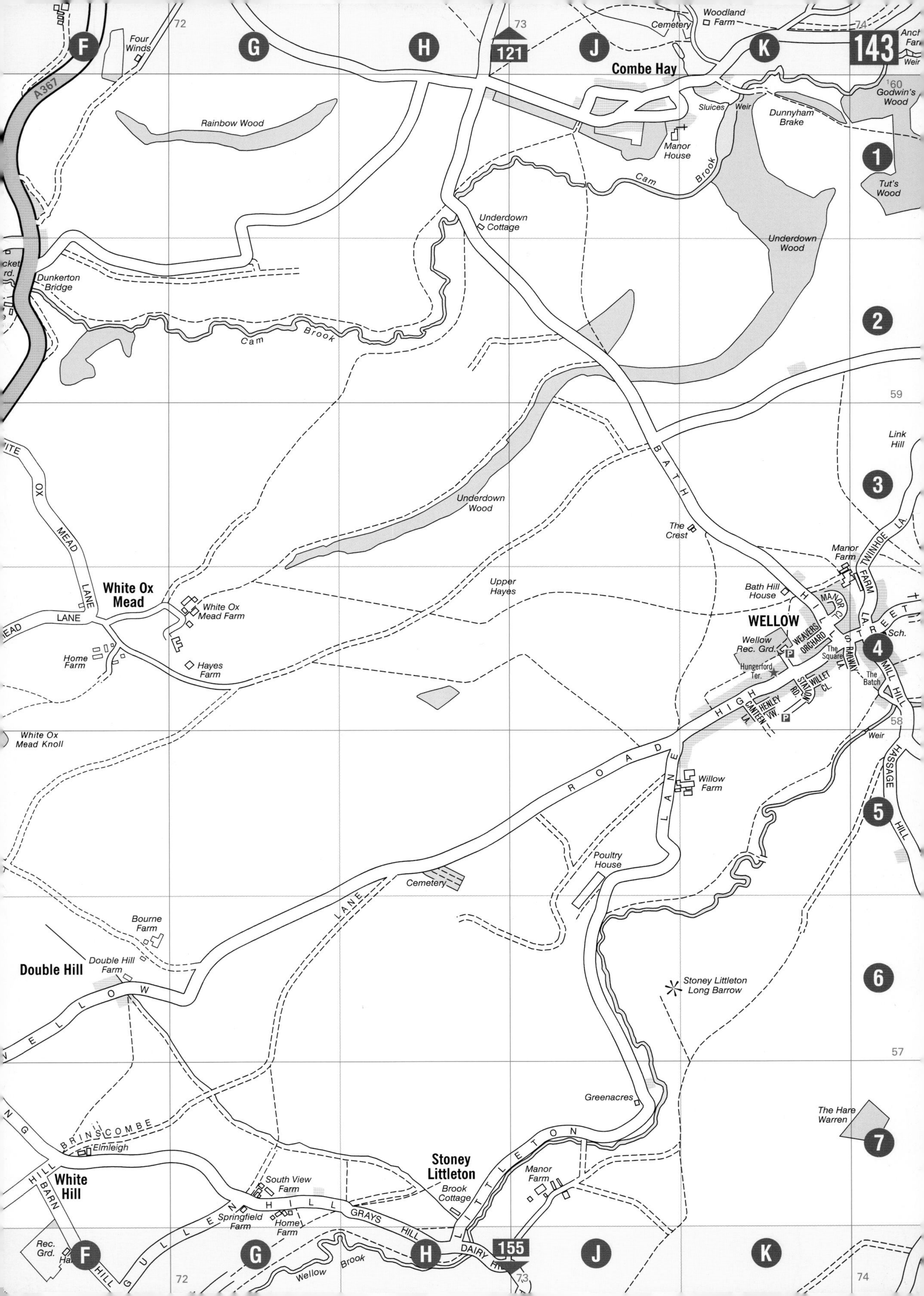
Combe Hay
Woodland Farm
Cemetery
Four Winds
Rainbow Wood
Sluices
Weir
Dunnyham Brake
Godwin's Wood
Manor House
Cam Brook
Tut's Wood
Underdown Cottage
Underdown Wood
Dunkerton Bridge
A367
Link Hill
BATH HILL
The Crest
WHITE OX MEAD LANE
White Ox Mead
White Ox Mead Farm
Upper Hayes
Manor Farm
TWINHOE LA.
FARM LA.
Bath Hill House
MANOR CL.
WELLOW
Wellow Rec. Grd.
WEAVERS ORCHARD
The Square
RAILWAY LA.
STREET
Sch.
MILL HILL
The Batch
Hungerford Ter.
WILLET CL.
STATION RD.
HENLEY VW.
CANTEEN LA.
HIGH ROAD
Home Farm
Hayes Farm
White Ox Mead Knoll
Weir
HASSAGE HILL
LANE
Willow Farm
Poultry House
Cemetery
Bourne Farm
Double Hill
Double Hill Farm
WELLOW LANE
Stoney Littleton Long Barrow
Greenacres
The Hare Warren
BRINSCOMBE
Elmleigh
White Hill
BARN HILL
Stoney Littleton
Manor Farm
Brook Cottage
South View Farm
Springfield Farm
Home Farm
GULLEN HILL
GRAYS HILL
LITTLETON
DAIRY HILL
Wellow Brook
Rec. Grd.
121
155
72
73
74
59
58
57
60
F
G
H
J
K
1
2
3
4
5
6
7

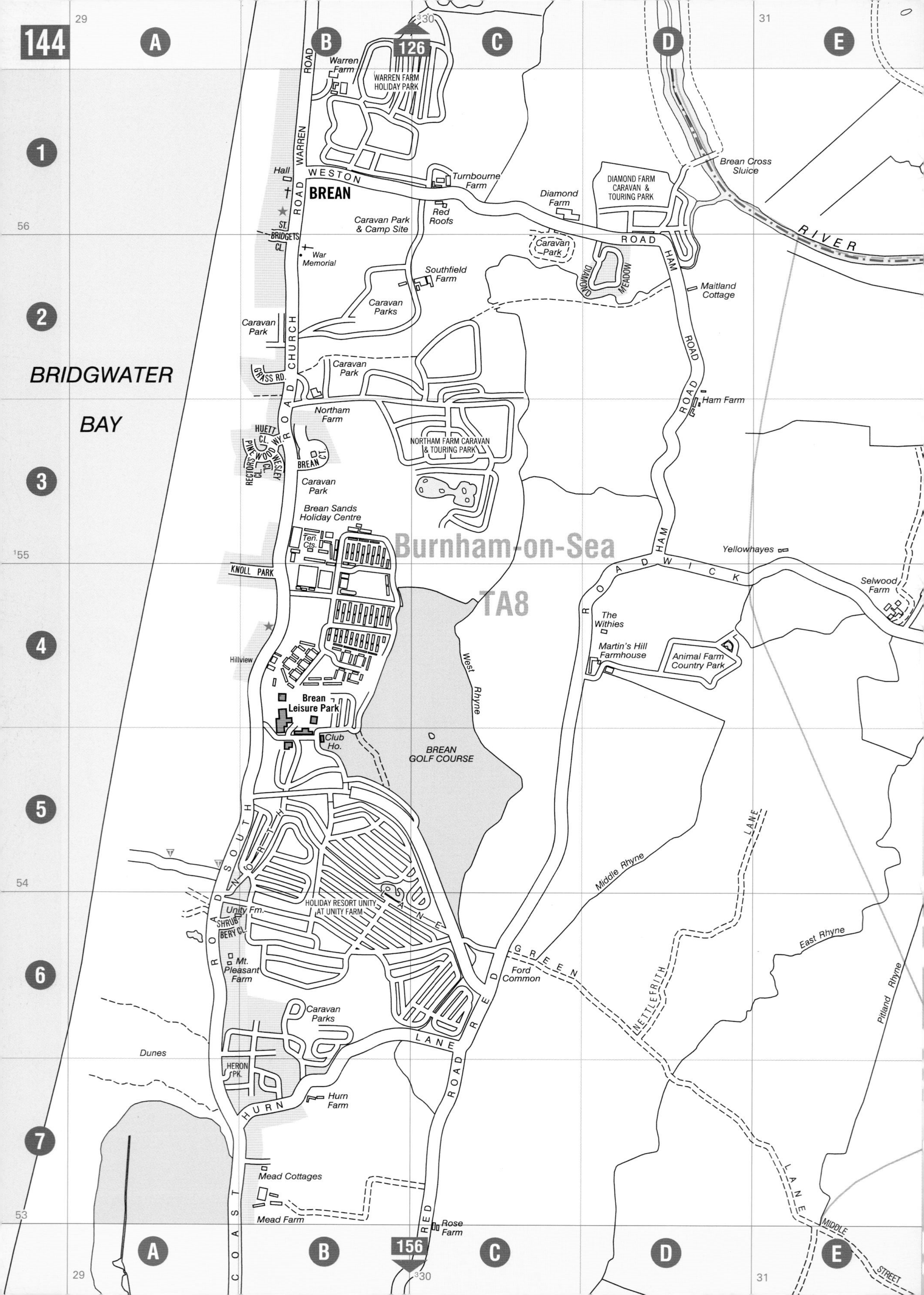

A **B** **C** **D** **E**

126

1

WARREN FARM
HOLIDAY PARK

Warren
Farm

56

Hall

WARREN ROAD

WESTON

BREAN

Turnbourne
Farm

Diamond
Farm

DIAMOND FARM
CARAVAN &
TOURING PARK

Brean Cross
Sluice

RIVER

ST.
BRIDGETS
CL.

Red
Roofs

Caravan Park
& Camp Site

Caravan
Park

ROAD

HAM ROAD

Maitland
Cottage

2

War
Memorial

Southfield
Farm

Caravan
Park

Caravan
Parks

CHURCH ROAD

Ham Farm

BRIDGWATER

BAY

CROSS RD.

Caravan
Park

Northam
Farm

NORTHAM FARM CARAVAN
& TOURING PARK

ROAD

3

HUETT
CL.

PINEWOOD CL.

RECTORY NY

KELSEY

BREAN
CT.

Caravan
Park

HAM

Brean Sands
Holiday Centre

Burnham-on-Sea
TA8

Yellowhayes

Selwood
Farm

155

Ten.
Cts.

KNOLL PARK

West
Rhyne

ADWICK ROAD

The
Withies

Martin's Hill
Farmhouse

Animal Farm
Country Park

4

Hillview

Brean
Leisure Park

Club
Ho.

BREAN
GOLF COURSE

5

SOUTH ROAD

NORTH

Middle Rhyne

LANE

54

Unity Fm.

SHRUB
BERY CL.

HOLIDAY RESORT UNITY
AT UNITY FARM

MIDDLE LANE

GREEN

East Rhyne

NETTLEFRITH

Pitland Rhyne

6

Mt.
Pleasant
Farm

Ford
Common

RED ROAD

LANE

Dunes

Caravan
Parks

HURN ROAD

HERON
PK.

LANE

7

Mead Cottages

Hurn
Farm

156

Rose
Farm

MIDDLE

53

STREET

COAST

A **B** **C** **D** **E**

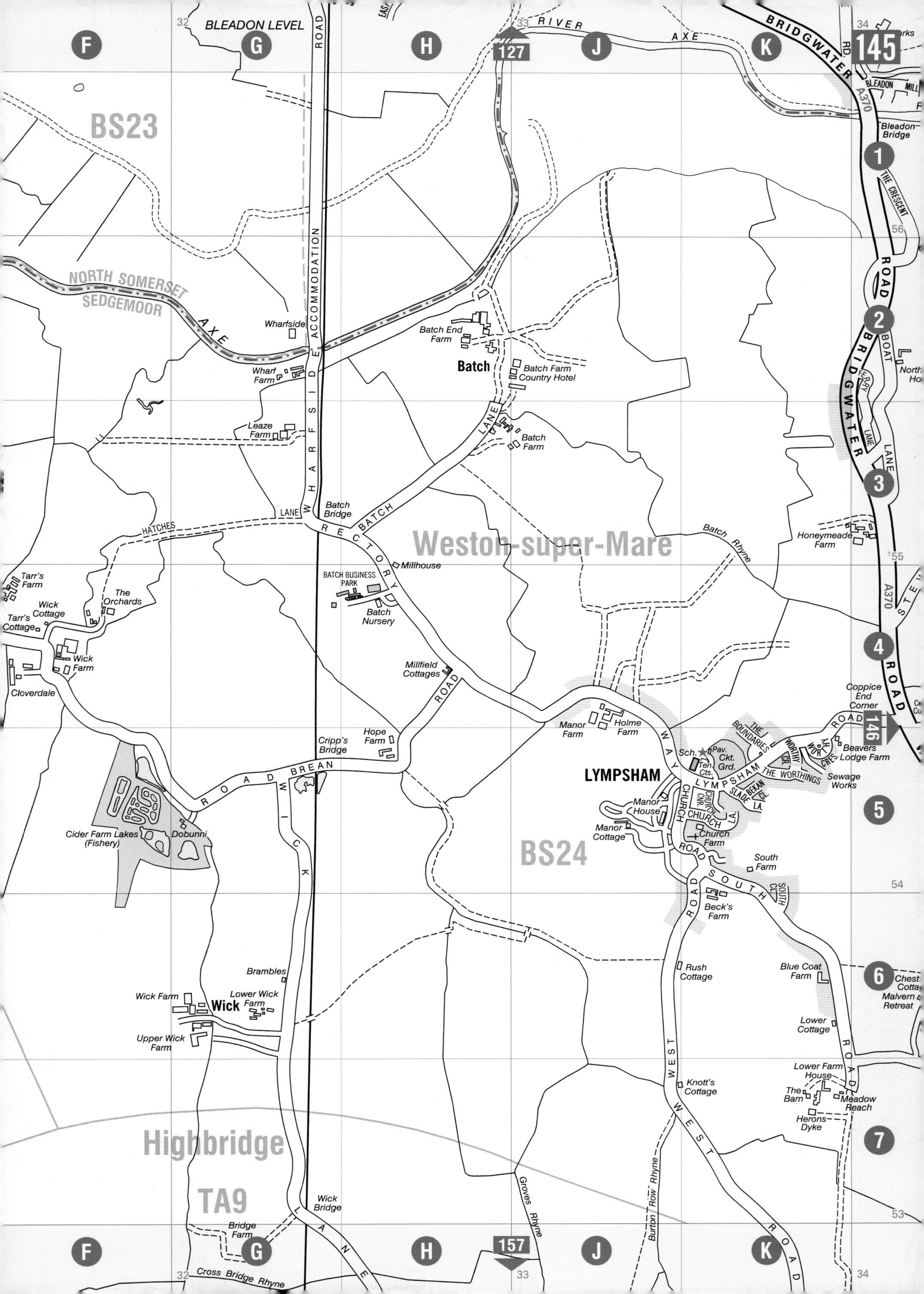

145
127
157
146
BLEADON LEVEL
RIVER AXE
BRIDGWATER ROAD
A370
Bleadon Bridge
THE CRESCENT
BS23
NORTH SOMERSET
SEDGEMOOR
AXE
ACCOMMODATION ROAD
WHARFSIDE
Wharfside
Wharf Farm
Leaze Farm
Batch End Farm
Batch
Batch Farm Country Hotel
Batch Farm
BATCH LANE
Batch Bridge
HATCHES LANE
RECTORY
Millhouse
BATCH BUSINESS PARK
Batch Nursery
Weston-super-Mare
Batch Rhyne
Honeymeade Farm
BOAT LANE
FERRY LANE
Tarr's Farm
The Orchards
Wick Cottage
Tarr's Cottage
Wick Farm
Cloverdale
Millfield Cottages
ROAD
Cripp's Bridge
Hope Farm
BREAN ROAD
Cider Farm Lakes (Fishery)
Dobunni
WICK LANE
Manor Farm
Holme Farm
WAY
LYMPSHAM
Sch.
Pav.
Ckt. Grd.
Ten. Cts.
THE BOUNDARIES
WORTHY CR.
WORTHY CRES.
THE WORTHINGS
Coppice End Corner
Beavers Lodge Farm
Sewage Works
LYMPSHAM ROAD
SLADE CL.
BEKAN LA.
CHURCH CNR.
CHURCH LA.
CHURCH ROAD
Manor House
Manor Cottage
Church Farm
South Farm
SOUTH ROAD
SOUTH CL.
Beck's Farm
BS24
Rush Cottage
Blue Coat Farm
Lower Cottage
Brambles
Wick Farm
Wick
Lower Wick Farm
Upper Wick Farm
WEST ROAD
WEST
Knott's Cottage
Lower Farm House
The Barn
Meadow Reach
Herons Dyke
Groves Rhyne
Burton Row Rhyne
Highbridge
TA9
Wick Bridge
Bridge Farm
Cross Bridge Rhyne
F
G
H
J
K
1
2
3
4
5
6
7
32
33
34
53
54
55
56

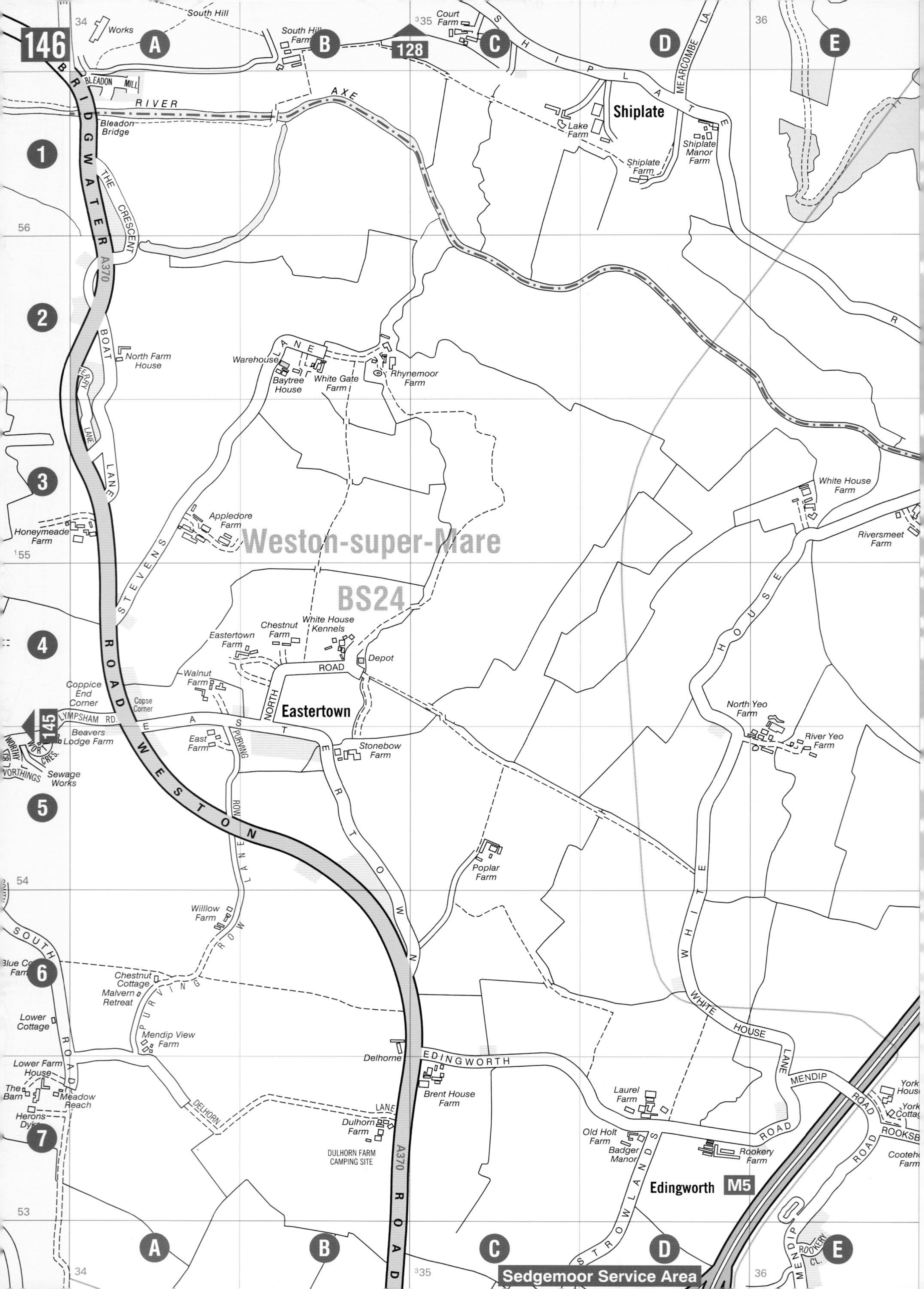

South Hill
Works
South Hill Farm
Court Farm
128
Shiplate
Lake Farm
Shiplate Manor Farm
Shiplate Farm
MEARCOMBE LA.
SHIPLATE
BLEADON MILL
RIVER AXE
Bleadon Bridge
THE CRESCENT
BRIDGWATER ROAD
A370
BOAT LANE
FERRY LANE
North Farm House
Warehouse
LANE
Baytree House
White Gate Farm
Rhynemoor Farm
Honeymeade Farm
Appledore Farm
STEVENS
Weston-super-Mare
BS24
White House Farm
Riversmeet Farm
WHITE HOUSE
Chestnut Farm
White House Kennels
Eastertown Farm
Depot
ROAD
Walnut Farm
NORTH
Eastertown
Coppice End Corner
Copse Corner
LYMPSHAM RD.
EAST
EASTERTOWN
145
Beavers Lodge Farm
East Farm
PURVING
Stonebow Farm
North Yeo Farm
River Yeo Farm
WORTHY CRES.
WORTHINGS
Sewage Works
WESTON ROAD
ROW LANE
Poplar Farm
Willlow Farm
SOUTH ROAD
PURVING ROW
Chestnut Cottage
Malvern Retreat
Lower Cottage
Mendip View Farm
WHITE HOUSE LANE
Delhorne
EDINGWORTH
Brent House Farm
Laurel Farm
MENDIP ROAD
York House
York Cottage
ROOKSB
Lower Farm House
The Barn
Meadow Reach
Herons Dyke
DELHORN
LANE
Dulhorn Farm
DULHORN FARM CAMPING SITE
A370 ROAD
Old Holt Farm
Badger Manor
STROWLANDS
Rookery Farm
Cootehe Farm
Edingworth
M5
MENDIP CL.
ROOKERY
Sedgemoor Service Area
A B C D E
1 2 3 4 5 6 7
34 335 36
56 55 54 53

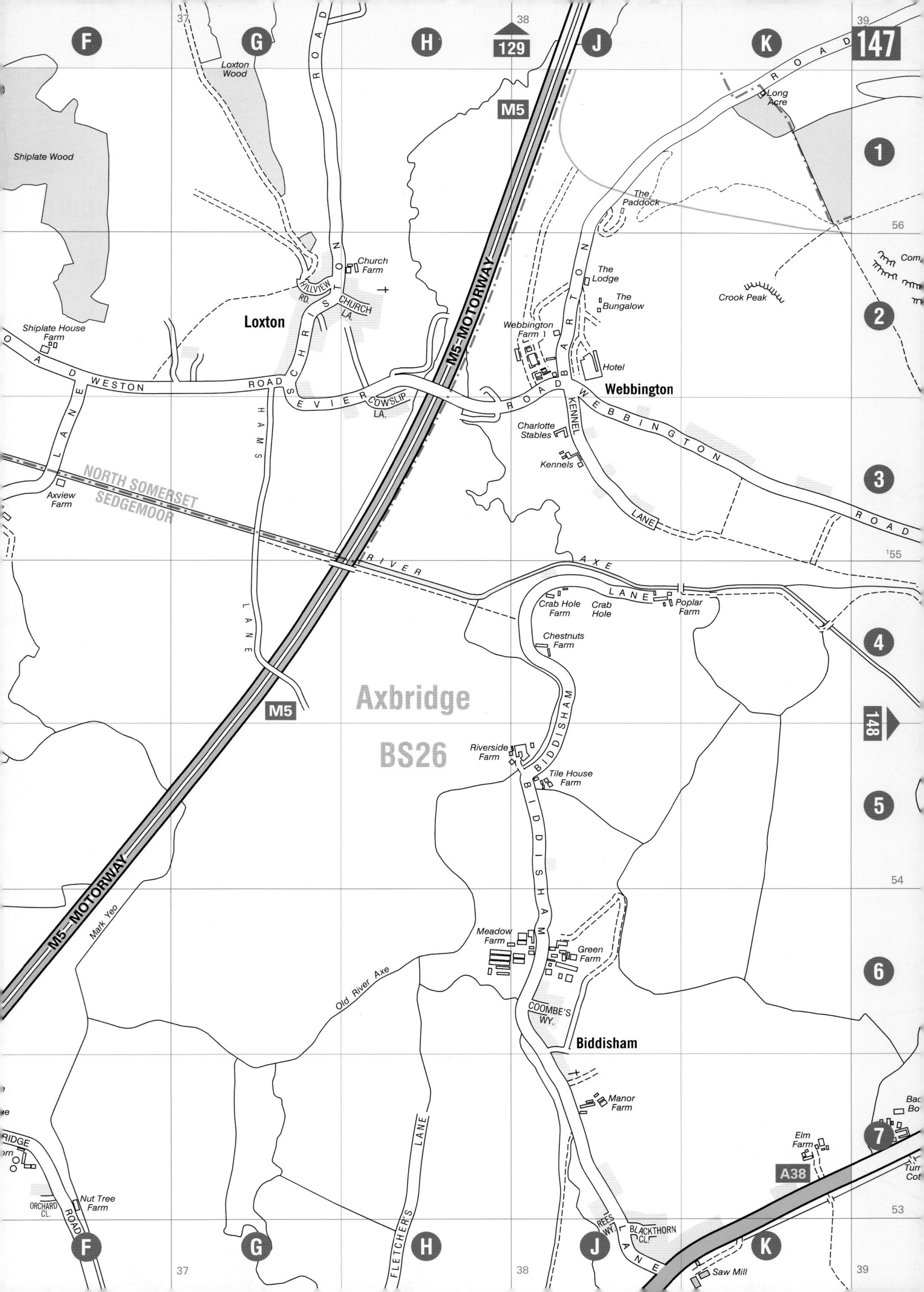

Shiplate Wood

Loxton Wood

Church Farm

Loxton

CHURCH LA.

HILLVIEW RD.

CHRIST

SEVIER ROAD

COWSLIP LA.

Shiplate House Farm

WESTON ROAD

HAMS LANE

Axview Farm

NORTH SOMERSET

SEDGEMOOR

M5 MOTORWAY

M5

The Paddock

The Lodge

The Bungalow

Crook Peak

Webbington Farm

Hotel

Webbington

BARTON ROAD

KENNEL LANE

WEBBINGTON ROAD

Charlotte Stables

Kennels

Long Acre

Com

RIVER AXE

AXE LANE

Crab Hole Farm

Crab Hole

Poplar Farm

Chestnuts Farm

Axbridge

BS26

M5

Mark Yeo

Old River Axe

Riverside Farm

Tile House Farm

BIDDISHAM

Meadow Farm

Green Farm

COOMBE'S WY.

Biddisham

Manor Farm

Elm Farm

FLETCHERS LANE

REES WY.

BLACKTHORN CL.

A38

Saw Mill

Turn Cot

Bad Bo

BRIDGE ROAD

ORCHARD CL.

Nut Tree Farm

148

56

55

54

53

1 · 2 · 3 · 4 · 5 · 6 · 7

37 · 38 · 39

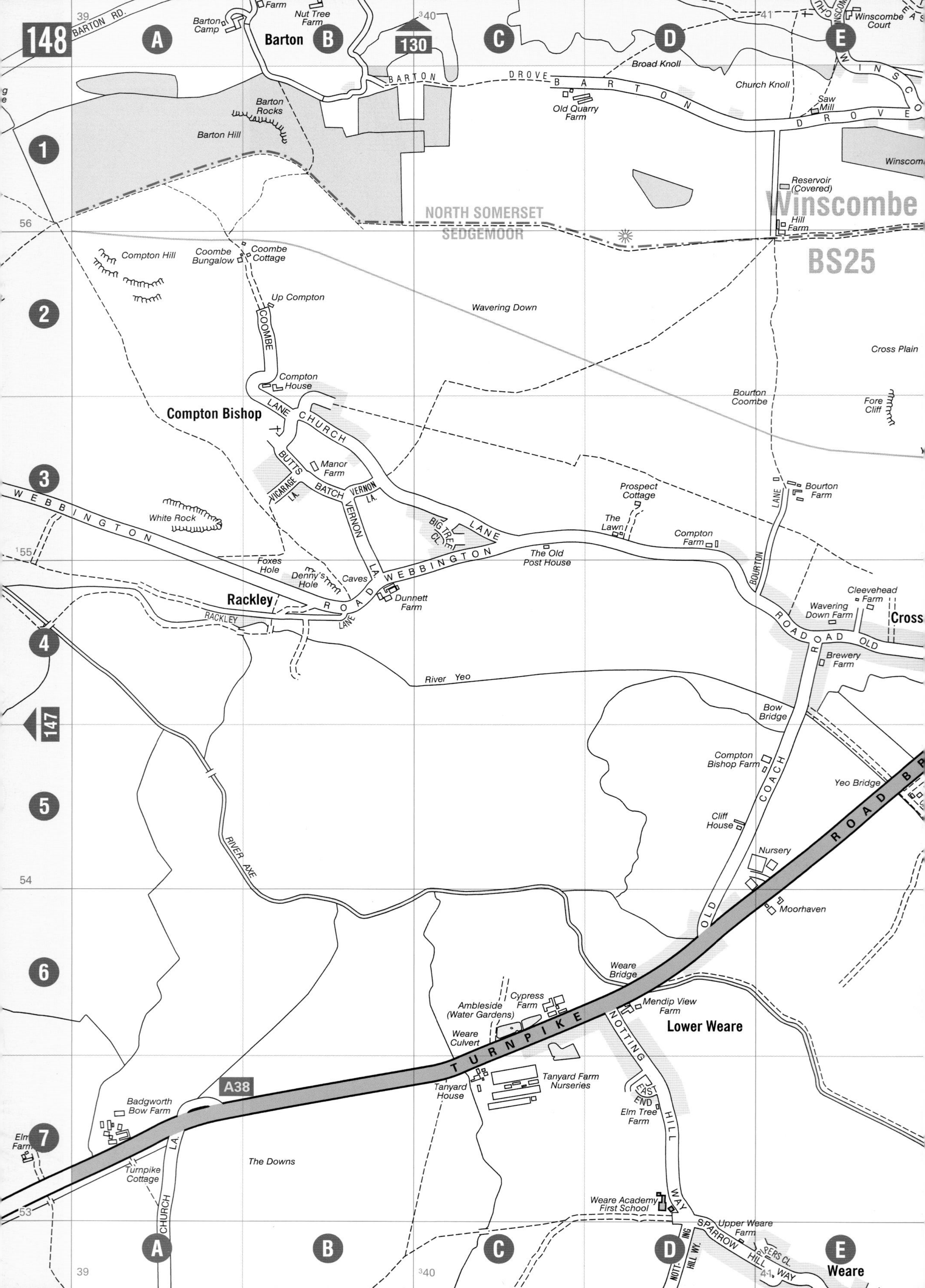
Barton Camp
Nut Tree Farm
Barton
130
Barton Rocks
Barton Hill
BARTON DROVE
Broad Knoll
Church Knoll
Old Quarry Farm
Saw Mill
Winscombe Court
Reservoir (Covered)
NORTH SOMERSET
SEDGEMOOR
Winscombe
Hill Farm
BS25
Compton Hill
Coombe Bungalow
Coombe Cottage
Up Compton
Wavering Down
COOMBE LANE
Compton House
Compton Bishop
CHURCH LANE
Manor Farm
BUTTS BATCH
VICARAGE LA.
VERNON LA.
BIG TREE CL.
Bourton Coombe
Cross Plain
Fore Cliff
Prospect Cottage
The Lawn
Compton Farm
Bourton Farm
BOURTON LANE
WEBBINGTON ROAD
White Rock
Foxes Hole
Denny's Hole
Caves
The Old Post House
Dunnett Farm
Rackley
RACKLEY LANE
Cleevehead Farm
Wavering Down Farm
Cross
OLD ROAD
Brewery Farm
River Yeo
Bow Bridge
147
Compton Bishop Farm
Yeo Bridge
OLD COACH ROAD
Cliff House
Nursery
Moorhaven
RIVER AXE
Weare Bridge
Cypress Farm
Ambleside (Water Gardens)
Mendip View Farm
Lower Weare
Weare Culvert
TURNPIKE ROAD
NOTTING HILL WAY
Tanyard Farm Nurseries
Tanyard House
EAST END
Elm Tree Farm
A38
Badgworth Bow Farm
Elm Farm
Turnpike Cottage
CHURCH LA.
The Downs
Weare Academy First School
Upper Weare Farm
SPARROW HILL WAY
PIPERS CL.
Weare
HILL WY.

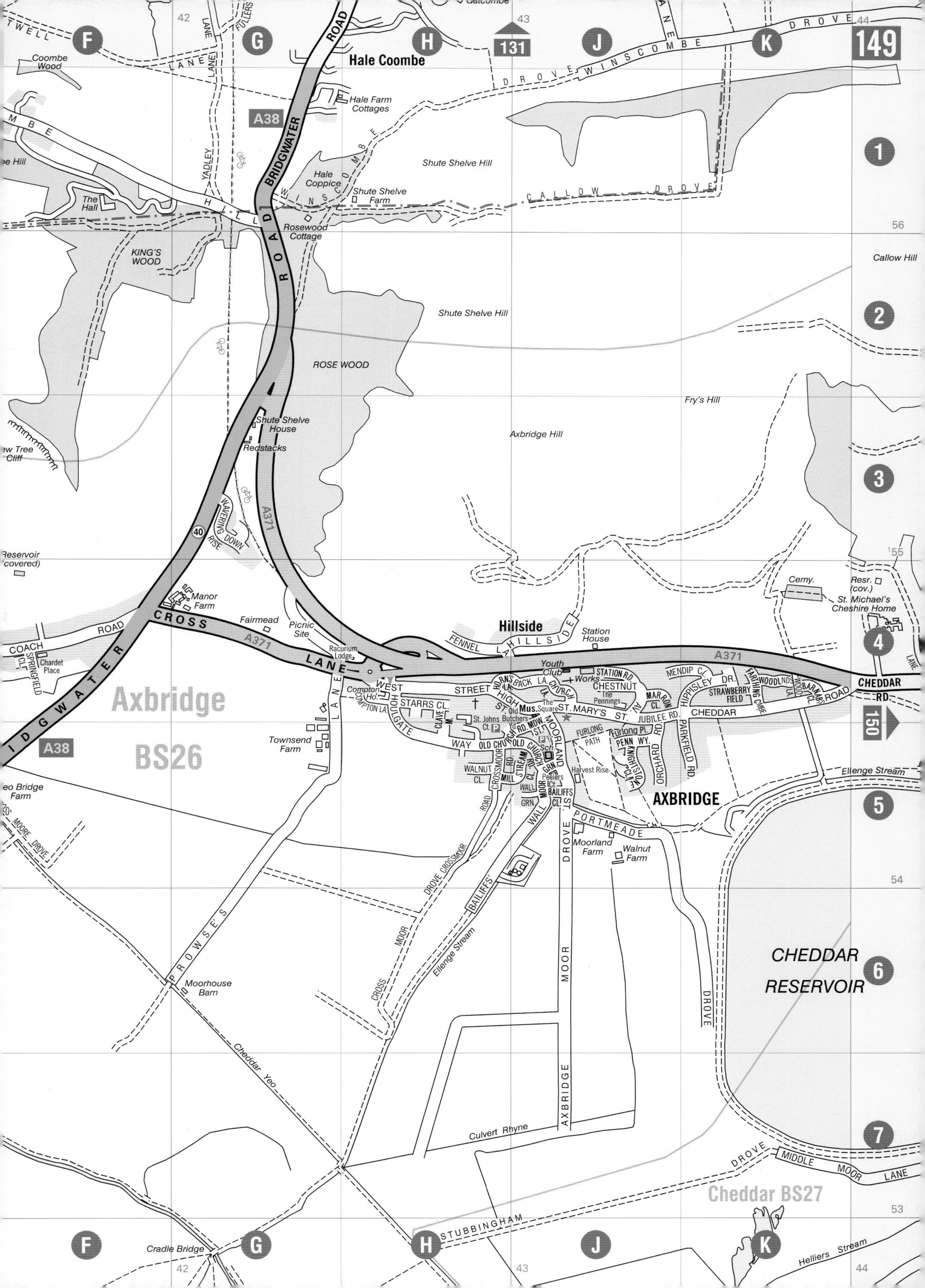

Hale Coombe

Coombe Wood

Hale Farm Cottages

Shute Shelve Hill

CALLOW DROVE

Callow Hill

The Hall

KING'S WOOD

Rosewood Cottage

Shute Shelve Farm

Hale Coppice

Shute Shelve Hill

ROSE WOOD

Fry's Hill

Axbridge Hill

Shute Shelve House

Redstacks

ew Tree Cliff

Reservoir (covered)

Manor Farm

Fairmead

Picnic Site

Racunium Lodge

Cemy.

Resr. (cov.)

St. Michael's Cheshire Home

COACH ROAD

Springfield

Chardet Place

CROSS LANE

Hillside

Station House

Fennel La

Youth Club

STATION RD.

Works

The Pennings

CHESTNUT

MENDIP CL

MARTON CL.

HIPPISLEY DR.

Strawberry Field

WOODLNDS

BARN

Road

CHEDDAR RD.

150

Axbridge

BS26

A38

Townsend Farm

Compton Ho.

WEST HOLGATE

STARRS CL.

CLAVE

St. Johns Butchers

Mus.

HIGH ST

HORNS LA

BACK LA

St. MARY'S ST

The Square

CHURCH

FURLONG PL.

PENN WY.

WINDMILL

ORCHARD RD.

PARKFIELD RD.

CHEDDAR

Street

Ellenge Stream

WALNUT CL.

WAY

OLD CHU

MILL

MOOR RD

OLD CHURCH

MOORLAND

Harvest Rise

FURLONG PATH

AXBRIDGE

Moorland Farm

Walnut Farm

eo Bridge Farm

Moorhouse Barn

PROWSES MOORE DROVE

CROSSMOOR DROVE

BAILIFFS

MOOR

AXBRIDGE MOOR

PORTMEADE

DROVE

CHEDDAR RESERVOIR

Cheddar Yeo

Culvert Rhyne

STUBBINGHAM

Cheddar BS27

Cradle Bridge

DROVE MIDDLE MOOR LANE

Helliers Stream

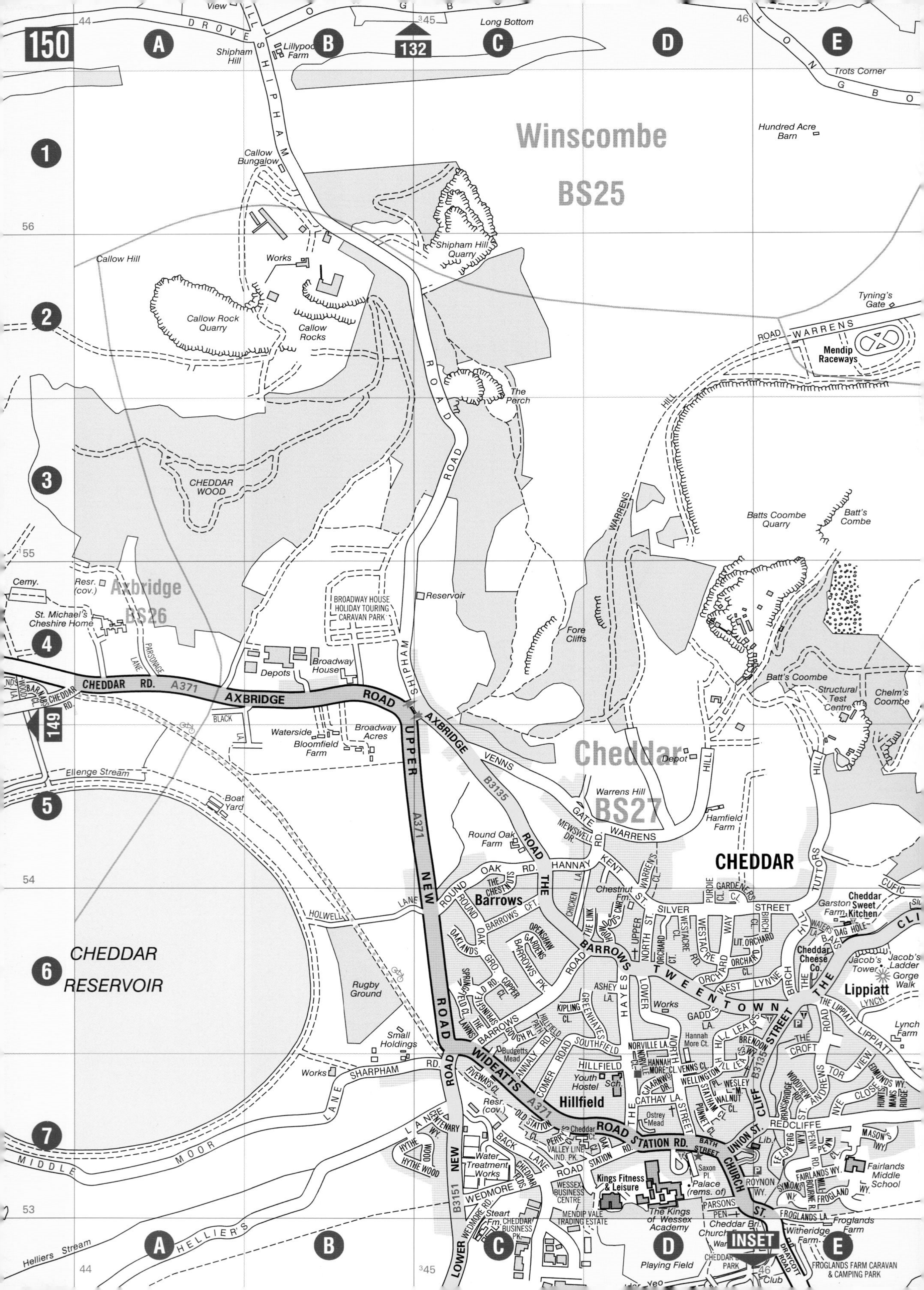
132
149
INSET
Winscombe
BS25
Axbridge
BS26
Cheddar
BS27
CHEDDAR
Shipham Hill
Lillypool Farm
Long Bottom
Trots Corner
Hundred Acre Barn
Callow Bungalow
Shipham Hill Quarry
Callow Hill
Works
Callow Rock Quarry
Callow Rocks
Tyning's Gate
Mendip Raceways
The Perch
CHEDDAR WOOD
Batts Coombe Quarry
Batt's Combe
Cemy.
Resr. (cov.)
St. Michael's Cheshire Home
BROADWAY HOUSE HOLIDAY TOURING CARAVAN PARK
Reservoir
Fore Cliffs
Depots
Broadway House
Batt's Coombe
Structural Test Centre
Chelm's Coombe
CHEDDAR RD.
A371
AXBRIDGE ROAD
BLACK LA.
Waterside
Bloomfield Farm
Broadway Acres
Depot
Ellenge Stream
Boat Yard
Warrens Hill
Hamfield Farm
Round Oak Farm
CHEDDAR RESERVOIR
Barrows
Hillfield
Lippiatt
Rugby Ground
Small Holdings
Works
Cheddar Sweet Kitchen
Garston Farm
Cheddar Cheese Co.
Jacob's Tower
Jacob's Ladder
Gorge Walk
Lynch Farm
Youth Hostel
Sch.
Resr. (cov.)
Water Treatment Works
WESSEX BUSINESS CENTRE
MENDIP VALE TRADING ESTATE
CHEDDAR BUSINESS PK.
Steart Fm.
Kings Fitness & Leisure
The Kings of Wessex Academy
Saxon Pl. Palace (rems. of)
Cheddar Br. Church
Ostrey Mead
Hannah More Ct.
Budgetts Mead
Valley Line Ind. Pk.
Fairlands Middle School
Froglands Farm
Witheridge Farm
FROGLANDS FARM CARAVAN & CAMPING PARK
Playing Field
CHEDDAR PARK
Lib.
Helliers Stream
B3151
B3135
A B C D E
1 2 3 4 5 6 7
44 345 46
56 55 54 53

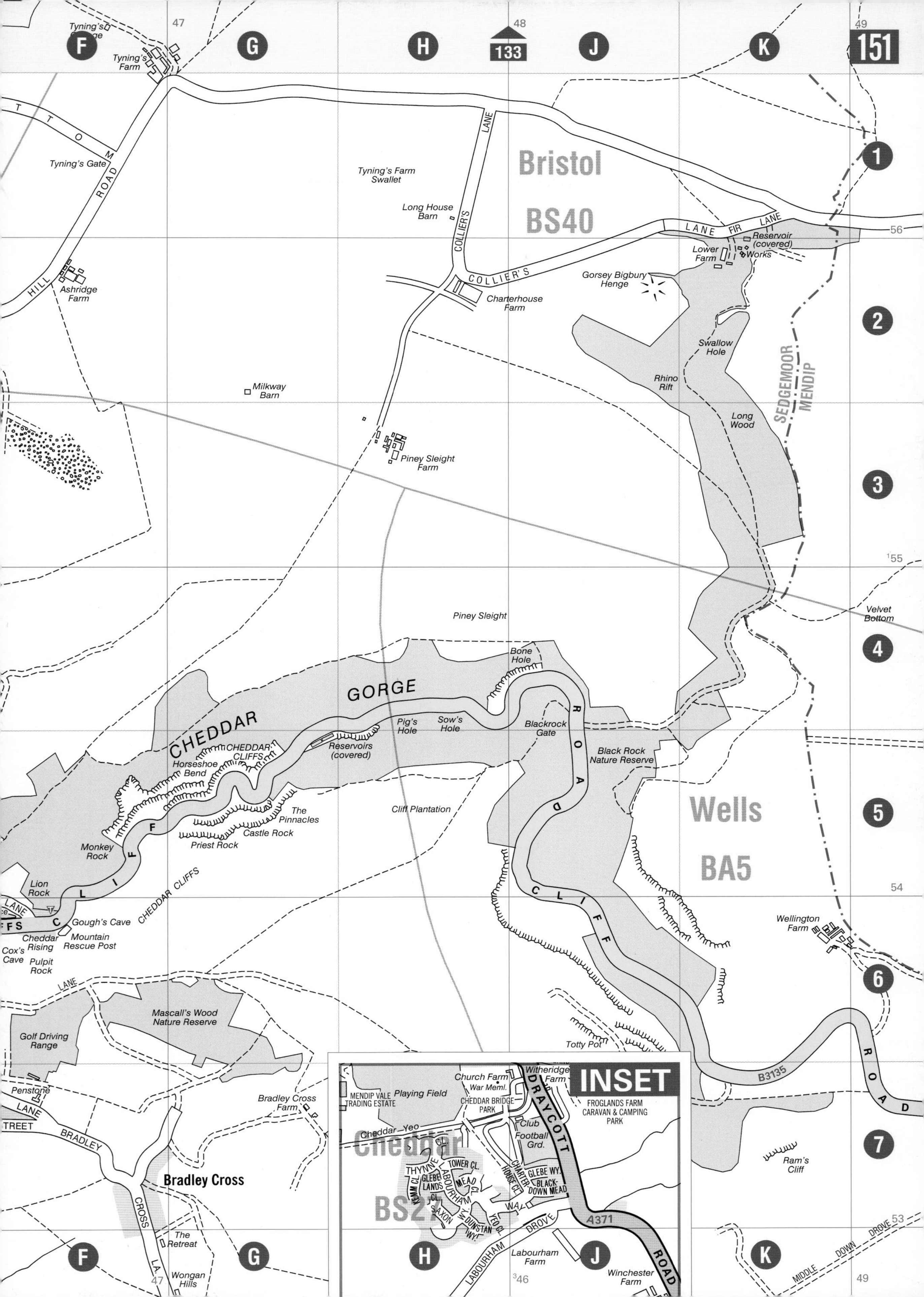
F
G
H
133
J
K
47
48
49
Tyning's Cottage
Tyning's Farm
TOTT MOOR
Tyning's Gate
HILL ROAD
Ashridge Farm
Tyning's Farm Swallet
Long House Barn
COLLIER'S LANE
Bristol
BS40
FIR LANE
Reservoir (covered)
Lower Farm
Works
Gorsey Bigbury Henge
Charterhouse Farm
Swallow Hole
Rhino Rift
Long Wood
SEDGEMOOR
MENDIP
Milkway Barn
Piney Sleight Farm
Piney Sleight
Velvet Bottom
Bone Hole
CHEDDAR GORGE
Pig's Hole
Sow's Hole
Blackrock Gate
Reservoirs (covered)
CHEDDAR CLIFFS
Horseshoe Bend
Black Rock Nature Reserve
The Pinnacles
Castle Rock
Priest Rock
Cliff Plantation
Wells
BA5
Monkey Rock
Lion Rock
CLIFF ROAD
CHEDDAR CLIFFS
Gough's Cave
Cheddar Rising
Mountain Rescue Post
Cox's Cave
Pulpit Rock
Wellington Farm
LANE
Mascall's Wood Nature Reserve
Golf Driving Range
Totty Pot
B3135
ROAD
Penstone
LANE
STREET
BRADLEY
Bradley Cross Farm
Bradley Cross
CROSS LA.
The Retreat
Wongan Hills
Ram's Cliff
MIDDLE DOWN DROVE
INSET
Church Farm
War Meml.
Witheridge Farm
MENDIP VALE TRADING ESTATE
Playing Field
CHEDDAR BRIDGE PARK
FROGLANDS FARM CARAVAN & CAMPING PARK
Cheddar Yeo
Cheddar
Club
Football Grd.
DRAYCOTT ROAD
THYNNE CL.
TOWER CL.
GLEBE LANDS
LABOURHAM WY.
MEAD CL.
CHARTERHOUSE CL.
GLEBE WY.
BLACKDOWN MEAD
KEMM CL.
BS27
SAXON
DUNSTAN WY.
YEO CL.
WA.
A371
DROVE
LABOURHAM DROVE
Labourham Farm
Winchester Farm
1
2
3
4
5
6
7
56
55
54
53
46

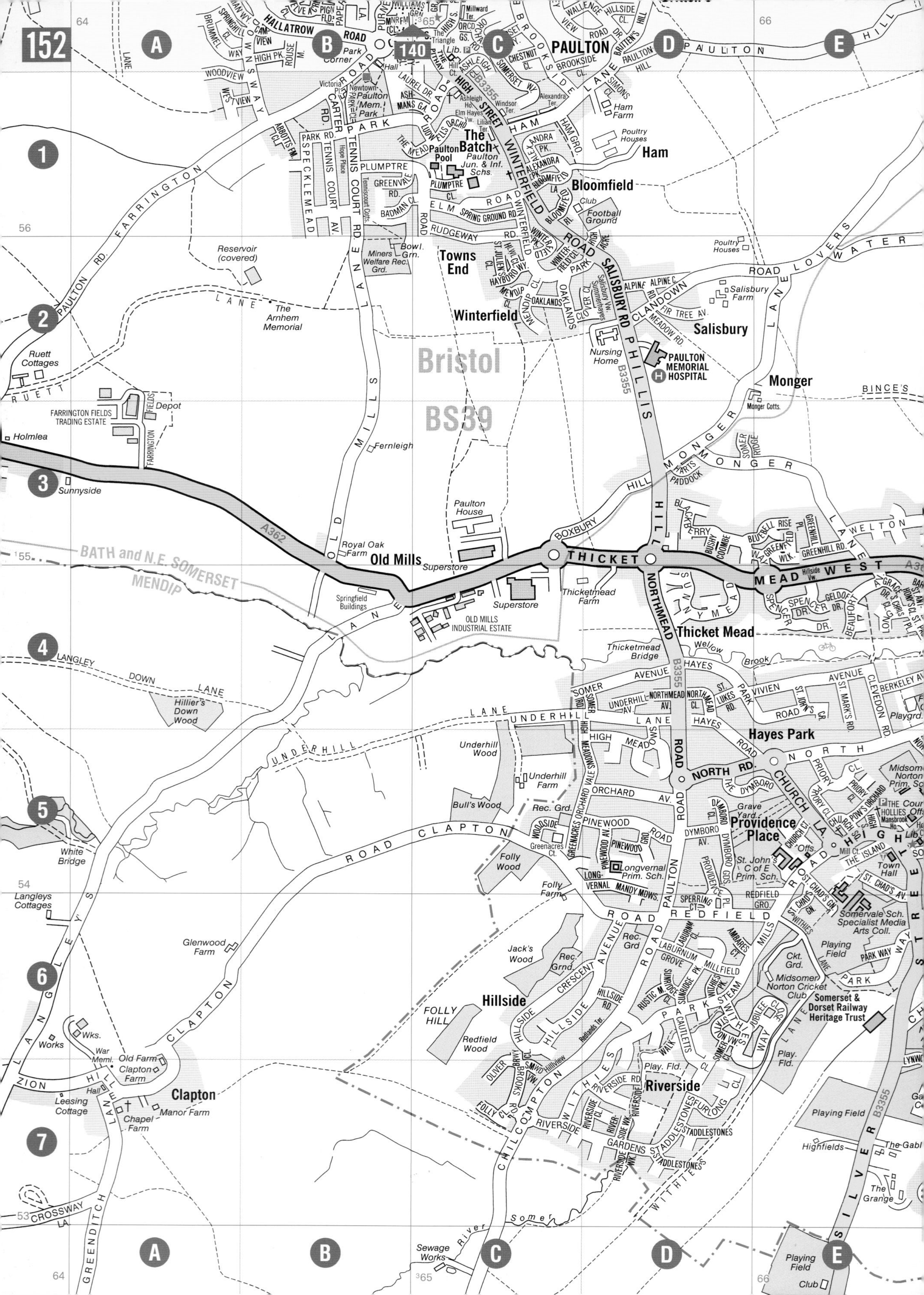

140
A
B
C
D
E
1
2
3
4
5
6
7
64
65
66
56
55
54
53
HALLATROW ROAD
PAULTON
PAULTON HILL
Park Corner
Newtown
Paulton Mem. Park
The Batch
Paulton Pool
Paulton Jun. & Inf. Schs.
HIGH STREET
WINTERFIELD ROAD
Ham
Ham Farm
Poultry Houses
Bloomfield
Football Ground
Towns End
Miners Welfare Rec. Grd.
Bowl. Grn.
Reservoir (covered)
The Arnhem Memorial
Winterfield
SALISBURY RD
Salisbury
Salisbury Farm
Nursing Home
PAULTON MEMORIAL HOSPITAL
Monger
Monger Cotts.
Bristol
BS39
FARRINGTON RD.
PAULTON RD.
Ruett Cottages
FARRINGTON FIELDS TRADING ESTATE
Depot
Holmlea
Sunnyside
A362
OLD MILLS LANE
Fernleigh
Paulton House
Royal Oak Farm
Old Mills
Superstore
Springfield Buildings
OLD MILLS INDUSTRIAL ESTATE
Thicketmead Farm
THICKET MEAD
BATH and N.E. SOMERSET
MENDIP
BOXBURY HILL
MONGER LANE
PHILLIS HILL
B3355
NORTHMEAD
Thicket Mead
MEAD WEST
WELTON
LOVERS LANE
WATER
LANGLEY DOWN LANE
Hillier's Down Wood
UNDERHILL LANE
Underhill Wood
Underhill Farm
Bull's Wood
HAYES PARK ROAD
Hayes Park
NORTH RD.
CHURCH LA.
Providence Place
St. John's C of E Prim. Sch.
Grave Yard
Longvernal Prim. Sch.
Rec. Grd.
Folly Wood
Folly Farm
Jack's Wood
CLAPTON ROAD
REDFIELD ROAD
PAULTON ROAD
Hillside
FOLLY HILL
Redfield Wood
Riverside
Play. Fld.
Playing Field
Ckt. Grd.
Midsomer Norton Cricket Club
Somerset & Dorset Railway Heritage Trust
Somervale Sch. Specialist Media Arts Coll.
Town Hall
Midsomer Norton Prim. Sch.
SILVER STREET
Highfields
The Grange
Glenwood Farm
Langleys Cottages
White Bridge
Works
Wks.
Old Farm
Clapton Farm
Clapton
Leesing Cottage
Chapel Farm
Manor Farm
ZION HILL
CROSSWAY LA.
GREENDITCH
CHILCOMPTON RD.
River Somer
Sewage Works
Wellow Brook
Thicketmead Bridge
Club

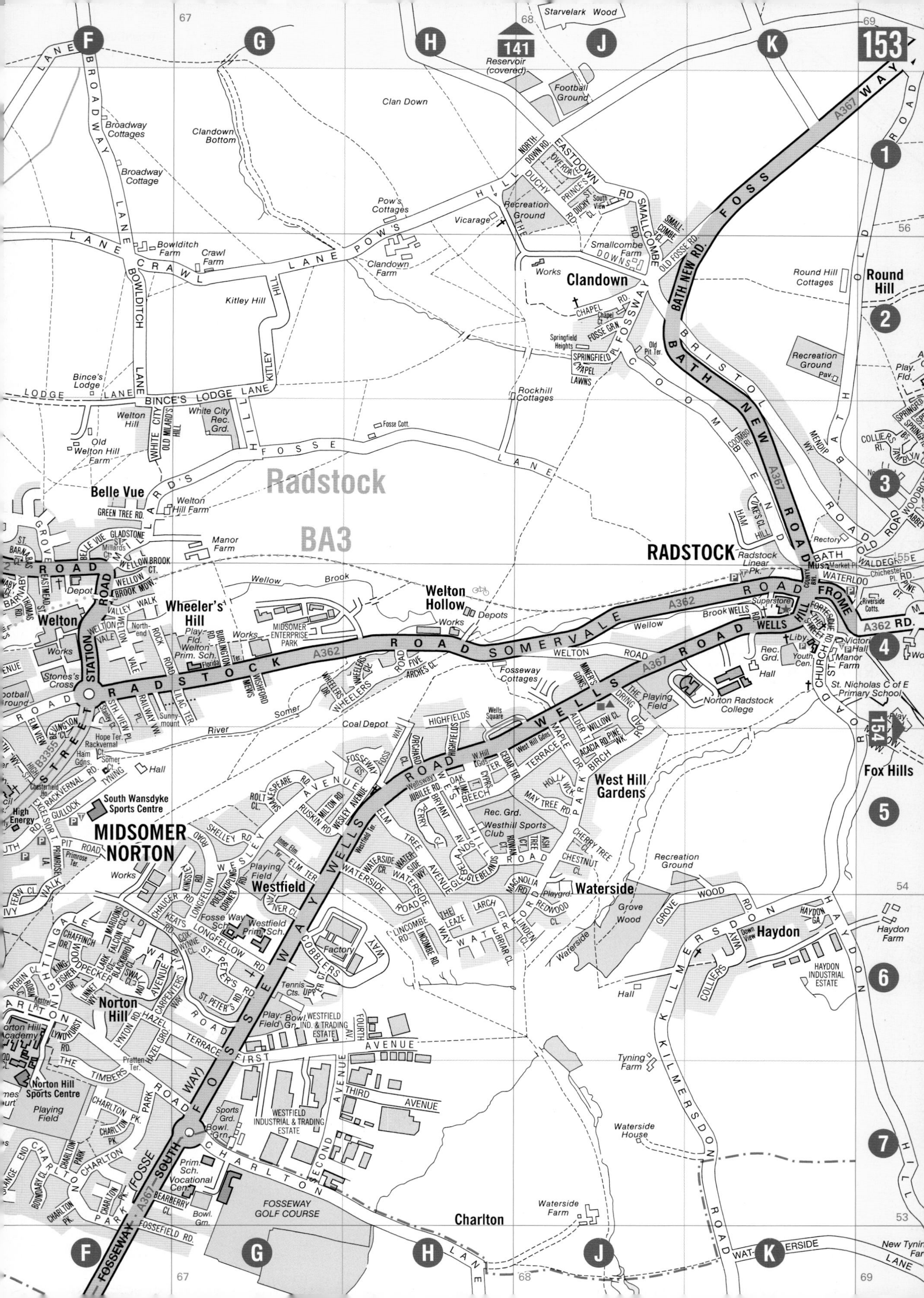

153
141
154
F
G
H
J
K
67
68
69
1
2
3
4
5
6
7
56
55
54
53
Starvelark Wood
Reservoir (covered)
Football Ground
Clan Down
Broadway Cottages
Broadway Cottage
Clandown Bottom
BROADWAY LANE
Pow's Cottages
POW'S HILL
Vicarage
Recreation Ground
NORTH DOWN RD.
EASTDOWN RD.
OVERDALE
DUCHY RD.
PRINCE'S
DUCHY ST. CL.
South View
SMALLCOMBE RD.
SMALL-COMBE CL.
Smallcombe Farm
DOWNS
OLD FOSSE RD.
FOSS WAY
A367
Bowlditch Farm
Crawl Farm
CRAWL LANE
POW'S LANE
Clandown Farm
Works
Clandown
Kitley Hill
KITLEY HILL
BOWLDITCH LANE
CHAPEL RD.
Chapel Ct.
FOSSE GRN.
FOSSWAY
Springfield Heights
Old Pit Ter.
SPRINGFIELD PL.
CHAPEL LAWNS
BATH NEW RD.
BRISTOL RD.
BATH NEW ROAD
Round Hill Cottages
Round Hill
Recreation Ground
Pav.
Play. Fld.
MENDIP WY.
BATH OLD ROAD
COLLIERS RI.
Bince's Lodge
LODGE LANE
BINCE'S LODGE LANE
Rockhill Cottages
Welton Hill
WHITE CITY
OLD MILLARD'S HILL
White City Rec. Grd.
Old Welton Hill Farm
Fosse Cott.
FOSSE LANE
COOMBE END
COOMBD RI.
Radstock
BA3
Belle Vue
GREEN TREE RD.
LARD'S
Welton Hill Farm
Manor Farm
GROVE
ST. BARNABAS CL.
BELLE VUE ST.
GLADSTONE ST.
Millards Ct.
MILL
WELLOW BROOK CT.
WELLOW BROOK MDW.
HAM
DYKE'S CL.
HILL
Rectory
RADSTOCK
Radstock Linear Pk.
Mus.
Market Pl.
BATH OLD RD.
WALDEGRAVE
WATERLOO RD.
Chichester Pl.
PINE CT.
ROAD
Depot
Wellow Brook
Welton Hollow
Depots
STATION ROAD
VALLEY WALK
Welton
Wheeler's Hill
North-end
ROCK ROAD
Play. Fld.
Welton Prim. Sch.
BURLINGTON ST.
Florida Ter.
Works
MIDSOMER ENTERPRISE PARK
A362
SOMERVALE ROAD
RADSTOCK ROAD
FIVE ARCHES CL.
Superstore
Brook WELLS RD.
WELLS HILL
COUNTY BRI.
FROME
Riverside Cotts.
A362 RD.
FORTESCUE RD.
CHEW ST.
Liby.
Victoria Hall
Manor Farm
Rec. Grd.
Youth Cen.
Hall
CHURCH ST.
St. Nicholas C of E Primary School
Play.
Works
Stones's Cross
WELTON VALE
RAILWAY VW.
LILAC TER.
WISHFORD MEWS
Sunny-mount
WHEELERS DR.
WHEELERS CL.
WELTON ROAD
Wellow
Fosseway Cottages
MINER'S GDNS.
THE DRING
Playing Field
Norton Radstock College
ELM VIEW
BEVINGTON CL.
Hope Ter.
Rackvernal Ct.
Ham Gdns.
Somer Ct.
TYNING
RACKVERNAL RD.
Somer River
Coal Depot
Hall
HIGHFIELDS
Wells Square
WELLS ROAD
WILLOW CL.
ALDER TER.
MAPLE DR.
PINE WK.
ACACIA RD.
BIRCH
ROAD
Fox Hills
B3355
HIGH STREET
South Wansdyke Sports Centre
FOSSEWAY GS.
SHAKESPEARE RD.
ROLT CL.
AVENUE
MILTON RD.
RUSKIN RD.
WESLEY AVENUE
ORCHARD CL.
Wellsway
JUBILEE RD.
BRYANT AV.
PERRY
W. Hill Gdns.
WEST HILL
OAK TER.
LIME
BEECH
CYPRS. TER.
CEDAR TER.
West Hill Gdns.
TERRACE
HOLLY WK.
PARK
West Hill Gardens
MAY TREE RD.
Rec. Grd.
Westhill Sports Club
High Energy
MIDSOMER NORTON
SHELLEY RD.
GULLOCK
PIT ROAD
Primrose Ter.
PRIMROSE WALK
Works
WESLEY
Inner Elm Ter.
ELM TER.
Westfield Ter.
Playing Field
Westfield
WATERSIDE CR.
WATERSIDE WY.
WATERSIDE
ROWAN CT.
TREE CT.
ASH
CHERRY TREE
CHESTNUT CL.
GLEBELANDS
Recreation Ground
MAGNOLIA RD.
Playgrd.
Waterside
IVY
FERN CL.
CHAUCER RD.
KEATS RD.
KIPLING
POETS CORNER
LONGFELLOW
KINGSLEY RD.
Fosse Way Sch.
Westfield Prim. Sch.
COX
WYNNE CL.
LONGFELLOW RD.
ST. PETER'S RD.
LINCOMBE RD.
THE LEAZE
LARCH
WATER
BRIAR CT.
LINDEN CL.
REDWOOD CL.
Grove Wood
GROVE
WOOD
Haydon
Down View
HAYDON GA.
Haydon Farm
HAYDON INDUSTRIAL ESTATE
HAYDON HILL
KILMERSDON ROAD
COLLIERS
Factory
COBBLERS
CHAFFINCH DR.
MARDONS CL.
FALCON CL.
LARK
BLACKBIRD
WOODPECKER
KINGFISHER DR.
SWALLOW
ROBIN CL.
LINNET WY.
Kestrel
Norton Hill
CARPENTERS
AVENUE
Tennis Cts.
UPPER
Play. Field
Bowl. Gn.
WESTFIELD IND. & TRADING ESTATE
FOURTH AV.
Hall
Norton Hill Academy
LYNDHURST RD.
LYNTON RD.
HAZEL
HAZEL GRO.
TERRACE
FIRST AVENUE
THE TIMBERS
Pratten Ter.
Tyning Farm
Norton Hill Sports Centre
Playing Field
CHARLTON PK.
PARK ROAD
THIRD AVENUE
SECOND AVENUE
WESTFIELD INDUSTRIAL & TRADING ESTATE
Sports Grd.
Bowl. Grn.
Waterside House
CHARLTON
SOUTH
A367
FOSSE WAY
FOSSEWAY
Prim. Sch.
Vocational Cen.
BEARBERRY CL.
Bowl. Grn.
FOSSEWAY GOLF COURSE
CHARLTON LANE
Charlton
Waterside Farm
WATERSIDE
New Tyning Farm
LANE
BOUNDARY CL.
FOSSEFIELD RD.
PARK

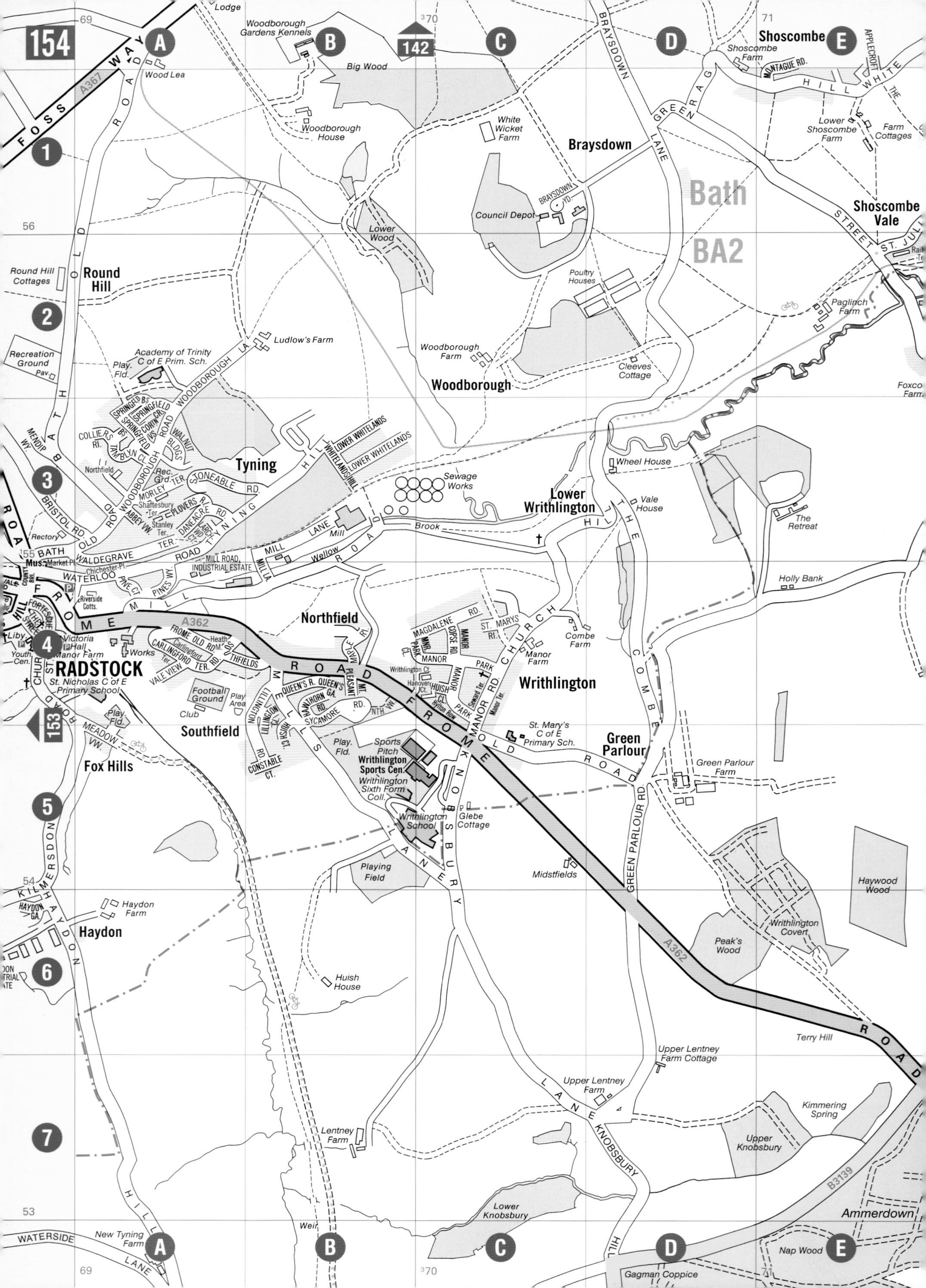

154

FOSS WAY A367

A
Wood Lea
Lodge
B Woodborough Gardens Kennels
Big Wood
142
C
White Wicket Farm
Braysdown
D Shoscombe Farm
Shoscombe **E**
Montague Rd.
Lower Shoscombe Farm
APPLECROFT
HILL
WHITE

1

BRAYSDOWN
GREEN LANE AG
Farm Cottages

56
Round Hill Cottages
Round Hill
Lower Wood
Council Depot
BRAYSDOWN YD.

Bath
BA2
STREET
Shoscombe Vale
ST. JUL
Rail Te

2
Recreation Ground Pav.
Academy of Trinity C of E Prim. Sch.
Play. Fld.
Ludlow's Farm
WOODBOROUGH LA.
Poultry Houses
Woodborough Farm
Woodborough
Cleeves Cottage
Paglinch Farm
Foxco Farm

3
Round Hill
BATH
MENDIP WY.
COLLIERS RI.
Northfield
SPRINGFD. BS.
SPRINGFIELD
SPRINGFIELD COMM. CEN.
BLDGS.
WALNUT
MORLEY
Tyning
STONEABLE RD.
SHAFTESBURY TER.
STANLEY TER.
DANECRE RD.
PLOVERS R.
Rec. Grd.
ABBEY VW.
WOODBOROUGH RD.
OLD RD.
TIMSBURY RD.
WOODBOROUGH RD.
LOWER WHITELANDS
WHITELANDS
LOWER WHITELANDS
WHITELANDS HILL
MILL LANE
Sewage Works
Brook
†
Lower Writhlington
Wheel House
Vale House
The Retreat
THE COMBE

4
BRISTOL RD.
Rectory
BATH
Mus.
Market Pl.
Chichester Pl.
WALDEGRAVE RD.
WATERLOO
Riverside Cotts.
FROME HILL
FORTESCUE
CHU. ST.
Liby.
Youth Cen.
Victoria Hall
Manor Farm
Works
CARLINGFORD TER.
VALE VIEW
THFIELDS
FROME OLD RD. M'S.
Heath Cottage
Carlingford
MILL RD.
MILL ROAD INDUSTRIAL ESTATE
Mill
Wellow
Northfield
MAYPLE RD.
MT. PLEASANT
MAGDALENE PARK
MNR. PARK CT.
COPSE RD.
MANOR RD.
ST. MARYS RD.
ST. MARYS
CHURCH RD.
Manor Farm
Combe Farm
Holly Bank

RADSTOCK
St. Nicholas C of E Primary School
A362
FROME OLD RD.
ROAD
Queen's R.
Queen's GA.
HANTHORN CT.
SYCAMORE RD.
HUISH
Hanover Ct.
Lytton Row
MANOR RD.
MANOR PARK
Medlar Tce.
Writhlington

153
MEADOW VW.
Play Fld.
Play Area
Football Ground
Club
Southfield
LILLINGTON RD.
CONSTABLE CT.
RD.
NTH.
Play. Fld.
Sports Pitch
Writhlington Sports Cen.
Writhlington Sixth Form Coll.
Writhlington School
St. Mary's C of E Primary Sch.
Speedwell
Green Parlour
Green Parlour Farm

5
KILMERSDON
Fox Hills
KNOBSBURY LANE
Glebe Cottage
Playing Field
Midstfields
GREEN PARLOUR RD.
Haywood Wood
Writhlington Covert

54
Haydon Farm
HAYDON GA.
Haydon
Peak's Wood

6
DON TRIAL ATE
Huish House
Upper Lentney Farm Cottage
Terry Hill
Kimmering Spring
A362
ROAD

7
Lentney Farm
Upper Lentney Farm
UPPER LENTNEY LANE
Upper Knobsbury
B3139

53
WATERSIDE
New Tyning Farm
HILL LANE
A
Weir
B
Lower Knobsbury
C
Gagman Coppice
D
Nap Wood
Ammerdown
E

69
370
370
71

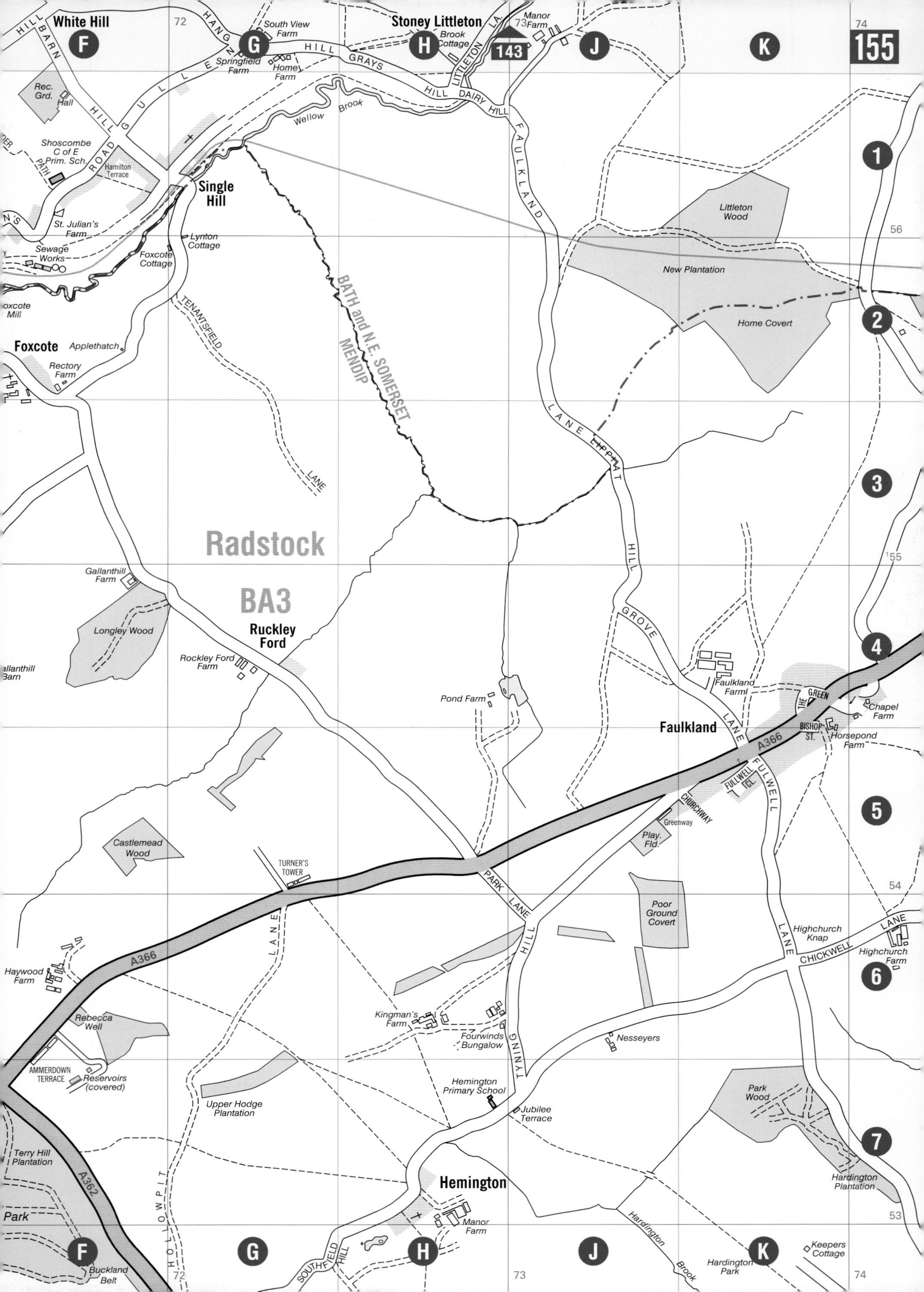
White Hill
Stoney Littleton
143
South View Farm
Manor Farm
Brook Cottage
Springfield Farm
Home Farm
Rec. Grd.
Hall
Shoscombe C of E Prim. Sch.
Hamilton Terrace
Single Hill
St. Julian's Farm
Sewage Works
Lynton Cottage
Foxcote Cottage
Foxcote
Applethatch
Rectory Farm
Wellow Brook
Littleton Wood
New Plantation
Home Covert
BATH and N.E. SOMERSET
MENDIP
Radstock
BA3
Gallanthill Farm
Longley Wood
Ruckley Ford
Rockley Ford Farm
Pond Farm
Faulkland
Faulkland Farm
Chapel Farm
Horsepond Farm
A366
Greenway
Play. Fld.
Castlemead Wood
TURNER'S TOWER
Poor Ground Covert
Highchurch Knap
Highchurch Farm
Haywood Farm
Rebecca Well
Kingman's Farm
Fourwinds Bungalow
Nesseyers
AMMERDOWN TERRACE
Reservoirs (covered)
Upper Hodge Plantation
Hemington Primary School
Jubilee Terrace
Park Wood
Terry Hill Plantation
A362
Hardington Plantation
Hemington
Manor Farm
Park
Buckland Belt
Hardington Brook
Hardington Park
Keepers Cottage

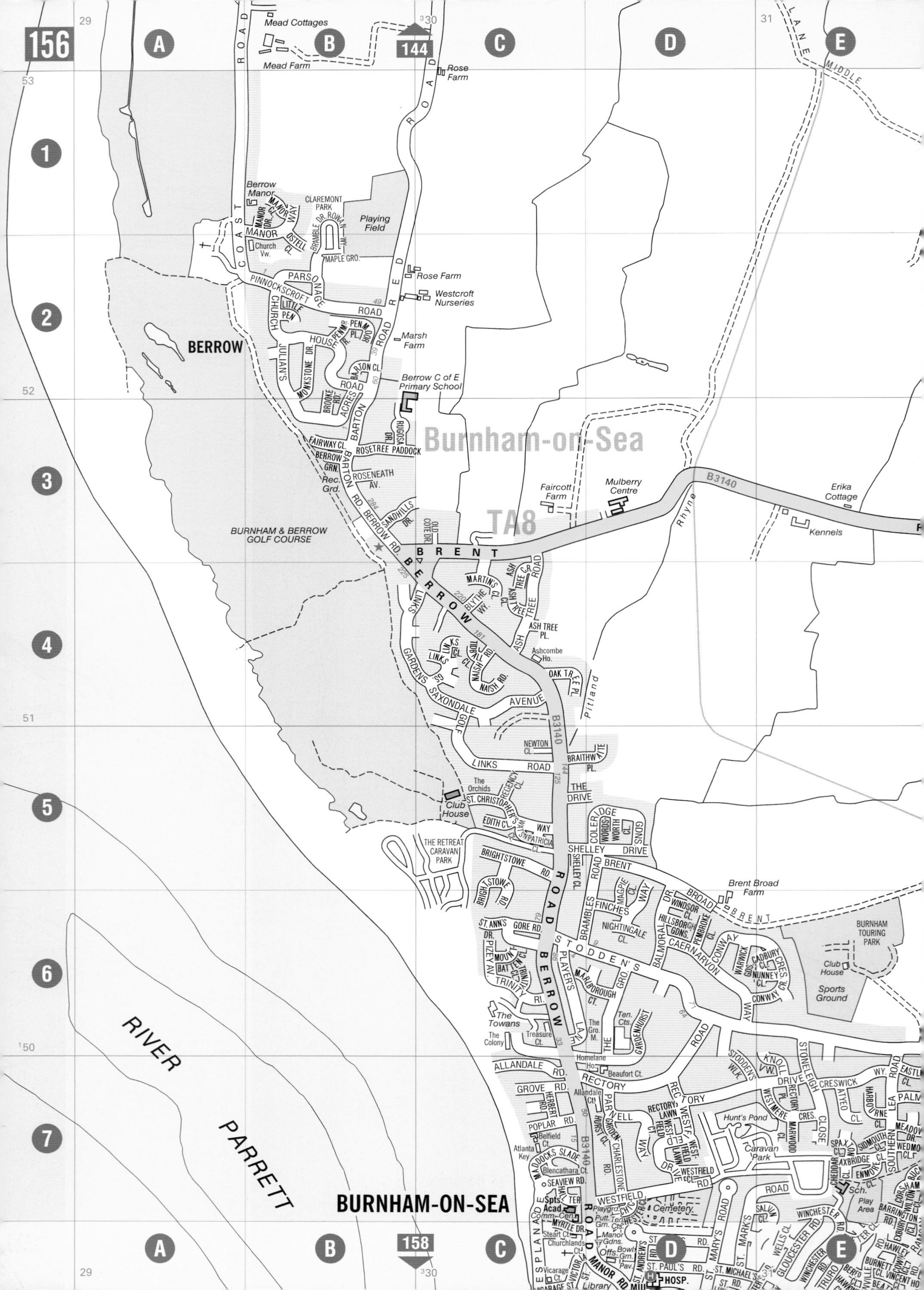

144
Mead Cottages
Mead Farm
Rose Farm
Berrow Manor
CLAREMONT PARK
Playing Field
Westcroft Nurseries
Marsh Farm
BERROW
Berrow C of E Primary School
Burnham-on-Sea
Faircott Farm
Mulberry Centre
B3140
Erika Cottage
Kennels
TA8
BURNHAM & BERROW GOLF COURSE
BRENT
BERROW
Ashcombe Ho.
Pitland
Rhyne
Club House
THE RETREAT CARAVAN PARK
Brent Broad Farm
BURNHAM TOURING PARK
Sports Ground
The Towans
RIVER PARRETT
Hunt's Pond
Caravan Park
Cemetery
BURNHAM-ON-SEA
158
HOSP.
Library

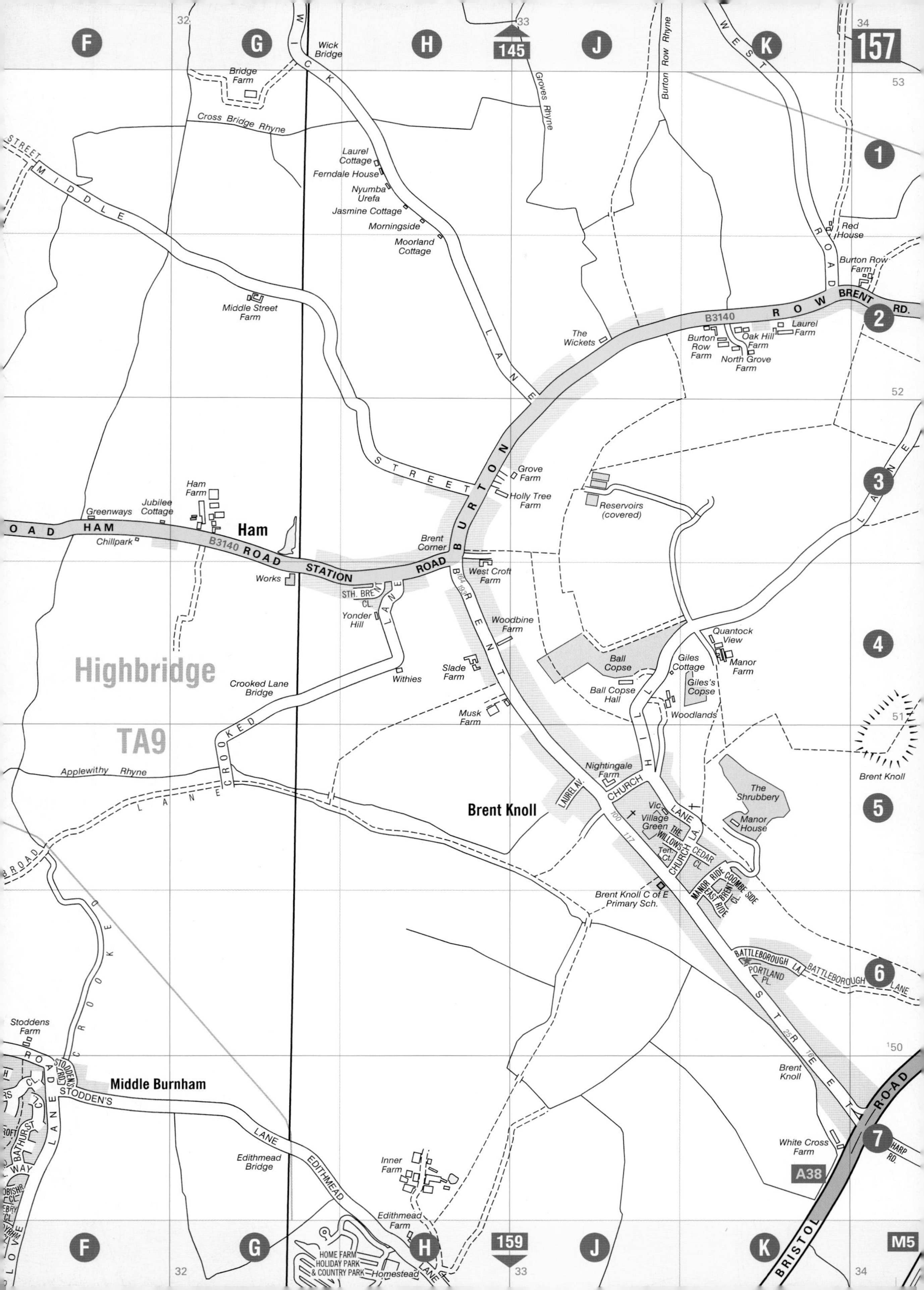

145
159
F
G
H
J
K
1
2
3
4
5
6
7
32
33
34
53
52
51
50
Wick Bridge
Bridge Farm
Cross Bridge Rhyne
Groves Rhyne
Burton Row Rhyne
WEST ROAD
MIDDLE STREET
WICK LANE
Laurel Cottage
Ferndale House
Nyumba Urefa
Jasmine Cottage
Morningside
Moorland Cottage
Red House
Burton Row Farm
BRENT RD.
B3140
ROW
Laurel Farm
Oak Hill Farm
Burton Row Farm
North Grove Farm
The Wickets
Middle Street Farm
BURTON
STREET
Grove Farm
Holly Tree Farm
Reservoirs (covered)
Ham Farm
Jubilee Cottage
Greenways
HAM ROAD
Ham
Chillpark
B3140 ROAD
STATION ROAD
Brent Corner
West Croft Farm
Works
STH. BRENT CL.
Yonder Hill
LANE
BRENT
Woodbine Farm
Quantock View
Manor Farm
Ball Copse
Giles Cottage
Giles's Copse
Ball Copse Hall
Woodlands
Highbridge
Crooked Lane Bridge
Withies
Slade Farm
Musk Farm
TA9
CROOKED LANE
Applewithy Rhyne
Nightingale Farm
HILL LANE
CHURCH LANE
LAUREL AV.
Brent Knoll
Vic.
Village Green
THE WILLOWS
Ten. Ct.
CHURCH LA.
CEDAR CL.
The Shrubbery
Manor House
Brent Knoll
MANOR RIDE
COOMBE SIDE
EAST BRENT CL.
Brent Knoll C of E Primary Sch.
BROAD
BATTLEBOROUGH LA.
BATTLEBOROUGH LANE
PORTLAND PL.
STREET
Stoddens Farm
STODDENS RD.
Middle Burnham
STODDEN'S LANE
BATHURST CL.
Brent Knoll
White Cross Farm
ROAD
HARP RD.
A38
BRISTOL
M5
Edithmead Bridge
EDITHMEAD LANE
Inner Farm
Edithmead Farm
HOME FARM HOLIDAY PARK & COUNTRY PARK
Homestead

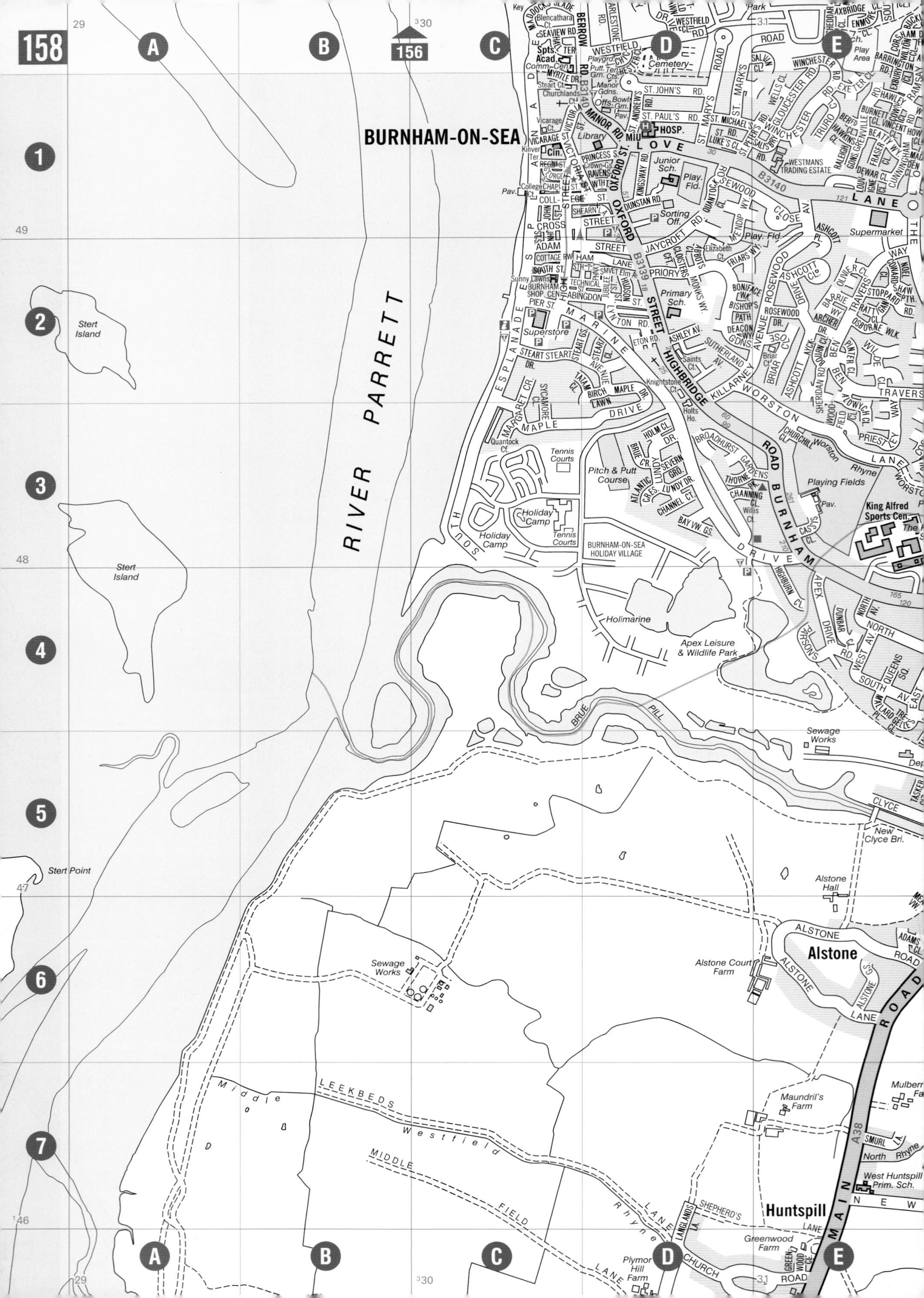

BURNHAM-ON-SEA

RIVER PARRETT

Stert Island

Stert Island

Stert Point

HIGHBRIDGE

King Alfred Sports Cen.

Apex Leisure & Wildlife Park

Sewage Works

Holimarine

BURNHAM-ON-SEA HOLIDAY VILLAGE

Holiday Camp

Supermarket

Cemetery

HOSP.

Alstone Hall

Alstone

Alstone Court Farm

New Clyce Bri.

Sewage Works

Maundril's Farm

West Huntspill Prim. Sch.

Huntspill

Greenwood Farm

Plymor Hill Farm

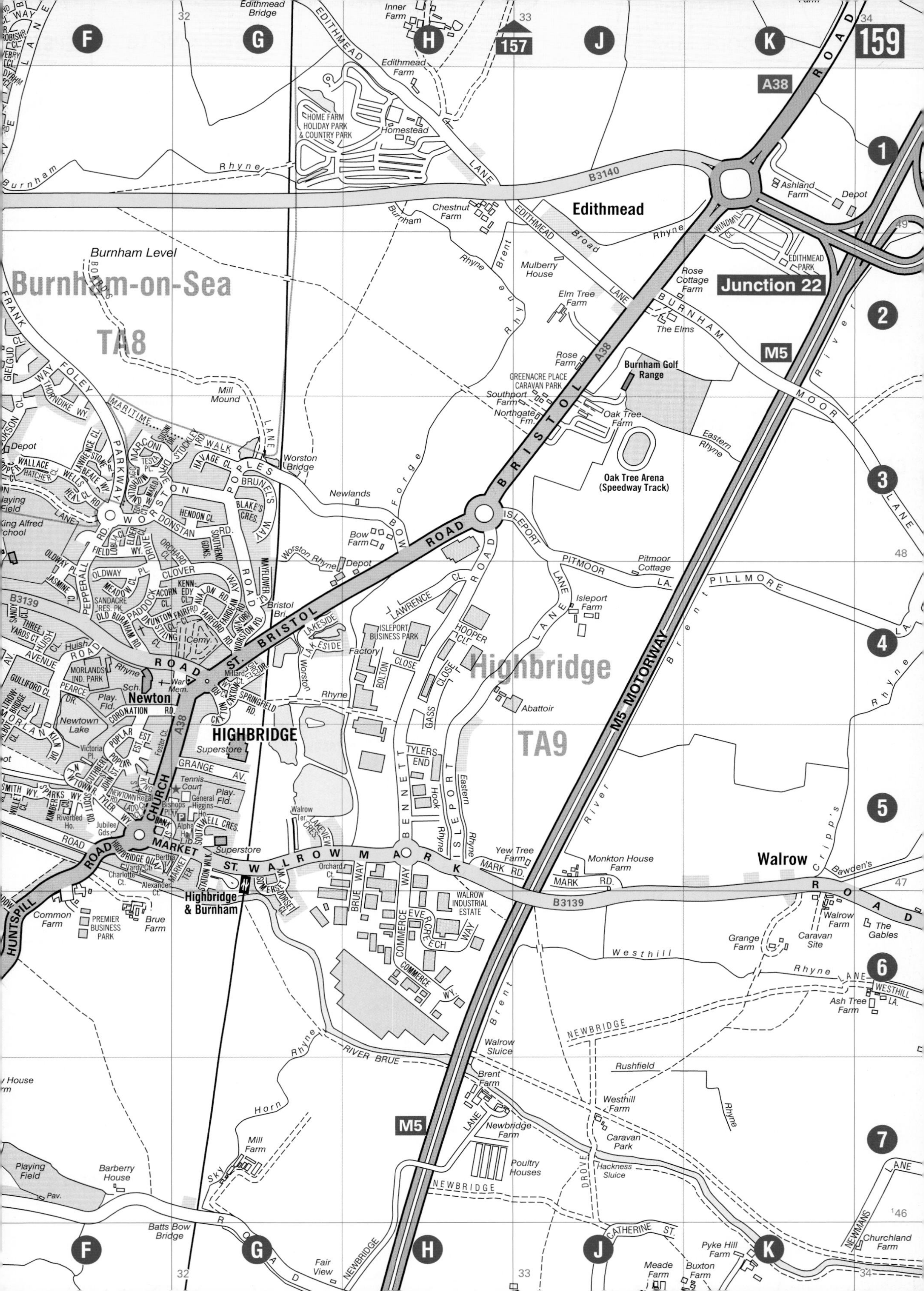
F
G
H
J
K
157
32
33
34
1
2
3
4
5
6
7
48
47
46
Edithmead Bridge
Inner Farm
Edithmead Farm
HOME FARM HOLIDAY PARK & COUNTRY PARK
Homestead
EDITHMEAD LANE
Rhyne
Burnham
B3140
A38
ROAD
Ashland Farm
Depot
Chestnut Farm
Edithmead
EDITHMEAD
Broad
Rhyne
WINDMILL CL.
EDITHMEAD PARK
Junction 22
Burnham Level
Burnham-on-Sea
TA8
Mulberry House
Rose Cottage Farm
Elm Tree Farm
BURNHAM
The Elms
M5
Rose Farm
GREENACRE PLACE CARAVAN PARK
Burnham Golf Range
Southport Farm
Northgate Fm.
Oak Tree Farm
MOOR
River
Eastern Rhyne
Oak Tree Arena (Speedway Track)
LANE
Mill Mound
Worston Bridge
Newlands
Forge
BRISTOL
ROAD
Bow Farm
Worston Rhyne
Depot
ISLEPORT
PITMOOR
Pitmoor Cottage
LA.
PILLMORE
Isleport Farm
LAWRENCE CL.
ISLEPORT BUSINESS PARK
Factory
HOOPER CL.
Highbridge
Abattoir
BOLTON CLOSE
CLOSE
GASS
TA9
M5 MOTORWAY
Brent
Rhyne
TYLERS END
Hook Rhyne
Eastern Rhyne
Cripp's
Walrow
Bawden's
Yew Tree Farm
Monkton House Farm
MARK RD.
MARK RD.
B3139
ROAD
Walrow Farm
The Gables
Caravan Site
Grange Farm
Westhill
Rhyne
LANE
WESTHILL LA.
Ash Tree Farm
WALROW INDUSTRIAL ESTATE
COMMERCE WAY
EVERCREECH WAY
COMMERCE WY.
NEWBRIDGE
Walrow Sluice
RIVER BRUE
Rushfield
Brent Farm
Westhill Farm
Rhyne
Newbridge Farm
Caravan Park
Poultry Houses
Hackness Sluice
DROVE
NEWBRIDGE
CATHERINE ST.
Pyke Hill Farm
Meade Farm
Buxton Farm
NEWMANS LANE
Churchland Farm
Horn
Mill Farm
Sky
Rhyne
Playing Field
Barberry House
Pav.
Batts Bow Bridge
ROAD
Fair View
NEWBRIDGE
FOLEY WAY
FRANK
GIELGUD CL.
THORNDIKE WY.
MARITIME WALK
PARKWAY
MARCONI DRIVE
TESLA PL.
STOCKLEY WALK
HAVAGE CL.
POPLES
BRUNEL'S WAY
BLAKE'S CRES.
WORSTON
HENDON CL.
DONSTAN
SOUTHEND GDNS.
RD.
Depot
WALLACE
LAWRENCE CL.
STONE
BEALE WY.
HATCHER CL.
WELLS
LANE
Playing Field
King Alfred School
OLDWAY PL.
JASMINE
PEPPERALL
FIELD
ELDER
WY.
DRIVE
ORCHARD CL.
OLDWAY PL.
MEADOW CL.
CLOVER
KENNEDY CL.
ON RD.
WAY
ROAD
MAYFLOWER CL.
PADDOCK
ACORN CL.
SANDACRE RES. PK.
OLD BURNHAM RD.
DAUNTON
FAIRFORD RD.
FAIRDEAN
WORSTON RD.
Bristol Bri.
B3139
THREE YARDS CT.
HUISH CL.
Huish
ROAD
AVENUE
MORLANDS IND. PARK
Rhyne
Sch.
ROAD
War Mem.
ST. BRISTOL
Cemy.
LAKESIDE
LAKESIDE
Worston
Millard Ct.
SPRINGFIELD RD.
Rhyne
GULLIFORD CL.
PEARCE DR.
Play. Fld.
Newton
CORONATION RD.
Newtown Lake
A38
HIGHBRIDGE
Superstore
EST.
POPLAR
Victoria Pl.
Foster Ct.
GRANGE AV.
CHURCH
Tennis Court
General Higgins Ho.
Play. Fld.
SMITH WY.
SPARKS WY.
KIMBER CL.
NEWTOWN R.
SCOTT RD.
TYLER WY.
JOHN ST.
Riverbed Ho.
Jubilee Gds.
Bishops Pk.
Alpha Ho.
Lib.
SOUTHWELL CRES.
Superstore
ROAD
MARKET
ROAD
HIGHBRIDGE QUAY
Bertha Ct.
Charlotte Ct.
Alexander Ct.
MARKET TER.
STATION WLK.
ST. WALROW MARK
Orchard Ct.
BRUE WAY
BENNETT WAY
ISLEPORT
Walrow Ter.
LAKEVIEW CRES.
SOMERSET
DORSET CL.
Highbridge & Burnham
HUNTSPILL
Common Farm
PREMIER BUSINESS PARK
Brue Farm

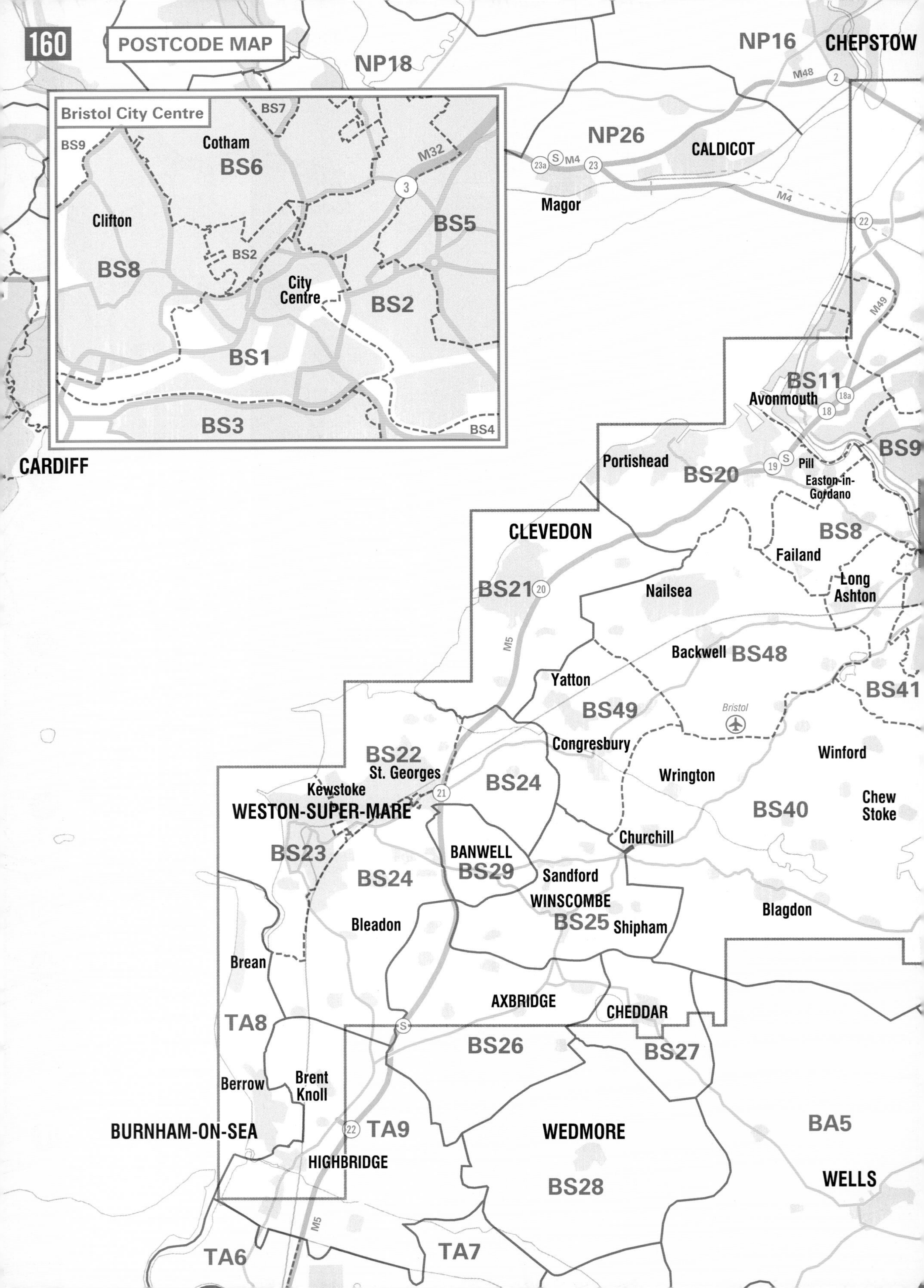

POSTCODE MAP

Bristol City Centre

BS9
Cotham
BS6
BS7
M32
Clifton
BS2
BS8
City Centre
BS2
BS5
BS1
BS2
BS3
BS4

CARDIFF

NP18

NP16   **CHEPSTOW**

M48
2

NP26   CALDICOT
23a S M4 23
M4
Magor
M4
22

M49

BS11
Avonmouth
18a
18
BS9

Portishead   **BS20**
19 S   Pill
Easton-in-Gordano

CLEVEDON

BS8
Failand

BS21 20
Nailsea
Long Ashton

Backwell   **BS48**

BS41

M5
Yatton

BS49
Bristol ✈
Congresbury

BS22
St. Georges
Kewstoke
21
BS24
Wrington
BS40
Winford

WESTON-SUPER-MARE
Churchill
Chew Stoke

BS23
BS24
BANWELL
BS29
Sandford
WINSCOMBE
BS25 Shipham
Blagdon

Bleadon

Brean

TA8
AXBRIDGE
CHEDDAR

Berrow   Brent Knoll
BS26
BS27
BA5

BURNHAM-ON-SEA
22   **TA9**
WEDMORE
WELLS

HIGHBRIDGE
BS28

M5

TA6   **TA7**

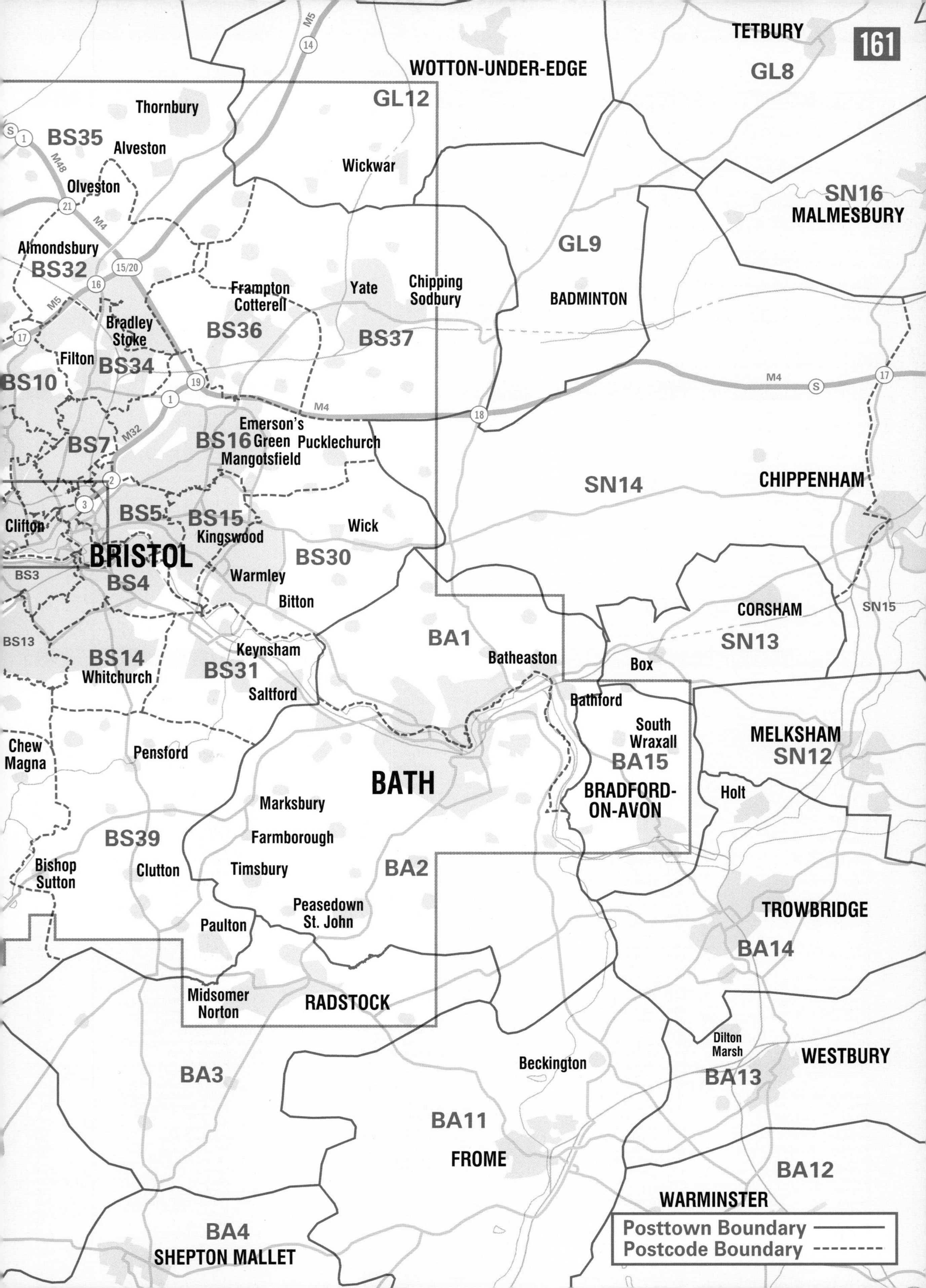

TETBURY
GL8

WOTTON-UNDER-EDGE
GL12

SN16
MALMESBURY

BS35
Thornbury
Alveston
Olveston

GL9
BADMINTON

Almondsbury
BS32
Frampton
Cotterell
Yate
Chipping
Sodbury

BS36
BS37

Bradley
Stoke
Filton
BS34

BS10

BS7

BS16 Emerson's
Green Pucklechurch
Mangotsfield

SN14
CHIPPENHAM

BS5
BS15
Kingswood
Wick

Clifton

BRISTOL
BS4
Warmley
BS30

BA1
Batheaston
Box

CORSHAM
SN15

BS3
Bitton

SN13

BS13
Keynsham

South
Wraxall
BA15
BRADFORD-
ON-AVON

MELKSHAM
SN12

BS14
Whitchurch
BS31
Saltford
Bathford

Holt

Chew
Magna
Pensford

BATH

BS39
Marksbury
Farmborough

TROWBRIDGE

Bishop
Sutton
Clutton
Timsbury
BA2
BA14

Paulton
Peasedown
St. John

Dilton
Marsh
WESTBURY

Midsomer
Norton
RADSTOCK

BA3
Beckington
BA13

BA11
FROME

BA12

WARMINSTER

BA4
SHEPTON MALLET

Posttown Boundary ———
Postcode Boundary - - - - -

INDEX

Including Streets, Places & Areas, Industrial Estates,
Selected Flats & Walkways, Service Areas, Stations and Selected Places of Interest.

HOW TO USE THIS INDEX

1. Each street name is followed by its Postcode District and then by its Locality abbreviation(s) and then by its map reference; e.g. **Abbey Rd.** BS9: W Trym . . . .2F **47** is in the BS9 Postcode District and the Westbury-on-Trym Locality and is to be found in square 2F on page **47**. The page number is shown in bold type.

2. A strict alphabetical order is followed in which Av., Rd., St., etc. (though abbreviated) are read in full and as part of the street name; e.g. **Abbey Ga.** appears after **Abbey Gdns.** but before **Abbey Ga. St.**

3. Streets and a selection of flats and walkways that cannot be shown on the mapping, appear in the index with the thoroughfare to which they are connected shown in brackets; e.g. **Abbey Chambers** BA1: Bath . . . .5G **7** (off York St.)

4. Addresses that are in more than one part are referred to as not continuous.

5. Places and areas are shown in the index in **BLUE TYPE** and the map reference is to the actual map square in which the town centre or area is located and not to the place name shown on the map; e.g. **ALMONDSBURY** 2C **26**

6. An example of a selected place of interest is **American Museum in Britain, The (Claverton Manor).** . . .6J **101**

7. Examples of stations are:
Avoncliff Station (Rail) . . . .7C **124**; **Bath Bus Station** . . . .6G **7** (6C **100**); **Bath Road (Park & Ride)** 2H **77**

8. Junction names and Service Areas are shown in the index in **BOLD CAPITAL TYPE**; e.g. **GORDANO SERVICE AREA** 4D **44**

9. Map references for entries that appear on large scale pages **4-7** are shown first, with small scale map references shown in brackets; e.g. **Abbey Ct.** BA2: Bath 3J **7** (4D **100**)

GENERAL ABBREVIATIONS

All. : Alley	**Cott.** : Cottage	**Info.** : Information	**Quad.** : Quadrant
App. : Approach	**Cotts.** : Cottages	**La.** : Lane	**Res.** : Residential
Arc. : Arcade	**Ct.** : Court	**Lit.** : Little	**Ri.** : Rise
Av. : Avenue	**Cres.** : Crescent	**Lwr.** : Lower	**Rd.** : Road
Bk. : Back	**Cft.** : Croft	**Mnr.** : Manor	**Rdbt.** : Roundabout
Blvd. : Boulevard	**Dr.** : Drive	**Mans.** : Mansions	**Shop.** : Shopping
Bri. : Bridge	**E.** : East	**Mkt.** : Market	**Sth.** : South
B'way. : Broadway	**Ent.** : Enterprise	**Mdw.** : Meadow	**Sq.** : Square
Bldg. : Building	**Est.** : Estate	**Mdws.** : Meadows	**Sta.** : Station
Bldgs. : Buildings	**Fld.** : Field	**M.** : Mews	**St.** : Street
Bungs. : Bungalows	**Flds.** : Fields	**Mt.** : Mount	**Ter.** : Terrace
Bus. : Business	**Gdn.** : Garden	**Mus.** : Museum	**Twr.** : Tower
Cvn. : Caravan	**Gdns.** : Gardens	**Nth.** : North	**Trad.** : Trading
C'way. : Causeway	**Ga.** : Gate	**No.** : Number	**Up.** : Upper
Cen. : Centre	**Gt.** : Great	**Pde.** : Parade	**Va.** : Vale
Chu. : Church	**Grn.** : Green	**Pk.** : Park	**Vw.** : View
Circ. : Circle	**Gro.** : Grove	**Pas.** : Passage	**Vs.** : Villas
Cir. : Circus	**Hgts.** : Heights	**Pl.** : Place	**Vis.** : Visitors
Cl. : Close	**Ho.** : House	**Pct.** : Precinct	**Wlk.** : Walk
Comn. : Common	**Ho's.** : Houses	**Prom.** : Promenade	**W.** : West
Cnr. : Corner	**Ind.** : Industrial		**Yd.** : Yard

LOCALITY ABBREVIATIONS

Abbots Leigh: BS8 . . . .Abb L	**Butcombe**: BS40 . . . .But	**Easton-in-Gordano**: BS20 . . . .Eas	**Kewstoke**: BS22 . . . .Kew
Abson: BS30 . . . .Abson	**Cadbury Heath**: BS30 . . . .C Hth	**East Rolstone**: BS24 . . . .E Rols	**Keynsham**: BS4,BS14,BS31 . . . .Key
Aldwick: BS40 . . . .Aldw	**Cameley**: BS39 . . . .Came	**Eastville**: BS5,BS7 . . . .Eastv	**Kilmersdon**: BA3 . . . .Kil
Almondsbury: BS32 . . . .Alm	**Camerton**: BA2 . . . .Cam	**Edingworth**: BS24 . . . .E'wth	**Kingsdown**: SN13 . . . .Kgdn
Alveston: BS32,BS35 . . . .A'ton	**Charfield**: GL12 . . . .Char	**Edithmead**: TA9 . . . .Edith	**Kingston Seymour**: BS21 . . . .Kings S
Ashton Gate: BS3 . . . .Ash G	**Charlcombe**: BA1 . . . .Charl	**Elberton**: BS35 . . . .Elbton	**Kingswood**: ,BS15,GL12 . . . .Kgswd
Ashton Vale: BS3 . . . .Ash V	**Charterhouse**: BS40 . . . .C'hse	**Elborough**: BS24 . . . .Elbgh	**Kington**: BS35 . . . .King
Ashwicke: SN14 . . . .Ash	**Cheddar**: BA5,BS27 . . . .Ched	**Emersons Green**: BS16,BS36 . . . .Emer G	**Knowle**: BS3-4 . . . .Know
Aust: BS35 . . . .Aust	**Chelvey**: BS48 . . . .Chelv	**Englishcombe**: BA2 . . . .Eng	**Langford**: BS40 . . . .L'frd
Avoncliff: BA15 . . . .Avonc	**Chelwood**: BS39 . . . .Chelw	**Failand**: BS8,BS48 . . . .Fail	**Langridge**: BA1 . . . .L'rdge
Avonmouth: BS10-11 . . . .A'mth	**Chew Magna**: BS39-41 . . . .Chew M	**Falfield**: GL12 . . . .Fal	**Lansdown**: BA1 . . . .L'dwn
Axbridge: BS26 . . . .Axb	**Chew Stoke**: BS40 . . . .Chew S	**Farmborough**: BA2 . . . .F'boro	**Lawrence Weston**: BS11 . . . .Law W
Backwell: BS48 . . . .Back	**Chipping Sodbury**: BS37 . . . .Chip S	**Farrington Gurney**: BS39 . . . .Far G	**Leigh Woods**: BS8 . . . .L Wds
Badgworth: BS26 . . . .Badg	**Chittening**: BS11 . . . .Chit	**Faulkland**: BA3 . . . .Faul	**Leyhill**: GL12 . . . .Ley
Bagstone: GL12 . . . .Bag	**Christon**: BS25-26 . . . .Chri	**Felton**: BS40 . . . .F'tn	**Limpley Stoke**: BA1-2 . . . .Lim S
Banwell: BS24-25,BS29 . . . .Ban	**Churchill**: BS25 . . . .C'hll	**Filton**: BS7,BS34 . . . .Fil	**Little Ashley**: BA15 . . . .Lit A
Barrow Gurney: BS48 . . . .Bar G	**Clandown**: BA3 . . . .Clan	**Fishponds**: BS16 . . . .Fish	**Little Stoke**: BS34 . . . .Lit S
Barrs Court: BS30 . . . .Bar C	**Clapton**: BA3 . . . .Clapt	**Flax Bourton**: BS48 . . . .Flax B	**Littleton-upon-Severn**: BS35 . . . .L Sev
Barton: BS25-26 . . . .Bart	**Clapton-in-Gordano**: BS20 . . . .Glap G	**Foxcote**: BA3 . . . .Fox	**Lockeaze**: BS7,BS16 . . . .L'lze
Barton Hill: BS5 . . . .Bar H	**Claverham**: BS49 . . . .C'ham	**Frampton Cotterell**: BS36 . . . .Fram C	**Long Ashton**: BS41,BS48 . . . .L Ash
Bath: BA1-2 . . . .Bath	**Claverton**: BA2 . . . .C'ton	**Frenchay**: BS16 . . . .Fren	**Longwell Green**: BS30 . . . .Long G
Bathampton: BA2 . . . .Batham	**Claverton Down**: BA2 . . . .C'ton D	**Freshford**: BA2 . . . .F'frd	**Lower Hamswell**: BA1 . . . .L Ham
Batheaston: BA1 . . . .Bathe	**Cleeve**: BS49 . . . .C've	**Gaunt's Earthcott**: BS32 . . . .Gau E	**Lower South Wraxall**: BA15 . . . .L Wrax
Bathford: BA1 . . . .Bathf	**Clevedon**: BS21 . . . .Clev	**Grovesend**: BS35 . . . .Grov	**Lower Weare**: BS26 . . . .L Wre
Beach: BS30 . . . .Beach	**Clifton**: BS1,BS8 . . . .Clftn	**Hallatrow**: BS39 . . . .Hall	**Loxton**: BS26 . . . .Lox
Beachley: NP16 . . . .Beach	**Clutton**: BS39 . . . .Clut	**Hallen**: BS10 . . . .H'len	**Lympsham**: BS24 . . . .Lym
Bedminster: BS3,BS13 . . . .Bedm	**Coalpit Heath**: BS36 . . . .Coal H	**Hall End**: GL12 . . . .H End	**Mangotsfield**: BS16 . . . .Mang
Berrow: TA8 . . . .Berr	**Codrington**: BS37 . . . .Cod	**Hambrook**: BS16,BS34 . . . .H'ook	**Marksbury**: BA2 . . . .Mark
Biddisham: BS26 . . . .Bidd	**Cold Ashton**: SN14 . . . .C Ash	**Hanham**: BS15,BS30 . . . .Han	**Midford**: BA2 . . . .Mid
Bishopston: BS6-7 . . . .Bishop	**Combe Down**: BA2 . . . .C Down	**Hartcliffe**: BS13-14 . . . .Hart	**Midsomer Norton**: BA3 . . . .Mid N
Bishop Sutton: BS39 . . . .Bis S	**Combe Hay**: BA2 . . . .C Hay	**Haydon**: BA3 . . . .Hay	**Monkton Combe**: BA2 . . . .Mon C
Bishopsworth: BS13 . . . .Bis	**Compton Bishop**: BS26 . . . .Comp B	**Hemington**: BA3 . . . .Hem	**Monkton Farleigh**: BA15 . . . .Mon F
Bitton: BS30 . . . .Bit	**Compton Dando**: BS39 . . . .Comp D	**Henbury**: BS10 . . . .Hen	**Nailsea**: BS21,BS48 . . . .Nail
Blagdon: BS40 . . . .Blag	**Compton Martin**: BS40 . . . .Comp M	**Henfield**: BS36 . . . .Henf	**Nempnett Thrubwell**: BS40 . . . .Nem T
Bleadon: BS23-24 . . . .B'don	**Congresbury**: BS24-25,BS40,BS49 . . . .Cong	**Hengrove**: BS14 . . . .H'gro	**Newton St Loe**: BA2 . . . .New L
Bourton: BS22,BS24 . . . .Bour	**Coombe Dingle**: BS9 . . . .C Din	**Henleaze**: BS6,BS9 . . . .Henle	**Northwick**: BS35 . . . .N'wick
Bower Ashton: BS3 . . . .Bwr A	**Corston**: BA2 . . . .Cor	**Hewish**: BS22,BS24 . . . .Hew	**North Wick**: BS41 . . . .N Wick
Bradley Leigh: BA2 . . . .Brad L	**Cotham**: BS6,BS8 . . . .Cot	**Highbridge**: TA9 . . . .Highb	**North Widcombe**: BS40 . . . .N Wid
Bradford-on-Avon: BA15 . . . .Brad A	**Cowhill**: BS35 . . . .C'hill	**High Littleton**: BA2,BS39 . . . .High L	**Norton Hawkfield**: BS39 . . . .Nor H
Bradley Stoke: BS16,BS32,BS34 . . . .Brad S	**Cromhall**: GL12 . . . .Crom	**Hinton**: SN14 . . . .Hin	**Norton Malreward**: BS14,BS39 . . . .Nor M
Brean: TA8 . . . .Brean	**Cross**: BS26 . . . .Cross	**Hinton Blewett**: BS39 . . . .Hin B	**Nye**: BS24 . . . .Nye
Brent Knoll: BS24,TA9 . . . .Bre K	**Dodington**: BS37 . . . .Dod	**Horfield**: BS6-7,BS10 . . . .Hor	**Odd Down**: BA2 . . . .Odd D
Brentry: BS10,BS34 . . . .Bren	**Downend**: BS16,BS36 . . . .Down	**Horton**: BS37 . . . .Hort	**Old Down**: BS32 . . . .Old D
Bridgeyate: BS30 . . . .B'yte	**Doynton**: BS30,SN14 . . . .Doy	**Hunstrete**: BA2,BS39 . . . .Huns	**Oldland Common**: BS30 . . . .Old C
Brislington: BS4,BS14 . . . .Brisl	**Dundry**: BS41 . . . .Dun	**Hutton**: BS24 . . . .Hut	**Old Sodbury**: BS37 . . . .Old S
Bristol: BS1-7 . . . .Bris	**Dunkerton**: BA2 . . . .Dunk	**Inglesbatch**: BA2 . . . .Ing	**Olveston**: BS35 . . . .Olv
Brockley: BS48 . . . .B'ley	**Dyrham**: SN14 . . . .Dyr	**Inglestone Common**: GL9 . . . .Ing C	**Patchway**: BS10,BS34-35 . . . .Pat
Broomhill: BS16 . . . .Bmhll	**Earthcott Green**: BS35 . . . .Ear G	**Ingst**: BS35 . . . .Ingst	**Paulton**: BS39 . . . .Paul
Buckover: GL12 . . . .Buck	**East Brent**: TA9 . . . .E Brnt	**Iron Acton**: BS37 . . . .Iron A	**Peasedown St John**: BA2 . . . .Pea J
Bulwark: NP16 . . . .Bul	**Easter Compton**: BS35 . . . .E Comp	**Itchington**: BS35 . . . .Itch	**Pensford**: BS39 . . . .Pens
Burnett: BS31 . . . .Burn	**East Harptree**: BS40 . . . .E Harp	**Iwood**: BS40,BS49 . . . .Iwood	**Pill**: BS20 . . . .Pill
Burnham-on-Sea: TA8 . . . .Bur S	**East Huntspill**: TA9 . . . .E Hunt	**Kelston**: BA1 . . . .Kel	**Pilning**: BS32,BS35 . . . .Piln
Burrington: BS40 . . . .Burr	**Easton**: BS2,BS5 . . . .E'ton	**Kenn**: BS21 . . . .Kenn	

5C Bus. Cen.—Alton Rd.

Portbury: BS20 ... P'bry
Portishead: BS20 ... P'head
Priston: BA2 ... Pris
Publow: BS39 ... Pub
Pucklechurch: BS16,BS30 ... Puck
Puxton: BS24 ... Pux
Queen Charlton: BS31 ... Q Char
Radstock: BA3 ... Rads
Rangeworthy: BS37 ... Rang
Redfield: BS5 ... Redf
Redhill: BS40 ... Redh
Redland: BS6 ... Redl
Redwick: BS35 ... Red
Regil: BS40 ... Regil
Rickford: BS40 ... R'frd
Rooksbridge: BS26 ... Rook
Rowberrow: BS25 ... Row
Rudgeway: BS35 ... Rudg
St Annes Park: BS4 ... St Ap
St Catherine: BA1 ... St C
St George: BS5,BS15 ... St G
St George's: BS22 ... St G
Saltford: BS31 ... Salt
Sandford: BS24-25 ... Sandf
Sea Mills: BS9 ... Sea M
Severn Beach: BS35 ... Sev B
Shipham: BS25 ... S'ham
Shirehampton: BS11 ... Shire
Shockerwick: BA1 ... Sho
Shortwood: BS16 ... Short
Shoscombe: BA2 ... Shos
Siston: BS15-16,BS30 ... Sis
Soundwell: BS15-16 ... Soun
Southmead: BS9-10 ... S'mead
Southstoke: BA2 ... S'ske
Speedwell: BS5 ... S'wll
Stanton Drew: BS39-40 ... Stan D
Stanton Prior: BA2 ... Stan P
Stanton Wick: BS39 ... Stan W
Staple Hill: BS16 ... Stap H
Stapleton: BS16 ... Stap
Star: BS25 ... Star
Stockwood: BS14 ... Stoc
Stoke Bishop: BS9 ... Stok B
Stoke Gifford: BS34 ... Stok G
Stoney Littleton: BA2 ... Ston L
Stowey: BS39 ... Stow
Stratton-on-the-Fosse: BA3 ... Stratt F
Swainswick: BA1 ... Swa
Swineford: BA1 ... S'frd
Tadwick: BA1 ... Tad
Temple Cloud: BS39 ... Temp C
Thornbury: BS35 ... T'bry
Tickenham: BS21 ... Tic
Timsbury: BA2-3,BS39 ... Tims
Tockington: BS32,BS35 ... Toc
Tunley: BA2 ... Tun
Turleigh: BA15 ... Tur
Tytherington: GL12 ... Tyth
Ubley: BS40 ... Ubl
Udley: BS40 ... Udl
Uphill: BS23 ... Uph
Upper South Wraxall: BA15 ... Up S Wra
Upper Strode: BS40 ... Up Str
Upper Swainswick: BA1 ... Up Swa
Upton Cheyney: BS30 ... Upton C
Walton-in-Gordano: BS21 ... Walt G
Warleigh: BA1 ... Warl
Warmley: BS15,BS30 ... Warm
Watchfield: TA9 ... Watch
Weare: BS26 ... Weare
Webbington: BS26 ... Webb
Webbs Heath: BS30 ... W Hth
Wellow: BA2 ... Well
Westbury-on-Trym: BS9-10 ... W Trym
Westerleigh: BS37 ... W'lgh
West Harptree: BS40 ... W Har
West Huntspill: TA9 ... W Hunt
Weston: BA1 ... W'ton
Weston-in-Gordano: BS20 ... W'ton G
Weston-super-Mare: BS22-24 ... W Mare
Weston Village: BS22,BS24 ... W'ton V
West Wick: BS22,BS24 ... W Wick
Whitchurch: BS14 ... Whit
Whitehall: BS5 ... W'hall
Wick: BS30 ... Wick
Wick St Lawrence: BS22 ... Wick L
Wickwar: GL12 ... Wickw
Willsbridge: BS30 ... Will
Windmill Hill: BS3-4 ... Wind H
Winford: BS40 ... Winf
Winscombe: BS25 ... Wins
Winsley: BA15 ... W'ley
Winterbourne: BS36 ... Wint
Winterbourne Down: BS36 ... Wint D
Withywood: BS13 ... Withy
Woollard: BS39 ... Wool
Woolley: BA1 ... Wool
Worle: BS22,BS24 ... Wor
Wraxall: BS20,BS48 ... Wrax
Wrington: BS40 ... Wrin
Writhlington: BA3 ... Writ
Yate: BS37 ... Yate
Yatton: BS24,BS49 ... Yat

5C Bus. Cen. BS21: Clev ... 1B 68
21 West *BS3: Bedm ... 6J 61*
(off Skypark Rd.)
51.02 BS1: Bris ... 1G 5 (1A 62)
100 Steps BS15: Han ... 4J 63

A

Abbey Apartments BS31: Key ... 4C 78
Abbey Chambers *BA1: Bath ... 5G 7*
(off York St.)
Abbey Chu. Ho. *BA1: Bath ... 5F 7*
(off Westgate Bldgs.)
Abbey Chu. Yd. *BA1: Bath ... 5G 7*
(off Stall St.)
Abbey Cl. BS31: Key ... 4D 78
Abbey Ct. BA2: Bath ... 3J 7 (4D 100)
BS4: St Ap ... 4H 63
Abbeydale BS36: Wint ... 1C 38
Abbeyfield Ho. BS37: Chip S ... 5H 31
Abbey Gdns. BS24: W'ton V ... 4C 106
Abbey Ga. BS9: Stok B ... 3E 46
Abbey Ga. St. BA1: Bath ... 5G 7 (5C 100)
Abbey Grn. BA1: Bath ... 5G 7 (5C 100)
Abbey Ho. BS37: Yate ... 7D 30
Abbey La. BS35: Grov ... 5A 12
Abbey Mill BA15: Brad A ... 6H 125
Abbey Pk. BS31: Key ... 4D 78
Abbey Retail Pk. BS34: Fil ... 5E 36
Abbey Rd. BS9: W Trym ... 2F 47
Abbey St. *BA1: Bath ... 5G 7*
(off York St.)
Abbey Vw. BA2: Bath ... 6K 7 (6D 100)
BA3: Rads ... 3A 154
Abbey Vw. Gdns. BA2: Bath ... 6J 7 (6D 100)
Abbeywood BS34: Fil ... 5D 36
Abbeywood Dr. BS9: Stok B ... 3C 46
Abbey Wood Nth. BS34: Stok G ... 4F 37
Abbots Av. BS15: Han ... 5A 64
Abbotsbury Rd. BS48: Nail ... 1F 71
Abbot's Cl. BS22: Wor ... 1E 106
Abbots Cl. BS14: Whit ... 7C 76
TA8: Bur S ... 2D 158
Abbotsford Rd. BS6: Cot ... 7H 47
Abbots Horn BS48: Nail ... 7F 57
ABBOTSIDE ... 2K 13
ABBOTS LEIGH ... 1A 60
Abbots Leigh Rd. BS8: Abb L, L Wds ... 1A 60
Abbots Rd. BS15: Han ... 6A 64
Abbots Way BS9: Henle ... 2K 47
Abbotswood BS15: Kgswd ... 2B 64
BS37: Yate ... 7D 30
Abbotswood Cl. BS31: Key ... 7B 78
Abbott Rd. BS35: Sev B ... 1A 24
Abbotts Farm Cl. BS39: Paul ... 1B 152
Aberdeen Rd. BS6: Cot ... 1H 61
Abi Clay Ct. *BS2: Bris ... 6B 48*
(off Sevier St.)
Abingdon Gdns. BA2: Odd D ... 4K 121
Abingdon Rd. BS16: Fish ... 5J 49
Abingdon St. TA8: Bur S ... 2C 158
Ableton Ct. BS35: Sev B ... 7A 16
Ableton La. BS10: H'len ... 6A 24
BS35: Sev B ... 7A 16
Ableton Wlk. BS9: Sea M ... 3C 46
Abona Ct. BS9: Sea M ... 2C 46
Abon Ho. BS9: Sea M ... 4C 46
Abraham Cl. BS5: E'ton ... 1D 62
Abraham Fry Ho. BS15: Kgswd ... 2C 64
ABSON ... 6D 52
Abson Rd. BS16: Puck ... 3C 52
BS30: Abson ... 5C 52
Acacia Av. BS16: Stap H ... 4A 50
BS23: W Mare ... 4K 105
Acacia Cl. BS16: Stap H ... 5B 50
Acacia Ct. BS31: Key ... 6A 78
Acacia Gro. BA2: Bath ... 1J 121
Acacia M. BS16: Stap H ... 4B 50
Acacia Rd. BA3: Rads ... 5J 153
BS16: Stap H ... 4B 50
Academy, The BA2: Bath ... 6E 6 (6B 100)
Access 18 BS11: A'mth ... 4H 33
Access 18 West BS11: A'mth ... 5G 33
Accolade Pk. BS11: A'mth ... 3G 33
Accommodation Rd. BS24: B'don ... 2G 145
Acer Cres. BS32: Alm ... 1G 27
Acer Village BS14: H'gro ... 3E 76
Achlles Path BS24: W Mare ... 1K 127
Aconite Cl. BS22: Wick L ... 6F 85
Acorn Cl. TA9: Highb ... 4F 159
Acorn Dr. BS16: Emer G ... 7G 39
Acorn Gro. BS13: Bis ... 4E 74
Acraman's Rd. BS3: Bedm ... 7D 4 (5J 61)
Acresbush Cl. BS13: Bis ... 5G 75
Acton Court ... 1H 29
Acton Rd. BS16: Fish ... 5J 49
Adams Cl. BA2: Pea J ... 5D 142
TA9: W Hunt ... 6E 158
Adams Ct. *BS8: Clftn ... 3F 61*
(off Cumberland Pl.)
Adams Hay BS4: Brisl ... 1F 77
Adams Land BS36: Coal H ... 7G 29
Adam St. TA8: Bur S ... 2C 158
Adastral Rd. BS24: Lock ... 1H 129
Adderly Ga. BS16: Emer G ... 1F 51
Addicott Rd. BS23: W Mare ... 6G 105
Addington Ct. BS23: W Mare ... 3E 104
Addiscombe Rd. BS14: Whit ... 5D 76
BS23: W Mare ... 1G 127
Addison Rd. BS3: Wind H ... 6A 62
Adelaide Pl. BA2: Bath ... 4K 7 (5D 100)
BS5: E'ton ... 1D 62
BS16: Fish ... 4H 49
Adelaide Ter. BS16: Fish ... 4J 49
Adelante Cl. BS34: Stok G ... 3J 37
Admiral Cl. BS16: Stap ... 1F 49
Admirals Wlk. BS20: P'head ... 3D 42
Admirals Yd. BS34: Lit S ... 1E 36
Admiralty Gdns. BS16: Fish ... 3J 49
Aelfric Mdw. BS20: P'head ... 4H 43
Aerospace Av. BS34: Fil ... 4C 36
Agate St. BS3: Bedm ... 6H 61
Aiken St. BS5: Bar H ... 3D 62
Ainslie's Belvedere *BA1: Bath ... 1F 7*
(off Caroline Pl.)
Aintree Dr. BS16: Down ... 6D 38
Air Balloon Rd. BS5: St G ... 2J 63
Airpoint BS3: Bedm ... 6J 61
Airport Rd. BS14: H'gro ... 3B 76
Aisecome Way BS22: W Mare ... 6A 106
Akeman Way BS11: Shire ... 7G 33
Alanscourt BS30: C Hth ... 4F 65
Alard Rd. BS4: Know ... 3B 76
Albany BS23: W Mare ... 3G 105
Albany Bldgs. BS3: Bedm ... 5J 61
Albany Ct. BA2: Bath ... 5H 99
Albany Ga. BS34: Stok G ... 2G 37
Albany Rd. BA2: Bath ... 5H 99
BS6: Bris ... 7B 48
Albany St. BS15: Kgswd ... 1A 64
Albany Way BS30: Old C ... 4G 65
Albermarle Row BS8: Clftn ... 3F 61
Albermarle Ter. *BS8: Clftn ... 3F 61*
(off Cumberland Pl.)
Albert Av. BA2: Pea J ... 6C 142
BS23: W Mare ... 6G 105
Albert Cl. BS30: Old C ... 4H 65
Albert Cres. BS2: Bris ... 4C 62
Albert Gro. BS5: St G ... 1H 63
Albert Gro. Sth. BS5: St G ... 1H 63
Albert Ho. BS1: Bris ... 5H 5
Albert Mill BS31: Key ... 6D 78
Alberton Rd. BS16: Bmhll ... 2H 49
Albert Pde. BS5: Redf ... 1F 63
Albert Pk. BS6: Bris ... 7B 48
Albert Pk. Pl. BS6: Bris ... 7A 48
Albert Pl. BA2: C Down ... 3E 122
BS3: Bedm ... 6J 61
BS9: W Trym ... 1G 47
BS20: P'head ... 4F 43
Albert Quad. BS23: W Mare ... 4G 105
Albert Rd. BS2: Bris ... 7K 5 (5C 62)
BS15: Han ... 4B 64
BS16: Stap H ... 4C 50
BS20: P'head ... 3F 43
BS21: Clev ... 6C 54
BS23: W Mare ... 6G 105
BS31: Key ... 5C 78
BS35: Sev B ... 7A 16
Albert St. BS5: Redf ... 1E 62
Albert Ter. BA2: Bath ... 5J 99
BS16: Fish ... 4H 49
Albion Bldgs. BA1: Bath ... 3B 6 (4K 99)
Albion Chambers BS1: Bris ... 3F 5
Albion Cl. BS16: Mang ... 3D 50
Albion Dockside Est. BS1: Bris ... 6B 4 (4H 61)
Albion Pl. BA1: Bath ... 3C 6 (4A 100)
BS2: Bris ... 3C 62
(Kingsland Rd.)
BS2: Bris ... 2J 5
(Lawford St.)
Albion Rd. BS5: E'ton ... 7D 48
Albion St. BS5: Redf ... 1E 62
Albion Ter. BA1: Bath ... 3C 6 (4A 100)
BS27: Ched ... 7D 150
(off Cliff St.)
BS34: Pat ... 5D 26
Albright Ct. BS20: P'head ... 2G 43
Alburys BS40: Wrin ... 1F 111
Alcove Rd. BS16: Fish ... 5G 49
Aldercombe Rd. BS9: C Din ... 7C 34
Alder Ct. BS14: H'gro ... 5D 76
Alderdown Cl. BS11: Law W ... 7A 34
Alder Dr. BS5: W'hall ... 7G 49
Alderley Rd. BA2: Bath ... 7G 99
Alderman Twr. *BS6: Redl ... 5J 47*
(off Redland Ct. Rd.)
Aldermoor Way BS30: Long G ... 5C 64
(not continuous)
Alderney Av. BS4: Brisl ... 5H 63
Alder Pl. *BS22: Kew ... 1J 105*
(in Ardnave Holiday Pk.)
Alders, The *BS16: Fren ... 6K 37*
(off Marlborough Dr.)
Alder Ter. BA3: Rads ... 4J 153
Alderton Rd. BS7: Hor ... 7A 36
Alder Way BA2: Odd D ... 4K 121
Aldhelm Ct. BA15: Brad A ... 7J 125
ALDWICK ... 5A 112
Aldwick Av. BS13: Hart ... 7J 75
Aldwick La. BS40: Aldw, But ... 5K 111
Aldwych Cl. TA8: Bur S ... 3E 158
Alec Ricketts Cl. BA2: Bath ... 6F 99
Alexander Bldgs. BA1: Bath ... 2D 100
Alexander Ct. TA9: Highb ... 5F 159
Alexander Hall BA2: Lim S ... 6A 124
Alexander Ho. BS1: Bris ... 4E 4
Alexander Way BS49: Yat ... 4H 87
Alexandra Apartments *BS6: Redl ... 5J 47*
(off Redland Ct. Rd.)
Alexandra Cl. BS16: Stap H ... 4B 50
Alexandra Ct. BS16: Fish ... 4H 49
BS21: Clev ... 5C 54
Alexandra Gdns. BS16: Stap H ... 4B 50
Alexandra Ga. BS8: Clftn ... 1H 61
Alexandra Ho. BS23: W Mare ... 1H 127
Alexandra Pde. BS23: W Mare ... 5G 105
Alexandra Pk. BS6: Redl ... 6J 47
BS16: Fish ... 4H 49
BS39: Paul ... 1C 152
Alexandra Pl. BA2: C Down ... 3E 122
BS16: Stap H ... 4B 50
Alexandra Rd. BA2: Bath ... 7G 7 (6C 100)
BS8: Clftn ... 1A 4 (1H 61)
BS10: W Trym ... 7J 35
BS13: Bis ... 3F 75
Alexandra Rd. BS15: Han ... 4B 64
BS21: Clev ... 5C 54
BS36: Coal H ... 7H 29
Alexandra Ter. BS39: Paul ... 1C 152
Alexandra Way BS35: T'bry ... 1K 11
Alford Rd. BS4: Brisl ... 7E 62
Alfred Ct. BS23: W Mare ... 5G 105
Alfred Hill BS2: Bris ... 1E 4 (1K 61)
Alfred Lovell Gdns. BS30: C Hth ... 5E 64
Alfred Pde. BS2: Bris ... 1E 4 (1K 61)
Alfred Pl. BS1: Bris ... 7F 5 (4K 61)
BS2: Bris ... 1D 4 (1J 61)
Alfred Rd. BS3: Wind H ... 6K 61
BS6: Henle ... 4G 47
Alfred St. BA1: Bath ... 2F 7 (4B 100)
BS2: Bris ... 3C 62
BS5: Redf ... 1E 62
BS23: W Mare ... 5G 105
Algars Dr. BS37: Iron A ... 3J 29
Algiers St. BS3: Wind H ... 6K 61
Alison Gdns. BS48: Back ... 3J 71
Allandale Rd. TA8: Bur S ... 7C 156
Allanmead Rd. BS14: H'gro ... 2D 76
Allans Way BS24: W'ton V ... 5D 106
Allendale Ct. TA8: Bur S ... 7C 156
Allen Ho. BS7: Bishop ... 4B 48
Allens La. BS25: S'ham ... 6B 132
Aller BS24: W Mare ... 3J 127
Aller Pde. BS24: W Mare ... 3J 127
Allerton Cres. BS14: Whit ... 6D 76
Allerton Gdns. BS14: H'gro ... 5D 76
Allerton Rd. BS14: Whit ... 6C 76
Allfoxton Rd. BS7: Eastv ... 5C 48
All Hallows Rd. BS5: E'ton ... 1D 62
Allington Dr. BS30: Bar C ... 5D 64
Allington Gdns. BS48: Nail ... 2E 70
Allington Rd. BS3: Bris ... 7C 4 (4J 61)
Allison Av. BS4: Brisl ... 6G 63
Allison Ct. BS8: Clftn ... 7G 47
Allison Rd. BS4: Brisl ... 6F 63
All Saints Cl. BS30: Long G ... 6E 64
All Saints Ct. BS1: Bris ... 3F 5 (3K 61)
All Saints Gdns. BS8: Clftn ... 1G 61
All Saints Ho. BS2: Bris ... 1G 5
All Saints La. BS1: Bris ... 3F 5 (2K 61)
BS21: Clev ... 5F 55
All Saints Pl. BA2: C'ton D ... 6F 101
All Saints Rd. BA1: Bath ... 3B 100
BS8: Clftn ... 1G 61
BS23: W Mare ... 3G 105
All Saints St. BS1: Bris ... 3F 5 (2K 61)
Alma Cl. BS15: Kgswd ... 1C 64
Alma Ct. BS8: Clftn ... 7H 47
Alma Rd. BS8: Clftn ... 1G 61
BS15: Kgswd ... 7C 50
Alma Rd. Av. BS8: Clftn ... 1H 61
Alma St. BS23: W Mare ... 5G 105
Alma Va. Rd. BS8: Clftn ... 1G 61
Almeda Rd. BS5: St G ... 3J 63
Almond Cl. BS22: Wor ... 3E 106
ALMONDSBURY ... 2C 26
Almondsbury Bus. Cen. BS32: Brad S ... 2F 27
Almond Wlk. BS13: Bis ... 4H 75
Almond Way BS16: Mang ... 3D 50
Almorah Rd. BS3: Wind H ... 6A 62
Alonzo Pl. BS21: Clev ... 5D 54
Alpha Centre, The BS37: Yate ... 3C 30
Alpha Ho. TA9: Highb ... 5G 159
Alpha Rd. BS3: Bedm ... 7E 4 (5K 61)
Alpine Cl. BS39: Paul ... 2D 152
Alpine Gdns. BA1: Bath ... 1G 7 (3C 100)
Alpine Rd. BS5: E'ton ... 7E 48
BS39: Paul ... 2D 152
Alsop Rd. BS15: Kgswd ... 1B 64
ALSTONE ... 6E 158
Alstone Gdns. TA9: W Hunt ... 6E 158
Alstone La. TA9: W Hunt ... 6E 158
Alstone Rd. TA9: W Hunt ... 6E 158
Alton Pl. BA2: Bath ... 7G 7 (6C 100)
Alton Rd. BS7: Hor ... 3B 48

Altringham Rd.—Avondale Bus. Cen.

Altringham Rd. BS5: W'hall 7F 49
Alverstoke BS14: H'gro 3B 76
ALVESTON 7J 11
ALVESTON DOWN 7H 11
Alveston Hill BS35: T'bry 6J 11
Alveston Rd. BS32: Old D 2E 18
Alveston Wlk. BS9: Sea M 1B 46
Alwins Ct. BS30: Bar C 5D 64
Ambares Ct. BA3: Mid N 6D 152
Amberey Rd. BS23: W Mare 7H 105
Amberlands Cl. BS48: Back 3J 71
Amberley Cl. BS16: Down 1B 50
BS31: Key 6C 78
Amberley Gdns. BS48: Nail 1F 71
Amberley Rd. BS16: Down 1B 50
BS34: Pat 6D 26
Amberley Way GL12: Wickw 1H 23
Amble Cl. BS15: Kgswd 2D 64
Ambleside Av. BS10: S'mead 6H 35
Ambleside Rd. BA2: Bath 2H 121
Ambra Ct. BS8: Clftn 3G 61
Ambra Ter. BS8: Clftn 3G 61
Ambra Va. BS8: Clftn 3G 61
Ambra Va. E. BS8: Clftn 3G 61
Ambra Va. Sth. BS8: Clftn 3G 61
Ambra Va. W. BS8: Clftn 3G 61
Ambrose Rd. BS8: Clftn 3G 61
Ambury BA1: Bath 6F 7 (6B 100)
Amelia Ct. BS1: Bris 4E 4 (3K 61)
Amercombe Wlk. BS14: Stoc 3F 77
American Museum in Britain, The
(Claverton Manor) 6J 101
Amery La. BA1: Bath 5F 7 (5C 100)
AMESBURY 3D 140
Amesbury Dr. BS24: B'don 7K 127
AMF Bowling
Weston-Super-Mare 5F 105
Amis Wlk. BS7: Hor 7C 36
Ammerdown Park 7E 154
Ammerdown Ter. BA3: Hem 7F 155
Anchorage BS1: Bris 7D 4 (4J 61)
Anchorage, The BS20: P'head 2G 43
Anchor Cl. BS5: St G 3H 63
Anchor Ho. BS4: Know 7D 62
Anchor La. BS1: Bris 5D 4 (3J 61)
Anchor Point BS1: Bris 5C 4 (3J 61)
Anchor Rd. BA1: W'ton 2H 99
BS1: Bris 5B 4 (3H 61)
BS15: Kgswd 7E 50
Anchor Sq. BS1: Bris 5D 4 (3J 61)
Anchor Way BS20: Pill 4H 45
Ancliff Sq. BA15: Avonc 7C 124
Andereach Cl. BS14: H'gro 2D 76
Andover Rd. BS4: Know 7B 62
Andrew Millman Ct. BS37: Yate 5F 31
Andruss Dr. BS41: Dun 1D 92
Angels Ground BS4: St Ap 3H 63
Angers Rd. BS4: Wind H 5B 62
Anglesea Pl. BS8: Clftn 6G 47
Anglo Office Pk. BS15: Kgswd 6K 49
Anglo Ter. BA1: Bath 1H 7
Animal Farm Country Pk. 4D 144
Ankatel Cl. BS23: W Mare 7J 105
Annaly Rd. BS27: Ched 7C 150
Annandale Av. BS22: Wor 3C 106
Annie Scott Cl. BS16: Fish 4H 49
Anson Cl. BS31: Salt 1H 97
Anson Rd. BS22: Kew 7B 84
BS24: Lock 6E 106
Ansteys Cl. BS15: Han 4K 63
Ansteys Rd. BS15: Han 4K 63
Anstey St. BS5: E'ton 7D 48
Anthea Rd. BS5: S'wll 6G 49
Antona Ct. BS11: Shire 1H 45
Antona Dr. BS11: Shire 1H 45
Antrim Rd. BS9: Henle 2H 47
Anvil Rd. BS49: C'ham 2B 88
Anvil St. BS2: Bris 4K 5 (3B 62)
Apex Ct. BS32: Brad S 3F 27
Apex Dr. TA9: Highb 4E 158
Apex Leisure & Wildlife Pk. 4D 158
Apollo Apartments BS1: Bris 4F 5
Apperley Cl. BS37: Yate 6D 30
Appleby Wlk. BS4: Know 3K 75
Applecroft BA2: Shos 7E 142
Appledore BS22: Wor 2D 106
Appledore Cl. BS14: H'gro 2D 76
Apple Farm La. BS24: W Wick 3F 107
Applegate BS10: Bren 4H 35
Applehayes Ri. BS20: Eas 5F 45
Appletree Ct. BS22: Wor 2F 107
Apple Tree Dr. BS25: Wins 5G 131
Appletree Gro. BS22: Kew 1J 105
(in Ardnave Holiday Pk.)
Appletree M. BS22: Wor 2F 107
Applin Grn. BS16: Emer G 2G 51
Approach Rd. BS1: Bris 6J 5 (4B 62)
Appsley Cl. BS22: W Mare 2A 106
Apseleys Mead BS32: Brad S 4E 26
Apsley Cl. BA1: Bath 4H 99
Apsley Ho. BS6: Bris 6A 48
Apsley Rd. BA1: Bath 4G 99
BS8: Clftn 7G 47
Apsley St. BS5: Eastv 6E 48
Apsley Vs. BS6: Bris 7K 47
Arbutus Dr. BS9: C Din 1C 46
Arbutus Wlk. BS9: C Din 6D 34
Arcade, The BS1: Bris 2G 5
Arch Cl. BS41: L Ash 1K 73
Archer Ct. BS30: Long G 6D 64
Archer Dr. TA8: Bur S 2E 158
Archer's Ct. BS21: Clev 5D 54
Archer Wlk. BS14: Stoc 4G 77
Archfield Rd. BS6: Cot 7J 47
Arch Gro. BS41: L Ash 1K 73
Architectural Cen., The BS1: Bris 6E 4
(off Narrow Quay)
Archway St. BA2: Bath 6J 7 (6D 100)
Ardagh Ct. BS7: Hor 1B 48
Arden Cl. BS22: Wor 1D 106
BS32: Brad S 1G 37
Ardenton Wlk. BS10: Bren 4G 35
Ardern Cl. BS9: C Din 7B 34
Ardnave Holiday Pk. BS22: Kew 1J 105
Argentina Pl. BS20: P'head 1H 43
Argus Ct. BS3: Bedm 7J 61
Argus Rd. BS3: Bedm 6J 61
Argyle Av. BS5: Eastv 6E 48
BS23: W Mare 1H 127
Argyle Ct. BS2: Bris 1A 62
Argyle Dr. BS37: Yate 2E 30
Argyle Pl. BS8: Clftn 5A 4 (3G 61)
Argyle Rd. BS2: Bris 1A 62
BS16: Fish 6K 49
BS21: Clev 4D 54
Argyle St. BA2: Bath 4H 7 (5C 100)
BS3: Bedm 5J 61
BS5: Eastv 6E 48
Argyle Ter. BA2: Bath 5J 99
Ariel Rowing Club 4H 63
Arkells Ct. GL12: Wickw 6G 15
Arley Cotts. BS6: Cot 7K 47
Arley Ct. BS6: Cot 7K 47
Arley Hill BS6: Cot 7K 47
Arley Pk. BS6: Cot 7K 47
Arley Ter. BS5: W'hall 7G 49
Arlingham Way BS34: Pat 5A 26
Arlington Ho. BA1: Bath 5F 7
(off Bath St.)
Arlington Mans. BS8: Clftn 1A 4
Arlington Rd. BA2: Bath 6B 6 (6K 99)
BS4: St Ap 3F 63
Arlington Vs. BS8: Clftn 2A 4 (2H 61)
Armada Ho. BS1: Bris 7A 48
Armada Pl. BS1: Bris 7A 48
Armada Rd. BS14: Whit 4C 76
Armes Ct. BA2: Bath 7H 7 (6C 100)
Armidale Av. BS6: Bris 7A 48
Armidale Pl. BS6: Bris 7A 48
Armoury Sq. BS5: E'ton 1C 62
Armstrong Cl. BS35: T'bry 5B 12
Armstrong Ct. BS37: Yate 3C 30
TA9: Highb 3F 159
(off Mulholland Way)
Armstrong Dr. BS30: C Hth 4F 65
Armstrong Way BS37: Yate 3A 30
Arnall Dr. BS10: Hen 6F 35
Arncliffe BS10: S'mead 7J 35
Arnold Ct. BS37: Chip S 5H 31
Arnold Rd. BS16: Mang, Sis 5F 51
Arnolds Fld. Est. GL12: Wickw 6G 15
Arnold's Way BS49: Yat 2F 87
Arnolfini 6E 4 (4J 61)
Arnor Cl. BS22: Wor 7E 84
Arno's St. BS4: Wind H 6C 62
ARNO'S VALE 5D 62
Arnside Rd. BS10: S'mead 6J 35
Arrowfield Cl. BS14: Whit 1C 94
Artemesia Av. BS22: W Mare 4C 106
Arthur Milton St. BS7: Bishop 4B 48
Arthurs Cl. BS16: Emer G 2G 51
Arthur Skemp Cl. BS5: Bar H 2D 62
Arthur St. BS2: Bris 4C 62
BS5: Redf 1E 62
Arthurswood Rd. BS13: Withy 6G 75
Arundel Cl. BS13: Hart 5H 75
Arundel Ct. BS7: Bishop 5K 47
Arundell Ct. BS23: W Mare 4G 105
Arundell Rd. BS23: W Mare 4G 105
Arundel Rd. BA1: Bath 2C 100
BS7: Bishop 5K 47
BS21: Clev 6D 54
Arundel Wlk. BS31: Key 5B 78
Ascension Ho. BA2: Bath 7K 99
Ascot Cl. BS16: Down 6D 38
Ascot Rd. BS10: S'mead 5K 35
Ashbourne Cl. BS30: Old C 3G 65
Ashburton Rd. BS10: S'mead 6J 35
Ashbury Dr. BS22: W Mare 2K 105
Ash Cl. BS16: Fish 5A 50
BS22: St G 2H 107
BS25: Wins 4G 131
BS34: Lit S 7F 27
BS37: Yate 3D 30
Ashcombe Cres. BS30: Old C 3G 65
Ashcombe Gdns. BS23: W Mare 3J 105
Ashcombe Ho. TA8: Bur S 4C 156
Ashcombe Pk. Rd. BS23: W Mare 3J 105
Ashcombe Pl. BS23: W Mare 5H 105
Ashcombe Rd. BS23: W Mare 5H 105
Ashcott BS14: H'gro 3B 76
Ashcott Cl. TA8: Bur S 2E 158
Ashcott Dr. TA8: Bur S 2E 158
Ashcott Pl. TA8: Bur S 1E 158
Ash Ct. BS14: Whit 4C 76
Ashcroft BS24: W Mare 3K 127
Ashcroft Av. BS31: Key 5B 78
Ashcroft Rd. BS9: Sea M 1C 46
Ashdene Av. BS5: Eastv 5F 49
Ashdene Rd. BS23: W Mare 3J 105
Ashdown Ct. BS9: W Trym 7F 35
(off Northover Cl.)
Ashdown Rd. BS20: P'head 2C 42
Asher La. BS2: Bris 2J 5 (2B 62)
Ashes La. BA2: F'frd 7H 123
Ashey La. BS27: Ched 6D 150
Ashfield M. BS6: Bris 7B 48
Ashfield Pl. BS6: Bris 7B 48
Ashfield Rd. BS3: Bedm 6H 61
Ashford Dr. BS24: W Mare 4J 127
Ashford Rd. BA2: Bath 7K 99
BS34: Pat 7C 26
BS40: Redh 7C 90
Ashford Way BS15: Kgswd 2E 64
ASHGROVE 5D 142
Ash Gro. BA2: Bath 7J 99
BS16: Fish 5A 50
BS21: Clev 5E 54
BS23: Uph 3G 127
Ashgrove BA2: Pea J 5D 142
BS35: T'bry 3A 12
Ashgrove Av. BS7: Bishop 4B 48
BS8: Abb L 2B 60
Ashgrove Cl. BS7: Bishop 4B 48
Ashgrove Ct. BA2: Pea J 5D 142
Ashgrove Pl. BS7: Bishop 4B 48
Ashgrove Rd. BS3: Bedm 6H 61
BS6: Redl 7H 47
BS7: Bishop 4B 48
Ash Hayes Dr. BS48: Nail 1G 71
Ash Hayes Rd. BS48: Nail 1G 71
Ashland Rd. BS13: Withy 6G 75
Ash La. BS32: Alm 3C 25
Ash Lea Ct. BS7: Hor 7B 36
Ashleigh Cl. BS23: W Mare 4J 105
BS39: Paul 7C 140
Ashleigh Cres. BS49: Yat 3H 87
Ashleigh Ho. BS39: Paul 1C 152
Ashleigh Rd. BS23: W Mare 4J 105
BS49: Yat 3H 87
Ashley BS15: Kgswd 1D 64
Ashley Apartments BS6: Bris 6B 48
Ashley Av. BA1: Bath 4J 99
TA8: Bur S 2D 158
Ashley Cl. BA15: Brad A 4F 125
(not continuous)
BS7: Bishop 4B 48
BS25: Wins 6G 131
Ashley Ct. BS6: Bris 7B 48
Ashley Ct. Rd. BS7: Bris 6B 48
ASHLEY DOWN 4B 48
Ashley Down Rd. BS7: Bishop, Bris 5B 48
BS7: Bishop, Hor 3A 48
Ashley Gro. Rd. BS2: Bris 6B 48
Ashley Hall BS7: Hor 3A 48
Ashley Hgts. BS7: Bishop 4B 48
Ashley Hill BS6: Bris 5B 48
BS7: Bris 5B 48
Ashley Hill Trad. Est. BS2: Bris 6B 48
Ashley La. BA15: W'ley 5D 124
BS40: Burr, L'frd 6H 111
Ashley Pde. BS2: Bris 6B 48
Ashley Pk. BS6: Bris 5B 48
Ashley Rd. BA1: Bathf 1A 102
(not continuous)
BA15: Brad A, Lit A 3F 125
BS6: Bris 7A 48
BS21: Clev 1B 68
Ashley St. BS2: Bris 7C 48
Ashley Ter. BA1: Bath 4J 99
Ashman Cl. BS5: E'ton 1C 62
Ashman Ct. BS16: Fish 5G 49
(off Marina Gdns.)
Ashmans Ga. BS39: Paul 1B 152
Ashmans Yd. BA1: Bath 5H 99
Ashmead BS39: Temp C 4G 139
Ashmead Ho. BS5: Bar H 2E 62
Ashmead Ind. Est. BS31: Key 5F 79
Ashmead Pk. BS31: Key 5F 79
Ashmead Rd. BS31: Key 5F 79
Ashmead Way BS1: Bris 4F 61
Ash Ridge Rd. BS32: Brad S 3D 26
Ash Rd. BS7: Hor 3A 48
BS29: Ban 2J 129
Ashton BS16: Fren 6A 38
(off Harford Dr.)
Ashton Av. BS1: Bris 4G 61
Ashton Cl. BS21: Clev 1B 68
Ashton Ct. BS41: L Ash 5D 60
Ashton Court Nature Reserve 5C 60
Ashton Court Vis. Cen. 5D 60
Ashton Cres. BS48: Nail 1F 71
Ashton Dr. BS3: Ash V 1E 74
ASHTON GATE 5G 61
Ashton Ga. Rd. BS3: Bris 5G 61
Ashton Gate Stadium 6F 61
Ashton Ga. Ter. BS3: Bris 5G 61
Ashton Ga. Trad. Est. BS3: Ash V 6E 60
Ashton Ga. Underpass
BS3: Ash V, Bwr A 5F 61
ASHTON HILL 3J 97
Ashton Hill BA2: Cor 4A 98
Ashton Pk. Sports Cen. 5E 60
Ashton Rd. BS3: Ash G 5E 61
BS3: Ash V 6F 61
BS41: L Ash 6C 60
ASHTON VALE 7F 61
Ashton Vale (Park & Ride) 7D 60
Ashton Va. Rd. BS3: Ash V 6E 60
Ashton Va. Trad. Est. BS3: Ash V 1F 75
ASHTON WATERING 2H 73
Ashton Way BS31: Key 4C 78
Ash Tree Cl. BS24: B'don 7A 128
TA8: Bur S 4C 156
Ash Tree Ct. BA3: Rads 5J 153
Ash Tree Cres. TA8: Bur S 4C 156
Ash Tree Pl. TA8: Bur S 4C 156
Ash Tree Rd. TA8: Bur S 4C 156
Ashvale Cl. BS48: Nail 7J 57
Ashville Pk. BS35: T'bry 5K 11
Ashville Rd. BS3: Ash G 5G 61
Ash Wlk. BS10: Bren 4H 35
Ashwell Cl. BS14: Stoc 4G 77
Ashwicke BS14: H'gro 4C 76
Ashwood BS40: E Harp 7K 137
Aspects Leisure Pk. 4C 64
Aspen Pk. Rd. BS22: W Mare 4C 106
Assembly Rooms & Fashion Mus.
2F 7 (4B 100)
Assembly Rooms La. BS1: Bris 5E 4 (3K 61)
Aston Ga. Depot BS3: Ash G 5F 61
Aston Ho. BS1: Bris 7G 5
Astry Cl. BS11: Law W 6A 34
Atchley St. BS5: Bar H 2D 62
Atherston BS30: Old C 4H 65
Athlone Wlk. BS4: Know 1A 76
Atholl Cl. BS22: Wor 1D 106
Atkins Cl. BS14: Stoc 4G 77
Atlanta Key TA8: Bur S 7C 156
Atlantic Bus. Pk. BS23: W Mare 3E 104
Atlantic Ct. BS23: W Mare 3E 104
Atlantic Cres. TA8: Bur S 3D 158
Atlantic Rd. BS11: Shire 7G 33
BS23: W Mare 3E 104
Atlantic Rd. Sth. BS23: W Mare 3E 104
Atlas Cl. BS5: S'wll 6J 49
Atlas Rd. BS3: Wind H 6A 62
Atlas St. BS2: Bris 4D 62
Atlay Ct. BS49: Yat 2H 87
Atrium, The BS1: Bris 5G 5
BS2: Bris 5K 5
(off Anvil St.)
Attewell Ct. BA2: Bath 7B 100
Atwell Cl. BS32: Alm 5D 26
Atwood Dr. BS11: Law W 5B 34
Atyeo Cl. BS3: Ash V 1E 74
TA8: Bur S 7E 156
Aubrey Meads BS30: Bit 2J 79
Aubrey Rd. BS3: Bedm 6H 61
Auburn Av. BS30: Long G 6F 65
Auburn Rd. BS6: Redl 6H 47
Auckland Cl. BS23: W Mare 2H 127
Auden Mead BS7: Hor 7C 36
Audley Av. BA1: Bath 2A 6 (4J 99)
Audley Cl. BA1: Bath 2A 6 (4K 99)
BS37: Rang 5A 22
Audley Gro. BA1: Bath 4J 99
Audley Lodge BA1: Bath 2A 6 (4K 99)
Audley Pk. Rd. BA1: Bath 1A 6 (3J 99)
Audrey Wlk. BS9: Henle 1K 47
Augusta Pl. BA1: Bath 3A 6 (4K 99)
Augustus Ho. BS5: St G 3K 63
Aumery Gdns. BS39: High L 4B 140
AUST 5G 9
Austen Dr. BS22: Wor 7F 85
Austen Gro. BS7: Hor 7C 36
Austen Ho. BS7: Hor 7C 36
Austen Pl. BS11: Shire 1J 45
Aust La. BS9: W Trym 7G 35
Aust Rd. BS35: Elbton, Olv 7K 9
BS35: N'wick 2D 16
Autumn M. BS24: W'ton V 4E 106
Avalon Cl. BS49: Yat 2G 87
Avalon Ho. BS48: Nail 1E 70
Avalon La. BS5: St G 3K 63
Avalon Rd. BS5: St G 4K 63
TA9: Highb 4G 159
Avebury Cl. TA8: Bur S 7F 157
Avebury Rd. BS3: Ash V 7E 60
Aveline's Hole 3H 133
Avening Cl. BS48: Nail 2H 71
Avening Rd. BS15: Kgswd 1J 63
Avenue, The BA2: C Down 3D 122
BA2: C'ton D 6G 101
(not continuous)
BA2: Tims 3F 141
BS5: St G 2G 63
BS7: Bishop 5A 48
BS8: Clftn 7F 47
BS9: Stok B 6D 46
BS16: Fren 6G 37
BS21: Clev 4D 54
BS22: St G 1G 107
BS25: Wins 5J 131
BS31: Key 4C 78
BS34: Lit S 1E 36
BS34: Pat 4D 26
BS37: Yate 5D 30
BS48: Back 3J 71
BS49: Yat 3H 87
Avenue Pl. BA2: C Down 3D 122
Averay Rd. BS16: Stap 4E 48
Averill Ct. BS21: Clev 5D 54
Avonbank Ind. Est.
BS11: A'mth 1F 45
Avonbridge Trad. Est.
BS11: Shire 7G 33
Avon Bus. Pk. BS16: Fish 5H 49
AVONCLIFF 7D 124
Avoncliff Station (Rail) 7C 124
Avon Cl. BA15: Brad A 7J 125
BS5: St G 3H 63
BS23: W Mare 3H 127
BS31: Key 4D 78
Avon Ct. BA1: Bathe 6J 83
BS8: Clftn 7G 47
BS16: Fish 3K 49
Avon Cres. BS1: Bris 4G 61
GL12: Wickw 6H 15
(not continuous)
Avondale Bldgs. BA1: Bath 1D 100
Avondale Bus. Cen. BS15: Kgswd 6A 50

Avondale Ct.—Bath Abbey

Avondale Ct. BA1: Bath .4H 99
BS9: Stok B .5D 46
BS30: Long G .6D 64
Avondale Rd. BA1: Bath .4H 99
Avondale Works BS15: Kgswd .6A 50
Avondown Cl. BS10: S'mead .5K 35
Avondown Ct. BS3: Bedm .7J 61
Avondown Ho. BA2: Bath .6H 99
Avonfield Av. BA15: Brad A .7J 125
Avon Gorge Ind. Est.
BS11: A'mth .1G 45
Avon Gro. BS9: Stok B .6D 46
Avon Hgts. BA2: Lim S .6A 124
Avon La. BS31: Salt .6K 79
Avonlea BS15: Han .4A 64
BS37: Yate .6D 30
Avonleaze BS9: Sea M .3B 46
Avonleigh Ct. BS3: Bedm .7H 61
Avonleigh Rd. BS3: Bedm .7H 61
Avonmead Ho. BS1: Bris .1G 5
Avon Meads BS2: Bris .4E 62
Avon Meads Shopping Pk.
BS2: Bris .4E 62
Avon Mill La. BS31: Key .4D 78
AVONMOUTH .6F 33
Avonmouth Distribution Cen.
BS35: Piln .1D 24
Avonmouth Dock .5D 32
Avonmouth Rd. BS11: A'mth .6F 33
BS11: Shire .7G 33
Avonmouth Station (Rail) .6F 33
Avonmouth Way BS10: Hen .4E 34
BS11: A'mth .6G 33
Avonmouth Way W.
BS11: A'mth .5F 33
Avon Pk. BA1: Bath .4G 99
BS5: Redf .2F 63
Avon Ring Rd.
BS4: Key .2A 78
BS15: Han .2A 78
BS15: Warm, Sis .1F 65
BS16: Down .6B 38
BS16: Emer G, Mang, Sis .5E 38
BS16: H'ook .5G 37
BS30: Bar C, Han .2A 78
BS30: Sis .6F 51
Avon Riverside Est. BS11: A'mth .1F 45
Avon Riverside Station
Avon Valley Railway .4J 79
Avon Rd. BS13: Bis .4G 75
BS20: Pill .3G 45
BS31: Key .5D 78
Avonside Ind. Est. BS2: Bris .3E 62
Avonside Ind. Pk. BS2: Bris .3E 62
Avonside Rd. BS2: Bris .3E 62
Avonside Way BS4: St Ap .3H 63
Avon Ski & Action Cen. .2J 131
Avonsmere Res. Pk.
BS34: Stok G .4E 36
Avon St. BA1: Bath .6F 7 (5B 100)
BS2: Bris .4J 5 (3B 62)
Avon Trad. Est. BS2: Bris .7K 5 (4C 62)
Avon Va. BS9: Stok B .4D 46
Avonvale Pl. BA1: Bathe .7H 83
Avonvale Rd. BS5: Bar H, Redf .3D 62
Avon Valley Adventure & Wildlife Pk.
.4G 79
Avon Valley Bus. Pk. BS4: St Ap .3G 63
Avon Valley Farm Bus. Pk.
BS31: Key .5H 79
Avon Valley Pk. .5K 63
Avon Valley Railway
Avon Riverside Station .4J 79
Bitton Station .1F 79
Oldland Common Station .5H 65
Avon Vw. BS15: Han .6K 63
Avon Way BS9: Stok B .3C 46
BS10: S'mead .7K 35
BS20: P'head .3D 42
BS35: T'bry .4A 12
Avonwood Cl. BS11: Shire .2J 45
Avon Works BS3: Bedm .7G 61
Awdelett Cl. BS11: Law W .6B 34
AWKLEY .5A 18
Awkley La. BS32: Toc .4A 18
BS35: Olv .4A 18
Awkward Hill BS40: Nem T .7H 113
AXBRIDGE .4J 149
Axbridge Cl. BS48: Nail .2G 71
TA8: Bur S .7E 156
Axbridge Moor Drove BS26: Axb .7J 149
Axbridge Mus. (King John's Hunting Lodge)
.4J 149
Axbridge Rd. BA2: C Down .2C 122
BS4: Know .7B 62
BS27: Ched .4A 150
Axe Cl. BS23: W Mare .7J 105
Axe Ct. BS35: T'bry .4K 11
Axford Way BA2: Pea J .5D 142
Axis BS14: Hart .5K 75
Ayckbourn Cl. TA8: Bur S .2E 158
Aycote Cl. BS22: W Mare .2K 105
Aylesbury Cres. BS3: Bedm .1H 75
Aylesbury Rd. BS3: Bedm .1H 75
Aylmer Cres. BS14: H'gro .4D 76
Aylminton Wlk.
BS11: Law W .5B 34
Ayr St. BA2: Bath .5A 6 (5K 99)
Azalea Rd. BS22: Wick L .6E 84
Azelin Av. BS13: Hart .5H 75
Azov Cl. BS7: Hor .1A 48
Aztec Cen., The BS32: Alm .4C 26
AZTEC WEST .4C 26
Aztec W. BS32: Alm .4C 26
Azure, The *BS6: Bris* .*7A 48*
(off Bath Bldgs.)

B

Backfields BS2: Bris .1G 5 (1A 62)
Backfields Ct. *BS2: Bris* .*1A 62*
(off Backfields La.)
Backfields La. BS2: Bris .1G 5 (1A 62)
Back La. BS16: Puck .4A 52
BS20: Pill .3G 45
(not continuous)
BS21: Kings S .5A 68
BS25: Row .4C 132
BS26: Axb .4J 149
BS27: Ched .7C 150
BS31: Key .4C 78
BS36: Coal H .1H 39
BS39: Pens .7G 95
GL12: Wickw .6G 15
SN14: Dyr .3H 53
Bk. of Kingsdown Pde. BS6: Bris .1K 61
Back Rd. BS3: Bris .5G 61
Bk. Stoke La. BS9: W Trym .2F 47
Back St. BS23: W Mare .5G 105
BACKWELL .4K 71
Backwell Bow BS48: Back .1K 71
BACKWELL COMMON .2J 71
Backwell Comn. BS48: Back .3J 71
BACKWELL GREEN .2B 72
BACKWELL HILL .6C 72
Backwell Hill Rd. BS48: Back .3B 72
Backwell Leisure Cen. .4K 71
Backwell Vw. BS48: Wrax .5A 58
Backwell Wlk. BS13: Bis .2F 75
Badenham Gro. BS11: Law W .7K 33
Baden Hill Rd. GL12: Tyth .7F 13
Baden Ho. BA1: Bath .1E 6
Baden Rd. BS5: Redf .2E 62
BS15: Kgswd .2E 64
BS15: Warm .1F 65
Bader Cl. BS37: Yate .3D 30
Badger Cl. BS30: Long G .6D 64
Badger Ri. BS20: P'head .5A 42
Badger Rd. BS35: T'bry .1B 12
Badgers, The BS22: St G .1G 107
Badgers Cl. BS32: Brad S .3F 27
Badgers Dr. BS10: Bren .3A 36
Badger Sett BS5: St G .2K 63
Badgers Holt BS14: H'gro .4E 76
Badger's La. BS32: Alm .3J 25
Badgers Wlk. BS4: Brisl .7F 63
Badgers Way BS24: W'ton V .4D 106
Badger Wlk. BS20: Eas .4F 45
Badgeworth BS37: Yate .1D 40
Badman Cl. BS39: Paul .1B 152
Badminton *BS16: Fren* .*6A 38*
(off Penn Dr.)
Badminton Cen. BS37: Yate .4C 30
Badminton Ct. BS37: Yate .4C 30
Badminton Gdns. BA1: Bath .3J 99
BS16: Down .7E 38
Badminton Rd. BS2: Bris .7B 48
BS16: Down .2C 50
BS36: Coal H, Wint, Wint D .5E 38
BS36: Fram C .6J 29
BS37: Chip S .6K 31
BS37: Yate .5E 38
Badminton Rd. Trad. Est. BS37: Yate .5B 30
Badminton Wlk. BS16: Down .1C 50
Badock Hall BS9: Stok B .4E 46
Baglyn Av. BS15: Soun .5D 50
Bagnell Cl. BS14: Stoc .5G 77
Bagnell Rd. BS14: Stoc .5G 77
BAGSTONE .2K 21
Bagstone Rd. GL12: Bag .3K 21
Bagworth Dr. BS30: Long G .6D 64
BAILBROOK .7F 83
Bailbrook Ct. BA1: Swa .7G 83
Bailbrook Gro. BA1: Swa .7F 83
Bailbrook La. BA1: Swa .7E 82
Baildon Ct. BS23: W Mare .1H 127
Baildon Cres. BS23: W Mare .1J 127
Baildon Rd. BS23: W Mare .1H 127
Bailey Cl. BS22: W Mare .4C 106
Bailey Ct. BS20: P'head .2H 43
Baileys Barn BA15: Brad A .7H 125
Baileys Ct. BS32: Brad S .1H 37
Baileys Ct. Rd. BS32: Brad S .1H 37
Baileys Mead Rd. BS16: Stap .3E 48
Bailiffs Cl. BS26: Axb .5J 149
Bailiffs' Wall BS26: Axb .6H 149
Baily Pl. BS16: L'lze .7E 36
Bainton Cl. BA15: Brad A .5J 125
Baker Cl. BS21: Clev .2B 68
Baker's Bldgs. BS40: Wrin .2F 111
Bakersfield BS30: Long G .6E 64
Bakers Ground BS34: Stok G .2H 37
Bakers Ho. BS1: Bris .2G 5
Bakers La. BS40: L'frd .4E 110
Bakers Pde. BA2: Tims .3F 141
Bakers Pk. BS13: Bis .4G 75
Baker St. BS23: W Mare .4G 105
Balaclava Ind. Est. BS16: Fish .5H 49
Balaclava Rd. BS16: Fish .5H 49
Baldwin Chambers *BS1: Bris* .*4E 4*
(off Baldwin St.)
Baldwin Lofts BS1: Bris .4E 4
Baldwin St. BS1: Bris .4E 4 (3K 61)
Balfour Rd. BS3: Ash G .6H 61
Ballance St. BA1: Bath .1F 7 (3B 100)
Ballance St. Nth. BA1: Bath .1F 7 (3B 100)
Ballantine Wlk. *TA9: Highb* .*3F 159*
(off Mulholland Way)
Ballard Cl. BS5: S'wll .6H 49
Ballast La. BS11: A'mth .5H 33
Balloon Ct. BS2: Bris .1H 5 (1A 62)
Balls Barn La. BS24: E Rols .3A 108
Ballstreet La. BS35: N'wick .4C 16
Balmain St. BS4: Wind H .5C 62
Balmoral Cl. BS34: Stok G .3F 37
Balmoral Ct. BS16: Mang .3E 50
Balmoral Dr. TA8: Bur S .6D 156
Balmoral Ho. BS1: Bris .6C 4
Balmoral Rd. BS7: Bris .6B 48
BS30: Long G .7D 64
BS31: Key .6C 78
Balmoral Way BS22: W Mare, Wor .2A 106
Baltic Pl. BS20: Pill .4H 45
Baltic Wharf Water Leisure Cen. .4G 61
Balustrade *BA1: Bath* .*2D 100*
(off London Rd.)
Bamfield BS14: H'gro, Whit .3B 76
Bampton BS22: Wor .2D 106
Bampton Cl. BS13: Bis .3H 75
BS16: Emer G .2G 51
Bampton Cft. BS16: Emer G .2G 51
Bampton Dr. BS16: Down .7B 38
Bancroft BA15: Brad A .5H 125
Banfield Cl. BS11: Law W .7A 34
Bangor Gro. BS4: St Ap .4H 63
Bangrove Wlk. BS11: Law W .7J 33
Banister Gro. BS4: Know .3K 75
Bank, The BS4: Wind H .5B 62
Bank Pl. BS20: Pill .4H 45
Bank Rd. BS15: Kgswd .1B 64
BS35: Piln .6D 16
Banks Cl. BS21: Clev .2D 68
Bankside BS16: Stap H .4D 50
Bankside Ho. BA1: Bath .1E 6
Bankside Rd. BS4: Brisl .6F 63
Bank St. TA9: Highb .5F 159
Bannatyne Health Club
Bristol .6K 47
Bannerdown Cl. BA1: Bathe .6K 83
Bannerdown Dr. BA1: Bathe .6J 83
Bannerdown Rd. BA1: Bathe .7J 83
Bannerleigh La. BS8: L Wds .3E 60
Bannerleigh Rd. BS8: L Wds .3E 60
Bannerman Rd. BS5: E'ton .1D 62
(not continuous)
Banner Rd. BS6: Bris .7A 48
Bannetts Tree Cres. BS35: A'ton .7J 11
Bantock Cl. BS4: Know .4K 75
Bantry Rd. BS4: Know .2A 76
BANWELL .2B 130
Banwell Cl. BS13: Bis .2G 75
BS31: Key .1E 96
Banwell Rd. BA2: Odd D .4K 121
BS3: Ash G .6G 61
BS24: Elbgh, Hut .3D 128
BS25: Chri .6J 129
BS25: Wins .4D 130
BS26: Chri .6J 129
BS29: Ban .6J 129
Banyard Rd. BS20: P'bry .3C 44
BAPTIST MILLS .6C 48
Baptist Mills Ct. BS5: E'ton .7C 48
Baptist St. BS5: E'ton .7C 48
Barberry Farm Rd. BS49: Yat .2H 87
Barbour Gdns. BS13: Hart .7K 75
Barbour Rd. BS13: Hart .7K 75
Barcroft Cl. BS15: Kgswd .1A 64
Barker Cl. BS24: W Wick .3G 107
Barkers Mead BS37: Yate .1F 31
Barker Wlk. BS5: E'ton .7C 48
Barkleys Hill BS16: Stap .4E 48
Barlands Ho. BS10: Hen .4F 35
Barley Cl. BS16: Mang .2E 50
BS36: Fram C .6G 29
Barley Cft. BS9: W Trym .3F 47
Barley Cross BS22: Wick L .6E 84
Barleyfields BS2: Bris .4K 5 (3B 62)
Barnabas Cl. BS26: Axb .4K 149
Barnabas St. BS2: Bris .7A 48
Barnaby Cl. BA3: Mid N .4E 152
Barnack Trad. Cen. BS3: Bedm .1J 75
Barnard Cl. BS49: Yat .3J 87
Barnard Wlk. BS31: Key .6B 78
Barn Cl. BS16: Emer G .2F 51
Barn Copsie BS16: Fren .7F 37
Barnes Ct. BS34: Stok G .3G 37
Barnes St. BS5: St G .1F 63
Barnfield Way BA1: Bathe .6K 83
Barn Hill BA2: Shos .7F 143
Barnhill Cl. BS37: Yate .2G 31
Barnhill Ct. BS37: Chip S .5H 31
Barnhill Rd. BS37: Chip S .5H 31
Barn La. BS39: Chelw .6J 117
Barn Owl Way BS34: Stok G .2H 37
Barn Piece BA15: Brad A .7H 125
Barn Pool BS25: S'ham .5B 132
Barns Cl. BS48: Bar G .6H 73
BS48: Nail .7G 57
Barns Ground BS21: Clev .2D 68
Barnstaple Ct. BS4: Know .2A 76
Barnstaple Rd. BS4: Know .2A 76
Barnstaple Wlk. BS4: Know .2B 76
Barnwell Cl. BS10: Bren .3G 35
Barnwood BS16: L'lze .7E 36
Barnwood Cl. BS15: Kgswd .1D 64
Barnwood Ct. BS48: Nail .1D 70
Barnwood Rd. BS37: Yate .7C 30
Baron Cl. BS30: Bit .2J 79
Barons Cl. BS3: Ash V .6F 61
Barossa Pl. BS1: Bris .6F 5 (4K 61)
Barracks La. BS11: Shire .7H 33
Barratt St. BS5: E'ton .7D 48
Barrie Way TA8: Bur S .2E 158
Barrington Cl. BS15: Soun .6D 50
Barrington Ct. BS4: Wind H .5B 62
BS15: Soun .7C 50
Barrington Rd. TA8: Bur S .7E 156
BARROW COMMON .6B 74
Barrow Ct. BS21: Tic .5B 56
Barrow Ct. La. BS48: Bar G .6F 73
BARROW GURNEY .6H 73
Barrow Hill BS30: Wick .3B 66
Barrow Hill Cres. BS11: Shire .1G 45
Barrow Hill Rd. BS11: Shire .2G 45
Barrow La. BS40: Winf .1J 91
Barrowmead Dr. BS11: Law W .7K 33
Barrow Rd. BA2: Odd D .3J 121
BS5: Bar H .2D 62
BS24: Hut .3C 128
BARROWS .6C 150
Barrows, The BS22: W Mare .5A 106
BS27: Ched .5C 150
Barrows Cl. BS25: C'hll .1K 131
Barrows Cft. BS27: Ched .6C 150
Barrows Pk. BS27: Ched .6C 150
Barrows Rd. BS27: Ched .6C 150
Barrow St. BS48: Bar G .4G 73
BARROW VALE .7B 118
Barrow Vw. BA2: F'boro .1F 141
BARRS COURT .4D 64
Barr's Ct. BS1: Bris .1G 5 (1A 62)
Barrs Ct. Av. BS30: Bar C .4E 64
Barrs Ct. Rd. BS30: Bar C .4E 64
Barry Cl. BS24: W Mare .4J 127
BS30: Bit .1G 79
Barry Rd. BS30: Old C .7G 65
Barstaple Almshouse BS10: Bren .4G 35
Barstaple Ho. BS2: Bris .3K 5
Barter Cl. BS15: Kgswd .1B 64
Bartholomew Row BA2: Tims .3F 141
Bartholomews Sq. BS7: Hor .1B 48
Bartletts Ct. BA2: Bath .7H 7
Bartlett's Rd. BS3: Bedm .7J 61
Bartlett St. BA1: Bath .3F 7 (4B 100)
Bartletts Way BS24: Lock .1F 129
Bartley Ct. BS5: St G .2F 63
Bartley St. BS3: Bedm .5K 61
BARTON .7B 130
Barton, The BA2: Cor .4A 98
BS15: Han .5A 64
BS24: B'don .7A 128
BS39: Stan D .1C 116
BS40: Comp M .6B 136
Barton Bldgs. BA1: Bath .3F 7 (4B 100)
Barton Cl. BA15: Brad A .6H 125
BS4: St Ap .3H 63
BS35: A'ton .7J 11
BS36: Wint .2C 38
TA8: Berr .2B 156
Barton Ct. *BA1: Bath* .*4G 7*
(off Up. Borough Walls)
BS5: Bar H .3E 62
Barton Drove BS25: Wins .1B 148
Barton Farm Country Pk. .7E 124
Barton Grn. BS5: Bar H .2D 62
BARTON HILL .3D 62
Barton Hill Rd. BS5: Bar H .3D 62
Barton Hill Rugby Club .6J 49
Barton Hill Trad. Est.
BS5: Bar H .3D 62
Barton Ho. BS1: Bris .1G 5 (1A 62)
BS5: Redf .3E 62
Bartonia Gro. BS4: Brisl .1F 77
Barton Mnr. BS2: Bris .4K 5 (3C 62)
Barton Mdw. Est. BS16: Fish .2A 50
Barton Orchard BA15: Brad A .6G 125
Barton Rd. BS2: Bris .5K 5 (3B 62)
BS25: Bart, Wins .2J 147
BS26: Bart, Webb .2J 147
TA8: Berr .3B 156
Barton St. BA1: Bath .4F 7 (5B 100)
BS1: Bris .1F 5 (1K 61)
Barton Va. BS2: Bris .4K 5 (3C 62)
(not continuous)
Barwick Ho. BS11: Shire .1J 45
Bassetts Pasture *BA15: Brad A* .*7H 125*
(off Southway Rd.)
BATCH .2H 145
BATCH, THE
BS39, BISHOP SUTTON .1K 137
BS39, PAULTON .1C 152
Batch, The BA1: Bathe .7H 83
BA2: F'boro .6E 118
BA2: Well .4K 143
BS25: C'hll .2B 132
BS31: Salt .7K 79
BS39: High L .4B 140
BS40: But .4E 112
BS40: Chew M .1H 115
BS40: Comp M .6A 136
BS40: R'frd .1K 133
BS48: Back .2B 90
(not continuous)
BS49: Yat .4H 87
Batch Bus. Pk. BS24: Lym .4G 145
Batches, The BS3: Bedm .7H 61
Batch La. BS24: Lym .3H 145
BS39: Clut .2H 139
Bates Cl. BS5: E'ton .1K 5 (1C 62)
BATH .4G 7 (5C 100)
Bath Abbey .4G 7 (5C 100)

Bath Abbey Heritage Vaults—Berkeley Gro.

Bath Abbey Heritage Vaults 4G 7
(within Bath Abbey)
BATHAMPTON 2H 101
Bathampton La. BA2: Batham 2G 101
Bath & Dundas Canal Vis. Cen. 3J 123
Bath Approach Golf Course 1C 6 (3A 100)
Bath Aqua Theatre of Glass 2G 7 (4C 100)
Bath Boating Station 1J 7 (3D 100)
Bath Bldgs. BS6: Bris 7A 48
Bath Bus. Pk. BA2: Pea J 6E 142
Bath Bus Station 6G 7 (6C 100)
Bath City Farm 6H 99
Bath City FC 5H 99
BATHEASTON .6H 83
Batheaston Swainswick By-Pass
BA1: Bath, Swa, Up Swa 4D 82
BA2: Batham 2F 101
BATHFORD 1A 102
Bathford Hill BA1: Bathf 1K 101
BS39: Comp D 5B 96
Bath Golf Course 5F 101
Bath Hill BA2: Well 3J 143
BS31: Key 4D 78
Bathings, The BS35: T'bry 4A 12
Bathite Cotts. BA2: Mon C 3F 123
Bath Marina & Cvn. Pk. BA1: Bath 3F 99
Bath New Rd. BA3: Clan, Rads 2J 153
Bath Old Rd. BA3: Rads 3K 153
Bath Pavilion 5H 7 (5C 100)
Bath Postal Mus. 4G 7
Bath Racecourse 4G 81
Bath Rd. BA1: Kel, S'frd 4A 80
BA2: Cor 5F 79
BA2: F'boro 1B 140
BA2: Pea J .6B 142
BA15: Brad A 3G 125
BS4: Bris, Wind H 7K 5 (4B 62)
BS4: Brisl 1G 77
(Bonville Rd.)
BS4: Brisl 7F 63
(Eagle Rd.)
BS25: C'hll 1B 132
BS30: B'yte, Old C 4H 65
BS30: Bit, Will 1F 79
BS30: Long G 5C 64
BS30: Wick .3E 66
BS31: Key, Salt 5D 78
BS35: T'bry .4K 11
BS39: Paul 7C 140
BS40: Blag .3C 134
BS40: L'frd 1B 132
BS40: N Wid, W Har 7E 136
Bath Road (Park & Ride) 2H 77
Bath Royal Literary & Scientific Institution
. . . . .4E 6 (5B 100)
Bath RUFC 4H 7 (5C 100)
Baths, The BS23: W Mare 4E 104
Bath's Original Theatre Royal & Masonic Mus.
. . . . .5G 7
Bath Spa Station (Rail) 6H 7 (6C 100)
Bath Spa University
Newton Pk. Campus 6A 98
Bath Spa University College 2A 100
Bath Sports & Leisure Cen. 4H 7 (5C 100)
Bath St. BA1: Bath 5F 7 (5B 100)
BS1: Bris 4G 5 (3A 62)
BS3: Ash G .5G 61
BS16: Stap H 4C 50
BS27: Ched 7D 150
Bathurst Cl. TA8: Bur S 7F 157
Bathurst Pde. BS1: Bris 7E 4 (4K 61)
Bathurst Rd. BS22: W Mare 3A 106
Bathurst Ter. BS1: Bris 7E 4
(off Commercial Rd.)
Bathview Pk. BA1: Up Swa 1C 82
Bathwell Rd. BS4: Wind H 6C 62
BATHWICK 2J 7 (4D 100)
Bathwick Hill
BA2: Bath, C'ton D 3J 7 (5D 100)
Bathwick Pl. BA2: Bath 3K 7 (4D 100)
Bathwick Ri. BA2: Bath 2K 7 (3E 100)
Bathwick St. BA2: Bath 1H 7 (3C 100)
Bathwick Ter. BA2: Bath 4K 7
(off Bathwick Hill)
Batley Ct. BS30: Old C 5H 65
Batstone Cl. BA1: Bath 1D 100
Batt Cl. BS32: Alm 1G 27
Battenburg Rd. BS5: St G 1J 63
Batten Ct. BS37: Chip S 5J 31
Batten Rd. BS5: St G 2K 63
Batten's La. BS5: St G 3J 63
Battersby Way BS10: Hen 5E 34
Battersea Rd. BS5: E'ton 1E 62
Battery La. BS20: P'head 2F 43
Battery Rd. BS20: P'head 2F 43
Battleborough La. TA9: Bre K 6K 157
Battle La. BS40: Chew M 1G 115
Battson Rd. BS14: Stoc 5G 77
Baugh Gdns. BS16: Down 6C 38
Baugh Rd. BS16: Down 6C 38
Baxter Cl. BS15: Kgswd 1D 64
Bay Gdns. BS5: Eastv 6E 48
Bayham Rd. BS4: Know, Wind H 6B 62
Bayleys Dr. BS15: Kgswd 3A 64
Baylie Av. BS24: W Wick 3G 107
Baynard Cl. BS40: Blag 3C 134
Baynham Ct. BS15: Han 4K 63
(off Henbury Rd.)
Baynton Ho. BS5: E'ton 2C 62
Baynton Mdw. BS16: Emer G 2G 51
Baynton Rd. BS3: Ash G 5G 61
Bay Rd. BS21: Clev 3D 54
Bays, The BS27: Ched 6E 150
Bayswater Av. BS6: Henle 4H 47
Bayswater Rd. BS7: Hor 1B 48
Bay Tree Cl. BS34: Pat 7B 26
Baytree Ct. BS22: W Mare 3A 106
Bay Tree Rd. BA1: Bath 1C 100
BS21: Clev .7E 54
Baytree Rd. BS22: W Mare 3A 106
Baytree Vw. BS22: W Mare 3B 106
Bay Vw. Ct. BS23: W Mare 3E 104
Bay Vw. Gdns. TA8: Bur S 3D 158
Bay Willow Dr. BS6: Redl 6H 47
BEACH 7C 66
Beach, The BS21: Clev 5C 54
Beach Av. BS21: Clev 7C 54
BS35: Sev B .6A 16
Beach Ct. BS23: W Mare 6F 105
Beach End Rd. BS23: Uph 3E 126
Beachgrove Gdns. BS16: Fish 4A 50
Beachgrove Rd. BS16: Fish 4K 49
Beach Hill BS20: P'head 2E 42
BS30: Bit 6J 65
Beach La. BS30: Beach 6B 66
BEACHLEY 1C 8
Beachley Rd. NP16: Beach 1B 8
Beachley Wlk. BS11: Shire 1H 45
Beach Rd. BS22: Kew 1H 105
BS23: W Mare 7F 105
BS35: Sev B .6A 16
Beach Rd. E. BS20: P'head 2F 43
Beach Rd. W. BS20: P'head 2E 42
BEACON HILL 2C 100
Beacon Ho. BS8: Clftn 2B 4
Beacon La. BS36: Wint 2A 38
Beaconlea BS15: Kgswd 3B 64
Beacon Rd. BA1: Bath 2C 100
Beaconsfield Cl. BS5: Bar H 3D 62
Beaconsfield Ct. BS8: Clftn 7G 47
(off Beaconsfield Rd.)
Beaconsfield Rd. BS4: Know 6D 62
BS5: St G 1G 63
BS8: Clftn 7G 47
BS21: Clev .7E 54
BS23: W Mare 5G 105
Beaconsfield St. BS5: Bar H 3D 62
Beale Cl. BS14: Stoc 4G 77
Beale Wlk. BA2: Bath 4C 6 (5A 100)
Beale Way TA8: Bur S 3F 159
BEAM BRIDGE 3F 111
Beam St. BS5: Redf 2E 62
Bean Acre, The BS11: Shire 7H 33
Beanhill Cres. BS35: A'ton 7J 11
Beanwood Pk. BS37: W'lgh 4E 40
Bearberry Cl. BA3: Mid N 7F 153
Bearbridge Rd. BS13: Withy 6F 75
Bear Cl. BA15: Brad A 5F 125
Bearfield Bldgs. BA15: Brad A 4G 125
BEAR FLAT 7A 100
Bear Yd. M. BS8: Clftn 3G 61
(off Charles Pl.)
Beatrix Pl. BS7: Hor 7C 36
Beatty Way TA8: Bur S 1E 158
Beauchamp Rd. BS7: Bishop 4K 47
Beaufighter Rd. BS24: W Mare 6B 106
Beauford Sq. BA1: Bath 4F 7 (5B 100)
Beaufort BS16: Fren 6A 38
(off Harford Dr.)
Beaufort All. BS5: St G 3H 63
Beaufort Av. BA3: Mid N 4E 152
BS37: Yate .4D 30
Beaufort Bldgs. BS8: Clftn 2F 61
Beaufort Cl. BS5: St G 2F 63
BS24: Elbgh 2G 129
Beaufort Ct. BS16: Down 7E 38
BS21: Clev .4C 54
TA8: Bur S .7D 156
Beaufort Cres. BS34: Stok G 3G 37
Beaufort E. BA1: Bath 2E 100
Beaufort Gdns. BS48: Nail 1F 71
Beaufort Hgts. BS5: St G 2G 63
Beaufort Ho. BS5: Bar H 2D 62
Beaufort M. BA1: Bath 2E 100
BS8: Clftn 2F 61
Beaufort Pk. BS32: Brad S 3F 27
Beaufort Pl. BA1: Bath 2E 100
BS5: E'ton .1C 62
BS16: Fren .6K 37
Beaufort Rd. BS5: St G 2F 63
BS7: Hor 2B 48
BS8: Clftn 7G 47
BS15: Kgswd 7A 50
BS16: Down 1E 50
BS16: Stap H 4C 50
BS23: W Mare 4H 105
BS36: Fram C 6E 28
BS37: Yate .4D 30
Beaufort St. BS3: Bedm 7J 61
BS5: E'ton .1C 62
Beaufort Trade Pk. BS16: Puck 3B 52
Beaufort Vs. BA1: Bath 2D 100
Beaufort Way BS10: S'mead 7K 35
Beaufort W. BA1: Bath 2D 100
Beau Ho. BA2: Bath 4C 6 (5A 100)
Beauley Rd. BS3: Bris 7B 4 (4H 61)
Beaumont Cl. BS23: W Mare 1H 127
BS30: Long G 6E 64
Beaumont Ct. BS7: Hor 1C 48
Beaumont St. BS5: E'ton 1C 62
Beaumont Ter. BS5: E'ton 1C 62
Beau St. BA1: Bath 5F 7 (5B 100)
Beaver Cl. BS36: Wint 7D 28
Beazer Cl. BS16: Soun 5B 50
Beazer Garden Maze 4H 7 (5C 100)
Beck Cl. BS16: Emer G 2G 51
Becket Ct. BS16: Puck 3B 52
Becket Dr. BS22: Wor 1E 106
Becket Rd. BS22: Wor 1E 106
Becket's La. BS48: Nail 2G 71
Beckford Ct. BA2: Bath 2K 7
(off Darlington Rd.)
Beckford Gdns. BA2: Bath 2K 7 (3D 100)
BS14: Whit .7C 76
Beckford Rd. BA2: Bath 2J 7 (4D 100)
Beckford's Tower & Museum 6K 81
Beckhampton Rd. BA2: Bath 7B 6 (6K 99)
Beck Ho. BS34: Pat 6C 26
Beckington BS24: W Mare 3J 127
Beckington Rd. BS3: Know 7B 62
Beckington Wlk. BS3: Know 7B 62
Becks Bus. Pk. BS23: W Mare 5J 105
Beckspool Rd. BS16: Fren 1K 49
Beddoe Cl. BA15: Brad A 7J 125
Bedford Ct. BA1: Bath 3C 100
Bedford Cres. BS7: Hor 3B 48
Bedford Pl. BS2: Bris 1E 4 (1K 61)
Bedford Rd. BS23: W Mare 1G 127
Bedford St. BA1: Bath 1J 7 (3C 100)
BEDMINSTER .6J 61
Bedminster Bri. BS1: Bris 7F 5 (4K 61)
BS3: Bris 7F 5 (4K 61)
BEDMINSTER DOWN 2G 75
Bedminster Down Rd.
BS13: Bedm, Bis 1G 75
Bedminster Pde. BS3: Bedm 5K 61
Bedminster Pl. BS3: Bedm 5K 61
Bedminster Rd. BS3: Bedm 1H 75
Bedminster Station (Rail) 5K 61
Bedminster Trade Pk. BS3: Bedm 6J 61
Bedwin Cl. BS20: P'head 4B 42
Beechacres BS35: T'bry 2A 12
Beech Av. BA2: C'ton D 6G 101
Beech Cl. BS25: S'ham 5B 132
BS30: Bar C 4E 64
BS35: A'ton .7J 11
Beech Ct. BS14: Whit 5C 76
Beech Cft. BS14: H'gro 5D 76
Beechcroft BS41: Dun 1D 92
Beechcroft Wlk. BS7: Hor 7C 36
Beech Dr. BS25: S'ham 5B 132
BS48: Nail 6J 57
BEECHEN CLIFF 7F 7 (6B 100)
Beechen Cliff Rd. BA2: Bath 7E 6 (6B 100)
Beechen Cliff Vs. BA2: Bath 7E 6 (6B 100)
Beechen Dr. BS16: Fish 6K 49
Beeches, The BA2: Odd D 3K 121
BS4: St Ap .4G 63
BS9: Stok B .5D 46
BS25: Sandf 1H 131
BS30: Old C .7G 65
BS32: Brad S 6F 27
Beeches Gro. BS4: Brisl 7F 63
Beeches Ind. Est. BS37: Yate 4B 30
Beechfield Cl. BS41: L Ash 7C 60
Beechfield Gro. BS9: C Din 7C 34
Beech Gro. BA2: Bath 7J 99
Beech Ho. BS16: Stap 3E 48
Beech Leaze BS35: A'ton 7J 11
Beechmount Cl. BS24: W Mare 4H 127
Beechmount Ct. BS14: H'gro 2D 76
Beechmount Dr. BS24: W Mare 4J 127
Beechmount Gro. BS14: H'gro 2D 76
Beech Rd. BS7: Hor 3A 48
BS25: S'ham 5B 132
BS31: Salt 7J 79
BS49: Yat 3J 87
Beech Ter. BA3: Rads 5H 153
Beech Vw. BA2: C'ton D 6F 101
Beechwood Av. BS15: Han 4B 64
BS24: Lock 7E 106
Beechwood Cl. BS14: Stoc 2E 76
Beechwood Dr. BS20: P'head 3A 42
Beechwood Ho. BS16: Fish 4J 49
Beechwood Rd. BA2: C Down 3D 122
BS16: Fish .4J 49
BS20: Eas 4E 44
BS20: P'head 3A 42
BS48: Nail 7F 57
Beehive Trad. Est. BS5: St G 2G 63
Beehive Yd. BA1: Bath 3G 7 (4C 100)
Beesmoor Rd.
BS36: Coal H, Fram C 7F 29
Begbrook Dr. BS16: Bmhll 2H 49
Begbrook La. BS16: Bmhll 2H 49
Begbrook Pk. BS16: Fren 7J 37
Beggar Bush La. BS8: Abb L, Fail 5H 59
Beggarswell Cl. BS2: Bris 1B 62
Belcombe Pl. BA15: Brad A 6G 125
Belcombe Rd. BA15: Brad A 6F 125
Belfast Wlk. BS4: Know 2A 76
Belfield Ct. TA8: Bur S 7C 156
Belfields La. BS16: Fren 6A 38
Belfry BS30: Warm 3F 65
Belfry All. BS5: St G 1J 63
Belfry Av. BS5: St G 1J 63
Belgrave Cres. BA1: Bath 3C 100
Belgrave Hill BS8: Clftn 6G 47
Belgrave Ho. BS8: Clftn 2A 4
Belgrave Pl. BA1: Bath 2C 100
BS8: Clftn 2G 61
Belgrave Rd. BA1: Bath 2D 100
BS8: Clftn 1B 4 (1H 61)
BS22: W Mare 4K 105
Belgrave Ter. BA1: Bath 2C 100
Bellamy Av. BS13: Hart 6J 75
Bellamy Cl. BS15: St G 4J 63
Belland Dr. BS14: Whit 6B 76
Bell Av. BS1: Bris 6F 5 (4K 61)
Bella Vista Rd. BA1: Bath 3B 100
Bell Barn Rd. BS9: Stok B 2D 46
Bell Cl. BA2: F'boro 6D 118
BS10: Hor 1A 48
Belle Ct. BS3: Wind H 5B 62
(off Bellevue Rd.)
BELLE VUE 3F 153
Belle Vue BA3: Mid N 3F 153
Bellevue BS8: Clftn 4A 4 (3H 61)
Belle Vue Cl. BA2: Pea J 5D 142
Bellevue Cl. BS15: Kgswd 2C 64
Bellevue Cotts. BS8: Clftn 5A 4 (3H 61)
BS9: W Trym 1G 47
Bellevue Ct. BS8: Clftn 4A 4 (3H 61)
Bellevue Cres. BS8: Clftn 4A 4 (3H 61)
Bellevue Mans. BS21: Clev 5D 54
Bellevue Pk. BS4: Brisl 7F 63
Belle Vue Rd. BS5: E'ton 6E 48
Bellevue Rd. BS4: Wind H 5B 62
BS5: St G 1J 63
BS15: Kgswd 2D 64
BS21: Clev .5D 54
Bellevue Ter. BS4: Brisl 7F 63
BS4: Wind H 5B 62
BS8: Clftn 4A 4 (3H 61)
Bellhanger Ct. BA1: Bath 1F 7
Bell Hill BS16: Stap 4E 48
Bell Hill Rd. BS5: St G 1J 63
Bellhouse Wlk.
BS11: Law W 6B 34
Bellifants BA2: F'boro 6E 118
Bell La. BS1: Bris 3E 4 (2K 61)
(not continuous)
BS32: Alm, Piln 1H 25
BS35: Piln .1H 25
Bellotts Rd. BA2: Bath 5A 6 (5J 99)
Bell Pit Brow BS48: Wrax 7K 57
Bell Rd. BS36: Coal H 7G 29
Bell Sq. BS40: Blag 2C 134
Bell's Wlk. BS40: Wrin 2G 111
BELLUTON 6E 94
Belluton La. BS39: Pens 6F 95
Belluton Rd. BS4: Know 6C 62
Belmont BA1: Bath 2F 7 (4B 100)
Belmont, The BS21: Clev 6D 54
Belmont Dr. BS8: Fail 6F 59
BS34: Stok G 2G 37
Belmont Hill
BS48: Fail, Flax B 1E 72
Belmont Pk. BS7: Fil 6B 36
Belmont Rd. BA2: C Down 3E 122
BS4: Brisl 5E 62
BS6: Bris 6A 48
BS25: Wins 5G 131
Belmont St. BS5: E'ton 7D 48
Belmore Gdns. BA2: Bath 1H 121
Beloe Rd. BS7: Hor 3A 48
Belroyal Av. BS4: Brisl 6H 63
Belsher Dr. BS15: Kgswd 3E 64
Belstone Wlk. BS4: Know 2J 75
Belton Ct. BA1: W'ton 1H 99
Belton Ho. BA1: W'ton 1H 99
Belton Rd. BS5: E'ton 7D 48
BS20: P'head 2C 42
Belvedere BA1: Bath 2F 7 (4B 100)
Belvedere Cres.
BS22: W Mare 3A 106
Belvedere Pl. BA1: Bath 1F 7
(off Morford St.)
Belvedere Rd. BS6: Redl 5G 47
Belvedere Vs. BA1: Bath 1F 7 (3B 100)
Belvoir Rd. BA2: Bath 7A 6 (6K 99)
BS6: Bris 6A 48
Bence Ct. BS15: Han 4K 63
(off Memorial Rd.)
Benches La. BS40: Winf 7H 91
Bendalls Bri. BS39: Clut 3G 139
Benford Cl. BS16: Fish 2A 50
Bengough's Almshouses
BS2: Bris 2D 4 (2J 61)
BENGROVE 4K 141
Bennett Rd. BS5: St G 2G 63
TA9: Highb 5H 159
Bennetts Ct. BS37: Yate 5F 31
Bennett's La. BA1: Bath 2C 100
Bennett's Rd. BA1: Swa 7E 82
Bennett St. BA1: Bath 2F 7 (4B 100)
Bennetts Way BS21: Clev 4E 54
Bennett Way BS8: Clftn 4F 61
Bensaunt Gro. BS10: Bren 3K 35
Bentley Cl. BS14: Whit 7B 76
Bentley Rd. BS22: Wor 1F 107
Ben Travers Way TA8: Bur S 2E 158
Benville Av. BS9: C Din 7C 34
Berchel Ho. BS3: Bedm 5J 61
Berenda Dr. BS30: Long G 6F 65
Beresford Cl. BS31: Salt 1J 97
TA8: Bur S 1E 158
Beresford Gdns. BA1: W'ton 7G 81
Berkeley Av. BA3: Mid N 4E 152
BS1: Clftn 3C 4 (2J 61)
BS7: Bishop 5K 47
Berkeley Cl. BS16: Down 7D 38
Berkeley Ct. BA2: Bath 4K 7 (5E 100)
BS5: E'ton .2D 62
BS7: Bishop 5K 47
BS34: Pat 5B 26
Berkeley Cres. BS8: Clftn 3B 4 (2H 61)
BS23: Uph 3E 126
Berkeley Gdns. BS31: Key 6B 78
Berkeley Grn. BS16: Fren 6K 37
Berkeley Grn. Rd. BS5: Eastv 6E 48
Berkeley Gro. BS5: Eastv 6E 48

Bower Wlk.—Broad St. Pl.

Bower Wlk. BS3: Wind H .6A 62
Bowlditch La. BA3: Mid N .2F 153
Bowling Hill BS37: Chip S .5G 31
Bowling Hill Bus. Pk. BS37: Chip S .5G 31
Bowling Rd. BS37: Chip S .6H 31
(not continuous)
Bowlplex
Kingswood .4C 64
Bow Mead BS14: Stoc .5G 77
Bowood BS16: Fren .6A 38
(off Avon Ring Rd.)
Bowring Cl. BS13: Hart .7J 75
Bowsland BS32: Brad S .4G 27
Bowsland Way BS32: Brad S .4E 26
Bowstreet La. BS35: E Comp .6G 25
Boxbury Hill BS39: Paul .3C 152
Box Bush La. BS24: E Rols .3C 108
Box Hedge La. BS36: Henf .4J 39
Box Rd. BA1: Bathf .7K 83
Box Wlk. BS31: Key .6A 78
Boyce Cl. BA2: Bath .6F 99
Boyce Dr. BS2: Bris .6C 48
Boyce's Av. BS8: Clftn .2G 61
Boyd Cl. BS30: Wick .2B 66
Boyd Rd. BS31: Salt .7H 79
BRABAZON .2A 36
Brabazon Office Pk. BS34: Fil .4B 36
Brabazon Rd. BS34: Fil .5D 36
Bracewell Gdns. BS10: Bren .3J 35
Bracey Dr. BS16: Fish .2A 50
Brackenbury Dr. BS34: Stok G .2H 37
Brackendene BS32: Brad S .5E 26
Brackenwood Gdns.
BS20: P'head .3B 42
Brackenwood Rd. BS21: Clev .3E 54
Bracton Dr. BS14: Whit .6C 76
Bradbury Ct. BS10: Hen .4E 34
Bradeston Gro. BS16: Bmhll .1J 49
Bradford Cl. BS21: Clev .1C 68
BRADFORD LEIGH .2K 125
BRADFORD-ON-AVON .6H 125
Bradford-on-Avon Golf Course .7J 125
Bradford-on-Avon Mus. .6H 125
Bradford-on-Avon Station (Rail) .6G 125
Bradford-on-Avon Swimming Pool .6G 125
Bradford Pk. BA2: C Down .2C 122
(not continuous)
Bradford Rd. BA1: Bathf, Warl .7K 83
BA2: C Down .3B 122
BA15: W'ley .6B 124
Bradford Wood La. BA15: Brad A .6K 125
Bradhurst St. BS5: Bar H .3D 62
Bradley Av. BS11: Shire .2J 45
BS36: Wint .2C 38
Bradley Ct. BS16: Down .3A 50
Bradley Cres. BS11: Shire .2J 45
BRADLEY CROSS .7F 151
Bradley Cross La. BS27: Ched .7F 151
Bradley Ho. BS1: Bris .4E 4
(off St Stephen's Av.)
Bradley Pavilions BS32: Brad S .4E 26
Bradley Rd. BS20: P'bry .3C 44
BS34: Pat .6B 26
BRADLEY STOKE .4E 26
Bradley Stoke Leisure Cen. .5G 27
Bradley Stoke Way BS32: Brad S .4D 26
Bradstone Rd. BS36: Wint .2B 38
Bradville Gdns. BS41: L Ash .2K 73
Bradwell Gro. BS10: S'mead .7J 35
Braemar Av. BS7: Fil .6A 36
Braemar Cres. BS7: Fil .6B 36
Brae Ri. BS25: Wins .5G 131
Brae Rd. BS25: Wins .5G 131
Bragg's La. BS2: Bris .2K 5 (2B 62)
Braikenridge Cl. BS21: Clev .1C 68
Braikenridge Rd. BS4: Brisl .5F 63
Brainsfield BS9: W Trym .2F 47
Braithwaite Pl. TA8: Bur S .5C 156
Brake, The BS36: Coal H .2G 39
BS37: Yate .1E 30
Brake Cl. BS15: Kgswd .2D 64
BS32: Brad S .7G 27
Brakewell Gdns. BS14: Whit .6C 76
Bramble Dr. BS9: Stok B .5C 46
TA8: Berr .2B 156
Bramble La. BS9: Stok B .5C 46
Brambles, The BS13: Hart .6J 75
BS22: St G .2H 107
BS31: Key .7B 78
(not continuous)
Brambles Rd. TA8: Bur S .6C 156
Bramble Way BA2: C Down .2D 122
Bramblewood BS49: Yat .2H 87
Bramblewood Rd. BS22: Wor .1C 106
Brambling La. BS20: P'head .2J 43
Brambling Wlk. BS16: Bmhll .2H 49
(not continuous)
Bramley Cl. BA2: Pea J .6D 142
BS20: Pill .4G 45
BS24: Lock .1E 128
BS25: Sandf .1G 131
BS35: Olv .2C 18
BS49: Yat .4H 87
Bramley Copse BS41: L Ash .2J 73
Bramley Ct. BS30: Bar C .5D 64
Bramley Dr. BS48: Back .5J 71
Bramleys, The BS20: P'head .4H 43
BS48: Nail .2D 70
Bramley Sq. BS49: Cong .1A 110
Brampton Way BS20: P'head .3F 43
Bramshill Dr. BS22: Wor .1D 106
Branche Gro. BS13: Hart .7K 75
Brandash Rd. BS37: Chip S .5J 31
Brandon Cotts. BS1: Bris .4C 4
Brandon Hill La. BS8: Clftn .3B 4 (2H 61)
Brandon Hill Nature Pk. .4B 4 (3H 61)
Brandon Ho. BS1: Bris .4C 4
BS8: Clftn .4A 4 (3H 61)
Brandon Steep BS1: Bris .4C 4 (3J 61)
Brandon Steps BS1: Bris .4C 4 (3J 61)
Brandon Vs. BS8: Clftn .4A 4 (3H 61)
Brangwyn Gro. BS7: L'lze .3D 48
Brangwyn Sq. BS22: Wor .2D 106
Branksome Cres. BS34: Fil .4D 36
Branksome Dr. BS34: Fil .4D 36
BS36: Wint .1C 38
Branksome Rd. BS6: Redl .5H 47
Bransby Way BS24: W'ton V .4E 106
Branscombe Rd. BS9: Stok B .4C 46
Branscombe Wlk. BS20: P'head .5B 42
Branwhite Cl. BS7: L'lze .1D 48
BRASSKNOCKER .2H 123
Brassknocker Hill
BA2: C'ton D, Mon C .1H 123
Brassmill Ent. Cen. BA1: Bath .4G 99
Brassmill La. BA1: Bath .3G 99
Brassmill La. Trad. Est. BA1: Bath .4G 99
Bratchel Ct. BS15: Han .4K 63
Bratton Rd. BS4: Know .3K 75
Braunton Rd. BS3: Bedm .6J 61
Braydon Av. BS34: Lit S .6E 26
Brayne Ct. BS30: Long G .6D 64
Braysbridge BS27: Ched .7E 150
BRAYSDOWN .1D 154
Braysdown Cl. BA2: Pea J .7B 142
Braysdown La. BA2: Pea J .6C 142
(not continuous)
Braysdown Yd. BA2: Pea J .1C 154
BREACH .6H 117
Breaches, The BS20: Eas .4F 45
Breaches Ga. BS32: Brad S .1H 37
Breaches La. BS31: Key .6E 78
BREACH HILL COMMON .1A 136
Breach Hill La. BS40: Chew S .7B 114
Breach La. BS48: Nail .2B 70
Breach Rd. BS3: Bedm .6G 61
Breachwood Vw. BA2: Odd D .2J 121
Breakneck BS48: Back .6K 71
BREAN .1B 144
Brean Ct. TA8: Brean .3B 144
Brean Down Av. BS9: Henle .3H 47
(not continuous)
BS23: W Mare .1F 127
Brean Down Rd. TA8: Brean .3B 126
Brean Gdns. BS3: Wind H .7A 62
Brean Golf Course .5B 144
Brean Leisure Pk. .4B 144
Brean Rd. BS24: Lym .5G 145
Brecknock Rd. BS4: Wind H .6C 62
Brecon Cl. BS9: Henle .2H 47
Brecon Ct. BS16: Fren .6F 37
Brecon Rd. BS9: Henle .2G 47
Brecon Vw. BS24: W Mare .4J 127
Bredon BS37: Yate .7D 30
Bredon Cl. BS15: Kgswd .2D 64
Bredon Nook Rd. BS10: W Trym .1J 47
Bree Cl. BS22: Wor .7E 84
Brendon Av. BS23: W Mare .3H 105
Brendon Cl. BS30: Old C .5G 65
Brendon Ct. BA2: C'ton D .5G 101
Brendon Gdns. BS48: Nail .1G 71
Brendon Rd. BS3: Wind H .6K 61
BS20: P'head .3C 42
Brendon Way BS27: Ched .6D 150
Brenner St. BS5: E'ton .6D 48
Brent Broad TA8: Bur S .5D 156
Brent Cl. BS24: W Mare .3K 127
TA9: Bre K .6K 157
BRENT KNOLL .5J 157
Brent Rd. BS7: Hor .3B 48
TA8: Bur S .3C 156
TA9: Bre K .3C 156
TA9: E Brnt .2K 157
BRENTRY .4H 35
Brentry Av. BS5: Bar H .2D 62
Brentry Hill BS9: W Trym .6G 35
Brentry Ho. BS10: Bren .4H 35
Brentry La. BS10: Bren .5G 35
Brentry Rd. BS16: Fish .4G 49
Brent St. TA9: Bre K .4H 157
Brereton Way BS30: C Hth .5F 65
Brewerton Cl. BS10: Bren .4J 35
Brewery Ct. BS3: Ash G .5G 61
Brewery Hill BS30: Upton C .3K 79
Brewhouse BS1: Bris .4G 5
Briar Cl. BA3: Rads .6H 153
BS48: Nail .7J 57
TA8: Bur S .2E 158
Briar Ct. BS20: Pill .5G 45
TA8: Bur S .2E 158
Briarfield Av. BS15: Han .4K 63
Briarlands Office Pk. BS35: Rudg .2J 19
Briarleaze BS35: Rudg .3H 19
Briar Mead BS49: Yat .2G 87
Briar Rd. BS24: Hut .2C 128
Briars, The BS48: Back .3H 71
Briars Ct. BA2: Bath .7G 99
Briarside Rd. BS10: Bren .4J 35
Briar Wlk. BS16: Fish .5A 50
Briar Way BS16: Fish .4K 49
Briarwood BS9: W Trym .2F 47
Briary Rd. BS20: P'head .3E 42
Briavels Gro. BS6: Bris .6B 48
Brick La. BS39: High L .4B 140
Brick St. BS2: Bris .2K 5 (2B 62)
Brickworks Cl. BS5: S'wll .7G 49
Bridewell La. BA1: Bath .4F 7 (5B 100)
BS24: Ban, Hut .5F 129
Bridewell St. BS1: Bris .2F 5 (2K 61)
Bridge Cl. BS14: Whit .6E 76
Bridge Farm Cl. BS14: Whit .7C 76
Bridge Farm Sq. BS49: Cong .7K 87
Bridge Farm Wlk. BS16: Mang .5F 51
Bridge Gdns. BA2: F'boro .6E 118
Bridge Ho. BS1: Bris .4F 5
Bridgeleap Rd. BS16: Down .7D 38
Bridge Lock M. BA2: Bath .6J 7
Bridge Pl. Rd. BA2: Cam .5J 141
Bridge Rd. BA2: Bath .7A 6 (6J 99)
BS5: Eastv .5D 48
BS8: L Wds .3D 60
BS15: Soun .5D 50
BS16: Short .4G 51
BS23: W Mare .6H 105
BS24: B'don .7K 127
BS37: Yate .4A 30
Bridge Rd. Ind. Est. BS15: Soun .5E 50
Bridges Ct. BS16: Fish .4K 49
Bridges Dr. BS16: Fish .2A 50
Bridge St. BA2: Bath .4G 7 (5C 100)
BA15: Brad A .6H 125
BS1: Bris .4F 5 (3A 62)
BS5: Eastv .6F 49
Bridge Valley Rd. BS8: Clftn .1E 60
Bridge Vw. BS35: Aust .4G 9
Bridge Vw. Cl. BS5: E'ton .7E 48
Bridge Wlk. BS7: Hor .7C 36
Bridge Way BS36: Fram C .6F 29
Bridge Yd. BA15: Brad A .6H 125
BRIDGEYATE .2H 65
Bridgman Gro. BS34: Fil .4D 36
Bridgwater Ct. BS24: W Mare .2J 127
Bridgwater Rd. BS13: Bis .3E 74
BS23: W Mare, B'don .2G 127
BS24: Lym .1A 146
BS25: Wins .1G 149
BS26: Axb, Cross .5E 148
BS40: F'tn .3E 90
BS41: Dun .1G 91
BS48: Bar G .1G 91
Bridle Way BS35: A'ton .1H 19
Bridleway Cl. BA3: Mid N .6C 152
Briercliffe Rd. BS9: Stok B .1D 46
Brierly Furlong BS34: Stok G .4F 37
Briery Leaze Rd. BS14: Whit .5C 76
Brighton Cres. BS3: Bedm .7H 61
Brighton M. BS8: Clftn .1H 61
Brighton Pk. BS5: E'ton .1D 62
Brighton Pl. BS15: Kgswd .7B 50
Brighton Rd. BS6: Redl .7J 47
BS23: W Mare .6G 105
BS34: Pat .6B 26
Brighton St. BS2: Bris .7A 48
Brighton Ter. BS3: Bedm .7H 61
Brightside Pk. BS35: Aust .4F 9
Brightstowe Rd. TA8: Bur S .5C 156
Bright St. BS5: Bar H .2D 62
BS15: Kgswd .1B 64
Brigstocke Rd. BS2: Bris .7A 48
Brigstowe St. BS1: Bris .2H 5 (2A 62)
Brimbles, The BS7: Hor .5D 36
Brimbleworth La. BS22: St G .1G 107
Brimridge Rd. BS25: Wins .5G 131
Brimsham Pk. Shop. Cen.
BS37: Yate .2E 30
Brinkmarsh La. GL12: Fal .1H 13
Brinkworthy Rd. BS16: Stap .2F 49
Brinmead Wlk. BS13: Withy .7F 75
Brins Cl. BS34: Stok G .3H 37
Brinscombe La. BA2: Shos, Ston L .7F 143
BRINSEA .4A 110
Brinsea Batch BS49: Cong .3A 110
Brinsea La. BS49: Cong .4A 110
Brinsea Rd. BS49: Cong .1K 109
Brinsham La. BS37: Yate .7G 23
Brinsmead Cres. BS20: Pill .4H 45
(off Heywood Rd.)
Briscoes Av. BS13: Hart .6J 75
BRISLINGTON .7G 63
Brislington Hill BS4: Brisl .7G 63
Brislington Retail Pk. BS4: Brisl .1G 77
Brislington Trad. Est. BS4: Brisl .7H 63
(not continuous)
BRISTOL .3F 5 (2K 61)
Bristol & Anchor Ho. BS5: W'hall .1F 63
(off Park Cres.)
Bristol & Bath Science Pk.
BS16: Emer G .6F 39
Bristol & Exeter M. BS1: Bris .6J 5 (4B 62)
Bristol Bri. Ho. BS1: Bris .4F 5 (3A 62)
Bristol Bus. Pk. BS16: Fren .6H 37
Bristol Bus Station .1F 5 (1K 61)
Bristol Cathedral .5D 4 (3J 61)
Bristol City FC .6F 61
Bristol Distribution Pk. BS32: Brad S .3F 27
Bristol Ga. BS8: Clftn .4F 61
Bristol Harbour Railway .6C 4 (4J 61)
Bristol Hill BS4: Brisl .7F 63
Bristol Hippodrome .4D 4 (3K 61)
Bristol Ho. BS1: Bris .4G 5
Bristol Ice Rink .3D 4 (2J 61)
Bristol Indoor Bowls Club .1E 74
BRISTOL AIRPORT .4D 90
Bristol North Baths .5K 47
Bristol Outdoor Pursuits .3C 118
Bristol Parkway Nth. BS34: Stok G .2J 37
Bristol Parkway Station (Rail) .3G 37
Bristol Resource Recovery Pk.
BS11: A'mth .3H 33
Bristol Rd. BA2: Cor, New L .3B 98
BA3: Rads .2K 153
BS14: Whit .5E 76
BS16: Fren, H'ook .7J 37
BS16: H'ook .4B 38
BS20: P'head .4F 43
BS22: St G, Wor .2F 107
BS24: W Wick .2F 107
BS25: C'hll .1B 132
BS25: Row, Star, Wins .6H 131
BS31: Key .4B 78
BS35: T'bry .5K 11
BS36: Fram C, Wint .7C 28
BS37: Iron A .3G 29
BS39: Far G, Hall .7H 139
BS39: Paul .7C 140
BS39: Pens, Pub .5F 95
BS40: But, Redh .7E 90
BS40: Chew S .4D 114
BS40: L'frd .1B 132
BS48: Wrax .6J 57
BS49: Cong .7K 87
GL12: Crom .2B 14
TA9: Bre K, Edith, Highb .4G 159
Bristol Rd. Lwr. BS23: W Mare .4F 105
Bristol Rovers FC .2B 48
Bristol RUFC .6F 61
Bristol Sth. End BS3: Wind H .7K 61
Bristol South Swimming Pool .5J 61
Bristol Sports Cen. .1E 62
Bristol Temple Meads Station (Rail)
.6K 5 (4B 62)
Bristol Va. Cen. for Industry
BS3: Bedm .1H 75
Bristol Va. Trad. Est. BS3: Bedm .2J 75
Bristol Vw. BA2: Odd D .4J 121
Bristol Zoo Gdns. .7F 47
Bristow B'way. BS11: A'mth .6G 33
Bristowe Ho. BS16: Fish .3K 49
Britannia Cl. BS36: Down .6E 38
Britannia Cres. BS34: Stok G .2F 37
Britannia Ho. BS34: Fil .5B 36
Britannia Rd. BS5: E'ton .7D 48
BS15: Kgswd .1A 64
BS34: Pat .6K 25
Britannia Way BS21: Clev .1C 68
British, The BS37: Yate .2B 30
British Rd. BS3: Bedm .6H 61
Brittan Pl. BS20: P'bry .5C 44
Britten Ct. BS30: Long G .5D 64
BRITTEN'S .7D 140
Brittens BS39: Paul .7D 140
Britten's Cl. BS39: Paul .7D 140
Britten's Hill BS39: Paul .7D 140
Britton Gdns. BS15: Kgswd .7A 50
Britton Ho. BS15: Warm .1F 65
Brixham Rd. BS3: Wind H .7J 61
Brixton Rd. BS5: E'ton .1D 62
Brixton Rd. M. BS5: E'ton .1D 62
Broadbury Rd. BS4: Know .2K 75
Broad Cft. BS32: Brad S .4E 26
BS34: Pat .1A 36
Broadcroft BS40: Chew M .1F 115
Broadcroft Av. BS49: C'ham .2B 88
Broadcroft Cl. BS49: C'ham .2B 88
Broadfield Av. BS15: Kgswd .1A 64
Broadfield Rd. BS4: Know .2C 76
Broadhurst Gdns. TA8: Bur S .3D 158
Broadlands BS21: Clev .6F 55
Broadlands Av. BS31: Key .4B 78
Broadlands Dr. BS11: Law W .7A 34
Broad La. BS36: Coal H .2H 39
BS37: W'lgh .3A 40
BS37: Yate .2B 30
(not continuous)
Broadleas BS13: Bis .3J 75
Broadleaze BS11: Shire .1H 45
Broadleaze Way BS25: Wins .3F 131
Broadleys Av. BS9: Henle .1J 47
BROAD MEAD .3D 36
BROADMEAD .3G 5 (2A 62)
Broadmead BS1: Bris .2G 5 (2A 62)
Broadmead Gallery BS1: Bris .2A 62
(within The Galleries)
Broad Mead La. BS40: Regil .1K 113
Broadmead La. BS31: Key .5F 79
Broadmead La. Ind. Est.
BS31: Key .3F 79
Broadmoor La. BA1: W'ton .6F 81
Broadmoor Pk. BA1: W'ton .1H 99
Broadmoor Va. BA1: W'ton .7G 81
Broadoak Hill BS41: Dun .1F 93
Broad Oak Rd. BS13: Withy .6F 75
Broadoak Rd. BS23: W Mare .2F 127
BS40: L'frd .7C 110
Broad Oaks BS8: L Wds .3E 60
Broadoak Wlk. BS16: Fish .4K 49
Broad Plain BS2: Bris .4J 5 (2B 62)
Broad Quay BA1: Bath .6F 7 (6B 100)
BS1: Bris .4E 4 (3K 61)
Broad Quay Ho. BS1: Bris .5E 4
Broad Rd. BS15: Kgswd .7A 50
BS40: Blag .5B 134
Broadstone La. BS21: Kings S .1K 85
Broadstones BA15: Mon F .4C 102
Broadstone Wlk. BS13: Hart .5K 75
Broad St. BA1: Bath .3G 7 (4C 100)
BS1: Bris .3F 5 (2K 61)
BS16: Stap H .4B 50
BS37: Chip S .5H 31
BS40: Wrin .2F 111
BS49: Cong .7K 87
Broad St. Pl. BA1: Bath .3G 7 (4C 100)

168 A-Z Bristol, Bath & North Somerset Atlas

Broad Wlk.—Calcott Rd.

Broad Wlk. BS4: Know ... 7B 62
BS20: P'head ... 1G 43
Broadwalk Shop. Cen.
BS4: Know ... 7D 62
Broadway BA2: Bath ... 5J 7 (5D 100)
BS24: Lock ... 1H 129
BS24: W Mare ... 3H 127
BS25: S'ham, Star ... 4K 131
BS31: Salt ... 7H 79
(not continuous)
BS37: Yate ... 4F 31
Broadway Av. BS9: Henle ... 2K 47
Broadway Ct. BA2: Bath ... 6H 7 (6C 100)
Broadway Ho. Holiday Touring Cvn. Pk.
BS27: Ched ... 4B 150
Broadway La. BA3: Rads ... 7F 141
Broadway Rd. BS7: Bishop ... 5K 47
BS13: Withy ... 5F 75
Broadways Dr. BS16: Bmhll ... 1H 49
Broad Weir BS1: Bris ... 3H 5 (2A 62)
Brock End BS20: P'head ... 5B 42
Brockhurst Gdns. BS15: Kgswd ... 1J 63
Brockhurst Rd. BS15: Kgswd ... 1J 63
BROCKLEY ... 1F 89
Brockley Cl. BS24: W Mare ... 4H 127
BS34: Lit S ... 7E 26
BS48: Nail ... 1F 71
Brockley Combe Rd. BS48: Back, B'ley ... 1G 89
Brockley Cres. BS24: W Mare ... 4H 127
Brockley La. BS48: B'ley, Chelv ... 5F 71
Brockley Rd. BS31: Salt ... 7H 79
Brockley Wlk. BS13: Bis ... 2G 75
Brockley Way BS48: B'ley ... 7C 70
BS49: C'ham, C've ... 1B 88
(not continuous)
Brockridge La. BS36: Fram C ... 7G 29
Brocks La. BS41: L Ash ... 1K 73
Brocks Rd. BS13: Hart ... 7J 75
Brock St. BA1: Bath ... 2E 6 (4B 100)
Brockway BS48: Nail ... 7H 57
Brockwood BA15: W'ley ... 5D 124
Brockworth BS37: Yate ... 1C 40
Brockworth Cres. BS16: Bmhll ... 2H 49
Bromfield Wlk. BS16: Emer G ... 1F 51
Bromley Dr. BS16: Down ... 7B 38
Bromley Farm BS16: Down ... 6B 38
BROMLEY HEATH ... 7C 38
Bromley Heath Av. BS16: Down ... 7B 38
Bromley Heath Rd. BS16: Down ... 1B 50
BS16: H'ook ... 5B 38
Bromley Rd. BS7: Hor ... 3B 48
BS39: Stan D ... 2B 116
Brompton Cl. BS15: Kgswd ... 1D 64
Brompton Ho. BA2: Bath ... 2H 7 (4C 100)
Brompton Rd. BS24: W Mare ... 3J 127
Broncksea Rd. BS7: Fil ... 6B 36
Bronte Cl. BS23: W Mare ... 1J 127
Bronte Wlk. BS7: Hor ... 7C 36
Brook Bus. Pk. BS30: C Hth ... 3F 65
Brook Cl. BS41: L Ash ... 1B 74
Brookcote Dr. BS34: Lit S ... 1F 37
Brook Ct. BS13: Bis ... 4G 75
BS32: Brad S ... 6G 27
Brookdale Rd. BS13: Bis ... 4H 75
Brooke Rd. TA8: Berr ... 3B 156
Brookfield Av. BS7: Bishop ... 5K 47
Brookfield Cl. BS37: Chip S ... 4J 31
Brookfield La. BS6: Cot ... 6K 47
Brookfield Pk. BA1: W'ton ... 1H 99
Brookfield Rd. BS6: Cot ... 6K 47
BS34: Pat ... 6D 26
Brookfield Wlk. BS21: Clev ... 6F 55
BS30: Old C ... 6G 65
Brookgate BS3: Ash V ... 1E 74
Brook Hill BS6: Bris ... 7B 48
Brook Ho. BS34: Lit S ... 6E 26
Brooking Mdw. BS48: Nail ... 1F 71
Brookland Rd. BS6: Henle ... 3K 47
BS22: W Mare ... 5K 105
Brooklands BA2: Dunk ... 2D 142
Brook La. BS6: Bris ... 7B 48
BS16: Bmhll ... 2G 49
Brooklea BS30: Old C ... 5F 65
Brookleaze BS9: Sea M ... 3C 46
Brookleaze Bldgs. BA1: Bath ... 1D 100
Brookleaze Pl. BA1: Bath ... 1D 100
Brook Lintons BS4: Brisl ... 6F 63
Brook Lodge Touring Cvn. & Camping Pk.
BS40: Redh ... 3K 111
Brooklyn BS40: Wrin ... 2F 111
Brooklyn Rd. BA1: Bath ... 1E 100
BS13: Bis ... 2H 75
Brookmead BS35: T'bry ... 5B 12
Brook Office Pk. BS16: Emer G ... 5F 39
Brookridge Ho. BS10: Hen ... 4F 35
Brook Rd. BA2: Bath ... 4A 6 (5K 99)
BS3: Bedm ... 5K 61
BS5: S'wll ... 7G 49
BS6: Bris ... 7B 48
BS15: Kgswd, Warm ... 1E 64
(not continuous)
BS15: Warm ... 1F 65
BS16: Fish ... 4J 49
(not continuous)
BS16: Mang ... 2D 50
Brookside BS20: Pill ... 5G 45
BS39: Paul ... 7C 140
BS40: Winf ... 4K 91
Brookside Cl. BA1: Bathe ... 5H 83
BS39: Paul ... 7C 140
Brookside Dr. BA2: F'boro ... 6D 118
BS36: Fram C ... 6F 29
Brookside Ho. BA1: W'ton ... 2H 99
Brookside Rd. BS4: Brisl ... 7G 63
Brook St. BS5: Redf ... 2E 62
BS37: Chip S ... 5G 31
Brookthorpe BS37: Yate ... 6D 30
Brookthorpe Av. BS11: Law W ... 6A 34
Brookthorpe Ct. BS37: Yate ... 6D 30
Brook Vw. BS10: Hen ... 4F 35
Brookview Wlk. BS13: Bis ... 3H 75
Brook Way BS32: Brad S ... 5E 26
Broom Farm Cl. BS48: Nail ... 2G 71
Broomground BA15: W'ley ... 5C 124
BROOM HILL ... 5H 63
BROOMHILL ... 2H 49
Broom Hill BS16: Bmhll ... 2G 49
Broom Hill La. BS39: High L ... 5C 140
Broomhill La. BS39: Clut ... 2G 139
Broomhill Rd. BS4: Brisl ... 6H 63
Brooms, The BS16: Emer G ... 5E 38
Brotherswood Ct. BS32: Brad S ... 3F 27
Brougham Hayes BA2: Bath ... 6B 6 (5K 99)
Brougham Pl. *BA1: Bath ... 1E 100*
(off St Saviours Rd.)
Broughton Ho. BS1: Bris ... 7H 5 (4A 62)
Brow, The BA2: Bath ... 6H 99
BA2: C Down ... 3E 122
Brow Hill BA1: Bathe ... 6H 83
Brow Hill Vs. BA1: Bathe ... 6H 83
Browne Ct. *BS8: Clftn ... 3F 61*
(off Cumberland Pl.)
Browning Ct. BS7: Hor ... 7D 36
Brownlow Rd. BS23: W Mare ... 1G 127
Brown's Folly Nature Reserve ... 2B 102
Broxholme Wlk. BS11: Law W ... 7K 33
Bruce Av. BS5: E'ton ... 7E 48
Bruce Rd. BS5: E'ton ... 7E 48
Brue Cl. BS23: W Mare ... 7J 105
Brue Cres. TA8: Bur S ... 3D 158
Brue Way TA9: Highb ... 6H 159
Brummel Way BS39: Paul ... 7A 140
Brunel Cl. BS24: W Mare ... 5H 127
BS30: Warm ... 2G 65
Brunel Ct. BS20: P'head ... 2F 43
BS37: Yate ... 4C 30
Brunel Gro. BS14: H'gro ... 3C 76
Brunel Ho. BA2: Bath ... 5G 99
BS1: Bris ... 4C 4 (3J 61)
Brunel Lock Rd. BS1: Bris ... 4F 61
Brunel Rd. BS13: Bis ... 2F 75
BS48: Nail ... 1D 70
Brunel Sq. BA1: Bath ... 6G 7
BS1: Bris ... 6B 4 (4H 61)
Brunel's SS Great Britain ... 6B 4 (4H 61)
Brunel's Way TA9: Highb ... 3G 159
Brunel Way BS1: Bris ... 4F 61
BS3: Ash G, Bwr A ... 5F 61
BS35: T'bry ... 5K 11
BS49: Yat ... 2F 87
Brunswick Ct. BS2: Bris ... 1G 5
Brunswick Pl.
BA1: Bath ... 2F 7 (4B 100)
BS1: Bris ... 4F 61
Brunswick Sq. BS2: Bris ... 1G 5 (1A 62)
Brunswick St. BA1: Bath ... 2D 100
BS2: Bris ... 1A 62
BS5: Redf ... 2E 62
Bruton BS24: W Mare ... 3J 127
Bruton Av. BA2: Bath ... 7E 6 (7B 100)
BS20: P'head ... 3C 42
Bruton Cl. BS5: St G ... 1H 63
BS48: Nail ... 2G 71
Bruton Pl. BS8: Clftn ... 3A 4 (2H 61)
Bryanson's Cl. BS16: Stap ... 4C 50
Bryant Av. BA3: Rads ... 5H 153
Bryant Gdns. BS21: Clev ... 1C 68
Bryants Cl. BS16: Fren ... 6A 38
Bryants Hill BS5: St G ... 3K 63
Brynland Av. BS7: Bishop ... 4A 48
BS2 Lofts *BS2: Bris ... 1A 62*
(off Lit. Bishop St.)
Buchanans Wharf Nth. BS1: Bris ... 5F 5
Buchanans Wharf Sth. BS1: Bris ... 5F 5
Buckingham Dr. BS34: Stok G ... 3F 37
Buckingham Gdns. BS16: Down ... 2C 50
Buckingham Ho. BS34: Fil ... 5B 36
Buckingham Pde. BS35: T'bry ... 3K 11
Buckingham Pl. BS8: Clftn ... 2A 4 (2G 61)
BS16: Down ... 2C 50
Buckingham Rd. BS4: Brisl ... 4F 63
BS24: W Mare ... 3K 127
Buckingham St. BS3: Bedm ... 7J 61
Buckingham Va. BS8: Clftn ... 7J 47
Buckland Cl. TA8: Bur S ... 7E 156
Buckland Grn. BS22: Wor ... 6E 84
Bucklands Batch BS48: Nail ... 2H 71
Bucklands Dr. BS48: Nail ... 2H 71
Bucklands End BS48: Nail ... 2H 71
Bucklands Gro. BS48: Nail ... 2H 71
Bucklands La. BS48: Nail ... 2H 71
Bucklands Vw. BS48: Nail ... 2J 71
Buckle Path BS24: W Wick ... 4G 107
Bucklewell Cl. BS11: Shire ... 2K 45
Buckleys Rd. BS34: Pat ... 7C 26
BUCKOVER ... 3E 12
Buckthorn Ct. BS37: Yate ... 1F 31
Budbury Circ. BA15: Brad A ... 5G 125
Budbury Cl. BA15: Brad A ... 5G 125
Budbury Pl. BA15: Brad A ... 5G 125
(not continuous)
Budbury Ridge BA15: Brad A ... 5G 125
Budbury Tyning BA15: Brad A ... 5F 125
Bude Av. BS5: St G ... 1J 63
Bude Cl. BS48: Nail ... 1J 71
Bude Rd. BS34: Fil ... 4D 36
Budgetts Mead BS27: Ched ... 6C 150
Building of Bath Collection ... 2F 7 (4C 100)
Bullens Cl. BS32: Brad S ... 4F 27
Buller Rd. BS4: Know ... 7E 62
Bullhouse La. BS40: Wrin ... 1F 111
(not continuous)
Bull La. BS5: St G ... 3H 63
BS20: Pill ... 4G 45
Bullocks La. BS21: Kings S ... 6C 68
Bull Pit BA15: Brad A ... 6H 125
Bull Wharf BS1: Bris ... 4G 5 (3K 61)
Bully La. BS37: Yate ... 4D 22
BULWARK ... 1A 8
Bumblebee Cl. BS13: Withy ... 6E 74
Bumper's Batch BA2: S'ske ... 4C 122
Bungay's Hill BA2: High L, Tims ... 4B 140
BS39: High L ... 4B 140
Bunting Ct. BS22: Wor ... 3C 106
Bunting La. BS20: P'head ... 2J 43
Burbank Cl. BS30: Long G ... 6E 64
Burbarrow La. BS37: Cod, W'lgh ... 4D 40
Burchells Av. BS15: Kgswd ... 7K 49
BURCHELLS GREEN ... 1K 63
Burchells Grn. Cl. BS15: Kgswd ... 7K 49
Burchells Grn. Rd. BS15: Kgswd ... 7K 49
Burchill Cl. BS39: Clut ... 2H 139
Burcombe Cl. BS36: Coal H ... 7H 29
Burcott Rd. BS11: A'mth ... 2G 33
Burden Cl. BS32: Brad S ... 1H 37
Burfoote Gdns. BS14: Stoc ... 6G 77
Burfoote Rd. BS14: Stoc ... 6G 77
Burford Av. BS34: Pat ... 6E 26
Burford Cl. BA2: Bath ... 1H 121
BS20: P'head ... 4G 43
Burford Gro. BS11: Shire ... 3K 45
Burgage Cl. BS37: Chip S ... 6H 31
Burgess Grn. Cl. BS4: St Ap ... 2G 63
Burghill Rd. BS10: W Trym ... 6G 35
Burghley Ct. BS36: Wint ... 2C 38
Burghley Rd. BS6: Bris ... 6A 48
Burgis Rd. BS14: Stoc ... 4F 77
Burleigh Gdns. BA1: Bath ... 3G 99
Burleigh Way GL12: Wickw ... 7H 15
(not continuous)
Burley Av. BS16: Mang ... 3D 50
Burley Crest BS16: Mang ... 2D 50
Burley Gro. BS16: Mang ... 2D 50
Burlington Ct. BS6: Redl ... 6H 47
BS20: P'head ... 2G 43
Burlington Pl. BA1: Bath ... 2E 6
Burlington Rd. BA3: Mid N ... 4G 153
BS6: Redl ... 6H 47
BS20: P'head ... 1G 43
Burlington St. BA1: Bath ... 1E 6 (3B 100)
BS23: W Mare ... 4G 105
Burltons, The GL12: Crom ... 2B 14
Burnbush Cl. BS14: Stoc ... 4G 77
Burnell Dr. BS2: Bris ... 1B 62
BURNETT ... 4F 97
Burnett Bus. Pk. BS31: Key ... 2F 97
Burnett Cl. TA8: Bur S ... 1E 158
Burnett Hill BS31: Burn, Key ... 2E 96
Burnett Ind. Est. BS40: Wrin ... 3G 111
Burney Way BS30: Long G ... 6E 64
Burnham & Berrow Golf Course ... 5C 156
Burnham Cl. BS15: Kgswd ... 7D 50
BS24: W Mare ... 4H 127
Burnham Dr. BS15: Kgswd ... 7D 50
BS24: W Mare ... 4H 127
Burnham Golf Range ... 2J 159
Burnham Moor La. TA9: Edith, Watch ... 2J 159
BURNHAM-ON-SEA ... 1C 158
Burnham-on-Sea Holiday Village
TA8: Bur S ... 3D 158
Burnham-on-Sea Swm & Sports Academy ... 7C 156
Burnham-on-Sea Tourist Info. Cen. ... 2C 158
Burnham Rd. BA2: Bath ... 5J 99
BS11: Shire ... 2H 45
TA8: Bur S ... 3E 158
TA9: Highb ... 3E 158
Burnham Shop. Cen. TA8: Bur S ... 2C 158
Burnham Touring Pk. TA8: Bur S ... 6E 156
Burnside Cl. BS10: S'mead ... 5J 35
Burnt Ho. Cotts. BA2: Odd D ... 4J 121
Burnthouse Ct. BA2: Odd D ... 4J 121
Burnt Ho. Rd. BA2: Odd D ... 4J 121
BURRINGTON ... 2H 133
Burrington Av. BS24: W Mare ... 4H 127
Burrington Cl. BS24: W Mare ... 4H 127
BS48: Nail ... 1G 71
Burrington Combe ... 4H 133
Burrington Combe BS40: Blag ... 4K 133
Burrington La. BS40: Burr ... 2J 133
Burrington Wlk. BS13: Bis ... 2G 75
Burrough Way BS36: Wint ... 2C 38
Burrows, The BS22: St G ... 1H 107
Burton Cl. BS1: Bris ... 7G 5 (4A 62)
Burton Ct. BS8: Clftn ... 3A 4 (2H 61)
BS16: Fish ... 5G 49
(off Marina Gdns.)
Burton Row TA9: Bre K ... 3H 157
Burton St. BA1: Bath ... 4G 7 (5C 100)
Burwalls Rd. BS8: L Wds ... 3E 60
Bury, The BS24: Elbgh, Lock ... 2E 128
Bury Ct. Cl. BS11: Law W ... 6A 34
Bury Hill BS16: H'ook ... 5C 38
BS36: Wint D ... 5C 38
Bury Hill La. BS37: Yate ... 6F 23
Bury Hill Vw. BS16: Down ... 6C 38
Bury La. BS30: Doy, Wick ... 3E 66
Bury Vw. BS36: Wint D ... 3C 38
Bush Av. BS34: Lit S ... 1E 36
Bush Ct. BS4: Wind H ... 6B 62
BS35: A'ton ... 7H 11
Bush Ind. Est. BS5: St G ... 1F 63
Bush La. BS3: Bris ... 5H 61
Bushy Coombe BA3: Mid N ... 3D 152
Bushy Ho. BS4: Wind H ... 6B 62
Bushy Leas BS16: Fren ... 7F 37
Bushy Pk. BS4: Wind H ... 6B 62
Bushy Rd. BS34: Pat ... 7B 26
Bushythorn Rd. BS40: Chew S ... 4E 114
BUTCOMBE ... 4E 112
Butcombe BS24: W Mare ... 3J 127
Butcombe La. BS40: But, Nem T ... 5F 113
Butcombe Wlk. BS14: Whit ... 5D 76
Butham La. BS40: Chew M ... 7G 93
Buthay, The GL12: Wickw ... 7G 15
Buthay La. GL12: Wickw ... 7G 15
Butlass Cl. BS39: High L ... 4B 140
Butler Ho. BS5: St G ... 1H 63
Butlers Cl. BS5: St G ... 3H 63
Butlers Wlk. BS5: St G ... 3H 63
Buttercliffe Ri. BS41: L Ash ... 6C 60
Buttercup Cres. BS22: Wor ... 7E 84
Buttercup Wlk. BS3: Ash V ... 1F 75
Butterfield Cl. BS10: Hor ... 1A 48
BS36: Fram C ... 1F 39
Butterfield Pk. BS21: Clev ... 1C 68
Butterfield Rd. BS10: Hor ... 1A 48
Buttermere Rd. BS23: W Mare ... 1J 127
Butterworth Ct. BS4: Know ... 3K 75
Butt La. BS35: T'bry ... 1A 12
Button Cl. BS14: Whit ... 4C 76
BUTT'S BATCH ... 3F 111
Butt's Batch BS40: Wrin ... 3F 111
Butts Batch BS26: Comp B ... 3B 148
Butt's La. BA15: Mon F ... 5D 102
BS39: Hall ... 7A 140
Butts Orchard BS40: Wrin ... 3F 111
Buxton Wlk. BS7: Hor ... 7C 36
Bye Mead BS16: Emer G ... 7E 38
Bye Pass BS40: L'frd ... 7D 110
Byeways La. BS25: Sandf ... 1J 131
Byfield BA2: C Down ... 3D 122
Byfield Bldgs. *BA2: C Down ... 3D 122*
(off Byfield Pl.)
Byfield Pl. BA2: C Down ... 3D 122
Byfields BS21: Clev ... 2C 68
Byron Cl. BS24: Lock ... 1E 128
Byron Ct. BS23: W Mare ... 4H 105
Byron Pl. BS8: Clftn ... 3B 4 (2H 61)
BS16: Stap H ... 4C 50
Byron Rd. BA2: Bath ... 7F 7 (7B 100)
BS23: W Mare ... 1J 127
BS24: Lock ... 1E 128
Byron St. BS2: Bris ... 7C 48
BS5: Redf ... 2E 62
Byways Pk. BS21: Clev ... 1C 68
Byzantine Ct. BS1: Bris ... 7E 4

C

Cabot Cir. BS1: Bris ... 2H 5 (2A 62)
Cabot Cl. BS15: Kgswd ... 2A 64
BS31: Salt ... 1H 97
BS37: Yate ... 5F 31
Cabot Ct. BS2: Bris ... 2K 5
BS7: Fil ... 6B 36
Cabot Grn. BS5: Bar H ... 2D 62
Cabot Ho. BS35: T'bry ... 4A 12
Cabot M. BS2: Bris ... 3J 5 (2B 62)
Cabot Pk. BS11: A'mth ... 1H 33
Cabot Ri. BS20: P'head ... 3C 42
Cabot Tower ... 4B 4 (3H 61)
Cabot Way BS8: Clftn ... 4F 61
BS20: Pill ... 5H 45
BS22: Wor ... 1E 106
Cabstand BS20: P'head ... 2F 43
Cadbury Camp ... 4C 56
Cadbury Camp La. BS20: Glap G ... 3D 56
BS21: Tic ... 3D 56
Cadbury Camp La. W. BS21: Tic ... 5J 55
Cadbury Cl. TA8: Bur S ... 6E 156
Cadbury Farm Rd. BS49: Yat ... 4H 87
Cadbury Gdns. BS30: C Hth ... 3F 65
Cadbury Halt BS20: W'ton G ... 7B 42
CADBURY HEATH ... 3F 65
Cadbury Heath Rd. BS30: C Hth ... 4E 64
Cadbury La. BS20: W'ton G ... 7B 42
Cadbury Rd. BS20: P'head ... 4F 43
BS31: Key ... 1E 96
Cadbury Sq. BS49: Cong ... 1K 109
Cadby Ho. BA2: Bath ... 5G 99
Caddick Cl. BS15: Kgswd ... 6D 50
Cade Cl. BS15: Kgswd ... 3D 64
BS34: Stok G ... 2G 37
Cadogan Gro. BS48: Back ... 4K 71
Cadogan Rd. BS14: H'gro ... 2C 76
Caen Rd. BS3: Wind H ... 6K 61
Caernarvon Cl. BS31: Key ... 5A 78
Caernarvon Rd. BS31: Key ... 6A 78
Caernarvon Way TA8: Bur S ... 6D 156
Caern Well Pl. BA1: Bath ... 1G 7
Caine Rd. BS7: Hor ... 1B 48
Cains Cl. BS15: Kgswd ... 3C 64
Cairn Cl. BS48: Nail ... 1J 71
Cairn Gdns. BS36: Wint D ... 3C 38
Cairns Ct. BS6: Redl ... 4J 47
Cairns Cres. BS2: Bris ... 7B 48
Cairns Rd. BS6: Henle, Redl ... 3H 47
Caister Cl. BS23: W Mare ... 7H 105
Cala Trad. Est. BS3: Ash V ... 6F 61
Calcott Rd. BS4: Know ... 7C 62

Caldbeck Cl.—Chapel Grn. La.

Caldbeck Cl. BS10: S'mead . . . 5K 35
Calder Cl. BS31: Key . . . 6E 78
Caldicot Cl. BS11: Law W . . . 5C 34
BS30: Will . . . 7F 65
Caledonia M. BS8: Clftn . . . 3F 61
Caledonian Rd. BA2: Bath . . . 5A 6 (5K 99)
BS1: Bris . . . 6B 4 (4H 61)
Caledonia Pl. BS8: Clftn . . . 3F 61
California Rd. BS30: Long G . . . 6E 64
Callard Ho. BS16: Fish . . . 4H 49
Callicroft Rd. BS34: Pat . . . 7C 26
Callington Rd. BS4: Brisl . . . 1D 76
BS14: H'gro . . . 1D 76
Callington Road Nature Reserve . . . 1E 76
Callow Drove BS25: Wins . . . 1J 149
Callowhill Ct. BS1: Bris . . . 2G 5 (2A 62)
Calluna Cl. BS22: Wick L . . . 6E 84
Calton Gdns. BA2: Bath . . . 7F 7 (6B 100)
Calton Rd. BA2: Bath . . . 7G 7 (6C 100)
Calton Wlk. BA2: Bath . . . 7F 7 (6B 100)
Camberley Dr. BS36: Fram C . . . 6D 28
Camberley Rd. BS4: Know . . . 2J 75
(not continuous)
Camberley Wlk. BS22: W Mare . . . 4C 106
Camborne Rd. BS7: Hor . . . 1C 48
Cambrian Dr. BS37: Yate . . . 3D 30
Cambrian Green Ct. BS37: Yate . . . 3E 30
CAMBRIDGE BATCH . . . 2G 73
Cambridge Ct. BS40: Wrin . . . 2F 111
Cambridge Cres. BS9: W Trym . . . 1G 47
Cambridge Gro. BS21: Clev . . . 4D 54
Cambridge Ho. *BA1: Bath . . . 5G 7*
(off Henry St.)
Cambridge Pk. BS6: Redl . . . 5H 47
Cambridge Pl. BA2: Bath . . . 7J 7 (6D 100)
BS23: W Mare . . . 4F 105
Cambridge Rd. BS7: Bishop . . . 4K 47
BS21: Clev . . . 4D 54
Cambridge St. BS3: Wind H . . . 5B 62
BS5: Redf . . . 2E 62
Cambridge Ter. BA2: Bath . . . 7J 7 (6D 100)
Cam Brook Cl. BA2: Cam . . . 5H 141
Cambrook Ho. BS39: Temp C . . . 5H 139
Camden Ct. BA1: Bath . . . 1F 7 (3B 100)
Camden Cres. BA1: Bath . . . 1F 7 (3B 100)
Camden Rd. BA1: Bath . . . 3C 100
BS3: Bris . . . 7B 4
Camden Row BA1: Bath . . . 1F 7 (3B 100)
Camden Ter. *BA1: Bath . . . 3C 100*
(off Camden Rd.)
BS8: Clftn . . . 3G 61
BS23: W Mare . . . 5G 105
CAMELEY . . . 5E 138
Cameley Cl. BS39: Temp C . . . 5G 139
Cameley Grn. BA2: Bath . . . 5F 99
Cameley La. BS39: Came, Hin B . . . 6B 138
Cameley Rd. BS39: Came, Temp C . . . 6D 138
Camelford Rd. BS5: E'ton . . . 7F 49
Camellia Dr. BS32: Alm . . . 1F 27
Cameron Wlk. BS7: L'lze . . . 2E 48
Cameroons Cl. BS31: Key . . . 6C 78
CAMERTON . . . 5J 141
Camerton Cl. BS31: Salt . . . 7J 79
Camerton Hill BA2: Cam . . . 5J 141
Camerton Rd. BA2: Cam . . . 3J 141
BS5: E'ton . . . 7F 49
Camomile Wlk. BS20: P'head . . . 3H 43
Campbell Farm Dr. BS11: Law W . . . 6K 33
Campbell St. BS2: Bris . . . 7A 48
Campian Wlk. BS4: Know . . . 4K 75
Campion Cl. BS22: W Mare . . . 5B 106
BS35: T'bry . . . 2B 12
Campion Dr. BS32: Brad S . . . 4F 27
Camplins BS21: Clev . . . 1C 68
Camp Rd. BS8: Clftn . . . 2F 61
BS23: W Mare . . . 3D 104
Camp Rd. Nth. BS23: W Mare . . . 3D 104
Campus, The . . . 4E 106
Camp Vw. BS36: Wint D . . . 3C 38
BS48: Nail . . . 7F 57
Camvale BA2: Pea J . . . 5B 142
Camview BS39: Paul . . . 7B 140
Camwal Ct. BS2: Bris . . . 4C 62
Camwal Ind. Est. BS2: Bris . . . 4C 62
Camwal Rd. BS2: Bris . . . 4C 62
Canada Coombe BS24: Hut . . . 3D 128
Canada Way BS1: Bris . . . 7A 4 (4G 61)
Canal Bri. BA2: Bath . . . 7J 7
Canal Path BA2: Batham . . . 1J 101
Canal Ter. BA2: Batham . . . 2H 101
Canal Vw. BA2: Cam . . . 5J 141
Canberra Cres. BS24: Lock . . . 6F 107
Canberra Gro. BS34: Fil . . . 3D 36
Canberra Rd. BS23: W Mare . . . 2H 127
Candlegrease La. *BS39: Paul . . . 7C 140*
(shown as Church La.)
Candy Ct. BS4: St Ap . . . 4F 63
Canford Crematorium BS9: W Trym . . . 1E 46
Canford La. BS9: W Trym . . . 1D 46
Canford Rd. BS9: W Trym . . . 7F 35
Cannans Cl. BS36: Wint . . . 7C 28
Cann La. BS30: B'yte, Old C . . . 3H 65
Cannons Ga. BS21: Clev . . . 2C 68
Cannon St. BS1: Bris . . . 1F 5 (1K 61)
BS3: Bedm . . . 5J 61
Canons Cl. BA2: Bath . . . 2H 121
Canons Ho. BS1: Bris . . . 6D 4 (4J 61)
CANON'S MARSH . . . 5C 4 (3J 61)
Canon's Rd. BS1: Bris . . . 5D 4 (3J 61)
(not continuous)
Canon St. BS5: Redf . . . 1E 62
Canon's Wlk. BS15: Soun . . . 6C 50
BS22: Wor . . . 2B 106
Canons Way BS1: Bris . . . 5C 4 (3J 61)
Canowie Rd. BS6: Redl . . . 5H 47
Canteen La. BA2: Well . . . 4K 143
Cantell Gro. BS14: Stoc . . . 5H 77
Canterbury Cl. BS22: Wor . . . 7E 84
BS37: Yate . . . 3E 30
Canterbury Rd. BA2: Bath . . . 6B 6 (6K 99)
Canterbury St. BS5: Bar H . . . 3D 62
Canters Leaze GL12: Wickw . . . 1H 23
Cantock's Cl. BS8: Clftn . . . 3C 4 (2J 61)
Canton Pl. BA1: Bath . . . 1H 7
Canvey Cl. BS10: Hor . . . 1A 48
Canynge Ho. BS1: Bris . . . 7G 5 (4A 62)
Canynge Rd. BS8: Clftn . . . 1F 61
Canynge Sq. BS8: Clftn . . . 1F 61
Canynge St. BS1: Bris . . . 5G 5 (3A 62)
Capel Cl. BS15: Warm . . . 1F 65
Capell Cl. BS22: W Mare . . . 4K 105
Capel Rd. BS11: Law W . . . 6B 34
Capenor Cl. BS20: P'head . . . 4E 42
Capgrave Cl. BS4: Brisl . . . 6J 63
Capgrave Cres. BS4: Brisl . . . 6J 63
Capital Edge BS8: Clftn . . . 5A 4 (4H 61)
Caple La. BS40: Chew S . . . 7B 114
Cappards Rd. BS39: Bis S . . . 1K 137
Capricorn Pl. BS8: Clftn . . . 5B 4 (3H 61)
Caraway Gdns. BS5: Eastv . . . 6E 48
Carberry Vw. BS24: W'ton V . . . 5E 106
Cardigan Cres. BS22: W Mare . . . 4A 106
Cardigan La. BS9: Henle . . . 2H 47
Cardigan M. BS9: Henle . . . 3H 47
Cardigan Rd. BS9: Henle . . . 2H 47
Cardill Cl. BS13: Bis . . . 2G 75
Cardinal Cl. BA2: Odd D . . . 4K 121
Carditch Drove BS49: Cong . . . 4H 109
Carey's Cl. BS21: Clev . . . 5F 55
Careys Way BS24: W'ton V . . . 5C 106
Carfax Ct. BS6: Redl . . . 5G 47
Carice Gdns. BS21: Clev . . . 2D 68
Carisbrooke Rd. BS4: Know . . . 2K 75
CARLINGCOTT . . . 4A 142
Carlingford Ter. BA3: Rads . . . 4A 154
Carlingford Ter. Rd. BA3: Rads . . . 4A 154
Carlow Rd. BS4: Know . . . 2A 76
Carlton Chambers *BS1: Bris . . . 4E 4*
(off St Stephen's St.)
Carlton Cl. BS39: Clut . . . 3H 139
Carlton Ct. BS9: W Trym . . . 1G 47
Carlton Mans. BS8: Clftn . . . 3A 4 (2G 61)
Carlton Mans. Nth. *BS23: W Mare . . . 5F 105*
(off Beach Rd.)
Carlton Mans. Sth. *BS23: W Mare . . . 5F 105*
(off Beach Rd.)
Carlton Pk. BS5: Redf . . . 1E 62
Carlton St. BS23: W Mare . . . 5F 105
Carlyle Rd. BS5: E'ton . . . 7E 48
Carmarthen Cl. BS37: Yate . . . 2F 31
Carmarthen Gro. BS30: Will . . . 1F 79
Carmarthen Rd. BS9: Henle . . . 2G 47
Carnarvon Rd. BS6: Redl . . . 6J 47
Carnival Ct. BS2: Bris . . . 1A 62
Carolina Ho. BS2: Bris . . . 1F 5 (1K 61)
Caroline Bldgs. BA2: Bath . . . 6J 7 (6D 100)
Caroline Cl. BS31: Key . . . 6A 78
BS37: Chip S . . . 4H 31
Caroline Pl. BA1: Bath . . . 1F 7 (3B 100)
BS48: Back . . . 5J 71
Carousel La. BS24: W'ton V . . . 5C 106
Carpenter Cl. BS23: W Mare . . . 5J 105
Carpenters La. BS31: Key . . . 5C 78
Carpenters Pl. *BS4: Know . . . 1A 76*
(off Leinster Av.)
Carpenters Shop La. BS16: Down . . . 2C 50
Carpenters Way BA3: Mid N . . . 6F 153
Carre Gdns. BS22: Wor . . . 7D 84
Carr Ho. BA2: Bath . . . 5G 99
BS2: Bris . . . 7B 48
Carriage Ct. BA1: Bath . . . 2E 6
Carriage Dr. BS10: Bren . . . 5H 35
Carrick Bus. Cen. BS4: Brisl . . . 1G 77
Carrick Ho. *BS8: Clftn . . . 3F 61*
(off Hotwell Rd.)
Carrington Rd. BS3: Ash G . . . 5G 61
Carroll Ct. BS16: Fren . . . 6G 37
Carrs Cl. BA2: Bath . . . 5G 99
Carsons Rd. BS16: Mang, Sis . . . 5F 51
Carter Rd. BS39: Paul . . . 1B 152
Carter's Bldgs. *BS8: Clftn . . . 2F 61*
(off Portland St.)
Carter Wlk. BS32: Brad S . . . 6F 27
Cart La. BS1: Bris . . . 5H 5 (3A 62)
Cartledge Rd. BS5: E'ton . . . 7E 48
Cashmore Ho. BS5: Bar H . . . 2D 62
Caslon Ct. BS1: Bris . . . 7H 5 (4A 62)
Cassell Rd. BS16:
Down, Fish . . . 3A 50
Cassey Bottom La. BS5: St G . . . 2J 63
Cassis Cl. TA8: Bur S . . . 3E 158
Casson Dr. BS16: Stap . . . 7G 37
Castle Cl. BS10: Hen . . . 5D 34
BS48: Flax B . . . 3D 72
Castle Coombe BS35: T'bry . . . 3A 12
Castle Ct. BS34: Stok G . . . 3J 37
BS35: T'bry . . . 3K 11
Castle Ct. M. BS5: Bar H . . . 2D 62
Castle Farm La. BS41: Dun . . . 1B 92
Castle Farm Rd. BS15: Han . . . 7K 63
Castle Gallery *BS1: Bris . . . 3G 5*
(within The Galleries)
Castle Gdns. BA2: Bath . . . 1A 122
Castlegate Ho. BS4: Brisl . . . 7G 63
Castle Hill BS29: Ban . . . 3C 130
Castle Ho. GL12: Wickw . . . 7H 15
Castlemead BS1: Bris . . . 2H 5
Castlemead Shop. Cen.
BS22: Wor . . . 6E 84
Castle M. GL12: Wickw . . . 7H 15
Castle Rd. BS15: Kgswd . . . 6B 50
BS16: Puck . . . 2C 52
BS21: Clev . . . 3D 54
BS22: Wor . . . 1C 106
BS30: Old C . . . 6G 65
Castle St. BS1: Bris . . . 3H 5 (2A 62)
BS35: T'bry . . . 2J 11
Castle Vw. BS24: W'ton V . . . 4D 106
Castle Vw. Rd. BS21: Clev . . . 4D 54
Castle Wharf BS1: Bris . . . 3G 5 (2A 62)
Castlewood BS21: Clev . . . 6F 55
Castlewood Cl. BS21: Clev . . . 4D 54
Caswell Hill BS20: Glap G . . . 1J 57
Caswell La. BS20: Glap G, P'bry . . . 7H 43
CATBRAIN . . . 1H 35
Catbrain Hill BS10: Pat . . . 1H 35
Catbrain La. BS10: Pat . . . 1H 35
Catemead BS21: Clev . . . 2C 68
Cater Bus. Pk. BS13: Bis . . . 4H 75
Cater Rd. BS13: Bis . . . 4G 75
Catharine Pl. BA1: Bath . . . 2E 6 (4B 100)
Cathay BS1: Bris . . . 7G 5
Cathay La. BS27: Ched . . . 7D 150
Cathcart Ho. BA1: Bath . . . 2C 100
Cathedral, The BS8: Clftn . . . 3A 4 (2H 61)
Cathedral Sq. BS1: Bris . . . 5D 4 (3J 61)
Cathedral Wlk. BS1: Bris . . . 6C 4 (4J 61)
Catherine Ct. *BS6: Bris . . . 7A 48*
(off Backfields La.)
Catherine Hill BS35: Olv . . . 3B 18
Catherine Mead St. BS3: Bedm . . . 5J 61
Catherine St. BS11: A'mth . . . 7G 33
TA9: E Hunt . . . 7J 159
Catherine Way BA1: Bathe . . . 6H 83
Catley Gro. BS41: L Ash . . . 1B 74
Cato St. BS5: E'ton . . . 6D 48
Catsley Pl. BA1: Swa . . . 7E 82
Cattistock Dr. BS5: St G . . . 3J 63
Cattlemarket Bus. Pk.
BS40: Winf . . . 5A 92
Cattle Mkt. Rd. BS1: Bris . . . 6J 5 (4B 62)
Cattybrook Rd. BS16: Short . . . 3H 51
Cattybrook Rd. Nth. BS16: Short . . . 3H 51
Cattybrook St. BS5: E'ton . . . 1D 62
Caulfield Rd. BS22: Wor . . . 7E 84
Causeway BS21: Nail, Tic . . . 6D 56
BS48: Nail . . . 7D 56
Causeway, The BS20: Glap G . . . 7G 43
BS36: Coal H . . . 7G 29
BS49: Cong . . . 7K 87
BS49: Yat . . . 4J 87
Causeway Vw. BS48: Nail . . . 7E 56
Causley Dr. BS30: Bar C . . . 4D 64
Cautletts Cl. BA3: Mid N . . . 6D 152
Cavan Wlk. BS4: Know . . . 1K 75
Cave Cl. BS16: Down . . . 2C 50
Cave Ct. BS2: Bris . . . 1H 5 (1A 62)
Cave Dr. BS16: Fish . . . 2B 50
Cave Gro. BS16: Emer G . . . 1F 51
Cavell Ct. BS21: Clev . . . 1C 68
Cavendish Cl. BS31: Salt . . . 1H 97
Cavendish Cres. BA1: Bath . . . 3A 100
Cavendish Gdns. BS9: Stok B . . . 4C 46
Cavendish Lodge BA1: Bath . . . 3A 100
Cavendish Pl. BA1: Bath . . . 1D 6 (3A 100)
Cavendish Rd. BA1: Bath . . . 1D 6 (3A 100)
BS9: Henle . . . 3G 47
BS34: Pat . . . 6B 26
Caveners Ct. BS22: W Mare . . . 3K 105
Caversham Dr. BS48: Nail . . . 7J 57
Cave St. BS2: Bris . . . 1H 5 (1A 62)
Caxton Ct. BA2: Bath . . . 3G 7 (4C 100)
Caxton Dr. TA9: Highb . . . 4G 159
Caxton Rd. TA9: Highb . . . 4G 159
Cecil Av. BS5: S'wll . . . 7H 49
Cecil Rd. BS8: Clftn . . . 1F 61
BS15: Kgswd . . . 1B 64
BS23: W Mare . . . 3G 105
Cedar Av. BS22: W Mare . . . 3A 106
Cedar Cl. BS30: Old C . . . 5F 65
BS34: Pat . . . 7B 26
BS41: L Ash . . . 1K 73
TA9: Bre K . . . 5K 157
Cedar Ct. BA15: Brad A . . . 4H 125
BS9: Stok B . . . 4C 46
BS16: Down . . . 2C 50
BS23: W Mare . . . 3F 105
Cedar Dr. BS31: Key . . . 6B 78
Cedar Gro. BA2: Bath . . . 1K 121
BS9: Stok B . . . 3D 46
Cedar Hall BS16: Fren . . . 7A 38
Cedar Hill Ct. BS16: Stap H . . . 4B 50
Cedarhurst Rd.
BS20: P'head . . . 5A 42
Cedarn Ct. BS22: Kew . . . 1K 105
Cedar Pk. BS9: Stok B . . . 3D 46
Cedar Row BS11: Shire . . . 2K 45
Cedars, The BS9: Stok B . . . 5D 46
BS40: Chew S . . . 4D 114
Cedars Way BS36: Wint . . . 2B 38
Cedar Ter. BA3: Rads . . . 5H 153
Cedar Vs. BA2: Bath . . . 7D 6 (6A 100)
Cedar Wlk. BA2: Bath . . . 6D 6 (6A 100)
Cedar Way BA2: Bath . . . 6D 6 (6A 100)
BS16: Puck . . . 3B 52
BS20: P'head . . . 4E 42
BS48: Nail . . . 7J 57
Cedern Av. BS24: Elbgh . . . 2G 129
Cedric Cl. BA1: Bath . . . 4J 99
Cedric Rd. BA1: Bath . . . 4J 99
Celandine Cl. BS35: T'bry . . . 2B 12
Celandine Ct. BS37: Yate . . . 1F 31
Celestine Rd. BS37: Yate . . . 3C 30
Celia Ter. BS4: St Ap . . . 3H 63
Celtic Way BS24: B'don . . . 5K 127
Cemetery La. BA15: Brad A . . . 5J 125
Cemetery Rd. BS4: Wind H . . . 6C 62
Cennick Av. BS15: Kgswd . . . 7C 50
Centaurus Rd. BS34: Pat . . . 7J 25
Centenary Way BS27: Ched . . . 7C 150
Central Av. BS10: H'len . . . 3A 24
BS15: Han . . . 4A 64
Central Hall *BS2: Bris . . . 3J 5*
(off Redcross St.)
Central Pk. BS14: H'gro . . . 2D 76
Central Quay Nth. BS1: Bris . . . 4E 4
Central Quay Sth. BS1: Bris . . . 4E 4
Central Rd. BS4: Bris . . . 5D 62
Central Trad. Est. BS4: Bris . . . 5D 62
Central Way BS21: Clev . . . 1D 68
Centre, The BS23: W Mare . . . 5G 105
BS31: Key . . . 5C 78
Centre Dr. BS29: Ban . . . 1J 129
Centre for Sport . . . 5G 37
Centre for Sport, Exercise and Health
. . . 1C 4 (1J 61)
Centre Ga. *BS1: Bris . . . 3E 4*
(off Colston Av.)
Centre Quay BS20: P'head . . . 1G 43
Centro BS1: Bris . . . 1F 5
Centrum BS5: E'ton . . . 1K 5 (1B 62)
Ceres Cl. BS30: Long G . . . 7D 64
Cerimon Ga. BS34: Stok G . . . 2G 37
Cerney Gdns. BS48: Nail . . . 7J 57
Cerney La. BS11: Shire . . . 3J 45
Cesson Cl. BS37: Chip S . . . 6J 31
Chadleigh Gro. BS4: Know . . . 3K 75
Chaffinch Dr. BA3: Mid N . . . 6F 153
Chaffins, The BS21: Clev . . . 7E 54
Chaingate La. BS37: Iron A . . . 7K 21
Chakeshill Cl. BS10: Bren . . . 4J 35
Chakeshill Dr. BS10: Bren . . . 4J 35
Chalcombe Cl. BS34: Lit S . . . 6E 26
Chalcroft Ho. BS3: Bris . . . 5G 61
Chalcroft Wlk. BS13: Withy . . . 6E 74
Chalet, The BS10: Hen . . . 4F 35
Chalfield Cl. BS31: Key . . . 1E 96
Chalfont Rd. BS22: W Mare . . . 4A 106
Chalford Cl. BS37: Yate . . . 6D 30
Chalk Farm Cl. BS39: Nor M . . . 4C 94
Chalks, The BS40: Chew M . . . 1H 115
Chalks Rd. BS5: St G . . . 1F 63
Challender Av. BS10: Hen . . . 5F 35
Challoner Ct. BS1: Bris . . . 6E 4 (4K 61)
Challow Dr. BS22: W Mare . . . 2K 105
Chamberlain Rd. BS24: Lock . . . 7G 107
Champion Ct. BS2: Bris . . . 2J 5
Champion Rd. BS15: Kgswd . . . 6D 50
Champion Sq. BS2: Bris . . . 2J 5 (2B 62)
Champneys Av. BS10: Hen . . . 4F 35
Champs Sur Marne BS32: Brad S . . . 6G 27
Chancel Cl. BS9: Stok B . . . 5D 46
BS48: Nail . . . 2F 71
Chancery St. BS5: Bar H . . . 2D 62
Chandag Rd. BS31: Key . . . 6D 78
Chandler Cl. BA1: Bath . . . 2H 99
Chandlers Ho. BS1: Bris . . . 7D 4 (4J 61)
Chandlery Sq. BS20: P'head . . . 2G 43
Chandos BS6: Redl . . . 6J 47
Chandos Bldgs. *BA1: Bath . . . 5F 7*
(off Westgate Bldgs.)
Chandos Ct. BS23: W Mare . . . 6F 105
Chandos Rd. BS6: Redl . . . 7H 47
BS31: Key . . . 3C 78
Chandos Trad. Est. BS2: Bris . . . 4C 62
Channel Ct. TA8: Bur S . . . 3D 158
Channel Hgts. BS24: W Mare . . . 4H 127
Channells Hill BS9: W Trym . . . 7G 35
Channel Rd. BS21: Clev . . . 3D 54
Channels Ct. BS16: Fish . . . 4H 49
Channel Vw. Cvn. Pk.
TA8: Brean . . . 6B 126
Channel Vw. Cres. BS20: P'head . . . 3D 42
Channel Vw. Rd. BS20: P'head . . . 3D 42
Channing Cl. TA8: Bur S . . . 3D 158
Channon's Hill BS16: Fish . . . 4H 49
Channon's Hill Retail Pk.
BS16: Fish . . . 4H 49
Chanterelle Pk. BA15: Brad A . . . 7G 125
Chantry Cl. BS48: Nail . . . 1E 70
Chantry Ct. *BS1: Bris . . . 4D 4*
(off Denmark St.)
Chantry Dr. BS22: Wor . . . 7D 84
Chantry Gro. BS11: Law W . . . 5C 34
Chantry La. BS16: Down . . . 6D 38
Chantry Mead Rd. BA2: Bath . . . 1A 122
Chantry Rd. BS8: Clftn . . . 7H 47
BS35: T'bry . . . 2K 11
Chapel Barton BS3: Bedm . . . 7H 61
BS39: High L . . . 4B 140
BS48: Nail . . . 7E 56
Chapel Cl. BS15: Warm . . . 1F 65
BS40: Chew S . . . 4E 114
BS40: Winf . . . 5A 92
BS48: Nail . . . 7G 57
Chapel Ct. *BA1: Bath . . . 5F 7*
(off Westgate Bldgs.)
BA3: Clan . . . 2J 153
BS4: Brisl . . . 7F 63
Chapel Fld. BA2: Pea J . . . 5E 142
Chapel Gdns. BS10: W Trym . . . 6G 35
Chapel Grn. La. BS6: Redl . . . 6H 47

Clyde Av.—Cotham Lawn Apartments

Clyde Av. BS31: Key 6D 78
Clyde Gdns. BA2: Bath 5H 99
BS5: St G 3K 63
Clyde Gro. BS34: Fil 5B 36
Clyde La. BS6: Redl 6H 47
Clyde M. BS6: Redl 6J 47
Clyde Pk. BS6: Redl 6H 47
Clyde Rd. BS4: Know 6C 62
BS6: Redl 6H 47
BS36: Fram C 6F 29
Clydesdale Cl. BS14: H'gro 4C 76
Clyde Ter. BS3: Bedm 6J 61
BS4: Know 6C 62
Clynder Gro. BS21: Clev 3E 54
Coach Ho., The BS2: Bris 1G 5
Coach Ho. La. *BS5: St G 1G 63*
(off Beaconsfield Rd.)
Coach Rd. BA15: Brad A 6G 125
Coachworks, The *BA1: Bath 1H 7*
(off Long Acre)
Coalbridge Cl. BS22: Wor 2D 106
Coaley Rd. BS11: Shire 3H 45
COALPIT HEATH 1G 39
Coalpit Rd. BA1: Bathe 6J 83
Coalsack La. BS36: Henf 4F 39
Coalville Rd. BS36: Coal H 7H 29
Coape Rd. BS14: Stoc 5H 77
Coast Rd. TA8: Berr 2A 156
Coates Gro. BS48: Nail 7J 57
Coates Wlk. BS4: Know 4K 75
Cobbler La. BS21: Clftn 6G 47
Cobblers Way BA3: Mid N 6G 153
Cobblestone M. BS8: Clftn 2G 61
Cob Ct. BS34: Stok G 4E 36
Cobden Cen., The BS16: Emer G 5E 38
Cobden St. BS5: Redf 2D 62
Coberley BS15: Kgswd 3A 64
Cobham Pde. BS24: W Mare 7K 105
Cobhorn Dr. BS13: Withy 6F 75
Cobley Cft. BS21: Clev 2C 68
Cobourg Rd. BS6: Bris 7B 48
Cobthorn Way BS49: Cong 6A 88
Coburg Vs. BA1: Bath 2C 100
Cock and Yew Tree Hill BS40: Regil 2A 114
Cockers Hill BS39: Comp D 7K 95
Cock La. SN14: Hin 3J 53
Cock Rd. BS15: Kgswd 3C 64
COCKSHOT HILL 6C 50
CODRINGTON 4H 41
Codrington Pl. BS8: Clftn 2G 61
Codrington Rd. BS7: Bishop 5K 47
BS37: W'lgh 4D 40
Cody Ct. BS15: Han 4K 63
Cody Wlk. BS24: W Mare 1A 128
Cogan Rd. BS16: Soun 5C 50
Cogmill La. BS36: Fram C 2D 28
BS37: Iron A 2D 28
Cogsall Rd. BS14: Stoc 4H 77
Coity Pl. BS21: Clev 5C 54
Coker Rd. BS22: Wor 2F 107
Colbourne Rd. BA2: Odd D 3K 121
Colchester Cres. BS4: Know 3K 75
Coldbath BA2: F'boro 6D 118
Coldharbour La. BS16: Fren, Stap 6G 37
BS23: W Mare 2F 127
Coldharbour Rd. BS6: Redl 5H 47
Coldpark Gdns. BS13: Withy 5E 74
Coldpark Rd. BS13: Withy 5E 74
Coldrick Cl. BS14: Whit 7B 76
Colebrook Rd. BS15: Kgswd 1A 64
Coleford Rd. BS10: S'mead 7K 35
Colehouse Farm Holiday Pk.
BS21: Clev 2C 68
Colehouse Holiday Village
BS21: Clev 3D 68
Colehouse La. BS21: Clev 2B 68
Cole Mead BS13: Bis 5H 75
Coleridge Ct. BS21: Clev 6D 54
Coleridge Gdns. TA8: Bur S 5D 156
Coleridge Rd. BS5: Eastv 5E 48
BS21: Clev 6C 54
BS23: W Mare 2H 127
Coleridge Va. Rd. E. BS21: Clev 6D 54
Coleridge Va. Rd. Nth. BS21: Clev 7C 54
Coleridge Va. Rd. Sth. BS21: Clev 7C 54
Coleridge Va. Rd. W. BS21: Clev 7C 54
Cole Rd. BS2: Bris 3D 62
Colesborne Cl. BS37: Yate 6D 30
Coleshill Dr. BS13: Hart 5H 75
Coley Rd. BS40: E Harp 6K 137
Colin Cl. BS35: T'bry 3K 11
College Av. BS16: Fish 3J 49
College Ct. BS8: Clftn 1G 61
BS16: Fish 3J 49
TA8: Bur S 1C 158
College Dr. BS10: Hen 6F 35
College Flds. BS8: Clftn 1F 61
College Grn. BS1: Bris 4D 4 (3J 61)
College Ho. *BS1: Bris 4D 4*
(off Orchard St.)
College La. BS1: Bris 4D 4
College Pk. Ct. BS10: Hen 6F 35
College Pk. Dr. BS10: Hen 6F 35
College Rd. BA1: L'dwn, Bath 1A 100
BS8: Clftn 1F 61
BS9: W Trym 1G 47
BS16: Fish 3J 49
College Sq. BS1: Bris 5C 4 (3J 61)
College Sq. Sth BS1: Bris 5C 4 (3J 61)
College St. BS1: Bris 5C 4 (3J 61)
TA8: Bur S 1C 158
College Vw. BA1: Bath 2C 100
College Way BS34: Fil 3C 36
Collett Cl. BS15: Han 4K 63
BS22: Wor 7G 85
Collett Way BS37: Yate 3C 30
Collier Cl. BA2: Cam 5H 141
Colliers Break BS16: Emer G 3F 51
Colliers Gdns. BS16: Fish 3K 49
Collier's La. BA1: Charl 6A 82
BS40: C'hse 2H 151
Collier's Pl. BS16: Soun 6B 50
Colliers Ri. BA3: Rads 3A 154
Colliers Wlk. BS48: Nail 7G 57
Colliers Way BA3: Hay 6K 153
Collingwood Av. BS15: Kgswd 7C 50
Collingwood Cl. BS22: Wor 7C 84
BS31: Salt 1J 97
Collingwood Rd. BS6: Redl 7H 47
Collin Rd. BS4: Brisl 5F 63
Collins Av. BS34: Lit S 1E 36
Collins Bldgs. BS31: Salt 7J 79
Collins Dr. BS35: Sev B 3C 24
Collinson Rd. BS13: Hart 5H 75
Collins St. BS11: A'mth 7F 33
Collier Cres. BS3: Bedm 7G 61
Collum La. BS22: Kew 4B 84
Colne Grn. BS31: Key 6E 78
Coln Sq. BS35: T'bry 4A 12
Colombo Cres. BS23: W Mare 2G 127
Colonnades, The BA1: Bath 5F 7
Colony, The TA8: Bur S 6C 156
Colston Av. BS1: Bris 4E 4 (3K 61)
Colston Cen. *BS1: Bris 3E 4*
(off Colston St.)
Colston Cl. BS16: Soun 5B 50
BS36: Wint D 3C 38
Colston Ct. BS7: Bishop 5K 47
Colston Dale BS16: Stap 4G 49
Colstone Ct. *BS16: Fish 5G 49*
(off Marina Gdns.)
Colston Fort *BS6: Bris 1E 4*
(off Montague Pl.)
Colston Hall 3E 4 (2K 61)
Colston Hill BS16: Stap 4F 49
Colston M. BS6: Bris 7A 48
Colston Pde. BS1: Bris 7G 5 (4A 62)
Colston Pl. BS1: Bris 5H 5 (3A 62)
Colston Rd. BS5: E'ton 7E 48
Colston's Almshouses BS2: Bris 2D 4
Colston St. BS1: Bris 3E 4 (2K 61)
BS16: Soun 5B 50
Colston Twr. BS1: Bris 3E 4
Colston Yd. *BS1: Bris 2E 4*
(off Colston St.)
Colthurst Dr. BS15: Han 4C 64
COLT'S GREEN 6K 31
Colwyn Rd. BS5: E'ton 7E 48
Combe, The BA3: Writ 3D 154
BS40: Burr 2H 133
Combe Av. BS20: P'head 2E 42
COMBE DOWN 3D 122
Combe Flds. BS20: P'head 2E 42
Combe Gro. BA1: Bath 3H 99
COMBE HAY 7J 121
Combe Hay La. BA2: C Hay, Odd D 6H 121
Combe La. BS39: Hall 7K 139
Combe Pk. BA1: Bath 4J 99
Combermere BS35: T'bry 4B 12
Combe Rd. BA2: C Down 3D 122
BS20: P'head 3F 43
Combe Rd. Cl. BA2: C Down 3D 122
Combe Royal Cres. BA2: C'ton D 6F 101
Combeside BA2: Bath 1C 122
BS48: Back 3J 71
Combfactory La. BS5: E'ton 1D 62
Comb Paddock BS9: W Trym 1H 47
Comer Rd. BS27: Ched 7C 150
Comfortable Pl. BA1: Bath 3C 6 (4A 100)
Commerce Way TA9: Highb 6H 159
Commercial Rd. BS1: Bris 7E 4 (4K 61)
Commercial Way BS22: Wor 2F 107
Common, The BS16: Fren 1K 49
BS34: Pat 5D 26
BS35: Olv 2B 18
Common E., The BS34: Brad S 5E 26
Commonfield Rd. BS11: Law W 6B 34
Common La. BS8: Fail 5F 45
BS20: Eas 5F 45
BS25: C'hll 6H 109
BS35: Aust 7G 9
Common Mead La. BS16: H'ook 6J 37
Common Rd. BS15: Han 6K 63
BS36: Wint 7D 28
Como Ct. *BS20: P'head 2E 42*
(off Kilkenny Pl.)
Compass Ct. BA1: Bath 2E 6
Compass Ho. BS3: Bedm 6J 61
COMPTON BISHOP 3B 148
COMPTON COMMON 7A 96
COMPTON DANDO 5B 96
Compton Dr. BS9: Sea M 1C 46
BS24: W'ton V 5C 106
COMPTON GREEN 6C 96
Compton Grn. BS31: Key 6C 78
COMPTON GREENFIELD 6F 25
Compton La. BS26: Axb 4H 149
Compton Lodge *BS6: Redl 7H 47*
(off Hampton Rd.)
COMPTON MARTIN 6A 136
Compton Martin Rd. BS40: W Har 7C 136
Compton Mead BS48: Bar G 6H 73
Compton St. BS5: Redf 2E 62
Comrade Av. BS25: S'ham 5A 132
Comyn Wlk. BS16: Fish 3J 49
CONCORDE 1C 36
Concorde Dr. BS10: S'mead 6H 35
BS21: Clev 1B 68
Concorde Ho. BS34: Fil 5B 36
Concorde Lodge BS34: Fil 5C 36
Concorde Rd. BS34: Pat 7A 26
Concorde St. BS1: Bris 2H 5 (2A 62)
Concourse, The BS4: Brisl 7G 63
Condor Cl. BS22: W Mare 4B 106
Condor Ho. BS7: L'lze 1E 48
Condover Rd. BS4: Brisl 6H 63
Conduit Pl. BS2: Bris 7C 48
Conduit Rd. BS2: Bris 7C 48
CONE, THE 1J 35
Coneygree BS13: Bis 5F 75
Conference Av. BS20: P'head 3G 43
Conference Cl. BS20: P'head 4H 43
Congleton Rd. BS5: W'hall 7F 49
CONGRESBURY 7K 87
CONHAM 4H 63
Conham Hill BS15: Han 4J 63
Conham Rd. BS5: St G 4H 63
BS15: Han, St G 4H 63
Conifer Cl. BS16: Fish 2B 50
BS36: Fram C 5E 28
Conifer Way BS24: Lock 7C 106
Conigre Hill BA15: Brad A 5G 125
Coniston Av. BS9: W Trym 2E 46
Coniston Cl. BS30: Old C 3H 65
Coniston Cres. BS23: W Mare 1H 127
Coniston Rd. BS34: Pat 6A 26
CONKWELL 3K 123
Connaught Mans. BA2: Bath 3H 7 (4C 100)
Connaught Pl. BS23: W Mare 4F 105
Connaught Rd. BS4: Know 2A 76
Connection Rd. BA2: Bath 5G 99
Constable Cl. BS31: Key 4D 78
Constable Dr. BS22: Wor 1D 106
Constable Rd. BS7: L'lze 2D 48
Constantine Av. BS34: Stok G 2G 37
Constellation Pk. BS11: A'mth 4G 33
Constitution Hill BS8: Clftn 4A 4 (3G 61)
Contemporis *BS8: Clftn 2G 61*
(off Merchants Rd.)
Convent Cl. BS10: Hen 4D 34
Convocation Av. BA2: C'ton D 5G 101
Conway Cres. TA8: Bur S 6D 156
Conway Grn. BS31: Key 7E 78
Conway Rd. BS4: Brisl 5E 62
Conygar Cl. BS21: Clev 4F 55
Conygre Grn. BA2: Tims 3F 141
Conygre Gro. BS34: Fil 3D 36
Conygre Ri. BA2: F'boro 6D 118
Conygre Rd. BS34: Fil 4C 36
Cook Cl. BS30: Old C 5G 65
Cook Ct. BS16: L'lze 7E 36
Cooke's Dr. BS35: E Comp 5G 25
Cooks Bridle Path BS48: Back 4B 90
Cooks Cl. BS32: Brad S 3E 26
Cooks Folly Rd. BS9: Stok B 5D 46
Cooks Gdns. BS48: Wrax 7K 57
Cook's Hill BS39: Clut 2G 139
Cook's La. BS29: Ban 1A 130
Cooks La. BS21: Clev 7G 55
BS36: Henf 4H 39
Cooksley Rd. BS5: Redf 1E 62
Cookson Cl. TA8: Bur S 3F 159
Cook St. BS11: A'mth 7F 33
Cookworthy Cl. BS5: Bar H 3D 62
Coombe, The BS40: Blag, R'frd 2K 133
BS40: Comp M 7A 136
Coombe Av. BS35: T'bry 2K 11
Coombe Bri. Av. BS9: Stok B 2D 46
Coombe Brook Cl. BS15: Kgswd 7K 49
Coombe Brook La. BS5: Eastv 6G 49
Coombe Cl. BS10: Hen 4D 34
BS20: P'head 3F 43
Coombe Dale BS9: Sea M 2C 46
BS48: Back 3E 90
COOMBE DINGLE 1D 46
Coombe Dingle Sports Complex 1E 46
Coombe Gdns. BS9: Stok B 2E 46
Coombe La. BS8: Fail 7D 44
BS9: Stok B, W Trym 1D 46
BS20: Eas 6E 44
BS26: Comp B 2B 148
BS40: E Harp 7J 137
Coombend BA3: Clan, Rads 2J 153
Coombend Ho. *BA3: Rads 3K 153*
(off Coombend)
Coombend Ri. BA3: Rads 3K 153
Coombe Orchard *BA3: Rads 3K 153*
(off Combend)
Coombe Rd. BS5: Eastv 6E 48
BS23: W Mare 4G 105
BS48: Nail 1F 71
Coombe Rocke BS9: Stok B 1D 46
Coombe Side TA9: Bre K 5K 157
Coombe's Way BS26: Bidd 6J 147
Coombe Way BS10: Hen 6F 35
BS30: Old C 5H 65
Cooperage La. BS3: Bris 7A 4 (4H 61)
Cooperage Rd. BS5: Redf 2F 63
Co-operation Rd. BS5: E'ton 7E 48
Cooper Rd. BS9: W Trym 1F 47
BS35: T'bry 5K 11
Coopers Ct. BS37: Yate 5D 30
Coopers Dr. BS37: Yate 1F 31
Coots, The BS14: Stoc 4G 77
Copeland Dr. BS14: Whit 5D 76
Cope Pk. BS32: Alm 1E 26
Copford La. BS41: L Ash 1B 74
Cophills La. BS35: L Sev 2A 10
Copley Ct. BS15: Han 4C 64
Copley Gdns. BS7: L'lze 2D 48
BS22: Wor 2D 106
Copley Ho. BS7: L'lze 2D 48
Copper Cl. BS27: Ched 6C 150
Copperfield Dr. BS22: Wor 7D 84
Coppice, The BS13: Withy 6E 74
BS32: Brad S 7G 27
Coppice Hill BA15: Brad A 5H 125
Coppice M. BS21: Clev 5C 54
Copse, The BS22: St G 2H 107
Copse Cl. BS24: W Mare 4J 127
Copse Cnr. BS24: Lym 4A 146
Copse End BS25: Wins 3F 131
Copseland BA2: C'ton D 6F 101
Copse Rd. BS4: Know 6D 62
BS21: Clev 5C 54
BS31: Salt 6G 79
Copthorne Cl. BS14: H'gro 5D 76
Copthorn La. BS40: Burr, L'frd 7H 111
Coralberry Dr. BS22: Wor 3D 106
Corbet Cl. BS11: Law W 5B 34
Corbett Cl. BS37: Yate 2F 31
Corbett Ho. BS5: Bar H 2E 62
Cordwell Wlk. BS10: Hor 1K 47
Corey Cl. BS2: Bris 7B 48
Corfe Cl. BS48: Nail 1F 71
Corfe Cres. BS31: Key 6C 78
Corfe Pl. BS30: Will 1F 79
Corfe Rd. BS4: Know 3K 75
Coriander Dr. BS32: Brad S 1J 37
Coriander Wlk. BS5: Eastv 6E 48
Corinthian Ct. BS1: Bris 6H 5 (4A 62)
Corinum Cl. BS16: Emer G 2G 51
Corkers Hill BS5: St G 3H 63
Cork Pl. BA1: Bath 3A 6
Cork St. BA1: Bath 2A 6 (4K 99)
Cork Ter. BA1: Bath 2A 6 (4K 99)
Cormorant Cl. BS22: Wor 3D 106
Corner Cft. BS21: Clev 1D 68
Cornfield Cl. BS32: Brad S 5E 26
Cornfields, The BS22: Wor 6D 84
Cornflower Cl. BS11: Law W 7A 34
Cornhill Dr. BS14: H'gro 3C 76
Cornish Gro. BS14: Stoc 4G 77
Cornish Rd. BS14: Stoc 4G 77
Cornish Wlk. BS14: Stoc 4G 77
Cornleaze BS13: Bis 5G 75
Corn St. BA1: Bath 5F 7 (5B 100)
BS1: Bris 4F 5 (3K 61)
Cornwall Cres. BS37: Yate 3F 31
Cornwallis Av. BS8: Clftn 3G 61
BS22: Wor 7C 84
Cornwallis Cres. BS8: Clftn 3F 61
Cornwallis Gro. BS8: Clftn 3F 61
Cornwallis Ho. BS8: Clftn 3G 61
Cornwall Rd. BS7: Bishop 4K 47
Coromandel Hgts. BA1: Bath 1F 7
Coronation Av. BA2: Bath 1J 121
BA15: Brad A 5J 125
BS16: Fish 4J 49
BS31: Key 6B 78
Coronation Cl. BS30: C Hth 4E 64
Coronation Cotts. BA1: Bathe 7H 83
Coronation Est. BS23: W Mare 2H 127
Coronation Pl. BS1: Bris 4F 5 (3K 61)
Coronation Rd. BA1: Bath 2A 6 (4K 99)
BS3: Ash G, Bris 7A 4 (5G 61)
BS15: Kgswd 2D 64
BS16: Down 3C 50
BS22: Wor 2C 106
BS24: B'don 7A 128
BS29: Ban 2A 130
BS30: C Hth 4E 64
TA9: Highb 4F 159
Coronation Vs. BA3: Rads 3A 154
Corondale Rd. BS22: W Mare 4B 106
Corridor, The BA1: Bath 4G 7 (5C 100)
Corsham Dr. TA8: Bur S 7E 156
Corsley Wlk. BS4: Know 2B 76
CORSTON 4B 98
Corston BS24: W Mare 3J 127
Corston Dr. BA2: New L 5B 98
CORSTON FIELDS 5G 97
Corston La. BA2: Cor 4A 98
Corston Vw. BA2: Odd D 2J 121
Corston Wlk. BS11: Shire 1H 45
Corum Office Pk. BS30: Warm 2G 65
Coryton BS22: Wor 2E 106
Cossham Cl. BS35: T'bry 2A 12
Cossham Rd. BS5: St G 1F 63
BS16: Puck 4C 52
Cossham St. BS16: Emer G, Mang 3E 50
Cossham Wlk. BS5: St G 7J 49
Cossington Rd. BS4: Know 1B 76
Cossins Rd. BS6: Redl 5H 47
Costers Cl. BS35: A'ton 7J 11
Costiland Dr. BS13: Bis 4F 75
Cote Bank Ho. BS9: W Trym 1H 47
Cote Dr. BS9: W Trym 4G 47
Cote Ho. La. BS9: W Trym 3F 47
Cote La. BS9: W Trym 3G 47
BS35: L Sev 4K 9
Cote Lea Pk. BS9: W Trym 1G 47
Cote Paddock BS9: W Trym 4F 47
Cote Pk. BS9: W Trym 2E 46
Cote Rd. BS9: W Trym 4G 47
COTHAM 7J 47
Cotham Brow BS6: Cot 7K 47
Cotham Gdns. BS6: Cot 7H 47
Cotham Gro. BS6: Cot 7K 47
Cotham Hill BS6: Cot 7H 47
Cotham Lawn Apartments *BS6: Cot 1J 61*
(off Cotham Lawn Rd.)

Cotham Lawn Rd.—Dalrymple Rd.

Cotham Lawn Rd. BS6: Cot 1J 61
Cotham Pk. BS6: Cot 7J 47
Cotham Pk. Nth. BS6: Cot 7J 47
Cotham Pl. BS6: Cot 7J 47
Cotham Rd. BS6: Cot 1J 61
Cotham Rd. Sth. BS6: Bris 1K 61
Cotham Side BS6: Cot 7K 47
Cotham Va. BS6: Cot 7J 47
Cotman Wlk. BS7: L'lze 2D 48
BS22: Wor 2D 106
Cotrith Gro. BS10: Hen 4E 34
Cotswold Cl. BS20: P'head 4G 43
Cotswold Ct. BS16: Fren 6G 37
BS37: Chip S 5H 31
Cotswold Rd. BA2: Bath 7K 99
BS3: Wind H 6K 61
BS37: Chip S 6H 31
Cotswold Rd. Nth. BS3: Wind H 6K 61
Cotswold Vw. BA2: Bath 6H 99
BS15: Kgswd 6B 50
BS34: Fil 4C 36
GL12: Wickw 6H 15
Cottage Ct. BS37: Yate 5D 30
Cottage Gdns. BS5: St G 2J 63
Cottage Pl. BA1: Bath 1E 100
BS2: Bris 1E 4 (1K 61)
Cottage Row TA8: Bur S 2C 158
Cottages, The BS40: Wrin 2F 111
BS48: Bar G 4K 73
Cotterell Ct. BA1: Bath 4E 6
(off Monmouth Pl.)
Cottington Ct. BS15: Han 4C 64
Cottisford Rd. BS5: Eastv 4D 48
Cottle Av. BA15: Brad A 4H 125
Cottle Gdns. BS14: Stoc 4H 77
Cottle Rd. BS14: Stoc 4H 77
Cottles La. BA15: Tur 6D 124
Cotton Mead BA2: Cor 4B 98
Cotton Mill La. BS5: Bar H 3E 62
Cottonwood Dr. BS30: Long G 7C 34
Cottrell Av. BS15: Kgswd 6K 49
Cottrell Rd. BS5: Eastv 5E 48
Coulson Dr. BS22: Wor 1F 107
Coulson Ho. BS7: Bishop 4B 48
Coulsons Cl. BS14: Whit 7C 76
Coulson's Rd. BS14: Whit 7B 76
Coulson Wlk. BS15: Kgswd 6A 50
Counterpool Rd. BS15: Kgswd 2A 64
Counterslip BS1: Bris 4G 5 (3A 62)
Counterslip Gdns. BS14: H'gro 4E 76
Countess of Huntingdon Chapel 2G 7
Countess Wlk. BS16: Stap 2F 49
County Bri. BA3: Rads 4K 153
County Court
Bath 4J 7 (5D 100)
County Ground, The
Bristol 4A 48
County St. BS4: Wind H 5C 62
County Way BS34: Stok G 3J 37
Court Av. BS34: Stok G 2H 37
BS49: Yat 4H 87
Court Cl. BS7: Hor 1A 48
BS20: P'head 4F 43
BS22: St G 2G 107
BS48: Back 5A 72
Court Dr. BS25: Sandf 1H 131
Courtenay Cres. BS4: Know 3K 75
Courtenay Rd. BS31: Key, Salt 1E 96
Courtenay Wlk. BS22: Wor 1E 106
Court Farm 7K 107
Court Farm Gdns. BS30: Long G 7C 64
Court Farm Rd. BS14: Whit 7B 76
BS30: Long G 1B 78
Courtfield Gro. BS16: Fish 4J 49
Court Gdns. BA1: Bathe 6J 83
Court Hay BS20: Eas 4E 44
Court Hill BS39: Comp D 6B 96
Courthouse Pl. BA1: Bath 3A 6
Courtlands BS31: Key 5C 78
BS32: Brad S 5E 26
Courtlands La. BS3: Bwr A 5E 60
Court La. BA1: Bathf 1K 101
BS16: Stap H 4C 50
BS21: Clev 6G 55
BS25: S'ham 6B 132
BS30: Wick 3B 66
Courtmead BA2: S'ske 5B 122
Courtney Pl. BS15: Kgswd 2C 64
Courtney Rd. BS15: Kgswd 2C 64
Courtney Vw. BS15: Kgswd 2C 64
Courtney Way BS15: Kgswd 2D 64
Court Pl. BS22: Wor 2D 106
Court Rd. BS7: Hor 1B 48
BS15: Kgswd 2B 64
BS30: Old C 6F 65
BS36: Fram C 6D 28
Courtrooms, The BS1: Bris 3E 4
(off Rupert St.)
Courtside BS15: Kgswd 2D 64
Courtside M. BS6: Cot 7J 47
Courtside Ter. BA15: Brad A 6H 125
(off Frome Rd.)
Court Vw. BS30: Wick 3C 66
Court Vw. Cl. BS32: Alm 1C 26
Courtyard, The BS21: Clev 2E 68
BS32: Brad S 3F 27
BS40: W Har 7E 136
BS48: Nail 7G 57
Courville Cl. BS35: A'ton 1J 19
Cousins Cl. BS10: Hen 4D 34
Cousins La. BS5: St G 2H 63
Cousins M. BS4: St Ap 3H 63
Cousins Way BS16: Emer G 7F 39
Couzens Cl. BS37: Chip S 4H 31
Couzens Pl. BS34: Stok G 2H 37
Cove, The 1B 116
Coventry Wlk. BS4: St Ap 3H 63
Cowan Cl. TA8: Bur S 1E 158
Cow Barton BS16: L'lze 7E 36
Cowdray Rd. BS4: Know 3K 75
COWHILL 1D 10
Cowhorn Hill BS30: Old C 4G 65
Cow La. BA1: Bath 2C 6 (4A 100)
Cowleaze La. BS40: W Har 7C 136
Cowler Wlk. BS13: Withy 6F 75
Cowling Dr. BS14: Stoc 5E 76
Cowling Rd. BS14: Stoc 5F 77
Cowmead Wlk. BS2: Bris 7C 48
Cowper Rd. BS6: Redl 7J 47
Cowper St. BS5: Redf 2E 62
Cowship La. GL12: Crom, Wickw 5B 14
Cowslip Cres. BS16: Emer G 7G 39
COWSLIP GREEN 4K 111
Cowslip Grn. BS40: Redh 4K 111
Cowslip La. BS24: E Rols, Hew 2K 107
BS26: Lox 3H 147
Cowslip Mead BS32: Alm 1F 27
Cox Ct. BS30: Bar C 5D 64
Coxgrove Hill BS16: Puck 1K 51
Coxley Dr. BA1: Bath 1D 100
Cox's Cave 6F 151
COX'S GREEN 3G 111
Cox's Grn. BS40: Wrin 3G 111
Coxway BS21: Clev 7E 54
Coxwynne Cl. BA3: Mid N 6G 153
Crabtree Cl. BS41: Dun 2D 92
Crabtree La. BS41: Dun 1C 92
Crabtree Pk. BS21: Clev 1C 68
Crabtree Path BS21: Clev 1C 68
Crabtree Wlk. BS5: Eastv 6F 49
Cradock Cl. BS30: C Hth 5E 64
Craftes Ct. BS5: S'wll 7G 49
Cranberry Wlk. BS9: C Din 7C 34
Cranbourne Chase BS23: W Mare 3J 105
Cranbourne Rd. BS34: Pat 7B 26
Cranbrook Rd. BS6: Redl 5K 47
Crandale Rd. BA2: Bath 6A 6 (6K 99)
Crandell Cl. BS10: Hen 3F 35
Crane Cl. BS15: Warm 1F 65
Cranford Cl. BS22: W Mare 3B 106
Cranford Ct. BS9: Henle 2H 47
Cranham BS37: Yate 7C 30
Cranham Cl. BS15: Soun 6D 50
Cranham Dr. BS34: Pat 5E 26
Cranham Rd. BS10: W Trym 7J 35
Cranhill Rd. BA1: W'ton 1B 6 (3K 99)
Cranleigh BA2: S'ske 4B 122
Cranleigh Ct. Rd. BS37: Yate 4D 30
Cranleigh Gdns. BS9: Stok B 4E 46
Cranleigh Rd. BS14: Whit 5D 76
Cranmoor Grn. BS35: Piln 6D 16
Cranmoor La. BS21: Kings S 1D 86
Cranmore BS24: W Mare 3J 127
Cranmore Av. BS31: Key 4B 78
Cranmore Cres. BS10: S'mead 6K 35
Cranmore Pl. BA2: Odd D 4K 121
Cranside Av. BS6: Redl 4J 47
Cransley Cres. BS9: Henle 1J 47
Crantock Av. BS13: Bis 2H 75
Crantock Dr. BS32: Alm 1D 26
Crantock Rd. BS37: Yate 5D 30
Cranwell Gro. BS14: Whit 5C 76
Cranwell Rd. BS24: Lock 7G 107
Cranwells Pk. BA1: W'ton 1A 6 (3K 99)
Crates Cl. BS15: Kgswd 1C 64
Craven Cl. BS30: Bar C 4D 64
Craven Way BS30: Bar C, C Hth 4D 64
Crawford Cl. BS21: Clev 1B 68
Crawl La. BA3: Mid N 2F 153
Craydon Gro. BS14: Stoc 5F 77
Craydon Rd. BS14: Stoc 5F 77
Craydon Wlk. BS14: Stoc 5F 77
CREATE Environment Cen. 4F 61
Crediton BS22: Wor 2E 106
Crediton Cres. BS4: Know 1B 76
Crescent, The BS1: Bris 6C 4 (4J 61)
BS9: Henle 2J 47
BS9: Sea M 2C 46
BS16: Fren 6H 37
BS16: Soun 5B 50
BS22: W Mare 3K 105
(Milton Brow)
BS22: W Mare 2K 105
(Worlebury Hill Rd.)
BS24: Lym 1A 146
BS30: Wick 2B 66
BS32: Old D 1F 19
BS39: Stan D 3B 116
BS40: Chew M 1H 115
BS48: Back 4J 71
Crescent Cen., The BS1: Bris 4H 5
Crescent Gdns. BA1: Bath 3D 6 (4A 100)
Crescent La. BA1: Bath 1D 6 (3A 100)
Crescent Office Pk. BA2: Bath 2J 121
Crescent Pl. M. BA2: Odd D 3K 121
Crescent Rd. BS16: Fish 2A 50
Crescent Vw. BA2: Bath 7E 6 (6B 100)
Cresswell Cl. BS22: Wor 2E 106
Crest, The BS4: Brisl 7E 62
Crest Hgts. BS20: P'head 4A 42
Creswicke Av. BS15: Han 4A 64
Creswicke Rd. BS4: Know 3K 75
Creswick Way TA8: Bur S 7E 156
Crewkerne Cl. BS48: Nail 1K 71
CREW'S HOLE 2H 63
Crews Hole Rd. BS5: St G 2G 63
CRIBBS CAUSEWAY 2G 35
Cribbs C'way. BS10: Hen, Pat 3F 35
BS10: Pat 7H 25
Cribbs C'way. Cen. BS10: Hen 2G 35
Cribbs C'way. Regional Shop. Cen.
BS34: Pat 1K 35
Cribbs C'way. Retail Pk. BS34: Pat 1J 35
Cribb's La. BS40: Redh 3B 112
Crickback La. BS40: Chew M 1G 115
Cricket Fld. Grn. BS48: Nail 7F 57
Cricket La. BS10: W Trym 7G 35
Cricklade Ct. BS48: Nail 1J 71
Cricklade Rd. BS7: Bishop 4A 48
Cripps Rd. BS3: Bedm 6J 61
Crispin La. BS35: T'bry 3K 11
Crispin Way BS15: Soun 6D 50
Crockbarton BA2: Tims 3F 141
Crockerne Dr. BS20: Pill 5G 45
Crockerne Ho. BS20: Pill 4G 45
(off Underbanks)
CROCOMBE 2G 141
Crocombe La. BA2: Tims 2G 141
Croft, The BA2: Mon C 3G 123
BS16: Mang 3D 50
BS21: Clev 5F 55
BS24: Hut 2C 128
BS27: Ched 6E 150
BS30: Old C 6G 65
BS48: Back 3J 71
Croft Av. BS16: Stap 4E 48
Croft Cl. BS30: Bit 2H 79
Crofters Wlk. BS32: Brad S 6F 27
Crofton Av. BS7: Hor 2B 48
Crofton Flds. BS36: Wint 1C 38
Crofton M. BS15: Kgswd 2C 64
Croft Rd. BA1: Bath 2D 100
CROFTS END 7G 49
Crofts End Ind. Est. BS5: S'wll 7G 49
Crofts End Rd. BS5: S'wll 7G 49
Croft Vw. BS9: Henle 2J 47
Crokeswood Wlk. BS11: Law W 6A 34
Crome Rd. BS7: L'lze 1D 48
Cromer Rd. BS5: E'ton 6E 48
BS23: W Mare 7G 105
CROMHALL 3A 14
CROMHALL COMMON 5A 14
Cromhall La. GL12: Crom, Fal 3G 13
Cromwell Ct. BS15: Han 4C 64
BS35: Olv 2C 18
Cromwell Dr. BS22: Wor 7E 84
Cromwell Rd. BS5: St G 1J 63
BS6: Bris 6K 47
Cromwells Hide BS16: Stap 3G 49
Cromwell St. BS3: Bedm 6J 61
Crooked La. TA8: Bur S 6F 157
TA9: Bre K 5G 157
Crooke's La. BS22: Kew 1J 105
CROOK'S MARSH 5A 24
Crookwell Drove BS49: Cong 3H 109
Croomes Hill BS16: Down 2B 50
Cropthorne Rd. BS7: Hor 6C 36
Cropthorne Rd. Sth. BS7: Hor 7C 36
Crosby Hall BS23: W Mare 4F 105
Crosby Row BS8: Clftn 3G 61
CROSS 4E 148
Crosscombe Dr. BS13: Hart 7H 75
Crosscombe Wlk. BS13: Hart 7H 75
Cross Elms La. BS9: Stok B 3E 46
Crossfield Rd. BS16: Soun 5C 50
Cross Hands Rd. BS35: Piln 6D 16
Crossing Cott. Est. BS37: Iron A 7G 21
Cross La. BS26: Axb, Cross 4G 149
Cross Lanes BS20: Pill 4F 45
Crossleaze Rd. BS15: Han 6A 64
Crossley Cl. BS36: Wint 7D 28
Crossley Farm Bus. Cen.
BS36: Wint 7C 28
Crossman Av. BS36: Wint 2C 38
Crossman Wlk. BS21: Clev 7F 55
Cross Moor Drove BS26: Axb 6H 149
Cross Moore Drove BS26: Cross 5F 149
Crossmoor Rd. BS26: Axb 5H 149
Crosspost La. BA2: Mark 7F 97
Cross St. BS15: Kgswd 7A 50
BS23: W Mare 5G 105
TA8: Bur S 1C 158
Cross Tree Gro. BS32: Brad S 6F 27
Cross Wlk. BS14: H'gro 4C 76
Crossway La. BA3: Clapt 7A 152
CROSS WAYS 1A 140
CROSSWAYS 2C 12
Crossways Bus. Pk. BS35: T'bry 2C 12
Crossways Ct. BS16: Down 2C 50
Crossways La. BA2: Dunk 6F 121
BS35: T'bry 2C 12
Crossways M. BS4: Know 1C 76
Crossways Pk. BA2: Dunk 7F 121
Crossways Rd. BS4: Know 1C 76
BS35: T'bry 3B 12
Crowe Hill BA2: F'frd, Lim S 6K 123
Crowe La. BA2: F'frd 7K 123
Crow La. BS1: Bris 4F 5 (3K 61)
BS10: Hen 5F 35
Crowley Way BS11: A'mth 5F 33
Crown & Anchor Ho.
BS2: Bris 4K 5 (3B 62)
Crown Court
Bristol 3E 4 (2K 61)
Crown Ct. BA15: Brad A 5J 125
Crowndale Rd. BS4: Know 6C 62
Crown Gdns. BS30: Warm 2F 65
TA8: Bur S 1D 158
Crown Glass Pl. BS48: Nail 7G 57
Crown Hill BA1: W'ton 2J 99
BS5: S'wll 1H 63
BS40: Winf 7K 91
Crown Hill Wlk. BS5: S'wll 7H 49
Crown Ho. BS48: Nail 1E 70
Crown Ind. Est. BS30: Warm 2G 65
Crown La. BS16: Soun 5B 50
Crownleaze BS16: Soun 5B 50
Crown Rd. BA1: W'ton 2H 99
BS15: Kgswd 6B 50
BS30: Warm 3G 65
Crown Way BS30: Warm 2G 65
Crows Gro. BS32: Brad S 3F 27
Crowther Pk. BS7: L'lze 4C 48
Crowther Rd. BS7: L'lze 4C 48
Crowthers Av. BS37: Yate 3E 30
Crowther St. BS3: Bedm 6H 61
Croxham Orchard BA1: Bathe 6H 83
Croydon Ho. BS5: E'ton 1D 62
Croydon St. BS5: E'ton 1D 62
Crunnis, The BS32: Brad S 1G 37
Crusader Ho. BS1: Bris 3E 4
Crusty La. BS20: Pill 3G 45
Crystal Way BS32: Brad S 6G 27
Cube Cinema
Bristol 1F 5 (1K 61)
Cubitt Cl. BS24: W Mare 1A 128
Cuck Hill BS25: S'ham 6A 132
Cuckoo La. BS36: Wint D 4D 38
BS39: Clut, High L 1K 139
BS48: Wrax 3J 57
Cuffington Av. BS4: Brisl 5F 63
Cufic La. BS27: Ched 5E 150
Culleysgate La. BS30: Doy 3F 67
Culverhay BS39: Comp D 5B 96
Culverhay Sports Cen. 2H 121
Culverhill Rd. BS37: Chip S 5G 31
Culver La. BS40: E Harp 7K 137
Culver Rd. BA15: Brad A 7J 125
Culvers Cl. BS31: Key 4C 78
Culvers Rd. BS31: Key 4C 78
Culver St. BS1: Bris 4D 4 (3J 61)
Culvert, The BS32: Brad S 6F 27
Culvert Av. BS37: Yate 5B 30
Culverwell Rd. BS13: Withy 6G 75
Culvery La. BS39: Pens 7F 95
Cumberland Basin 4F 61
Cumberland Basin Rd. BS8: Clftn 4F 61
Cumberland Cl. BS1: Bris 7A 4 (4G 61)
Cumberland Ct. BS1: Bris 7C 4 (4H 61)
Cumberland Gro. BS6: Bris 6B 48
Cumberland Ho. BA1: Bath 4D 6
Cumberland Pl. BS8: Clftn 3F 61
Cumberland Rd. BS1: Bris 7A 4 (4F 61)
Cumberland Row BA1: Bath 4E 6 (5B 100)
Cumberland St. BS2: Bris 1G 5 (1A 62)
Cumbria Cl. BS35: T'bry 3C 12
Cunningham Gdns. BS16: Fish 3K 49
Cunningham Rd. TA8: Bur S 1E 158
Cunnington Cl. BS30: Will 1E 78
Curland Gro. BS14: Whit 5D 76
Curlew Cl. BS16: Bmhll 2H 49
Curlew Gdns. BS22: Wor 3D 106
Curlew Pl. BS20: P'bry, P'head 2H 43
Currells La. BS40: F'tn 2F 91
Curtis La. BS34: Stok G 4J 37
Curzon Community Cinema, The 6D 54
Custom Cl. BS14: H'gro 3C 76
Custom Ho., The BS1: Bris 6F 5
Cuthbert St. TA9: Highb 5F 159
Cutler Rd. BS13: Bis 4F 75
Cutlers Ho. BS1: Bris 2H 5 (2A 62)
Cutters Row BS3: Bedm 7H 5
Cuttsheath Rd. GL12: Buck 3E 12
GL12: Fal 3G 13
Cygnet Cres. BS22: Wor 3D 106
Cynder Way BS16: Emer G 6E 38
Cynthia Rd. BA2: Bath 7A 6 (6J 99)
Cynthia Vs. BA2: Bath 6J 99
Cypress Ct. BS9: Stok B 5D 46
Cypress Gdns. BS8: L Wds 3E 60
Cypress Gro. BS9: Henle 2J 47
Cypress Ter. BA3: Rads 5H 153
Cyrus Ct. BS16: Emer G 1F 51

D

Dafford's Bldgs. BA1: Bath 1E 100
Dafford's Pl. BA1: Bath 1E 100
(off Dafford St.)
Dafford St. BA1: Bath 1E 100
Dag Hole BS27: Ched 6E 150
Daglands, The BA2: Cam 5H 141
Dahlia Gdns. BA2: Bath 2K 7 (4D 100)
Dahl Wlk. BS7: Hor 7D 36
Daines Ct. BS16: Fish 5G 49
(off Marina Gdns.)
Dairy Cl. BS49: Yat 2G 87
Dairy Hill BA2: Ston L 1H 155
Dairy Way BS40: Chew S 4E 114
Daisy Bank BA2: Bath 7D 100
Daisy Cl. BS31: Key 7B 78
Daisy Rd. BS5: E'ton 6E 48
Daisy Wlk. BS16: Emer G 7G 39
Dakin Cl. BS4: Know 1A 76
Dakota Dr. BS14: Whit 6C 76
Dalby Av. BS3: Bedm 5K 61
Daldry Gdns. BS35: Olv 2C 18
Dale St. BS5: St G 1H 63
Daley Cl. BS22: Wor 1F 107
Dalkeith Av. BS15: Kgswd 7A 50
Dalrymple Rd. BS2: Bris 7A 48

Dalston Rd.—Druid Woods

Dalston Rd. BS3: Bris 5H **61**
Dalton Sq. BS2: Bris 1A **62**
Dalwood BS22: Wor 2E **106**
Dame Ct. Cl. BS22: Wor 7D **84**
Dampier Rd. BS3: Ash G 6G **61**
Damson Orchard BA1: Bathe 6J **83**
Damson Rd. BS22: W Mare 4C **106**
Danbury Cres. BS10: S'mead 6J **35**
Danbury Wlk. BS10: S'mead 6J **35**
Danby Ho. BS7: L'lze 3C **48**
Danby St. BS16: L'lze 7E **36**
Dancey Mead BS13: Bis 3F **75**
Dandy's Mdw. BS20: P'head 3G **43**
Daneacre Rd. BA3: Rads 3A **154**
Dane Cl. BA15: W'ley 5C **124**
Dane Ri. BA15: W'ley 5C **124**
Dangerfield Av. BS13: Bis 4F **75**
Daniel Cl. BS21: Clev 6F **55**
Daniel M. BA2: Bath 2J **7** (4D **100**)
Daniel St. BA2: Bath 2J **7** (4D **100**)
Dapp's Hill BS31: Key 5D **78**
Dapp's La. BS31: Key 5D **78**
Dapwell La. BS31: Q Char 2J **95**
Dark La. BA2: Batham 2H **101**
BA2: F'frd 7K **123**
BS9: W Trym 7G **35**
BS29: Ban 2C **130**
BS40: Blag 2C **134**
BS40: Chew M 1F **115**
BS48: Back 4K **71**
Darley Cl. BS10: Hen 4D **34**
Darlington M. BA2: Bath 3J **7** (4D **100**)
Darlington Pl. BA2: Bath 5K **7** (5D **100**)
Darlington Rd. BA2: Bath 2K **7** (4D **100**)
Darlington St. BA2: Bath 3J **7** (4D **100**)
Darlington Wharf BA2: Bath 1K **7** (3D **100**)
Darmead BS24: W'ton V 3F **107**
Darnley Av. BS7: Hor 2B **48**
Dart Cl. BS35: T'bry 4K **11**
Dartmoor St. BS3: Bedm 5H **61**
Dartmouth Av. BA2: Bath 6J **99**
Dartmouth Cl. BS22: Wor 2E **106**
Dartmouth Wlk. BS31: Key 6B **78**
Dart Rd. BS21: Clev 1D **68**
Darwin Cl. BS30: C Hth 5E **64**
Daubeny Cl. BS16: Fish 3K **49**
Daubeny Ct. BS1: Bris 7E **4**
Daunton Cl. TA9: Highb 4F **159**
Davenport Cl. BS30: Long G 7E **64**
Daventry Rd. BS4: Know 1A **76**
Davey St. BS2: Bris 7B **48**
David Lloyd Leisure
Bristol 6E **60**
Bristol Westbury 7H **35**
David's Cl. BS35: A'ton 1J **19**
David's La. BS35: A'ton 1J **19**
Davidson Rd. BS10: S'mead 5K **35**
David's Rd. BS14: H'gro 3E **76**
David St. BS2: Bris 3J **5** (2B **62**)
David Thomas Ho. BS6: Bris 6A **48**
David Thomas La. *BS6: Bris* *6A **48***
(off Effingham Rd.)
Davies Dr. BS4: St Ap 4H **63**
Davin Cres. BS20: Pill 5G **45**
Davis Cl. BS30: Bar C 4D **64**
Davis Ct. BS35: T'bry 2A **12**
Davis La. BS21: Clev 2D **68**
Davis St. BS11: A'mth 7F **33**
Dawes Cl. BS21: Clev 1D **68**
Dawes Ct. *BS8: Clftn* *3F **61***
(off Cumberland Pl.)
Dawley Cl. BS36: Wint 7C **28**
Dawlish Rd. BS3: Wind H 7K **61**
Dawn Ri. BS15: Kgswd 7D **50**
Daws Ct. BS16: Fish 4K **49**
Day Cres. BA2: Bath 5F **99**
Days La. BS2: Bris 2C **62**
Day's Rd. BS2: Bris 3C **62**
BS5: Bar H 3C **62**
Days Rd. Commercial Cen. BS2: Bris 3C **62**
Deacon Cl. BS36: Wint 2C **38**
Deacons Cl. BS22: Wor 2C **106**
Deacon Way TA8: Bur S 2D **158**
Deadmill La. BA1: Swa 7E **82**
Dean Av. BS35: T'bry 2A **12**
Dean Cl. BS15: Han 4J **63**
BS22: Wor 1F **107**
Dean Ct. BS37: Yate 3B **30**
Dean Cres. BS3: Bedm 5J **61**
(not continuous)
Deanery Cl. BS15: Warm 1F **65**
Deanery Rd. BS1: Bris 5C **4** (3J **61**)
BS15: Warm 1E **64**
Deanery Wlk. BA2: Lim S 6A **124**
DEAN HILL 1F **99**
Deanhill La. BA1: W'ton 1F **99**
Dean La. BS3: Bedm 7D **4** (5J **61**)
Deanna Ct. BS16: Down 2C **50**
Dean Rd. BS11: A'mth 2G **33**
BS37: Yate 3C **30**
Deans, The BS20: P'head 4D **42**
Dean's Ct. BS1: Bris 4C **4** (3J **61**)
Deans Dr. BS5: S'wll 6J **49**
Deans Mead BS11: Law W 7A **34**
Dean St. BS2: Bris 1H **5** (1A **62**)
BS3: Bedm 5J **61**
Debeccas La. BS20: Eas 4F **45**
De Clifford Rd. BS11: Law W 5C **34**
Deco Building, The *BS4: Bris* *5D **62***
(off Paintworks)
Decoypool Drove BS49: C'ham 5J **69**
Deep Coombe Rd. BS3: Bedm 7G **61**
Deep Pit Rd. BS5: S'wll 7G **49**
Deep St. BS1: Bris 2F **5** (2K **61**)
Deerhurst BS15: Kgswd 6C **50**
BS37: Yate 6C **30**
Deering Cl. BS11: Law W 6B **34**
Deerleap BS25: S'ham 5B **132**
Deer Mead BS21: Clev 1B **68**
Deerswood BS15: Soun 6E **50**
Delabere Av. BS16: Fish 3K **49**
Delapre Rd. BS23: W Mare 2F **127**
De La Warre Ct. BS4: St Ap 3H **63**
Delhorn La. BS24: E'wth 7A **146**
Delius Gro. BS4: Know 3K **75**
Dell, The BS9: W Trym 3F **47**
BS22: Wor 7C **84**
BS30: Old C 4G **65**
BS32: Brad S 7G **27**
BS48: Nail 7F **57**
Delvin Rd. BS10: W Trym 7J **35**
De Montalt Pl. BA2: C Down 3D **122**
Denbigh Dr. NP16: Bul 1A **8**
Denbigh St. BS2: Bris 7B **48**
Dene Cl. BS31: Key 7D **78**
Dene Rd. BS14: Whit 6E **76**
Denleigh Cl. BS14: Whit 6C **76**
Denmark Av. BS1: Bris 4D **4** (3J **61**)
Denmark Pl. BS7: Bishop 5A **48**
Denmark Rd. BA2: Bath 5A **6** (5K **99**)
Denmark St. BS1: Bris 4D **4** (3J **61**)
Denning Ct. BS22: Wor 7F **85**
Dennisworth BS16: Puck 3B **52**
Dennor Pk. BS14: H'gro 3D **76**
Denny Cl. BS20: P'head 3C **42**
Denny Isle Dr. BS35: Sev B 7A **16**
Denny La. BS40: Chew M 4G **115**
Denny Vw. BS20: P'head 3B **42**
Dennyview Rd. BS8: Abb L 1K **59**
Denston Dr. BS20: P'head 4G **43**
Denston Wlk. BS13: Bis 3G **75**
Denton Patch BS16: Emer G 1F **51**
Dentwood Gro. BS9: C Din 1B **46**
Denys Ct. BS35: Olv 2B **18**
Derby Rd. BS7: Bishop 5A **48**
Derby St. BS5: St G 1F **63**
Derham Cl. BS49: Yat 3H **87**
Derham Ct. BS49: Yat 3H **87**
Derham Pk. BS49: Yat 3H **87**
Derham Rd. BS13: Bis 5G **75**
Dermot St. BS2: Bris 7B **48**
Derricke Rd. BS14: Stoc 4H **77**
Derrick Rd. BS15: Kgswd 1B **64**
Derry Rd. BS3: Bedm 7H **61**
Derwent Cl. BS34: Pat 6D **26**
Derwent Ct. BS35: T'bry 4B **12**
Derwent Gro. BS31: Key 5E **78**
Derwent Rd. BS5: S'wll 7H **49**
BS23: W Mare 1J **127**
De Salis Pk. BS24: W Wick 4H **107**
Devaney Cl. BS4: St Ap 4H **63**
Deverell Ct. BA15: Brad A 7J **125**
Deveron Gro. BS31: Key 6E **78**
De Verose Ct. BS15: Han 5C **64**
Devil's La. GL12: Char 2F **15**
Devon Gro. BS5: E'ton 1E **62**
Devon Rd. BS5: E'ton 7E **48**
Devonshire Bldgs. BA2: Bath 7B **100**
(not continuous)
BS3: Bedm 7G **5**
Devonshire Ct. BS23: W Mare 1G **127**
Devonshire Dr. BS20: P'head 3B **42**
Devonshire M. *BA2: Bath* *1B **122***
(off Devonshire Bldgs.)
Devonshire Pl. BA2: Bath 7B **100**
Devonshire Rd. BA2: Batham 2G **101**
BS6: Henle 4H **47**
BS23: W Mare 2G **127**
Devonshire Vs. BA2: Bath 1B **122**
Dewar Cl. TA8: Bur S 1E **158**
Dewfalls Dr. BS32: Brad S 5F **27**
Dial Hill Rd. BS21: Clev 4C **54**
Dial La. BS16: Down 2B **50**
BS40: F'tn 2G **91**
Diamond Batch BS24: W'ton V 3F **107**
Diamond Ct. BS24: Wor 3F **107**
Diamond Farm Cvn. & Touring Pk.
TA8: Brean 1D **144**
Diamond Mdw. TA8: Brean 2D **144**
Diamond Rd. BS5: St G 2H **63**
Diamond St. BS3: Bedm 6J **61**
Diamonite Ind. Pk. BS16: Fish 5J **49**
Diana Gdns. BS32: Brad S 6G **27**
Dibden Cl. BS16: Down 7E **38**
Dibden Ct. BS16: Emer G 1F **51**
Dibden La. BS16: Emer G 1E **50**
Dibden Rd. BS16: Down 7E **38**
Dickens Cl. BS7: Hor 7C **36**
Dickenson Rd. BS23: W Mare 6G **105**
Dickensons Gro. BS49: Cong 1A **110**
Dickinsons Flds. BS3: Wind H 7K **61**
Didsbury Cl. BS10: Hen 6F **35**
Dighton Ct. BS2: Bris 1F **5**
Dighton Ga. BS34: Stok G 2G **37**
Dighton St. BS2: Bris 1F **5** (1K **61**)
Dillon Ct. BS5: St G 2F **63**
Dinder Cl. BS48: Nail 1G **71**
DINGHURST 1A **132**
Dinghurst Rd. BS25: C'hll 1K **131**
Dingle, The BS9: C Din 1D **46**
BS36: Wint D 3C **38**
BS37: Yate 2F **31**
Dingle Cl. BS9: Sea M 2C **46**
Dingle Ct. BS13: Bis 3F **75**
Dingle Rd. BS9: C Din 1D **46**
Dingle Vw. BS9: Sea M 1C **46**
Dinglewood Cl. BS9: C Din 1D **46**
Dingley La. BS37: Yate 1F **31**
DINGS, THE 4C **62**
Dings Wlk. BS2: Bris 4K **5** (3C **62**)
Dipland Gro. BS40: Blag 3D **134**
Dirac Cres. BS16: Emer G 7F **39**
Dirac Rd. BS7: Bishop 4B **48**
Disbrey M. BS24: Lock 7G **107**
DISTRICT CENTRE RDBT. 6G **27**
District Probate Registry
Bristol *4G **5***
(off Redcliff St.)
Dixon Gdns. BA1: Bath 2B **100**
Dixon Rd. BS4: Brisl 7H **63**
Dock Ga. La. BS8: Clftn 5G **61**
Dockside BS8: Clftn 6A **4**
Doctor White's Cl. BS1: Bris 7G **5** (4A **62**)
Dodington La. BS37: Dod 1H **41**
Dodington Rd. BS37: Chip S 7H **31**
Dodisham Wlk. BS16: Fish 2K **49**
Dodmore Crossing BS37: W'lgh 3B **40**
Dodsmoor La. BS35: A'ton 1A **20**
Dog La. BS10: H'len 3C **34**
Dogwood Rd. BS32: Alm 1F **27**
Doleberrow BS25: C'hll 2B **132**
Dolebury Hill Fort 2B **132**
Dolebury Warren Nature Reserve 2B **132**
Dolemoor La. BS49: Cong 7G **87**
(Old Weston Rd.)
BS49: Cong 1G **109**
(The Causeway)
Dolman Cl. BS10: Hen 4E **34**
Dolphin Sq. BS23: W Mare 5F **105**
Dominion Rd. BA2: Bath 5G **99**
BS16: Fish 5H **49**
Donald Rd. BS13: Bis 3F **75**
Donal Early Way BS7: Hor 7A **36**
Doncaster La. BS10: S'mead 7K **35**
Doncaster Rd. BS10: S'mead 6H **35**
Donegal Rd. BS4: Know 1K **75**
Dongola Av. BS7: Bishop 4A **48**
Dongola Rd. BS7: Bishop 4A **48**
Don John Ho. BS5: St G 1G **63**
Donnington Wlk. BS31: Key 6B **78**
Donstan Rd. TA9: Highb 3F **159**
Doone Rd. BS7: Hor 7B **36**
Dorcas Av. BS34: Stok G 2H **37**
Dorchester Cl. BS48: Nail 2F **71**
Dorchester Rd. BS7: Hor 1C **48**
Dorchester St. BA1: Bath 6G **7** (6C **100**)
Dorester Cl. BS10: Bren 3J **35**
Dorian Cl. BS7: Hor 1A **48**
Dorian M. BS7: Hor 1A **48**
Dorian Rd. BS7: Hor 1A **48**
Dorian Way BS7: Hor 7A **36**
Doric Ho. BA2: Bath 4C **6** (5A **100**)
Dormeads Vw. BS24: W'ton V 5D **106**
Dormer Cl. BS36: Coal H 1H **39**
Dormer Rd. BS5: Eastv 5D **48**
Dorset Cl. BA2: Bath 5B **6** (5K **99**)
TA9: Highb 6G **159**
Dorset Cotts. BA2: C Down 3E **122**
Dorset Gro. BS2: Bris 6C **48**
Dorset Ho. BA2: Bath 1K **121**
Dorset Rd. BS9: W Trym 2H **47**
BS15: Kgswd 7B **50**
Dorset St. BA2: Bath 5A **6** (5K **99**)
BS3: Bedm 6H **61**
Dorset Way BS37: Yate 3G **31**
DOUBLE HILL 6F **143**
Doudney Ct. BS3: Bedm 5A **62**
Douglas Ct. BS23: W Mare 7H **105**
Douglas Rd. BS7: Hor 1B **48**
BS15: Kgswd 2B **64**
BS23: W Mare 7H **105**
Douglas Rd. Ind. Pk. BS15: Kgswd 2B **64**
Doulton Way BS14: Whit 5D **76**
Dovecote BS37: Yate 6E **30**
Dovedale BS35: T'bry 5B **12**
Dove La. BS2: Bris 1J **5** (1B **62**)
BS5: Redf 2E **62**
Dovercourt Rd. BS7: Hor 3C **48**
Dover Ho. BA1: Bath 3C **100**
Dover Pl. BA1: Bath 3C **100**
BS8: Clftn 3A **4** (2H **61**)
Dover Pl. Cotts. BS8: Clftn 3A **4** (2H **61**)
Dovers La. BA1: Bathf 1A **102**
(not continuous)
Dovers Pk. BA1: Bathf 1A **102**
Dover Ter. *BA1: Bath* *3D **100***
(off London Rd.)
Dove St. BS2: Bris 1F **5** (1K **61**)
Dove St. Sth. BS2: Bris 1F **5** (1K **61**)
Doveswell Gro. BS13: Withy 6G **75**
Dovetail Dr. BS23: W Mare 5J **105**
Dovey Ct. BS30: Old C 4G **65**
Dowdeswell Cl. BS10: Hen 4F **35**
Dowding Cl. BS37: Chip S 4J **31**
Dowding Rd. BA1: Bath 2D **100**
Dowding Vs. BA1: Bath 2D **100**
Dower Ho. BS16: Stap 1G **49**
(not continuous)
Dowland BS22: Wor 2E **106**
Dowland Gro. BS4: Know 4K **75**
Dowling Rd. BS13: Hart 7J **75**
Down, The BS32: Old D 2F **19**
BS35: A'ton 7H **11**
Down Av. BA2: C Down 3C **122**
Downavon BA15: Brad A 7H **125**
Down Cl. BS20: P'head 3B **42**
DOWNEND 2C **50**
Downend Pk. BS7: Hor 3B **48**
Downend Pk. Rd. BS16: Down 3B **50**
Downend Rd. BS7: Hor 3B **48**
BS15: Kgswd 7B **50**
BS16: Down 3A **50**
BS16: Fish 3K **49**
Downend Sports Cen. 1D **50**
Down Farm Ho. BS36: Wint 1B **38**
Downfield BS9: Sea M 1C **46**
BS31: Key 5B **78**
Downfield Cl. BS35: A'ton 7H **11**
Downfield Dr. BS36: Fram C 6F **29**
Downfield Lodge BS8: Clftn 7G **47**
Downfield Rd. BS8: Clftn 7G **47**
Downland Cl. BS48: Nail 1F **71**
Down La. BA2: Batham 2H **101**
Down Leaze BS35: A'ton 7J **11**
Downleaze BS9: Stok B 5F **47**
BS16: Down 7B **38**
BS20: P'head 3C **42**
Downleaze Dr. BS37: Chip S 6G **31**
Downman Rd. BS7: L'lze 3C **48**
Down Rd. BS20: P'head 5A **42**
BS35: A'ton 7H **11**
BS36: Wint D 3C **38**
Downs, The BA3: Clan 1J **153**
BS20: P'head 4D **42**
GL12: Wickw 5F **15**
Downs Cl. BA15: Brad A 5F **125**
BS22: Wor 3D **106**
BS34: Pat 7C **26**
BS35: A'ton 7J **11**
Downs Cote Av. BS9: W Trym 2F **47**
Downs Cote Dr. BS9: W Trym 2F **47**
Downs Cote Gdns. BS9: W Trym 2G **47**
Downs Cote Pk. BS9: W Trym 2G **47**
Downs Cote Vw. BS9: W Trym 2G **47**
DOWNSIDE 2B **90**
Downside BS20: P'head 3E **42**
Downside Cvn. Pk. BS48: Back 2D **90**
Downside Cl. BA2: Batham 2H **101**
BS30: Bar C 4D **64**
Downside Ct. *BS8: Clftn* *7G **47***
(off Downside Rd.)
Downside Rd. BS8: Clftn 7G **47**
BS23: W Mare 1H **127**
BS48: Back 2A **90**
Downs Pk. E. BS6: Henle 3G **47**
Downs Pk. W. BS6: Henle 3G **47**
Downs Rd. BS9: W Trym 2G **47**
(not continuous)
BS41: Dun 1D **92**
Downs Rd., The GL12: Wickw 5G **15**
Downs Vw. BA15: Brad A 5F **125**
Downsway BS39: Paul 7B **140**
Downton Rd. BS4: Know 1K **75**
Down Vw. BA3: Hay 6K **153**
BS7: Bishop 5B **48**
Dowry M. *BS8: Clftn* *3G **61***
(off Hotwell Rd.)
Dowry Pl. BS8: Clftn 4F **61**
Dowry Rd. BS8: Clftn 3G **61**
Dowry Sq. BS8: Clftn 3F **61**
DOYNTON 7G **53**
Doynton La. BS30: Doy 7G **53**
SN14: Dyr 7G **53**
Dragon Ct. BS5: S'wll 7G **49**
Dragonfly Cl. BS15: Kgswd 2B **64**
Dragon Rd. BS36: Wint 2B **38**
Dragons Hill Cl. BS31: Key 5D **78**
Dragons Hill Ct. BS31: Key 5D **78**
Dragons Hill Gdns. BS31: Key 5D **78**
Dragons Well Rd. BS10: Hen 5G **35**
Dragon Wlk. BS5: St G 7H **49**
Drake Av. BA2: C Down 2B **122**
Drake Cl. BS22: Wor 7D **84**
BS31: Salt 1H **97**
Drake Ho. *BS1: Bris* *3F **5***
(off Rupert St.)
Drake Rd. BS3: Ash G 6G **61**
Drakes Way BS20: P'head 3C **42**
Dram La. BS5: St G 3J **63**
Dramway Footpath, The BS36: Coal H 3H **39**
Dransfield Way BA2: Bath 7J **99**
Draycot Pl. BS1: Bris 7E **4** (4K **61**)
Draycott Ct. BA2: Bath 2H **7** (4C **100**)
Draycott Rd. BS7: Hor 3B **48**
BS27: Ched 7J **151**
Draydon Rd. BS4: Know 2J **75**
Drayton BS24: W Mare 3J **127**
Drayton Cl. BS14: H'gro 2D **76**
Drayton Rd. BS9: C Din 7C **34**
Drews Orchard GL12: Crom 2B **14**
Dr Fox's BS23: W Mare 4E **104**
Dring, The BA3: Rads 4J **153**
Drive, The BS9: Henle 2H **47**
BS14: H'gro 4E **76**
BS23: W Mare 4H **105**
BS25: C'hll 1A **132**
BS25: S'ham 5A **132**
BS31: Key 4C **78**
BS39: Stan D 3B **116**
TA8: Bur S 5C **156**
Drove, The BS20: P'bry 1A **44**
Drove Ct. BS48: Nail 6G **57**
Drove Rd. BS23: W Mare 7G **105**
BS49: Cong 1K **109**
Drovers Way BS37: Chip S 5G **31**
Drove Way BS24: Nye 4E **108**
Druett's Cl. BS10: Hor 1A **48**
Druid Cl. BS9: Stok B 3E **46**
Druid Hill BS9: Stok B 3E **46**
Druid Rd. BS9: Stok B 4D **46**
Druid Stoke Av. BS9: Stok B 3C **46**
Druid Woods BS9: Stok B 3C **46**

Drumhead Way, The—Elmgrove Pk.

Drumhead Way, The BS25: S'ham 5A 132
Drummond Ct. BS30: Long G 5D 64
Drummond Rd. BS2: Bris 7A 48
BS16: Fish 5H 49
Drungway BA2: Mon C 3G 123
DRY ARCH 6B 102
Dryleaze BS31: Key 3C 78
BS37: Yate .1E 30
Dryleaze Rd. BS16: Bmhll 2H 49
Drysdale Cl. BS22: W Mare 3B 106
Dubber's La. BS5: Eastv 6G 49
Dublin Cres. BS9: Henle 2H 47
Duchess Rd. BS8: Clftn 7G 47
Duchess Way BS16: Stap 3F 49
Duchy Cl. BA3: Clan 1J 153
Duchy Rd. BA3: Clan 1J 153
Ducie Cl. GL12: Crom 2B 14
Ducie Rd. BS5: Bar H 2D 62
BS16: Stap H 3C 50
Ducie Rd. Bus. Pk. *BS5: Bar H* *2D 62*
(off Lawrence Hill)
Duckett Flds. BS10: Hor 1K 47
Duck La. BS21: Kenn 3G 69
BS22: Wick L 3E 84
BS40: L'frd .4C 110
Duckmoor Rd. BS3: Ash G, Bedm 5G 61
Duckmoor Rd. Ind. Est.
BS3: Ash G .5F 61
Duck St. BS25: C'hll 7J 109
GL12: Tyth .7F 13
Ducrow Ct. BS2: Bris 1G 5
Dudley Cl. BS31: Key 6C 78
Dudley Ct. BS30: Bar C 5D 64
Dudley Gro. BS7: Hor 7C 36
Dugar Wlk. BS6: Redl 5J 47
Duicie Ct. BS16: Stap H 4C 50
Duke St. BA2: Bath 5H 7 (5C 100)
Dulhorn Farm Camping Site
BS24: E'wth 7B 146
Dulverton Rd. BS7: Bishop 4K 47
Dumaine Av. BS34: Stok G 2G 37
Dumfries Pl. BS23: W Mare 7G 105
Dumpers La. BS40: Chew M 2G 115
Dunbar Cl. TA9: Highb 4E 158
Duncan Gdns. BA1: W'ton 7G 81
Duncan M. BS8: Clftn 2G 61
Duncombe La. BS15: Kgswd 6J 49
Duncombe Rd. BS15: Kgswd 7K 49
Dundas Aqueduct 2J 123
Dundas Cl. BS10: Hen 5E 34
Dundee Dr. BS16: Fish 3A 50
Dundonald Rd. BS6: Redl 5H 47
Dundridge Gdns. BS5: St G 3J 63
Dundridge La. BS5: St G 3J 63
DUNDRY 1D 92
Dundry Cl. BS15: Kgswd 3B 64
Dundry La. BS40: Winf 4A 92
BS41: Dun .6B 74
Dundry Vw. BS4: Know 1C 76
Dunedin Way BS22: St G 7G 85
Dunford Rd. BS3: Wind H 6K 61
Dungarvon Rd. BS24: W'ton V 5D 106
Dunkeld Av. BS34: Fil 5B 36
Dunkerry Rd. BS3: Wind H 6K 61
DUNKERTON 2E 142
Dunkerton Hill BA2: Dunk, Pea J 4D 142
Dunkery Cl. BS48: Nail 1G 71
Dunkery Rd. BS23: W Mare 3H 105
Dunkirk Rd. BS16: Fish 5H 49
Dunkite La. BS22: Wor 7D 84
Dunlin Dr. BS20: P'bry, P'head 2H 43
Dunmail Rd. BS10: S'mead 5J 35
Dunmore St. BS4: Wind H 5B 62
Dunsford Pl. BA2: Bath 4K 7 (5D 100)
Dunstan M. BS13: Bedm 7H 61
Dunstan Rd. TA8: Bur S 1D 158
Dunstan Way BS27: Ched 7H 151
Dunster Ct. BS25: Wins 5F 131
Dunster Cres. BS24: W Mare 3H 127
Dunster Gdns. BS30: Will 7F 65
BS48: Nail .1G 71
Dunster Ho. BA2: C Down 2C 122
Dunster Rd. BS4: Know 2B 76
BS31: Key .6B 78
Dunsters Rd. BS49: C'ham 2B 88
Durban Rd. BS34: Pat 6B 26
Durban Way BS49: Yat 2H 87
Durbin Pk. Rd. BS21: Clev 4D 54
Durbin Wlk. BS5: E'ton 1C 62
Durcott La. BA2: Cam, Tims 5G 141
Durdham Ct. BS6: Redl 5G 47
Durdham Hall BS9: Stok B 4F 47
Durdham Pk. BS6: Redl 5G 47
Durham Gro. BS31: Key 6B 78
Durham Rd. BS2: Bris 6C 48
Durleigh Cl. BS13: Bis 4G 75
Durley Hill BS31: Key 2K 77
Durley La. BS31: Key 3A 78
Durley Pk. BA2: Bath 7A 100
BS31: Key .3A 78
Durnford Av. BS3: Ash G 5G 61
Durnford St. BS3: Ash G 5G 61
Durnhill BS40: Comp M 6K 135
Dursley Cl. BS37: Yate 5E 30
Dursley Rd. BS11: Shire 3H 45
Durston BS24: W Mare 3J 127
Durville Rd. BS13: Bis 4H 75
Durweston Wlk. BS14: Stoc 2E 76
Dutton Cl. BS14: Stoc 4F 77
Dutton Rd. BS14: Stoc 4F 77
Dutton Wlk. BS14: Stoc 4F 77
DW Fitness
Whitchurch 4J 75
Dyers Cl. BS13: Hart 6K 75
Dyer's La. BS37: Iron A 7A 22
Dylan Thomas Ct. BS30: Bar C 4E 64
Dymboro, The BA3: Mid N 5D 152
Dymboro Av. BA3: Mid N 5D 152
Dymboro Cl. BA3: Mid N 5D 152
Dymboro Gdns. BA3: Mid N 5D 152
DYRHAM 4K 53
Dyrham *BS16: Fren* *6A 38*
(off Harford Dr.)
Dyrham Cl. BS9: Henle 2K 47
BS15: Kgswd 1D 64
BS35: T'bry .1A 12
TA8: Bur S .1F 159
Dyrham Ct. BS8: Clftn 1G 61
Dyrham Pde. BS34: Pat 6E 26
Dyrham Park
Gloucestershire 4K 53
Dyrham Rd. BS15: Kgswd 1D 64
Dyrham Vw. BS16: Puck 4C 52
Dysons Cl. BS49: Yat 3H 87

E

Eagle Cl. BS22: W Mare 4B 106
Eagle Cotts. BA1: Bathe 5H 83
Eagle Cres. BS16: Puck 4C 52
Eagle Dr. BS34: Pat 6A 26
Eagle Pk. BA1: Bathe 5H 83
Eagle Rd. BA1: Bathe 5H 83
BS4: Brisl .7F 63
Eagles, The BS49: Yat 3H 87
Eagles Wood Bus. Pk. BS32: Brad S 3E 26
Earl Cl. BS34: Stok G 3J 37
Earlesfield BS48: Nail 1E 70
Earlham Gro. BS23: W Mare 5H 105
Earl Russell Way BS5: E'ton 2D 62
Earls Mead BS16: Stap 4G 49
Earlstone Cl. BS30: C Hth 5E 64
Earlstone Cres. BS30: C Hth 5E 64
Earl St. BS1: Bris 1F 5 (1K 61)
EARTHCOTT GREEN 6C 20
Earthcott Rd. BS35: A'ton, Ear G, Itch . . .5C 20
Easedale Cl. BS10: S'mead 5K 35
East Av. TA9: Highb 4E 158
Eastbourne Av. BA1: Bath 2D 100
Eastbourne Rd. BS5: E'ton 1D 62
Eastbourne Vs. BA1: Bath 2D 100
Eastbury Cl. BS35: T'bry 3A 12
Eastbury Rd. BS16: Fish 4J 49
BS35: T'bry .3A 12
EAST CLEVEDON 6F 55
E. Clevedon Triangle BS21: Clev 5E 54
Eastcliff BS20: P'head 1G 43
East Cl. BA2: Bath 6G 99
Eastcombe Gdns. BS23: W Mare 3H 105
Eastcombe Rd. BS23: W Mare 3H 105
Eastcote Pk. BS14: Whit 5D 76
East Ct. BS3: Ash V 6F 61
Eastcourt Rd. BS39: Temp C 5G 139
East Cft. BS9: Henle 1J 47
Eastcroft BS40: Blag 3C 134
Eastcroft Cl. BS40: Blag 3D 134
Eastdown Pl. *BA3: Clan* *1J 153*
(off Eastdown Rd.)
Eastdown Rd. BA3: Clan 1J 153
EAST DUNDRY 2G 93
E. Dundry La. BS41: Dun 1F 93
E. Dundry Rd. BS14: Whit 1B 94
EAST END
BS40 . . . . .3C 134
BS48 . . . . .1J 71
East End BS26: L Wre 7D 148
EASTER COMPTON 4G 25
Easter Ct. BS37: Yate 5A 30
Eastermead La. BS29: Ban 2C 130
Eastern Drove BS49: C'ham 4K 69
Eastern Ho. BS23: W Mare 4G 105
EASTERTOWN 4B 146
Eastertown BS24: Lym 4A 146
EASTFIELD 1J 47
Eastfield BS9: W Trym 1H 47
Eastfield Av. BA1: W'ton 7H 81
Eastfield Dr. BS37: Yate 1E 30
Eastfield Gdns. BS23: W Mare 3H 105
Eastfield La. BS35: N'wick 2D 16
Eastfield Pk. BS23: W Mare 3G 105
Eastfield Rd. BS6: Cot 6K 47
BS9: W Trym 1G 47
BS24: Hut .3C 128
E. Fields Rd. BS16: Fren 7F 37
Eastfield Ter. BS9: Henle 2H 47
Eastgate Cen. BS5: Eastv 5D 48
Eastgate Office Cen. BS5: Eastv 5D 48
Eastgate Rd. BS5: Eastv 5D 48
East Gro. BS6: Bris 7B 48
EAST HARPTREE 7K 137
EAST HEWISH 5B 86
Eastlake Cl. BS7: L'lze 1D 48
Eastland Av. BS35: T'bry 2A 12
Eastland Rd. BS35: T'bry 2A 12
Eastlea BS21: Clev 1B 68
E. Lea Rd. BA1: Bath 3G 99
Eastleigh Cl. BS16: Soun 4E 50
TA8: Bur S .7E 156
Eastleigh Rd. BS10: S'mead 6K 35
BS16: Soun .5C 50
Eastlyn Rd. BS13: Bis 2H 75
Eastmead BA3: Mid N 4F 153
Eastmead Ct. BS9: Stok B 4E 46
E. Mead Drove BS24: B'don 7H 127
Eastmead La. BS9: Stok B 4E 46
Eastnor Rd. BS14: Whit 7C 76
Easton Bus. Cen. BS5: E'ton 1D 62
Easton Hill Rd. BS35: T'bry 2B 12
Easton Ho. BA1: Bath 2E 100
EASTON-IN-GORDANO 4E 44
Easton Leisure Cen. 1C 62
Easton Rd. BS5: E'ton 2C 62
BS20: Pill 4G 45
Easton Way BS5: E'ton 7C 48
Eastover Cl. BS9: W Trym 7G 35
Eastover Gro. BA2: Odd D 3J 121
Eastover Rd. BS39: High L 4B 140
East Pde. BS9: Sea M 2C 46
East Pk. BS5: Eastv 6E 48
East Pk. Dr. BS5: Eastv 6E 48
East Pk. Trad. Est. BS5: E'ton, W'hall 7F 49
E. Priory Cl. BS9: W Trym 1G 47
East Ride TA9: Bre K 6K 157
Eastridge Dr. BS13: Bis 5F 75
EAST ROLSTONE 3B 108
East Shrubbery BS6: Redl 6H 47
East St. BS3: Bedm 6J 61
BS11: A'mth .6E 32
BS29: Ban .2B 130
East St. M. *BS3: Bedm* *5K 61*
(off East St.)
E. Tucker St. BS1: Bris 4G 5 (3A 62)
EAST TWERTON 5B 6 (5K 99)
East Vw. BS16: Mang 2D 50
EASTVILLE 5E 48
Eastville BA1: Bath 2D 100
East Wlk. BS37: Yate 5E 30
East Way BA2: Bath 6G 99
Eastway BS48: Nail 6F 57
Eastway Cl. BS48: Nail 7F 57
Eastway Sq. BS48: Nail 6G 57
Eastwell La. BS25: Wins 7E 130
Eastwood BA2: C'ton D 5G 101
Eastwood Cl. BS39: High L 3B 140
Eastwood Cres. BS4: Brisl 5H 63
Eastwood Pl. BS20: P'head 1F 43
Eastwood Rd. BS4: Brisl 5H 63
Eastwoods BA1: Bathf 7K 83
Eaton Cl. BS14: Stoc 5G 77
BS16: Fish .4K 49
Eaton Cres. BS8: Clftn 1A 4 (1G 61)
Eaton St. BS3: Bedm 6J 61
Ebden Lodge BS22: Wor 2E 106
EBDON 5E 84
Ebdon Ct. BS22: Wor 2E 106
Ebdon La. BS22: Bour, Wick L 5E 84
Ebdon Rd. BS22: Wick L, Wor 6D 84
Ebenezer La. BS9: Stok B 2D 46
(not continuous)
Ebenezer St. BS5: St G 2F 63
Ebenezer Ter. BA2: Bath 6H 7
Eccleston Ho. BS5: Bar H 3D 62
Eckweek Gdns. BA2: Pea J 5D 142
Eckweek La. BA2: Pea J 5D 142
Eckweek Rd. BA2: Pea J 5D 142
Eclipse BS1: Bris 2H 5
Eclipse Office Pk. BS16: Stap H 4A 50
Eddington Ct. BS23: W Mare 6F 105
Eden Apartments BS23: W Mare 3F 105
Eden Cft. BS24: W'ton V 4C 106
Eden Gro. BS7: Hor 6B 36
Eden Pk. Cl. BA1: Bathe 6J 83
Eden Pk. Dr. BA1: Bathe 6J 83
Eden Ter. BA1: Bath 1D 100
Eden Vs. *BA1: Bath* *1E 100*
(off Dafford's Bldgs.)
Edgar Bldgs. BA1: Bath 3F 7
Edgarley Ct. BS21: Clev 4C 54
Edge, The BS15: Kgswd 1A 64
Edgecombe Av. BS22: W Mare 2B 106
Edgecombe Cl. BS15: Kgswd 7D 50
Edgecumbe Rd. BS6: Redl 6K 47
Edgefield Cl. BS14: Whit 7B 76
Edgefield Rd. BS14: Whit 7B 76
Edgehill Rd. BS21: Clev 3D 54
Edgeware Rd. BS3: Bris 5J 61
BS16: Stap H 4B 50
Edgewood Cl. BS14: H'gro 2D 76
BS30: Long G 6E 64
Edgeworth BS37: Yate 1C 40
Edgeworth Rd. BA2: Bath 2J 121
Edinburgh Pl. BS23: W Mare 4F 105
Edinburgh Rd. BS31: Key 6C 78
Edington Gro. BS10: Hen 5G 35
EDINGWORTH 7D 146
Edingworth Rd. BS24: E'wth 6C 146
Edison Ct. TA9: Highb 3F 159
Edith Cl. TA8: Bur S 5C 156
EDITHMEAD .1J 159
Edithmead La. TA9: Edith 7G 157
Edithmead Pk. TA9: Edith 2K 159
Edmund Cl. BS16: Down 2B 50
Edmund Ct. BS16: Puck 2B 52
Edmund Rd. BS14: H'gro 3C 76
Edmunds Way BS27: Ched 7E 150
Edna Av. BS4: Brisl 6G 63
Edward Bird Ho. BS7: L'lze 1D 48
Edward Rd. BS4: Bris 5D 62
BS15: Kgswd 1C 64
BS21: Clev .4E 54
Edward Rd. Sth. BS21: Clev 4E 54
Edward Rd. W. BS21: Clev 3E 54
Edwards Ct. *BS5: Redf* *2F 63*
(off Victoria Av.)
Edward St. BA1: Bath 3A 6 (4J 99)
BA2: Bath 3J 7 (4D 100)
BS5: Eastv .6F 49
BS5: Redf 1E 62
Edwin Short Cl. BS30: Bit 2J 79
Effingham Rd. BS6: Bris 6A 48
Egerton Brow BS7: Bishop 4K 47
Egerton Ct. *BS7: Bishop* *4A 48*
(off Gloucester Rd.)
Egerton La. BS7: Bishop 4K 47
Egerton Rd. BA2: Bath 7A 100
BS7: Bishop .4K 47
Eggshill La. BS37: Yate 5D 30
Egg Theatre, The 4F 7
Eglin Cft. BS13: Withy 6H 75
Eighteen Acre Dr. BS34: Pat 1C 36
Eighth Av. BS7: Hor 7D 36
BS14: H'gro 3C 76
Eirene Ter. BS20: Pill 4H 45
ELBERTON 7B 10
Elberton BS15: Kgswd 1E 64
Elberton Rd. BS9: Sea M 1B 46
BS35: Elbtn, Olv 6B 10
ELBOROUGH 2G 129
Elborough Av. BS49: Yat 3H 87
Elborough Gdns. BS24: Elbgh 2G 129
Elbridge Ho. BS2: Bris 2J 5
Elbury Av. BS15: Kgswd 6A 50
Elderberry Wlk. BS10: S'mead 5J 35
BS22: Wor *3D 106*
(off Silverberry Rd.)
Elderberry Way BS32: Alm 1F 27
Elder Cl. TA9: Highb 3F 159
Elderwood Dr. BS30: Long G 6E 64
Elderwood Rd. BS14: H'gro 3D 76
Eldon Pl. BA1: Bath 1D 100
Eldon Ter. BS3: Wind H 6K 61
Eldonwall Trad. Est. BS4: Brisl 4E 62
Eldon Way BS4: Brisl 4E 62
Eldred Cl. BS9: Stok B 3D 46
Eleanor Cl. BA2: Bath 6F 99
Eleventh Av. BS7: Hor 6D 36
Elfin Rd. BS16: Fish 3J 49
Elgar Cl. BS4: Know 4K 75
BS21: Clev .1E 68
Elgin Av. BS7: Fil 6B 36
Elgin Pk. BS6: Redl 6H 47
Elgin Rd. BS16: Fish 6K 49
Eliot Cl. BS7: Hor 6C 36
BS23: W Mare 2J 127
Elizabeth Cl. BS24: Hut 2B 128
BS35: T'bry .4B 12
Elizabeth Ct. BS13: Withy 6F 75
TA8: Bur S .2D 158
Elizabeth Cres. BS34: Stok G 3G 37
Elizabeth's M. BS4: St Ap 3H 63
Elizabeth Way BS16: Mang 5F 51
Elkstone Wlk. BS30: Bit 7G 65
Ella Cl. BS16: Fish 2A 50
Ellacombe Rd. BS30: Long G 7C 64
Ellan Hay Rd. BS32: Brad S 1J 37
Ellbridge Cl. BS9: Stok B 3D 46
Ellenborough Cres. BS23: W Mare 6G 105
Ellenborough Ho. BS8: Clftn 5A 4
Ellenborough Mnr. BS23: W Mare 6G 105
Ellenborough Pk. Nth. BS23: W Mare . . .6F 105
Ellenborough Pk. Rd. BS23: W Mare . . .6G 105
Ellenborough Pk. Sth.
BS23: W Mare 6F 105
Ellen Ho. BA2: Bath 6G 99
Ellesmere BS35: T'bry 4A 12
Ellesmere Rd. BS4: Brisl 2F 77
BS15: Kgswd 1B 64
BS23: Uph .3F 127
Ellfield Cl. BS13: Bis 4F 75
Ellick Rd. BS40: Blag 5A 134
Ellicks Cl. BS32: Brad S 4G 27
Ellicott Rd. BS7: Hor 2B 48
Ellinghurst Cl. BS10: Bren 5G 35
Elliott Av. BS16: Fren 6A 38
Ellis Av. BS13: Bis 2G 75
Ellis Pk. BS22: St G 1G 107
Elliston Dr. BA2: Bath 7H 99
Elliston La. BS6: Redl 6J 47
Elliston Rd. BS6: Redl 6J 47
Elloytt Ct. *BS16: Fish* *5G 49*
(off Marina Gdns.)
Ellsbridge Cl. BS31: Key 5F 79
Ellsworth Rd. BS10: Hen 5F 35
Elm Av. TA8: Bur S 2D 158
Elmbrook BA1: W'ton 1A 6 (3K 99)
Elm Cl. BS11: Law W 6K 33
BS25: Star .4K 131
BS29: Ban .1J 129
BS34: Lit S .7F 27
BS37: Chip S 5G 31
BS48: Nail .1E 70
BS49: Yat 4H 87
Elm Ct. BS6: Redl 6H 47
BS14: Whit .4C 76
BS31: Key .6A 78
Elmcroft BA1: Bath 1E 100
Elmcroft Cres. BS7: L'lze 4C 48
Elmdale Cres. BS35: T'bry 3A 12
Elmdale Gdns. BS16: Fish 4J 49
Elmdale Rd. BS3: Bedm 7H 61
BS8: Clftn 1B 4 (1H 61)
Elmfield BA15: Brad A 5G 125
BS15: Kgswd 3C 64
Elmfield Cl. BS15: Kgswd 3C 64
Elmfield Rd. BS9: S'mead 7G 35
Elm Gro. BA1: Swa 1E 100
BA2: Bath 7J 99
BS24: Lock 1D 128
Elmgrove Av. BS5: E'ton 1D 62
Elmgrove Dr. BS37: Yate 4F 31
Elmgrove Pk. BS6: Cot 7K 47

Elmgrove Rd.—Fiennes Cl.

Elmgrove Rd. BS6: Cot 7K 47
BS16: Fish 5G 49
Elmham Way BS24: W'ton V 3F 107
Elm Hayes BS13: Bis 4F 75
Elm Hayes Vw. BS39: Paul 1C 152
Elmhirst Gdns. BS37: Yate 4G 31
Elmhurst Av. BS5: Eastv 5F 49
Elmhurst Est. BA1: Bathe 6J 83
Elmhurst Gdns. BS41: L Ash 1K 73
Elmhurst Rd. BS24: Hut 3C 128
Elmhyrst Rd. BS23: W Mare 4H 105
Elming Down Cl. BS32: Brad S 1F 37
Elm La. BS6: Redl 6H 47
Elmlea Av. BS9: W Trym 3F 47
Elmleigh Av. BS16: Mang 3F 51
Elmleigh Cl. BS16: Mang 3F 51
Elmleigh Rd. BS16: Mang 3E 50
Elm Lodge Rd. BS48: Wrax 6J 57
Elmore BS15: Soun 6D 50
BS37: Yate 6D 30
Elmore Rd. BS7: Hor 2C 48
BS34: Pat 5B 26
Elm Pk. BS34: Fil 5C 36
Elm Pl. BA2: Bath 7B 100
Elm Rd. BS7: Hor 3A 48
BS15: Kgswd 3C 64
BS39: Paul 1C 152
Elms, The BA1: Bath, Swa 1E 100
BA2: Tims 3F 141
BA15: Brad A 4F 125
BS16: Fren 6A 38
BS16: Stap H 5B 50
Elms Cross Dr. BA15: Brad A 7G 125
Elms Gro. BS34: Pat 5D 26
Elmsleigh Rd. BS23: W Mare 1F 127
Elmsley La. BS22: Kew 4A 84
Elm Ter. BA3: Rads 5G 153
Elm Tree Av. BA3: Rads 5H 153
BS21: Tic 5C 56
Elmtree Av. BS16: Mang 1E 50
Elmtree Cl. BS15: Kgswd 7B 50
Elmtree Dr. BS13: Withy 6F 75
Elm Tree Pk. BS20: P'bry 4B 44
Elm Tree Rd. BS21: Clev 7D 54
BS24: Lock 7D 106
Elmtree Way BS15: Kgswd 7B 50
Elmvale Dr. BS24: Hut 2D 128
Elm Vw. BA3: Mid N 4F 153
Elm Wlk. BS20: P'head 4E 42
BS49: Yat 4H 87
Elmwood BS37: Yate 6E 30
Elsbert Dr. BS13: Bis 4E 74
Elstree Rd. BS5: W'hall 7G 49
Elton Ho. BS2: Bris 2K 5
Elton La. BS7: Bishop 6K 47
Elton Mans. BS7: Bishop 5K 47
Elton Rd. BS7: Bishop 5K 47
BS8: Clftn 2B 4 (2H 61)
BS15: Kgswd 7K 49
BS21: Clev 6B 54
BS22: Wor 7F 85
Elton St. BS2: Bris 1K 5 (1B 62)
Elvard Cl. BS13: Withy 6G 75
Elvard Rd. BS13: Withy 5G 75
Elvaston Rd. BS3: Wind H 6A 62
Elwell La. BS40: Winf 2K 91
Ely Gro. BS9: Sea M 1B 46
Embassy Ho. BS8: Clftn 2B 4 (2H 61)
Embassy La. BS5: W'hall 7G 49
Embassy Rd. BS5: W'hall 7G 49
Embassy Wlk. BS5: W'hall 7G 49
Embercourt Dr. BS48: Back 4J 71
Embleton Rd. BS10: S'mead 5H 35
Emerald Ct. BS9: Henle 4H 47
EMERSON'S GREEN 2F 51
Emersons Grn. La. BS16: Emer G 2E 50
(Blackhorse Pl.)
BS16: Emer G 2G 51
(Johnson Rd.)
Emerson Sq. BS7: Hor 7C 36
Emerson Way BS16: Emer G 7F 39
Emery Ga. BS29: Ban 2B 130
Emery Rd. BS4: Brisl 7H 63
Emet Gro. BS16: Emer G 2F 51
Emet La. BS16: Emer G 2F 51
Emley La. BS40: Aldw, Burr, L'frd 1J 133
Emlyn Cl. BS22: Wor 7F 85
Emlyn Rd. BS5: E'ton 6E 48
Emma Chris Way BS34: Fil 5E 36
Emmanuel Ct. BS8: Clftn 1G 61
Emmett Wood BS14: Whit 7D 76
Empire, The *BA2: Bath* 4G 7
(off Grand Pde.)
Empire Cres. BS15: Han 5C 64
Empress Menen Gdns. BA1: Bath 3G 99
Emra Cl. BS5: St G 7H 49
Enderleigh Gdns. BS25: C'hll 1B 132
Enfield Rd. BS16: Fish 5J 49
ENGINE COMMON 7C 22
Engine Comn. La. BS37: Yate 6C 22
Enginehouse La. BS31: Q Char 6J 77
Engine La. BS48: Nail 1D 70
England's Cres. BS36: Wint 7C 28
England Way BA2: Pea J 5E 142
ENGLISHCOMBE 2F 121
Englishcombe La. BA2: Bath 1H 121
ENGLISHCOMBE PARK 7J 99
Englishcombe Ri. BA2: Bath 1G 121
Englishcombe Rd. BA2: Eng 2F 121
BS13: Hart 7J 75
Englishcombe Way BA2: Bath 1A 122
Enmore BS24: W Mare 3J 127
Enmore Cl. TA8: Bur S 7E 156
Ennerdale Cl. BS23: W Mare 7J 105
Ennerdale Rd. BS10: S'mead 5K 35
Enterprise Trade Cen.
BS4: Know 3A 76
Entry Hill BA2: Bath, C Down 1B 122
Entry Hill Dr. BA2: Bath 1B 122
Entry Hill Gdns. BA2: Bath 1B 122
Entry Hill Golf Course 2B 122
Entry Hill Pk. BA2: C Down 2B 122
Entry Ri. BA2: C Down 3B 122
Epney Cl. BS34: Pat 5B 26
Epsom Cl. BS16: Down 6D 38
Epworth Rd. BS10: Bren 4G 35
Equinox BS32: Brad S 3E 26
Equus Ho. BA1: L'dwn 7A 82
Erin Wlk. BS4: Know 2K 75
Ermine Way BS11: Shire 1G 45
Ermleet Rd. BS6: Redl 6J 47
Ernest Barker Cl. BS5: Bar H 2D 62
Ernest Ct. BS7: Hor 5D 36
Ernestville Rd. BS16: Fish 5H 49
Esgar Ri. BS22: Wor 1C 106
Eskdale BS35: T'bry 5B 12
Eskdale Cl. BS22: W Mare 4B 106
Esmond Gro. BS21: Clev 5D 54
Esplanade TA8: Bur S 2C 158
Esplanade Rd. BS20: P'head 2E 42
Esporta Health & Fitness
Stoke Gifford 3H 37
Essery Rd. BS5: E'ton 6E 48
Esson Rd. BS15: Kgswd 7K 49
Estcourt Gdns. BS16: Stap 3F 49
Estelle Pk. BS5: Eastv 6E 48
Estoril BS37: Yate 5F 31
Estuary Ho. BS20: P'head 1G 43
Estune Bus. Pk. BS41: L Ash 2J 73
Estune Wlk. BS41: L Ash 7A 60
Etloe Rd. BS6: Henle 4G 47
Eton La. BS29: Ban 5H 107
Eton Rd. BS4: Brisl 6J 63
TA8: Bur S 2D 158
Ettlingen Way BS21: Clev 7E 54
Ettricke Dr. BS16: Fish 2K 49
Eugene Flats BS2: Bris 1E 4
Eugene St. BS2: Bris 1F 5 (1K 61)
BS5: E'ton 1K 5 (1B 62)
Evans Cl. BS4: St Ap 4H 63
Evans Rd. BS6: Redl 6H 47
Eva Turner Cl. BS14: H'gro 4E 76
Eveleigh Av. BA1: Swa 7F 83
Eveleigh Ho. *BA2: Bath* 3G 7
(off Grove St.)
Evelyn La. BS11: A'mth 6F 33
Evelyn Rd. BA1: Bath 3H 99
BS10: W Trym 7J 35
Evelyn Ter. BA1: Bath 2C 100
Evenlode Gdns. BS11: Shire 3K 45
Evenlode Way BS31: Key 7E 78
Evercreech Rd. BS14: Whit 6C 76
Evercreech Way TA9: Highb 6H 159
Everest Av. BS16: Fish 4G 49
Everest Rd. BS16: Fish 4G 49
Evergreen Cl. BS25: Wins 4F 131
Eve Rd. BS5: E'ton 7D 48
Ewart Rd. BS22: W Mare 4A 106
Ewell Rd. BS14: H'gro 4D 76
Exbourne BS22: Wor 2E 106
Exbury Cl. TA8: Bur S 1E 158
Excelsior St. BA2: Bath 6H 7 (6D 100)
Excelsior Ter. BA3: Mid N 5F 153
Excel Tennis in the Park 3E 6 (4B 100)
Exchange Av. BS1: Bris 4F 5 (3K 61)
Exeter Bldgs. BS6: Redl 6H 47
Exeter Cl. TA8: Bur S 1E 158
Exeter Rd. BS3: Bris 5H 61
BS20: P'head 4G 43
BS23: W Mare 7G 105
Exford Cl. BS23: W Mare 3H 127
Exley Cl. BS30: Old C 4G 65
Exmoor Rd. BA2: C Down 2B 122
Exmoor St. BS3: Bedm 5H 61
Exmouth Rd. BS4: Know 1B 76
Explore-at-Bristol 5D 4 (3J 61)
Explore La. BS1: Bris 5D 4 (3J 61)
Exton BS24: W Mare 3J 127
Exton Cl. BS14: Whit 5D 76
Eye, The BS2: Bris 4J 5 (3B 62)
Eyer's La. BS2: Bris 2J 5 (2B 62)
Eyers Rd. BS24: W'ton V 5D 106

F

Faber Gro. BS13: Hart 6J 75
Fabian Dr. BS34: Stok G 2G 37
Factory Rd. BS36: Wint 7D 28
FAILAND 5F 59
Failand Cres. BS9: Sea M 3C 46
Failand La. BS8: Fail 6C 44
BS20: P'bry 6C 44
Failand Wlk. BS9: Sea M 2C 46
Fairacre Cl. BS7: L'lze 3D 48
BS24: Lock 1F 129
Fairacres Cl. BS31: Key 5C 78
Fairdean Rd. TA9: Highb 4G 159
Fairfax St. BS1: Bris 3F 5 (2K 61)
Fairfield BA2: Tun 2A 142
Fairfield Av. BA1: Bath 1C 100
Fairfield Cl. BS22: W Mare 3K 105
BS48: Back 3B 72
Fairfield Mead BS48: Back 3B 72
FAIRFIELD PARK 1C 100
Fairfield Pk. Rd. BA1: Bath 1B 100
Fairfield Pl. BS3: Bedm 5H 61
Fairfield Rd. BA1: Bath 2C 100
BS3: Bedm 5J 61
BS6: Bris 6B 48
Fairfield Ter. BA1: Bath 1C 100
BA2: Pea J 6C 142
Fairfield Vw. BA1: Bath 1C 100
Fairfield Way BS48: Back 4A 72
Fairfoot Rd. BS4: Wind H 6C 62
Fairford Cl. BS15: Soun 6D 50
TA9: Highb 4G 159
Fairford Cres. BS34: Pat 6E 26
Fairford Rd. BS11: Shire 1H 45
TA9: Highb 4G 159
Fair Furlong BS13: Withy 6G 75
Fairhaven BS37: Yate 5F 31
Fairhaven Cotts. BA1: Bathe 4J 83
Fairhaven Rd. BS6: Bishop 4J 47
Fair Hill BS25: S'ham 5B 132
Fairholm BS31: Key 7D 78
Fairlands Way BS27: Ched 7E 150
Fair Lawn BS30: Old C 5E 64
Fairlawn BS16: Stap H 4B 50
Fairlawn Rd. BS6: Bris 6B 48
Fairleigh Rd. BS21: Clev 1A 68
Fairlyn Dr. BS15: Soun 5D 50
Fairoaks BS30: Long G 6E 64
Fairseat Ind. Est. BS40: Chew S 5E 114
Fairview BS22: Wor 7D 84
Fairview Ct. BS15: Kgswd 3B 64
Fairview Dr. BS6: Redl 6J 47
Fairview Rd. BS15: Kgswd 1D 64
Fairview Ter. BS37: Iron A 2H 29
Fairway BS4: Brisl 1F 77
Fairway Apartments BS4: Brisl 2F 77
Fairway Cl. BS22: W Mare 2K 105
BS30: Old C 5F 65
TA8: Berr 3B 156
Fairway Ind. Cen. BS34: Fil 4B 36
Fairways BS31: Salt 1J 97
Fairy Hill BS39: Comp D 5B 96
Falcon Cl. BA3: Mid N 6F 153
BS9: W Trym 7F 35
BS20: P'head 4F 43
BS34: Pat 6A 26
Falcon Ct. BS9: W Trym 2G 47
BS15: Kgswd 7C 50
Falcon Cres. BS22: W Mare 4B 106
Falcondale Rd. BS9: W Trym 1F 47
Falcondale Wlk. BS9: W Trym 7G 35
Falcon Dr. BS34: Pat 6A 26
Falconer Rd. BA1: W'ton 7G 81
Falcons Ga. BS37: Yate 3B 30
Falcon Wlk. BS34: Pat 5A 26
Falcon Way BS35: T'bry 2B 12
Falfield Rd. BS4: Brisl 6E 62
Falfield Wlk. BS10: S'mead 7J 35
Falkland Rd. BS6: Bris 6B 48
Fallodon Ct. BS9: Henle 3H 47
Fallodon Way BS9: Henle 3H 47
Fallowfield BS22: Wor 7D 84
BS30: Old C 4G 65
BS40: Blag 3B 134
Falmouth Cl. BS48: Nail 1J 71
Falmouth Rd. BS7: Bishop 4K 47
Fane Cl. BS10: Bren 5G 35
Fanshawe Rd. BS14: H'gro 3C 76
Faraday Rd. BS8: Clftn 4F 61
Farendell Rd. BS16: Emer G 6F 39
Far Handstones BS30: C Hth 5E 64
Farington Rd. BS10: W Trym 1K 47
Farlands BS16: Puck 2B 52
FARLEIGH 3B 72
Farleigh Ct. BS48: Flax B 2F 73
Farleigh La. GL12: Crom 2B 14
Farleigh Ri. BA1: Bathf 2B 102
BA15: Mon F 2B 102
(not continuous)
Farleigh Rd. BS31: Key 6B 78
BS48: Back 4K 71
Farleigh Vw. *BA1: Bath* 2C 100
(off Richmond La.)
Farleigh Wlk. BS13: Bis 2G 75
FARLEIGH WICK 7C 102
Farler's End BS48: Nail 2H 71
(not continuous)
Farley Cl. BS34: Lit S 6E 26
Farleys Yd. *BS3: Ash G* 5G 61
(off Coronation Rd.)
FARMBOROUGH 6E 118
Farm Cl. BS16: Emer G 2F 51
BS22: St G 7G 85
Farm Ct. BS16: Down 1C 50
Farmer Rd. BS13: Withy 6E 74
Farm Gdns. BS16: Down 1C 50
Farmhouse Cl. BS48: Nail 1G 71
Farm La. BA2: Well 4K 143
BS35: E Comp 4D 24
Farm Rd. BS16: Down 1C 50
BS22: W Mare 3K 105
BS24: Hut 3C 128
Farmwell Cl. BS13: Hart 5H 75
Farnaby Cl. BS4: Know 3J 75
Farnborough Rd. BS24: Lock 7G 107
Farndale Rd. BS5: St G 3J 63
BS22: W Mare 4B 106
Farne Cl. BS9: Henle 3H 47
Farrant Cl. BS4: Know 4K 75
Farriers Ct. BS16: Mang 1E 50
Farringford Ho. BS5: Eastv 6F 49
Farrington Flds. BS39: Far G 3A 152
Farrington Flds. Trad. Est.
BS39: Far G 3A 152
Farrington Rd. BS39: Far G, Paul 1A 152
Farr's La. BA2: C Down 2D 122
Farrs La. BS1: Bris 5E 4 (3K 61)
Farr St. BS11: A'mth 7F 33
Farthing Combe BS26: Axb 4K 149
FAULKLAND 4J 155
Faulkland La. BA2: Ston L 1J 155
BA3: Faul, Fox 1J 155
Faulkland Rd. BA2: Bath 7A 6 (6K 99)
Faulkland Vw. BA2: Pea J 6E 142
Favell Ho. BS1: Bris 4F 5
Faversham Dr. BS24: W Mare 4J 127
Fawkes Cl. BS15: Warm 1F 65
Fearnville Est. BS21: Clev 7C 54
Featherbed La. BS39: Clut, Stan W 5D 116
BS40: Regil 1K 113
Featherstone Rd. BS16: Fish 4H 49
Fedden Bldgs. BS7: L'lze 2E 48
Fedden Village BS20: P'head 3B 42
Feeder Rd. BS2: Bris 6K 5 (4B 62)
Felix Ct. *BS15: Kgswd* 1B 64
(off Downend Rd.)
Felix Rd. BS5: E'ton 1D 62
Felsberg Way BS27: Ched 7E 150
Felstead Rd. BS10: S'mead 6A 36
Feltham Ct. BS34: Fil 5B 36
Feltham Rd. BS16: Puck 3C 52
FELTON 3G 91
FELTON COMMON 4G 91
Felton Gro. BS13: Bis 2F 75
Felton La. BS40: F'tn, Winf 4H 91
Felton St. BS40: F'tn 4G 91
Fenbrook Cl. BS16: H'ook 6K 37
Feniton BS22: Wor 2E 106
Fennel Dr. BS32: Brad S 7J 27
Fennel La. BS26: Axb 4H 149
Fennell Gro. BS10: Hen 5G 35
Fennel Rd. BS20: P'head 2H 43
Fenners BS22: Wor 7F 85
Fenns La. BS41: L Ash 1J 73
Fenshurst Gdns. BS41: L Ash 2K 73
Fenswood Cl. BS41: L Ash 1J 73
Fenswood Ct. BS41: L Ash 1J 73
Fenswood Mead BS41: L Ash 1J 73
Fenswood Rd. BS41: L Ash 1J 73
Fenton Cl. BS31: Salt 7H 79
Fenton Rd. BS7: Bishop 4K 47
Ferenberge Cl. BA2: F'boro 6E 118
Fermaine Av. BS4: Brisl 6H 63
Fernbank Rd. BS6: Redl 6J 47
Ferncliffe BS8: L Wds 2E 60
Fern Cl. BA3: Mid N 6F 153
BS10: Bren 4H 35
Ferndale Av. BS30: Long G 6D 64
Ferndale Cl. BS32: Alm 6F 19
Ferndale Grange BS9: Henle 2H 47
Ferndale Rd. BA1: Swa 7E 82
BS7: Hor 5C 36
BS20: P'head 2F 43
Ferndene BS32: Brad S 4E 26
Ferndown BS25: S'ham 5A 132
BS37: Yate 5E 30
Ferndown Cl. BS11: Law W 1A 46
Fern Gro. BS32: Brad S 6F 27
BS48: Nail 2E 70
Fernhill BS32: Alm 5D 18
Fernhill La. BS11: Law W 6B 34
Fernhurst Rd. BS5: S'wll 7H 49
Fern Lea BS24: B'don 7K 127
Fernlea Gdns. BS20: Eas 4F 45
Fernlea Rd. BS22: W Mare 5A 106
Fernleaze BS36: Coal H 1G 39
Fernleigh Ct. BS6: Redl 5H 47
Fern Lodge BS23: W Mare 6F 105
Fern Rd. BS16: Down 3B 50
Fernside BS48: Back 3J 71
Fernsteed Rd. BS13: Bis 4F 75
Fern St. BS2: Bris 7B 48
Ferry Ct. BA2: Bath 5J 7 (5D 100)
Ferry La. BA2: Bath 5H 7 (5C 100)
BA2: C'ton 6A 102
BS24: Lym 2A 146
Ferryman's Ct. BS2: Bris 4H 5
Ferry Rd. BS15: Han 1B 78
Ferry Steps Ind. Est. BS2: Bris 5C 62
Ferry St. BS1: Bris 5G 5 (3A 62)
Fersfield BA2: Bath 1D 122
Feynman Way Central BS16: Emer G 7G 39
Feynman Way Nth. BS16: Emer G 6G 39
Feynman Way Sth. BS16: Emer G 7G 39
Fiddes Rd. BS6: Redl 4J 47
Fiddlers Wood La. BS32: Brad S 6G 27
Fielders, The BS22: Wor 7F 85
Fieldfare BS16: Emer G 5E 38
Fieldfare Av. BS20: P'head 2J 43
Field Farm Cl. BS34: Stok G 3H 37
Fieldgardens Rd. BS39: Temp C 4H 139
Fieldgrove La. BS30: Bit 2G 79
Fielding Ho. BA2: Bath 5G 99
Fieldings Rd. BA2: Bath 5J 99
Fieldins BA15: W'ley 5C 124
Field La. BS30: Long G 6C 64
BS35: Itch 2C 20
BS35: L Sev 4B 10
Field Marshal Slim Ct.
BS2: Bris 2J 5 (2B 62)
Field Rd. BS15: Kgswd 7A 50
Fields, The BS22: St G 2H 107
Field Vw. BS5: E'ton 1C 62
Field Vw. Dr. BS16: Fish 2A 50
Field Way TA9: Highb 3F 159
Fieldway BS25: Sandf 1H 131
Fiennes Cl. BS16: Stap H 4C 50

Gallivan Cl.—Grange La.

Gallivan Cl. BS34: Lit S 6D 26
Galway Rd. BS4: Know 1A 76
Gander Cl. BS13: Hart 5H 75
Gang Wall BS24: Yat 5F 87
Gannet Rd. BS22: Wor 3D 106
Gaolferry Steps BS1: Bris 7D 4 (4J 61)
Garamond Ct. BS1: Bris 7H 5 (4A 62)
Garden Cl. BS9: Sea M 3C 46
BS22: Wor 2C 106
Garden Ct. BS8: Clftn 1G 61
Gardeners Cl. BS27: Ched 5D 150
Gardeners Wlk. BS41: L Ash 1B 74
Gardenhurst TA8: Bur S 6D 156
Gardenhurst Cl. TA8: Bur S 7D 156
Gardens, The BA2: Tun 1A 142
BS16: Fren 6G 37
BS16: Stap H 5C 50
BS30: C Hth 3G 65
Gardens Rd. BS21: Clev 5C 54
Garden Walls GL12: Wickw 7H 15
Gardner Av. BS13: Bis 3F 75
Gardner Rd. BS20: P'head 2F 43
Garfield Ct. *BS5: St G* *1H 63*
(off Orchard Rd.)
Garfield Rd. BS5: St G 1J 63
Garfield Ter. BA1: Bath 1E 100
Garland Av. BS24: Lock 7G 107
Garner Ct. BS22: Wor 7F 85
Garnet St. BS3: Bedm 6H 61
Garnett Pl. BS16: Down 1D 50
Garonor Way BS20: P'bry 3D 44
Garre Ho. BA2: Bath 6F 99
Garrett Dr. BS32: Brad S 7F 27
Garrick Rd. BA2: Bath 6F 99
Garsdale Rd. BS22: W Mare 4B 106
Garston Cotts. BS40: Blag 2C 134
Garston La. BS40: Blag 2C 134
Garstons BA1: Bathf 1B 102
BS21: Clev 2B 68
BS40: Wrin 3G 111
Garstons, The BS20: P'head 4E 42
Garstons Cl. BS40: Wrin 2G 111
BS48: Back 4H 71
Garstons Orchard BS40: Wrin 3F 111
Garth Rd. BS13: Bis 2G 75
Gascoigns Way BS34: Pat 7C 26
Gas Ferry Rd. BS1: Bris 7B 4 (4H 61)
Gaskins, The BS7: L'lze 3C 48
Gas La. BS2: Bris 5K 5 (3C 62)
Gass Cl. TA9: Highb 4H 159
Gaston Av. BS31: Key 4D 78
Gastons BS11: Law W 7A 34
Gastons, The BS11: Law W 7A 34
Gasworks La. BS1: Bris 5B 4 (3H 61)
Gatcombe Dr. BS34: Stok G 3G 37
Gatcombe La. BS48: Flax B 2G 73
Gatcombe Rd. BS13: Hart 5H 75
Gatecombe Farm Ind. Est. BS40: Udl 7E 88
Gate House, The BS2: Bris 2K 5
Gatehouse Av. BS13: Withy 5G 75
Gatehouse Cen. BS13: Withy 5H 75
Gatehouse Cl. BS13: Withy 5G 75
Gatehouse Ct. BS13: Withy 5G 75
Gatehouse Way BS13: Withy 5G 75
Gatesby Mead BS34: Stok G 2G 37
Gateway Ter. BS20: P'head 2G 43
Gathorne Cres. BS37: Yate 4D 30
Gathorne Rd. BS3: Bris 5H 61
Gator Ct. BS24: W Wick 3G 107
Gatton Rd. BS2: Bris 7C 48
Gaunts Cl. BS20: P'head 4B 42
GAUNT'S EARTHCOTT 1K 27
Gaunt's Earthcott La. BS32: Gau E 1K 27
Gaunts La. BS1: Bris 4D 4 (3J 61)
Gaunts Rd. BS37: Chip S 6H 31
Gay Ct. BA1: Bathe 7G 83
Gay Elms Rd. BS13: Withy 6G 75
Gayner Rd. BS7: Fil 6C 36
Gay's Hill BA1: Bath 3C 100
Gay's Rd. BS15: Han 5K 63
Gay St. BA1: Bath 3F 7 (4B 100)
Gaywood Ho. BS3: Bedm 6H 61
Gazelle Rd. BS24: W Mare 2K 127
Gazzard Cl. BS36: Wint 7C 28
Gazzard Rd. BS36: Wint 7C 28
Gee Moors BS15: Kgswd 2D 64
Gefle Cl. BS1: Bris 7A 4 (4H 61)
Geldof Dr. BA3: Mid N 4E 152
General Higgins Ho. TA9: Highb 5G 159
Gentian Cl. BS16: Emer G 7G 39
Geoffrey Cl. BS13: Bis 4E 74
George & Dragon La. *BS5: St G* *1F 63*
(off Church Rd.)
BS5: St G *2F 63*
(off Claremont Ter.)
George Cl. BS48: Back 3B 72
George Ct. *BS6: Redl* *7H 47*
(off Hampton Pk.)
George Jones Rd. BS2: Bris 2C 62
George's Bldgs. BA1: Bath 1G 7 (3C 100)
Georges Ho. BA2: Bath 4K 7
George's Pl. BA2: Bath 4K 7
George's Rd. BA1: Bath 2C 100
Georges Sq. BS1: Bris 4G 5 (3A 62)
George St. BA1: Bath 3F 7 (4B 100)
BA2: Bath 4K 7 (5D 100)
BS5: Redf 1E 62
BS20: P'head 6E 42
BS23: W Mare 5G 105
TA8: Bur S 1C 158
George White St. BS1: Bris 2H 5 (2A 62)
Georgian Garden 3E 6 (4B 100)
Georgian House 4C 4 (3J 61)
Georgian Ho. BA2: Bath 5H 7
Georgian Vw. BA2: Bath 1J 121
Gerald Rd. BS3: Ash G 6G 61
Gerard Rd. BS23: W Mare 4G 105
Gerrard Bldgs. BA2: Bath 3J 7 (4C 100)
Gerrard Cl. BS4: Know 3K 75
Gerrish Av. BS5: Redf 1E 62
BS16: Mang 3D 50
Gibbet La. BS14: Whit 2E 94
Gibbsfold Rd. BS13: Hart 7J 75
Gibson Rd. BS6: Cot 7K 47
Gielgud Cl. TA8: Bur S 2F 159
Giffard Ho. BS34: Lit S 1F 37
Gifford Cl. BS37: Rang 5A 22
Gifford Ct. BS34: Stok G 5F 37
Gifford Cres. BS34: Lit S 1E 36
Gifford Rd. BS10: Hen 3F 35
Giffords Pl. BS13: Bis 3G 75
Gilbeck Rd. BS48: Nail 7E 56
Gilbert Rd. BS5: Redf 1E 62
BS15: Kgswd 7B 50
Gilberyn Dr. BS22: Wor 1F 107
Gilda Cl. BS14: H'gro 5E 76
Gilda Cres. BS14: H'gro 4D 76
Gilda Pde. BS14: H'gro 5E 76
Gilda Sq. E. BS14: H'gro 5E 76
Gilda Sq. W. BS14: H'gro 5D 76
(not continuous)
Gillard Cl. BS15: Kgswd 1K 63
Gillard Rd. BS15: Kgswd 1K 63
Gill Av. BS16: Fish 3K 49
Gillebank Cl. BS14: Stoc 5F 77
Gillet's Hill La. BS39: Temp C 5G 139
Gillham Ho. *BS7: Bishop* *6K 47*
(off Claremont Rd.)
Gillingham Hill BS5: St G 4K 63
Gillingham Ter. BA1: Bath 2D 100
GILLINGSTOOL 3A 12
Gillingstool BS35: T'bry 4A 12
Gill M. BS22: Wor 7E 84
Gillmore Cl. BS22: W Mare 3B 106
Gillmore Rd. BS22: W Mare 3B 106
Gillson Cl. BS24: Hut 3B 128
Gilpin Cl. BS15: Kgswd 7D 50
Gilray Cl. BS7: L'lze 2D 48
Gilroy Cl. BS30: Long G 6F 65
Gilslake Av. BS10: Bren 4H 35
Gilton Ho. BS4: Brisl 7G 63
Gimblett Rd. BS22: Wor 7F 85
Gingell's Grn. BS5: St G 1J 63
Gipsies Plat BS35: Sev B 7B 16
Gipsy Patch La. BS34: Lit S 1D 36
Glades, The BS5: Eastv 6G 49
Gladstone Dr. BS16: Soun 5B 50
Gladstone La. BS36: Fram C 7G 29
Gladstone Pl. BA2: C Down 3E 122
Gladstone Rd. BA2: C Down 2E 122
BS14: H'gro 4D 76
BS15: Kgswd 7B 50
Gladstone St. BA3: Mid N 3F 153
BS3: Bedm 6H 61
BS5: Redf 2F 63
BS16: Soun 5B 50
Glaisdale Rd. BS16: Fish 3J 49
Glanville Dr. BS39: Hin B 7A 138
Glanville Gdns. BS15: Kgswd 2C 64
Glasscutter *BS14: H'gro* *2D 76*
(off Petherton Rd.)
Glass Ho. BS1: Bris 2H 5
Glass Ho. La. BS2: Bris 4D 62
Glass Wlk. BS1: Bris 2H 5
Glass Wharf BS2: Bris 5J 5 (3B 62)
Glastonbury Cl. BS30: Bar C 4D 64
BS48: Nail 1K 71
Glastonbury Way BS22: Wor 2E 106
Glaze BS5: St G 2J 63
Glebe, The BA2: F'frd 7K 123
BA2: Tims 2F 141
BS35: Piln 6C 16
BS40: Wrin 2F 111
Glebe Av. BS20: P'head 4G 43
Glebe Cl. BS41: L Ash 7B 60
Glebe Crest BS5: St G 2J 63
Glebe Fld. BS32: Alm 1C 26
Glebe Ho. *BA2: Bath* *7J 7*
(off Widcombe Hill)
BS23: W Mare 4F 105
Glebelands BA3: Rads 5H 153
Glebelands Cl. BS27: Ched 7H 151
Glebelands Rd. BS34: Fil 4C 36
Glebe Rd. BA2: Bath 7H 99
BS5: St G 1G 63
BS20: P'head 4G 43
BS21: Clev 7C 54
BS23: W Mare 4G 105
BS41: L Ash 1C 74
Glebes, The *BS5: St G* *1G 63*
(off Glebe Rd.)
Glebe Wlk. BS31: Key 6A 78
Glebe Way BS27: Ched 7J 151
Gledemoor Dr. BS36: Coal H 7H 29
Glen, The BS6: Redl 5H 47
BS15: Han 5K 63
BS22: W Mare 2K 105
BS31: Salt 2K 97
BS37: Yate 4E 30
Glena Av. BS4: Know 7D 62
Glenarm Rd. BS4: Brisl 7G 63
Glenarm Wlk. BS4: Brisl 7G 63
Glen Av. BS8: Abb L 1K 59
Glenavon Ct. BS9: Stok B 4C 46
Glenavon Pk. BS9: Stok B 4C 46
Glenburn Rd. BS15: Kgswd 7K 49
Glencairn Ct. BA2: Bath 4J 7 (5D 100)
Glencoe Bus. Pk. BS23: W Mare 5J 105
Glencoyne Sq. BS10: S'mead 5J 35
Glencroft Way BS22: Wor 1C 106
Glendale BS8: Clftn 3F 61
BS16: Down 7C 38
BS16: Fish 5A 50
Glendare St. BS5: Bar H 3E 62
Glendevon Rd. BS14: Whit 7C 76
Glen Dr. BS9: Stok B 4D 46
Gleneagles BS37: Yate 5E 30
Gleneagles Cl. BS22: Wor 1D 106
BS48: Nail 1J 71
Gleneagles Dr. BS10: Hen 4D 34
Gleneagles Rd. BS30: Warm 3F 65
Glenfall BS37: Yate 7D 30
Glenfrome Ho. BS5: Eastv 6D 48
Glenfrome Rd. BS2: Bris 6C 48
BS5: Eastv 5D 48
Glen La. BS4: Brisl 7F 63
Glen Pk. BS5: Eastv 6E 48
BS5: St G 1J 63
Glen Pk. Gdns. BS5: St G 1J 63
Glenroy Av. BS15: Kgswd 7K 49
Glenside Cl. BS16: Fish 1A 50
Glenside Hospital Mus. 3G 49
Glenside Pk. BS16: Stap 3G 49
Glentworth Rd. BS6: Redl 6J 47
BS8: Clftn 5A 4 (3H 61)
Glenview Rd. BS4: Brisl 7F 63
Glenwood BS16: Fish 5A 50
Glenwood Dr. BS30: Old C 5F 65
Glenwood Ri. BS20: P'head 3B 42
Glenwood Rd. BS10: W Trym 1J 47
Glen Yeo Ter. BS49: Cong 7J 87
Glevum Cl. BS16: Emer G 1G 51
Glider Av. BS24: W Mare 1K 127
Gloster Av. BS5: Eastv 5F 49
Gloster Vs. BA1: Bath 1G 7 (3C 100)
Gloucester Cl. BS34: Stok G 2F 37
Gloucester Ho. BS2: Bris 2K 5
Gloucester La. BS2: Bris 2K 5 (2B 62)
Gloucester Mans. BS7: Bishop 6K 47
Gloucester Pl. *BS2: Bris* *2E 4*
(off St Michael's Hill)
Gloucester Rd. BA1: Bath, Swa 5E 82
BA1: Up Swa 1B 82
BS7: Bishop, Hor 6K 47
BS11: A'mth 6E 32
BS16: Soun 5C 50
BS32: Alm, Brad S 1D 26
BS34: Pat 7C 26
BS35: A'ton, Grov, Rudg 4G 19
BS35: T'bry 3K 11
GL12: Fal 1D 12
TA8: Bur S 1E 158
Gloucester Rd. Nth. BS7: Fil 6B 36
BS34: Fil 4C 36
Gloucester Row BS8: Clftn 2F 61
Gloucestershire County Cricket Club 4A 48
Gloucester St. BA1: Bath 2E 6 (4B 100)
BS1: Bris 1H 5 (1A 62)
BS2: Bris 1H 5 (1A 62)
BS5: Eastv 5F 49
BS8: Clftn 2F 61
BS23: W Mare 5F 105
Gloucester Ter. BS35: T'bry 3K 11
Glovers Fld. BS25: S'ham 6B 132
Glyn Va. BS3: Know 1K 75
Goblin Combe Nature Reserve 4G 89
Goddard Dr. BS22: Wor 7F 85
Goddard Way BS10: W Trym 6G 35
Godfrey Ct. BS30: Long G 5D 64
Goding La. BS29: Ban 2B 130
Godwin Dr. BS48: Nail 7E 56
Goffenton Dr. BS16: Fish 2K 49
Goldcrest Rd. BS37: Chip S 7F 31
Goldcrest Way BS20: P'head 2J 43
BS35: E Comp 3D 24
GOLDEN HILL 3J 47
Golden Hill BS6: Bishop 3K 47
Golden Lion Ct. BS1: Bris 5G 5
Golden Valley La. BS30: Bit 2J 79
Goldfinch Way BS16: Puck 4C 52
Goldney Av. BS8: Clftn 3G 61
BS30: Warm 2G 65
Goldney Cl. BS39: Temp C 4G 139
Goldney Ct. *BS16: Fish* *5G 49*
(off Marina Gdns.)
Goldney Hall BS8: Clftn 3G 61
Goldney La. BS8: Clftn 3G 61
Goldney Rd. BS8: Clftn 3G 61
Goldney Way BS39: Temp C 4G 139
Goldsbury Wlk. BS11: Law W 6A 34
GOLD'S CROSS 6A 116
Goldsmiths Ho. BS2: Bris 4J 5 (3B 62)
Golf Club La. BS31: Salt 1J 97
Golf Course La. BS34: Fil 4B 36
Golf Course Rd. BA2: Bath 5E 100
Golf Links Rd. TA8: Bur S 4C 156
Gooch Ct. BS30: Old C 6G 65
Gooch Way BS22: Wor 1F 107
Goodeve Pk. BS9: Stok B 5D 46
(not continuous)
Goodeve Rd. BS9: Stok B 5D 46
Goodhind St. BS5: E'ton 1K 5 (1C 62)
Goodneston Rd. BS16: Fish 5J 49
Goodrich Cl. BS37: Yate 5A 30
Goodring Hill BS11: Law W 6A 34
Good Shepherd Cl. BS7: Bishop 4J 47
Goodwin Dr. BS14: Whit 6B 76
Goodwood Gdns. BS16: Down 6D 38
Goold Cl. BA2: Cor 3A 98
Goolden St. BS4: Wind H 6C 62
Goosard La. BS39: High L 5B 140
Goose Acre BS32: Brad S 1H 37
Gooseberry La. BS31: Key 5D 78
GOOSE GREEN
BS30 7G 51
BS37 2E 30
Goose Grn. BS30: Sis 7G 51
BS36: Fram C 6G 29
BS37: Yate 2E 30
Goose Grn. Way BS37: Yate 2C 30
Gooseham Mead BS49: Cong 7K 87
Gooseland Cl. BS14: Whit 7B 76
Goosey Drove BS24: Pux 7D 86
Goosey La. BS22: St G 2G 107
Gordano Ct. BS20: P'head 3G 43
Gordano Gdns. BS20: Eas 4F 45
Gordano Ga. Bus. Pk.
BS20: P'head 3G 43
Gordano Rd. BS20: P'bry 7B 32
GORDANO SERVICE AREA 4D 44
Gordano Sports Cen. 4E 42
Gordano Vw. BS20: P'head 3E 42
Gordano Way BS20: P'bry 3D 44
Gordon Av. BS5: W'hall 7F 49
Gordon Bldgs. *BA3: Rads* *3A 154*
(off Woodborough Rd.)
Gordon Cl. BS5: W'hall 7G 49
Gordon Rd. BA2: Bath 7J 7 (6D 100)
BA2: Pea J 5D 142
BS2: Bris 7B 48
BS5: W'hall 7F 49
BS8: Clftn 3A 4 (2H 61)
BS23: W Mare 5H 105
Gore Rd. BS3: Bedm 6G 61
TA8: Bur S 6C 156
Gore's Marsh Rd. BS3: Bedm 7G 61
Gores Pk. BS39: High L 3K 139
Gorge Walk 6E 150
Gorham Cl. BS11: Law W 5C 34
Gorlands Rd. BS37: Chip S 5J 31
Gorlangton Cl. BS14: H'gro 3C 76
Gorse Cover Rd. BS35: Sev B 7A 16
Gorse Covert Local Nature Reserve 6A 26
Gorse Hill BS16: Fish, Stap H 5K 49
Gorse La. BS8: Clftn 4A 4 (3H 61)
BS30: Doy 3J 67
SN14: Dyr 3J 67
Gosforth Cl. BS10: S'mead 6H 35
Gosforth Rd. BS10: S'mead 5H 35
Goshawk Dr. BS20: P'head 1H 43
Goslet Rd. BS14: Stoc 5G 77
Goss Barton BS48: Nail 1F 71
Goss Cl. BS48: Nail 1E 70
Goss La. BS48: Nail 1E 70
Goss Vw. BS48: Nail 1E 70
Gotley Rd. BS4: Brisl 7F 63
Gott Dr. BS4: St Ap 4F 63
Gough Pl. BS27: Ched 6C 150
Gough's Cave 6F 151
Gould Cl. BS13: Hart 5K 75
Goulston Rd. BS13: Bis 5G 75
Goulston Wlk. BS13: Bis 4G 75
Goulter St. BS5: Bar H 3D 62
Gourney Cl. BS11: Law W 5B 34
Governors Ho. BA2: Bath 5A 6 (5K 99)
Gover Rd. BS15: Han 6A 64
Govier Way BS35: Sev B 2C 24
Grace Apartments BS7: Bishop 4B 48
Grace Cl. BS37: Chip S 5J 31
BS49: Yat 3H 87
Grace Ct. BS16: Down 2B 50
Grace Dr. BA3: Mid N 4E 152
BS15: Kgswd 7D 50
Grace Pk. Rd. BS4: Brisl 1F 77
Grace Rd. BS16: Down 3A 50
BS22: Wor 7F 85
Gradwell Cl. BS22: Wor 1F 107
Graeme Cl. BS16: Fish 4J 49
Graham Rd. BS3: Bedm 6J 61
BS5: E'ton 7D 48
BS16: Down 2D 50
BS23: W Mare 5G 105
Grainger Ct. BS11: Shire 1J 45
Grain Loft, The *BS1: Bris* *5F 5*
(off Queen Sq. Av.)
Graitney Cl. BS49: C've 3C 88
Grampian Cl. BS30: Old C 5G 65
Granary, The *BS1: Bris* *5F 5*
(off Queen Charlotte St.)
Granby Ct. BS8: Clftn 3F 61
Granby Hill BS8: Clftn 3F 61
Grandmother's Rock La. BS30: Beach 7D 66
Grand Pde. BA2: Bath 4G 7 (5C 100)
Grand Pier 5F 105
Granfield Gdns. BS40: L'frd 7C 110
Grange, The BS9: C Din 1D 46
BS48: Flax B 3D 72
Grange Av. BS15: Han 4A 64
BS34: Lit S 1E 36
TA9: Highb 5G 159
Grange Cl. BS23: Uph 4G 127
BS32: Brad S 4E 26
BS34: Stok G 3J 37
Grange Cl. Nth. BS9: W Trym 2H 47
Grange Ct. BS9: Henle 2H 47
BS15: Han 4B 64
BS20: P'head 4F 43
Grange Ct. Rd. BS9: Henle 2G 47
Grange Dr. BS16: Fish 2A 50
Grange End BA3: Mid N 7F 153
Grange Farm Rd. BS49: Yat 2G 87
Grange La. BS13: Withy 6F 75

Grange Pk.—Hammond Apartments

Grange Pk. BS9: W Trym 2H 47
BS16: Fren 7A 38
Grange Rd. BS8: Clftn 2G 61
BS13: Bis 5G 75
BS23: Uph 4G 127
BS31: Salt 1G 97
Grange Vw. BA15: Brad A 5J 125
Grangeville Cl. BS30: Long G 6F 65
Grangewood Cl. BS16: Fish 2A 50
Granny's La. BS15: Han 3C 64
Grantham Apartments BS15: Kgswd 1A 64
(off Two Mile Hill Rd.)
Grantham Ct. BS15: Kgswd 1A 64
(off Grantham Rd.)
Grantham Ho. BS15: Kgswd 7A 50
Grantham La. BS15: Kgswd 1A 64
Grantham Rd. BS15: Kgswd 1A 64
Grantson Cl. BS4: Brisl 7G 63
Granville Cl. BS15: Han 6K 63
Granville Rd. BA1: L'dwn 7A 82
Granville St. BS5: Bar H 3E 62
Grasmere Cl. BS10: S'mead 7G 35
Grasmere Dr. BS23: W Mare 1H 127
Grasmere Gdns. BS30: Old C 3H 65
Grassington Dr. BS37: Chip S 6G 31
Grass Meers Dr. BS14: Whit 6C 76
Grassmere Rd. BS49: Yat 3H 87
Grass Rd. TA8: Brean 2B 144
Gratitude Rd. BS5: E'ton 7E 48
Gravel Hill BS40: Up Str, Chew S 6K 113
Gravel Hill Rd. BS37: Yate 2F 31
(not continuous)
Gravel Hill Rd. (Nth.) BS37: Yate 2G 31
Gravel Wlk. BA1: Bath 2D 6 (4A 100)
Graveney Apartments BS7: Bishop 4B 48
Graveney Cl. BS4: Brisl 1F 77
Gray Cl. BS10: Hen 5E 34
Grayle Rd. BS10: Hen 5G 35
Grays Hill BA2: Ston L 7H 143
Gt. Ann St. BS2: Bris 2K 5 (2B 62)
GREAT ASHLEY 3E 124
Gt. Bedford St. BA1: Bath 1E 6 (3B 100)
Great Brockeridge BS9: W Trym 2F 47
Gt. Copsie Way BS16: L'lze 7E 36
Great Dowles BS30: C Hth 5E 64
Gt. Eastern Ho. BS1: Bris 6B 4
Gt. George St. BS1: Bris 4C 4 (3J 61)
BS2: Bris 2J 5 (2B 62)
Gt. Hayles Rd. BS14: H'gro 3B 76
Great Leaze BS30: C Hth 5E 64
Great Meadow Rd. BS32: Brad S 7H 27
Great Pk. Rd. BS32: Brad S 3E 26
Gt. Pulteney St. BA2: Bath 3H 7 (4C 100)
Gt. Stanhope St. BA1: Bath 4D 6 (5A 100)
GREAT STOKE 2H 37
Gt. Stoke Way BS34: Stok G 5F 37
(Filton Rd.)
BS34: Stok G 2J 37
(Winterbourne Rd.)
Greatstone La. BS40: Winf 7K 91
Gt. Swanmoor Cl. BS34: Stok G 4E 36
Gt. Western Bus. Pk. BS37: Yate 3B 30
(not continuous)
Gt. Western Ct. BS34: Stok G 3H 37
Gt. Western Ho. BS1: Bris 6B 4
Gt. Western La. BS5: Bar H 3E 62
Gt. Western Rd. BS21: Clev 6D 54
Gt. Wood Cl. BS13: Hart 6J 75
Green, The BA2: Odd D 3K 121
BA3: Faul 4K 155
BS11: Shire 2J 45
BS15: Soun 6C 50
BS20: Pill 4H 45
(not continuous)
BS24: Lock 1E 128
BS25: Wins 5F 131
BS30: Wick 4B 66
BS34: Stok G 3G 37
BS35: Olv 3C 18
BS39: Comp D 6B 96
BS48: Back 5H 71
GL12: Crom 4B 14
Greenacre BS22: W Mare 2K 105
Greenacre Pl. Cvn. Pk. TA9: Edith 2J 159
Green Acre Rd. BS14: Whit 7C 76
Greenacres BA1: W'ton 7H 81
BA3: Mid N 5C 152
BS9: W Trym 1E 46
Green Acres Cvn. Site BS35: Aust 5G 9
Greenacres Ct. BA3: Mid N 5C 152
Greenacres Pk. BS36: Coal H 2H 39
Greenbank Av. E. BS5: E'ton 7E 48
Greenbank Av. W. BS5: E'ton 7D 48
Greenbank Gdns. BA1: W'ton 2H 99
Greenbank Rd. BS3: Bris 7A 4 (4G 61)
BS5: E'ton 7E 48
BS15: Han 5B 64
Greenbank Vw. BS5: Eastv 6E 48
BS15: Kgswd 2C 64
Green Cl. BS7: Hor 7C 36
BS39: Paul 7C 140
Green Cotts. BA2: C Down 3E 122
Green Ct. BS35: Olv 3C 18
Green Cres. BS36: Fram C 1F 39
Green Cft. BS5: S'wll 7J 49
Greendale Rd. BS3: Wind H 6A 62
BS6: Redl 4H 47
Green Dell Cl. BS10: Hen 4D 34
Greenditch Av. BS13: Hart 5J 75
Greenditch La. BA3: Clapt 7A 152
Greenditch St. BS35: Olv, Toc 4A 18
BS35: Piln, Toc 4J 17
Greendown BS5: St G 2J 63
Greendown Pl. BA2: C Down 3C 122
Green Dragon Rd. BS36: Wint 2B 38
Green Farm Bus. Pk. BS37: Iron A 1E 28
Greenfield Av. BS10: S'mead 7K 35
Greenfield Cres. BS48: Nail 6G 57
Greenfield Pk. BS20: P'head 5E 42
Greenfield Pl. BS23: W Mare 4E 104
Greenfield Rd. BS10: S'mead 6K 35
BS31: Key 7B 78
Greenfields Av. BS29: Ban 2A 130
Greenfield Wlk. BA3: Mid N 3E 152
Greenfinch Lodge BS16: Bmhll 2H 49
Greengage Cl. BS22: W Mare 4C 106
Greenhayes BS27: Ched 6D 150
BS37: Chip S 6J 31
Greenhill BS35: A'ton 1J 19
Greenhill Cl. BS22: Wor 1E 106
BS48: Nail 7F 57
Greenhill Cft. BS25: Sandf 1H 131
Greenhill Down BS35: A'ton 1J 19
Greenhill Gdns. BS35: A'ton 1J 19
Greenhill Gro. BS3: Bedm 7G 61
Greenhill La. BS11: Law W 6C 34
BS25: Sandf 1H 131
BS35: A'ton 2H 19
Greenhill Pde. BS35: A'ton 7J 11
Greenhill Pl. BA3: Mid N 3E 152
Greenhill Rd. BA3: Mid N 3E 152
BS25: Sandf 1G 131
BS35: A'ton 7J 11
Greenland Mills BA15: Brad A 6J 125
Greenland Rd. BS22: W Mare 3B 106
Greenlands Av. BA2: Pea J 5C 142
BS10: Hen 3E 34
Greenlands Way BS10: Hen 4E 34
Greenland Vw. BA15: Brad A 6J 125
Green La. BA15: Tur 6D 124
BS8: Fail 5G 59
BS11: A'mth 7F 33
BS35: Red, Sev B 6A 16
BS36: Wint 1A 38
BS39: Far G, Hall 7G 139
(not continuous)
BS40: Blag, Comp M 6F 135
BS40: But 5E 112
BS40: Redh, Winf 7E 90
GL12: Bag 3A 22
GL12: Buck 3F 13
TA8: Berr 6C 144
Greenleaze BS4: Know 1D 76
Greenleaze Av. BS16: Down 6B 38
Greenleaze Cl. BS16: Down 6B 38
Greenmore Rd. BS4: Know 7D 62
Green Oak Cres. BS5: E'ton 7F 49
Greenore BS15: Kgswd 2A 64
Green Pk. BA1: Bath 5D 6
BS30: Old C 3H 65
Green Pk. Ho. BA1: Bath 5E 6
Green Pk. M. BA1: Bath 5D 6 (5A 100)
Green Pk. Rd. BA1: Bath 5E 6 (5B 100)
Greenpark Rd. BS10: S'mead 6A 36
Green Pk. Sta. BA1: Bath 4E 6 (5A 100)
GREEN PARLOUR 5D 154
Green Parlour Rd. BA3: Writ 5D 154
Green Pastures Rd. BS48: Wrax 6J 57
Greenridge BS39: Clut 2H 139
Greenridge Cl. BS13: Withy 6E 74
GREENSBROOK 2H 139
Greens Hill BS16: Fish 5G 49
Greenside BS16: Mang 2E 50
Greenside Cl. BS10: Hen 4D 34
Greenslade Gdns. BS48: Nail 6F 57
Green St. BA1: Bath 4F 7 (5B 100)
BA2: Shos 1D 154
BS3: Wind H 5B 62
Green Tree Rd. BA3: Mid N 3F 153
GREENVALE 4F 141
Greenvale Cl. BA2: Tims 4F 141
Greenvale Dr. BA2: Tims 4F 141
Greenvale Rd. BS39: Paul 1B 152
Greenview BS30: Long G 7E 64
Green Wlk. BS4: Know 1C 76
GREENWAY 7B 138
Greenway BA3: Faul 5J 155
Greenway, The BS16: Fish 5A 50
Greenway Bush La. BS3: Bris 7A 4 (5G 61)
Greenway Ct. BA2: Bath 7B 100
Greenway Dr. BS10: S'mead 6K 35
Greenway La. BA2: Bath 1B 122
BS10: S'mead 6K 35
SN14: C Ash 5K 67
Greenway Pk. BS10: S'mead 7K 35
BS21: Clev 6F 55
Greenway Rd. BS6: Redl 6H 47
Greenways BS15: Kgswd 7E 50
Greenways Rd. BS37: Yate 3D 30
Greenwell La. BS40: L'frd 5E 110
Greenwich Apartments BS6: Redl 5J 47
(off Redland Ct. Rd.)
Greenwood Cl. BS7: Hor 1A 48
TA9: W Hunt 7E 158
Greenwood Dr. BS35: A'ton 1H 19
Greenwood Rd. BS4: Know 7C 62
BS22: Wor 2C 106
Gregory Ct. BS30: C Hth 3E 64
Gregory Mead BS49: Yat 2G 87
Gregorys Gro. BA2: Odd D 4K 121
Gregory St. BS5: Bar H 2D 62
Gregory's Tyning BS39: Paul 7C 140
Greinton BS24: W Mare 3J 127
Grenville Av. BS24: Lock 1E 128
Grenville Chapel BS8: Clftn 4F 61
(off Lit. Caroline Pl.)
Grenville Cl. BS5: St G 1H 63
Grenville Pl. BS1: Bris 4F 61
(off Brunel Lock Rd.)
Grenville Rd. BS6: Bris 5A 48
TA8: Bur S 1E 158
Greve Ct. BS30: Bar C 5D 64
Greville M. BS3: Bris 5H 61
Greville Rd. BS3: Bris 5H 61
Greville St. BS3: Bedm 5J 61
GREYFIELD 3A 140
Greyfield Comn. BS39: High L 3A 140
Greyfield Rd. BS39: High L 3A 140
Greyfield Vw. BS39: Temp C 4H 139
Greyfriars BS1: Bris 2E 4 (2K 61)
Grey Hollow BS40: E Harp 7K 137
Greyhound Wlk. BS1: Bris 3G 5
(within The Galleries)
Greylands Rd. BS13: Bis 3F 75
Greystoke Av. BS10: S'mead 7G 35
Greystoke Bus. Cen. BS20: P'head 4F 43
Greystoke Gdns. BS10: S'mead 7H 35
(not continuous)
Greystones BS16: Down 6C 38
Grib La. BS40: Blag 3D 134
Griffen Rd. BS24: W'ton V 5C 106
Griffin Cl. BS22: Wor 2E 106
Griffin Ct. BA1: Bath 5E 6
Griffin Rd. BS21: Clev 6D 54
Griggfield Wlk. BS14: H'gro 3B 76
Grimes La. BS1: Bris 4G 5 (3A 62)
Grimsbury Rd. BS15: Kgswd 1E 64
Grindell Rd. BS5: St G 2F 63
Grinfield Av. BS13: Hart 6J 75
Grist Ct. BA15: Brad A 6H 125
Grittleton Rd. BS7: Hor 7A 36
Grosvenor Bri. Rd. BA1: Bath 2E 100
Grosvenor Ct. BS6: Redl 7H 47
BS9: W Trym 1G 47
Grosvenor Pk. BA1: Bath 2E 100
Grosvenor Pl. BA1: Bath 2E 100
Grosvenor Rd. BS2: Bris 7B 48
Grosvenor Ter. BA1: Bath 1E 100
Grosvenor Vs. BA1: Bath 2D 100
Grove, The BA1: W'ton 2J 99
BS1: Bris 6E 4 (4K 61)
BS21: Clev 1B 68
BS25: Wins 4F 131
BS30: C Hth 5E 64
BS34: Pat 7D 26
BS37: Rang 5A 22
BS39: Hall 6K 139
BS40: Blag 3C 134
BS48: Wrax 6A 58
TA8: Bur S 6J 75
Grove Av. BS1: Bris 6F 5 (4K 61)
BS9: C Din 1C 46
BS16: Fish 4H 49
Grove Bank BS16: Fren 6A 38
Grove Ct. BS9: W Trym 3E 46
Grove Dr. BS22: W Mare 3A 106
Grove Ho. BA2: Bath 4J 7
BS8: Clftn 3G 61
(off Cornwallis Gro.)
Grove Ind. Est., The BS34: Pat 6D 26
Grove La. BA3: Faul 4J 155
BS23: W Mare 4F 105
SN14: Hin 2J 53
Grove Leaze BA15: Brad A 6F 125
BS11: Shire 2G 45
Grove Mews, The BS36: Wint 7C 28
TA8: Bur S 6D 156
Grove Orchard BS40: Blag 3C 134
Grove Pk. BS4: Brisl 7F 63
BS6: Redl 6J 47
Grove Pk. Av. BS4: Brisl 7F 63
Grove Pk. Ct. BS4: Brisl 7F 63
Grove Pk. Rd. BS4: Brisl 7F 63
BS23: W Mare 3F 105
Grove Pk. Ter. BS16: Fish 4H 49
Grove Rd. BS6: Redl 6G 47
BS9: C Din 7C 34
BS16: Fish, Stap 4G 49
BS22: W Mare 3A 106
BS23: W Mare 4F 105
BS29: Ban 1J 129
TA8: Bur S 7C 156
Groves, The BS13: Hart 6K 75
GROVESEND 5C 12
Grovesend Rd. BS35: Grov, T'bry 4A 12
BS35: T'bry 3K 11
Grove Sports Cen. 2F 71
Grove St. BA2: Bath 3G 7 (4C 100)
Grove Vw. BS16: H'ook 4A 38
BS16: Stap 2G 49
Grove Wood Rd. BA3: Hay 6J 153
Guardian Ct. BS8: Clftn 2F 61
(off Clifton Down)
Guernsey Av. BS4: Brisl 5H 63
Guest Av. BS16: Emer G 1F 51
Gug, The BS39: High L 3A 140
Guild Ct. BS1: Bris 6G 5 (3A 62)
Guildford Rd. BS4: St Ap 4G 63
Guildhall Market 4G 7 (5C 100)
Guillemot Rd. BS20: P'head 2H 43
Guinea La. BA1: Bath 2F 7 (4B 100)
BS16: Fish 3J 49
Guinea St. BS1: Bris 7F 5 (4K 61)
Gullen BA2: Shos, Ston L 1F 155
Gulliford Cl. TA9: Highb 4F 159
Gulliford's Bank BS21: Clev 2E 54
Gullimore Gdns. BS13: Hart 6H 75
Gullivers Pl. BS37: Chip S 6G 31
Gullock Tyning BA3: Mid N 5F 153
Gullons Cl. BS13: Bis 4G 75
Gullon Wlk. BS13: Withy 5F 75
Gully, The BS36: Wint 7D 28
Gullybrook La. BS5: Bar H 3D 62
Gumhurn La. BS35: Piln 5E 16
Gunning Cl. BS15: Kgswd 3B 64
Gunter's Hill BS5: St G 3J 63
Guthrie Rd. BS8: Clftn 1F 61
Gwilliam St. BS3: Wind H 6K 61
Gwyn St. BS2: Bris 7A 48
Gypsy La. BS16: Puck 5J 39
BS31: Key 3E 96
BS36: Henf 5J 39

H

Haberfield Hill BS8: Abb L 6J 45
Haberfield Ho. BS8: Clftn 3F 61
(off Hotwell Rd.)
HACKET, THE 3C 12
Hacket BS35: T'bry 3C 12
Hacket Hill BS35: T'bry 4D 12
Hacket La. BS35: Grov 5D 12
BS35: T'bry 3B 12
(not continuous)
Haddrell Ct. BS35: A'ton 7H 11
Hadley Ct. BS30: C Hth 3F 65
Hadley Rd. BA2: C Down 2D 122
Hadrian Cl. BS9: Stok B 4C 46
Hadrians Wlk. BS16: Emer G 2G 51
Hadwells Rd. BS34: Pat 7B 26
Hafner Grn. BS24: W Mare 1A 128
Ha Ha, The BA2: Tims 3E 140
Haig Cl. BS9: Sea M 1B 46
Halbrow Cres. BS16: Fish 3A 50
Haldon Cl. BS3: Wind H 1K 75
Hale Cl. BS15: Han 5B 64
HALE COOMBE 7H 131
Hales Horn Cl. BS32: Brad S 1F 37
Half Acre Cl. BS14: Whit 7C 76
Half Acre La. BS14: Whit 7D 76
Half Yd. BS40: L'frd 5E 110
Halifax Rd. BS37: Yate 2D 30
Hallam Rd. BS21: Clev 5C 54
Hallards Cl. BS11: Law W 7K 33
HALLATROW 6K 139
Hallatrow Bus. Pk. BS39: Hall 7J 139
Hallatrow Hill BS39: High L 5A 140
Hallatrow Rd. BS39: Hall, Paul 6K 139
HALLEN 3C 34
Hallen Cl. BS10: Hen 4D 34
BS16: Emer G 2G 51
HALL END 3D 22
Hall End La. GL12: H End 4C 22
Hallen Dr. BS9: Sea M 1C 46
Hallen Ind. Est. BS10: H'len 7A 24
Hallen Rd. BS10: H'len, Hen 3C 34
Halletts Way BS20: P'head 3F 43
Halliwell Rd. BS20: P'head 4A 42
Hall La. BA1: L Ham, Tad 7H 67
Halls Gdn. BS34: Stok G 3J 37
Halls Rd. BS15: Kgswd 1B 64
Hall St. BS3: Bedm 7H 61
Hall Ter. TA8: Bur S 7C 156
Halsbury Rd. BS6: Henle, Redl 4H 47
Halstock Av. BS16: Fish 5H 49
Halston Dr. BS2: Bris 1B 62
Halswell Gdns. BS13: Hart 6H 75
Halswell Rd. BS21: Clev 1D 68
Halt End BS14: Whit 7E 76
Halwyn Cl. BS9: Stok B 3D 46
Halyard Way BS20: P'head 1H 43
HAM
BS39 . . . . . 1D 152
TA9 . . . . . 3G 157
Hamble Cl. BS35: T'bry 4A 12
Hambledon Rd. BS22: St G 7G 85
HAMBROOK 5A 38
Hambrook La. BS16: H'ook 4H 37
BS34: Stok G 4H 37
Ham Cl. BS39: Temp C 4H 139
Ham Farm La. BS16: Emer G 2F 51
Ham Gdns. BA1: Bath 5G 7 (5C 100)
BA3: Mid N 5F 153
HAM GREEN 5H 45
Ham Grn. BS20: Pill 4H 45
Ham Gro. BS39: Paul 1C 152
Ham Hill BA3: Rads 3K 153
Hamilton Ct. BS1: Bris 1F 5
Hamilton Ho. BA1: L'dwn 7K 81
Hamilton Lodge BS2: Bris 1F 5
(off Dighton St.)
Hamilton Rd. BA1: Bath 1A 100
BS3: Bris 5H 61
BS5: E'ton 1D 62
BS23: W Mare 3E 104
Hamilton Ter. BA2: Shos 1F 155
Hamilton Way BS14: Whit 7F 77
Ham La. BS16: Bmhll 2G 49
(not continuous)
BS21: Kings S 1J 85
BS30: Doy 7E 52
BS39: Bis S 7J 115
BS39: Paul 1C 152
BS41: Dun 7D 74
BS48: Wrax 5J 57
BS49: Yat 7F 69
TA8: Bur S 2D 158
Hamlet, The BS48: Nail 6J 57
Ham Link BS40: Burr 2H 133
Hammersmith Rd. BS5: St G 1F 63
Hammond Apartments BS7: Bishop 4B 48

Hammond Cl.—Henfield Bus. Pk.

Hammond Cl. BS4: Brisl 1F 77
Hammond Gdns. BS9: W Trym 1E 46
Hammond Rd. BS34: Pat 7B 26
Hampden Cl. BS37: Yate 2D 30
Hampden Rd. BS4: Know 6D 62
BS22: Wor 2C 106
Hampshire Way BS37: Yate 2F 31
Hampstead Rd. BS4: Brisl 6E 62
Hampton Cl. BS30: C Hth 4E 64
Hampton Cnr. BS11: Shire 2J 45
Hampton Ct. BS6: Redl 7H 47
Hampton Ho. BA1: Bath 2E 100
Hampton La. BS6: Cot 7H 47
Hampton Pk. BS6: Redl 7H 47
Hampton Rd. BS6: Cot, Redl 6H 47
Hampton Row BA2: Bath 1K 7 (3D 100)
Hampton St. BS15: Kgswd 7B 50
Hampton Vw. BA1: Bath 2D 100
Ham Rd. TA8: Berr 2D 144
TA9: Bre K 3F 157
Hams La. BS26: Lox 3G 147
Hamwood Cl. BS24: W Mare 3K 127
Hanbury Cl. BS15: Han 4B 64
Hanbury Ct. BS8: Clftn 1G 61
Hanbury Rd. BS8: Clftn 1A 4 (1G 61)
Handel Av. BS5: St G 2F 63
Handel Cossham Ct. BS15: Kgswd 7A 50
Handel Rd. BS31: Key 5B 78
Handford Way BS30: Long G 6F 65
Hanford Ct. BS14: Stoc 3F 77
Hangar Way BS14: H'gro 5B 76
Hang Hill BA2: Shos, Ston L 7E 142
Hangstone Wlk. BS21: Clev 6C 54
HANHAM 4A 64
Hanham Bus. Pk. BS15: Han 5K 63
HANHAM GREEN 6K 63
Hanham La. BS39: Paul 6D 140
Hanham Mills BS15: Han 1B 78
Hanham Mt. BS15: Kgswd 3B 64
Hanham Rd. BS15: Kgswd 3B 64
Hanham Way BS48: Nail 7D 56
Hanna Cl. BA2: Bath 5G 99
Hannah Dr. BS24: Lock 7G 107
Hannah More Cl. BS27: Ched 7D 150
BS40: Wrin 2G 111
Hannah More Ct. BS27: Ched 6D 150
Hannah More Rd. BS48: Nail 1E 70
Hannay Rd. BS27: Ched 5C 150
Hannover Quay BS1: Bris 6C 4
Hanny's La. BS40: Chew M 1J 115
Hanover Cl. BS22: Wor 7E 84
Hanover Ct. BA1: Bath 2D 100
BA3: Writ .4B 154
BS1: Bris 2H 5 (1A 62)
BS34: Fil 4C 36
Hanover Ho. BS2: Bris 2C 62
Hanover La. BS8: Clftn 3A 4 (2H 61)
Hanover Pl. *BA1: Bath 3D 100*
(off London Rd.)
BS1: Bris 7B 4 (4H 61)
Hanover St. BA1: Bath 2D 100
BS1: Bris 4E 4
BS5: Redf 2E 62
Hanover Ter. *BA1: Bath 2D 100*
(off Gillingham Ter.)
Hansford Cl. BA2: C Down 3A 122
Hansford M. BA2: C Down 3B 122
Hansford Sq. BA2: C Down 3A 122
Hansons Way BS21: Clev 7C 54
Hans Price Cl. BS23: W Mare 4G 105
Hans Price Sports Cen. 7H 105
Hantone Hill BA2: Batham 3H 101
Hapgood St. BS5: Bar H 2D 62
Hapil Cl. BS25: Sandf 1F 131
Happerton La. BS20: Eas 6G 45
Happy La. BS7: Bishop, Bris 5B 48
Hapsburg Cl. BS22: Wor 7E 84
Harbour Ct. BS1: Bris 5C 4
Harbour Cres. BS20: P'head 3G 43
Harbour Ho. *BS8: Clftn 6A 4*
(off Hotwell Rd.)
Harbourne Cl. TA8: Bur S 7E 156
Harbour Rd. BS20: P'head 2F 43
Harbour Rd. Trad. Est. BS20: P'head 2G 43
Harbour's Edge BS8: Clftn 5B 4 (3H 61)
Harbourside Wlk. BS1: Bris 6B 4
Harbour Wlk. BS1: Bris 7C 4
Harbour Wall BS9: Sea M 4C 46
Harbour Way BS1: Bris 6C 4 (4J 61)
Harbury Rd. BS9: Henle 1J 47
Harbutts BA2: Batham 2H 101
Harcombe Hill BS36: Wint D 3C 38
Harcombe Rd. BS36: Wint 2B 38
Harcourt Av. BS5: St G 3J 63
Harcourt Cl. BS31: Salt 1J 97
Harcourt Gdns. BA1: W'ton 1H 99
Harcourt Hill BS6: Redl 5J 47
Harcourt Rd. BS6: Redl 4H 47
Hardenhuish Rd. BS4: Brisl 4F 63
Harden Rd. BS14: Stoc 5G 77
Harding Pl. BS31: Key 5F 79
Harding Rd. BS34: H'ook 5H 37
Hardings Ter. *BS5: St G 1H 63*
(off Clovelly Rd.)
Hardington Dr. BS31: Key 1E 96
Hardwick BS37: Yate 7C 30
Hardwick Cl. BS4: Brisl 6G 63
BS30: Old C 4H 65
Hardwick Rd. BS20: Pill 3G 45
Hardy Av. BS3: Ash G 5G 61
Hardy Ct. BS30: Bar C 4D 64
Hardy La. BS32: Toc 5B 18
Hardy Rd. BS3: Bedm 7H 61
Hareclive Rd. BS13: Hart 5H 75
Harefield Cl. BS15: Han 7A 64
Hare Knapp BA15: Brad A 6F 125
Harescombe BS37: Yate 7E 30
Harewood Rd. BS5: S'wll 7J 49
Harford Cl. BS9: C Din 1C 46
Harford Dr. BS16: Fren 6A 38
Harford Sq. BS40: Chew M 1H 115
Harington Ct. BA2: New L 6B 98
Harington Pl. BA1: Bath 4F 7 (5B 100)
Harlech Cl. BS31: Key 6A 78
Harlech Way BS30: Will 7F 65
Harlequin Office Pk. BS16: Emer G 5E 38
Harleston St. BS5: E'ton 1K 5 (1C 62)
Harley Ct. BS8: Clftn 2F 61
Harley La. BS21: Clev 3J 55
Harley M. BS8: Clftn 2F 61
Harley Pl. BS8: Clftn 2F 61
Harley St. BA1: Bath 1E 6 (3B 100)
Harmer Cl. BS10: Hen 4F 35
Harmony Dr. BS20: P'head 4B 42
Harnhill Cl. BS13: Hart 6H 75
Harolds Way BS15: Kgswd 3A 64
Harper Ho. BS6: Redl 6G 47
Harp Rd. TA9: Bre K 7K 157
Harptree BS24: W Mare 3J 127
Harptree Cl. BS48: Nail 2F 71
Harptree Ct. BS30: Bar C 5E 64
Harptree Gro. BS3: Bedm 7H 61
Harptree Hill BS40: W Har 7B 136
Harratz Pl. BS1: Bris 5J 5 (3B 62)
Harrier Path BS22: Wor 4C 106
Harriet's Yd. BS31: Key 5C 78
Harrington Av. BS14: Stoc 4G 77
Harrington Cl. BS30: Bit 2J 79
Harrington Gro. BS14: Stoc 4G 77
Harrington Rd. BS14: Stoc 5F 77
Harrington Wlk. BS14: Stoc 4G 77
Harris Barton BS36: Fram C 7F 29
Harris Ct. *BA1: Bath 6G 7*
(off Newark St.)
BS30: Long G 5D 64
Harris Gro. BS13: Hart 7H 75
Harris Ho. BS5: Bar H 2E 62
Harris La. BS8: Abb L 1K 59
Harrison Cl. BS16: Emer G 2F 51
Harrowdene Rd. BS4: Know 6D 62
Harrow Rd. BS4: Brisl 6F 63
HARRY STOKE 5G 37
Harry Stoke Rd. BS34: Stok G 5G 37
HARTCLIFFE .6J 75
Hartcliffe Rd. BS4: Know 2A 76
Hartcliffe Wlk. BS4: Know 2B 76
Hartcliffe Way BS3: Bedm 1J 75
BS13: Bis 1J 75
BS13: Hart .5K 75
Hart Cl. BS20: Pill 4J 45
Hartfield Av. BS6: Cot 7J 47
Hartgill Cl. BS13: Hart 7H 75
Hartington Pk. BS6: Redl 6H 47
Hartland BS22: Wor 2E 106
HARTLEY 4C 124
Hartley Cl. BS37: Chip S 5J 31
Harts Cft. BS37: Yate 2F 31
Hart's La. BS39: Hall 6J 139
Harts Paddock BA3: Mid N 3D 152
Harvest Cl. BS32: Brad S 5F 27
Harvest La. BS22: W Wick 4F 107
Harvest Ri. BS26: Axb 5J 149
Harvest Way BS22: Wor 6E 84
Harvey Cl. BS22: Wor 7E 84
Harvey's La. BS5: St G 1H 63
Harwood Grn. BS22: Kew 1C 106
Harwood Ho. BS5: Bar H 2D 62
Harwood Sq. BS7: Hor 3A 48
Haselbury Gro. BS31: Salt 1J 97
Haskins Ct. BS30: Bar C 5E 64
Haslands BS48: Nail 2F 71
Haslemere Ind. Est. BS11: A'mth 5G 33
Hassage Hill BA2: Well 5K 143
Hassell Dr. BS2: Bris 2C 62
Hastings Cl. BS3: Bedm 1J 75
Hastings Rd. BS3: Bedm 1J 75
Hatcher Cl. TA8: Bur S 3F 159
Hatches La. BS24: E Rols 2A 108
BS24: Lym 3F 145
Hatchet La. BS34: Stok G 3G 37
Hatchet Rd. BS34: Stok G 2F 37
Hatchmere BS35: T'bry 4B 12
Hatfield Bldgs. BA2: Bath 7J 7 (6D 100)
Hatfield Rd. BA2: Bath 1A 122
BS23: W Mare 4J 105
Hathaway Ho. *BS2: Bris 1K 61*
(off Dove St. Sth.)
Hatherley BS37: Yate 7E 30
Hatherley Rd. BS7: Bishop 4A 48
Hathway Wlk. BS5: E'ton 1C 62
Hatters Cl. BS36: Wint 7C 28
Hatters La. BS37: Chip S 5H 31
Hatton Rd. BS16: L'lze 7E 36
HAUGH 3C 124
Havage Cl. TA9: Highb 3G 159
Havage Drove BS24: E Rols 4C 108
Haven, The BS15: Kgswd 7C 50
Haven Vw. BS20: P'head 3G 43
Haversham Cl. BS22: W Mare 3B 106
Haverstock Rd. BS4: Wind H 6C 62
Haviland Gro. BA1: W'ton 7G 81
Haviland Ho. BS2: Bris 2K 5
Haviland Pk. BA1: W'ton 1H 99
Havory BA1: Bath 2E 100
Havyatt Bus. Pk. BS40: Wrin 3G 111
HAVYATT GREEN 6G 111
Havyatt Rd. BS40: L'frd, Wrin 4G 111
Havyatt Trad. Est. BS40: Wrin 3G 111
Hawarden Ter. BA1: Bath 2D 100
Hawburn Cl. BS4: Brisl 7F 63
Haweswater BS10: S'mead 5H 35
Haweswater Cl. BS30: Old C 3H 65
Hawke Rd. BS22: Kew 7C 84
Hawkesbury Rd. BS16: Fish 5G 49
Hawkesley Dr. BS34: Lit S 1F 37
(not continuous)
Hawkesworth Rd. BS37: Yate 3C 30
Hawkfield Bus. Pk. BS14: Hart 5K 75
Hawkfield Cl. BS14: Hart 5K 75
Hawkfield Rd. BS13: Hart 5K 75
Hawkfield Way BS14: Hart 5K 75
Hawkins Cl. BS30: Old C 5G 65
TA8: Bur S .1E 158
Hawkins Cres. BS32: Brad S 6F 27
Hawkins La. BS1: Bris 4G 5 (3A 62)
Hawkins St. BS2: Bris 3J 5 (2B 62)
Hawkley Dr. BS32: Brad S 3F 27
Hawkridge Dr. BS16: Puck 3C 52
Hawksmoor Cl. BS14: H'gro 4C 76
Hawksmoor La. BS16: Stap 7G 37
Hawksworth Dr. BS15: Han 4K 63
BS22: Wor 7G 85
Haw La. BS32: Old D 3C 18
BS35: Olv 3C 18
Hawleys La. GL12: Crom 3C 14
Hawley Way TA8: Bur S 1E 158
Hawthorn Av. BS15: Han 4K 63
Hawthorn Cl. BS16: Puck 3C 52
BS20: P'head 3B 42
BS34: Pat 6A 26
Hawthorn Coombe BS22: Wor 1B 106
Hawthorn Ct. BS31: Key 5C 78
Hawthorn Cres. BS35: T'bry 2A 12
BS49: Yat 2G 87
Hawthorne Gdns. BS16: Stap H 4D 50
Hawthorne Ri. BS10: Bren 4J 35
Hawthornes, The BS16: Stap H 4D 50
Hawthorne St. BS4: Wind H 6C 62
Hawthorn Gdns. BS22: Wor 2B 106
Hawthorn Gro. BA2: C Down 3B 122
Hawthorn Hgts. BS22: Wor 1B 106
Hawthorn Hill BS22: Wor 2B 106
Hawthorn Ho. BS5: St G 1G 63
Hawthorn La. BS22: St G 2G 107
Hawthorn Pk. BS22: Wor 1C 106
Hawthorn Rd. BA3: Rads 4B 154
Hawthorns, The BS8: Clftn 1C 4 (1J 61)
BS21: Clev .6C 54
Hawthorns La. BS31: Key 5C 78
Hawthorn Way BS16: Emer G 7G 39
BS34: Stok G 2G 37
BS48: Nail .7H 57
Hayboro Way BS39: Paul 2C 152
Haycombe BS14: H'gro 4B 76
Haycombe Crematorium
BA2: Bath 7F 99
Haycombe Dr. BA2: Bath 6G 99
Haycombe La. BA2: Eng 1F 121
Haycroft Rd. BS34: Fil 4B 36
Hayden Cl. BA2: Bath 7D 6 (6A 100)
Haydock Cl. BS16: Down 6D 38
HAYDON 6K 153
Haydon Gdns. BS7: L'lze 3D 48
Haydon Ga. BA3: Hay 6K 153
Haydon Hill BA3: Hay 6K 153
Haydon Ind. Est. BA3: Hay 6K 153
Hayeley Dr. BS32: Brad S 1G 37
Hayes, The BS27: Ched 7D 150
Hayes Cl. BS2: Bris 2C 62
Hayes Ct. BS34: Pat 7D 26
Hayesfield Pk. BA2: Bath 7D 6 (6B 100)
HAYES PARK 4D 152
Hayes Pk. Rd. BA3: Mid N 4D 152
Hayes Pl. BA2: Bath 7E 6 (7B 100)
Hayes Rd. BA3: Mid N 4D 152
Hayes Way BS34: Pat 1B 36
Hayeswood Rd. BA2: Tims 1B 140
Hay Field La. BS7: Hor 1C 48
Hayfield La. BS6: Cot 7J 47
Haygarth Ct. BA1: Bath 1F 7 (3B 100)
Hay Hill BA1: Bath 2F 7 (4B 100)
Hay La. BS40: Winf 5H 91
Hay Leaze BS37: Yate 2D 30
Hayleigh BS3: Bedm 6H 61
Hayleigh Ho. BS13: Hart 6J 75
Haymans Ct. *BS15: Kgswd 6A 50*
(off Cherrytree Cres.)
Haymarket, The BS1: Bris 2F 5 (2K 61)
Haymarket Wlk. *BS1: Bris 1F 5*
(off Cannon St.)
Haynes La. BS16: Stap H 3B 50
Haythorne Ct. *BS16: Fish 5G 49*
(off Marina Gdns.)
BS16: Stap H 3D 50
Haytor Pk. BS9: C Din 2D 46
Hayward Av. BS24: W Wick 4F 107
Hayward Cl. BS21: Clev 1C 68
Hayward Ind. Est. BS16: Soun 5B 50
Hayward Rd. BS5: Redf 2E 62
BS16: Stap H 4B 50
Haywood Cl. BS24: W Mare 4J 127
Haywood Gdns. BS24: W Mare 4J 127
Hazel Av. BS6: Redl 6H 47
Hazel Barrow BS40: Comp M 6A 136
Hazel Brook Gdns. BS10: Hen 2G 35
Hazelbury Cl. BS48: Nail 7G 57
Hazelbury Dr. BS30: Old C 4G 65
Hazelbury Rd. BS14: H'gro 2E 76
BS48: Nail .1F 71
Hazel Cl. BS37: Yate 1F 31
Hazel Cote Rd. BS14: Whit 6D 76
Hazel Cres. BS35: T'bry 3B 12
Hazeldene Rd. BS23: W Mare 4J 105
BS34: Pat 7C 26
Hazel Gdns. BS35: A'ton 1H 19
Hazel Gro. BA2: Bath 7K 99
BA3: Mid N 6F 153
BS7: Hor 7C 36
Hazelgrove BS36: Wint 2B 38
Hazel La. BS32: A'ton 2F 19
BS35: A'ton, Rudg 2F 19
Hazell Cl. BS21: Clev 1E 68
Hazel Ter. BA3: Mid N 6F 153
Hazelton Rd. BS7: Bishop 5K 47
Hazel Way BA2: Odd D 4K 121
Hazelwood Cl. BS16: Stap H 3D 50
Hazelwood Ct. BS9: Stok B 5D 46
Hazelwood Rd. BS9: Stok B 5D 46
Hazleton Gdns. BA2: C'ton D 1H 123
Head Cft. BS48: Flax B 2F 73
Headford Av. BS5: St G 2K 63
Headford Rd. BS4: Know 1K 75
Headington Cl. BS15: Han 5B 64
Headland, The NP16: Bul 1A 8
Headley Ct. BS13: Bis 4H 75
Headley La. BS13: Bis 4G 75
HEADLEY PARK 3H 75
Headley Pk. Av. BS13: Bis 4H 75
Headley Pk. Rd. BS13: Bis 3G 75
Headley Rd. BS13: Bis 4G 75
Headley Wlk. BS13: Bis 3H 75
Heal Cl. TA8: Bur S 3F 159
Healey Dr. SN14: Hin 2J 53
Heart Meers BS14: H'gro 5D 76
Heath Cl. BS36: Wint 1C 38
Heathcote Dr. BS36: Coal H 7H 29
Heathcote La. *BS36: Coal H 7H 29*
(off Boundary Rd.)
Heathcote Rd. BS16: Fish 6K 49
BS16: Stap H 3C 50
Heathcote Wlk. BS16: Fish 6A 50
Heath Ct. BS16: Down 1B 50
HEATH END 4B 14
Heather Av. BS36: Fram C 1F 39
Heather Cl. BS15: Kgswd 1K 63
Heatherdene BS14: H'gro 3B 76
Heather Dr. BA2: Odd D 4K 121
Heathfield Cl. BA1: W'ton 7G 81
BS31: Key 5A 78
Heathfield Cres. BS14: Whit 6C 76
Heathfield Rd. BS48: Nail 7G 57
Heathfields BS16: Down 7B 38
Heathfield Way BS48: Nail 7G 57
Heath Gdns. BS16: Down 7B 38
BS36: Coal H 1G 39
Heathgate BS49: Yat 3H 87
Heath Gates *BS48: Nail 7H 57*
(off Heath Rd.)
Heathgates BS23: W Mare 1F 127
Heath Ho. La. BS16: Stap 4D 48
Heath M. BA3: Rads 4A 154
Heath Ridge BS41: L Ash 7A 60
Heath Ri. BS30: C Hth 4F 65
Heath Rd. BS5: Eastv 5D 48
BS15: Han 5K 63
BS16: Down .1B 50
BS48: Nail .6H 57
(not continuous)
Heath St. BS5: Eastv 5E 48
Heath Wlk. BS16: Down 1B 50
Heber St. BS5: Redf 2E 62
Hebron Rd. BS3: Bedm 6J 61
Hector Cl. BS24: Lock 1H 129
Hedge Cl. BS22: W Wick 3F 107
Hedgemead Cl. BS16: Stap 3F 49
Hedgemead Ct. BA1: Bath 1G 7
Hedgemead Vw. BS16: Stap 3G 49
Hedgerows, The BS32: Brad S 5F 27
Hedgers Cl. BS3: Bedm 7G 61
Hedges, The BS22: St G 2G 107
Hedges Cl. BS21: Clev 1B 68
Hedwick Av. BS5: St G 2G 63
Hedwick St. BS5: St G 2G 63
Heggard Cl. BS13: Bis 5G 75
Helens Rd. BS25: Sandf 1H 131
Helicopter Mus., The 7C 106
Heligan Wlk. BS24: W'ton V 5C 106
Hellier Wlk. BS13: Hart 7J 75
Helston Rd. BS48: Nail 1J 71
HEMINGTON 7H 155
Hemmings Pde. BS5: Bar H 2D 62
Hemming Way BS24: Hut 2C 128
Hemplow Cl. BS14: Stoc 3F 77
Hempton Fld. Dr. BS34: Pat 7C 26
Hempton La. BS32: Alm 4C 26
Henacre Rd. BS11: Law W 7K 33
HENBURY 5E 34
Henbury Ct. BS10: Hen 4E 34
Henbury Gdns. BS10: Hen 5E 34
Henbury Hill BS9: W Trym 7F 35
Henbury Leisure Cen. 4E 34
Henbury Rd. BS9: W Trym 7F 35
BS10: Hen 5E 34
BS15: Han 4K 63
Hencliffe Rd. BS14: Stoc 3F 77
Hencliffe Way BS15: Han 6K 63
Hencliffe Wood 7K 63
Henderson Rd. BS15: Han 4K 63
Hendon Cl. TA9: Highb 3G 159
Hendre Rd. BS3: Bedm 7G 61
HENFIELD 4H 39
Henfield Bus. Pk. BS36: Henf 5H 39

Henfield Cres.—Holcombe Gro.

Henfield Cres. BS30: Old C 5F 65
Henfield Rd. BS36: Coal H, Henf 3G 39
Hengaston St. BS3: Bedm 7H 61
HENGROVE 4D 76
Hengrove Av. BS14: H'gro 2D 76
Hengrove Farm La. BS14: H'gro 2C 76
Hengrove La. BS14: H'gro 2C 76
Hengrove Leisure Pk. BS14: H'gro 4A 76
Hengrove Pk. Leisure Cen. 5A 76
Hengrove Promenade BS14: H'gro 5A 76
Hengrove Rd. BS4: Know 7C 62
Hengrove Way BS13: Bis 4H 75
BS14: H'gro 4K 75
HENLEAZE 2H 47
Henleaze Av. BS9: Henle 3G 47
Henleaze Gdns. BS9: Henle 3G 47
Henleaze Pk. BS9: Henle 3J 47
Henleaze Pk. Dr. BS9: Henle 2H 47
Henleaze Rd. BS9: Henle 3G 47
Henleaze Ter. BS9: Henle 1H 47
Henley Gro. BS9: Henle 3H 47
Henley La. BS49: Yat 4K 87
SN13: Kgdn 1F 103
Henley Lodge BS49: Yat 4K 87
Henley Pk. BS49: Yat 4J 87
Henley Vw. BA2: Well 4K 143
Hennessy Cl. BS14: Whit 7B 76
Henrietta Ct. BA2: Bath 1H 7 (3C 100)
Henrietta Gdns. BA2: Bath 2H 7 (4C 100)
Henrietta M. BA2: Bath 3H 7 (4C 100)
Henrietta Pl. BA2: Bath 3G 7 (4C 100)
Henrietta Rd. BA2: Bath 2H 7 (4C 100)
Henrietta St. BA2: Bath 3H 7 (4C 100)
BS2: Bris 1D 4 (1J 61)
BS5: E'ton 7D 48
Henrietta Vs. BA2: Bath 2H 7 (4C 100)
Henry Butt Ho. BS23: W Mare 4G 105
(off Boulevard)
Henry Ho. BS13: Withy 6F 75
Henry St. BA1: Bath 5G 7 (5C 100)
BS3: Wind H 5B 62
Henry Williamson Ct. BS30: Bar C 4D 64
Henshaw Cl. BS15: Kgswd 6A 50
Henshaw Rd. BS15: Kgswd 6A 50
Henshaw Wlk. BS15: Kgswd 6A 50
Hensley Gdns. BA2: Bath 7A 100
Hensley Rd. BA2: Bath 7A 100
Hensman's Hill BS8: Clftn 3G 61
Hepburn Rd. BS2: Bris 1A 62
Herald Cl. BS9: Stok B 3D 46
Herapath St. BS5: Bar H 3E 62
Herbert Cres. BS5: Eastv 5F 49
Herbert Rd. BA2: Bath 7A 6 (6K 99)
BS21: Clev 5D 54
TA8: Bur S 7C 156
Herbert St. BS3: Bedm 5J 61
(not continuous)
BS5: W'hall 1E 62
Hercules Cl. BS34: Lit S 1F 37
Hereford Rd. BS2: Bris 6C 48
Hereford St. BS3: Bedm 6K 61
Heritage, The BA2: Cam 5J 141
Heritage Cl. BA2: Pea J 5D 142
Herkomer Cl. BS7: L'lze 1D 48
Herluin Way BS22: W Mare 5B 106
BS23: W Mare 6J 105
Hermes Cl. BS31: Salt 1H 97
Hermitage Cl. BS11: Shire 1J 45
Hermitage Rd. BA1: Bath 2A 100
BS16: Stap H 3B 50
Hermitage Wood Rd. BS16: L'lze 7E 36
Hern La. BS48: Bar G 5J 73
Heron Cl. BS22: W Mare 3C 106
Heron Gdns. BS20: P'head 4G 43
Heron Pk. TA8: Berr 7A 144
Heron Rd. BS5: E'ton 7D 48
HERONS GREEN 2C 136
Heron Way BS37: Chip S 7F 31
Herridge Cl. BS13: Hart 6H 75
Herridge Rd. BS13: Hart 6H 75
Herschel Mus. of Astronomy, The 4E 6 (5B 100)
Herschel Pl. BA2: Bath 2J 7 (4C 100)
Herschel Ter. BA2: Bath 4C 6
Hersey Gdns. BS13: Withy 7E 74
Hesding Cl. BS15: Han 6A 64
Hestercombe Cl. BS24: W'ton V 5C 106
Hestercombe Rd. BS13: Bis 4H 75
Hester Wood BS37: Yate 2F 31
Hetling Ct. BA1: Bath 5F 7 (5B 100)
HEWISH 6B 86
Hewlands Ct. BS11: Law W 5C 34
Hexagon, The BA2: Odd D 3A 122
Heyford Av. BS5: Eastv 4D 48
Heyron Wlk. BS13: Hart 6H 75
Heywood Rd. BS20: Pill 4G 45
Heywood Ter. BS20: Pill 4G 45
Hiatt Baker Hall BS9: Stok B 4F 47
Hicking Ct. BS15: Kgswd 7B 50
Hickory La. BS32: Alm 1F 27
Hicks Av. BS16: Emer G 7F 39
Hick's Barton BS5: St G 1H 63
HICKS COMMON 1D 38
Hicks Comn. Rd. BS36: Wint 3C 38
Hicks Ct. BS5: St G 1H 63
BS30: Long G 5D 64
HICKS GATE 2K 77
Hicks Ga. Ho. BS31: Key 2K 77
Hidcote M. BS24: W'ton V 5C 106
Hide Mkt. BS2: Bris 3K 5 (2B 62)
High Acre BS39: Paul 2D 152
Higham St. BS4: Wind H 5B 62
High Bannerdown BA1: Bathe 6K 83
HIGHBRIDGE 5G 159
Highbridge & Burnham Station (Rail) 5G 159
Highbridge Quay TA9: Highb 5F 159
Highbridge Rd. TA8: Bur S 2D 158
Highburn Cl. TA8: Bur S 4E 158
Highbury Farm Bus. Pk. BS39: Hall 5J 139
Highbury Pde. BS23: W Mare 3E 104
Highbury Pl. BA1: Bath 2C 100
Highbury Rd. BS3: Bedm 1J 75
BS7: Hor 1B 48
BS23: W Mare 3E 104
BS39: Hall 5K 139
Highbury Ter. BA1: Bath 2C 100
Highbury Vw. BS39: Temp C 4H 139
Highbury Vs. *BA1: Bath* 2C 100
(off Highbury Pl.)
BS2: Bris 1C 4 (1J 61)
High Corner BS10: Hen 6F 35
High Cft. BS30: Old C 3G 65
Highcroft Ct. BS40: Blag 3C 134
Highdale Av. BS21: Clev 6D 54
Highdale Cl. BS14: Whit 6D 76
Highdale Rd. BS21: Clev 6D 54
High Elm BS15: Kgswd 3C 64
High Energy Fitness Studio 5F 153
Highett Dr. BS5: E'ton 7C 48
Highfield Av. BS15: Han 4B 64
Highfield Cl. BA2: Bath 6H 99
Highfield Dr. BS20: P'head 5A 42
Highfield Gdns. BS30: Bit 7G 65
Highfield Gro. BS7: Hor 3K 47
Highfield La. BS40: Comp M 7A 136
Highfield Rd. BA2: Pea J 5C 142
BA15: Brad A 5H 125
BS24: W Mare 4J 127
BS31: Key 1D 96
BS37: Chip S 5G 31
Highfields BA3: Rads 4H 153
BS39: Stan D 3B 116
Highfields Cl. BS34: Stok G 4H 37
Highgate BA2: Bath 4B 6 (5A 100)
High Gro. BS9: Sea M 2B 46
Highgrove St. BS4: Wind H 5C 62
Highgrove Wlk. BS24: W'ton V 4E 106
High Kingsdown BS2: Bris 1D 4 (1J 61)
Highland Cl. BS22: W Mare 2K 105
Highland Cres. BS8: Clftn 6G 47
Highland Pl. BS8: Clftn 6G 47
Highland Rd. BA2: Bath 6H 99
Highlands La. BS24: W'ton V 4E 106
Highland Sq. BS8: Clftn 6G 47
Highlands Rd. BS20: P'head 3D 42
BS41: L Ash 7A 60
Highland Ter. BA2: Bath 5A 6 (5K 99)
High La. BS36: Wint 6A 28
(not continuous)
High Leaze Rd. BS34: Pat 7B 26
Highleaze Rd. BS30: Old C 5G 65
HIGH LITTLETON 4B 140
Highmead Gdns. BS13: Withy 6E 74
BS39: Bis S 2K 137
High Mdws. BA3: Mid N 5D 152
Highmore Ct. BS7: L'lze 1D 48
Highmore Gdns. BS7: L'lze 1E 48
Highnam Cl. BS34: Pat 5D 26
High Pk. BS14: H'gro 1D 76
BS39: Paul 7B 140
Highpoint Ho. *BS15: Kgswd* 7A 50
(off Lodge Rd.)
HIGHRIDGE
BS13 5E 74
BS41 6D 74
Highridge Ct. BS13: Bis 3F 75
Highridge Cres. BS13: Bis 5F 75
Highridge Grn. BS13: Bis 3E 74
Highridge Pk. BS13: Bis 4F 75
Highridge Rd. BS3: Bedm 7H 61
BS13: Bis, Withy 6E 74
BS41: Dun 7C 74
Highridge Wlk. BS13: Bis 3E 74
High St. BA1: Bath 4G 7 (5C 100)
BA1: Bathe 7H 83
BA1: Bathf 1A 102
BA1: W'ton 1H 99
BA1: Wool 4B 82
BA2: Bath 5G 99
BA2: Batham 2H 101
BA2: F'frd 7K 123
BA2: Tims 3F 141
BA2: Well 4K 143
BA3: Mid N 5E 152
BS1: Bris 3F 5 (2K 61)
BS5: E'ton 7D 48
BS8: Clftn 6G 47
BS9: W Trym 1G 47
BS11: Shire 1H 45
BS15: Han 4A 64
BS15: Kgswd 1C 64
BS15: Warm 1F 65
BS16: Stap H 4A 50
BS20: P'bry 5B 44
BS20: P'head 4F 43
BS22: Wor 3C 106
BS23: W Mare 4F 105
(not continuous)
BS26: Axb 4H 149
BS29: Ban 3J 129
BS30: Bit 2J 79
BS30: Doy 7F 53
BS30: Old C 6G 65
BS30: Wick 3C 66
High St. BS31: Key 4C 78
BS31: Salt 7J 79
BS35: T'bry 4K 11
BS36: Wint 1B 38
BS37: Chip S 5H 31
BS37: Iron A 2H 29
BS39: High L 4A 140
BS39: Paul 7C 140
(not continuous)
BS39: Pens 7F 95
BS40: Blag 2B 134
BS40: Chew M 1G 115
BS40: E Harp 6K 137
BS40: Winf 4K 91
BS40: Wrin 1F 111
BS48: Nail 7G 57
BS49: C'ham 2B 88
BS49: Cong 7K 87
BS49: Yat 2H 87
GL12: Wickw 6G 15
TA8: Bur S 2C 158
High Vw. BS20: P'head 4C 42
Highview BA2: Bath 7D 6 (6A 100)
Highview Rd. BS15: Soun 6C 50
Highwall La. BS31: Q Char 2H 95
Highway BS37: Yate 4F 31
Highwood La. BS10: Pat 7H 25
Highwood Pk. BS34: Pat 1A 36
Highwood Rd. BS34: Pat 1A 36
Highworth Cres. BS37: Yate 6D 30
Highworth Rd. BS4: St Ap 4F 63
Hilcot Gro. BS22: W Mare 3K 105
Hildesheim Bri. BS23: W Mare 5G 105
Hildesheim Cl. BS23: W Mare 5H 105
Hildesheim Ct. *BS23: W Mare* 5G 105
(off Station Rd.)
Hill, The BA2: F'frd 7A 124
BS4: Bris 5D 62
BS32: Alm 2D 26
Hill Av. BA2: C Down 3B 122
BS3: Wind H 6A 62
Hillbrook Rd. BS35: T'bry 4B 12
Hill Burn BS9: Henle 2J 47
Hillburn Rd. BS5: St G 2J 63
Hill Cl. BS16: Emer G 7F 39
Hillcote BS24: W Mare 5K 127
Hillcote Mans. BS23: W Mare 3E 104
Hill Ct. BS39: Paul 7C 140
HILLCREST 1F 117
Hill Crest BS4: Know 1D 76
BS49: Cong 6A 88
Hillcrest BA2: Pea J 5C 142
BS35: T'bry 3K 11
BS39: Pens 1G 117
Hillcrest Cl. BS13: Bis 4G 75
BS48: Nail 1G 71
Hillcrest Dr. BA2: Bath 7H 99
Hillcrest Flats BA15: Brad A 5J 125
Hillcrest Rd. BS20: P'head 4A 42
BS48: Nail 1G 71
Hillcroft Cl. BS15: Han 5C 64
BS22: W Mare 2J 105
Hilldale Rd. BS48: Back 5K 71
Hill Dr. BS8: Fail 6G 59
HILLEND 3H 129
Hill End BS22: Wor 1C 106
Hill End Dr. BS10: Hen 4D 34
HILLFIELD 7C 150
Hillfield BS27: Ched 7D 150
Hillfield Path BS27: Ched 6C 150
HILLFIELDS 5K 49
Hillfields Av. BS16: Fish 6A 50
Hill Gay Cl. BS20: P'head 4B 42
Hill Gro. BS9: Henle 2J 47
Hillgrove St. BS2: Bris 1A 62
Hillgrove St. Nth. BS2: Bris 1K 61
Hillgrove Ter. BS23: Uph 4F 127
Hillhouse BS9: Sea M 2C 46
BS16: Stap H 4D 50
Hill Ho. Rd. BS16: Stap H 2D 50
Hillier's La. BS25: C'hll 1K 131
Hill La. BS20: W'ton G 7B 42
BS21: Tic 5J 55
BS25: Row 4C 132
TA9: Bre K, E Brnt 5J 157
Hill Lawn BS4: Brisl 6F 63
Hill Lea Gdns. BS27: Ched 6D 150
Hillmead BS40: L'frd 7C 110
Hillmer Ri. BS29: Ban 2K 129
Hill Moor BS21: Clev 7E 54
Hill Pk. BS49: Cong 6A 88
Hill Path BS29: Ban 3B 130
Hill Rd. BS21: Clev 5C 54
BS22: Wor 2C 106
BS23: W Mare 4H 105
BS25: Sandf 2F 131
BS41: Dun 1D 92
Hill Rd. E. BS22: Wor 2C 106
Hills Barton BS13: Bis 1G 75
Hillsborough Flats BS8: Clftn 3G 61
Hillsborough Gdns. TA8: Bur S 6D 156
Hillsborough Ho. BS23: W Mare 1J 127
Hillsborough Rd. BS4: Brisl 5E 62
Hills Cl. BS31: Key 5E 78
Hillsdon Rd. BS9: W Trym 7F 35
HILLSIDE
BA3 6C 152
BS26 4J 149
Hillside BS6: Cot 1J 61
BS8: Clftn 4A 4 (3H 61)
BS16: Mang 3D 50
BS20: P'bry 5B 44
BS26: Axb 4J 149
Hillside Av. BA3: Mid N 6C 152
BS15: Kgswd 1A 64
Hillside Cl. BS36: Fram C 7G 29
BS39: Paul 7D 140
Hillside Cotts. BA2: Mid 6D 122
Hillside Ct. BS5: St G 2K 63
Hillside Cres. BA3: Mid N 6C 152
Hillside Gdns. BS22: W Mare 3K 105
BS39: Bis S 2J 137
Hillside La. BS36: Fram C 7G 29
Hillside Rd. BA2: Bath 7K 99
BA3: Mid N 6D 152
BS5: St G 2J 63
BS20: P'head 4A 42
BS21: Clev 6D 54
BS24: B'don 5K 127
BS41: L Ash 7B 60
BS48: Back 5J 71
Hillside St. BS4: Wind H 5C 62
Hillside Vw. BA2: Pea J 5C 142
BA3: Mid N 4E 152
Hillside W. BS24: Hut 2D 128
Hill St. BS1: Bris 3C 4 (2J 61)
BS3: Wind H 5B 62
BS5: St G 1H 63
BS15: Kgswd 1D 64
Hilltop BS20: P'head 4C 42
Hilltop Gdns. BS5: St G 2J 63
BS16: Soun 6B 50
(not continuous)
Hilltop Rd. BS16: Soun 6B 50
Hilltop Vw. BS5: St G 2J 63
Hill Vw. BA2: Mark 3F 119
BS8: Clftn 4A 4 (3H 61)
BS9: Henle 2J 47
BS16: Emer G 7E 38
BS16: Soun 6B 50
BS34: Fil 4C 36
Hillview BA2: Tims 4F 141
BA3: Mid N 7C 152
TA8: Brean 4A 144
Hillview Av. BS21: Clev 7D 54
Hill Vw. Cl. BS30: Old C 5G 65
Hill Vw. Ct. BS22: W Mare 4B 106
Hillview Gdns. BS40: F'tn 3G 91
Hill Vw. Ho. *BS15: Kgswd* 7A 50
(off Lodge Rd.)
Hillview Pk. Homes BS22: W Mare 4B 106
BS40: F'tn 2F 91
Hill Vw. Rd. BA1: Bath 1D 100
BS13: Bis 2G 75
BS23: W Mare 5J 105
Hillview Rd. BS16: Puck 3C 52
BS26: Lox 2G 147
Hillyfield Rd. BS13: Bis 4G 75
Hillyfields BS25: Wins 5H 131
Hillyfields Way BS25: Wins 5G 131
Hilton Ct. BS5: E'ton 1D 62
Hinckley Cl. BS22: St G 1G 107
Hind Pitts BS25: S'ham 6A 132
HINTON 2J 53
Hinton BS24: W Mare 3J 127
HINTON BLEWETT 7A 138
Hinton Cl. BA2: Bath 5F 99
BS31: Salt 7J 79
Hinton Dr. BS30: Old C 3G 65
Hinton La. BS8: Clftn 3F 61
Hinton Rd. BS5: E'ton 7E 48
BS16: Fish 4J 49
BS16: Puck 2D 52
Hippisley Dr. BS26: Axb 4K 149
Hiscocks Cl. BA2: New L 5B 98
Hiscocks Dr. BA2: Bath 7A 100
Hitchings Leaze BS34: Pat 7C 26
Hither Bath Bri. BS4: Brisl 2E 76
Hither Grn. BS21: Clev 7F 55
Hither Grn. Ind. Est. BS21: Clev 7F 55
Hither Mead BS36: Fram C 1F 39
Hi-Ways Cvn. Pk. BS10: H'len 3B 34
Hi-Ways Pk. BS10: H'len 3B 34
HMP Bristol BS7: Bishop 4K 47
HMYOI Ashfield BS16: Puck 4B 52
Hobart Rd. BS23: W Mare 2H 127
Hobbiton Rd. BS22: Wor 6E 84
Hobbs Ct. BS48: Nail 7H 57
Hobbs La. BS1: Bris 4D 4 (3J 61)
BS30: Sis 7F 51
BS48: Bar G 6J 73
HOBB'S WALL 7C 118
Hobb's Wall BA2: F'boro 7C 118
Hobhouse Cl. BA15: Brad A 7J 125
BS9: Henle 1J 47
Hobwell La. BS41: L Ash 7C 60
Hockey's La. BS16: Fish 4J 49
Hockley Ct. BA1: W'ton 2K 99
Hodden La. BS16: Puck 3C 52
Hodshill BA2: S'ske 6B 122
Hogarth M. BS22: Wor 1E 106
Hogarth Wlk. BS7: L'lze 7D 36
BS22: Wor 1E 106
Hogues Wlk. BS13: Hart 6H 75
Holbeach Way BS14: Whit 7C 76
Holbrook BS39: Stan D 2C 116
HOLBROOK COMMON 1B 66
Holbrook Cres. BS13: Hart 6K 75
Holbrook La. BS30: Wick 2A 66
Holburne Museum, The 2J 7 (4D 100)
Holburne Pl. BA2: Bath 2H 7 (4C 100)
Holcombe BS14: H'gro 5C 76
Holcombe Cl. BA2: Batham 2H 101
Holcombe Grn. BA1: W'ton 1H 99
(not continuous)
Holcombe Gro. BS31: Key 5B 78

Iron Acton—King La.

IRON ACTON .2H 29
Iron Acton Way BS37: Yate .3A 30
Ironchurch Rd. BS11: A'mth .3F 33
Iron Hogg La. GL12: Fal .1G 13
Ironmould La. BS4: Brisl .7J 63
Irons Way BS24: W Wick .4G 107
Irving Cl. BS16: Stap H .4C 50
BS21: Clev .6F 55
Irving Ho. BS1: Bris .3C 4
Isabella Cotts. BA2: C Down .3D 122 (off Rock La.)
Isabella M. BA2: C Down .3D 122
Isabella Rd. BS14: H'gro .3C 76
Isambard Wlk. BS1: Bris .5J 5 (3B 62)
Island, The BA3: Mid N .5E 152
Island Gdns. BS16: Stap .4E 48
Island Trade Pk. BS11: A'mth .6G 33
Isleport Bus. Pk. TA9: Highb .4H 159
Isleport La. TA9: Highb .3J 159
Isleys Ct. BS30: Long G .6D 64
Islington Rd. BS3: Bris .7B 4 (5H 61)
Ison Hill BS10: Hen .4D 34
Ison Hill Rd. BS10: Hen .4D 34
ITCHINGTON .2D 20
Itchington Rd. BS35: Grov, Itch .6C 12
GL12: Tyth .2E 20
Ivo Peters Rd. BA2: Bath .5D 6 (5A 100)
Ivor Rd. BS5: W'hall .1E 62
IVORY HILL .3E 38
Ivy Av. BA2: Bath .7J 99
Ivy Bank Pk. BA2: C Down .2B 122
Ivybridge BS22: Wor .2E 106
Ivy Cl. BS48: Nail .1F 71
Ivy Cotts. BA2: S'ske .5B 122
Ivy Ct. BS20: P'head .3B 42
Ivy Gro. BA2: Bath .7J 99
Ivy La. BA15: L Wrax .6J 103
BS16: Fish .5J 49
BS24: W'ton V .4E 106
Ivy Pl. BA2: Bath .7J 99
Ivy Ter. BA15: Brad A .5H 125
BS37: W'lgh .3B 40
Ivy Vs. BA2: Bath .7J 99
Ivy Wlk. BA3: Mid N .6F 153
BS29: Ban .1J 129
Ivywell Rd. BS9: Stok B .5E 46
IWOOD .1C 110
Iwood La. BS40: Iwood .3C 110

J

Jack Knight Ho. BS7: Hor .3B 48
JACKLANDS .5G 57
Jack Price Cl. BS13: Hart .7J 75
Jackson Cl. BS35: Piln .6D 16
Jacob Bldg., The BS8: Clftn .3A 4
Jacob Ct. BS2: Bris .3K 5 (2B 62)
Jacobs Brewery BS8: Clftn .4A 4
Jacobs Ct. BS1: Bris .5C 4
Jacob's Ladder .6E 150
Jacob's Mdw. BS20: P'head .4H 43
Jacob's Tower .6E 150
Jacob St. BS2: Bris .3J 5 (2B 62) (Hawkins St.)
BS2: Bris .3H 5 (2A 62) (Tower Hill)
Jacob's Wells Rd. BS8: Clftn .4A 4 (3H 61)
Jaguar Ho. BA1: Bath .2F 7 (off Julian Rd.)
Jamaica St. BS2: Bris .1F 5 (1A 62)
James Cl. BS16: Soun .4C 50
James Counsell Way BS34: H'ook .5H 37
James Pl. BS8: Clftn .2F 61 (off Portland St.)
James Rd. BS16: Soun .5C 50
James St. BS2: Bris .6C 48
BS5: E'ton .1K 5 (1B 62)
James St. W. BA1: Bath .4D 6 (5A 100)
Jane Austen Cen. .3F 7
Jane St. BS5: E'ton .2D 62
Jarratts Rd. BS10: S'mead .5K 35
Jarvis St. BS5: Bar H .3D 62
Jasmine Cl. BS22: Wor .3E 106
TA9: Highb .4F 159
Jasmine La. BS49: C'ham .7B 70
Jasmine Way BS24: W'ton V .3E 106
Jasmin Gro. BS11: Law W .5C 34
Jasper St. BS3: Bedm .6H 61
Jaycroft Rd. TA8: Bur S .2D 158
Jays, The GL12: Tyth .6F 13
Jays Cl. BS15: Kgswd .3B 64
Jay Vw. BS23: W Mare .7J 105
Jean Rd. BS4: Brisl .7G 63
Jeffery Ct. BS30: C Hth .3F 65
Jeffreys Ct. BS16: Fish .5G 49 (off Marina Gdns.)
JEFFRIES HILL .4K 63
Jeffries Hill Bottom BS15: St G .4K 63
Jekyll Cl. BS16: Stap .7G 37
Jellicoe Av. BS16: Stap .7G 37
Jellicoe Ct. BS22: Wor .7C 84
Jena Ct. BS31: Salt .7H 79
Jenner Blvd. BS16: Emer G .6F 39
Jenner Cl. BS37: Chip S .6K 31
Jennings Ct. BS3: Bris .7A 4
Jenny La. BS10: S'mead .5K 35
Jersey Av. BS4: Brisl .5H 63
Jesmond Rd. BS21: Clev .6C 54
BS22: St G .7G 85
Jesse Hughes Ct. BA1: Bath .1E 100
Jessop Apartments BS7: Bishop .4B 48
Jessop Ct. BS1: Bris .5G 5 (3A 62)
Jessop Cres. BS10: W Trym .6G 35
Jessop Underpass BS3: Ash G .5F 61
Jew's La. BA2: Bath .5J 99
Jews La. BS25: C'hll .1B 132
Jill's Garden .4F 105
Jim O'Neil Ho. BS11: Shire .1H 45
Jinty La. BS16: Sis .6F 51
Jobbins Cl. BS37: Chip S .6G 31
Jocelin Dr. BS22: Wor .7D 84
Jocelyn Rd. BS7: Hor .1B 48
Jockey La. BS5: St G .2J 63
John Cabot Ct. BS1: Bris .6A 4 (4G 61)
John Carr's Ter. BS8: Clftn .4B 4 (3H 61)
John Chiddy Cl. BS15: Han .6A 64
John Cozens Ho. BS2: Bris .2K 5
John Fosters Almshouses
BS10: Hen .4G 35
John Hall Cl. BS14: H'gro .3D 76
John James Ct. BS7: L'lze .1D 48
Johnny Ball La. BS2: Bris .2E 4 (2K 61)
John Rennie Cl. BA15: Brad A .7J 125 (off Moulton Dr.)
John Repton Gdns. BS10: Bren .5H 35
John Sebastian Quay BS1: Bris .7E 4 (4K 61)
John Slessor Ct. BA1: Bath .1F 7 (3B 100)
Johnson Dr. BS30: Bar C .4D 64
Johnson Rd. BS16: Emer G .2G 51
Johnsons La. BS5: W'hall .7F 49
Johnsons Rd. BS5: W'hall .7E 48
Johnstone St. BA2: Bath .4H 7 (5C 100)
John St. BA1: Bath .3F 7 (4B 100)
BS1: Bris .3F 5 (2K 61)
BS2: Bris .6C 48
BS15: Kgswd .1A 64
BS34: Stok G .5F 37
TA8: Bur S .1C 158
TA9: Highb .5F 159
John St. Sth. TA8: Bur S .1C 158
John Wesley Rd. BS5: St G .3K 63
BS15: St G .3K 63
John Wesley's Chapel .2G 5 (2A 62)
John Wood Ho. BA1: Bath .5F 7 (off Westgate Bldgs.)
Jones Cl. BS49: Yat .2F 87
Jones Hill BA15: Brad A .7F 125
Jordan Wlk. BS32: Brad S .6F 27
Jorrocks Ind. Est. BS37: W'lgh .3C 40
Joyce Cl. BS7: Hor .7C 36
Joy Hill BS8: Clftn .3F 61
Jubilee Cl. BA3: Mid N .6E 152
Jubilee Cotts. BS13: Bis .2F 75
Jubilee Ct. BS4: Brisl .6G 63
BS23: W Mare .4H 105
Jubilee Cres. BS16: Mang .1E 50
Jubilee Dr. BS8: Fail .5F 59
BS35: T'bry .3B 12
Jubilee Gdns. BS37: Yate .4G 31
TA9: Highb .5F 159
Jubilee Ho. BS34: Lit S .6E 26
Jubilee La. BS40: L'frd .6C 110
GL12: Crom .5A 14
Jubilee Path BS22: W Mare .3A 106
Jubilee Pl. BS1: Bris .6F 5 (4K 61)
BS15: Kgswd .2E 64
BS21: Clev .1D 68
Jubilee Rd. BA2: Pea J .7C 142
BA3: Rads .5H 153
BS2: Bris .7C 48
BS4: Know .7E 62
BS5: St G .2H 63
BS15: Soun .5C 50
BS23: W Mare .5G 105
BS26: Axb .4J 149
Jubilee Row BS2: Bris .7C 48 (off Ashley St.)
Jubilee St. BS2: Bris .4K 5 (3B 62)
TA8: Bur S .2D 158
Jubilee Swimming Pool .7D 62
Jubilee Ter. BA1: Bath .2D 100
BS39: Paul .7C 140
Jubilee Way BS11: A'mth .5F 33
BS22: St G .1G 107
Julian Cl. BS9: Stok B .5E 46
Julian Cotts. BA2: Mon C .3G 123
Julian Ct. BS9: Stok B .5E 46
Julian Rd. BA1: Bath .1E 6 (3B 100)
BS9: Stok B .5E 46
Julian's Acres TA8: Berr .2B 156
Julier Ho. BA1: Bath .1G 7
Julius Cl. BS16: Emer G .2G 51
Julius Rd. BS7: Bishop .5K 47
Junction Av. BA2: Bath .7C 6 (6A 100)
Junction Cut BS11: A'mth .6E 32
Junction Rd. BA2: Bath .6C 6 (6A 100)
BA15: Brad A .6H 125
BS4: Brisl .5E 62
Junction Way BS16: Soun .5E 50
Juniper Ct. BS5: Eastv .6E 48
Juniper Pl. BS22: Wor .7D 84
Juniper Way BS32: Brad S .7H 27
Jupiter Rd. BS34: Pat .7K 25
Justice Av. BS31: Salt .7J 79
Justice Rd. BS16: Fish .5H 49
Jutland Rd. BS11: A'mth .6F 33

K

Karen Cl. BS48: Back .6J 71
Karen Dr. BS48: Back .5J 71
Kathdene Gdns. BS7: Bris .5B 48
Kaynton Mead BA1: Bath .5H 99
Keats Ct. BS7: Hor .7C 36
Keats Ho. BS23: W Mare .1H 127 (off Lonsdale Av.)
Keats Rd. BA3: Rads .6F 153
Keble Av. BS13: Withy .6F 75
Keed's La. BS41: L Ash .7J 59
Keedwell Hill BS41: L Ash .1K 73
Keel Av. BS20: P'head .1H 43
Keel Cl. BS5: St G .3H 63
Keel's Hill BA2: Pea J .5C 142
Keene's Way BS21: Clev .7C 54
Keen's Gro. BS35: Piln .6C 16
Keep, The BS22: Wor .1E 106
BS30: Old C .4H 65
Keepers La. BS7: Bris .5B 48
Keg Store, The BS1: Bris .4G 5 (3A 62)
Keinton Wlk. BS10: Hen .5G 35
Kelbra Cres. BS36: Fram C .1F 39
Kellaway Av. BS6: Bishop, Hor .3J 47
BS7: Hor .3J 47
Kellaway Ct. BS6: Bishop .3K 47
Kellaway Cres. BS9: Henle .2K 47
Kellways BS48: Back .6J 71
Kelso Pl. BA1: Bath .3A 6 (4K 99)
KELSTON .7C 80
Kelston Cl. BS31: Salt .7H 79
BS37: Yate .7D 30
Kelston Gdns. BS10: W Trym .7K 35
BS22: Wor .6F 85
Kelston Gro. BS15: Han .3C 64
Kelston M. BS10: W Trym .7K 35
Kelston Rd. BA1: Bath .2E 98
BS10: W Trym .7K 35
BS22: Wor .7F 85
BS31: Key .5B 78
Kelston Vw. BA2: Bath .6F 99
BS31: Salt .7H 79
Kelston Wlk. BS16: Fish .4A 50
Kelting Gro. BS21: Clev .7F 55
Kemble Cl. BS15: Kgswd .3C 64
BS48: Nail .1J 71
Kemble Gdns. BS11: Shire .3J 45
Kemm Cl. BS27: Ched .7H 151
Kemperleye Way BS32: Brad S .7F 27
Kempes Cl. BS41: L Ash .7A 60
Kempe Way BS24: W'ton V .5C 106
Kempthorne La. BA2: Odd D .3A 122
Kempton Cl. BS16: Down .6D 38
BS35: T'bry .1K 11
Kemys Cl. BS16: Fish .3K 49
Kencot Wlk. BS13: Withy .7H 75
Kendall Cl. BS37: Yate .5B 30
Kendall Gdns. BS16: Stap H .4B 50
Kendall Rd. BS16: Stap H .4B 50
Kendal Rd. BS7: Hor .1C 48
KENDLESHIRE .4E 38
Kendon Dr. BS10: Hor .1K 47
Kendon Way BS10: S'mead .7K 35
Kenilworth BS37: Yate .6F 31
Kenilworth Cl. BS31: Key .6B 78
Kenilworth Ct. BA1: Bath .3D 100 (off Snow Hill)
Kenilworth Dr. BS30: Will .7F 65
Kenilworth Rd. BS6: Cot .7J 47
Kenmare Rd. BS4: Know .1A 76
Kenmeade Cl. BS25: S'ham .5A 132
Kenmore Cres. BS7: Hor .6A 36
Kenmore Dr. BS7: Hor .6A 36
Kenmore Gro. BS7: Hor .6A 36
KENN .3F 69
Kennard Cl. BS15: Kgswd .2A 64
Kennard Ri. BS15: Kgswd .1A 64
Kennard Rd. BS15: Kgswd .1A 64
Kennaway Path BS21: Clev .7E 54
Kennaway Rd. BS21: Clev .7D 54
Kenn Bus. Pk. BS21: Clev .2E 68
Kenn Cl. BS23: W Mare .7J 105
Kenn Ct. BS4: Know .3A 76
Kennedy Cl. TA9: Highb .4G 159
Kennedy Ho. BS37: Yate .5F 31
Kennedy Way BS37: Chip S, Yate .5E 30
Kennel La. BS26: Webb .3J 147
Kennel Lodge Rd. BS3: Bwr A .5E 60
BS41: L Ash .5D 60
Kenn Est. BS21: Kenn .2G 69
Kennet Gdns. BA15: Brad A .7H 125
Kenneth Rd. BS4: Brisl .7F 63
Kennet Pk. BA2: Batham .2G 101
Kennet Rd. BS31: Key .6E 78
Kennet Way BS35: T'bry .4B 12
Kennford BS22: Wor .2D 106
Kennington Av. BS7: Bishop .4A 48
BS15: Kgswd .7B 50
Kennington Rd. BA1: Bath .4H 99
Kennion Rd. BS5: St G .2J 63
Kennmoor Cl. BS30: C Hth .3E 64
Kenn Moor Dr. BS21: Clev .1E 68
Kenn Moor Rd. BS49: Yat .2H 87
Kennmoor Rd. BS21: Clev, Kenn .3G 69
Kenn Pier BS21: Clev .2G 69
Kenn Rd. BS5: St G .2J 63
BS21: Clev, Kenn .1D 68
Kenn St. BS21: Kenn .4F 69
Kensal Av. BS3: Wind H .6A 62
Kensal Rd. BS3: Wind H .6A 62
Kensington, The BS8: Clftn .2G 61 (off Kensington Pl.)
Kensington Apartments BS6: Redl .5J 47 (off Redland Ct. Rd.)
Kensington Cl. BS35: T'bry .2K 11
Kensington Ct. BA1: Bath .2D 100
BS8: Clftn .2G 61
Kensington Gdns. BA1: Bath .2D 100
KENSINGTON HILL .7F 63
Kensington Ho. BS5: St G .1J 63 (off Kensington Rd.)
KENSINGTON PARK .6E 62
Kensington Pk. BS5: E'ton .7C 48
Kensington Pk. Rd. BS4: Brisl .7E 62
Kensington Pl. BA1: Bath .3D 100
BS8: Clftn .2G 61
Kensington Rd. BS5: St G .1J 63
BS6: Redl .7J 47
BS16: Stap H .4B 50
BS23: W Mare .7H 105
Kent Av. BS24: W Wick .4G 107
BS37: Yate .3F 31
Kent Cl. BS34: Stok G .3F 37
Kent La. BA1: Up Swa .4D 82
Kent M. BS16: Stap .1G 49
Kenton M. BS9: Henle .3J 47
Kent Rd. BS7: Bishop .5A 48
BS49: Cong .6K 87
Kents Grn. BS15: Kgswd .6C 50
Kentshare La. BS40: Winf .5A 92
Kent St. BS3: Bedm .6J 61
BS27: Ched .5D 150
Kent Way BS22: Wor .7F 85
Kenwood Cl. BS15: Kgswd .7D 50
Keppel Cl. BS31: Salt .1H 97
Kerry Rd. BS4: Know .1A 76
Kersteman Rd. BS6: Redl .6J 47
Kestrel Cl. BS34: Pat .6A 26
BS35: T'bry .2B 12
BS37: Chip S .6F 31
Kestrel Ct. BS20: P'head .2G 43
Kestrel Dr. BS16: Puck .4C 52
BS22: W Mare .3C 106
Kestrel Pl. BA3: Mid N .6F 153
Keswick Wlk. BS10: S'mead .5J 35
Ketch Rd. BS3: Wind H .6B 62
Kew Rd. BS23: W Mare .3G 105
Kewside BS22: Kew .1K 105
KEWSTOKE .1K 105
Kewstoke Rd. BA2: C Down .2C 122
BS9: Stok B .4E 46
BS22: Kew .1J 105
Kew Wlk. BS4: Brisl .2E 76
Keyes Path BS22: Wor .7D 84
KEYNSHAM .4C 78
Keynsham By-Pass BS31: Key .2A 78
Keynsham Leisure Cen. .5D 78
Keynsham Rd. BS30: Will .4D 78
BS31: Key .4D 78
Keynsham Station (Rail) .4D 78
Key Point BS32: Brad S .2F 27
Keys Av. BS7: Hor .1B 48
Kielder Dr. BS22: Wor .1D 106
Kilbirnie Rd. BS14: Whit .7C 76
Kilburn St. BS5: E'ton .1D 62
Kildare BA2: Bath .3K 7 (4D 100)
Kildare Rd. BS4: Know .1K 75
Kilkenny La. BA2: Eng, Ing, Odd D .5E 120
Kilkenny Pl. BS20: P'head .2E 42
Kilkenny St. BS2: Bris .4K 5 (3B 62)
Killarney Av. TA8: Bur S .2D 158
Kilmersdon Rd.
BA3: Hay, Kil, Rads .6J 153
BS13: Hart .6H 75
Kilminster Cl. BS34: Lit S .1F 37
Kilminster Rd. BS11: Shire .1H 45
Kiln, The BS3: Bedm .5H 61
Kiln Cl. BS15: Kgswd .6K 49
Kiln Dr. TA9: Highb .5F 159
Kilnhurst Cl. BS30: Long G .7D 64
Kiln Pk. BS23: W Mare .6J 105
Kilve BS24: W Mare .3H 127
Kilvert Cl. BS4: Brisl .4F 63
Kimber Cl. TA9: Highb .5F 159
Kimberley Av. BS16: Fish .3A 50
Kimberley Cl. BS16: Down .1D 50
Kimberley Ct. BS34: Pat .5B 26
Kimberley Cres. BS16: Fish .3A 50
Kimberley Rd. BS15: Kgswd .7B 50
BS16: Fish .3A 50 (not continuous)
BS21: Clev .7C 54
Kinber Cl. BA1: W'ton .7G 81
Kinema Ho. BS4: Brisl .5E 62 (off Belmont Rd.)
King Alfred Sports Cen. .3E 158
King Alfred Way BA15: W'ley .5B 124
Kingcott Mill Farm Caravans
BS48: Flax B .2F 73
King Dick's La. BS5: St G .1H 63
Kingdom Ho. BS1: Bris .6B 4
Kingdom Vw. BS3: Bedm .7H 61
KINGDOWN .6H 91
Kingdown La. BS40: Winf .5G 91
Kingdown Rd. BS40: Redh, Winf .7E 90
King Edward Cl. BS14: H'gro .4C 76 (not continuous)
King Edward Rd. BA2: Bath .7B 6 (6K 99)
Kingfisher Cl. BS10: Bren .3H 35
BS32: Brad S .4G 27
BS35: T'bry .2B 12
Kingfisher Ct. BA2: Lim S .6A 124
Kingfisher Dr. BA3: Mid N .6F 153
BS16: Bmhll .2G 49
Kingfisher Rd. BS20: P'bry, P'head .1H 43
BS22: Wor .4D 106
BS37: Chip S .6G 31
King George V Pl. BS1: Bris .5E 4 (3K 61)
King George's Rd. BS13: Bis .5F 75
King Georges Rd. BA2: Bath .6J 99
King John's Rd. BS15: Kgswd .6K 49
King La. BS39: Clut .7H 117

King Rd.—Laphams Ct.

King Rd. BS4: Know 1E 76
BS25: C'hll 6K 109
King Rd. Av. BS11: A'mth 5E 32
Kingrove Cres. BS37: Chip S 6J 31
Kingrove La. BS37: Chip S 7J 31
Kings Av. BS7: Bishop 4J 47
BS15: Han 5K 63
Kings Bus. Pk. BS2: Bris 3E 62
King's Chase Shop. Cen.
BS15: Kgswd 1B 64
Kingscote BS37: Yate 1D 40
Kingscote Pk. BS5: St G 3K 63
Kingscott Mill Farm BS48: Flax B 2F 73
King's Ct. BS13: Withy 6F 75
Kings Ct. *BA1: Bath 4F 7*
(off Parsonage La.)
BS1: Bris 5F 5
BS2: Bris 2K 5 (2B 62)
(Braggs La.)
BS2: Bris 1G 5 (1A 62)
(Jamaica St.)
BS3: Bedm 5J 61
BS15: Kgswd 2B 64
BS34: Lit S 1E 36
Kingscourt Cl. BS14: Whit 5C 76
Kings Cft. BS41: L Ash 1J 73
KINGSDOWN
BS2 1D 4 (1J 61)
SN13 1D 102
Kingsdown Golf Course 1F 103
Kingsdown Gro. SN13: Kgdn 1D 102
Kingsdown Pde. BS6: Bris 1E 4 (1K 61)
Kingsdown Sports Cen. 1J 61
Kingsdown Vw. BA1: Bath 2C 100
King's Dr. BS7: Bishop 3J 47
Kings Dr. BS15: Han 5K 63
BS34: Stok G 3J 37
Kings Fld. BS37: Rang 5A 22
Kingsfield BA2: Bath 1J 121
BA15: Brad A 5H 125
Kingsfield Cl. BA15: Brad A 5H 125
BS30: Wick 3D 66
Kingsfield Grange Rd.
BA15: Brad A 5J 125
Kingsfield La. BS15: Han 4C 64
(not continuous)
BS30: Long G 5C 64
Kings Head La. BS13: Bis 3E 74
KING'S HILL 7E 56
Kingshill BS48: Nail 7E 56
Kingshill Gdns. BS48: Nail 7E 56
Kingshill La. BS40: Chew S 7B 114
Kingshill Rd. BS4: Know 1D 76
Kingsholme Ct. BS23: W Mare 3G 105
Kingsholme Rd. BS15: Kgswd 7B 50
Kingsholm Rd. BS10: S'mead 7K 35
Kings Ho. BS2: Bris 1D 4 (1J 61)
Kingsland Cl. BS2: Bris 4K 5 (3C 62)
Kingsland Rd. BS2: Bris 3C 62
Kingsland Rd. Bri. BS2: Bris 4K 5 (3C 62)
Kingsland Trad. Est. BS2: Bris 3K 5 (2B 62)
King's La. BS23: W Mare 4G 105
Kings La. BS16: Puck 3K 51
BS21: Clev 4D 54
Kingsleigh Ct. BS15: Kgswd 2D 64
Kingsleigh Gdns. BS15: Kgswd 2D 64
Kingsleigh Pk. BS15: Kgswd 2D 64
Kingsley BA2: Bath 6C 6
Kingsley Ho. BS2: Bris 4K 5 (3B 62)
Kingsley Pl. *BS3: Bris 5J 61*
(off Beauley Rd.)
Kingsley Rd. BA3: Rads 5G 153
BS5: E'ton 7E 48
BS6: Cot 6K 47
BS21: Clev 7D 54
BS23: W Mare 2H 127
Kingsmarsh Ho. BS5: E'ton 2D 62
Kingsmead BS48: Nail 7E 56
Kingsmead Ct. *BA1: Bath 5E 6*
(off Kingsmead Nth.)
Kingsmead E. BA1: Bath 5E 6 (5B 100)
Kingsmead Ho. BA1: Bath 4E 6
Kingsmead Leisure Complex 5E 6
Kingsmead Nth. BA1: Bath 5E 6 (5B 100)
Kingsmead Rd. BS5: S'wll 7J 49
Kingsmead Sq. BA1: Bath 5F 7 (5B 100)
Kingsmead St. BA1: Bath 4F 7 (5B 100)
Kingsmead Ter. BA1: Bath 5F 7
Kingsmead Wlk. BS5: S'wll 7J 49
Kingsmead W. BA1: Bath 5E 6 (5B 100)
Kings M. BS6: Bris 1K 61
Kingsmill BS9: Stok B 3D 46
Kings Oak Mdw. BS39: Clut 3G 139
Kings of Wessex Leisure Cen. 7D 150
Kings Orchard BS2: Bris 3H 5 (2A 62)
Kings Pde. Av. BS8: Clftn 7H 47
Kings Pde. M. BS8: Clftn 7G 47
Kings Pk. Av. BS2: Bris 3E 62
King Sq. BS2: Bris 1F 5 (1K 61)
(not continuous)
King Sq. Av. BS2: Bris 1F 5 (1K 61)
Kings Sq. Studios *BS1: Bris 1F 5*
(off Dighton St.)
Kings Quarter Apartments BS1: Bris 1F 5
King's Rd. BS4: Brisl 6E 62
BS8: Clftn 2G 61
BS20: P'head 4B 42
BS21: Clev 4D 54
Kings Rd. BS40: Wrin 3F 111
Kings Sq. BS30: Bit 2H 79
Kingston Av. BA15: Brad A 7J 125
BS21: Clev 6E 54
BS31: Salt 1G 97
Kingston Bldgs. *BA1: Bath 5G 7*
(off York St.)
Kingston Cl. BS16: Mang 1E 50
Kingston Dr. BS16: Mang 1E 50
BS48: Nail 2E 70
Kingston La. BS40: Winf 4J 91
Kingston Mead *BS40: Winf 4K 91*
(off Felton La.)
Kingston Pde. *BA1: Bath 5G 7*
(off York St.)
Kingston Rd. BA1: Bath 5G 7 (5C 100)
BA15: Brad A 6H 125
BS3: Bedm 5J 61
BS48: Nail 2E 70
KINGSTON SEYMOUR 1C 86
Kingston Sq. BA15: Brad A 6H 125
Kingston Way BS48: Nail 2E 70
Kingstree St. BS4: Wind H 5C 62
King St. BS1: Bris 5E 4 (3K 61)
BS5: E'ton 7E 48
BS11: A'mth 6E 32
BS15: Kgswd 1K 63
TA9: Highb 5F 159
King's Wlk. BS13: Bis 3E 74
Kingsway BA2: Bath 1J 121
BS5: St G 2K 63
BS15: Kgswd 1K 63
BS20: P'head 4B 42
BS34: Lit S 1E 36
Kingsway Av. BS5: St G 1K 63
BS15: Kgswd 1K 63
Kingsway Cvn. Pk. BS20: P'head 2F 43
Kingsway Ct. BS15: Kgswd 1K 63
Kingsway Cres. BS15: Kgswd 1A 64
Kingsway Pk. BS30: Warm 3F 65
Kingsway Rd. TA8: Bur S 1D 158
Kingsway Shop. Pct. BS5: St G 3K 63
Kingswear BS22: Wor 2E 106
Kingswear Rd. BS3: Know 1K 75
Kings Weston Av. BS11: Shire 1H 45
Kingsweston Down Nature Reserve 6C 34
Kings Weston La.
BS11: A'mth, Law W 3G 33
Kings Weston Rd. BS10: Hen 1A 46
BS11: Law W 1A 46
KINGSWOOD 1B 64
Kingswood Douglas Est.
BS15: Kgswd 2B 64
Kingswood Fountain Est.
BS15: Kgswd 1A 64
Kingswood Hgts. BS15: Kgswd 7B 50
Kingswood Heritage Mus. 3F 65
Kingswood Ind. Est. BS30: Long G 5D 64
Kingswood Leisure Cen. 5B 50
Kingswood Theatre 1A 100
Kingswood Trad. Est. BS15: Kgswd 7B 50
KINGTON 3G 11
Kington La. BS35: King, T'bry 3G 11
Kington Rd. BS35: King 1G 11
Kingwell Vw. BS39: High L 3B 140
King William Av. BS1: Bris 5F 5 (3K 61)
King William St. BS3: Bedm 5H 61
Kinsale Rd. BS14: H'gro 3E 76
Kinsale Wlk. BS4: Know 1A 76
Kinvara Rd. BS4: Know 2A 76
Kinver Ter. TA8: Bur S 1C 158
Kipling Av. BA2: Bath 7B 100
Kipling Rd. BA3: Rads 5G 153
BS7: Hor 6D 36
BS23: W Mare 2J 127
Kirkby Rd. BS11: Law W 6A 34
Kirkstone Gdns. BS10: S'mead 5J 35
Kirtlington Rd. BS5: Eastv 5D 48
Kite Hay Cl. BS16: Stap 3G 49
Kites Cl. BS32: Brad S 4E 26
Kites Farm La. BS30: Upton C 2A 80
Kite Wlk. BS22: Wor 4C 106
Kitland La. BS40: L'frd 5D 110
Kitley Hill BA3: Mid N 2G 153
Kittiwake Dr. BS20: P'head 1H 43
Knapp, The BS37: Yate 1F 31
Knapp La. GL12: Crom 1B 14
Knapp Rd. BS35: T'bry 4A 12
Knapps Cl. BS25: Wins 5F 131
Knapps Dr. BS25: Wins 5F 131
Knapps La. BS5: S'wll 6G 49
Kneller Cl. BS11: Law W 7A 34
Knighstone Beacon BS23: W Mare 4E 104
Knight Cl. BS22: Wor 6E 84
KNIGHTCOTT 2J 129
Knightcott Gdns. BS29: Ban 2K 129
Knightcott Ind. Est. BS29: Ban 2J 129
Knightcott Pk. BS29: Ban 2A 130
Knightcott Rd. BS8: Abb L 1K 59
BS29: Ban 2J 129
Knighton Rd. BS10: S'mead 6A 36
Knights Acres BS29: Ban 2K 129
Knightsbridge Pk. BS13: Hart 6A 76
Knights Cl. BS9: Henle 2H 47
Knightstone C'way. BS23: W Mare 4E 104
Knightstone Cl. BA2: Pea J 5B 142
BS26: Axb 5J 149
Knightstone Ct. BS21: Clev 1D 68
BS23: W Mare 3F 105
TA8: Bur S 2D 158
Knightstone Gdns. *BS4: Know 7D 62*
(off Oakmeade Pk.)
BS23: W Mare 7F 105
Knightstone Ho. BS2: Bris 1D 4
BS23: W Mare 4F 105
(off Bristol Rd. Lwr.)
Knightstone Lodge *BS6: Cot 7K 47*
(off Archfield Rd.)
Knightstone Mt. *BS5: St G 3J 63*
(off Nicholas La.)
Knightstone Pk. BS23: W Mare 7G 105
Knightstone Pl. BA1: W'ton 2H 99
BS15: Han 6K 63
BS22: Wor 2D 106
Knightstone Rd. BS23: W Mare 4E 104
Knightstone Theatre BS23: W Mare 4E 104
Knightstone Wlk. *BS2: Bris 1D 4*
(off Portland St.)
Knightswood BS48: Nail 6F 57
Knightwood Rd. BS34: Stok G 2H 37
Knobsbury Hill BA3: Rads 7D 154
Knobsbury La. BA3: Writ 5C 154
Knole Cl. BS32: Alm 2B 26
Knole La. BS10: Bren 4G 35
Knole Pk. BS32: Alm 3B 26
Knoll, The BS20: P'head 1F 43
Knoll Ct. BS9: Stok B 5D 46
Knoll Hill BS9: Stok B 5D 46
Knoll Pk. TA8: Brean 4B 144
Knoll Vw. TA8: Bur S 7E 156
Knovill Cl. BS11: Law W 5B 34
KNOWLE 7D 62
Knowle Golf Course 2F 77
KNOWLE HILL 5J 115
KNOWLE PARK 1D 76
Knowle Rd. BS4: Wind H 6B 62
Knowles Rd. BS21: Clev 7C 54
Knowle W. Health Pk. BS4: Know 1K 75
Knowsley Rd. BS16: Fish 5G 49
Knyfton Cl. BS23: Uph 3G 127
Komedia Bath *4F 7*
(off Westgate St.)
Kyght Cl. BS15: Warm 1E 64
Kylross Av. BS14: H'gro 5D 76
Kynaston Vw. BS15: Han 5B 64
Kynges Mill Cl. BS16: Bmhll 1J 49
Kyngstone Ct. BS16: Fish 5G 49
Kyrle Gdns. BA1: Bathe 7H 83

L

Labbott, The BS31: Key 5C 78
Labourham Drove BS27: Ched 7H 151
Labourham Way BS27: Ched 7H 151
Laburnum Cl. BA3: Mid N 6D 152
Laburnum Ct. BS23: W Mare 5K 105
Laburnum Gro. BA3: Mid N 6D 152
BS16: Fish 4K 49
Laburnum Rd. BS15: Han 4A 64
BS23: W Mare 5J 105
Laburnum Ter. BA1: Bathe 7H 83
Laburnum Wlk. BS31: Key 7A 78
Lacey Rd. BS14: Stoc 4G 77
Lacock Dr. BS30: Bar C 4D 64
Ladd Cl. BS15: Kgswd 2D 64
TA9: Highb 5F 159
Ladden Ct. BS35: T'bry 4A 12
Laddon Mead BS37: Yate 2D 30
Ladies Mile BS9: Stok B 7F 47
Ladman Gro. BS14: Stoc 4G 77
Ladman Rd. BS14: Stoc 4G 77
Ladycroft BS21: Clev 2A 68
Ladye Bay BS21: Clev 2D 54
Ladye Wake BS22: Wor 7D 84
Ladymead BS20: P'head 3H 43
Ladymeade BS48: Back 3J 71
Ladymead Ho. BA1: Bath 2G 7 (4C 100)
Ladymead La. BA25: C'hll 1B 132
BS40: L'frd 1B 132
Ladysmith Rd. BS6: Henle 4H 47
Ladywell BS40: Wrin 2F 111
Laggan Gdns. BA1: Bath 2A 100
Lake La. GL12: Crom 3C 14
Lakemead Gdns. BS13: Withy 6F 75
Lakemead Gro. BS13: Bis 4F 75
Lake Rd. BS10: W Trym 1J 47
BS20: P'head 2E 42
Lakeshore BS13: Bis 4J 75
Lake Shore Dr. BS13: Bis 4J 75
Lakeside BS16: Fish 5G 49
TA9: Highb 4G 159
Lakeside Cl. BS40: Nem T 7G 113
Lakeside Ct. BS24: W'ton V 3F 107
Lake Vw. BS16: Fish 5H 49
Lakeview Cres. TA9: Highb 5G 159
Lake Vw. Rd. BS5: St G 1F 63
Lakewood Cres. BS10: W Trym 7H 35
Lakewood Rd. BS10: W Trym 7H 35
Lalonde Ho. BS8: Clftn 2B 4
Lambert Pl. BS4: Know 4K 75
Lamb Hill BS5: St G 2H 63
Lambley Rd. BS5: St G 1G 63
Lambourn Cl. BS3: Wind H 6K 61
Lambourne Way BS20: P'head 4H 43
Lambourn Rd. BS31: Key 6E 78
LAMBRIDGE 2E 100
Lambridge Bldgs. BA1: Bath 1D 100
Lambridge Bldgs. M. *BA1: Bath 2E 100*
(off Salisbury Rd.)
Lambridge Grange BA1: Bath 1E 100
Lambridge M. BA1: Bath 2E 100
Lambridge Pl. BA1: Bath 2E 100
Lambridge St. BA1: Bath 2E 100
Lambrook Rd. BS16: Fish 4J 49
Lamb St. BS2: Bris 2K 5 (2B 62)
Lamb Yd. BA15: Brad A 6H 125
Lamington Cl. BS13: Bis 4F 75
Lamont Ho. BA1: Bath 1E 100
Lamord Ga. BS34: Stok G 2G 37
Lampards Bldgs. BA1: Bath 1F 7 (3B 100)
Lampeter Rd. BS9: W Trym 1F 47
Lampley Rd. BS21: Kenn, Kings S 1C 86
Lampton Av. BS13: Hart 7A 76
Lampton Gro. BS13: Hart 7A 76
Lampton Rd. BS41: L Ash 1K 73
Lanaway Rd. BS16: Fish 2K 49
Lancashire Rd. BS7: Bishop 5A 48
Lancaster Cl. BS34: Stok G 3F 37
Lancaster Rd. BS2: Bris 6C 48
BS37: Yate 3E 30
Lancaster St. BS5: Redf 2E 62
Lancelot Rd. BS16: Stap 7G 37
Land, The BS36: Coal H 7G 29
Landemann Cir. BS23: W Mare 4G 105
Landemann Path BS23: W Mare 4G 105
Landing Lights BS14: H'gro 5A 76
Land La. BS49: Yat 4J 87
Landmark Ct. BS1: Bris 7C 4
Landrail Wlk. BS16: Bmhll 2H 49
Landseer Av. BS7: L'Ize 2D 48
Landseer Cl. BS22: Wor 1D 106
Landseer Rd. BA2: Bath 5H 99
Lane, The BS35: E Comp 4F 25
Lanercost Rd. BS10: S'mead 5J 35
Lanesborough Ri. BS14: Stoc 3F 77
Lanes End BS4: Brisl 1E 76
Laneys Drove BS24: Lock 7C 106
Langdale Ct. BS34: Pat 6C 26
Langdale Rd. BS16: Fish 4H 49
Langdon Rd. BA2: Bath 7H 99
Langfield Cl. BS10: Hen 4E 34
LANGFORD GREEN 2G 133
Langford La. BS40: Burr, L'frd 7G 111
Langford Pl. Gdns. BS40: L'frd 6F 111
Langford Rd. BS13: Bis 2F 75
BS23: W Mare 6J 105
BS40: L'frd 7D 110
Langford's La. BS39: High L 5A 140
Langford Way BS15: Kgswd 2C 64
Langham Rd. BS4: Know 7E 62
Langhill Av. BS4: Know 3J 75
Langlands La. TA9: W Hunt 7D 158
Langley Cres. BS3: Ash V 1E 74
Langley Down La. BA3: Mid N 4A 152
Langley Mow BS16: Emer G 1F 51
Langley's La. BA3: Clapt, Mid N 6A 152
BS39: Paul 6A 152
Langport Gdns. BS48: Nail 2G 71
Langport Rd. BS23: W Mare 6G 105
LANGRIDGE 2A 82
Langridge La. BA1: L'rdge, L'dwn 3H 81
Langthorn Cl. BS36: Fram C 7G 29
Langton Ct. BA2: New L 6B 98
BS16: Fish 5G 49
(off Marina Gdns.)
Langton Ct. Rd. BS4: St Ap 4F 63
Langton Ho. BS2: Bris 2J 5
Langton Pk. BS3: Bedm 5J 61
Langton Rd. BS4: St Ap 4F 63
Langton Way BS4: St Ap 3H 63
LANSDOWN 4H 81
Lansdown BS23: W Mare 4H 105
BS37: Yate 6E 30
Lansdown Cl. BA1: Bath 2A 100
BS15: Kgswd 6B 50
Lansdown Club, The 2B 100
Lansdown Cres. BA1: Bath 2B 100
BA2: Tims 3G 141
Lansdowne *BS16: Fren 6A 38*
(off Avon Ring Rd.)
Lansdowne Ct. BS5: E'ton 1C 62
Lansdown Gdns. BS22: Wor 6F 85
Lansdown Golf Course 4G 81
Lansdown Gro. BA1: Bath 1F 7 (3B 100)
Lansdown Gro. Ct. BA1: Bath 1F 7
Lansdown Gro. Lodge BA1: Bath 1F 7
Lansdown Hgts. BA1: Bath 1B 100
Lansdown Ho. BS15: Kgswd 6B 50
Lansdown La. BA1: L'dwn, W'ton 1H 99
BS30: Upton C 1B 80
Lansdown Lawn Tennis
& Squash Racquets Club *2B 100*
(within The Lansdown Club)
Lansdown Mans. *BA1: Bath 3B 100*
(off Lansdown Rd.)
Lansdown M. BA1: Bath 3F 7 (4B 100)
Lansdown Pk. BA1: L'dwn 7A 82
Lansdown (Park & Ride) 5J 81
Lansdown Pl. BS8: Clftn 2G 61
BS16: Emer G 1F 51
BS39: High L 4A 140
Lansdown Pl. E. BA1: Bath 3B 100
Lansdown Pl. W. BA1: Bath 2B 100
Lansdown Rd.
BA1: Bath, L'dwn 1F 7 (4H 81)
BS5: E'ton 7C 48
BS6: Redl 7J 47
BS8: Clftn 2G 61
BS15: Kgswd 6B 50
BS16: Puck 2C 52
BS31: Salt 7J 79
Lansdown Ter. *BA1: Bath 1F 7*
(off Lansdown Rd.)
BA1: W'ton 2J 99
BS6: Henle 3K 47
Lansdown Vw. BA2: Bath 6J 99
BA2: Tims 3G 141
BS15: Kgswd 1C 64
Lansdown Vs. BA1: Bath 1F 7
Lanson Roberts Rd.
BS35: Sev B 1C 24
Lanthony Cl. BS24: W'ton V 4E 106
Laphams Ct. BS30: Long G 5D 64

Lapwing Cl.—Lodge St.

Lapwing Cl. BS20: P'bry, P'head 2H 43
BS32: Brad S 4F 27
Lapwing Gdns. BS16: Bmhll 2H 49
BS22: Wor 3D 106
Larch Cl. BS16: Puck 7H 39
BS40: L'frd 7C 110
BS48: Nail 7J 57
Larch Ct. BA3: Rads 6H 153
Larches, The BS22: Wor 1E 106
Larchgrove Cres. BS22: Wor 3D 106
Larchgrove Wlk. *BS22: Wor* *3E 106*
(off Chestnut Av.)
Larch Rd. BS15: Soun 5C 50
Larch Way BS34: Pat 7A 26
Larchwood Ct. BA3: Rads 3A 154
Lark Cl. BA3: Mid N 6F 153
Larkfield BS36: Coal H 7H 29
LARKHALL 1D 100
Larkhall Bldgs. *BA1: Bath* *1E 100*
(off St Saviours Rd.)
Larkhall Pl. BA1: Bath 1E 100
Larkhall Sq. BA1: Bath 1E 100
Larkhall Ter. BA1: Bath 1E 100
Larkhill Rd. BS24: Lock 6F 107
Larkin Pl. BS7: Hor 6C 36
Lark Pl. BA1: Bath 3A 6
Lark Ri. BS37: Yate 2E 30
Lark Rd. BS22: Wor 3D 106
Larks Fld. BS16: Stap 3G 49
Lark's La. BS37: Iron A 6F 21
Larksleaze Rd. BS30: Long G 7C 64
Larkspur Cl. BS35: T'bry 3B 12
La Sainte BS20: P'head 2E 42
Lasbury Gro. BS13: Hart 5J 75
Latchmoor Ho. BS13: Bis 2G 75
Late Broads BA15: W'ley 5B 124
Latimer Cl. BS4: Brisl 5G 63
LATTERIDGE 7E 20
Latteridge La. BS35: A'ton, Itch 3D 20
BS37: Iron A 3D 20
Latteridge Rd. BS37: Iron A 7E 20
Latton Rd. BS7: Hor 7B 36
Launceston Av. BS15: Han 4K 63
Launceston Rd. BS15: Kgswd 7K 49
Laura Pl. BA2: Bath 3H 7 (4C 100)
Laureate, The BS1: Bris 1F 5
Laurel Av. TA9: Bre K 5J 157
Laurel Dr. BS16: Emer G 7G 39
BS23: Uph 3G 127
BS39: Paul 1B 152
BS48: Nail 7H 57
Laurel Gdns. BA2: Tims 4F 141
BS49: Yat 2H 87
Laurels, The BA2: Mid 7E 122
BS10: Hen 1G 35
BS16: Mang 2E 50
BS25: C'hll 2B 132
Laurel St. BS15: Kgswd 1B 64
Laurel Ter. BS49: Yat 2H 87
Laurie Cres. BS9: Henle 2K 47
Laurie Lee Ct. BS30: Bar C 4E 64
Lavender Cl. BS22: Wick L 6E 84
BS35: T'bry 3B 12
Lavender Ct. BS5: S'wll 7H 49
Lavender Way BS32: Brad S 7H 27
Lavenham Rd. BS37: Yate 4B 30
Lavers Cl. BS15: Kgswd 3C 64
Lavington Cl. BS21: Clev 1A 68
Lavington Rd. BS5: St G 3K 63
Lawders Orchard BS40: Wrin 2G 111
Lawford Av. BS34: Lit S 1E 36
Lawford M. BS2: Bris 3K 5 (2B 62)
Lawfords Ga. BS2: E'ton 2K 5 (2B 62)
BS5: E'ton 1K 5 (1B 62)
Lawfords Ga. Ho. *BS2: Bris* *3K 5*
(off Lawford St.)
Lawford St. BS2: Bris 2K 5 (2B 62)
Law Gro. BS24: W Wick 4H 107
Lawn Av. BS16: Fish 3K 49
Lawn Cl. BS16: L'lze 7E 36
Lawn Rd. BS16: Fish 3K 49
Lawns, The BS11: Shire 1J 45
BS22: Wor 1F 107
BS27: Ched 6C 150
BS37: Yate 4E 30
BS49: Yat 2G 87
Lawnside BS48: Back 5K 71
Lawns Rd. BS37: Yate 4E 30
Lawnwood Rd. BS5: E'ton 1D 62
Lawnwood Rd. Ind. Est. BS5: E'ton 1D 62
Lawrence Av. BS5: E'ton 7D 48
Lawrence Cl. BS15: Soun 6E 50
BS22: Wor 2C 106
TA8: Bur S 3F 159
TA9: Highb 4H 159
Lawrence Dr. BS37: Yate 4B 30
Lawrence Gro. BS9: Henle 3H 47
Lawrence Hill BS5: Bris 2C 62
BS5: E'ton 2D 62
Lawrence Hill Ind. Pk. BS5: E'ton 1D 62
LAWRENCE HILL RDBT. 2C 62
Lawrence Hill Station (Rail) 2D 62
Lawrence La. BS9: Henle 3H 47
Lawrence M. BS22: Wor 2C 106
Lawrence Rd. BS22: Wor 2C 106
BS40: Wrin 2G 111
LAWRENCE WESTON 6A 34
Lawrence Weston Meadows Nature Reserve
4B 34
Lawrence Weston Rd.
BS11: A'mth, Law W 2J 33
(not continuous)
BS11: Law W 5B 34
Laws Dr. BS24: W'ton V 5D 106
Lawson Cl. BS31: Salt 1G 97
Laxey Rd. BS7: Hor 1B 48
Laxton Cl. BS35: Olv 2C 18
Laxton Way BA2: Pea J 6D 142
Lays Dr. BS31: Key 5A 78
Lays Farm Bus. Cen. BS31: Key 6A 78
Lays Farm Trad. Est. BS31: Key 6A 78
Lays La. BS40: Blag 1B 134
Leach Cl. BS21: Clev 1C 68
Lea Cft. BS13: Withy 5G 75
Leader St. BS16: L'lze 1E 48
Leading Edge BS8: Clftn 5A 4 (3H 61)
Leafy Way BS24: Lock 1F 129
Leagrove Rd. BS21: Clev 5C 54
Leaholme Gdns. BS14: Whit 7C 76
Leaman Cl. BS37: Chip S 5G 31
Leap Va. BS16: Down 7E 38
Leap Valley Cres. BS16: Down 7D 38
Lear Cl. BS30: C Hth 4F 65
Leawood Ct. BS23: W Mare 3E 104
Leaze, The BA3: Rads 6H 153
BS37: Yate 4D 30
Leaze Cl. BS35: T'bry 4K 11
Leaze La. BS40: Blag 5C 134
Leda Av. BS14: H'gro 3C 76
Ledbury Rd. BS16: Fish 4A 50
Leechpool Way BS37: Yate 1E 30
Lee Cl. BS34: Pat 6B 26
Leedham Rd. BS24: Lock 7F 107
Leekbeds La. TA9: W Hunt 7B 158
Leeming Way BS11: Shire 7G 33
Lees Hill BS15: Soun 7C 50
Leeside BS20: P'head 3E 42
Lees La. BS30: Old C 4H 65
Leewood Rd. BS23: W Mare 3H 105
Leg La. BS40: R'frd 2K 133
Leicester Sq. BS16: Soun 5B 50
Leicester St. BS3: Bedm 5K 61
Leicester Wlk. BS4: St Ap 4H 63
Leigh Cl. BA1: Bath 1C 100
Leigh Ct. Bus. Cen. BS8: Abb L 6A 46
LEIGH GROVE 3J 125
Leigh La. BS37: W'lgh 6B 40
Leigh Pk. Rd. BA15: Brad A 4H 125
Leigh Rd. BA15: Brad L, Brad A 4J 125
BS8: Clftn 1A 4 (1H 61)
Leigh Rd. W. BA15: Brad A 3G 125
Leigh St. BS3: Bris 5G 61
Leighton Cres. BS24: W Mare 5J 127
Leighton Rd. BA1: W'ton 7G 81
BS3: Bris 7B 4 (5H 61)
BS4: Know 7D 62
Leigh Vw. Rd. BS20: P'head 1F 43
Leighwood Dr. BS48: Nail 1D 70
LEIGH WOODS 3D 60
Leigh Woods Forest Walks 7D 46
Leigh Woods Ho. BS8: L Wds 3D 60
Leigh Woods National Nature Reserve
1C 60
Leinster Av. BS4: Know 3K 75
Leisure Box, The 7J 49
Leisure Rd. BS15: Kgswd 4C 64
Lemon La. BS2: Bris 1J 5
Lena Av. BS5: E'ton 7E 48
Lena St. BS5: E'ton 7D 48
Lenover Gdns. BS13: Hart 6H 75
Leonard La. BS1: Bris 3E 4
Leonard Rd. BS5: Redf 2E 62
Leonard's Av. BS5: E'ton 7E 48
Leopold Bldgs. BA1: Bath 1G 7
Leopold Rd. BS6: Bris 6A 48
Les Brown Ct. BS2: Bris 4K 5 (3B 62)
Lescren Way BS11: A'mth 6H 33
Lester Dr. BS22: Wor 1E 106
Lewington Rd. BS16: Fish 4A 50
Lewins Mead BS1: Bris 3E 4 (2K 61)
Lewin St. BS5: St G 2F 63
Lewis Cl. BS16: Emer G 3G 51
BS30: Old C 4H 65
Lewis Ct. BS22: Wor 2D 106
Lewisham Gro. BS23: W Mare 5J 105
Lewis Rd. BS13: Bis 2G 75
Lewis St. BS2: Bris 4D 62
Lewton La. BS36: Wint 7C 28
LEYHILL 1B 14
Leyland Wlk. BS13: Withy 6F 75
Ley La. BS35: Olv 2B 18
Leys, The BS21: Clev 1B 68
Leyton Vs. BS6: Redl 6H 47
Liberty Gdns. BS1: Bris 6C 4 (4J 61)
Liberty Ind. Pk. BS3: Ash V 1G 75
Liberty La. BS40: Blag 3C 134
Library Apartments, The *BS7: Bishop* *5K 47*
(off Gloucester Rd.)
Lichfield Rd. BS4: St Ap 3G 63
Lightbox La. *BS4: Bris* *5D 62*
(off River Rd.)
Lilac Cl. BS10: S'mead 6J 35
Lilac Ct. BS31: Key 7A 78
Lilac Dr. BS16: Emer G 7G 39
Lilac Ter. BA3: Mid N 4G 153
Lilac Way BS22: Wick L 6E 84
Lilian Ter. BS39: Paul 1C 152
Lillian St. BS5: Redf 1E 62
Lillington Cl. BA3: Rads 4B 154
Lillington Rd. BA3: Rads 4B 154
LILLIPUT 6G 31
Lilliput Av. BS37: Chip S 6G 31
Lilliput Ct. *BA1: Bath* *5G 7*
(off North Pde. Pas.)
BS37: Chip S 6G 31
Lilstock Av. BS7: Bishop 4B 48
Lilton Wlk. BS13: Bis 1G 75
Lilymead Av. BS4: Wind H 6B 62
Lilypool Drove BS21: Kenn 3H 69
BS49: C'ham 6H 69
Limebreach Wood BS48: Nail 6F 57
Limeburn Hill BS40: Chew M 1E 114
Lime Cl. BS10: Bren 4H 35
BS22: Wor 3E 106
BS24: Lock 1F 129
Lime Ct. BS31: Key 6A 78
Lime Cft. BS37: Yate 2G 31
Lime Gro. BA2: Bath 5J 7 (5D 100)
BS35: A'ton 7H 11
Lime Gro. Gdns. BA2: Bath 5J 7 (5D 100)
Lime Kiln Cl. BS34: Stok G 5F 37
Lime Kiln Gdns. BS32: Brad S 3F 27
Lime Kiln La. BS21: Clev 6D 54
Limekiln La. BA2: C'ton D 7H 101
Lime Kiln Rd. BS1: Bris 5B 4 (3H 61)
Limekiln Rd. BS37: Rang, Yate 4C 22
Limekilns Cl. BS31: Key 5D 78
Limerick Rd. BS6: Redl 6J 47
Lime Rd. BS3: Bris 5H 61
BS15: Han 4J 63
Limes, The *BS16: Fren* *6K 37*
(off Wellington Pl.)
Limestone La. BS37: Chip S 4G 31
Lime Ter. BA3: Rads 5H 153
Lime Tree Gro. BS20: Pill 5H 45
Lime Trees Rd. BS6: Henle 2K 47
Lime Wlk. *BS22: Kew* *1J 105*
(in Ardnave Holiday Pk.)
LIMPLEY STOKE 6J 123
Limpley Stoke Rd. BA15: W'ley 5A 124
Lincoln Cl. BS31: Key 6A 78
Lincoln Gdns. BS5: Bar H 2D 62
Lincoln La. BS24: W Mare 1K 127
Lincoln St. BS5: Bar H 2D 62
Lincombe Av. BS16: Down 2B 50
Lincombe Rd. BA3: Rads 6H 153
BS16: Down 3A 50
Lincott Vw. BA2: Pea J 5C 142
Linden Av. BS23: W Mare 4K 105
Linden Cl. BA3: Rads 6J 153
BS14: Stoc 4G 77
BS16: Fish 6J 49
BS36: Wint 1C 38
Linden Ct. BS15: Kgswd 7K 49
Linden Dr. BS32: Brad S 6G 27
Linden Gdns. BA1: W'ton 1A 6 (3K 99)
Linden Grange BS6: Redl 5J 47
Linden Ho. BS15: Kgswd 1C 64
BS16: Stap 3E 48
Linden Rd. BS6: Henle, Redl 4H 47
BS21: Clev 5D 54
Lindens, The BS22: Wor 7C 84
Linder Quarter *BS3: Bedm* *6J 61*
(off Cromwell St.)
Lindisfarne Cl. BA15: W'ley 5C 124
Lindon Ho. BS4: Brisl 6G 63
Lindrea St. BS3: Bedm 6H 61
Lindsay Rd. BS7: L'lze 4C 48
Lindsey Cl. BS20: P'head 4B 42
Linear Pk. BS2: Bris 3B 62
Linemere Cl. BS48: Back 4A 72
Linen Wlk. BA1: Swa 1E 100
Lines Way BS14: Whit 7E 76
Lingfield Pk. BS16: Down 6D 38
Link, The BS27: Ched 6D 150
Link La. BA15: Mon F 2E 102
BS40: Burr 3G 133
Link Rd. BS20: P'head 3E 42
BS34: Fil 4B 36
(New Rd.)
BS34: Fil 5C 36
(Springfields)
BS37: Yate 5F 31
BS48: Nail 7H 57
Link Rd. W. BS10: Pat 1H 35
Links Cl. TA8: Bur S 4C 156
Links Gdns. TA8: Bur S 4C 156
Linkside BS21: Clev 3E 54
Links Rd. BS23: Uph 3E 126
Linley Cl. BA2: Bath 6G 99
Linleys, The BA1: Bath 2A 6 (4J 99)
Linne Ho. BA2: Bath 6G 99
Linnell Cl. BS7: L'lze 2D 48
Linnet Cl. BS22: W Mare 3C 106
BS34: Pat 6A 26
Linnet Gdns. BS20: P'head 2H 43
Linnet Way BA3: Mid N 6F 153
BS14: Stoc 3F 77
Lintern Cres. BS30: C Hth 3F 65
Lintham Dr. BS15: Kgswd 3D 64
Lintons Wlk. BS14: H'gro 3C 76
Lion Cl. BS7: L'lze 1D 48
BS48: Nail 7F 57
Lipgate Pl. BS20: P'head 5F 43
Lippiat Hill BA3: Faul 3J 155
LIPPIATT 6E 150
Lippiatt, The BS27: Ched 6E 150
Lippiatt La. BA2: Tims 3F 141
BS25: S'ham 5B 132
BS27: Ched 6E 150
Lisburn Rd. BS4: Know 1A 76
Lisle Rd. BS22: Wor 7E 84
Litfield Pl. BS8: Clftn 2F 61
Litfield Rd. BS8: Clftn 1F 61
Lit. Ann St. BS2: Bris 2K 5 (2B 62)
LITTLE ASHLEY 3E 124
Lit. Birch Cft. BS14: Whit 7C 76
Lit. Bishop St. BS2: Bris 1A 62
LITTLE BRISTOL 1H 15
Lit. Bristol La. GL12: Char 2H 15
Littlebrook BS39: Paul 7C 140
Lit. Caroline Pl. BS8: Clftn 4F 61
Littlecross Ho. BS3: Bris 7A 4 (5H 61)
Littledean BS37: Yate 7E 30
Little Dowles BS30: C Hth 5E 64
Littlefields Av. BS29: Ban 2A 130
Littlefields Ri. BS29: Ban 2B 130
Littlefields Rd. BS29: Ban 2B 130
Lit. George St. BS2: Bris 1K 5 (1B 62)
BS23: W Mare 5G 105
Little Green BS32: Brad S 5F 27
Lit. Green La. BS35: Sev B 6A 16
Little Halt BS20: P'head 4A 42
Little Ham BS21: Clev 2C 68
Little Hayes BS16: Fish 2K 49
Lit. Headley Cl. BS13: Bis 3H 75
Little Hill BA2: Bath 5G 99
Lit. John St. BS1: Bris 3F 5 (2K 61)
Lit. King St. BS1: Bris 5F 5 (3K 61)
Little La. BA2: F'boro 6E 118
Lit. Locky Cl. BS16: L'lze 6E 36
Little Mead BS11: Law W 6B 34
Lit. Mead Cl. BS24: Hut 2C 128
Lit. Meadow BS32: Brad S 1J 37
Lit. Meadow End BS48: Nail 1G 71
Little Orchard BS23: Uph 4F 127
BS27: Ched 6D 150
Little Paradise BS3: Bedm 5K 61
Lit. Parr Cl. BS16: Stap 3E 48
Lit. Paul St. BS2: Bris 1D 4 (1J 61)
Little Pen TA8: Berr 2B 156
LITTLE SOLSBURY 6G 83
Little Solsbury Hill Fort 6F 83
Little Southgate *BA1: Bath* *6G 7*
(within Southgate Shop. Cen.)
Lit. Stanhope St. BA1: Bath 4D 6 (5A 100)
LITTLE STOKE 1F 37
Lit. Stoke La. BS34: Lit S 6E 26
Lit. Stoke Rd. BS9: Stok B 4E 46
Lit. Stony Leas BS16: Fren 7F 37
Lit. Thatch Cl. BS14: H'gro 4E 76
Little Theatre & Cinema 5F 7
Lit. Thomas La. BS1: Bris 4G 5 (3A 62)
LITTLETON 7C 92
Littleton Ct. BS34: Pat 5A 26
Littleton La. BA2: Ston L, Well 7H 143
BS40: Chew M, Winf 6C 92
BS41: Dun 2C 92
Littleton Rd. BS3: Wind H 7K 61
Littleton St. BS5: E'ton 7E 48
LITTLETON-UPON-SEVERN 3A 10
Lit. Wall Drove BS49: Cong 7G 87
Lit. Withey Mead BS9: W Trym 2E 46
Littlewood Cl. BS14: Whit 7D 76
Littlewood La. BS49: C've 7D 70
Litton BS24: W Mare 3J 127
Litton La. BS39: Hin B 7B 138
Livingstone Rd. BA2: Bath 6A 6 (6K 99)
Livingstone Ter. BA2: Bath 7C 6 (6K 99)
Livingston M. BS3: Bedm 6J 61
Llewellyn Ct. BS9: W Trym 7G 35
Llewellyn Way BS22: Wor 1F 107
Lobelia Cl. TA9: Highb 3F 159
Lockemor Rd. BS13: Hart 6B 76
Lockes Paddock BS22: St G 1G 107
Lock Gdns. BS13: Bis 3E 74
LOCKING 1E 128
Locking Castle Bus. Pk.
BS24: W Wick 3G 107
Locking Farm Ind. Est. BS24: Lock 7E 106
Locking Head Drove BS24: Lock 5E 106
BS24: W'ton V 4E 106
Locking Moor Rd. BS22: W Mare 4A 106
BS24: Lock, W Mare 6C 106
LOCKING PARKLANDS 6F 107
Locking Rd. BS22: W Mare 4A 106
BS23: W Mare 5G 105
Lockingwell Rd. BS31: Key 5A 78
LOCKLEAZE 1D 48
Lockleaze Rd. BS7: Hor 2C 48
Lockleys Way BS16: Fren 7F 37
Locksacre BS35: A'ton 6K 11
Locksbrook Ct. BA1: Bath 5H 99
Locksbrook Pl. BA1: Bath 4J 99
Locksbrook Rd. BA1: Bath 5H 99
BS22: Wor 6F 85
Locksbrook Rd. Trad. Est. BA1: Bath 5H 99
Lockside BS20: P'head 1G 43
Lockside Sq. BS20: P'head 1G 43
Lock's La. BS37: Iron A 2C 28
Locks Yd. Cvn. Site BS3: Bedm 1H 75
Loddon Way BA15: Brad A 7J 125
Lodge C'way. BS16: Fish 5H 49
Lodge C'way. Trad. Cen. BS16: Fish 5H 49
Lodge Cl. BS49: Yat 3H 87
Lodge Ct. BS9: Stok B 4E 46
Lodge Dr. BS23: W Mare 3J 105
BS30: Old C 7G 65
BS41: L Ash 7B 60
Lodge Gdns. BA2: Odd D 3K 121
Lodge Hill BS15: Kgswd 6A 50
Lodge La. BS48: Nail, Wrax 6J 57
Lodge Pl. BS1: Bris 3D 4 (2K 61)
Lodge Rd. BS15: Kgswd 6A 50
BS30: Abson, Wick 1A 66
BS37: Yate 3B 30
(North Rd.)
BS37: Yate 3A 30
(Yate Rd.)
Lodgeside Av. BS15: Kgswd 7A 50
Lodgeside Gdns. BS15: Kgswd 7A 50
Lodge St. BS1: Bris 3D 4 (2J 61)

Lodge Wlk.—Mallard Wlk.

Lodge Wlk. BS16: Down 2B 50
Lodore Rd. BS16: Fish 5H 49
LODWAY 3G 45
Lodway BS20: Eas, Pill 4F 45
Lodway Cl. BS20: Pill 3G 45
Lodway Gdns. BS20: Pill 4G 45
Lodway Rd. BS4: Brisl 7E 62
Logan Rd. BS7: Bishop 5K 47
Logus Ct. BS30: Long G 5D 64
Lombard St. BS3: Bedm 5K 61
Lombardy Cl. BS22: W Mare 4C 106
Lomond Rd. BS7: Fil 6B 36
London Rd. BA1: Bath 1G 7 (3C 100)
BS2: Bris 7B 48
BS30: B'yte, Warm 2G 65
BS30: Wick 3E 66
London Rd. E. BA1: Bathe, Bathf 7H 83
London Rd. W. BA1: Bath, Bathe 2E 100
London Sq. BS20: P'head 1G 43
London St. BA1: Bath 1G 7 (3C 100)
BS15: Kgswd 1B 64
Long Acre BA1: Bath 1H 7 (3C 100)
Longacre BS21: Clev 2B 68
Longacre Ho. BA1: Bath 3C 100
Long Acre Rd. BS14: Whit 7C 76
Long Acres Cl. BS9: C Din 1D 46
LONG ASHTON 1K 73
Long Ashton Bus. Pk. BS41: L Ash 1B 74
Long Ashton By-Pass BS41: L Ash 2B 74
BS48: Flax B, L Ash 3F 73
Long Ashton Rd. BS41: L Ash 1A 74
Long Av. BS21: Clev 7B 54
Long Barnaby BA3: Mid N 4E 152
Long Beach Rd. BS30: Long G 6E 64
Longbottom BS25: S'ham 7B 132
BS40: C'hse 7B 132
Longbrook Trad. Est. BS3: Ash V 6E 60
Long Cl. BS16: Fish 2A 50
BS32: Brad S 1G 37
Long Cft. BS37: Yate 2D 30
Long Cross BS11: Law W 7J 33
BS40: F'tn .4H 91
Longcross GL12: Crom 3B 14
Longden Rd. BS16: Down 2D 50
Long Down Av. BS16: L'lze 7E 36
BS34: Stok G 6E 36
Longdown Dr. BS22: Wor 7F 85
Long Eaton Dr. BS14: H'gro 2D 76
Longfellow Av. BA2: Bath 7B 100
Longfellow Rd. BA3: Rads 6G 153
Longfield Rd. BS7: Bishop 5A 48
Longford BS37: Yate 6C 30
Longford Av. BS10: S'mead 7K 35
Long Fow Mnr. BS4: Brisl 1J 77
Long Ground Rd. BS34: Pat 7C 26
Long Handstones BS30: C Hth 5E 64
Long Hay Cl. BA2: Bath 6H 99
Longhills Hostel BS5: S'wll 6J 49
LONGHOUSE 7D 120
Longlands Ho. BS5: Bar H 2E 62
Long La. BS40: F'tn, Redh 5F 91
BS40: Redh, Wrin 2H 111
BS48: Back 7K 71
Longleat Cl. BS9: Henle 3J 47
Longleaze Gdns. BS24: Hut 2D 128
Long Mead BS37: Yate 1E 30
Longmead Av. BS7: Hor 3K 47
Longmead Cft. BS13: Withy 6F 75
Long Mdw. BS16: Stap 3F 49
Longmeadow Rd. BS31: Key 6A 78
Longmead Rd. BS16: Emer G 6F 39
Longmead Ter. BA2: Bath 4C 6 (5K 99)
Longmoor Ct. BS3: Bedm 7G 61
Longmoor Rd. BS3: Bedm 7G 61
Longney Pl. BS34: Pat 5B 26
Longreach BS31: Salt 6G 79
Longreach Gro. BS14: Stoc 3F 77
Longridge Way BS24: W'ton V 5C 106
Long Rd. BS16: Mang 3E 50
Long Row BS1: Bris 5G 5 (3A 62)
Longs Dr. BS37: Yate 4C 30
Longs Yd. BA15: Brad A 6H 125
Longthorn BS48: Back 4H 71
Longthorne Pl. BA2: C Down 2B 122
Long Thorn La. BS40: Nem T, Up Str . . .4H 113
Longton Gro. Rd. BS23: W Mare 4G 105
Longton Ind. Est. BS23: W Mare 6H 105
Long Valley Rd. BA2: Bath 6F 99
Longvernal BA3: Mid N 5D 152
Longway Av. BS14: Whit 6B 76
LONGWELL GREEN 6D 64
Longwell Grn. Gallagher Trade Pk.
BS30: Long G 5C 64
Longwell Green Leisure Cen. 4C 64
Longwell Ho. BS30: Long G 6D 64
Longwood BS4: Brisl 7J 63
Longwood La. BS8: Fail 5K 59
Long Wood Mdws. BS16: L'lze 1E 48
Long Wood Rd. BS16: L'lze 7E 36
Lonsdale Av. BS23: W Mare 7H 105
Lonsdale Bus. Cen. BS15: Kgswd 6A 50
Loop Rd. BA1: Bath 3G 7 (4C 100)
BS16: Soun 5E 50
Lorain Wlk. BS10: Hen 5F 35
Lorne Rd. BA2: Bath 5B 6 (5K 99)
Lorton Cl. BS10: S'mead 6H 35
Lorton Rd. BS10: S'mead 6H 35
Lotts Av. BS48: Back 5K 71
Loughman Cl. BS15: Kgswd 1C 64
Louisa St. BS2: Bris 4K 5 (3B 62)
Louise Av. BS16: Mang 3E 50
Louvigne Cl. TA8: Bur S 1E 158
Love La. BS35: E Comp 6H 25
BS37: Chip S 6G 31
BS37: Yate .2G 31
TA8: Bur S 1D 158
Lovelinch Gdns. BS41: L Ash 1K 73
Lovell Av. BS30: Old C 5H 65
Lovell Dr. BS39: Bis S 1K 137
Lovells, The BS20: Eas 4F 45
Lovells Hill BS15: Han 4K 63
BS39: Bis S 1K 137
Loveridge Ct. BS36: Fram C 7F 29
Loveringe Cl. BS10: Hen 3F 35
Lovers La. BS39: Paul 2E 152
Lover's Wlk. BS21: Clev 4C 54
Lovers' Wlk. BS6: Cot, Redl 6J 47
(not continuous)
BS23: W Mare 4F 105
Love's Hill BA2: Tims 4E 140
Love's La. BA2: F'boro 6C 118
Lowbourne BS14: H'gro 4B 76
LOWER ALMONDSBURY 1C 26
Lower App. Rd. BS1: Bris 6J 5 (4B 62)
Lwr. Ashley Rd. BS2: Bris 7B 48
BS5: E'ton .7C 48
Lower Batch BS40: Chew M 1H 115
Lwr. Borough Walls BA1: Bath . . .5F 7 (5B 100)
Lwr. Bristol Rd. BA2: Bath 4A 6 (3F 99)
BS39: Clut 2H 139
Lwr. Burlington Rd. BS20: P'head 2G 43
Lwr. Camden Pl. BA1: Bath 3C 100
LOWER CANADA 3D 128
Lwr. Castle St. BS1: Bris 2H 5 (2A 62)
Lwr. Chapel La. BS36: Fram C 1G 39
Lwr. Chapel Rd. BS15: Han 4A 64
Lwr. Cheltenham Pl. BS6: Bris 7B 48
Lwr. Church La. BS2: Bris 3D 4 (2K 61)
Lwr. Church Rd. BS23: W Mare 4F 105
LOWER CLAVERHAM 1B 88
Lower Claverham BS49: C'ham 1A 88
Lwr. Clifton Hill BS8: Clftn 4A 4 (3G 61)
Lwr. Cock Rd. BS15: Kgswd 2D 64
Lwr. College St. BS1: Bris 5C 4 (3J 61)
Lwr. Conham Va. BS15: St G 4H 63
(not continuous)
Lower Ct. Rd. BS32: Alm 1C 26
Lwr. Down Rd. BS20: P'head 3E 42
Lwr. East Hayes BA1: Bath 3D 100
LOWER EASTON 7D 48
LOWER FAILAND 1E 58
Lwr. Fallow Cl. BS14: Whit 6B 76
Lwr. Farm La. BA2: Cor 4B 98
Lwr. Gay St. BS2: Bris 1K 61
Lower Gro. Rd. BS16: Fish 4G 49
Lwr. Guinea St. BS1: Bris 7F 5 (4K 61)
LOWER HAMSWELL 6J 67
Lwr. Hanham Rd. BS15: Han 4A 64
LOWER HAZEL 2H 19
Lwr. Hedgemead Rd.
BA1: Bath 1G 7 (3C 100)
Lwr. High St. BS11: Shire 7H 33
Lower Ho. BS34: Fil 4D 36
Lower Ho. Cres. BS34: Fil 3D 36
Lwr. Kewstoke Rd. BS22: Kew, Wor 1C 106
Lwr. Kingsdown Rd. SN13: Kgdn 1C 102
Lwr. Knole La. BS10: Bren 4G 35
LOWER KNOWLE 7A 62
Lwr. Knowles Rd. BS21: Clev 7C 54
Lwr. Lamb St. BS1: Bris 5C 4 (3J 61)
LOWER LANGFORD 7D 110
Lwr. Linden Rd. BS21: Clev 6D 54
Lwr. Maudlin St. BS1: Bris 2F 5 (2K 61)
Lwr. Moor Rd. BS37: Yate 2E 30
Lwr. Myrtle Hill BS20: Pill 3G 45
Lwr. New Rd. BS27: Ched 7C 150
Lower Northend BA1: Bathe 5H 83
Lwr. North St. BS27: Ched 6D 150
Lwr. Norton La. BS22: Kew 1K 105, 7A 84
(Kewside)
BS22: Kew .7C 84
(Queen's Way)
Lwr. Oldfield Pk. BA2: Bath 6B 6 (6K 99)
Lwr. Parade Ground Rd. BS24: Lock 7F 107
Lwr. Park Row BS1: Bris 3E 4 (2K 61)
LOWER PEASEDOWN 5B 142
Lwr. Queen's Rd. BS21: Clev 6D 54
Lwr. Redland M. BS6: Redl 6H 47
Lwr. Redland Rd. BS6: Redl 6H 47
Lower Rd. BS39: Hin B 7A 138
Lwr. Sidney St. BS3: Bris 5G 61
LOWER SOUNDWELL 6D 50
Lwr. Station Rd. BS16: Fish 4J 49
BS16: Stap H 4A 50
Lower Stoke BA2: Lim S 3J 123
Lwr. Stone Cl. BS36: Fram C 6G 29
Lower St. SN14: Dyr 4K 53
LOWER STRODE 5A 114
Lower Strode BS40: Up Str 4K 113
Lwr. Strode Rd. BS21: Clev 3A 68
LOWER SWAINSWICK 1E 100
Lwr. Thirlmere Rd. BS34: Pat 6C 26
Lwr. Tockington Rd. BS32: Toc 5D 18
LOWER WEARE 6D 148
LOWER WESTON 4J 99
Lower Whitelands BA3: Rads 3B 154
Lower Woods Nature Reserve 1K 23
LOWER WRAXALL 6J 103
LOWER WRITHLINGTON 3C 154
Lowlis Cl. BS10: Hen 4F 35
Lowry Gro. BS16: L'lze 7E 36
Lowther Rd. BS10: S'mead 5J 35
Loxley Gdns. BA2: Bath 7J 99
LOXTON 2G 147
Loxton Dr. BA2: Bath 5H 99
Loxton Rd. BS23: W Mare 2H 127
Loxton Sq. BS14: H'gro 4C 76
Lucas Cl. BS4: Brisl 1F 77
Luccombe Hill BS6: Redl 6H 47
Luccombe Quarry BA15: Brad A 5J 125
Luckington Rd. BS7: Hor 6A 36
Lucklands Rd. BA1: W'ton 2J 99
Luckley Av. BS13: Hart 5J 75
Luckwell Rd. BS3: Bedm 6H 61
Lucky La. BS3: Bedm 7E 4 (5K 61)
Ludlow Cl. BS2: Bris 7B 48
BS30: Will .7F 65
BS31: Key .5B 78
Ludlow Ct. BS30: Will 1F 79
Ludlow Rd. BS7: Hor 1C 48
Ludwell Cl. BS36: Wint 2B 38
Ludwells Orchard BS39: Paul 1C 152
Luke's Cl. BA3: Rads 3K 153
Lullington Rd. BS4: Know 7D 62
LULSGATE BOTTOM 3E 90
Lulsgate Rd. BS13: Bis 2G 75
Lulworth Cres. BS16: Down 7D 38
Lulworth Rd. BS31: Key 6C 78
Lundy Dr. TA8: Bur S 3D 158
Lundy Ga. BS20: P'head 2H 43
Lunty Mead BS48: Back 4H 71
Lupin Cl. BS16: Emer G 7G 39
Lurgan Wlk. BS4: Know 1K 75
Lutyens Cl. BS16: Stap 7F 37
Luvers La. BS40: Blag 4A 134
Lux Furlong BS9: Sea M 1B 46
Luxton St. BS5: E'ton 1D 62
Lychgate Pk. BS24: Lock 1E 128
Lydbrook Cl. BS37: Yate 6D 30
Lyddieth Ct. BA15: W'ley 5C 124
Lyddington Rd. BS7: Hor 6A 36
Lyddon Rd. BS22: Wor 1F 107
LYDE GREEN .7H 39
LYDE GREEN RDBT. 7F 39
Lydford Wlk. BS3: Wind H 7K 61
Lydia Ct. BS7: Bishop 4B 48
Lydiard Cft. BS15: Han 5A 64
Lydney Rd. BS10: S'mead 7K 35
BS16: Stap H 4C 50
Lydstep Ter. BS3: Bedm 5J 61
LYE CROSS .3A 112
Lye Cross Rd. BS40: Redh 3A 112
Lyefield Rd. BS22: Kew, Wor 7C 84
LYE GREEN .7E 124
LYE HOLE 2B 112
Lye Hole La. BS40: Redh 2B 112
Lye Mead BS40: Winf 5A 92
Lyes, The BS49: Cong 1K 109
Lyme Gdns. BA1: Bath 4H 99
Lyme Rd. BA1: Bath 4H 99
Lymore Av. BA2: Bath 7A 6 (6J 99)
Lymore Cl. BA2: Bath 7J 99
Lymore Gdns. BA2: Bath 6J 99
Lymore Ter. BA2: Bath 7A 6 (7J 99)
LYMPSHAM .5K 145
Lympsham Grn. BA2: Odd D 3K 121
Lympsham Rd. BS24: Lym 5K 145
Lynbrook BS41: L Ash 1K 73
Lynbrook La. BA2: Bath 1B 122
Lynch, The BS25: Wins 6F 131
Lynch Cl. BS22: Wor 1D 106
Lynch Ct. BS30: Long G 5D 64
Lynch Cres. BS25: Wins 6F 131
Lynch La. BS27: Ched 6E 150
Lynchmead BS25: Wins 6F 131
Lyncombe Dr. BS25: Sandf 1J 131
LYNCOMBE HILL 7C 100
Lyncombe Hill BA2: Bath 7H 7 (6C 100)
Lyncombe La. BS25: C'hll, Sandf 3K 131
LYNCOMBE VALE 1C 122
Lyncombe Va. BA2: Bath 7C 100
Lyncombe Va. Rd. BA2: Bath 1C 122
Lyncombe Wlk. BS16: Fish 6K 49
Lyndale Av. BS9: Stok B 3D 46
Lyndale Rd. BS5: St G 1F 63
BS37: Yate .5D 30
Lynde Cl. BS13: Hart 6H 75
Lyndhurst Bungs. BA15: Brad A 6H 125
Lyndhurst Pl. BA1: Bath 3C 100
Lyndhurst Rd. BA2: Bath 5J 99
BA3: Mid N 6F 153
BS9: W Trym 1F 47
BS23: W Mare 1G 127
BS31: Key .7D 78
Lyndhurst Ter. BA1: Bath 3C 100
Lynfield Pk. BA1: W'ton 1J 99
Lynmouth Cl. BS22: Wor 2E 106
Lynmouth Rd. BS2: Bris 6B 48
Lynn Rd. BS16: Stap 3F 49
Lynton BS15: Kgswd 1E 64
Lynton Cl. BS20: P'head 4G 43
Lynton Pl. BS5: Redf 1E 62
Lynton Rd. BA3: Mid N 6F 153
BS3: Wind H 1J 75
TA8: Bur S 2D 158
Lynton Way BS16: Fren 6K 37
Lynwood Cl. BA3: Mid N 6E 152
Lynwood Ct. BS13: Bis 4G 75
Lynwood Rd. BS3: Bedm 7H 61
Lynx Cres. BS24: W Mare 2K 127
Lyons Ct. BS23: W Mare 5H 105
Lyons Ct. Rd. BS14: Stoc 3F 77
Lyppiatt Rd. BS5: Redf 1F 63
Lyppincourt Rd. BS10: Bren 4G 35
Lypstone Cl. BS24: W'ton V 4E 106
Lypstone Farm BS24: W'ton V 4E 106
Lysander Rd. BS10: Pat 1H 35
BS34: Pat .1H 35
Lysander Wlk. BS34: Stok G 2G 37
Lytchet Dr. BS16: Down 7D 38
Lytes Cary Rd. BS31: Key 1E 96
Lytham Ho. BS4: Brisl 1F 77
Lytton Gdns. BA2: Bath 7H 99
Lytton Gro. BS7: Hor 7C 36
BS31: Key .5E 78
Lyveden Gdns. BS13: Hart 5H 75
Lyvedon Way BS41: L Ash 1B 74

M

Mabberley Cl. BS16: Emer G 3G 51
McAdam Way BS1: Bris 4F 61
Macaulay Bldgs. BA2: Bath 7E 100
Macauley Rd. BS7: Hor 7C 36
McCrae Rd. BS24: Lock 7F 107
Macdonald Wlk. BS15: Kgswd 1B 64
Macey's Rd. BS13: Hart 7K 75
Macfarlane Chase BS23: W Mare 7J 105
Machin Cl. BS10: Hen 4F 35
Machin Ct. BS10: Hen 4F 35
Machin Gdns. BS10: Hen 4G 35
Machin Ri. BS10: Hen 4F 35
Machin Rd. BS10: Hen 4F 35
Machins M. BS10: Hen 4F 35
Macies, The BA1: W'ton 7H 81
Mackie Av. BS34: Fil 5D 36
Mackie Gro. BS34: Fil 5D 36
Mackie Rd. BS34: Fil 5D 36
McLaren Rd. BS11: A'mth 6F 33
Macleod Cl. BS21: Clev 7A 54
Macquarie Farm Cl. BS49: Yat 2G 87
Macrae Ct. BS15: Kgswd 1C 64
Macrae Office Pk. BS20: Pill 4J 45
Macrae Rd. BS20: Pill 4J 45
Madam La. BS22: Wor 2D 106
(Orchard Cl.)
BS22: Wor 1E 106
(Wynter Cl.)
Madam's Paddock BS40: Chew M 2H 115
Madden Cl. TA8: Bur S 1E 158
Maddocks Slade TA8: Bur S 7C 156
Madeira Ct. BS23: W Mare 4E 104
Madeira Rd. BS21: Clev 6D 54
BS23: W Mare 3E 104
Madeline Rd. BS16: Fish 6H 49
Madison Cl. BS37: Yate 4D 30
Maesbury BS15: Kgswd 3C 64
Maesbury Rd. BS31: Key 1E 96
Maesknoll La. BS14: Nor M, Whit 3C 94
BS39: Nor M 3C 94
Maesknoll Rd. BS4: Know 6C 62
Magdalena Ct. BS1: Bris 6G 5 (4A 62)
Magdalen Av. BA2: Bath 7E 6 (6B 100)
Magdalene Pl. BS2: Bris 7B 48
Magdalene Rd. BA3: Writ 4C 154
Magdalen Rd. BA2: Bath 7E 6 (6B 100)
Magdalen Way BS22: Wor 1E 106
Magellan Cl. BS22: Wor 7D 84
Maggs Cl. BS10: S'mead 4K 35
Maggs Hill BA2: Tims 3F 141
Maggs La. BS5: S'wll 6G 49
BS14: Whit 6D 76
Magistrates' Court
Bath 4J 7 (5D 100)
Bristol 1F 5 (1K 61)
Flax Bourton 2F 73
North Somerset 2G 107
Magnolia Av. BS22: Wor 3E 106
Magnolia Cl. BS22: W Mare 5C 106
Magnolia Gdns. BS32: Alm 1G 27
Magnolia Grange BS22: Wor 2D 106
Magnolia M. *BS22: Kew* *1J 105*
(in Ardnave Holiday Pk.)
Magnolia Rd. BA3: Rads 5J 153
Magnon Rd. BA15: Brad A 5F 125
Magpie Bottom La. BS5: St G 3K 63
BS15: Kgswd 3A 64
Magpie Cl. BS22: Wor 4C 106
TA8: Bur S 6D 156
MAIDEN HEAD 2F 93
Maidenhead Rd. BS13: Hart 7K 75
Maiden Way BS11: Shire 1G 45
Maidstone Gro. BS24: W Mare 4J 127
Maidstone St. BS3: Wind H 6B 62
MAINES BATCH 1F 111
Main Rd. BS16: Short 3G 51
BS24: Hew .6B 86
BS24: Hut 3B 128
BS35: E Comp 4F 25
BS48: Back, B'ley 4C 88
BS48: Flax B 3C 72
BS49: C've .4C 88
TA9: W Hunt 7E 158
Main Vw. BS36: Coal H 7H 29
Maisemore BS37: Yate 1D 40
Maisemore Av. BS34: Pat 5D 26
Makin Cl. BS30: Old C 4G 65
Malago Greenway BS13: Bis 3G 75
Malago Rd. BS3: Bedm 6J 61
Malago Va. Est. BS3: Bedm 6J 61
Malago Wlk. BS13: Withy 6E 74
Malden Mead BS14: Whit 5C 76
Maldowers La. BS5: St G 7J 49
Malin Pde. BS20: P'head 2H 43
Mall, The BS8: Clftn 2F 61
BS32: Brad S 5G 27
Mallard Cl. BS5: S'wll 7H 49
BS32: Brad S 4F 27
BS37: Chip S 6G 31
Mallard Pl. TA9: Highb 4E 158
Mallard Wlk. BS22: W Mare 4C 106

A-Z Bristol, Bath & North Somerset Atlas 187

Mallow Cl.—Mead Way

Mallow Cl. BS21: Clev 7E 54
BS35: T'bry 2B 12
Malmains Dr. BS16: Fren 6K 37
Malmesbury Cl. BS6: Redl 4J 47
BS30: Bar C 4D 64
Malpass Dr. BS15: Han 5A 64
Malt Ho. BS1: Bris 4G 5
Malthouse, The BS6: Bris 6B 48
Maltings, The BA15: Brad A 7H 125
BS6: Bris 6B 48
(off Fairlawn Rd.)
BS22: Wor 2D 106
Maltings Ind. Estate, The
BA1: Bath 4G 99
Maltlands BS22: W Mare 5B 106
Malvern Bldgs. BA1: Bath 1C 100
Malvern Ct. BS5: St G 2G 63
Malvern Dr. BS30: Old C 4G 65
BS35: T'bry 4B 12
Malvern Rd. BS4: Brisl 6F 63
BS5: St G 2H 63
BS23: W Mare 7G 105
Malvern Ter. BA1: Bath 2C 100
Malvern Vs. *BA1: Bath 2C 100*
(off Camden Rd.)
Mancroft Av. BS11: Law W 1J 45
Mandy Mdws. BA3: Mid N 5D 152
MANGOTSFIELD 3E 50
Mangotsfield Rd.
BS16: Mang, Stap H 4D 50
Manilla Cres. BS23: W Mare 3E 104
Manilla Pl. BS23: W Mare 3E 104
Manilla Rd. BS8: Clftn 2G 61
Manmoor La. BS21: Clev 1G 69
Manor Cl. BA2: F'frd 7A 124
BA2: Well 4K 143
BS20: Eas 4E 44
BS20: P'head 3C 42
BS32: Toc 4D 18
BS36: Coal H 1G 39
TA8: Berr 1B 156
Manor Cl., The BS8: Abb L 1A 60
Mnr. Copse Rd. BA3: Writ 4C 154
Manor Ct. *BS5: E'ton 7D 48*
(off St Mark's Gro.)
BS16: Stap 4G 49
BS23: W Mare 4J 105
BS24: Lock 1E 128
BS48: Back 5J 71
Manor Ct. Dr. BS7: Hor 1A 48
Manor Dr. BA1: Bathf 1A 102
TA8: Berr 1B 156
Mnr. Farm Cvn. Pk. BS23: Uph 4G 127
Mnr. Farm Cl. BS24: W Mare 3K 127
BS39: Paul 7B 140
Mnr. Farm Cotts. BS32: Brad S 5E 26
Mnr. Farm Cres.
BS24: W Mare 3K 127
BS32: Brad S 6F 27
MANOR FARM RDBT. 6F 27
Manor Gdns. BA2: F'boro 6D 118
BA15: Brad A 4H 125
BS22: Kew 1K 105
BS24: Lock 1E 128
Manor Gdns. Ho. BS16: Fish 3H 49
Manor Grange BS24: B'don 6K 127
Manor Gro. BS16: Mang 4E 50
BS34: Pat 4D 26
Manor Hall BS8: Clftn 3A 4 (2H 61)
Manor Ho. BS2: Bris 2D 4
Manor Ho. Ct. BS14: H'gro 4E 76
Manor Ho. La. BS14: H'gro 5E 76
Manor La. BS8: Abb L 1K 59
BS36: Wint 7D 28
Manor Pk. BA1: Bath 3H 99
BA3: Writ 4C 154
BS6: Redl 5H 47
BS32: Toc 3D 18
Manor Pk. Cl. BA3: Writ 4C 154
Manor Pl. BS16: Fren 6A 38
BS34: Stok G 3J 37
Manor Ride TA9: Bre K 5K 157
Manor Rd. BA1: W'ton 2J 99
BA3: Writ 4C 154
BS7: Bishop 4A 48
BS8: Abb L 3K 59
BS13: Bis 4F 75
BS16: Fish 3H 49
BS16: Mang 4E 50
BS23: W Mare 3H 105
BS30: Wick 3C 66
BS31: Key, Salt 7D 78
BS37: Rang, Yate 6K 22
TA8: Bur S 1D 158
Manor Ter. BA3: Writ 4C 154
Manor Valley BS23: W Mare 3J 105
Manor Vs. BA1: W'ton 2J 99
Manor Wlk. BS35: T'bry 1K 11
Manor Way BS8: Fail 6G 59
BS37: Chip S 5J 31
TA8: Berr 1B 156
Mansbrook Ho. BA3: Mid N 5E 152
Mansel Cl. BS31: Salt 7G 79
Mansfield Av. BS23: W Mare 4K 105
Mansfield Cl. BS23: W Mare 4K 105
Mansfield St. BS3: Bedm 7H 61
Manston Cl. BS14: Stoc 3E 76
Mantle Cl. BS21: Clev 7E 54
Manvers St. BA1: Bath 5G 7 (5C 100)
Manworthy Rd. BS4: Brisl 6F 63
Manx Rd. BS7: Hor 1B 48
Maple Av. BS16: Fish 5A 50
BS35: T'bry 3A 12
Maple Cl. BS14: Stoc 5F 77
BS23: W Mare 4J 105
BS30: Old C 5F 65
BS34: Lit S 7E 26
Maple Ct. BS15: Kgswd 7B 50
BS23: W Mare 3E 104
Maple Dr. BA3: Rads 5J 153
TA8: Bur S 2D 158
Maple Gdns. BA2: Bath 7A 100
Maple Grange BS9: W Trym 2H 47
Maple Gro. BA2: Bath 7A 100
TA8: Berr 2B 156
Maple Ho. BS2: Bris 1F 5
Maple Leaf Ct. BS8: Clftn 3A 4 (2H 61)
Mapleleaze BS4: Brisl 6F 63
Maplemeade BS7: Bishop 4J 47
Maple Pk. BS14: H'gro 3E 76
Mapleridge La. BS37: Hort, Yate 5H 23
Maple Ri. BA3: Rads 4B 154
Maple Rd. BS4: St Ap 4F 63
BS7: Hor 3K 47
Maples, The BS48: Nail 1E 70
Maples, The (Mobile Home Pk.)
BS37: Hort 6K 23
Maplestone Rd. BS14: Whit 7C 76
Mapleton La. BS25: Star 3K 131
Maple Vw. *BS22: Kew 1J 105*
(in Ardnave Holiday Pk.)
Maple Wlk. BS16: Puck 3C 52
BS31: Key 6B 78
Mapstone Cl. BS16: H'ook 4K 37
Map Stone Ri. BS30: Long G 6C 64
Marbeck Rd. BS10: S'mead 6H 35
Marchfields Way BS23: W Mare 6H 105
Marconi Cl. BS23: W Mare 5K 105
Marconi Dr. TA9: Highb 3F 159
Marconi Rd. BS20: P'head 3B 42
Mardale Cl. BS10: S'mead 5J 35
Marden Rd. BS31: Key 6E 78
Mardon Rd. BS4: St Ap 1G 63
Mardons Cl. BA3: Mid N 6F 153
Mardyke Ferry Rd. BS1: Bris 6A 4 (4H 61)
Margaret Cres. TA8: Bur S 3C 158
Margaret Rd. BS13: Withy 6F 75
Margaret's Bldgs. BA1: Bath 2E 6 (4B 100)
Margaret's Hill BA1: Bath 1G 7 (3C 100)
Margaret's St. BA15: Brad A 6H 125
Margate St. BS3: Wind H 6B 62
Marguerite Rd. BS13: Bis 3F 75
Marigold Wlk. BS3: Bedm 7G 61
Marina Gdns. BS16: Fish 5G 49
Marindin Dr. BS22: Wor 7F 85
Marine Dr. TA8: Bur S 2D 158
Marine Hill BS21: Clev 4C 54
Marine Pde. BS20: Pill 3G 45
BS21: Clev 5C 54
BS23: W Mare 7F 105
(Beach Rd.)
BS23: W Mare 3D 104
(Claremont Cres.)
Mariner's Cl. BS22: W Mare 3B 106
Mariners Cl. BS48: Back 4J 71
Mariner's Dr. BS9: Stok B 4D 46
Mariners Dr. BS48: Back 4J 71
Mariner's Path BS9: Stok B 4D 46
Mariners Path BS20: P'head 3A 42
Mariners Way BS20: Pill 3G 45
Marion Rd. BS15: Han 6K 63
Marion Wlk. BS5: St G 2J 63
Marissal Cl. BS10: Hen 4E 34
Marissal Rd. BS10: Hen 4D 34
Marisston Way BS30: Old C 3G 65
Maritime Heritage Cen. 6B 4 (4H 61)
Maritime Wlk. TA9: Highb 3F 159
Marjoram Pl. BS32: Brad S 7H 27
Marjoram Way BS20: P'head 3H 43
Market Av. BS22: St G 1G 107
Marketgate BS1: Bris 2J 5
Market Ind. Est. BS49: Yat 2H 87
Market La. BS23: W Mare 4F 105
Market Pl. BA3: Rads 3K 153
BS40: Winf 4K 91
Marketside BS2: Bris 5C 62
Market Sq. BS16: Fish 5A 50
BS35: T'bry 4K 11
Market Steps BS1: Bris 4F 5
Market St. BA15: Brad A 5H 125
TA9: Highb 5G 159
Market Ter. TA9: Highb 5G 159
Marklands BS9: Stok B 5E 46
Mark La. BS1: Bris 4D 4 (3J 61)
Mark Rd. TA9: Highb, Watch 5H 159
MARKSBURY 3F 119
Marksbury Ga. BA2: Cor 7F 97
Marksbury Rd. BS3: Bedm, Wind H 7J 61
Marlborough Av. BS16: Fish 5G 49
Marlborough Bldgs.
BA1: Bath 2D 6 (4A 100)
Marlborough Ct. BA2: C'ton D 5G 101
TA8: Bur S 6D 156
Marlborough Dr. BS16: Fren 6K 37
BS22: Wor 2E 106
Marlborough Flats BS2: Bris 1E 4
Marlborough Hill BS2: Bris 1E 4 (1K 61)
Marlborough Hill Pl. BS2: Bris 1E 4 (1K 61)
Marlborough Ho. BS2: Bris 1E 4
Marlborough La. BA1: Bath 3D 6 (4A 100)
Marlborough St. BA1: Bath 1D 6 (3A 100)
BS1: Bris 1F 5 (1K 61)
BS2: Bris 1F 5 (1K 61)
BS5: Eastv 5G 49
Marlepit Gro. BS13: Bis 4E 74
Marle Pits BS48: Back 4H 71
Marlfield Wlk. BS13: Bis 3E 74
Marling Rd. BS5: St G 1H 63
Marlowe Ho. *BS23: W Mare 1H 127*
(off Lonsdale Av.)
Marlwood Dr. BS10: Bren 4G 35
Marmaduke St. BS3: Wind H 6B 62
Marmalade La. BS4: Brisl 1E 76
Marmion Cres. BS10: Hen 4E 34
Marne Cl. BS14: Stoc 5F 77
Marron Cl. BS26: Axb 4J 149
Marsden Rd. BA2: Bath 1H 121
Marshacre La. BS35: Elbton 5B 10
Marshall Ho. BS16: Fish 4H 49
Marshall Wlk. BS4: Know 3K 75
Marsham Way BS30: Bar C, Long G 4C 64
Marsh Cl. BS36: Wint 3C 38
MARSH COMMON 2E 24
Marsh Comn. Rd. BS35: E Comp, Piln 7D 16
Marshfield La. BS30: Upton C 2A 80
Marshfield Pk. BS16: Down 7A 38
Marshfield Rd. BS16: Fish 4K 49
Marshfield Way BA1: Bath 2C 100
Marsh Ho. BS1: Bris 4E 4 (3K 61)
Marsh La. BS3: Bedm 7G 61
BS5: Redf 3E 62
BS20: Eas 1C 44
BS39: Clut, Hall 3H 139
Marsh La. Ind. Est. BS20: Eas 2C 44
Marsh Rd. BS3: Ash G 6F 61
BS49: Yat 4H 87
Marsh St. BS1: Bris 5E 4 (3K 61)
BS11: A'mth 7G 33
Marshwall La. BS32: Alm 7A 18
Marson Rd. BS21: Clev 6D 54
Marston Rd. BS4: Know 7D 62
Martcombe Rd. BS20: Eas 5E 44
Martha's Orchard BS13: Bis 3E 74
Martin Cl. BS34: Pat 6A 26
Martin Ct. *BS16: Fish 5G 49*
(off Marina Gdns.)
Martindale Ct. BS22: W Mare 4B 106
Martindale Rd. BS22: W Mare 4B 106
Martingale Rd. BS4: Brisl 5F 63
Martingale Way BS20: P'head 2G 43
Martins, The BS20: P'head 2J 43
Martin's Cl. TA8: Bur S 4C 156
Martins Cl. BS15: Han 4A 64
Martins Gro. BS22: Wor 2C 106
Martin's Rd. BS15: Han 4A 64
Martin St. BS3: Bedm 6H 61
Martock BS24: W Mare 3H 127
Martock Cres. BS3: Bedm 1J 75
Martock Rd. BS3: Bedm 1J 75
BS31: Key 7E 78
Marwood Cl. TA8: Bur S 7E 156
Marwood Rd. BS4: Know 2A 76
Marybush La. BS2: Bris 3H 5 (2A 62)
Mary Carpenter Pl. BS2: Bris 7B 48
Mary Ct. *BS5: Redf 1F 63*
(off Alfred St.)
Marygold Leaze BS30: C Hth 5E 64
Mary Seacole Ct. *BS2: Bris 6C 48*
(off Mercia Dr.)
Mary St. BS5: Redf 1F 63
Mascall's Wood Nature Reserve 6F 151
Mascot Rd. BS3: Wind H 6K 61
Masefield Way BS7: Hor 2C 48
Maskelyne Av. BS10: Hor 1K 47
Masonpit Pool La. BS36: Wint 6A 28
Masons La. BA15: Brad A 5H 125
Masons Vw. BS36: Wint 1D 38
Mason's Way BS27: Ched 7E 150
Matchells Cl. BS4: St Ap 3G 63
Materman Rd. BS14: Stoc 5G 77
Matford Cl. BS10: Bren 3K 35
BS36: Wint 2C 38
Matthews Cl. BS14: Stoc 4H 77
Matthews Rd. BS5: Redf 2E 62
Maules Gdns. BS34: H'ook 5H 37
Maules La. BS16: H'ook 5H 37
Maunsell Rd. BS11: Law W 5B 34
BS24: W'ton V 5C 106
Maurice Rd. BS6: Bris 6A 48
Mautravers Cl. BS32: Brad S 7F 27
Mawdeley Ho. *BS3: Bedm 5J 61*
(off Catherine Mead St.)
Max Mill La. BS25: Ban, Wins 4B 130
Maxse Rd. BS4: Know 6D 62
Maxwell Dr. TA9: Highb 3F 159
Maybank Rd. BS37: Yate 5D 30
Maybec Gdns. BS5: St G 3J 63
Maybourne BS4: Brisl 7J 63
Maybrick Rd. BA2: Bath 7A 6 (6K 99)
Maycliffe Pk. BS6: Bris 6B 48
Mayfair Av. BS48: Nail 1G 71
Mayfield Av. BS16: Fish 6J 49
BS22: Wor 3C 106
Mayfield Ct. BS16: Fish 6J 49
Mayfield M. BA2: Bath 7A 6 (6J 99)
MAYFIELD PARK 6J 49
Mayfield Pk. BS16: Fish 6J 49
Mayfield Pk. Nth. BS16: Fish 6J 49
Mayfield Pk. Sth. BS16: Fish 6J 49
Mayfield Rd. BA2: Bath 7A 6 (6K 99)
Mayfields BS31: Key 5C 78
Mayflower Cl. BS9: C Din 1C 46
Mayflower Ct. BS16: Stap H 3C 50
TA9: Highb 4G 159
Mayflower Gdns. BS48: Nail 7J 57
May La. BA1: Bath 3H 99
Maynard Cl. BS13: Hart 5J 75
BS21: Clev 6F 55
Maynard Rd. BS13: Hart 5J 75
Maynard Ter. BS39: Clut 2H 139
Mayors Bldgs. BS16: Fish 3K 49
Maypole Cl. BS39: Clut 2G 139
Maypole Sq. BS15: Han 4A 64
Mays Cl. BS36: Coal H 7H 29
Maysfield Cl. BS20: P'head 5F 43
MAY'S GREEN 7B 86
Maysgreen La. BS24: Hew 7B 86
MAYSHILL 5J 29
Mays Hill BS36: Fram C 5J 29
May's La. BS24: Hew, Pux 1B 108
(not continuous)
Maysmead La. BS40: L'frd 6E 110
May St. BS15: Kgswd 7A 50
Maytree Av. BS13: Bis 3H 75
May Tree Cl. BS48: Nail 1E 70
Maytree Cl. BS13: Bis 3H 75
May Tree Rd. BA3: Rads 5J 153
Maytrees BS5: Eastv 6E 48
May Tree Wlk. BS31: Key 7A 78
Mayville Av. BS34: Fil 4C 36
Maywood Av. BS16: Fish 4K 49
Maywood Cres. BS16: Fish 4K 49
Maywood Rd. BS16: Fish 4A 50
Maze St. BS5: Bar H 3D 62
Mead, The BA2: F'boro 6E 118
BA2: Tims 2G 141
BA15: W'ley 5C 124
BS25: S'ham 5A 132
BS31: Key 7B 78
BS34: Fil 3D 36
BS35: A'ton 7J 11
BS39: Clut 2G 139
(not continuous)
BS39: Paul 1B 152
BS41: Dun 1D 92
Mead Cl. BA2: Bath 1A 122
BS11: Shire 2J 45
BS27: Ched 7H 151
Mead Ct. BS36: Wint 1C 38
Mead Ct. Bus. Pk. BS35: T'bry 5K 11
Meade Ho. BA2: Bath 6G 99
Meadgate BS16: Emer G 1F 51
MEADGATE EAST 3J 141
MEADGATE WEST 3H 141
Meadlands BA2: Cor 4B 98
Mead La. BS24: Nye, Sandf 7D 108
BS25: Sandf 1E 130
BS31: Salt 6K 79
BS32: Brad S 1G 37
BS35: Olv 3K 17
(not continuous)
BS40: Blag 2C 134
Meadowbank BS22: Wor 1D 106
Meadow Cl. BS16: Down 1D 50
BS48: Back 4K 71
BS48: Nail 6G 57
TA9: Highb 4F 159
Meadow Ct. BA1: Bath 4G 99
Meadow Ct. Dr. BS30: Old C 6G 65
Meadow Cft. BS24: W Mare 3K 127
Meadowcroft BS16: Down 7E 38
Meadowcroft Dr. TA8: Bur S 7E 156
Meadow Dr. BA2: Odd D 4K 121
BS20: W'ton G 7B 42
BS24: Lock 1F 129
Meadowfield BA15: Brad A 6F 125
Meadow Gdns. BA1: Bath 2G 99
Meadow Gro. BS11: Shire 1H 45
Meadowland BS49: Yat 2G 87
Meadowland Rd. BS10: Hen 3E 34
Meadowlands BS22: St G 2G 107
Meadow La. BA2: Batham 2F 101
Meadow Lea BS39: Hall 7J 139
Meadow Mead
BS36: Fram C 6F 29
BS37: Yate 1E 30
Meadow Pk. BA1: Bathf 7K 83
Meadow Pl. BS22: St G 1H 107
Meadow Rd. BS21: Clev 6E 54
BS37: Chip S 5G 31
BS39: Paul 2D 152
GL12: Ley 1B 14
Meadows, The BS15: Han 5B 64
Meadows Cl. BS20: P'head 3B 42
Meadows End BS25: C'hll 1K 131
Meadow Side BS37: Iron A 2H 29
Meadowside BS35: T'bry 4B 12
Meadowside Dr. BS14: Whit 7C 76
Meadow St. BS11: A'mth 3E 32
BS23: W Mare 5G 105
BS26: Axb 5J 149
Meadowsweet Av. BS34: Fil 4D 36
Meadowsweet Ct. *BS16: Stap 3G 49*
(off Foxglove Cl.)
Meadow Va. BS5: St G 7J 49
Meadow Vw. BA3: Rads 5A 154
BS36: Fram C 7G 29
TA9: Highb 6E 158
Meadow Vw. Cl. BA1: Bath 3G 99
Meadow Vs. *BS23: W Mare 4G 105*
(off Prospect Pl.)
Meadow Way BS32: Brad S 7G 27
Mead Ri. BS3: Bris 7J 5 (5B 62)
Mead Rd. BS20: P'head 6E 42
BS34: Stok G 1G 37
BS37: Chip S 6J 31
Meads, The BS16: Down 1D 50
(not continuous)
Mead St. BS3: Bris 7J 5 (5B 62)
Mead Va. BS22: W Mare, Wor 3C 106
Mead Way BS9: Sea M 2C 46
BS35: T'bry 5K 11

Meadway—Moorland Pk.

Meadway BA2: F'boro 6E **118**
BS39: Temp C 4G **139**
Meadway Av. BS48: Nail 7F **57**
Mearcombe La. BS24: B'don 1D **146**
Meardon Rd. BS14: Stoc 4G **77**
Meare BS24: W Mare 3H **127**
Meare Rd. BA2: C Down 2B **122**
MEARNS 3C **140**
Mecca Bingo
Bristol 2D **62**
Mede Cl. BS1: Bris 7G **5** (4A **62**)
Media Ho. BS8: Clftn 3A **4**
Medical Av. BS2: Bris 3D **4** (2J **61**)
Medina Cl. BS35: T'bry 5A **12**
Medlar Cl. BS10: Pat 1H **35**
Medway Cl. BS31: Key 7E **78**
Medway Ct. BS35: T'bry 4B **12**
Medway Dr. BS31: Key 7E **78**
BS36: Fram C 7F **29**
Meere Bank BS11: Law W 6B **34**
Meer Wall BS24: Cong 1F **109**
BS25: Cong 1F **109**
Meeting Ho., The BS1: Bris 2H **5**
Meeting Ho. La. BS49: C'ham, C've 1C **88**
Meg Thatchers Gdns. BS5: St G 2K **63**
Meg Thatcher's Grn. BS5: St G 2K **63**
Melbourne Dr. BS37: Chip S 5H **31**
Melbourne Rd. BS7: Bishop 4K **47**
Melbourne Ter. BS21: Clev 7D **54**
Melbury Rd. BS4: Know 7B **62**
Melcombe Ct. BA2: Bath 7A **6** (7K **99**)
Melcombe Rd. BA2: Bath 7A **6** (6K **99**)
Melita Rd. BS6: Bris 5A **48**
Mellent Av. BS13: Hart 7J **75**
Mells Cl. BS31: Key 1E **96**
Mells La. BA3: Rads 4B **154**
Melrose Av. BS8: Clftn 1H **61**
BS37: Yate 4F **31**
Melrose Cl. BS37: Yate 4G **31**
Melrose Gro. BA2: Bath 1H **121**
Melrose Pl. BS8: Clftn 1H **61**
Melrose Ter. BA1: Bath 1C **100**
Melton Cres. BS7: Hor 7C **36**
Melville Rd. BS6: Redl 7H **47**
Melville Ter. BS3: Bedm 6J **61**
Melvin Sq. BS4: Know 1A **76**
Memorial Cl. BS15: Han 5K **63**
Memorial Cotts. BA1: W'ton 2J **99**
Memorial Rd. BS15: Han 4K **63**
BS40: Wrin 2G **111**
Memorial Stadium 2B **48**
Mendip Av. BS22: Wor 2C **106**
Mendip Cl. BS26: Axb 4J **149**
BS31: Key 5B **78**
BS39: Paul 2C **152**
BS48: Nail 1G **71**
BS49: Yat 4H **87**
Mendip Ct. BS16: Fren 6G **37**
Mendip Cres. BS16: Down 1E **50**
Mendip Edge BS24: W Mare 5H **127**
Mendip Gdns. BA2: Odd D 4K **121**
BS49: Yat 4H **87**
Mendip Model Motor Racing Circuit 7H **127**
Mendip Raceways 2F **151**
Mendip Ri. BS24: Lock 1F **129**
Mendip Rd. BS3: Wind H 6K **61**
BS20: P'head 3C **42**
BS23: W Mare 5J **105**
BS24: E'wth 7E **146**
BS24: Lock 1G **129**
BS26: Rook 7E **146**
BS49: Yat 3G **87**
Mendip Va. Trad. Est. BS27: Ched 7C **150**
Mendip Vw. BS30: Wick 2C **66**
Mendip Vw. Av. BS16: Fish 5J **49**
Mendip Vw. Bus. Pk. BS24: Hew 6C **86**
Mendip Vs. BS40: Comp M 6K **135**
Mendip Way BA3: Rads 3K **153**
TA8: Bur S 1D **158**
Menhyr Gro. BS10: Bren 4H **35**
Menlea BS40: Blag 2B **134**
Mercer Ct. BS14: H'gro 2D **76**
Merchants Academy Community Sports
& Facilities Cen. 5G **75**
Merchants Almshouses BS1: Bris 5E **4**
Merchants Ct. BS8: Clftn 4G **61**
Merchant Sq. BS20: P'head 2G **43**
Merchants Quay BS1: Bris 6E **4** (4K **61**)
Merchants Rest BS2: Bris 3J **5**
Merchants Rd. BS8: Clftn 4G **61**
(Nova Scotia Pl.)
BS8: Clftn 2G **61**
(Victoria Sq.)
Merchants Row BS1: Bris 7C **4**
Merchants Trade Pk. BS2: Bris 3E **62**
Merchant St. BS1: Bris 2G **5** (2A **62**)
Mercia Dr. BS2: Bris 6C **48**
Mercier Cl. BS37: Yate 4F **31**
Merebank Rd. BS11: A'mth 3H **33**
Meredith Ct. BS1: Bris 7A **4** (4G **61**)
Merfield Rd. BS4: Know 7D **62**
Meriden BA1: W'ton 1B **6** (3K **99**)
Meridian Pl. BS8: Clftn 3A **4** (2H **61**)
Meridian Rd. BS6: Cot 7J **47**
Meridian Ter. BS7: Bishop 5A **48**
Meridian Va. BS8: Clftn 3A **4** (2H **61**)
Meriet Av. BS13: Hart 6H **75**
Merioneth St. BS3: Wind H 6B **62**
Meriton St. BS2: Bris 4D **62**
Merlin Cl. BS9: W Trym 7F **35**
BS22: Wor 4C **106**
Merlin Ct. BS10: W Trym 1H **47**
Merlin Pk. BS20: P'head 4B **42**
Merlin Ridge BS16: Puck 4C **52**
Merlin Rd. BS10: Pat 7H **25**
Merlin Way BS37: Chip S 6F **31**
Merrett Ct. BS7: L'lze 2D **48**
Merrick Ct. BS1: Bris 6E **4** (4K **61**)
Merrimans Rd. BS11: Shire 7H **33**
Merritt Way BS16: Mang, Soun 5E **50**
Merryfield Rd. BS24: Lock 6F **107**
Merryhole La. BS32: Old D 2F **19**
Merryweather Cl. BS32: Brad S 6F **27**
Merryweathers BS4: Brisl 7G **63**
Merrywood Cl. BS3: Bedm 5J **61**
Merrywood Ct. *BS4: Know 7D 62*
(off Maxse Rd.)
Merrywood Mills *BS3: Bedm 5J 61*
(off Merrywood Rd.)
Merrywood Rd. BS3: Bedm 5J **61**
Merstham Rd. BS2: Bris 6C **48**
Merton Dr. BS24: W'ton V 4E **106**
Merton Rd. BS7: Hor 3A **48**
Mervyn Rd. BS7: Bishop 4A **48**
Meryl Ct. BS6: Redl 7H **47**
Metford Gro. BS6: Redl 5H **47**
Metford Pl. BS6: Redl 5J **47**
Metford Rd. BS6: Redl 5H **47**
Methuen Cl. *BA15: Brad A 7J 125*
(off Southway Rd.)
Methwyn Cl. BS22: W Mare 5A **106**
Metropolitan, The *BS1: Bris 6G 5*
(off Redcliff Backs)
Mews, The BA1: Bath 3G **99**
BS7: Hor 2K **47**
Mewswell Dr. BS27: Ched 5C **150**
Mezellion Pl. *BA1: Bath 2D 100*
(off Camden Rd.)
Michaels Mead BA1: W'ton 1H **99**
Michael Tippett Cen. 6B **98**
Middle Av. BS1: Bris 5E **4** (3K **61**)
Middle Bri. Bus. Pk. BS20: P'head 5G **43**
MIDDLE BURNHAM 7F **157**
Middle Down Drove BA5: Ched 7K **151**
Middle Fld. La. TA9: W Hunt 7B **158**
Middleford Ho. BS13: Hart 6J **75**
Middle Hope Nature Reserve 2A **84**
Middle La. BA1: Bath 2D **100**
BS21: Kings S 7A **68**
Middle Moor La. BS27: Ched 7K **149**
Middlepiece La. BS31: Burn 4F **97**
Middle Rank BA15: Brad A 5G **125**
Middle Rd. BS15: Soun 5C **50**
BS39: Hin B 7A **138**
Middle Stoke BA2: Lim S 6H **123**
Middle St. BS40: E Harp 7K **137**
TA9: Bre K 1E **156**
Middleton Rd. BS11: Law W 7K **33**
MIDDLETOWN 5A **56**
Middleway La. BS41: Dun 1F **93**
Middlewood Cl. BA2: Odd D 2J **121**
Middle Yeo Grn. BS48: Nail 6F **57**
MIDFORD 6D **122**
Midford BS24: W Mare 3H **127**
Midford Hill BA2: Mid 6E **122**
Midford La. BA2: Lim S, Mid 6E **122**
Midford Rd.
BA2: C Down, Odd D, S'ske, Mid 3A **122**
Midhaven Ri. BS22: Wor 7C **84**
Midland Bri. Rd.
BA1: Bath 5D **6** (5A **100**)
BA2: Bath 5D **6** (5A **100**)
Midland Cl. BA15: Brad A 6G **125**
Midland M. BS2: Bris 3K **5** (2B **62**)
Midland Rd. BA1: Bath 4B **6** (4K **99**)
BA2: Bath 4B **6** (5K **99**)
(not continuous)
BS2: Bris 3K **5** (2B **62**)
BS16: Stap H 4B **50**
Midland St. BS2: Bris 4K **5** (3B **62**)
Midland Ter. BS16: Fish 5H **49**
Midland Way BS35: T'bry 4K **11**
Midland Way Bus. Pk. BS35: T'bry 4K **11**
Midsomer Ent. Pk. BA3: Mid N 4G **153**
MIDSOMER NORTON 5E **152**
Midsomer Norton South Station
Somerset & Dorset Railway
Heritage Trust 6E **152**
Midsummer Bldgs. BA1: Bath 1D **100**
Milburn Rd. BS23: W Mare 5H **105**
Milbury Gdns. BS22: W Mare 2K **105**
MILBURY HEATH 3F **13**
Mildred St. BS5: Redf 2E **62**
Miles Cl. BS20: Pill 5J **45**
Miles Ct. BS8: Clftn 7G **47**
BS30: Bar C 5D **64**
Miles Rd. BS8: Clftn 7G **47**
Miles's Bldgs. BA1: Bath 3F **7** (4B **100**)
Miles St. BA2: Bath 6H **7** (6C **100**)
Milestone Ct. BS22: St G 2H **107**
Mile Wlk. BS14: H'gro 4C **76**
Milford Av. BS30: Wick 2B **66**
Milford St. BS3: Bedm 5J **61**
Milk St. BA1: Bath 5F **7** (5B **100**)
BS1: Bris 2H **5**
Mill, The BS39: Hall 5J **139**
Millard Cl. BS10: S'mead 5J **35**
Millards Ct. BA3: Mid N 3F **153**
Millard's Hill BA3: Mid N 3F **153**
Millar Ho. BS8: Clftn 3G **61**
Mill Av. BS1: Bris 5F **5** (3K **61**)
Millbank Cl. BS4: Brisl 6G **63**
Millbourn Cl. BA15: W'ley 5B **124**
Millbourne Rd. BS27: Ched 7E **150**
Millbrook Av. BS4: Brisl 6H **63**
Millbrook Cl. BS30: Old C 3G **65**
Millbrook Ct. BA2: Bath 7H **7**
Millbrook La. BA2: Bath 7H **7** (6C **100**)
Millbrook Pl. BA2: Bath 7H **7** (6C **100**)
Millbrook Rd. BS37: Yate 4B **30**
Mill Cl. BS20: P'bry 6B **44**
BS36: Fram C 7G **29**
Mill Ct. BA3: Mid N 5E **152**
BS5: St G 2F **63**
Mill Cres. BS37: W'lgh 3B **40**
Millcross BS21: Clev 2C **68**
Millennium Cl. BS36: Coal H 7H **29**
Millennium M. BS49: Cong 7A **88**
Millennium Prom. BS1: Bris 6C **4** (4J **61**)
Millennium Sq. BS1: Bris 6D **4** (4J **61**)
Miller Cl. BS23: W Mare 4H **105**
Miller Ct. BS13: Bis 4H **75**
Millers Cl. BS20: Pill 4G **45**
Millers Dr. BS30: Old C 4G **65**
Miller's Ri. BS22: Wor 7E **84**
Miller Wlk. BA2: Batham 2G **101**
Millfield BA3: Mid N 6D **152**
BS35: T'bry 2A **12**
Millfield Dr. BS30: Old C 3G **65**
Millground Rd. BS13: Withy 6E **74**
Mill Hill BA2: Well 4K **143**
Mill Ho. BS5: E'ton 7C **48**
Mill Ho., The BA15: Brad A 6H **125**
BS1: Bris 5F **5**
Millier Rd. BS49: C've 3C **88**
Milliman Cl. BS13: Hart 5K **75**
Mill La. BA2: Bath 5H **99**
BA2: Batham 1H **101**
BA2: Ing, Pris 6A **120**
(not continuous)
BA2: Mon C 4G **123**
BA2: Tims 4F **141**
BA3: Rads 3B **154**
BA15: Brad A 6H **125**
BS3: Bedm 5K **61**
BS16: H'ook 4A **38**
BS20: P'bry 5C **44**
BS30: Bit 2J **79**
BS30: Bit, Upton C 1K **79**
BS30: C Hth, Old C 4F **65**
BS30: Doy 7F **53**
BS32: Toc 4C **18**
BS36: Fram C 5F **29**
BS37: Chip S 5G **31**
BS37: Old S 1K **41**
BS39: Wool 6J **95**
BS40: But 5E **112**
BS40: Chew S 4D **114**
BS40: Comp M 6A **136**
BS40: Wrin 3G **111**
BS49: Cong 7K **87**
Mill Leg BS49: Cong 7K **87**
Millmead Ho. BS13: Hart 6J **75**
Millmead Rd. BA2: Bath 6A **6** (6J **99**)
Mill Paddock BS13: Hart 5H **75**
Millpill Cl. BS9: Stok B 3D **46**
Millpond St. BS5: E'ton 7C **48**
Millpool Ct. BS10: S'mead 6H **35**
Mill Rd. BA3: Rads 4A **154**
BS36: Wint D 3B **38**
Mill Rd. Ind. Est. BA3: Rads 3A **154**
Mill Steps BS36: Wint D 4C **38**
Millstone Cl. BS24: W'ton V 4D **106**
Mill Stream Cl. BS26: Axb 5H **149**
Mill Stream Works GL12: Wickw 5H **15**
Millward Gro. BS16: Fish 4A **50**
Millward Ter. BS39: Paul 7C **140**
Milner Grn. BS30: Bar C 4E **64**
Milner Rd. BS7: Hor 3B **48**
Milsom Apartments *BA1: Bath 3G 7*
(off Milsom Pl.)
Milsom Pl. BA1: Bath 3F **7** (4B **100**)
Milsom St. BA1: Bath 3F **7** (4B **100**)
BS5: E'ton 1K **5** (1C **62**)
MILTON 3A **106**
Milton Av. BA2: Bath 7B **100**
BS23: W Mare 4J **105**
Milton Brow BS22: W Mare 3K **105**
Milton Cl. BS37: Yate 4D **30**
BS48: Nail 6G **57**
Milton Grn. BS22: W Mare 3A **106**
MILTON HILL 1K **105**
Milton Hill BS22: W Mare 2K **105**
Milton Pk. BS5: Redf 2E **62**
Milton Pk. Rd. BS22: W Mare 3A **106**
Milton Ri. BS22: W Mare 3K **105**
Milton Rd. BA3: Rads 5G **153**
BS7: Hor 2A **48**
BS22: W Mare 4H **105**
BS23: W Mare 4H **105**
BS37: Yate 4D **30**
Miltons Cl. BS13: Hart 6K **75**
Milverton BS24: W Mare 3H **127**
Milverton Gdns. BS6: Bris 6B **48**
Milward Rd. BS31: Key 4C **78**
Mina Rd. BS2: Bris 5C **48**
Minehead Rd. BS4: Know 1B **76**
Miners Cl. BS41: L Ash 7K **59**
Miner's Gdns. BA3: Rads 4J **153**
Miners Wlk. BA2: Pea J 7C **142**
Minerva Ct. BA2: Bath 2H **7** (4C **100**)
Minerva Gdns. BA2: Bath 6J **99**
Minor's La. BS10: H'len 6A **24**
Minsmere Rd. BS31: Key 7E **78**
Minster Ct. BS37: Yate 7D **30**
Minster Way BA2: Bath 3E **100**
Minton Cl. BS14: Whit 5D **76**
Minto Rd. BS2: Bris 6B **48**
Minto Rd. Ind. Cen. BS2: Bris 6B **48**
Mirage BS20: P'head 2G **43**
Mission Rd. BS37: Iron A 2A **30**
Mission Theatre, The 5F **7**
Mitchell Ct. BS1: Bris 5G **5** (3A **62**)
Mitchell La. BS1: Bris 5G **5** (3A **62**)
Mitchell Wlk. BS30: B'yte 2H **65**
Mivart St. BS5: E'ton 6D **48**
Mizzen Ct. BS20: P'head 1G **43**
Mizzymead Cl. BS48: Nail 1F **71**
Mizzymead Recreation Cen. 1G **71**
Mizzymead Ri. BS48: Nail 1F **71**
Mizzymead Rd. BS48: Nail 1G **71**
Modecombe Gro. BS10: Hen 4F **35**
Mogg St. BS2: Bris 6C **48**
Molesworth Cl. BS13: Withy 6G **75**
Molesworth Dr. BS13: Withy 6G **75**
Molly Cl. BS39: Temp C 5G **139**
Mollyfriend La. BA2: Mark 5E **118**
MONGER 2E **152**
Monger Cotts. BS39: Paul 3E **152**
Monger La. BA3: Mid N 3D **152**
BS39: Paul 3D **152**
Monk Rd. BS7: Bishop 4K **47**
Monks Av. BS15: Kgswd 1K **63**
Monksdale Rd. BA2: Bath 7B **6** (7K **99**)
Monks Hill BS22: Kew, W Mare 1K **105**
Monks Ho. BS37: Yate 7D **30**
Monk's Pk. Av. BS7: Hor 6A **36**
Monks Pk. Way BS10: S'mead 7A **36**
Monkstone Dr. TA8: Berr 2B **156**
Monks Way TA8: Bur S 2D **158**
Monkton Av. BS24: W Mare 3J **127**
MONKTON COMBE 3G **123**
MONKTON FARLEIGH 4D **102**
Monkton Rd. BS15: Han 5K **63**
Monmouth Cl. BS20: P'head 4B **42**
Monmouth Ct. *BA1: Bath 4D 6*
(off Monmouth Pl.)
BS20: Pill 3G **45**
Monmouth Hill BS32: Alm 2K **25**
Monmouth Pl. BA1: Bath 3D **6** (4A **100**)
(not continuous)
Monmouth Rd. BS7: Bishop 4K **47**
BS20: Pill 3G **45**
BS31: Key 5B **78**
Monmouth St. BA1: Bath 4E **6** (5B **100**)
BS3: Wind H 6B **62**
Monsdale Cl. BS10: Hen 4G **35**
Monsdale Dr. BS10: Hen 4G **35**
Mont, The *BS6: Bris 7A 48*
(off St Andrew's Rd.)
Montacute Cir. BS24: W'ton V 4D **106**
Montague Cl. BS34: Stok G 2G **37**
Montague Ct. BS2: Bris 1F **5**
Montague Flats BS2: Bris 1E **4**
Montague Hill BS2: Bris 1E **4** (1K **61**)
Montague Hill Sth. BS2: Bris 1F **5**
Montague Pl. BS6: Bris 1E **4** (1K **61**)
Montague Rd. BA2: Shos 1E **154**
BS31: Salt 1G **97**
Montague St. BS2: Bris 1F **5** (1K **61**)
Montgomery St. BS3: Wind H 5B **62**
MONTPELIER 7A **48**
Montpelier BA1: Bath 2F **7** (4B **100**)
BS23: W Mare 3H **105**
Montpelier Central *BS6: Bris 7A 48*
(off Station Rd.)
Montpelier Ct. BS6: Bris 6A **48**
Montpelier E. BS23: W Mare 3H **105**
Montpelier Path BS23: W Mare 4G **105**
Montpelier Station (Rail) 6A **48**
Montreal Av. BS7: Hor 7B **36**
Montreux Ho. BS5: St G 2J **63**
Montrose Av. BS6: Cot 7J **47**
Montrose Cotts. BA1: W'ton 2J **99**
Montrose Dr. BS30: Warm 3F **65**
Montrose Pk. BS4: Brisl 7F **63**
Montroy Cl. BS9: Henle 2J **47**
Moon St. BS2: Bris 1G **5** (1A **62**)
Moor Cft. Dr. BS30: Long G 5D **64**
Moorcroft Rd. BS24: Hut 2C **128**
Moordell Cl. BS37: Yate 5D **30**
Moor Drove BS49: Cong 3J **109**
MOOREND 5C **38**
Moorend Farm Av.
BS11: A'mth 2J **33**
Moorend Gdns. BS11: Law W 1K **45**
Moorend Rd. BS16: H'ook 4B **38**
Moor End Spout BS48: Nail 6F **57**
Moorfield Ho. *BS5: Redf 2E 62*
(off Church Rd.)
Moorfield Rd. BS48: Back 3H **71**
MOORFIELDS 1E **62**
Moorfields Cl. BA2: Bath 7K **99**
BS5: Redf 2E **62**
Moorfields Ct. BS48: Nail 7F **57**
Moorfields Dr. BA2: Bath 7K **99**
Moorfields Ho. BS48: Nail 7E **56**
Moorfields Rd. BA2: Bath 7K **99**
BS48: Nail 7F **57**
Moor Ga. BS20: P'head 4H **43**
Moor Grn. BS26: Axb 5J **149**
Moor Gro. BS11: Law W 7K **33**
Moorgrove Ho. BS9: C Din 7C **34**
Moorham Rd. BS25: Wins 4G **131**
Moorhill St. BS5: E'ton 7D **48**
Moorhouse Cvn. Pk.
BS10: A'mth 3A **34**
Moorhouse La. BS10: H'len 2K **33**
BS11: A'mth 2K **33**
Moorings, The BA2: Bath 4K **7** (5D **100**)
BS20: Pill 4G **45**
Moorland Pk. BS24: Hew 6F **87**

A-Z Bristol, Bath & North Somerset Atlas 189

Moorland Rd.—Norbin

Moorland Rd. BA2: Bath 6A 6 (6K 99)
BS23: W Mare 1F 127
BS37: Yate 5D 30
MOORLANDS 7K 99
Moorlands, The BA2: Bath 1K 121
Moorlands Cl. BS48: Nail 7F 57
Moorlands Rd. BS16: Fish 5H 49
(not continuous)
Moorland St. BS26: Axb 5J 149
Moor La. BS20: Glap G 7G 43
BS21: Clev 7E 54
(Beaconsfield Rd.)
BS21: Clev 7F 55
(Cook's La.)
BS21: Tic 5B 56
BS21: Walt G 2H 55
BS22: Wor 3D 106
BS24: Hut 1B 128
BS24: W'ton V 5C 106
BS32: Toc 5A 18
BS48: Back 4H 71
Moorlay Cres. BS40: Winf 3K 91
MOORLEDGE 3K 115
Moorledge La. BS39: Stan D 4B 116
BS40: Chew M 3J 115
Moorledge Rd. BS40: Chew M 2H 115
Moor Pk. BS21: Clev 7E 54
(not continuous)
Moorpark Av. BS37: Yate 5C 30
Moor Rd. BS29: Ban 4K 107
BS49: Yat 7H 69
Moorsfield BS39: Clut 2H 139
Moorside BS49: Yat 2H 87
Moorside Ct. BS21: Clev 7E 54
Moravian Bus. Pk. BS15: Kgswd 1B 64
Moravian Ct. BS15: Kgswd 1B 64
Moravian Pl. *BA2: Bath 7J 99*
(off Coronation Av.)
Moravian Rd. BS15: Kgswd 1B 64
Morden Wlk. BS14: Stoc 3F 77
Moreton Cl. BS14: Whit 6C 76
Moreton La. BS40: Comp M 3D 136
Morford St. BA1: Bath 2F 7 (3B 100)
Morgan Cl. BS22: W Wick 4F 107
BS31: Salt 1H 97
Morgan Pl. BS48: Flax B 2F 73
Morgans Hill Cl. BS48: Nail 2F 71
Morgan St. BS2: Bris 7B 48
Morgan Way BA2: Pea J 6D 142
Morland Rd. TA9: Highb 4F 159
Morlands Ind. Pk. TA9: Highb 4F 159
Morley Av. BS16: Mang 4E 50
Morley Cl. BS16: Soun 4B 50
BS34: Lit S 7E 26
Morley Pl. BS16: Soun 5B 50
Morley Rd. BS3: Bedm 5J 61
BS16: Soun 4B 50
Morley Sq. BS7: Bishop 4A 48
Morley St. BS2: Bris 7B 48
BS5: Bar H 2D 62
Morley Ter. BA2: Bath 4A 6 (5K 99)
BA3: Rads 3A 154
BS15: Kgswd 7B 50
Mornington Rd. BS8: Clftn 6G 47
Morpeth Rd. BS4: Know 2K 75
Morris Cl. BA1: Bathf 7K 83
Morris La. BA1: Bathf 7K 83
Morris Rd. BS7: L'lze 3C 48
Morse Rd. BS5: Redf 2E 62
Morston Ct. BS22: W Mare 5A 106
Mortimer Cl. BA1: W'ton 1H 99
Mortimer Rd. BS8: Clftn 2G 61
BS34: Fil 6D 36
MORTON 2B 12
Morton St. BS5: Bar H 2D 62
Morton Way BS35: T'bry 1B 12
Moseley Gro. BS23: Uph 3G 127
Motorway Distribution Cen.
BS11: A'mth 5G 33
Moulton Dr. BA15: Brad A 7H 125
Mountain Ash BA1: W'ton 2K 99
Mountain M. BS5: St G 2J 63
Mountain's La. BA2: F'boro 5B 118
Mountain Wood BA1: Bathf 1A 102
Mountbatten Cl. BS22: Kew 7C 84
BS37: Yate 3D 30
TA8: Bur S 6C 156
Mount Beacon BA1: Bath 2C 100
Mt. Beacon Pl. BA1: Bath 2B 100
Mt. Beacon Row BA1: Bath 2C 100
Mount Cl. BS36: Fram C 6D 28
Mount Cres. BS36: Wint 2C 38
Mounteney's La. GL12: Wickw 6K 15
Mount Gdns. BS15: Kgswd 3B 64
Mount Gro. BA2: Bath 1H 121
MOUNT HILL 3C 64
Mount Hill Rd. BS15: Han, Kgswd 3A 64
Mt. Pleasant BA2: Mon C 3F 123
BA3: Rads 4B 154
BA15: Brad A 5H 125
BS10: H'len 3C 34
BS20: Pill 4H 45
Mt. Pleasant Cl. BS30: Long G 6C 64
Mt. Pleasant Ter. BS3: Bedm 5J 61
Mount Rd. BA1: Bath 3B 100
BA2: Bath 7G 99
Mount Vw. *BA1: Bath 2C 100*
(off Beacon Rd.)
BA2: Bath 1H 121
Mow Barton BS13: Bis 4F 75
BS37: Yate 4D 30
Mowbray Rd. BS14: H'gro 3E 76
Mowcroft Rd. BS13: Hart 6J 75
Moxham Dr. BS13: Hart 6H 75
M Shed 7E 4 (4K 61)
Muddy La. BS22: Wick L 2E 84
Mud La. BS49: C'ham 1K 87
Muirfield BS30: Warm 3E 64
BS37: Yate 6E 30
Mulberry Av. BS20: P'head 3G 43
Mulberry Cl. BS15: Kgswd 1C 64
BS20: P'head 3H 43
BS22: Wor 3D 106
BS48: Back 4J 71
Mulberry Ct. BS4: Brisl 5F 63
Mulberry Cres. BS37: Yate 5F 31
Mulberry Dr. BS15: Kgswd 7D 50
Mulberry Gdns. BS16: Soun 5B 50
Mulberry Gro. BS16: Soun 5B 50
Mulberry La. BS24: B'don 7A 128
Mulberry Rd. BS49: Cong 1A 110
Mulberry Wlk. BS9: C Din 7C 34
Mulholland Way TA9: Highb 3F 159
Muller Av. BS7: Bishop 4B 48
Muller Ho. BS7: Bishop 4B 48
Muller Rd. BS5: Eastv 5E 48
(not continuous)
BS7: Hor 2B 48
Mulready Cl. BS7: L'lze 2E 48
Mumbleys La. BS35: T'bry 6G 11
Munscroft Ct. BS23: W Mare 4H 105
Murdoch Sq. BS7: Hor 7B 36
Murford Av. BS13: Hart 5H 75
Murford Wlk. BS13: Hart 6H 75
MURHILL 6A 124
Murray St. BS3: Bedm 5J 61
Museum of Bath at Work 1F 7 (3B 100)
Museum of East Asian Art 2F 7 (4B 100)
Musgrove Cl. BS11: Law W 5C 34
Musthay Flds. BS32: Toc 3D 18
Myrtleberry Mead BS22: Wick L 6E 84
Myrtle Ct. *BS3: Bedm 5H 61*
(off Exmoor St.)
BS3: Bedm 5H 61
(off Myrtle St.)
Myrtle Dr. BS11: Shire 3J 45
TA8: Bur S 1C 158
Myrtle Gdns. BS49: Yat 3J 87
Myrtle Hill BS20: Pill 4G 45
Myrtle Rd. BS2: Bris 1D 4 (1J 61)
Myrtles, The BS24: Hut 3B 128
Myrtle St. BS3: Bedm 5H 61
Mythern Mdw. BA15: Brad A 7J 125

N

Nags Head Hill BS5: St G 2J 63
NAILSEA 7G 57
Nailsea & Backwell Station (Rail) 3H 71
Nailsea Cl. BS13: Bis 3G 75
Nailsea Moor La. BS48: Nail 3B 70
Nailsea Pk. BS48: Nail 7H 57
Nailsea Pk. Cl. BS48: Nail 6H 57
Nailsea Wall BS21: Clev 2G 69
BS48: Nail 2G 69
Nailsea Wall La. BS48: Nail 3A 70
Nailsworth Av. BS37: Yate 5E 30
NAILWELL 6D 120
Naishcombe Hill BS30: Wick 3C 66
Naishes Av. BA2: Pea J 5D 142
Naish Hill BS20: Glap G 7H 43
Naish Ho. BA2: Bath 5G 99
Naish La. BS48: Bar G 7G 73
Naish Rd. TA8: Bur S 4C 156
Nanny Hurn's La.
BS39: Came, Clut 3C 138
Napier Ct. BS1: Bris 7A 4 (4H 61)
Napier Miles Rd. BS11: Law W 7A 34
Napier Rd. BA1: W'ton 7G 81
BS5: Eastv 6D 48
BS6: Redl 6H 47
BS11: A'mth 6F 33
Napier Sq. BS11: A'mth 6E 32
Napier St. BS5: Bar H 3D 62
Narroways Rd. BS2: Bris 5C 48
Narrow La. BS16: Soun 5C 50
Narrow Lewins Mead BS1: Bris 2E 4 (2K 61)
Narrow Plain BS2: Bris 4H 5 (3A 62)
Narrow Quay BS1: Bris 6E 4 (4K 61)
(not continuous)
Narrow Quay Ho. BS1: Bris 5E 4 (3K 61)
Narrow Weir BS1: Bris 2H 5 (2A 62)
Naseby Wlk. BS5: S'wll 7H 49
Nash Cl. BS31: Key 5E 78
Nash Dr. BS7: L'lze 1E 48
Nates La. BS40: Wrin 3H 111
Naunton Way BS22: W Mare 2K 105
Navigators Ct. BS20: P'head 2H 43
Neads Dr. BS30: Old C 4G 65
Neale La. BS11: A'mth 6G 33
Neate Ct. BS34: Pat 6E 26
Neath Rd. BS5: W'hall 1F 63
Nelson Bldgs. BA1: Bath 1H 7 (3C 100)
Nelson Ct. BS22: Wor 7C 84
Nelson Ho. BA1: Bath 3D 6 (4A 100)
BS1: Bris 3F 5
(off Rupert St.)
BS16: Stap H 3B 50
Nelson La. BA1: Bath 3D 6 (4A 100)
Nelson Pde. BS3: Bedm 7F 5 (5K 61)
Nelson Pl. BA1: Bath 1G 7 (3C 100)
Nelson Pl. E. BA1: Bath 1G 7
Nelson Pl. W. BA1: Bath 4D 6 (5A 100)
Nelson Rd. BS16: Stap H 3B 50
(not continuous)
Nelson St. BS1: Bris 3E 4 (2K 61)
BS3: Bedm 7G 61
Nelson Vs. BA1: Bath 4C 6 (5A 100)
Nempnett St. BS40: Nem T 6G 113
NEMPNETT THRUBWELL 7H 113
Neston Wlk. BS4: Know 2B 76
NETHAM 3F 63
Netham Ct. *BS5: Redf 2F 63*
(off Netham Rd.)
Netham Gdns. BS5: Redf 2F 63
Netham Ind. Pk. BS5: Redf 3F 63
Netham Rd. BS5: Redf 2F 63
Netham Vw. Ind. Pk. BS5: Redf 2F 63
Netherton Wood La. BS48: Nail 4B 70
Netherways BS21: Clev 1B 68
Nettlefrith La. TA8: Berr 6D 144
Nettlestone Cl. BS10: Hen 3E 34
Nevalan Dr. BS5: St G 3J 63
Neva Rd. BS23: W Mare 6G 105
Nevill Ct. BA2: New L 6B 98
Neville Rd. BS15: Kgswd 6C 50
Nevil Rd. BS7: Bishop 4A 48
Nevinson Pl. BS7: L'lze 3D 48
Newark St. BA1: Bath 6G 7 (6C 100)
New Bond Ho. BS2: Bris 1H 5
New Bond St. BA1: Bath 4F 7 (5B 100)
New Bond St. Bldgs. *BA1: Bath 4F 7*
(off New Bond St.)
New Bond St. Pl. BA1: Bath 4G 7
Newbourne Rd. BS22: W Mare 5A 106
Newbrick Rd. BS34: Stok G 2J 37
NEWBRIDGE 3G 99
Newbridge Cl. BS4: St Ap 3F 63
Newbridge Ct. BA1: Bath 4H 99
Newbridge Drove TA9: E Hunt 7H 159
Newbridge Gdns. BA1: Bath 3G 99
Newbridge Hill BA1: Bath 3G 99
Newbridge La. TA9: E Hunt 7H 159
(not continuous)
Newbridge (Park & Ride) 3F 99
Newbridge Rd. BA1: Bath 3F 99
BA2: Bath 3F 99
BS4: St Ap 3F 63
Newbridge Trad. Est. BS4: St Ap 4F 63
New Bristol Rd. BS22: Wor 3C 106
New Brunswick Av. BS5: St G 2K 63
NEW BUILDINGS 6B 142
New Bldgs. BS16: Fish 4H 49
Newbury Rd. BS7: Hor 1C 48
New Charlotte St. BS3: Bedm 7F 5 (5K 61)
New Charlton Way BS10: Pat 1G 35
NEW CHELTENHAM 7C 50
New Cheltenham Rd. BS15: Kgswd 7B 50
New Church Rd. BS23: Uph 3F 127
Newclose La. BS40: Comp M 4D 136
Newcombe Dr. BS9: Stok B 4C 46
Newcombe La. BS25: Wins 6H 131
Newcombe Rd. BS9: W Trym 1F 47
New Cut Bow BS21: Kings S 5A 68
Newditch La. BS40: F'tn 2G 91
Newdown La. BS41: Dun 2H 93
New Ear La. BS24: Hew 7J 85
New Engine Rank BS36: Henf 4H 39
Newent Av. BS15: Kgswd 2K 63
Newfields BS40: Blag 4A 134
New Fosseway Rd. BS14: H'gro 4D 76
Newfoundland Cir. BS2: Bris 1J 5 (1B 62)
Newfoundland Rd. BS2: Bris 1J 5 (1B 62)
Newfoundland St. BS2: Bris 1J 5 (1B 62)
Newfoundland Way BS2: Bris 1J 5 (1B 62)
BS20: P'head 2G 43
Newgate BS1: Bris 3G 5 (2A 62)
New Grove BS16: Fish 4H 49
Newhaven Pl. BS20: P'head 4A 42
Newhaven Rd. BS20: P'head 5A 42
New John St. BS3: Bedm 6J 61
New Kings Ct. BS7: Bishop 4J 47
New Kingsley Rd. BS2: Bris 4J 5 (3B 62)
New King St. BA1: Bath 4D 6 (5B 100)
Newland Dr. BS13: Withy 6G 75
Newland Gro. BS31: Key 5C 78
Newland Rd. BS13: Withy 6G 75
BS23: W Mare 6H 105
Newlands, The BS16: Fren 1K 49
Newlands Av. BS36: Coal H 7G 29
Newlands Cl. BS20: P'head 3E 42
Newlands Grn. BS21: Clev 1E 68
Newlands Hgts. *BS7: Bris 6B 48*
(off Hurlingham Rd.)
Newlands Hill BS20: P'head 4E 42
Newlands La. BS16: Emer G 7G 39
Newlands Rd. BS31: Key 6B 78
Newland Wlk. BS13: Withy 7G 75
New La. BS35: A'ton 7A 12
BS40: Regil, Winf 6H 91
NEWLEAZE 5D 36
New Leaze BS32: Brad S 3E 26
Newleaze Ho. BS34: Fil 5D 36
Newlyn Av. BS9: Stok B 3D 46
Newlyn Wlk. BS4: Know 1D 76
Newlyn Way BS37: Yate 4F 31
Newman Cl. BS37: W'lgh 3B 40
Newmans La. BA2: Tims 3F 141
TA9: E Hunt 7K 159
New Marchants Pas.
BA1: Bath 6G 7 (6C 100)
Newmarket Av. BS1: Bris 3F 5 (2K 61)
Newmarket Row *BA2: Bath 4G 7*
(off Grand Pde.)
New Mdws. BS14: H'gro 4C 76
Newminster Ho. BS1: Bris 4E 4
Newnham Cl. BS14: Stoc 3F 77
Newnham Pl. BS34: Pat 5B 26
New Orchard St. BA1: Bath 5G 7 (5C 100)
NEW PASSAGE 4A 16
New Passage Rd. BS35: Red 4A 16
New Pit BS39: Paul 7D 140
New Pit La. BS30: Bit 6J 65
Newport Cl. BS20: P'head 4B 42
BS21: Clev 7C 54
Newport Rd. BS20: Pill 3G 45
Newport St. BS3: Wind H 6A 62
Newquay Rd. BS4: Know 1B 76
New Queen St. BS3: Bedm 5A 62
BS15: Kgswd 7K 49
New Rd.
BA1: Bathf 1B 102
BA2: F'frd 7K 123
BA2: Tims 3A 140
BA15: Brad A 5H 125
BS20: Pill 4G 45
BS21: Clev 7D 54
BS25: C'hll 2B 132
BS25: Row, S'ham 5A 132
BS29: Ban 1J 129
BS34: Fil 4B 36
BS34: Fil, Stok G 5E 36
BS35: Olv 3C 18
BS37: Rang 5A 22
(not continuous)
BS39: High L, Tims 3A 140
BS39: Pens 1F 117
BS40: Redh 7D 90
GL12: Tyth 7F 13
TA9: E Hunt, W Hunt 7E 158
New Rd. Ct. BA15: Brad A 5J 125
Newry Wlk. BS4: Know 1A 76
Newsome Av. BS20: Pill 4G 45
New Stadium Rd. BS5: Eastv 6D 48
New Station Rd. BS16: Fish 4J 49
New Station Way BS16: Fish 4J 49
New St. BA1: Bath 5F 7 (5B 100)
BS2: Bris 2J 5 (2B 62)
New Thomas St. BS2: Bris 3J 5 (3B 62)
NEWTON 4F 159
Newton Cl. BS15: Kgswd 7E 50
BS40: W Har 7E 136
TA8: Bur S 5C 156
Newton Dr. BS30: C Hth 4E 64
Newton Grn. BS48: Nail 2E 70
Newton Mill Camping & Cvn. Pk.
BA2: New L 5E 98
Newton Park 5B 98
Newton Rd. BA2: Bath 6F 99
BS23: W Mare 7G 105
BS30: C Hth 4E 64
NEWTON ST LOE 5D 98
Newtons Rd. BS22: Kew, Wor 7C 84
(not continuous)
Newton St. BS5: E'ton 1K 5 (1C 62)
Newton Wlk. BS24: W Wick 4G 107
NEWTOWN
BS2 2C 62
BS40 5K 115
Newtown BA15: Brad A 6G 125
BS39: Paul 1B 152
Newtown Rd. TA9: Highb 5F 159
(not continuous)
New Tyning Ter. *BA1: Bath 2D 100*
(off Fairfield Rd.)
New Villas BA2: Bath 7C 100
New Wlk. BS15: Han 4K 63
New Walls BS4: Wind H 5B 62
New Workshops BA1: Bath 2G 7
Niblett Cl. BS15: Kgswd 3D 64
Niblett's Hill BS5: St G 3H 63
NIBLEY 5A 30
Nibley Bus. Pk. BS37: Yate 5A 30
Nibley La. BS37: Iron A, Yate 3J 29
BS37: W'lgh, Yate 5A 30
Nibley Rd. BS11: Shire 3H 45
Nicholas La. BS5: St G 3J 63
Nicholas Rd. BS5: E'ton 7D 48
Nicholas St. BS3: Bedm 5A 62
Nicholettes BS30: Old C 4H 65
Nicholls Ct. BS36: Wint 1C 38
Nicholls La. BS36: Wint 7C 28
Nicholl's Pl. *BA1: Bath 2F 7*
(off Lansdown Rd.)
Nichol's Rd. BS20: P'head 2B 42
Nigel Pk. BS11: Shire 1J 45
Nightingale Cl. BS4: St Ap 3G 63
BS22: Wor 3C 106
BS35: T'bry 2B 12
BS36: Fram C 1E 38
TA8: Bur S 6D 156
Nightingale Ct. BS4: Brisl 6F 63
BS22: Wor 3C 106
Nightingale Gdns. BS48: Nail 7E 56
Nightingale La. BS36: Wint 6E 28
Nightingale Ri. BS20: P'head 5B 42
Nightingale Valley BS4: St Ap 4G 63
Nightingale Way BA3: Mid N 6F 153
Nile St. BA1: Bath 4D 6 (5A 100)
NINE ELMS 4G 137
Ninetree Hill BS1: Bris 7A 48
Ninth Av. BS7: Hor 6D 36
Nippors Way BS25: Wins 5F 131
Nithsdale Rd. BS23: W Mare 1G 127
Noah's Ark Zoo Farm 2K 57
Noble Av. BS30: Old C 5G 65
Noel Coward Cl. TA8: Bur S 2E 158
Noels Sidings Ind. Est.
BS22: St G 1H 107
Nomis Pk. BS49: Cong 2A 110
NORBIN 2K 103

Norden—Old Orchard, The

Norden BA15: Brad A 6H 125
Nordrach La. BS40: Comp M 7H 135
Nore Gdns. BS20: P'head 2E 42
Nore Pk. Dr. BS20: P'head 2B 42
Nore Rd. BS20: P'head 4A 42
Norewood Gro. BS20: P'head 3B 42
Norfolk Av. BS2: Bris 1H 5 (1A 62)
BS6: Bris 6A 48
Norfolk Bldgs. BA1: Bath 4D 6 (5A 100)
Norfolk Ct. BA1: Bath 3C 6
Norfolk Cres. BA1: Bath 4D 6 (5A 100)
Norfolk Gro. BS31: Key 6A 78
Norfolk Hgts. *BS2: Bris 1H 5*
(off Norfolk Av.)
Norfolk Ho. BS1: Bris 4H 5
Norfolk Pl. BS3: Bedm 6J 61
Norfolk Rd. BS20: P'head 4G 43
BS23: W Mare 7H 105
Norland Rd. BS8: Clftn 1F 61
Norley Rd. BS7: Hor 1B 48
Normanby Rd. BS5: E'ton 7D 48
Normandy Dr. BS37: Yate 6F 31
Norman Gro. BS15: Kgswd 6B 50
Norman Rd. BS2: Bris 6C 48
BS30: Warm 7F 51
BS31: Salt 7H 79
Normans, The BA2: Batham 2H 101
Normans Way BS20: Eas 1C 44
Normanton Rd. BS8: Clftn 6G 47
Norrisville Rd. BS6: Bris 7A 48
Northam Farm Cvn. & Touring Pk.
TA8: Brean 3C 144
Northampton Bldgs. BA1: Bath 1E 6 (3B 100)
Northampton St. BA1: Bath 1E 6 (3B 100)
Northanger Ct. *BA2: Bath 3G 7*
(off Grove St.)
North Av. TA9: Highb 4E 158
Nth. Bristol Pk. BS34: Lit S 2D 36
Nth. Chew Ter. BS40: Chew M 1H 115
NORTH COMMON 3H 65
North Contemporis *BS8: Clftn 2G 61*
(off Merchants Rd.)
NORTH CORNER 5D 28
North Cnr. *BS3: Bedm 6H 61*
(off North St.)
Northcote Rd. BS5: St G 1G 63
BS8: Clftn 7F 47
BS16: Down, Mang 2D 50
Northcote St. BS5: E'ton 7D 48
North Ct. BS32: Brad S 3F 27
North Cft. BS30: Old C 5H 65
Nth. Devon Rd. BS16: Fish 3J 49
Nth. Down Cl. BS25: S'ham 5B 132
Nth. Down La. BS25: S'ham 5B 132
Northdown Rd. BA3: Clan 1J 153
North Drove BS48: Nail 1K 69
North East Rd. BS35: T'bry 2A 12
NORTH END
BA1 5H 83
BS39 7G 117
BS49 7F 69
North End BS49: Yat 7F 69
Northend BA3: Mid N 4F 153
Northend Av. BS15: Kgswd 6B 50
Northend Cotts. BA1: Bathe 5H 83
Northend Gdns. BS15: Kgswd 6B 50
North End Rd. BS49: Yat 7F 69
Northend Rd. BS15: Kgswd 6C 50
Northern Path BS21: Clev 6F 55
Northern Way BS21: Clev 7E 54
NORTHFIELD 4B 154
Northfield BA2: Tims 2G 141
BA3: Rads 3A 154
BA15: W'ley 5D 124
BS37: Yate 6D 30
Northfield Av. BS15: Han 4B 64
Northfield Ho. BS3: Bedm 5J 61
Northfield Rd. BS5: St G 2K 63
BS20: P'head 5A 42
Northfields BA1: Bath 2B 100
Northfields Cl. BA1: Bath 2B 100
Northgate St. BA1: Bath 4G 7 (5C 100)
Northgate Yd. *BA1: Bath 4G 7*
(off Northgate St.)
North Grn. St. BS8: Clftn 3F 61
North Gro. BS20: Pill 4G 45
North Hills Cl. BS24: W Mare 3K 127
North La. BA2: C'ton D 6F 101
BS23: W Mare 5G 105
(off Meadow St.)
BS48: Nail 1D 70
TA8: Berr 5B 144
Northleach Wlk. BS11: Shire 3K 45
North Leaze BS41: L Ash 7B 60
Northleigh BA15: Brad A 3J 125
Northleigh Av. BS22: W Mare 3A 106
Northmead Av. BA3: Mid N 4D 152
Northmead Cl. BA3: Mid N 4D 152
Northmead La. BS37: Iron A 1H 29
North Mdws. BA2: Pea J 5D 142
Northmead Rd. BA3: Mid N 4D 152
Northover Cl. BS9: W Trym 6F 35
Northover Ct. BS35: Piln 7E 16
Northover Rd. BS9: W Trym 6F 35
North Pde. BA1: Bath 5H 7 (5C 100)
BA2: Bath 5H 7 (5C 100)
BS37: Yate 4E 30
North Pde. Bldgs. *BA1: Bath 5G 7*
(off Abbey Ga. St.)
North Pde. Pas. BA1: Bath 5G 7 (5C 100)
North Pde. Rd. BA2: Bath 5H 7 (5C 100)
North Pk. BS15: Kgswd 7C 50
North Quay BS1: Bris 4H 5
North Rd. BA2: Bath, C'ton D 2K 7 (4E 100)
BA2: C Down 3D 122
BA2: Tims 3F 141
BA3: Mid N 5D 152
BS3: Ash G 5G 61
BS6: Bris 6K 47
BS8: L Wds 2C 60
BS24: Lym 4B 146
BS29: Ban 2A 130
BS34: Stok G 3G 37
BS35: T'bry 2A 12
BS36: Wint 7D 28
BS37: Yate 7B 22
Nth. Side Rd. BS48: Back 3C 90
NORTH STOKE 3C 80
Nth. Stoke La. BS30: Upton C 2A 80
North St. BS1: Bris 1G 5 (1A 62)
BS3: Ash G, Bedm 5G 61
BS16: Down 3B 50
BS23: W Mare 4F 105
BS30: Old C 5G 65
BS48: Nail 1D 70
GL12: Wickw 6G 15
Northumberland Bldgs. *BA1: Bath 4F 7*
(off Barton St.)
Northumberland Pl.
BA1: Bath 4G 7 (5C 100)
Northumberland Rd. BS6: Redl 6J 47
Northumbria Dr. BS9: Henle 3H 47
North Vw. BA2: Pea J 5C 142
BA3: Rads 4B 154
BS6: Henle 4G 47
BS16: Soun 4B 50
BS16: Stap H 3C 50
North Vw. Cl. BA2: Bath 6H 99
North Vw. Dr. BS29: Ban 3K 129
NORTHVILLE 6D 36
Northville Ct. BS7: Hor 6B 36
Northville Rd. BS7: Hor 6B 36
North Wlk. BS37: Yate 4E 30
North Way BA2: Bath 6G 99
BA3: Mid N 5E 152
Northway BS34: Fil 3D 36
Northwell Ho. *BS6: Bris 6K 47*
(off Cromwell Rd.)
NORTH WESTON 5E 42
NORTH WICK 3J 93
NORTHWICK 3D 16
Northwick Gdns. BS39: Bis S 1K 137
Northwick Rd. BS7: Hor 7B 36
BS35: N'wick, Piln 3D 16
BS39: Nor H 4K 93
BS41: N Wick 4K 93
NORTH WIDCOMBE 5H 137
Northwood Pk. BS36: Wint 7J 27
Northwoods Wlk. BS10: Bren 4K 35
Nth. Worle Shop. Cen. BS22: Wor 2F 107
NORTON 7A 84
Norton Cl. BS15: Kgswd 2D 64
BS40: Chew M 1H 115
Norton Farm Rd. BS10: Hen 4D 34
NORTON HAWKFIELD 5A 94
NORTON HILL 6F 153
Norton Hill Sports Cen. 7F 153
Norton Ho. BS1: Bris 7G 5
Norton La. BS14: Whit 2E 94
BS22: Kew 7A 84
BS39: Chew M, Nor H, Nor M 5A 94
BS40: Chew M 1H 115
NORTON MALREWARD 4C 94
Norton Rd. BS4: Know 7C 62
NORTON'S WOOD 4J 55
Nortons Wood La. BS21: Clev 4F 55
Norville Cl. BS27: Ched 7D 150
Norville La. BS27: Ched 6D 150
Norwich Dr. BS4: St Ap 3G 63
Norwood Av. BA2: C'ton D 7G 101
Notgrove Cl. BS22: W Mare 2K 105
Nottingham Rd. BS7: Bishop 5A 48
Nottingham St. BS3: Wind H 6A 62
Notting Hill Way
BS26: L Wre, Weare 6D 148
Nova Distribution Cen. BS11: A'mth 6F 33
Nova Scotia Pl. BS1: Bris 4G 61
Nova Way BS11: A'mth 6F 33
Nover's Cres. BS4: Know 2J 75
Nover's Hill BS3: Know, Wind H 1J 75
BS4: Know 1J 75
Nover's Hill Trad. Est. BS3: Bedm 1J 75
Nover's La. BS4: Know 2J 75
Nover's Pk. Cl. BS4: Know 1J 75
Nover's Pk. Dr. BS4: Know 2J 75
Nover's Pk. Rd. BS4: Know 2K 75
Nover's Rd. BS4: Know 2J 75
Nowhere La. BS48: Nail 1H 71
Nuffield Health
Bristol 2B 4
Nugent Hill BS6: Cot 7K 47
No. 1 Royal Crescent 2E 6 (4B 100)
Nunney Cl. BS31: Key 1E 96
TA8: Bur S 6E 156
Nupdale La. BS35: King 4F 11
Nurseries, The GL12: Tyth 7F 13
Nursery, The BS3: Bedm 6H 61
Nursery Gdns. BS10: Bren 4G 35
Nutfield Gro. BS34: Fil 5D 36
Nutfield Ho. BS34: Fil 6D 36
Nutgrove Av. BS3: Wind H 6A 62
Nutgrove La. BS40: Chew M 1G 115
Nuthatch Dr. BS16: Bmhll 2H 49
Nuthatch Gdns. BS16: Bmhll 2H 49
Nutwell Rd. BS22: Wor 2C 106
Nutwell Sq. BS22: Wor 2C 106
NYE 4E 108
Nye Cl. BS27: Ched 7E 150
Nye Drove BS24: E Rols, Nye 6C 108
BS29: Ban 6C 108
Nye Rd. BS25: Sandf 7F 109
Nympsfield BS15: Kgswd 6C 50

O

Oak Av. BA2: Bath 1J 121
Oak Cl. BS27: Ched 7D 150
BS34: Lit S 7F 27
BS37: Yate 2D 30
Oak Ct. BS14: Whit 4C 76
BS22: St G 1G 107
BS23: W Mare 3F 105
Oakdale Av. BS16: Down 7B 38
Oakdale Cl. BS16: Down 7C 38
Oakdale Ct. BS16: Down 7B 38
Oakdale Gdns. BS22: Wor 2D 106
Oakdale Rd. BS14: H'gro 2C 76
BS16: Down 7C 38
Oakdale Wlk. BS16: Down 1C 50
Oakdene Av. BS5: Eastv 5F 49
Oak Dr. BS20: P'head 4D 42
Oakenhill Rd. BS4: Brisl 7G 63
Oakenhill Wlk. BS4: Brisl 7G 63
Oak Farm Touring Pk. BS49: Cong 7H 87
Oakfield Bus. Pk. BS15: Kgswd 2B 64
Oakfield Cl. BA1: Bath 1A 6 (3K 99)
Oakfield Ct. BS8: Clftn 1A 4 (1H 61)
Oakfield Gro. BS8: Clftn 1A 4 (1H 61)
Oakfield Pl. BS8: Clftn 1A 4 (1H 61)
Oakfield Rd. BS8: Clftn 1A 4 (1G 61)
BS15: Kgswd 2B 64
BS31: Key 7D 78
Oakford Av. BS23: W Mare 4H 105
Oakford La. BA1: Bathe 4J 83
SN14: Ash 3J 83
Oak Gro. BS20: Eas 4G 45
Oakhanger Dr. BS11: Law W 6A 34
Oakhill BS24: W Mare 3J 127
Oakhill Av. BS30: Bit 7G 65
Oakhill Cl. BS48: Nail 1K 71
Oakhill La. BS10: H'len 3C 34
Oakhill Rd. BA2: C Down 2B 122
Oak Ho. BS13: Hart 6K 75
Oakhurst Rd. BS9: W Trym 3F 47
Oakland Dr. BS24: Hut 2C 128
Oakland Rd. BS5: St G 1G 63
BS6: Redl 7H 47
Oaklands BS21: Clev 5C 54
BS27: Ched 6C 150
BS39: Paul 2C 152
BS39: Temp C 4G 139
Oaklands Bus. Pk. BS37: Yate 3B 30
Oaklands Cl. BS16: Mang 3F 51
Oaklands Dr. BS16: Bmhll 1J 49
BS30: Old C 7G 65
BS32: Alm 2C 26
Oaklands Rd. BS16: Mang 3E 50
Oak La. BS5: S'wll 6H 49
Oak Leaze BS34: Pat 1B 36
Oakleaze BS36: Coal H 7H 29
Oakleaze Rd. BS35: T'bry 3A 12
Oakleigh Av. BS5: W'hall 1F 63
Oakleigh Cl. BS48: Back 5K 71
Oakleigh Gdns. BS30: Old C 7G 65
Oakley BA2: C'ton D 6G 101
BS21: Clev 2B 68
OAKLEY GREEN 4A 40
Oakley Green Farm La. BS37: W'lgh 4K 39
Oakley Rd. BS7: Hor 1B 48
Oak Lodge *BS16: Fish 2A 50*
(off Partridge Dr.)
Oakmeade Pk. BS4: Know 7D 62
Oakridge Cl. BS15: Kgswd 2E 64
BS25: Wins 6H 131
Oakridge La. BS25: Wins 6H 131
Oak Rd. BS7: Hor 3A 48
BS25: Wins 4G 131
Oaks, The BS7: Bishop 4A 48
BS40: Winf 4K 91
BS48: Nail 7J 57
Oaksey Gro. BS48: Nail 7J 57
Oak St. BA2: Bath 6E 6 (6B 100)
Oak Ter. BA3: Rads 5H 153
Oak Tree Arena (Speedway Track) 3J 159
Oaktree Av. BS16: Puck 3B 52
Oak Tree Cl. BS16: Down 1E 50
Oaktree Cl. BS15: Han 7A 64
Oaktree Ct. BS11: Shire 1J 45
Oaktree Cres. BS32: Brad S 4D 26
Oaktree Gdns. BS13: Withy 5E 74
Oaktree Pk. BS24: Lock 7C 106
Oaktree Pk. (Cvn. Site) BS24: Lock 1C 128
Oak Tree Pl. TA8: Bur S 4C 156
Oaktree Pl. BS22: St G 1G 107
Oak Tree Wlk. BS31: Key 6B 78
Oakwood Av. BS9: Henle 2H 47
Oakwood Bus. Pk. BS24: W Mare 2J 127
Oakwood Gdns. BA2: C'ton D 6F 101
BS36: Coal H 7J 29
Oakwood Pk. BS16: Fish 5J 49
Oakwood Rd. BS9: Henle 2H 47
Oatfield BS48: Back 2D 90
Oatlands Av. BS14: Whit 4C 76
Oatley Ho. BS9: W Trym 3G 47
Oberon Av. BS5: S'wll 6G 49
Observatory Fld. BS25: Wins 5H 131
October La. BS7: Hor 3C 48
ODD DOWN 3K 121
Odd Down (Park & Ride) 4J 121
Odeon Cinema
Bath 5E 6 (5B 100)
Bristol 3F 5 (2K 61)
Weston-Super-Mare 5G 105
Odins Rd. BA2: Odd D 3K 121
Office Village, The BA2: Pea J 6E 142
Okebourne Cl. BS10: Bren 3H 35
Okebourne Rd. BS10: Bren 4H 35
Old Acre Rd. BS14: Whit 7C 76
Old Ashley Hill BS6: Bris 6B 48
Old Aust Rd. BS32: Alm 7E 18
Old Bakery Ct., The *BS6: Bris 7B 48*
(off Brook Rd.)
Old Banwell Rd. BS24: Lock 1F 129
Old Barn La. BS40: Redh 6E 90
Oldbarn La. BS40: Comp M 4D 136
Old Barrow Hill BS11: Shire 1H 45
Old Batch, The BA15: Brad A 4F 125
Old Bell Ct. BS40: Wrin 2F 111
Old Bond St. BA1: Bath 4F 7 (5B 100)
Old Bread St. BS2: Bris 4J 5 (3B 62)
Oldbridge Rd. BS14: Whit 7E 76
Old Bristol Rd. BS22: Wor 2E 106
BS31: Key 3A 78
Old Burnham Rd. TA9: Highb 4F 159
Oldbury Chase BS30: Will 7E 64
Oldbury Ct. Dr. BS16: Fish 2K 49
Oldbury Ct. Rd. BS16: Fish 3J 49
Oldbury La. BS30: Wick 4D 66
Old Butchers Yd. BS26: Axb 4J 149
Old Chapel BA1: Bath 1H 7
Old Chapel, The BS23: W Mare 1F 127
Old Chelsea La. BS8: Fail 5G 59
Old Church Rd. BS21: Clev 7A 54
BS23: Uph 3F 127
BS26: Axb 5H 149
BS48: Nail 2F 71
Old Cider Mill Est. GL12: Wickw 5H 15
Old Coach Cl. NP16: Beach 1C 8
Old Coach Rd. BS26: Cross, L Wre 6D 148
NP16: Beach 1C 8
Old Cote Dr. TA8: Bur S 3C 156
Old Cottage Row BS48: Nail 6J 57
Old Ct. BA15: Brad A 6J 125
Old Dairy, The BA2: Bath 7A 6 (7K 99)
Old Dairy Ct. BS21: Clev 6E 54
OLD DOWN 2E 18
Old Down Hill BS32: Old D, Toc 3D 18
Old Drill Hall, The BS2: Bris 3J 5
Old England Way BA2: Pea J 5D 142
Old Exchange, The BS2: E'ton 2C 62
Old Farm La. BS5: St G 3K 63
Old Ferry Rd. BA2: Bath 5J 99
Oldfield BS21: Clev 2E 68
Oldfield La. BA2: Bath 7B 6, 7C 6 (7K 99)
OLDFIELD PARK 6C 6 (6A 100)
Oldfield Park Station (Rail) 5A 6 (5K 99)
Oldfield Pl. BA2: Bath 6D 6 (6A 100)
BS8: Clftn 4F 61
Oldfield Rd. BA2: Bath 7C 6 (6A 100)
BS8: Clftn 4G 61
Oldfields La. BS32: Gau E 1K 27
BS35: Ear G 6A 20
Old Fire Sta. Ct. BS48: Nail 7E 56
Old Forge M. BS49: Yat 3K 87
Old Forge Way BA2: Pea J 5E 142
Old Fosse Rd. BA2: Odd D 2J 121
BA3: Clan 2J 153
Old Frome Rd. BA2: Odd D 4A 122
Old Gaol BA2: Bath 3G 7 (4C 100)
Old Gloucester Rd. BS16: Fren, H'ook 6K 37
BS16: H'ook 2K 37
BS35: A'ton 7K 11
BS35: Ear G 5K 27
BS36: Wint 5K 27
GL12: Buck, Fal 2F 13
Old Hill BS40: F'tn, Winf 4H 91
BS40: Wrin 1H 111
Old Junction Rd. BS23: W Mare 7K 105
Old King St. BA1: Bath 3F 7 (4B 100)
Old King St. Ct. BS1: Bris 2G 5 (2A 62)
Old Lamb Cl. BS5: St G 2H 63
OLDLAND 5G 65
OLDLAND COMMON 6G 65
Oldland Common Station
Avon Valley Railway 5H 65
Oldland Halt BS30: Old C 5H 65
Oldlands Av. BS36: Coal H 1G 39
Old La. BA2: F'boro 6E 118
BS16: Emer G 2G 51
BS21: Tic 4E 56
Old Malthouse, The *BA1: Bath 1H 7*
(off Clarence St.)
BS5: E'ton 1K 5
Old Market St. BS1: Bris 3H 5 (2A 62)
BS2: Bris 3J 5 (2B 62)
Oldmead Wlk. BS13: Bis 3E 74
Old Methodist Church, The BA2: Bath 6A 6
Old Midford Rd. BA2: S'ske 5C 122
Old Millard's Hill BA3: Mid N 3F 153
Old Mill Cl. BS37: W'lgh 3B 40
Old Mill Rd. BS20: P'head 2F 43
OLD MILLS 3B 152
Old Mills Ind. Est. BS39: Paul 4C 152
Old Mills La. BS39: Paul 3B 152
Old Mill Way BS24: W'ton V 4D 106
OLDMIXON 3J 127
Oldmixon Cres. BS24: W Mare 2J 127
Oldmixon Rd. BS24: Hut, W Mare 4J 127
Old Newbridge Hill BA1: Bath 3G 99
Old Orchard BA1: Bath 2G 7 (4C 100)
Old Orchard, The BS16: Mang 3F 51

Old Orchard St.—Park St.

Old Orchard St. BA1: Bath 5G 7 (5C 100)
Old Park BS2: Bris 3D 4 (2J 61)
Old Park Hill BS2: Bris 3D 4 (2J 61)
Old Pk. Rd. BS11: Shire 1H 45
BS21: Clev 4D 54
OLD PASSAGE 6F 9
Old Pit Rd. BA3: Mid N 6F 153
Old Pit Ter. BA3: Clan 2J 153
Old Pooles Yd. BS4: Brisl 7G 63
(off Brookside Rd.)
Old Post Office La. BS23: W Mare 4F 105
Old Print Works Rd. BS39: Paul 7B 140
Old Priory Rd. BS20: Eas 4F 45
Old Quarry BA2: Odd D 2K 121
Old Quarry Gdns. BS16: Mang 4D 50
Old Quarry Ri. BS11: Shire 1J 45
Old Quarry Rd. BS11: Shire 1H 45
Old Rd. BA3: Writ 5C 154
BS39: Pens 1G 117
Old School, The BA1: Bath 1E 6
Old School Cl. BS25: C'hll 1B 132
BS30: Warm 2H 65
Old School Hill BA2: S'ske 5B 122
Old School Ho. BA1: Bath 1G 7 (4C 100)
BS4: Know 7D 62
(off Maxse Rd.)
Old School Ho., The BS2: Bris 1J 5 (1B 62)
Old School La. BS8: Clftn 5A 4 (3H 61)
BS13: Bis 1G 75
BS24: B'don 7A 128
Old Smiths Yd. BS15: Han 4B 64
Old Sneed Av. BS9: Stok B 4D 46
Old Sneed Cotts. BS9: Stok B 4D 46
Old Sneed Pk. BS9: Stok B 4D 46
Old Sneed Rd. BS9: Stok B 4D 46
Old Station Bus. Pk. BS39: Hall 6J 139
Old Station Cl. BS27: Ched 7C 150
BS40: Wrin 3F 111
Old St. BS21: Clev 6D 54
Old Tarnwell BS39: Stan D 2C 116
Old Temple St. BS1: Bris 4G 5 (3A 62)
Old Track BA2: Lim S 5H 123
Old Vicarage BS8: Clftn 4F 61
(off Lit. Caroline Pl.)
Old Vicarage, The BS6: Bris 6A 48
Old Vicarage Cl. BS20: Pill 4G 45
Old Vicarage Ct. BS14: Whit 6E 76
Old Vicarage Grn. BS31: Key 4G 78
Old Vicarage Pl. BS8: Clftn 6G 47
Oldville Av. BS21: Clev 7D 54
Old Walcot School, The BA1: Bath 2G 7
(off Guinea La.)
Old Water Gdns., The BS40: Blag 3C 134
Oldway Pl. TA9: Highb 3F 159
(not continuous)
Old Wells Rd. BA2: Bath 1B 122
Old Weston Rd. BS48: Flax B 3F 73
BS49: Cong 6G 87
Oldwood La. BS37: Rang, Yate 4B 22
Old Workhouse, The BS5: St G 1G 63
Old Yd., The BS8: Fail 5F 59
Olive Gdns. BS35: A'ton 1H 19
Oliver Brooks Rd. BA3: Mid N 7C 152
Olivier Cl. TA8: Bur S 2E 158
OLVESTON 2C 18
Olveston Rd. BS7: Hor 3A 48
Olympus Cl. BS34: Lit S 1F 37
Olympus Rd. BS34: Pat 6K 25
One Castlepark BS2: Bris 3H 5
Onega Cen. BA1: Bath 3C 6
Onega Ter. BA1: Bath 3C 6 (4A 100)
Oolite Gro. BA2: Odd D 3K 121
Oolite Rd. BA2: Odd D 3K 121
Openshaw Gdns. BS27: Ched 6C 150
Oram Ct. BS30: Bar C 5D 64
Orange Gro. BA1: Bath 4G 7 (5C 100)
Orange St. BS2: Bris 1J 5 (1B 62)
Orchard, The BA2: C Down 3D 122
BA2: Cor 3B 98
BA2: F'frd 7A 124
BA15: L Wrax 6J 103
BS9: W Trym 2G 47
BS24: Lock 7D 106
BS29: Ban 2A 130
BS34: Stok G 2H 37
BS36: Fram C 6G 29
BS39: Pens 7G 95
BS39: Stan D 2C 116
GL12: Tyth 7F 13
Orchard Av. BA3: Mid N 5D 152
BS1: Bris 4D 4 (3J 61)
BS21: Tic 4A 56
BS35: T'bry 3A 12
Orchard Blvd. BS30: Old C 5F 65
Orchard Cl. BA3: Rads 5H 153
BS9: W Trym 3F 47
BS15: Kgswd 1C 64
BS20: P'head 3F 43
BS22: Kew 1K 105
BS22: Wor 2D 106
BS26: Rook 7F 147
BS27: Ched 6D 150
BS29: Ban 2B 130
BS31: Key 4A 78
BS32: Alm 1D 26
BS36: Wint 1C 38
BS37: Yate 4F 31
BS39: Bis S 2J 137
BS40: F'tn 3G 91
BS40: Wrin 1G 111
BS48: Flax B 2E 72
BS49: Cong 7K 87
TA9: Highb 3F 159
Orchard Close, The BS24: Lock 1D 128
Orchard Cnr. BS15: Kgswd 1C 64
Orchard Ct. BS1: Bris 4D 4
BS5: Redf 2F 63
BS9: Stok B 5C 46
BS27: Ched 6D 150
BS34: Fil 5C 36
(off Gloucester Rd. Nth.)
BS37: Yate 3B 30
BS49: C'ham 2B 88
TA9: Highb 4G 159
(Caxton Dr.)
TA9: Highb 5G 159
(Walrow Rd.)
Orchard Cres. BS11: Shire 1H 45
Orchard Dr. BS13: Bis 5G 75
BS25: Sandf 1G 131
BS35: Aust 5G 9
Orchard End BS40: E Harp 7K 137
Orchard Gdns. BA15: Brad A 6H 125
(off Up. Regents Pk.)
BS15: Kgswd 1D 64
BS39: Paul 7C 140
Orchard Ga. BS32: Brad S 4E 26
Orchard Grange BS35: T'bry 2K 11
Orchard Ho. BS5: St G 1H 63
Orchard La. BS1: Bris 4D 4 (3J 61)
BS9: Stok B 4D 46
Orchard Lea BS20: Pill 4H 45
BS35: A'ton 7J 11
Orchard Lodge BA2: Batham 3H 101
BS30: Old C 3H 65
Orchard Pk. (Mobile Homes Pk.)
BS14: Whit 6F 77
Orchard Pl. BS23: W Mare 5G 105
Orchard Ri. BS35: Olv 3C 18
Orchard Rd. BS5: St G 1H 63
BS7: Bishop 4A 48
BS15: Kgswd 1C 64
BS16: Puck 3B 52
BS21: Clev 7D 54
BS24: Hut 3B 128
BS26: Axb 5J 149
BS36: Coal H 7H 29
BS39: Paul 7C 140
BS41: L Ash 1K 73
BS48: Back 4J 71
BS48: Nail 1E 70
Orchards, The BS11: Shire 2J 45
BS15: Kgswd 2D 64
BS20: Pill 4G 45
Orchard Sq. BS5: Redf 2F 63
Orchard St. BS1: Bris 4D 4 (3J 61)
BS23: W Mare 5G 105
Orchard Ter. BA2: Bath 5H 99
Orchard Va. BA3: Mid N 5C 152
BS15: Kgswd 1D 64
Orchard Wlk. BS25: C'hll 1A 132
Orchard Way BA2: Pea J 6D 142
BS27: Ched 6D 150
Orchid Dr. BA2: Odd D 3J 121
BS31: Key 7C 78
Orchids, The TA8: Bur S 5C 156
Oriel Gdns. BA1: Swa 1E 100
Oriel Gro. BA2: Bath 7H 99
Orion Dr. BS34: Lit S 1F 37
Orland Way BS30: Long G 6E 64
Orlebar Gdns. BS11: Law W 5B 34
Orme Dr. BS21: Clev 4D 54
Ormerod Rd. BS9: Stok B 4E 46
Ormonds Cl. BS32: Brad S 4G 27
Ormsley Cl. BS34: Lit S 6E 26
Orpen Gdns. BS7: L'lze 3D 48
Orpen Pk. BS32: Brad S 3D 26
Orpheus Av. BS32: Brad S 1F 37
Orwell Dr. BS31: Key 6D 78
Orwell St. BS3: Wind H 6A 62
Osborne Av. BS7: Bris 5B 48
BS23: W Mare 5H 105
Osborne Cl. BS34: Stok G 3F 37
Osborne Rd. BA1: Bath 5H 99
BS3: Bris 7C 4 (5J 61)
BS8: Clftn 7G 47
BS23: W Mare 5H 105
BS35: Sev B 6A 16
Osborne Ter. BS3: Bedm 7H 61
Osborne Vs. BS2: Bris 1C 4 (1J 61)
Osborne Wlk. TA8: Bur S 2E 158
Osmond Rd. BS24: W'ton V 5D 106
Osprey Ct. BS14: Hart 5K 75
Osprey Gdns. BS22: Wor 3D 106
Osprey Pk. BS35: T'bry 1B 12
Osprey Rd. BS5: Redf 2E 62
Ostlings La. BA1: Bathf 1K 101
Ostrey Mead BS27: Ched 7D 150
Otago Ter. BA1: Bath 1E 100
Ottawa Rd. BS23: W Mare 2H 127
Otterford Cl. BS14: H'gro 5D 76
Otter Rd. BS21: Clev 1E 68
Ottery Cl. BS11: Law W 6A 34
Ottery Way BS35: T'bry 1B 12
Ottrells Mead BS32: Brad S 3E 26
OVAL, THE 7J 99
Oval, The BA2: Bath 7J 99
OVER 5K 25
Overcombe Ho.
BS23: W Mare 3F 105
Over Ct. M. BS32: Alm 5K 25
Overdale BA2: Tun 2K 141
BA3: Clan 1J 153
Over Dr. BS34: Pat 7A 26
OVERHILL 5H 45
Overhill BS20: Pill 5G 45
Over La. BS32: Alm 4A 26
BS35: E Comp 6H 25
Overndale Rd. BS16: Down 3A 50
Overnhill Ct. BS16: Down 3B 50
Overnhill Rd. BS16: Down 3A 50
Overnhurst Ct. BS16: Down 3B 50
Overstables La. BS21: Clev 6D 54
Overton Rd. BS6: Bris 6A 48
Owen Dr. BS8: Fail 5F 59
Owen Gro. BS9: Henle 3H 47
Owen Henry Ho. BS2: Bris 7C 48
(off Conduit Pl.)
Owen St. BS5: E'ton 1E 62
Owls Head Rd. BS15: Kgswd 3C 64
Oxbarton BS34: Stok G 2H 37
Oxenham Ct. BS5: St G 1F 63
Oxen Leaze BS32: Brad S 4G 27
Oxford Pl.
BA2: C Down 2E 122
BS5: E'ton 7D 48
BS8: Clftn 3F 61
BS23: W Mare 5F 105
Oxford Row BA1: Bath 2F 7 (4B 100)
Oxford Sq. BS24: Lock 6F 107
Oxford St. BS2: Bris 5K 5 (3B 62)
(Anvil St.)
BS2: Bris 1J 61
(Cotham Rd.)
BS3: Wind H 5B 62
BS5: Redf 2E 62
BS23: W Mare 5F 105
TA8: Bur S 1D 158
Oxford Ter. BA2: C Down 2E 122
Oxhouse Gdns. BS10: Hen 4E 34
Oxhouse La. BS8: Fail 2F 59
BS40: Winf 4H 91
Oxleaze BS13: Hart 6K 75
Oxleaze La. BS41: Dun 7D 74
Oxleigh Way BS34: H'ook 4H 37
Oxney Pl. BA2: Pea J 6C 142
Ozenhay BS39: Hin B 7A 138
Ozleworth BS15: Kgswd 1E 64

P

Packgate Rd. BS11: A'mth 3K 33
PACKGATE RDBT. 3K 33
Pack Horse La. BA2: S'ske 5B 122
Pacquet Ho's. BS20: Pill 3H 45
(off Underbanks)
Paddock, The BA2: Cor 4B 98
BA15: Brad A 6H 125
BS20: P'head 4F 43
BS21: Clev 7D 54
BS29: Ban 2A 130
Paddock Cl. BS16: Emer G 2F 51
BS32: Brad S 4F 27
Paddock Dr. TA9: Highb 4F 159
Paddock Gdn. BS14: Whit 6B 76
Paddock Gdns. BS35: A'ton 7J 11
Paddock Pk. Homes
BS22: Wor 2F 107
Paddocks, The BA2: C Down 3D 122
BS23: Uph 3F 127
BS25: Sandf 1J 131
BS35: T'bry 3B 12
BS36: Down 6E 38
Paddock Woods BA2: C Down 2F 123
Padfield Cl. BA2: Bath 6H 99
PADLEIGH 2G 121
Padleigh Hill BA2: Bath 2G 121
Padmore Ct. BS5: St G 2F 63
Padstow Rd. BS4: Know 2B 76
Pagans Hill
BS40: Chew M, Chew S 2D 114
Page Cl. BS16: Stap H 4D 50
Page Ct. BS16: Stap H 4D 50
Page Rd. BS16: Stap H 4B 50
Pages Ct. BS3: Bedm 6H 61
(off Ireton Rd.)
BS49: Yat 3J 87
Pages Mead BS11: A'mth 7G 33
Painswick Av. BS34: Pat 6D 26
Painswick Dr. BS37: Yate 5E 30
Paintworks BS4: Bris 5D 62
Palace Yd. M. BA1: Bath 4E 6 (5B 100)
Palairet Cl. BA15: Brad A 7H 125
Palladian BA2: Bath 4C 6 (5A 100)
Palmdale Cl. BS30: Long G 6E 64
Palmer Av. BS35: Sev B 3C 24
Palmer Dr. BA15: Brad A 4H 125
Palmer Row BS23: W Mare 4G 105
Palmers Cl. BS30: Bar C 3D 64
TA8: Bur S 7E 156
PALMER'S ELM 7A 86
Palmers Leaze BS32: Brad S 7J 27
Palmerston Rd. BS6: Redl 4H 47
Palmerston St. BS3: Bedm 6J 61
Palmer St. BS23: W Mare 4G 105
Palmers Way BS24: Hut 3B 128
Palmyra Rd. BS3: Bedm 7H 61
PANBOTTOM 2B 134
Panorama Wlk. BS15: Han 5J 63
Panoramic, The BS1: Bris 3D 4 (2J 61)
Paper La. BS39: Paul 7B 140
Parade, The BA2: Bath 5H 99
BA2: C'ton D 5G 101
BS11: Shire 2J 45
BS13: Bis 4G 75
BS14: H'gro 2C 76
BS34: Pat 5B 26
BS37: Chip S 5G 31
Parade Ct. BS5: S'wll 7H 49
Paragon, The BA1: Bath 3G 7 (4C 100)
BS8: Clftn 3F 61
Paragon Ct. BS23: W Mare 3E 104
Paragon Rd. BS23: W Mare 3E 104
Parbrook Ct. BS14: H'gro 5D 76
Parfitts Hill BS5: St G 3H 63
Parish, The BS3: Bris 7B 4
Parish Brook Rd. BS48: Nail 1D 70
Parish Wharf Leisure Cen. 2G 43
Park, The BS15: Kgswd 1B 64
BS16: Fren 6K 37
BS20: P'head 3H 43
BS30: Will 1F 79
BS31: Key 4C 78
BS32: Brad S 3E 26
BS49: Yat 2H 87
Park & Ride
Ashton Vale 7D 60
Bath Road 2H 77
Lansdown 5J 81
Newbridge 3F 99
Odd Down 4J 121
Portway 1G 45
Park Av. BA2: Bath 7E 6 (6B 100)
BS3: Wind H 6A 62
BS5: Eastv 5F 49
BS5: St G 1G 63
BS32: Alm 4B 26
BS36: Fram C 1F 39
BS36: Wint 1C 38
BS49: Yat 2H 87
Park Batch BS40: Blag 3C 134
Park Cl. BS15: Kgswd 2C 64
BS30: C Hth 4F 65
BS31: Key 5B 78
BS39: Paul 1B 152
PARK CORNER 7J 123
Park Ct. BS23: W Mare 7G 105
Park Cres. BS5: W'hall 1F 63
BS16: Fren 6A 38
BS30: C Hth 4F 65
Park Edge BS5: St G 1G 63
Park End BS29: Ban 1J 129
Parkers Av. BS30: Wick 2C 66
Parkers Barton BS5: Bar H 3D 62
Parkers Cl. BS10: Bren 3K 35
Parker St. BS3: Bedm 6H 61
Parkes Av. BS24: Lock 1H 129
Parkes Rd. BS24: Lock 7G 107
Park Farm Bus. Pk. BS40: F'tn 4F 91
Park Farm Ct. BS30: Long G 5D 64
PARKFIELD 2A 52
Parkfield BS26: Axb 5K 149
Parkfield Av. BS5: St G 2F 63
Parkfield Gdns. BS39: Bis S 2K 137
Parkfield Rank BS16: Puck 1A 52
Parkfield Rd. BS16: Puck 2A 52
Park Gdns. BA1: Bath 1A 6 (3K 99)
Park Gro. BS6: Henle 3H 47
BS9: Henle 3H 47
Park Hill BS11: Shire 2J 45
Park Home Est. BS48: Flax B 2F 73
Park Ho. BA2: Bath 7A 100
BS1: Bris 4D 4
Parkhouse La. BS31: Key 1A 96
(not continuous)
Parkhurst Av. BS16: Fish 4K 49
Parkhurst Rd. BS23: W Mare 5J 105
Parklands BS8: Cot 1C 4 (1J 61)
BS15: Kgswd 1C 64
BS39: High L 3B 140
Parklands Av. BS22: Wor 7D 84
Parklands Rd. BS3: Bwr A 5E 60
Parkland Way BS35: T'bry 1K 11
Park La. BA1: Bath 1B 6 (3K 99)
BA3: Hem 5H 155
BS2: Bris 2D 4 (2J 61)
BS36: Fram C, Wint 3E 38
BS40: Blag 1C 134
Park Leaze BS34: Pat 5A 26
Park Mans. BA1: Bath 1D 6 (3A 100)
Park Pl. BA1: Bath 1D 6 (3A 100)
BA2: C Down 3D 122
BS2: Bris 2D 4 (2J 61)
BS5: Eastv 5G 49
BS8: Clftn 2A 4 (2H 61)
BS23: W Mare 4F 105
Park Rd. BA1: Bath 4H 99
BS3: Bris 7B 4 (4H 61)
BS7: Hor 6C 36
BS11: Shire 2J 45
BS15: Kgswd 7B 50
BS16: Stap 3F 49
BS16: Stap H 3C 50
BS21: Clev 5D 54
BS30: C Hth 4F 65
BS31: Key 5C 78
BS35: T'bry 2J 11
BS39: Paul 1B 152
BS49: Cong 1A 110
GL12: Ley 1B 14
Park Row BS1: Bris 3C 4 (2J 61)
BS36: Fram C 6E 28
Parkside Av. BS36: Wint 1B 38
Parkside Ct. BS4: Brisl 6E 62
Parkside Gdns. BS5: Eastv 4D 48
Parkstone Av. BS7: Hor 2B 48
Park St. BA1: Bath 1D 6 (3A 100)
BS1: Bris 3C 4 (2J 61)
BS4: Wind H 5C 62
BS5: St G 1H 63
BS37: Iron A 2H 29

Park St. Av.—Pleasant Pl.

Park St. Av. BS1: Bris 3C 4 (2J 61)
Park St. M. BA1: Bath 1D 6 (3A 100)
Park Vw. BA1: Bath 3B 6
BA2: Bath 4B 6 (5K 99)
BS15: Kgswd 2C 64
Park Vw. Av. BS35: T'bry 2A 12
Park Vw. Ter. BS5: St G 1G 63
Park Vs. BS23: W Mare 4F 105
Park Wlk. BS20: Pill 4H 45
Parkwall Cres. BS30: Bar C 5D 64
Parkwall Rd. BS30: C Hth 5D 64
PARKWAY 4G 37
Park Way BA3: Mid N 6E 152
BS22: Wor 3F 107
BS30: C Hth 4F 65
Parkway BA2: Cam 3J 141
BS2: Bris 7C 48
BS5: Eastv 5E 48
BS16: Fren, H'ook 7J 37
Parkway La. BA2: Cam 1H 141
Parkway Trad. Est. BS2: Bris 6B 48
Parkwood Cl. BS14: Whit 6B 76
Parliament St. BS4: Wind H 5C 62
Parnall Cres. BS37: Yate 3C 30
Parnall Rd. BS16: Fish 5J 49
Parnall Rd. Ind. Est. BS16: Fish 5J 49
Parnell Rd. BS16: Stap 1G 49
BS21: Clev 6D 54
Parnell Way TA8: Bur S 7D 156
Parry Cl. BA2: Bath 7H 99
Parry's Cl. BS9: Stok B 3E 46
Parrys Gro. BS9: Stok B 3E 46
Parrys La. BS9: Stok B, W Trym 3E 46
Parslows Barton BS5: St G 2J 63
Parsonage Cl. BS40: W Har 7E 136
BS40: Winf 5K 91
Parsonage Ct. BS20: P'head 4F 43
BS40: Winf 4K 91
Parsonage La. BA1: Bath 4F 7 (5B 100)
BS26: Axb 4A 150
BS39: Pens, Pub 6F 95
BS40: Winf 6J 91
Parsonage Rd. BS41: L Ash 7C 60
TA8: Berr 2B 156
Parsons Av. BS34: Stok G 2H 37
Parson's Grn. BS22: Wor 1E 106
Parsons Grn. BS21: Clev 2C 68
Parsons Mead BS48: Flax B 3D 72
Parsons Paddock BS14: H'gro 3C 76
Parsons Pen BS27: Ched 7D 150
Parsons Rd. TA9: Highb 4E 158
Parson St. BS3: Bedm 7H 61
Parson Street Station (Rail) 7H 61
Parsons Wlk. BS30: B'yte 2H 65
Parsons Way BS25: Wins 6D 130
Partis College BA1: Bath 3G 99
Partis Way BA1: Bath 3G 99
Partition St. BS1: Bris 5C 4 (3J 61)
Partridge Cl. BS22: Wor 3D 106
BS37: Yate 2F 31
Partridge Dr. BS16: Fish 2A 50
Partridge Rd. BS16: Puck 4C 52
Passage Leaze BS11: Shire 2H 45
Passage Rd. BS9: W Trym 6G 35
BS10: Hen 2G 35
BS10: Hen, W Trym 4F 35
BS35: Aust 7E 8
Passage St. BS2: Bris 4H 5 (3A 62)
Pasture, The BS32: Brad S 5F 27
Pastures Av. BS22: St G 2G 107
Patch Ct. BS16: Emer G 7E 38
Patch Cft. BS21: Clev 2C 68
Patch Elm La. BS37: Rang 6J 21
Patch La. BS37: Rang 5A 22
PATCHWAY 1E 36
Patchway Sports Cen. 5C 26
Patchway Station (Rail) 1E 36
Patchway Trad. Est. BS34: Pat 6A 26
(Britannia Rd.)
BS34: Pat 7K 25
(Olympus Rd.)
Patricia Cl. TA8: Bur S 5C 156
Patterson Ho. BS1: Bris 7G 5
Paul Alan Ho. *BS5: Redf 2E 62*
(off Witchell Rd.)
Paulman Gdns. BS41: L Ash 2K 73
Paulmont Ri. BS39: Temp C 4G 139
Paul's C'way. BS49: Cong 7K 87
Paul St. BS2: Bris 1D 4 (1J 61)
Paulto' Hill BS39: Paul 7D 140
PAULTON 7C 140
Paulton Dr. BS7: Bishop 4J 47
Paulton La. BA2: Cam 6H 141
Paulton Pool 1C 152
Paulton Rd. BA3: Mid N 5D 152
BS39: Far G 2A 152
Paultow Av. BS3: Wind H 6A 62
Paultow Rd. BS3: Wind H 6A 62
Paulwood Rd. BS39: Temp C 4G 139
Pavey Cl. BS13: Hart 6J 75
Pavey Rd. BS13: Hart 6J 75
Pavilion Rd. NP16: Beach 2C 8
Pavilions, The BS4: Brisl 1E 76
BS13: Bis 2E 74
Pawlett BS24: W Mare 3J 127
Pawlett Rd. BS13: Hart 7H 75
Pawlett Wlk. BS13: Hart 7J 75
Paxton BS16: Stap 7G 37
Paxton Dr. BS3: Ash G 5F 61
Paybridge Rd. BS13: Withy 6F 75
Payne Dr. BS5: E'ton 2D 62
Payne Rd. BS24: Hut 3B 128
Paynes Orchard Cvn. Pk. BS10: Bren 3K 35
Paynes Way BS23: W Mare 3H 127
Peache Ct. BS16: Down 2C 50
Peache Rd. BS16: Down 2C 50
Peacock Lodge BS16: Fish 3J 49
Peacocks La. BS15: Kgswd 1A 64
Pearce Cl. BS35: T'bry 4A 12
Pearce Dr. TA9: Highb 4F 159
Pearces Hill BS16: Fren 1K 49
Pearl St. BS3: Bedm 6H 61
Pearsall Rd. BS30: Long G 7C 64
Pearse Cl. BS22: Wor 6F 85
Peart Cl. BS13: Withy 5E 74
Peart Dr. BS13: Withy 6E 74
Pear Tree Av. BS41: L Ash 2J 73
Peartree Cl. BS13: Hart 6H 75
Peartree Fld. BS20: P'head 3H 43
Peartree Gdns. BS24: B'don 6K 127
Pear Tree Hey BS37: Yate 1E 30
Pear Tree Ind. Est. BS40: L'frd 1E 132
Pear Tree La. BS5: St G 3K 63
Peartree La. BS15: Soun 6D 50
Pear Tree Rd. BS32: Brad S 4E 26
Pear Tree Way BS16: Puck 7H 39
PEASEDOWN ST JOHN 6C 142
Peasedown St John By-Pass
BA2: Pea J 4E 142
Peats Hill BS39: Pub 6G 95
Pedder Rd. BS21: Clev 1D 68
Peelers Ct. BS26: Axb 5J 149
Peel St. BS5: E'ton 1B 62
Pegasus Ct. BS20: P'head 3F 43
BS23: W Mare 7F 105
BS48: Nail 7G 57
Pegasus Lodge BS23: W Mare 7F 105
Pegasus Pk. BS34: Lit S 1D 36
Pegasus Pl. BS25: Sandf 1F 131
Pegasus Rd. BS34: Pat 7K 25
Peg Hill BS37: Yate 2F 31
Peg La. BS16: Puck 1A 52
Pegwell Cl. BS34: Pat 1A 36
Pelican Cl. BS22: Wor 4D 106
Pemberton Ct. BS16: Fish 3K 49
Pembery Rd. BS3: Bedm 6H 61
Pembroke Av. BS11: Shire 2J 45
Pembroke Cl. TA8: Bur S 6D 156
Pembroke Ct. BS2: Bris 1H 5
BS21: Clev 5C 54
Pembroke Ga. BS8: Clftn 7G 47
Pembroke Gro. BS8: Clftn 2G 61
Pembroke Lodge BS8: Clftn 2A 4
Pembroke Mans. BS8: Clftn 1A 4 (1G 61)
Pembroke Pl. BS8: Clftn 4G 61
Pembroke Rd. BS3: Bris 5J 61
BS8: Clftn 7G 47
BS11: Shire 2J 45
BS15: Kgswd 5C 50
BS20: P'head 5A 42
BS23: W Mare 7H 105
Pembroke St. BS2: Bris 1H 5 (1A 62)
Pembroke Va. BS8: Clftn 2A 4 (1G 61)
Penard Way BS15: Kgswd 2D 64
Penarth Dr. BS24: W Mare 4J 127
Pendennis Av. BS16: Stap H 3B 50
Pendennis Ho. BS16: Stap H 3B 50
Pendennis Pk. BS4: Brisl 7F 63
BS16: Stap H 4B 50
Pendennis Rd. BS16: Stap H 3B 50
Pendlesham Gdns. BS23: W Mare 3J 105
Pendock Cl. BS30: Bit 1G 79
Pendock Ct. BS16: Emer G 1F 51
Pendock Rd. BS16: Fish 2K 49
BS36: Wint 2C 28
Penfield Ct. BS2: Bris 6C 48
Penfield Rd. BS2: Bris 6C 48
Penlea Ct. BS11: Shire 1H 45
Penmoor Pl. TA8: Berr 2B 156
Penmoor Rd. TA8: Berr 2B 156
Pennant Pl. BS20: P'head 1H 43
Pennard BS24: W Mare 3J 127
Pennard Ct. BS14: Whit 5D 76
Pennard Grn. BA2: Bath 5G 99
Penn Cl. BS27: Ched 7E 150
Penn Dr. BS16: Fren 6A 38
Penn Gdns. BA1: Bath 3G 99
Penngrove BS30: Long G 6E 64
Penn Hill Rd. BA1: Bath, W'ton 3G 99
Pennine Gdns. BS23: W Mare 3J 105
Pennine Rd. BS30: Old C 5G 65
Pennings, The BS26: Axb 4J 149
Pennlea BS13: Bis 3J 75
Penn Lea Ct. BA1: Bath 3H 99
(not continuous)
Penn Lea Rd. BA1: Bath 2G 99
Pennon Ri. BS1: Bris 6C 4
Penn Rd. BS27: Ched 7E 150
Penns, The BS21: Clev 7E 54
Penn St. BS1: Bris 2H 5 (2A 62)
Penn Way BS26: Axb 5J 149
Pennycress BS22: W Mare 5B 106
Pennycress Cl. BS16: Emer G 7H 39
Penny La. BS15: Soun 5D 50
Pennyquick BA2: New L 4C 98
Pennyquick Vw. BA2: Bath 5F 99
Pennyroyal Gro. BS16: Stap 3G 49
Pennywell Ct. BS5: E'ton 1K 5
Pennywell Grn. BS5: E'ton 1K 5
Pennywell Rd. BS5: E'ton 1K 5 (1B 62)
Pen Pk. Rd. BS10: S'mead 4J 35
Pen Pk. Sports Pavilion 5K 35
Penpole Av. BS11: Shire 2J 45
Penpole Cl. BS11: Shire 1H 45
Penpole La. BS11: Shire 1H 45
Penpole Pk. BS11: Shire 1J 45
Penpole Pl. BS11: Shire 2J 45
Penrice Cl. BS22: W Mare 2A 106
Penrith Gdns. BS10: S'mead 6K 35
(not continuous)
Penrose BS14: H'gro 3B 76
Penrose Dr. BS32: Brad S 7F 27
Pensfield Pk. BS10: Bren 3K 35
PENSFORD 7F 95
Pensford Ct. BS14: Stoc 5F 77
Pensford Hill BS39: Pens 6F 95
Pensford La. BS39: Stan D 2C 116
Pensford Lock Up 7G 95
Pentagon, The BS9: Sea M 2B 46
Penthouse Hill BA1: Bathe 7H 83
Pentire Av. BS13: Bis 4G 75
Pentland Av. BS35: T'bry 4C 12
Pepperall Rd. TA9: Highb 4F 159
Peppershells La. BS39: Comp D 5A 96
Pepys Cl. BS31: Salt 1H 97
Pera Pl. BA1: Bath 3C 100
Pera Rd. BA1: Bath 1G 7 (3C 100)
Percival Ct. BS8: Clftn 1F 61
Percival Rd. BS8: Clftn 1F 61
Percy Pl. BA1: Bath 2D 100
Percy St. BS3: Bedm 5K 61
Percy Walker Ct. BS16: Down 2A 50
Peregrine Cl. BS22: Wor 3D 106
Perfect Vw. BA1: Bath 2C 100
Pero's Bridge 6E 4 (3K 61)
Perrett Ho. *BS2: Bris 2J 5*
(off Redcross St.)
Perretts Ct. BS1: Bris 7D 4 (4J 61)
Perrett Way BS20: Pill 4J 45
Perrin Cl. BS39: Temp C 5G 139
Perrings, The BS48: Nail 1G 71
Perrinpit Rd. BS36: Fram C, Wint 2B 28
Perrott Rd. BS15: Kgswd 7E 50
Perry Cl. BA3: Rads 5H 153
BS36: Wint 2B 38
Perrycroft Av. BS13: Bis 4G 75
Perrycroft Rd. BS13: Bis 4G 75
Perrymans Cl. BS16: Fish 2J 49
BS30: Doy 1G 67
PERRYMEAD 1D 122
Perrymead BA2: Bath 7D 100
BS22: Wor 6F 85
Perrymead Pl. BA2: Bath 7D 100
Perry Rd. BS1: Bris 3D 4 (2J 61)
BS41: L Ash 1K 73
Perry's Cl. BS27: Ched 7C 150
Perrys Lea BS32: Brad S 4F 27
Perry St. BS5: E'ton 1C 62
Pesley Cl. BS13: Withy 6G 75
Petercole Dr. BS13: Bis 4G 75
Peterside BS39: Temp C 6G 139
Peterson Av. BS13: Hart 7J 75
Peterson Sq. BS13: Hart 7J 75
(not continuous)
Peter's Ter. BS5: Bar H 2D 62
Petersway Gdns. BS5: St G 3J 63
Petherbridge Way BS7: Hor 3C 48
Petherton Cl. BS15: Kgswd 2C 64
Petherton Gdns. BS14: H'gro 3D 76
Petherton Rd. BS14: H'gro 2D 76
Petticoat La. BS1: Bris 4H 5 (3A 62)
Pettigrove Gdns. BS15: Kgswd 2C 64
Pettigrove Rd. BS15: Kgswd 3C 64
Pevensey Wlk. BS4: Know 3K 75
Peverell Cl. BS10: Hen 4F 35
Peverell Dr. BS10: Hen 4F 35
Phase One
Bath 3C 6 (4A 100)
Philadelphia St. BS1: Bris 2G 5 (2A 62)
Philfare La. BS25: Row 4B 132
Philippa Cl. BS14: H'gro 3C 76
Philippa Ho. BA2: Bath 6A 6
Philips Ho. *BS2: Bris 1A 62*
(off Dove St. Sth.)
Philip St. BA1: Bath 5G 7
BS2: Bris 4D 62
BS3: Bedm 5K 61
Phillips Rd. BS23: W Mare 6J 105
Phillis Hill BA3: Mid N 2D 152
BS39: Paul 2D 152
Phippen St. BS1: Bris 6G 5 (4A 62)
Phipps Barton BS15: Kgswd 1K 63
Phipps St. BS3: Bris 7A 4 (5H 61)
Phoenix Bus. Pk. BS3: Bedm 7G 61
Phoenix Ct. BS2: Bris 2J 5
Phoenix Gro. BS6: Henle 3J 47
BS16: Soun 5B 50
Phoenix Ho. BA1: Bath 1E 6
BS1: Bris 6F 5 (4K 61)
BS5: Bar H 3D 62
Phoenix St. BS5: Bar H 3D 62
Phoenix Ter. TA8: Bur S 2D 158
Phoenix Way BS20: P'bry, P'head 1H 43
Piccadilly Pl. BA1: Bath 2D 100
Pickwick Rd. BA1: Bath 1C 100
Picton La. BS6: Bris 7A 48
Picton M. BS6: Bris 7A 48
Picton St. BS6: Bris 7A 48
Pier Cl. BS20: P'head 1G 43
Pierrepont Pl. BA1: Bath 5G 7 (5C 100)
Pierrepont St. BA1: Bath 5G 7 (5C 100)
Pier Rd. BS20: P'head 1F 43
Pier St. TA8: Bur S 2C 158
Pigeon Fld. BS39: Paul 7B 140
Pigeon Ho. Dr. BS13: Hart 6K 75
Pigeon La. BS40: Redh 3B 112
Pigott Av. BS13: Withy 6G 75
PILE MARSH 2F 63
Pilemarsh BS5: St G 2F 63
Pilgrims Way BS11: Shire 1G 45
BS16: Down 7B 38
BS22: Wor 2C 106
BS40: Chew S 4D 114
Pilgrims Wharf BS4: St Ap 2G 63
Pilkington Cl. BS34: Fil 5E 36
PILL 4G 45
Pillengers Pl. *BS8: Clftn 5A 4*
(off Hotwell Rd.)
Pillingers Gdns. BS6: Redl 6H 47
Pillingers Rd. BS15: Kgswd 2A 64
Pillmore La. TA9: Watch 4K 159
Pill Rd. BS8: Abb L 6J 45
BS20: Pill 5H 45
Pill St. BS20: Pill 4G 45
Pill Way BS21: Clev 7B 54
PILNING 6D 16
Pilning Station (Rail) 1F 25
Pilning St. BS32: Piln, Toc 7F 17
BS35: Piln 7F 17
Pimm's La. BS22: W Mare 1K 105
(not continuous)
Pimpernel Mead BS32: Brad S 7G 27
PINCKNEY GREEN 6C 102
Pincots La. GL12: Wickw 2G 23
Pine Cl. BS22: Wor 2B 106
BS35: T'bry 3A 12
Pine Ct. BA3: Rads 4A 154
BS31: Key 6A 78
BS40: Chew M 1H 115
Pinecroft BS14: H'gro 3B 76
BS20: P'head 2B 42
Pine Gro. BS7: Fil 6C 36
Pine Gro. Pl. BS7: Bishop 5K 47
Pine Hill BS22: Wor 2B 106
Pine Lea BS24: B'don 6K 127
Pine Ridge Cl. BS9: Stok B 4C 46
Pine Rd. BS10: Bren 4H 35
Pines, The BS9: Stok B 5D 46
BS16: Soun 6E 50
Pinesgate BA2: Bath 5C 6 (5A 100)
Pines La. BS32: Old D 2F 19
Pines Rd. BS30: Bit 1G 79
Pines Way BA2: Bath 5C 6 (5A 100)
BA3: Rads 4A 154
Pines Way Ind. Est. BA2: Bath 5D 6
Pinetree Rd. BS24: Lock 1H 129
Pine Wlk. BA3: Rads 5J 153
Pinewood BS15: Kgswd 7D 50
Pinewood Av. BA3: Mid N 5D 152
Pinewood Cl. BS9: W Trym 1H 47
Pinewood Gro. BA3: Mid N 5D 152
Pinewood Rd. BA3: Mid N 5D 152
Pinewood Way TA8: Brean 3B 144
Pinghay La. BS40: Regil, Winf 6A 92
Pinhay Rd. BS13: Bis 4H 75
Pinkers Ct. BS35: Rudg 3H 19
Pinkers Mead BS16: Emer G 2G 51
Pinkhams Twist BS14: Whit 5C 76
Pinnell Gro. BS16: Emer G 1G 51
Pinnockscroft TA8: Berr 2B 156
Pinter Cl. TA8: Bur S 2E 158
Pioneer Av. BA2: C Down 3B 122
Pioneer Pk. BS4: Brisl 4E 62
PIPEHOUSE 7H 123
Pipehouse La. BA2: F'frd 7G 123
Pipe La. BS1: Bris 4D 4 (3J 61)
Piper Rd. BS37: Yate 3E 30
Pipers Cl. BS26: Weare 7E 148
Piplar Ground BA15: Brad A 7H 125
Pippin Cl. BA2: Pea J 6D 142
Pippin Ct. BS30: Bar C 5D 64
Pippins, The BS20: P'head 3H 43
Pitch & Pay La. BS9: Stok B 5E 46
Pitch & Pay Pk. BS9: Stok B 5E 46
Pitchcombe BS37: Yate 7C 30
Pitchcombe Gdns. BS9: C Din 1D 46
Pitch La. BS6: Cot 7K 47
Pithay, The BS1: Bris 3F 5 (2K 61)
BS39: Paul 7C 140
Pithay Ct. BS1: Bris 3F 5 (2K 61)
Pit La. BS40: Nem T 1J 135
BS40: Nem T, Up Str 6J 113
BS48: Back 6J 71
Pitlochry Cl. BS7: Hor 6B 36
Pitman Ct. BA1: Bath 1E 100
Pitman Ho. BA2: Bath 1K 121
Pitman Rd. BS23: W Mare 6G 105
Pitmoor La. TA9: Highb 3J 159
Pit Rd. BA3: Mid N 5F 153
Pitt Rd. BS7: Hor 3A 48
Pitt's La. BS40: Chew M 3H 115
Pittville Cl. BS35: T'bry 1A 12
Pitville Pl. BS6: Cot 1H 61
Pixash Bus. Cen. BS31: Key 5F 79
Pixash La. BS31: Key 5F 79
Pizey Av. BS21: Clev 7B 54
TA8: Bur S 6C 156
Pizey Av. Ind. Est. BS21: Clev 7B 54
Pizey Cl. BS21: Clev 7B 54
Plain, The BS35: T'bry 3K 11
Planetarium, The 6D 4 (3J 61)
PLASTER'S GREEN 6K 113
Platform, The BS6: Bris 6A 48
Platts Wood BS16: Fren 7F 37
Players Cl. BS16: H'ook 3K 37
Player's La. TA8: Bur S 6C 156
Playford Gdns. BS11: Law W 7J 33
Playhouse Theatre
Weston-Super-Mare 4F 105
Plaza, The BS2: Bris 4K 5
Pleasant Ho. BS16: Stap H 3B 50
Pleasant Pl. BA1: Bathf 1B 102

Pleasant Rd.—Quayside La.

Pleasant Rd. BS16: Stap H 3B 50
Pleshey Cl. BS22: Wor 2B 106
Plimsoll Ho. BS1: Bris 7G 5
Ploughed Paddock BS48: Nail 1F 71
Plough Ho. BS13: Bedm 7H 61
Plover Cl. BS22: Wor 3D 106
BS37: Yate 4C 30
Plovers Ri. BA3: Rads 3A 154
Plowright Ho. BS15: Han 4K 63
Plumers Cl. BS21: Clev 1E 68
Plumley Ct. BS23: W Mare 7F 105
Plumley Cres. BS24: Lock 1E 128
PLUMMER'S HILL 7B 140
Plummer's Hill BS5: S'wll, St G 1G 63
Plumpton Ct. BS16: Down 6D 38
Plumptre Cl. BS39: Paul 1C 152
Plumptre Rd. BS39: Paul 1B 152
Plum Tree Cl. BS25: Wins 4G 131
Plum Tree Rd. BS22: W Mare 4C 106
Plunder St. BS49: C've 4D 88
Podgers Dr. BA1: W'ton 1H 99
Podium, The BA1: Bath 3G 7 (5C 100)
Poet's Cl. BS5: W'hall 1F 63
Poets Cnr. BA3: Rads 6G 153
Poet's Wlk. BS21: Clev 7A 54
Point 4 Distribution Cen. BS11: A'mth 6H 33
Polden Cl. BS48: Nail 1G 71
Polden Ct. BA2: C'ton D 5F 101
Polden Ho. BS3: Wind H 6K 61
Polden Rd. BS20: P'head 3D 42
(not continuous)
BS23: W Mare 4H 105
Polestar Way BS24: W'ton V 4E 106
Police La. BS39: Pens 1G 117
Pollard Rd. BS24: W'ton V 4D 106
Polly Barnes Cl. BS15: Han 4K 63
Polly Barnes Hill BS15: Han 4K 63
BS15: St G 4K 63
Polygon, The *BS8: Clftn 3F 61*
(off Polygon Rd.)
BS11: A'mth 6H 33
Polygon La. BS8: Clftn 3F 61
Polygon La. Sth. *BS8: Clftn 3F 61*
(off Polygon Rd.)
Polygon Rd. BS8: Clftn 3F 61
Pomfrett Gdns. BS14: Stoc 5G 77
POMPHREY 3F 51
Pomphrey Hill BS16: Emer G 3F 51
Pond Cl. BS34: Pat 5D 26
Pond Head Ct. *BS20: Pill 4H 45*
(off Eirene Ter.)
Ponsford Rd. BS4: Know 2D 76
Ponting Cl. BS5: S'wll 7J 49
Pool Barton BS31: Key 4C 78
Pool Cnr. BS32: Toc 3D 18
Poole Cl. BS13: Hart 5J 75
Poole Ct. BS37: Yate 4E 30
Poole Ct. Dr. BS37: Yate 4E 30
Poole Ho. BA2: Bath 6F 99
Poolemead Rd. BA2: Bath 6F 99
Poole St. BS11: A'mth 7F 33
Pooles Wharf BS8: Clftn 4G 61
Pooles Wharf Ct. BS8: Clftn 4G 61
Pool Ho. BS34: Pat 6C 26
Pool La. BS40: Regil 2A 114
Pool Rd. BS15: Soun 3C 50
Poor Hill BA2: F'boro 6D 118
Pope Ct. BA2: New L 6B 98
Popes Wlk. BA2: Bath, C Down 7D 100
Poplar Av. BS9: Stok B 2D 46
Poplar Cl. BA2: Bath 7K 99
BS22: Kew 1J 105
(in Ardnave Holiday Pk.)
BS30: Old C 3G 65
Poplar Dr. BS16: Puck 3B 52
Poplar Est. TA9: Highb 5F 159
Poplar Flds. BS30: Old C 3H 65
Poplar La. GL12: Wickw 1H 23
Poplar Pl. BS16: Fish 5J 49
BS23: W Mare 4G 105
Poplar Rd. BA2: Odd D 4K 121
BS5: S'wll 7H 49
BS13: Bis 3F 75
BS15: St G 4J 63
BS30: Old C 4G 65
TA8: Bur S 7C 156
POPLAR RDBT. 2J 33
Poplars, The BS20: Eas 4F 45
BS22: Wor 3D 106
Poplar Ter. BS15: Kgswd 1D 64
Poplar Wlk. BS24: Lock 7C 106
Poplar Way E. BS11: A'mth 2J 33
Poplar Way W. BS11: A'mth 1H 33
Poples Bow TA9: Highb 3G 159
Pople Wlk. BS7: Bishop 5B 48
Poppy Cl. BS22: Wick L 6E 84
Poppy Mead BS32: Brad S 7G 27
Porlock Cl. BS21: Clev 1E 68
BS23: W Mare 3H 127
Porlock Gdns. BS48: Nail 1G 71
Porlock Rd. BA2: C Down 3C 122
BS3: Wind H 6K 61
Portal Rd. BS24: Lock 1H 129
PORTBURY 5B 44
Portbury Comn. BS20: P'head 4G 43
Portbury Gro. BS11: Shire 2H 45
Portbury Hundred, The BS20: P'bry 4H 43
Portbury La. BS20: P'bry 6C 44
Portbury Wlk. BS11: Shire 2H 45
Portbury Way BS20: P'bry 3B 44
PORTBURY WHARF 2J 43
PORTISHEAD 3F 43
Portishead Bus. Pk. BS20: P'head 3F 43
Portishead Lodge BS20: P'head 2F 43
Portishead Rd. BS22: Wor 7F 85
Portishead Swimming Pool 1E 42
Portishead Way BS3: Ash V, Bwr A 6E 60
Portland Cl. BS48: Nail 1F 71
Portland Ct. BS1: Bris 6A 4 (4G 61)
BS16: Soun 5B 50
Portland Dr. BS20: P'head 4G 43
Portland Hgts. BS2: Bris 1H 5
Portland Lofts *BS2: Bris 1H 5*
(off Wilson St.)
Portland Mans. *BS2: Bris 1H 5*
(off Portland Sq.)
Portland Pl. BA1: Bath 1E 6 (3B 100)
BS16: Stap H 5B 50
TA9: Bre K 6K 157
Portland Rd. BA1: Bath 1E 6
Portland Sq. BS2: Bris 1H 5 (1A 62)
Portland St. BS2: Bris 1D 4 (1J 61)
BS8: Clftn 2F 61
BS16: Soun, Stap H 5B 50
Portland Ter. *BA1: Bath 1E 6*
(off Harley St.)
Portmeade Drove BS26: Axb 5J 149
Portmeirion Cl. BS14: Whit 5D 76
Port Side Cl. BS5: St G 3H 63
Port Vw. BS20: Pill 3G 45
Portview Ho. *BS11: A'mth 6F 33*
(off Portview Rd.)
Portview Rd. BS11: A'mth 6F 33
Portwall La. BS1: Bris 6G 5 (4A 62)
Portwall La. E. BS1: Bris 6H 5 (4A 62)
Portwall Pl. BS1: Bris 6G 5 (4A 62)
Portway BS9: Sea M, Stok B 3B 46
BS11: Shire 7G 33
Portway La. BS37: Chip S 4J 31
Portway (Park & Ride) 1G 45
PORTWAY RDBT. 7G 33
Post Office La. BS5: St G 1G 63
BS40: Blag 2B 134
BS48: Flax B 3C 72
Post Office Rd. BS23: W Mare 4F 105
BS24: Lock 7F 107
Poston Way BA15: W'ley 5C 124
POTTERS HILL 2F 91
POTTERSWOOD 2K 63
Potterswood Cl. BS15: Kgswd 2B 64
Pottery Cl. BS23: W Mare 6J 105
Pottery Farm Cl. BS13: Hart 6J 75
Potts Cl. BA1: Bathe 6H 83
Poulton BA15: Brad A 7H 125
Poulton La. BA15: Brad A 7J 125
Pound, The BS32: Alm 1C 26
BS40: Redh 1B 112
Pound Dr. BS16: Fish 3H 49
Pound La. BA15: Brad A 6G 125
BS16: Fish 4H 49
BS48: Nail 7E 56
Pound Mead BS40: F'tn 3G 91
Pound Rd. BS15: Kgswd, Soun 6D 50
Pountney Dr. BS5: E'ton 1D 62
Powell Ct. BS30: Doy 7E 52
Powells Acres BS21: Clev 6E 54
Powis Cl. BS22: W Mare 2A 106
Powlett Ct. BA2: Bath 2J 7 (4D 100)
Powlett Rd. BA2: Bath 1J 7 (3D 100)
Pow's Hill BA3: Clan 2H 153
Pow's Orchard BA3: Mid N 5E 152
Pow's Rd. BS15: Kgswd 2B 64
Poyntz Ct. BS30: Long G 6D 64
Poyntz Rd. BS4: Know 2B 76
Praedium, The BS6: Redl 6H 47
Prattens La. BS16: Stap H 4B 50
Pratten Ter. BA3: Mid N 6F 153
Preacher Cl. BS5: St G 3K 63
Preanes Grn. BS22: Wor 2E 106
Precinct, The BS20: P'head 3F 43
Preddy's La. BS5: St G 3J 63
Premier Bus. Pk. TA9: Highb 6F 159
Prescot Cl. BS22: W Mare 2K 105
Prescott BS37: Yate 6D 30
Press Moor Dr. BS30: Bar C 5D 64
Prestbury BS37: Yate 6D 30
Preston Wlk. BS4: Know 1C 76
Prestwick Cl. BS4: Brisl 1F 77
Pretoria Rd. BS34: Pat 6B 26
Prewett St. BS1: Bris 7G 5 (4A 62)
Priddy Cl. BA2: Bath 6H 99
(not continuous)
Priddy Ct. BS14: Whit 5D 76
Priddy Dr. BS14: Whit 5D 76
PRIEST DOWN 5H 95
Priestley Way TA8: Bur S 3E 158
Priest Path BS31: Q Char 7J 77
Priests Way BS22: Wor 3B 106
Priestwood Cl. BS10: Hen 4G 35
Primrose Cl. BS15: Kgswd 1A 64
BS32: Brad S 4F 27
Primrose Dr. BS35: T'bry 2B 12
PRIMROSE HILL 2K 99
Primrose Hill BA1: W'ton 2K 99
Primrose La. BA3: Mid N 5F 153
BS15: Kgswd 7A 50
Primrose Ter. BA3: Mid N 5F 153
BS15: Kgswd 7A 50
Primrose Wlk. BS31: Key 7B 78
Prince Rupert Ho. BS8: Clftn 1B 4 (1H 61)
Prince's Bldgs. BS8: Clftn 3F 61
Princes Bldgs. *BA1: Bath 3F 7*
(off George St.)
Princes Ct. BS30: Long G 5D 64
Prince's La. BS8: Clftn 3F 61
Prince's Pl. BS7: Bishop 5A 48
Prince's Rd. BS21: Clev 6D 54
Princess Cl. BS31: Key 6C 78
Princess Gdns. BS16: Stap 2F 49
Princess Row BS2: Bris 1F 5
Princess Royal Gdns. BS5: Redf 1E 62
Princess St. BS2: Bris 3C 62
BS3: Bedm 5A 62
TA8: Bur S 1D 158
Prince's St. BA3: Clan 1J 153
BS2: Bris 1B 62
Princes St. BA1: Bath 4F 7 (5B 100)
Princess Victoria St. BS8: Clftn 3F 61
Prince St. BS1: Bris 6E 4 (4K 61)
Prince's Wharf 7D 4 (4J 61)
Prinknash Ct. BS37: Yate 7D 30
Prior Pk. Bldgs. BA2: Bath 7J 7 (6D 100)
Prior Pk. Cotts. BA2: Bath 7J 7 (6C 100)
Prior Pk. Gdns. BA2: Bath 7J 7 (6D 100)
Prior Pk. Landscape Garden 1E 122
Prior Pk. Rd. BA2: Bath 7J 7 (6D 100)
Priors Hill BA2: Tims 4D 140
Prior's Hill Flats BS6: Bris 7K 47
Priors Lea BS37: Yate 5D 30
Priory Av. BS9: W Trym 1G 47
Priory Cl. BA2: C Down 1D 122
BA3: Mid N 5E 152
BA15: Brad A 5G 125
Priory Ct. BS15: Han 6A 64
Priory Ct. Rd. BS9: W Trym 1G 47
Priory Dene BS9: W Trym 1G 47
Priory Farm Trad. Est. BS20: P'bry 5B 44
Priory Gdns. BS7: Hor 7B 36
BS11: Shire 1H 45
BS20: Eas 4F 45
TA8: Bur S 2D 158
Priory M. BS23: W Mare 5K 105
Priory Pk. BA15: Brad A 5H 125
Priory Rd. BS4: Know 7D 62
BS8: Clftn 1B 4 (1H 61)
BS11: Shire 2H 45
BS20: Eas 4F 45
BS20: P'bry 5B 44
BS23: W Mare 5J 105
BS31: Key 3C 78
Priory Wlk. BS20: P'bry 5B 44
PRISTON 7A 120
Priston Cl. BS22: Wor 6F 85
Priston La. BA2: Pris 1K 141
Priston Mill 4B 120
Priston Rd. BA2: Ing 6C 120
Pritchard St. BS2: Bris 1H 5 (1A 62)
Privet Dr. BS13: Hart 5J 75
Probyn Cl. BS16: Bmhll 1J 49
Pro-Cathedral La. BS8: Clftn 3B 4 (2H 61)
Proctor Cl. BS4: Brisl 1F 77
Proctor Dr. BS24: W Mare 1K 127
Proctor Ho. BS1: Bris 7H 5 (4A 62)
Promenade, The BS7: Bishop 6K 47
BS8: Clftn 1F 61
Prospect Av. BS2: Bris 1E 4 (1K 61)
BS15: Kgswd 7K 49
Prospect Bldgs. BA1: Bathe 5H 83
Prospect Cl. BS35: E Comp 4F 25
BS36: Fram C 6D 28
BS36: Wint D 3C 38
Prospect Cres. BS15: Soun 6D 50
Prospect Gdns. BA1: Bathe 5H 83
Prospect La. BS36: Fram C 6D 28
Prospect Pl. BA1: Bath 2C 100
BA1: Bathf 1B 102
BA1: W'ton 1J 99
BA2: Bath 7E 6 (6B 100)
BA2: C Down 3D 122
BS5: W'hall 1E 62
BS6: Cot 6K 47
BS23: W Mare 4G 105
Prospect Rd. BA2: Bath 7E 100
BS35: Sev B 1A 24
Prospect Ter. BS3: Bedm 6J 61
Protheroes Ho. *BS1: Bris 4D 4*
(off Hobbs La.)
PROUD CROSS 7J 137
PROVIDENCE 7K 59
Providence La. BS41: L Ash 6K 59
PROVIDENCE PLACE 5D 152
Providence Pl. BA3: Mid N 5D 152
BS2: Bris 4J 5 (3B 62)
BS3: Bedm 6K 61
BS5: Redf 2E 62
BS40: Chew S 4D 114
Providence Ri. BS41: L Ash 7K 59
Providence Vw. BS41: L Ash 1A 74
Prowse Cl. BS35: T'bry 3A 12
Prowse's La. BS26: Axb 6G 149
Prudential Bldg. BS1: Bris 3F 5
Prudham St. BS5: E'ton 7E 48
Pruen Ho. BS23: W Mare 4E 104
PUBLOW 6G 95
Publow La. BS39: Pens, Pub, Wool 7F 95
(not continuous)
PUCKLECHURCH 3B 52
Pucklechurch Trad. Est. BS16: Puck 4B 52
Pudding Pie Cl. BS40: L'frd 6C 110
Pudding Pie La. BS40: L'frd 6C 110
Puffin Cl. BS22: Wor 4D 106
Pullin Ct. BS30: Old C 5H 65
Pullins Grn. BS35: T'bry 3K 11
Pulteney Av. BA2: Bath 5J 7 (5D 100)
Pulteney Bridge 4G 7 (4C 100)
Pulteney Bri. BA2: Bath 4G 7 (5C 100)
Pulteney Ct. BA2: Bath 6J 7 (6D 100)
Pulteney Gdns. BA2: Bath 5J 7 (5D 100)
Pulteney Gro. BA2: Bath 6J 7 (6D 100)
Pulteney M. BA2: Bath 4H 7 (4C 100)
Pulteney Rd. BA2: Bath 6J 7 (6D 100)
Pulteney Ter. *BA2: Bath 5J 7*
(off Pulteney Rd.)
Pump House, The BS4: St Ap 4H 63
Pump Ho. La. BS4: St Ap 4H 63
Pump La. BA1: Bathf 2K 101
BS1: Bris 6G 5 (4A 62)
BS32: Old D 1F 19
BS40: Redh 2B 112
Pump Room 4F 7 (5C 100)
Pump Sq. BS20: Pill 3H 45
Punnet Cl. BS27: Ched 7D 150
Purcell Wlk. BS4: Know 3K 75
Purdie Cl. BS27: Ched 6D 150
Purdown Rd. BS7: Hor 3B 48
Purdue Cl. BS22: Wor 1F 107
Purdy Ct. BS16: Fish 4J 49
Purifier Ho. BS1: Bris 5B 4
Purlewent Dr. BA1: W'ton 1J 99
PURN 6J 127
Purnell Way BS39: Paul 7B 140
Purn Holiday Pk. BS24: B'don 7J 127
Purn La. BS24: B'don, W Mare 5J 127
Purn Rd. BS24: W Mare 5H 127
Purn Way BS24: B'don 6J 127
Pursey Dr. BS32: Brad S 1H 37
Purton Cl. BS15: Kgswd 3C 64
Purton Rd. BS7: Bishop 6K 47
Purving Row BS24: Lym 5A 146
Purving Row La. BS24: Lym 6A 146
Puttingthorpe Dr. BS22: W Mare 5A 106
Puxley Cl. BS14: Stoc 4G 77
PUXTON 1D 108
Puxton La. BS24: E Rols, Hew, Pux 7D 86
Puxton Park 2B 108
Puxton Rd. BS24: E Rols, Pux 4B 108
PYE CORNER 4B 38
Pye Cft. BS32: Brad S 3G 27
Pyecroft Av. BS9: Henle 1H 47
Pylewell La. BS25: Star 3K 131
Pylle Hill Cres. BS3: Wind H 5B 62
Pyne Point BS21: Clev 6C 54
Pynne Cl. BS14: Stoc 4H 77
Pynne Rd. BS14: Stoc 5G 77
Pyracantha Wlk. BS14: H'gro 4C 76

Q

QEH Theatre 3B 4 (2H 61)
Quadrangle, The BS37: W'lgh 3C 40
Quadrant BS32: Brad S 3D 26
Quadrant, The BS2: Bris 4K 5
BS6: Redl 5H 47
BS32: Alm 3C 26
Quadrant E. BS16: Fish 5A 50
Quadrant W. BS16: Fish 5A 50
Quadrilles, The *BS35: Sev B 7A 16*
(off Ableton La.)
Quaker Ct. *BS35: T'bry 3K 11*
(off Quaker La.)
Quaker La. BS35: T'bry 3K 11
Quakers Cl. BS16: Down 7B 38
Quakers' Friars BS1: Bris 2G 5 (2A 62)
Quakers Ho. BS1: Bris 2H 5
Quakers' La. BS1: Bris 2G 5 (2A 62)
Quakers Rd. BS16: Down 6B 38
Quantock Cl. BS30: Old C 4G 65
TA8: Bur S 1D 158
Quantock Ct. BS16: Fren 6G 37
TA8: Bur S 3C 158
Quantock Rd. BS3: Wind H 6K 61
BS20: P'head 3D 42
BS23: W Mare 1F 127
Quantocks BA2: C Down 3C 122
Quarries, The BS32: Alm 1D 26
Quarrington Rd. BS7: Hor 3A 48
Quarry Bank BS37: Chip S 4G 31
Quarry Barton BS16: H'ook 3A 38
Quarry Cl. BA2: C Down 3B 122
BA2: Lim S 6B 124
BA15: W'ley 6B 124
Quarry Hay BS40: Chew S 4D 114
Quarry La. BS11: Law W 6C 34
BS36: Wint D 3C 38
Quarrymans Ct. BA2: C Down 3D 122
Quarry Mead BS35: A'ton 7H 11
Quarry Ri. BS10: Bren 4J 35
BS24: W Mare 5H 127
Quarry Rd. BA2: C'ton D 6F 101
BS8: Clftn 6G 47
BS15: Kgswd 3B 64
BS16: Fren 1K 49
BS20: P'head 4E 42
BS25: Sandf 3G 131
BS35: A'ton 7H 11
BS37: Chip S 5G 31
Quarry Rock Gdns. BA2: C'ton D 7G 101
Quarry Steps BS8: Clftn 6G 47
Quarry Va. BA2: C Down 3D 122
Quarry Way BS16: Emer G 6E 38
BS16: Stap 3G 49
BS48: Nail 7F 57
Quarter Mile All.
BS15: Kgswd 7B 50
Quasar BA1: Bath 6F 7 (6B 100)
Quay Point BS1: Bris 5C 4 (3J 61)
Quays, The BS1: Bris 7D 4 (4J 61)
Quays Av. BS20: P'head 3G 43
Quay Side BS1: Bris 4H 5 (3A 62)
Quayside BS8: Clftn 5A 4 (3H 61)
Quayside La. BS5: St G 3H 63

Quayside Wlk.—Ripley Rd.

Quayside Wlk. BS1: Bris . . . 5F 5 (off Redcliff Backs)
Quays Office Pk. BS20: P'head . . . 3G 43
Quay St. BS1: Bris . . . 3E 4 (2K 61)
Quebec BA2: Bath . . . 5G 99
Quedgeley BS37: Yate . . . 6C 30
Queen Ann Rd. BS5: Bar H . . . 3D 62
Queen Charlotte St. BS1: Bris . . . 4F 5 (3K 61)
QUEEN CHARLTON . . . 7J 77
Queen Charlton La. BS14: Whit . . . 7F 77
BS31: Q Char . . . 7F 77
Queen Quay BS1: Bris . . . 5F 5 (3K 61)
Queens Apartments BS8: Clftn . . . 3C 4
Queen's Av. BS8: Clftn . . . 2B 4 (2H 61)
Queens Av. BS20: P'head . . . 3E 42
Queenscote BS20: P'head . . . 3H 43
Queen's Ct. BS8: Clftn . . . 2A 4 (2H 61)
Queensdale Cres. BS4: Know . . . 1C 76
Queensdown Ct. BS4: Brisl . . . 6E 62
Queensdown Gdns. BS4: Brisl . . . 6E 62
Queen's Dr. BA2: C Down . . . 3C 122
BS7: Bishop . . . 4J 47
Queens Dr. BS15: Han . . . 5K 63
Queen's Ga. BA3: Rads . . . 4B 154
Queens Gate BS9: Stok B . . . 3D 46
Queenshill Rd. BS4: Know . . . 1C 76
Queensholm Av. BS16: Down . . . 6C 38
Queensholm Cl. BS16: Down . . . 6C 38
Queensholm Cres. BS16: Down . . . 6B 38
Queensholm Dr. BS16: Down . . . 6C 38
Queens Mans. BS8: Clftn . . . 2A 4 (1H 61)
Queen's Pde. BS1: Bris . . . 5B 4 (3H 61)
Queens Pde. BA1: Bath . . . 3E 6 (4B 100)
Queens Pde. Pl. BA1: Bath . . . 3F 7 (4B 100)
Queens Pl. BA2: Bath . . . 6J 7 (6D 100)
Queen Sq. BA1: Bath . . . 3F 7 (4B 100)
BS1: Bris . . . 5E 4 (3K 61)
BS31: Salt . . . 7K 79
Queen Sq. Apartments BS1: Bris . . . 6F 5
Queen Sq. Av. BS1: Bris . . . 5F 5 (3K 61)
Queen Sq. Ho. BS1: Bris . . . 5F 5
Queens Sq. Pl. BA1: Bath . . . 3E 6 (4B 100)
Queen's Rd. BA3: Rads . . . 4B 154
BS5: St G . . . 1H 63
BS8: Clftn . . . 3A 4 (2G 61)
BS13: Bis, Withy . . . 7F 75
BS16: Puck . . . 3B 52
BS20: P'head . . . 4A 42
BS21: Clev . . . 6D 54
BS23: W Mare . . . 3F 105
BS48: Nail . . . 1E 70
Queens Rd. BS4: Know . . . 1E 76
BS7: Bishop . . . 4B 48
BS29: Ban . . . 2A 130
BS30: C Hth . . . 5E 64
BS31: Key . . . 6B 78
Queens Sq. BS21: Clev . . . 6D 54 (off Station Rd.)
TA9: Highb . . . 4E 158
Queen St. BA1: Bath . . . 4F 7 (5B 100)
BS2: Bris . . . 3H 5 (2A 62)
BS5: Eastv . . . 5F 49
BS11: A'mth . . . 6E 32
BS15: Kgswd . . . 2K 63
Queens Wlk. BS35: T'bry . . . 1K 11
Queen's Way BS20: Kew, St G, Wor . . . 7C 84
Queens Way BS20: P'head . . . 4A 42
Queensway BS34: Lit S . . . 1E 36
Queensway Cen. BS22: Wor . . . 2F 107
Queen Victoria Rd. BS6: Henle . . . 4G 47
Queen Victoria St. BS2: Bris . . . 3C 62
Queenwood Av. BA1: Bath . . . 2C 100
Quickthorn Cl. BS14: Whit . . . 4C 76
Quiet St. BA1: Bath . . . 4F 7 (5B 100)
Quilter Gro. BS4: Know . . . 3K 75
Quinton Cl. BS34: Stok G . . . 5F 37
Quorum, The BS2: Bris . . . 3J 5

R

Raby M. BA2: Bath . . . 3J 7 (4D 100)
Raby Pl. BA2: Bath . . . 3J 7 (4D 100)
Raby Vs. BA2: Bath . . . 3K 7 (4D 100)
Rackfield Pl. BA2: Bath . . . 5H 99
Rackham Cl. BS7: L'lze . . . 2D 48
Rackhay BS1: Bris . . . 4F 5 (3K 61)
RACKLEY . . . 4A 148
Rackley La. BS26: Comp B . . . 4A 148
Rackvernal Ct. BA3: Mid N . . . 5F 153
Rackvernal Rd. BA3: Mid N . . . 5F 153
Racurium Lodge BS26: Axb . . . 4G 149
RADFORD . . . 5G 141
Radford Hill BA2: Tims . . . 3G 141 (not continuous)
BA3: Rads, Tims . . . 6G 141
Radley Rd. BS16: Fish . . . 4K 49
Radnor Rd. BS7: Hor . . . 3K 47
BS9: Henle . . . 3H 47
RADSTOCK . . . 4K 153
Radstock Linear Pk. . . . 3K 153
Radstock Mus. . . . 4K 153
Radstock Rd. BA3: Mid N . . . 4F 153
Raeburn Rd. BS5: St G . . . 2K 63
Rag Hill BA2: Shos . . . 1D 154
Raglan Cl. BA1: Bath . . . 1C 100 (off Ragland La.)
Ragland La. BA1: Bath . . . 1C 100
Ragland St. BA1: Bath . . . 1C 100
Rag La. GL12: Wickw . . . 6D 14
Raglan La.
BS5: St G . . . 2J 63
BS40: Winf . . . 4J 91
Raglan Pl. BS7: Bishop . . . 5K 47
BS23: W Mare . . . 4E 104
BS35: T'bry . . . 4K 11
Raglan Rd. BS7: Bishop . . . 5K 47
Raglan Ter. BA1: Bath . . . 1C 100
Raglan Vs. BA1: Bath . . . 2C 100
Raglan Wlk. BS31: Key . . . 6B 78
Railton Jones Cl. BS34: Stok G . . . 4G 37
Railway La. BA2: Well . . . 4K 143
Railway Pl. BA1: Bath . . . 6H 7 (6C 100)
Railway St. BA1: Bath . . . 6G 7 (6C 100)
Railway Ter. BA2: Shos . . . 2E 154
BS16: Fish . . . 4A 50
Railway Vw. BS16: H'ook . . . 4B 38 (off Moorend Rd.)
Railway Vw. Pl. BA3: Mid N . . . 4F 153
Railway Wlk. BS25: Wins . . . 4F 131
Rainbow Ct. BS37: Yate . . . 3B 30
Rainham Ct. BS23: W Mare . . . 3E 104
Rains Batch BS40: C'hse . . . 7B 134
Raja Rammohun Roy Wlk.
BS16: Stap . . . 4E 48
Raleigh Cl. BS31: Salt . . . 1G 97
Raleigh Gdns. TA8: Bur S . . . 1E 158
Raleigh Ri. BS20: P'head . . . 2D 42
Raleigh Rd. BS3: Ash G, Bris . . . 7B 4 (6G 61)
Ralph Allen Dr. BA2: Bath, C Down . . . 7D 100
Ralph M. BS8: Clftn . . . 1C 4
Ralph Rd. BS7: Bishop . . . 4B 48
RAM HILL . . . 2H 39
Ram Hill BS36: Coal H . . . 2G 39
Ram Hill Bus. Pk. BS36: Coal H . . . 2H 39
Ram Hill Rd. BS36: Henf . . . 3H 39
Ramsay Cl. BS22: Wor . . . 7C 84
Ramsay Way TA8: Bur S . . . 1E 158
Ramscombe La. BA1: Bathe . . . 4G 83
Ramsey Rd. BS7: Hor . . . 1B 48
Rams Leaze BS34: Pat . . . 7C 26
Ranchway BS20: P'head . . . 4B 42
Randall Cl. BS15: Soun . . . 6D 50
Randall Rd. BS8: Clftn . . . 5A 4 (3G 61)
Randolph Av. BS13: Hart . . . 5H 75
BS37: Yate . . . 1D 30
Randolph Cl. BS13: Hart . . . 5H 75
Rangers Wlk. BS15: Han . . . 5A 64
RANGEWORTHY . . . 4K 21
Rankers La. BS39: Comp D . . . 6A 96
Rannoch Rd. BS7: Fil . . . 5B 36
Ranscombe Av. BS22: Wor . . . 2B 106
Ransford BS21: Clev . . . 1B 68
Raphael Ct. BS1: Bris . . . 7H 5 (4A 62)
Rapide Way BS24: W Mare . . . 1K 127
Ratcliffe Ct. BS2: Bris . . . 4K 5
Ratcliffe Dr. BS34: Stok G . . . 2G 37
Rathbone Cl. BS36: Coal H . . . 2G 39
Rattigan Cl. TA8: Bur S . . . 2E 158
Raven Cl. BS22: W Mare . . . 3C 106
Ravendale Dr. BS30: Long G . . . 6F 65
Ravenglass Cres. BS10: S'mead . . . 5J 35
Ravenhead Dr. BS14: H'gro . . . 2D 76
Ravenhill Av. BS3: Know . . . 7B 62
Ravenhill Rd. BS3: Wind H . . . 6B 62
Ravenscourt Rd. BS34: Pat . . . 7D 26
Ravenswood BS30: Long G . . . 6E 64
Ravenswood Rd. BS6: Cot . . . 7J 47
Ravensworth Ter. TA8: Bur S . . . 1D 158
Rawlins Av. BS22: Wor . . . 6E 84
Rawnsley Ho. BS5: E'ton . . . 7C 48
Rayens Cl. BS41: L Ash . . . 1K 73
Rayens Cross Rd. BS41: L Ash . . . 1K 73
Rayleigh Rd. BS9: W Trym . . . 1D 46
Raymend Rd. BS3: Wind H . . . 6A 62
Raymend Wlk. BS3: Wind H . . . 7A 62
Raymill BS4: Brisl . . . 7J 63
Raymore Ri. BS41: L Ash . . . 2K 73
Raynes Rd. BS3: Ash G . . . 6G 61
Rayneswood BS23: W Mare . . . 4H 105
Reade Cl. BS15: Han . . . 5B 64
Reading Ct. BS15: Kgswd . . . 1K 63
Reads Gdn. BS26: Axb . . . 4H 149 (off Old Church Rd.)
Recreation Ground . . . 4H 7 (5C 100)
Rector's Cl. TA8: Brean . . . 3B 144
Rectors Way BS23: W Mare . . . 6H 105
Rectory Cl. BA2: F'boro . . . 6E 118
BS37: Yate . . . 3F 31
BS48: Wrax . . . 7J 57
Rectory Dr. BS49: Yat . . . 4J 87
TA8: Bur S . . . 7D 156
Rectory Gdns. BS10: Hen . . . 5E 34
Rectory La. BA2: Tims . . . 3F 141
BS24: B'don . . . 7A 128
BS34: Fil . . . 4C 36
BS40: Comp M . . . 7B 136
GL12: Crom . . . 3A 14
Rectory Lawn TA8: Bur S . . . 7D 156
Rectory Pl. TA8: Bur S . . . 7E 156
Rectory Rd. BS20: Eas . . . 5F 45
BS36: Fram C . . . 6E 28
TA8: Bur S . . . 7D 156
Rectory Way BS24: Lym . . . 3G 145
BS49: Yat . . . 4J 87
Redacre BS40: Redh . . . 1B 112
Redcar Ct. BS16: Down . . . 6D 38
Redcatch Rd. BS3: Know . . . 6B 62
BS4: Know . . . 6B 62
Redcliff Backs BS1: Bris . . . 5G 5 (3A 62)
Redcliff Cres. BS3: Bris . . . 7H 5
REDCLIFFE BAY . . . 4A 42
Redcliffe Cl. BS20: P'head . . . 5A 42
Redcliffe Pde. E. BS1: Bris . . . 6F 5 (4K 61)
Redcliffe Pde. W. BS1: Bris . . . 6F 5 (4K 61)
Redcliffe Point BS1: Bris . . . 6G 5
Redcliffe St. BS27: Ched . . . 7E 150
Redcliffe Way BS1: Bris . . . 6F 5 (4K 61)
Redcliffe Wharf . . . 6F 5 (4K 61)
Redcliff Hill BS1: Bris . . . 7G 5 (4A 62)
Redcliff Mead La. BS1: Bris . . . 6H 5 (4A 62)
Redcliff Quay BS1: Bris . . . 5G 5 (3K 61)
Redcliff St. BS1: Bris . . . 4G 5 (3A 62)
Redcroft BS40: Redh . . . 1B 112
Redcross Ct. BS2: Bris . . . 3J 5 (off Redcross St.)
Redcross La. BS2: Bris . . . 2J 5
Redcross M. BS2: Bris . . . 3J 5 (2B 62)
Redcross St. BS2: Bris . . . 3J 5 (2B 62)
Redding Pit La. BS40: Winf . . . 6J 91
Redding Rd. BS5: Eastv . . . 6D 48
Reddings, The BS15: Soun . . . 6D 50
BS40: Comp M . . . 6B 136
REDFIELD . . . 1F 63
Redfield Gro. BA3: Mid N . . . 5E 152
Redfield Hill BS30: Bit, Old C . . . 5H 65
Redfield Ho. BS34: Pat . . . 7D 26
Redfield Leisure Cen. . . . 2E 62
Redfield Rd. BA3: Mid N . . . 6D 152
BS34: Pat . . . 7D 26
Redford Cres. BS13: Withy . . . 7E 74
Redford La. BS30: Doy, Puck . . . 4C 52
Redford Trad. Est. BS3: Bedm . . . 1J 75
Redford Wlk. BS13: Withy . . . 7F 75
Redgrave Theatre . . . 1F 61
Redham La. BS35: Piln . . . 5E 16
REDHILL . . . 1B 112
Red Hill BA2: Cam . . . 5J 141
BS40: Redh . . . 3A 112
Redhill Cl. BS16: Fish . . . 5G 49
Redhill Dr. BS16: Fish . . . 5G 49
Redhill Farm Bus. Pk. BS35: Elbton . . . 6B 10
Redhill La. BS35: Elbton . . . 7K 9
Red Ho. La. BS9: W Trym . . . 2E 46
BS32: Alm . . . 2D 26
REDLAND . . . 6H 47
Redland Av. BS20: Eas . . . 2D 44
Redland Ct. Rd. BS6: Redl . . . 5J 47
Redland Green . . . 5H 47
Redland Grn. Rd. BS6: Redl . . . 6H 47
Redland Gro. BS6: Cot, Redl . . . 6J 47
Redland Hill BS6: Redl . . . 6G 47
Redland La. BS39: Stow . . . 7A 116
Redland Pk. BA2: Bath . . . 5F 99 (not continuous)
BS6: Redl . . . 6H 47
Redland Rd. BS6: Cot, Redl . . . 5G 47
Redland Station (Rail) . . . 6J 47
Redlands Ter. BA3: Mid N . . . 6D 152
Redland Ter. BS6: Redl . . . 6H 47
Red Lion Works BS4: Know . . . 1D 76
Red Lodge Bus. Pk.
BS24: W Wick . . . 2H 107
Red Lodge Mus. . . . 3D 4 (2J 61)
Redlynch La. BS31: Key . . . 1K 95
Redpoint Climbing Cen. . . . 7H 61
Redpoll Dr. BS20: P'head . . . 2J 43
RED POST . . . 6B 142
Red Post Ct. BA2: Pea J . . . 6B 142
Red Rd. TA8: Berr . . . 2B 156
Redshank Wlk. BS11: Law W . . . 6A 34
Redshard La. BS40: L'frd . . . 5D 110
Redshelf Wlk. BS10: Bren . . . 4J 35
REDWICK . . . 5B 16
Redwick Cl. BS11: Law W . . . 5C 34
Redwick Gdns. BS35: Piln . . . 6C 16
Redwick Rd. BS35: Piln, Red . . . 5C 16
Redwing Dr. BS22: Wor . . . 3D 106
Redwing Gdns. BS16: Bmhll . . . 2G 49
Redwood Cl. BA3: Rads . . . 6J 153
BS30: Long G . . . 6E 64
BS48: Nail . . . 7J 57
Redwood Ho. BS13: Hart . . . 7K 75
Redwood La. BS48: Bar G, L Ash . . . 3G 73 (not continuous)
Redwoods, The BS31: Key . . . 4B 78
Reed Cl. BS10: Hor . . . 2K 47
Reed Ct. BS30: Long G . . . 6D 64
Reedley Rd. BS9: Stok B, W Trym . . . 3E 46
Reedling Cl. BS16: Bmhll . . . 2G 49
Reed Way BS22: St G . . . 1G 107
Rees Way BS26: Bidd . . . 7J 147
Refinery, The BS2: Bris . . . 3J 5
Regal Ct. TA9: Highb . . . 5F 159
Regency Cl. TA8: Bur S . . . 5C 156
Regency Dr. BS4: Brisl . . . 7J 63
Regent Rd. BS3: Bedm . . . 5K 61
Regents, The BS31: Key . . . 4C 78
Regents Apartments BS6: Redl . . . 5J 47 (off Redland Ct. Rd.)
Regents Cl. BS35: T'bry . . . 1K 11
Regents Fld. BA2: Batham . . . 3F 101
Regents Pl. BA15: Brad A . . . 6H 125
Regent St. BS8: Clftn . . . 3G 61
BS15: Kgswd . . . 1B 64
BS23: W Mare . . . 5F 105
TA8: Bur S . . . 1C 158
REGIL . . . 2K 113
Regil La. BS40: Winf . . . 5A 92
Regil Rd. BS40: Regil . . . 1K 113
Regina, The BA1: Bath . . . 2F 7
Regus Ho. BS1: Bris . . . 5J 5
Remenham Dr. BS9: Henle . . . 3H 47
Remenham Pk. BS9: Henle . . . 3H 47
Rendcomb Cl. BS22: W Mare . . . 2K 105
Rene Rd. BS5: E'ton . . . 7D 48
Rennie Cl. BA2: Bath . . . 5J 7 (5D 100)
Repton Hall BS10: Bren . . . 5H 35
Repton Rd. BS4: Brisl . . . 6E 62
Retail Ter. BS32: Brad S . . . 5F 27
Retford Ho. BA2: C'ton D . . . 7G 101
Retreat Cvn. Park, The TA8: Bur S . . . 5C 156
Reubins, The BS5: S'wll . . . 6J 49
Reynold's Cl. BS31: Key . . . 5E 78
Reynolds Ct. BS7: Hor . . . 7C 36
Reynolds Wlk. BS7: Hor . . . 1C 48
Rhode Cl. BS31: Key . . . 7E 78
Rhododendron Wlk. BS10: Hen . . . 6E 34
Rhodyate BS40: Blag . . . 4B 134
Rhodyate, The BS29: Ban . . . 3C 130
Rhodyate Hill BS49: C've, Cong . . . 6A 88
Rhodyate La. BS49: C've . . . 4B 88
Rhymes Pl. BA1: Swa . . . 7E 82
Rhyne Ter. BS23: Uph . . . 3F 127
Rhyne Vw. BS48: Nail . . . 1D 70
Ribblesdale BS35: T'bry . . . 4A 12
Richards Cl. BS22: Wor . . . 7F 85
Richardson Pl. BA2: C Down . . . 3E 122
Richeson Cl. BS10: Hen . . . 5F 35
Richeson Wlk. BS10: Hen . . . 5F 35
Richmond Apartments BS6: Redl . . . 5J 47 (off Redland Ct. Rd.)
Richmond Av. BS6: Bris . . . 6B 48
BS34: Stok G . . . 2G 37
Richmond Cl. BA1: Bath . . . 2B 100
BS20: P'head . . . 3G 43
BS31: Key . . . 6B 78
Richmond Ct. BS3: Wind H . . . 5B 62
BS8: Clftn . . . 6G 47 (off Richmond Dale)
BS34: Pat . . . 5B 26
Richmond Dale BS8: Clftn . . . 6G 47
Richmond Grn. BS48: Nail . . . 1H 71
Richmond Hgts. BA1: Bath . . . 1B 100
BS8: Clftn . . . 2A 4
Richmond Hill BA1: Bath . . . 2B 100
BS8: Clftn . . . 2A 4 (2H 61)
Richmond Hill Av. BS8: Clftn . . . 3A 4 (2H 61)
Richmond La. BA1: Bath . . . 2B 100
BS8: Clftn . . . 3A 4 (2G 61)
Richmond M. BS8: Clftn . . . 2G 61
Richmond Pk. Rd. BS8: Clftn . . . 2G 61
Richmond Pl. BA1: Bath . . . 2B 100
Richmond Rd. BA1: Bath . . . 1B 100
BS5: St G . . . 1G 63
BS6: Bris . . . 7A 48
BS16: Mang . . . 3E 50
Richmond St. BS3: Wind H . . . 5B 62
BS23: W Mare . . . 5F 105
Richmond Ter. BA1: Bath . . . 2C 100 (off Claremont Bldgs.)
BS8: Clftn . . . 3A 4 (2G 61) (not continuous)
BS11: A'mth . . . 6E 32
Richmond Vs. BS11: A'mth . . . 6E 32
Ricketts La. BS22: Wor . . . 2E 106
Rickfield BA15: Brad A . . . 6F 125
RICKFORD . . . 2J 133
Rickford La. BS40: Burr . . . 2H 133
Rickford Ri. BS40: Burr . . . 2J 133
Rickford Rd. BS48: Nail . . . 1H 71
Ricklands, The BS40: Winf . . . 5A 92
Rickyard Rd. BS40: Wrin . . . 2G 111
Ride, The BS15: Kgswd . . . 6E 50
RIDGE, THE . . . 4F 31
Ridge, The BA15: Brad A . . . 5J 125
BS11: Shire . . . 1J 45
BS14: H'gro . . . 5E 76
BS36: Coal H . . . 7G 29
BS49: Yat . . . 3H 87
Ridge Cl. BS20: P'head . . . 4C 42
Ridge Cres. BS40: W Har . . . 7E 136
Ridge Grn. Cl. BA2: Odd D . . . 4K 121
Ridgehill BS9: Henle . . . 2J 47
Ridge La. BS40: W Har . . . 7D 136
Ridgemeade BS14: Whit . . . 6D 76
Ridgemount Gdns. BS14: Whit . . . 5D 76
Ridge Vw. BS41: L Ash . . . 7B 60
RIDGEWAY . . . 6H 49
Ridgeway BS36: Coal H . . . 7H 29
BS37: Yate . . . 4F 31
BS48: Nail . . . 1E 70
Ridgeway, The BS10: W Trym . . . 6G 35
BS22: W Mare . . . 2K 105
Ridgeway Av. BS23: W Mare . . . 6G 105
Ridgeway Cl. BS40: W Har . . . 7E 136
Ridgeway Ct. BS10: W Trym . . . 6G 35
BS14: Whit . . . 5E 76
Ridgeway Gdns. BS14: Whit . . . 5E 76
Ridgeway Ind. Cen. BS5: S'wll . . . 6G 49
Ridgeway La. BS14: Whit . . . 6D 76
Ridgeway Pde. BS5: Eastv . . . 5G 49
Ridgeway Rd. BS16: Fish . . . 5G 49
BS41: L Ash . . . 1A 74
Ridgewood BS9: Stok B . . . 6D 46
BS37: Yate . . . 5F 31
Riding Barn Hill BS30: Wick . . . 3K 65
Riding Cotts., The BS37: Chip S . . . 4H 31
Ridingleaze BS11: Law W . . . 6A 34
Ridings, The BS13: Withy . . . 6E 74
BS36: Coal H . . . 1G 39
Ridings Cl. BS37: Chip S . . . 5J 31
Ridings Rd. BS36: Coal H . . . 1G 39
Ridley Av. BS16: Soun . . . 5E 50
Ringsfield La. BS34: Pat . . . 7B 26
Ringspit La. BS14: Whit . . . 3G 95
BS39: Pub . . . 4F 95
Ringswell Gdns. BA1: Bath . . . 2D 100
Ringwood Cres. BS10: S'mead . . . 6J 35
Ringwood Gro. BS23: W Mare . . . 3J 105
Ringwood Rd. BA2: Bath . . . 5J 99
Ripley Rd. BS5: St G . . . 7J 49

Ripon Ct.—Ruthven Rd.

Ripon Ct. BS16: Down 5D 38
Ripon Rd. BS4: St Ap 3G 63
Ripple, The BS21: Tic 5F 57
Rippleside BS20: P'head 3E 42
Rippleside Rd. BS21: Clev 4E 54
Risdale Rd. BS3: Ash V 1E 74
Risedale Rd. BS25: Wins 5G 131
Ritz Cinema, The
Burnham-on-Sea 1C 158
Riva Bingo
Knowle 7D 62
Rivendell BS22: Wor 7E 84
Riverbed Ho. TA9: Highb 5F 159
Rivergate BS1: Bris 5J 5 (3B 62)
Riverland Dr. BS13: Withy 6F 75
Riverleaze BS9: Sea M 3B 46
BS20: P'head 2B 42
River Mead BS21: Clev 2D 68
BS37: Yate 3C 30
River Path BS21: Clev 6D 54
(Arundel Rd.)
BS21: Clev 1E 68
(Claremont Gdns.)
BS21: Clev 2B 68
(River Mead)
River Pl. BA2: Bath 5H 99
River Rd. BS20: P'bry 6C 32
BS37: Chip S 5J 31
RIVERSIDE 7D 152
Riverside BS29: Ban 6B 108
Riverside Bus. Pk. BA2: Bath 5E 6 (5B 100)
BS4: St Ap 3F 63
Riverside Cl. BA3: Mid N 7D 152
BS11: Shire 3K 45
BS21: Clev 7B 54
BS22: St G 1G 107
Riverside Cotts. BA3: Rads 4A 154
Riverside Ct. BA2: Bath 6E 6 (5B 100)
BS4: St Ap 3H 63
Riverside Dr. BS16: Fish 1A 50
Riverside Gdns. BA1: Bath 5E 6
BA3: Mid N 7C 152
Riverside Ho. BS1: Bris 4F 5
Riverside Leisure Cen.
Bristol 1K 5 (1B 62)
Riverside Leisure Club 7E 26
Riverside M. BS4: St Ap 3H 63
Riverside Pk. BS35: Sev B 7A 16
Riverside Pk. Homes BS21: Clev 2D 68
Riverside Rd. BA2: Bath 5D 6 (5A 100)
BA3: Mid N 7D 152
Riverside Steps BS4: St Ap 2G 63
Riverside Wlk. BA3: Mid N 7D 152
(not continuous)
BS5: St G 3H 63
Riverside Way BS15: Han 6A 64
Rivers Rd. BA1: Bath 3B 100
(not continuous)
Rivers St. BA1: Bath 2E 6 (4B 100)
Rivers St. M. BA1: Bath 2E 6 (4B 100)
Rivers St. Pl. BA1: Bath 2F 7
River St. BS2: Bris 2J 5 (2B 62)
River Ter. BS31: Key 5D 78
River Vw. BS16: Bmhll 3G 49
River Wlk. BS22: St G 2H 107
Riverway BS48: Nail 6H 57
Riverwood Rd. BS16: Fren 6A 38
Riviera Cres. BS16: Soun 4C 50
Riviera Way BS34: Stok G 3J 37
Road Two BS10: H'len 4A 24
Roath Rd. BS20: P'head 3F 43
Robbins Cl. BS32: Brad S 1H 37
Robbins Ct. BS16: Emer G 2F 51
Robel Av. BS36: Fram C 6D 28
Robert Ct. BS8: L Wds 3E 60
BS16: Emer G 1F 51
Robert Nightingale Ct.
BS23: W Mare 6H 105
Robertson Dr. BS4: St Ap 3H 63
Robertson Rd. BS5: E'ton 6D 48
Robert St. BS5: Bar H 2D 62
BS5: Eastv 6D 48
Robin Cl. BA3: Mid N 6F 153
BS10: Bren 5H 35
BS14: Stoc 4F 77
BS22: W Mare 4C 106
Robin Ct. BS5: E'ton 1C 62
Robin Cousins Sports Cen. 7G 33
Robin Dr. BS24: Hut 3C 128
Robin Hood La. BS2: Bris 2D 4 (2J 61)
Robinia Wlk. BS14: H'gro 3B 76
Robin La. BS21: Clev 4D 54
Robin Pl. BS20: P'head 2J 43
Robinson Bldg., The *BS3: Bedm 6J 61*
(off Norfolk Pl.)
Robinson Cl. BS48: Back 5J 71
Robinson Dr. BS5: E'ton 1C 62
Robinson Way BS48: Back 5J 71
Robin Way BS37: Chip S 7F 31
Rob-Lynne Ct. BS25: Wins 5F 131
Rochester Cl. BS24: W Mare 4J 127
Rochester Rd. BS4: St Ap 4G 63
Rochfort Ct. BA2: Bath 1J 7 (3D 100)
Rochfort Pl. BA2: Bath 1H 7 (3C 100)
Rock, The BS4: Brisl 6G 63
Rock Av. BS48: Nail 7E 56
Rock Cl. BS4: Brisl 7G 63
Rock Cotts. BA2: C Down 3D 122
Rockdale Ct. BS4: Brisl 6E 62
Rockeries Dr. BS25: Wins 5F 131
Rockfield Cotts. BS22: W Mare 3K 105
Rock Hall Cotts. BA2: C Down 3D 122
Rock Hall Ho. BA2: C Down 3D 122
Rock Hall La. BA2: C Down 3D 122
Rockhill Est. BS31: Key 6D 78
Rock Ho. BS10: Bren 4J 35
Rockingham Gdns. BS11: Law W 7A 34
Rockingham Gro. BS23: W Mare 3J 105
ROCKINGHAM RDBT. 1G 33
Rockland Cl. BS16: Down 1A 50
Rockland Gro. BS16: Stap 2F 49
Rockland Rd. BS16: Down 1A 50
Rock La. BA2: C Down 3D 122
BS34: Stok G 2H 37
Rockleaze BS9: Stok B 6E 46
Rockleaze Av. BS9: Stok B 5E 46
Rockleaze Ct. BS9: Stok B 5E 46
Rockleaze Rd. BS9: Stok B 5E 46
Rockliffe Av. BA2: Bath 1K 7 (3D 100)
Rockliffe Rd. BA2: Bath 1J 7 (3D 100)
Rock of Ages 3H 133
Rock Rd. BA3: Mid N 4F 153
BS30: Wick 2C 66
BS31: Key 5C 78
BS49: Yat 4J 87
ROCKS, THE 2F 31
Rockside Av. BS16: Down 7D 38
Rockside Dr. BS9: Henle 2H 47
Rockside Gdns. BS16: Down 7D 38
BS36: Fram C 6G 29
Rocks La. BS40: F'tn, Winf 2H 91
Rockstowes Way BS10: Bren 4K 35
Rock St. BS35: T'bry 4K 11
Rockwell Av. BS11: Law W 6B 34
Rockwell Wood Ct. BS36: Fram C 1E 38
Rockwood Ho. BS37: Yate 2G 31
Rocky La. BS29: Ban 3B 130
Rodborough BS37: Yate 7C 30
Rodborough Way BS15: Kgswd 2E 64
Rodbourne Rd. BS10: Hor 1K 47
RODFORD 7D 30
Rodfords Mead BS14: H'gro 3C 76
Rodford Way BS37: Yate 7C 30
Rodmead Wlk. BS13: Withy 6G 75
Rodmoor Rd. BS20: P'head 2F 43
Rodney BS24: W Mare 3J 127
Rodney Av. BS15: Kgswd 1J 63
Rodney Cres. BS34: Fil 3C 36
Rodney Ho. BA2: Bath 5G 99
BS8: Clftn 2G 61
(off Clifton Down Rd.)
Rodney Pl. BS8: Clftn 2G 61
Rodney Rd. BS15: Kgswd 7J 49
BS31: Salt 1J 97
BS48: Back 4J 71
Rodney Wlk. BS15: Kgswd 7J 49
Rodway Ct. BS16: Mang 2E 50
RODWAY HILL 4E 50
Rodway Hill BS16: Mang 4E 50
Rodway Hill Rd. BS16: Mang 3E 50
Rodway Rd. BS16: Mang 3E 50
BS34: Pat 7B 26
Rodway Vw. BS15: Soun 5D 50
Roebuck Cl. BS22: Wor 7E 84
Roegate Dr. BS4: St Ap 3G 63
Roegate Ho. BS5: S'wll 7H 49
Rogers Cl. BS30: C Hth 4F 65
BS39: Clut 2F 139
Rogers Ct. BS15: Han 5A 64
BS37: Chip S 5J 31
Rogers Wlk. BS30: B'yte 2H 65
Rokeby Av. BS6: Cot 7J 47
ROLSTONE 2K 107
Roman Baths 5G 7 (5C 100)
Roman Farm Ct. BS11: Law W 5C 34
Roman Farm Rd. BS4: Know 3A 76
Roman Ho. BA1: Bath 1H 7 (3C 100)
Roman Rd. BA2: Eng, Odd D 4J 121
BS5: E'ton 7D 48
BS24: W Mare, B'don 5J 127
BS25: Sandf 1F 131
Roman Wlk. BS4: Brisl 6E 62
BS34: Stok G 2G 37
Roman Way BA2: Pea J 6E 142
BS9: Stok B 4C 46
BS15: Han 5A 64
BS39: Paul 7A 140
Romney Av. BS7: L'lze 3D 48
Romney Gdns. *BS7: L'lze 3C 48*
(off Romney Av.)
Romo Ct. BS16: Stap H 4A 50
Ronald Rd. BS16: Bmhll 2H 49
Ronaldson BS30: Bit 7G 65
Ronayne Wlk. BS16: Fish 2A 50
Rondo Theatre, The 2E 100
Rookery Cl. BS21: Kings S 1C 86
BS22: Wor 1C 106
BS26: Rook 7E 146
Rookery La. BS35: Piln 7G 17
SN14: Doy 2F 53
SN14: Hin 2F 53
Rookery Rd. BS4: Know 7B 62
Rookery Way BS14: Whit 6B 76
Rooksbridge Rd. BS26: Rook 7E 146
Rooksbridge Wlk. BA2: Bath 5J 99
Roper's La. BS40: Wrin 1F 111
Rope Wlk. BS1: Bris 4J 5 (3B 62)
BS48: Back 5J 71
Ropewalk, The BA15: Brad A 6G 125
Rope Wlk. Ho. BS2: Bris 2J 5
Rosa Parks La. BS6: Bris 7B 48
Rosary, The BS34: H'ook 5G 37
Rosary Rdbt., The BS16: Emer G 1H 51
Rose Acre BS10: Bren 4G 35
Rosebay Mead BS16: Stap 4G 49
Roseberry Pk. BS5: St G 1F 63
Roseberry Pl. BA2: Bath 4A 6 (5K 99)
Roseberry Rd. BA2: Bath 4A 6 (5J 99)
BS5: Redf 2E 62
Rosebery Av. BS2: Bris 7C 48
Rosebery Ct. BS2: Bris 7C 48
Rosebery Ter. BS8: Clftn 4B 4 (3H 61)
Rose Cl. BS36: Wint D 3C 38
Rose Cotts. BA2: Odd D 4J 121
BA2: S'ske 5B 122
Rose Ct. BS15: Kgswd 3B 64
Rosedale Av. BS23: W Mare 5J 105
Rosedale Rd. BS16: Fish 5K 49
Rosedown Dr. BS34: H'ook 5H 37
Rose Gdns. BS22: Wor 7F 85
ROSE GREEN 7G 49
Rose Green Cen. 7F 49
Rose Grn. BS5: Eastv 6F 49
Rose Grn. Cl. BS5: S'wll 6G 49
Rose Grn. Rd. BS5: S'wll 6F 49
Rose Hill BA1: Bath, Swa 1D 100
(not continuous)
BS20: P'head 2E 42
Roseland Cl. BA1: Swa 7E 82
Roseland Gdns. BS15: Warm 1F 65
Rose La. BS36: Coal H 1H 39
Roselarge Gdns. BS10: Bren 5G 35
Rosemary Cl. BS32: Brad S 1H 37
Rosemary Cres. BS20: P'head 3H 43
Rosemary La. BS5: Eastv 6E 48
Rosemary Wlk. *BA15: Brad A 5G 125*
(off Newtown)
Rose Mead BS7: Hor 1C 48
Rose Mdw. Vw. BS3: Ash V 1E 74
Rosemeare Gdns. BS13: Bis 3E 74
Rosemont Ter. BS8: Clftn 3G 61
Rosemount Ct. BS15: Kgswd 1K 63
Rosemount La. BA2: Bath 7D 100
Rosemount Rd. BS48: Flax B 2F 73
Roseneath Av. TA8: Berr 3B 156
Rose Oak Dr. BS36: Coal H 7H 29
Rose Oak La. BS36: Coal H 7H 29
Rose Rd. BS5: St G 2G 63
Rosery, The BS16: Fish 5A 50
Rosery Cl. BS9: W Trym 7G 35
Rose Ter. BA2: C Down 2E 122
BS8: Clftn 3A 4 (2H 61)
Rosetree Paddock TA8: Berr 3B 156
Rosevear BS2: Bris 2C 62
Roseville Av. BS30: Long G 7E 64
Rose Wlk. BS16: Fish 5A 50
Rosewarn Cl. BA2: Bath 7G 99
Rosewell Ct. BA1: Bath 4E 6 (5B 100)
Rosewood Av. BS35: A'ton 7H 11
TA8: Bur S 2E 158
Rosewood Ct. TA8: Bur S 1D 158
Rosewood Dr. TA8: Bur S 2E 158
Roshni Ghar E. *BS5: E'ton 7D 48*
(off Woodborough St.)
Roshni Ghar Nth. *BS5: E'ton 7D 48*
(off Woodborough St.)
Rosling Rd. BS7: Hor 2A 48
Roslyn Av. BS22: W Mare 3A 106
Roslyn Rd. BS6: Redl 7J 47
Rossall Av. BS34: Lit S 1E 36
Rossall Rd. BS4: Brisl 6F 63
Ross Cl. BS37: Chip S 5H 31
Rossendale Cl. BS22: Wor 1D 106
Rossetti Way BS7: L'lze 2E 48
Rossini Cotts. BA1: Bath 1G 7
Rossiter Grange BS13: Withy 6F 75
Rossiter Rd. BA2: Bath 6H 7 (6C 100)
Rossiter's La. BS5: St G 3J 63
Rossiter Wood Ct. BS11: Law W 5B 34
Rosslyn Cl. BA1: Bath 4H 99
Rosslyn Rd. BA1: Bath 4H 99
Rosslyn Way BS35: T'bry 1A 12
ROTCOMBE 3B 140
Rotcombe La. BS39: High L 4B 140
Rotcombe Va. BS39: High L 3B 140
Rougemont Gro. NP16: Bul 1A 8
Rounceval St. BS37: Chip S 5J 31
ROUND HILL 2A 154
Roundhill Gro. BA2: Bath 1H 121
Roundhill Pk. BA2: Bath 7G 99
Roundmoor Cl. BS31: Salt 7H 79
Roundmoor Gdns. BS14: Stoc 4F 77
Round Oak Gro. BS27: Ched 6C 150
Round Oak Rd. BS27: Ched 6C 150
Roundways BS36: Coal H 1G 39
Rousham Rd. BS5: Eastv 5C 48
Row, The BS35: Aust 5G 9
Rowacres BA2: Bath 1H 121
BS14: H'gro 4B 76
Rowan Cl. BS16: Fish 6J 49
BS48: Nail 7J 57
Rowan Ct. BA3: Rads 5H 153
BS5: Bar H 2D 62
BS22: Kew 1J 105
(in Ardnave Holiday Pk.)
BS37: Yate 3C 30
Rowan Ho. BS13: Hart 6K 75
Rowan Pl. BS24: W'ton V 3F 107
Rowans, The BS16: Fren 6K 37
BS20: P'head 4D 42
Rowan Wlk. BS31: Key 6A 78
Rowan Way BS15: Han 6K 63
BS40: L'frd 7C 110
TA8: Berr 1B 156
ROWBERROW 4C 132
Rowberrow BS14: H'gro 3B 76
ROWBERROW BOTTOM 5D 132
Rowberrow La. BS25: Row, S'ham 3B 132
Rowberrow Way BS48: Nail 1G 71
Rowland Av. BS16: Stap 4F 49
Rowlands Cl. BA1: Bathf 1A 102
Rowlandson Gdns. BS7: L'lze 2D 48
Rowley St. BS3: Bedm 6J 61
Rownham Cl. BS3: Bwr A 5E 60
Rownham Ct. BS8: Clftn 4G 61
Rownham Hill BS8: L Wds 3D 60
Rownham Mead BS8: Clftn 4G 61
Row of Ashes La. BS40: Redh 7C 90
Rows, The BS22: Wor 2C 106
Royal Albert Rd. BS6: Henle 4G 47
Royal Av. BA1: Bath 2D 6 (4A 100)
Royal Cl. BS10: Hen 4D 34
Royal Ct. *BS23: W Mare 1F 127*
(off Royal Sands)
Royal Crescent 2D 6 (4A 100)
Royal Cres. BA1: Bath 2D 6 (4A 100)
BS23: W Mare 4F 105
Royal Edward Dock BS11: A'mth 5D 32
Royal Fort Rd. BS2: Bris 2D 4 (2J 61)
Royal Oak Av. BS1: Bris 5E 4 (3K 61)
Royal Oak Ho. BS1: Bris 6E 4
Royal Pde. BS8: Clftn 2B 4 (2H 61)
BS23: W Mare 4F 105
Royal Pk. BS8: Clftn 2G 61
Royal Pk. M. BS8: Clftn 2G 61
Royal Pier Apartments BS21: Clev 5C 54
Royal Portbury Dock 7C 32
Royal Portbury Dock Rd. BS20: P'bry 2C 44
Royal Rd. BS16: Mang 2E 50
Royal Sands BS23: W Mare 1F 127
(not continuous)
Royal Victoria Pk. BS10: Bren 5H 35
Royal York Cres. BS8: Clftn 3F 61
Royal York Ho. *BS8: Clftn 3G 61*
(off Royal York Vs.)
Royal York M. BS8: Clftn 3G 61
Royal York Vs. BS8: Clftn 3G 61
Royate Hill BS5: Eastv 6F 49
Roycroft Rd. BS34: Fil 5D 36
Roy King Gdns. BS30: C Hth 3G 65
Roynon Way BS27: Ched 7E 150
Royston Wlk. BS10: S'mead 5K 35
Rozel Rd. BS7: Hor 3A 48
RPS, The 7D 6 (7A 100)
Rubens Cl. BS31: Key 5E 78
Rubens Ct. BS22: Wor 1D 106
Ruby St. BS3: Bedm 6H 61
RUCKLEY FORD 4G 155
Ruddymead BS21: Clev 7D 54
Rudford Cl. BS34: Pat 5D 26
Rudge Cl. BS15: Soun 6D 50
RUDGEWAY 4H 19
Rudgeway Pk. BS35: Rudg 4G 19
Rudgeway Rd. BS39: Paul 1C 152
Rudgewood Cl. BS13: Hart 6K 75
Rudgleigh Av. BS20: Pill 4G 45
Rudgleigh Rd. BS20: Pill 4G 45
Rudhall Grn. BS22: Wor 1F 107
Rudhall Gro. BS10: Hor 1A 48
Rudmore Pk. BA1: Bath 4G 99
Rudthorpe Rd. BS7: Hor 3A 48
Ruett La. BS39: Far G 2A 152
Ruffet Rd. BS36: Coal H 4E 38
Rugby Rd. BS4: Brisl 6F 63
Rugosa Dr. TA8: Berr 3B 156
Runnymead Av. BS4: Brisl 1F 77
Runnymede BS15: Kgswd 7C 50
Runswick Rd. BS4: Brisl 6E 62
Rupert Ho. BS2: Bris 1D 4
Rupert St. BS1: Bris 3E 4 (2K 61)
BS5: Redf 3E 62
Rush Cl. BS32: Brad S 4F 27
Rushen La. BS35: L Sev 3K 9
Rushey La. BA15: Brad L, L Wrax 7K 103
Rushgrove Gdns. BS39: Bis S 1J 137
RUSH HILL 2H 121
Rush Hill BA2: Bath 2H 121
Rushmead La. BA15: L Wrax 6J 103
Rushmoor BS21: Clev 1A 68
Rushmoor Gro. BS48: Back 5J 71
Rushmoor La. BS48: Back 5J 71
Rushton Dr. BS36: Coal H 7H 29
Rushway BS40: Burr 1H 133
Rushy BS30: C Hth 5E 64
Rushy Leaze BS34: Pat 7C 26
Rushy Way BS16: Emer G 6E 38
Ruskin Gro. BS7: Hor 7C 36
Ruskin Rd. BA3: Rads 5G 153
Russell Av. BS15: Kgswd 2C 64
BS24: Lock 7G 107
Russell Cl. BS40: Winf 5A 92
Russell Gro. BS6: Henle 3J 47
Russell M. BS37: Chip S 5H 31
Russell Rd. BS6: Henle 4H 47
BS16: Fish 6K 49
BS21: Clev 6C 54
BS24: Lock 6F 107
Russell St. BA1: Bath 2F 7 (4B 100)
RUSSELL TOWN 2D 62
Russell Town Av. BS5: E'ton 1D 62
Russell Town Av. Ind. Cen. *BS5: Redf 2E 62*
(off Russell Town Av.)
Russet Cl. BS35: Olv 2C 18
Russets, The BS20: P'head 4H 43
Russett Cl. BS48: Back 4K 71
Russett Gro. BS48: Nail 2E 70
Russet Way BA2: Pea J 6D 142
Russ La. BS21: Kenn 4E 68
Russ St. BS2: Bris 4J 5 (3B 62)
Rustic Pk. Cvn. Site BS35: Sev B 7A 16
Rutherford Cl. BS30: Long G 6E 64
Ruthven Rd. BS4: Know 2A 76

Rutland Av.—Salmons Way

Rutland Av. BS30: Will .7E 64
Rutland Cl. BS22: W Mare .4A 106
Rutland Ho. *BS8: Clftn .3F 61*
(off Granby Hill)
Rutland Rd. BS7: Bishop .5A 48
Rydal Av. BS24: Lock .1D 128
Rydal Rd. BS23: W Mare .1H 127
Ryde Rd. BS4: Know .7D 62
Rye Cl. BS13: Bis .4E 74
Ryecroft Av. BS22: Wor .2C 106
Ryecroft Ri. BS41: L Ash .1B 74
Ryecroft Rd. BS36: Fram C .6G 29
Ryedown La. BS30: Bit .1G 79
Ryeleaze BS11: Shire .3J 45
Ryland Pl. BS2: Bris .6C 48
Rylestone Cl. BS36: Fram C .6D 28
Rylestone Gro. BS9: W Trym .3F 47
Rysdale Rd. BS9: W Trym .2F 47

S

Sabin Cl. BA2: Bath .1H 121
Sabrina Way BS9: Stok B .4C 46
Saco Ho. *BA1: Bath .5F 7*
(off St James's Pde.)
BS1: Bris .5H 5 (3A 62)
Sadbury Cl. BS22: Wor .7F 85
Sadlers Ct. BS15: Kgswd .7B 50
Sadlier Cl. BS11: Law W .7K 33
Saffron Ct. BA1: Bath .3C 100
Saffron Gdns. BS5: W'hall .1E 62
Saffrons, The BS22: Wor .7F 85
Sage Cl. BS20: P'head .4A 42
Sages Mead BS32: Brad S .6F 27
St Agnes Av. BS4: Know .7B 62
St Agnes Cl. BS48: Nail .1J 71
St Agnes Gdns. BS4: Know .7B 62
St Agnes Wlk. BS4: Know .7B 62
St Aidans Cl. BS5: St G .3K 63
St Aidans Rd. BS5: St G .3J 63
St Albans Rd. BS6: Henle .4H 47
St Aldams Dr. BS16: Puck .3B 52
St Aldhelm Rd. BA15: Brad A .7J 125
St Aldwyn's Cl. BS7: Hor .7B 36
ST ANDREWS .5A 48
St Andrews BS30: Warm .3F 65
BS37: Yate .6E 30
St Andrew's Cl. BS48: Nail .1J 71
BS49: Cong .7J 87
St Andrews Cl. BS22: Wor .1D 106
St Andrews Dr. BS21: Clev .7A 54
ST ANDREWS GATE RDBT. .5F 33
St Andrews Ho. BS11: A'mth .6E 32
St Andrew's Pde. BS23: W Mare .1H 127
St Andrew's Rd. BS6: Bris .7A 48
BS11: A'mth .5F 33
BS48: Back .5K 71
TA8: Bur S .1D 158
St Andrews Rd. BS27: Ched .7E 150
St Andrew's Road Station (Rail) .3F 33
St Andrews Ter. BA1: Bath .3F 7 (4B 100)
St Andrews Trad. Est. BS11: A'mth .5G 33
St Andrew's Wlk. BS8: Clftn .3G 61
ST ANNE'S .4F 63
St Annes Av. BS31: Key .4B 78
St Annes Cl. BS5: St G .3H 63
BS30: C Hth .5F 65
St Anne's Ct. BS4: St Ap .4F 63
BS31: Key .4B 78
St Anne's Dr. BS30: Wick .2B 66
BS36: Coal H .2G 39
St Annes Dr. BS30: Old C .7G 65
ST ANNE'S PARK .4G 63
St Annes Pk. Rd. BS4: St Ap .4G 63
St Anne's Rd. BS4: St Ap .3F 63
BS5: St G .3K 63
St Anne's Ter. BS4: St Ap .4G 63
St Ann's Dr. TA8: Bur S .6C 156
St Ann's Pl. BA1: Bath .4E 6
St Ann's Way BA2: Bath .4K 7 (5D 100)
St Anthony's Cl. BA3: Mid N .4E 152
St Anthony's Dr. BS30: Wick .2B 66
St Aubin's Av. BS4: Brisl .6H 63
St Aubyn's Av. BS23: Uph .3F 127
St Augustines BS9: W Trym .3G 47
St Augustine's Cl. BS20: P'head .4A 42
St Augustine's Pde. BS1: Bris .4E 4 (3K 61)
St Augustine's Pl. BS1: Bris .4E 4 (3K 61)
St Augustines Yd. BS1: Bris .4D 4
St Austell Cl. BS48: Nail .2J 71
St Austell Rd. BS22: W Mare .4K 105
St Barnabas Cl. BA3: Mid N .3F 153
BS4: Know .1B 76
BS30: Warm .2G 65
St Bartholomew's Rd. BS7: Bris .5B 48
St Bede's Rd. BS15: Kgswd .6A 50
St Bernards Rd. BS11: Shire .2J 45
St Brandons Ho. BS1: Bris .4C 4
St Brelades Gro. BS4: St Ap .4G 63
ST BRENDANS RDBT. .6F 33
St Brendans Trad. Est. BS11: A'mth .5F 33
St Brendans Way BS11: A'mth .6F 33
St Briavels Dr. BS37: Yate .6D 30
St Bridgets Cl. TA8: Brean .2B 144
St Cadoc Ho. BS31: Key .5D 78
ST CATHERINE .1H 83
St Catherine's Cl. BA2: Bath .4K 7 (5E 100)
St Catherine's Ct. BS3: Bedm .6K 61
St Catherines Ct. BS8: Clftn .3B 4
St Catherines Hospital BA1: Bath .5G 7
St Catherine's Ind. Est. *BS3: Bedm .5K 61*
(off Whitehouse La.)
St Catherine's Mead BS20: Pill .5H 45
St Catherine's Pl. BS3: Bedm .5K 61
St Catherine's Ter. *BS3: Bedm .6K 61*
(off Church La.)
St Chad's Av. BA3: Mid N .5E 152
St Chad's Grn. BA3: Mid N .5E 152
St Charles Cl. BA3: Mid N .4E 152
St Christopher's Cl. BA2: Bath .4E 100
St Christophers Ct. BS21: Clev .4C 54
St Christopher's Way TA8: Bur S .5C 156
St Clement's Ct. BS31: Key .6C 78
St Clements Ct. BA1: W'ton .2J 99
BS2: Bris .1J 5
(off Wilson St.)
BS16: Soun .5B 50
BS21: Clev .5C 54
BS22: Wor .2E 106
St Clement's Rd. BS31: Key .5C 78
(not continuous)
St Congards Way BS49: Cong .7A 88
St David M. BS1: Bris .5C 4
St David's Av. BS30: C Hth .4E 64
St David's Cl. BS22: W Mare .2K 105
St David's Ct. BS21: Clev .2E 68
St David's Cres. BS4: St Ap .3H 63
St David's Rd. BS35: T'bry .3A 12
St Dunstans Cl. BS31: Key .4C 78
St Dunstan's Rd. BS3: Bedm .7J 61
St Edward's Rd. BS8: Clftn .5A 4 (3H 61)
St Edyth's Rd. BS9: Sea M .2B 46
St Fagans Ct. BS30: Will .7F 65
St Francis Dr. BS30: Wick .2B 66
BS36: Wint .1D 38
St Francis Rd. BS3: Ash G .5G 61
BS31: Key .4A 78
St Gabriel's Bus. Pk. BS5: E'ton .1D 62
St Gabriel's Rd. BS5: E'ton .1D 62
ST GEORGE .1J 63
ST GEORGES .2H 107
St Georges Av. BS5: St G .3H 63
St George's Bristol .4C 4 (3J 61)
St Georges Bldgs. *BA1: Bath .3D 6*
(off Up. Bristol Rd.)
St Georges Cl. BS20: Eas .5E 44
St Georges Ct. BS22: St G .7G 85
St Georges Gate *BS5: St G .1F 63*
(off Church Rd.)
St Georges Hgts. BS5: Redf .2F 63
St George's Hill BA2: Batham .3F 101
St Georges Hill BS20: Eas .5E 44
St Georges Ho. BS5: St G .1G 63
St Georges Ind. Est. BS11: A'mth .4F 33
St Georges La. BS20: Eas .4F 45
St Georges Pl. *BA1: Bath .3D 6*
(off Up. Bristol Rd.)
St George's Rd. BS1: Bris .5B 4 (3H 61)
BS20: P'bry .1C 44
St Georges Rd. BS31: Key .4B 78
St Giles Ct. BS1: Bris .3E 4
St Gregory's Rd. BS7: Hor .7B 36
St Helena Rd. BS6: Henle .4H 47
St Helens Dr. BS30: Old C .7G 65
BS30: Wick .2C 66
St Helen's Wlk. BS5: St G .7J 49
St Helier Av. BS4: Brisl .5H 63
St Hilary Cl. BS9: Stok B .3D 46
St Ivel Way BS30: Warm .3G 65
St Ives Cl. BS48: Nail .1J 71
St Ives Rd. BS23: W Mare .1J 127
St James' Barton BS1: Bris .1G 5 (1A 62)
St James Cl. BS35: T'bry .1A 12
St James Ct. BS1: Bris .2F 5
BS32: Brad S .3E 26
St James' Pde. BS1: Bris .2F 5 (2K 61)
St James Pl. BS16: Mang .3E 50
St James's Pde. BA1: Bath .5F 7 (5B 100)
St James's Pk. BA1: Bath .1E 6 (3B 100)
St James's Pl. BA1: Bath .1E 6 (3B 100)
St James's Sq. BA1: Bath .1D 6 (3A 100)
St James's St. BA1: Bath .1E 6 (3B 100)
St James St. BS16: Mang .3E 50
BS23: W Mare .5F 105
St John's BA1: Bath .3H 99
St John's Av. BS21: Clev .6D 54
St John's Cl. BA2: Pea J .6B 142
BS23: W Mare .3F 105
St John's Ct. BS3: Wind H .7K 61
BS31: Key .4C 78
St Johns Ct. BA2: Bath .2G 7 (4C 100)
BS16: Fish .5J 49
BS26: Axb .4H 149
St John's Cres. BA3: Mid N .4E 152
BS3: Wind H .7A 62
St Johns Hospital *BA1: Bath .5F 7*
(off Westgate Bldgs.)
St John's La. BS3: Bedm, Wind H .6J 61
St John's Pl. BA1: Bath .4F 7 (5B 100)
St John's Rd. BA1: Bath .3A 6 (4J 99)
BA2: Bath .3G 7 (4C 100)
BS3: Bedm .7E 4 (5K 61)
(Lombard St.)
BS3: Bedm .6J 61
(St John's St.)
BS8: Clftn .7G 47
BS21: Clev .6D 54
BS48: Back .5K 71
TA8: Bur S .1D 158
St Johns Rd. BA2: Tims .4F 141
St John's Steep *BS1: Bris .3F 5*
(off All Saints St.)
St John's St. BS3: Bedm .6J 61
St John St. BS35: T'bry .3K 11
St John's Way BS37: Chip S .4H 31
St Joseph's Rd. BS10: Bren .4H 35
BS23: W Mare .3G 105
St Judes BS2: Bris .2K 5 (2B 62)
St Judes Ter. BS22: W Mare .3A 106
St Julian's Rd. BA2: Shos .2E 154
St Julien's Cl. BS39: Paul .2C 152
St Katherine's Quay BA15: Brad A .7H 125
St Keyna Ct. BS31: Key .5D 78
St Keyna Rd. BS31: Key .5C 78
St Kilda's Rd. BA2: Bath .7A 6 (6K 99)
St Ladoc Rd. BS31: Key .5B 78
St Laud Cl. BS9: Stok B .3D 46
St Laurence Rd. BA15: Brad A .7J 125
St Lawrence Ct. BS11: Law W .7J 33
St Lawrence St. BA1: Bath .5G 7 (5C 100)
St Leonard's Rd. BS5: E'ton .6E 48
BS7: Hor .2A 48
St Loe Cl. BS14: Whit .7B 76
St Lucia Cl. BS7: Hor .1A 48
St Lucia Cres. BS7: Hor .1A 48
St Luke's Cl. TA8: Bur S .1D 158
St Lukes Cl. BS16: Emer G .1G 51
St Luke's Ct. BS3: Bedm .7H 5 (5A 62)
St Luke's Cres. BS3: Wind H .5B 62
St Luke's Gdns. BS4: Brisl .7G 63
St Lukes Ho. BS16: Emer G .1G 51
St Luke's M. BS4: Brisl .7G 63
St Luke's Rd. BA2: Bath .1B 122
BS3: Bris, Wind H .7H 5 (5A 62)
St Lukes Rd. BA3: Mid N .4D 152
St Luke's Steps BS3: Wind H .5A 62
St Margaret's Cl. BS31: Key .4B 78
BS48: Back .5J 71
St Margaret's Ct. BA15: Brad A .6H 125
St Margaret's Dr. BS9: Henle .3J 47
St Margaret's Hill BA15: Brad A .6H 125
St Margarets La. BS48: Back .5J 71
St Margaret's Pl. BA15: Brad A .6H 125
St Margaret's Steps *BA15: Brad A .6H 125*
(off St Margaret's Hill)
St Margaret's Ter. BS23: W Mare .4F 105
St Margaret's Vs. BA15: Brad A .6H 125
St Mark's Av. BS5: E'ton .6E 48
St Marks Cl. BS31: Key .4C 78
St Marks Gdns. BA2: Bath .7G 7 (6C 100)
St Mark's Gro. BS5: E'ton .7D 48
St Mark's Pl. BA1: Bath .2D 100
St Mark's Rd. BA2: Bath .7G 7 (6C 100)
BA3: Mid N .4E 152
BS5: E'ton .7D 48
BS22: Wor .7D 84
TA8: Bur S .1D 158
St Mark's Ter. BS5: E'ton .7D 48
St Martins BS41: L Ash .1A 74
St Martin's Cl. BS4: Know .5E 76
St Martin's Ct. BA2: Odd D .3A 122
BS2: Bris .3D 62
St Martins Ct. BS16: Soun .5B 50
BS22: Wor .1C 106
St Martin's Gdns. BS4: Know .1D 76
St Martins Ind. Pk. BS11: A'mth .2K 33
St Martin's Rd. BS4: Know .7D 62
St Martin's Wlk. BS4: Know .1D 76
St Mary Redcliffe Church .6G 5
St Mary's Bldgs. BA2: Bath .6F 7 (6B 100)
St Mary's Cl. BA2: Bath .4K 7 (5D 100)
BA2: Tims .3F 141
BS24: Hut .3B 128
St Marys Cl. BS30: C Hth .3F 65
St Mary's Ct. BS24: W Mare .3J 127
St Mary's Gdns. BS40: L'frd .7D 110
St Mary's Grn. BA2: Tims .3F 141
St Mary's Gro. BS48: Nail .3E 70
St Mary's Pk. BS48: Nail .2E 70
St Mary's Pk. Rd. BS20: P'head .4E 42
St Marys Ri. BA3: Writ .4C 154
St Mary's Rd. BS8: L Wds .3D 60
BS11: Shire .1G 45
BS20: P'head .4E 42
BS24: Hut .3B 128
TA8: Bur S .1D 158
St Mary's St. BS26: Axb .4J 149
St Mary St. BS35: T'bry .4K 11
St Mary's Wlk. BS11: Shire .2H 45
St Mary's Way BS37: Yate .4F 31
St Marys Way BS35: T'bry .3K 11
St Matthews Av. BS6: Bris .7K 47
St Matthew's Cl.
BS23: W Mare .3F 105
St Matthews Pl. BA2: Bath .6J 7 (6D 100)
St Matthew's Rd. BS6: Bris .1E 4 (1K 61)
St Matthias Ho. BS2: Bris .2J 5
St Matthias Pk. BS2: Bris .2J 5 (2B 62)
St Michael's Av. BS21: Clev .1D 68
BS22: Wor .1E 106
St Michael's Cl. BS36: Wint .7C 28
St Michaels Cl. BS7: Bishop .4A 48
St Michael's Ct. BS15: Kgswd .1K 63
St Michaels Ct. BA2: Mon C .4G 123
St Michael's Hill BS2: Bris .1C 4 (1J 61)
St Michael's Pk. BS2: Bris .1C 4 (1J 61)
St Michael's Pl. BA1: Bath .5F 7 (5B 100)
St Michael's Rd. BA1: Bath .2A 6 (4K 99)
BA2: Bath .6G 99
TA8: Bur S .1D 158
St Monica Ct. BS9: W Trym .3G 47
St Nicholas Almshouses
BS1: Bris .4F 5
St Nicholas Cl. BA15: W'ley .5B 124
St Nicholas Ct. BA2: Batham .2H 101
St Nicholas Ho. BS1: Bris .4F 5
St Nicholas Mkt. BS1: Bris .4F 5 (3K 61)
St Nicholas Pk. BS5: E'ton .7D 48
St Nicholas Rd. BS2: Bris .7B 48
BS14: Whit .6E 76
BS23: Uph .3F 127
St Nicholas Steps BS1: Bris .4F 5
St Nicholas St. BS1: Bris .4F 5 (3K 61)
St Nicholas Way BS48: B'ley .1F 89
St Oswald's Ct. BS6: Redl .5H 47
St Oswald's Rd. BS6: Redl .5H 47
St Patrick's Ct. BA2: Bath .4K 7 (5D 100)
BS31: Key .5C 78
St Patricks Vw. BS5: St G .2F 63
ST PAUL'S .1C 62
St Pauls Ho. *BS3: Bedm .5K 61*
(off New Charlotte St.)
St Paul's Pl. BA3: Mid N .4E 152
St Pauls Pl. BA1: Bath .4E 6
St Paul's Rd. BS3: Bedm .5K 61
BS8: Clftn .2A 4 (2H 61)
BS23: W Mare .7G 105
TA8: Bur S .1D 158
St Paul St. BS2: Bris .1H 5
St Peter's Av. BS23: W Mare .3F 105
St Peter's Ct. *BA2: Bath .5B 6*
(off Dorset Cl.)
St Peters Ct. *BS3: Bedm .5K 61*
(off Bedminster Pde.)
St Peter's Cres. BS36: Fram C .6F 29
St Peter's Ho. BS8: Clftn .5B 4
St Peters Lodge BS20: P'head .4F 43
St Peter's Pl. BA2: Bath .5B 6 (5K 99)
St Peter's Ri. BS13: Bis .3G 75
St Peter's Rd. BA3: Mid N .6G 153
BS20: P'head .4F 43
TA8: Bur S .1D 158
St Peter's Ter. BA2: Bath .5B 6 (5K 99)
St Peter's Wlk. BS9: Henle .2H 47
St Philips C'way. BS2: Bris .2C 62
BS4: Bris .2C 62
BS5: Bar H .2C 62
St Philips Central Ind. Est.
BS2: Bris .7K 5 (4C 62)
ST PHILIP'S MARSH .4D 62
St Philips Rd. BS2: Bris .3K 5 (2B 62)
St Philips Trade Pk. BS2: Bris .5D 62
St Pierre Dr. BS30: Warm .3F 65
St Ronan's Av. BS6: Cot .7J 47
St Saviours Chu. BS23: W Mare .5H 105
St Saviours Ho. BS4: Know .7B 62
St Saviours Ri. BS36: Fram C .1F 39
St Saviours Rd. BA1: Bath, Swa .2D 100
St Saviour's Ter. BA1: Bath .2D 100
St Saviours Way BA1: Bath .2E 100
Saints Ct. BS5: E'ton .1K 5
TA8: Bur S .2D 158
St Silas Ct. BS14: Stoc .5E 76
St Stephen's Av. BS1: Bris .4E 4 (3K 61)
St Stephens Bus. Cen. *BS30: Old C .4G 65*
(off Poplar Rd.)
St Stephen's Cl. BA1: Bath .2B 100
BS10: S'mead .5J 35
BS16: Soun .5C 50
St Stephen's Ct. BA1: Bath .3B 100
St Stephen's Ho. *BS1: Bris .4E 4*
(off Colston Av.)
St Stephen's Pl. BA1: Bath .3B 100
St Stephen's Rd. BA1: Bath .1F 7 (3B 100)
BS16: Soun .6B 50
St Stephen's St. BS1: Bris .3E 4 (2K 61)
St Swithin's Pl. BA1: Bath .1G 7 (3C 100)
St Swithin's Yd. BA1: Bath .2G 7
St Tecla Cl. BS11: Shire .1H 45
St Thomas Ct. BS1: Bris .5G 5
St Thomas Pl. BS1: Bris .5G 5 (3A 62)
St Thomas Rd. BA3: Mid N .4F 153
St Thomas St. BS1: Bris .4G 5 (3A 62)
St Thomas St. E. BS1: Bris .5G 5 (3A 62)
St Vincent's Hill BS6: Redl .6G 47
St Vincents Rd. BS8: Clftn .3G 61
St Vincents Trad. Est. BS2: Bris .3E 62
Saint Way BS34: Stok G .3J 37
St Werburghs City Farm .5B 48
St Werburgh's Pk. BS2: Bris .6C 48
St Werburgh's Rd. BS2: Bris .6B 48
St Whytes Rd. BS4: Know .2K 75
St Winifred's Dr. BA2: C Down .2F 123
St Wulfstan Av. BS10: W Trym .7G 35
Salcombe Gdns. BS22: Wor .1E 106
Salcombe Rd. BS4: Know .1B 76
Salem Rd. BS36: Wint .7D 28
SALISBURY .2D 152
Salisbury Av. BS15: Kgswd .1K 63
Salisbury Dr. BS16: Down .2C 50
Salisbury Gdns. BS16: Down .3C 50
Salisbury Ho. BS6: Redl .5J 47
Salisbury Pk. BS16: Down .2C 50
Salisbury Rd. BA1: Bath .1D 100
BS4: St Ap .4F 63
BS6: Redl .6K 47
BS16: Down .2C 50
BS22: W Mare .3A 106
BS39: Paul .2D 152
TA8: Bur S .1E 158
Salisbury St. BS5: Bar H .3D 62
BS5: St G .2G 63
Salisbury Ter. BS23: W Mare .4F 105
Salisbury Vw. BS39: Paul .2D 152
Sally Barn Cl. BS30: Long G .7C 64
Sally Hill BS20: P'head .1G 43
Sally Lunn's House .5G 7 (5C 100)
Sallysmead Cl. BS13: Hart .6H 75
Sallys Way BS36: Wint .7D 28
Salmon Cl. BS35: Sev B .7A 16
Salmons Way BS16: Emer G .7E 38

Salters Brook—Showering Cl.

SALTERS BROOK . . . 1F 117
SALTFORD . . . 7J 79
Saltford Ct. BS31: Salt . . . 7J 79
Saltford Golf Course . . . 2J 97
Salthouse Farm Cvn. Pk. BS35: Sev B . . . 5A 16
Salthouse Rd. BS21: Clev . . . 7B 54
Salthrop Rd. BS7: Bishop . . . 4A 48
Saltings Cl. BS21: Clev . . . 7B 54
Saltmarsh Dr. BS11: Law W . . . 6A 34
Saltwell Av. BS14: Whit . . . 5E 76
Salway Cl. BS40: Chew S . . . 3E 114
Sambourne La. BS20: Pill . . . 3G 45
Samian Way BS34: Stok G . . . 2G 37
Sampson Ho. Bus. Pk. BS10: H'len . . . 7D 24
Sampsons Rd. BS13: Hart . . . 6K 75
Samuel Barnett Cl. BS4: Know . . . 2A 76
Samuel Cft. La. SN14: Hin . . . 2H 53
Samuel Rodgers Cres. NP16: Bul . . . 1A 8
Samuel St. BS5: Redf . . . 1E 62
Samuel White Rd. BS15: Han . . . 6K 63
Samuel Wright Cl. BS30: Old C . . . 4H 65
SAN ANDREAS . . . 1K 35
Sanctuary, The BS20: Pill . . . 4J 45
Sanctuary Gdns. BS9: Stok B . . . 5D 46
Sandacre Res. Pk. TA9: Highb . . . 4F 159
Sandbach Rd. BS4: Brisl . . . 5F 63
Sandbed Rd. BS2: Bris . . . 6C 48
Sandburrows Rd. BS13: Bis . . . 4E 74
Sandburrows Wlk. BS13: Bis . . . 4F 75
Sand Cl. BA15: Brad A . . . 5J 125
Sandcroft BS14: H'gro . . . 4B 76
Sandcroft Av. BS23: Uph . . . 3F 127
Sanderling Pl. BS20: P'head . . . 2H 43
Sanders Cl. BS3: Ash V . . . 7E 61
SANDFORD . . . 1G 131
SANDFORD BATCH . . . 3F 131
Sandford Cl. BS21: Clev . . . 1B 68
Sandford Rd. BS8: Clftn . . . 4G 61
BS23: W Mare . . . 5H 105
BS25: Wins . . . 3F 131
Sandgate Rd. BS4: Brisl . . . 6F 63
Sand Hill BS4: Brisl . . . 5E 62
Sandhills Dr. TA8: Bur S . . . 3B 156
Sandholme Cl. BS16: Down . . . 7C 38
Sandholme Rd. BS4: Brisl . . . 5E 62
Sandhurst BS37: Yate . . . 6D 30
Sandhurst Cl. BS34: Pat . . . 5D 26
Sandhurst Rd. BS4: Brisl . . . 5F 63
Sandling Av. BS7: Hor . . . 1C 48
Sandmead Rd. BS25: Sandf . . . 1G 131
Sandown Cl. BS16: Down . . . 6D 38
Sandown Rd. BS4: Brisl . . . 5F 63
BS34: Fil . . . 4E 36
Sandpiper Dr. BS22: Wor . . . 3D 106
Sandringham Av. BS16: Down . . . 7C 38
Sandringham Ct. BS23: W Mare . . . 7H 105
Sandringham Pk. BS16: Down . . . 7C 38
Sandringham Rd. BS4: Brisl . . . 6F 63
BS23: W Mare . . . 7H 105
BS30: Long G . . . 7D 64
BS34: Stok G . . . 2F 37
Sand Rd. BS22: Kew . . . 6A 84
Sands Hill SN14: Dyr . . . 4K 53
Sands La. BS36: Fram C . . . 5D 28
Sandstone Ri. BS36: Wint . . . 3C 38
Sandwich Rd. BS4: Brisl . . . 5F 63
Sandy Cl. BS32: Brad S . . . 1G 37
TA9: Highb . . . 4F 159
Sandy La. BS5: Eastv . . . 5E 48
BS8: Abb L, Fail . . . 7E 44
BS35: Aust . . . 4G 9
(not continuous)
BS39: Stan D . . . 1A 116
BS40: Chew M, Stan D . . . 1J 115
Sandy Leaze BA15: Brad A . . . 6G 125
Sandyleaze BS9: W Trym . . . 1E 46
Sandy Lodge BS37: Yate . . . 6E 30
Sandy Pk. Rd. BS4: Brisl . . . 5E 62
Sarabeth Dr. BA2: Tun . . . 1A 142
Saracens, The BS7: Hor . . . 3A 48
Saracen St. BA1: Bath . . . 3G 7 (4C 100)
Sarah St. BS5: Bar H . . . 2D 62
Sargent St. BS3: Bedm . . . 5A 62
Sark Cl. BS4: Brisl . . . 5G 63
Sarum Cl. BS16: Emer G . . . 2G 51
Sarum Cres. BS10: S'mead . . . 6J 35
Sassoon Ct. BS30: Bar C . . . 4D 64
Satchfield Cl. BS10: Hen . . . 5F 35
Satchfield Ct. BS10: Hen . . . 5F 35
Satchfield Cres. BS10: Hen . . . 5F 35
Satellite Bus. Pk. BS5: St G . . . 2F 63
Sates Way BS9: Henle . . . 2J 47
Saunders Rd. BS16: Stap H . . . 4C 50
Saunton Wlk. BS4: Know . . . 2A 76
Savages Wood Rd.
BS32: Brad S . . . 6F 27
Savernake Rd. BS22: Wor . . . 1D 106
Saville Ct. Bus. Cen.
BS8: Clftn . . . 2G 61
Saville Cres. BS22: W Mare . . . 4A 106
Saville Ga. Cl. BS9: Stok B . . . 4F 47
Saville M. BS6: Bris . . . 1K 61
Saville Pl. BS8: Clftn . . . 3G 61
Saville Rd. BS9: Stok B . . . 5F 47
BS22: W Mare . . . 4A 106
Saville Row BA1: Bath . . . 2F 7 (4B 100)
Savoy, The BS11: Shire . . . 2J 45
Savoy Ct. BS4: Brisl . . . 5E 62
Savoy Rd. BS4: Brisl . . . 5F 63
Sawclose BA1: Bath . . . 4F 7 (5B 100)
Saw Mill La. BS35: T'bry . . . 3K 11
Sawyers Cl. BS48: Wrax . . . 7J 57
Sawyers Ct. BS21: Clev . . . 6E 54
Saxby Cl. BS21: Clev . . . 1B 68
BS22: Wor . . . 7F 85
Saxon Ct. BS22: St G . . . 1H 107
Saxondale Av. TA8: Bur S . . . 4C 156
Saxon Pl. BS27: Ched . . . 7D 150
Saxon Rd. BS2: Bris . . . 6C 48
BS22: W Mare . . . 4A 106
Saxon St. BS40: L'frd . . . 6F 111
Saxon Way BA2: Pea J . . . 5E 142
BA15: W'ley . . . 5D 124
BS27: Ched . . . 7H 151
BS32: Brad S . . . 5E 26
Sayer Pl. BS10: Hor . . . 1A 48
Says La. BS40: L'frd . . . 7C 110
Say Wlk. BS30: B'yte . . . 2H 65
SBI Cen. BS15: Han . . . 4K 63
Scafell Cl. BS23: W Mare . . . 3J 105
Scandrett Cl. BS10: Hen . . . 5E 34
Scantleberry Cl.
BS16: Down . . . 6B 38
Scaurs, The BS22: Wor . . . 2D 106
School Cl. BS5: Eastv . . . 5F 49
BS14: Whit . . . 6B 76
BS29: Ban . . . 2B 130
BS34: Pat . . . 6E 26
School Ct. BS34: Stok G . . . 3J 37
School La. BA1: Bathe . . . 6H 83
BS16: Stap . . . 3G 49
BS21: Clev . . . 6E 54
(off Old St.)
BS22: Wick L . . . 4F 85
BS25: Row . . . 4C 132
BS29: Ban . . . 2B 130
BS39: Chelw . . . 3J 117
BS40: Chew S . . . 4D 114
BS40: F'tn . . . 3E 90
BS48: Bar G . . . 5H 73
School Rd. BS4: Brisl . . . 7G 63
BS4: Wind H . . . 6C 62
BS15: Kgswd . . . 1A 64
BS30: C Hth . . . 5E 64
BS30: Old C . . . 6F 65
BS36: Fram C . . . 6D 28
BS40: Wrin . . . 2G 111
School Vw. BS48: Wrax . . . 7K 57
School Wlk. BS5: W'hall . . . 7F 49
BS37: Yate . . . 4E 30
School Way BS35: Sev B . . . 7A 16
Scobell Ri. BS39: High L . . . 3A 140
Scop, The BS32: Alm . . . 1D 26
Score, The BS40: Blag . . . 3C 134
Score La. BS40: Blag . . . 4C 134
Scornfield La. BS40: Chew S . . . 5D 114
Scotch Horn Cl. BS48: Nail . . . 7H 57
Scotch Horn Leisure Cen. . . . 7H 57
Scotch Horn Way BS48: Nail . . . 7H 57
Scot Elm Dr. BS24: W Wick . . . 3G 107
Scotland La. BS4: Brisl . . . 2H 77
BS14: Brisl . . . 4H 77
Scot La. BS40: Chew S . . . 3D 114
Scots Pine Av. BS48: Nail . . . 7H 57
Scott Ct. BS30: Bar C . . . 4D 64
Scott Lawrence Cl. BS16: Bmhll . . . 1J 49
Scott (Orpheus) Cinema
Bristol . . . 4H 47
Scott Rd. BS23: W Mare . . . 1J 127
TA9: Highb . . . 5F 159
Scott Wlk. BS30: B'yte . . . 2H 65
Scott Way BS37: Yate . . . 6F 31
Scumbrum La. BS39: High L . . . 2A 140
Sea Bank Rd. BS20: P'bry . . . 6C 32
Seabrook Rd. BS22: W Mare . . . 3B 106
Seacole St. BS7: Hor . . . 1A 48
Seagry Cl. BS10: S'mead . . . 6A 36
SEA MILLS . . . 2C 46
Sea Mills La. BS9: Sea M . . . 4C 46
Sea Mills Station (Rail) . . . 4B 46
SeaQuarium . . . 6F 105
Searle Ct. BS21: Clev . . . 6E 54
Searle Ct. Av. BS4: Brisl . . . 5G 63
Searle Cres. BS23: W Mare . . . 6J 105
Seaton Rd. BS5: E'ton . . . 7E 48
Seavale Rd. BS21: Clev . . . 5C 54
Seaview Rd. BS20: P'head . . . 4B 42
TA8: Bur S . . . 7C 156
Seawalls BS9: Stok B . . . 6D 46
Sea Walls Rd. BS9: Stok B . . . 6D 46
Second Av. BA2: Bath . . . 7B 6 (7K 99)
BA3: Mid N . . . 7G 153
BS14: H'gro . . . 3D 76
Second Severn Crossing BS35: Sev B . . . 5A 16
Second Way BS11: A'mth . . . 6H 33
Seddon Rd. BS2: Bris . . . 6C 48
Sedgefield Gdns. BS16: Down . . . 6D 38
Sedgemoor Cl. BS48: Nail . . . 2F 71
Sedgemoor Rd. BA2: C Down . . . 3B 122
BS23: W Mare . . . 3H 105
SEDGEMOOR SERVICE AREA . . . 7D 146
Sedgemoor Ter. BA2: C Down . . . 2C 122
Sedgewick Ho. BS11: Shire . . . 1J 45
Sefton Pk. Rd. BS7: Bishop . . . 5A 48
Sefton Sq. BS24: W'ton V . . . 4E 106
Selborne Rd. BS7: Hor . . . 3B 48
Selbourne Cl. BA1: Bath . . . 3G 99
Selbourne Rd. BS23: W Mare . . . 1G 127
Selbrooke Cres. BS16: Fish . . . 2K 49
Selby Rd. BS5: S'wll . . . 7H 49
Selden Rd. BS14: Stoc . . . 5G 77
Selkirk Rd. BS15: Kgswd . . . 7A 50
Selley Wlk. BS13: Bis . . . 5G 75
Selway Ct. BA2: C Down . . . 2D 122
Selwood Cl. BS22: W Mare . . . 5A 106
Selworthy BS15: Kgswd . . . 2C 64
Selworthy Cl. BS31: Key . . . 5B 78
Selworthy Gdns. BS48: Nail . . . 1G 71
(off Mizzymead Rd.)
Selworthy Ho. BA2: C Down . . . 2B 122
Selworthy Rd. BS4: Know . . . 7D 62
BS23: W Mare . . . 1H 127
Selworthy Ter. BA2: C Down . . . 2B 122
Seneca Pl. BS5: St G . . . 2F 63
Seneca St. BS5: St G . . . 2F 63
Septimus Bldgs. BS14: Hart . . . 5K 75
(off Hawkfield Cl.)
Serbert Cl. BS20: P'head . . . 3G 43
Serbert Rd. BS20: P'head . . . 3G 43
Serbert Way BS20: P'head . . . 3G 43
Sercombe Pk. BS21: Clev . . . 1E 68
Serlo Ct. BS22: Wor . . . 7D 84
Serridge La. BS36: Coal H . . . 3G 39
Sevastopol Rd. BS7: Hor . . . 1A 48
Seven Acres, The BS24: W'ton V . . . 5D 106
Seven Acres La. BA1: Bathe . . . 5H 83
Seven Dials BA1: Bath . . . 4F 7 (5B 100)
Seventh Av. BS7: Hor . . . 6D 36
BS14: H'gro . . . 3C 76
Seven Ways BS2: Bris . . . 2J 5
Severn Av. BS23: W Mare . . . 7G 105
SEVERN BEACH . . . 7A 16
Severn Beach Station (Rail) . . . 7A 16
Severn Bridge Vis. Cen. . . . 5A 16
Severn Dr. BS35: T'bry . . . 2K 11
Severn Grange BS10: Hen . . . 4D 34
Severn Gro. TA8: Bur S . . . 3D 158
Severn Ho. BS10: Hen . . . 4D 34
Severn Leigh Gdns. BS9: Stok B . . . 5F 47
Severnmead BS20: P'head . . . 3B 42
Severn Point BS10: Hen . . . 3G 35
(off Wyck Beck Rd.)
Severn Rd. BS10: H'len . . . 6A 24
BS11: Chit . . . 6A 24
BS11: Shire . . . 2H 45
BS20: P'head . . . 3E 42
BS20: Pill . . . 3G 45
BS23: W Mare . . . 7F 105
BS35: N'wick, Piln . . . 6C 16
BS35: Sev B . . . 2A 24
NP16: Beach . . . 2D 8
Severnside Trad. Est. BS11: A'mth . . . 2G 33
Severn Vw. BS11: Law W . . . 6C 34
Severn Vw. Ind. Pk. BS10: H'len . . . 3A 24
Severn Vw. Rd. BS35: T'bry . . . 2A 12
SEVERN VIEW SERVICE AREA . . . 4F 9
Severn Way BS31: Key . . . 6D 78
BS34: Pat . . . 5B 26
Severnwood Gdns. BS35: Sev B . . . 1A 24
Sevier Rd. BS26: Lox, Webb . . . 3G 147
Sevier St. BS2: Bris . . . 6B 48
Seville Ct. BS20: P'head . . . 1G 43
Seville Rd. BS20: P'head . . . 1G 43
Seward Ter. BA3: Writ . . . 4C 154
Sewell Ho. BS25: Wins . . . 5G 131
Seymour Av. BS7: Bishop . . . 4A 48
Seymour Cl. BS21: Clev . . . 6E 54
BS22: Wor . . . 7D 84
Seymour Pl. BS36: Fram C . . . 1F 39
Seymour Rd. BA1: Bath . . . 3C 100
BS5: E'ton . . . 7C 48
BS7: Bishop . . . 4A 48
BS15: Kgswd . . . 7B 50
BS16: Stap H . . . 4B 50
Seyton Wlk. BS34: Stok G . . . 2G 37
Shackel Hendy M.
BS16: Emer G . . . 3G 51
Shackleton Av. BS37: Yate . . . 6F 31
Shadow Wlk. BS24: Elbgh . . . 2G 129
Shadwell Rd. BS7: Bishop . . . 5K 47
Shaftesbury Av. BA1: Bath . . . 4J 99
BS6: Bris . . . 7A 48
Shaftesbury Cl. BS48: Nail . . . 2F 71
Shaftesbury Crusade BS2: Bris . . . 3C 62
(off Union Rd.)
Shaftesbury M. BA2: Bath . . . 7B 6 (6K 99)
Shaftesbury Rd. BA2: Bath . . . 7B 6 (6K 99)
BS23: W Mare . . . 4K 105
Shaftesbury Ter. BA3: Rads . . . 3A 154
BS5: St G . . . 2F 63
BS6: Bris . . . 7A 48
(off Ashley Rd.)
Shaft Rd. BA2: C Down, Mon C . . . 2F 123
BS35: Sev B . . . 5A 16
Shakespeare Av. BA2: Bath . . . 7B 100
BS7: Hor . . . 7C 36
Shakespeare Ct. BS23: W Mare . . . 3H 127
Shakespeare Rd. BA3: Rads . . . 5G 153
Shaldon Rd. BS7: L'lze . . . 4C 48
Shallows, The BS31: Salt . . . 7K 79
Shambles, The BA15: Brad A . . . 5H 125
Sham Castle La. BA2: Bath . . . 3K 7 (4D 100)
Shamrock Rd. BS5: Eastv . . . 5F 49
Shanklin Dr. BS34: Fil . . . 4D 36
Shannaways Cl. BS16: Fish . . . 4H 49
Shannon Ct. BS1: Bris . . . 4F 5
BS35: T'bry . . . 4B 12
Shannon Wlk. BS20: P'head . . . 2H 43
Shapcott Cl. BS4: Know . . . 1D 76
Shaplands BS9: Stok B . . . 4F 47
Sharland Cl. BS9: Stok B . . . 5E 46
Sharland Gro. BS13: Hart . . . 6J 75
Sharpham Rd. BS27: Ched . . . 7B 150
Sharples Cl. BS16: L'lze . . . 7E 36
Shaw Cl. BS5: E'ton . . . 1D 62
BS16: Mang . . . 5F 51
Shaw Gdns. BS14: H'gro . . . 2C 76
Shaw Path TA8: Bur S . . . 2E 158
Shaws Way BA2: Bath . . . 5F 99
Shaymoor La. BS35: Piln . . . 2F 25
Shearmore Cl. BS7: Hor . . . 1C 48
Shearn La. TA8: Bur S . . . 1D 158
Shearwater Ct. BS16: Bmhll . . . 2H 49
(off Begbrook La.)
Sheaves Pk. BS10: S'mead . . . 5K 35
Sheene Ct. BS3: Bedm . . . 6J 61
Sheene Rd. BS3: Bedm . . . 6J 61
Sheene Way BS3: Bedm . . . 6J 61
Sheephouse Cvn. Pk. BS20: Eas . . . 1C 44
Sheepscroft BS13: Withy . . . 6G 75
SHEEPWAY . . . 3A 44
Sheepway BS20: P'bry, P'head . . . 4H 43
Sheepway La. BS20: P'bry . . . 2A 44
Sheepwood Cl. BS10: Hen . . . 5G 35
Sheepwood Rd. BS10: Hen . . . 5G 35
Sheldare Barton BS5: St G . . . 2K 63
Sheldon Cl. BS21: Clev . . . 7F 55
Sheldrake Dr. BS16: Bmhll . . . 2G 49
Shellard Rd. BS34: Fil . . . 5C 36
Shellards La. BS35: A'ton . . . 1A 20
Shellards Rd. BS30: Long G . . . 6D 64
Shelley Av. BS21: Clev . . . 7D 54
Shelley Cl. BS5: St G . . . 1H 63
TA8: Bur S . . . 5C 156
Shelley Dr. TA8: Bur S . . . 5C 156
Shelley Rd. BA2: Bath . . . 7F 7 (6B 100)
BA3: Rads . . . 5G 153
BS23: W Mare . . . 1J 127
Shelley Way BS7: Hor . . . 7C 36
Shellmor Av. BS34: Pat . . . 5D 26
Shellmor Cl. BS34: Pat . . . 5E 26
Shepherds Cl. BS16: Stap H . . . 3C 50
Shepherd's La. TA9: W Hunt . . . 7D 158
Shepherd's Wlk. BA2: C Down . . . 3B 122
Shepherds Wlk. BS32: Brad S . . . 5F 27
Shepherd's Way BS22: St G . . . 2G 107
Sheppard Rd. BS16: Fish . . . 2A 50
Sheppards Gdns. BA1: W'ton . . . 1H 99
Sheppy's Mill BS49: Cong . . . 6K 87
Shepton BS24: W Mare . . . 3J 127
Shepton Wlk. BS3: Bedm . . . 7J 61
Sherbourne Av. BS32: Brad S . . . 1G 37
Sherbourne Cl. BS15: Soun . . . 6D 50
Sherbourne St. BS5: St G . . . 1G 63
Sheridan Rd. BA2: Bath . . . 6F 99
BS7: Hor . . . 6C 36
TA8: Bur S . . . 3E 158
Sheridan Way BS30: Long G . . . 7E 64
Sherrings, The BS34: Pat . . . 6D 26
Sherrin Way BS13: Withy . . . 6E 74
Sherston Cl. BS16: Fish . . . 3K 49
BS48: Nail . . . 1J 71
Sherston Rd. BS7: Hor . . . 7A 36
Sherwell Rd. BS4: Brisl . . . 6G 63
Sherwood Cl. BS31: Key . . . 5C 78
Sherwood Cres. BS22: Wor . . . 1D 106
Sherwood Rd. BS15: Kgswd . . . 7K 49
BS31: Key . . . 5C 78
Shetland Rd. BS10: S'mead . . . 6K 35
Shetland Way BS48: Nail . . . 1J 71
Shickle Gro. BA2: Odd D . . . 3J 121
Shield Retail Cen. BS34: Fil . . . 4C 36
Shields Av. BS7: Hor . . . 5C 36
Shiels Dr. BS32: Brad S . . . 7F 27
Shilton Cl. BS15: Kgswd . . . 3C 64
Shimsey Cl. BS16: Fish . . . 2A 50
Shiners Elms BS49: Yat . . . 3G 87
SHIPHAM . . . 5B 132
Shipham Cl. BS14: Whit . . . 5D 76
BS48: Nail . . . 2H 71
Shipham Ct. BS23: W Mare . . . 5J 105
Shipham La. BS25: Wins, Star . . . 4F 131
Shipham Rd. BS25: S'ham . . . 7B 132
BS27: Ched . . . 4B 150
Ship Hill BS15: Han . . . 4K 63
Ship La. BS1: Bris . . . 7G 5 (4A 62)
SHIPLATE . . . 1D 146
Shiplate Rd. BS24: B'don . . . 7A 128
BS26: Lox . . . 7A 128
Shipley Mow BS16: Emer G . . . 2F 51
Shipley Rd. BS9: W Trym . . . 7G 35
Shire Gdns. BS11: Shire . . . 7H 33
SHIREHAMPTON . . . 2J 45
Shirehampton Rd.
BS9: Sea M, Stok B . . . 1B 46
BS11: Shire . . . 2K 45
Shirehampton Sailing Club . . . 3H 45
Shirehampton Station (Rail) . . . 3H 45
Shires Yd. BA1: Bath . . . 3F 7 (4B 100)
Shire Way BS37: Yate . . . 7C 30
Shockerwick La. BA1: Bathf . . . 6K 83
Shoe La. BS39: Paul . . . 7B 140
Shophouse Rd. BA2: Bath . . . 5H 99
Shoreditch BS40: Chew S . . . 5C 114
Shorland Ho. BS8: Clftn . . . 7G 47
Shorthill Rd. BS37: W'lgh . . . 3C 40
Shortlands Rd. BS11: Law W . . . 6A 34
Short La. BS41: L Ash . . . 7A 60
Short St. BS2: Bris . . . 4C 62
Short Way BS8: Fail . . . 6F 59
BS35: T'bry . . . 5K 11
SHORTWOOD . . . 3H 51
Shortwood Hill BS16: Short . . . 3H 51
Shortwood Rd. BS13: Hart . . . 7A 76
BS16: Puck . . . 4K 51
Shortwood Vw. BS15: Kgswd . . . 1D 64
Shortwood Wlk. BS13: Hart . . . 7A 76
SHOSCOMBE . . . 7E 142
SHOSCOMBE VALE . . . 1E 154
Showcase Cinema
Bristol . . . 4E 62
Showering Cl. BS14: Stoc . . . 5F 77

Showering Rd.—Spinners End

Showering Rd. BS14: Stoc 5F 77
Shrewsbury Bow BS24: W'ton V 4E 106
SHROWLE 7H 137
Shrubbery, The BA1: Bath 1E 6 (3B 100)
Shrubbery Av. BS23: W Mare 3E 104
Shrubbery Cl. TA8: Berr 6A 144
Shrubbery Cotts. BS6: Redl 6H 47
Shrubbery Ct. BS16: Stap H 3B 50
Shrubbery Rd. BS16: Stap H 3B 50
BS23: W Mare 3F 105
Shrubbery Ter. BS23: W Mare 3E 104
Shrubbery Wlk. BS23: W Mare 3F 105
Shrubbery Wlk. W. BS23: W Mare 3F 105
Shums Ct. *BA1: Bath 4G 7*
(off Cheap St.)
Shuter Rd. BS13: Withy 5F 75
Sibland BS35: T'bry 4B 12
Sibland Cl. BS35: T'bry 4B 12
Sibland Rd. BS35: T'bry 3B 12
Sibland Way BS35: T'bry 4A 12
SIDCOT 6H 131
Sidcot BS4: Brisl 7J 63
Sidcot Dr. BS25: Wins 6G 131
Sidcot La. BS25: Wins 6G 131
Sideland Cl. BS14: Stoc 4G 77
Sidelands Rd. BS16: Fish 2A 50
Sidelings, The BS40: Ubl 5H 135
Sidings, The BS16: Sis 6F 51
BS34: Fil 5E 36
BS39: Clut 2H 139
Sidmouth Ct. TA8: Bur S 7E 156
Sidmouth Gdns. BS3: Wind H 7K 61
Sidmouth Rd. BS3: Wind H 7K 61
Signal Rd. BS16: Stap H 4C 50
Silbury Ri. BS31: Key 1E 96
Silbury Rd. BS3: Ash V 7E 60
Silcox Rd. BS13: Hart 6J 75
Silklands Gro. BS9: Sea M 2C 46
Silverberry Rd. BS22: Wor 3D 106
Silver Birch Cl. BS34: Lit S 7F 27
Silvercombe BS23: W Mare 7F 105
Silver Ct. BS48: Nail 7F 57
Silverhill Brake BS35: Rudg 4G 19
Silverhill Rd. BS10: Hen 4E 34
Silverlow Rd. BS48: Nail 7F 57
Silver Mead BS49: Cong 2K 109
Silver Moor La. BS29: Ban 6J 107
Silverstone Way BS49: Cong 1K 109
Silver St. BA3: Mid N, Stratt F 7E 152
BA15: Brad A 6H 125
BS1: Bris 2F 5 (2K 61)
BS20: W'ton G 7A 42
BS27: Ched 6D 150
BS35: T'bry 3K 11
BS40: Chew M 1H 115
BS40: Wrin 2F 111
BS48: Nail 7E 56
BS49: Cong 2K 109
Silverthorne La. BS2: Bris 4C 62
Silverthorne Wharf BS2: Bris 3C 62
Silverton Ct. BS4: Know 1B 76
Simmonds Bldgs. BS16: H'ook 4A 38
Simmonds Vw. BS34: Stok G 2H 37
Simons Cl. BS22: Wor 2E 106
BS39: Paul 1D 152
Sinclair Ho. BS8: Clftn 4A 4 (3H 61)
Singapore Rd. BS23: W Mare 2G 127
SINGLE HILL 1G 155
Sion Ct. BS8: Clftn 2F 61
SION HILL 2A 100
Sion Hill BA1: Bath 2A 100
BS8: Clftn 2F 61
Sion Hill Pl. BA1: Bath 2A 100
Sion Ho. *BS8: Clftn 2F 61*
(off Sion Pl.)
Sion La. BS8: Clftn 2F 61
Sion Pl. BA2: Bath 4K 7 (5D 100)
BS8: Clftn 2F 61
Sion Rd. BA1: Bath 2A 100
BS3: Bedm 6J 61
Sir Bevil Grenville Monument 1G 81
Sir John's La. BS5: Eastv 4D 48
(not continuous)
BS16: L'lze 4D 48
Sir Johns Wood BS48: Nail 6F 57
Siskin Cl. BS20: P'head 2H 43
Siskin Wlk. BS22: Wor 4D 106
SISTON 5K 51
Siston Cen. BS15: Soun 6E 50
Siston Cl. BS15: Soun 6E 50
SISTON COMMON 6E 50
Siston Comn. BS15: Sis 6E 50
(not continuous)
BS30: Sis 6E 50
Siston Hill BS30: Sis 7E 50
(not continuous)
Siston La. BS16: Sis 4K 51
BS30: W Hth 1J 65
Siston Pk. BS15: Soun 6E 50
Sixpence BS39: High L 3B 140
Sixth Av. BS7: Hor 6D 36
BS14: H'gro 3C 76
Sixty Acres Cl. BS8: Fail 6F 59
Six Ways BS21: Clev 5D 54
Skinners Cft. BS34: Pat 7C 26
Skinner's Hill BA2: Cam 6J 141
Skinners La. BS25: C'hll 1B 132
Skippon Ct. BS15: Han 4C 64
Skypark Rd. BS3: Bedm 6J 61
Slad, The BS35: Grov 6C 12
Sladacre La. BS40: Blag 3C 134
SLADEBROOK 1J 121
Sladebrook Av. BA2: Bath 1J 121
Sladebrook Ct. BA2: Bath 1H 121
Sladebrook Rd. BA2: Bath 7H 99
Slade Cotts. BA2: Mon C 3G 123
Slade La. BS25: Lym 5K 145
BS48: Bar G 6F 73
Slade Rd. BS20: P'head 3F 43
Sladesbrook BA15: Brad A 5H 125
Sladesbrook Cl. BA15: Brad A 4H 125
Slades Ct. BS48: Back 4J 71
Slate La. BS31: Q Char 3J 95
BS39: Comp D 3J 95
Slaughter La. BS30: Upton C 7D 66
Sleep La. BS14: Whit 7F 77
Sleight Vw. BA2: Tims 2F 141
Slimbridge Cl. BS37: Yate 7F 31
Slimeridge Farm Cvn. Pk.
BS23: Uph 3E 126
Slingsby Gdns. BS24: W Mare 1A 128
Sloan St. BS5: St G 1F 63
Sloe Cl. BS22: W Mare 5B 106
Sloe Way BS34: H'ook 4H 37
Slymbridge Av. BS10: Bren 4G 35
Smallbrook La. BS39: Comp D, Wool 5J 95
Smallcombe Cl. BA3: Clan 1J 153
Smallcombe Rd. BA3: Clan 1J 153
Small Down End BS25: Wins 3F 131
Small La. BS16: Stap 3G 49
Small St. BS1: Bris 3E 4 (2K 61)
BS2: Bris 4C 62
Smallway BS49: Cong 5K 87
Smallwood Vw. BA3: Mid N 7C 152
Smarts Grn. BS37: Chip S 6J 31
Smeaton Rd. BS1: Bris 4F 61
Smithcourt Dr. BS34: Lit S 1E 36
Smithmead BS13: Hart 5H 75
Smiths Complex BS34: Pat 6C 26
Smith's Forge Ind. Est. BS49: Yat 7F 69
Smith Way TA9: Highb 5F 159
Smoke La. BS11: A'mth, Chit 1G 33
Smoke La. Ind. Est. BS11: A'mth 1G 33
Smurl La. TA9: W Hunt 7E 158
Smythe Cft. BS14: Whit 7C 76
Smythe Ter. *BS3: Bris 5J 61*
(off Beauley Rd.)
Smyth Rd. BS3: Bedm 6G 61
Smyths Cl. BS11: A'mth 6F 33
SNEYD PARK 5D 46
Sneyd Pk. Ho. BS9: Stok B 5D 46
Snowberry Cl. BS22: Wor 3E 106
BS32: Brad S 6G 27
Snowberry Wlk. BS5: W'hall 7G 49
Snowdon Cl. BS16: Fish 4H 49
Snowdon Rd. BS16: Fish 3H 49
Snowdon Va. BS23: W Mare 3J 105
Snowdrop Cl. BS22: Wick L 6E 84
Snow Hill BA1: Bath 3C 100
Snow Hill Ho. BA1: Bath 3C 100
Soapers La. BS35: T'bry 4K 11
Soaphouse Ind. Est. BS5: St G 1G 63
Sodbury La. BS37: W'lgh 2E 40
Sodbury Rd. GL12: Wickw 2G 23
Sodbury Va. BS37: Chip S 4H 31
Solent Way BS35: T'bry 5B 12
Solsbury Ct. BA1: Bathe 6H 83
BA2: C'ton D 5H 101
Solsbury La. BA1: Bathe 6G 83
Solsbury Vw. BA2: Batham 2H 101
Solsbury Way BA1: Bath 1B 100
(not continuous)
Somer Av. BA3: Mid N 4D 152
Somerby Cl. BS32: Brad S 7F 27
Somer Cl. BA3: Mid N 6D 152
Somer Ct. BA3: Mid N 5F 153
SOMERDALE 3C 78
Somerdale Av. BA2: Odd D 2J 121
BS4: Know 2B 76
BS22: W Mare 4A 106
Somerdale Cl. BS22: W Mare 4A 106
Somerdale Vw. BA2: Bath 2J 121
Somerford Ct. *BS9: W Trym 6F 35*
(off Northover Cl.)
Somer La. BS3: Bedm 1J 75
Somermead BS3: Bedm 1J 75
Somer Ridge BA3: Mid N 3D 152
Somer Rd. BA3: Mid N 4D 152
Somerset & Dorset Railway Heritage Trust
Midsomer Norton South Station 6E 152
Somerset Av. BS22: W Wick 5C 106
BS24: W Wick, W'ton V 5C 106
BS37: Yate 3F 31
Somerset Cres. BS34: Stok G 2H 37
Somerset Folly BA2: Tims 3F 141
Somerset Ho. BA2: Bath 1K 121
BS2: Bris 2K 5
Somerset La. BA1: Bath 2A 100
Somerset M. BS20: P'head 4F 43
BS23: W Mare 7H 105
Somerset Pl. BA1: Bath 2A 100
Somerset Rd. BS4: Know 6C 62
BS20: P'head 3B 42
BS21: Clev 6E 54
Somerset Sq. BS1: Bris 7G 5 (4A 62)
BS48: Nail 7G 57
Somerset St.
BA1: Bath 6F 7 (6C 100)
BS1: Bris 7H 5 (4A 62)
BS2: Bris 1E 4 (1K 61)
Somerset Ter. BS3: Wind H 6K 61
Somerset Way BS39: Paul 7C 140
TA9: Highb 5G 159
Somerton BS24: W Mare 3J 127
Somerton Cl. BS15: Kgswd 2C 64
Somerton Rd. BS7: Hor 2A 48
BS21: Clev 1E 68
Somervale Rd. BA3: Rads 4H 153
Somerville Cl. BS31: Salt 1J 97
Somerville Rd. BS25: Sandf 2G 131
Sommerville BS10: W Trym 7G 35
Sommerville Rd. BS6: Bris 5A 48
BS7: Bishop, Bris 5A 48
Sommerville Rd. Sth.
BS6: Bris 6B 48
BS7: Bris 6B 48
Soper Gdns. BS4: Know 3K 75
Sophia Gdns. BS22: Wor 7F 85
Sorbus Cl. BS32: Alm 1G 27
Sorrel Cl. BS35: T'bry 2B 12
Sorrel Gdns. BS20: P'head 3H 43
Sorrel Pl. BS34: H'ook 4H 37
SOUNDWELL 5D 50
Soundwell Rd. BS15: Kgswd 7A 50
BS16: Soun 6B 50
Sour Mead BS16: Fren 7F 37
Southampton Gdns.
BS7: Bishop 3B 48
Southampton M. BS7: Bishop 3B 48
South Av. BA2: Bath 6A 6 (6K 99)
BS20: P'head 2F 43
BS37: Yate 5B 30
TA9: Highb 4E 158
Southblow Ho. BS3: Ash G 6G 61
Southbourne Gdns. BA1: Bath 2D 100
Southbourne Mans.
BA2: Bath 5H 7 (5C 100)
Sth. Brent Cl. TA9: Bre K 4H 157
Sth. Bristol Bus. Pk. BS4: Know 3A 76
Sth. Bristol Crematorium & Cemetery
BS13: Bis 2F 75
Sth. Bristol Retail Pk. BS3: Ash G 6F 61
South Bristol Skills Academy 5A 76
Sth. Bristol Trade Pk. BS3: Ash V 6F 61
South Cl. BS24: Lym 5K 145
South Combe BS24: B'don 7K 127
Southcot Pl. BA2: Bath 7H 7 (6C 100)
South Ct. BS32: Brad S 3F 27
South Cft. BS9: Henle 1J 47
BS25: Wins 3F 131
South Dene BS9: Stok B 2E 46
SOUTH DOWN 1H 121
Southdown BS22: Wor 7D 84
Southdown Av. BA2: Bath 1H 121
Southdown Rd. BA2: Bath 7H 99
BS9: W Trym 7F 35
Southdowns BS8: Clftn 7G 47
Southend Gdns. GL12: Wickw 7G 15
TA9: Highb 3G 159
Southend Ho. GL12: Wickw 7H 15
Southend Rd. BS23: W Mare 1G 127
Southernhay BS8: Clftn 5A 4
BS16: Stap H 4A 50
Southernhay Av. BS8: Clftn 5A 4 (3H 61)
Southernhay Cres. BS8: Clftn 5A 4 (3H 61)
Southern Lea Rd. TA8: Bur S 7E 156
Southern Ring Path BS21: Clev 1C 68
(Braikenridge Cl.)
BS21: Clev 7E 54
(Hill Moor, not continuous)
Southern Way BS21: Clev 7B 54
South Esplanade TA8: Bur S 3C 158
Southey Av. BS15: Kgswd 7C 50
Southey Ct. BS15: Kgswd 7B 50
Southey Rd. BS21: Clev 7D 54
Southey St. BS2: Bris 6B 48
SOUTHFIELD 4A 154
Southfield BS27: Ched 6D 150
Southfield Av. BS15: Kgswd 7C 50
Southfield Cl. BS23: Uph 3F 127
BS48: Nail 6G 57
Southfield Ct. BS9: W Trym 1G 47
Southfield Hill BA3: Hem 7G 155
Southfield Rd. BS6: Cot 7K 47
BS9: W Trym 1G 47
BS48: Nail 6G 57
(not continuous)
Southfield Rd. Trad. Est. BS48: Nail 6H 57
Southfields BA3: Rads 4A 154
Southfield Way BS37: Yate 2G 31
Southgate Pl. BA1: Bath 5G 7
Southgate Shop. Cen.
BA1: Bath 6G 7 (6C 100)
Southgate St. BA1: Bath 5G 7 (5C 100)
South Grn. St. BS8: Clftn 3F 61
South Gro. BS6: Henle 3J 47
BS20: Pill 4G 45
South Hayes BS5: Eastv 4D 48
South Hill BS25: Wins 3F 131
Southlands BA1: W'ton 1G 99
(not continuous)
BS4: Know 1D 76
GL12: Tyth 1F 21
Southlands Dr. BA2: Tims 4F 141
Southlands Way BS49: Cong 6K 87
South Lawn BS24: Lock 1D 128
Sth. Lawn Cl. BS24: Lock 1D 128
Sth. Lea Rd. BA1: Bath 3G 99
Southleaze BS25: Wins 7G 131
Southleigh BA15: Brad A 7G 125
Southleigh Rd. BS8: Clftn 1A 4 (1H 61)
Sth. Liberty La.
BS3: Ash V, Bedm 1E 74
South Lodge BS9: Stok B 2D 46
SOUTH LYNCOMBE 1B 122
SOUTHMEAD 6J 35
Southmead BS25: Wins 5G 131
South Mdws. BS40: Wrin 2G 111
Southmead Rd. BS9: W Trym 1J 47
BS10: S'mead, W Trym 1J 47
BS22: W Mare 5K 105
BS34: Fil 1J 47
Southmead Way BS10: S'mead 7K 35
Southover Cl. BS9: W Trym 7G 35
Southover Rd. BS39: High L 4B 140
South Pde. BA2: Bath 5H 7 (5C 100)
BS8: Clftn 1A 4 (1H 61)
BS23: W Mare 4F 105
BS37: Yate 5E 30
BS40: Chew M 1H 115
South Pde. Cotts. *BA2: C Down 3E 122*
(off Tyning Rd.)
Sth. Plaza BS1: Bris 1F 5 (1K 61)
South Quay BS1: Bris 4H 5 (3A 62)
Southridge Hgts. BS24: W Mare 5J 127
South Rd. BA2: Tims 4F 141
BA3: Mid N 5E 152
BS3: Bedm 6J 61
BS6: Redl 6J 47
BS15: Kgswd 1B 64
BS20: P'head 1F 43
BS23: W Mare 3E 104
BS24: Lym 5K 145
BS32: Alm 7F 19
TA8: Berr, Brean 5A 144
Southsea Rd. BS34: Pat 7C 26
Southside BS23: W Mare 4G 105
BS49: Cong 6A 88
Southside Cl. BS9: C Din 7B 34
SOUTH STOKE 5B 122
Southstoke La. BA2: S'ske 5B 122
Southstoke Rd. BA2: C Down 3B 122
South St. BS3: Bedm 6H 61
TA8: Bur S 2C 158
Sth. St. M. BS3: Bedm 6H 61
South Ter. BS6: Redl 6H 47
BS23: W Mare 4F 105
TA8: Bur S 2C 158
SOUTH TWERTON 7A 6 (6K 99)
South Vw. *BA1: Bath 2C 100*
(off Camden Rd.)
BA2: C'ton D 2H 123
BA2: Mon C 3G 123
BA2: Tims 3F 141
BA3: Clan 1J 153
BS2: Bris 1E 4
BS16: Stap H 3C 50
BS20: P'head 1F 43
BS36: Fram C 7F 29
BS39: Paul 7C 140
Southview Cl. BS24: Hut 3C 128
South Vw. Cres. BS36: Coal H 1H 39
South Vw. Pl. BA2: Odd D 4J 121
BA3: Mid N 4F 153
South Vw. Ri. BS36: Coal H 1G 39
South Vw. Rd. BA2: Bath 5A 6 (5K 99)
South Vw. Ter. BS49: Yat 2H 87
SOUTHVILLE 5J 61
Southville Cl. BA15: Brad A 7J 125
Southville Pl. BS3: Bedm 5K 61
Southville Rd. BA15: Brad A 7J 125
BS3: Bedm 7D 4 (5J 61)
BS23: W Mare 1G 127
Southville Ter. BA2: Bath 7D 100
South Wlk. BS37: Yate 5E 30
South Wansdyke Sports Cen. 5F 153
Southway Ct. BS21: Clev 1D 68
Southway Dr. BS30: Old C 4H 65
Southway Rd. BA15: Brad A 7H 125
Southwell Cres. TA9: Highb 5G 159
Southwell St. BS2: Bris 1D 4 (1J 61)
SOUTH WIDCOMBE 7H 137
Southwood Av. BS9: C Din 7C 34
Southwood Dr. BS9: C Din 1B 46
Southwood Dr. E. BS9: C Din 7C 34
SOUTH WRAXALL 5J 103
Sovereign Shop. Cen. BS23: W Mare 4F 105
Spa, The
Bath 3K 7 (4E 100)
Space BS3: Bedm 1H 75
Space Health & Fitness 7E 6 (6B 100)
Spa La. BA1: Swa 1E 100
Spalding Cl. BS7: Eastv 5C 48
Spaniorum Vw. BS35: E Comp 4F 25
Sparks Way TA9: Highb 5F 159
Spar Rd. BS37: Yate 4D 30
Sparrowbill Way BS34: Pat 7C 26
Sparrow Hill Way BS26: Weare 7D 148
Sparrow La. BS20: P'head 2J 43
Spartley Dr. BS13: Bis 4F 75
Spartley Wlk. BS13: Bis 4F 75
Spaxton Cl. TA8: Bur S 7E 156
Specklemead BS39: Paul 1B 152
Spectrum Ho. BS2: Bris 1H 5 (1A 62)
SPEEDWELL 7J 49
Speedwell Av. BS5: St G 2F 63
Speedwell Cl. BS35: T'bry 2B 12
Speedwell Rd. BS5: S'wll 7H 49
BS15: Kgswd 7H 49
Spencer Dr. BA3: Mid N 4E 152
BS22: Wor 1F 107
Spencer Ho. BS1: Bris 7G 5
Spencers Belle Vue
BA1: Bath 1F 7 (3B 100)
Spencers Ct. BS35: A'ton 6K 11
Spencers Orchard BA15: Brad A 7H 125
Sperring Ct. BA3: Mid N 6D 152
Spey Cl. BS35: T'bry 4A 12
Spider La. BS23: W Mare 4F 105
Spindleberry Gro. BS48: Nail 7J 57
Spinners End BS22: Wor 7F 85

A-Z Bristol, Bath & North Somerset Atlas 199

Thatchers Cl.—Tyning

Thatchers Cl. BS5: St G . . . 2K 63
The . . . .
Names prefixed with 'The' for example 'The Academy' are indexed under the main name such as 'Academy, The'
Theatre Royal
Bristol . . . 4E 4 (3K 61)
Theatre Royal (Ustinov Studio)
Bath . . . 4F 7
There & Back Again La.
BS8: Clftn . . . 3C 4 (2J 61)
Theresa Av. BS7: Bishop . . . 4A 48
Thermae Bath Spa . . . 5F 7
Theynes Cft. BS41: L Ash . . . 1A 74
Thicket Av. BS16: Fish . . . 6K 49
THICKET MEAD . . . 4D 152
Thicket Rd. BS16: Fish . . . 4A 50
Thicket Wlk. BS35: T'bry . . . 3A 12
Thiery Rd. BS4: Brisl . . . 7E 62
Thingwall Pk. BS16: Fish . . . 5G 49
Third Av. BA2: Bath . . . 7B 6 (6K 99)
BA3: Mid N . . . 7H 153
BS7: Hor . . . 6C 36
BS14: H'gro . . . 3D 76
Third Way BS11: A'mth . . . 5F 33
Thirlmere Ct. BS30: Old C . . . 3H 65
Thirlmere Rd. BS23: W Mare . . . 1J 127
BS34: Pat . . . 6C 26
Thistle St. BS3: Bedm . . . 6H 61
Thomas Av. BS16: Emer G . . . 7F 39
Thomas Blount M. BS3: Bedm . . . 7D 4 (5J 61)
Thomas Cl. BS29: Ban . . . 2A 130
Thomas Ct. BS1: Bris . . . 5G 5
Thomas La. BS1: Bris . . . 5G 5 (3A 62)
Thomas La. Apartments BS1: Bris . . . 5G 5
Thomas Pring Wlk. BS5: St G . . . 7J 49
Thomas St. BA1: Bath . . . 1H 7 (3C 100)
BS1: Bris . . . 1A 62
BS2: Bris . . . 7B 48
BS5: Bar H . . . 2D 62
Thomas St. Nth. BS2: Bris . . . 7K 47
Thomas Way BS16: Stap . . . 1G 49
Thompson Rd. BS14: Stoc . . . 4G 77
Thompson Way BS24: W Wick . . . 4G 107
Thomson Rd. BS5: E'ton . . . 1D 62
Thornbank Gdns. BA2: Bath . . . 6E 6 (6B 100)
Thornbank Pl. BA2: Bath . . . 6D 6 (6A 100)
THORNBURY . . . 3K 11
Thornbury & District Mus. . . . 4K 11
Thornbury Dr. BS23: Uph . . . 3E 126
Thornbury Hill BS35: A'ton . . . 6J 11
Thornbury Ind. Pk. BS35: T'bry . . . 5K 11
Thornbury Leisure Cen. . . . 5K 11
THORNBURY PARK . . . 2K 11
Thornbury Rd. BS23: Uph . . . 3E 126
BS35: A'ton . . . 7J 11
Thorn Cl. BS22: Wor . . . 3F 107
BS37: Yate . . . 5D 30
Thorndale BS8: Clftn . . . 1G 61
Thorndale Cl. BS22: W Mare . . . 4B 106
Thorndale Ct. BS8: Clftn . . . 7G 47
Thorndale M. BS8: Clftn . . . 1G 61
Thorndike Way TA8: Bur S . . . 2F 159
Thorne Pk. TA8: Bur S . . . 3D 158
Thorneycroft Cl. BS7: L'lze . . . 1D 48
Thornhayes Cl. BS36: Fram C . . . 6E 28
Thornhills, The BS16: Fish . . . 2K 49
Thornleigh Rd. BS7: Hor . . . 3A 48
Thornmead Gro. BS10: Bren . . . 4G 35
Thorns Farm BS37: Yate . . . 5E 30
Thorpe Lodge *BS6: Bris* . . . *7K 47*
(off St Matthew's Rd.)
Three Brooks La. BS32: Brad S . . . 6G 27
Three Brooks Local Nature Reserve . . . 6H 27
Three Kings Ct., The BS1: Bris . . . 3E 4 (2K 61)
Three Oaks Cl. BS16: Fish . . . 4A 50
Three Queens' La. BS1: Bris . . . 5G 5 (3A 62)
Three Wells Rd. BS13: Withy . . . 6F 75
Three Yards Ct. TA9: Highb . . . 4F 159
Thrissell St. BS5: E'ton . . . 1C 62
Throgmorton Rd. BS4: Know . . . 2B 76
Thrubwell La. BS40: Redh . . . 7F 91
Thrush Cl. BS22: Wor . . . 4C 106
Thunderbolt Sq. BS1: Bris . . . 5E 4
Thunderbolt Steps BS4: Wind H . . . 5C 62
Thurlestone BS14: H'gro . . . 4B 76
Thurlow Rd. BS5: E'ton . . . 6E 48
Thurston's Barton BS5: W'hall . . . 7G 49
Thyme Cl. BS20: P'bry, P'head . . . 3H 43
Thynne Cl. BS27: Ched . . . 7H 151
Tibberton BS15: Kgswd . . . 1E 64
Tibbott Rd. BS14: Stoc . . . 5F 77
Tibbott Wlk. BS14: Stoc . . . 5E 76
Tichborne Rd. BS5: Redf . . . 2E 62
BS23: W Mare . . . 3G 105
TICKENHAM . . . 5C 56
Tickenham Drove BS21: Tic . . . 7K 55
Tickenham Hill BS21: Tic . . . 5F 57
Tickenham Rd. BS21: Clev . . . 6F 55
Ticket Mead BA3: Mid N . . . 3D 152
Tidball Cl. TA8: Bur S . . . 4C 156
Tide Gro. BS11: Law W . . . 7A 34
Tidenham Way BS34: Pat . . . 5B 26
Tiffany Ct. BS1: Bris . . . 6H 5 (4A 62)
Tiledown BS39: Temp C . . . 4H 139
Tiledown Cl. BS39: Temp C . . . 4H 139
Tileyard, The BS5: S'wll . . . 7G 49
Tilley Cl. BA2: F'boro . . . 6E 118
BS31: Key . . . 1E 96
Tilley La. BA2: F'boro . . . 7D 118
Tilling Rd. BS10: Hor . . . 1A 48
Tilling Wlk. BS10: Hor . . . 1A 48
Tilting Rd. BS35: T'bry . . . 2K 11
Timber Dene BS16: Stap . . . 4F 49
Timbers, The BA3: Mid N . . . 7F 153
Timberscombe Wlk. BS14: Whit . . . 5D 76
TIMSBURY . . . 3F 141
TIMSBURY BOTTOM . . . 4D 140
Timsbury Ind. Est. BA2: Tims . . . 2D 140
Timsbury Rd. BA2: F'boro . . . 6E 118
BS3: Know . . . 7A 62
BS39: High L . . . 4B 140
Timsbury Wlk. BS3: Know . . . 7A 62
Timswell Batch BS40: Blag . . . 2C 134
Tindell Ct. BS30: Long G . . . 5D 64
Tinding Dr. BS16: Fren . . . 7F 37
Tinker's La. BS40: Comp M . . . 6B 136
BS48: Back . . . 7D 72
Tintagel Cl. BS31: Key . . . 5B 78
Tintern Av. BS5: St G . . . 1F 63
Tintern Cl. BS30: Bar C . . . 3D 64
Tippetts Rd. BS15: Kgswd . . . 3B 64
Tirley Way BS22: W Mare . . . 2K 105
Titan Barrow BA1: Bathf . . . 1A 102
Tithe Barn
Bradford-on-Avon . . . 7G 125
Tiverton Gdns. BS22: Wor . . . 2E 106
Tiverton Rd. BS21: Clev . . . 1E 68
Tiverton Wlk. BS16: Fish . . . 6J 49
Tivoli Ho. BS23: W Mare . . . 4G 105
Tivoli La. BS23: W Mare . . . 4G 105
Tobacco Factory, The . . . 5G 61
Tobias Gdns. BS37: Yate . . . 5D 30
TOCKINGTON . . . 4D 18
Tockington Grn. BS32: Toc . . . 4D 18
Tockington La. BS32: Alm . . . 1C 26
Tockington Pk. La. BS32: Alm . . . 5G 19
Toddington Cl. BS37: Yate . . . 6D 30
Toghill La. BS30: Doy . . . 7G 53
Tolland BS24: W Mare . . . 3J 127
Toll Bri. Rd. BA1: Bathe . . . 7G 83
Toll Ho. Ct. BS3: Ash G . . . 5G 61
Toll House Gallery . . . 5C 54
Toll Rd. BS23: B'don . . . 5H 127
Tone Rd. BS21: Clev . . . 1D 68
Top Rd. BS25: S'ham . . . 6B 132
Top Yard Cotts. BA2: Bath . . . 1K 7
Tor Cl. BS22: Wor . . . 2E 106
Tormarton Cres. BS10: Hen . . . 3F 35
Tormynton Rd. BS22: Wor . . . 2C 106
Toronto Rd. BS7: Hor . . . 7B 36
Torpoint Rd. BS3: Wind H . . . 1K 75
Torrance Cl. BS30: Old C . . . 3H 65
Torridge Rd. BS31: Key . . . 6E 78
Torrington Av. BS4: Know . . . 2B 76
Torrington Cres. BS22: Wor . . . 1E 106
Tortworth Rd. BS7: Hor . . . 3A 48
Tor Vw. BS27: Ched . . . 7E 150
Tory BA15: Brad A . . . 6G 125
Tory Pl. BA15: Brad A . . . 6G 125
Totnes Cl. BS22: Wor . . . 2E 106
Totshill Dr. BS13: Hart . . . 7A 76
Totshill Gro. BS13: Hart . . . 6A 76
Tottenham Pl. BS8: Clftn . . . 3A 4 (2H 61)
TOTTERDOWN . . . 5B 62
Totterdown Bri. Trad. Est.
BS2: Bris . . . 5C 62
Totterdown La. BS24: W Mare . . . 5J 127
Totterdown Rd. BS23: W Mare . . . 1G 127
Touchstone Av. BS34: Stok G . . . 2H 37
Tourist Info. Cen.
Bath . . . 5G 7 (5C 100)
Bradford-on-Avon . . . 6H 125
Bristol . . . 5E 4 (3K 61)
Chipping Sodbury . . . 5H 31
Thornbury . . . 3K 11
Weston-Super-Mare . . . 4F 105
Tovey Cl. BS22: Kew . . . 7C 84
Tower, The BS1: Bris . . . 4G 5
Tower Cl. BS27: Ched . . . 7H 151
TOWERHEAD . . . 1E 130
Towerhead Rd. BS25: Sandf . . . 2C 130
BS29: Ban . . . 2C 130
Tower Hill BS2: Bris . . . 3H 5 (2A 62)
BS24: Lock . . . 1H 129
Tower Ho. La. BS48: Wrax . . . 4H 57
Tower La. BS1: Bris . . . 3F 5 (2K 61)
(not continuous)
BS30: Warm . . . 3E 64
Tower La. Bus. Pk. BS30: Warm . . . 3F 65
Towerleaze BS9: Stok B . . . 5D 46
Tower Rd. BS15: Kgswd . . . 7A 50
BS20: P'head . . . 4C 42
Tower Rd. Nth. BS30: Warm . . . 2F 65
Tower Rd. Sth. BS30: C Hth . . . 3F 65
Tower St. BS1: Bris . . . 5H 5 (3A 62)
Tower Wlk. BS23: W Mare . . . 3F 105
TOWNS END . . . 2C 152
TOWNSEND
BS40, CHEW STOKE . . . 4E 114
BS40, EAST HARPTREE . . . 6K 137
Townsend BS32: Alm . . . 2B 26
Townsend Cl. BS14: Stoc . . . 5H 77
Townsend La. BS32: Alm . . . 2B 26
Townsend Rd. BS14: Stoc . . . 5H 77
Townshend Rd. BS22: Wor . . . 6E 84
Town Sq. BS32: Brad S . . . 6F 27
TOWNWELL . . . 2B 14
Toynbee Rd. BS4: Know . . . 2A 76
Tozer's Hill BS4: Know . . . 7E 62
Tracy Cl. BS14: H'gro . . . 3B 76
(not continuous)
Trafalgar Ct. BS23: W Mare . . . 5G 105
Trafalgar Rd. BA1: W'ton . . . 2H 99
Trafalgar Ter. BS3: Bedm . . . 7H 61
Trafalgar Wlk. BS1: Bris . . . 2F 5 (2K 61)
Tralee Wlk. BS4: Know . . . 1K 75
Tramshed, The BA1: Bath . . . 3G 7 (4C 100)
Tramway Rd. BS4: Brisl . . . 6E 62
Tranmere Av. BS10: Bren . . . 3G 35
Tranmere Gro. BS10: Bren . . . 4G 35
Transom Ho. BS1: Bris . . . 5H 5
Tratman Wlk. BS10: Hen . . . 4F 35
Travers Cl. BS4: Know . . . 4K 75
Travers Wlk. BS34: Stok G . . . 2H 37
Trawden Cl. BS23: W Mare . . . 3J 105
Treasure Ct. TA8: Bur S . . . 6C 156
Tredegar Rd. BS16: Fish . . . 5K 49
Treefield Pl. BS2: Bris . . . 6C 48
Treefield Rd. BS21: Clev . . . 7D 54
Treeleaze BS37: Yate . . . 4F 31
Tregarth Rd. BS3: Ash V . . . 1F 75
Tregelles Ct. TA9: Highb . . . 4E 158
Trelawn Cl. BS22: St G . . . 2H 107
Trelawney Av. BS5: St G . . . 1F 63
Trelawney Pk. BS4: Brisl . . . 6F 63
Trelawney Rd. BS6: Cot . . . 7J 47
Trelissick Gdns. BS24: W'ton V . . . 4D 106
Trellick Wlk. BS16: Stap . . . 7G 37
Tremlett M. BS22: Wor . . . 7F 85
Trenchard Rd. BS24: Lock . . . 1H 129
BS31: Salt . . . 7H 79
Trenchard St. BS1: Bris . . . 3E 4 (2J 61)
Trench La. BS32: Alm . . . 4G 27
BS36: Wint . . . 4G 27
Trendlewood Pk. BS16: Stap . . . 4G 49
Trendlewood Way BS48: Nail . . . 7J 57
Trenleigh Dr. BS22: Wor . . . 1D 106
Trent Dr. BS35: T'bry . . . 5B 12
Trent Gro. BS31: Key . . . 6E 78
Trentham Cl. BS2: Bris . . . 6C 48
Trescothick Cl. BS31: Key . . . 4B 78
Trescothick Dr. BS30: Old C . . . 5H 65
Tresham Cl. BS32: Brad S . . . 4F 27
Trevelyan Rd. BS23: W Mare . . . 5H 105
Trevelyan Wlk. BS10: Hen . . . 4F 35
BS34: Stok G . . . 2J 37
Trevenna Rd. BS3: Ash V . . . 1F 75
Treverdowe Wlk. BS10: Hen . . . 4D 34
Trevethin Cl. BS15: Kgswd . . . 2A 64
Trevisa Gro. BS10: Bren . . . 3J 35
Trewartha Cl. BS23: W Mare . . . 4H 105
Trewartha Pk. BS23: W Mare . . . 4H 105
Trewint Gdns. BS4: Know . . . 2B 76
Triangle, The
BS20: P'head . . . 3D 42
BS21: Clev . . . 6D 54
BS39: Paul . . . 7C 140
BS40: Wrin . . . 2F 111
Triangle Ct. BA2: Bath . . . 6A 6
Triangle E. BA2: Bath . . . 6A 6 (6K 99)
Triangle Nth. BA2: Bath . . . 6A 6 (5K 99)
Triangle Sth. BS8: Clftn . . . 3B 4 (2H 61)
Triangle Vs. BA2: Bath . . . 6A 6 (6K 99)
Triangle Wlk. BS8: Clftn . . . 3B 4
Triangle W. BA2: Bath . . . 6A 6 (6K 99)
BS8: Clftn . . . 3B 4 (2H 61)
Trident Cl. BS16: Down . . . 6E 38
Trim Bri. BA1: Bath . . . 4F 7 (5B 100)
Trim St. BA1: Bath . . . 4F 7 (5B 100)
Trinder Rd. BS20: Eas . . . 4F 45
Trinity Cl. BA1: Bath . . . 5E 6 (5B 100)
BS39: Paul . . . 7B 140
TA8: Bur S . . . 6C 156
Trinity Ct. BS15: Kgswd . . . 1C 64
BS48: Nail . . . 1E 70
Trinity La. BS37: Chip S . . . 4J 31
Trinity M. BS2: Bris . . . 3J 5
Trinity Office Pk. BS7: Hor . . . 1B 48
Trinity Pl. BA1: Bath . . . 4E 6 (5B 100)
BS8: Clftn . . . *3G 61*
(off Charles Pl.)
BS23: W Mare . . . 3E 104
(not continuous)
Trinity Quay BS2: Bris . . . 4J 5 (3B 62)
Trinity Ri. TA8: Bur S . . . 6C 156
Trinity Rd. BA2: C Down . . . 2D 122
BS2: Bris . . . 2K 5 (2C 62)
BS23: W Mare . . . 3E 104
BS48: Nail . . . 1E 70
Trinity St. BA1: Bath . . . 5F 7 (5B 100)
BS1: Bris . . . 5D 4 (3J 61)
BS2: Bris . . . 2C 62
Trinity Theological College . . . 4E 46
Trinity Wlk. BS2: Bris . . . 2K 5 (2B 62)
Trin Mills BS1: Bris . . . 6F 5 (4K 61)
Tripps Cnr. BS49: Yat . . . 4K 87
Tripps Row BS41: L Ash . . . 1A 74
Troon BS37: Yate . . . 6E 30
Troon Dr. BS30: Warm . . . 3F 65
Trooper's Hill Rd. BS5: St G . . . 3H 63
Tropical Bird Garden . . . 3B 126
Trossachs Dr. BA2: Bath . . . 3F 101
Trowbridge Cl. TA9: Highb . . . 4F 159
Trowbridge Rd.
BA15: Brad A . . . 6H 125
BS10: S'mead . . . 6J 35
Trowbridge Wlk. BS10: S'mead . . . 6J 35
Trubshaw Cl. BS7: Hor . . . 2B 48
Trumpet La. BS5: St G . . . 2K 63
Truro Cl. TA8: Bur S . . . 1E 158
Truro Rd. BS3: Ash G . . . 6H 61
BS48: Nail . . . 2J 71
Trym Cross Rd. BS9: Sea M . . . 3C 46
Trym Leaze BS9: Sea M . . . 3C 46
Trym Rd. BS9: W Trym . . . 7G 35
Trym Side BS9: Sea M . . . 3C 46
Trymwood Cl. BS10: Hen . . . 5F 35
Trymwood Pde. BS9: Stok B . . . 2D 46
TT Trad. Est. BS37: Chip S . . . 5H 31
Tucker's La. BS40: Ubl . . . 4J 135
Tucker St. BS2: Bris . . . 2J 5 (2B 62)
Tuckett Ho. BS16: Fren . . . 1A 50
Tuckett La. BS16: Fren . . . 1A 50
Tuckingmill La. BS39: Comp D . . . 6C 96
Tuckmill BS21: Clev . . . 1B 68
Tudor Cl. BS30: Old C . . . 6G 65
Tudor Rd. BS2: Bris . . . 7B 48
BS5: E'ton . . . 7E 48
BS15: Han . . . 4A 64
BS20: P'head . . . 4G 43
BS22: Wor . . . 7E 84
Tuffley Rd. BS10: W Trym . . . 7J 35
Tufton Av. BS11: Law W . . . 7A 34
Tugela Rd. BS13: Bis . . . 3F 75
Tumps Nature Area, The . . . 5B 26
Tunbridge Cl. BS40: Chew M . . . 2H 115
Tunbridge Rd. BS40: Chew M . . . 1H 115
Tunbridge Way BS16: Emer G . . . 7E 38
TUNLEY . . . 2A 142
Tunley Hill BA2: Cam . . . 3J 141
Tunley Rd. BA2: Tun . . . 1B 142
Tunstall Cl. BS9: Stok B . . . 4E 46
TURLEIGH . . . 6D 124
Turley Rd. BS5: E'ton . . . 7F 49
Turnberry BS30: Warm . . . 3F 65
BS37: Yate . . . 6E 30
Turnberry Wlk. BS4: Brisl . . . 1F 77
Turnbridge Cl. BS10: Bren . . . 4J 35
Turnbridge Rd. BS10: Bren . . . 4J 35
Turnbury Av. BS48: Nail . . . 1J 71
Turnbury Cl. BS22: Wor . . . 1D 106
Turner Cl. BS31: Key . . . 5E 78
Turner Ct. BS22: Wor . . . 1D 106
Turner Dr. BS37: Yate . . . 5B 30
Turner Gdns. BS7: L'lze . . . 2D 48
Turners Ct. BS30: Long G . . . 5D 64
Turner's Twr. BA3: Hem . . . 5G 155
Turner Wlk. BS30: B'yte . . . 2H 65
Turner Way BS21: Clev . . . 1B 68
Turnock Gdns. BS24: W Wick . . . 4G 107
Turnpike Cl. BS25: C'hll . . . 1B 132
BS37: Yate . . . 4E 30
Turnpike Ga. GL12: Wickw . . . 6G 15
Turnpike Rd. BS25: S'ham . . . 5A 132
BS26: L Wre . . . 7C 148
Turnstone Av. BS20: P'head . . . 2H 43
Turtlegate Av. BS13: Withy . . . 6E 74
Turtlegate Wlk. BS13: Withy . . . 6E 74
Turville Dr. BS7: Hor . . . 2C 48
Tuscany Ho. BS6: Redl . . . 5G 47
Tutton Way BS21: Clev . . . 2D 68
Tuttors Hill BS27: Ched . . . 5E 150
Tweed Cl. BS35: T'bry . . . 4A 12
Tweed Rd. BS21: Clev . . . 1C 68
Tweed Rd. Ind. Est.
BS21: Clev . . . 1C 68
Tweentown BS27: Ched . . . 6D 150
Tweeny La. BS30: Old C . . . 3H 65
Twelveacres Cl. BS39: Paul . . . 7B 140
Twelve O'Clock La.
BA2: New L . . . 2B 120
Twenty Acres Rd.
BS10: S'mead . . . 5H 35
TWERTON . . . 5A 6 (6J 99)
Twerton Farm Cl. BA2: Bath . . . 5H 99
TWERTON HILL . . . 1G 121
Twerton Pk. . . . 6H 99
Twickenham Rd. BS6: Henle . . . 3J 47
Twinhoe La. BA2: Well . . . 3K 143
Twinnell Ho. BS5: E'ton . . . 1C 62
Two Acres Rd. BS14: H'gro . . . 2C 76
Two Mile Ct. BS15: Kgswd . . . 1K 63
TWO MILE HILL . . . 1K 63
Two Mile Hill Rd. BS15: Kgswd . . . 1J 63
Two Stones La. BS37: Chip S . . . 6J 31
Two Trees BS40: Blag . . . 4B 134
Twynings, The BS15: Kgswd . . . 6C 50
Tybalt Way BS34: Stok G . . . 2G 37
Tydeman Rd. BS20: P'head . . . 3H 43
Tydings Cl. BS41: L Ash . . . 1A 74
Tyler Cl. BS15: Han . . . 4C 64
Tyler Grn. BS22: Wor . . . 7F 85
Tylers End TA9: Highb . . . 5H 159
Tylers Farm BS37: Yate . . . 2F 31
Tylers La. BS16: Stap H . . . 3B 50
Tyler St. BS2: Bris . . . 3C 62
Tylers Way BS37: Yate . . . 1F 31
Tyler Way TA9: Highb . . . 5F 159
Tyndale Av. BS16: Fish . . . 4K 49
BS37: Yate . . . 3D 30
Tyndale Ct. *BS6: Redl* . . . *7H 47*
(off Chertsey Rd.)
Tyndale Rd. BS15: Soun . . . 6C 50
Tyndale Vw. BS35: T'bry . . . 4K 11
Tyndall Av. BS8: Clftn . . . 2C 4 (2J 61)
Tyndall Ho. BS2: Bris . . . 2J 5
Tyndall Rd. BS5: E'ton . . . 1D 62
TYNDALL'S PARK . . . 2B 4 (2H 61)
Tyndalls Pk. M.
BS2: Bris . . . 1C 4 (1J 61)
Tyndall's Pk. Rd.
BS8: Clftn . . . 1B 4 (1H 61)
Tyndalls Way
BS10: S'mead . . . 7A 36
Tyne Gro. BS20: P'head . . . 2H 43
Tyne Path BS7: Bishop . . . 6K 47
Tyne Rd. BS7: Bishop . . . 5K 47
Tyne St. BS2: Bris . . . 6C 48
TYNING
BA2 . . . 3E 140
BA3 . . . 3A 154

Tyning, The—Walkers Dr.

Tyning, The BA2: Bath 7K 7 (6D 100)
BA2: F'frd 7K 123
Tyning Cl. BS14: H'gro 3C 76
BS37: Yate 4E 30
Tyning End BA2: Bath 6K 7 (6D 100)
Tyning Hill BA3: Hem 7J 155
BA3: Rads 3A 154
Tyning La. BA1: Bath 2D 100
BS39: Stan D 2A 116
Tyning Pl. BA2: C Down 2E 122
Tyning Rd. BA2: Batham 1H 101
BA2: C Down 2E 122
BA2: Pea J 6C 142
BA15: W'ley 5C 124
BS3: Wind H 6B 62
BS31: Salt 1J 97
Tynings BS39: Clut 2F 139
Tynings, The BS20: W'ton G 7B 42
BS21: Clev 1A 68
Tyning's La. BS36: Wint 4A 28
Tynings M. BS23: W Mare 1G 127
Tynings Way BS39: Clut 2G 139
Tyning Ter. *BA1: Bath 2D 100*
(off Fairfield Rd.)
Tynte Av. BS13: Hart 7K 75
Tyntesfield 5D 58
Tyntesfield Park 6D 58
Tyntesfield Rd. BS13: Bis 3G 75
Tyrone Wlk. BS4: Know 2A 76
Tyrrel Way BS34: Stok G 2G 37
TYTHERINGTON 7F 13
Tytherington Rd. BS35: Grov 5D 12
GL12: Tyth 5D 12

U

UBLEY 4H 135
Ubley Drove BS40: Blag 7E 134
BS40: Ubl 5G 135
UBLEY SIDELING 5H 135
UDLEY 7E 88
Ullswater Cl. BS23: W Mare 1J 127
BS30: Old C 3H 65
BS37: Yate 3E 30
Ullswater Dr. BA1: Bath 1C 100
Ullswater Rd. BS10: S'mead 6H 35
Uncombe Cl. BS48: Back 3B 72
Underbanks BS20: Pill 4H 45
Underdown Ho. BS1: Bris 7F 5 (4K 61)
Underhill Av. BA3: Mid N 4D 152
Underhill Dr. BS23: Uph 3F 127
Underhill La. BA3: Mid N 5B 152
Under Knoll BA2: Pea J 4E 142
Under La. BS40: Redh 3B 112
Underleaf Way BA2: Pea J 6D 142
Undertown BS40: Comp M 6A 136
Undertown La. BS40: Comp M 6A 136
Underwood Av. BS22: W Mare 3K 105
Underwood Cl. BS35: A'ton 1J 19
Underwood End BS25: Sandf 1G 131
Underwood Rd. BS20: P'head 5E 42
Unicorn Bus. Pk. BS4: Brisl 4F 63
Unicorn Pk. Av. BS4: Brisl 4E 62
Union Pas. BA1: Bath 4G 7 (5C 100)
Union Pl. BS23: W Mare 5F 105
Union Rd. BS2: Bris 4K 5 (3C 62)
(not continuous)
Union St. BA1: Bath 4G 7 (5C 100)
BS1: Bris 2F 5 (2K 61)
BS23: W Mare 5F 105
BS27: Ched 7D 150
BS48: Nail 7E 56
Union Ter. BA2: Bath 6F 7
Unite Ho. BS1: Bris 4D 4
Unity Ct. BS31: Key 5E 78
Unity Rd. BS31: Key 5E 78
(not continuous)
Unity St. BS1: Bris 4D 4 (3J 61)
BS2: Bris 3J 5 (2B 62)
BS15: Kgswd 1A 64
University Cl. BS9: Stok B 4F 47
University Hall BS9: Stok B 4F 47
University of Bath 6G 101
University of Bath Sports Training Village 6H 101
University of Bristol
Botanic Garden 4F 47
Cantock's Cl. 2D 4 (2J 61)
Canynge Hall 7H 47
(off Whatley Rd.)
Cobham House 1J 61
Department of Clinical Veterinary Science 6D 110
Dorothy Hodgkin Building 1F 5
Graduate School of Education 3C 4 (2J 61)
Hampton House 1J 61
ILRT 3B 4 (2H 61)
Library 1D 4
Priory Rd. Complex 1B 4 (1H 61)
Queen's Rd. 3C 4 (2J 61)
School of Medical Sciences 1D 4 (1J 61)
The Victoria Rooms 2A 4 (2H 61)
University of the West of England
Bower Ashton Campus 5D 60
Frenchay Campus 7G 37
Glenside Campus 3G 49
University Rd. BS8: Clftn 3C 4 (2J 61)
University Wlk. BS8: Clftn 2C 4 (2J 61)
UPHILL 3F 127
Uphill Dr. BA1: Bath 1D 100
Uphill Pk. Homes BS23: Uph 4G 127
Uphill Rd. BS7: Hor 3B 48
Uphill Rd. Nth. BS23: W Mare 1F 127
Uphill Rd. Sth. BS23: Uph 2F 127
Uphill Way BS23: Uph 3F 127
Upjohn Cres. BS13: Hart 7K 75
Uplands, The BS48: Nail 3E 70
Uplands Cl. BA2: Lim S 5H 123
Uplands Dr. BS31: Salt 1K 97
Uplands Rd. BS16: Fish 5A 50
BS31: Salt 1J 97
Up. Bath Rd. BS35: T'bry 4K 11
Up. Belgrave Rd. BS8: Clftn 6G 47
Up. Belmont Rd. BS7: Bishop 5A 48
Up. Berkeley Pl. BS8: Clftn 3B 4 (2H 61)
Up. Bloomfield Rd. BA2: Odd D 4J 121
Up. Borough Walls BA1: Bath 4F 7 (5B 100)
Up. Bristol Rd. BA1: Bath 3A 6 (4J 99)
BS22: W Mare 3J 105
BS39: Clut 3F 139
Upper Bldgs. BA2: S'ske 5B 122
Up. Byron Pl. BS8: Clftn 3B 4 (2H 61)
Up. Camden Pl. BA1: Bath 3C 100
UPPER CANADA 4E 128
Up. Chapel La. BS36: Fram C 7G 29
Up. Cheltenham Pl. BS6: Bris 7A 48
Up. Church La. BS2: Bris 3D 4 (2J 61)
BS24: Hut 4B 128
Up. Church Rd. BS23: W Mare 4E 104
Up. Church St. BA1: Bath 2E 6 (4B 100)
Up. Conham Va. BS15: St G 4J 63
Upper Ct. BA3: Mid N 6G 153
Up. Cranbrook Rd. BS6: Henle, Redl 4H 47
Up. East Hayes BA1: Bath 2D 100
UPPER EASTON 1D 62
UPPER EASTVILLE 5G 49
Upper Furlong BA2: Tims 2F 141
Up. Green La. BS40: But 4E 112
Up. Hedgemead Rd.
BA1: Bath 1F 7 (3B 100)
Up. Kewstoke Rd. BS23: W Mare 3D 104
Up. Kingsdown Rd. SN13: Kgdn 1D 102
UPPER KNOWLE 6D 62
Up. Lambridge St. BA1: Bath 1E 100
UPPER LANGFORD 1D 132
Up. Lansdown M. BA1: Bath 2B 100
UPPER LITTLETON 5C 92
Up. Maudlin St. BS2: Bris 2E 4 (2K 61)
Upper Mill BA15: Brad A 6J 125
UPPER MORTON 1B 12
Up. Myrtle Hill *BS20: Pill 4G 45*
(off Myrtle Hill)
Up. New Rd. BS27: Ched 5B 150
Upper Nth. St. BS27: Ched 6D 150
Up. Oldfield Pk. BA2: Bath 6C 6 (6A 100)
Up. Perry Hill BS3: Bris 7C 4 (5J 61)
UPPER RADFORD 5F 141
Up. Regents Pk. BA15: Brad A 6H 125
Upper Rd. BS39: Hin B 7A 138
Up. Sandhurst Rd. BS4: Brisl 5F 63
UPPER SOUNDWELL 5B 50
Upper Stanton BS39: Stan D 2B 116
UPPER STANTON DREW 2C 116
Up. Station Rd. BS16: Stap H 4A 50
Up. Stone Cl. BS36: Fram C 7G 29
Upper St. BS4: Wind H 5C 62
SN14: Dyr 4K 53
Upper Strode BS40: Up Str 6J 113
UPPER SWAINSWICK 5D 82
Up. Sydney St. BS3: Bedm 6H 61
Up. Tockington Rd. BS32: Toc 3C 18
UPPER TOWN 3G 91
Up. Town La. BS40: F'tn 3G 91
Up. Wells St. BS1: Bris 3D 4 (2J 61)
UPPER WESTON 7H 81
Up. York St. BS2: Bris 1G 5 (1A 62)
Upton BS24: W Mare 3J 127
UPTON CHEYNEY 2A 80
Upton La. BS41: Dun 2F 93
Upton Rd. BS3: Bris 5H 61
Urchinwood La. BS49: Cong 1B 110
Urfords Dr. BS16: Fish 2A 50
Usk Ct. BS35: T'bry 4A 12

V

Valda Rd. BS22: W Mare 2A 106
Vale Ct. BS8: Clftn 1G 61
Vale Cres. BS22: St G 2G 107
Vale End BS48: Nail 1F 71
Vale Foundry La. BS3: Ash V 7F 61
Vale La. BS3: Bedm 2J 75
Vale Mill Way BS24: W'ton V 4D 106
Valentine Cl. BS14: H'gro 5D 76
Valerian Cl. BS11: Shire 2K 45
Vale St. BS4: Wind H 6C 62
Valetta Cl. BS23: W Mare 2H 127
Vale Vw. BA3: Rads 4A 154
Vale Vw. Pl. BA1: Bath 2D 100
Vale Vw. Ter. BA1: Bathe 7H 83
Valley Cl. BS48: Nail 7G 57
Valley Ct. BS20: P'head 5A 42
Valley Gdns. BS16: Down 7D 38
BS48: Nail 7G 57
Valley Hgts. BS13: Bis 3G 75
Valley Line Ind. Pk. BS27: Ched 7C 150
Valley Rd. BS8: L Wds 2C 60
BS13: Bis 2G 75
BS16: Mang 3E 50
BS20: P'head, W'ton G 5A 42
BS21: Clev 4F 55
BS30: Old C 3H 65
Valley Vw. BS39: Clut 2G 139
Valley Vw. Cl. BA1: Bath 1D 100
Valley Vw. Rd. BA1: Charl, Swa 7D 82
BS39: Paul 7C 140
Valley Wlk. BA3: Mid N 4F 153
Valley Way Rd. BS48: Nail 6G 57
Valls, The BS32: Brad S 1H 37
Valma Rocks BS5: St G 3J 63
Vanbrugh Gdns. BS11: Law W 7K 33
Vanbrugh La. BS16: Stap 1G 49
Van Diemen's La. BA1: L'dwn 1A 100
Vandyck Av. BS31: Key 4D 78
Vane St. BA2: Bath 3J 7 (4D 100)
Vantage Ct. Office Pk. BS16: Brad S 1J 37
Vantage Office Pk. BS16: Brad S 1J 37
Vardy Ct. TA9: Highb 5F 159
Varsity Way BS24: Lock 6F 107
Vassall Ct. BS16: Fish 3K 49
Vassall Rd. BS16: Fish 3K 49
Vattingstone La. BS35: A'ton 7G 11
Vaughan Cl. BS10: Hen 4F 35
Vauxhall Av. BS3: Bris 5G 61
Vauxhall Ter. BS3: Bris 5G 61
Vauxhall Vs. *BS3: Bris 5G 61*
(off Walter St.)
Vayre Cl. BS37: Chip S 5J 31
Veale, The BS24: B'don 7A 128
Vee La. BS40: F'tn, Winf 3H 91
Vellore La. BA2: Bath 3K 7 (4D 100)
Venns Cl. BS27: Ched 7D 150
Venns Ga. BS27: Ched 5C 150
Ventnor Av. BS5: St G 1H 63
Ventnor Rd. BS5: S'wll, St G 7H 49
BS34: Fil 4D 36
Venton Ct. *BS15: Han 4K 63*
(off Henbury Rd.)
Venue, The BS10: Pat 1J 35
Venus La. BS39: Clut 3G 139
Venus St. BS49: Cong 2A 110
Vera Rd. BS16: Fish 6H 49
Verbena Way BS22: Wor 3E 106
Verde Cl. BS16: Soun 6B 50
Verdigris BS2: Bris 3J 5
Vereland Rd. BS24: Hut 2C 128
Verlands BS49: Cong 6A 88
Vernham Gro. BA2: Odd D 3J 121
Vernhamwood Cl. BA2: Odd D 3J 121
Vernon Cl. BS31: Salt 7H 79
Vernon La. BS26: Comp B 3B 148
Vernon Pk. BA2: Bath 5J 99
Vernon St. BS4: Wind H 5B 62
Vernon Ter. BA2: Bath 5J 99
Vernslade BA1: W'ton 1G 99
Verona Ho. BS16: Fish 4K 49
Verrier Rd. BS5: Redf 2E 62
Verwood Dr. BS30: Bit 1G 79
Vestry Hall BS5: E'ton 1K 5
Vestry La. BS5: E'ton 1K 5 (1B 62)
Vian End BS22: Wor 7D 84
Vibe BS2: Bris 2K 5
Viburnum Rd. BS32: Alm 1F 27
Vicarage Cl. BS22: Wor 1E 106
Vicarage Ct. *BS5: Redf 2E 62*
(off Victoria Av.)
BS15: Han 4K 63
TA8: Bur S 1C 158
Vicarage Gdns. BA2: Pea J 6B 142
Vicarage La. BS26: Comp B 3B 148
BS32: Old D 2C 18
BS35: Olv 2C 18
BS39: Comp D 5B 96
BS48: Bar G 4G 73
Vicarage Rd. BS3: Bris 5H 61
BS5: E'ton 1E 62
BS8: L Wds 3D 60
BS13: Bis 4F 75
BS15: Han 4K 63
BS35: Piln 6C 16
BS36: Coal H 2G 39
Vicarage St. TA8: Bur S 1C 158
Vicars Cl. BS16: Fish 4K 49
Victor Ho. BS34: Lit S 7E 26
Victoria Art Gallery 4G 7 (5C 100)
Victoria Av. BS5: Redf 2E 62
Victoria Bri. Ct. BA1: Bath 3C 6
Victoria Bri. Rd. BA1: Bath 3C 6 (5A 100)
BA2: Bath 4C 6 (5A 100)
Victoria Bldgs. BA2: Bath 4B 6 (5K 99)
Victoria Bldgs. M. BA2: Bath 4B 6
Victoria Cl. BA2: Bath 6J 99
BS20: P'head 3F 43
BS35: T'bry 1K 11
Victoria Ct. BS6: Redl 6G 47
BS20: P'head 3F 43
Victoria Cres. BS35: Sev B 7A 16
Victoria Gdns. BA1: Bathe 7H 83
BS6: Cot 7K 47
Victoria Gro. BS3: Bedm 5A 62
Victoria Ho. BA1: W'ton 1A 6 (3K 99)
BS31: Key 6D 78
Victoria Pde. BS5: Redf 1E 62
VICTORIA PARK 1A 4 (1H 61)
Victoria Pk. BS15: Kgswd 1B 64
BS16: Fish 3J 49
BS23: W Mare 3F 105
Victoria Pk. Bus. Cen.
BA1: Bath 3A 6 (4K 99)
Victoria Pk. Ct. *BS3: Wind H 6B 62*
(off St Johns La.)
Victoria Pl. *BA1: Bath 2E 100*
(off St Saviours Rd.)
BA2: C Down 3E 122
BA2: S'ske 5B 122
Victoria Pl. BS3: Bedm 5J 61
BS5: St G 2F 63
(off Pilemarsh)
BS23: W Mare 4F 105
BS39: Paul 1B 152
TA9: Highb 5F 159
Victoria Quad. BS23: W Mare 4G 105
Victoria Rd. BA2: Bath 5B 6 (5K 99)
BS2: Bris 4C 62
(not continuous)
BS11: A'mth 7F 33
BS15: Han 4A 64
BS21: Clev 6C 54
BS30: Old C 4G 65
BS31: Salt 7H 79
Victoria Sq. BS8: Clftn 2G 61
BS20: P'head 3F 43
BS23: W Mare 5F 105
Victoria St. BS1: Bris 4G 5 (3A 62)
BS16: Stap H 4B 50
TA8: Bur S 1C 158
Victoria Ter. BA2: Bath 5B 6 (5K 99)
BS2: Bris 4D 62
BS8: Clftn 3F 61
BS39: Paul 7C 140
Victoria Wlk. BS6: Bris, Cot 7K 47
Victor Rd. BS3: Bedm 6J 61
Victor St. BS2: Bris 7K 5 (5C 62)
BS5: Bar H 3D 62
View, The BS23: W Mare 3G 105
Vigor Rd. BS13: Hart 5H 75
VILLA FIELDS 3D 100
VILLAGE, THE 4B 10
Village, The BS16: Emer G 1G 51
Village Cl. BS37: Yate 5D 30
Village Farm BS35: E Comp 4G 25
Villa Rosa BS23: W Mare 3E 104
Villice La.
BS40: Chew S, Comp M, Ubl 6A 136
Villiers Rd. BS5: E'ton 7D 48
Vilner La. BS35: T'bry 5K 11
Vimpany Cl. BS10: Hen 4F 35
Vimpennys La. BS35: E Comp 5D 24
Vincent Cl. BS11: Law W 5C 34
TA8: Bur S 1E 158
Vincent Ct. BS16: Soun 5B 50
Vine Acres BS7: Hor 3C 48
Vine Cotts. BA15: Brad A 6G 125
Vine Gdns. BS22: Wor 2E 106
Vinery, The BS25: Wins 6G 131
Vines Ind. Est. BS48: Nail 6J 57
Vineyards BA1: Bath 2G 7 (4C 100)
Vining Wlk. BS5: E'ton 1D 62
Vinney La. BS37: Hort 4K 23
Vinny Av. BS16: Down 1E 50
VINNY GREEN 1E 50
Vintery Leys BS10: W Trym 1H 47
Virginia Cl. BS37: Chip S 5G 31
Vision BS6: Henle 4G 47
Vivian St. BS3: Wind H 6K 61
Vivien Av. BA3: Mid N 4E 152
Vowell Cl. BS13: Withy 6H 75
Vowles Cl. BS48: Wrax 6J 57
Voyager Cl. BS34: Stok G 3J 37
Vue Cinema
Cribbs Causeway 1J 35
Kingswood 4C 64
Vulcan Ho. BA2: Bath 2H 7 (4C 100)
Vynes Cl. BS48: Nail 1J 71
Vynes Way BS48: Nail 1J 71
Vyvyan Rd. BS8: Clftn 2G 61
Vyvyan Ter. BS8: Clftn 2G 61

W

Wade Ct. BS2: Bris 1K 5 (1B 62)
Wadehurst Ind. Pk. BS2: Bris 2C 62
Wade Rd. BS37: Iron A 3A 30
Wades Rd. BS34: Fil 4D 36
Wade St. BS2: Bris 1J 5 (1B 62)
Wadham Dr. BS16: Fren 6K 37
Wadham Gro. BS16: Emer G 3F 51
Wadham St. BS23: W Mare 4F 105
Wagtail Cres. BS20: P'head 2J 43
Wagtail Gdns. BS22: Wor 4C 106
Wainblade Ct. BS37: Yate 1F 31
Wainbridge Cres. BS35: Piln 6C 16
Wainbrook Dr. BS5: Eastv 6F 49
Wains Cl. BS21: Clev 7C 54
Wainwright Cl. BS22: Wor 7F 85
Waits Cl. BS29: Ban 2K 129
Wakedean Gdns. BS49: Yat 2G 87
Wakeford Rd. BS16: Down 1E 50
Wakeford Way BS30: B'yte 2H 65
Wakehurst Gdns. BS24: W'ton V 5C 106
Walcot Bldgs. BA1: Bath 1H 7 (3C 100)
Walcot Ct. BA1: Bath 1H 7 (3C 100)
Walcot Ga. BA1: Bath 1G 7 (3C 100)
Walcot Ho. BA1: Bath 3C 100
Walcot Pde. BA1: Bath 1G 7
Walcot St. BA1: Bath 3G 7 (4C 100)
Walcot Ter. BA1: Bath 1H 7 (3C 100)
Waldegrave Rd. BA1: Bath 2A 100
Waldegrave Ter. BA3: Rads 3A 154
Walden Rd. BS31: Key 6E 78
Walford Av. BS22: St G, Wor 7F 85
Walk, The GL9: Ing C 7K 15
GL12: Wickw 7K 15
Walker Cl. BS5: E'ton 1D 62
BS16: Down 1E 50
BS37: Yate 5B 30
Walkers Dr. BS24: W'ton V 5D 106

SAFETY CAMERA INFORMATION

PocketGPSWorld.com's CamerAlert is a self-contained speed and red light camera warning system for
SatNavs and Android or Apple iOS smartphones/tablets. Visit www.cameralert.com to download.

Safety camera locations are publicised by the Safer Roads Partnership which operates them in order to encourage drivers to comply
with speed limits at these sites. It is the driver's absolute responsibility to be aware of and to adhere to speed limits at all times.

By showing this safety camera information it is the intention of Geographers' A-Z Map Company Ltd. to encourage
safe driving and greater awareness of speed limits and vehicle speed. Data accurate at time of printing.

HOSPITALS, HOSPICES and selected HEALTHCARE FACILITIES covered by this atlas.

N.B. Where it is not possible to name these facilities on the map,
the reference given is for the road in which they are situated.

BATH BMI CLINIC 2F **123**
Claverton Down Road
Combe Down
BATH
BA2 7BR
Tel: 01225 835555

BLACKBERRY HILL HOSPITAL 3H **49**
Manor Road
Fishponds
BRISTOL
BS16 2EW
Tel: 0117 3784441

BRISTOL DENTAL HOSPITAL 2E **4** (2K **61**)
Lower Maudlin Street
BRISTOL
BS1 2LY
Tel: 0117 342 4383

BRISTOL EYE HOSPITAL 2F **5** (2K **61**)
Lower Maudlin Street
BRISTOL
BS1 2LX
Tel: 0117 9230060

BRISTOL HAEMATOLOGY & ONCOLOGY CENTRE
. . . . .2E **4** (2K **61**)
Horfield Road
BRISTOL
BS2 8ED
Tel: 0117 923 0000

BRISTOL HOMEOPATHIC HOSPITAL 5B **76**
Whitchurch Lane
BRISTOL
BS14 0DE
Tel: 0117 342 9832

BRISTOL NUFFIELD HOSPITAL AT THE CHESTERFIELD
. . . . .3G **61**
Upper Byron Place
BRISTOL
BS8 1BN
Tel: 01179 119587

BRISTOL PRIORY GRANGE HOSPITAL 4D **48**
Heath House Lane
Stapleton
BRISTOL
BS16 1EQ
Tel: 0117 952 5255

BRISTOL ROYAL HOSPITAL FOR CHILDREN 2E **4** (2K **61**)
Upper Maudlin Street
BRISTOL
BS2 8BJ
Tel: 0117 342 8460

BRISTOL ROYAL INFIRMARY 1E **4** (1K **61**)
Upper Maudlin Street
BRISTOL
BS2 8HW
Tel: 0117 923 0000

BRISTOL SPIRE HOSPITAL 6G **47**
Redland Hill
Redland
BRISTOL
BS6 6UT
Tel: 0117 980 4000

BROADWAY LODGE 4J **127**
37 Totterdown Lane
WESTON-SUPER-MARE
BS24 9NN
Tel: 01934 812319

BURNHAM-ON-SEA WAR MEMORIAL HOSPITAL 1D **158**
6 Love Lane
BURNHAM-ON-SEA
TA8 1ED
Tel: 01278 773100

CALLINGTON ROAD HOSPITAL 1E **76**
Marmalade Lane
BRISTOL
BS4 5BJ
Tel: 0117 919 5600

CHILDREN'S HOSPICE S.W. CHARLTON FARM 1A **58**
Charlton Drive
Wraxall
BRISTOL
BS48 1PE
Tel: 01275 866600

CIRCLE BATH HOSPITAL 7E **142**
Foxcote Avenue
Bath Business Park
PEASEDOWN ST JOHN
BA2 8SQ
Tel: 01761 422222

CLEVEDON HOSPITAL 6E **54**
Old Street
CLEVEDON
BS21 6BS
Tel: 01275 872212

COSSHAM MEMORIAL HOSPITAL 6A **50**
Lodge Road
BRISTOL
BS15 1LF
Tel: 0117 3408400

DOROTHY HOUSE HOSPICE CARE 6B **124**
Winsley
BRADFORD-ON-AVON
BA15 2LE
Tel: 01225 722988

FRENCHAY HOSPITAL 7K **37**
Frenchay Park Road
BRISTOL
BS16 1LE
Tel: 0117 970 1212

KEWSTOKE CYGNET HOSPITAL 1J **105**
Beach Road
Kewstoke
WESTON-SUPER-MARE
BS22 9UZ
Tel: 01934 428989

MINOR INJURIES UNIT (BURNHAM-ON-SEA) 1D **158**
Burnham-on-Sea War Memorial Hospital
6 Love Lane
BURNHAM-ON-SEA
TA8 1ED
Tel: 01278 773100

MINOR INJURIES UNIT (CLEVEDON) 6E **54**
Clevedon Hospital
Old Street
CLEVEDON
BS21 6BS
Tel: 01275 872212

NHS WALK-IN CENTRE (BRISTOL - SOUTH) 5B **76**
Whitchurch Lane
BRISTOL
BS14 0DE
Tel: 0117 3429692

NHS WALK-IN CENTRE (BROADMEAD MEDICAL CENTRE)
. . . . .2G **5**
59 Broadmead
BRISTOL
BS1 3EA
Tel: 0117 9549828

PAULTON MEMORIAL HOSPITAL 2D **152**
Salisbury Road
Paulton
BRISTOL
BS39 7SB
Tel: 01761 412315

ROBERT SMITH UNIT DAY HOSPITAL 2G **61**
12 Mortimer Road
BRISTOL
BS8 4EX
Tel: 0117 973 5004

ROYAL NATIONAL HOSPITAL FOR RHEUMATIC DISEASES
. . . . .4F **7** (5B **100**)
Upper Borough Walls
BATH
BA1 1RL
Tel: 01225 465941

ROYAL UNITED HOSPITAL 3H **99**
Combe Park
BATH
BA1 3NG
Tel: 01225 428331

SOUTH BRISTOL COMMUNITY HOSPITAL 5B **76**
Whitchurch Lane
BRISTOL
BS14 0DE
Tel: 0117 9643300

SOUTHMEAD HOSPITAL .7K **35**
Southmead Road
Westbury-on-Trym
BRISTOL
BS10 5NB
Tel: 0117 950 5050

ST MARTIN'S HOSPITAL 3A **122**
Midford Road
BATH
BA2 5RP
Tel: 01225 831500

ST MICHAEL'S HOSPITAL 1D **4** (1J **61**)
Southwell Street
BRISTOL
BS2 8EG
Tel: 0117 342 5325

ST PETERS HOSPICE 7C **62**
St Agnes Avenue
BRISTOL
BS4 2DU
Tel: 0117 915 9200

ST PETER'S HOSPICE (BRENTRY) 5H **35**
Charlton Road
Brentry
BRISTOL
BS10 6NL
Tel: 0117 915 9400

THORNBURY HOSPITAL .3A **12**
Prowse Close
Thornbury
BRISTOL
BS35 1DN
Tel: 01454 412636

URGENT CARE CENTRE (BATH) 3H **99**
Royal United Hospital
Combe Park
BATH
BA1 3NG
Tel: 01225 428331

URGENT CARE CENTRE (BRISTOL) 5B **76**
South Bristol Community Hospital
Whitchurch Lane
BRISTOL
BS14 0DE
Tel: 0117 3429692

URGENT CARE CENTRE (WESTERN-SUPER-MARE) 3G **127**
Western General Hospital
Grange Road,
Uphill
WESTON-SUPER-MARE
BS23 4TQ
Tel: 01934 636363

WESTON GENERAL HOSPITAL 3G **127**
Grange Road
Uphill
WESTON-SUPER-MARE
BS23 4TQ
Tel: 01934 636363

WESTON HOSPICECARE .3F **127**
Jackson-Barstow House
28 Thornbury Road
Uphill
WESTON-SUPER-MARE
BS23 4YQ
Tel: 01934 423900